T5-AXI-747

# On Language

# On Language

## Selected Writings of

## JOSEPH H. GREENBERG

Edited by Keith Denning and Suzanne Kemmer

Stanford University Press, Stanford, California
1990

Stanford University Press
Stanford, California



Printed in the United States of America

CIP data appear at the end of the book

*Linguae docent*

# Acknowledgments

We would like to thank Charles Ferguson, John Ohala, Elizabeth Traugott, and William Croft for useful suggestions regarding this volume, and for their helpful comments on an earlier draft of the Introduction. Thanks are also due to Eve Clark for discussion of portions of the materials included under Psycholinguistics. Special thanks to William Carver and Peter Kahn of Stanford University Press for encouragement and support in getting this volume to press. We would also like to acknowledge the contribution of the National Science Foundation for its support of Keith Denning in the form of a Graduate Fellowship, and the Center for the Study of Language and Information at Stanford University for making its facilities available to Suzanne Kemmer. Thanks to Laura Jones and Laura Leach-Palm for assisting in the preparation of the Bibliography, to Bonnie McElhinny for collating footnotes and endnotes, and to the Department of Anthropology, Stanford University, for aid of various kinds. Most of all, we thank Joseph H. Greenberg, our teacher and guide, for sanctioning this project. He gave generously of his valuable time and energy during the preparation of this volume, discussing issues raised in the articles, helping to identify potential errors, and especially, checking the diverse linguistic data.

Special thanks to Merritt Ruhlen for his generous help in resolving many outstanding problems at the galley stage.

We also gratefully acknowledge the institutions and individuals named below for their permission to reprint the articles in this volume, which are listed in order of date of original publication.

"Swahili prosody." *Journal of the American Oriental Society* 67: 24–30 (1947). Reprinted with permission of the American Oriental Society.

"Hausa verse prosody." *Journal of the American Oriental Society* 69: 125–35 (1949). Reprinted with permission of the American Oriental Society.

Review of *The Classification of the Bantu Languages*, by Malcolm Guthrie. *Word* 5: 81–83 (1949). Reprinted with permission of the International Linguistic Association.

"The patterning of root morphemes in Semitic." *Word* 6: 162–81 (1950). Reprinted with permission of the International Linguistic Association.

"A quantitative approach to the morphological typology of language." In *Method and Perspective in Anthropology: Papers in Honor of Wilson D. Wallis*, ed. R. F. Spencer, 192–220. Minneapolis: University of Minnesota Press, 1954. Reprinted with permission of the publisher.

Review of *Languages of West Africa*, by D. Westermann and M. A. Bryan. *Language* 30: 302–9 (1954). Reprinted with permission of the Linguistic Society of America.

"Internal *a*-plurals in Afroasiatic (Hamito-Semitic)." *Afrikanistische Studien* 26: 198–204 (Diedrich Westermann zum 80.en Geburtstag gewidmet). Berlin: Akademie-Verlag, 1955. Reprinted with permission of the publisher.

"The nature and uses of linguistic typologies." *International Journal of American Linguistics* 23: 68–77 (1957). Reprinted with permission of the University of Chicago Press and the editors of *IJAL*.

"The labial consonants of Proto-Afro-Asiatic." *Word* 14: 295–302 (1958). Reprinted with permission of the International Linguistic Association.

"The origin of the Masai passive." *Africa* 29: 171–76 (1959). Reprinted with permission of the International African Institute.

"Linguistic evidence for the influence of the Kanuri on the Hausa." *Journal of African History* 1: 205–12 (1960). ©1960 by Cambridge University Press. Reprinted with permission of Cambridge University Press.

"A survey of African prosodic systems." In *Culture in History*, ed. Stanley Diamond, 925–50. New York: Columbia University Press, 1960. Reprinted with permission of the publisher.

"The interpretation of the Coptic vowel system." *Journal of African Languages* 1: 22–29 (1962). Reprinted with permission of Joseph H. Greenberg.

"Some universals of grammar with particular reference to the order of meaningful elements." In *Universals of Language*, ed. J. H. Greenberg, 58–90. Cambridge, Mass.: M.I.T. Press, 1963. Reprinted from the second edition, 1966, 73–113, with permission of the publisher.

(With James J. Jenkins). "Studies in the psychological correlates of the sound system of American English." Parts I and II, *Word* 20: 157–77 (1964); Parts III and IV, *Word* 22: 207–42 (1966). Reprinted with permission of the International Linguistic Association and the co-author, James J. Jenkins.

"Some methods of dynamic comparison in linguistics." In *Substance and Structure of Language*, ed. J. Puhvel, 147–203. Berkeley and Los Angeles:

University of California Press, 1969. ©1969 by the Regents of the University of California. Reprinted with permission of the publisher.

Review of *The Problems in the Classification of the African Languages*, by I. Fodor. *Language* 45: 427–32 (1969). Reprinted with permission of the Linguistic Society of America.

"Some generalizations concerning glottalic consonants, especially implosives." *International Journal of American Linguistics* 36,2 (Part I): 123–45 (1970). Reprinted with permission of the University of Chicago Press and the editors of *IJAL*.

"The role of typology in the development of a scientific linguistics." In *Theoretical Problems of Typology and the Northern Eurasian Languages*, ed. L. Dezsö and P. Hajdu, 11–24. Budapest: Akadémiai Kiadó, 1970. Reprinted with permission of the publisher.

"On the 'language of observation' in linguistics." *Working Papers on Language Universals* 4, G1–G15 (1970). Stanford: Department of Linguistics, Stanford University. Reprinted with permission of the Stanford University Department of Linguistics.

"Linguistic evidence regarding Bantu origins." *Journal of African History* 13: 189–216 (1972). ©1972 by Cambridge University Press. Reprinted with permission of Cambridge University Press.

"Numeral classifiers and substantival number: Problems in the genesis of a linguistic type." In *Proceedings of the Eleventh International Congress of Linguistics*, ed. Luigi Heilmann. Bologna: Società Editrice il Mulino, 1974. ©1974 by Società Editrice il Mulino. Reprinted with permission of the publisher. (First appeared in *Working Papers on Language Universals* 9: 1–39 (1972). Stanford: Department of Linguistics, Stanford University.)

"Studies in numerical systems, I: Double numeral systems." *Working Papers on Language Universals* 14: 75–89 (1974). Stanford: Department of Linguistics, Stanford University. Reprinted with permission of the Stanford University Department of Linguistics.

"The relation of frequency to semantic feature in a case language (Russian)." *Working Papers on Language Universals* 16: 21–45 (1974). Stanford: Department of Linguistics, Stanford University. ©1975 by the Board of Trustees of the Leland Stanford Junior University. Reprinted with permission of Stanford University and the Stanford University Department of Linguistics.

"Dynamic aspects of word order in the numeral classifier." In *Word Order and Word Order Change*, ed. Charles Li, 27–43. Austin: University of Texas Press, 1975. Reprinted with permission of the publisher.

"How does a language acquire gender markers?" In *Universals of Human Language*, ed. Joseph H. Greenberg, Charles A. Ferguson, and Edith A. Moravcsik. Vol. 3, 47–82. Stanford: Stanford University Press, 1978.

©1978 by the Board of Trustees of the Leland Stanford Junior University. Reprinted with permission of Stanford University Press.

"Generalizations about numeral systems." In *Universals of Human Language*, ed. Joseph H. Greenberg, Charles A. Ferguson, and Edith A. Moravcsik. Vol. 3, 249–95. Stanford: Stanford University Press, 1978. © 1978 by the Board of Trustees of the Leland Stanford Junior University. Reprinted with permission of Stanford University Press.

"Rethinking linguistics diachronically." *Language* 55: 275–90 (1979). Reprinted with permission of the Linguistic Society of America.

"Types of linguistic models in other disciplines." *Proceedings of the American Philosophical Society* 124: 35–40 (1980). Reprinted with permission of the American Philosophical Society.

"Universals of kinship terminology: Their nature and the problem of their explanation." In *On Linguistic Anthropology, Essays in Honor of Harry Hoijer*, ed. Jacques Maquet, 9–32. Malibu, Calif.: Undena Publications, 1980. ©1980 by Joseph H. Greenberg. Reprinted by author's permission.

"Nilo-Saharan moveable *k*- as a Stage III article (with a Penutian typological parallel)." *Journal of African Languages and Linguistics* 3: 105–12 (1981). Reprinted with permission of Foris Publications.

"Some areal characteristics of African languages." In *Current Approaches to African Linguistics*, ed. Ivan Dihoff. Vol. I, 3–21. Providence, R.I., and Dordrecht: Foris, 1983. Reprinted with permission of the publisher.

"Some iconic relationships among place, time, and discourse deixis." In *Iconicity in Syntax*, ed. John Haiman, 271–87. (Typological Studies in Language 6.) Amsterdam and Philadelphia: John Benjamins, 1985. Reprinted with permission of the publisher.

"Were there Egyptian koines?" In *The Fergusonian Impact*, ed. Joshua A. Fishman et al. Vol. I, 271–90. Berlin, New York, Amsterdam: Mouton de Gruyter, 1986. Reprinted with permission of the publisher.

"The first person inclusive dual as an ambiguous category." *Studies in Language* 12: 1–18 (1988). Reprinted by permission of John Benjamins B.V.

"Two approaches to language universals." In *New Vistas in Grammar: Invariance and Variation*, ed. Linda Waugh. Amsterdam and Philadelphia: John Benjamins, in press. Reprinted by permission of publisher and editor.

For permission to reprint the map of African language families entitled "Summary of Classification" from the final page of J. H. Greenberg, *The Languages of Africa* (Indiana University and Mouton and Co., 1963), we would like to thank Mouton de Gruyter.

K. D.
S. K.

# Contents

## Part IV: Psycholinguistics



## Part V: Linguistic Models and Linguistic Explanation

# Introduction

*Suzanne Kemmer and Keith Denning*

The papers collected in this volume represent a broad selection of Joseph Greenberg's linguistic work spanning the last four decades. There already exists one collection of previously published articles, *Language, Culture, and Communication* (1971a), which contains some of Greenberg's contributions to sociolinguistics; in addition, a number of articles, at the time newly published, appeared in *Essays in Linguistics* (1957). However, there is a large body of his work that has never been collected. Some of this work is not easily accessible, such as articles that initially appeared in small specialist journals or in books that have since gone out of print. This book is intended to fill the need for a representative collection of Greenberg's writings.

Choosing from the wealth of material available was not an easy task. In making our selections, we attempted to strike a balance between judgments of intrinsic worth, on the one hand, and considerations external to the works themselves, on the other. The external criteria included such issues as availability, overlap with material in other articles reprinted here, representativeness of Greenberg's main currents of thought, impact on the field, and relevance to current work in linguistics. The overall goal was to bring together in convenient form a mix of classic, well-known studies and works that we feel deserve wider recognition.

Inevitably, our choices to some extent also reflect our own personal scholarly interests. We are both diachronic typologists; but Denning's work concentrates on phonology and African historical linguistics, while Kemmer focuses on the semantics underlying grammatical categories.

The papers fall into a number of areas, not all mutually exclusive but nevertheless useful to distinguish. We have divided the book into the following parts: (I) typology and language universals; (II) studies in languages of Africa and the Near East; (III) verse prosody; (IV) psycholinguistics, and (V) linguistic models and linguistic explanation. In what follows, we offer remarks on some of the leading ideas in each part, historical observations where relevant, and a few notes on the choice of inclusions.

The first and largest of the five parts contains work on typology and language universals. Greenberg's impact on the field of typology and universals research has been immense. He was the first American linguist to recognize the importance of studying universals and to promote research in that area. He organized the Dobbs Ferry Conference on Language Universals (April 1961), which took place at a time when prevailing attitudes among American linguists were decidedly anti-universalistic.[1] The outcome of this conference was the volume *Universals of Language* (Greenberg 1963a), the first important milestone of universals research. Greenberg also provided the main impetus for the Stanford Project on Language Universals (1967–76), which he and Charles Ferguson jointly directed. The research results of this project appeared in *Working Papers on Language Universals* (1969–76) and the four volumes of *Universals in Human Language* (Greenberg et al. 1978). The project provided the training grounds for a large number of American universals researchers, as well as sparking a parallel project in Cologne that continues to thrive. In addition, typological research in the Soviet Union has been heavily influenced by Greenberg. The influence of Greenberg's approach to typology/universals can be clearly seen in the following books: Uspenskii 1968, Li 1975, Juilland 1976, W. Lehmann 1978, Comrie 1981, Mallinson and Blake 1981, Hawkins 1983, Seiler 1983, Givón 1984, Maddieson 1984, C. Lehmann 1984, Solntseva 1985, Stassen 1985, Ruhlen (forthcoming), and works that have appeared in the Benjamins series *Typological Studies in Language*, e.g. Craig 1985.

Part I contains what we consider the best of Greenberg's articles in this field, excluding, however, several papers that appeared in *Universals of Human Language*. The reason for the omission of these articles is that they are easily available and in some cases overlap considerably with some less well-known papers that we wished to include. We did, however, choose to reprint two papers from *Universals of Human Language*, namely "How Does a Language Acquire Gender Markers?" and "Generalizations About Numeral Systems," since both of these papers constitute major breakthroughs in the areas that they treat.

One notable characteristic of the work in this part is the integration of typological investigation with research on language universals. These two

[1] For the historical context of the Dobbs Ferry Conference, see Ferguson 1978. Of historical as well as theoretical interest is the "Memorandum Concerning Language Universals" (Greenberg, Osgood, and Jenkins 1963, written for presentation at the conference in 1961).

areas of endeavor were once thought to have rather opposite goals (viz., typology: the discovery of the differences among languages; universals: the study of what languages have in common). Greenberg's approach, however, shows how typological comparison can be used as a powerful tool for the discovery of universals. The two *Universals* papers are paradigmatic examples of this technique.

A related theme recurring throughout Part I is the close connection between implicational universals and marking theory. Prague School scholars showed that asymmetry within categories is a pervasive phenomenon in human language; linguistic categories tend to have one member that stands out with respect to a particular cluster of properties. These properties together define markedness. In the course of exploring markedness in various linguistic domains, Greenberg substantially extended classical marking theory. Among other innovations, he was the first to point out the significance of diachronic processes to synchronic marking relations. Previously, the only application of marking theory to historical linguistics had been as a kind of touchstone for the plausibility of linguistic reconstructions. An extensive discussion of marking theory and some results of its application in the investigation of language universals are found in Greenberg's 1966 monograph *Language Universals, with Special Reference to Feature Hierarchies*. (For more recent contributions to marking theory following Greenberg's general approach, see Eckman, Moravcsik, and Wirth 1986.)

Aside from the major contributions to the field of typology and universals found in the work in this part, there are a number of ideas developed in these papers that are of more general applicability in other areas of linguistics. Here we will just mention a few.

One area of relevance to current work is Greenberg's attention to the semantic side of particular linguistic systems. His discussion of the semantics underlying numeral classifiers, gender markers, and deictic systems, for example, informed as it is by observation of recurrent typological patterns and diachronic developments, provides an excellent basis on which to build general theories of number, definiteness, deixis, and anaphora.

An important point regarding semantic change is found in "The First Person Dual Inclusive as an Ambiguous Category." Greenberg's analysis makes reference to a Gestalt-like shift of focus from one semantic property to another, thus highlighting the fact that semantic complexity can play a crucial role in language change. Furthermore, this paper illustrates the general point that typological change can be the result of a semantic change undergone by a particular element.

Applicable to current work in morphology is Greenberg's early paper "A Quantitative Approach to the Morphological Typology of Language." Here he presents a method of quantifying the traditional morphological typologies of languages (isolating vs. agglutinative vs. inflective and synthetic vs. analytic). His numerical scales, particularly those for degree of synthesis and degree of fusion, are potentially of great empirical value for testing correlations with other typological properties. Despite the fact that morphological typology in the above sense has been out of fashion for the greater part of this century, there is a growing suspicion among some linguists that the morphological structure of the word is of fundamental importance to many aspects of linguistic structure (see for example Bybee 1985).

Part II represents Greenberg's substantial contributions to African and Near Eastern linguistics. Greenberg's influence on the field of African language studies is pervasive; most notably, his African language classification has become standard for the field. The works included in this section cover a number of areas, including classification, synchronic analysis of particular linguistic systems, areal linguistics, typology, language contact, and historical linguistics.

Many papers in this part are elegant, self-contained studies that deserve a wider audience than they initially received. One such is "Linguistic Evidence for the Influence of the Kanuri on the Hausa," which is a model of how to apply linguistic evidence to determine the direction of lexical borrowing. Two others of note are "The Origin of the Masai Passive" and "Nilo-Saharan Moveable *k*- as a Stage III Article." These will be of considerable interest to typologists as well as general historical linguists, since they illustrate recurrent diachronic processes that give rise to particular construction types. "The Labial Consonants of Proto-Afro-Asiatic" is a classic illustration of how a traditional problem becomes amenable to solution once reference is made to languages in a larger genetic grouping than had previously been perceived.

In addition to research papers, this part contains several reviews of books on African language classification. They were included not only because we found them entertaining (they contain some of Greenberg's most trenchant writing) but also because they set forth some basic principles of linguistic classification that may not have been fully appreciated by some stock specialists. We hope in particular that the fallacies regarding classification that these reviews expose (e.g., use of typological criteria in classification, the assumption that reconstructions are "proof" of genetic relationships, etc.) may not reemerge in future work in genetic classification.[2]

To aid the non-specialist reader in keeping track of the genetic relationships referred to in the articles and reviews in this part, we have included a map of the distribution of the major language families and subgroups in Africa. Since

[2]See Greenberg 1987, chap. 1, and Ruhlen 1987 for discussion of these fallacies and of the general principles of genetic classification.

Greenberg's African classification underwent various modifications over the years, particularly before 1963 when it reached its present degree of comprehensiveness, some references to the classification of particular languages and language groups in the papers included here are outdated.[3] Rather than attempting to update such references, which are in all cases immaterial to the basic content of the articles, we refer the interested reader to Greenberg's major works on African linguistic classification (Greenberg 1955 and 1963b).

Part III includes three works on African verse prosody. These studies are notable for their originality and their synthesizing character, as they brought together a body of previously scattered observations. Two are in-depth analyses of particular prosodic systems, while the third, "A Survey of African Prosodic Systems," was the first general characterization of verse prosodic devices in African languages. Taken together, these studies have considerable significance for a general theory of verse prosody. In addition, they are important contributions to the study of the linguistic history of Africa (for example in their identification of native vs. Arabic-influenced poetic devices). Greenberg's results in this area reveal the great potential of the comparative study of verse prosody for historical investigation.

An area of research for which Greenberg is less well-known today is psycholinguistics. This was at one time one of his major research interests; in the early 1960's he was a member of the Social Science Research Council Committee on Linguistics and Psychology, which sponsored a large number of research projects over the years (see Osgood and Sebeok 1965). The first paper in Part IV, "Studies in the Psychological Correlates of the Sound System of American English," contains four reports of psycholinguistic experiments conducted by Greenberg and James J. Jenkins. These studies, which constitute the earliest psycholinguistic experiments by American psychologists and linguists working in collaboration, are concerned with a variety of phenomena, including the psychological distance of nonsense words from English norms; relationships between distinctive sounds in psychological space; and the application of the semantic differential to measure similarity between speech sounds. In addition, this part includes a paper that has never before appeared in print, "A Linguistic Approach to the Meaningfulness of Nonsense Syllables." This study presents a non-experimental, language-internal method of determining the proximity of nonsense syllables to English. The index of meaningfulness thus derived, it turns out, correlates highly with measures of psychological distance arrived

[3]The two main cases of outdated information are references in early papers to Songhai as an unaffiliated language (Songhai was later incorporated into Nilo-Saharan) and references to a Chari-Nile group of Niger-Congo (cf. footnote 4 in "Some Areal Characteristics of African languages" [in Part II below]).

at in previous experimental studies. The article, originally planned as a collaborative paper with Jenkins, was written in 1965 by Greenberg and has been revised for publication here. The types of empirical investigations represented by the work in this part have been the subject of renewed interest by a number of linguists and psychologists, and we hope that the articles included here will be a further stimulus to research in this area.

The papers in Part V deal with models and explanation. In these papers, linguistics is placed in the broader context of scientific endeavor as a whole. The comparisons between linguistics and other sciences that are drawn serve to illuminate particular historical trends in linguistics.

The promotion of physics as a "model science" for linguistics has become commonplace since the rise of the generative school. In "Types of Linguistic Models in Other Disciplines," Greenberg shows that the direction of influence has flowed the other way, from linguistics to other disciplines, at various points in the nineteenth and twentieth centuries. In "On the 'Language of Observation' in Linguistics," he calls attention to a level of scientific discourse that has not explicitly received recognition in linguistics, and points to ways this 'language of observation' can be utilized as a universal basis for comparable language descriptions. The remarks found in this paper on the essentially relative nature of observational and theoretical levels foreshadow the discussion of levels of explanation in "Rethinking Linguistics Diachronically" and "Two Approaches to Language Universals." These papers should lay to rest the fallacious idea that it is possible or desirable to draw an absolute dichotomy between "description" and "explanation."

"Rethinking Linguistics Diachronically" focuses on a matter of central concern to Greenberg: the reintegration of diachrony into general linguistic theory. In this paper it becomes clear why so much of Greenberg's work in typology/universals is integrally diachronic. His view can be summed up as follows: However useful the distinction between synchrony and diachrony may be as a heuristic, the two are ultimately inseparable from the point of view of explanation—diachronic facts are indispensable to the understanding of synchronic phenomena, and vice versa. Implicit in this view is the assumption, repeatedly borne out by the findings of cross-linguistic research, that the same factors—semantic, pragmatic, cognitive, and, for phonology, articulatory, perceptual, and acoustic—underlie both synchronic typological patterns and the recurrent diachronic developments associated with them.

Perhaps one of the reasons that historical linguistics became ancillary to synchronic descriptive linguistics in this century was that it was felt to be overly particularistic and not amenable to generalization. Greenberg has often pointed out that there is no necessary incompatibility between historically oriented research and law-seeking scientific investigation in linguistics.

This is probably stated best in "Some Methods of Dynamic Comparison in Linguistics," a paper from Part I: "There exists the possibility of a more comprehensive mode of diachronic comparison which shares with synchronic typology the attribute of generality. The individual items of such comparisons are not the cognate forms, but the changes themselves . . . occurring in historically independent cases, and hence subject to classification . . . and generalization" (p. 74).

"Two Approaches to Language Universals" (written nearly a decade ago but first published only recently) continues and extends the theme of the necessity for a broad conception of linguistic theory that embraces generalizations lying outside the realm of grammar. Here Greenberg warns against the prevailing tendency to arbitrarily limit the concerns of linguistics to the specific problems of synchronic grammatical theory. Of particular importance is the broadening of the notion of what constitutes explanation. Greenberg's approach to explanation is far more eclectic than that found in current generative approaches. In his view, the search for explanations for many linguistic phenomena will ultimately take us outside the realm of linguistics proper and into cognitive and other domains.

One area of linguistic scholarship that is left unrepresented in this book is Greenberg's work on language classification outside Africa. Greenberg has published important work on the classification of non-Austronesian languages of the Pacific ("The Indo-Pacific Hypothesis," 1971) and the New World (*Language in the Americas*, 1987). In addition, he is currently at work on a book elaborating his hypothesis of the existence of a large language family that subsumes Indo-European, a number of major linguistic stocks in Asia, and Eskimo-Aleut (tentatively titled *Indo-European and Its Closest Relatives: The Eurasiatic Language Family*). We felt that his work on American Indian and on Eurasiatic is best left represented by complete book-length treatments, rather than partial explications in article form. "The Indo-Pacific Hypothesis" is not reprinted here because of its length and the fact that it consists mostly of citations of data, difficult to interpret for those not familiar with the languages treated.

A number of other areas of inquiry were also intentionally omitted. To keep this book to a reasonable size, we restricted ourselves to those of Greenberg's writings that are most centrally concerned with language structure. Another volume could be filled with his writings on anthropology, culture history, macrosociolinguistics, and the philosophy of science, all attesting to the breadth of Greenberg's interest and scholarship.

We have tried to keep editorial intrusion to a minimum, largely confining ourselves to correcting errors in the original published versions. Articles have in most respects been left in their original editorial format; in a few cases, notes and bibliographic entries have been updated. We also made a few stylistic modifications in consultation with the author.

A full bibliography of Joseph Greenberg's work to date has been included at the end of this volume. Since Greenberg continues to be immensely productive, it will probably be somewhat out of date before this book appears. In looking forward to future work, we anticipate many more new and challenging ideas from one of the foremost linguistic scholars of the twentieth century.

## References Cited

Bybee, Joan. 1985. *Morphology: A Study of the Relation between Meaning and Form*. Amsterdam and Philadelphia: John Benjamins.

Comrie, Bernard. 1981. *Language Universals and Linguistic Typology*. Oxford: Basil Blackwell.

Craig, Collette, ed. 1985. *Noun Classes and Categorization*. (Typological Studies in Language 7). Amsterdam and Philadelphia: John Benjamins.

Eckman, Fred R., Edith A. Moravcsik, and Jessica R. Wirth, eds. 1986. *Markedness*. Proceedings of the Twelfth Annual Linguistics Symposium of the University of Wisconsin-Milwaukee 1983. New York: Plenum Press.

Ferguson, Charles. 1978. "The historical background of universals research." In Greenberg et al. 1978, Vol. I.

Givón, Talmy. 1984. *Syntax: A Functional-Typological Introduction*. Vol. I. Amsterdam and Philadelphia: John Benjamins.

Greenberg, Joseph H. 1955. *Studies in African Linguistic Classification*. New Haven, Conn.: Compass Press.

———. 1957. *Essays in Linguistics*. Chicago: University of Chicago Press.

———. 1963a, ed. *Universals of Language*. Cambridge, Mass.: M.I.T. Press.

———. 1963b. *The Languages of Africa. International Journal of American Linguistics*, 29: 1, Part II. (Publication of the Indiana University Research Center in Anthropology, Folklore, and Linguistics 25.) Bloomington: Indiana University, and The Hague: Mouton.

———. 1966. *Language Universals, with Special Reference to Feature Hierarchies* (Janua Linguarum Series Minor 59). The Hague: Mouton.

———. 1971a. *Language, Culture, and Communication*. Essays by Joseph H. Greenberg. Selected and introduced by Anwar S. Dil. Stanford: Stanford University Press.

———. 1971b. "The Indo-Pacific hypothesis." *Current Trends in Linguistics* 8: 808–71.

———. 1987. *Language in the Americas*. Stanford: Stanford University Press.

———. Forthcoming. *Indo-European and Its Closest Relatives: The Eurasiatic Language Family*. Stanford: Stanford University Press.

Greenberg, Joseph H., Charles Osgood, and James Jenkins. 1963. "Memorandum concerning language universals." In Greenberg 1963a.

Greenberg, Joseph H., Charles A. Ferguson, and Edith A. Moravcsik, eds. 1978. *Universals of Human Language*. 4 vols. Stanford: Stanford University Press.

Hawkins, John. 1983. *Word Order Universals*. New York: Academic Press.

Juilland, Alphonse, ed. 1976. *Linguistic Studies Offered to Joseph Greenberg on the Occasion of His Sixtieth Birthday*. 3 vols. Saratoga, Cal.: Anma Libri.

Lehmann, Christian. 1984. *Der Relativsatz: Typologie seiner Strukturen, Theorie seiner Funktionen, Kompendium seiner Grammatik*. (Language Universals Series 3.) Tübingen: Günter Narr.

Lehmann, Winfred, ed. 1978. *Syntactic Typology. Studies in the Phenomenology of Language*. Austin: University of Texas Press.

Li, Charles, ed. 1975. *Word Order and Word Order Change*. Austin: University of Texas Press.

Maddieson, Ian. 1984. *Patterns of Sounds*. Cambridge: Cambridge University Press.

Mallinson, Graham, and Barry Blake. 1981. *Language Typology: Crosslinguistic Studies in Syntax*. Amsterdam and New York: North Holland.

Osgood, Charles E., and Thomas A. Sebeok, eds. 1965. *Psycholinguistics: A Survey of Theory and Research Problems*. Bloomington and London: Indiana University Press.

Ruhlen, Merritt. 1987. *A Guide to the World's Languages*. Vol. I, Classification. Stanford: Stanford University Press.

———. Forthcoming. *A Guide to the World's Languages*. Vol. III, Language Universals. Stanford: Stanford University Press.

Seiler, Hansjakob. 1983. *Possession as an Operational Dimension of Language*. (Language Universals Series vol. 2.) Tübingen: Günter Narr.

Solntseva, Nina V. 1985. *Problemy Tipologii Izoliruiushchikh Iazykov* [Problems in the typology of isolating languages]. Moscow: Nauka.

Stassen, Leon. 1985. *Comparison and Universal Grammar*. New York: Basil Blackwell.

Uspenskii, Boris A. 1968. *Printsipy Strukturnoi Tipologii*. (Principles of Structural Typology.) (Janua Linguarum Series Minor 62.) The Hague, Paris: Mouton.

PART I

# TYPOLOGY AND LANGUAGE UNIVERSALS

# A Quantitative Approach to the Morphological Typology of Language

One of the steps which any science must take if it is to realize the potentialities of the scientific method is to advance beyond mere description to comparison and classification of the objects it studies. That linguistics has taken this step is indicated by the very existence of a subject matter called "comparative linguistics," one which is, moreover, of respected standing among the sciences dealing with man. However, the methods of comparative linguistics represent but one of two fundamental methods by which languages may be compared. The second method, which may be called the typological, is the subject of the present paper. It has had a more checkered career than the historic-genetic method which characterizes comparative linguistics. It is important to distinguish as clearly as possible the differences between the two methods. Each is legitimate in its own sphere, but a confusion between the two methods, as when typological criteria are employed to establish genetic relationships, has had harmful effects in the past.

The genetic-historical method classifies languages into "families" which have a common historic origin. A familiar example is the descent of the modern forms of Romance speech, French, Spanish, Portuguese, Italian, Rumanian, etc., from an original unified Latin as the result of changes of the same speech form in distinct areas. When this diversification has not been so remote in time as to remove all evidential traces, comparison will reveal characteristic resemblances among languages which have such a common origin. What is chiefly relevant for such comparisons is the resemblance between individual forms in language, both with respect to sound and meaning. For example, English *nose* and German *Nase* have similar sounds and both have virtually identical meanings, 'nose'; English *hound* and German *Hund*, 'dog', are similar in sound and similar though not identical in meaning. Any language consists of thousands of forms with both sound and meaning, the relation between the two being arbitrary. In principle, any sound whatever can express any meaning whatever. Therefore, if two languages agree in a considerable number of such items, as do German and English, and if—a problem not discussed here—the resemblances cannot be explained by borrowing, we necessarily draw a conclusion of common historic origin. Such genetic classifications are not arbitrary, in the sense that there is no room for the establishment of varied criteria leading to different results. This is because such classifications reflect historic events, which must either have happened or not have happened. Either the speakers of German and English speak a language transmitted from an original unified proto-Germanic speech community or they do not. The analogy here to biological classification is extremely close as, indeed, the use of such terms as *family*, *related*, and *genetic* might suggest. Just as in biology we classify species in the same genus or high unit because the resemblances are such as to suggest a hypothesis of common descent, so with genetic hypotheses in language.

One can, however, compare languages which cannot be shown to be related genetically and this either with respect to some features of sound only or meaning only. The two following examples will serve at once to illustrate this possibility and to show that, in this way, legitimate scientific problems arise. All languages must express comparison—the fact, for example, that one thing is larger than another. If we compare all the languages of the world in this respect, we discover that the number of methods is limited—e.g., a special, inflected form of the adjective (English *greater*), the use of a preposition meaning *from* (Semitic), the use of a verb meaning *surpasses* (as widely used in Africa)—and that of these some are far more frequent than others and have definite geographical distributions which disregard genetic boundaries. All these are surely data of real interest which require an explanation. The phenomenon just discussed is semantic. In the area of sound patterns, the independent appearance of a system of five vowels with two degrees of length—a, a:, e, e:, i, i:, o, o:, u, u:—in classical Latin, Hausa in West Africa, Yokuts, an Indian language of California, and doubtless elsewhere—is surely worthy of attention. Indeed, such phenomena have been studied by Trubetskoy and others in an attempt to discover what types of vowel and consonant systems are possible and their relative frequency and area of appearance.

If genetic comparison establishes classes of languages, i.e., language families in the accepted sense, does not typological classification do this also? The answer, of course, is that it can but that, as opposed to genetic classification, it has no specific historic implications and is arbitrary, i.e., will lead to different results depending on the criterion or combination of criteria selected.

In this respect it is like racial classification based on a number of arbitrarily selected traits. If, for example, we select such a purely phonetic criterion as the presence or absence of lip rounding as a feature distinguishing pairs of vowel phonemes, the languages of the world will fall into two groups, those that avail themselves of this particular principle of contrast and those that do not. English and Italian, which do not, will fall in class A with innumerable other languages; and French and German, along with a smaller number of other languages from different parts of the world, will fall into class B. If some other typological trait is selected, say the position of the dependent genitive relative to the noun, again two classes of languages will emerge, but they will not coincide with those obtained by the criterion of rounded versus unrounded vowel. Taking both factors into consideration, there will be four classes. Certain characteristics will allow of more than two classes. If languages are classified semantically on the basis of their numerical system, we shall obtain a number of classes of languages: binary, quinary, decimal, duodecimal, and no doubt others as well. In short, in contrast to genetic classification, the number of language groups and their membership will differ with the number and particular selection of linguistic traits utilized for the comparison. At one extreme, if some such feature as the presence of a vowel system is employed as the sole criterion, the languages of the world will fall into two groups, those with (and this group will include all the languages of the world) and those without. This latter class will, of course, have no member. At the other extreme, one can specify so many traits that each language becomes the only member of a specific type.

Many such classifications, as should be evident from the examples just cited, are not very useful. We seek to establish typologies which involve characteristics of fundamental importance in language and which are useful for a variety of reasons. Such a classification does exist, the nineteenth-century division of languages which, in its classical version, was threefold: isolating, agglutinative, and inflective types.

This *trop fameuse classification*, to use Meillet's trenchant phrase, betrays fundamental weaknesses which have inevitably led to its present state of disrepute. Yet the problem itself *is* of sufficient importance for Sapir, in the only major contribution to the subject since the nineteenth century, to have made it the central topic of his book *Language*. However inadequate the nineteenth-century discussion of this topic now appears, the major virtue of the schemes advanced remains. Something of fundamental importance to the over-all characterization of a language, the morphological structure of the word, was instinctively seized upon as the basis of classification, and Sapir's contribution simply continued this essential feature of the earlier approach, in revised form. Other typologies, particularly phonological, are possible, and these latter have been the chief center of interest in typological discussions in recent years. However, the problem of a morphological typology remains, as evidenced by Rulon Wells's recent statement, "It is shocking that there is no established taxonomy of the languages of the world" (1950: 31). The revived interest in this topic is further evidenced by the virtually simultaneous and independent development by Charles Hockett of Cornell and myself of the ideas presented in this paper.[1] In short, the time seems propitious to re-examine the nineteenth-century approach to the problem, discarding what the intervening period of linguistic criticism has demonstrated as invalid and incorporating recent methodological advances in order to reformulate the hypotheses along more rigorous lines. A brief critical review of earlier attempts may serve to place the present treatment in its proper perspective.

The germ of all later classifications is found in the distinction, first set forth by Friedrich von Schlegel in his essay "*Über die Sprache und Weisheit der Indier*" (1808), between languages with affixes and languages with inflections. The valuational attitudes so prominent throughout the later history of the theory are already present in this earliest formulation. The affix-languages express relations through a merely mechanical process. In a striking figure they are likened to a "heap of atoms which every wind of chance scatters or sweeps together" (p. 51). Only Indo-European languages are inflectional, but Semitic is tending in that direction.

This twofold classification was elaborated into a tripartite one by Friedrich's brother, August von Schlegel. In an essay "*Sur la littérature provençale*" (1818), Schlegel describes three classes of languages: "languages without grammatical structure, affixing and inflectional languages" (p. 559). Of his first class, called by later writers isolating or root languages, he says, "One might say that all their words are roots, but sterile roots which produce neither plants nor trees" (p. 159). To create a literature of science in such a language is a *tour de force*. The affixing languages use added elements ("affixes") to express the relations and nuances of the root ideas, but these affixes still have an independent meaning. Regarding inflectional languages in which such affixes are meaningless (i.e., devoid of concrete meaning), we learn that to them can be attributed a kind of organic life ("organisme") in that "they contain a vital principle of development and growth" (p. 159). As with later writers, Chinese is his model of a root-language; only the Semitic

[1] The same basic approach was presented by Charles Hockett in an unpublished paper read at the annual meeting of the Linguistic Society of America, Philadelphia, 1949, and in a talk I gave before the Linguistic Circle of New York at Columbia University, January 1950.

and Indo-European languages belong to the inflectional group; all the others belong to the vast and heterogeneous intermediate or agglutinative class. The inconvenient fact that the Indo-European languages have tended to lose their inflection bothers him as it did other later writers. He therefore introduces a further subdivision of his inflectional languages, the earlier synthetic and later analytic. All analytic languages we know result from the decomposition of synthetic languages. Passing over other writers who discussed the topic in much the same terms as Schlegel, we come to Wilhelm von Humboldt who, in his essay "*Über die Verschiedenheit des menschlichen Sprachbaues*" (1836), placed this type of analysis at the very heart of his approach to language. Von Humboldt viewed each language as a distinct self-revelation of the spirit (*Geist*). Such self-revelations, while each a valid expression in its own right, exhibit lesser or greater degrees of perfection. There are four classes of languages in von Humboldt's scheme. He adds a fourth, incorporating type to the by now traditional threefold classification in order to accommodate certain American Indian languages whose very complex word-patterns include instances in which the object of a verb is incorporated in the same word as the verb root. Von Humboldt is explicit in rejecting any historical evolutionary interpretation in which higher types evolve out of lower types. These are ideal types involving different degrees of the unfolding of form. The isolating languages are "formless," the incorporating languages, through their over-elaboration, betray no true sense of form. As might be expected, only the inflected languages, by their harmonious fusion of root and affix in a true unity, are credited with a true sense of form.

The definitive exposition of the theory is found in the writings of A. Schleicher, who stood under the twin influences of Darwin and Hegel. The classes of languages are now interpreted as so many historical evolutionary phases of the development of languages. The types are limited to three, which are equated to the stages of the Hegelian dialectic. The inflectional class of languages becomes a higher synthesis arising out of a previous opposition. The decay of inflection in historic times introduces a new phase of the *Geist* in which the material side of language no longer counts. In accord with the intellectual currents of the age, and equipped with an impressive set of quasi-algebraic formulas to indicate the various relations of the root to subordinate elements, Schleicher's version of the theory won wide acceptance and provided the basis for the exposition by those two great popularizers of linguistic science, Max Müller in Europe and William Dwight Whitney in the United States. Later versions such as that of Steinthal-Misteli, which added to the complications of the scheme without any compensating advantages, never became as popular as Schleicher's, which thus established itself as the basic form of the theory.

During this whole period criticism of the ethnocentrism and vagueness of these typologies was by no means lacking. To cite but one instance, Whitney, who was by no means as enthusiastic about the Schleicherian typology as his European contemporary, Max Müller, declares "*loved* from *love* is as good a preterite as *led* from *lead* or *sang* from *sing*" (1876: 362). *Loved* is, of course, an example of agglutinative technique, while *led* and *sang* are inflective. Still, in regard to isolating languages he talks of "this lack of resources possessed by more happily developed languages; . . . thought is but brokenly represented and feebly aided by its instrument." Others, particularly at a later date, were highly critical or even contemptuous, as, for example, Mauthner, according to whom ". . . the valuation [of languages] according to whether their inflections are more or less transparent is as foolish as if one judged the merit of European armies according to the greater or lesser visibility of their trouser seams" (1923: 309).

Sapir's treatment of the topic in his book *Language* (1921) marks an epoch. He firmly rejects both the valuative and evolutionary aspects of the theory. There is no real reason to suppose that Chinese or Hungarian is not as effective an instrument of thought as Latin or English. "When it comes to linguistic form, Plato walks with the Macedonian swineherd, Confucius with the head-hunting savage of Assam" (p. 234). Man must have had language for at least 500,000 years; hence, if there is indeed a line of development—isolating, agglutinative, inflective—present-day isolating languages cannot possibly represent the primitive stage. Indeed, the evidence of human paleontology and glacial geology had made this assumption long since untenable. Chinese, the classic instance of an isolating language, was known by Sapir's time to have formerly possessed a more complex morphological system, both from earlier records of the language and comparison with Tibetan and other related languages.

Perhaps more significant than these no longer tenable assumptions were other logical defects which had been pointed out from time to time. The distinctive criteria of the various types had never been either defined with clarity or applied with objectivity. In reading Steinthal-Misteli, one has the feeling that the writer is playing with loaded dice. Whenever, on the basis of his own showing, a non-Aryan, non-Semitic language appears to have a praiseworthy feature, a tacit shift in definition shows that the "true form" or "true inflection" is not involved. The definitions were not only vague but partly referred to quite different things, so that a language might well belong to several of the supposedly mutually exclusive classes simultaneously. For example, agglutination was usually taken as referring to a technique of mechanical affixation, so that, in Max Müller's words, "The difference between Aryan and Turanian is somewhat the same as between good and bad mosaic. The Aryan words seem made of one piece, the Turanian words clearly show the sutures and fissures where the small stones are cemented together" (1890: 292). The contrary term should be *inflection*. But the term *inflection* was also used to indicate the presence of affixes without concrete meaning to denote relations among words of the sentence; e.g., by case endings in the noun or person-number terminations in the verb. On this basis Turkish is both agglutinational (on the basis of technique) and inflectional (because of its case and verb conjugational systems).

A further defect, as was pointed out by some critics, was that a language had to be assigned to a single category, although the features employed might be present to a greater or lesser degree. A term like *agglutinative* applies primarily to a single construction. A language may well and indeed usually does contain some agglutinational as well as some nonagglutinational constructions. In other words, it is a matter of over-all tendency rather than absolute presence or absence of the diagnostic traits. Sapir, by distinguishing among the various criteria which were unconsciously being employed in a confused way in the classical theory, constructs a more complex system in which languages are classified by a number of independent criteria and in which the traditional terms are retained, but in well-defined uses which are often on different axes so that they are no longer mutually exclusive.

One such axis distinguished by Sapir may be said to relate to the gross complexity of the word, i.e., the degree of complexity exhibited on the basis of the number of subordinate meaningful elements it contains. The terms employed here by Sapir are *analytic*, *synthetic*, and *polysynthetic*, in ascending order of complexity. The theoretic extreme of analysis is represented by languages in which each word consists of only one meaningful unit and thus has no internal structure. Languages which actually approach this extreme are Chinese, Annamite, and Ewe (in West Africa). These are the languages traditionally called isolating, but, as we shall see, Sapir reserved this term for another use. Languages like English with words of little complexity were included by Sapir in the analytic group. However, the degree of synthesis is but one criterion and a relatively superficial one, since it does not tell us in what the complexity of the word consists. A second and quite different consideration refers to technique of construction. The contrast is, roughly, between languages in which the subordinate elements are added to the root elements mechanically, i.e., without either of the elements being modified (the most common meaning of agglutination in the classical scheme), and those involving a process of fusion by which the constituent elements become difficult to recognize and separate. To quote Sapir's examples: *good* + *ness* in English is agglutinative, *dep* + *th*, fusional. After treating this topic several times with varying conclusions, Sapir finally sets up a fourfold division: *a*, isolating; *b*, agglutinative; *c*, fusional; *d*, symbolic. Isolation, by which Sapir means significant order of elements, is included here because he thinks of this rubric as concerned with techniques of relating elements. Just as we know that in "John hit Bill" "John" is in construction with "hit" as the subject of the verb by the fact that it precedes the verb, so in *dep-th*, the modification of *deep* to *dep-* indicates that it is in construction with *-th*. Since the agglutination-fusion contrast refers merely to the mechanics of expression rather than to what is being related, Sapir considers this scale likewise somewhat superficial, though useful as a supplementary criterion.

The division which appears to Sapir the most basic rests on the following considerations. There are two types of concepts which all languages must express, a stock of roots with concrete meanings, e.g., *table*, *eat*, and pure relational ideas which "serve to relate the concrete elements of the proposition to each other," thus giving it definite syntactic form; e.g., Latin *-um* as a mark of the verb object. As constituting the two extremes of concrete and abstract, Sapir puts these two classes at the ends of his scale as I (concrete), IV (pure relational). Between these, he places two groups of concepts which are dispensable, since some languages have them and others do not. Type II consists of derivational concepts which "differ from type I in expressing ideas irrelevant to the proposition as a whole but that give a radical element a particular increment of significance and that thus are related in a specific way to concepts of type I." Sapir's example is the suffix *-er* in *farmer*, which gives an increment of meaning to *farm-* but is not concerned with the structure of the rest of the sentence. A language which does not have concepts of type II would employ a single unanalyzable element to convey the meaning *farmer*. Concepts of type III (concrete relational concepts) lead over to type IV (pure relational), insofar as they help to relate members of a sentence to each other, but differ in that they have an element of the concrete in their meaning. Examples are the elements indicating gender in a language like German. The *-er* of *d-er* in "der Bauer tötet das Entelein" (the farmer kills the duckling) relates *d-* to *Bauer* by agreement in number, gender, and case. It thus indicates that *d-* modifies *Bauer* and that *Bauer* is singular and subject of the sentence. It does this, however, with the material alloy of the indication of sex gender, in this case, masculine.

Such concepts are called by Sapir concrete-relational. Since we have four types of concepts, of which I and IV are necessary in all languages, but II and III are dispensable, we set up the following four classes of languages. Group A consists of those with I and IV only. These Sapir calls Simple Pure-Relational Languages, e.g., Chinese. Group B contains those with II as well as the indispensable I and IV. These are Complex (i.e., Deriving) Pure-

Relational Languages. Group C is constituted by languages which have I, III, and IV, but not II. These are Simple Mixed-Relational Languages. In Group D, finally, we have those languages which have all four types of concepts, i.e., Complex Mixed-Relational Languages. Of the two considerations, the presence or absence of II (derivational) and presence or absence of III (concrete-relational), Sapir considers the latter, which aligns types A and B versus C and D, as the more fundamental. In his final table of classifications, Sapir takes a number of languages and, employing the sets of criteria already discussed, first assigns a particular language to one of the "fundamental types" A, B, C, and D just mentioned. He likewise indicates degree of synthesis.

The third factor, technique, is specified separately for each of the groups of concepts II, III (when they are present), and IV, using the above mentioned scale: *a*, isolating; *b*, agglutinative; *c*, fusional; *d*, symbolic. Sapir often mentions two and sometimes three techniques. If weakly developed, he encloses the symbol in parentheses. He then gives an overall estimate of the dominant technique of the language, often using compound terms such as agglutinative-fusional to indicate roughly equal use of these two techniques. Note that Sapir does not use the term *inflectional* anywhere in his finished classification. He defines *inflection* as the use of fusional techniques in the sphere of syntactic relations. He believes that, so defined, it is not of sufficient importance to figure as a fundamental term in his classification. The presence of inflection is, therefore, indicated by the appearance of *c*, indicating fusion, or *c* and *d*, indicating fusion and symbolism, in association with the concepts of group III (mixed-relational). As an example of Sapir's total scheme, let us take his classification of Semitic. These languages are assigned as a group to D, i.e., complex-mixed relational languages with all four types of concepts present. They are synthetic. In the area of derivational concepts (II) the techniques are listed as *d*, *c*, in that order, i.e., symbolic and fusional. In the area of mixed-relational concepts (III) the techniques are given as *c*, *d*, fusional, symbolic. Under IV the technique is (*a*), isolation, i.e., significant word order, the parentheses indicating its weak development. There is finally an overall estimate of technique as symbolic-fusional.

The present method utilizes the Sapir classification in revised form. The basic criticisms of Sapir, already voiced by Most (1948: 183–90), boil down to two. The first and most significant is that in his classification into four basic types, Sapir seems to be talking about concepts, but in reality his test is a formal, not a semantic one, a fact which leads to some difficulties in exposition. For example, Sapir discusses the concept of the plural, which he considers highly abstract. However, it can be assigned anywhere along the scale I–IV in a particular language, as he points out. His test, then, as to whether the plural is a root concept (I), a derivational one (II), or relational (III or IV) depends upon which formal class a particular language assigns it to. Sapir recognizes this disparity. "It is because our conceptual scheme is a sliding scale rather than a philosophical analysis of experience that we cannot say in advance just where to put a given concept" (1921: 113). In the typology presented here, the approach is formal. It is recognized that there is, in fact, a tendency for meanings of root morphemes (Sapir's I) to be more concrete in meaning than derivational (Sapir's II) or inflectional morphemes (III or IV), but this is too vague to constitute a valid procedure. Here, as elsewhere in modern linguistics, we isolate our distinctive units by a formal, not a semantic, test for purely practical reasons. The second criticism relates to Sapir's scale: *a*, isolating; *b*, agglutinative; *c*, fusional; *d*, symbolic. Isolating is a technique of relating, as are the other devices, but applies almost only between words, relative order being rarely significant within the word. It is therefore out of place here, and this betrays itself in the asymmetry of its occurrence in Sapir's scheme, for it only appears as a technique under IV (pure relational concepts) and does not refer to relations within the word as with the other techniques, but between words.

The method of classification proposed here is fundamentally that of Sapir, with certain modifications in the light of these criticisms. Moreover in place of intuitive estimates based on overall impressions, an attempt is made to define each feature involved in this classification in terms of a ratio of two units, each defined with sufficient rigor and by the calculation of a numerical index based on the relative frequency of these two units over stretches of text. Five bases of classification are set up in place of Sapir's three, and a set of one or more indices is established to measure the place of any language in regard to each of them. The first of these parameters is the degree of synthesis or gross complexity of the word. Since Sapir's time the minimum meaningful sequence of phonemes in a language has come to be called the morpheme in American linguistics. For example, the English *sing-ing* contains two morphemes but forms one word. The ratio M/W where M equals morpheme and W equals word, is a measure of this synthesis and may be called the synthetic index. Its theoretical lower limit is 1.00, since every word must contain at least one meaningful unit. There is no theoretical upper limit, but in practice values over 3.00 are infrequent. Analytic languages will give low results on this index, synthetic higher, and polysynthetic the highest of all.

The second parameter refers to technique. At one extreme are languages in which the meaningful elements are joined with slight or no modification. This is the classic meaning of *agglutination*. The opposite phenomenon is reciprocal modification or merging of the elements. Actually a number of types of constructions can be distinguished, and thus a more subtle typology might be developed. For purposes of the present paper an alternative is selected which seems to correspond most closely to the intent of Sapir and of the usual nineteenth-century analyses. To use contemporary terminology, what is involved is the degree of morpho-phonemic alternation. The meaningful stretch actually found in an utterance is called a "morph." A number of related morphs are subsumed under a single fundamental unit, the morpheme. The various morphs are then said to be in alternation. For example, in English we relate the morph *lijf* ('leaf') with the morph *lijv-*, which only occurs with the plural morph *-z* to form *lijvz* ('leaves'). *Lijf* and *lijv-* are morphs which alternate within the same morphemic unit. The rules for the statement of this alternation belong to the morpho-phonemic section of the description of English. Where there are no variations among the constituent morphs of a morpheme or where the variations which exist are all automatic, the morpheme itself is said to be automatic. By an automatic alternation is meant one in which all the alternants can be derived from a base form by a set of rules of combination that holds in all similar instances throughout the language. This matter will be discussed in greater detail below. If both morphs in a construction belong to morphemes which are automatic, the construction is called agglutinative.

The index of agglutination is the ratio of agglutinative constructions to morph juncture. There is necessarily always one less morph juncture in a word than the number of morphs. Thus *leaves* has two morphs but one morph juncture. The index of agglutination is A/J, where A equals the number of agglutinative constructions and J equals the number of morpheme junctures. A language with a high value for this index will be agglutinational, one with a low value fusional. In general, the lower the first, or synthetic, index, the fewer the morph junctures which occur and the less the importance of this second index in characterizing the language. If a language reaches the theoretic lower limit of the synthetic index 1.00, this second index becomes impossible of calculation because no morpheme junctures occur; that is, the agglutinational index becomes 0/0, which is meaningless. In calculating this index the differences between the degree of agglutination which might be found in constructions involving Sapir's concepts of groups II, III, and IV and which, as we have seen, figures in Sapir's final formulation, have been ignored. Such indices might be calculated on the basis of the distinctions between root, derivational, and inflectional morpheme classes described below, since it is these features which correspond most closely to Sapir's division of concepts. They were not set up, partly in order to avoid too great over-all complications in the typology, partly because of the considerable labor involved in their calculation.

The third parameter corresponds most closely to what for Sapir was the most fundamental basis of classification in languages, the presence or absence of derivational and concrete-relational concepts. Since, as has been seen, an approach in terms of the meaning of concepts is too vague to handle with any degree of rigor, the present treatment is based on the possibility of the exhaustive division of morphemes into three classes, root, derivational, and inflectional. Every word must have at least one root morpheme and many words in many languages have no more. The existence of more than one root morpheme in a word is called compounding. This is a significant feature in which languages differ from each other considerably. There are languages which cannot compound at all, or only very sparingly. Others again compound freely, while most languages are somewhere between. It is remarkable that Sapir nowhere seems to take this into account in his typology. It can easily be measured by a compositional index R/W, where R equals number of root morphemes and W equals number of words. The second class of morphemes is the derivational. Examples of derivational morphemes in English are *re-* in *re-make*, *-ess* in *lion-ess*, *-er* in *lead-er*. The derivational index is D/W, the ratio of derivational morphemes to words. Languages with a high D/W will belong to Sapir's Complex or Deriving subtypes and will thus fit into classes B or D in his scheme. The inflectional morphemes are the third class. Examples in English are *-s* of *eats* and the *-es* of *houses*.

The inflectional index is I/W, i.e., the proportion of inflectional morphemes to words. This does not quite cover Sapir's concepts of type III (concrete relational), as will be shown. However, a language which has these concepts and so belongs to Sapir's mixed-relational types C and D necessarily has a fairly high value for the inflectional index; the inverse relation does not necessarily hold.

The fourth parameter refers to a topic discussed by Sapir as important for the morphological structure of a language but not included in his final formulation. This is the order of subordinate elements in relation to the root. The main distinction here is between the use of prefixes and suffixes. The prefixial index, P/W, is the ratio of prefixes to the number of words, and the suffixial, S/W, is the ratio of suffixes to the number of words. An index of infixing, that is, of the number of subordinate elements which are incorporated within the root could likewise have been calculated, but the occurrence of infixes was so rare in the particular languages investigated that it seemed justifiable to omit it. There are an indefinite number of further types of relative position of subordinate elements to the root, for example, containment, as in the Arabic imperfective prefix of the second person feminine which surrounds the verb morpheme, e.g., *taqtuli·*, 'thou (fem.) killest', in which the second person feminine morpheme is *ta----i·* while 'kill' is *-q-t-l* and 'imperfect tense' is *-u-*. There is likewise intercalation, again found in

Semitic, in which a portion of the subordinate element precedes or follows the root and another portion is incorporated. All these devices are so rare that, at least for the languages treated, it did not seem worth while to calculate indices. Sapir's symbolism, which he considers a kind of technique along with isolation, agglutination, and fusion, really belongs here. Sapir's symbolism or internal change is, in my opinion, simply the infixing of an inflective element, e.g., the preterite *-a-* in *sang*. When the elements are derivational, as in Indonesian languages, the process is usually called infixing. This brings out the fact that there are two distinct considerations involved in Sapir's use of the term symbolism, position and regularity. An infixing process might well be regular, in which case the construction would be agglutinative. In fact, though, this hardly ever occurs.

The final parameter has to do with the devices employed for relating words to each other. It therefore brings in syntactical as well as morphological considerations. There are three devices that languages may use, inflectional morphemes without concord, significant order, or concord (agreement).

Languages using the first two devices belong to Sapir's pure-relational category, while those using concord are mixed-relational. The inflectional index discussed above would include both nonconcordial and concordial inflectional morphemes. This index, which may be called the index of gross inflection, is therefore of limited use for the present problem. It might seem that by distinguishing between concordial and nonconcordial inflectional morphemes and by assigning the words without inflectional morphemes to the isolating class, it would be possible to make a clear threefold division. The extent of isolating, inflectional, and concordial techniques could then be calculated by three indices based on the ratio of each of these types to the total number of words. There are a number of complications that prevent such a simple procedure. Many languages, for example, Latin, merge concordial and nonconcordial features in the same inflectional morpheme. Thus, the *-um* of the Latin masculine accusative singular of adjectives has two concordial features, gender and number, and a pure inflectional one, case. In such cases, the procedure adopted is to count the same morpheme a number of times, one for each distinct feature. Another difficulty arises in regard to order. Order probably always has some value in relating elements even where inflection exists. We relate the accusative to the nearest verb even where the order is not fixed. Order may even be fixed although other means are present to indicate which words are in construction. This is largely true of German, for example. Significant order should perhaps be restricted to cases where a change of order produces a change of constructional meaning. The criterion employed was closest to this latter one, but easier of application. The absence of an inflectional morpheme in a word was taken as an indication that the method of relating it was order. If we call each instance of the use of a principle to indicate relations between words in the sentence a nexus, then three indices, O/N, Pi/N, and Co/N were calculated, where O = order, Pi = pure inflection, Co = concord, and N = nexus.

The following, in summary, are the typological indices which have been described: (1) M/W = index of synthesis; (2) A/J = index of agglutination; (3) R/W = compounding index; (4) D/W = derivational index; (5) I/W = gross inflectional index; (6) P/W = prefixial index; (7) S/W = suffixial index; (8) O/N = isolational index; (9) Pi/N = pure inflectional index; (10) Co/N = concordial index.

The validity of these indices assumes that we can define the units employed consistently and in such a manner that they may be applied to all languages. In fact, there is hardly one of the units employed in the above formulas which does not admit of a number of alternative definitions. The choices made here are dependent on the particular purposes of the study. We always ask what it is that we want to measure. In certain cases there seems to be no good reason for the choice of one alternative over the other from this point of view, and a purely arbitrary choice was made since some basis of decision had to be reached. It may be of some comfort to note that the theoretically wide range of choice of definitions for certain units only bore on decisions for a relatively small proportion of difficult instances. As evidence of this, the results of the indices calculated for a passage of 100 words of English in 1951, and arrived at by methods no longer fully recoverable by introspection, may be compared with indices for a 100-word passage done recently in accordance with the methods outlined here.

| | 1951 | 1953 |
|---|---|---|
| Synthesis | 1.62 | 1.68 |
| Agglutination | .31 | .30 |
| Compounding | 1.03 | 1.00 |
| Prefixing | 1.00 | 1.04 |
| Suffixing | .50 | .64 |
| Gross inflection | .64 | .53 |

It should be emphasized that other alternatives than those chosen here for the definition of units are equally possible and probably preferable for certain other purposes, for example, writing a grammar of a language.

In the following section the chief problems encountered in defining the units employed in the indices are discussed. These refer to the morph, the morpheme, agglutinative constructions, the distinction of root, derivational and inflectional morphemes, and the word. Nothing approaching an exhaustive treatment of the problems is attempted here. The purpose of the present discussion is merely to point out the chief problems encountered in this study and the reasons for the particular solutions which were adopted.

Basic to the synthetic index as well as most of the others is the possibility of segmenting any utterance in a language into a definite number of meaningful sequences which cannot be subject to a further division. Such a unit is called a morph. There are clearly divisions which are completely justified and which every analyst would make. For example, everyone would divide English *eating* into *eat-ing* and say that there were two units. There are other divisions which are just as clearly unjustified. For example, the analysis of *chair* into *ch-*, 'wooden object', and *-air*, 'something to sit on', would be universally rejected. There is, however, an intermediate area of uncertainty in which opinions differ. Should, for example, English *deceive* be analyzed into *de-* and *-ceive*? It is this intermediate area with which we must be able to deal. We start with a set of forms that will be hereafter called a square. A square exists when there are four meaningful sequences in a language which take the form AC, BC, AD, BD. An example is the English *eating* : *sleeping* :: *eats* : *sleeps*, where A is *eat-*, B is *sleep-*, C is *-ing* and D is *-s*.[2] Where a square exists with corresponding variation of meaning, we are justified in segmenting each of the sequences of which it is composed. Once it has been segmented, each of its segments may then be tested to discover if it also is a member of a square. If it is, it in turn will be segmented into two morphs. If it is impossible, then we have reached the limit of analysis and cannot divide further. A test of correspondence of meaning is applied to avoid such squares as *hammer* : *ham* :: *badger* : *badge*. A square conforming to these conditions described will always give us valid, generally acceptable analyses. It is too severe, however, in that it excludes some segmentations which everyone would want to accept. The first extension which we make is the following. A sequence which occurs with a member of a square is also recognized elsewhere if with regard to this member (a) the sequence of phonemes is identical except for automatic changes (for which see below) and (b) if the meaning is the same. On this basis we recognize a segmentation of *huckleberry* into *huckle* plus *berry*, since *berry* itself is a morph elsewhere. This leaves *huckle-* also as a morph although it never occurs in a square. If now *huckle-* were to occur in some other combination, we would recognize a segmentation there also and so add a new morph. This process is continued until we reach a sequence that does not recur in any other combination. In this instance we have reached it with *huckle-*.

[2]One of the four elements may be zero provided the sequences in which it occurs are free forms, i.e., may occur in isolation. For example, *hand* : *hands* :: *table* : *tables* is a valid square, in which A is *hand*, B is *table*, C is *zero*, and D is *-s*.

A further extension must be made in the case of what might be called a formally defective square. We should like to analyze *men* into two morphs, one with the meaning 'man' and the other 'plural', but there is no square into which it can be put. For example, *man* : *men* :: *boy* : *boys* is defective. We set up the following rule. If there can be found a square like the one just cited in which *boy* : *boys* itself is a pair in another valid square, e.g., *boy* : *boys* :: *lad* : *lads*, and if *man* may always substitute for *boy* and *men* for *boys* and produce a grammatical (even though at times semantically improbable) sentence, then *man* : *men* may be subjected to a segmentation analogous to that of *boy* : *boys*, and *men* may be considered two morphs. In the case of *sheep* : *sheep* :: *goat* : *goats* we recognize two morphs for the plural of sheep, one of which is a zero. Such analyses are not to be confused with segmentations into two or more semantic categories, where no valid square exists for substitution. In Latin, for example, we cannot analyze *-us* nominative singular into two morphemes, nominative and singular. The square *-us* : *ō* :: *ī* : *īs*—nominative singular : dative singular :: nominative plural : dative plural—does not have a pair which can be substituted for members of a formally perfect square, and hence the segmentation of these forms is not permitted. Corresponding to formally defective squares we have those which are semantically defective. Here, if there are parallel non-automatic variations, the analysis is permitted even though definite meanings cannot be assigned to the morphs. Thus, the sets *deceive* : *receive* :: *decep-tion* : *recep-tion* :: *decei-t* : *recei(p)t* justify the segmentations *de* + *ceive* and *re* + *ceive*. This rule permits the usual assumption of morphs for derived forms of the verb in Semitic. In view of the variety of meanings in instances of this kind, it would be difficult to operate without it.

There are certain extensions of the morph concept which are rejected here as inconsistent with the purposes of this study, although entirely legitimate for other purposes. No discontinuous morphs which contain segments in two different words are accepted. This is understandable, since we wish to measure the ratio of morphemes to words and we therefore want each word to contain a definite number of morphemes restricted to the word itself. We likewise do not include meaningful units simultaneous with grammatical stretches longer than the word, e.g., intonation patterns of the sentence. The reason again is clear. We wish morphemes to be parts of words and this they cannot be if they are simultaneous with an entire sequence of words. In this connection it should be noted that neither the index of synthesis nor any of the others utilized in the present study is a general measure of total complexity of a language. Intonational patterns and certain other items which contribute to the overall complication of a language are not included.

The next step to be taken after the identification of morphs is the establishment of more complex units, morphemes, with morphs as their members. It is this aspect of the problem which has been most frequently discussed in the literature as the chief subject matter of morphemic analysis by Harris, Hockett, Bloch, Nida, and others. In general, the principles set forth by Nida are adequate (1948: 414–41). These involve the generally recognized criteria of sameness of meaning (here applied strictly) and of complementary distribution and the requirement that if morphs of varying phonemic shape are to be assigned to the same morphemic unit, there must be at least one nonvarying unit with at least as wide a distribution.

On this point, however, for reasons to be explained, it is inadvisable to accept the complementations allowed by Nida in accordance with his rule that "complementary distribution in tactically different environments constitutes a basis for combining different forms into one morpheme only on the following condition: that some other morpheme—belonging to the same distribution class, and having either a single phonemic shape or phonologically defined alternant shapes—occurs in all the tactically different environments where the forms in question are found" (p. 421). For example, in Arabic there are pronominal suffixes indicating possession when added to the noun and another set indicating the verb object when added to the verb. These are tactically different: i.e., the verb in general could not be substituted for the noun or vice versa. The existence of *-ka*, 'second person singular masculine', and other phonemically identical forms in both series would, on the basis of Nida's rule, allow us to unite the morphs of the first person singular: *-ī* and *-ya*, noun possessive, and *-nī*, verb object, as constituent morphs of the same morpheme. This alternation is, of course, irregular and in reckoning our agglutinative index, if we accepted this alternative, we should have to call any construction involving one of the first person singular suffix forms irregular, or nonagglutinative. We should thus be penalizing Arabic, as it were, for some degree of regularity in these forms. In a language with two totally different sets of pronouns in these uses, Nida's rule would not allow complementation; hence there would be no irregular alternations from this source, although, on a common-sense basis, we should call this the more irregular situation. Hence only members of the same structural set, i.e., those substitutable for each other in the same tactical environment, are considered as possible alternants of the same morpheme.

Given certain morphs as alternants of the same basic morpheme units, we can define an agglutinative construction. It seems consistent with the traditional use of the term to consider its basic reference to be to morphological regularity. However, the term regular has been used in a number of different ways. In the discussions of Bloomfield, Wells, and others it is now usual to distinguish types and degrees of regularity and irregularity. The definition of regularity adopted here is that which appears to be closest to actual usage in typological discussion. This is the requirement that all the varying phonemic shapes of the morph be derivable from a nonfictive (i.e., actually occurring) base form by rules of combination which hold for all similar combinations throughout the language. This is usually called automatic alternation. The case of a morpheme which does not have alternating morphs, i.e., which involves the same phonemic sequence in all occurrences, is a limiting instance which is, of course, also reckoned as automatic. Sometimes one choice of a base form gives automaticity, i.e., predictability from base forms, while another does not. In cases of doubt those base forms are chosen which give the greatest degree of automaticity for the total description of the language. This is admittedly not a very precise rule, but in practice this does not prove to be a major difficulty.

We define automaticity as the property of the entire morpheme where every morph is in automatic alternation with every other. The morphs may often be grouped in subalternating sets. It is not sufficient for these to be in automatic alternation. The English plural morpheme has the statistically most frequent subset *-s -z -ez*, which are in automatic alternation. However, there are other alternants, e.g., *-en*, *-zero*, etc., which are not in automatic alternation with *-s -z -ez* as a whole. Hence the English plural morpheme is not automatic.

The possibility of calculating compounding, derivational, and inflectional indices depends on our ability to distinguish root, derivational, and inflectional morphemes. Of these the root class is probably the most difficult of formal definition, but the easiest of recognition. By this is meant that in actual practice, there is virtually complete agreement as to which morphemes are to be regarded as root morphemes. The root position in the word is characterized by a large and easily extendible membership and concreteness of meanings. The contrast with inflectional morphemes is greatest in these respects, since these latter tend to be few in number and relational as well as abstract in meaning. Another characteristic would generally be agreed on. Every word must have at least one root morpheme. Hence in a one-morpheme word, that morpheme is necessarily a root. In contrast, derivational and inflectional morphemes need not occur, and there are some languages, so-called root or isolating languages, in which derivational and inflectional morphemes are rare or perhaps do not occur at all. Derivational morphemes may be defined as morphemes which, when in construction with a root morpheme, establish a sequence which may always be substituted for some particular class of single morpheme in all instances without producing a change in the construction. If the class of single morphemes for which the derivational sequence may substitute contains one of the morphemes in the derivational sequence itself, we call the sequence endocentric; if not, then it is exocentric.

For example, *duckling* in English is a derivational sequence, since it may be substituted anywhere for *goose*, *turkey*, etc. without change of constructional meaning. Since *duck* is included in this class of single morphemes for which *duckling* may substitute, *-ling* is here an endocentric derivational morpheme. *Singer* is an exocentric sequence, since the class of single morpheme sequences for which *singer* may substitute consists of single-morpheme nouns only, and does not include the verb *sing*. Hence *-er* is an exocentric derivational morpheme.

We can now define the inflectional morpheme simply as a nonroot, nonderivational morpheme making the three classes exhaustive and mutually exclusive. Inflectional morphemes, like derivational, need not occur at all in any particular language. When one is part of a word pattern, however, its appearance in the appropriate position is compulsory like that of the root. One member of the class is frequently zero. In these instances, the absence of an overt phonemic sequence shows itself as significant because the word in this form has definite syntactic limitations on its uses, e.g., the nominative singular in Turkish or the noun singular in English.

We finally reach what is in some ways the most difficult problem, the definition of the word unit. It is clearly fundamental to the purpose of the present study inasmuch as all the indices involve the number of words. In most instances this is explicit; sometimes it is tacit, as in the index of agglutination, in which the number of morpheme junctures is always one less than the number of words. There is at present no general agreement on this topic. Some deny the validity of the word as a linguistic unit. Others admit it, but deny that it need be taken into account in the description of a particular language. Some say the word is definable only for each language in a separate *ad hoc* fashion. Some define it in phonological, others in morphological terms. In practice, however, the word continues to be the key unit of most actual language descriptions. Of the two basic types of overall definitions of the word, the phonological and the morphological, the former is clearly insufficient for the purposes of the present study. In phonological definitions, we define the word in terms of some single phonological characteristic, or through a combination of characteristics which serve as markers. These markers are usually stresses or boundary modifications of phonemes, i.e. junctures. Besides the fact that the use of phonological markers to define the word sometimes leads to the isolation of individual units which we should not wish to call words on other grounds, many languages do not have such phenomena, so that a phonological procedure cannot lead to a universal definition. The other basis has been called morphological, since it is based on the distribution of meaningful elements. Of definitions of this kind, Bloomfield's characterization of the word as the minimum free form is the most satisfactory in that it is universally applicable and points in the right direction to freedom or absence of freedom, that is, bondage as the basic criterion. The actual test of freedom, ability to occur in isolation, is, however, difficult to apply in practice and leads to unusual results. For example, *the* in English would not be a word by Bloomfield's test.

The procedure adopted here can only be briefly outlined. It has led to results satisfactory for this study in the relatively few doubtful cases regarding the existence or nonexistence of a word boundary in the languages under consideration. Instead of asking whether a particular minimal form is bound or free in general, as is usually done, the present treatment is in terms of morphs in particular contexts. This allows us, for example, in Latin to make *ab*, 'from', a free form as a preposition but a bound form as a verb prefix in *abduco*, 'I lead away'. What is specified as bound or free is not a morph as such but a contextually determined class of mutually substitutable morphs. Such a class is here called a morph substitution class (MSC). This notion is expanded to include a sequence of morpheme substitution classes which may in all circumstances be substituted for a particular MSC and none of whose members are identical in membership with it.[3] It is convenient to use the term *nucleus* to cover both individual MSC's and such substitutable sequences. Having broken up an utterance into nuclei in this manner, we now test each nucleus boundary to see if it is a word boundary or not. A nucleus boundary is a word boundary if it is possible to insert an indefinitely long sequence of nuclei. If it is an intraword boundary, either no nucleus can be inserted or a fixed maximum number can be. For example, in the sentence "the farmer killed the ugly duckling" there are nine morphemes: (1) the (2) farm (e) er (4) kill (5) ed (6) the (7) ugly (8) duck (9) ling; seven nuclei: (1) the (2) farmer (3) kill (4) ed (5) the (6) ugly (7) duckling; and six words: (1) the (2) farmer (3) killed (4) the (5) ugly (6) duckling. There is an intraword boundary at 'kill-ed' because no nucleus may be inserted. On the other hand at the boundary between 'farmer' and 'killed' there is no fixed maximum number of insertable nuclei. We may talk of the "farmer who killed the man who killed the man who . . . killed the ugly duckling." The contradiction with the phonological word is in certain cases merely apparent. Thus in Latin the

[3] This is necessary in order to exclude endocentric phrases in which a sequence of words can always be substituted for the head or chief number. A sequence of adjectives followed by a single-morph noun would be a nucleus were it not for the proviso of dependence among its members. Adjectives are not bound to nouns in English, for example, because they occur in predicative adjective constructions also. For the basic ideas of the MSC and the derivational sequence, I am largely indebted to the stimulus of the writings of Zellig S. Harris and Rulon S. Wells. The resemblance to the notions of focus class and expansion of the latter writer is particularly close. See especially R. Wells 1947: 81–117.

*Table 1*

| | Sanskrit | Anglo-Saxon | Persian | English | Yakut | Swahili | Annamite | Eskimo |
|---|---|---|---|---|---|---|---|---|
| Synthesis | 2.59 | 2.12 | 1.52 | 1.68 | 2.17 | 2.55 | 1.06 | 3.72 |
| Agglutination | .09 | .11 | .34 | .30 | .51 | .67 | ... | .03 |
| Compounding | 1.13 | 1.00 | 1.03 | 1.00 | 1.02 | 1.00 | 1.07 | 1.00 |
| Derivation | .62 | .20 | .10 | .15 | .35 | .07 | .00 | 1.25 |
| Gross inflection | .84 | .90 | .39 | .53 | .82 | .80 | .00 | 1.75 |
| Prefixing | .16 | .06 | .01 | .04 | .00 | 1.16 | .00 | .00 |
| Suffixing | 1.18 | 1.03 | .49 | .64 | 1.15 | .41 | .00 | 2.72 |
| Isolation | .16 | .15 | .52 | .75 | .29 | .40 | 1.00 | .02 |
| Pure inflection | .46 | .47 | .29 | .14 | .59 | .19 | .00 | .46 |
| Concord | .38 | .38 | .19 | .11 | .12 | .41 | .00 | .38 |

enclitic *-que*, 'and', which is reckoned as a syllable with any preceding sequence in locating the stress which serves as a phonological word marker, is also part of the word by the present test. *Dō'minus*, 'the lord', and *dō'minu's* in *dō'minu'sque*, 'and the lord', are not members of the same MSC because they are not substitutable for each other. *Dó'minu's-* belongs to the same nucleus as *legātu's-*, *pue'r*, and this class is dependent on the class of the following *-que*, *-ve* since it must be followed by it and hence belongs to the same word. Even with monosyllables, where there is no stress shift, *mū's*, 'mouse', and the *mūs* of *mū's-que*, 'and the mouse', are members of different nuclei, since the former can be substituted only by *dō'minus*, *pue'r*, etc., the latter only by the class of *dō'minu's-*, *pue'r-*.

Table 1 shows the calculated indices. The languages selected are chiefly those frequently cited as examples of specific types in the existing literature in typology, subject to the limitations of my own knowledge of specific languages. Instead of Turkish, the related Yakut was selected as an example of an agglutinating language, since the extensive Arabic borrowings in Osmanli Turkish have led to irregularities in the vowel harmony and in other respects to such an extent as to render it untypical. Two ancient Indo-European languages, Anglo-Saxon and Sanskrit, were chosen, and two modern languages of the same Germanic and Indo-Iranian branches, modern English and Persian, were also selected to illustrate long-term change in type. Annamite was selected as a representative root isolating language, Eskimo as polysynthetic, and Swahili as an agglutinative, concordial Bantu language.[4]

[4] The passages selected were 100 words long for each language, as follows: Sanskrit, *Hitopadeśa*, ed. Max Mueller, p. 5, *varam ekas*, ff.; Anglo-Saxon, *An Anglo-Saxon Reader*, J. W. Bright (New York 1917), p. 5, *hit gelamp gio*, ff.; Persian, I. Pizzi, *Chrestomathie Persane* (Turin, 1889), p. 107, *ruzi Ibrahimi*, ff.; English, *New Yorker*, December 13, 1952, p. 29, *Anyone who*, ff.; Yakut, *Über die Sprache der Yakuten* (St. Petersburg, 1851), p. 29, *min bäyäsä*, ff.; Swahili,

On the basis of counts such as these, the next step would be to define terms like analytic, synthetic, agglutinative, and prefixing after plotting a frequency distribution curve. There are too few languages here to make this procedure feasible. However, even cursory inspection of the indices set forth here shows that, if we define an analytic language as one with a synthetic index of 1.00–1.99, synthetic as 2.00–2.99, and polysynthetic as 3.00+, the results would conform to the usual nonquantitative judgments. Similarly we might call a language agglutinative if its agglutination index is over 0.50 and similarly for the others.

The present results should also be confirmed by further counts, since they were obtained only for single passages of 100 words each, besides which the probable error should be calculated for each. One might well suspect differences based on the style of the passages selected. The synthetic index was calculated in English and German for a number of passages of varying style, however, with remarkably concordant results.

| English | | German | |
|---|---|---|---|
| *Ladies' Home Journal*, Jan. 1950, p. 55 | 1.62 | Baumann, *Nama Folk-tale* | 1.90 |
| R. Linton, *Study of Man*, p. 271 | 1.65 | Ratsel, *Anthropogeographie*, p. 447 | 1.92 |
| O. J. Kaplan, *Mental Disorders in Later Life*, p. 373 | 1.60 | Cassirer, *Philosophie der symbolischen Formen*, p. 1 | 2.11 |

This, of course, is no substitute for statistical evaluation. Another topic that can be studied by the present method is the general direction of historical changes in language over an extended period. The coincidences between Sanskrit and Anglo-Saxon on the one hand, and Persian and English on the other hand, are striking. The direction of change for virtually every index is the same from the older to the more recent language. Were more conservative Indo-European languages such as the Slavonic chosen, the results might well be different.

The present study is to be evaluated as purely a preliminary attempt. Some indices may well have to be eliminated and others substituted. The specific definitional choices may likewise be subject to alternation in future studies. However, the general method of the calculation of indices based on text ratios

---

C. Sacleux *Grammaire Swahilie* (Paris, 1909), p. 321, *Kiyana mmoja*, ff.; Annamite, M. B. Emeneau, *Studies in Vietnamese (Annamese) Grammar* (Berkeley and Los Angeles, 1951), p. 226, *mot hom*, etc.; Eskimo, W. Thalbitzer in *Handbook of American Indian Languages*, Part I, ed. Franz Boas (Washington, 1911), p. 1066, *kaasasurujuŋuaq*, ff. (phonemicized and slightly normalized to conform to Kleinschmidt's grammatical description).

of carefully defined linguistic elements has, I believe, definite value for typological studies.

## References Cited

Humboldt, Wilhelm von. 1836. *Über die Verschiedenheit des menschlichen Sprachbaues*. Reprinted Darmstadt, 1949.
Mauthner, F. 1923. *Beiträge zu einer Kritik der Sprache*, 3rd ed., vol. 2. Leipzig.
Most, M. 1948. In *Actes du sixième Congrès International des Linguistes*. Paris.
Müller, M. 1890. *Lectures on the Science of Language*. New York (from 2nd London ed., rev.).
Nida, E. 1948. "The Identification of Morphemes," *Language*, vol. 24.
Sapir, E. 1921. *Language*. New York.
Schlegel, A. von. 1818. *Sur la littérature provençale*. (Printed as pp. 149–209 in vol. 2 of his collected French works, edited by Edouard Börking, Leipzig, 1846. The quoted passage occurs on p. 159 of this edition.)
Schlegel, F. von. 1808. *Über die Sprache und Weisheit der Indier*. Leipzig.
Wells, R. 1947. "Immediate Constituents," *Language*, vol. 23.
———. 1950. *The State and Prospects of Semantics*. Lithographed.
Whitney, William D. 1876. *Language and the Study of Language*, 5th ed. New York.

# The Nature and Uses of Linguistic Typologies

## 1. Preliminary Remarks

As contrasted with the other two main methods of linguistic classification, the areal and the genetic, typological procedures have tended to an uncertain and marginal status in linguistic science. In view of recent stirrings which appear to indicate renewed interest in typological procedures in linguistics as well as other fields, it seems appropriate to consider the general logic of typological classifications with particular reference to linguistics, to survey the kinds of linguistic typologies both potential and actual, and to evaluate the possible uses of typological analyses. This latter consideration is of particular importance in view of the common imputation of arbitrariness to typological as opposed to genetic classifications in linguistics.

It is of some interest to note that the term 'type' in the period prior to modern theories of evolution had a connotation opposite to arbitrariness to the highest possible degree. A type was a class sharing essential, not merely accidental, properties and was a true constituent of the very ground plan of the universe. With the appearance of evolutionary interpretations, however, the explanation of similarities as the result of common origin led to a new conception of classes, whether of species in biology or languages in linguistics, as groups whose members were connected through the historical process of generation. With these discoveries and the appropriation of the terms 'family', 'relationship', etc., in linguistics as the analogues of biological processes, only genetic classifications came to be considered as truly founded in the nature of things insofar as they reflected actual historical relationships. The word 'type', then, became a kind of relict applied to all classifications involving non-historical criteria and which therefore were, by their very nature, felt to be arbitrary. The one prominent attempt to apply typological criteria during the nineteenth century, the well-known classification of languages into isolating, agglutinative, and inflective in the attempt to avoid the charge of arbitrariness was either given an untenable evolutionary interpretation or fell into a basic confusion of typological and genetic considerations by the assertion, for example, that all agglutinative languages might be expected to be related.

In fields other than linguistics the meanings of the terms 'type' and 'typology' have been roughly similar to those just outlined for linguistics, and analogous problems arise regarding the formulation of non-arbitrary criteria for classification and the possible significance of typological resemblances. Such terms as 'feudal society', 'patrilineal land organization', 'industrial society', etc., refer to types of societies which may well occur in historically independent instances, and questions may be raised concerning the precision of the criteria utilized and the usefulness of comparing, for example, feudal China with feudal Europe. In similar fashion, archeologists have traditionally used designations such as Mousterian for implements of certain forms wherever they appear and regardless of chronology and presence or absence of concrete historical connections. Some discussions have emphasized the search for typological criteria which are non-arbitrary in the sense that they possess real historical implications, but it would appear that the prevailing use of the term in practice continues to be close, in principle, to its employment in linguistics.[1]

## 2. The Logic of Typological Classification

Any kind of classification involves the consideration of two factors: a set of entities which are to count as the individuals in the universe subject to classification, and one or more attributes in accordance with which each individual can be placed in a class or assigned a rank order or an absolute number as a measure of the extent to which the given individual possesses the attribute.

What is an individual for purposes of a particular classification must be defined in each instance. There are no absolute individuals, and what functions as an individual in one classification may function as a constituent of an individual or as a class of individuals in another classification. For example, in race classification we may take human beings or whole populations defined, perhaps, by geographical boundaries. In linguistics, the language is usually the individual entity figuring in classification, typological or otherwise; but as will appear later, there are other possibilities. A first requirement for

[1] The attempt to give historical significance to typological concepts in archaeology is especially marked in Alex Krieger, "The typological concept," *American Anthropologist* 9: 271–87 (1944), but archaeological terminological practice does not seem to coincide with Krieger's proposals.

rigor in any classification is the definition of the entities to be considered as individuals. Language, of course, is a somewhat vague term; but major difficulties do not seem to arise from this fact.

Attributes may be classified as predicates, comparative concepts, and numerical concepts.[2] Predicates are attributes whose presence in a given individual is susceptible of a yes-no answer. Logically, it is of predicate form, whence the name, e.g., *x* is red. We often encounter a number of predicates referring to the same attribute; for example, skin color in the early Blumenbach classification of races into black, brown, red, yellow, and white; but these are always logically restatable as choices between black and not-black, brown and not-brown, etc. It is this restatability which provides the logical basis for the contention that all linguistic predicates are binary.

A comparative concept is of the form *x* is ——er than *y*. Since it contains two variables, it is, from the logical point of view, a relation. A comparative concept gives rise to a serial order rather than a segregation into mutually exclusive classes. An example of a comparative concept is hardness in minerals. *X* is harder than *y* holds if and only if *x* scratches *y* and *y* does not scratch *x*. A numerical concept assigns to each individual a number as an expression of the degree to which the individual is invested with attributes. A common example is weight as given in pounds. It is clear that, other things being equal, numerical concepts are more exact than comparative concepts and comparative concepts more than simple predicates. If it is convenient, a numerical concept can be reduced to a comparative and a comparative one to a simple predicate, though with loss of information in each case. For example, '*x* weighs 12 pounds and *y* weighs 10 pounds' can be reduced to '*x* is heavier than *y*'. If we call a person weighing more than 200 pounds heavy, then the numerical concept of weight can be reduced to a choice between the simple predicates heavy and not-heavy.

In linguistics, comparative concepts do not play a significant role in typologies. The distinction between predicates and numerical concepts as attributes can be illustrated by Sapir's and Greenberg's morphological typologies, respectively. In the latter scheme certain reductions of quantitative to predicate attributes were suggested; for example, that the predicate polysynthetic be applied to a language if its index of synthesis is 3.00 or larger.

A further principle of classifying attributes leads directly to the distinction between typological and non-typological classifications. This principle

[2] For a discussion of these three kinds of attributes see C. G. Hempel and P. Oppenheim, *Der Typusbegriff im Lichte der Neuen Logik* (1936) and P. F. Lazarsfeld, "Some remarks on the typological procedures in social research," *Zeitschrift für Sozialforschung* 6: 119–39 (1937).

pertains to the manner in which distinct individuals may be said to be the same or similar with reference to a particular attribute. This aspect of classification will be called mode. There are three modes: the formal, the functional, and the processual. In the widest sense, the distinction between the formal and functional modes rests logically on the difference between internal and external attributes. This distinction can be illustrated by the following example. Let us suppose that a factory produces two implements of cast iron which are indistinguishable, not as yet having acquired any differences resulting from use, e.g., scratches or stains. By 'indistinguishable' is meant that an observer would not be able to tell them apart consistently. Let us say that one belongs to a consignment to be sent to Cleveland and the other to Chicago. These two pieces of iron at this point share all internal predicates, but one has the external predicate 'to be shipped to Chicago' but does not have the external predicate 'to be shipped to Cleveland', and the other piece of iron *vice versa*. Again, if one is being handled at time T by someone while the other is not, it will have the external predicate 'handled at time T'.

The classification of artifacts into cutting tools, scraping tools, etc., is based on external predicates involving relationships to other things and is therefore functional. Examples from biology would include a classification of species into fresh water, salt water, and land animals, and ecological classifications in general. In linguistics the predicates 'national', 'substandard', 'spoken by wavy-haired people' are all predicates in the functional mode. The term 'pidgin' as generally used is ambiguous, being applied partly because of internal properties, e.g., simplicity of morphological structure, and partly because of external properties, e.g., not being the first language of any population, used as an auxiliary means of communication. There is often, of course, some degree of causal connection between internal and external properties, which remains to be investigated, but the distinction between formal and functional classifications is, in general, a clear one. There may be cases in which what is first interpreted as an external predicate is later, with deeper knowledge, considered to be internal. For example, the fact that a person becomes involved in an automobile accident was generally regarded as an external property, but recent investigations tend to show that 'accident-prone' may be considered an internal property of certain persons.

The distinction between the formal and the processual modes involves two distinct methods of comparison, the difference between which is crucial in linguistics and certain other fields. In formal comparison a particular attribute is defined, and the individuals are assigned to the class depending on whether they have the attribute or not. It is thus a very straightforward procedure. If we compare processually, however, we do not demand formal coincidence in the properties used as criteria, but merely similarity. Such judgments of similarity are based on the possibility of the two individuals being plausible resultants of formally identical originals through differential changes. Therefore, although synchronic in appearance, such a comparison always involves theories concerning possible kinds of changes—that is, processes—and is implicitly diachronic. We may define typological, historical, and functional classification as involving formal, processual, and functional modes of comparison, respectively.

A particular attribute applied typologically may be called a typological criterion. By a typology, however, we usually indicate a "system" of distinct typological criteria, each of which involves a separate attribute in an attribute space. Thus, in various phonologic typologies, point of articulation and manner of articulation of consonants comprise two of the attributes in an attribute space in terms of which any consonant can be located. Traditional terminologies often imply elaborate, hitherto unanalyzed attribute spaces, usually vague and at points inconsistent in formulation. The process of discovering and reformulating in a more precise form the underlying attribute space of such an implicit typology has been called substruction.[3] In this sense the phonologic typologies of Trubetskoy, Hockett, and Voegelin are substructions of the rather vague terminology of traditional phonetics. In such a process another logical stage is sometimes reached in which the presence of certain relationships among the attributes themselves or classes of these attributes are employed as criteria. An example of the former is Trubetskoy's use of the term quadrangular and triangular for vowel systems and of the latter, some terms of Jakobson, Fant, and Halle's analysis; for example, grave and acute, each of which contains several classes which are distinct from the articulatory point of view.

Finally, we may distinguish language typologies in which the individuals of the universe to be typologized are languages, from linguistic typologies in general, of which they are a subclass. Ordinarily we are concerned with language typologies and other linguistic typologies; some of those which will be illustrated below would, perhaps, not be considered typologies in prevailing usage.

## 3. Linguistic Typologies

Starting, then, with language typologies, one principle of classification will refer to the above-mentioned division of attributes into predicates, comparative concepts, and numerical variables. Since comparative concepts in the case of linguistics hardly play a role, our fundamental distinction here will be between non-quantitative attributes (predicates) and quantitative attributes

[3] This is the term employed by Lazarsfeld (1937) and, following him, A. Barton, *The concept of property space in the language of social research* (Glencoe, Ill., 1955).

(numerical variables). Quantitative attributes, in turn, can be treated either on the basis of occurrences in the system (systemic) or in actual usage, e.g., texts (pragmatic). This is a general extension of the notion of lexicon vs. text frequency employed in studies of vocabulary frequency. Thus, to say that vowel-consonant ratio in Italian is 7 : 22 because there are seven vowels and twenty-two consonants in the phonologic system is a systemic quantitative statement, whereas to give the ratio of vowels to consonants in a text is a pragmatic quantitative statement. All typological criteria may be considered, then, to be non-quantitative, systemic quantitative, or pragmatic quantitative.

It is clear, also, that an important basis of classification has to do with the particular aspect of language with which we are concerned, for example, phonology or morphology. In fact, all typologies hitherto proposed have dealt only with a single aspect. It will prove convenient to distinguish six classes of typologies from this point of view: phonologic, morphologic, syntactic, those pertaining to canonic form, semantic, and symbolic.

The area of phonology, along with morphology, has been the most frequently treated from a typological point of view. The most common approach stems from Trubetskoy and is based on the presence or absence of certain phonetic features as principles of phonemic distinction in particular languages. Thus a comprehensive system such as that of Jakobson, Fant, and Halle would assign every language in the world to one of a maximum of $2^n$ typological classes, where $n$ is the number of principles of binary opposition enumerated. Actually, fewer than $2^n$ classes occur because the use of certain binary oppositions excludes that of certain others.

Non-quantitative typologies based on phoneme sequences are likewise possible and are implied by the common use of such terms as open syllable, closed syllable, consonant cluster, etc. Thus languages can be classified according to the syllable types or consonantal and vocalic sequences which occur. One simple scheme would divide languages into those which always have an initial non-peak consisting of one phoneme only, and those which allow clusters in this position, and as the second axis of classification those which permit phonemes after the peak and those which do not. Yokuts and Classical Arabic would then belong to the same class, since in both languages every syllable contains a single non-peak, and a maximum of one phoneme is allowed after the peak within the syllable.

An example of a systemic quantitative phonologic typology is the measurement of degree of symmetry of a sound system by calculating the ratio of combinations of sound features utilized to the total combinational possibilities of the phonemic system, as suggested by Saporta.[4] Here belong also measures of vowel-consonant ratio based on occurrence in the system.

[4] Sol Saporta in C. E. Osgood and T. A. Sebeok, eds., *Psycholinguistics* (Bloomington: Indiana University Publications, Anthropology and Linguistics, 1954).

The foregoing systemic typologies have pragmatic counterparts based on text counts. The consonant-vowel ratio is a simple instance of such a typological criterion. It is also possible to count the relative frequency of different syllable types or of phoneme sequences based on comparable features in different languages. After compiling frequency data for phonemes or phoneme sequences, it is possible to measure the entropy of the system and thus compare various languages from the point of view of entropy or economy in the use of the system of phonemes and phoneme sequences.[5]

Morphologic typologies, the next to be considered, have employed criteria based on the internal structure of the word. Thus the traditional nineteenth-century typology considered such factors as the number of morphemes in the word and the existence or absence of irregular morphophonemic alterations, though without explicit statement. Sapir's discussion is essentially an attempt to define and reformulate in a more precise manner the implicit attribute space. Sapir's use of phrases such as "slightly polysynthetic" and "strongly fusional" comes nearest to a comparative concept found anywhere among linguistic typologies and, in so doing, replaces the nineteenth-century predicate attributes by which languages were, for example, either analytic or synthetic but not more or less so. My typology is a pragmatic quantitative approach using Sapir's attribute space with some modification. A systemic quantitative approach is also possible for some of these indices, for example, the agglutinative; a comparison of the results of such an approach with corresponding pragmatic indices would be of interest in showing the manner in which the morphological resources of a language are employed in actual practice.[6]

Some of Sapir's categories and the corrresponding indices in Greenberg's treatment skirt the borderline of syntax, e.g., the indices of concord and gross inflection. There are several possible types of a purely syntactic nature. One is the measurement of the degree of freedom of word order. One might take each word and consider it free or bound, depending upon whether it could be moved to another part of the sentence, other things being held constant, without changing the construction. The relative order of modifier and modified can also be considered by both quantitative and non-quantitative means. This particular feature has been employed by Bally in his contrasting typological characterizations of French and German.[7]

A further area of research is possible in the domain of word classes. If

[5] An example is written English in C. E. Shannon and W. Weaver, *The mathematical theory of communication* (Urbana: University of Illinois Press, 1949).

[6] This problem is raised in regard to Yokuts in Stanley Newman, "Semantic problems in grammatical systems and lexemes: A search for method in language in culture," in *Conference on the Interrelations of Language and Other Aspects of Culture. Language in Culture*, ed. H. Hoijer (University of Chicago Press, 1954): 82–91.

[7] C. Bally, *Linguistique générale et linguistique française*, 2nd ed. (Berne: Francke, 1944).

objective cross-linguistically valid definitions could be developed, then languages might be classified by the presence or absence of particular classes. At present, essentially typological judgments of an imprecise nature are made in this regard. If, for example, there are languages without distinct noun and verb classes, which is subject to real doubt, then these languages would form a typological class against those that make the distinction. Similarly, there are said to be languages in which adjectives are absent as a class. Another type of study is that of relative word frequencies such as those conducted by Zipf. These, like some of the above-mentioned morphologic studies, lead to measures of entropy.

For want of an existing term, Hockett's phrase "canonic form" is here extended to all studies dealing with the phonemic make-up of grammatical units. The phonemic structure of morphemes, for which Hockett has employed this term, constitutes one subdivision of this general field. The triliteralism of Semitic root morphemes and the pattern of Penutian disyllabic roots with identical vowels in both syllables are examples of canonic form in Hockett's sense. Menzerath and his collaborators have developed this subdivision of typological studies.[8] Number of phonemes per morpheme or number of phonemes per word are possible subjects of investigation employing either pragmatic or systemic quantitative methods.

With more specific reference to the phonetic characteristics of the phonemes, we may have typological criteria by which languages are classified as having or not having vowel or consonantal harmony of particular types. An example of a systemic quantitative study here is my study of the patterning of root morphemes in Semitic and related languages.[9] Using the syllable as a phonologic unit, the traditional term "monosyllabic language" implies a quantitative ratio between number of syllables to words either pragmatically or systematically. These are but a few of the actual and possible types of study in the area of canonic form.

In semantic typologies we consider certain meaning categories and examine the varying methods by which languages express these meanings. An obvious instance is numerical systems. The classification of languages according to whether their terminology of numerals has a binary, quinary, decimal, duodecimal, or some other base is an example of a semantic typological procedure. Likewise, kinship systems may be analyzed by componential procedures as suggested by Lounsbury and then compared typologically.[10]

[8] P. Menzerath, "Typology of languages," *Journal of the Acoustic Society of America* 22: 698–700 (1950); P. Menzerath and W. Meyer-Eppler, *Sprachtypologische Untersuchungen I.* (Lund, 1950).

[9] J. H. Greenberg, "Patterning of root morphemes in Semitic," *Word* 6: 162–84 (1950).

[10] F. G. Lounsbury, "A Semantic Analysis of the Pawnee Kinship Usage," *Language* 32: 158–94 (1956).

Quantitative methods in this area are probably not feasible at the present time and perhaps would not accomplish anything not more easily attainable by purely qualitative methods. However, comparative concepts may here prove of some value. Thus one might want to be able to state that one language has a more elaborate and specialized vocabulary pertaining to zoological terms than another. Another area to be explored is comparative metaphor. For example, one might use a standard set of directional terms (above, below, in back of, etc.), and compare the extent to which languages utilize terms derived from body parts to express these ideas. Here a comparative scale, or even a systemic quantification, seems possible. Still another subject of investigation is semantic vagueness and homonymy. Is it true that certain languages tolerate more homonymy than others? Vagueness might be measured for certain terms by tests in which a series of objects more and more unlike the average specimen of a class and tending towards a class designated by another term are presented to subjects to be named. The degree of intersubjective agreement and uncertainty can then be measured.[11] If one took a set of roughly equivalent terms for a number of different languages, a measure of average vagueness for each language could be calculated. There are, of course, many difficulties still to be overcome in investigations of this sort, but a beginning has already been made with color terms.[12] The writer's a priori expectation would be that no significant differences among languages would appear in this respect, but doubtless some genetically oriented psychologists would expect otherwise and would offer an evolutionary interpretation by which more "primitive" languages would be expected to show greater areas of vagueness. A related problem is the extent of generic terms as opposed to specific terms in certain areas of lexicon for which no satisfactory procedure of measurement has as yet been suggested.

Thus far all criteria considered have involved sound without meaning or meaning without sound. Indeed it would be possible in practice to define typologies for linguistics on this basis since, typically, it is comparison of this kind which, by its disregard of one or the other factor, is, in general, without historical implications and which provides a conveniently small set of typological classes. Thus, if languages in a phonological typology are called similar if they employ phonemes of tone, that is, are assigned to a class of tonal languages in disregard of the meanings of the forms in which the tones figure, then only two classes of language result. If we specify the phonemes of tones as level or contour in addition, only four classes result; in this case

[11] Max Black, *Language and Philosophy* (Ithaca, N.Y.: Cornell University Press, 1949). See particularly pp. 52–53.

[12] E. H. Lenneberg and J. M. Roberts, *The language of experience* (Bloomington: Indiana University Publications, Anthropology and Linguistics, 1956).

we have: (1) non-tonal, (2) level tones, (3) contour tones, (4) both level and contour tones. Even if we elaborate further, the number of classes will be small, and membership in the same typological class will have no necessary historical implications. Likewise, a purely semantic classification of languages into those which employ body part metaphors for spatial relations and those which do not, will involve meaning without sound since we will not consider the phonemic sequences by which the body-part terms are characterized. On the other hand, were we to classify languages into those which expressed the notion of 'dog' by the phoneme sequence /dɔg/, those which expressed it by /kane/, etc., we would arrive at thousands of classes and membership in the same class would have historical implications. A somewhat transitional zone is constituted by comparisons involving order and meaning. Order is a formal principle but its possibilities of variations are few. Thus the fact that two languages both express pronominal subjects by a prefix to the verb has relatively insignificant historical implications and leads to a viable typology with a small number of classes. One might therefore define a typological criterion in language as one that does not employ sound and meaning simultaneously. However, apart from the fact that such a definition tends to obscure the points of contact between typology in linguistics and in other subject matters, it excludes at least one possible type of classification to be discussed shortly, the symbolic, which would be generally felt to be typological in nature. This possibility arises as follows: As we reduce the specificity of the requirements of phonetic resemblance of the form expressing some particular meaning, we diminish the historical significance of the resemblance and by the same token reduce the number of possible types producing a more usable typological criterion. For example, we put all languages which have a nasal consonant in the word for 'mother' in the same class. The clustering of a large number of languages in this typological class is a manifestation of what is usually called sound symbolism. A typology emerges when a sound symbolic connection has been determined in this manner for the equivalents of a number of concepts. A language may then be called more or less symbolic depending on the extent to which it belongs to the classes with the largest membership. All this represents a somewhat arduous procedure which has never yet been carried out in practice to this writer's knowledge. As with measures of semantic vagueness, certain psychologists would expect significant differences among languages in this regard, the more "primitive" languages showing a higher degree of symbolism.

All the possibilities considered thus far have been language typologies as defined above; namely, typologies in which the individuals to be classified are languages. There is at least one possible typological area, however, in which diachronic changes rather than languages might figure as individuals. One talks of types of linguistic change, particularly phonetic change, and the usual terminology of conditioned change, unconditioned change, assimilatory change, dissimilatory change, etc., implies a typology. A class of diachronic changes based on conformity to the same typological criteria is usually called a process. Such typologies might be qualified also as diachronic as opposed to all those previously mentioned which are synchronic. Here again, although the individuals themselves are historical changes, membership in the same typological class involves no necessary historical connection among the changes themselves. For example, the Chwana languages in South Africa have undergone a series of consonantal shifts remarkably parallel to those described by Grimm's law for Germanic but obviously in a historically independent manner. Diachronic typologies are subject to much the same divisions as synchronic typologies: phonological, morphological, syntactic, semantic, canonic form, but probably not symbolic which, as has been seen, stands apart from the other categories in that it involves sound and meaning simultaneously.

## 4. Use of Typologies

The foregoing review is, of course, far from exhaustive. Moreover, it is realized that many of the types of studies discussed or suggested would not usually be called typological. Insofar as all of them involve comparison in which historical significance is entirely lacking or indifferent to the purpose of the study they exhibit a certain unity and the term typological seems the most suited by traditional usage to designate them in an overall way. For the most part, also, they involve individual typological criteria rather than a comprehensive typology defined by a significant attribute space. The application of individual criteria can be looked upon as a preliminary step to the development of full-fledged typologies in such instances.

The establishment of typological criteria sufficiently rigorous for application has a certain incidental usefulness, which is nevertheless of some importance for linguistics. In effect every descriptive scheme is typological and the very notion that the techniques of descriptive linguistics can be taught and can be employed on new and hitherto unknown languages requires the use of criteria, non-historic in their nature, which can be applied to any language. This is a commonplace in phonology, where terms such as stop consonant, vowel, etc. are employed cross-linguistically and automatically define typological criteria. In other areas of description, however, this is only partially the case. There is perhaps even the feeling that parts of speech and such units as the morpheme and the word involve different procedures for each language and are therefore not comparable. The application of typological criteria and the ultimate development of rigorous typologies in these areas has therefore the heuristic value of stimulating us to seek for cross-linguistically valid definitions and procedures.

It should be noted that this does not involve imposing on any language a set of descriptive categories which do not conform to the facts of the language. We distinguish between the procedure and the results of the application of the procedure in individual instances. Thus the fact that there are universally applicable definitions of what is a vowel and for defining phonemes does not lead to the analytic result that all languages have the same phonemic vowel system nor would it prevent us from saying that a particular language has no vowels if such a language were to be discovered. In the same way it is clear that terms like *adjective*, *word*, and *phrase* are of universal significance but that we are here usually far less clear about what they have in common in diverse instances than is the rule for phonological concepts. But the delineation of such procedures is forced upon us in typological work if languages are to be validly compared in these respects.

The formulation and application of individual typological procedures has a further value in that non-random distribution of languages among typological classes or in respect to quantitative attributes leads to the discovery of facts of universal scope concerning language and such facts constitute linguistic data of general significance for psychology, logic, physiology, and perhaps other fields. For example, a typological study of subject, object, and verb word order would doubtless show a non-random membership of languages in reference to the six logically possible arrangements and constitute a fundamental datum on the psychology of human thinking. It has been suggested in tentative fashion that the apparent predominance of suffixing over prefixing can be understood in the light of certain results of learning theory in psychology.[13] The frequency of types of vowel phonemic systems with only one low vowel and the rarity of such systems for mid and high vowels has physiological correlates. The index of synthesis based on text counts of morpheme-word ratios has a normal distribution about a mean of approximately 2.2; this is again a fundamental though as yet unexplained datum regarding human speech behavior.[14] Again, in diachronic typologies the prevalence of anticipatory regular change over lag phenomena can be plausibly connected with certain well-known results of learning theory in psychology. These are but a few examples of possible results which may accrue from the widespread application of individual typological criteria.

[13] Osgood and Sebeok, eds., *Psycholinguistics* (1954).

[14] J. H. Greenberg, "A quantitative approach to the morphological typology of language," in *Method and perspective in anthropology*, ed. R. Spencer (Minneapolis, 1954).

A further step, as has been already noted, is the simultaneous application of a set of individual criteria, a process which can be conveniently conceptualized in terms of a multidimensional attribute space. The attributes will presumably be chosen in that they represent closely related aspects of the same general class of phenomena which may reasonably be expected to reveal significant mutual connections. The number of typological classes is in general larger, of course, for typologies than for individual criteria and consists of the product of the number of classes for each individual criterion. Here again, non-chance distribution of memberships in the various classes or, in quantitative typologies, significant positive or negative correlations among indices constitute significant data which require explanation. Unlike those mentioned above in the case of individual criteria, non-random distribution of languages among typological classes suggests in the first instance a connection among linguistic traits themselves, but such relationships may ultimately require explanation by reference to non-linguistic psychological, logical, or other factors. To illustrate, the presumed lesser frequency of prefixing as opposed to suffixing was mentioned above. It has been further suggested not only that prefixing is less frequent but that it is more irregular than suffixing. This would manifest itself in a multidimensional typology by the rarity of prefixing-agglutinating languages as compared with prefixing-fusional. Likewise, Schmidt's contention that there are languages which in general put the modifier before the modified and others which place the modified before the modifier[15] is in effect a multiple series of suggestions of the form: If in a given language the adjective is placed before the noun, it is likely with more than chance probability that adverbs are placed before the verb, etc.

In all these cases, then, we have a clustering of certain combinations of attributes while for others few or no languages exist which exhibit the combinations in question. In such instances a few salient types may emerge by a process discussed by Lazarsfeld under the name of reduction.[16] This can be accomplished by merging similar classes and disregarding classes with extremely small membership.

Finally, typologies can be utilized as a tool in the study of changes of types. In the nineteenth century, morphological typology was generally connected in the minds of its adherents with a universal evolutionary scheme of change of type from isolating to agglutinative to inflective. There was even an attempt by Max Müller at one time to connect these three types with hunting, pastoral, and agricultural stages of economy, respectively, an assertion not repeated in later writings or accepted by any other writer. The

[15] W. Schmidt, *Die Sprachfamilien und Sprachenkreise der Erde* (Heidelberg, 1926).

[16] P. F. Lazarsfeld, "Some remarks on the typological procedures in social research," *Zeitschrift für Sozialforschung* 6: 119–39 (1937).

question here raised does not concern such unilineal schemes but rather a careful study of changes of type in order to establish what limitations in the successions of types exist. Such knowledge clearly adds to our understanding of linguistic historical change and our predictive power since from a given synchronic system certain developments will be highly likely, others have less probability, and still others may be practically excluded.

The obvious method to be employed is the typological comparison of the same language at different chronological periods and the comparison of genetically related languages. The first results of such comparison in the latter case is a test of the phenomena of drift, or similar changes in related languages. Where the indices are quantitative a measure of this drift becomes possible. For example, in my morphological typology, for all of the ten indices changes in the same direction occur for Sanskrit-Persian and Anglo-Saxon-English. Additional unpublished data made available by Samuel Martin show the same results for Latin-French. The comparison of historically independent cases in different parts of the world would show whether there are overall tendencies in such matters or whether this is an Indo-European peculiarity.

# Some Universals of Grammar with Particular Reference to the Order of Meaningful Elements

## 1. Introduction

The tentative nature of the conclusions set forth here should be evident to the reader. Without much more complete sampling of the world's languages, the absence of exceptions to most of the universals asserted here cannot be fully assured. As indicated by the title, attention has been concentrated largely, but by no means exclusively, on questions concerning morpheme and word order. The reason for this choice was that previous experience suggested a considerable measure of orderliness in this particular aspect of grammar. In the body of this paper a number of universals are proposed. A large proportion of these are implicational; that is, they take the form, "given $x$ in a particular language, we always find $y$." When nothing further is said, it is understood that the converse, namely, "given $y$, we always find $x$," does not hold. Where the two sets of characteristics are binary, the typical distribution in a tetrachoric table is a zero as one of the four entries.[1] From the point of view of scientific methodology, there is nothing to apologize for in such results, and this is so for two reasons. First, the lowest-level laws as described in manuals of scientific method take precisely this form.[2] Second, what seem to be nonimplicational universals about language are in fact tacitly implicational since they are implied by the definitional characteristics of language.[3] Further, to assert the definitional characteristics themselves is obviously tautologous.

[1] I am indebted to the work of Roman Jakobson for directing my attention to the importance of implicational universals. I would also like to thank Fred Householder and Charles F. Hockett for making helpful critical comments on the earlier version of this paper.

[2] See, for example, the remarks of R. B. Braithwaite, *Scientific Explanation* (Cambridge, Eng., 1953), concerning scientific laws. "The one thing upon which everyone agrees is that it always includes a generalization, i.e., a proposition asserting a universal connection between properties" (p. 9).

[3] That is, empirically, not logically, implied. All languages are observed to have the characteristics in question. It should be added that universals in the sense of nondefinitional

It is perhaps worthwhile to point out that a number of universals of the second type—that is, those implied by the definitional characteristics of language—although not usually formally stated in this paper, are in fact involved in the notion of the general comparability of languages in the grammatical sphere which underlies the specific statements found here. For example, a whole series of universals in the usual sense are assumed in such a statement as the following: If a language has verb-subject-object as its basic word order in main declarative clauses, the dependent genitive always follows the governing noun. It is here assumed, among other things, that all languages have subject-predicate constructions, differentiated word classes, and genitive constructions, to mention but a few. I fully realize that in identifying such phenomena in languages of differing structure, one is basically employing semantic criteria. There are very probably formal similarities which permit us to equate such phenomena in different languages. However, to have concentrated on this task, important in itself, would have, because of its arduousness, prevented me from going forward to those specific hypotheses, based on such investigation, which have empirical import and are of primary interest to the nonlinguist. Moreover, the adequacy of a cross-linguistic definition of 'noun' would, in any case, be tested by reference to its results from the viewpoint of the semantic phenomena it was designed to explicate. If, for example, a formal definition of 'noun' resulted in equating a class containing such glosses as 'boy', 'nose', and 'house' in one language with a class containing such items as 'eat', 'drink', and 'give' in a second language, such a definition would forthwith be rejected and that on semantic grounds. In fact, there was never any real doubt in the languages treated about such matters. There is every reason to believe that such judgments have a high degree of validity. If, for example, someone were to dispute the specific assignment of order type of a genitive construction given in this paper, it is quite clear on what evidence such an assignment would be accepted or rejected.

For many of the statements in this paper, a sample of the following 30 languages has been utilized: Basque, Serbian, Welsh, Norwegian, Modern Greek, Italian, Finnish (European); Yoruba, Nubian, Swahili, Fulani, Masai, Songhai, Berber (African); Turkish, Hebrew, Burushaski, Hindi, Kannada, Japanese, Thai, Burmese, Malay (Asian); Maori, Loritja (Oceanian); Maya, Zapotec, Quechua, Chibcha, Guarani (American Indian).

This sample was selected largely for convenience. In general, it contains languages with which I had some previous acquaintance or for which a reasonably adequate grammar was available to me. Its biases are obvious,

characteristics, if found only in language, do have the additional logical property of implying as well as being implied by the definitional properties.

although an attempt was made to obtain as wide a genetic and areal coverage as possible. This sample was utilized for two chief purposes. First, it seemed likely that any statement which held for all of these 30 languages had a fair likelihood of complete or, at least, nearly complete universal validity. Second, less reliably, it serves to give some notion of the relative frequency of association of certain grammatical traits. In this respect, of course, it is not to be taken literally. On some questions, I have gone well outside the sample.

The main section of the paper, which follows, is concerned with the establishment of universals on the basis of the empirical linguistic evidence. These are presented with a minimum of theoretical comment. The final section is exploratory, seeking to discover what general principles may exist from which at least some of the generalizations of the earlier sections might be deduced. For convenience of exposition, the universals scattered through the text are repeated for cross reference in Appendix III. The theoretical section is far more speculative and uncertain than the sections devoted to the universals themselves. In a certain sense we would prefer to have as few universals as possible, not as many. That is, we would like to be able to deduce them from as small a number of general principles as possible. However, the establishment of a relatively large number of empirical generalizations must, on the whole, come first. For one thing, it would be embarrassing to deduce a particular universal from what seemed like a valid general principle, only to discover that the generalization was not empirically valid.

## 2. The Basic Order Typology

Linguists are, in general, familiar with the notion that certain languages tend consistently to put modifying or limiting elements before those modified or limited, while others just as consistently do the opposite.[4] Turkish, an

[4] Some of the ideas regarding the basic order typology are found in nineteenth-century linguistic literature. For example, the relation between genitive position and prepositions versus postpositions and the hypothesis that some languages favor the order modifier-modified and others the opposite order is already a familiar notion in R. Lepsius' introduction to his *Nubische Grammatik* (Berlin, 1880).

The most systematic treatment is that of W. Schmidt in *Die Sprachfamilien und Sprachenkreise der Erde* (Heidelberg, 1926) and in several other works. Schmidt's basic conclusions may be summarized here. Prepositions go with nominative-genitive order and postpositions with the reverse order. The nominative-genitive order tends to appear with verb before nominal object and genitive-nominative with object-verb. Schmidt says nothing of subject-verb order so that types I and II as treated in this paper are not distinguished. Further, nominative-genitive is associated with noun-adjective and genitive-nominative with adjective-noun. This last correlation, particularly the latter half, is much weaker than the others. Schmidt gives figures based on a world sample which show good general agreement with the results

example of the former type, puts adjectives before the nouns they modify, places the object of the verb before the verb, the dependent genitive before the governing noun, adverbs before adjectives which they modify, etc. Such languages, moreover, tend to have postpositions for concepts expressed by prepositions in English. A language of the opposite type is Thai, in which adjectives follow the noun, the object follows the verb, the genitive follows the governing noun, and there are prepositions. The majority of languages, as for example English, are not as well marked in this respect. In English, as in Thai, there are prepositions, and the noun object follows the verb. On the other hand, English resembles Turkish in that the adjective precedes the noun. Moreover, in the genitive construction both orders exist: 'John's house' and 'the house of John'.

More detailed consideration of these and other phenomena of order soon reveals that some factors are closely related to each other while others are relatively independent. For reasons which will appear in the course of the exposition, it is convenient to set up a typology involving certain basic factors of word order. This typology will be referred to as the basic order typology. Three sets of criteria will be employed. The first of these is the existence of prepositions as against postpositions. These will be symbolized as Pr and Po, respectively. The second will be the relative order of subject, verb, and object in declarative sentences with nominal subject and object. The vast majority of languages have several variant orders but a single dominant one. Logically, there are six possible orders: SVO, SOV, VSO, VOS, OSV, and OVS. Of these six, however, only three normally occur as dominant orders. The three which do not occur at all, or at least are excessively rare, are VOS, OSV, and OVS. These all have in common that the object precedes the subject. This gives us our first universal:

> *Universal 1.* In declarative sentences with nominal subject and object, the dominant order is almost always one in which the subject precedes the object.[5]

This leaves us with three common types: VSO, SVO, and SOV. These will be symbolized as I, II, and III, respectively, reflecting the relative position of the verb.

The third basis of classification will be the position of qualifying adjectives (i.e., those designating qualities) in relation to the noun. As will be seen later,

---

from the thirty-language sample utilized here. It should be added that Schmidt's chief interest in this topic is as a vehicle for the interpretation of culture history. His results there verge on the fantastic.

[5] Siuslaw and Coos, which are Penutian languages of Oregon, and Coeur d'Alene, a Salishan language, are exceptions.

*Table 1*

| | I | II | III |
|---|---|---|---|
| Po-A | 0 | 1 | 6 |
| Po-N | 0 | 2 | 5 |
| Pr-A | 0 | 4 | 0 |
| Pr-N | 6 | 6 | 0 |

the position of demonstratives, articles, numerals, and quantifiers (e.g., 'some', 'all') frequently differs from that of qualifying adjectives. Here again there is sometimes variation, but the vast majority of languages have a dominant order. Dominant order with adjective preceding noun will be symbolized by A and dominant order with noun preceding adjective by N. We thus arrive at a typology involving 2 × 3 × 2, that is, twelve logical possibilities. The 30 languages of the sample are distributed among these twelve classes as shown in Table 1.[6]

The table has been arranged so that the 'extreme' types Po-A and Pr-N are in the first and fourth row, respectively. It is evident that with respect to these extremes, I and III are polar types, the former being strongly correlated with Pr-N and the latter with Po-A. Type II is more strongly correlated with Pr-N than with Po-A. It is also clear that adjective position is less closely related to types I, II, and III than is the Pr/Po contrast. The table is, I believe, a fair representation of the relative frequency of these alternatives on a world-wide basis. Type II is the most frequent; type III almost as common; type I is a definite minority. This means that the nominal subject regularly precedes the verb in a large majority of the world's languages.

Turning for a moment to genitive order, we note that this characteristic might fittingly have been utilized for typological purposes. The reason for not employing it is its extremely high correlation with Pr/Po, a fact generally known to linguists. It would thus virtually have duplicated the latter criterion. It was not chosen because Pr/Po on the whole is slightly more highly correlated with other phenomena. Of the present sample of 30 languages, 14 have postpositions, and in every one of these the genitive order is genitive followed by governing noun. Of the 16 prepositional languages, 15 have the genitive following the governing noun. In Norwegian, the genitive may precede or follow. Thus, 29 of the 30 cases conform to the rule. If anything, 1/30 is an overestimation of the proportion of exceptions on a world-wide basis. We therefore have the following universal:

[6]The manner in which each language has been assigned can be determined from the data of Appendix I.

*Universal 2*. In languages with prepositions, the genitive almost always follows the governing noun, while in languages with postpositions it almost always precedes.

Turning once more to the data of Table 1, we find striking evidence of lawful relationships among the variables in that of the 12 possibilities 5, or almost half, are not exemplified in the sample. All of these types are either rare or nonexistent.[7] For type I, we see that all 6 languages of the sample are Pr/N. This holds with extremely few exceptions on a world-wide basis. There are, however, a few valid examples of I/Pr/A, the mirror image, so to speak, of the fairly frequent III/Po/N. On the other hand, there are, so far as I know, no examples of either I/Po/A or I/Po/N. Hence we may formulate the following universal:

*Universal 3*. Languages with dominant VSO order are always prepositional.

Languages of type III are, as has been seen, the polar opposites of type I. Just as there are no postpositional languages in type I, we expect that there will be no prepositional languages in type III. This is overwhelmingly true, but I am aware of several exceptions.[8] Since, as has been seen, genitive position correlates highly with Pr/Po, we will expect that languages of type III normally have GN order. To this there are some few exceptions. However, whenever genitive order deviates, so does adjective order, whereas the corresponding statement does not hold for Pr/Po.[9] We therefore have the following universals:

*Universal 4*. With overwhelmingly greater than chance frequency, languages with normal SOV order are postpositional.

*Universal 5*. If a language has dominant SOV order and the genitive follows the governing noun, then the adjective likewise follows the noun.

An important difference may be noted between languages of types I and III. In regard to verb-modifying adverbs and phrases as well as sentence adverbs, languages of type I show no reluctance in placing them before the verb so that the verb does not necessarily begin the sentence. Further, all VSO

[7] For details, see Appendix II.

[8] Iraqw, a southern Cushitic language, Khamti, a Thai language, standard Persian, and Amharic.

[9] The single case where it does not hold seems to be Amharic, which has SOV, GN, and AN, but is prepositional.

languages apparently have alternative basic orders among which SVO always figures. On the other hand, in a substantial proportion, possibly a majority, of type III languages, the verb follows all of its modifiers, and if any other basic order is allowed, it is OSV. Thus the verb, except possibly for a few sentence modifiers (e.g., interrogative particles), is always at the end in verbal sentences. It is not logically required, of course, that languages all of whose basic orders involve the verb in the third position should also require all verb modifiers to precede the verb, but this seems to hold empirically. Thus, languages in which the verb is always at the end may be called the "rigid" subtype of III. In the present sample, Burushaski, Kannada, Japanese, Turkish, Hindi, and Burmese belong to this group, while Nubian, Quechua, Basque, Loritja, and Chibcha do not.[10] These considerations permit us to state the following as universals:

> *Universal 6.* All languages with dominant VSO order have SVO as an alternative or as the only alternative basic order.

> *Universal 7.* If in a language with dominant SOV order, there is no alternative basic order, or only OSV as the alternative, then all adverbial modifiers of the verb likewise precede the verb. (This is the rigid subtype of III.)

## 3. Syntax

Having defined the basic order typology and stated some of the universals that can be most immediately derived from the consideration of its defining properties, we turn to a number of syntactic universals, many but not all of which are associated with this typology. One set of criteria employed in this typology was the order of nominal subject, nominal object, and verb in declarative sentences. One reason for stating the criteria in this manner was that interrogative sentences tend to exhibit certain characteristic differences as compared to declarative statements. There are two main categories of questions, those of the yes-no variety and those involving specific question words. A common method of differentiating yes-no questions from the corresponding statement is by a difference of intonational pattern, as in English. Our knowledge of these patterns still leaves much to be desired. However, the following statement seems to be sufficiently documented:

> *Universal 8.* When a yes-no question is differentiated from the corresponding assertion by an intonational pattern, the distinctive

[10] However, Householder informs me that in Azerbaijani, and in most types of spoken Turkish, it is allowable to have one modifier, especially a dative or locative noun phrase after the verb.

*Table 2*

| | I | II | III |
|---|---|---|---|
| Initial particle | 5 | 0 | 0 |
| Final particle | 0 | 2 | 5 |

intonational features of each of these patterns are reckoned from the end of the sentence rather than from the beginning.

For example, in English a yes-no question is marked by a rise in pitch in the last stressed syllable of the sentence and the corresponding statement by falling pitch. The reckoning of distinctive patterns from the end of the sentence may well hold for all intonational patterns.

Yes-no questions may likewise be signaled by a question particle or affix. Some languages use both this method and intonation as alternatives. The position of such question markers is fixed by either reference to some specific word, most frequently the verb or the emphasized word of the question, or it may be fixed by position in the sentence as a whole. In languages of the rigid subtype III, it is of course impossible to distinguish between position after the verb and position at the end of the sentence. In the present sample, there are 12 languages with such initial or final particles. With reference to the basic order typology, these 12 examples are distributed as shown in Table 2.[11]

The two examples of a final particle in group II are prepositional languages (Thai and Yoruba). The table includes only cases where there is a single such particle or affix in the language, or there are several following the same rule. In two of the languages in the samples, there is more than one such element, each with differing rules. Zapotec (I/Pr) has either an initial particle alone or this same particle in conjunction with a final particle. Songhai (II/Po) has three such particles, two of them an initial and one a final particle. These complications as well as the fact that at least one language outside of the sample belonging to (II/Po), namely, Lithuanian, has an initial particle suggest the following rather cautious statement:

> *Universal 9*. With well more than chance frequency, when question particles or affixes are specified in position by reference to the sentence as a whole, if initial, such elements are found in prepositional languages, and, if final, in postpositional.

Where specification depends on some particular word, the particle almost always follows. Such particles are found in 13 languages of the present

[11] Languages of type I—Berber, Hebrew, Maori, Masai, and Welsh; II—Thai, Yoruba; III—Burmese, Burushaski, Japanese, Kannada, Nubian. For Yoruba, see further note 12.

sample.[12] Examples of the rigid subtype III are counted in both this and the previous category. Of these 13, 12 are suffixed. They include both prepositional and postpositional languages, but none in group I. The following, therefore, probably holds:

> *Universal 10.* Question particles or affixes, when specified in position by reference to a particular word in the sentence, almost always follow that word. Such particles do not occur in languages with dominant order VSO.

The other basic kind of question, that involving an interrogative word, likewise shows a definite relationship to the basic order typology. In such sentences, many languages have a different word order than that of the corresponding declarative sentence. Characteristically, the question word comes first, except for the possible retention of normal order within smaller units (e.g., phrases). This holds in English, for example, where the question word is first in 'What did he eat?' as against the statement, 'He ate meat'. The second point is illustrated by 'With whom did he go?' as against 'He went with Henry', where the question phrase comes first but the order within the phrase itself is not disturbed. Many languages which put interrogatives first likewise invert the order of verb and subject (e.g., German 'Wen sah er?'). Such languages sometimes invert for yes-no questions (e.g., 'Kommt er?'). It appears that only languages with interrogatives always initially invert, and only languages which invert in interrogative word questions invert for yes-no questions.[13]

In the present sample, 16 languages put the interrogative word or phrase first. They are distributed as shown in Table 3.

A definite relationship thus appears, and we have the following universals:

> *Universal 11.* Inversion of statement order so that verb precedes subject occurs only in languages where the question word or phrase is normally initial. This same inversion occurs in yes-no questions only if it also occurs in interrogative word questions.

> *Universal 12.* If a language has dominant order VSO in declarative sentences, it always puts interrogative words or phrases first in interrogative word questions; if it has dominant order SOV in declarative sentences, there is never such an invariant rule.

[12] In the following languages the affix or particle follows: II—Finnish, Guarani, Malay, Maya, Serbian; III—Basque, Burmese, Japanese, Kannada, Nubian, Turkish, Quechua. It precedes in Yoruba, but may be accompanied by a final particle.

[13] The question word is first in Berber, Finnish, Fulani, Greek, Guarani, Hebrew, Italian, Malay, Maori, Masai, Maya, Norwegian, Serbian, Welsh, Yoruba, and Zapotec.

*Table 3*

| | I | II | III | Pr | Po |
|---|---|---|---|---|---|
| Question word first | 6 | 10 | 0 | 14 | 2 |
| Question and statement order identical | 0 | 3 | 11 | 2 | 12 |

Verbal subordination to verb will be considered next. Semantically, the concepts to be considered here include time, cause, purpose, and condition. Formally, we have one or more of the following: introductory words (i.e., "conjunctions"); and verbal inflections, whether finite, involving categories of person and number (e.g., subjunctives) or nonfinite forms such as verbal nouns and gerundives. It seems probable that conjunctions are more frequent in prepositional languages, nonfinite verb forms in postpositional languages, and that finite verb forms are found in both, but this point was not investigated. In accordance with the overall emphasis of the paper, attention was directed to the question of the relative order of subordinate and main verbal forms. Since the subordinate verb qualifies the main verb, we would expect it to precede the main verb in all languages of the rigid subtype of III. Since this subtype was defined merely in terms of the invariable precedence of noun object, the question remains for empirical verification. In fact, this turns out to be true for all the languages of this subtype in the sample and, no doubt, holds generally.[14] In languages of other types certain characteristics of individual constructions appear. The normal order everywhere is for the protasis of conditional constructions to precede the apodosis, that is, for the condition to precede the conclusion. This is true for all 30 languages of the sample. In languages of the rigid subtype of III the protasis never follows, but in other languages it will do so occasionally.

On the other hand, in expressions of purpose and volition the normal order is for these to follow the main verb except in languages of the rigid subtype of III. Here again there are no exceptions in the sample. We have therefore the following universals:

> *Universal 13*. If the nominal object always precedes the verb, then verb forms subordinate to the main verb also precede it.
>
> *Universal 14*. In conditional statements, the conditional clause precedes the conclusion as the normal order in all languages.
>
> *Universal 15*. In expressions of volition and purpose, a subordinate verbal form always follows the main verb as the normal order

[14] Again, this only holds for literary Turkish, according to Householder. See note 10.

*Table 4*

| | I | II | III | Pr | Po |
|---|---|---|---|---|---|
| Auxiliary precedes verb | 3 | 7 | 0 | 9 | 1 |
| Auxiliary follows verb | 0 | 1 | 8 | 0 | 9 |

*Table 5*

| | I | II | III | Pr | Po |
|---|---|---|---|---|---|
| NA | 6 | 8 | 5 | 12 | 7 |
| AN | 0 | 5 | 6 | 4 | 7 |

except in those languages in which the nominal object always precedes the verb.

Another relation of verb to verb is that of inflected auxiliary to main verb. For present purposes, such a construction will be defined as one in which a closed class of verbs (the auxiliaries) inflected for both person and number is in construction with an open class of verbs not inflected for both person and number. For example, in English 'is going' is such a construction. This definition, of course, excludes the possibility of such a construction in languages in which the verb has no category of person and number (e.g., Japanese). In the sample of 30 languages, 19 have such inflected auxiliaries. They are distributed among the order types as shown in Table 4.[15]

These data suggest the following universal:

*Universal 16.* In languages with dominant order VSO, an inflected auxiliary always precedes the main verb. In languages with dominant order SOV, an inflected auxiliary always follows the main verb.

Uninflected auxiliaries will be considered later in connection with verb inflections.

In nominal phrases, the position of attributive adjectives in relation to the noun modified is a key factor. The position of the qualifying adjective shows a definite though only statistical relation to the two other bases of the typology. A summary of these data for the languages of the sample is given in Table 5.

In general, then, the tendency is for adjectives to follow the noun in prepositional languages, and most strongly so in languages of type I, which

[15] Auxiliary precedes verb in Finnish, Greek, Italian, Masai, Maya, Norwegian, Serbian, Swahili, Welsh, Zapotec. Auxiliary follows verb in Basque, Burushaski, Chibcha, Guarani, Hindi, Kannada, Nubian, Quechua, Turkish.

are always prepositional as has been noted. There are a few rare exceptions, not in the sample, of languages of type I with adjective before the noun, as was noted earlier. Hence, we have the following *near* universal:

> *Universal 17.* With overwhelmingly more than chance frequency, languages with dominant order VSO have the adjective after the noun.

From the data of Table 5, it will also be noticed that there are 19 languages with adjective after the noun, as against 11 with the adjective before the noun. This is representative of a general tendency which very nearly overrides the opposite rule to be expected in languages of type III.

The position of demonstratives and numerals is related to that of descriptive adjectives in individual languages. However, these items show a marked tendency to precede even when the descriptive adjective follows. On the other hand, when the descriptive adjective precedes, then the demonstratives and numerals virtually always precede the noun likewise. The data from the sample languages are given in Table 6.

In one language, Guarani, numbers may either precede or follow the noun, and this case was not included in the table. In Guarani, the adjective follows the noun, as would be expected. In the case of numbers, it should be noted that for languages with numeral classifiers, it was the position of the numeral in relation to the classifier which was taken into account.[16] There seems to be no relation between the position of the numeral and the demonstrative outside of that mediated by adjective position. Languages in which the adjective follows the noun may have numeral preceding while demonstrative does not, demonstrative preceding while numeral does not, both preceding or neither preceding. Outside of the sample, however, there are a small number of instances (e.g., Efik) in which the demonstrative follows while the adjective precedes. It may be noted that other quantifiers (e.g., 'some', 'all') and interrogative and possessive adjectives show this same tendency to precede the noun, as evidenced, for example, in the Romance languages, but those cases were not studied. We have then the following universal:

> *Universal 18.* When the descriptive adjective precedes the noun, the demonstrative and the numeral, with overwhelmingly more than chance frequency, do likewise.

An additional related observation may be noted:

> *Universal 19.* When the general rule is that the descriptive adjective follows, there may be a minority of adjectives which usually

[16] For details, see Appendix 1.

*Table 6*

| | NA | AN |
|---|---|---|
| Dem.-Noun | 12 | 7 |
| Noun-Dem. | 11 | 0 |
| Num.-Noun | 8 | 10 |
| Noun-Num. | 11 | 0 |

*Table 7*

| | AN | NA |
|---|---|---|
| Adverb-Adjective | 11 | 5 |
| Adjective-Adverb | 0 | 8 |
| Adj.-Adv. and Adv.-Adj. | 0 | 2 |

> precede, but when the general rule is that descriptive adjectives precede, there are no exceptions.

This last universal is illustrated by Welsh and Italian in the present sample.

The order within the noun phrase is subject to powerful constraints. When any or all of the three types of qualifiers precede the noun, the order among them is always the same: demonstrative, numeral, and adjective, as in English, 'these five houses'.

When any or all follow, the favorite order is the exact opposite: noun, adjective, numeral, demonstrative. A less popular alternative is the same order as that just given for the instances in which these elements precede the noun. An example of the latter is Kikuyu, a Bantu language of East Africa, with the order, 'houses these five large', instead of the more popular 'houses large five these'. We have, then, a universal:

> *Universal 20*. When any or all of the items (demonstrative, numeral, and descriptive adjective) precede the noun, they are always found in that order. If they follow, the order is either the same or its exact opposite.

The order of adverbial qualifiers of adjectives in relation to the adjective will now be considered. This order also shows a definite relation to that between the descriptive adjective and the noun, as shown by Table 7. In the third row are cases in which certain adverbs precede and others follow.[17]

From Table 7 it can be seen that there is a tendency for the adverb to precede the adjective, which can be overridden only in some cases when the adjective follows the noun. The situation thus far is similar to that obtaining with regard to demonstratives and numerals. However, if we look further,

[17] Languages with adjective-noun and adverb-adjective order are Burushaski, Finnish, Greek, Hindi, Japanese, Kannada, Maya, Norwegian, Quechua, Serbian, Turkish. Languages with noun-adjective and adverb-adjective order are Basque, Burmese, Chibcha, Italian, Loritja. Languages with noun-adjective and adjective-adverb order are Fulani, Guarani, Hebrew, Malay, Swahili, Thai, Yoruba, and Zapotec. Languages with noun-adjective and the rule that certain adverbs precede and certain follow the adjective are Maori and Welsh. Berber, Masai, Nubian, and Songhai—no data.

we note that all of those languages in which some or all adverbs follow the adjective not only have the noun followed by the adjective, but also are all of types I and II. Thus we have a universal:

> *Universal 21.* If some or all adverbs follow the adjective they modify, then the language is one in which the qualifying adjective follows the noun and the verb precedes its nominal object as the dominant order.

One other topic concerning the adjective to be considered is that of comparisons, specifically that of superiority as expressed, for example in English, by sentences of the type '*X* is larger than *Y*'. A minority of the world's languages have, like English, an inflected comparative form of the adjective. More frequently a separate word modifies the adjective, as in English '*X* is more beautiful than *Y*', but in many languages this is optional or does not exist at all. On the other hand, there is always some element which expresses the comparison as such, whether word or affix, corresponding to English 'than' and obviously both the adjective and the item with which comparison is made must be expressed. We thus have three elements whose order can be considered, as in English *larg(er) than Y*. These will be called adjective, marker of comparison, and standard of comparison. The two common orders are: adjective, marker, standard (as in English); or the opposite order: standard, marker, adjective. These two alternatives are related to the basic order typology, as shown by Table 8.[18] A number of languages are not entered in this table because they utilize a verb with general meaning 'to surpass'. This is particularly common in Africa (e.g., Yoruba): '*X* is large, surpasses *Y*'. Loritja, an Australian language which has '*X* is large, *Y* is small', is likewise not entered.

> *Universal 22.* If in comparisons of superiority the only order, or one of the alternative orders, is standard-marker-adjective, then the language is postpositional. With overwhelmingly more than chance frequency if the only order is adjective-marker-standard, the language is prepositional.

A clear relation to the basic order typology is likewise found in constructions of nominal apposition, particularly those involving a common along with a proper noun. A number of semantic and formal subtypes are involved (e.g.,

[18] Languages with adjective-marker-standard are Berber, Fulani, Greek, Hebrew, Italian, Malay, Maori, Norwegian, Serbian, Songhai, Swahili, Thai, Welsh, Zapotec. Languages with standard-marker-adjective are Basque, Burmese, Burushaski, Chibcha, Guarani, Hindi, Japanese, Kannada, Nubian, Turkish. Both constructions are found in Finnish.

*Table 8*

| | I | II | III | Pr | Po |
|---|---|---|---|---|---|
| Adjective-Marker-Standard | 5 | 9 | 0 | 13 | 1 |
| Standard-Marker-Adjective | 0 | 1 | 9 | 0 | 10 |
| Both | 0 | 1 | 0 | 0 | 1 |

*Table 9*

| | I | II | III | GN | NG |
|---|---|---|---|---|---|
| Common Noun-Proper Noun | 2 | 7 | 0 | 1 | 8 |
| Proper Noun-Common Noun | 0 | 2 | 6 | 8 | 0 |

titles of address 'Mr. X', as against appellations 'Avenue X'). The latter type is, in certain cases, assimilation to the genitive, and may therefore be expected to show a similar order (e.g., 'the city of Philadelphia'). English is somewhat ambivalent, doubtless because of adjective-noun order, as can be seen from '42nd Street' versus 'Avenue A', or 'Long Lake' versus 'Lake Michigan'. Most languages, however, have a single order (e.g., French, 'Place Vendôme', 'Lac Genève', 'Boulevard Michelet'). My data here are incomplete because grammars often make no statement on the subject, and I was dependent on text examples.[19]

In Table 9, contrary to usual practice, the genitive construction is used instead of Pr/Po since it gives more clear-cut results.

> *Universal 23*. If in apposition the proper noun usually precedes the common noun, then the language is one in which the governing noun follows its dependent genitive. With much better than chance frequency, if the common noun usually precedes the proper noun, the dependent genitive follows its governing noun.

As the concluding item in the discussion of nominal construction, we take the relative clause which modifies a noun (e.g., English, 'I saw the man who came', 'I saw the student who failed the examination'). Here again there is considerable diversity of formal means from language to language. All that will be considered here is the order as between nominal antecedent and the verb of the relative clause (e.g., 'man' and 'came' in the first sentence).

Once more the distribution of the rules of order, as set forth in Table 10,

[19] Languages with common noun–proper noun are Greek, Guarani, Italian, Malay, Serbian, Swahili, Thai, Welsh, Zapotec. Those with proper noun–common noun are Basque, Burmese, Burushaski, Finnish, Japanese, Norwegian, Nubian, and Turkish.

*Table 10*

| | I | II | III | Pr | Po |
|---|---|---|---|---|---|
| Relational expression precedes noun | 0 | 0 | 7 | 0 | 7 |
| Noun precedes relational expression | 6 | 12 | 2 | 16 | 4 |
| Both constructions | 0 | 1 | 1 | 0 | 2 |

shows a clear relation to the categories of the basic order typology.[20]

From Table 10 it is clear that if the relational expression precedes the noun either as the only construction or as alternate construction, the language is postpositional. However, outside of the sample there is at least one exception, Chinese, a prepositional language in which the relational expression precedes the noun. It is plausible to explain this deviation as connected with the fact that in Chinese the adjective precedes the noun. As with adjective-noun order there is a pronounced general tendency for the relative expression to follow the noun it qualifies. This tendency is sometimes overcome but only if (1) the language is prepositional or (2) if the qualifying adjective precedes the noun.

> *Universal 24*. If the relative expression precedes the noun either as the only construction or as an alternate construction, either the language is postpositional, or the adjective precedes the noun, or both.

Thus far nothing has been said about pronouns. In general, pronouns exhibit differences regarding order when compared with nouns. This was the reason for specifying nominal subject and nominal object in the definitions of the basic typology. One peculiarity of pronominal order is illustrated by French where we have, 'Je vois l'homme' but 'Je le vois'; that is, the pronominal object precedes, whereas the nominal object follows. Similar examples are found in a number of languages of the sample. In Italian, Greek, Guarani, and Swahili, the rule holds that the pronominal object always precedes the verb, whereas the nominal object follows. In Italian and Greek, however, the pronoun follows just as does the nominal object with imperatives. In Berber the pronoun objects, direct or indirect, precede the verb when the verb is accompanied by the negative or future particle. In Loritja, the pronominal object may be an enclitic added to the first word of the sentence. In Nubian, the usual nominal order is SOV, but the alternative SVO is fairly

[20] The relational expression precedes the noun in Basque, Burmese, Burushaski, Chibcha, Japanese, Kannada, Turkish. The noun precedes the relational expression in Berber, Fulani, Greek, Guarani, Hebrew, Hindi, Italian, Malay, Maori, Masai, Maya, Norwegian, Quechua, Serbian, Songhai, Swahili, Thai, Welsh, Yoruba, Zapotec. Both orders are found in Finnish and Nubian. In Finnish the construction with the relational expression preceding the noun is in imitation of literary Swedish (personal communication of Robert Austerlitz).

frequent. For pronominal object, this alternative never occurs. In other words, the pronominal object always precedes the verb, whereas the nominal object may either precede or follow. In Welsh, in an alternative order with emphasis on the pronoun subject, the pronoun subject comes first in the sentence. In such sentences the pronominal object precedes the verb, but the nominal object follows. Finally, in Masai, whereas normal order for nominal object is VSO, a pronominal object precedes a nominal subject and immediately follows the verb.

No contrary instances occur in the sample of a pronominal object regularly following the verb while a nominal object precedes. We may therefore state the following universal:

> *Universal 25*. If the pronominal object follows the verb, so does the nominal object.

## 4. Morphology

Before proceeding to the question of inflectional categories, which will be the chief topic of this section, certain general considerations relating to morphology will be discussed. Morphemes within the word are conventionally divided into root, derivational, and inflectional. As elsewhere in this paper, no attempt at definition of categories will be attempted. Derivational and inflectional elements are usually grouped together as affixes. On the basis of their order relation to the root, they may be classified into a number of categories. By far the most frequent are prefixes and suffixes. Infixing, by which a derivational or inflectional element is both preceded and followed by parts of the root morpheme, may be grouped with other methods involving discontinuity. Examples of such other methods are intercalation, as in Semitic, and what might be called ambifixing, where an affix has two parts, one of which precedes the entire root, while the other follows. All such discontinuous methods are relatively infrequent, and some languages do not employ any of them. The following universal on this topic is probably valid:

> *Universal 26*. If a language has discontinuous affixes, it always has either prefixing or suffixing or both.

As between prefixing and suffixing, there is a general predominance of suffixing. Exclusively suffixing languages are fairly common, while exclusively prefixing languages are quite rare. In the present sample, only Thai seems to be exclusively prefixing. Here again (see Table 11) a relationship with the basic order typology appears.[21]

[21] The exclusively suffixing languages are Basque, Burmese, Chibcha, Finnish, Hindi, Japanese, Kannada, Loritja, Nubian, Quechua, Songhai, Turkish.

*Table 11*

| | I | II | III | Pr | Po |
|---|---|---|---|---|---|
| Exclusively prefixing | 0 | 1 | 0 | 1 | 0 |
| Exclusively suffixing | 0 | 2 | 10 | 0 | 12 |
| Both | 6 | 10 | 1 | 15 | 2 |

> *Universal 27*. If a language is exclusively suffixing, it is postpositional; if it is exclusively prefixing, it is prepositional.

Where both derivational and inflectional elements are found together, the derivational element is more intimately connected with the root. The following generalization appears plausible:

> *Universal 28*. If both the derivation and inflection follow the root, or they both precede the root, the derivation is always between the root and the inflection.

There are probably no languages without either compounding, affixing, or both. In other words, there are probably no purely isolating languages. There are a considerable number of languages without inflections, perhaps none without compounding and derivation. The following probably holds:

> *Universal 29*. If a language has inflection, it always has derivation.

Turning now to verb inflectional categories, we can state that since there are languages without inflection, there will obviously be languages in which the verb has no inflectional categories. In the far more frequent cases in which the verb has inflectional categories, a partial implicational hierarchy exists.

> *Universal 30*. If the verb has categories of person-number or if it has categories of gender, it always has tense-mode categories.

The greater externality of gender categories in the verb can be seen from the following generalization:

> *Universal 31*. If either the subject or object noun agrees with the verb in gender, then the adjective always agrees with the noun in gender.

Gender agreement between noun (usually noun subject) and verb is far less frequent than agreement in person and number; yet examples of the former without the latter do occur (e.g., in some Daghestan languages of the Caucasus). However, where such gender categories appear, they always seem to be associated with number also. Therefore we have the following:

*Universal 32*. Whenever the verb agrees with a nominal subject or nominal object in gender, it also agrees in number.

A further observation about noun-verb agreement in number may be made. There are cases in which this agreement is regularly suspended. In all such cases, if order is involved, the following seems to hold:[22]

*Universal 33*. When number agreement between the noun and verb is suspended and the rule is based on order, the case is always one in which the verb precedes and the verb is in the singular.

Such phenomena as the suspension of agreement are analogous to that of neutralization in phonemics. The category which does not appear in the position of neutralization, in this case the plural, may be called the marked category (as in classical Prague School phonemic theory). Similar phenomena will be encountered in the subsequent discussion.

The three most common nominal inflectional categories are number, gender, and case. Among systems of number, there is a definite hierarchy which can be stated in the following terms:

*Universal 34*. No language has a trial number unless it has a dual. No language has a dual unless it has a plural.

Nonsingular number categories are marked categories in relation to the singular, as indicated in the following universal:

*Universal 35*. There is no language in which the plural does not have some nonzero allomorphs, whereas there are languages in which the singular is expressed only by zero. The dual and the trial are almost never expressed only by zero.

The marked character of the nonsingular numbers as against the singular can also be seen when number occurs along with gender. The interrelations of these two sets of categories are stated in the following universals:

*Universal 36*. If a language has the category of gender, it always has the category of number.

*Universal 37*. A language never has more gender categories in nonsingular numbers than in the singular.

[22] The reason for specifying order is that there are instances of neutralization of number agreement in which the order of the item is not involved. For example, in classical Greek the neuter plural goes with a singular verb without regard to order.

This latter statement may be illustrated from Hausa, which has a masculine and feminine gender distinction in the singular but not in the plural. The opposite phenomenon, to my knowledge, never occurs.

Case systems may occur with or without gender systems and with or without the category of number. The unmarked categories of case systems are the subject case in nonergative systems and the case which expresses the subject of intransitive and the object of transitive verbs in ergative systems. Hence we have the following universal:

> *Universal 38.* Where there is a case system, the only case which ever has only zero allomorphs is the one which includes among its meanings that of the subject of the intransitive verb.

As between number and case, where there is a distinct morpheme boundary, the following relation almost always holds:

> *Universal 39.* Where morphemes of both number and case are present and both follow or both precede the noun base, the expression of number almost always comes between the noun base and the expression of case.

The following general statement may be made about agreement between adjectives and nouns:

> *Universal 40.* When the adjective follows the noun, the adjective expresses all the inflectional categories of the noun. In such cases the noun may lack overt expression of one or all of these categories.

For example, in Basque, where the adjective follows the noun, the last member of the noun phrase contains overt expressions of the categories of case and number and it alone has them.

Case systems are particularly frequent in postpositional languages, particularly those of type III. In the present sample, all the languages of this type have case systems. There are a few marginal cases or possible exceptions.

> *Universal 41.* If in a language the verb follows both the nominal subject and nominal object as the dominant order, the language almost always has a case system.

Finally, pronominal categories may be briefly considered. In general, pronominal categories tend to be more differentiated than those of the noun, but almost any specific statement in this regard will have some exceptions. As a general statement we have the following universals:

*Universal 42*. All languages have pronominal categories involving at least three persons and two numbers.

*Universal 43*. If a language has gender categories in the noun, it has gender categories in the pronoun.

Gender categories show certain relations to categories of person in pronouns, as might be expected.

*Universal 44*. If a language has gender distinctions in the first person, it always has gender distinctions in the second or third person, or in both.

There is likewise a relation to the category of number.

*Universal 45*. If there are any gender distinctions in the plural of the pronoun, there are some gender distinctions in the singular also.

## 5. Conclusion: Some General Principles

No attempt is made here to account for all of the universals described in the preceding sections and repeated in Appendix III. Some general principles, however, are proposed which seem to underlie a number of different universals and from which they may be deduced. Attention is first directed to those universals which are most closely connected with the basic order typology and the closely associated genitive construction. Two basic notions, that of the dominance of a particular order over its alternative and that of harmonic and disharmonic relations among distinct rules of order, are introduced. This latter concept is very obviously connected with the psychological concept of generalization.

We may illustrate the reasoning involved by reference to Universal 25, according to which, if the pronominal object follows the verb, the nominal object does so likewise. In other words, in the tetrachoric table resulting from the alternative for each of the combinations there is a single blank. Since the nominal object may follow the verb whether the pronoun object precedes or follows, while the nominal object may precede the verb only if the pronoun precedes, we will say that VO is dominant over OV since OV only occurs under specified conditions, namely when the pronominal object likewise precedes, while VO is not subject to such limitations. Further, the order noun object-verb is harmonic with pronoun object-verb but is disharmonic with verb-pronoun object since it does not occur with it. Likewise verb-noun object order is harmonic with verb-pronoun object and disharmonic with pronoun object-verb. We may restate our rule, then, in terms of these concepts as follows:

> A dominant order may always occur, but its opposite, the recessive, occurs only when a harmonic construction is likewise present.

Note that the notion of dominance is not based on its more frequent occurrence but on the logical factor of a zero in the tetrachoric table. It is not difficult to construct an example in which one of the recessive alternatives is more frequent than the dominant. Dominance and harmonic relations can be derived quite mechanically from such a table with a single zero. The entry with zero is always the recessive one for each construction, and the two constructions involved are disharmonic with each other.

Harmonic and disharmonic relations, as noted earlier, are examples of generalization. In similar constructions, the corresponding members tend to be in the same order. The basis for the correspondence in the present instance is obvious, in that pronoun and noun are both objects of the verb, and the other pair verb-verb is identical. In regard to harmonic and disharmonic relations, a fair amount of freedom will be exercised based on transformational and other relations among constructions, not merely the occurrence of a zero in a tetrachoric table.

Proceeding on this basis, we now consider Universal 3. It will be noted that this universal amounts to an assertion of the non-existence of postpositional languages of type I. Since in all of the types, I, II, and III, S precedes O, this is irrelevant for the present context. This leads to the following conclusions:

> Prepositions are dominant over postpositions, and SV order is dominant over VS order. Further, prepositions are harmonic with VS and disharmonic with SV, while postpositions are harmonic with SV and disharmonic with VS.

What distinguishes type II from type III is that in type II the object follows the verb, a characteristic shared with type I. On the other hand, type III has the object before the verb. From Universal 4, which states that with overwhelmingly more than chance frequency SOV is associated with postpositions, the conclusion is drawn that OV is harmonic with postpositions while VO is harmonic with prepositions. The constructional analogies which support this are discussed later with reference to the closely associated genitive constructions. For the moment it may be noted that the relations between types I, II, and III and Pr/Po may now be recapitulated in these terms: Type I has VS which is harmonic with prepositions, and SO which is likewise harmonic with prepositions. Further, prepositions are dominant. All languages of type I, in fact, are prepositional. Type II has SV which is harmonic with postpositions and VO which is harmonic with prepositions, and prepositions are dominant. In fact, a definite majority of languages of type II have prepositions. Type III has SV and OV, both of which are harmonic with postpositions. However, prepositions are dominant. In fact, the preponderant majority of languages which have type III have postpositions, with but a handful of exceptions.

From the overwhelming association of prepositions with governing noun-genitive order and of postpositions with genitive-governing noun order but with a small number of exceptions of both types, the conclusion is drawn that prepositions are harmonic with NG and postpositions with GN.

The close connection between genitive order and Pr/Po is a simple instance of generalization. The relation of possession is assimilated to other relational notions, for example, spatial relations. In English, 'of' which marks possession is a preposition with the same order properties as 'under', 'above', etc. Further, such spatial and temporal relations are often expressed by nouns or nounlike words, for example, English 'in back of'. In many languages 'behind' = 'the back + genitive'; hence: '*X*'s back' = 'in back of *X*' parallels '*X*'s house'; and 'back of *X*' = 'in back of *X*' parallels 'house of *X*'.

The connection between these genitives and the analogous prepositional or postpositional phrases on the one hand, and subject-verb and object-verb constructions on the other, is via the so-called subjective and objective genitive. Note that in English 'Brutus' killing of Caesar started a civil war' has the same truth value as 'The fact that Brutus killed Caesar started a civil war'. The order of elements is likewise similar. In other words, in such transformations, the noun subject or object corresponds to the genitive, and the verb to the governing noun. In fact, there are languages in which the subject or the object of the verb is in the genitive. For example, in Berber *argaz* 'man' is the general form of the noun, and *urgaz* is either the dependent genitive or the subject of the verb, provided it follows immediately. Thus *iffeɣ urgaz*, 'went out the man', exactly parallels *axam urgaz*, 'the house of the man'. Berber, it will be noted, is a language of type I, and the genitive follows the noun. It likewise has prepositions rather than postpositions.

A further relationship among the variables of the basic order typology may be posited, that between genitive order and adjective order. Both the genitive and qualifying adjectives limit the meaning of the noun. There are further facts to support this. There are languages like Persian, in which both adjective and genitive dependence are marked by exactly the same formal means. Where pronominal possession is involved, some languages use a derived adjective, while others use a genitive of the pronoun. There are even instances where adjectives are used in the first and second person, while a genitive is used in the third person (e.g., Norwegian).

We may summarize these results by stating that all of the following are directly or indirectly harmonic with each other: prepositions, NG, VS, VO, and NA. We have here a general tendency to put modified before modifier, and the most highly "polarized" languages in this direction are those of type I with NG and NA, a considerable group of languages. The opposite type is based on harmonic relations among postpositions, GN, SV, OV, and AN. This is also a very widespread type, as exemplified by Turkish and others in the present sample. On the other hand, the general dominance of NA order tends to make languages of the Basque type (i.e., III/Po/NA with GN order) very nearly as common as the Turkish type. It should also be pointed out that languages being highly complex structures, there are other factors at work in individual cases not included among the five factors cited at this point. One of them, demonstrative-noun order, has already been mentioned.

It is more difficult to account for the dominances than for the harmonic relations, to explain, for example, why the adjective tends to follow the noun. It may be suggested, however, that noun-adjective predominance arises from the same factor as that which makes subject-verb the dominant order. In Hockett's terminology, there is a general tendency for comment to follow topic. There is some evidence that noun-adjective does parallel subject-verb in this way. In many languages all adjectival notions are treated as intransitive verbs. The qualifying adjective is then a relative or participle of the verb. The tendency of relative clauses, it has been seen, is even stronger than that of adjectives to follow the noun. In some languages such as Arapesh in New Guinea, 'The good man came' would be literally translated 'The man is-good that-one he came'. Adjective-noun order, then, is somewhat ambivalent since analogies with other constructions involving modifiers make it indirectly harmonic with VS while the factor of topic-comment order makes it analogous with SV.

All this is far from a complete theory. Nevertheless, it does suggest that one should examine instances in which, contrary to the prevailing rules, the genitive construction is disharmonic with Pr/Po. One would reason that in such cases the genitive construction is, as it were, being attracted by the adjective-noun construction which, as has been seen, has sources of determination that are to some extent outside of the general framework of harmonic relations connected with the order of modifier and modified. For example, if, in spite of the general rule, we find genitive-governing noun order with prepositions, the reason might be the opposing pull of order adjective-noun which is harmonic with genitive-governing noun. Otherwise stated, the genitive construction should only be disharmonic with Pr/Po when

Pr/Po is disharmonic with the adjective-noun order. One may include here cases in which a language has two genitive orders, indicating a probable change of type since one must, in all likelihood, be older than the other. One may further conjecture that if there are exceptions, they will be in type II, which, having both SV and VO which are disharmonic, can provide an anchor in either case for deviant genitive order.

It will be noted that Universal 5, insofar as it refers to postpositional languages of type III (the vast majority), gives a particular instance of this hypothesis; for this statement asserts that a language of type III if it has NG will also have NA. If such a language is postpositional, then NG will be disharmonic with postpositions but harmonic with NA. If we include languages with both genitive orders, then there are at least six cases, all favorable (i.e., with NA rather than AN). These are Somali and Maba with both genitive orders, and Kanuri, Galla, Teda, and Sumerian which have SOV, postpositions, NG, and NA.

This hypothesis will, however, produce some further predictions. For prepositional languages of type III, the hypothesis will be that with varying genitive order or with GN, which is disharmonic with prepositions, the adjective-noun order will be AN. I know of only two cases, Tigrinya with both genitive orders, and Amharic with GN. Both have AN in accordance with our hypothesis. For languages of type II which are prepositional and which have GN, and should therefore have AN, we have Danish, Norwegian, and Swedish (possibly a single case), and English with two genitive orders. Both fulfill the hypothesis in that they have AN. Among postpositional languages of type II, we have the Moru-Madi group in the Sudan and the fairly distantly related Mangbetu, both of which, with alternative genitive orders, have the predicted NA. We now encounter the only exceptions of which I am aware, Araucanian in Chile, with both genitive orders; and a group of Daghestan languages in the Caucasus, including some like Rutulian with NG, and others like Tabassaran with both genitive orders. Apparently all those languages of the Daghestan group which are of type III have only GN harmonizing with both postpositions and AN. If so, this is an important indication of the general validity of our hypothesis. Finally, since all languages of type I are prepositional, we have only a single case to consider, prepositional languages with GN. I know of only one example, the Milpa Alta dialect of Nahuatl described by Whorf. It has AN as expected.

A different type of relation from those that have just been considered is illustrated by Universals 20 and 29. These may be called proximity hierarchies. What we have is a rule that certain elements must be closer to some central element than some other satellite. The central element may be the root morpheme or base of a word or the head-word of an endocentric construction. Such a proximity hierarchy is likely to be related to an implicational hierarchy in the instance of inflectional categories. Just as the category of number is almost always closer to the base than expressions of case, so there are many languages with the category of number but without the category of case, and very few with case but without number. Since, by the proximity hierarchy, number is closer, it is more likely to become amalgamated with the base and so become an inflection. These hierarchies are presumably related to degrees of logical and psychological remoteness from the center, but no analysis is attempted here.

These phenomena are likewise related to those of neutralization. The more proximate category, or the implied category, tends to be more elaborate, and it is the less proximate or the implying categories which tend to be neutralized in its presence. Universals 36 and 37 are related in this manner. Number is the implied category. Gender categories are often neutralized in the marked number (i.e. nonsingular). It is much rarer for number to be neutralized in some particular gender (e.g., the neuter in Dravidian languages). With regard to number and case, number is, as has been seen, more proximate and generally present when case is present, while the opposite relation holds far more rarely. It is likewise common for certain case distinctions to be neutralized in number, while the opposite phenomenon perhaps never occurs.

Another principle is evident from Universal 34. We do not have such systems as the following: a particular grammatical category for the trial, while another embraces the dual and all numbers larger than three. In other words, disjunctiveness or lack of continuity in this respect is never tolerated.

Universals 14 and 15 possibly illustrate the same principle. The order of elements in language parallels that in physical experience or the order of knowledge. In the instance of conditionals, although the truth relations involved are timeless, logicians have always symbolized in the order implying, implied exactly as in spoken language. If *modus ponens* is used in proof, then we have a pragmatic example which follows the order of reasoning. No one thinks to write a proof backwards.

Universals 7, 8, and 40, although superficially very different, seem to be examples of the same general tendency to mark the end of units rather than the beginning. For example, in rigid subtype III, the verb marks the end of the sentence. When the inflections occur only with the final member of the noun phrase, this marks the end of the phrase. This is probably related to the fact that we always know when someone has just begun speaking, but it is our sad experience that without some marker we don't know when the speaker will finish.

The existence of a rigid subtype III, whereas there are no examples of a rigid subtype of I, is probably related to still another factor. In general the initial position is the emphatic one, and while there are other methods of emphasis (e.g., stress), the initial position always seems to be left free so that an element to which attention is directed may come first. Here Universal 12 is an example. It seems probable that in all languages expressions of time and place may appear in the initial positions in the sentence.

The discontinuity of the predicate, which commonly appears in such instances (e.g., German, 'Gestern ist mein Vater nach Berlin gefahren'), illustrates a further principle. On the whole, the higher the construction in an immediate constituent hierarchy, the freer the order of the constituent elements. It has been seen that practically all languages have some freedom of order regarding subject and predicate as a whole; whereas only a small minority have variant order in genitive constructions, and then almost always along with other differences, not merely a difference of order. Within morphological constructions, order is the most fixed of all. On the whole, then, discontinuous constituents are far less frequent than continuous ones.

As indicated in the initial section of this paper, the principles described in this section are to be viewed as no more than suggestive. It is hoped that some of them at least will prove useful for further investigation.

## *Appendix I*

Table of Basic Data on the 30-Language Sample

| | VSO | Pr | NA | ND | N Num |
|---|---|---|---|---|---|
| Basque | III | — | X | X | — |
| Berber | I | X | X | X | — |
| Burmese | III | — | X[a] | — | —[b] |
| Burushaski | III | — | — | — | — |
| Chibcha | III | — | X | — | X |
| Finnish | II | — | — | — | — |
| Fulani | II | X | X | X | X |
| Greek | II | X | — | — | — |
| Guarani | II | — | X | — | 0 |
| Hebrew | I | X | X | X | — |
| Hindi | III | — | — | — | — |
| Italian | II | X | X[c] | — | — |
| Kannada | III | — | — | — | — |
| Japanese | III | — | — | — | —[b] |
| Loritja | III | — | X | X | X |
| Malay | II | X | X | X | —[b] |
| Maori | I | X | X | — | — |
| Masai | I | X | X | — | X |
| Maya | II | X | — | — | —[b] |
| Norwegian | II | X | — | — | — |
| Nubian | III | — | X | — | X |
| Quechua | III | — | — | — | — |
| Serbian | II | X | — | — | — |
| Songhai | II | — | X | X | X |

*Appendix I (continued)*

| | VSO | Pr | NA | ND | N Num |
|---|---|---|---|---|---|
| Swahili | II | X | X | X | X |
| Thai | II | X | X | X | —[b] |
| Turkish | III | — | — | — | — |
| Welsh | I | X | X[c] | X | — |
| Yoruba | II | X | X | X | X |
| Zapotec | I | X | X | X | — |

NOTE: In the first column, I indicates that normal word order is verb-subject-object, II indicates subject-verb-object, and III subject-object-verb. In the second column, X indicates that the language has prepositions, and — that it has postpositions. In the third column, X indicates that the noun precedes its modifying adjective, and — that it follows. In the fourth column, X indicates that the noun precedes its modifying demonstrative, and — that it follows. In the fifth column, X indicates that the noun precedes its modifying numeral, and — that it follows. In any column, 0 means that both orders are found.

[a] Participial adjective/verb, however, precedes and is probably as common as adjective following.

[b] Numeral classifiers following numerals in each case. The construction numeral + classifier precedes in Burmese and Maya, follows in Japanese and Thai, and either precedes or follows in Malay.

[c] In Welsh and Italian a small number of adjectives usually precede.

## *Appendix II*

## Distribution of Basic Order Types

1. I/Pr/NG/NA. Celtic languages; Hebrew, Aramaic, Arabic, Ancient Egyptian, Berber; Nandi, Masai, Lotuko, Turkana, Didinga; Polynesian languages and probably other Austronesian languages; Chinook, Tsimshian; Zapotec, Chinantec, Mixtec, and probably other Oto-Mangue languages.
2. I/Pr/NG/AN. Tagabili and probably other Philippine Austronesian languages; Kwakiutl, Quileute, Xinca.
3. I/Pr/GN/AN. Milpa Alta Nahuatl.
4. I/Pr/GN/NA. No examples.
5. I/Po/NG/NA. No examples.
6. I/Po/NG/AN. No examples.
7. I/Po/GN/AN. Papago.
8. I/Po/GN/NA. No examples.
9. II/Pr/NG/NA. Romance languages, Albanian, Modern Greek; West Atlantic languages, Yoruba, Edo group, most languages of Benue-Congo group including all Bantu languages; Shilluk, Acholi, Bari, most languages of Chad group of Hamito-Semitic but not Hausa; Neo-Syriac, Khasi, Nicobarese, Khmer, Vietnamese, all Thai languages except Khamti; many Austronesian languages including Malay; Subtiaba.
10. II/Pr/NG/AN. German, Dutch, Icelandic, Slavonic, Efik, Kresh, Maya, Papiamento.
11. II/Pr/GN/AN. Swedish, Danish.
12. II/Pr/GN/NA. Arapesh (New Guinea).
13. II/Po/NG/NA. No examples.
14. II/Po/NG/AN. Rutulian and other Daghestan languages in the Caucasus.
15. II/Po/GN/AN. Finnish, Estonian, Ijo, Chinese, Algonquian (probably), Zoque.
16. II/Po/GN/NA. Most Mandingo and Voltaic languages, Kru, Twi, Gã, Guang, Ewe, Nupe, Songhai, Tonkawa, Guarani.
17. III/Pr/NG/NA. Persian, Iraqw (Cushitic), Khamti (Thai), Akkadian.
18. III/Pr/NG/AN. No examples.
19. III/Pr/GN/AN. Amharic.
20. III/Pr/GN/NA. No examples.

*Appendix II (continued)*

21. III/Po/NG/NA. Sumerian, Elamite, Galla, Kanuri, Teda, Kamila-roi and other southeastern Australian languages.
22. III/Po/NG/AN. No examples.
23. III/Po/GN/AN. Hindi, Bengali, and other Aryan languages of India; Modern Armenian, Finno-Ugric except Finnish group; Altaic, Yukaghir, Paleo-Siberian, Korean, Ainu, Japanese, Gafat, Harari, Sidamo, Chamir, Bedauye, Nama Hottentot; Khinalug, Abkhaz and other Caucasian languages; Burushaski, Dravidian; Newari and other Sino-Tibetan languages; Marind-Anim, Navaho, Maidu, Quechua.
24. III/Po/GN/NA. Basque, Hurrian, Urartian, Nubian, Kunama, Fur, Sandawe, Burmese, Lushei, Classical Tibetan, Makasai, Bunak (Timor), Kate (New Guinea), most Australian languages, Haida, Tlingit, Zuni, Chitimacha, Tunica, Lenca, Matagalpa, Cuna, Chibcha, Warrau.

NOTES: *Languages with object before subject:* Coeur d'Alene: VOS/Pr/NG/NA; Siuslaw, Coos: VOS and OVS/Po/GN/AN. *Languages with variant constructions:* Geez, Bontoc Igorot, 1, 2; Tagalog 1, 2, 3, 4; Sango 9, 10; English, Norwegian 10, 11; Lithuanian 11, 15 (prepositions more numerous); Mangbetu, Araucanian 12, 13; Takelma 12, 16 (prepositions more frequent); Moru-Madi 13, 16; Tabassaran 14, 15; Luiseño 15, 16; Tigre 17, 18, 19, 20; Tigrinya 18, 19; Somali, Maba 21, 24; Afar, Ekari 23, 24.

## *Appendix III*

## Universals Restated

1. In declarative sentences with nominal subject and object, the dominant order is almost always one in which the subject precedes the object.
2. In languages with prepositions, the genitive almost always follows the governing noun, while in languages with postpositions it almost always precedes.
3. Languages with dominant VSO order are always prepositional.
4. With overwhelmingly greater than chance frequency, languages with normal SOV order are postpositional.
5. If a language has dominant SOV order and the genitive follows the governing noun, then the adjective likewise follows the noun.
6. All languages with dominant VSO order have SVO as an alternative or as the only alternative basic order.
7. If in a language with dominant SOV order there is no alternative basic order, or only OSV as the alternative, then all adverbial modifiers of the verb likewise precede the verb. (This is the "rigid" subtype of III.)
8. When a yes-no question is differentiated from the corresponding assertion by an intonational pattern, the distinctive intonational features of each of these patterns is reckoned from the end of the sentence rather than the beginning.
9. With well more than chance frequency, when question particles or affixes are specified in position by reference to the sentence as a whole, if initial, such elements are found in prepositional languages and, if final, in postpositional.
10. Question particles or affixes, specified in position by reference to a particular word in the sentence, almost always follow that word. Such particles do not occur in languages with dominant order VSO.
11. Inversion of statement order so that verb precedes subject occurs only in languages where the question word or phrase is normally initial. This same inversion occurs in yes-no questions only if it also occurs in interrogative word questions.
12. If a language has dominant order VSO in declarative sentences, it always puts interrogative words or phrases first in interrogative word questions; if it has dominant order SOV in declarative sentences, there is never such an invariant rule.

*Appendix III (continued)*

13. If the nominal object always precedes the verb, then verb forms subordinate to the main verb also precede it.
14. In conditional statements, the conditional clause precedes the conclusion as the normal order in all languages.
15. In expressions of volition and purpose, a subordinate verbal form always follows the main verb as the normal order except in those languages in which the nominal object always precedes the verb.
16. In languages with dominant order VSO, an inflected auxiliary always precedes the main verb. In languages with dominant order SOV, an inflected auxiliary always follows the main verb.
17. With overwhelmingly more than chance frequency, languages with dominant order VSO have the adjective after the noun.
18. When the descriptive adjective precedes the noun, the demonstrative and the numeral, with overwhelmingly more than chance frequency, do likewise.
19. When the general rule is that the descriptive adjective follows, there may be a minority of adjectives which usually precede, but when the general rule is that descriptive adjectives precede, there are no exceptions.
20. When any or all of the items—demonstrative, numeral, and descriptive adjective—precede the noun, they are always found in that order. If they follow, the order is either the same or its exact opposite.
21. If some or all adverbs follow the adjective they modify, then the language is one in which the qualifying adjective follows the noun and the verb precedes its nominal object as the dominant order.
22. If in comparisons of superiority the only order or one of the alternative orders is standard-marker-adjective, then the language is postpositional. With overwhelmingly more than chance frequency, if the only order is adjective-marker-standard, the language is prepositional.
23. If in apposition the proper noun usually precedes the common noun, then the language is one in which the governing noun follows its dependent genitive. With much better than chance frequency, if the common noun usually precedes the proper noun, the dependent genitive follows its governing noun.
24. If the relative expression precedes the noun either as the only construction or as an alternative construction, either the language is postpositional or the adjective precedes the noun or both.
25. If the pronominal object follows the verb, so does the nominal object.
26. If a language has discontinuous affixes, it always has either prefixing or suffixing or both.
27. If a language is exclusively suffixing, it is postpositional; if it is exclusively prefixing, it is prepositional.
28. If both the derivation and inflection follow the root, or they both precede the root, the derivation is always between the root and the inflection.
29. If the language has inflection, it always has derivation.
30. If the verb has categories of person-number or if it has categories of gender, it always has tense-mode categories.
31. If either the subject or object noun agrees with the verb in gender, then the adjective always agrees with the noun in gender.
32. Whenever the verb agrees with a nominal subject or nominal object in gender, it also agrees in number.
33. When number agreement between the noun and verb is suspended and the rule is based on order, the case is always one in which the verb precedes and the verb is in the singular.
34. No language has a trial number unless it has a dual. No language has a dual unless it has a plural.
35. There is no language in which the plural does not have some nonzero allomorphs, whereas there are languages in which the singular is expressed only by zero. The dual and the trial are almost never expressed only by zero.
36. If a language has the category of gender, it always has the category of number.

*Appendix III (continued)*

37. A language never has more gender categories in nonsingular numbers than in the singular.
38. Where there is a case system, the only case which ever has only zero allomorphs is the one which includes among its meanings that of the subject of the intransitive verb.
39. Where morphemes of both number and case are present and both follow or both precede the noun base, the expression of number almost always comes between the noun base and the expression of case.
40. When the adjective follows the noun, the adjective expresses all the inflectional categories of the noun. In such cases the noun may lack overt expression of one or all of these categories.
41. If in a language the verb follows both the nominal subject and nominal object as the dominant order, the language almost always has a case system.
42. All languages have pronominal categories involving at least three persons and two numbers.
43. If a language has gender categories in the noun, it has gender categories in the pronoun.
44. If a language has gender distinctions in the first person, it always has gender distinctions in the second or third person or in both.
45. If there are any gender distinctions in the plural of the pronoun, there are some gender distinctions in the singular also.

# Some Methods of Dynamic Comparison in Linguistics

The comparative method, or more accurately stated, comparative methods, since a multiplicity of them exist, have a fundamental place in the disciplines concerned with man in his social and cultural aspects. These disciplines, in contrast with the physical and biological sciences, never encounter in pure form the phenomena concerning which they seek for understanding and the formulation of regularities. Such entities as culture, society, religion, or language are always encountered in the concrete form of particular, historically conditioned cultures, societies, religions, languages, and so on. One basic approach is, therefore, the comparative one; and a fundamental purpose often served by such an approach is the uncovering of constancies of structure or of developmental tendencies underlying the individual variant forms. Hence we may study culture by means of cultures and language by means of languages.

In linguistics there are two generally recognized methods of comparison, the genetic and the typological. Both of these are associated with language classification, but the classification may be considered essentially a by-product of the application of fundamentally different criteria of resemblance. The classificational aspect is even more a subordinate matter when considered in relation to the overall purposes of the two methods. In the context of the present investigation, in which certain additional types of comparison are proposed, since these types do not lead to further kinds of language classification, the two aspects referred to above—namely the criteria of resemblance and the overall goal of comparison—are all the more important.

In regard to both of these, the contrast between the genetic and typological modes of comparison is of a basic nature. What constitutes a similarity for genetic investigation is determined by some theory of process, that is, a theory regarding the classes of possible changes. Thus the acceptance of Latin *sex* as a cognate of Greek *hex* involves, among other things, the assumption of certain sound changes. In this instance one assumption is that Latin continues an earlier **s* in essentially unchanged form, while in Greek there has been a change **s* > *h*. Where identity is involved, it is merely the limiting case of change (i.e., zero change or stability).[1] Such a method of comparison may be classified as dynamic because it involves, in an essential way, hypotheses about change, while methods in which this feature is absent may be called static.

Of course, often the hypothesis regarding change was arrived at later in order to explain previously noted similarities; but its being so does not nullify the fact that some such hypothesis is integrally a part of the method in that the resemblance is not theoretically accounted for until a satisfactory hypothesis of change has been proposed. It will also generally hold that the genetically accounted for resemblance involves items that are highly similar, so that they could be classified together in some acceptable static scheme. But this is merely a consequence, although in practice a highly important one, of the fact that the outcomes of historical process are, on the basis of static resemblance, similar to their antecedents.

In contrast, typological criteria of resemblance involve no such hypotheses of change. Accordingly as the relevant properties are defined more widely or more narrowly, the degree of resemblance necessary to assign languages to a typological class is greater or less. Once defined, however, providing the definition meets the necessary logical requirements, a language is declared either to have the property or not to have it, without reference to considerations of change, that is, on a purely synchronic basis. Thus, if the criterion is the existence of tone as a distinctive feature of individual segments, then Chinese, Vietnamese, and Yoruba share a common class membership in the class of tone languages.

The differing concepts of resemblance inherent in these two methods are related to their general goals. The genetic comparison of individually related forms, that is, cognates, leads to the positing of reconstructed forms as the source of the later reflexes or the resultants of changes. Inasmuch as, in satisfactory applications of the method, the hypotheses are not *ad hoc* but bring together apparently disparate instances under a single formulation, historical explanations constitute acceptable answers to certain questions and exhibit the common hallmark of satisfactory explanations, namely, generalizing

[1] From the purely phonetic point of view, the data over a time span are practically never sufficient for us to posit an identity. It is often possible, however, to assert with some confidence that phonetic feature specifications have not altered through a given period, and this lack of change in phonetic feature specifications is what is intended by "phonetic identity" in the present context.

power as shown in the subsuming of particulars under some general rule. Thus the "irregular" plurals of internal change in English (e.g., *tooth–teeth*, *mouse–mice*, *man–men*), can be shown to arise from the same succession of changes, fronting of a vowel before *i* of the following syllable in the prehistoric nominative-accusative plural termination, followed by loss of final vowel and subsequent unrounding of the *y* [ü:] of *mȳs* and the [ö:] of **tōþ*, respectively. As is characteristic of satisfactory explanations, it "unexpectedly" also accounts for other phenomena, for example, the variation in the comparative and superlative in *old–elder–eldest* and of certain derived nouns in relation to the underlying adjective, for example, *long–length*, *strong–strength*.

Typological comparison has had a much more marginal position in linguistics, precisely because, unlike the genetic method, its overall purpose was not easily apparent; however, it now seems clear that the chief value of such comparison is its role as a heuristic for the formulation of universally valid relations among properties of language. Whenever a logically possible class of some typology is null, this same fact is logically equivalent to some statement about languages in general. So-called unrestricted universals, for example, the assertion that all languages have some phonetic segments with the vocalic feature, are merely limiting cases in which the typology is the simplest possible, that is, where there is a single predicate that takes on two values, the presence or absence of some specified property. Thus, corresponding to the above statement regarding the universality of the vocalic feature is a typology in which all languages are assigned to one of two classes defined by the presence or absence of the vocalic feature, and in which the latter class is null. The logical equivalence of null membership of certain classes in more complex typologies to implicational universals has been sufficiently illustrated elsewhere.[2]

Thus both genetic and typological comparison lead to generalizations; however, there is at least one important way in which the two types of generalization differ and in respect to which, on the usual view, the explanations arising from typological procedures would be adjudged superior. The generalizations that flow from typologies approach more closely the notion of scientific law in that they are asserted to hold under general, rather than "proper-name," conditions. With regard to genetic explanatory laws, it is commonplace that regular phonetic changes, actually the only kind of linguistic regularities to which the name "law" has ever been commonly attached (e.g., Grimm's Law), hold in each instance for some specified language, or group of languages, and for a specified chronological span. This limitation would cease to exist

[2] See Greenberg 1966a: 9–10.

if it were possible to specify in general terms, in principle applicable to all languages, the conditions under which changes such as those codified in Grimm's statement take place. Such general specification, of course, has not been possible.

In contrast, such an implicational universal as the one discussed later in this paper, namely that whenever a language has voiceless low vowels it always has voiceless high vowels, has the class of all languages as its scope. Its logical form may be paraphrased as follows. If we take any language, if that language has property $\alpha$ it has property $\beta$. Because it applies to any language, its limiting conditions are merely the definitional characteristics of language and do not involve specific constants of time and space. Hence such universals conform to the usual requirements of generality for scientific laws, while those based on genetic comparisons do not.

This distinction is no mere quibble about the use of the word "law" with its honorific connotations. Given that the conditions of application of synchronically derived universals are general, when one encounters a new language it is possible, from certain characteristics, to predict others. Such fresh data will also constitute an empirical test of the validity of the hypothesis. On the other hand, it makes no sense to ask such questions as whether there are any languages in the world which violate Grimm's Law, since it only applies to a given language during a specified chronological period.

These results would seem to be a particular exemplification within linguistics of the well-known dichotomy, described, for example, by Windelband in the nineteenth century, between idiographic, historical, particularizing disciplines and nomothetic, generalizing sciences. Within anthropology, the structuralist-functionalist school of A. R. Radcliffe-Brown has similarly divided anthropology into two disciplines, a law-seeking, scientific, social anthropology and a particularistic, historically oriented ethnology, with an undisguised superior evaluation of the former.[3]

This contrast, however, as I will attempt to show, is merely an apparent one. There exists the possibility of a more comprehensive mode of diachronic comparison which shares with synchronic typology the attribute of generality. The individual items of such comparisons are not the cognate forms, but the changes themselves, as formulated in rules and occurring in historically independent cases, and hence subject to classification (corresponding to synchronic typology) and generalization without proper-name restriction. For reasons that will presently appear, it is appropriate to call such comparison

[3] It should be pointed out, however, that others, notably Kroeber, accept this division in principle but claim that anthropology is basically history rather than science, without viewing this as a defect.

processual. That this type of comparison has received only marginal and unexplicit attention rests at least partly on the preemption of the term "comparative" to particular applications of the genetic method, so that diachronic linguistics has appeared already to possess its own comparative method.

Unlike the genetic and the typological methods, the classification involved in the processual approach is not one of languages but of changes. A classificatory scheme exists, although it still stands in need of systematic reformulation, namely the traditional terminology of process, since a process is simply a class of similar changes. Such rubrics as analogical change, dissimilation of liquids, and palatalization each define a class of changes, individual members of which occur in different languages and at different times. As with synchronic typologies, we may have classificatory criteria of lesser or greater breadth. Just as the class of languages with level tones only is a subset of the tonal languages, so palatalization, umlauting, and the like are subprocesses in relation to regular, conditioned sound change.

In this study, processual generalizations are not investigated in isolation from the static universals arising from the application of typological methods. Four methods of processual comparison are proposed here, and each is illustrated by an extended example. Their status as distinct methods, as will appear from later consideration, is more pragmatic than logical, but such a classification should prove useful in the initial stages of development. The four methods are called here the dynamicization of typologies, the dynamicization of subtypologies, intergenetic processual comparison, and intragenetic processual comparison, respectively.

Since the first of these, the *dynamicization of typologies*, has been discussed elsewhere, though not under the same name, it will be treated with relative brevity.[4] Consider any typology in which there are at least two nonempty classes among those defined by the typology. Then, for every pair of nonempty classes, we can ask a processual question regarding the mechanism of change of type in either direction. If, for example, a certain typology contains, among its defined classes of languages, three nonempty ones, $A$, $B$, and $C$, we can ask how a language of type $A$ becomes a language of type $B$, how a language of type $B$ becomes a language of type $A$, and so on. The number of such processual questions is evidently $n(n - 1)$, in the present instance, 6. Not all these processes need occur, however. For example, given three types $A$, $B$, and $C$, investigation might show that a language cannot change directly from $A$ to $C$, but must first change from $A$ to $B$ and then from $B$ to $C$. It is even theoretically possible, though in practice

[4] Greenberg 1966b.

unlikely, that none of the classes can change into each other. Then, if there are *n* such classes in existence, there must be at least *n* protolanguages for mankind, so that no language in one type could have a common progenitor with a language of another type. The assumption of such fixity for any typological criterion is highly improbable and can be refuted in very many instances. For example, the relation of Persian, a non-sex-gender language, to Hindi, a sex-gender language, shows that change in at least one direction is possible in this instance.

A theory that states the set of changes by which a language can move from one typological class to another may be called a theory of relative origin because it applies to the origin of a specific type of language, a type that, in general, arises in a multiplicity of language families and chronological periods. To arrive at such a theory, we will have to compare diverse and historically independent examples which are themselves the results of comparative genetic studies in the ordinary sense. If a single, typical set of changes is found to occur in each instance, we may say that we have a theory of exclusive relative origin. Such theories are obviously the most useful, but theories of multiple origin can also be useful, as will be shown later.

We may illustrate the dynamicization of typologies by means of the following example. Consider the synchronic typology in accordance with which languages are classified by the simultaneous application of two criteria, the presence or absence of nasal vowels and the presence or absence of oral vowels. There will then be four logically possible typological classes of languages: (1) oral and nasal vowels both present; (2) oral vowels present but nasal vowels absent; (3) nasal vowels present but oral vowels absent; and (4) oral and nasal vowels both absent.

Of the four classes thus defined, classes 3 and 4 are empty as far as present knowledge goes. Corresponding to this fact, we have the unrestricted universal that all languages have oral vowels, and the implicational universal that the presence of nasal vowels implies the presence of oral vowels but not vice versa. Because there are two nonempty classes, 1 and 2, we have two questions regarding relative origins. The first of these is concerned with change from class 1 to class 2: How do languages with both oral vowels and nasal vowels become languages with only oral vowels? In other words, how are nasal vowels lost? The second question relates to the manner in which languages of class 2 become languages of class 1: How do languages without nasal vowels acquire them?

We shall be chiefly concerned with this second question. Ferguson has already suggested a hypothesis in the form of the following diachronic universal. This hypothesis asserts that a nasal vowel "apart from borrowings and analogical innovations, always results from the loss of a primary nasal consonant."[5] The typical course of events is as follows. A previously oral vowel becomes nasalized nondistinctively through a preceding and/or following nasal consonant. With the loss of the nasal consonant, which is the conditioning factor, a phonological contrast between oral and nasal vowel comes into existence. Where the nasal consonant follows the vowel, the sequence of changes may be schematized as follows: $VN \rightarrow \tilde{V}N \rightarrow \tilde{V}$.

It should be noted that in such diachronic universals of exclusive relative origin, no assertion is made about the period of time in which the change takes place. Indeed, if *VN* remained in some language indefinitely, it would not refute this thesis. It is not even refuted by the fact that, in certain languages (e.g., Polish), in certain environments (normally before stops), nasalized vowels have changed back into sequences of oral vowel + homorganic nasal consonant (e.g., *ẽb* = > *emb* =). All that is asserted is that, if a language has nasal vowels, at some time in its past, if their origin can be discovered, they arise from the loss of nasal consonants in the environment of nondistinctively nasalized vowels. Such universals might be considered diachronic implications, in which certain facts about a language at time $t_2$ imply certain other facts about the same language at time $t_1$, provided $t_1$ precedes $t_2$ at some unspecified interval. Since the implied is the hierarchically superior in an implication, the statement in terms of which certain facts at a specified time imply certain facts at a previous time, but not vice versa, is in accord with the historian's intuitive feeling that events of an earlier period explain those of a later period, and not the other way around.

The connection between synchronic and diachronic universals can be illustrated by showing how a specific synchronic universal about the relationship of oral and nasal vowels can be explained in the sense of logical deduction from a set of premises which includes the diachronic hypothesis of relative origin which has just been stated. For simplicity of exposition, I confine the illustration here to the situation in which nasalized vowels developed from the phonetic nasalization of oral vowels with a following nasal consonant, but what will be said is applicable *mutatis mutandis* to instances in which it precedes, or both precedes and follows.

The synchronic universal with which I am concerned is again one already stated by Ferguson and voiced still earlier by Hockett.[6] It is particularly well attested, and I know of no contrary instances. It is the thesis that the number of nasalized vowel phonemes in a language is always less than or equal to the number of oral vowels.

The most frequent situation before loss of the following nasal consonant will be that in which the set of vowels which occurs with following nasal

[5] Ferguson 1963.

[6] Ferguson 1963: 46; Hockett 1955: 90.

consonants is identical with the set of vowels which occurs in all other environments. If this condition holds, then, to begin with, each oral vowel will be matched by a corresponding nasal vowel. Hence the number of oral vowels is here equal to the number of nasal vowels.

Sometimes the number of vowels which may be followed by a nasal consonant is smaller. If this condition holds, then the number of nasal vowels will, in their initial period of autonomous existence, be fewer in number than the oral vowels. On the other hand, no instance is known to me of a language in which the number of vowels which may be followed by nasal consonants is greater than that of vowels which may occur in all other environments. We may, therefore, consider that a synchronic universal asserting that the number of distinct oral vowels preceding nasal consonants is always less than or equal to the oral vowels occurring in any other environment will be another premise in deducing the universal under discussion.

To this premise we must add a further diachronic factor, namely that merger among nasal vowels seems to occur more often than merger among oral vowels. A strong statement may be cast in the form of a further diachronic hypothesis. Merger between any pair of oral vowels implies the preceding merger of the corresponding nasals if they exist. Thus in contemporary French *œ̃* has become *ɛ̃* for many speakers, merging with the latter, while the corresponding oral vowels *œ* and *ɛ* have shown no such tendency. From this diachronic universal it follows that there is a mechanism that will decrease the number of nasal vowels relative to the number of oral ones, but there is none working in the opposite direction. The various generalizations just described, both synchronic and diachronic, seem sufficient as premises to deduce the synchronic universals regarding the relation of nasal to oral vowels and may, therefore, be said to explain them.

It has been noted that, in considering the problems of change of type to and from the two classes of languages under consideration, that is, those with oral but without nasal vowels, and those with both oral and nasal vowels, the two types were not, as it were, treated symmetrically. A change from the first type to the second was considered as a theory of the acquisition of nasal vowels, and from the second to the first, as a loss of the same property. In fact, it appears to be more than an arbitrary terminological convention that nasality is treated as a property and nonnasality as its negation, rather than vice versa. There is an obvious phonetic justification here. On this basis a great many instances of change of type may be viewed as coming under the general heading of acquisition and loss of contingent properties, such as nasality in vowels. Usually the proportion of languages with a contingent property is a relative minority of the world's languages.

The second method to be discussed is the intensive comparison of the languages which have such a property. It thus corresponds to the method of "comparison within the type" advocated by functional theorists in the social sciences. In applying this method, termed the *dynamicization of a subtypology*, we first consider such languages with a view to the formulation of synchronic universals concerning the property in question. We then "dynamicize" the results by procedures to be described later, in order to establish developmental courses of events typical of the subtype.

The example chosen to illustrate this method is a study of languages that have phonetically voiceless vowels. This type is one that occurs within a typology embracing all languages based on the criteria of presence or absence of voiced vowels and presence or absence of unvoiced vowels. In such a typology the class of languages with voiced vowels only constitutes the vast majority, the languages with both unvoiced and voiced vowels is a minority, and the class of languages with voiceless vowels only and the class without either voiced or voiceless vowels are both null. The universals associated with the parent typology are then the following: All languages have vowels. The presence of voiceless vowels implies the presence of voiced vowels.

This study, which makes no claim to exhaustiveness, deals with approximately fifty languages.[7] In most of these the feature of voicelessness in vowels is nondistinctive. There are a number of languages, however, including the Keresan languages of Santa Ana and Santo Domingo, the Shoshonean languages Comanche and Ute, Mayan Chontal and Galla, and Teso and Bagirmi in Africa, in which a phonemic contrast between voiced and voiceless vowels exists.[8] On the basis of this sample, we will first seek to establish synchronic generalizations relating to voiceless vowels, and then illustrate the process of dynamicization.

Before proceeding further, however, some discussion of phonetic matters is called for.[9] In general, languages have been considered to have voiceless vowels if this term is used in the phonetic description; but, as will presently

[7]The sources regarding languages with voiceless vowels are enumerated in Section B of the bibliography. Footnote references to titles in this section of the bibliography are marked B. The phenomenon of voiceless vowels is probably more widespread than would appear from the literature. It is reported from every major world area. The apparent predominance of occurrence in American Indian languages is probably a by-product of the phonetic training of linguists involved in this area. It should be noted that, for certain languages listed in the bibliography, the information is too vague to be utilized for some, or even all, of the general statements proposed here, as is tacitly indicated by their omission.

[8]The existence of phonemic contrasts of voice in vowels was denied by Jakobson but asserted by Comanche specialists. On this matter see especially Canonge 1957-B. Since that time further examples have been adduced. Recently Harms 1966-B, in a binary transformationally oriented restatement of Southern Paiute phonology, has treated voicing in vowels as phonemic (I believe incorrectly).

[9]I am particularly indebted to Paul Postal for several comments regarding voiceless vowels raised during the discussion of this paper as given orally at the 1966 Linguistic Institute at the University of California, Los Angeles.

appear, this criterion is not entirely adequate. The problem concerns the relation between voiceless vowels and whispered vowels on the one hand, and aspiration and *h*-sounds on the other. Presumably voiceless vowels have an open glottis with the same adjustment as for voiceless consonants, while whispered vowels involve a different glottal adjustment which includes the closing of the arytenoid part of the glottis.[10] An early investigator, Harrington, in his description of Ute draws a clear distinction along these lines: "Voiceless sounds are not whispered. Whispering requires a special adjustment of the larynx."[11] It is evident, however, from some of the descriptions that many linguists consider the terms "voiceless vowels" and "whispered vowels" to be synonymous. Thus Andrzejewski, after describing four Galla vowels that "have no voicing," states that "several alternative terms could be suggested . . . voiceless vowels, semi-mute vowels, or whispered vowels."[12] In regard to Bannack, Liljeblad refers to certain vowels as unvoiced, and in a passage immediately following and obviously alluding to the same sound, calls them whispered vowels.[13] Furthermore, Yamagiwa refers to vowels of Japanese which other writers have generally called voiceless as "devocalized (whispered)."[14] In view of this apparent equivalence of usage, a few instances have been included in this study; for example, Karok, for which the only source describes certain vowels as whispered. Moreover, Holmer's description of Goajiro, which contains the statement that ". . . final short vowels are usually voiceless (or whispered) . . . ," is susceptible to interpretation either as a synonymous use of the two terms, or as free variation between voiceless and whispered.[15]

In contrast to *h*-sounds, voiceless vowels should theoretically show a lack of glottal friction. And, indeed, several sources indicate phonetic differences along this line. For example, Chontal Mayan is stated to have final segments of vowels in the utterance-final position containing "light aspiration." The same phonetic symbolization is employed here as for vowels in medial position explicitly stated to be unvoiced. It is then stated that "this aspiration is much lighter than that which is interpreted as phonemic *h*."[16] In Kaiwa, aspiration and devoicing are stated to be in free variation in final unaccented

[10] Smalley (1962), especially pp. 392–93 and the accompanying tapes. The study reported in Lehiste 1964: 150–59, supports the acoustic distinctness of *h* and whispered vowels in American English.

[11] Harrington 1910-B: 22.

[12] Andrzejewski 1957-B: 264.

[13] Liljeblad 1950-B: 130.

[14] Yamagiwa 1942-B: 2.

[15] Holmer 1949-B: 51. Also the remarks of Heffner 1964: 85, indicate the precariousness of the distinction.

[16] Keller 1959-B: 45.

syllables. They are thus treated as being distinct phonetically. A further statement concerns Cayuvava in which "voiceless trailoff" of a vowel is called "slight aspiration." Further, "this aspiration differs markedly in quality and distribution from the sound that is interpreted as phonemic *h*. It is more lenis and does not have the friction of the *h*."[17]

It is well known, however, that *h* as a phonetic symbol is frequently used to represent voiceless vowels of the same quality as adjacent voiced vowel segments. In this instance the difference is purely distributional. Such a view is clearly expressed by Lounsbury in reference to Oneida. "Voiceless vowels are assigned to the |h| phoneme in those positions in which their vowel color is environmentally determined but their voicelessness is not. They are assigned to the respective vowel phonemes in those cases . . . in which their voicelessness is environmentally determined but their vowel color is not."[18]

If we conclude, as appears necessary, that sounds assigned to the |h| phoneme in some languages in existing descriptions are, in fact, voiceless vocalic segments, then there are four possible cases: (1) Vowel color is predictable but voicelessness is not. Here we have *h*. (2) Vowel color is not predictable but voicelessness is. These are nonphonemic voiceless vowels of the quality of the corresponding voiced segments. (3) Neither vowel color nor voicing is predictable. Such segments are likewise considered voiceless vowels but phonemically distinct from their voiced counterparts, as is true of Comanche. (4) Both voicelessness and vowel color are predictable, as is true in Secoya, a language in which strongly stressed vowels have a voiceless final mora which is of the same quality as the initial voiced portion, and which only appears as a free variant before a following voiceless consonant. Such a voiceless vowel segment is to be considered an *h* because its quality is predictable, and in traditional phonemic analysis it is eliminated as nonphonemic.

We have chosen as our definitional feature for voiceless vowel, as distinct from *h*, absence of predictability of vowel quality from an immediately adjacent voiced vowel segment.[19] Wherever this condition does not hold, we do not consider the sound in question to be a voiceless vowel, unless there is an explicit indication of phonetic difference from an *h* in the same language. On this basis only one instance in which the existing description specifies a

[17] Key 1964-B: 146.

[18] Lounsbury 1953-B: 30n.

[19] On the basis of this definition, voiceless segments constituting "echo" vowels after the glottal stop are considered voiceless vowels because they are not immediately adjacent to the voiced vowel with which they agree in quality. Huasteco, in which there is only terminal unvoicing of the vowel segment, is considered to have voiceless vowels for present purposes, as these sounds are stated to be less fortis than the *h* that occurs in the language (Larsen and Pike 1949-B: 275). For the merely heuristic value of the present definition, see note 62, below.

voiceless vowel has been eliminated from the sample, namely, that of Secoya, just mentioned. It seems likely that, because the voiceless vowel segment in this language is always followed by a voiceless consonant, this example is to be assimilated to that of preaspirated consonants which are always unvoiced and medial.

The consistent application of this criterion eliminates one possible universal, namely, that which would assert that the existence of voicelessness in the initial portion of a vocoid implies its presence throughout the segment. What would be forbidden by this statement would include sequences of the type *ḁa*. These do occur but are everywhere analyzed as *ha* in practice and according to the above definition. The universals proposed here are valid, to my knowledge, for the sample considered here and do not rest on the unlawfulness of combinations that occur phonetically, but are to be analyzed as containing occurrences of segments labeled *h* according to the present definition.

We turn now to a consideration of synchronic universals relating to voiceless vowels. Basically we are looking for hierarchical preferences regarding properties associated with voiceless vowels. These may be properties pertaining to the voiceless vowel segments themselves, to sequential characteristics, or to prosodic features over longer stretches. For example, among the present results, preference for low stress over high stress refers to properties of the voiceless segments as such, the preference for adjoining voiceless consonants is sequential, while that for voicelessness of the final vowel in a statement over a question intonation is prosodic. These synchronic results are summarized in a series of numbered universals, each of which is accompanied by discussion of the supporting evidence.

The first set which, in accordance with the foregoing division, refers to features simultaneous with vocalic voicelessness, has as a common motif the preference of voiceless vowels for nonculminative features, that is, weak stress, short length, and low pitch. By culminative features are meant those that figure in rules of the following type, taking stress as an example. Every phonological word has exactly one occurrence of strong stress. No such rules seem to exist for the opposite, nonculminative feature. Thus there is no language in which every word has one and only one weak stress.

1. In languages with stress, every vocalic segment that is voiceless has the weakest degree of stress.

There are explicit statements regarding the co-occurrence of the weakest stress with all voiceless vowels for the following languages: Acoma, Chama, Comanche, Dagut, Kaiwa, Nyangumata, Oneida, Papago, Southern Paiute, Tadjik, Tunica, Uzbek, and Yana. Arizona Tewa, Bagirmi, Galla, Japanese, and Teso are tonal or tonal accentual, and they are not described as possessing stress phenomena. The Yaitepec dialect of Chatino, the only one with voiceless vowels, is a tonal language with automatic stress on the final syllable. The rules are so stated that the vowel of this stressed syllable cannot be voiceless. For Totonac and Korean, neither stress nor tone is mentioned.

Cayuvava, which has been included in the sample on the strength of the statement quoted earlier that the voiceless vowel is distinct from the stronger aspiration of a true *h*, has certain occurrences of the voiceless vowel as the terminal portion of a stressed syllabic. The transcription is neutral regarding the participation in stress of the voiceless portion. There are a number of languages in which the rules as stated do not necessarily exclude stress in voiceless vowels. Nowhere, however, in the literature examined was there an example cited in which a voiceless vowel is unambiguously marked as stressed. The above generalization is considered highly probable on this basis. The absence of stress on voiceless vowels may, of course, rest merely on the physical impossibility of a voiceless vowel having sufficient prominence to produce the acoustic impression of stress.

> 2. In languages with distinctive vowel length, the existence of voiceless long vowels implies that of voiceless short vowels but not vice versa.

For a number of languages with distinctive vowel length, there are explicit or easily deducible statements regarding the nonoccurrence of voiceless long vowels. These include Bannack, Comanche, Galla, Goajiro, Japanese, Karok, Nyangumata, Oneida, Santa Ana, Southern Paiute, Tadjik, and Yana. In other cases there is no statement explicitly denying their existence, but no examples are cited. In Acoma there is a cited example of a voiceless long vowel. For all the languages with vowel quantity, however, the presence of short voiceless vowels is well attested; hence, the above implication holds. Unlike stress, there is no question of physical impossibility, as shown by the Acoma example.

We would correspondingly expect voicelessness to be favored for low-pitched, as against high-pitched, vowels. Because few of the languages with voiceless vowels are pitch languages, the evidence is necessarily limited. In view of the close relation between voicelessness and whisper in vowels, alluded to above, we have a phonetic issue closely allied to the much-discussed question regarding the preservation of distinctive pitch in whispered speech. There is a corresponding difference of opinion in the literature on the present topic. Thus McKaughan mentions voiceless allophones of *i* and *u* in Chatino "whose tone registers (if indeed they exist), have not been discovered."[20] In

[20] McKaughan 1954-B: 27.

regard to Arizona Tewa, it is stated that, when a vowel or vowel cluster is completely devoiced, it has no tone.[21] On the other hand, Tucker and Bryan give tone markings for all three levels found in the languages for the voiceless vowels of Galla, Teso, and Bagirmi. What evidence there is wholly favors low pitch over high pitch for voiceless vowels, as exemplified most clearly in Japanese, for which Han says that the "vowels *i* and *u* in low pitched *onsetsu* are regularly unvoiced between voiceless consonants."[22] For Cheyenne, it is stated that single short vowels not characterized by high pitch are voiceless in final position.[23] In other languages, for example, Karok and Chama, the unstressed vowels that are voiceless are stated to have low pitch as a concomitant feature. Such linguistic evidence appears definite enough to support the following statement:

3. If any language has high-pitched voiceless vowels, it has low-pitched voiceless vowels.

We now consider the quality of voiceless vowels.

4. To every voiceless vowel in any language there is a corresponding voiced vowel of the same quality, but not necessarily vice versa.

This statement implies that the number of voiceless vowels never exceeds the number of voiced vowels in any language, and parallels the relationship of nasal to oral vowels. The present statement is, however, stronger in that one fairly commonly finds nasal vowels that do not match any oral vowel in quality, whereas in our sample every voiceless vowel can be matched by a voiced vowel of the same quality.

5. The existence of voiceless vowels of less than the maximal degree of vowel height implies the existence of some vowels of the maximal degree.

The favoring of high vowels with regard to voicelessness is apparent in Table 1, which includes all the languages of the present sample in which voiceless vowels do not occur with all the qualities of voiced vowels.

[21] Yegerlehner 1959-B: 5.

[22] Han 1962-B: 51. *Onsetsu* means, roughly, "mora." Compare also the statement of Doke (1931-B: 33): "A common occurrence in the Bantu languages is the devocalization (almost whispering) of final vowels, particularly *i*, when the tone in careful pronunciation would be a very low one." Trager (1940-B: 29) describes the final vowel in Serbo-Croatian disyllables with falling accent pattern and hence low final pitch as "very weak—often voiceless."

[23] Davis 1962-B: 36. The inference here is that low-pitched final short vowels have *become* voiceless. There is no indication that these voiceless vowels have distinguishable pitch.

*Table 1*

High Vowels and Voicelessness

| Language | Voiceless and voiced | Voiced only |
|---|---|---|
| Awadhi | *i, u, e* | *a, o* |
| Campa | *i* | *o, e, a* |
| Chatino | *i, u* | *o, e, a* |
| Dagur | *i, u, e*[1] | *o, a* |
| Huichol | *i, ʌ, e*[2] | *u, a* |
| Serbo-Croatian | *i, u*[3] | *o, e, a* |
| Tadjik | *i, u, a* | *e*(:), *o*(:), *ú*(:)[4] |
| Tunica | *u* | *i, e, ɛ, a, ɔ, o* |
| Uzbek | *i, u* | *e, ɔ, o, a* |

[1] I follow Martin's symbolization here: *e* is phonetically [ə].

[2] Huichol /ʌ/ is described as a high, central, unrounded vowel in McIntosh 1945b.

[3] Trager (1940b) seems to imply, however, that all Serbo-Croatian vowels may be voiceless under certain accentual conditions.

[4] Since the investigations of Polivanov, it has become customary to categorize the Tadjik vowels *e, o, ú as stable in contrast to i, u,* and *a,* which are categorized as unstable. Traditionally the former were considered long, and the latter, short; and the comparative evidence suggests that this was formerly true phonetically. The stable vowels do not differ in length from the unstable in stressed syllables. In unstressed syllables the unstable vowels are subject to voicelessness in an unvoiced consonantal environment and quantitative reduction or loss in general, while the stable vowels are only slightly shorter than in stressed syllables. We may conjecture that the unstable vowels became voiceless in a period when the phonetic distinction was still one of length in all environments.

Additional evidence for the favoring of high vowels can be found in some instances in which voiceless vowels exist with all the same qualities as voiced. In Japanese and Papago, the high vowels are devoiced in a more extensive set of environments than low vowels. Regarding Japanese, Gensen Mori states that ". . . *a* is subject to devocalization in a lesser degree than *i* or *u*. Those who regularly devocalize *i* and *u* in certain positions will not always do the same with *a*."[24] For Comanche and Nyangumata there are explicit statements that the lowest vowel *a* is much more rarely devoiced than the others. In Shawnee, of the four vowels *i*, *e*, *a*, and *o*, all of which are pausally devoiced, only *i* exerts a further regressive force in devoicing a vowel of the preceding syllable under certain conditions.

We now consider some environmental limitations on the appearance of voiceless vowels.

> 6. Every voiceless vowel is either preceded or followed by silence or a voiceless plain (i.e., nonglottalic) sound.

[24] Mori 1929-B: 41.

For example, no voiceless vowel occurs between two voiced consonants. In some languages the stronger statement holds that every voiceless vowel is both preceded and followed by a voiceless plain sound or silence. Silence almost always follows, rather than precedes, because, as will be shown later, a favorite position for voiceless vowels is utterance final, while occurrences in utterance, or indeed in word initial are excessively rare.[25] Among the languages for which this stronger statement holds are: Acoma, Cayuvava, Chama, Chatino, Chontal, Comanche, Huasteco, Japanese, Nyangumata, Pame, Serbo-Croatian, Tadjik, Tunica, Ute, and Yana.[26] In some of these languages, voiceless allophones of otherwise voiced nasals, liquids, and semivowels are found adjacent to voiceless vowels.

The preceding statement also excludes the occurrence of voiceless vowels flanked by two glottalized consonants, glottal stop and glottalized consonant, voiced consonant and glottalized consonant, or voiced consonant and glottal stop. There is additional evidence regarding the disfavoring of voiceless vowels adjacent to glottalic sounds. In Acoma only plain consonants occur before final unvoiced vowels, and nonfinal vowels are devoiced only when neither preceded nor followed by glottalic consonants.[27] In Chatino *i* and *u* are unvoiced in unstressed syllables, provided the following consonant is not a glottal stop. In Papago *i* and *ɨ* are voiceless in pause, except after a laryngeal. In Southern Paiute after a glottal stop preceded by a vowel, a final vowel is said to be only partly reduced in voice, becoming a "murmured" vowel.

The tendency of vowels to voicelessness is particularly powerful in the final of words and of longer units such as sentence or utterance. For many of the languages, voiceless vowels can only occur in the final position of some such unit. Thus, in the following languages, voiceless vowels appear only in the final position of utterance, sentence, or some extensive intonational contour: Arabela, Arizona Tewa, Basque, Galla, Hawaiian, Huichol, Ignaciana, Kaiwa, Karok, Maori, Nyangumata, Oneida, Shawnee, Tunica, and Yana. Languages such as Shawnee, in which voicelessness extends to nonfinal vowel under specified conditions and only when the final vowel is itself voiceless, have been included here.

In most of the languages of the foregoing list, there are further limitations, so that finals are unvoiced only under certain conditions. These limitations are usually in terms of variables already mentioned. For example, in some languages

[25] The only examples encountered were in Southern Paiute.

[26] It is not clear from Harrington's description whether voiced consonants occur adjacent to voiceless vowels in Ute.

[27] More precisely, a final vowel can be devoiced only if the preceding consonant is a plain aspirated occlusive or /h/. A short, unaccented vowel that does not come after the last accent is optionally devoiced if it is preceded and followed by plain obstruents (Miller 1965-B: 16–17).

only unstressed final vowels are devoiced, or only high final vowels, and so on. For another considerable group of languages, voiceless vowels occur only in the word-final position, thus embracing *a fortiori* final position in longer units. These include Bagirmi, Bannack, Campa, Chama, Cofan, Huasteco, Serbo-Croatian, Teso, and Totonac. Most of the remaining languages of the sample have voiceless vowels in both word-medial and word-final positions. Where they do, final occurrences are more frequent, sometimes overwhelmingly so. There are, however, four languages, Mayan Chontal, Chatino, Tadjik, and possibly Japanese,[28] in which voiceless vowels occur in initial and medial position, but not in word-final position. Chatino and Tadjik share the feature of regular final stress, and it has been seen that voicelessness is incompatible with loud stress. Mayan Chontal has most commonly, but not exclusively, final stress. Japanese will be considered later for its methodological interest. For the moment, we consider it a possible exception to the following generalization.

> 7. If a language does not regularly have high stress on the word-final syllabics, then, if it has voiceless vowels in word initial, it has them in word medial; if in word medial, then in word final; if in word final, then in the final of some longer unit or units such as an intonational contour, sentence, or utterance.

The disfavoring of laryngeal sounds, including the glottal stop in the environment of voiceless vowels, was discussed earlier. In sentence-final position, a special relationship of opposition sometimes exists between glottalization and voicelessness. For example, in Chama, "the plain glottal stop distinguishes the open juncture terminally when it is preceded by a primary stressed vowel or when the final vowel is not unvoiced under weak stress."[29] In other words, a final, unstressed vowel varies between voicelessness and voicing followed by the glottal stop. In Arabela, a nondistinctive glottal stop appears in most sentence finals and is incompatible with voicelessness of the preceding vowel. In Karok, whereas a short final vowel is optionally devoiced, a long vowel is voiced and glottalized. In Bannack, final unstressed vowels vary freely between voicelessness and voicing. In the latter instance, the preceding consonant is glottalized. In Oneida, in pause a final glottal stop is lost, and the preceding, now final, vowel becomes voiceless. In some instances, the two alternatives of voicelessness and glottal closure are connected with types of sentence intonation. In Nyangumata, in which most sentences

[28] Japanese is included on the basis of Bloch's analysis; however, some earlier accounts indicate the presence of voiceless vowels in word final, e.g., Lange 1903: xvii.

[29] Firestone 1955-B: 53.

end in voiceless vowels, glottalization occurs in place of voicelessness most commonly in questions and accompanied by rising intonation. In Walapai, there is a similar opposition, though without concomitant glottalization. Terminal statement juncture has decrease in stress, pitch, and voicing. Question final juncture is characterized by a sharp rise in pitch and amplitude, and there is no devoicing. A parallel situation exists in Galla. Those short, final vowels that are subject to voicelessness have this characteristic in statement-final position but keep their voicing in the corresponding yes-no question. Those short final vowels that are not subject to devoicing retain it in statements and are replaced by the paired long vowel in the corresponding yes-no question. In Mikasuki, a Muskoghean language without voiceless vowels, "the glottal catch occurs most frequently with questions of the type 'Is it a ____?' and 'Is he ____ing?,' in which a tone change often combines with glottal catch to change a statement to a question."[30] The further observation is made that a terminal vowel with falling tone indicates "rest" or "completion," while level tone with following glottal stop indicates "nonfinality." These phenomena are evidently allied with the "rhetorical lengthening" described by Sapir for Southern Paiute. "Final vowels, instead of being elided or unvoiced, are sometimes, for reasons of rhetorical emphasis, lengthened and generally followed by a glottal stop."[31]

Just as the preferred position for voiceless vowels is final, so that for glottal stop is initial. The existence of glottal attack for the vocalic sentence-initial or word-initial position is a well-known phenomenon. A particularly striking example in the present sample is Totonac, in which all word-initial vowels are laryngealized, and all sentence-final short vowels are voiceless. Corresponding to the preference of voiceless vowels for nonculminative prosodic elements is the widely reported occurrence of glottal accent in which glottalization fulfills the function of a culminative pitch accent. This complex of oppositions is diagramed in Table 2. The manifold connections involved in Table 2 suggest a number of possible universals. In the present connection, only those involving voicelessness are considered. The connections between voicelessness and final position, and weak stress and shortness in vowels have already been stated. The following additional universal holds on the basis of the evidence just cited.

> 8. The presence of voiceless vowels in the final of yes-no questions implies their presence in the corresponding statements.

As a final observation concerning synchronic generalizations about voiceless vowels, it may be pointed out that in Yana voiceless vowels occur in

[30] West 1962: 86.
[31] Sapir 1930-B: 20–21.

*Table 2*

Complex of Oppositions Between Voiceless Vowels and Glottal Stops

| Marked | Unmarked |
|---|---|
| Initial | Final |
| Glottalization | Voicelessness |
| Question | Statement |
| Emphatic statement | Normal statement |
| Rising pitch | Falling pitch |
| Strong stress | Weak stress |
| Vowel length | Vowel shortness |

"woman's speech" but not in "men's speech." What is meant here by woman's speech is that of women talking to women, men to women, or women to men. Men's speech comprises only those instances in which men speak to men.

Thus far, the method of subtypologies has been applied in a purely synchronic manner. Comparison of a set of languages containing voiceless vowels has led to the formulation of a number of synchronic universals concerning them; however, every implication in which both the implying and implied have empirical exemplification can be mapped into a diachronic process by which the former develops from the latter. For example, from the synchronic universal that voiceless vowels of lower tongue heights imply those of the highest tongue height, we can frame the hypothesis that voicelessness in vowels begins with those of the highest level and then spreads to the others. This statement is a hypothesis, because there is nothing contradictory involved in the assumption that in some languages only the high vowels become voiceless, while in others all of the vowels become voiceless through a single change. What is excluded, though, is the hypothesis that low vowels are the first to become voiceless and that voicelessness subsequently spreads to high vowels. If this latter statement were so, such languages in the initial stages would have low voiceless vowels without having high ones and thus contradict the original universal.

The relevance of the proviso that both implier and implied must have empirical exemplification can be shown by reference to the universal regarding stressed and unstressed voiceless vowels. The implication that every language with stressed voiceless vowels has unstressed voiceless vowels holds. There are, as has been seen, no authenticated examples of stressed voiceless vowels. Hence we cannot hypothesize that languages first have unstressed voiceless vowels, and that voicelessness then extends to stressed vowels because this, as a limiting case, is a hypothetical stage that is never reached.

Purely synchronic evidence can be relevant in demonstrating that the

*Table 3*
Free Variation and Style Assumptions

| Vowel type | Speech style: Lento | Allegro |
|---|---|---|
| Low | $a$ | $a > A$ |
| High | $I < i$ | $I > i$ |

hypothesized succession does take place. There are, here, two assumptions which, for phonological change at least, receive considerable support outside of the present examples. The first of these is that, whenever a sound change takes place, the older form and the innovating form are, for a period of time, in free variation, with the innovating free variant increasing in frequency until the change is accomplished. Hence, if in one environment variation is free, while in another complimentary distribution shows that the change has been accomplished, change in the first environment must be more recent. The other assumption has to do with style. The situation is no doubt more complex than the mere coexistence of two styles, lento and allegro; however, it is only in reference to this distinction that a large body of data exists which can be exploited for theoretical purposes. There is much evidence in the area of phonology which shows that the allegro form is the innovating form which only later spreads to the lento style. Both the free variation and style assumptions can be neatly documented from the detailed observations regarding voicelessness in Japanese vowels made by Bloch and summarized in Table 3.
Here, *a*, *A*, *i*, and *I* represent voiced low vowels, voiceless low vowels, voiced high vowels, and voiceless high vowels, respectively. The symbol > means "more frequent than," and < means "less frequent than."

The information in Table 3 may be stated as follows: The voiceless high vowels are more frequent than voiced high vowels in allegro, less frequent in lento. The low vowels are voiced only in lento. They occur in allegro; but, unlike the high vowels, the voiceless variants are less frequent than the voiced. We may translate these assertions into dynamic terms as follows: The high vowels have progressed further in becoming voiceless than the low vowels, inasmuch as they have penetrated into lento from allegro, although they are still less frequent in the former style than the latter. The voiceless low vowels have not yet penetrated the lento style, and even in the allegro style, unlike the voiceless high vowels, they are still less frequent than their voiced variant.

Note that these data constitute an empirical confirmation of the thesis that innovations first appear in allegro, then in lento. The hypothesis arrived at independently of the present evidence from a variety of languages was that voicelessness in vowels could not begin with low vowels because such a beginning would produce, in the first stages, a nonexistent language type. Had, for example, low vowels in voiceless form been found in lento but not in allegro, or had low voiceless vowels been more frequent than their voiced correlates in either lento or allegro, while the reverse held for high vowels, our thesis about the relation between lento and allegro styles would have been empirically refuted.

In these instances, in which the nonpreferred or implicating state is not known to exist, we must construct our historical theory in such a manner that we do not assume its existence at any stage. Thus, as was pointed out earlier, the language state mentioned in the *implicans* of the universal that stressed voiceless vowels imply unstressed voiceless vowels has no empirical realization. As far as appears from the present materials at least, there are no instances of stressed voiceless vowels. An application of this principle can be made in Southern Paiute. In this language internal evidence shows that an original system of high stress in alternate syllables existed before the unvoicing of certain vowels. Stress is now found in the syllable preceding that of the voiceless vowel in those instances where the general rule would predict a stress on the voiceless vowel. It is evidently inadmissible here to posit the following sequence of events: voiced stressed vowel, unvoiced stressed vowel, shift of high stress to preceding syllable leaving the voiceless vowel with low stress. We must rather posit a simultaneous change in stress and voicing, so that the historical sequence is that a voiced, high stressed vowel becomes an unvoiced, low stressed vowel, and the stress moves back to the preceding syllable. In such instances, we may talk of correlated changes, that is, of unvoicing with simultaneous change from high to low stress in vowels.

Since the aim of this study is primarily methodological, I do not propose to treat all of the changes in unstressed vowels which may be investigated by means of comparison within the subtype of languages with voiceless vowels. In addition to those already mentioned, it is of interest to note the existence of evidence in the form of free and style variation that voiceless vowels tend to be replaced by zero (i.e., lost). In Shoshone, voiceless vowels maintained in careful speech (i.e., lento) are suppressed in ordinary conversational style, whether intervocalic or final.[32] In North Carolina Cherokee, without reference to style difference, vowels preceding phrase boundary are often "whispered or dropped."[33] In Goajiro, they are "whispered and eventually suppressed."[34]

[32] Shimkin 1949-B: 175.
[33] Bender and Harris 1945-B: 17.
[34] Holmer 1949-B: 49.

In Dagur, the vowels subject to unvoicing (*i*, *u*, *e*) "often seem to disappear, especially in rapid speech."[35] As noted by Gensen Mori for Japanese, "from devocalization to complete elimination is but a single step."[36] According to Yamagiwa, once more in reference to Japanese, "*i* and *u* are often 'devocalized' (whispered) or lost between two voiceless consonants."[37]

In Cheyenne, a voiceless front vowel following *t*, *s*, *š*, *m*, *n*, or *w* is "very unstable." Forms that in careful speech contain a vowel in this position often lose the vowel in rapid speech. This loss is normally accompanied by a compensatory lengthening of the previous consonant, for example, *néše*~*néš·*.[38]

It was noted earlier that Japanese was the only language that constituted an exception to the universal according to which languages with voiceless vowels in word-medial position also possess them in word-final position. In view of the evidence just cited regarding the tendency to loss of voiceless vowels, the explanation is now evident. Voiceless *i* and *u* formerly existed in word final but have already been lost precisely because this position is the one that is favored and the one in which they are likely to appear first.

In such forms as *x·tots·* ("one"), and *arimas·* ("is"), cited by Bloch, there is both internal evidence in the form of a distributional gap (the nonappearance of word-final **tsu* and **su* in Bloch's material), and external evidence from the kana orthography, of the loss of final *u* after an unvoiced consonant. Bloch gives *hatš·* ("eight") as an allegro form in alternation with *hatši*. That these final vowels were formerly devoiced is made likely by the coincidence of the conditioning factor with that operative in word medial in present free variations, and from the earlier observation of Gensen Mori regarding devoicing, particularly of *u*, "at the termination of a breath-group." Moreover, Mori gives examples like *moši̥* and *mainitši̥*. For a still earlier period, R. Lange observes that "final *ssu* usually loses the vowel and becomes *ss*, and the vowel in final *tsu*, *shi*, and *chi* is barely audible."[39] It may be noted that the consonantal length specified by Bloch in instances where a following voiceless vowel has been lost is exactly parallel to the situation in Cheyenne already referred to.

As can be seen in Japanese, the true regularity lies in the dynamic tendency rather than in the static situation. It is not merely that an exception is "explained" by reference to historical process. The implication is that the valid generalization pertains to the form and the conditions in which a historical change occurs.

[35] Martin 1961-B: 16.
[36] Mori 1929-B: 22.
[37] Yamagiwa 1942-B: 2.
[38] Davis 1962-B: 36.
[39] Lange 1903-B: x.

Reverting to the tendency to loss of voiceless vowels, the suggestion may be advanced that, in many historical instances of loss of vowels, there was, in fact, a period of voicelessness which could not find expression in the orthography. A number of conditions fit quite exactly. The greater tendency of final vowels, unstressed vowels, and short vowels to loss hardly needs documentation. There is also some evidence that high vowels are more easily lost than low vowels, and such loss is a well-known phenomenon in Romance languages. Meyer-Lübke summarizes the situation regarding final vowels in the statement that "l'*a* est la plus résistante des voyelles finales."[40]

The only important respect in which a real difference seems to exist between the conditions for voicelessness in vowels and the conditions for vowel loss is in the preference for a voiceless consonantal environment for the former which does not appear in most formulations regarding vowel loss. The fact is that the rule for vowel loss in modern Japanese requires a previous voiceless consonant as a conditioning factor, and in this instance we can be sure that loss was preceded by voicelessness of the final vowel. This fact suggests that there might be two types of vowel loss: one with a stage of vowel voicelessness and another without. In some instances of final vowel loss, the preceding consonant has become voiceless. For example, in most of Slavic at least the obstruents that preceded the disappearing final *jers* (*ĭ* and *ŭ*) appear as unvoiced in word final (e.g., *rogŭ* > *rog* > *rok*, "horn" in Russian). The *jers* would seem to be good candidates for voicelessness before loss, since it is precisely the high and shortest vowels in word final which are affected.[41] Considering the frequency of regressive spread of voicelessness, it is reasonable to assume, instead of the succession of events as described above in accordance with the usual formula, rather *rogŭ* > *rogŭ̥* > *rog̥ŭ̥* > *rog̥* > *rok*. Since the voiceless *g* was lenis, it would still be distinguishable for a time from *k*, and would hence be retained in orthographies. In languages such as Serbo-Croatian, voicing could have been restored analogically from forms in which it was never lost (e.g., from *roga* [genitive singular]).

The detailed instrumental phonetic observations of Sokolova on Tadjik, however, show that whereas unstressed short vowels in an unvoiced environment varied between voicelessness and complete loss, in a voiced environment the same vowels varied between a fully voiced variant and loss, though such loss was substantially less frequent.[42] This fact perhaps indicates that under otherwise favorable conditions for vowel voicelessness this loss occurs in

[40] Meyer-Lübke 1890–1906: I, 260.

[41] The *jers* are always lost in word final. They were also lost in so-called weak position word internally, that is whenever there was a full vowel (non-*jer*) in the next syllable.

[42] Sokolova 1949-B. In voiced environments, in addition to less frequent loss of unstable vowels, where these vowels are not lost, their duration is significantly greater. The greater length

a voiceless consonantal environment, while loss without a stage of vocalic voicelessness takes place in a voiced consonantal environment.

Further investigation is obviously required in this instance, but the theoretical point to be made is that the vast literature of synchronic description, with its numerous instances of free and style variation, is capable of throwing important light on the phonetic nature of sound changes of the past which are only known from documentary sources. The principles involved may be illustrated by another example. Even if we had no historical evidence of an intermediate *h*-stage, in considering the correspondence of *s* in Romance and other Indo-European languages with modern Greek zero (e.g., Italian *sette*, Modern Greek *eftá*, seven), we should assume ($s > h >$ zero) for Greek, rather than, directly, $s >$ zero. There are well-attested instances of free variation $s \sim h$ and $h \sim$ zero in contemporary languages but apparently none of $s \sim$ zero.[43]

We may briefly compare the two methods that have been discussed up to now, the dynamicization of typologies and of subtypologies. In both we are interested in the establishment of lawful successions of types. This statement was not made explicitly with regard to the subtypological method but should be evident. For example, the statement that voiceless low vowels imply voiceless high vowels but not vice versa, and the dynamic evidence that there are instances in which voicelessness spreads from high to low vowels but not vice versa, can be restated in terms of typology. The language type defined by the presence of voiceless high vowels may be succeeded by the type in which all vowels may occur voiceless, but the opposite succession of types is excluded. In the subtypological method, however, the pragmatic emphasis was on the discovery of significant types and their successions based on typological comparison. In the first method, the types were treated as given, and the mechanism of change of type was investigated. A further difference was the emphasis on the use of the comparative and direct historical approach in the

---

of vowels in voiced environments, particularly before voiced consonants, is a widely known phenomenon.

A supporting instance for the hypothesis that final vowels are more likely to be lost after unvoiced consonants may be found in the German loss of final unstressed vowel. Modern Standard German is rather irregular in this regard, but Paul noted that there was a preference for the retention of the vowel after *b*, *d*, *g*, and *z* (Paul and Stolte 1951: 74).

Furthermore, Whiteley's material on Ci-miini, a dialect of Swahili, indicates that *i* and *u* have been lost before unvoiced, and not before voiced, consonants (Whiteley 1965).

[43] Of course free variation is not the only source of internal evidence for sound change. Complementary distribution resulting from accomplished conditioned change, and morphophonemic alternations representing still older processes, are also relevant. Free variation, however, is the only internal source regarding unconditioned merger, and it also provides the most direct information about the phonetic conditions of change because there has been, as yet, no chance for intervening phonetic changes.

first method. The origin of nasal vowels was to be investigated chiefly by comparing the results of historically independent instances of reconstruction and of historically documented examples of change. In the subtypological method, the emphasis was on the use of internal change phenomena for individual languages without essential regard for their genetic connections. In fact, both methods can be utilized for either case, for internal reconstruction with regard to nasal vowels and for the comparative study of voiceless vowels. For the latter, comparative study of the Keresan and Shoshonean languages, which has already been initiated, is a potential source of enlightenment regarding the problems considered here.[44]

The third method that will be illustrated is that of *intergenetic processual comparison*. Historical independent reconstructions are compared as a test of the extent to which they are mutually corroborative, and to help in the selection among mutually exclusive hypotheses in individual instances by reference to other typologically similar cases. As with the other methods with which we are concerned, the emphasis here is dynamic, that is, we compare lines of development rather than reconstructions viewed statically. It has been proposed, as a basic contribution of synchronic typology to historical linguistics, that synchronic universals serve as a touchstone for the validity of reconstructed systems.[45] And it is certainly true that a violation of principles, valid for directly documented languages, precisely for an only indirectly attested language is always a suspicious circumstance which throws doubt on the reconstruction.

This criterion has been applied to Proto-Indo-European; but the question we shall ask here is not the one hitherto and quite justly asked, namely, whether the reconstructed Indo-European phonological inventory conforms to the universal norms of such systems. Instead we will ask whether the sequence of changes in the key instance of laryngeals is plausible when considered with reference to other reconstructible or historically documented instances of change. A study that would illustrate this method should ideally be complete in that all instances of changes in systems of laryngeals accessible to internal reconstruction, direct historical documentation, and comparative reconstruction should be included. In keeping with the present purpose, however, which is merely illustrative, a single non-Indo-European instance will be considered, that of Coptic, and only in limited detail. There will also be occasional reference to non-Coptic materials.

The Coptic data are of special interest from the methodological point of view for the following reason. They have come down to us in the form of

[44] See Davis 1966-B and Voegelin, Voegelin, and Hale 1962-B: 48, for Uto-Aztecan; see Miller and Davis 1963-B for Keresan.

[45] Cf. Jakobson 1958.

five literary dialects, from the comparison of which it is possible to construct at least the general outlines of a Proto-Coptic. The Coptic dialects do not have laryngeal consonants; but, as will be shown here, a comparative study will lead to the reconstruction of several consonants not known in existing dialects. In this instance earlier Egyptian, as written in the hieroglyphic script and the structurally equivalent hieratic and later demotic, attests their actual existence where they would be postulated on the basis of Coptic, and the comparative evidence of Semitic and other Afro-Asiatic languages, as well as the transcription of Semitic words of an earlier period, gives evidence regarding their phonetic nature.

The results presented here are part of a more extensive reconstruction effort. All previous work has been in terms of tracing the Egyptian antecedents of items found in Coptic. It has doubtless been done with substantial correctness, and the changes posited here do not differ in essentials from those usually assumed. Such an independent comparison of Coptic dialects in relation to Ancient Egyptian is similar in procedure to that of Romance linguistics in relation to Classical Latin. This approach is even more justified in the present instance because of the defective and arbitrary nature of hieroglyphic and demotic orthography.

We shall be chiefly concerned with two Proto-Coptic vowels symbolized here as *ɔ́ and *ɛ, and we shall proceed by the discussion of a number of instances of correspondences among the dialects. The five standard literary dialects will be indicated by their usual abbreviations, and forms will be cited in accordance with a transcription system described in the accompanying footnote.[46]

1) SBɔ́, AA²F *á*. *ɔ́

Every Coptic word has a single high stress on one of the last two syllabics. All other vowels are reduced, and in reduced position only a limited set occurs, for example, never *ɔ*, *o*, or *e* in any dialect in native words. When, as for example in compounds, a form with *Vy* or *Vw* diphthong occurs with low or (possibly) intermediate stress, the vowel may be lost and the *y* or *w* become

[46] The abbreviations used for the dialects are as follows: S, Sahidic; B, Bohairic; A, Achmimic; A², Subachmimic; F, Fayumic. The transcription is self-explanatory except for the following: The vowel symbols *epsilon* and *eta* are rendered as ɛ and *e*, respectively, and *omicron* and *omega* as *ɔ* and *o*. Geminate vowel writings are transcribed by length. For a justification of both of these interpretations, see Greenberg 1962. The supralinear stroke that apparently symbolizes a reduced vowel is transcribed *ə*. *Beta* is rendered by *b*, although its phonetic value seems to have been a bilabial unrounded semivowel. For a standard account of vowel changes from Egyptian to Coptic, see Steindorff 1951. What is said here regarding the development of Egyptian laryngeals is subject to the qualification that it is not impossible that laryngeals still survived in Coptic, particularly in Achmimic. On this see Till 1929.

syllabic. Compare, in S, *stɔ́j* ("smell") with *stì-núfə* (lit. "smell-good," i.e., "perfume").

The above correspondence never occurs in word-final position, and it never occurs before certain consonantal correspondences. Examples containing 1 are:

1*a*) SB *sɔ́n*, AA²F *sán* ("brother"). **sɔ́n*.

1*b*) S *sɔ́tməf*, B *sɔ́thmɛf*, AA²F *sátmɛf* ("to hear him"). **sɔ́tm(ə)f*.
1*b* contains the third person masculine dependent form -(*ə*)*f*. The aspiration in Bohairic *th* is automatic before any sonant.

2) SBAA² *á*, F *έ*. **ɔ́*

Correspondence 2, unlike 1, is not restricted to nonfinal position. When nonfinal and followed by a consonant, it is limited to environments in which one of the three following consonant correspondences occurs, these being precisely the environments in which 1 is not found. These three correspondences are:

3) SBAA²F *h*. **h*

4) SA²F *h*, BA *x*. **x*

5) SBA²F *š*, A *x*. **ç*

That 1 and 2 represent the same protophoneme is shown not only from this complementary distribution but from morphophonemic alternations. No verb of the same class as **sɔ́tm(ə)f* (1*b* above) occurs with correspondence 1 before **h*, **x*, and **ç*, but instead correspondence 2 makes its appearance. The following is an example in which 2 is followed by **h*.

2*a*) S *náhməf*, BAA² *náhmɛf*, F *nέhmɛf* ("to save him"). **nɔ́hm(ə)f*.

All of the dialects except B have long vowels indicated orthographically by geminate vowel symbols. Long vowels occur only as the syllabic of stressed syllables, and they never appear in word-final position. Among the correspondences involving long vowels is the following:

6) SAA² *á:*, B *á*, F *έ:*

An example of this correspondence is:

6*a*) SAA² *ká:f*, B *kháf*, F *kέ:f* ("to put him").

Correspondence 6 is evidently the same as correspondence 2, except for vowel length, in those dialects in which this feature occurs. Moreover it is found in verb forms with the same formation as that of 1*b* and 2*a*. The present example belongs more exactly to the most important class of verb stems with two consonants. It is thus parallel to the following form:

6*b*) S *bɔ́ləf*, B *bɔ́lɛf*, AA²F *bálɛf* ("to loosen him"). We therefore have reason to see here an occurrence of the protophoneme **ɔ*. Moreover, it cannot be accidental that, except for length, 6 is identical with 2, the form that **ɔ* takes before **h*, **x*, and **ç*. The natural conclusion is that the same conditioning factor (i.e., a back continuant) must have been present. Note that Proto-Coptic has front continuants *s, *š, and *f* which do not exercise this effect. That the last conditioning factor should be voiceless is not a necessary assumption because all the reconstructed fricatives are voiceless and the distinctive features need only be fricativity and back articulation. Because, when consonants are lost, it frequently happens that the preceding vowel is lengthened, we may consider the long vowels of the dialects other than B to be the historical continuation of *ɔ plus the lost consonant. We will symbolize this consonant as $H_2$ and thus reconstruct 6*a* as *$k\acute{ɔ}H_2f$*. Further evidence for the second mora of a long vowel in 6 representing a consonant at an earlier stage is that in A, one of the Coptic dialects, a final unstressed vowel written *ε* develops after a sequence of final consonant plus sonant. For example, A has *satmε* as the qualitative (i.e., stative) of the verb "to hear" corresponding to S *sɔ́təm* (**sɔ́t(ə)m*). A similarly has final *ε* when a long vowel precedes a sonant, for example, A *yɔ́:rε* ("canal") as contrasted with S *yɔ́:r*. A therefore treats the last mora of a long vowel as though it were a consonant.

It was noted earlier that the long vowels do not normally appear in word-final position; therefore, where correspondence 2 occurs in word final, we should also assume the disappearance of $H_2$. Hence we reconstruct the following word as *$lɔH_2$*:

6*c*) SAA²B *lá*, F *lέ* ("slander").

Compare 6*d*) SA² *sáh*, AB *sáx*, F *sεh*. **sɔx* ("scribe").

The absence of vocalic length preceding word-final, as contrasted with length before word-medial, preconsonantal $H_2$ can be accounted for in two ways. Either $VH_2 > V$: in all environments originally and word-final long vowels were shortened, or word-final $H_2$, unlike medial $H_2$, was lost without lengthening the preceding vowel.[47]

The identity of correspondences in vowel quality between internal long vowels and final stressed vowel is not confined to correspondence 2 but is general throughout Coptic. This fact can hardly be an accident. We, therefore, interpret the pairs of internal long vowels and final stressed short vowels as representing the same vowel in each instance. Whether length in every instance results from loss of a consonant remains provisionally undecided. The evidence outlined below regarding the same vowel *ɔ, however, strongly suggests a second lost consonant.

We find another matching pair of correspondences between word interior long vowel and final short vowel as follows:

7) SAA² *ɔ́:*, B *ɔ́*, F *á*:

8) SBAA² *ɔ́#*, F *á#*

[47] Medial $H_2$ usually occurs before a following consonant. Where, however, it is intervocalic, it is normally reflected by a short (i.e., nongeminated) vowel in Coptic.

Examples of 7 and 8 are:

7*a*) SAA² *bɔ́:nɛ*, B *bɔ́ni*, F *bá:ni* ("be bad").

8*a*) SBAA² *rɔ́*, F *lá* ("mouth").

Besides the phonetic resemblance of this correspondence to 1, we have morphophonemic evidence that 8, and hence 7, must involve **ɔ́*. In the independent pronominal forms of the second and third person, we have a uniform base followed by the pronominal suffixes already quoted in 1*b* and 6*a*. This base appears before an overt consonant in the third masculine singular and elsewhere.

8*b*) S *(ə)ntɔ́f*, B *(ə)nthɔ́f*, AA²F *(ə)ntáf*. **(ə)ntɔ́f* ("he").

The stressed vowel here shows correspondence 1 and is, therefore, reconstructed as **ɔ́*. The second person feminine pronoun, however, displays a final stressed vowel with correspondence 8.

8*c*) SAA² *(ə)ntɔ́*, B *(ə)nthɔ́*, F *(ə)ntá*.

We therefore interpret it as containing the same vowel **ɔ*. Since correspondence 8 differs from 2 which we interpreted in final position as $*H_2$, the consonant involved must be a different one. We symbolize it as $*H_1$, and hence reconstruct 7*a*, 8*a*, 8*b*, and 8*c* as **bɔ́*$H_1$*nə*, **rɔ́*$H_1$, **(ə)ntɔ́f*, and **(ə)ntɔ́*$H_1$, respectively.

We now consider the front vowel corresponding to **ɔ́*. The following correspondence of stressed internal short vowel is frequently found:

9) SB *á*, AA²F *ɛ́*.

It is possible to cite at least one minimal contrast with **ɔ*:

9*a*) SB *bɔ́l*, AF *bál*. **bɔ́l* ("outside").

9*b*) SB *bál*, AA²F *bɛ́l* ("eye").

We symbolize this new vowel as **ɛ*, hence **bɛ́l* ("eye").

For **ɛ*, we find a contrast between other second and third person suffixes and the second person feminine suffix parallel to that for **ɔ* cited in 8*b* and 8*c*.

10) SBAA² *ɛ́*, F *é*.

The pair of contrasting forms just alluded to are:

10*a*) SB *náf*, AA²F *nɛ́f*. **nɛ́f* ("to him").

10*b*) SBAA² *nɛ́*, F *né* ("to you [f]").

In 10*a* we naturally reconstruct **ɛ́* since it represents correspondence 9 as above. In view of the parallelism with **(ə)ntɔ́*$H_1$ ("you [f]"), we posit **nɛ́*$H_1$ as the protoform for 10*b*.

We should now expect a correspondence word internally involving long vowels and identical in quality with 10, representing *ɛ́*$H_1$, in this position as follows:

11) SAA² *ɛ́:*, B *ɛ́*, F *é:*

It is in fact found, as in the following example:

11*a*). SAA[2] *mέ:rə*, B *mέri*, F *mé:ri*. *$*m\acute{\varepsilon}H_1r\partial$*. We have now found correspondences representing $*\acute{ɔ}H_2$, $*\acute{ɔ}H_1$, and $*\acute{\varepsilon}H_1$. We have yet to find evidence for $*\acute{\varepsilon}H_2$. Here there are apparently no morphophonemic clues; however, we do find another pair of correspondences identical in quality, one involving long vowels in word medial, the other, short stressed final vowels.

12) S *á:*, B *á*, AA[2]F *έ:*

13) SB *á#*, AA[2]F *έ#*

13*a*) S *má:tə*, B *máti*, AA[2] *mέ:tε*, F *mέ:ti*. $*m\acute{\varepsilon}H_2t\partial$ ("to reach").

13*b*) S *wá*, AA[2]F *wε* ("one"). $*w\varepsilon H_2$.

Several observations, however, are to be made regarding 12 and 13. It will be noted that 13 is, in fact, identical with 9, and 12 is also identical with 9, except for vowel length. Thus, *ε, unlike *ɔ, does not show special protoallophones before those back fricatives that survive in the existing dialects. Hence it is not surprising that before presumed $H_2$ it only shows length in word medial and is identical in word final. The other observation to be made is that examples of 13 are difficult to find and the one cited was probably, as shown by Bohairic *wai*, not word final. This form should probably be reconstructed as $*w\acute{\varepsilon}H_2j\partial$. The rarity of $H_2$ in word final suggests that perhaps $*H_2\# > *H_1\#$ at an earlier stage. With this reservation, as indicated by parentheses, the results thus far are summarized in Table 4.

We now consider evidence for the existence and identity of $H_1$ and $H_2$ when not immediately following a stressed vowel. In poststressed syllables, which are always final syllables, only one vowel phoneme is reconstructible. It appears as *ε* or *ə* (the supralinear stroke) when followed by final consonant, and as SAA[2] *ε*, BF *i*, when immediately followed by word boundary. In both instances in the earlier examples it is symbolized as *ə. There is evidently no chance of distinguishing $H_1$ from $H_2$ in this position.[48]

In prestressed position, a considerable variety of correspondences is found involving absence of vowel, or differing patterns of occurrences of *a* or *ε*. In addition we find unstressed *i* and *u* which can be shown to represent syllabic forms of *j* and *w* in reduced syllables. Earlier the example of S *stɔ́j* ("smell") and *stìnúfe* ("smell-good," i.e., "perfume") was cited. We may add here S *hɔ́w* ("day") as compared with *hù-mísə* ("birthday," lit. "day of birth"). There are also instances of liquids and nasals in reduced forms, that is, preceded by the supralinear stroke here transcribed *ə*. In such instances, some scholars interpret *ər* as syllabic *r*, and analogously for other liquids and nasals.[49] An

[48] However, as Polotsky 1931 shows, $H_2$ is under certain statistically rare conditions reflected as Fayumic *ε* instead of *i*.

[49] On this point see Till 1951 and the literature cited there.

*Table 4*

Summary of Reconstructed Proto-Coptic Forms

| Reconstructed protoform | Corresponding forms in existing dialects | | | | | Remarks |
|---|---|---|---|---|---|---|
| | S | B | A | A² | F | |
| **ɔ́* | *ɔ́* | *ɔ́* | *á* | *á* | *á* | Except before *h*, *x*, *ç*, and *H* |
| **ɔ́*$H_2$*#* | *á* | *á* | *á* | *á* | *ɛ́* | Before unvoiced back fricatives as well as before $H_2$# |
| **ɔ́*$H_2$ | á: | á | á: | á: | *ɛ́:* | |
| **ɔ́*$H_1$*#* | *ɔ́* | *ɔ́* | *ɔ́* | *ɔ́* | *á* | |
| **ɔ́*$H_1$ | *ɔ́:* | *ɔ́* | *ɔ́:* | *ɔ́:* | *á:* | |
| **ɛ´* | *á* | *á* | *ɛ́* | *ɛ́* | *ɛ́* | |
| (**ɛ́*$H_2$*#*) | (á) | (á) | (*ɛ́*) | (*ɛ́*) | (*ɛ́*) | |
| **ɛ*$H_2$ | *á:* | *á* | *ɛ́:* | *ɛ́:* | *ɛ́:* | |
| **ɛ́*$H_1$*#* | *ɛ́* | *ɛ́* | *ɛ́* | *ɛ́* | *é* | |
| **ɛ́*$H_1$ | *ɛ́:* | *ɛ́* | *ɛ́:* | *ɛ́:* | *é:* | |

example is S *sór* ("to scatter") as an independent verbal form, and the reduced form *sə̀r-* (interpreted by some as phonetically *sṛ̀-*) with the following nominal object.

Where in prestressed syllables there is evidence for $H_1$ or $H_2$, we find a reduced vowel appearing as *a* and *ɛ* in different dialects in a variety of patterns not yet fully accounted for. That, however, a reduced vowel followed by $H_2$ may appear as *a* in all dialects is shown by the verbal forms with final stem $H_2$. Thus, parallel to such alternations as S *sór* ("to scatter"), *sɔ́r-əf* ("to scatter him"), *sə̀r-* ("to scatter [something]"), we have S *jó* ("to wash"); *já:f* ("to wash him"); *jà-* ("to wash [something]"). The second of these, *já:f*, shows correspondence 6 as indicated by its form in other dialects, and is, therefore, to be reconstructed as **jɔ́*$H_2$*f*. Hence *jà-*, which takes this form in all the dialects, goes back to *j*(ə̀)$H_2$-. We shall number this correspondence 14.

14) SBAA²F *a* (with low or secondary stress).

At this point we resort to the causative formations with prefixed *t-* to give us information regarding the reflexes of $H_1$ and $H_2$ in prestressed syllables. A verb such as **çópə* ("to become") has a causative which, on the basis of correspondences previously cited, is *tçpɔ́*$H_1$. Hence, when we find SB *ašáj*, AA²F *ašɛ́j* ("to be many"), alongside its causative SBAA² *tašɔ́*, F *tašá*, we may, in conformity with our interpretation of *ja-* with vowel correspondence 14 as *j*(ə)$H_2$, reconstruct *(ə)$H_2$*šɛ́j* and **t*(ə)$H_2$*šɔ́*$H_1$, respectively. A different correspondence, 15, is found in other causatives:

15) SBF *a*, AA² *ɛ*

An example is SB *takɔ́*, AA² *tɛkɔ́*, F *taká* ("to destroy"), for which the non-causative simplex does not exist in Coptic. Since nonlaryngeals have either zero or the supralinear stroke *ə*, it seems reasonable to attribute this correspondence to our missing $H_1$. Hence we posit **t(ə)$H_1$kɔ́$H_1$* in this and similar instances.

All verbs that appear in noncausatives with initial vowel without preceding consonant, when they have causatives, show either 14 or 15 in the initial syllable. Thus S *ón(ə)h* ("to live") has the causative in S *tanhɔ́*, in which the initial syllable shows correspondence 14. Hence it seems reasonable to reconstruct the simplex as $H_2$*ón(ə)x*, and the hypothetical noncausative of **t(ə)$H_1$kó$H_1$* ("to destroy") as *$H_1$*ók* ("to perish"). Evidently initial $H_1$ or $H_2$ is lost before a stressed vowel.

Since we may consider the specific set of verbs which have a *t-* causative as a reasonable sample of Coptic verbs, the fact that every verb with initial stressed vowel in Coptic displays reflexes of either $H_1$ or $H_2$ when it has a *t-* causative leads to the conclusion that all initial stressed vowels in Coptic formerly had *H* initially; but, of course, where no alternation exists we can only reconstruct with a cover symbol *H* because we cannot tell which of the two it is.

Because, in the form *(ə)$H_2$*šɛ́j* ("to be many"), $H_2$ appears as correspondence 14, we may expect examples of 15 in similar position to reflect (ə)$H_1$*CV* . . . ; as in the following examples:

15*a*) SB *awán*, AA² *ɛwɛ́n*, F *awɛ́n* ("color").

We accordingly reconstruct *(ə)$H_1$*wɛ́n*.

A further fairly common initial unstressed vowel correspondence preceding *CV́* . . . is the following:

16) SBAA²F ɛ

as is found, for example, in

16*a*) SBAA²F *ɛsét* ("ground").

Because we have not accounted for initial sequences in which the laryngeal is in the second position and have seen that before an initial stressed vowel *H* is simply zero, we may suspect that 16*a* represents an earlier **(ə)sHét*. Here again, before a stressed vowel there is no way in the absence of alternations to decide between $H_1$ and $H_2$. Evidently $H_1$ and $H_2$ may modify the quality and length of preceding vowels but exercise no such effect on the succeeding vowel.

We have gone about as far as it is possible to go with Coptic alone. The reconstructed units symbolized here as $H_1$ and $H_2$ appear consistently in earlier Egyptian as consonants that can be considered phonetically a glottal stop (ʔ) and voiced pharyngeal ('), respectively.[50] The only real point of discrepancy is

[50] Such at least seems to be the situation not long prior to the Coptic period. However, ʔ represents two apparently different Egyptian sounds, one *y*-like and the other possibly a glottal

that, in all dialects, forms with prestressed *a*, which, on the basis of alternations in causatives, was reconstructed as $(ə)H_2$, reflects $(ə)H_1$ in a fair number of instances; for example, SB *anɔ́k*, AA[2]F *anák*, which goes back to Egyptian (*ə*)*ʔnɔ́k*, rather than to *(*ə*)*ʿnɔ́k* = $(ə)H_2nɔ́k$.

We may summarize the reflexes of $H_1$ and $H_2$ in the following list; its parallelism to the most commonly posited developments of the Indo-European laryngeals should be obvious.

1) Nonfinal laryngeals following a stressed vowel are lost and produce length.

2) Final laryngeals are lost without producing length.

3) Laryngeals preceding a vowel do not produce length.

4) Certain laryngeals change the vowel quality of certain preceding vowels.

5) Laryngeals in reduced syllables are accompanied by reduced vowels which survive where vowels with nonlaryngeals under the same accentual condition are lost.

6) For this reduced vowel, it is impossible to tell which vowel has been reduced (e.g., *ɛ or *ɔ), but the laryngeal involved is identifiable in certain forms (e.g., the causatives).

7) An initial sequence of nonlaryngeal consonant plus laryngeal plus vowel develops a preceding, low-stressed shwa, whereas sequences of nonlaryngeals have no initial vowel.

8) Long vowels developing from laryngeals followed by *w* or *y* display a marked tendency to shorten the resulting long diphthong. (This point has not been illustrated. Compare Indo-European treatment of *e:u* and similar combinations.)

9) Laryngeals tend strongly to metathesis, which usually results in their preceding consonants they formerly followed. (An example is S *šópɛ* ["become"] < *$šóp(ə)H_1$, as compared with the qualitative *šɔ́:p* < *$šɔ́H_1p$ in which Egyptian indicates that the original sequence was $š\text{-}p\text{-}H_1$.

10) Intervocalic laryngeals are lost without producing vowel length, but they often change preceding vowel color. (This point, likewise, was not illustrated here.)

11) All words that begin in the existing dialects with a stressed vowel originally had an initial laryngeal.

With regard to the development of vowel length in sequences consisting of vowel plus laryngeal plus consonant, it may be pointed out that the common formulation of this process as "compensatory," implying perhaps a feeling of

---

stop. Both of these may appear in Coptic as *i* in stressed syllables but under further conditions that cannot be specified on the basis of present evidence. In addition, some instances of Proto-Coptic $H_1$ arise from earlier *r* and *t* which sometimes apparently become ʔ.

collective guilt at having repressed a consonant, conceals the phonetic problem involved. Here the evidence of Hebrew is valuable because it shows, precisely before consonants but not when the consonant is word final, the development of an extra vocalic segment with the same vowel quality as that of the vowel preceding the laryngeals. These are the so-called *Hatephs* or "hurried shwas," for example, *ya‘$^{a}$móδ* ("he stands") < **ya‘móδ*. The sequence *ya‘$^{a}$móδ* < *ya:móδ* as a possible further development is easily understandable; and this development actually occurred with regard to the glottal stop in Hebrew in the prehistoric period, for example, *yo:mér* ("he speaks") < **ya:mér* < *yaʔmér*. Compare also Western transcriptions of Arabic words such as *Kaaba* = Arabic *ka‘ba* and the existence of "echo vowels" in some Amerindian languages after ʔ.

As a final principle of dynamic comparison, we consider the *intragenetic* mode. The following may serve as a preliminary characterization. The comparison is confined to a genetically delimited group of languages. Empirical hypotheses of a diachronic nature are advanced. They are empirical in the sense that it is clearly stated what would constitute a violation. They are diachronic in that they refer to linguistic changes within the family. Typically they take on one of two forms. Either they state that, of two or more mutually exclusive changes, only one may take place (although the change is not inevitable, its alternatives are denied) or that, of several changes, one must take place earlier than the others.[51] Here again, it is not stated as inevitable that the change *will* take place. Only the order of their occurrence is predicted if they do materialize. Although the hypotheses are stated in terms of properties of a particular language family (e.g., they may mention such categories as "weak verbs in English," "palatalized consonants in Celtic"), they may be viewed as exemplifications of universal diachronic hypotheses in which the variables have been filled in with proper name specifications.

Intragenetic comparison is illustrated here with reference to the Slavic system of nominal declension. Attention was initially directed to this topic, because of a problem that arose in connection with the well-known overall tendency in languages for certain categories (the so-called unmarked) to receive zero expression, while opposing marked categories typically have overt expression. Apparently contravening this principle is the well-known existence in some Slavic languages of extensive classes of nouns (basically the hard feminines and neuters) which show the opposite of the expected phenomenon. Although the singular is to be considered unmarked as against the plural, and the direct cases (nominative, accusative) as unmarked in

[51] These two types of statements are equivalent to the diachronic universals discussed in Greenberg 1966b.

comparison with the oblique cases (genitive, dative, instrumental, locative), these languages have, in certain classes of nouns, an overt desinence for the doubly unmarked nominative singular and a zero for the doubly marked genitive plural. This fact may be illustrated by the following examples from Standard Czech: *žena* (nom. sing.), *žen* (gen. pl., "woman [f]"); *město* (nom. sing.), *měst* (gen. pl., "city [n]"). On the other hand, there is also an extensive set of nouns which does show the expected type of ending, for example, *hrad* (nom. sing.), *hradů* (gen. pl., "castle [m]"). Hence Czech and the other Slavic languages that show analogous phenomena do not constitute exceptions to the principles stated provided one specifies that in no language does a marked category have zero as a sole allomorph; but such a statement is not really satisfactory because it is well known that the zeroes in both instances, where predicted, as in the nominative singular, and contraindicated, as in the genitive plural, arose by the same sound change, the loss of the *jers* (*ŭ* and *ĭ*) still found in Old Church Slavonic. Thus the present nominative singular *hrad* and genitive plural *žen* at an earlier period possessed overt endings as seen in the corresponding Old Church Slavonic forms *gradŭ* and *ženŭ*.

The loss of *ĭ* and *ŭ* in all word-final and certain word-medial positions conforms to certain typical conditions for vowel loss, as was pointed out in the earlier discussion of unvoiced vowels. As a phonological phenomenon it therefore makes sense; but it is, of course, but an illustration of what has been a commonplace since the time of the neogrammarians. Its effects on the morphological system are random, producing by the very same change zeroes in categories where they are both expected and unexpected. If this were the whole story, how would one find the extensive conformity to certain synchronically stated principles, such as the preference of unmarked categories for zero and marked categories for overt expression, which in fact exists?

The answer may be expected to lie in the direction of certain dynamic selective tendencies. Synchronic regularities are merely the consequences of such forces. It is not so much again that "exceptions" are explained historically, but that the true regularity is contained in the dynamic principles themselves.

These principles, where morphology is concerned, may be expected to lie chiefly in the area of analogical change viewed as the spread of one allomorph at the expense of another. The loss of final *jers* in Slavic produced, in effect, a laboratory situation in that it resulted in zero allomorphs both in a category in which they should be favored (nominative singular) and disfavored (genitive plural). We may now consider the situation resulting from the loss of *jers* separately for each of these two categories, beginning with the genitive plural.

Because the ending of the genitive plural was *ŭ* in most declensional classes, the dropping of final *ŭ* produced a situation in which zero was by far the most common allomorph occuring in all three genders and in the most numerous classes in each; however, after this change, there did remain two overt endings. The masculine *u*-stems, a very restricted class, had in Old Church Slavonic the ending *-ovŭ*, historically the same ending as *ŭ*, since *-ov-* derives from an original *o*-grade (actually, *ov-ŭ* or *ev-ŭ*) in stemfinal *u/w* nouns. This *-ovŭ*, of course, became *-ov*. The *i*-stems, which were chiefly feminine but included some masculines in Old Church Slavonic, had an ending *-ĭjĭ* from earlier *-ĭjŭ*. With loss of final *-ĭ*, this ending became *-ĭj*, which takes various forms in the Slavic languages. When the *-ĭj* was stressed, it became *-éj* in Russian, and I shall use *-ej* as the citation form for this allomorph. To summarize, with loss of final *jers* the genitive plural had three allomorphs zero ~ *ov* ~ *ej*, of which the first was by far the most frequent.

In the nominative singular, both *-ŭ* and *-ĭ* existed in certain extensive categories of nouns. When *-ĭ* was lost, it left a trace in the palatalization of the previous consonant (unless this was already "soft" because of an earlier *-i-*). The ending *-ŭ* existed in the nominative singular of hard *o*-stems, the dominant category in masculine nouns, and in *u*-stems, a limited group, as has been seen. In masculine soft stems (i.e., those historically with stem final *-i*), by a regular prehistoric change already exemplified above for the genitive plural of *i*-stems (*-ĭjĭ* < **ĭjŭ*), the nominative singular had *-ĭ*. An example is the word for "man" in Old Church Slavonic, which, in the nominative singular, is *mǫžĭ* < **mǫgjĭ* < *mǫgjŭ*. In addition the *i*-stems, whether masculine or feminine, had the ending *-ĭ* in the nominative and accusative singular. All of these categories, therefore, had zero after the loss of the *jers*. On the other hand, no neuter had *-ŭ* or *-ĭ* (most had *-o* for hard stems, *-e* for soft stems), and the dominant feminine class of *a*-stems had the overt ending *-a* in the nominative singular. In the nominative singular, then, after the loss of *jers*, zero was the dominant ending in masculine nouns, was present in a substantial minority of feminines (the *i*-stems), and occurred not at all in the neuter. The alternants for the nominative singular were, then, *a* ~ *o* ~ *e* ~ zero.[52] Hence, after the loss of the *jers*, zero was the dominant allomorph in the category in which it should not be expected (genitive plural), and only one of several common allomorphs in a category in which it should be expected (nominative singular and the accusative singular of inanimates that are, in Slavic, identical in the nominative and accusative).

With regard to the genitive plural, we hypothesize that of the three alternants

[52] I have not included here the various forms of the nominative singular (or the neuter nominative-accusative singular) which involve truncation of the stem common to the remaining cases, for example, the feminine *u*-stems that have nominative singular *-y* and, in the remaining cases, *-ov* plus the usual consonant stem endings. Such truncations behave like nonzeroes. All of these classes have a severely restricted membership.

zero, *-ov*, and *-ej*, the first will never replace the second or third. If there are any instances of analogical spread, it will be at the expense of the zero allomorph. The historical evidence is, in fact, in favor of this hypothesis. In particular, *-ov* has tended to spread at the expense of the zero ending. In one language, Upper Lusatian, except for a small remnant with zero, all of the nouns in the language have *-ov*. In Russian dialects, *-ov* has spread to hard feminines and neuters (e.g., *knígov*, *mestóv*) so that practically all nouns have overt genitive plural endings. In the Serbo-Croatian literary language, all nouns have nonzero genitive plural endings, the dominant form being *-a*: of still mysterious origin, but with *-í* < *ej* also in certain nominal classes. It is fair to say that, in every single Slavic dialect or standard language, zero has lost ground. Nowhere is it now the dominant allomorph, and in some instances it has almost completely disappeared. The only exception to the spread of nonzero endings of which I am aware is that in Polish, from the fifteenth to the eighteenth century, a small number of *i*-stems replaced their inherited ending by zero (e.g., *myszy* [gen. pl., "mice"] with *-y* < *-ej* was replaced by *mysz*).[53] This trend was subsequently reversed, and modern Polish has *myszy*.

The inverse hypothesis concerning the nominative singular is, of course, that the nonzero allomorphs will not gain ground at the expense of the zero allomorph. If there is any change, it should be in the opposite direction. This hypothesis appears to be verified by the historical evidence from Slavic languages without exception. I do not know of a single instance in which the zero of the masculine basic *o-/jo*-stems and *u*-stems, or that of the *i*-stems, has been replaced by an overt ending. At the same time, the overt endings *-a* for the feminine, *-o/-e* for the neuter have in general been maintained, since they have a function within the gender system, marking the feminine and neuter as against the zero of the masculine. The situation in the nominative singular in Slavic after the loss of *jers* is represented in Table 5 for the major declensional classes.

Nevertheless, where there has been change in this relatively stable situation, it has been in the direction of the spread of zero to the feminine *a*-stems, rather than vice versa. This change has taken place in West Slavic and has gone farthest in Upper Lusatian and in Slovak. Here the *i*-stems have coalesced with the soft *a*-stems; and, in the merged declension, it is precisely the zero of the nominative-accusative which has been carried over from the *i*-stems, whereas all the other inflections come from the *a*-stems. The same tendencies are noticeable in Polish and in Czech. In the latter, an intermediate declension has arisen (e.g., *dlaň*, "palm of the hand") alongside the *a* and *i* feminine declensions with the zero of the nominative-accusative singular from the

[53] Klemensiewicz et al. 1955: 299.

*Table 5*

Slavic Nominative Singular After Loss of *Jers*

| Gender | Hard | Soft |
|---|---|---|
| Masculine | zero | 'zero |
| 1. Feminine (*a*-stems) | *a* | '*a* |
| 2. Feminine (*i*-stems) | — | 'zero |
| Neuter | *o* | '*e* |

NOTE: The symbol ' indicates palatalization of the preceding consonant.

*i*-stems and the remaining forms from the *a* declension. These are former *a*-stems that have replaced their overt endings of the nominative and accusative singular with zero, and not former *i*-stems that have acquired the remainder of their inflection from the *a*-stems.

Both hypotheses then, the favoring of the zero alternant in the nominative singular and the overt alternant in the genitive plural, are verified by the historical linguistic data.

We have seen that, in the genitive plural, after the loss of the *jers*, there were three alternants: zero ~ *ov* ~ *ej*. Our first hypothesis stated that zero was disfavored as against the two overt allomorphs. We may now inquire whether it is possible to set up any hypothesis regarding the relation between *-ov* and *-ej*.

There are certain expectations based on the observation of these and similar instances. Thus, other things being equal, we may hypothesize that *-ov*, which was originally the genitive plural of a masculine "hard" (nonpalatalized) declension, will more easily spread into a masculine than a feminine or neuter declension, and into a hard declension than a soft declension. Such statements are easily converted into refutable diachronic implications. Spread of *-ov* into a feminine or neuter class implies previous spread into a masculine class, and so on.

In the present instance, there is just one declensional class, the masculine *o*-stems, which agrees in gender and nonpalatality with the *u*-stems. We may, therefore, advance the hypothesis that spread to any other class implies previous spread to this class. Because the third genitive plural alternant *-ej* belongs initially to a soft declension which is predominantly feminine with a few marginal masculines, *-ov* will be favored over *-ej* for the masculine *o*-stems.

Such is, in fact, the case, in that wherever else it may spread, it is also found in this class, and that where it is found in several declensions, the direct historical evidence shows its prior presence in the masculine *o*-stems; however, this development is not an independent event in the various Slavic languages.

These two declensions have already largely merged in Old Church Slavonic, the original *u*-stems being distinguishable on the whole by greater frequency of inflectional variants stemming historically from the *u*-declension. Hence, the process started before the loss of *jers* with the consequent zero allomorph in the genitive plural of the *o*-stems. The initial conditions for this merger were the resemblance in gender and nonpalatality, but it may be conjectured that the agreement of both declensions in having *-ŭ* in the most frequent (unmarked) cases, the nominative and accusative singular, was a precipitating factor in the merger.[54] I shall return to this point later.

In the course of the merger, individual Slavic languages often retained inflections inherited from both declensions, sometimes with secondary redistributions of function. Nevertheless, the inflections of the far more numerous *o*-class were normally dominant. It is precisely in the genitive plural, where the Slavic languages, after the loss of final *ŭ*, inherited a zero from the more numerous *o*-stems and *-ov* from the *u*-stems, that the triumph of the *u*-stem inflection was most widespread and complete. Thus, Vaillant summarizes the result of the merger insofar as it concerns the survival of original *u*-stem inflections in the following terms: "L'extension de ces désinences est très limitée. Elle est plus notable au nominatif et surtout au génitif pluriels."[55]

We may seek to generalize concerning the factors involved in declensional merger which were seen to operate in the instance of the hard *o*- and *u*-stems. Agreement in palatality, gender, and identity of inflection in the nominative and accusative singular may be conjectured to be necessary and sufficient conditions for merger; and, where other factors such as marking do not intervene, the forms of the more frequent declension will triumph. Such a thesis involves, of course, factors that, while not exclusively confined to Slavic (e.g., gender and the distinction of palatal and nonpalatal stems), are sometimes absent in other instances; therefore, it would have to be restated for certain other families of languages.

This particular thesis is verified in a whole series of instances in Slavic; however, statement in the form of necessary and sufficient conditions is not an empirical formulation, as can be shown from the following example. There were in early Slavic three classes of neuter consonant stems, all small in number and having as a common feature the possession of two forms of stem, a shorter in the nominative and accusative singular (in neuters, the nominative and accusative are the same in all numbers), and a longer, containing what is, from the synchronic point of view, an "extension" for the remaining cases of

[54] Josselson 1953 reports for conversational Russian a text frequency of 50.7 percent for the combined nominative and accusative singular and 49.3 percent for all remaining cases.

[55] Vaillant 1950–58: II, 91.

*Table 6*

| | Case | | |
|---|---|---|---|
| Stem ending | Nominative-Accusative Singular | Genitive Singular | Definition |
| *-en* | *vremę* | *vremen-e* | "time" |
| *-ent* | *otročę* | *otročęt-e* | "infant" |
| *-es* | *slovo* | *sloves-e* | "word" |
| *-o* | *sel-o* | *sel-a* | "village" |

the singular and the entire plural. On the basis of these extensions, we may call them the *en-*, *ent-*, and *es*-stems.

In Table 6 the shorter stem of the nominative-accusative singular is given along with the genitive singular to exemplify the extended stem. In addition the hard thematic *o*-stem neuters, the dominant neuter class, and one without extensions, are included. The forms cited are from Old Church Slavonic. The conditions for merger between the *es-* and *o*-stems are evidently present because, in addition to gender and nonpalatality, there is the factor of agreement in the nominative-accusative singular *-o*. We likewise hypothesize that the more frequent *o*-stems will triumph, so that we may expect that, as the result of merger, words like *slovo* will have genitive singular *slova* in place of *slovese*, and will similarly coincide with *selo* in the remaining forms of their declension. Here again the process has already commenced in Old Church Slavonic, and the dominance of *o*-stems is clear in that, on the whole, only original *es*-stems have variant forms from the two declensions. The process is complete in practically all contemporary languages; however, that Old Church Slavonic probably represents the merger in incipient form not yet carried through everywhere in Slavic territory is shown by modern Slovene, which still retains the distinction between *o-* and *es*-stems. We can always say that the merger will eventually take place in Slovene also, but we have waited roughly 1,000 years and it has not occurred. Hence predictions of this kind without a stated time limit are not empirically refutable. We can always wait longer for it to occur. On the other hand, Slovene has also kept the other neuter consonant declensions separate from the *o*-stems; hence, the familiar implicational thesis holds here as elsewhere in Slavic and can be stated in the following terms: Merger of the *en-* and *ent*-stems with the *o*-stems implies previous merger of the *es*-stems with the *o*-stems. The decisive importance of identity in the nominative-accusative singular is further shown by the occurrence of merger of these other classes with the *o*-stem, or its palatalized counterpart, the *e*-stems, when further phonetic change produces identity in the unmarked nominative-accusative singular (e.g., *en*-stems in Ukrainian).

We may note that in the three neuter consonant classes we are once again close to a "laboratory" situation in which *cetera* are indeed *paria*. The three consonant classes agree in gender and nonpalatality but differ in the factor of identity in the unmarked cases with the thematic neuter declension.

Because the combined frequency of the oblique singular together with the entire plural is roughly equal to that of the nominative-accusative singular, we might have expected that, in merging with the *o*-stems, the *es*-stems could have analogized in the opposite direction, generalizing the extended stem to produce a declension **sloveso* (nom.-acc. sing.), **slovesa* (gen. sing.), and so on. In fact, such a development has taken place rather widely with just one noun of the *es*-class, namely *kolo* ('wheel'). Russian, Ukrainian, Lower Lusatian, and Slovak all agree in generalizing the extended stem in just this word, and Upper Lusatian has *koleso* and *kolo* as doublets. Kuznetsov conjectures that the survival of the *-es* form in this word in Russian is the result of the frequency of its use in the plural.[56] If his conjecture is correct, then the nominative and accusative plural may be expected to be the most frequent cases, and these, of course, have the *-es* extension.

Thanks to the data provided by Steinfeldt, who gives the frequencies for individual inflectional categories of all the more frequent nouns in modern Russian, it is now possible to test this thesis, at least insofar as it pertains to Russian.[57] In Table 7 are listed all words that have survived in modern Russian of the words cited by Diels in his Old Church Slavonic grammar as belonging to the *-es* declension.[58] We see, indeed, that *kolo* is most frequent in the plural.[59] Generalizing the example of *kolo*, we may say that a set of relative frequencies can be mapped into a chain of diachronic implicational hypotheses. Of course, due regard would have to be given to the statistical significance of the frequency differences. Thus, if any word on this list generalizes the *es*-stem, it should be *kolo*. The generalization of the *es*-stem in *slovo* implies its generalization in *derevo* and *kolo*, and so on.

It will not be possible in the present connection to illustrate the further series of intragenetic hypotheses verified by the historical evidence even in

[56] Kuznetsov 1953: 83.

[57] Steinfeldt 1965.

[58] Diels 1932: 169.

[59] Slovak has doublets *telo-teleso* and *slovo-sloveso*. For both pairs, the forms in *-eso* are neologisms, of lesser frequency and with specialized technical meanings, as noted in Stanislav 1957–58: II, 231. The same is true in Czech. Thus *telo* is 'body' in the ordinary sense, *teleso* is a solid in geometry; *slovo* is 'word', but *sloveso* is a modern coinage meaning 'verb'. It should likewise be noted that the modern representatives of Old Church Slavonic, *nebo* ('sky') and *cudo* ('miracle') often have *-es* extensions in the plural only, which is recognized as an example of Old Church Slavonic influence.

*Table 7*

Russian Survivals of *-es* Declension

| Modern Russian word belonging to *-es* declension | Frequencies according to Steinfeldt | | Definition |
|---|---|---|---|
| | Singular | Plural | |
| *nebo* | 97 | 3 | "sky" |
| *telo* | 95 | 5 | "body" |
| *lico* | 84 | 16 | "face" |
| *delo* | 75 | 25 | "thing" |
| *čudo* | 54 | 46 | "miracle" |
| *slovo* | 53 | 47 | "word" |
| *derevo* | 44 | 56 | "tree" |
| *koleso* | 16 | 84 | "wheel" |

this one relatively restricted domain of morphological change. Other areas of change, not touched on at all, include, for example, the elimination of inflectional categories as such by merger or by replacement through syntactic constructions. An instance of the application to another linguistic family of one of the principles discussed here in reference to Slavic is the following: In Old High German, through phonetic change, the dominant allomorph of both the neuter singular nominative-accusative and the neuter plural nominative-accusative was zero. The single overt allomorph for the plural involved the suffix *-ir* and internal vowel change (e.g., OHG *lamb*/*lembir*), and it was restricted to a handful of nouns. Its subsequent spread would be predicted as a further instance of the principle involved in the expansion of *-ov* and *-ej* in the Slavic genitive plural. Ultimately all German neuter plurals acquired overt marking.

Although I believe that the specific examples presented here are novel, I do not imply that the application of such modes of comparison has been completely lacking in the previous literature.[60] What I believe to be an innovation is the attempt to indicate in a systematic way the manner in which such studies transcend the comparative method in the usual sense and the proposal to study some particular phenomenon, for example, vowel nasalization or voiceless vowels, by bringing in all the evidence available on a worldwide scale and in historically independent instances. None of the present extended examples could, for obvious reasons, be presented as an exhaustive study. It may be hoped, however, that the details presented are sufficient for illustrative purposes.

In summary, the four approaches described here are basically similar in that they involve, in varying combinations and from varying points of view,

[60] For example, Allen 1957–58, Kuryłowicz 1964, and Manczak 1957–58.

the deployment of the methods of internal reconstruction, comparative reconstruction, and direct historical documentation in order to arrive at universal diachronic principles. These take the form of theories of relative origin (e.g., of nasalized vowels, tonal systems, gender), or of implicational relations among changes (e.g., that low vowels do not become voiceless earlier than high vowels). Synchronic typologies function merely as heuristic, though often indispensable, devices in defining the problems and in assembling the relevant data.[61] Thus it makes sense, I would maintain, to compare all the languages exhibiting some particular phenomenon (e.g., voiceless vowels, laryngeals, nominal case systems, etc.). So, likewise, the method of synchronic universals, which is inextricably involved with typological comparisons, has limitations, as has already been pointed out in the body of this paper by the citation of several instances where it was seen that the true regularity lies in the dynamic tendencies, that is, the diachronic universals.

We may illustrate this dominance and the purely auxiliary role to be assigned to synchronic static regularities, at least in regard to contingent linguistic phenomena, by reverting once more to one of the problems raised in connection with voiceless vowels. It was pointed out that we could not state as a synchronic universal that voicelessness in an earlier portion of a vowel implied voicelessness in the remainder because, at least on the hypothesis that *h*-sounds were, in some instances, voiceless vowels, the sequence forbidden by this law exists but is generally interpreted as *h* + vowel (e.g., *ḁa* = *ha*). If, however, we state the hypothesis as a diachronic implication, it will be true as far as the evidence with which I am familiar goes that when vowels *become* voiceless this process may initially affect only the latter part of the vowel but never merely the initial. On one phonetic assumption, at least, that some sounds labeled *h* are merely voiceless vowels, the difference between the two is that *h* arises from previous consonants, and *V* from previous vowels.[62] This difference would sometimes, at least, appear in a generative grammar in the

[61] For a discussion of some of the limitations of typologies, see Greenberg 1966a: 82.

[62] Voiceless vowels seem to be exceptional in that definitions based solely on articulatory and/or acoustic phenomena without regard to distribution or historical origin are normally adequate at least for the heuristic purposes of defining typologically a set of languages within which generalizing comparisons can be carried out. The definition of voiceless vowel given earlier seems adequate for a singling out of the set of languages within which comparison may operate insofar as it delineates the property "to have a voiceless vowel." It is unrevealing, however, in the following respect: Where a voiceless vowel in accordance with the definition occurs, say in final, but in its regressive spread only affects the terminal portion of the vowel of the previous syllable, this latter segment has predictable quality and is, hence, *h* rather than a voiceless vowel by the earlier definition. This definition is clearly unsatisfactory, although it does serve the initial purpose of classifying the language itself as having a voiceless vowel.

form of the rules in the phonological component. This general topic is reserved for later treatment.[63]

Finally, three types of limitations in the present treatment of diachronic hypotheses should be pointed out. The first pertains to the possibility of explaining (i.e., deducing) these from more general phonetic or semantic principles. Such explanations are often feasible, or at least reasonable suggestions may be made. For example, high voiceless vowels are probably more easily distinguishable than low voiceless vowels. Moreover, previous consonants often have initially redundant palatalization or labialization which carries most of the burden of differentiation and may ultimately carry all of it after the loss of the vowels. This limitation of interpretation was purposely adopted as not within the scope of the present paper.

A second limitation is that diachronic changes were studied only in relation to immediate conditioning factors and to the hierarchy among obviously connected changes, not in relation to the rest of the system. Thus we did not ask what other characteristics might exist in languages which might serve to explain why nasalized vowels develop in some languages but not in others. Virtually all languages have the initial conditions, namely nasal consonants adjacent to vowels, which might lead to the genesis of nasalized vowels. It is the largely unfulfilled promise of structuralism that such conditions exist. They deserve continued investigation, but it seemed preferable as a matter of scientific tactics to investigate first those areas in which success seems more likely and is indeed a probable prerequisite for the wider problem. Until we know what hierarchies of change exist in fact, we cannot investigate the synchronic structural conditions of their appearance.

The third limitation is very likely an extension of the one just mentioned. It has been aptly named by Weinreich, Labov, and Herzog the riddle of actualization.[64] Why does a specific type of expectable change materialize in one language and not in another, and why does it come into being at one

[63] The following remarks are of a provisional nature. In phonology, at least insofar as generative rules restate sound changes of the past, regularities in the form of limitations in the types of possible changes can be stated as conditions on such rules as they appear in descriptions. It is, however, not clear in practice to what extent higher level representations are required to represent earlier lower level realizations. Thus Harms, in his treatment of Southern Paiute (1966-B), at one stage of representation puts stress on every syllabic including voiceless vowels and then erases some of them, including those on the voiceless vowels. Perhaps this is not a satisfactory generative phonology. If we are to prefer other analyses of the same weak generative power, the evaluation criteria employed will come from the phonetic plausibility of both the representations and the changes, and these are subject to independent verification by the evidence of ordinary phonetics and the well-established methods of internal reconstruction and comparative linguistics proper.

[64] U. Weinreich, W. Labov, and M. Herzog 1968.

period of a particular language and not another? Thus we hypothesized that the Slavic *es*-declension would merge with the *o*-declension neuters sooner than certain other declensions; but why have they all remained distinct in Slovene to the present day, while other Slavic languages merged them at earlier dates? When stated in this form, our problem admits of a wider search for relevant variables than the internal structural factors mentioned earlier. We might turn to possible sociolinguistic and cultural conditions, though here also the search has heretofore been largely profitless, and it may be that, in the words of Du Bois Raymond, we must, in the end, say *ignorabimus*.

## References Cited

*Abbreviations*

| | |
|---|---|
| *AL* | *Anthropological Linguistics* |
| *BSOAS* | *Bulletin of the School of Oriental and African Studies* |
| *IJAL* | *International Journal of American Linguistics* |
| *WZKM* | *Wiener Zeitschrift für die Kunde des Morgenlandes* |
| *ZPAS* | *Zeitschrift für Phonetik und allgemeine Sprachwissenschaft* |

*A. References Exclusive of Data on Voiceless Vowels*

Allen, W. S. 1957–58. "Some Problems of Palatalization in Greek," *Lingua* 7: 113–33.
Diels, Paul. 1932. *Altkirchenslavische Grammatik*. Vol. 1: *Grammatik*. Heidelberg.
Ferguson, Charles A. 1963. "Assumptions about Nasals: A Sample Study in Phonological Universals." In *Universals of Language*, ed. J. H. Greenberg (Cambridge, Mass.), pp. 42–47.
Greenberg, Joseph H. 1962. "The Interpretation of the Coptic Vowel System," *Journal of African Languages* 1: 22–29.
———. 1966a. *Language Universals, with Special Reference to Feature Hierarchies*. The Hague and Paris.
———. 1966b. "Synchronic and Diachronic Universals in Phonology," *Language* 42: 508–17.
Heffner, R. M. S. 1964. *General Phonetics*. Madison, Wisc.
Hockett, Charles F. 1955. *Manual of Phonology*. Baltimore.
Jakobson, R. 1958. "Typological Studies and Their Contribution to Historical Comparative Linguistics," *Proceedings of the Eighth International Congress of Linguists*. Oslo. Pp. 17–25.
Josselson, Harry Hirsch. 1953. *The Russian Word Count and Frequency Analysis of Grammatical Categories in Standard Literary Russian*. Detroit.
Klemensiewicz, A., T. Lehr-Spławinski, and S. Urbanczyk. 1955. *Gramatyka historyczna języka polskiego*. Warsaw.
Kuryłowicz, Jerzy. 1964. *The Inflectional Categories of Indo-European*. Heidelberg.
Kuznetsov, P. S. 1953. *Istoricheskaja grammatika russkogo jazyka: Morfologija*. Moscow.
Lehiste, Ilse. 1964. *Acoustical Characteristics of Selected English Consonants*. Baltimore.

Manczak, W. 1957–58. "Tendances générales des changements analogiques," *Lingua* 7: 298–323, 387–420.
Meyer-Lübke, W. 1890–1906. *Grammaire des langues romaines*. Paris. 4 vols.
Paul, H., and H. Stolte. 1951. *Kurze deutsche Grammatik* (2d ed.). Tübingen.
Polotsky, H. J. 1931. "Zur koptischen Lautlehre. I," *Zeitschrift für Ägyptische Sprache und Altertumskunde* 67: 74–77.
Samarin, William J. 1966. *The Gbeya Language*. Berkeley and Los Angeles.
Smalley, William A. 1962. *Manual of Articulatory Phonetics*. 2 pts. Tarrytown, N.Y.
Stanislav, Jan. 1957–58. *Dejiny slovenskeho jazyka*. Bratislava. 3 vols.
Steindorff, Georg. 1951. *Lehrbuch der koptischen Grammatik*. Chicago.
Steinfeldt, E. 1965. *Russian Word Count*. Moscow.
Till, Walter. 1929. "Altes aleph und 'ajin im Koptischen," *WZKM* 36: 186–96.
———. 1951. "Der Mittelzungenvokal im Koptischen," *Le Muséon* 64: 63–69.
Vaillant, André. 1950–58. *Grammaire comparée des langues slaves*. Lyon. 2 vols.
Weinreich, U., W. Labov, and M. Herzog. 1968. "Empirical Foundations for a Theory of Language Change." In *Directions in Historical Linguistics*, ed. W. Lehmann and Y. Malkiel (Austin, Texas).
West, John David. 1962. "The Phonology of Mikasuki," *Studies in Linguistics* 16: 77–91.
Whiteley, W. H. 1965. "Notes on the Ci-miini Dialect of Swahili," *African Language Studies* 6: 67–72.

### *B. References on Voiceless Vowels*

Andrzejewski, B. W. 1957. "Some Preliminary Observations on the Borana Dialect of Galla," *BSOAS* 30: 354–74.
Aschmann, Herman P. 1945. "Totanaco Phonemes," *IJAL* 12: 34–43.
Bender, Ernest, and Zellig S. Harris. 1945. "The Phonemes of North Carolina Cherokee," *IJAL* 12: 14–21.
Biggs, Bruce. 1961. "The Structure of New Zealand Maori," *AL* 3, no. 3: 1–54.
Bloch, Bernard. 1950. "Studies in Colloquial Japanese IV. Phonemics," *Language* 26: 86–125.
Borman, M. B. 1962. "Cofan Phonemes," *Studies in Ecuadorian Indian Languages* (Norman, Okla.) I: 45–59.
Bridgeman, Loraine. 1961. "Kaiwa Phonology," *IJAL* 27: 329–34.
Bright, William. 1957. *The Karok Language*. Berkeley and Los Angeles.
Canonge, Elliot D. 1957. "Voiceless Vowels in Comanche," *IJAL* 23: 63–67.
Casagrande, Joseph. 1954. "Comanche Linguistic Acculturation I," *IJAL* 20: 140–51.
Davis, Irvine. 1962. "Phonological Function in Cheyenne," *IJAL* 28: 36–42.
———. 1964. "The Language of Santa Ana Pueblo," *Bureau of American Ethnology Bulletin* (Washington) 191: 53–190.
———. 1966. "Numic Consonantal Correspondences," *IJAL* 32: 124–40.
deAngulo, Jaime. 1932. "The Chichimeco Language," *IJAL* 7: 152–94.
Dirks, Sylvester. 1953. "Campa Phonemes," *IJAL* 19: 30–44.
Doke, Clement M. 1931. *A Comparative Study in Shona Phonetics*. Johannesburg.
Firestone, Homer. 1955. "Chama Phonology," *IJAL* 21: 52–55.
Gibson, Lorna F. 1956. "Pame Phonemics and Morphophonemics," *IJAL* 22: 242–65.
Gleason, Henry Allan. 1962. *Workbook in Descriptive Linguistics* (New York). Esp. p. 62 (Chatino).

Haas, Mary. 1946. "A Grammatical Sketch of Tunica," In *Linguistic Structures of Native America*, ed. H. Hoijer (New York).

Halpern, A. M. 1946. "Yuma. I. Phonemes," *IJAL* 12: 25–33.

Han, Mieko S. 1962. "Internal Juncture in Japanese," *Studies in Linguistics* 16: 49–61.

Harms, Robert T. 1966. "Stress, Voice, and Length in Southern Paiute," *IJAL* 32: 228–35.

Harrington, J. P. 1910. "The Phonetic System of the Ute Language," *University of Colorado Studies* 8: 199–222.

Hodge, Carlton T. 1946. "Serbo-Croatian Phonemes," *Language* 22: 112–20.

Holmer, Nils M. 1949. "Goajiro (Arawak) I. Phonology," *IJAL* 15: 45–56.

Jimbo, K. 1925. "The Word-Tone of the Standard Japanese Language," *BSOAS* 3: 659–67.

Johnson, Orville E., and Catherine Peeke. 1962. "Phonemic Units in the Secoya Word," *Studies in Ecuadorian Indian Languages* (Norman, Okla.) I: 78–95.

Keller, Kathryn. 1959. "The Phonemes of Chontal," *IJAL* 25: 44–53.

Key, Harold. 1964. "Phonotactics of Cayuvava," *IJAL* 30: 143–50.

Lange, Rudolf. 1903. *A Text-book of Colloquial Japanese*. Eng. ed. by Christopher Ness (Tokyo).

Larsen, Raymond S., and Eunice Pike. 1949. "Huasteco Intonation and Phonemes," *Language* 25: 268–77.

Liljeblad, Sven. 1950. "Bannack. I. Phonemes," *IJAL* 12: 126–31.

Lochak, Dorita. 1960. "Basque Phonemics," *AL* 2, no. 3: 12–31.

Lounsbury, F. 1953. *Oneida Verb Morphology*. New Haven, Conn.

McIntosh, John B. 1945. "Huichol Phonemes," *IJAL* 11: 31–35.

McKaughan, Howard. 1954. "Chatino Formulas and Phonemes," *IJAL* 20: 23–27.

Martin, Samuel E. 1951. "Korean Phonemics," *Language* 27: 519–33.

———. 1961. *Dagur Mongolian Grammar, Texts and Lexicon*. Bloomington, Ind.

Miller, Wick R. 1965. *Acoma Grammar and Texts*. Berkeley and Los Angeles.

Miller, Wick R., and Irvine Davis. 1963. "Proto-Keresan Phonology," *IJAL* 29: 310–30.

Mori, Masatoshi Gensen. 1929. *The Pronunciation of Japanese*. Tokyo.

O'Grady, Geoffrey. 1964. *Nyangumata Grammar*. Sydney.

Ott, Willis, and Rebecca Ott. 1959. *Fonemas de la lengua Ignaciana*. La Paz.

Polivanov, E. D. 1928. "Karšinskij govor," *Doklady Akademii Nauk SSSR* (Uzbek), no. 5.

Preuss, K. Th. 1932. "Grammatik der Cora-Sprache," *IJAL* 7: 1–84.

Pride, Kitty. 1961. "Numerals in Chatino," *AL* 3, no. 2: 1–106.

———. 1963. "Chatino Tonal Structure," *AL* 5, no. 2: 19–28.

Ramanujan, A. K., and C. Masica. 1966. "Toward a Phonological Typology of the Indian Linguistic Area" (Awadhi). Unpublished MS.

Ransom, Jay Ellis. 1945. "Duwanish Phonology and Morphology," *IJAL* 11: 204–10.

Rich, Furne. 1963. "Arabela phonemes and High-level Phonology," *Studies in Peruvian Indian Languages* (México) I, 193–206.

Redden, James E. 1966. "Walapai. I. Phonology," *IJAL* 32: 1–16.

Riggs, Venda. 1949. "Alternate Phonemic Analyses of Comanche," *IJAL* 15: 229–33.

Sapir, Edward. 1930. "The Southern Paiute Language," *Proceedings of the American Academy of Arts and Sciences* 65, no. 1: 1–296.

Saxton, Dean. 1963. "Papago Phonemes," *IJAL* 29: 29–35.

Seiler, Hansjakob. 1957. "Die phonetischen Grundlagen der Vokalphoneme des Cahuilla," *ZPAS* 10: 204–223.
———. 1965. "Accent and Morphophonemics in Cahuilla and in Uto-Aztecan," *IJAL* 31: 50–59.
Shimkin, D. B. 1949. "Shoshone. I. Linguistic Sketch and Text," *IJAL* 15: 175–88.
Sjoberg, Andrée F. 1963. *Uzbek Structural Grammar*. Bloomington, Ind.
Smith, William B. S. 1949. "Some Cheyenne Forms," *Studies in Linguistics* 7: 77–85.
Sokolova, V. S. 1949. *Fonetika tadžikskogo jazyka*. Moscow and Leningrad.
Trager, George L. 1940. "Serbo-Croatian Accents and Quantities," *Language* 16: 29–32.
Tucker, A. N., and M. A. Bryan. 1966. *Linguistic Analyses: The Non-Bantu Languages of North-Eastern Africa* (Galla, Teso, Bagirmi). International African Institute, London.
Voegelin, C. F. 1935. "Shawnee Phonemes," *Language* 11: 23–37.
Voegelin, C. F., and F. M. Voegelin. 1964. "Indo-Pacific, Fascicle Two," *AL* 6, no. 7: 20–56 (Hawaiian).
Voegelin C. F., F. M. Voegelin, and Kenneth L. Hale. 1962. *Typological and Comparative Grammar of Uto-Aztecan. I. (Phonology)*. Baltimore.
Wurm, Stephen. 1947. "The Uzbek Dialect of Qïzïl Qujaš," *BSOAS* 12: 86–105.
———. 1949. "The (Kara-) Kirghiz Language," *BSOAS* 13: 97–120.
Yamagiwa, Joseph K. 1942. *Modern Conversational Japanese*. New York and London.
Yegerlehner, John. 1959. "Arizona Tewa. I. Phonemes," *IJAL* 25: 1–7.

# Some Generalizations Concerning Glottalic Consonants, Especially Implosives

[1]

J. C. Catford, in a now classic paper (1939) distinguished two types of glottalic consonants: (1) ejectives (or explosives) involving the raising of the larynx and the subsequent expulsion of the air compressed in the supraglottal cavity, and (2) injectives (or implosives) utilizing the opposite mechanism of lowering the larynx, thus rarefying the air in the supraglottal cavity so that, on release of the oral closure, an ingressive flow of external air is immediately succeeded by egressive lung air.

For purposes of the present study of these two classes of sounds, approximately 150 phonological descriptions have been examined.[1] This sampling is perhaps close to exhaustive for the implosives with which this paper is more particularly concerned. For the more widely distributed ejectives, the sample is far less complete. The appended bibliography lists all the sources consulted whether cited in the body of this paper or not.

A more thorough review of the literature at a later stage of the study showed that some of the conclusions regarding implosives had been anticipated by Haudricourt (especially 1950). Reference is made to those conclusions where appropriate. The present study is perhaps still of interest even for these questions, since it presents additional data not considered by Haudricourt, whether because they referred to languages outside his area of specialization (Southeast Asia) or because their appearance was subsequent to his publications. This evidence serves to confirm the essential correctness

[1] The research on which this paper is based was carried out as part of the NSF Project on Language Universals (Grant No. GS-1880) at Stanford University. This support is gratefully acknowledged. I am also grateful for the assistance of Dorothy Kaschube in earlier phases of this work.

of practically all his theses. Wang (1968) also presents some generalizations regarding both implosives and ejectives, some of which likewise duplicate Haudricourt's conclusions without citing them. This work appeared subsequent to my earlier investigations. Like Haudricourt's hypotheses these are also in basic agreement with my own observations and are cited where appropriate.

The approach employed here may be called 'processual'. Besides its possible substantive interest, the present study is designed to illustrate further the methodology outlined and exemplified in Greenberg 1969. In accordance with this approach, the article consists of two main sections. The first is essentially synchronic, while the second sets forth dynamic and comparative evidence bearing on the more typical diachronic processes in which glottalic consonants participate. The division is not rigid since it has not been possible, even had it been desirable, to segregate completely the synchronic and diachronic factors.

In the following section a number of important respects in which generalizations concerning ejective and implosive consonants are distinguishably different, or indeed, in some instances, involve polar oppositions, are considered. These include the temporal relation between oral and glottal releases, the relation to voicing, preferences regarding point and manner of articulation, effect on the pitch of adjoining vowel segments, and marked-unmarked relations to the plain series.

[2]

*1*. The phonological opposition in individual languages between ejectives and injectives applies effectively only to obstruents, and is neutralized for sonants and semi-vowels. The typical ejective obstruent is unvoiced and has abrupt onset (i.e., is a stop or affricate). Segments with this latter property will be referred to as non-continuants. These are the sounds commonly referred to as 'glottalized' in phonetic descriptions. The typical injective obstruent is, on the other hand, a voiced stop.

For the obstruent ejective, as is often pointed out in the phonetic literature, the glottal occlusion is normally released after the oral occlusion. For example, Hockett (1955: 33) observes that "typically the oral closure is released first . . . and then the glottis is opened." He goes on to point out, "But various timings are possible, and various degrees of pressure before release." This situation is mirrored in the most common phonetic symbolization of this class of sounds, e.g. [p'] in which the glottalization symbol follows that of the oral articulation. Not uncommonly in phonemic analyses glottalic ejectives are analyzed as phonemic sequences of an unvoiced obstruent and a glottal stop. In such cases the glottal stop symbol is invariably written second.

The opposite situation obtains in regard to the imploded obstruents. As Ladefoged (1968) correctly indicates, there are no less than three related phonetic possibilities, truly implosive sounds in which the larynx is lowered and ingressive air follows the oral release, sounds with laryngealized voicing, and preglottalized sounds. These may be symbolized as ɓ, b̰, and ˀb respectively. However, there are a number of reasons why, in spite of their phonetic distinguishability, they have to be considered as variants of the same basic type. Both phonetic and phonological considerations enter. For the first two of these three possibilities, implosives and laryngealized sounds, as Ladefoged himself points out, where there is implosion it is often accompanied by laryngealized voicing and where there is laryngealized voicing there is often simultaneous implosion, although 'pure' realizations of both types do occur.

For West Africa, Ladefoged cites Hausa as a typical example of a language with laryngealized voiced consonants (e.g. b̰). However, an earlier instrumental phonetic study of the Hausa sounds in question (Von Essen 1962), showed as one of its results that there was consistently negative oral pressure indicating actual implosion.

As for the distinction between laryngealized and preglottalized sounds, we are in an even more difficult situation, if we wish to assign languages to one or the other type with consistency. As Ladefoged points out (1968: 16): "Because I have not been able to distinguish consistently between voiced consonants with accompanying glottal stop and similar consonants marked by laryngealization, I have symbolized both by a prefixed ˀ." Hence, Ladefoged in his phonemic inventories of West African languages distinguishes two, not three, sound types, and even here it is noted that for Kambari there is free variation (1968: 60).

Even if one wished to distinguish two types, the implosive and the preglottalized/laryngealized, this would not be possible from the existing literature, with the exception of the examples listed in Ladefoged 1968. Even accomplished practical phoneticians have chosen to ignore these differences. Thus Westermann and Ward (1933) recognize only one sound type symbolized ɓ etc. Much more recently, Tucker and Bryan (1966), treating of the languages covering a vast area within Africa and with a large explicit apparatus for symbolizing phonetic types, lump all examples under such transcriptions as 'b. Crazzolara (1960: 5) goes so far as to say, "Consonants preceded by a glottal stop have also been called 'implosive consonants'."

Outside of Ladefoged's recent book, the only sources which distinguish more than one phonetic type occur in the reports of field workers with SIL training. In these accounts the differences are never distinctive. Sometimes there is free variation. In Southeast Asia, Thomas (1962) describes preglottalized and implosive consonants in free variation in Chrau, while Smalley (1954) indicates that in Sre there is free variation between preglottalized and laryngealized realizations. The fact that in the French literature on this area these sounds are uniformly described as preglottalized shows once more that a clean separation is not obtainable on the basis of existing accounts.

In other instances, most conspicuously for the Mayan languages, there is conditional variation in which, characteristically, preglottalized variants occur intervocalically and implosive and laryngealized types initially. An example is Aguacatec (McArthur and McArthur 1956) with ɓ initially and ˀb intervocalically. In Movima (Judy and Judy 1962), a language of Bolivia, implosive actualizations are described for initial and preglottalized for medial position.

There is thus no evidence, as far as can be seen, of phonologically distinctive contrast among laryngealized, preglottalized, and implosive obstruents. This is likewise the conclusion of Ladefoged (1968: 19), ". . . in fact no language uses the difference between these possibilities." Just as importantly for present purposes, it seems that all the generalizations to be discussed in subsequent sections apply equally to all these types. However, the possibility of distinctive opposition within a language or differences in respect to relevant generalizations should not be completely foreclosed in view of the presumed future accumulation of more exact phonetic information.

Because of these equivalences, the term 'injective' will be used as a cover term for all three phonetic types where their distinction is not relevant, and such symbolizations as ˀb, ˀd will be used for typographic convenience except where the phonetics is the explicit topic of discussion.

The foregoing discussion has been concerned exclusively with obstruents. Glottalic sonants resemble injective obstruents in that they tend to preglottalization. An implosive sonant is presumably a phonetic impossibility. There is however for sonants the same phonetic ambivalence and phonological equivalence between laryngealization and preglottalization which has been noted for obstruents, and here also there is presumably no hard and fast phonetic boundary between the two. Similarly free or conditional variation among the various phonetic types is sometimes reported. Thus for Khmu, an Austroasiatic language, Smalley (1961) notes free variation between actualizations which he symbolizes as m̓ and ˀm̓ and which he analyzes phonemically as a sequence of glottal stop and sonant. In a well-known paper, Sapir (1933) described how for his Nootka informant, sonants with glottal preceding oral release and the ordinary obstruent glottalic pressure stops with glottal release following oral release, were of the same type, so that having learned to write according to the then prevalent transcription p!, t!, etc., he spontaneously wrote m!, n!, etc. also, contrary to phonetic fact. It will be shown later that glottalic sonants, which are probably from the phonetic point of view the same type everywhere, may be functionally or historically the glottalic equivalents of either injective or ejective obstruents, depending on the language.

*2*. The next question to be considered is that of voicing in relation to glottalic consonants. Once more obstruents and sonants have to be considered separately. The ejective obstruent appears always to be unvoiced. Indeed, voicing for these sounds is probably a phonetic impossibility. On the other hand, for all the varieties of injective discussed in the preceding paragraph, preglottalized, laryngealized, or true implosive, voicing is normal. For this reason Wolff (1959) in his feature analysis of a set of Nigerian languages utilizes a single feature, glottalic, for both injectives and ejectives and distinguishes them by the presence of the features voiceless and voiced respectively. The present writer, in an early discussion of Hausa phonology, treated ejectives and injectives as members of the same series (Greenberg 1941).

However, voiceless implosives do occur. With the exception of most Munda languages, which have a full set of four injective unvoiced stops in final position, they are practically always bilabial and, as will be shown later, this is the preferred point of articulation for implosives in general. In most forms of Maya, a single implosive bilabial phoneme is found with a variety of allophones, voiceless, voiced, and sometimes nasal or with a nasal release. The unvoiced allophone occurs typically in final position, e.g., in the stress group (Aguacatec [McArthur and McArthur 1956]), or in syllable final (Chontal [Keller 1958], and Pocomchi [Mayers 1960]). In Tojolabal (Supple and Douglass 1949), the bilabial implosive is voiceless in all occurrences. In still other forms of Mayan, e.g., Tzeltal (Berlin 1962), the bilabial implosive is voiced in all its manifestations. It seems then that voicing contrast for the bilabial implosive is never distinctive in Mayan. However, a few Mayan languages have a contrast between an ejective p' and an implosive in the same position. When this occurs the implosive is generally voiced in all its realizations so that a contrast based solely on injection versus ejection without accompanying voicing contrasts does not usually exist. Examples of this situation are furnished by Tsotsil (Weathers 1947), Chorti (Mayers 1966), and Mopan (Mayers 1966).

However, it seems that in Chontal (Keller 1958) a voiceless bilabial implosive does contrast with a voiceless ejective in word final. In other positions the co-allophones of the implosive are voiced nonimplosive stops.

Iraqw, a southern Cushitic language (Whiteley 1958), like some Mayan languages, has a bilabial implosive which is devoiced in word final. This is also reported for Basa, a Bantu language of Cameroun (Bôt Ba Njock 1962). Unvoiced bilabial implosives are likewise found in Mangbetu and in Lendu, both Central Sudanic languages, according to Tucker and Bryan (1966). Both these languages are described as having voiced bilabial implosives, but existing sources do not show whether there is a contrast.

There remains, however, one reported but doubtful instance of which I am aware in which there is a voicing contrast in an implosive consonant. This is Igbo, in which Carnochan (1948) and subsequently other investigators report that the consonants written kp and gb in the standard orthography are velarized bilabial implosives differing only in voice. However, Ladefoged (1968: 11) notes that ". . . only Igbo has *ɓ* (but not *gb*) in contrast to *kp*," thus suggesting that there is a further difference in the presence of a velar occlusion in the voiceless member of the opposition.

A contrast between voiceless and voiced true labial velars, both described as implosive, is reported by Knappert (1962) in regard to Alur, a Western Nilotic language. However, as will be mentioned in later discussion, it is at the least doubtful whether sounds described as implosive labial velars should be included in the group of sounds which forms the topic of the present paper, since they involve a velaric airstream.

An instance was noted of a voiceless implosive without a bilabial component, once more from Igbo, for the Owerri dialect (Armstrong 1967) and for a dialect of the same group, in Swift, Agaghotu, and Ugorji (1962). Both these sources describe an implosive voiceless dental. An earlier source, Ward (1936), describes the Owerri dialect as having the common voiced implosives ˀb and ˀd without mention of a voiceless type. A further example of a voiceless nonlabial implosive is to be found in Galla (Andrzejewski 1957), where the only implosive, a retroflex ˀd, is reported, like the other voiced consonants, to have a voiceless allophone before a voiceless vowel allophone.

In view of these facts one might at least tentatively accept the thesis that the contrast between injection and ejection need not be accepted as autonomous for general phonetic theory. The implosive is normally voiced, but voicelessness occurs typically in word final where ordinary 'voiced' obstruents are subject to devoicing. It seems likely, therefore, that the constant feature here is also laxness. Hence one might have a common feature glottalic that is concomitantly injective with the lax feature and ejective with the tense feature.[2]

[2]This conclusion is similar to, but not identical with, that of Jakobson (1962, especially p. 655, and 1968). There is agreement that a single checked or glottalic feature is sufficient and

The relative laxness of the voiced injective stop as compared with the plain is noted several times in the literature (for Dan [Bearth and Zemp 1967: 13], Basa [Bôt Ba Njock 1962: 49], and Wolio [Anceaux 1952: 5]). The voiceless injectives of Kharia are explicitly described as lax by Pinnow (1959: 30).

With regard to sonants, corresponding to the absence of injective/ejective opposition, there is quite surely no phonological contrast of voicing. The recent study of Aoki (1968) sheds important light on this subject. In Klamath there is apparently laryngealized voicing intervocalically while in final position the sonant is voiceless after an initial period of glottal occlusion. Once more, then, phonetically at least, the glottalic sonant is rather more like the injective than the ejective obstruent.

*3*. Preferences regarding point of articulation for glottalic obstruents are summarized in the following formula: injectives tend to have front articulation, ejectives to have back articulation.[3] This is shown most strikingly in a number of languages which have both injectives and ejectives. An instance in point is Hausa, which has two voiced implosives which are bilabial and alveolar and two voiceless ejectives s' (or ts' depending on dialect) and k'. In addition there is a laryngealized or preglottalized ʔy which, as will be shown later, is the palatal representative of the implosive series. Thus the injective set has no member in the velar position and the ejective has none in the bilabial.

A gap in the class of ejectives at the bilabial point of articulation is found in a number of world areas. A considerable number of Amerind languages have this characteristic. In North America, probably all the Athabaskan languages (which are, however, also defective in the bilabial series for other sound types), Haida, Tlingit, Tillamook, Tonkawa, Zuni, Western Miwok, and Otomi are among the languages which may be listed here. Far to the south in Bolivia, Itonama, a Macro-Chibchan language, has t', c', and k' but no p'. In Africa, Gwamba, a Bantu language (van Warmelo 1930), has k' and various affricates ts', tl', etc. but neither t' nor p'. In Ethiopia, a number of Cushitic and Semitic languages show a similar gap in their series of ejective consonants. An example is Bilin, a Central Cushitic language (Palmer 1958), with the ejectives t', c', k', and $k^w$'. In Amharic and some other Semitic languages in the same area, p' occurs only in a few loan words from Ge'ez.

---

that there is no necessity for separate ejective and injective features. On the other hand, the facts cited here in regard to Mayan languages, Iraqw, and especially the Munda languages, suggest that implosives are to be considered checked and lenis, rather than checked and voiced. Cases such as Andi with fortis and lenis voiceless ejectives are then to be analyzed as checked, voiceless, and tense or lax, respectively.

[3] This was noted by Haudricourt (1950) insofar as it concerns injectives, and for both series by Wang (1968).

In Ge'ez p' is likewise of exotic origin as a rendering of Greek p. As in other Semitic languages, the Greek unaspirated stops are represented by 'emphatic' consonants.

Korana Hottentot (Beach 1938) has only one ejective in inherited words, the velar affricate kxʔ. It also has ts' in Nama loan words (once more a sound which does not occur in Nama itself) but no labial ejective.

Some Caucasian languages of the Northeast group, namely Avar, Andi, and Lak (Trubetskoy 1926), have an extensive series of glottalic ejectives which once more show a gap at the bilabial position.

Further indication of the favoring of back articulation of ejectives is the fact that in Amharic and other Semitic Ethiopian languages, the ejective corresponding to the velar nonejective k is the back velar ejective q'.

For injectives, on the other hand, the bilabial is clearly the favored point of articulation. Excluding for the moment labial velars which are a special case, it very nearly holds that if a language has one injective obstruent, it is ʔb; if it has two they are ʔb and ʔd (the most common pattern); if there are three they are ʔb, ʔd, and ʔɟ (the latter a palatal stop, often replaced, however, by ʔy); and if four they are ʔb, ʔd, ʔɟ, and ʔg. I know of no language with more than four injective obstruents.[4]

A number of qualifications are to be made regarding the foregoing statements. There are a few languages whose sole injective is ʔd. All these are in Africa and the surest examples are from Eastern Cushitic, where it is reported from Galla (Andrzejewski 1957), Baiso (Fleming 1964), and Rendille (Fleming 1964). In Somali there is apparently dialectical and free individual variation between implosive and nonimplosive d (L. E. Armstrong 1934). In Fök, a language of Cameroun, Meyer (1950: 271) describes a single implosive ʔd but observes "Ich kann nicht mit Sicherheit sagen dass das *d* . . . implosiv ist. . . ." There is, to my knowledge, only a single exception to the generalization that the presence of at least one posterior (compact) injective implies the presence of at least one anterior (diffuse) injective. This is Kinga, a Bantu language (R. Wolff 1905) which is reported to have as its only implosive a voiced velar ʔg.

As will be noted in greater detail in a subsequent section, the expected palatal stop implosive is rather unstable and tends to be replaced by a preglottalized or laryngealized sonant ʔy. The velar implosive is a very infrequent sound, and with the exception of Kinga, as noted above, always

[4] The Gutob, Remo, Pareng group of Munda languages for which Pinnow (1959: 44) lists the usual Indian five points of articulation for implosives in his table of phonemes, is probably not a real exception since it is based on phonetically unreliable data, and Pinnow specifically mentions the distinction between dental and retroflex as a point of uncertainty.

seems to imply the presence of bilabial, apical, and palatal members of the series. Examples of this pattern are Angas, a Chadic language of Nigeria, Swahili, Masai, Sindhi, and Papago (allophonically before voiceless vowels).

We have yet to consider labiovelars. In individual language descriptions, labiovelarity is often considered as a complex point of articulation. Labiovelars which are confined to Africa and to a restricted region in Melanesia (including part of New Guinea) are in some recent descriptions designated as injectives. For most languages, however, we cannot tell whether we are dealing with injectives or not. Here, once again, the pioneering instrumental phonetic research of Ladefoged (1968) has thrown new light on the subject. His investigations have concentrated on the phonetic variants associated with sounds generally symbolized as kp. He distinguishes three types from the phonetic point of view. The first of these, and in his observations the least commonly encountered, involves the superposition of two simultaneous closures on a pulmonic egressive airstream. This can also occur with voicing. There is obviously no basis for considering this sound type to be an injective. In the second type, which is found, for example, in Yoruba and is stated to be the most frequent, an ingressive airstream in the mouth is produced chiefly by retracting the back part of the tongue as in click sounds.

This variety involves a combination of an ingressive velaric airstream and an egressive pulmonic airstream in which the velar closure is released first, whence the common symbolization kp. It would seem to differ from a bilabial click such as is found in some southern Bushmen languages only in the order of velar and labial releases. In click sounds in general the velar release follows that of the closure interior to the velum in consonance with the common symbolizations //g, etc. This variety, then, like the first, does not qualify as an implosive in the ordinary sense, since there is no movement of the larynx and no ingressive glottalic airstream.

The third type, however, which is less frequent than that just described, has some claim to be considered as an injective. It combines velaric and glottalic ingressive air mechanisms. As usual with glottalic implosives, the descending vocal chords vibrate, or at least in this instance in their later phase as indicated by such symbolizations as Abraham's kb for Tiv. Ladefoged considers this third type as a form of kp. Here there is apparently only one type with respect to voicing.

Once again, however, it is not possible to categorize languages on the basis of these types. Thus Ladefoged (1968: 9) in a single utterance in Bini found all three types and in the phonemic inventories of languages the only symbols employed are kp, gb, or, for the corresponding nasal consonant, ŋm. A single instance, however, was noted in which a contrast between an implosive and a nonimplosive labiovelar was posited; the language is Balese (Vorbichler 1965). For these reasons labiovelars have not been considered here as injectives and the generalizations presented in this paper are to be considered in this light. As will appear later, however, in addition to the phonetic evidence just discussed there is evidence of a diachronic relationship between labiovelars and bilabial injectives.

*4*. A recurrent feature of injectives which deserves special mention and treatment is that the injective corresponding to a noninjective dental is often retracted to the alveolar or alveopalatal position and is consistently apical, often with accompanying retroflexion.[5] The examples in the sample were so numerous that this property can be considered normal and one may suspect that it is present in some instances without being noted in the phonetic description. The following are some examples. In Cambodian, t is dental, but ˀd is described as post-alveolar (Henderson 1952), and is represented in the orthography by a symbol of the Devanagari retroflex series. In Lendu, a Central Sudanic language (Tucker 1940) the nonimplosive t and d are dental while ˀd is alveolar retroflex. With regard to the Moru-Madi languages, also Central Sudanic, Tucker and Bryan (1966: 102) state that "the retroflex tongue position is in fact a more distinguishing feature than the manner of articulation, which hardly seems implosive at all." Armstrong (1934) makes a similar observation in regard to Somali.

This retraction and the frequently accompanying retroflexion often leads in a further stage of development to a preglottalized sonant ˀr (e.g. Sara-Mbay) or ˀl̥ (e.g. Mamvu). This development is parallel to, but far less frequent than, replacement of a palatal voiced imploded stop by the corresponding laryngealized or preglottalized sonant ˀy to be considered in the next section.

*5*. It is a striking parallelism between Africa and Southeast Asia that languages with the characteristic three implosive patterns, bilabial, alveolar, and palatal, have ˀy in place of the expected palatal stop. This holds for Sre (also called Koho), a Moi language of the Austroasiatic family, and for Li's reconstructed proto-Tai (1943). In Africa this is particularly common in languages of the Northern branch of West Atlantic (e.g. Konyagi, Pajade). It also occurs in Chadic languages; an example is Hausa with ˀb, ˀd, and ˀy as well as a set of ejectives. This same pattern is found much farther east in certain languages for the Moru-Madi group of Central Sudanic. For example, Logo has exactly the same series of voiced injective consonants as Hausa.

There is a body of evidence that demonstrates that in such cases ˀy is indeed the representative of the injective series at the palatal point of articulation and derives from an earlier injective voiced stop. In Fula, most

[5] This was noted in Haudricourt 1950.

dialects display the widespread ˀb, ˀd, ˀy pattern, but the extreme western dialects (e.g. that of the Futa Djallon) have a voiced injective palatal stop corresponding to the ˀy of other dialects. In the closely related Serer Sin as noted by Pichl (1963) there is similar dialect variation. Here the common pronunciation is that of the stop, but it is noted that in the dialect of Saloum this is sometimes pronounced ˀy.

In the system of initial consonantal alternations involving three grades which is common to Fula and a number of other languages of the Northern West Atlantic subgroup of Niger-Congo, the voiced injective consonants of Fula and Serer Sin do not alternate. However, in certain other languages of this group, these sounds participate in the consonant gradation system and may thus provide evidence that ˀy is the palatal representative of the voiced injective series.

One example is Bedik (Ferry 1968). In this and in other discussions of the languages of this group, the grades will be numbered as follows: (1) fricative, (2) stop, (3) prenasalized. These designations are historical and do not always agree with the synchronic data. Following is a relevant portion of the table of initial consonant alternation of Bedik.

| | | | | | | | | | | |
|---|---|---|---|---|---|---|---|---|---|---|
| 1. | f | w | ˀb | s | r | l | š | y | ˀy | . . . |
| 2. | p | b | ˀb | t | d | ˀd | č | ǰ | ˀy | . . . |
| 3. | p | mb | m | t | nd | n | č | nǰ | ɲ | . . . |

From this tabulation it is clear that ˀy is both the stop and fricative representative of the palatal series as shown by the occurrence of ɲ in series 3. We note that ˀb is to m as *ˀɟ is to ɲ. It may be noted in passing that here the nonimplosive series involves an alveopalatal affricate where the injective series has a palatal stop or sonant. Indeed, as will be discussed in further detail in the next section, injective affricates do not occur at all, while palatal noninjective stops have a strong tendency to be replaced by alveopalatal affricates.

Evidence similar to that of Bedik for the status of ˀy may also be found in the consonantal alternation system of Pajade and Konyagi in the same group of languages, but it is not considered here. (See J. D. Sapir 1971, and Wilson 1965.)

*6.* We now come to the question of manner preferences of ejective and injective obstruents. It has been seen that stop articulations are common in both sets of sounds. There is a difference, however, in that for injectives the stop is the normal—indeed the nearly exclusive type. As noted by Wang (1968: 8) affricate implosives do not occur. Once again we have to do with what is probably a phonetic impossibility. Preglottalized or implosive voiced spirants do occur but are excessively rare. In the present study only two examples were noted. A bilabial sound described as an implosive β (i.e. bilabial voiced spirant) is reported as occurring in Bongo, a Central Sudanic language (Tucker and Bryan 1966: 62). It is apparently in free variation with the common implosive ˀb of this language. Fang-Kwei Li (1965) reports a preglottalized voiced velar spirant ˀɣ in Sui of Li-Ngam, a Tai language. This sound seems to be the velar representative, absent in the vast majority of instances, of an injective series symbolized ˀb, ˀd, ˀɟ (i.e. the preglottalized semivowel), and ˀɣ.

For the ejective, spirants are also relatively infrequent and always imply the presence of some ejectives with abrupt onset (i.e. stop or fricatives). The greatest difference between ejectives and injectives is shown, however, in regard to affricates. They have been seen to be nonexistent for injectives. For ejectives, however, they are quite frequent and stable. In fact, in two languages within the sample all the glottalic consonants are affricate ejectives. These are (Hokan) Chontal (Waterhouse and Morrison 1950) and Korana Hottentot (Beach 1938). Further, for the palatal region in particular, it appears that the optimal ejective is the alveopalatal affricate č rather than a stop. This is true also for the plain obstruent, but in the case of the ejective this is even more the case. In the total sample, no example of an ejective palatal stop was found. In this matter, then, ejectives and injectives are in marked contrast.

*7*. Thus far, all the discussion has concerned glottalic consonants taken in isolation. We now consider certain properties of these sounds in regard to sound sequences and to syllabic position. In general it may be noted that both ejectives and injectives, particularly the latter, tend to be more limited in their combinational possibilities than plain consonants. Syllable initial position is favored for glottalic consonants in general. In almost every language studied they occur in syllable initial position, while in many they do not occur in syllable final even when the corresponding plain consonants do. However, most Munda languages are a striking exception to this generalization since injectives occur *only* in word or syllable final where they are always unvoiced lenis.

Similarly, injectives are found in word initial as against word medial intervocalic position. Examples are the following: In Kpelle (Welmers 1962: 77) ɓ "occurs intervocalically, but not commonly and, in that position, is frequently [ƀ], a bilabial resonant without the lip-rounding characteristic of *w*." Zulu ˀb is stated to be a kind of fricative between vowels (Panconcelli-Calzia 1923: 290). In Gurma, a Voltaic language, in which there is no distinctive opposition between ˀb and b, it is noted that ˀb occurs in word initial while implosion is nonexistent or at least less strong in intervocalic position (Chantoux, Gontier, and Prost 1968: 16). A similar relation is found in Sara-Mbay (Tubiana 1962: 336) between the preglottalized ˀr which is the apical representative of the injective series and a flapped r, the former occurring word initially, the latter intervocalically.

In general glottalic consonants are far less free in their clustering than plain consonants. Not a single example of a cluster containing both an injective and an ejective was found in the present material, for obvious phonetic reasons. Injectives tend not to cluster with plain consonants. The only instances of tautosyllabic combinations involving obstruents noted were in Mon (Luce 1965) where such syllable initial combinations as kɗ and tɓ occurred, and in Khmer (Henderson 1952).[6] These conform to what might be called the 'law of the voiced syllabic center' (Greenberg 1965); namely, that voicing, at least for obstruents, is not interrupted by an unvoiced segment and then voiced again within the domain of the same syllable. In Tsotsil, a Mayan language, the phoneme ˀb has a non-imploded allophone when preceded by a stop (Weathers 1947: 108). In Aguacatec, another Mayan language (McArthur and McArthur 1956), the phoneme ˀb has a plain voiced b as a final member of a consonant cluster.

The most conspicuous single fact, however, about combinations with injectives is that, in contrast with the highly favored status of nasal followed by homorganic plain voiced stop, there is an avoidance of corresponding sequences with injective voiced stops, i.e. combinations of the type mˀb, etc.

With one probable exception, to be noted later, all occurrences of the sequences of this type involve an intervening syllable boundary. The following typical phenomena recur in all major world areas in which injectives are found. In some languages the normal variant of voiced stops are injective; and noninjective allophones occur only after the homorganic nasal. Examples include Mazahau, an Otomi language, Jeh, Katu, Mnong, and Sre in Southeast Asia, Sindhi in India, and numerous examples in Africa including widely scattered Niger-Congo languages (e.g. Fula, Swahili, Konde, Kpelle, Mondunga) and Nilo-Saharan languages (Moru, Ngambay-Mundu, Masai). In Bantu languages one finds alternations such as Konde ulu-ɓafu/imbafu *rib/ribs*.

In those languages of the West Atlantic and Mande branches of Niger-Congo which have initial consonant mutation, in all those cases where the system would lead us to expect *ᵐˀb, etc., it is never found. In its place we may find mb (Biafada, Konyagi), ˀb (Fula, Serer Sin) or m (Kpelle, Basari). The only exception noted to the nonoccurrence of tautosyllabic nasal and homorganic voiced implosive is, apparently, Vai (Von Essen 1935–36), which has syllable initial ᵐˀb but no ᵐb. In Sedang nonimplosive voiced stops

[6]However, in Shorto's dictionary of Mon (1962) these clusters do not occur and the corresponding forms have a vowel ə between the initial non-injective and the injective consonant.

occur only in prenasalized form and "Voiced stops lose their nasalization when preglottalized" (Smith 1968: 55).

In contrast, the unvoiced ejective occurs freely after a homorganic nasal and in some languages replaces an expected plain unvoiced stop or affricate in that position. In Zulu, which like so many other languages has a voiced stop ʔb which is injective except in the tautosyllabic sequence mb, the unvoiced stops and affricates are aspirated except when prenasalized, in which case they are affricated ejectives. Thus for the bilabials ʔb is to ᵐb as p' is to mpɸ'. A strikingly similar situation is found in Mazahua (Spotts 1953). Two voiced stops, b and d, are injective except when preceded by a nasal consonant which is always homorganic. The ejectives t', k', ts', tš', kʷ', and s' (note the typical gap in the bilabial position) are analyzed as sequences tʔ, etc., and these sequences occur after the homorganic nasal consonant.

Finally, it may be noted that whereas injectives preceded by a nasal are highly disfavored, the injective may have a nasal release producing a unitary complex sound in which the nasal is generally described as not forming a separate syllable. There are well-attested examples of this in Mayan languages. In Pocomchi (Meyers 1960) the injective ʔb has ʔbm, ʔp, and ʔpᵐ in free variation before terminal junctures. Aguacatec (McArthur and McArthur 1956) has similar voiceless variants in free variation with pᵐ, i.e. p with a voiceless nasal release. This is evidently the source of Tsotsil ʔm as the allophone of ʔb in syllable final when not utterance final and ʔm̥ in utterance final.

*8*. There is evidence from areas as distant as New Guinea, Southeast Asia, and distinct areas of Africa that consonants affect the pitch of adjacent vowels, particularly those which immediately follow. The most important principle is that plain voiced or breathy voiced consonants, particularly obstruents, lower the pitch of the entire vowel segment or that portion which is immediately adjacent so that, for example, a following high tone becomes a rising tone.

On the other hand, a voiceless plain or aspirated segment has no such lowering effect. An ejective likewise fails to lower pitch. A voiced injective stop here has an effect identical with or more similar to that of voiceless and ejective consonants than to ordinary breathy or voiced consonants, i.e. it does not lower tone. All of these nonlowering sound types may even on occasion raise pitch.

The clearest evidence concerning this comes from languages in which tone variation is still allophonic so that neither internal reconstruction nor an application of the comparative method is necessary to establish the conditioning factors. There are several examples in Africa of languages in which tones have lowered allophones depending on the preceding consonant. One is Bassa

(Hobley 1964), a Kru language of Liberia in which the consonants are divided into two mutually exclusive sets. After the first set, which may be called the lowering set, a following high tone becomes a low-high glide, and a following mid-tone becomes a low-mid glide, and a following low tone is unaffected. After the second set, high and mid tones are unaffected but a following low tone is replaced by a mid-low falling tone. There is also a high-low glide which is apparently unaffected by the preceding consonant. Unfortunately Hobley's account is unaccompanied either by a chart or a phonetic description. The lowering set consists of the following consonants: b, d, g, gb, gm, h, hw, j, v, z; the raising set, of č, f, k, kp, s, t, xw, ɓ, ɖ, dy, m, n, ny, w. Most germane to the present purpose is that ɓ, apparently the only implosive, patterns with the unvoiced obstruents and the sonants in that it raises tone. It may be conjectured, on the basis of other cases, that h and hw have breathy voice (i.e. are 'voiced'). The symbol gm is probably intended to represent a nasal labiovelar. The retroflex ɖ is tone-raising rather than tone-lowering and contrasts in point of articulation with the dental or alveolar t and d. Among the group raising tone is likewise dy, which is a palatal stop and thus differs from the alveopalatal affricates č and j. These illustrate the points made in sections *4* and *5*, respectively. Such considerations suggest strongly that ɖ and dy are former implosives. We started with the typical three implosive pattern ˀb, ˀd, and ˀɟ; the implosion has been retained only in the most anterior implosive ˀb in accordance with the observation of section *3* regarding point of articulation preferences among implosives.

Important evidence regarding the effect of consonants on tone is also forthcoming from the closely related Nguni Bantu languages of South Africa, Zulu and Xhosa. Here, as first pointed out by Beach for Xhosa, voiced ɦ and the breathy voiced obstruents and sonants lower pitch, whereas the voiceless aspirated obstruents, the simple implosive ˀb, and the non-breathy voiced sonants do not lower pitch. A single plain voiced obstruent, g (i.e. without breathy voice), likewise lowers pitch and therefore presumably formerly had breathy voice.

There are a considerable number of examples from Southeast Asia of languages in which tonal modifications of vowels can be shown, on internal and/or comparative grounds, to have arisen from adjacent consonants. In some instances injectives are involved and it can be shown that they do not exercise the tone-lowering effects of the voiced plain consonants. Sometimes they act partially like voiced and partially like unvoiced, though more like the latter. Haudricourt in a fundamental study (1961) describes a considerable number of instances in Southeast Asia of tone modification based on the manner type of the preceding consonants. These involve languages in all major families of the area: Thai-Kadai, Austronesian, Miao-Yao, Sino-

Tibetan, and Austroasiatic. In most instances, as in Africa, consonants may be divided into two sets, those which exercise a tone-lowering effect and those that maintain or raise tone. Fairly frequently there is a third intermediate set which behaves predominantly like the second, but sometimes like the first. There has frequently been consonant merger after tonal differentiation so that the earlier situation has to be reconstructed by comparative evidence and internal reconstruction, sometimes abetted by analysis of the orthographic system which may reflect an earlier state of affairs (e.g. Siamese, Cambodian, Mon). From these data in Haudricourt and from other sources it is possible to construct a hierarchy of consonant types which may be symbolized in the following manner using symbols for alveolar consonants as type indicators: th, ʔn, hn ≥ t, ≥ ʔd > d, n. The symbol sequence hn indicates voiceless sonants. By X > Y is meant that X always exercises a smaller tone-lowering effect, and by X ≥ Y that X never exercises a greater tone-lowering effect than Y. Since none of these languages has voiceless ejectives it is not possible to place these sounds within the hierarchy by Southeast Asian evidence.

It will be noted that voiced injective stops, as in Africa, are always less productive of tone lowering than the corresponding plain voiced stops. The glottal stop always seems to have the same tonal effects as the voiced injective stops (Li 1943).

*9*. Finally it may be observed that the hierarchical relation between the normally voiced injective stops and the corresponding plain voiced stops is not parallel to that between the voiceless ejective and voiceless plain stops. The latter is a classic instance of a marked/unmarked relationship in that unvoiced ejectives never exist without plain stops. Indeed, the latter type is found, to present knowledge, in all languages. On the other hand, there are instances in which the entire voiced series is imploded to the exclusion of the plain voiced type. Examples are Maidu, Mazahua, Lotuxo, and Teso. Rather more numerous are the instances, like Masai and Swahili, in which the 'normal' allophone of the voiced stop series is implosive, while the nonimplosive occurs only when preceded by a homorganic nasal consonant. However, as Ladefoged (1967, 1968) emphasized, laryngeal phonation types form a continuous series in which the boundary between implosive and plain voiced stop is to some extent arbitrary. As pointed out by Fischer-Jørgensen (1963: 33), it has been observed in French, not normally regarded as having voiced implosive stops, that there is a lowering of the larynx in the production of these sounds. The difference between these sounds and true implosives would rest on a difference in the speed and vigor of the larynx lowering that is involved.

For sonants, of course, the picture is quite different. Here the voiced is clearly the unmarked type in relation either to the laryngealized types which function as representatives of both injective and ejective obstruents or to the voiceless type.

Sometimes, as has been seen for example in Hausa and in many Mayan languages, there is a single glottalic series, injective for front consonants and ejective for back. A contrast between an injective and an ejective series is rare but does occur, e.g. Montol (Jungraithmayr 1965) and Maidu.

## [3]

*1*. On the basis of the essentially static considerations concerning the properties of glottalic consonants developed in section [2] above, we now seek to depict the course of events by which these consonants originate and undergo characteristic developments which often result in loss of the glottalic feature. The treatment of this topic is of a merely preliminary nature. It is basically limited to the injectives, with some attention also to laryngealized sonants. Ideally, all languages with these sounds should be subject to the application of the diachronic methods of internal reconstruction, comparative study, and direct historical evidence, where this is available. This is far more than can be attempted here. Moreover, in many cases, essential data are lacking.

From the conclusions of section *9* of [2] above regarding the lack of marked/unmarked relation between plain and injective voiced stops, it is possible to derive the general diachronic hypothesis that at least one source of injectives might be a sound shift from voiced plain to voiced implosive stops, since such a change would result in a system of an attested type, namely one in which there were injective but not plain voiced stops. There is at least one historically documented example of this development, namely Sindhi (Bailey 1922 and R. L. Turner 1924), in which an injective series derives from earlier plain voiced stops. It was noted earlier that the maximum number of injective stops found is four, that the dental or alveolar member tends to be retracted and/or retroflex, and that the palatal member never becomes an affricate. All this occurs in Sindhi, so that the injective series exhibits what might be called phonetic optimality in striking disregard of the remainder of the noncontinuant system, which shows the typical Indic pattern of five positions of articulation with an alveopalatal affricate rather than a palatal stop. This pattern is shown in the usual four series consisting of unvoiced non-aspirates, unvoiced aspirates, voiced nonaspirates, and breathy voiced (i.e. 'voiced aspirate') consonants (Bordie 1958).

In other instances such a development can be inferred from comparative or internal evidence. Given the factors discussed in section *3* above concerning the hierarchy of preferences for forward points of articulation and that of section *7* concerning the disfavoring of combinations of nasal and injective, we may derive the following further hypotheses. Sometimes only forward members of the voiced plain series will become injectives while back members will remain or undergo other developments. If nasal and voiced plain stop combinations existed these might be expected to survive the shift of plain voiced stops to injectives so that the change would become conditioned. Both these hypotheses are verified in a number of Bantu languages. For example, in the central and eastern dialects of Shona (Doke 1931), b and d have become ˀb and ˀd, except in the combinations mb and nd, while j and g have not undergone a change to injectives. Similarly, in Vietnamese b and d have become injectives while g did not undergo this development.

Moreover, it is not necessary that the shift to voiced injectives take place simultaneously in all positions. If there is an order in which this takes place it can be expected to reflect the characteristic hierarchy of points of articulation already discussed. We may further postulate a reverse hierarchy of dissolution by which the least favored positions will undergo loss of the glottalic feature first. This is not unlike the well-known Jakobsonian hierarchy of acquisition in child language and loss in aphasia (Jakobson 1941). It may not always be possible to determine whether we are dealing with the formation of a new system or the dissolution of an old one. A few examples from the material examined in the present study will now be considered from this point of view.

A probable instance of an incipient development of an implosive and, as expected, at the bilabial point of articulation, is found in the Kalenjin languages of East Africa, forming the main body of South Nilotic languages. There are two divisions of Kalenjin: Päkot (also called Suk) and Nandi-Kipsigis. In the latter, "p is pronounced very softly, alternating initially with b (and occasionally with ɓ) with some speakers" (Tucker 1964a: 199). It will be noted that this takes place in initial position which, as has been seen in section 7 of [2] above, is the favored position for injectives. Tucker (1960) has made a similar observation for Konza, a Bantu language of East Africa, regarding what appears to be an incipient pronunciation of b as an implosive.

In Kirma (also called Gouin), a language of the Voltaic subgroup of Niger-Congo, "*b* initiale est prononcé parfois avec préglottalisation . . ." (Prost 1964: 21). Here again it is the initial position which is favored. In both instances the comparative evidence shows that the injective pronunciation is an innovation.

In several languages with two injectives, ˀb and ˀd, the former shows greater stability. None of these, however, appears to be an instance in which implosion has started with b and spread to d. In Alur, a Western Nilotic language, both injective and noninjective b and d exist, as well as kp and gb, both described as injectives. Whereas ɓ is stable, "ɗ is often interchanged with alveolar *d*" (Knappert 1963). A similar situation appears to exist in the Wanning dialect of Hainan where ˀb is stable but there is free variation between d and ˀd (Egerod 1967, referring to a paper by Chan). On the other hand, the only contrary evidence noted to the tendency for the greater stability of ˀb and ˀd is likewise from Hainan where it is reported for the Haik'ou dialect that for the younger generation the tendency is ɓ > p while ɗ appears to be stable (ibid., reporting on a paper by Liao).

When, in accordance with section *4* of [2] above, the injective in the dental or alveolar position has become retracted and/or retroflex, there is a tendency for its glottalic feature to be lost since it has become redundant. According to Tucker (1940: 102), in the Moru-Madi the retroflex tongue position is more important than the implosion, which may be lost.

The Sara group, which is, like Moru-Madi, part of the Central Sudanic subfamily, shows various stages of the loss of implosion in the former *ɗ which from retroflexion has usually gone on to ˀr. For Mbay, Fortier (1967: 51) states explicitly: "Le mbaï à la différence du ngambaï . . . ne possède qu'une injective: /ɗ/ a disparu." The remaining injective is, of course, ɓ. According to Vandame (1963), Ngambay does have two implosives but they are in the process of losing their implosion, ɓ merging with the previous b and ɗ with previous r. It is noted that the youngest generation prefers b and r. In the form of Sara described by Hillaire and Robinne (1955–59: 13), the oldest generation usually has ˀr with r as a less frequent variant, while children most frequently have r. In regard to Mbay, the favoring of initial position for injective pronunciations is also evident. For those speakers who have not replaced all cases of former ˀr with r, ˀr is initial while a flapped r occurs in medial position (Tubiana 1962).

A further example of the greater stability of the bilabial as compared with the dental-alveolar injective is furnished by Bedik, a West Atlantic language (Ferry 1968). In the system of initial consonant alternations, the continuant grade of ɓ remains as ɓ while ˀd becomes l.

The tendency of the palatal injective to become a laryngealized ˀy was discussed in section *5* of [2]. The positional hierarchy is further exemplified by the fact that none of the languages considered had shifted *ɗ to ˀr while still retaining the palatal injective as a stop. Thus there are no systems of the type ɓ, ˀr, ˀɟ, while systems of the type ɓ, ɗ, 'y are common.

The morphophonemics of Katu (Costello 1966) gives strong evidence of the former existence of a three-term system in which ɓ and ɗ still exist, but ˀɟ has lost its glottalic feature: ɓec *to sleep*, banec *bed*; ɗah *to eat meat*, danah *meat for eating*; dyiik *to clear ground*, janiik *cleared ground*. Here the former injective has retained its stop articulation whereas the plain stop has, as so often, become an alveopalatal affricate.

In section *8* of [2] it was pointed out that in Bassa ɓ, ɖ, and dy all had the same tone-raising effect as the unvoiced consonants. It is possible therefore to infer that ḍ < *ɗ and dy < ʔɟ, with ɓ once more showing the greatest persistence.

The instability and relatively rare occurrence of the velar injective, which is least favored, is so great that it is difficult to discover its usual course of development. A number of instances have already been cited in which the other voiced stops became implosive while g remained. In most instances, however, we have a gap in the velar position for the injectives, in contrast to a plain voiced series without such a gap. There is evidence from Semang-Sakai (Pinnow 1959: 66) that *ʔg has become ʔ. In Kharia, a Munda language, the lenis unvoiced injectives ʔb̥, ʔd̥, ʔɟ̊, which occur only in word or syllable final, alternate with the unvoiced aspirate pʻ, tʻ čʻ before the suffix oʔ of the past (Biligiri 1965: 54). In the same environment the injective corresponding to kʻ is ʔ, showing that the latter originated from *ʔg̊. It may be suspected that when ʔg does arise as part of a complete series, in many instances it becomes ʔ and then zero. Sui, which has ʔy along with ʔb, ʔd, and ʔy (as well as wʔ and laryngealized nasals), may give evidence of a transitional stage between ʔg and ʔ.

Thus far only one source of voiced injectives has been considered, namely acquisition of the glottalic feature by a previous plain voiced stop. There are, however, at least two other processes by which languages may come to have voiced injectives. One of these relates to ɓ only. There is evidence that ɓ can arise from a previous gb (presumably implosive) by loss of the velar closure. This possibility is illustrated by some of the Southwestern Mande languages and can be deduced once more from initial consonant alternatives. In Loma (Sadler 1958) there is a two-grade system and there are a number of clear instances in which unvoiced/voiced is the principle of distinction. The voiced equivalent of kp, however, is not *gb, as would be expected, but ɓ. In Loko, also a Southwestern Mande language, with initial consonants kp : gb alternation exists parallel with p : b and k : g. Innes (1964: 116) noted, however, that one informant who worked with Meeusen had a voiced implosive in place of gb. The common Igbo pronunciation as a velarized labial is quite possibly a transitional stage between between gb and ʔb. Some Igbo dialects, as noted by Ward (1936: 6) and by R. G. Armstrong (1967) for Ukwaali, have velar occlusion which may represent the earlier stage within Igbo. Evidence for the other common source of injective stops is from a cluster consisting of a voiced plain consonant and a glottal stop. The evidence in this case comes from the group of Austronesian languages spoken in Vietnam containing Cham, Rade, Jarai, and Chru. These languages have generally reduced the typical Austroasian canonical form CVCVC to the monosyllabic regional norm by reduction or loss of the first vowel. When the second consonant is the Austronesian laryngeal ʔ and the first is a voiced stop, the result is a voiced injective.[7] For example, the reflexes of PMP *buˀuk *hair* include Rade ˀbuk, Jarai ˀbuˀ, ˀbuk, and Chru ˀbuˀ (Thomas 1964). Less frequently, if the laryngeal is the first consonant the same result ensues. Thus from PMP *ˀijuN *nose*, Thomas gives Jarai, Chru ˀadun, Rade ˀdun or ˀadun. An unusual case for which no parallel can be cited is Päkot, a language with an already established ˀd in which, according to Tucker (1964b: 448) "The implosive [ɗ] is also found occasionally as the result of the combination |ɣ| + |t|."

A final possible source of injectives is found in Papago (Saxton 1963) where the plain voiced stops have preglottalized or voiceless consonant allophone. There is a possible parallel in the instance cited by Wenck (1954: 176) of the Japanese dialect of Southern Kyūshū in which, after the loss of final i and u (presumably after a stage of voicelessness), preceding stops have become implosives.

In regard to further changes of injectives once they have been established, again there are other possibilities beside loss of the glottalic feature. The supraglottal articulation may be lost so that only a glottal stop remains. Westermann and Ward (1933: 96) note regarding Bari, an Eastern Nilotic language, that "with certain speakers the mouth articulation of [sc. implosive] b and d is often omitted and the glottal articulation alone remains." Pichl (1966: 4) observed a similar tendency in regard to Serer, one of the Cangin languages of the West Atlantic subgroup of Niger-Congo, in which ˀ often replaces ɗ. In Margi (Hoffman 1963), ˀ may replace ɓ before u. A related phenomenon is reported by Klingenheben (1963: 8) in the Fula of Adamawa where ˀy may replace ɓ and ɗ before front vowels. Here a palatal glide replaces the stops while the glottal articulation remains.

In earlier discussion of Mayan languages it was noted that the bilabial ejective might have a nasal offglide in final position. In some instances this has developed into a laryngealized m. In Chalchihuitacàn Tzotzil (Hopkins 1967), /ɓ/ has ˀm̓ as a prejunctural allophone and m̓ before consonants.

In Jarai (Haudricourt 1950), ˀm corresponds to and has arisen from ˀb found in other languages of the Vietnamese Austronesian subgroup, and similarly ˀñ may correspond to ˀɟ. Similar developments have been noted in Thai languages with subsequent loss of glottalization. Thus the dialect of Po-ai (Li 1959) has m, n, and y as reflexes of the proto-Thai injective series, and certain Burmese Shan dialects have m and l as reflexes of ɓ and ɗ (Li 1943). In Vietnamese m and n have as one source earlier ɓ and ɗ. Thus Ferguson's query regarding the source of new nasals receives an answer, although from a worldwide perspective this is hardly a major one (Ferguson 1966).

[7] Dyen's *q and *h give h and ˀ, respectively, in these languages. I have, therefore, modified his reconstructions accordingly (Dyen 1953).

2. The double status of laryngealized sonants as corresponding to both injective and ejective sonants was noted at the very beginning of the discussion. We have just seen that laryngealized nasals may replace corresponding voiced injectives. Laryngealized nasals may also develop from the corresponding non-nasal voiced injective stops when preceding nasal vowels. According to Samarin (personal communication) the ʔm and ʔn of Gbeya which he formerly considered independent phonemes are allophones of ʔb and ʔd before nasalized vowels. Morphophonemic alternation in Margi (Hoffman 1965) shows that laryngealized y and w may arise from the sequence glottal stop + nonsyllabic i and u respectively.

When an ejective series exists, as Aoki (1968) shows for Nez Perce, laryngealized sonants may morphophonemically replace the sequence sonant + ʔ in a manner parallel to that by which unvoiced stop + ʔ produces an ejective unvoiced stop.

## [4]

The considerations adduced in sections [2]–[3] above obviously bear on the problems of comparative reconstruction. When for any class of sounds we can develop an overall theory concerning their patterning, phonetic characteristics, and dynamic tendencies, we will have made a contribution toward more accurate, realistic, and phonetically detailed reconstruction. For present purposes we will consider only one example in which such an approach helps to resolve an existing problem.

The case is that of Cham, an Austronesian language of Vietnam. This language, like the closely related Jarai, Rade, and Chru mentioned earlier, has tended toward loss or reduction of the vowel of the first syllable, thus producing extensive monosyllabism. Unlike the other languages of this group, however, Cham has also followed another regional tendency, lowering of pitch after originally voiced obstruents. The ensuing shift of voiced sounds to voiceless merging with previous voiceless sounds has caused a hitherto atonal language to generate a tonal system of two levels, rather than to double the number of preexisting tones as in other languages of Southeast Asia.

This development, along with others, is treated in Blood (1962). Thus PMP *beliʔ *to buy* > Cham plèy with low tone, but PMP *puluh *ten* > Cham plúh with high tone. However, Blood's material gives three exceptions in which PMP *b is not reflected in p followed by low tone but in b followed by high tone. Judging from the observations of the present study, we suspect that in these cases b has developed from a voiced injective. This is both because *ʔb would not be expected to have the same tone-lowering effects as *b and because ʔb, as has been seen, often changes to b but, as far as can be seen, never to p, at least directly. Hence a sequence of shifts *b > p followed by *ˀb > b may be posited, with low-pitch allophones on the following vowel only in the first case. Of the three Cham words in question, given by Blood as buq (i.e. buˀ) *hair*, bew *odor*, and blaq (blaˀ) *to open the eyes*, the first two have Dyen's h which, as has been seen, acts like ˀ, to which it had apparently shifted in languages of this group. Hence we may posit, parallel to developments in other languages of the Vietnamese Austronesian group, the following sequence of changes: PMP (or better, pre-Vietnamese Austronesian) *buˀuk *hair* > ˀbuk, and *baˀuˀ *odor* > ˀbew.

It may be presumed that Blood's material is phonetically accurate. Cham orthography, based on an Indian source, gives decisive evidence that the interpretation in the preceding paragraph is correct. The dictionary of Aymonier and Cabaton (1906) presumably gives a modified transcription of the orthography rather than the actual phonetics of that period. Here, as in other orthographies of the region, the letters of the Sanskrit unaspirated voiced series are used where the present language has an unvoiced consonant followed by a low-pitched vowel and, correspondingly, the voiced aspirate letters where an unvoiced aspirate is followed by a low tone. The following examples show that in Cham, as in other languages of the same group, *h (i.e. Dyen's q) gives rise to aspirated consonants just as *ˀ (Dyen's h) produces injectives. Aymonier and Cabaton's transcriptions follow Cham orthography. However, besides b and d, two additional symbols in Cham orthography resemble these in form. Aymonier and Cabaton transcribe these as ḅ and ḍ and describe them as ḅ and ḍ 'douce'. The first of these occurs in all three words which show the irregular correspondence in Blood. The following tabulation includes these three as well as a few other examples to show the correspondence among PMP, Cham orthography, and Blood's transcription.

| | Aymonier & Cabaton | Blood | *PMP |
|---|---|---|---|
| branch | dhan | thàn | d/Dahan (cf. Rade dhon) |
| four | pak | páˀ | *(em)pat |
| moon | bulan | pelàn | *bulan |
| hair | ḅak, ḅuk | búˀ | *buˀuk |
| odor | ḅau | béw | *baˀuˀ |
| open (the eyes) | ḅlak | bláˀ | *bulat |

## [5]

It was originally intended to discuss fully the phonetic factors underlying the phonological conclusions of this paper.[8] However, after further

[8] I have benefited greatly from discussion of these questions with William S.-Y Wang, and some of the following observations were suggested in discussion with him.

consideration, it seems more advisable to limit considerably this aspect of the discussion. It is probably more constructive to leave such matters to those whose professional specialization is in instrumental phonetics and the physiology of speech. It is to be hoped that the conclusions of the present paper, based as they are almost entirely on the field observations of phonetically trained linguists rather than on the product of laboratory investigation, may stimulate a search for phonetic explanations. For the most part, what might be offered here is either so obvious as not to require mention, or so problematical that it should not be mentioned. Nevertheless, observations on a few points may be offered.

Haudricourt (1950) already conjectured that two of the phenomena noted here, the tendency towards retroflexion and retraction in apical injectives and the tendency towards replacement by nasal consonants, could both be attributed to the rarefication of the air in the supraglottal cavity caused by the descending larynx. The relative vacuum thus produced would tend to suck in the mobile tongue tip and the velum. This explanation is somewhat strengthened by the existence of the phenomenon, not known to Haudricourt, of nasal off-glide of injectives, which is a possible transitional stage in the change to a nasal consonant. The velum would tend to be lowered somewhat late as the descending larynx increased the rarefication. However, whether the pressure difference is really great enough to cause these phenomena still remains to be investigated.

The point of articulation hierarchies of ejectives and injectives are obviously based on preference for a small and large air chamber, respectively. It is also clear that with the same thoracic pressure it is easier to build up compression in a smaller chamber. Injectives are usually voiced and involve leakage of air through the descending chords; such leakage is more easily tolerated from a larger chamber.

Certain aspects of the present paper which have a bearing on broader theoretical problems and which have remained implicit or have received only passing notice in the body of this paper may be briefly considered here.

The example of the four Sindhi injectives was discussed earlier as a striking instance in which phonetic optimality triumphs over what might be thought an irresistible systemic pull of four separate series of stops, all at the same five points of articulation. Not only is there a gap among the Sindhi injectives, but their phonetic realizations differ in several instances. The Sindhi injectives are thus far more easily comparable to those of other languages such as Angas, with four implosives embedded in a very different consonantal system, than to the remainder of the Sindhi system.

Although such clear instances are, indeed, rather rare and, in general, a considerable amount of symmetry reigns in phonological systems, it should be pointed out that where symmetry obtains it is basically a byproduct of diachronic processes by which the feature rather than the individual phoneme is the unit of change. Where it is cross-cut by a powerful graded hierarchy such as that of the positional preferences of implosives, the result is often asymmetrical. Thus in many languages only ʔb and ʔd exist as injectives, or only ʔb, while other series are more extensive. Symmetry and asymmetry are therefore, it may be submitted, most easily understood as resultants of diachronic forces.

In general this paper is intended to illustrate a methodology in which synchronic systems, and diachronic generalizations regarding change, are mutually supportive, and in which historical comparison and reconstruction enter in an integral way. In developing such a synchronic-diachronic account, historical linguistics makes a central contribution to the overall picture. The view set forth here thus differs in regard to the relation between these two fundamental branches of linguistics from what has been prevalent since the rise of structuralism. In all these developments the center of theoretical interest has been synchronic, and each synchronic theory in its heyday has sought to restructure or to reinterpret diachrony in its own terms. While real contributions have thus been made, it might be contended that they were merely peripheral to the basic enterprises of diachronic linguistics which, in its general aspect, seeks regularities regarding processes of change, and in its particularistic studies of individual language change has its own principles of historical explanation which are not coincident with or exhausted by synchronic analysis.

Finally, it may be pointed out that in the present investigation the notion of point of articulation was indispensable for the statement of generalizations. Yet in current theories this concept has been rather obscured. Further, the hierarchy of positions of articulation which is correlated with the size of the air chamber is most naturally expressed by an ordering, and such orderings, where more than two values on a dimension are involved, require an additional logical principle not deducible from unordered sets of binary oppositions. This same problem is involved in the analysis of pitch levels in tonal languages, which may require an ordering of as many as five levels.

The tentative nature of the present study should be obvious. In general it would seem that numerous and more complete studies of individual aspects of phonology should be carried out, independent of an excessively rigid framework of features. Only then will we be in a position to construct an overall system for the phonology of the world's languages.

## References Cited

The following journal abbreviations are used in the list of references below.

*AL* *Anthropological Linguistics*
*ALS* *African Language Studies*

| | |
|---|---|
| *AuÜ* | *Afrika und Übersee* |
| *BEFEO* | *Bulletin de l'École Française de l'Extrème-Orient* |
| *BSLP* | *Bulletin de la Société Linguistique de Paris* |
| *BSOAS* | *Bulletin of the School of Oriental and African Studies, London University* |
| *JAL* | *Journal of African Languages* |
| *JSA* | *Journal de la Société des Africanistes* |
| *JWAL* | *Journal of West African Languages* |
| *Lg* | *Language* |
| *LP* | *Lingua Posnaniensis* |
| *SIL* | *Studies in Linguistics* |
| *ZPSK* | *Zeitschrift für Phonetik, Sprachwissenschaft und Kommunicationsforschung* |

Anceaux, J. G. 1952. *The Walio Language*. The Hague.

Andrew, H. 1949. "Phonemes and morphophonemes of Temoayan Otomí," *JAL* 15, 2: 13–22.

Andrzejewski, B. W. 1957. "Some preliminary observations on the Borana dialect of Galla," *BSOAS* 19: 354–74.

Aoki, H. 1968. "A note on glottalized consonants." *Project on Linguistic Analysis, Reports*, Second Series, No. 7, A1-A13. (Phonology Lab., Dept. of Linguistics, U.C. Berkeley.)

Armstrong, L. E. 1934. "The phonetic structure of Somali," *Mitteilungen des Seminars für Orientalische Sprachen* 37: 116–61.

Armstrong, R. G. 1967. *A Comparative Wordlist of Five Igbo Dialects*. Ibadan.

Aymonier, E., and A. Cabaton. 1966. *Dictionnaire Cam-Français*. Paris.

Bailey, T. G. 1922. "The Sindhi implosives." *BSOAS* 2: 835–36.

Basker, M. E. 1963. "Proto-Vietnamuong initial labial consonants," *Van-Hoa Nguyet-San* 12: 491–500.

Beach, D. M. 1924. "The science of tonetics and its application to Bantu languages," *Bantu Studies* 1: 75–106.

———. 1938. *The phonetics of the Hottentot language*. Cambridge, England.

Bearth, T., and H. Zemp. 1967. "The phonology of Dan (Santa)," *JAL* 6: 9–29.

Berlin, B. 1962. "Esbozo de la fonología del Tzeltal de Tenejapa, Chiapas," *Estudios de Cultura Maya* 2: 17–36 (Mexico).

Biligiri, H. S. 1965. *Kharia (Phonology, Grammar, and Vocabulary)*. Poona.

Blood, D. W. 1962. "Reflexes of proto-Malayo-Polynesian in Cham," *AL* 4, 9: 11–20.

Blood, H., and E. Blood. 1966. "The pronoun system of Uon Njuñ Mnong Rolom," *Mon-Khmer Studies* II: 103–11 (Saigon).

Bordie, John G. 1958. "A descriptive Sindhi phonology." U. of Texas dissertation.

Bôt Ba Njock, H. M. 1962. "La description phonologique du ɓasa (Mbene)." Sorbonne thesis.

Bouquiaux, L. 1964. "À propos de la phonologie du Sara," *JAL* 3: 260–72.

Carnochan, J. 1948. "A study in the phonology of an Igbo speaker," *BSOAS* 12: 417–26.

Catford, J. C. 1939. "On the classification of stop consonants." *Le Maître Phonétique*, 3rd series, 65: 2–5.

———. 1964. "Phonation types: The classification of some laryngeal components of speech production," *In Honor of Daniel Jones*, ed. D. Abercrombie et al., 26–37 (London).

Chantoux, A., A. Gontier, and A. Prost. 1968. *Grammaire Gourmantché*. IFAN, Dakar.
Cohen, M. 1936. *Traité de langue amharíque*. Paris.
Condominas, G. 1954. "Enquête linguistique parmi les populations Montagnardes du Sud Indochinois," *BEFEO* 46: 573–97.
Cooper, J., and N. Cooper. 1966. "Halăng phonemes," *Mon-Khmer Studies* II: 87–98 (Saigon).
Costello, N. A. 1966. "Affixes in Katu," *Mon-Khmer Studies* II: 63–86 (Saigon).
Crazzolara, J. P. 1960. *A Study of the Logbara (Ma'di) Language*. London.
DeBoeck, L. B. 1952. *Grammaire du Mondunga (Lisala, Congo Belge)*. Brussels.
Doke, C. M. 1931. *A Comparative Study in Shona Phonetics*. Johannesburg.
———. 1954. *The Southern Bantu Languages*. Oxford Press.
Dunstan, Elizabeth, and G. E. Igwe. 1966. "Two views of the phonology of the Ọh̃ụh̃ụ dialect of Igbo," *JWAL* 3, 2: 71–76.
Dyen, I. 1953. *The Proto-Malayo-Polynesian Laryngeals*. Baltimore.
Edel, M. M. 1939. "The Tillamook language," *IJAL* 10: 1–57.
Egerod, Søren. 1967. "Chinese dialectology," in *Current Trends in Linguistics* II, ed. T. Sebeok, 89–129 (The Hague).
Ferguson, C. F. 1966. "Some assumptions about nasals," in J. H. Greenberg, ed. *Universals of Language* (2nd ed.), 53–60 (Cambridge, Mass.).
Ferry, M. P. 1968. "L'alternance consonantique en Bedik," *JWAL* 5: 91–96.
Fischer-Jørgensen, E. 1963. "Stimmhaftigkeit und intraoraler Luftdruck," *ZPSK* 16: 19–36.
Fleming, H. 1964. "Baiso and Rendille: Somali outliers," *Rassegna di Studi Etiopici* 20: 35–96.
Fortier, J. 1967. *Le mythe et les contes de Sou en pays Mbaï-Moissala*. Paris.
Freeland, L. S. 1947. "Western Miwok texts with linguistic sketch," *IJAL* 13: 31–46.
Garvin, P. 1948. "Kutenai I: phonemics," *IJAL* 14: 37–42.
Gibson, L. 1956. "Pame (Otomi) phonemics and morphophonemics," *IJAL* 22: 242–65.
Gradin, D. 1966. "Consonantal tone in Jeh phonemics," *Mon-Khmer Studies* II: 41–62 (Saigon).
Greenberg, J. H. 1941. "Some problems in Hausa phonology," *Lg.* 17: 316–23.
———. 1965. "Some generalizations concerning initial and final consonant clusters," *Linguistics* 3: 5–34.
———. 1969. "Methods of dynamic comparison in linguistics," in *Substance and Structure of Language*, Jaan Puhvel, ed. (Los Angeles and Berkeley), 147–204.
Haas, M. R. 1958. "The tones of four Tai dialects," *Bulletin of the Institute of History and Philology, Academia Sinica* 29: 817–26.
Haudricourt, A. G. 1942–45. "Restitution du Karen commun," *BSLP* 42: 103–11.
———. 1950. "Les consonnes préglottalisées en Indochine," *BSLP* 46: 172–82.
———. 1961. "Bipartition et tripartition dans les systèmes de tons," *BSLP* 56: 163–80.
———. 1963. "Remarques sur les initiales complexes de la langue Sek," *BSLP* 58: 156–63.
———. 1965. "Les mutatíons consonantiques des occlusives initiales en Mon-Khmer," *BSLP* 60: 160–72.
Henderson, E. J. A. 1952. "The main features of Cambodian pronunciation," *BSOAS* 149–74.

Hillaire, T., and J. Robinne. 1955–59. *Dictionnaire Sara-Français*. Kroumra-Fourvière.
Hobley, J. 1964. "A preliminary analysis of the Bassa language," *JWAL* 1, 2: 51–55.
Hockett, C. F. 1955. *A Manual of Phonology*. Baltimore.
Hoffman, C. 1963. *A grammar of the Margi language*. London.
———. 1965. "A word list of central Kambari," *JWAL* 2, 2: 7–31.
Hoijer, H. H. 1946. "Tonkawa," in *Linguistic Structures of Native America*, C. Osgood, ed. (New York), 289–311.
Hopkins, N. A. 1967. "A short sketch of Chalchihuitán Tzotzil," *AL* 9, 4: 9–25.
Hudgins, C. V., and R. H. Stetson. 1935. "Voicing of consonants by depression of the larynx," *Archives Neérlandaises de Phonétique Experimentale* 11: 1–28.
Innes, G. 1964. "An outline grammar of Loko with texts," *ALS* 5: 115–73.
Jakobson, R. 1941. *Kindersprache, Aphasie und allgemeine Lautgesetze*. Uppsala.
———. 1962. "Retrospect," in *Collected Writings I. Phonetic Studies* (The Hague), 631–58.
———. 1968. "Extrapulmonic consonants (ejectives, implosives, clicks)," Research Laboratory of Electronics (MIT), *Quarterly Progress Reports* 90: 221–7.
Jones, Robert B. 1961. *Karen Linguistic Studies*. Berkeley and Los Angeles.
Judy, R., and J. E. Judy. 1962. *Fonemas del Movima: con atención especial a la serie glotal*. Cochabamba.
Jungraithmayr, H. 1964–65. "Texte und Sprichwörter im Angas von Kabwir (Nordnigerien)," *AuÜ* 48: 17–35, 114–27.
———. 1965. "Materialen zur Kenntnis des Chip, Montol, Gerka, und Burrum," *AuÜ* 48: 161–82.
———. 1967. "Specimens of the Pa'a ('Afa') and Warja languages," *AuÜ* 50: 194–205.
Kähler-Meyer, E. 1953. "Sprachproben aus der Landschaft Bembe im Bezirk Bamenda, Kamerun," *AuÜ* 37: 109–18.
Keller, K. C. 1958. "The phonemes of Chontal (Mayan)," *IJAL* 25: 44–53.
Klingenheben, A. 1925. "Vai-Texte," *AuÜ* 16: 58–133.
———. 1963. *Die Sprache der Ful (Dialekt von Adamaua)*. Hamburg.
Knappert, J. 1962. "The tonological behaviour of the word in Alur," *ZPSK* 15: 93–101.
———. 1963. "The verb in Dhó-Álùr̀," *JAL* 2: 100–27.
Labouret, H. 1952. *La langue des Peuls ou Foulbé*. Dakar.
Lacroix, P. F. 1962. "Note sur la langue Galke ($^{n}$dáí)," *JAL* 1: 94–121.
Ladefoged, P. 1967. "Linguistic phonetics," *Working Papers in Phonetics* 6, Phonetics Laboratory, UCLA.
———. 1968. *A Phonetic Study of West African Languages*. 2nd ed., Cambridge, England.
Leslau, W. 1956. *Étude descriptive et comparative du Gafat (Ethiopien méridional)*. Paris.
Li, Fang Kuei. 1943. "The hypothesis of a pre-glottalized series of consonants in primitive Tai," *Bulletin of the Institute of History and Philology, Academia Sinica* 11: 177–88.
———. 1946. "Chipewyan," in *Linguistic Structures of Native America*, C. Osgood, ed. (New York): 398–423.
———. 1948. "The distribution of tones and initials in the Sui language," *Lg* 24: 160–67.

———. 1959. "Classification by vocabulary: Tai dialects," *AL* 1, 2: 15–21.
———. 1960. "A tentative classification of Tai dialects," in *Culture in History, Essays in Honor of Paul Radin*, Stanley Diamond, ed. (New York): 951–59.
———. 1965. "Tai and the Kam-Sui languages," *Lingua* 14: 148–79.
Liccardi, M., and J. Grimes. 1961. *Entonación y fonemas del Itonama (Cochabamba).*
Luce, G. H. 1965. "Danaw, a dying Austroasiatic language," *Lingua* 14: 98–129.
Lukas, J. 1965. "Das Hitkalanci, eine Sprache von Gwoza (Nordostnigerien)," *AuÜ* 48: 81–114.
Martini, F. 1946. "Aperçu phonologique du cambodgien," *BSLP* 42: 112–31.
Mayers, M. K. 1960. "The phonemes of Pocomchi," *AL* 2, 9: 1–39.
———. 1966. *Languages of Guatemala*. The Hague.
McArthur, H., and L. McArthur. 1956. "Aguacatec (Mayan) phonemes within the stress group," *IJAL* 22: 72–76.
Meinhof, C., and N. J. van Warmelo. 1932. *Introduction to the Phonology of the Bantu Languages*. Berlin.
Meyer, E. 1950. "Bemerkungen zum Fök im Hochland von Mittel-Kamerun," *AuÜ* 35: 264–80.
Milewski, Tadeusz. 1955. "Langues caucasiennes et américaines," *LP* 5: 136–65.
Minor, E. E. 1956. "Witoto vowel clusters," *IJAL* 22: 131–37.
Moore, B. R. 1962. "Correspondences in South Barbocoan Chibcha," *Studies in Ecuadorean Linguistics* I: 270–89.
Needham, D., and M. Davis. 1946. "Cuicateco phonology," *IJAL* 12: 139–46.
Newman, P. 1964. "A word list of Tera," *JWAL* 1: 33–50.
Oswalt, R. L. 1964. "A comparative study of two Pomo languages," in *Studies in Californian Linguistics*, W. Bright, ed. (Berkeley and Los Angeles): 149–62.
Palmer, F. R. 1957. "The verb in Bilin," *BSOAS* 19: 131–59.
——— 1958. "The noun in Bilin," *BSOAS* 21: 376–91.
———. 1962. *The morphology of the Tigre noun*. London.
Panconcelli-Calzia, G. 1920. "Experimentalphonetische Untersuchungen," *AuÜ* 11: 182–88.
———. 1923. "Objective Untersuchungen über die Stimmhaftigkeit der Explosive im Zulu," *AuÜ* 14: 287–90.
Pichl, W. J. 1963. "La permutation et l'accord en Sérèr," in *Actes du second colloque international de linguistique Negro-Africaine*. Dakar.
———. 1966. *The Cangin group: A Language Group in Northern Senegal*. Pittsburgh.
Pike, K. L., and E. V. Pike. 1947. "Immediate constituents of the Mazateco syllable," *IJAL* 13: 78–91.
Pike, K. L., and D. E. Sinclair. 1948. "Tonemes of Mesquital Otomi," *IJAL* 14: 91–98.
Pinnow, H. J. 1959. *Versuch einer historischen Lautlehre der Kharia-Sprache*. Wiesbaden.
Prost, André. 1964. *Contribution à l'étude des langues Voltaïques*. IFAN-Dakar.
Sadler, W. 1958. *Untangled Loma*. Monrovia.
Samarin, W. J. 1966. *The Gbeya Language*. Berkeley and Los Angeles.
Santandrea, S. 1963. *A Concise Grammar Outline of the Bongo Language*. Rome.
———. 1966. "The Birri language," *AuÜ* 49: 81–105.
Sapir, E. 1923. "The phonetics of Haida," *IJAL* 2: 143–58.
———. 1933. "La réalité psychologique des phonèmes," *Journal de Psychologie Normale et Pathologique* 30: 247–65.

———. 1938. "Glottalized continuants in Navaho, Nootka, and Kwakiutl (with a note on Indo-European)," *Lg* 14: 248–74.

Sapir, J. D. 1971. "West Atlantic: an inventory of the languages, their noun class systems and consonant alternations," *Current Trends in Linguistics*, VII: 45–112 (The Hague).

Saxton, D. 1963. "Papago phonemes," *IJAL* 29: 29–35.

Sebeok, T. 1943. "Phonemic analysis of Santali," *Journal of the American Oriental Society* 63: 66–67.

Shipley, W. F. 1964. *Maidu Grammar*. Berkeley and Los Angeles.

Shorto, H. L. 1962. *A Dictionary of Modern Spoken Mon*. London.

Smalley, W. A. 1954. "Sre phonemes and syllables," *Journal of the American Oriental Society* 74: 217–22.

———. 1961. *Outline of Khmu Structure*. New Haven.

Smith, Kenneth D. 1968. "Laryngealization and de-Laryngealization in Sedang Phonemes," *Linguistics* 38: 52–69.

Spotts, H. 1953. "Vowel harmony and consonant sequences in Mazahua (Otomí)," *IJAL* 19: 253–58.

Supple, J., and C. M. Douglass. 1949. "Tojolabal (Mayan): phonemes and verb morphology," *IJAL* 15: 168–74.

Swift, L., A. Ahaghotu, and E. Ugorji. 1962. *Igbo Basic Course*. Washington.

Thomas, D. 1962. "Remarques sur la phonologie du chrau," *BSLP* 57: 175–91.

———. 1966. "Chrau intonation," *Mon-Khmer Studies* II: 1–13 (Saigon).

Thomas, D. M. 1964. "Proto-Malayo-Polynesian reflexes in Rade, Jarai and Chru," *SIL* 7: 59–76.

Thompson, L. C. 1959. "Saigon phonemics," *Lg* 35: 454–76.

Trubetskoy, N. 1926. "Studien auf dem Gebiete der vergleichenden Lautlehre der nordkaukasischen Sprachen I. Die 'Kurzen' und 'Geminierten' Konsonanten der Awarandischen Sprächen," *Caucasica* 3: 7–36.

———. 1931. "Die Konsonantensysteme der ostkaukasischen Sprachen," *Caucasica* 8: 1–52.

Tubiana, J. 1962. "A propos d'un dictionnaire Mbay-Français," *JSA* 32: 332–39.

Tucker, A. N. 1940. *The Eastern Sudanic Languages*. Oxford.

———. 1949. "Sotho-Nguni orthography and tone-marking," *BSOAS* 13: 200–224.

———. 1951. "Notes on Murle ('Beir')," *AuÜ* 36: 99–109.

———. 1960. "Notes on Kanzo," *ALS* 1: 16–41.

———. 1962. "Noun classification in Kalenjin: Päkot," *ALS* 3: 137–81.

———. 1964a. "Noun classification in Kalenjin: Nandi-Kipsigis," *ALS* 5: 192–247.

———. 1964b. "Kalenjin Phonetics," in *In Honour of Daniel Jones*, ed. D. Abercrombie et al., 445–70 (London).

Tucker, A. N., and M. A. Bryan. 1966. *Linguistic Analyses, the Non-Bantu Languages of Northeastern Africa*. Oxford.

Tucker, A. N., and J. Mpaayei. 1955. *A Maasai Grammar*. Oxford.

Turner, P. 1967. "Highland Chontal phonemics," *AL* 9, 4: 26–32.

Turner, R. L. 1924. "The Sindhi recursives or voiced stops preceded by glottal closure," *BSOAS* 3: 301–15.

Uldall, H. J. 1954. "Maidu phonetics," *IJAL* 20: 8–16.

van Warmelo, N. J. 1930. "Zur Gwamba-Lautlehre," *AuÜ* 20: 221–37.

———. 1931. "Gitonga," *AuÜ* 22: 16–46.

Vandame, C. 1963. *Le Ngambay-Moundou*. IFAN, Dakar.

Von Essen, O. 1935–36. "Stimmhafte Implosive im Vai," *AuÜ* 26: 150–59.
———. 1962. "Implosive Verschlusslaute im Hausa," *AuÜ* 45: 285–91.
Vorbichler, A. 1965. *Die Phonologie und Morphologie des Balese (Ituri-Urwald, Kongo)*. Glückstadt.
———. 1967. "Erzählungen in der Mamvu-Sprache," *AuÜ* 50: 244–78.
Wallace, J. M. 1966. "Katu personal pronouns," *Mon-Khmer Studies* II: 55–62 (Saigon).
Wang, William S.-Y. 1968. "The basis of speech," *Project on Linguistic Analysis, Reports*, Second Series, No. 4, January 1968 (Phonology Lab., Dept. of Linguistics, U.C. Berkeley).
Ward, Ida C. 1936. *An Introduction to the Ibo Language*. Cambridge, England.
Waterhouse, V., and M. Morrison. 1950. "Chontal phonemes," *IJAL* 16: 35–39.
Watson, R. 1964. "Pacŏh phonemes," *Mon-Khmer Studies* I, 135–48 (Saigon).
Weathers, N. 1947. "Tsotsil phonemes with special reference to allophones of *b*," *IJAL* 13: 108–12.
Welmers, W. E. 1952. "Notes on the structure of Saho," *Word* 8: 145–62.
———. 1962. "The phonology of Kpelle," *JAL* 1: 69–93.
Wenck, G. 1954. *Japanische Phonetik, Band I*. Wiesbaden.
Westermann, D., and I. C. Ward. 1933. *Practical Phonetics for Students of African Languages*. Oxford.
Whiteley, W. H. 1958. *A Short Description of Item Categories in Iraqw*. Kampala.
Wilson, W. A. A. 1965. "A reconstruction of the Pajade mutation system," *JWAL* 2: 15–20.
Wolff, H. 1954. *Nigerian Orthography*. Zaria.
———. 1959. "Subsystem typologies and area linguistics," *AL* 1, 7: 1–88.
Wolff, R. 1905. *Grammatik der Kinga-Sprache (Deutsch-Ostafrika, Nyassagebiet)*. Berlin.

# The Role of Typology in the Development of a Scientific Linguistics

The history of linguistic typological studies has an obvious dramatic quality. Initially it shared the stage on practically equal terms with the new comparative linguistics of the nineteenth century and counted among its practitioners figures of the eminence of the two Schlegels, von Humboldt, Schleicher, and Max Mueller. Towards the end of the nineteenth century and well into the twentieth, however, it fell into neglect and even disrepute. It was perhaps kept from complete extinction during this period merely by the fact that as celebrated a linguist as Sapir judged the topic to be of sufficient significance to merit extended treatment in his one work intended for a general audience. It revived during the last two decades to attain a modest but definite position within linguistics.

Two other characteristics of this history may be pointed out in addition to these striking vicissitudes. One is the remarkable tenacity shown in its survival even through days of deep degradation founded on the apprehension, dim though at times it may have been, that the problem of type is indeed a fundamental one.

The other characteristic of its history has been its adaptability and hence its changing character in different historical periods. While still retaining sufficient continuity to be recognizably the same basic subject, it has in recent decades sloughed off its nineteenth-century accoutrements of linguistic ethnocentrism, simplistic universal evolutionism, and loose methodology and developed anew, incorporating the more rigorous methods and the basic viewpoints of the structuralist approaches which came to dominate linguistics in the second quarter of the twentieth century. Signs are not wanting that with the most recent developments in general linguistic theory, typology may be facing a new crisis and that its role within linguistics once more stands in need of re-evaluation and may require the formulation of novel goals and new outlooks while still, as in the past, retaining essential bonds of continuity with its own earlier orientations. It is to a consideration of these problems that the present paper addresses itself.

The fact that the most recent revival of typology took place within a period in which structuralism in one or another of its variants held virtually undisputed sway in linguistics made it inevitable that it should have incorporated some of its most basic assumptions. Two of these are of particular importance in the present context. The first is the emphasis on the description of each language in terms of categories inherent in the language itself so that its internal structure might be made manifest. This was a reaction against *grammaire générale* with its imposition from sources external to the language, as it were, of *a priori* schemes believed to derive from the very nature of coherent discourse and to have a basis in universal logic. Such schemes turned out on closer examination to be thinly disguised versions of parochial European models. The structuralist emphasis on the essential integrity of each language and the necessity of dealing with it in its own terms leads easily to an emphasis on the uniqueness of each language and a concentration on differences rather than similarities among languages. Approached from this angle, the task of typology becomes that of catching the essential spirit of each language by showing how it exhibits some pervasive underlying pattern revealing, as it were, its true genius which distinguishes it from other languages. The prime examples of this approach are to be found in the work of men like Whorf and Weisgerber. Whorf is in a fact a typologist in so far as he contrasts what he calls the SAE (Standard Average European) worldview as revealed in European languages with that inherent in the Hopi language. Such an approach as that of Whorf's is indeed consonant with one of the most fundamental aspects of the structuralist approach and its vogue can largely be explained on these grounds. However, it would be more accurate to say that the question of uniqueness of individual language structure as against the demands of the scientific method for comparability of diverse structures constituted rather a source of inherent tension within structuralism and that the more sober typological methods of Trubetskoy and Hockett, confined also as they were to phonology were, in effect, an attempt within the structuralist framework to do justice to both the integrity of individual languages and their comparability. Languages differ in certain essential ways as can be seen from their assignment to different types. At the same time, the typology itself is based on criteria of universal applicability and also, and with equal inevitability, shows that individual languages are in certain respects also similar to each other in so far as they belong to the same type.

The other salient feature of more recent typology which reflects its development within a structuralist matrix is its essentially synchronic nature. This is, of course, not unconnected with the first characteristic of structuralism considered here, its concentration on the description of each language in its own terms. Not only is the structure an organized whole in its own right not in need of illumination from alien linguistic sources, but it can also be considered in abstraction from its own past. It can be understood in its own terms and the historical mode of explanation which seemed the only possible one in the traditional genetic approach, while not repudiated, is seen as but one among the possible types of explanation. The great contribution of de Saussure was that he, whose credentials as an Indo-European specialist were beyond cavil, proclaimed the autonomy of synchronic linguistics. Indeed, it is the study of synchronic states which becomes the central topic of the science of linguistics and the area in which to search for regularities. The essentially random effects of sound change are repaired by analogy and this process reveals the deepest drives of the speakers towards coherence of linguistic structure.

Here also typology performed a basic service for the new structuralism. In place of the older comparative method of diachronic linguistics, it offered its own type of comparison, typological comparison, and its own method of classification, typological as distinct from genetic. This distinction has, of course, been widely viewed as a kind of opposition between two incompatible approaches. In recent years, however, the view has become widely accepted that there is in fact no incompatibility between the two approaches, that each has its separate and legitimate goals. The essentially synchronic nature of contemporary typology can be seen, however, in the fact that discussion of the relation between typology and historical linguistics has tended to emphasize that the basic importance of typology in diachronic studies is as a kind of synchronic touchstone for the validity of the reconstructions of proto-languages. Does the reconstructed language viewed as a possible synchronic state exhibit typological characteristics found in directly documented languages?

Recent developments, both within and outside of the framework of generative grammar, place both of the questions raised here in a somewhat different light. In regard to the first, it is clear that the tendency to stress differences among languages and the individual genius of each one has been giving way to a renewed interest in the topic of universals. That it was, so to speak, "in the air" is shown by the fact that it developed both from within the earlier typological approaches, as can be seen from the papers presented at the S.S.R.C. sponsored Conference on Universals held in Dobbs Ferry in 1961, and in the context of generative grammar shortly thereafter.

It is obvious that the other basic characteristic of recent typology which derives from its structural matrix, namely its essentially synchronic nature, also stands in need of fundamental reconsideration. The separation of synchronic and diachronic studies never has been, in fact, nor could it be as complete as required by the de Saussure doctrine. Here once again the generative approach has raised fundamental questions. The very rules of synchronic description show an internal ordering which in many instances are in an obvious relation with the past history of the language which is not, however, one of identity. This is most obvious in phonology.

I shall now consider these two topics, the relationship of typology to universals and to diachronic linguistics, in greater detail.

Once seen, the relationship between typology and universals is indeed obvious. They become in fact logically interconvertible methods of making the same statements of universal scope. In the simplest case, that of unrestricted universals, we are asserting that all languages possess the typological characteristic corresponding to the universal and that the type which does not have the characteristic, while logically conceivable, has been shown empirically not to exist. Thus to state that all languages have a set of unvoiced stops is logically equivalent to saying that, in this respect, all languages belong to the type defined by that property and no languages belong to the type defined by its absence. In more complex instances where several characteristics are involved simultaneously and only certain of their combinations lack empirical exemplification the statement in terms of types is once more interconvertible with statements of universal scope which are, however, correspondingly conditional, i.e. implicational. Jakobson deserves great credit for having seen and emphasized the importance of such implicational relations with their implicit hierarchy of linguistic features, such as the relation between marked and unmarked features, at an early stage of development of the Prague School.

Considered in this relationship to universals, typology has then a vital contribution to make, one which relates to the most fundamental goals of linguistics, as to any other science, the development of a structure of interrelated generalizations or laws. In assigning a central role to the study of language universals and in asserting a basic role for typology in this search, one is in no way repudiating the fundamental insights of structuralism nor denigrating its vast contributions. It is rather a fulfillment of one of the implicit goals of structuralism. Its most outstanding proponents always considered the comparability of languages in their structural aspects as fundamental and did not hesitate to generalize on occasion about language. One need only allude once more to that classic of Prague structuralism, the *Grundzüge* of Trubetskoy with its typology of phonological systems and its generalizations about such systems.

Such an approach in no wise denies the individuality of each language which remains a unique combination and configuration of typological characteristics. Yet it retains its comparability with other languages through its typological similarities and dissimilarities. Each language is thus a realization of one particular concatenation of the typological possibilities which in their entirety comprise the concept of a "possible human language."

Indeed, it might be maintained that the actual practice of the experienced and successful field worker embodies in essential fashion typological assumptions which have remained for the most part implicit rather than explicit. The mythology is that the field worker records everything he hears in a phonetic transcription and then applies the procedures of phonemic theory without any prepossessions about what the language might turn out to be like. The facts are probably more like the following. The process of linguistic field work consists in the setting up and testing of typological hypotheses. For example, the field worker in African languages seeks first of all to answer such questions as whether the language is tonal and whether it has noun classes. Each of these is a typological hypothesis and the process of field work is to decide among these hypotheses and gradually narrow the choices among possible types of languages to which the language he is investigating belongs. Were this not so, his field work would founder for lack of directive hypotheses.

What the field linguist derives from previous direct experience of languages and the reading of grammars is not merely greater technical skill in transcribing or in working with informants, although this is, of course, part of the story, but an ever clearer conception of what may be expected to occur in languages, often enough somewhat circumscribed through his concentration of effort in one geographical area or language family. It is always valuable to bring forth and make explicit what has hitherto been merely implicit. One way of stating the goals of the study of universals through typology is that we are attempting, in a systematic and more complete and hence in more reliable fashion, to delimit the concept of "possible human language" which in far more inchoate form in fact guides and informs effective linguistic field work.

So far from such a viewpoint distorting the essential structure of a given language, one might rather claim that the universal illuminates the particular and that general considerations are, in any event, as has been seen, unavoidable in the investigation of specific languages.

The next step in this area would seem to be the systematic processing of the truly enormous empirical data regarding natural languages that is now at our disposal. As things stand we must all rely on personal and hence very limited and accidental samples of data if we wish to make more precise, for any aspect of language, what is the range of typological variation and what possible generalizations exist. Except perhaps for some aspects of phonology, notably vowel systems which have been the topics of typological surveys in the past, this is in general the situation. Even in these cases, enlightening and useful as are the work of Trubetskoy and Hockett, both these studies are largely out of date because of the mass of new phonological data which has accumulated in the meantime.

It is with the ultimate purpose of storing in retrievable form basic information on a large, ideally, a complete sample of the world's languages, that Professor Ferguson and myself at Stanford University have, with support from the National Science Foundation, organized a project on Universals which began work at the beginning of the current calendar year. The project is very modest in scope and designed to be chiefly exploratory with special attention to the methodological problems involved. At the same time we hope that the projects undertaken in this way will also produce results of substantive interest. We are aware that the varying reliability and the differing theoretical approaches employed in linguistic descriptions pose a very real problem. We hope also that one of the results of this project will be to specify in detail a good many aspects of language concerning which current descriptive practices tend to be inadequate and incomplete.

In this initial stage the work of the project primarily takes the form of individual or collaborative studies of topics of medium scope, that is neither so restricted as to be trivial nor so global as to be impracticable, e.g., the study of phonological systems in general. It will perhaps be of interest to present just one facet of some preliminary results of one of these projects. The subject of this particular study in which I have collaborated with Professor Dorothea Kaschube of the University of Colorado is word prosodic systems, a topic that has been largely neglected from the theoretical standpoint since the pioneer article of George Trager on the theory of accentual systems which appeared in 1941.

In our work on this subject we have gone through existing grammars, particularly phonologic descriptions, of well over 100 languages thus far, excerpting the relevant information for the files of the project and providing brief sketches of the salient characteristics of these systems. We are also in the process of revising an initial questionnaire on the subject drawn up in a fashion that would facilitate coding for computer processing. We have reached the conclusion, however, that while such coded information will doubtless be useful, the exigencies of a coding system tend to restrict the full range of relevant information that can be made available and that the method of discursive summary of the basic features of such systems is in fact a much more revealing one.

One particular aspect of the results of this project on word prosody is selected for discussion here because it serves to illustrate the theoretical point that has just been advanced. I believe that the results presented here will show that in the present instance systems of individual languages, presented in quite varying, and on the surface, diverse fashions, are representative of a single fairly widespread kind of word prosodic system which has not up to now received full recognition as a type. Moreover, I believe that in this case our understanding of individual occurrences is enhanced when we view them as particular exemplifications of a general type.

The type of word prosodic system to which I am alluding might be characterized as having culminative decrescendo and might be called, after its best studied example, the Japanese type. However, to place it properly in the perspective of the overall study of word prosodic systems, it will be necessary to preface its discussion by the consideration of certain more general aspects of word prosodic systems.

In such an investigation we are concerned with the phonetic properties of the phonologic word. Three features have generally been considered to be of central or even defining importance: stress, length, and tone. However, the subject of word prosodic features cannot be merely the study of these three features in relation to the phonologic word. To begin with, these features are themselves of cardinal importance within a prosodic hierarchy of which the word is but one level. Below the word is the syllable and above it there is at least a phrase and sentence intonational level. Further, it is important to distinguish whatever physical phonetic properties these may have in common from their distribution and function within the word. The distinction between form and function may be illustrated as follows. Stress is said to have a culminative function if it occurs (except possibly for clitics) once and only once in every word, but its position is not predictable from phonological information alone. Languages in which stress functions in this manner are often said to have free stress (e.g. Russian). Now there are languages, e.g. Nimboran in New Guinea, for which exactly the same distributional statement can be made for high tone. Hence the phonetically different features of stress and tone have the same culminative function in Russian and Nimboran. We may therefore raise the following question concerning phonetic features in general. Which ones may have culminative function? Are there languages, for example, in which consonantal voicing is culminative? In such a language every word would have one and just one voiced consonant whose position in the word would not be phonologically predictable. In similar fashion, the demarcative function of stress in languages like Hungarian and Czech may be defined as a compulsory single occurrence of the feature within the word but in a phonologically predictable position. Both the culminative and demarcative functions in Trubetskoy's well-known treatment of the subject may be subsumed under a single property, namely the occurrence of a particular feature just once in a word. In accordance with generally accepted terminology such a feature may be called accentual. On this basis it seems that it is just the three features stress, length, and pitch (with the possible addition of that remarkable feature glottalization) which may occur as accents, and no others.

It is possible to broaden the concept of accent in the following way. We can say that a feature is accentual in reference to the phonologic word if it occurs not just once, but a maximum of once, i.e. if it occurs zero or one time in each word. In such cases, which are particularly common in regard to length, we have a basic opposition between accentless words, those with zero occurrence of the feature in question, and accented words, those with exactly one occurrence. The decision to call such systems accentual, which is not motivated merely by the *ad hoc* expediency of applying it to this particular case, will turn out in the subsequent discussion to have a direct relevance to Japanese.

The phonologic properties of the word are not confined to accent. For example, in languages with vowel harmony involving an opposition between front vowels and back vowels 'to have front vowels' is a property of words as units. As indicated by this example, and as could be illustrated by reference to "nasal harmony" in certain languages of South America and Africa, unlike accentual properties, these harmonic properties normally involve features other than stress, length, and pitch.

However, for a tonal language of the usual type, for example, Yoruba which would usually be described as having tone as a word prosodic feature, the relation of tone to the word is neither accentual nor harmonic. Any syllable in the word may have any tone which thus, as it were, recurs at repeated intervals. Metaphorically compared to verbal aspect, one may say that accentual features are punctual, harmonic are durative, and for Yoruba and similar cases the tone feature is iterative.

Let us return once more to the question of the relation between form and function. As with the somewhat allied problem of the arbitrariness of the linguistic sign in regard to the relation between sound and meaning, the question turns out on closer examination to involve interesting complexities. On the one hand, as has been already done, it is important to distinguish form and function clearly. Two different forms may function in the same manner, as illustrated by the example of a culminative pitch language like Nimboran in which pitch functions in the same fashion as stress in many other languages. Likewise the same form may function differently in two different languages. Once more to keep to the examples already mentioned, tone in Nimboran functions like a culminative accent whereas the same phonetic feature in Yoruba functions iteratively in the word occurring once in each syllable.

Indeed tone may function harmonically also, parallel in principle to vowel harmony. In Jabem, an Austronesian language of New Guinea, every word has all high tones or all low tones.

In spite of the independence of form and function as shown by the preceding illustrative examples, the relation is not one of pure arbitrariness, which I would take in this context to mean a purely random or chance relationship between form and function. Stress is typically accentual in that it functions as an accent in the vast majority of languages in which it is found. We may say indeed that stress is 'monarchical'. There is normally one heaviest stress in the word and it tends to tolerate even secondary rivals only at a remove of at least one syllable. If stress is monarchical, then tone in the great majority of tone languages is democratic. Most commonly every syllable has all the tonal possibilities and no culminative hierarchy is established within the word. Where all the tonal possibilities are neutralized in certain syllables, i.e. where we have the so-called neutral tone, it is precisely the arch-rival of tone, stress, which is invariably present and the neutralization of tone in unstressed syllables is but a further instance of the neutralizations of other phonetic properties in the same environment, e.g. vowel quality and vowel quantity.

We are now ready to consider the case of Japanese. All modern descriptions of Japanese by qualified linguists are in agreement in attributing definite pitch to each voiced syllabic and in dismissing stress as a factor. However, it is also clear that Japanese tone does not function in the iterative fashion of typical tonal languages. On the other hand high pitch also does not function like loud stress in the usual stress language. It is not true that every word has just one high pitch or even a maximum of one high pitch in Japanese. Hence our earlier definition of accent will not allow us to say that high pitch functions as an accent. Approached in this fashion Japanese is not a pitch accent language.

However, there is a pitch phenomenon which patterns culminatively in the Japanese word in that it occurs either zero or once in every Japanese word and that is the sequence of a high tone followed by a low tone. Such a high tone is called an accent in the currently accepted analyses of Japanese. The tone of all tonal bearing moras before the accent are phonetically high except that an initial unaccented mora is mid. All tones following the accent are low. For example, in *ikimásita* 'went', which is accented on the third mora, the initial tone is mid, the second and third (the latter of which bears the accent) are high, and the fourth and fifth are low.

A few further observations regarding Japanese accent will be relevant in subsequent discussion. Since the accent consists of a high tone which is immediately followed by a low tone a sequence with an accented final mora will be indistinguishable from an unaccented sequence. Both will have automatically initial mid and following high tones. If something is added then the difference will appear since the tone of the subsequent mora will drop if there is a final accent but will remain high if there is not. For example, the word *otokó* 'male' with basic final accent will have the same pitch sequence in its final form as *otaku* 'home' which is basically accentless, i.e. [ōtókó] and [ōtákú] respectively. Followed by the particle *no*, however, the difference will appear [ōtókó nò] as opposed to [ōtákú nó] in which the accent on the final syllable of *otokó* makes its appearance with the drop in pitch from [kó] to [nò]. A further observation concerns vowel length. Japanese has phonetic long vowels analyzed as geminate vowel clusters. If the accent rests on the first mora of a long vowel then, in accordance with the general rule, the drop in pitch will be on the second mora of the same long vowel. Phonetically we will have a long vowel with a falling tone. An example is *obáasan* 'grandmother' which is phonetically [ōbâ:sàn].

It has been my own experience with tonal languages that the point of greatest perceptual prominence, likely to be interpreted as strong stress by a speaker of a stress language, is a high tone followed by a low tone, or a falling tone within a single syllable. Thus in a Hausa word such as *túkúnyàà* 'pot' the second high tone on *kú* will be perceived as more prominent than the first on *tú* and American students of Hausa will interpret this word as being stressed on the second syllable.

Hence the Japanese or accentual decrescendo type language may be interpreted as involving a kind of modification of form in terms of function. In utilizing pitch for culminative purposes the optimum perceptual effect is attained by transforming the high-low sequence into an accent which patterns functionally like stress in a culminative stress language.

Once one has become aware of this as a possible type, other instances of the same general character, though of course with difference in details, can be found. An example is Karok, a Hokan language of California. This is described by Bright as having a combination of pitch with concomitant stress. In his analysis there are two accents, an acute and a circumflex. There are, as in Japanese, unaccented words. Every accented word has just one accent and the circumflex can only occur on a long vowel. Abstracted from prejunctural phenomena it turns out that the acute is a high level tone accompanied by loud stress and the circumflex is a falling tone accompanied by loud stress. Abstracting from certain conditional variations the general rule is that syllables preceding the accent are high in pitch and those following are low. Just as in Japanese an initial unaccented syllable is lowered, here however to mid only if it has a long vowel, otherwise to low. The falling circumflex, which, as has been seen, can only occur on long vowels, is easily reinterpreted as in Japanese as involving the accent on the first mora of the long vowel. We thus need only one accent and the system is in essential respects of the same type as Japanese. The following Karok words followed by transcriptions indicating the phonetic tonal levels will illustrate this similarity.

(1) *puʔuumára* (Bright *puʔu·mára* [pùʔú·márà] 'he didn't arrive';

(2) *ʔasuúxara* (Bright *ʔasú·xara*) [ʔàsú·xàrà] 'fasting';

(3) *ʔifučtíimič* (Bright *ʔifučtîmič*) [ʔìfúčtî·mìč] 'last'.

It will be noted that a long vowel with the acute accent is quite naturally interpreted as accented on the second mora while one with a circumflex is interpreted as being accented on the first mora.

A number of other Amerind languages have been noted as probable examples of this type. Perhaps the most startling reanalysis is that which might be suggested for the Keresan language of Santa Ana pueblo. Time does not allow for the presentation of this complex case. In Davis' description there are no less than four accents. Every word except for some unaccented monosyllables has at least one of these but may have a larger number. If, however, one is willing to abstract from certain Spanish loanwords it becomes possible to reanalyze in terms of a single accent which, except for a few morphemically complex words, can only occur once in any word and which patterns in accordance with the same basic Japanese type.

These results may be viewed as at least suggestive for problems of early Indo-European accent. The Greek system, just like Karok, involves two accents. As in Karok the circumflex can only occur on long vowels or diphthongs. The possible application to Sanskrit is even more striking. If the Sanskrit system was of the Japanese type this would explain why it is not the accented syllable itself which is marked whereas the falling tone in the following syllable is indicated by the *svarita*. The essential feature of the system would indeed be the fall in pitch and, as in Japanese, if the accented syllable is final it cannot be marked because there is no following syllable to carry the descent in pitch. Some of the more recent work on Slavic accent suggests a similar type for Proto-Slavic. Thus Kuryłowicz in 1958 in an article in *Rocznik Slawistyczny* noted that accented words had phonetically high pitch on the syllable preceding the accent and low on those following and that there is a distinction between accented and unaccented words. The typological resemblance of this latter characteristic to Japanese was already noted by Jakobson and mentioned once more in his paper at the Fifth International Congress of Slavists in 1963.

We may recapitulate the basic argument thus far in the following manner. Typology in its more recent forms has displayed certain natural consequences of the fact that its revival took place during the period in which structuralism became the dominant trend in linguistics. Two of these have been mentioned, the tendency to emphasize the uniqueness of the structure of each individual language and the essentially synchronic nature of contemporary typology. With regard to the first of these, the attempt was made to show that generalizing trends were indeed also inherent in structuralism and that typological studies have an essential role in the study of language universals. For to discover what is valid for all languages is nothing more or less than to give concrete form to the concept 'possible human language'. And a 'possible human language' may in turn be considered to be a language of a possible type. By pointing to certain actual investigations in the area of word prosodic systems the attempt also was made to show that the general may illuminate and help us to understand the particular case, so that typological classification might be looked upon, not as detracting from, but as helping in the attainment of certain traditional and legitimate aims of structuralism.

We turn, therefore, to the other question raised in initial discussion, the relation of typology to diachronic studies. Here also, as I shall try to show, typology has a fundamental contribution to make in relation to the most comprehensive overall goals of linguistics as a science. This is because language like all human institutions can be approached from two distinct but complementary and related viewpoints. Every given language, like every human institution or cultural form, is one of the possible expressions open to man given his capacities in their full generality, what has traditionally been called 'human nature'. The study of linguistic universals as a study of possible types of synchronic language states makes here a major potential contribution to the understanding of language from this point of view, whose importance hardly needs to be underlined. But a specific language is not merely a particular exemplification of one among the empirically possible types of language. It is also a specific historical product. To say regarding some particular language that it represents a particular combination of typological characteristics whose range is specified by a general theory of universals is indeed a vast step forward. This is far from fully accomplished but one can begin to foresee the lines of development through which it may ultimately be attained. If one asks, however, why a particular language embodies one rather than another of the possible human types of language a universal theory of the kind envisioned will not provide an answer. It cannot say why a particular language is, for example, tonal rather than non-tonal. It would usually be said that the explanation in such cases is historical. We must understand the antecedent conditions from which it arose and this history both of internal development and external influences is within the province of historical and comparative linguistics.

It has been usual, however, to consider historical linguistics as a kind of particularistic study which reconstructs earlier, often undocumented language states, so-called proto-languages, and which specifies the changes from some particular proto-language forward in time to the contemporary synchronic states. Structuralism here produced an important advance when it substituted, by means of its key concept of structure, for the older neo-Grammarian notion of isolated changes the idea that diachronic changes are to be understood in terms of their effects on a system, on their structural consequences.

There exists, however, the possibility of a more comprehensive mode of diachronic comparison which shares with synchronic typology the attribute of generality. The individual items of such comparison are not cognate forms but the changes themselves which occur in historically independent cases and hence are subject to classification and generalization. Such comparison may be called processual. That this type of comparison has received only marginal and largely unexplicit attention rests at least partly on the preemption of the term comparative to particular applications of the genetic method so that diachronic linguistics already appeared to possess its own comparative method.

Such processual comparison involves a generalization of the traditional comparative method in that individually reconstructed instances, themselves the result of the application of the comparative method or of internal reconstruction in specific languages or language families, enter into a more comprehensive mode of comparison by which such historically independent cases are in turn compared with each other to arrive at general formulations regarding processes of change.

In such an approach typology has once more a central place. Just as there are, in accordance with universal principles, possible states so there are possible changes of state and each such change is a change of type. Hence the universal principles of dynamic change will be concerned with the lawful succession of synchronic states. Just as our understanding of a specific language is deepened when we see in it a particular exemplification of the synchronically given typological possibilities, so our understanding of it as a product of historical forces is enhanced when we comprehend it is as a result of processes which are of a general nature and have taken place in other languages in other periods.

Within the overall framework of the study of process a number of methods may be distinguished, at least on a pragmatic basis. They do not differ essentially but involve varying degrees of attention to internal reconstruction, the classical comparative method, and the use of direct historical documentation. It is convenient to distinguish a number of such methods. The first of these may be called the dynamicization of typologies. It involves the development of a theory which states the set of changes by which a language can move from one typological class to another. Such a theory may be called one of relative origin since it applies to the origin of a specific type of language, a type which in the general case arises independently in a multiplicity of language families and chronological periods. An example would be a theory regarding the origin of the type of language which has nasal vowels as well as oral vowels from the type which has oral vowels only. Ferguson has already suggested such a theory in his article "Some Assumptions about Nasals" in the volume *Universals of Language*. This theory asserts that nasal vowels "apart from borrowings and analogical innovations always result from the loss of a primary nasal consonant." The typical course of events is as follows. A previously oral vowel becomes nasalized non-distinctively by an adjacent nasal consonant. The conditioning factor in the form of the nasal consonant is lost and a phonological contrast between oral and nasal vowels comes into existence.

To verify such a theory we will have to compare diverse and historically independent cases each of which incorporates the comparative method in the ordinary sense. If the result of our study, which should ideally consider all available cases, shows that the mechanism just described is the sole way in which nasal vowels arise, then we may say that we have a theory of exclusive relative origin. Considered typologically, if this holds, then we have a lawful succession of types in which our stages are now conceptualized as types themselves. A language which belongs typologically to the class of those with nasalized vowels arises from a type in which there is nonphonemic nasalization of vowels adjacent to nasal consonants, and this type in turn arises from one in which there are phonetically no nasal vowels. Once more there is a relation to universals, in this case to diachronic universals. Each state implies the previous state at some earlier though not exactly specifiable time. We cannot state the implication in the other direction. Given a language with oral vowels only, as far as present knowledge goes, it may or may not develop nasalized allophones adjacent to nasal consonants. The implied is always past and this reflects a typical characteristic of all historical explanation. Earlier states explain later states and not vice versa.

Another at least pragmatically different method may be called, in distinction from the dynamicization of typologies just mentioned, the dynamicization of subtypologies. It tends to employ internal reconstruction to a greater degree than the former method. Let us consider a typological characteristic involving a contingent property of language, that is, one possessed by only a minority of the world's languages, and then undertake an intensive comparison of the languages which possess this property. It thus corresponds to the method 'comparison within the type' advocated by functional theorists in the social sciences. In applying this method we first consider such languages with a view to the formulation of synchronic universals concerning the property in question. We then 'dynamicize' these results in order to establish a developmental course of events typical of the subtype. The principle may be briefly illustrated by reference to one particular aspect of a study of language with phonetic voiceless vowels. In this study I utilized published materials regarding voiceless vowels from approximately 50 languages. From a comparison of these examples eight synchronic universals were formulated. One of these was the following. The existence of voiceless vowels of less than the maximal degree of vowel height implies the existence of at least one voiceless vowel of the maximal degree. This statement was based on the following type of evidence. For most languages with voiceless vowels one finds that the number of voiceless vowels is exactly the same as that of the voiced and that they match each other in quality. Some languages, however, have fewer voiceless than voiced vowels, none more. Ten languages with fewer voiceless than voiced vowels were found in the sample all with a basically similar pattern, namely a favoring of high voiceless over low voiceless vowels.

An example is Uzbek with six voiced vowels *i*, *e*, *ə*, *ɔ*, *o*, and *u*. Of these six only the two of minimum aperture *i* and *u* occur voiceless. Thus far we have a purely synchronic universal which is equivalent to an assertion of the non-existence of languages of a certain type, namely those with low voiceless vowels but not high ones. If a language with five voiced vowels *a*, *e*, *i*, *o*, *u* were found which had three voiceless vowels and these were *a*, *e*, and *o*, but not *i* or *u*, our assertion would be refuted.

However, every synchronic implication in which both the implying and the implied states have empirical exemplification can be mapped into a diachronic process by which the former develops from the latter. Thus in the present instance from the synchronic universal just stated, that voiceless vowels of lower tongue heights imply at least one of the greatest tongue height, we can frame the diachronic hypothesis that, where all vowel qualities do not undergo simultaneous devoicing, voicelessness starts first with the high vowels and later, if at all, spreads to the low vowels. We exclude the diachronic hypothesis that low vowels could first become voiceless, followed by the subsequent spread of voicelessness to the high vowels. For this to take place the initial state would be one which violates the synchronic implicational universal stated above. Our diachronic statement is evidently one concerning the permitted or non-permitted sequences of certain types of language and therefore pertains to change of type.

A third method of processual comparison may be called intergenetic. Historically independent reconstructions are compared as a test of the extent to which they are mutually corroborative and to help in the selection among diverse possibilities by reference to other typologically similar examples. As with the other methods discussed here the emphasis is dynamic. We compare lines of development rather than reconstruction viewed statically.

Thus with regard to the hypothesized laryngeals of Indo-European we ask not the question hitherto and quite justly asked, namely, whether a Proto-Indo-European reconstructed with laryngeals conforms to universal synchronic norms. We ask rather whether the sequence of changes posited is plausible when compared to other reconstructible or historically documented instances of change. The question has been considered in another publication in which it is pointed out that a comparison of the Coptic dialects would lead to the reconstruction of several lost consonants and that the series of changes implied by this reconstruction shares a number of important resemblances to those generally assumed to occur with the loss of laryngeals in Indo-European languages. [The paper referred to, "The Interpretation of the Coptic Vowel System," appears in Part II of this volume—eds.]

Still other methods of processual comparison exist but their discussion is not within the scope of the present paper. With regard to these matters, it should be made clear that all of them have in the past been utilized to some extent by historical linguists. Just as the experienced field worker utilizes a largely inexplicit background of universals in order to produce realistic hypotheses concerning the structure of the language he is studying, so the first rate historical linguist makes use of a similar, unexplicit set of generalizations about the nature of change. Thus, even though historical linguistics in recent times has tended to exclude such assumptions from its theoretical framework, in fact all historical linguists consider certain types of sound change far more plausible than others and make constant use of these and other processual assumptions in their work.

What is believed to be an innovation is the attempt to indicate the way in which such studies transcend the comparative method in the usual sense and the proposal to study such questions systematically and by the comparison of all available cases.

In summary then, typological methods have a central role in two of the most crucial long-range goals of linguistics as a science, the detailed specification of the universal principles to which linguistic synchronic states must conform and a similar specification of the possible sequences of changes in type through which these synchronic states come into being.

# Numeral Classifiers and Substantival Number: Problems in the Genesis of a Linguistic Type

The data and hypotheses presented here are part of a broader investigation concerned with numeral classifier systems considered both as representatives of a type of nominal classification and in relation to the problems of quantification in language.[1] What is meant by quantification in this connection is the manner in which languages express the fact that reference is being made to a quantitatively delimited amount of the thing mentioned.[2]

Such a typological approach involves both synchronic and diachronic considerations. Initially, we take into account an extensive, ideally, an exhaustive sample of languages which is based on preliminary notions regarding the definitional characteristics of the type. A comparison of such languages leads to a number of synchronic generalizations, usually implicational in form. The second major aim is to uncover the dynamic principles, that is the recurrent types of change in historically independent instances involved in the rise, subsequent expansion, and ultimate dissolution of the type.[3] In carrying out this part of the investigation our methods include deductions based on internal reconstruction within individual languages, the comparative method within linguistic stocks, and direct historical documentation where this is available.

[1] The present research was supported by the National Science Foundation as part of the Language Universals Project at Stanford University.

[2] The somewhat vague term 'thing mentioned' is used here because although the present study is basically confined to nominal phrases, verbal action can also be quantified. This is briefly discussed in the final section of the paper.

[3] For discussion and exemplification of these methods, see Greenberg 1966, 1969, 1970a, 1970b.

As noted initially, the tentative conclusions presented here are but a portion of a broader study which is in progress. In the present study the emphasis will be on questions relating to the initial conditions under which numeral classifier systems may be conjectured to arise. In the final section, in order to place the present study within the more general perspective of the study as a whole, a series of other problems and in some cases hypotheses regarding them will be outlined without pursuing them in detail.

One limitation should be mentioned at the outset. Systems of the type with which we are concerned here have undoubtedly, in some instances, arisen under conditions of language contact. For example, in those Dravidian languages which have such systems it seems clear that they have developed in general as a result of contact with Indo-Aryan languages.[4] Any theory of origin will ultimately have to take into account both the conditions under which pristine systems arise and those in which contact is a major factor. In the study in the present form, the predominant emphasis is on the former.

As mentioned earlier the sample is not exhaustive and this, of course, adds still further to the tentative nature of the results. Nevertheless the hypotheses presented here are based on quite extensive data.[5] They are presented here in the hope that they may provide at least a basis for conclusions that can be tested and modified in the light of both raw data and more penetrating theoretical analysis.

We begin with an attempt at a preliminary definition of what constitutes a numeral classifier language in terms of the existence of a particular syntactic construction. A considerable number of the world's languages including almost all of those in Southeast Asia exhibit the following characteristic. An English phrase such as 'five books' is rendered in translation by a phrase containing, outside of possible grammatical markers, not two but three elements. The kind of literal translation often supplied in grammars of such

[4] On this topic see especially Emeneau 1956.

[5] A list of languages in my sample follows. In a few instances the numeral classifier system is very marginal, e.g., Bulgarian, because of the use of *duši* 'soul' used in enumerating persons, and Hungarian, because it has a numeral series used only with persons: Ahom, Ainu, Assamese, Banggais, Bengali, Black Thai, Bodo, Breton (Medieval), Bribri, Brou, Bulgarian, Burmese, Cebuano, Chinese (Archaic, Mandarin, Hakka, Cantonese), Chiripo, Cholon, Chontal (Mayan), Cuna, Day, Dioi, Engenni, Egyptian Arabic, Empeo, Fijian, Garo, Gilbertese, Gilyak, Guaymi, Haida, Hausa, Hungarian, Hupa, Iban, Ibibio, Irish, Ishkashim, Jacaltec, Japanese, Kachin, Karen, Karo-Batak, Katu, Kei, Khamti, Khariya, Khasi, Khmer, Khmu, Kiriwina, Kolami, Korean, Kurukh, Laotian, Lisu, Malay, Malto, Man, Maru, Merir, Mikir, Miri, Mon, Mota, Muchik, Nahuatl (Classical and Tetelcingo), Nauru, Ojibwa, Omani Arabic, Ossete, Palau, Palaung, Parji, Pashto, Persian, Pocomchi, Ponape, Pur, Rawang, Samoan, Shan, Sonsorol, Tajik, Taraon, Tarascan, Tat, Thai, Tho, Tlingit, Toba-Batak, Totonac, Trukese, Tsimshian, Turkish, Tzeltal, Tzotzil, Uvea, Uzbek, Vietnamese, White Thai, Wolio, Yurok.

languages might be something like 'five flat-object book'.[6] The second item in such a phrase is often called a numeral classifier in allusion both to its occurrence in a numeral phrase and to its providing a semantic classification of the head noun.

Implicit in the terminology 'numeral classifier', there is, then, a quite straightforward definition of the syntactic construction in which the classifier appears, the occurrence of which could be criterial for a language to be considered a numeral classifier language. For example, the following statement by Burling (1965: 244) might provide the basis for a definition along these lines, "In many languages of Southeast Asia, a number is never used without being accompanied by one of the special morphemes known as classifiers."

However, while a useful starting point for discussion, it is clear that simply rephrasing this statement as a definition would leave unsolved a number of questions, questions which require settlement before a definition can be applied. This becomes particularly obvious when confronted with the variabilities and complexities of languages usually assigned to the type. For example, such a definition might be interpreted to require that every noun which in a language like English may be preceded by a number, should, in a classifier language, have a classifier. On such a view it is not excessive to state that there are no numeral classifier languages. There are in fact particular classes of nouns, e.g. measures, units of time, and the word 'time' in such phrases as 'three times' which hardly ever occur with classifiers. In some languages, always considered to be numeral classifier languages, the group of nouns which do not take classifiers is still more extensive (e.g. Vietnamese).

In many languages the classifiers are not compulsory even for the restricted set of nouns that have them. This holds for example in Khmer in which, we are told, the expression without the classifier is stylistically less formal.[7]

Sometimes the restrictions on the classifier construction pertain to the numbers with which the classifiers may co-occur. For example, in Khasi and Tat they do not appear with the number 'one', while in Malto they only occur with numbers larger than two, in this case with the numbers borrowed along with the classifier system from Indo-Aryan. It is particularly common for classifiers not to occur with higher units of the numerical system and their multiples, e.g. 10, 20, 60, 100, 300.

Syntactically also there is variability in that the classifiers need not be confined to numerical constructions. In Mandarin and other languages the classifier is required with demonstratives even in non-numeral phrases. In

[6] Of course, other word orders are possible.

[7] According to Jacob (1965: 148).

other languages it may occur in such phrases usually with some difference in meaning between instances in which the classifier does or does not appear (e.g. Thai). In Thai it may also occur with qualifying adjectives under the same general circumstances as with demonstratives. In Kiriwina it is required with demonstratives and certain adjectives while it may not occur with certain other adjectives. In some languages it may occur with the noun in the absence of any modifiers, numeral or otherwise, and is thus a kind of article (e.g. in Dioi, a Thai language). In one Mayan language at least, Jacaltec, the classifier can occur as the sole constituent of a substantive phrase in its function as an anaphoric substitute, i.e. as a pronoun. It is indeed universal in languages with numeral classifier constructions that the head noun may be deleted either when it has been previously mentioned or can be supplied from the non-linguistic context. In instances like Dioi and Jacaltec we may legitimately ask whether, synchronically considered, these should be considered numeral classifier systems as distinct from some other type of nominal classification.[8]

If all this creates difficulties in establishing precise criteria based on syntactic function in numerical phrases, even graver problems arise in regard to classification as a definitional criterion. It is clear that many of the items that are listed as classifiers in grammars of numeral classifier languages cannot, on any reasonable view, be said to classify. In our initial example, we employed a gloss of the type frequently found in grammars of such languages, namely, 'five flat-object book'; taking such a translation at its face value, we can justifiably state that we have classification in the semantic sense because, indeed, a book is a kind of flat object. The word for 'tail' is sometimes used as a classifier for animals (e.g. *ekor* in Malay) but we cannot consider a dog a kind of tail though of course we can devise a property 'having a tail'. On the other hand we could define the class meaning of *ekor* in Malay as that which is common to all nouns which take *ekor* as a classifier. This is, of course, what is usually done in describing class meanings in noun-class languages. These two alternatives bring out an interesting difference between numeral classifier and the noun class languages with which they have sometimes been compared. In the former, in the majority of instances, the classifier is itself a noun with its own lexical meaning and may, in fact, have its own classifier when it functions as the head of a noun phrase.

But even the approach based on the meaning of the items with which a classifier co-occurs and which disregards the lexical meaning of the classifier itself, runs into difficulties which are similar to those incidental to the

[8] Diachronically, from the evidence of related languages, they have in all probability arisen from systems in which the classifiers were confined to numeral constructions.

establishment of class meanings in noun-class languages. For example in Thai *tua* is used with animals in general but it also occurs with other nouns, e.g. *sya* 'a coat'.[9]

Furthermore in some languages such as Burmese and Thai, there are a fair number of words which are, as it were, their own classifiers. An example is Burmese *ʔein ta-ʔein* 'house one-house' in which *ʔein* in its first occurrence is a head noun and in its second occurrence a 'classifier'. In this limiting case the approach through the lexical meaning of the classifier and the semantic properties of the co-occurring noun fall together but give the somewhat fatuous result that *ʔein* as a classifier means 'the property of being a house'.

At the other end of the logical spectrum there are examples like *buʔuk* 'piece' in Cebuano, a language of the Philippines, which is used with any classifiable noun so that we would have to assign it the meaning 'having the property of being a classified noun'.

All this does not, of course, destroy the notion that, in a purely formal sense common co-occurrence with the same classifier determines a classification of those head nouns which occur with classifiers even though such a classification is often formal rather than semantic, is non-exhaustive in relation to the nouns of the language, is frequently overlapping in that the same noun occurs with more than one classifier and that classes with one member (Burmese) or overall classifications with only one class (Cebuano) may be found.

The considerations just cited in regard to classification have, in fact, been widely appreciated so that many who have been engaged in the description of these languages have consciously eschewed the term 'classifier' in favor of some semantically more neutral term. Such terms are legion, e.g. numerical coefficient (Anceaux, Wolio); numeral adjunct (Fraser, Lisu); numerical determinative (Milner, Palaung); while in the Russian literature *numerativ* has been widely adopted for this purpose.

The foregoing considerations might be held to destroy the very notion of languages with numerical classifiers as a valid linguistic type. Nevertheless, there is still an important difference between languages which are generally held to belong to this type and those which are not although our initial discussion has failed to capture it.

In order to isolate what is distinctive about these languages, we may first consider a range of facts which have not yet engaged our attention. In general, grammars of such languages as Burmese, Thai, and Mandarin

[9]Noss (1964: 106) seeks to define *tua* as occurring with non-humans with anthropomorphic characteristics, e.g., animals, coats, trousers, and tables, the last three because they have arms or legs.

subsume under the same basic construction of numeral + classifier + noun not only such examples as five + flat-object + book, but also many others in which, in contradistinction from this one, the item corresponding to the classifier requires translation into languages like English. Moreover, in languages like Khmer for which it is stated as the general rule that classifiers are optional in these other instances classifiers are *not* optional.[10]

The most important class of such instances is probably the measure construction which occurs most characteristically with mass nouns.[11] In non-classifier languages in which a grammatical mass/count distinction exists, a central characteristic of mass nouns is that they normally do not enter into a direct construction with a numeral but require an intervening measure, e.g. 'one cup of water', 'two gallons of water'.

What has impressed students of languages such as Thai is the evident parallelism between such expressions as (1) *ka·fɛ· sɔ̌ŋ thûaj* 'coffee two cup' and (2) *bùrì sɔ̌ŋ muan* 'cigarette two long-object'. Most linguists who have described these languages have felt that these are at best subtypes of the same fundamental construction. Most commonly they have used some common expression for all constructions of this same general type and then distinguished a series of subtypes, one of which is exemplified by the second of the above phrases.

In the foregoing examples the contrast was between a measure and a count construction. The following set of contrasts, once more from Thai, will show that, as exemplified by the first two constructions, certain count constructions display the same property as measure constructions in that the elements in the classifier position require translation into English and cannot be dispensed with in languages like Khmer: (1) *bùrì sɔ̌ŋ sɔ·ŋ* 'cigarette two pack'; (2) *bùrì sɔ̌ŋ lǒ* 'cigarette two dozen'; (3) *bùrì sɔ̌ŋ muan* 'cigarette two long-object'.

Evidently what is peculiar to languages like Thai is the overt expression of one particular mode of quantification, namely counting by units. This manner of quantifying is evidently the 'unmarked' method in that, in the absence of an overt indication, unit counting is assumed.[12]

The point noted here is not novel. Some analysts have understood its special status and have employed such expressions as 'unit counters' or

[10] Jacob (1965: 145).

[11] Of course, measures of weight can occur with all kinds of physical objects including countables.

[12] I have encountered just one instance of non-unit counting as the preferred form. According to Bataillon (1932: 10), in Uvea counting is most commonly by twos. There are unit classifiers when counting by units is intended. Even here, however, counting by twos also requires an overt indicator, e.g., *ufi lua gafua* 'yam two classifier' 'two yams'; *ufi lua gahoa* 'yam two pair' 'four yams'.

'individual classifiers' to mark out this particular class of expressions.[13] If we reserve the term 'classifier' for such unit counters we may now, in a closer approximation (but nevertheless as we shall see later only an approximation) to the definition of the characteristic numeral classifier construction, delimit it in terms of the overt expression of unit counting.

We may say then, that in even the most elaborate system, all the classifiers are from the referential point of view merely so many ways of saying 'one' or, more accurately, 'times one'. The latter expression is to be preferred because, taken pragmatically there is a difference between numerals proper and modes of quantifying even when the latter involve a number. 'Two dozen' and 'twelve pairs' represent different kinds of quantification acts even though the identity of the final numerical result is guaranteed by the commutative law of multiplications. Hence unit counting is to be distinguished from 'one' as a numeral although the connection between the two is a close one.

It was noted earlier that analysts of numeral classifier languages have often felt that unit counters in these languages are essentially no different from other quantifiers in these languages, that the difference is not intrinsic to the language being analyzed but is imported from considerations of differences of translation into languages not belonging to this type.

However, there is some evidence that both formally and psychologically the unit-counter is a unique type in these languages even though it is, in general, affiliated with the more inclusive type. For example, Chao, at once an eminent linguist and a native Mandarin speaker, classifies unit counters as a special type of measure under the term 'individual classifier' and notes that they do not co-occur with mass nouns (Chao 1968: 503). Burling reports in regard to the most common unit counter of Burmese (1965: 262), the so-called general classifier *-khù*, that it is included by some Burmese speakers "in the same series as the classifiers for the powers of ten . . . *-khù* indicating only one individual object." It was noted earlier that multiples of higher numerical units often do not take classifiers. This also occurs in Burmese and shows clearly the function of the unit classifier as meaning 'times one'. Thus in Burmese 'two-ten book' = '20 books', i.e. '2 × 10 books', while, following the interpretation by native speakers just cited, 'two-*khù* (classifier) book' = '2 books', i.e., '2 × 1 books'. Many analysts consider words for 'ten', 'hundred', etc. in these languages as a subtype of classifiers.

In a few languages there are grammatical peculiarities which distinguish count from measure constructions without there usually being sufficient

[13] The earliest statement along these lines that I have encountered is that of Emeneau (1951: 53) who gives as the class meaning of classifiers "one unit quantity or number of that denoted by the noun it precedes." Note, however, that measures are included here (i.e. 'quantity').

information to decide whether this separates unit counting from all other types of quantification or simply counting as against measuring. For example, measures take a different linking particle in Cebuano.

In spite of these few instances, the overwhelming impression is that of at least surface conformity of all quantifying constructions in these languages in such matters as word order and syntactic markers. This is so much the case that the first and simplest general diachronic hypothesis would be that they have modelled the unit counting construction after preexistent measure and non-unit count constructions.[14]

Nevertheless, the definition of a numeral classifier language as one which contains a construction in which counting by units receives overt expression raises some further problems. Such a formulation, since it primarily defines a construction and only indirectly a language type, taken by itself leaves unresolved such questions as whether a language in which the classifier is always optional or in which there are only isolated instances of it, e.g. English, because of expressions like 'two head of cattle', is to be considered a numeral classifier language. From the dynamic point of view, however, this is not our major concern, which is rather the genesis, spread, and loss of such constructions within languages.

There remains still another problem and this pertains to the adequacy of the definition of the construction itself as one in which unit counting receives overt expression. This stands in need of further elucidation regarding what is to be considered a unit counter. When writers of grammars in English seek to explain the notion of numeral classifier their stock example is 'head of cattle'. Yet other types of expressions occur in English which, it might be argued, involve unit counters, for example, 'sheet of paper'. The existence of a contrast between 'sheet of paper' and 'ream of paper', the latter being defined as equivalent to 480 sheets, seems to suggest the status of 'sheet' as a unit counter. Similar considerations hold regarding expressions such as 'slice of bread', 'piece of meat', and many others. They are countable and contrast as units to such non-unit counters as 'bunch' in 'bunch of carrots'. Yet their presence in English and in many other languages is not, in itself, generally considered a basis for considering the language a numeral classifier language. On the other hand, the nouns themselves in English are grammatically mass nouns in these constructions, but so is 'cattle'.

Is there any basis for this intuitive feeling? It may be proposed that there is a certain arbitrariness as to what constitutes an individual in such instances

[14] The same basic hypothesis seems to be stated in Sen-Gupta (1970, especially 677–78) as indicated in the following remark, "We consider MW [i.e. measure word] as the basis of NuCl [i.e. numeral classifier]."

which underlies this reaction, an arbitrariness not present in such instances as 'one dog' or 'one automobile'. A homely conceptual experiment may serve to pinpoint this difference. If I cut a piece of meat in two, I have two pieces of meat, but if I cut a dog in two, I still have only one dog, a dead one. The property that distinguishes dogs and automobiles in these cases is evidently internal organization into an integrated and organic whole, whether natural in the case of the dog or artificial in the case of the automobile. We might call this feature ± structured.

There is still another kind of borderline case which can be illustrated by English phrases such as 'grain of sand', 'blade of grass', and 'strand of hair'. Once more we see types of phrases which are widespread in non-classifier languages and which could not in themselves lead one to classify them as numeral classifier languages. They would also not be employed as pedagogical examples in languages like English in order to exemplify the notion of numeral classifier. Yet, as with the instances in the preceding paragraph they are unit items and countable. Moreover, they are, as it were, given in nature and do not have the same arbitrariness as 'piece' in 'piece of meat'. For this class of counters what makes them untypical is, it may be conjectured, their smallness and lack of individuality so that they are almost never used in actual counting. In this respect, the superordinates, e.g. rice, grass, approach the status of liquids and other items which form the basis for the grammatical category of mass nouns. These "particulates" as we might call them are almost exclusively used with 'one' or the indefinite article and particularly frequent in negative statements, e.g. 'In many stretches of the Sahara you will not find even one blade of grass'. In this respect their quantification is frequently like that of mass items such as 'water' in that in non-measured constructions the universe of numeration is confined to an opposition between 'one' or 'a' and 'none', in construction with items such as 'bit' or such other indefinites as 'some'.[15]

The two types of counters just considered have an equivocal status in that even analysts who have come to apprehend the difference among unit counters, non-unit counters, and measures and the special status of the first of these in relation to the concept of numeral classifier find difficulty in deciding in specific instances which of these morphemes are to be considered unit classifiers.[16] The reason for this uncertainty in practice is not merely that the

[15] In some descriptions such words are considered classifiers of mass nouns. But then they have the peculiarity that they can only occur with one. An example is Bengali *ṭuku* as in *ek-ṭuku jal* 'a bit of water' as analyzed in Ferguson 1964.

[16] An instance in point is Winstedt (1945, 1957) who lists certain nouns as classifiers in his grammar of Malay but not in his dictionary and vice versa. These seem generally to be quasi-unit classifiers, e.g. *potong* 'slice'.

analysis of the preceding section has not been carried out but because in many instances the same classifier has both 'true' unit uses as well as the marginal meanings which would be excluded from consideration as numeral classifier constructions in a non-classifier language. For example, Mandarin *chang* stated generally to be a classifier for fairly extensive flat objects is used with 'paper' where it is to be translated as 'sheet' and with 'table' where there is no English translation equivalent involved. Words like 'grain' are widely used both in the meaning of small particle and as a true classifier for small round or even large round objects. Indeed, these two classes of borderline items play a prominent role as sources for true classifiers in the course of the dynamic development of such systems. Where necessary the two foregoing types will be referred to as 'quasi-unit counters'.

For purposes of the present study the terminology 'unit counter' will continue to be employed with the understanding that quasi-unit counters are not included.

The discussion up to this point indicates that the languages commonly called numeral classifier languages can be considered from two points of view, either as involving the overt expression of a particular mode of quantification, or as imposing a classification on the head nouns in numerical constructions. In effect, such languages may be said to belong to two typological classes simultaneously and, in this, there is no logical contradiction since anything can belong to more than one class simultaneously. Both of these approaches are legitimate and both are utilized in the broader study of which this is a part. However, the former of these will turn out to be more relevant for questions of type genesis while the latter becomes valuable in considering further stages of dynamic development. In the light of our preliminary definition in terms of quantification we now turn to a more detailed consideration of the problem of type origin.

We might state our aim in terms of possible answers to the following question. What are the initial conditions in the form of other structural characteristics characteristic of languages which develop numeral classifiers? In putting our question in this form we are, at the most, asking for necessary, not sufficient conditions, that is we are not in the position to assert that, given certain linguistic properties, a language will inevitably develop classifiers. This is surely beyond our powers. Even the more modest goal of necessary conditions, that is conditions which must be present for classifiers to arise, might be too ambitious if by this we mean a single set of conditions. We may indeed have to deal with more than one type of origin. But this in turn should help understanding of these systems, since different origins usually imply different subtypological characteristics.

Our preliminary definition in terms of overt expression of unit counting and our observation regarding the virtually complete syntactic identity of all counting and measuring constructions in these languages leads quite directly to a hypothesis which is negative in form. In spite of this it represents a kind of progress because it narrows the class of languages which have properties relevant to the rise of numeral classifier systems.

It is our working hypothesis that unit counters are modelled after the construction of mass nouns which cannot stand directly with numerals but require a measure or quasi-unit counter as an intermediary. Now such non-unit counters are found in virtually all the languages in the areas and linguistic stocks with which most linguists are concerned and it might be thought that they are universal. In fact, this seems not to be so. In particular there are a considerable number of Amerind languages as well as some elsewhere, for example, in New Guinea which do not have measure constructions. Numerals occur directly both with nouns designating mass as well as countable objects. Hence no model exists in these languages for the development we postulate. Whorf (1941: 80) describes such a situation for Hopi. Unlike English with its grammatical distinction of mass and count nouns, Hopi "has a formally distinguished class of nouns. But this class has no formally distinguished class of mass nouns. . . . One says not 'a glass of water' but *kə·yí* 'a water' . . . not 'a piece of meat' but *sik$^{w}$í* 'a meat'."

There is evidently here a correlation between language and culture but not, I submit, in Whorf's terms of the philosophic non-existence of a Western worldview based on the Aristotelian dichotomy of form and matter. It is rather the absence of precise measures and their relatively infrequent employment which allows them to remain unexpressed since they can be deduced from context. This happens in special instances in languages like English in restricted situations. Thus, in a restaurant, one can say 'We want three coffees and one tea' and it will be understood that the unexpressed measures are 'cups'.

Although an evolutionary factor is involved here, it would be well to note in passing that the absence of a sufficient body of contrastive measures to require an explicit terminology is not correlated in any simple way with economic stages. While it is striking that Mayan and Nahuatl figure among the Amerind numeral-classifying languages we also find them in such languages as that of the Yurok of California who have no domesticated plants or animals. The absence of agriculture does not preclude under certain circumstances a considerable accumulation of material goods and, as in the case of the Yurok, the existence of a standard measure of value (dentalium shells).[17]

The foregoing hypothesis can also be stated as a synchronic implicational

[17] The Yurok have been described as 'primitive capitalists'—see Goldschmidt 1951.

universal. The presence of unit counters implies the presence of measure and other non-unit counter type constructions.[18] To suppose then, diachronically, that there might be a development of unit counters in a language without overtly expressed non-unit counter types would be to hypothesize the genesis of what would be, if this is valid, a non-existent type.

We turn now to that vast majority of the world's languages which have measure constructions as well as various non-unit and quasi-unit count constructions. They therefore by hypothesis possess a model in accordance with which unit classifiers might come into existence. The question is whether there are any properties in addition to these which are relevant to such a development.

A number of synchronic generalizations can be made about numeral classifier languages some of which will be treated in due course in this paper. There is one, however, which is merely statistical, that is, has exceptions although it holds very widely. It will, I believe, shed light on the problem under discussion. Indeed it is precisely the study of the exceptions in this case which proves most useful.

Numeral classifier languages generally do not have compulsory expression of nominal plurality, but at most facultative expression. This has already been observed by Sanches (1971) in an unpublished paper. She states her hypothesis as follows: "If a language includes in its basic mode of forming quantitative expressions numeral classifiers, then it will also have facultative expression of the plural. In other words it will *not* have obligatory marking of the plural on nouns." Sanches makes an additional valuable observation, namely, that the classified noun itself is normally singular. She includes in this such instances as English 'cattle' in 'head of cattle'. As will appear in the discussion, it is advantageous to reinterpret this observation in the sense not of the singular but in that of lack of marking for number.

In addition to the handful of possible exceptions, some of them valid, others marginal, noted in her paper there are a few others from languages which happen not to figure in her sample, e.g. Ossete and certain modern Arabic dialects. Those latter are of particular interest since numerical classifiers do not occur in Classical Arabic. Hence by studying these examples we can perhaps develop some insight into the conditions of their appearance. I have noted two fairly extensive systems in modern Arabic dialects, in Oman-Zanzibar and in Egyptian Arabic.[19] The present discussion

[18] By measure construction is meant here those of the type quantity + measure + noun. Amerind languages which lack this construction still express measure by using a verb 'to measure' with a numeral, the precise kind of measure being deducible from context.

[19] For Oman-Zanzibar Arabic see Reichardt 1894, especially p. 85, and for Egyptian Arabic, Mitchell 1956: 94. Brockelmann (1908–13, II: 280), in addition to Omani, gives an example

is confined essentially to Oman-Zanzibar which will hereafter be called Omani.

In this form of Arabic as described by Reichardt, a number of animals (described as *schlachtbar*), root crops, and the word for 'slave' are classified by *ra:s* 'head', a number of 'horn-shaped' edibles by *qarn* 'horn', fruits by *šo:b*, and 'flowers' by *'o:d* 'branch'. The system is therefore fairly extensive.

In Omani, which has no case system, corresponding to the classical construction of 3-10 with the genitive plural, the plural is used with these numbers. With the other numbers except 'two' which employs either the dual or the number 'two' with the plural, the singular is used, reflecting two classical constructions, one involving the accusative singular and the other the genitive singular.

In the Omani classifying construction the numeral precedes the classifier, agrees with it in gender, and governs it for number in accordance with the above rules. In this, the construction is entirely like that of a numeral with an unclassified noun. In the classifier construction the classified noun follows the classifier and is not affected by the syntax of the preceding construction. Examples with *finda:l* 'potato(es)', classified by *ra:s* 'head' will illustrate these rules. It should be noted that with the singular and dual the numerals 'one' and 'two' are not commonly employed. Thus we have *ra:s finda:l* 'one potato, a potato', *ra:se:n* (dual of *ra:s*) *finda:l* 'two potatoes', *thala:thit rwa:s* (plural of *ra:s*) *finda:l* 'three potatoes', *'ashri:n ra:s finda:l* 'twenty potatoes'.

What of *finda:l* which remains unchanged throughout? It is singular in form but is a collective and would in other contexts be translated 'potatoes'. In fact practically all of the words listed by Reichardt as taking this construction are collectives.[20] On the other hand not all collectives take this construction. The alternative corresponds to the use of the so-called 'noun of unity' (*ʔismu 'l waḥdati*) of Classical Arabic. This is in Classical Arabic a formation from the collective by the suffixation of the feminine suffix *-at(un)* (Omani *-a*, *-e*) with a regular sound plural in *a:t(un)*, Omani *a:t*.[21] Where the collective has

---

from Maltese in which *ruḥ* 'soul' is used in counting persons and 'head' for oxen and sheep in Modern Syriac.

[20] Except *'abi:d* 'slaves', which is an ordinary broken plural. There are several 'psychological' parallels to this Omani treatment of 'slave' as the only personal term with a classifier and in fact the same classifier as that used with animals. Vinogradov (1934: 94) states that in upper-class Russian speech of the eighteenth century the collective numerals were used with words designating humans only when members of the lower social classes were involved. One would say *dva arxiereja* 'two archbishops' and not e.g. *dvoje arxierejov* with the collective numeral. In the Early Archaic Chinese text in Dobson 1962 in which classifiers are optional, it may be noted that the classifier for persons tends to be used with words for subordinates, slaves, and captives.

[21] Classical Arabic substantives are conventionally cited in the numerative singular indefinite, usually ending in *-un*. I enclose this suffix in parentheses.

a noun of unity it is required both in Classical and Omani Arabic that it be used with numbers, the plural with 3-10 and the singular and the dual, usually without a numeral, for one and two respectively. An example of this alternative construction is Omani *be'u:d* 'gnats' (coll.) which may not occur with a numeral. Based on the noun of unity *be'u:da* we have *be'u:da* 'one gnat'; *thala:th be'u:da:t* 'three gnats', etc. In at least one instance there is a choice of the two constructions. From *baqar* 'cattle' there is a noun of unity *baqra* 'a cow' but it can also be classified by *ra:s* in which case the collective, of course, is used. Thus 'one cow' is either *baqra* or *ra:s baqar* and 'three cows' is either *thala:th baqra:t* or *thala:thit rwa:s baqar*. In Omani the basic consideration is that a numeral cannot occur directly with a collective. Either a classifying noun, itself a non-collective, is interposed and is in direct syntactic construction with the numeral or the 'noun of unity' is used in its stead.

In Classical Arabic as in Omani there were collectives which did not have a noun of unity. Like other collectives they could not be governed directly by a number. The Classical grammarians prescribe that in such instances the preposition *min* 'from' must intervene. Thus with *'ibl*, a collective meaning 'camels', one had to say *thala:thatu mina 'l 'ibli* 'three of the camels'.[22] What has happened in Omani and to a certain extent elsewhere is that the construction with *min* has been replaced by the use of a non-collective, we might say an individualized noun, as a classifier with the numeral while the collective follows as a kind of opposition.

The term 'singulative' was first employed in Celtic by Zeuss, for the derivational formation which corresponds in these languages to the Arabic 'noun of unity'. We may then talk of a 'three term system' in such instances in which a collective which cannot be used with numerals is opposed to a singulative with its own singular and plural (or, in addition dual as in Arabic). The plural of the singulative is thus distinct from the collective in such systems.[23]

In connection with the main thesis of the modelling of count nouns after mass nouns in quantitative constructions, it may be noted that there is an obvious analogy between mass nouns and collectives. In three term systems, the collective, in addition to its central use in distinguishing genus from

[22] The example is from Gaudefroy-Demombynes (1952: 372). He translates 'trois (individus) des chameaux'.

[23] It is of interest to note that such three-term systems also appear in Niger-Congo noun-class languages as in Banyun and the Mombar dialect of Senufo (Sauvageot 1967) in which nouns may appear in three classes, a singular, a 'limited' plural, and an 'unlimited plural'. With numerals only the former of these plurals may be used in Banyun which is described by Sauvageot as 'chiffrable' as distinguished from the unlimited plural which is 'pas chiffrable'. Sauvageot translates the unlimited plural of the word for a 'leaf' by collective 'le feuillage'.

individual for organic species and human ethnic groupings, tends to be used also in some instances for nouns designating materials and even liquids, in which case the singulative designates quasi-units in the sense described earlier. For instance, in Classical Arabic there are examples such as *khashab(un)* 'wood' with *khashabat(un)* as its noun of unity meaning 'a piece of wood' and similar examples in modern dialects. In Welsh alongside *dwfr* 'water' one finds a singulative *diferyn* 'a drop of water'.

In Classical Arabic there were two other systems besides that of the 'noun of unity' whose essential similarity with the noun of unity was noted by the grammarians. The noun of unity is only used with non-humans. For humans, in particular ethnic and occupational groups, from a basic unmarked collective there was derived a singulative by suffixing *-iyy(un)* used in a manner exactly parallel to the noun of unity, e.g. *ru:m(un)* 'Greeks (coll.)'; *ru:miyy(un)* 'a Greek', *thala:thatu ru:miyyi:na* 'three Greeks'. In addition the so-called *nomina vicis* (*ʔismu 'l marrati*) were derived from verbal nouns by the feminine singular suffix exactly as with the noun of unity to derive nouns designating individual acts. This also occurs in Omani, e.g. *ḍöḥk* 'laughter', *ḍöḥka* 'a laugh'.

A basically similar three term system is found in Russian in the period centering about the sixteenth century and has been described particularly by Unbegaun (1935). It developed on the basis of a Pan-Slavic collective formation in which yet another method of avoiding a direct construction between numerals and collectives had evolved, namely the use of a derivative of the numeral, the so-called collective numeral, governing the genitive of the collective.[24] In the Russian of the period under consideration there was once more a three term system in which as an alternative to the more general Slavic use of the collective numeral, a singulative could occur with the ordinary (non-collective numerals). Most of the collectives were declined in the plural rather than the singular. Alongside these collectives there were singulatives either by derivation or sometimes with lexically distinct forms. As in modern Russian numbers larger than four governed the genitive plural in nominative constructions or nominative-accusative with inanimates, and in the other cases agreed with the plural in case. In these instances if the non-collective numerals were used, they required the plural of the singulative

[24] With this we may compare the Classical Arabic construction with *min* 'from' cited above. It is of interest to note that Classical Arabic lexicons quote examples of *raʔs* 'head' and collectives without nouns of unity designating animals and root crops but with *min* intervening. Hence this is a kind of transition between *min*+genitive prescribed by the Arab grammarians and *ra:s*+numerated noun of Omani and other dialects. An example cited in Freytag (1830–35) is *raʔsun mina 'lkhaili* lit. 'a head from the horses' in which *khail(un)* is a collective which also occurs in Omani with *ra:s* (*ra:s khe:l*).

which in fact had no employment except in constructions with numbers. Where the collective was grammatically a singular as e.g. *bratĭja* 'brothers' (fem. sing.) the collective numeral could not be employed. As in Arabic there was a special singulative suffix, in this case *-in* used for ethnic and occupational names.

For example, there was a collective with plural inflection *krestĭjane* 'peasants' (coll.) with a singulative *krestĭjanin*. For 'five peasants' in the nominative one could have either *pjatero krestĭjan*, the collective numeral with the genitive of the collective noun, or *pjat' krestĭjaninov*, the ordinary (non-collective) numeral with the genitive plural of the singulative. However, as noted by Unbegaun, the first construction was uncommon. The most commonly employed was actually a third alternative for numerical constructions with personals and this corresponds to the use of an individualized classifying noun in Omani. In this construction the noun *čelověk* 'person' occurred preceding the ordinary non-collective cardinal number, followed by the personal collective in the dependent genitive. Thus alongside, and in fact more often than the two alternative constructions given above, for expressing 'five peasants' one could have *pjat' čelověk krestĭjan*. The word *čelověk* was itself a singulative corresponding to the collective *ljudi* 'people'. This relationship of course still survives in contemporary Russian in that only *čelověk* may occur with numbers and its use in the plural is confined to numeral constructions.

To sum up, what is common to the Russian and Arabic examples (and others, e.g., Celtic, that might have been considered) is that, where there is a system of collectives, the direct construction of the numeral with a collective is avoided. Among the alternatives is the use of one or more non-collectives in construction with the numeral and more loosely joined syntactically to the collective which is in apposition or is a dependent (partitive) genitive.[25] In view of these and similar instances we may suggest as a hypothesis that when a language is an exception to the implicational universal that numeral classifiers imply the absence of compulsory plurals, what is involved is a subsystem of such a singular/plural language within which the basic opposition is collective/singulative rather than singular/plural.

A collective is sometimes defined as a noun which is grammatically singular but semantically plural. An example is Bielfeldt (1961: 296) in his grammar of Old Church Slavonic who defines collective noun as follows,

[25] A further method of individuation besides those mentioned in the text is exemplified by Ibibio (Kaufman 1972) in which a phrasal compound of an individualizing noun plus the enumerated noun occurs, e.g. *ákpɔ ífíà kèèt* 'stalk (of) firewood one'. Cf. English 'one rice grain' = 'one grain of rice'.

"Kollektivum-Subst., das in der grammatischen Form des Sg. eine Mehrheit von Gegenständen bezeichnet." However, the notion of collective in the Arabic and Russian instances just considered and which is relevant to the present problem does not conform to this kind of formulation which seeks to define collective in terms of the categories of singular and plural, that is, as singular in form but plural in meaning.

Regarding the first of these criteria, singularity of form, we have seen that in sixteenth-century Russian most of the collectives have plural inflection. It would seem in fact that the typical life history of the collective is that it starts out as a singular but with plural agreements or variation between singular and plural in more remote syntactic constructions and tends to become a morphological plural in the course of time. This is an interesting topic which will not be pursued here.

In regard to meaning, if this is simply plural, then wherein does the distinction lie between the quantitative reference of the plural of the singulative and the collective? It would seem that the 'true collective' is semantically neither singular nor plural. It is a transnumeral category which is neutral in respect to number as opposed to the singulative which involves countability or, as stated by Unbegaun (1935: 262), it implies "l'opposition entre la collectivité et l'unité extraite de cette collectivité."

The generic noun (*ʔismu 'ljansiyyu*) of Arabic, whose noun of unity is derived from it either by *-at*(*un*) as in *tamr*(*un*) 'dates (collective)', *tamrat*(*un*) 'a date' or by *-iyy*(*un*) as in *ru:m* 'Greeks (collective)', *ru:miyy*(*un*) 'a Greek', is excluded by the famous thirteenth-century grammarian Ibn al-Ḥājib from his definition of plural since as he says, "the expression is not constituted to express units but what contains the special quiddity (*ma:hiyyat*(*un*) lit. 'whatness') whether it be singular or plural." Concerning this passage, the commentator Raḍīuddīn says, ". . . to which we will add that the generic noun is applied to the few and the many. . . . So that if you eat a date, or two dates or deal with a Greek or two Greeks you may still say *'akaltu 'ttmra* ['I ate the dates (coll.)'] and *'a:maltu 'rru:ma* ['I dealt with the Greeks (collect.)'] whereas if they were plural this would not be allowable, as *rija:l*(*un*) [the ordinary broken plural of *rajul*(*un*) 'man'] is not applied to 'a man' or 'two men'."[26] The lack of relevance of specific number to collectives is also expressed by Maretić, a native speaker of Serbo-Croatian, a language with extensive and productive collective formations. In his grammar of Serbo-Croatian (1910: 450) he says, "Therefore one cannot say, for example, *deset kamenja* ['ten stones (coll.)'] or *petnaest perja* ['fifteen feathers (coll.)'] etc., but instead *deset kamena*, *petnaest pera* [i.e.

[26] These passages are quoted from Howell (1880–1900: 1054–55).

with the gen. plural singulative], because when someone mentions a definite number, he then thinks of individual things; but for that which forms a collectivity [*što je u hrpi*, lit. 'is in a heap'] the number is not known."

It should be noted that in English the most commonly cited example of a numeral classifier construction 'head of cattle' involves a collective. There exists in English what might be called a miniature system of collective/singulative, e.g. Irish//Irishman/Irishmen, police//policeman/policemen. I have tried the following sentence on a number of native speakers of English. "Last night I was picked up by the police." They all denied that they would be surprised to learn that only one policeman was involved. My own reaction to constructions of numbers with these collectives is that small numbers seem definitely ungrammatical but fairly large numbers seem fairly natural. A meeting of twenty police or one hundred faculty seems acceptable, but the phrase 'a meeting of three police' is definitely strange.[27]

The development of the construction *čelověk* in Russian with collectives and the fairly extensive system found in Omani and elsewhere in Arabic suggests that classifiers in the large majority of classifier languages without plural inflections are performing the same individualizing function as both classifiers and singulative affixes in languages with collectives. We should expect then that in the typical classifier language, the classifiable noun when not accompanied by a classifier should show the same lack of numerical determination that we have found with collectives in languages like Arabic.

Emeneau (1951: 85) describes the Vietnamese noun when unaccompanied by a classifier in terms quite reminiscent of Raḍīuddīn in regard to the generic noun of Arabic: "A non-numerated substantive phrase . . . lacks any indication of number or individuation; that is when there is no explicit indication of number, a noun is entirely free of reference to the number category. For example, *tôi muốn mua sách* 'I want to buy book(s)'. There is absolutely no indication how many books are intended."

A considerable number of classifier languages (e.g. many Iranian and Turkic languages, Korean) have what are generally described as plural affixes. However, closer examination seems to show that in almost every instance the 'unmarked' singular is in fact a form which, like the collective in languages with a compulsory plural, is non-committal in regard to number.[28] For an

[27] Actually there exists a variety of uses of collectives which should be distinguished. These are heterogeneous and all that they have in common is that they do not involve the results of counting. These uses include true generic uses in generalizations, 'hypothetical' uses in such sentences as 'He went hunting for deer', and references to actual collections which are either so large as not to be practically countable or potentially countable but not actually counted, or counted where the numerical result is irrelevant. This topic is not pursued in this paper.

[28] Possible exceptions include Ossete, Pashto, and Tlingit.

explicit statement to this effect, parallel to those in regard to the other linguistic types we have been considering, reference may be made to Kononov (1960: 75) who states concerning Uzbek that words like 'girl' and 'bird' without any grammatical indication do not contain any indication of number. They represent an undivided (*nečlenimoje*) totality. When the suffix of plurality *-lar* is added they become a totality consisting of individual members (*členimoje*). What is hypothesized, then, is that in the usual classifier language (i.e. without inflection for number), classifiable nouns in their isolated form, that is when not accompanied by a classifier or a plural marker, are like collectives in their semantic non-specification of number and in their avoidance of a direct number construction. The classifier is an individualizer which performs the same function as a singulative derivational affix in languages with the collective/singulative opposition.

In two grammatical descriptions of classifier languages I have found a point of view similar to the one expressed here. One is Dobson's work on Early Archaic Chinese in which he states (1962: 28): "It is not a feature of 'substantival quality' that it distinguishes class and member, between the genus itself and 'an instance of' or instances of. . . . In EAC certain of the distinctions are made when a noun occurs in a syntagma in which the elements are distributed as enumerated noun/number/quantification. . . ." By quantification is here indicated what is usually called a classifier.

Another statement is that of Grjunberg (1963: 46) in his grammar of North Azerbaijanian Tat, an Iranian language: "As has been already indicated, what is formally in Tat the singular is the expression of an undivided multitude (*množestvo*) of objects and almost always has a particular kind of collective meaning. . . . In order to supply such a substantive expression with a quantitative meaning by means of a number, it is first necessary to select a unit for counting. For this reason the numeral does not usually stand immediately before the substantive. Between them one places a word indicating such a unit of calculation."

If the general point of view expressed here is taken in at least a working hypothesis, one of the further problems to be considered is the following. It was seen that in Arabic and Russian, the use of a noun as a classifier was but one of a series of functional alternatives such as a derived singulative of the enumerated noun or a special derived form of the numeral. One might conjecture that the choice of a noun itself as an individuator rests on the fact that, as a general rule, these languages have a very weak or even non-existent development of derivation. In general they use syntagmatic structures consisting of full words. This, it would seem, is what is meant by the traditional notion of isolating languages as a type.

We have seen what might be called, anthropomorphically, the aversion of collectives to direct construction with a numeral and the intervention of an individuated noun, the classifier, as one of the devices to avoid this direct confrontation. This aversion has, therefore, as its natural counterpart, the corresponding attraction to the classifier and an immediate constituent structure in which the numeral goes directly with the classifier while the numeral + classifier combination as a whole enters into a more remote construction with the enumerated noun. In languages with substantival inflection for number and a singulative/collective opposition it was noted that the numeral governs the classifier in respect to such categories as number and case, while the enumerated noun is in apposition to or stands in an adnominal construction (essentially partitive) to this combination.

This arrangement underlies a number of synchronic generalizations that may be made regarding classifier languages proper. We may summarize these as follows.

1. Of the six possible word orders among the three elements Q (quantifier), Cl (classifier), N (enumerated noun), only four occur: (1) Q-Cl-N; (2) N-Q-Cl; (3) Cl-Q-N; (4) N-Cl-Q.[29] The two non-occurring orders Cl-N-Q and Q-N-Cl have the property that the quantifier and the classifier are separated by the head noun.

2. There is frequent variation within languages between orders 1 and 2 or between 3 and 4. In other words the relative order of quantifier and classifier remains unchanged but the combination of the two may vary between placement before or after the head noun. The rare variation between Q-Cl and Cl-Q is of three kinds. In Bodo, a Sino-Tibetan language, there are two distinct subsystems, the indigenous (Cl-Q) and that borrowed from Assamese (Q-Cl). In Bengali, according to Chatterji (1926: 777), the usual order Q-Cl may be reversed to express numerical approximation. In most Thai languages the Q-Cl order generally holds but the order with the number 'one' is Cl-Q.

3. The connection between the numeral and the classifier is so close prosodically that they may have one accent, in which case it is on the numeral and there may be fused forms such that analysis becomes difficult. In this case, e.g. the Micronesian languages, the numerals are generally said to form a number of series. In many languages, analysts consider the numeral + classifier construction to be a single word.

4. The Q-Cl combination may often be separated in certain constructions from the enumerated noun.

[29] Q for 'quantifier' is used here because not only numerals but also the numerical interrogative 'how many?' and less frequently indefinite quantifiers such as 'few', 'many' occur in the same position as the numeral in classifier constructions. An apparent exception is Ibibio with Cl-Q-N (see footnote 25 above). Note, however, that the numeral here is really in construction not with the enumerated noun as such but with the phrasal compound.

5. The anaphoric construction of Q-Cl without overt expression of the noun occurs in all of these languages.

These facts and the general structuring which they exhibit have a bearing on the question of the interpretation of those instances cited in an earlier section of this paper of nouns which commonly appear without classifiers. These include words like 'day', 'month', 'time' (in phrases corresponding to English 'three times'), 'foot', 'mile', and currency expressions. As can be seen, these can all be interpreted as measures. In addition the words for 'person' and 'thing' may sometimes occur both with other items as classifiers of very general scope but also in their lexical meaning without previous mention in the context (e.g. for 'person' in many Thai languages). In these instances, then, where one might have expected 'person' to act as its own classifier we merely find the translational equivalent 'three person' rather than repetition, e.g. 'person three-person'.

Two interpretations of these phenomena have been offered by writers of grammars sometimes regarding the same language. For example Burling (1961: 266) in his grammar of Garo analyzes these words as classifiers without head nouns while noting that in previous grammars of the language they were analyzed as head nouns without classifiers. Burling's analysis would seem to be more justified. In such instances the same close syntactic construction between numeral and 'unclassified noun' is formed as between the numeral and the numeral classifier in the tripartite construction. Cuna (Sherzer 1976) provides here a particularly striking confirmation. As often elsewhere the classifier forms a single word with the numeral while the head noun is separate. This is shown here by the stress pattern, e.g. *óme wár-po* 'woman classifier-two'. In expressions such as 'one day', 'day' is seen to be a classifier from the stress pattern *ípa-k$^w$en* 'day one' rather than **ípa k$^w$én*.

Moreover, where the word order is noun + numeral classifier, these phrases invariably have numeral + 'unclassified noun' rather than the opposite order and similarly where the tripartite order is classifier + numeral + noun the order of these phrases is 'unclassified' noun + numeral. It could be maintained that in measure phrases, the place of the head noun is essentially taken by a verb; it is the verbal action that is being quantified. For example, 'he traveled two days' is equivalent to 'he performed two days of travel'.[30] There are both measure and count verbal constructions. For most languages a single lexical item, the equivalent of the English word 'time' is used with numerals or a special set of numerals is used (e.g. Latin), but another alternative which is found, for example, in Arabic, is the 'cognate' verbal noun meaning a single instance of an act and which may then co-occur with

[30] A few linguists have used such terms as verbal measures, e.g. Smalley (1961).

numerals. It was noted earlier in passing that in Arabic the so-called *maṣdar* or 'infinitive' is a verbal noun which may then take the same feminine suffix of the noun of unity when subject to count construction and that the Arabic grammarians noted the essential parallelism, collective noun : noun of unity = verbal noun (*maṣdar*) : *nomen vicis*. Similar phenomena occur in languages without the collective/singulative contrast. In Bodo there are examples such as *pay-tam pay* 'comings-three came'. There is also the use of nouns which are neither general for all verbs like 'time' in English nor cognate verbal nouns, e.g. Mandarin *kànle liáng-yěn* 'looked two eyes' = 'looked twice'.

The logical possibility exists, then, that a language might have a system of verbal classifiers each of which would be used with a particular class of verbs and an accompanying numeral. However, this possibility never seems to be realized in the systematic way in which it so often is for nouns. The distinction between mass and count then applies to verbal action and is related to aspect. Durative : punctual = measure : count, 'He has been laughing for two minutes', versus 'He laughed twice'.[31] There is the widespread phenomenon of 'plural verbs' marking plural action as against a single act. Once again the abstract possibility of incorporating count distinction beyond the singular/plural dichotomy in the verb exists, e.g. a verbal form meaning 'to perform X three times' which does not seem to occur anywhere.

The 'attraction' of the individuated noun to numerical expression, as contrasted with the 'aversion' of the collective noun, has already been discussed. The relation of 'measures' to numerical expression which we have hypothesized as a model for count construction is in a sense even closer than that of the individuated noun and is somewhat different in nature. They are syncategorematic with quantifiers in that they have no reality without them. A word like 'ounce' when used, not merely mentioned, has its *raison d'être* in being accompanied by a quantitative expression. Only perhaps in metalinguistic discourse—e.g. *an ounce is a measure noun* or *the Imperial gallon is larger than the usual American gallon*—can it be abstracted from quantity. Ounces are not counted like apples. If I have a set of six apples, I can ask about physical characteristics of the apples in abstraction from their number, e.g. their color, but not so with 6 ounces. I can imagine a large finite number of all past, present, and future apples but I cannot number ounces in the same way. Similarly, when a physical object like a cup is being used as

[31] For a discussion of the mass/count distinction in relation to verbs cf. Leech (1969: 134–35). He notes that ". . . not only noun meanings but verb meanings can include the factor 'countability'."

a measure, *three cups full of tea* is different from *three cups of tea*. I might indeed use the same cup three times. Not being physical objects they are not susceptible of the distinction between collective and individual. A further example of the contrast between abstract measures and concrete objects is the difference between monetary value and actual coins or bills. *Twenty-five cents* and *a quarter* as a coin are not the same thing.

This is perhaps why measures in many languages with inflected singular and plural tend to use measures in the unmarked singular. Note the distinction in German between *zehn Pfennig* as an amount and *zehn Pfennige* with the plural of the noun as ten coins each worth one Pfennig.

This brings us to a final consideration regarding substantival number in the numeral classifier constructions. As one might expect in languages of this kind, with singular and plural the number frequently has the same construction with classifiers as it does with other nouns, e.g. plural with 3-10 in Omani Arabic. However, in classifier languages without inflectional plurals neither counters nor measures ever take plural markers and, unlike typical noun class systems, the classifiers themselves practically never vary lexically for number. The only exception I have encountered is in Guaymi, a Chibchan language (Alphonse 1956: 13), in which *i* 'person' is used as a classifier with 'one' and *ni* 'people' with numbers greater than one.

In languages in which the demonstratives occur with classifiers there seems invariably to be a single 'plural' classifier replacing the ordinary classifier but only in the demonstrative construction, not in the numerical construction. For example in Mandarin the classifier *běn* required with *shu* 'book' with any number (e.g. *i běn shu* 'one book', *san běn shu* 'three books') occurs with the demonstrative also (*chè běn shu* 'this book') but only in the singular. For all nouns, the ordinary classifier is replaced by *hsie* 'some' to form the plural with demonstratives, *chè hsie shu* 'these books'. Basically similar are the Bengali, Assamese, etc. 'definitives' which are suffixed to the noun to make them definite as well as occurring with the numerals as classifiers, e.g. Bengali *pãnc-khana boi* 'five flat-object book', *boi-khana* 'the book'. In the plural definite all classifiers are replaced by the plural *gulo*, e.g. *boi-gulo* 'the books'. This plural marker cannot occur with numbers. Unit counters, then, behave very much like the measures which have been hypothesized here as their models. The notion of 'unit' seems to take on this same abstractness which characterizes measures and tends to make them take an unmarked invariable form with numbers. For the counters, whose lexical source is generally transparent, are like the singulative in containing two semantic moments, the concrete lexical meaning 'head', 'piece', 'grain', or whatever it may be, and the notion of 'unit of counting' as such. It is evidently the latter that tends to assume the same abstractness of meaning that is inherent in measures.

Finally, in order to place the present paper within the framework of the more general study of which it is a part, four other basic topics will be briefly considered and in some instances hypotheses will be outlined.

1. From the fact that certain languages have developed the numeral classifier system, it by no means follows that it must have appeared in a single step in all numerical constructions and compulsorily. There is some evidence that it tends to appear first as focus particularly in answers to quantitative WH- questions and later spreads to other constructions.

There is indeed a general problem here in relation to the main thesis of this paper. If some method of individualization with specific quantity is required where the noun has a general unmarked form, how is it that languages may have certain syntactic constructions requiring this and others not, and how can the construction be optional in other languages? This is part of the broader problem as to why the implicational relation between classifiers and lack of compulsory number in the substantive is just that and not a mutual implication, that is, a logical equivalence. There seem to be languages without compulsory number inflection, which likewise have measure constructions and yet do not have classifiers. In other words, as explained in the initial section of this paper, we have at best necessary but not sufficient conditions.

2. Another basic problem relates to the lexical sources of classifiers and their semantic relation to the head nouns. There seem here to be three main types: (a) superordinate terms such as 'person' as a classifier for humans and 'tree' for individual 'species'; (b) items in one-to-one relation to the objects being counted, among the most common of which are 'head' for animates and 'trunk' or 'stalk' for trees; (c) words which themselves designate arbitrary or insignificant units like 'piece', 'grain', etc. It was seen earlier that these exist quite generally in languages which have measures and having somewhat equivocal status, they are capable of spreading semantically to structured items. For non-structured units these terms often relate to the verbal action required to produce them, analogous to English *slice* in *slices of bread.*

3. This last example brings up a further major area of investigation, the semantic changes of the classifiers in terms of changes in the nouns that they classify. Here a thoroughgoing comparison with semantic changes of class indicators in other types of numeral classification systems is of value. These processes are in many respects similar to those involved in ordinary lexical semantic change. However, they are, so to speak, more unrestrained in their capacity of generalization because in the vast majority of instances they

are semantically redundant. The rôle of shape in classification has been singled out for particular attention by some analysts. It is indeed a recurrent phenomenon that we find classifiers which co-occur with groups of nouns which have as their common semantic feature one of the following: (a) long narrow object (one-dimensional), often subdivided into cylindrical and non-cylindrical; (b) flat object (two dimensional); (c) round object (three-dimensional). This latter tends to include large bulky objects of whatever shape. These classifiers apply primarily to inanimates but they sometimes include various categories of animates. For example 'snakes' or larger quadrupeds are often classified as long, narrow objects.

Insofar as classification is applied basically to countable, concrete objects it is not difficult to see that semantic criteria of shape provide the broadest possibilities for generalization as being that which otherwise heterogeneous physical objects have in common. In many instances the same lexical item used as a classifier has in diverse languages become one of the basic shape classifiers, notably 'stalk' or 'trunk', an item in one-to-one relation with plants and trees, for long narrow objects and 'grain', a 'quasi-unit classifier' for round objects.

The frequent occurrence of what is sometimes called the general classifier is to be interpreted in dynamic terms as the ultimate result of semantic generalization of one of the widespread classifiers, generally one of the shape classifiers and most typically the round object classifier to the point at which it not only itself co-occurs with a very large and heterogeneous group of nouns, but may be used as an alternative to almost any other classifier. There is evidence in some instances regarding the diachronic expansion of these classifiers. Often the spread of such classifiers is confined to inanimates. For example, in regard to Vietnamese, Thompson (1965: 196) notes that "In modern Vietnamese the general classifier *cái* is coming to be used more and more at the expense of other specific classifiers, especially with nouns denoting inanimate objects which in traditional usage go with one of the rarer classifiers. . . ." In other instances, e.g. Mandarin *gè*, the general classifier is used also with persons.

There is an enlightening parallel here with the process of consolidation and simplification found in noun-class languages. In Niger-Congo languages there is a tendency for one of the non-personal classes to become the 'general' class paralleling in its semantics that of the general classifier in heterogeneity of meaning, statistical frequency, and tendency to be used in place of other non-personal classes.

A similar phenomenon is found in what might be called possessive classificational systems. In many Oceanic and Amerind languages the very common contrast between intimate and non-intimate possession has been elaborated through the split of the latter into classes based on the use of various classifying nouns which take the possessive affixes in place of the noun designating the possessed item which is then placed in apposition. For example, in Mataco, a language of the Chaco, 'my dog' is, literally, 'my-animal dog' and 'my house' is 'my-property house'. Such systems also tend to develop a 'general' class. For example, in Sonsorol, a language of Micronesia which like many Oceanic languages has simultaneously possessive and numeral classifier systems which are independent of each other, one of the noun bases of the possessive system *ja-* is described as signifying "general possession, not covered by any other class" (Capell 1948: 13).

4. One of the lines of development of such systems is by syntactic spread to other constructions than the numeral classifier construction proper. The synchronic universal seems to hold that whenever a numeral classifier construction is also used in non-quantifier constructions, the construction with demonstratives is one of these, often the only one. The use of numeral classifiers with demonstratives occurs in a number of geographically separate areas and some of these instances at least must be historically independent, e.g. Thai, Vietnamese, Modern Chinese, Bengali, Nauru (Micronesia), and Kiriwina (Trobriand Islands east of New Guinea and geographically distant from Nauru). Demonstratives would seem to have, like numbers, a special relation to individuated non-collective expressions but the details of this process remain to be investigated.

Throughout this paper I have emphasized the tentativeness of the conclusions advanced and that it is to be viewed more in the light of a progress report than a definitive statement. Its value, it may be hoped, is to show that the method of dynamic typological comparison can help in investigating significant problems which have, on the whole, not been discussed very much in recent linguistics, and can also, by the consideration of empirical linguistic data from a great variety of languages at least, open the possibility of rational solutions to such traditional problems as the origin of gender and noun classificational systems in general.

## References Cited

Alphonse, E. S. 1956. *Guaymí Grammar and Dictionary*. Washington.

Bataillon, M. 1932. *Langue d'uvea*. Paris.

Bielfeldt, H. H. 1961. *Altslawische Grammatik*. Halle.

Brockelmann, C. 1908–13. *Grundriss der vergleichenden Grammatik der semitischen Sprachen*. Berlin.

Burling, R. 1961. *A Garo Grammar*. Poona.

———. 1965. "How to choose a Burmese numeral classifier." In *Context and Meaning in Cultural Anthropology* (*Festschrift Hallowell*), ed. M. Spiro, 243–64. New York.

Capell, A. 1948. *Grammar and Vocabulary of the Sonsoral-Tobi Language*. Washington.

Chao, Y. R. 1968. *A Grammar of Spoken Chinese*. Berkeley and Los Angeles.

Chatterji, S. K. 1926. *The Origin and Development of the Bengali Language*. Calcutta.

Dobson, W. A. C. H. 1962. *Early Archaic Chinese*. Toronto.

Emeneau, Murray B. 1951. *Studies in Vietnamese (Annamese) Grammar*. Berkeley and Los Angeles.

———. 1956. "India as a linguistic area." *Language* 32: 3–16.

Ferguson, C. A. 1964. "The basic grammatical categories of Bengali." In *Proceedings of the Ninth International Congress of Linguists*, ed. Horace Lunt, 881–90. The Hague.

Freytag, G. V. 1830–35. *Lexicon Arabico-Latinum*. Berlin.

Gaudefroy-Demombynes, M. 1952. *Grammaire de l'arabe classique*. 3d rev. ed. Paris.

Goldschmidt, W. 1951. "Ethics and the structure of society: an ethnological contribution to the sociology of knowledge." *American Anthropologist* 53: 506–24.

Greenberg, Joseph H. 1966. "Synchronic and diachronic universals in phonology." *Language* 42: 508–17.

———. 1969. "Some methods of dynamic comparison in linguistics." In *Substance and Structure of Language*, ed. J. Puhvel, 147–203. Berkeley and Los Angeles.

———. 1970a. "Some generalizations concerning glottalic consonants, especially implosives." *International Journal of American Linguistics* 36: 123–45.

———. 1970b. "The role of typology in the development of a scientific linguistics." In *Theoretical Problems of Typology and Northern Eurasian Languages*, ed. L. Dezsö and P. Hajdú, 11–24. Budapest.

Grjunberg, A. L. 1963. *Jazyk severoazerbajdzhanskix tatov*. Leningrad.

Howell, M. S. 1880–1900. *A Grammar of the Classical Arabic Language*. Allahabad.

Jacob, J. M. 1965. "Notes on the numerals and numerical coefficients in Old, Middle and Modern Khmer." *Lingua* 15: 143–62.

Kaufmann, E. M. 1972. *Ibibio Dictionary*. Office of Education. Washington, D.C.

Kononov, A. N. 1960. *Grammatika sovremennogo uzbekskogo literaturnogo jazyka*. Moscow-Leningrad.

Leech, G. N. 1969. *Towards a Semantic Description of English*. Bloomington and London.

Maretić, T. 1910. *Grammatika i stilistika hrvatskoga ili srpskoga književnoga jezika*. Zagreb.

Mitchell, T. F. 1956. *An Introduction to Egyptian Colloquial Arabic*. Oxford.

Noss, R. B. 1964. *Thai Reference Grammar*. Washington.

Reichardt, C. 1894. *Ein arabischer Dialekt gesprochen in Oman und Zanzibar*. Berlin.

Sanches, M. 1971. "Numeral Classifiers and Plural Marking: An Implicational Universal." Unpublished manuscript.

Sauvageot, S. 1967. "Note sur la classification nominale en bainouk." In *La classification nominale dans les langues Nègre-Africaines*, 225–36. Paris.

Sherzer, J. 1976. "Cuna numeral classifiers." In *Linguistic and Literary Studies in Honor of A. A. Hill*, eds. Mohammed Ali, Jazayery, and Werner Winter, 2: 331–38. Lisse, Belgium.

Sen-Gupta, S. 1970. "Genesis of the numeral classifier and its function as a morphological category." In *Proceedings of the Tenth International Congress of Linguists*, Vol. 3, 675–82. Bucharest.
Smalley, W. A. 1961. *Outline of Khmu Structure*. New Haven.
Thompson, L. C. 1965. *A Vietnamese Grammar*. Seattle.
Unbegaun, B. 1935. *La langue russe au XVIe siècle (1500–1550). I, La flexion des noms*. Paris.
Vinogradov, V. V. 1934. *Očerki po istorii russkogo literaturnogo jazyka, XVII–XIX vv*. Moscow.
Whorf, B. L. 1941. "The relation of habitual thought and behavior to language." In *Language, Culture and Personality, Essays in Memory of Edward Sapir*, ed. L. Spier et al., 75–93. Menasha.
Windstedt, R. 1945. *Colloquial Malay*. Revised edition. London.
———. 1957. *An Unabridged Malay-English Dictionary*. 2d edition. Singapore.

# Studies in Numerical Systems I: Double Numeral Systems

A recent paper, Denney and Odjig 1973, entitled "The meaning of *ninkotw* 'one' and *pešikw* 'one' in Ojibwa" discusses in some detail the constructions in which one or the other of these two lexically distinct forms for 'one' are used in the Ojibwa language.[1] A remarkable parallel is to be found in another language halfway around the globe from Ojibwa, namely Khasi, an Austroasiatic language spoken in Assam. Both Ojibwa and Khasi are numeral classifier languages. Khasi, like Ojibwa, has two lexically distinct numbers for 'one', *shii* and *wey*. A detailed comparison shows that in a whole series of uses Khasi *shii* corresponds to Ojibwa *ninkotw* and Khasi *wey* to Ojibwa *pešikw*. The main points of agreement are set forth schematically in Table 1 in which, as in the remainder of this paper, *shii*/*ninkotw* and forms corresponding in usage in other languages are called A-forms and those congruent with *wey*/*pešikw* are called B-forms. Similar facts have been noted in three other languages both classifier (Yurok) and non-classifier (Javanese, Burushaski). These five languages will be considered in detail in this paper. Similar phenomena no doubt occur elsewhere and some cases not exactly the same but suggestively similar are also considered at least in passing.

In the first section of this paper, the basic facts concerning the place of the A/B distinction and the syntactic structure of each of these five languages are presented with a minimum of theoretical discussion. Thereafter each of the categories of Table 1 and certain additional facts from these and other languages not easily presentable in a table are considered. In the final section

[1] Earlier treatment of the same topic in Ojibwa by the same authors are Denney and Odjig (1972a, b, c) all in less generably available publications. For Ojibwa I have also used Baraga 1876–78 and Verwyst 1901.

*Table 1*

| | T | M | V | U | I | H | G | F | SD | S | CN | C | D | P | PC |
|---|---|---|---|---|---|---|---|---|---|---|---|---|---|---|---|
| Khasi | A | A | A | A | A | A | A | A | A | A | B | B | B | B | B |
| Ojibwa | A | A | B | A | A | A | A | — | A | A | B | B | B | B | A |
| Yurok | (A) | A | B | A | A | A | A | — | — | — | B | — | B | B | — |
| Javanese | A | A | A | A | B | A | — | A | A | — | B | B | B | B | B |
| Burushaski | A | A | A | A | A | A | A | — | — | A | B | A | B | — | A |

NOTE: Parenthesized entries and blanks are explained in the text.

KEY: T = time periods; M = measures of length, area, volumes, and weight; V = measures of monetary value; U = unstandardized measures (e.g., 'cupful'); I = iteratives; H = multipliers in higher numeral units (e.g., 'three' in 'three tens' = 'thirty'); G = group measures (e.g., 'set', 'herd'); F = fractions; SD = syntactic dependence; S = singular in associated noun; CN = count noun construction; C = cardinal counting; D = distributive; P = predication; PC = punctual time expressions.

an attempt will be made to consider the deeper and more general principles that may be conjectured as underlying the empirically observed clusters of characteristics described in the earlier sections of the paper.

The first of the languages to be considered is Khasi. It has only two classifiers, *ŋut* used with human beings and *tilii* with non-humans. These are used with numbers larger than 'one'. In the classifier construction the order is numeral-classifier-noun. The noun is in most instances preceded by a non-generic article. This latter is part of a system of gender classification only marked in the article and relative pronoun. The "articles" are *ʔuu* 'masc. sing.', *ka* 'fem. sing', and *ki* 'plural, both genders'. There is also a minor "diminutive" gender marked by *ʔi* which has no number distinction. An example of the classifier construction is *ʔaar ŋut ki briw* 'two CLASSIFIER PLURAL man', i.e. 'two men'. However, this classifier construction is only used with numbers larger than one. For 'one' we find the two forms mentioned earlier *shii* (A) and *wei* (B). The former is used in those constructions marked by A in Table 1 and the latter in those marked by B. An example of the former is *shii poor* 'one time', i.e. 'once', and of the latter *ʔuu wei ʔuu briw* 'one man'. Note in the last phrase the absence of the classifier *ŋut* and the repetition of the singular article.

The basic facts for Ojibwa are those of the Odawa dialect as described in Denney and Odjig 1972, 1974. In Ojibwa the numeral as so often in Amerind languages fuses with the classifier into a single word within which, however, the order "numeral followed by classifier" is easily discernible. The quantified noun follows producing the same basic order as in Khasi numeral-classifier-noun. Ojibwa has a much larger variety of classifiers than Khasi involving to a considerable extent shape as the principle of classification, as is common in many classifier languages. In one further important respect Ojibwa differs from Khasi. Unlike Khasi, Ojibwa uses classifiers with 'one' in this case.[2] The following are illustrative examples:[3] *ninkot -onak ciiman* 'one [A form] CLASSIFIER canoe'; *nisso -minak mishiminak* 'two CLASSIFIER potatoes'.

Yurok, an Algonkian-Ritwan language of California, is, like Khasi and Ojibwa, a numeral classifier language. As in Ojibwa there are fused forms analyzable into numeral followed by classifier. However, the combination is less transparent than in Ojibwa. Hence, as is often the case with languages which exhibit such forms the combinations with each particular numeral is said to form a distinct series of numerals. One of these series, called by Robins (1958) the Times Series, has a set of uses which, as can be seen from Table 1, agree closely with the A forms of Khasi and Ojibwa. The other series in their usage correspond with the B forms of Khasi and Ojibwa, the choice among them resting on such semantic characteristics as shape and animacy. There are further important differences in that the distinction between A and B is extended to all numbers, not just 'one' and that 'one' only exhibits a single basic lexical form. Illustrative examples from Yurok are *nahksemi noˀoy* 'three + CLASSIFIER [fused form with time series] shoe', i.e. 'three pairs of shoes' (A form); *niˀit pegək* 'two + CLASSIFIER [fused form with personal series] man', i.e. 'two men' (B form).

The fourth language to be discussed, Javanese, unlike those previously mentioned, is not a numeral classifier language. It has however two series of numerals called in Horn (1961) the dependent and independent. The former of these is so called because it always immediately precedes a governing item and therefore cannot stand in isolation. This dependent form has predominantly A uses while the independent form has B uses. The A form usually ends in *-ng* but not always and there may be other phonetic differences, e.g. *rong* 'two' (A form); *loro* 'two' (B form). An example of a contrastive use of A and B forms is *rong djam* 'two hours'; *djam loro* 'two clocks' or 'two o'clock'.

The last language of Table 1 is Burushaski, a genetically unclassified language of Kashmir. Burushaski does not have numeral classifiers. There is a gender classification which consists of four categories in positions of maximum differentiation. These are defined and symbolized by Lorimer as follows: (1) *h* (human), (2) *f* (feminine, basically a subcategory of *h*), (3) *x* (animals and some inanimates), (4) *y* (remaining inanimates). With numerals there is, as elsewhere, considerable neutralization among these gender

[2] In some of the examples given, numerical constructions classifiers are not present but no rules are given.

[3] The last example has been adapted to Denney and Odjig's orthography from Verwyst (1910: 404) since Denney and Odjig are very sparing of examples.

categories. Nowhere in the numerals does *f* appear as a distinct category, being merged with *h*. The threefold *h*, *x*, *y* distinction only appears in the number 'two'. In 'one' and 'three' the opposition between *x* and *y* is neutralized so that these numerals have two forms, *h* and *x-y*. The numerals 3–10 have only a single form neutralizing all gender distinction. However, besides these *h*, *x*, and *y* gender forms, there is an additional form in all numerals called by Lorimer the *z* form. It is not lexically distinct from the gendered forms but is marked by a distinct inflectional suffix, e.g., 'three': *isken* (h); *usko* (x, y); *iski* (z). The *z* forms are called 'abstract numerals' in the grammar of Klimov and Edel'man. It is this *z* abstract form which corresponds in its uses to the A forms already considered. An example of an A construction (i.e. using the *z* form of the numeral) is *iski badan* 'two steps or paces'; of B constructions *isken gušiyents* 'three women' (*h* form used with *f* noun); *usko huyes* 'three goats' (*x*, *y* form used with *x* noun) and *usko hakičay* 'three houses' (*x*, *y* form with *y* noun).

After thus considering briefly that part of the basic morphological system in each of the five languages within which the A/B distinction is embedded, we now turn to a more detailed consideration of the various uses of these forms following the categories as given in Table 1 in the order employed there but with the addition of some relevant facts not easily summarized in a table. Accordingly we begin with the A uses.

1. T in the Table symbolizes 'time'. The expressions involved are those in which a number is accompanied by a unit of temporal duration as in English 'three years'. The only exception here is that in Yurok for 'month' but not for 'day' or 'year', the number takes one of the B form classifiers, namely, the one for 'round objects' in obvious reference to the shape of the moon.

2. M indicates measure and here are included those of length, area, volume, and weight. There are no deviations in this category.

3. V stands for 'value' in monetary systems. Both Ojibwa and Yurok are exceptions and the factors involved are similar. Ojibwa has here a B form, the classifier for hard objects, because, according to Denney and Odjig, "one dollar was originally one hard object, i.e. a silver dollar." In Yurok the round object classifier among the B forms is used in monetary expressions, e.g. *kohtonak* 'one round object', i.e. a coin or piece of money.

4. The fourth category of A form uses is that of "unstandardized measures."[4] By an unstandardized measure is meant one involving some item which is also a physical object. The object involved then can be referred to in

[4] I do not consider the term "unstandardized measure" a fully satisfactory one, since such measures may become standardized. Presumably Detroit car manufacturers do not match teams of horses pulling motorless cars against cars with motors to measure horsepower.

two different ways, *qua* measure or *qua* physical object. We may illustrate this from English: 'a cup of tea' (unstandardized measure), 'a yellow cup' (physical object). All five languages represented in Table 1 have here minimal contrasts in which the A forms indicate measure and the B forms physical object. An example is Javanese *rong sendoq* 'two spoonfuls' (A) and *sendoq loro* 'two spoons' (B). The term "unstandardized" measure is used here in distinction from something that might be called an "occasional measure." This latter notion can be illustrated by remarkably parallel examples from Khasi and Ojibwa. In Khasi we have *shi ing* 'one (A form) house' glossed by Roberts as 'a whole house or family', while in Ojibwa we find *ninko-tote*, 'one (A form) house' translated 'one family, household'. Such examples may be distinguished from the "unstandardized measures" just mentioned in that (1) they are not, so to speak, "serious measures" (unlike 'spoonful' or 'cupful' there is no fixed number, however rough, corresponding to the amounts involved in measure); (2) connected with this they are only used with the number 'one'.[5]

5. The next category, I, is that of iteratives, i.e. 'so many times'. In this category Javanese is deviant. It uses the B form with a word meaning 'time', e.g. 'three times' is *ping telu*, or *kaping telu*. For 'once' and 'twice' the forms are irregular *kapisan*, *sapisan* 'once'; *kapiṇḍo* or *piṇḍo* 'twice'. The *ka* which may be prefixed to *-ping* is evidently the derivative prefix which generally in Austronesian languages combines with a suffix *-an* to form iteratives. The same formation *ka...an* may be used to form abstracts in general. This combination *ka...an* is presumably found in *ka-pis-an* 'once', cited above.

There is a special agreement in this category between Yurok and Burushaski. In Yurok numerals of the A form when used in isolation have iterative meaning. This is why Robins calls them the Times Series. The same holds in Burushaski. Thus *hik*, the A form of 'one' in Burushaski, means 'once' when used in isolation.

6. In the sixth column of Table 1, H indicates "higher numeral units." By this is meant the use of a numeral to form higher numbers by functioning as multipliers of units of the system, e.g. English 'six' in 'six hundred'. All the languages being considered use the A forms here, e.g. Ojibwa *ninko-twākk* '100' which contains the A form of 'one' as its initial element.

7. G designates what are often called group counters, e.g. English 'herd'. In a broader category of such counters we may distinguish several semantic dimensions. One of these is numerically definite as against numerically indefinite, e.g. 'herd' (indefinite); 'score' (definite). Another basic dimension

[5] The term "occasional measure" has been taken from Chao 1968.

involves specialization of application. Once more English 'herd' and 'score' contrast on this dimension likewise, 'herd' being specialized and 'score' non-specialized. Khasi provides some good examples of the combination of numerical definiteness with specialization, e.g. *pen* 'a group of 80' but only applied to oranges and bamboos. There appears to be a tendency in language change towards generalization of application of counters whether numerically definite or indefinite. According to Roberts, Khasi *gynda* borrowed from Bengali *gāndā* in the monetary meaning *anna* = 4 *pice* is becoming generalized to mean any group of 'four'. Such counters are thus sources of designation of higher units in the general numerical system.

8. F in Table 1 symbolizes 'fractions'. The blanks in the table indicate absence of data. The only fractions reported are Javanese *se-tengah* '1/2' containing *se-* the bound A form for 'one' and Khasi *shii phiah* '1/2 rupee', literally 'one split', *shii teng* '1/2', and *shi-pawa* '1/4'.

9. This category SD 'syntactic dependence' is different in nature from those mentioned previously in that it does not refer to the nature of the item which is counted. There is a correlative tendency of the A form to be syntactically dependent and the B form to be independent. We have already seen that the A forms are called 'dependent numerals' in Horn's grammar of Javanese because they cannot stand alone but must be immediately followed by the item counted. In addition in Javanese the A form of 'one' *se- s-* is always bound to the following item as part of the same word. In Ojibwa, the A form of 'one' likewise always occurs bound to the following item. We have seen that the A forms occur independently in Burushaski and Yurok with iterative meaning. The corresponding tendency of B forms to be independent is illustrated below by their use in the categories of abstract counting and independent predication.

10. The characteristic of A forms which forms the basis of the tenth category is its tendency to be associated with the singular (s) as the unmarked number category. In Khasi the item counted or measured by the A form of 'one' is always in the singular as indicated by the use of the singular non-generic article, e.g. *shii kanii ˀuu kwaay* 'one [A form] group of 400 SG ART betel nuts'. However, where the intervening counter is itself a higher number the plural is used, e.g. in the expression for 'one hundred soldiers'. In Burushaski the item which follows the A form of the numeral is usually singular, e.g. with measures it will be rather the measure which is singular than what is measured unless the latter is a mass noun. The same rule holds at least in the form of Ojibwa described by Verwyst. In Javanese there is no morphological category of number so this category has no applicability. In Yurok only a few nouns have plurals and their use is not compulsory and in fact described as "very careful" (Robins 1958: 23). It seems likely that none

of the nouns with plurals would figure in A constructions so that for Yurok also this category is not applicable.

We now consider the part of Table 1 in which the constructions involving B forms are enumerated. These include the following:

1. Use with Count Nouns (CN). In all of the languages enumerated in the Table, B forms are used in the construction of a cardinal number directly with a count noun.

2. The next category is Counting (C). Here the data are not complete. It is explicitly indicated that B forms are used in counting in Khasi, Ojibwa, and Javanese. For Burushaski Lorimer states that the A form is employed. For Yurok I have not found any information on this point. One should no doubt draw a distinction between "abstract counting" with which in all probability usage in mathematical discourse agrees and "concrete counting" where specific objects are involved. There is some evidence that in numeral classifier languages when concrete objects are counted the numerals always occur with the appropriate classifiers. Only one of the sources used here makes this distinction. Rabel in her grammar of Khasi notes that in simple counting *wey* (B form) is used without a gender article but when used with a noun it agrees in gender. Presumably in these cases the noun actually occurs, e.g. 'one potato', 'two potatoes'.

3. All the languages in the table agree in using the B forms in distributive constructions (D). As is the case in many other languages, this involves complete reduplication as in Khasi and Burushaski or partial reduplication in Ojibwa, e.g. Burushaski *alta alta rupia* 'two rupees apiece'.

4. Except for Burushaski, for which I have no data, these languages agree in using the B forms in predication (P). An example is Javanese *anaqku loro*, 'my children two', i.e. I have two children. In Yurok the B form may be used as the stem of a verb in the meaning 'be alone'; in Ojibwa likewise it forms verbs, e.g. *pešiko* 'he is alone', based on the form of 'one'.

5. As a final category, there has been included one in which, unlike the others, there is no clear predominance of A or B forms. This is temporal punctuality as contrasted with duration. However there is some question here as to whether the examples which have been found are strictly comparable. In Khasi we find B forms as punctual contrasting with A as durative (cf. for the latter the category T 'time' above), e.g. *ka wey ka shii* '(on) one day'; *ka wey ka poor* 'at one time, once upon a time'. With this we may compare Javanese *djam loro* (B form) 'two o'clock' as contrasted with *rong djam* (A form) 'two hours'. On the other hand Ojibwa has *ninko-tink* (A form) in the meaning 'formerly', 'at one time'. Burushaski uses the A forms in instances such as *iski-ər* 'at the third time, on the third occasion'. For Yurok I have not found any evidence regarding punctual time expressions.

Throughout the previous exposition, I have sedulously avoided general formulations regarding the basic nature of the A/B distinction. However, any one of several of the more obvious possibilities must already have occurred to any but the most somnolent reader.

One such hypothesis would be simply that the distinction involved is that between measuring (A) and counting (B) which is in turn correlated with the opposition between mass noun (A) and count noun (B) in the quantified substance. We might also perhaps extend this contrast to the mathematics involved, continuous (A) versus discrete (B). The attractiveness of this proposal lies in the exceptionless contrast between the use of A forms in measure constructions and B forms in count constructions in the languages considered here. Moreover, the distinction between measuring and counting is evidently a fundamental one.

But one may object that certain A constructions on which all of the languages agree cannot be reasonably subsumed under measuring as usually understood and do not involve a continuous as opposed to a discrete mathematics. These negative instances include especially the A uses with group counters, in the formation of higher numeral units, and in iterative constructions.

Still, this first characterization is not completely valueless if we note the parallelism between A and B constructions on the one hand and those numerical constructions in numeral classifier languages which, respectively, do not use and do use what may be called classifiers in the proper and restricted sense of the term.[6] By classifiers proper are meant items which occur in count noun constructions, typically classified by shape or animacy and which are shown to be redundant when translation into a non-numeral classifier language like English is carried out. Thus a phrase like 'five-round object-orange' in a classifier language is translated simply as 'five oranges' in English.

These examples contrast with others in which items figure which often are somewhat loosely called classifiers in grammars of such languages because of their syntactic similarity in such matters as word order. In this second type of construction in contrast to the first, the item in the classifier position is not denotatively redundant and requires translation into non-classifier languages. Since measure constructions are prominent in this group, some grammars of classifier languages subdivide the overall classifier construction into those employing classifiers proper and those involving measures. Thus we may contrast 'five-round object-orange' with 'five-ounce-cheese' which are

[6]This and the following summarize conclusions already stated in Greenberg 1972, to which the reader is referred for greater detail and supporting evidence.

syntactically parallel in classifier languages but for which 'ounce' requires translation into English while 'round-object' does not. We may also note that 'ounce' which is itself morphologically a noun in English does not have a classifier in its construction with a numeral. There is no such thing as 'five-round object-ounce' in such languages.

However, while measures are prominent among such non-classifier constructions in these languages they are far from exhausting them. Such expressions as 'three-pairs-shoes' and 'one-herd-cattle' also do not take the classifiers proper and here also, such nouns as 'pair', 'herd' may be viewed as not having classifiers in association with numerals. We see then that our category G (group counters) which takes an A construction does not use classifiers proper in classifier languages.

Further, it is typical in classifier languages that certain other words which are morphologically nouns apparently do not take classifiers. These are such words as 'day', 'month', and 'time' in phrases like 'three times'. In the grammars of classifier languages it is generally stated that these nouns do not take classifiers. However, as I have argued elsewhere, an alternative more plausible analysis is that nouns like 'day', 'time' are themselves quantifiers and therefore like 'ounce', 'pair', etc. do not appear with classifiers. The place of the apparently omitted head noun is then taken by a verb since these are quantifiers of verbal action. We have seen that the categories T (time) and I (iterative) take A forms so these are once more parallel to the absence of classifiers in classifier languages.

Finally the use of A forms as multipliers to form higher numeral units likewise has its parallel in numeral classifier languages. In such languages, numerals formed by multiplication of units or the numeral system with other numbers often do not take classifiers. Thus 'five-round object-orange', with the classifier, but 'five-ten-orange' without a classifier.

There is then a broad equivalence between the use of A forms and the absence of classifiers proper in classifier languages and the use of B forms and their presence. We may note that there is a further congruity between this situation and the facts of Yurok, a language both with numeral classifiers and an A/B distinction. What are listed as numeral classifiers in Robins' grammar can be dichotomized into a particular one, that of the times series, which has, as we have seen, numerous idiosyncratic uses, and the remainder which function like the ordinary classifiers of classifier languages in that they are subdivided on the basis of such semantic criteria as shape and animacy and occur in count-noun constructions. The same holds for Ojibwa in which the B form of 'one' occurs with the ordinary classifiers while the A form does not.

The parallel just drawn between A and B forms on the one hand and the non-use and use of classifiers in classifier languages, while it broadens our perspective in the problem of the basis of the distinction, does not in itself solve it. It remains to investigate the basis of both these distinctions since we have seen that a formulation in terms of measuring versus counting is not adequate.

What does appear to be involved in B uses and in the use of classifiers proper in numeral classifier languages is most easily seen if we elaborate somewhat the example given above which shows the use of multipliers for higher units. When in a language like Burmese we have a phrase like 'fifty-three oranges' it is expressed as follows: 'five ten three round-object orange', that is '(five tens and three round-object) orange'. Now, viewed denotatively, this is simply $((5\times10) + (3\times1))$ oranges. This view was, as a matter of fact expressed by some of Burling's Burmese informants for whom the general classifier *khù* was included "in the same series as the classifiers for the powers of ten . . . *-khù* indicating only one individual object" (Burling 1965: 262). In other words, the B construction and the classifier construction may be characterized as indicating counting by ones, i.e. unit counting as opposed to all other forms of quantification including measuring but also counting by pairs, tens, groups, etc. In fact there is at least one classifier language in which there is only one "classifier" which therefore does not classify nouns. This is Cebuano which has a word *buquk* glossed as 'piece' used in unit counting but not used for any other mode of quantification.

Most languages, unlike numeral classifier languages, do not have an overt indicator of unit counting, which is therefore the unmarked mode of quantification. In classifier languages it is marked but opposed globally to all other types. We are reminded of the remark of the eminent nineteenth-century mathematician Leopold Kronecker, "God made the natural numbers. Everything else is man's invention."

It is possible, however, to characterize A uses in a non-negative way, that is not merely as a cover term for all forms of quantifying except the 'natural' method of counting by ones. Since a few languages, at least those considered in this paper, have a uniform method of indicating these uses it is plausible to seek for a more unified account.

There are two observations regarding the languages considered in this paper that should prove crucially important in reference to this question. One is the existence in all of them of the construction with non-standard measures using A numerals in minimal contrast with the construction using the same physical object with B numerals, e.g. 'five cupfuls' (A construction) versus 'five cups' (B construction). This corresponds exactly to the situation in numeral classifier languages which have the contrast 'five cup sugar' versus 'five round-object cup'. The other strategic fact is that the A numeral in isolation in Yurok and Burushaski means 'x-times'. This seems to be the only meaning that an A form ever has when it occurs independently. This suggests that the iterative notion must somehow play a major role.

Jespersen noted long ago that one need not have three cups in order to have three cupfuls of something. One may use the same cup three times. Likewise there is a distinction between 'three cups full of tea' and 'three cupfuls of tea'.

This suggests a new approach in place of the counting versus measuring frequently found in the literature. It also provides us with our second 'straw man' since though it is an improvement it is still not entirely adequate.

Denney and Odjig have a number of different but related formulations regarding Ojibwa which may be cited as being along the lines just sketched. "*Ninkotw* is used because measures are not conceived as static permanently existing units but as actions." (1972c: 5). Denney and Odjig again (*ibid.*: 1–2) in speaking of the B form: "The most important of these contexts is when referring to a single object, whereas *ninkotw* is usually retained when referring to an event or action." It is true indeed that for the Ojibwa measuring involves repeating an action which marks off the unit, so that 'five feet' is, as it were, 'five times a foot'. However, not all A uses involve actual repeated physical actions. One would be forced into saying that for higher numerals, for group counters, and for terms like 'pair', one goes through the actions mentally rather than physically. Interestingly, Classical Greek does use iteratives to form higher units above 1,000. Thus 2,000 is *diskhílioi* literally 'two times thousand' so this view is not entirely implausible.

However, a different formulation also by Denney and Odjig is, I believe, more adequate and more closely attains the objective of characterizing A-type uses in a single formulation. This is when they say "*Ninkotw* appears to convey the notion of one action, as in the act of measuring or the action of forming a new unit such as a pair; whereas *peshikw* conveys the notion of a single object" (1972a: 2).

I would put the emphasis here on forming a new unit with the physical action being incidental even though being actually present in many cases. In other words in all of these uses we form a unit, whether discrete, continuous, numerically definite, or numerically indefinite. The number applies not directly to the object quantified but only mediately in that it gives the number of these units, not that of the object. It is therefore the units that are being counted.

One can see a number of other characteristics which arise from this unit-creating aspect. One is the tendency for syntactic dependence of the A forms. Except in metamathematical discourse, the unit makes no sense unless accompanied by a number. The *raison d'être* of 'ounce' is that it be combined with a number. Unlike oranges, ounces have no independent existence except by their role in quantification. This is the basis also for the characterization of the Burushaski A forms by Klimov and Edel'man as abstract. So also 25 cents is not the same as five nickels. Two dimes and a nickel are equally 25 cents but so is the remainder in my bank account if it has $237.25. One could run out of physical quarters but not out of the possibility of instantiation of the value concept '25 cents'. With this "abstract" nature of the A form is probably also to be connected the tendency for it to be used with the singular form of the measure or other unit. As the unmarked number category, the singular tends to be used here since an actual plurality of physical objects is not involved. This is a widespread phenomenon outside of the languages considered here, cf. German _fünf Pfennig_ 'five cents' (sg.) and _fünf Pfennige_ (pl.) 'five pennies', and English 'six-foot tall', etc.

If we now turn back to the phenomenon discussed in this paper with the foregoing analyses in mind, the languages considered are unusual among the world's languages in that this process of unit-formation is expressed overtly. Consider for example Burushaski _iski ser brʌs_ 'two ser of rice'. Here, unlike the vast majority of the world's languages, not only does the measure 'ser' receive overt expression but also the fact that it is a non-natural unit is expressed by the choice of a separate inflected form of the numeral. These languages with the A/B distinction are the obverse of numeral classifier languages. They overtly indicate non-natural quantification while the latter indicate unit counting, the one 'natural' method of quantifying. There are even, as we have seen, at least three languages in the world—Khasi, Yurok, and Ojibwa—which realize the fourth typological possibility by expressing both. There are thus languages which express neither (English), natural unit counting (Mandarin), artificial unit formation (Burushaski, Javanese), or both (Khasi, Yurok, Ojibwa).

Finally it may be of interest to call attention to the possibility of the existence of phenomena at least suggestive of this distinction in Indo-European. In Indo-European two numbers for 'one' are reconstructed. These are _*oi-_ usually accompanied by suffixed _-n_, e.g. Latin _ūn-us_ < _*oi -n-us_ or _-k-_ Sanskrit _ekas_ < _*oik-os_ and _*sm̥/sem_ seen in Ancient Greek _heís_ (masc. sing. nom.) for _*hens_ < _*sem-s_ and Armenian _mi_. The latter form _*sm̥_ seems to have some uses parallel to A uses, e.g. in forming iteratives such as Latin _sem-el_, Greek _há-paks_, Sanskrit _sa-kr̥t_ 'once' and as a multiplier in higher numerals, e.g. Sanskrit _sa-hasra_ 'one thousand', Greek _hé-katon_ 'one hundred'. Further investigation will doubtless uncover still other instances of various types and degrees of overt expression of the distinction expressed by what have been called here dual numeral systems.

## References Cited

Baraga, F. 1876–78. _A Dictionary of the Otchipwe Language_. Montreal.

Burling, R. 1965. "How to choose a Burmese numeral classifier." In _Context and Meaning in Cultural Anthropology (Festschrift Hollowell)_, M. Spira, ed., 243–64. New York.

Chao, Y. R. 1968. _A Grammar of Spoken Chinese_. Berkeley and Los Angeles.

Denney, J. P., and L. Odjig. 1972a. "Note on Ojibway numeral classifiers." Ojibway Maths Project, Working Paper No. 2.

———. 1972b. "A semantically organized list of Ojibwa numeral classifiers." Research Bulletin No. 239, Department of Psychology. University of Western Ontario. London, Canada.

———. 1972c. "The semantics of *ninkotw* 'one' and *pešikw* 'one' in Ojibwa." Research Bulletin No. 240, Department of Psychology. University of Western Ontario. London, Canada.

———. 1973. "The meaning of *ninkotw* 'one' and *pešikw* 'one' in Ojibway." *International Journal of American Linguistics* 39, 2: 95–97.

Greenberg, J. H. 1972. "Numeral classifiers and substantival number: problems in the genesis of a linguistic type." *Working Papers on Linguistic Universals* 9: 1–39.

Horn, E. C. 1961. *Beginning Javanese*. New Haven.

Klimov, G. A., and D. I. Edel'man. 1970. *Jazyk Burushaski*. Moscow.

Lorimer, D. L. R. 1876–1962. *The Burushaski Language*. 3 vols. Cambridge, Mass.

Rabel, L. 1951. *Khasi, a Language of Assam*. Baton Rouge.

Roberts, H. 1891. *A Grammar of the Khassi Language*. London.

Robins, R. H. 1958. *The Yurok Language*. Berkeley and Los Angeles.

Verwyst, C. 1901. *Chippewa Exercises*. Harbor Springs, Michigan.

# The Relation of Frequency to Semantic Feature in a Case Language (Russian)

In reading a traditional grammar of a language with a case system, one derives the impression that, like the law in Iolanthe, "it has no flaw at all," that is, that every noun exists in every case. At the most, there is a short list of "defective" nouns which do not occur in particular cases. One consideration, however, almost immediately presents itself. This apparent symmetry has been gained by relegating a whole series of forms which might be analyzed as nouns occurring in cases limited to a small number of nouns, to that traditional junk heap, the class of adverbs and eliminating these particular cases from the general case system. This refuse of the case system consists largely of locative, time, and manner expressions. Particularly with regard to the first two of these, place and time, there is an obvious implication of affinity between particular delimited classes of nouns and particular cases. Many instances are known in Indo-European languages in which such adverbs are indeed survivals of nouns in case forms once much more widely distributed over nouns and thus formerly full-fledged members of the case system.

In fact, the notion of a connection between cases and substantive semantic features is by no means a novel one. For example Jakobson (1936) in his now-classic study of the Russian case system opposes the nominative to the accusative and the dative to the instrumental, with the former of each pair characterized as animate, the latter inanimate. More recently the development by Fillmore of the notion of a case grammar has tended to refocus interest on these problems. In his well-known essay "The Case for Case" (1968) he also points to the redundancy between nominal semantic features and case and attributes the feature animate to his deep-structure agent and dative cases and non-animate to the instrumental. In an article which appeared not long after this (Maher 1969) and which has given rise to continuing discussion since, it is proposed that Italian *serpe* 'snake', which comes from the Latin nominative rather than the accusative as is usual with nouns in Western Romance, does so because animacy is involved. There is indeed a fairly extensive literature on Indo-European languages regarding the semantic characteristics of forms which represent survivals of case forms when a case system is partly or completely broken down. Nor is it difficult to find examples elsewhere. For example, Hebrew *yomam* 'by day', generally analyzed as an adverb, is historically a survival of the accusative indefinite of the formerly functioning case system.

It is not merely in regard to the differential frequency with which specific semantically defined subclasses of nouns occur in particular cases that the monolithic appearance of case systems is illusory. Even though in fact where there is a case system almost all nouns can occur in all cases which from the synchronic view are still functioning members of the system, this conceals another factor of major synchronic and diachronic importance. It is generally assumed that the "same" noun in different cases has the same lexical meaning. In the traditional lexicography of a language like Latin it is assumed that a single lexical entry, say *vir* 'man', can be assigned a single overall lexical meaning so that, for example, its meaning is the same in the nominative and the ablative. The meaning of *virō*, the dative singular, is assumed to be a combination of an unvarying lexical meaning 'man' and a dative and, one should add, a singular meaning. While by and large this holds, there are frequently complications. Most commonly perhaps the occurrence in one case rather than another may disambiguate several meanings which are listed by lexicographers as distinct but related and often such relations are recurrent and systematic in the language. Thus in a case language like Russian the word *fabrika* 'factory' in the nominative in a sentence like "The factory buzzed with rumors" means "the people in the factory" rather than the place. Moreover we will expect the same possibility to recur in other names of place-institutions like 'school', 'library', etc. Now either we may attribute polysemy to the noun and say that the case form helps to disambiguate it or we can assume that in some sense the meaning as a place is more fundamental and that the interpretation as a set of people is not part of its lexical meaning but part of pragmatic interpretation or performance. In such instances it is generally possible to produce a paraphrase in which the noun occurs in another case, e.g. "Rumors were rife in the factory." Albert Sechehaye in his stimulating book *La Structure logique de la phrase* (1950) discusses such phenomena at length and applies the term "transposition" to such relationships. In examples of the kind just discussed, if we take the second of the above alternatives, i.e. with a fundamental meaning given in the lexicon as part of the overall linguistic description and disambiguation occurring pragmatically, we may say that for nouns with a particular semantic feature, e.g. place, it is usual for the basic meaning to occur in constructions in which it occurs in one particular case (here a locative) and transferred or metaphorical meaning in another case (here the nominative). Paralleling the relation of basic and transferred senses peculiar to metaphor is a case shift which makes its contribution to the transfer of sense. A shift to the nominative in examples such as the one just given tends to produce a particular kind of metaphor, personification. Thus, in the sentence "Revenge took possession of him," 'revenge' is, as it were, personified.

Since in general one will expect that basic non-transferred uses will be more frequent, it is plausible to hypothesize that, for example, a place noun will be used more frequently in cases in which such non-metaphorical basic meanings are more usual. Hence nouns with a basic feature like 'place' may be conjectured to occur more commonly in cases like locatives than in nominatives.

A frequency study of Russian (Shtejnfel'dt 1963) presents one of the infrequent opportunities to explore these questions from already assembled data. This work contains for the 961 common (i.e. not proper) nouns with a range greater than a specified minimum, the frequency of each noun in each case.

Shtejnfel'dt counted 400,000 words distributed over 350 texts of approximately equal length. Of the 400,000 words, 102,173 were noun tokens. She gives totals for the relative frequency of each Russian case among these tokens. This information is given on line 1 of Table 1. Six cases are distinguished: nominative, genitive, dative, accusative, instrumental, and prepositional.

The first method employed to test the hypothesis that there are significant correlations between the semantic feature of nouns and relative distribution over the cases was to classify the nouns into certain semantic categories and calculate the average frequency of each group for each case. The results of this investigation are to be found in Table 1.

Of the 961 noun types for which case frequencies are given, 448 fell with reasonable clarity into one or another of the twelve categories which were distinguished (lines 4–15). A listing of these nouns with their English glosses is found in Appendix I.

Of these 448 noun types, 119 were classified as personal, common, individual (as opposed to collective). The results for this category (line 4 of Table 1) may be summarized as follows. The nominative was by far the most frequent case (54.1) and a higher value was found for this case than for any

*Table 1*

Russian Case Frequencies

| | No. of types | No. of tokens | N | G | D | A | I | P |
|---|---|---|---|---|---|---|---|---|
| 1. All nouns | 9,073* | 102,173 | 33.6% | 24.6% | 05.1% | 19.5% | 07.8% | 09.4% |
| 2. Common nouns | 9,073 | 89,384 | 28.3 | 26.0 | 05.0 | 21.8 | 08.6 | 10.3 |
| 3. Proper nouns | ? | 12,789 | 76.3 | 13.5 | 05.5 | 01.1 | 01.4 | 02.2 |
| 4. Personal common individual | 119 | 11,769 | 54.1 | 22.5 | 06.9 | 07.0 | 08.0 | 01.5 |
| 5. Personal collective | 29 | 2,565 | 23.9 | 48.0 | 04.2 | 09.6 | 06.2 | 08.3 |
| 6. Animal | 9 | 746 | 35.6 | 28.4 | 03.8 | 21.6 | 06.0 | 04.6 |
| 7. Body parts | 31 | 3,318 | 18.2 | 09.9 | 03.2 | 36.5 | 20.3 | 11.9 |
| 8. Concrete count | 116 | 5,475 | 23.0 | 20.7 | 04.3 | 32.0 | 09.4 | 10.5 |
| 9. Concrete mass | 25 | 1,565 | 21.3 | 31.6 | 02.2 | 24.3 | 13.6 | 06.9 |
| 10. Non-enduring objects | 31 | 2,127 | 34.5 | 19.0 | 04.1 | 21.5 | 10.8 | 08.8 |
| 11. Abstract qualities | 21 | 1,295 | 33.3 | 24.9 | 03.8 | 17.4 | 12.3 | 09.0 |
| 12. Place nouns | 87 | 7,747 | 11.8 | 30.6 | 06.0 | 24.4 | 03.3 | 23.8 |
| 13. Place institutions | 17 | 2,445 | 13.0 | 40.9 | 02.3 | 17.8 | 01.8 | 24.1 |
| 14. Time periods | 8 | 2,998 | 12.8 | 37.5 | 02.0 | 36.0 | 03.4 | 08.3 |
| 15. Measures | 7 | 480 | 02.7 | 85.4 | 00.8 | 05.2 | 01.2 | 04.6 |
| 16. First and second person pronouns | 4 | 15,901 | 51.8 | 21.8* | 14.5 | 09.5 | 02.2 | 00.2 |

*Approximate.

NOTE: The figures for line 3 are deduced; those for lines 4–15 are only with a range > 13.

other category except proper nouns. On the other hand the accusative was strikingly lower than the general average (07.0 as against 19.5). The dative which in the overall count of nouns has the lowest frequency of all the cases shows here a higher value than for any other semantic category of nouns. The instrumental on the other hand is substantially lower while the drop in the value for the prepositional is very marked (01.5 as against the general average of 09.4 for this case). We see then that there are substantial differences between individual personal nouns and the general averages and that they are in the expected direction. The nominative and dative are specified as [+animate] and the accusative is specified as [−animate] in Jakobson's analysis. The prepositional case, so called because it is only used with prepositions, is largely a locative case. Hence its low value for personals.

If we turn to the place nouns we would therefore expect the prepositional to show a high value. In this and other respects these nouns differ drastically from the personal common individual nouns just discussed. Examples of nouns selected include *gora* 'mountain', *stancija* 'station', and *komnata* 'room'. Place names which function as institutions, e.g. *klub*, were excluded and assigned to a separate group (line 13), although the decision was often a difficult one. The place names (line 12) may be characterized as having a low nominative, a high accusative, and, as would be expected, a very high prepositional frequency, far higher than that in any other category.

The group of place-institutions which typically may either indicate an actual place or an institution might be expected to show some resemblance both to place names and to personal common collectives (line 5), words such as 'army' and 'brigade'. In fact it turns out to be much more similar to place names and also to have a genitive value higher than that of either collective or place names. Except in certain particular instances, the uses of the Russian genitive are so heterogeneous (in adnominal relations, and with a variety of prepositions and government by certain verbs) that it is usually difficult to assign reasons for the frequency associated with it.

We now turn to categories of physical objects. These were divided into two groups, count (line 8) and mass (line 9). Body parts were excluded and assigned to a separate category. Common to both mass and count concrete nouns are, roughly speaking, the properties of being tangible and either solid or liquid. Thus such words as *veter* 'wind' and *šum* 'noise' were not included here but put in a separate category of non-enduring objects (line 10). Examples of the concrete, count category are *stol* 'table' and *kniga* 'book' and of the concrete mass category are *moloko* 'milk' and *pesok* 'sand'. The most striking difference between these categories are in the genitive and the accusative. The mass nouns have a relatively high genitive value presumable because of their partitive uses. The accusative values for both categories are well above the general average but much higher in count nouns. Probably the lower accusative value for mass nouns is simply a reflection of their partitive use as direct object in the negative.

A relatively easily delimitable group is that of body parts, including here a few animal body parts, e.g. *xvost* 'tail'. The following comments can be made regarding the results for this category (line 6). As with other non-personals there is a relatively low nominative and high accusative, the latter being approximately twice as frequent as the former. Other characteristics are the low values for the dative and the genitive, the latter possibly because body parts are typically possessed rather than possessors. The most salient characteristic is, however, the high value in the instrumental, by far the largest of any of the groups in this study.

Having examined a number of non-animate classes we may now turn back to personal collectives (line 5). Included here are such words as *vojsko* 'army' and *narod* 'people'. The most striking here is the extremely high value for the genitive, one for which I cannot offer an explanation. Otherwise, as might be expected, it shows values intermediate between personal and 'thing' categories, but somewhat closer to the former. Thus the high nominative and low accusative aligns these words with the personal individual group but the low dative and high prepositional with physical objects.

It might be conjectured that words for animals might show a similar intermediate position. However there were only 9 words in this category, for the most part a function of the kinds of texts used, largely school readers. Thus *komsomol* 'Young Communist League' had a relatively high frequency while the word for 'cat' was not sufficiently frequent to be included in the list of words for which case frequencies were given.

The smallness of the sample of nouns in this category of course impairs its reliability. However, for what they may be worth, the values in Table 1 may be considered. As might have been predicted, the nominative is more frequent than the accusative but intermediate in this respect between the personal individual and the personal collective. It is again intermediate to these two categories in the prepositional case. Once more, as might be expected, it is lower than either personal categories in the dative and instrumental.

The numerous remaining nouns are all essentially non-concrete except perhaps for the category of "non-enduring objects" (line 10). In general this class was intended to include phenomena with a material basis but which were not enduring solid or liquid bodies. Among words included here were, for example, 'noise', 'shadow'. Also included were "ideal objects", e.g., 'fire', words which may in some contexts have reference to type and in others to specific realization. The results for this category are definitely closer to that for the various animate categories than the two categories of concrete objects, count and mass. This is shown by a higher frequency in the nominative than for the concrete categories (34.5 as against 23.0 and 21.3 for count and mass nouns respectively), a lower accusative value (21.5 as compared to 32.0 and 24.3) while in other cases the frequencies are similar to those for concrete nouns.

Among the essentially non-concrete nouns which make up the remainder, there is a heavy incidence of polysemy of the type found generally in the equivalent English terms. Very commonly the same term can refer to two or more of the following categories depending on context: (a) an activity in general, (b) a concrete instance of such an activity, sometimes in permanent or semi-permanent form, (c) individuals engaged in the activity. Thus *tvorčestvo* 'creating' or 'creation' can be used in senses (a) and (b); *redakcija* 'editorship' in (a), (b), and (c), etc. In view of this a relatively small group was isolated which are definitely abstract, often derived from adjectives of quality, e.g. *skorost'* 'speed', since these seemed relatively free of such polysemy. This is the group of line 11 (abstract qualities). These turned out on the whole to be similar to the preceding category of non-enduring objects.

Finally, two small and semantically distinctive groups were isolated. One of these was that of time periods (line 14), words such as 'hour', 'month'. The other was that of units of measure, e.g. 'kilometer', 'hectare' (line 15). These two groups have the lowest occurrence of the dative of all of the groups included in the table. The time period category is conspicuously high in the accusative and genitive. This is to be expected on the basis of the time constructions of duration (accusative) and the use with numerals which are used with the genitive, e.g. *tri goda* 'three years'.

The frequency of use of the genitive in constructions of measure with numerals reaches its high point in the category of measures in which no less than 85.4 percent of the occurrences are in the genitive—by far the most salient frequency characteristic of this group.

In addition to the categories of common nouns just considered, the relative frequency of cases for proper nouns is given on line 3. Shtejnfel'dt does not list these individually so although the number of tokens can be calculated the number of types cannot. Since she gives the overall totals for all common nouns (line 2) and of all nouns (line 1) it is possible to deduce the number of proper nouns and their frequency in each case by subtracting the latter figures from the former. The results are reduced to percentages. These proper names presumably include both personal and place names but it may be conjectured that the bulk of the occurrences belong to the first of these categories. This category shows in general the frequency characteristics of the personal individual nouns in extreme form particularly in the overwhelming frequency of the nominative (76.3). The very low value for the instrumental (01.4) as compared with that for common personal individual nouns can perhaps be attributed to the fact that the predicate instrumental, e.g. *on stal oficerom* (instrumental) would find no applicability to the category of proper names. The higher result for the prepositional is probably due to the proper place names in this group.

Another category which like personal proper names might be expected to show a distribution like that of personal common nouns is constituted by the first and second person pronouns (line 16). Since the Russian finite verb is inflected for person, the pronoun may be omitted, although it usually is not. This may explain the somewhat lower, though still very substantial, proportion of nominative occurrences (51.8) when compared with the personal common nouns (54.1) and proper names (76.3). For these pronouns, the dative (14.5) has the highest frequency of any category in Table 1, a frequency even higher than that for the accusative (09.5).

The manner in which the figures in line 16 were derived requires some explanation, as they are not given in the same manner as those for the common nouns. The range and frequency is given by Shtejnfel'dt for each phonologically distinct pronominal form. This is adequate in some instances (e.g. *mnoj* which is the instrumental of the first person pronouns). However, where there is homonymity, e.g. *vas* which is at once the genitive, accusative, and prepositional of *vy* the second person plural intimate and the polite form for both singular and plural, only a single figure is given. However, it is possible, in these instances, to arrive at an approximation because of other data given by Shtejnfel'dt, namely the frequency of each individual preposition + pronoun combination provided it occur at least seven times in the entire sample. For example the frequency of *ot nas* 'from us' is given as 9. Since the combination of preposition + pronoun is generally unambiguous for case (e.g. *ot* only occurs with the genitive) it is possible to determine the total for each of the prepositional uses of the first and second person pronouns. Further, the prepositional uses are the *only* uses in the prepositional case. This leaves as the only ambiguity the genitive/accusative homonymity for the non-prepositional uses. Since the genitive relation is expressed by the adjectives *moj* 'my', etc., the only genitive uses without prepositions are with a very few verbs like *dobivatsja* 'strive for' which govern the genitive. Hence all these occurrences were assigned to the accusative. Finally, since the possessive adjectives are the functional means of expressing the possessive relationship in the first and second person pronouns,

*Table 2*

"Pure" (i.e. Non-Prepositional) Frequencies of Noun Use

| | N | G | D | A | I | P |
|---|---|---|---|---|---|---|
| All nouns | 50.1% | 26.0% | 02.6% | 15.9% | 05.3% | 00.0% |
| First- and second-person pronouns | 58.2 | 16.8 | 15.0 | 09.7 | 00.3 | 00.0 |

NOTE: All values are deduced and approximate.

the totals for these were included in the genitive. Here also there was only an approximation because individual case forms were only listed if their frequency was larger than 7. However, these approximations seem to produce reasonable results, high nominative, low accusative, and very low prepositional frequencies as for the personal noun categories.

One other set of calculations of possible theoretical interest was undertaken, the results of which are to be found in Table 2. It was noted earlier that Shtejnfel'dt gives the frequency of every individual combination of preposition + pronoun occurring more than 7 times. She also gives overall frequencies of each preposition, thus including occurrences with both pronouns and nouns. Moreover, uses with different cases are distinguished, e.g. *na* with accusative 3834, *na* with prepositional 3509. By subtracting all the pronominal uses as noted above, it becomes possible to approximate the prepositional frequencies of nouns with each case. By subtracting these figures in turn from the overall frequency of all the nouns with each case one can calculate the proportion of use with each case in its "pure" uses, i.e. without prepositions. Table 2 excludes all prepositional uses and gives the relative frequency of the entire set of nouns in their pure uses. The second line gives the corresponding values for the first and second persons. Since all uses of the nominative are pure uses, its relative frequency will naturally increase. Since the prepositional case, as its name indicates, occurs only with prepositions, it has no pure uses. Hence the entries for this category are zero on both lines of Table 2 and it must be excluded from the comparison. Consideration of the other five cases in their pure uses and taking the first and second person pronouns as representative *par excellence* of the personal category shows more clearly than any of the data previously presented that, in accordance with Jakobson's analysis, which was in fact based on pure case uses, the nominative and dative are personal cases and the accusative and instrumental non-personal.

The status of the dative as personal and the accusative as non-personal is probably relevant to such diachronic development as the survival of the former dative in English in pronouns like 'him', 'her', 'them' in the functions of the former dative and accusative. Some of the Romance Languages have separate conjunctive forms for certain dative and accusative pronouns, distinct from disjunctive forms used with prepositions, thus corresponding to the "pure uses" just discussed in regard to Russian.

All of the results described thus far were obtained by testing hypotheses based on fairly rough semantic classifications based on prior assumptions. It would obviously be of interest to undertake an analysis in which no prior classification is imposed on the data. For this purpose a cluster analysis seemed to be the most appropriate among the reasonably simple mathematical procedures which were available.[1]

Since the computer used, an IBM 360/57, did not have a memory sufficient to store all of the 961 nouns in Stejnfel'dt's work along with the case frequency of each, they were split on a random basis into two groups. Each group was subject to the identical program, which with one set of nouns will be called the A program and with the other the B. The percentage frequency for a particular noun was employed rather than the absolute value. The nature of the cluster analysis applied to these data may be described as follows. Each of the 485 nouns in program A is assigned a point in a six-dimensional space, whose coordinates are the percentage of its occurrence with each of the six cases. The computer first calculates the matrix of the distance of each of these 485 points to each other using the generalized Euclidean distance formula

$$\sqrt{[(a_1 - b_1)^2 + (a_2 - b_2)^2 + (a_3 - b_3)^2 \ldots]}$$

where $a_1, a_2, a_3 \ldots$ are the coordinates of one point and $b_1, b_2, b_3 \ldots$ of another. The cluster analysis then proceeds as follows. At the first pass, the two points with the smallest distance are consolidated to form a group and the midpoint between them becomes the centroid which represents the group in subsequent clustering. In the present instance, then, after one pass there are 483 groups with one member and one group with two members. At the second pass, the two of the 484 points which remain which are closest to each other are once more consolidated to form a new group, so that we now have 483 points and 483 groups of which either 2 have 2 members while the remaining 481 have one member, or possibly one group has 3 members and the remaining 482 groups have one member. The process goes on until the 484th pass when all the nouns are in one group.

Obviously the early passes have too little clustering to produce significant

[1] I wish to express my great appreciation for the assistance given me in regard to the following cluster analysis by Professor Herbert Solomon who first suggested this procedure and to the programmer Jim Stein who was largely responsible for carrying it out.

overall semantic clustering while the very late passes have virtually consolidated all nouns so that these results are also relatively unenlightening. Hence the 225th pass was chosen for both programs and the clustering at this point is given in detail in Appendix II.

We may first consider the results of program A at this stage of the clustering. There is, to begin with, a large and heterogeneous group with 62 members (group 1). This is not surprising since one would expect such a grouping to develop putting together items which are close to the general average for case distribution. If the total distribution is a normal one, then there will be a clustering of values about the mean. Still it is worth noting that even this large group has no words which are primarily place words, only 2 personal collectives, 2 time words, and only 6 of the very large group of individual personal nouns. Words indicating concrete objects and actions predominate.

The category of personal individual nouns shows up clearly in group 5 (16 out of 18, plus 'bird', 'army'), group 7 (9 out of 12); group 10 (9 out of 10, plus 'officialdom') and group 21 (3 out of 4). It is of interest to note that the very next pass (no. 226) unites two of these groups, group 5 and 21, to produce a new group with 19 out of 22 personal individual nouns, and in the pass after that (no. 227), group 10 picks up the one-member group which consists of 'schoolchild' (*škol'nik*).

The category of individual personal nouns is thus the most clearly distinguished. Two groups have a substantial number of place nouns, group 4 (9 out of 32) and group 8 (5 out of 10).

The results of program B are, as would be expected, basically similar to those of program A, though with a few interesting points of difference. One of these is that there is no single group corresponding to the large and heterogeneous group 1 of program A. In program B there are three extensive groups which correspond to this group of 62 members in program A, group 2 (16 members), group 4 (16 members), and group 11 (27 members). Even more striking than in group 1 of program A is the absence in these three groups of personal individual and collective nouns and of place nouns. Except for guest (*gost'*) in group 11, there are no examples of any of these semantic categories in these three groups. Another difference is the existence of a group with a large membership of personal collective nouns, group 15, in which 8 out of 14 nouns belong to this category. There are 4 predominantly personal individual groupings, group 3 (9 out of 10; the only non-personal is 'wild beast' *zver'*, often metaphorical in Communist literature), group 5 (14 out of 19), group 12 (7 out of 12), and group 28 (3 out of 4). On the 227th pass groups 28 and 3 consolidate, producing a group with 12 out of 14 personals. There are two predominantly place groups, group 1 (11 out of 17) and 20 (3 out of 3). Group 14 has 4 members of which 2 are time periods. Group 24 has two month names.

From the data presented here, it seems fair to draw the minimum conclusion that the distribution of frequency over the cases is far from random in relation to the semantic characteristics of the noun. In the light of these results, certain further questions of method and theory may be raised.

One question that might be raised is why the results, though obviously significant, are not, so to speak, perfect. We could imagine a situation in which groupings based on some technique of cluster analysis would move from the most fine-grained semantically definable groupings in an ascending hierarchy to the most general and basic features. Outside of the inevitable variability due to sampling in any text frequency studies, there are certain other obvious factors which detract from the neatness of the results. Some of these relate to the nature of Shtejnfel'dt's study. As unique and valuable as her data are, they have certain limitations since, as in practically all frequency studies, they were undertaken with primarily applied pedagogical problems in mind.

Since her cut-off point is range 13, no data are given regarding relative case frequencies for many fairly frequent nouns. For example, only five of the month names appear. While the size of the sample is adequate for other purposes, where we are concerned as in this study with individual nouns, the number of occurrences of even fairly frequent nouns is small in relation to the six case categories.

Further, Shtejnfel'dt does not distinguish singular from plural for the individual cases, nor does she distinguish first and second genitives or first and second locatives even though minimal contrasts exist for these case forms (e.g. *pfunt saxaru* 'a pound of sugar' [second genitive]; *vkus saxara* 'the taste of sugar' [first genitive]). Including this distinction would probably help to delimit mass from count nouns. With regard to number there are instances in which certain constructions only occur in one number. An example is the construction of *po* with the dative plural of time words (e.g. *rabotat' po nočam* 'to work nights').

Finally, Shtejnfel'dt does not distinguish between proper names of persons and those of places. Other measures that would improve the results are rather due to the limitations of the techniques applied than to shortcomings in the data. Only the most simple method of cluster analysis was applied. More subtle methods, or perhaps other mathematical techniques, might give better results.

Further, the semantic analysis was fairly crude and unsystematic. For example, many physical objects if of sufficient bulk also occur in place constructions, e.g. 'table'. A larger and more complex and subtle set of semantic features would probably improve the results.

Even given all these, however, there is an important factor beyond sampling problems that would always prevent "perfect" results. This is precisely the tendency in case systems to reduce the redundancies based on correlation between case and semantic categories by developing specialized meanings for individual cases. Paralleling the inherent variety of semantic features in the lexical meanings of the individual nouns, there is a large and heterogeneous set of uses for individual case forms which is greatly abetted by the development of prepositions. There is also, as pointed out earlier, the factor of polysemy of individual nouns to a great extent disambiguated by case. Given these factors, the absence of complete correlation between case and the semantics of individual nouns is not surprising. Perhaps what is surprising, in view of this, is the extent to which, as I believe is shown in this study, there is at least a statistical correlation. If the present study presents valid results it would seem to indicate that, at the least, the observation of, and the attempt to explain, variations in frequency has a certain heuristic value in directing attention to problems which might otherwise tend to escape our notice.

From a more general point of view, we may raise the basic question as to the role and significance of frequency studies for linguistic theory. To begin with, it should be pointed out that the impossibility of generating the grammatical utterances of a language from transitional probabilities (a possibility never entertained, as far as my knowledge extends, by linguists, as distinct from engineers), while it has contributed to a general negative feeling towards frequency, is obviously irrelevant. On the general question perhaps the following basic positions might be sketched.

1. Linguistics is the study of *langue*, not *parole*. Frequency belongs to *parole*, therefore it is not part of linguistics. As a further justification for this position it might be argued that frequency is, so to speak, an epiphenomenon. Once we have done a complete syntactic and semantic analysis, the frequency phenomena could be deduced from this analysis.

2. A more moderate position would be that while frequency phenomena are not completely deducible, they are still essentially trivial, thus without theoretical interest. This position derives from the notion that current dominant theory does not include text frequency in any substantive way. Since it is not included in theory, it has no theoretical interest.

3. A third position would be that frequency phenomena are not only not to be relegated to the status of an epiphenomenon, but are of real theoretical interest. This is the position that I believe is the most tenable.

To begin with, it seems clear enough that frequency is not a mere predictable epiphenomenon. For example when of two paraphrase constructions one is taken as basic and the other is derivative one cannot predict how often the transformation will occur. Of course it might be unpredictable but still of no real interest if it fails to show significant connections with anything else. However, there is by now considerable evidence that frequency is at the very least symptomatic of important things like marking hierarchies and, in the present instance, the connection of case with semantic features.

It appears, however, that frequency is of importance at still deeper levels. The linguist's intuitions about what is likely to be basic as against what is to be derived seems to be guided largely by frequency knowledge which is present without actual counting. This seems to be so for example in regard to basic word order. The investigation of the connections between what is basic and what is frequent would seem to be a topic of fundamental theoretic interest.

Further, there are several important types of problems which cannot be investigated without some reference to frequency. This is most notably the case in regard to the study of style, insofar as it involves the relative frequency of paraphrase alternatives and historical changes, which resolves itself to a considerable extent into a study of frequency fluctuations among alternatives over time. Considered synchronically such frequency fluctuations have important sociolinguistic correlates as shown by the pioneering work of Labov in this area.

Finally, applied uses, with which frequency studies have been up to now almost exclusively allied, are not to be despised. In this field, even if the future should see the development of theories involving a greater variety of parameters than at present, it is clear that frequency inevitably will continue to play an essential role in relation to pedagogical strategies of second language learning.

## Appendix I

*Group 1. Personal Common Individual Names*: people (ljudi); children (rebjata); comrade (tovarišč); friend (drug); person (čelovek); boy (mal'čik); girl (devuška); worker (rabočij); girl (devočka); mother (mat'); children (deti); mother (mama); brother (brat); boss (načal'nik); guest (gost'); woman (ženščina); lad (paren'); artisan (master); pioneer (pioner); chairman (predsedatel'); schoolchild (škol'nik); pupil (učenik); komsomol member (komsomolec); boss (xozjain); wife (žena); father (otec); engineer (inžener); son (syn); worker (rabotnik); assistant (pomoščnik); director (direktor); youth (junoša); leader (rukovoditel'); old man (starik); student (student); hero (geroj); builder (stroitel'); captain (kapitan); commander (komandir); locksmith (slesar'); teacher (učitel'); child (rebënok); neighbor (sosed); uncle (djadja); participant (učastnik); husband (muž); enemy (vrag); parent (roditel'); sister (sestra); chauffeur (šofër); female teacher (učitel'nica); physician (vrač); grandmother (babuška); friend (podruga); brigadier (brigadir); boy (mal'čiška); man (mužčina); young child (malyš); fine person (molodec); girl (devčonka); author (avtor); reader (čitatel'); female pupil (učenica); artist (xudožnik); soldier (soldat); communist (kommunist); sportsman (sportsmen); fighter (boec); Fascist (fašist); artist (artist); peasant (xrest'janin); female worker (rabotnica); sailor (morjak); citizen (graždanin); aunt (tëtja); officer (oficer); agronomist (agronom); tractor driver (traktorist); specialist (specialist); inhabitant (žitel'); female neighbor (sosedka); doctor (doktor); general (general); German (nemec); spectator (zritel'); daughter (doč'); mistress (xozjajka); mechanic (mexanik); pedagogue (pedagog); pilot (šturman); sailor (matros); mister (gospodin); hunter (oxotnik); scout (razvedčik); representative (predstavitel'); daughter (dočka); opponent (protivnik); writer (pisatel'); grandfather (ded); technician (texnik); radio operator (radist); professor (professor); victor (pobeditel'); friend (prijatel'); fool (durak); deputy (deputat); passenger (passažir); lieutenant (lejtenant); old woman (staruxa); candidate (kandidat); correspondent (korrespondent); journalist (žurnalist); pilot (lëtčik); father (papa); brigade leader (brigadir).

*Group 2. Personal Collective*: people (narod); youth (molodëž'); party (partija); family (sem'ja); Young Communist League (komsomol); army (armija); committee (komitet); brigade (brigada); collective (kollektiv); circle (kružok); society (obščestvo); staff (štab); crowd (tolpa); District Committee (rajkom); chorus (xor); population (naselenie); academy (akademija); commission (komissija); orchestra (orkestr); faculty (fakul'tet); ministry (ministerstvo); authorities (načal'stvo); detachment (otrjad); state (gosudarstvo); generation (pokolenie).

*Group 3. Animals*: bird (ptica); horse (lošad'); fish (ryba); dog (sobaka); animal (životnoe); cow (korova); wild animal (zver'); horse (kon'); pigeon (golub').

*Group 4. Body Parts*: eye (glaz); hand (ruka); face (lico); head (golova); foot (noga); shoulder (plečo); heart (serdce); nose (nos); back (spina); hair (volos); chest (grud'); finger (palec); tooth (zub); forehead (lob); ear (uxo); lip (guba); cheek (ščeka); neck (šeja); mouth (rot); wing (krylo); eyebrow (brov'); elbow (lokot'); knee (koleno); nape (zatylok); face, appearance (oblik); chin (podborodok); tail (xvost); paw (lapa); palm (ladon'); fist (kulak).

*Group 5. Concrete Count Nouns*: table (stol); machine (mašina); book (kniga); letter (pis'mo); picture (kartina); box (jaščik); sheet of paper, leaf (list); book (knižka); gate (vorota); board (doska); airplane (samolët); bell (zvonok); stone (kamen'); telephone (telefon); present (podarok); dress (plat'e); bench (stanok); bed (krovat'); boat (korabl'); chair (stul); page (stranica); train, car (vagon); desk (parta); necktie (galstuk); armchair (kreslo); notebook (tetrad'); bed (postel'); eyeglasses (očki); pen (pero); sleeve (rukav); bottle (butylka); wardrobe (škaf); tractor (traktor); lamp (lampa); branch (vetka); pillow (poduška); bench (skamejka); crockery (posuda); ticket (bilet); trunk (čemodan); shirt (rubaška); ship (sudno); ball (mjač); apple (jabloko); wheel (koleso); pencil (karandaš); textbook (učebnik); cord (verëvka); plate (tarelka); flag (flag); key (ključ); bus (avtobus); sack (mešok); trolley (tramvaj); plant (rastenie); shovel (lopata); pine tree (sosna); knife (nož); clothing (odežda); leaflet (listok); instrument (instrument); glass (stakan); curtain (zanaves); stove (pečka); automobile (avtomobil'); weapons (oružie); bag (sumka); mirror (zerkalo); ribbon (lenta); steamer (paroxod); cage (kletka); ball (šar); cloud (oblako); rocket (raketa); telegram (telegramma); note (zapiska); briefcase (portfel'); brick (kirpič); boat (lodka); poster (plakat); lantern (fonar'); journal (dnevnik); leg (nožka); stick (palka); cloud (tuča); jacket (kurtka); fruit (plod); chain (cep'); football (futbol); tent (palatka); badge (značok); boot (botinok); lid (kryška); notebook (tetradka); stove (plita); microphone (mikrofon); hammer (molotok); side-board (bufet); column (stolb); toy (igruška); handle (ručka); motor (motor); card (karta); belt (pojas); stove (pec'); flower (cvetok); shawl (platok); train (poezd); watch (časy); suit (kostjum); boot (sapog); cap (šapka); pipe (truba).

*Group 6. Concrete Mass*: water (voda); bread (xleb); paper (bumaga); money (den'gi); snow (sneg); milk (moloko); tear (sleza); glass (steklo); paint (kraska); rain (dozd'); grass (trava); sand (pesok); tea (čaj); butter (maslo); grain (zerno); meat (mjaso); blood (krov'); wood (drova); iron (železo); ice (lëd); corn (kukuruza); hay (seno); ink (černila); vodka (vodka); leather (koža).

*Group 7. Abstract Qualities*: strength (sila); truth (pravda); joy (radost'); friendship (družba); power (vlast'); art (iskusstvo); glory (slava); pride (gordost'); age (vozrast); meaning (značenie); height (vysota); difficulty (trudnost'); speed (skorost'); stillness (tišina); cleanliness (čistota); depth (glubina); gratitude (blagodarnost'); youth (molodost'); health (zdorov'e); beauty (krasota); curiosity (ljubopytstvo).

*Group 8. Transient Objects*: voice (golos); name (imja); song (pesnja); glance (vzgljad); story (rasskaz); wind (veter); light (svet); fire (ogon'); air (vozdux); noise (šum); speech (reč'); dream (mečta); verse (stix); tone (ton); trace (sled); darkness (temnota); spirit (dux); wave (volna); ray (luč); frost (moroz); sleep (son); shadow (ten'); smell (zapax).

*Group 9. Place Nouns*: place (mesto); house (dom); side (storona); city (gorod); room (komnata); earth (zemlja); street (ulica); road (doroga); path (put'); country (strana); world (mir); shore (bereg); sky (nebo); field (pole); corner (ugol); apartment (kvartira); district (rajon); sea (more); garden (sad); mountain (gora); edge (kraj); floor (pol); building (zdanie); shop (cex); fatherland (rodina); workshop (masterskaja); hall (zal); river (reka); kitchen (kuxnja); corridor (koridor); village (derevnja); world (svet); station (stancija); public square (ploščad'); platform (ploščadka); threshold (porog); village (selo); cottage (domik); stairs (lestnica); region (oblast'); roof (kryša); center (centr); store (magazin); lodging (pomeščenie); camp (lager'); exposition (vystavka); corner (ugolok); floor (ètaž); side (bok); exit (vyxod); board (bort); dining room (stolovaja); park (park); bridge (most); shelf (polka); lake (ozero); ceiling (potolok); station (vokzal); kitchen garden (ogorod); island (ostrov); stream (potok); electric plant (elektrostancija); palace (dvorec); warehouse (sklad); wall (stenka); territory (territorija); town (gorodok); small window (okoško); farm (ferma); barn (saraj); rear (tyl); office (kontora); boundary (granica); porch (kryl'co); middle (seredina); stadium (stadion); locality (mestnost'); surface (poverxnost'); wilderness (pustynja); paved road (šosse); capital (stolica); ground (počva); valley (dolina); forest (les).

*Group 10. Institutions*: school (škola); factory (zavod); institute (institut); collective farm (kolxoz); republic (respublika); factory (fabrika); combine (kombinat); club (klub); theater (teatr); school (učilišče); technical school (texnikum); university (universitet); hospital (bol'nica); academy (akademija); museum (muzej); tribunal (sud); hotel (gostinica).

*Group 11. Time Periods*: year (god; let (g.pl.)); day (den'); hour (čas); month (mesjac); week (nedelja); century (vek); second (sekunda); minute (minuta).

*Group 12. Measures*: kilometer (kilometr); ruble (rubl'); meter (metr); kilogram (kilogramm); hectare (gektar); ton (tonna); percent (procent).

## Appendix II

*Program A: Groups after pass 225*

*Group 1*: matter (delo); face (lico); person (čelovek); book (kniga); water (voda); heart (serdce); children (deti); plan (plan); letter (pis'mo); story (rasskaz); step (šag); movement (dviženie); tree, wood (derevo); experience (opyt); detachment, detail (otrjad); snow (sneg); occupation (zanjatie); hair (volos); problem (zadača); feeling (čuvstvo); right, law (pravo); noise (šum); knowledge (znanie); victory (pobeda); line (linija); success (uspex); tear (sleza); hero (geroj); profession (professija); piece (kusok); airplane (samolët); glass (steklo); lip (guba); material (material); gift (podarok); winter (zima); husband (muž); education (obrazovanie); parent (roditel'); art (isskustvo); friend (podruga); dance (tanec); pipe (truba); document (dokument); notebook (tetrad'); motor (motor); pen (pero); star (zvezda); smell (zapax); cow (korova); wood (drova); apple (jabloko); wheel (koleso); textbook (učebnik); beauty (krasota); key (ključ); sack (mešok); anniversary (godovščina); skill (masterstvo); combine (kombajn); vodka (vodka); leather (koža).

*Group 2*: eye (glaz); shawl (platok); impression (vpečatlenie); shovel (lopata); knife (nož); confidence (uverennost').

*Group 3*: time (vremja); head (golova); transmission (peredača); calling (zvanie); moment (moment); suitcase (čemodan); half-hour (polčasa).

*Group 4*: life (žizn'); work (rabota); class (klass); plant (zavod); newspaper (gazeta); world (mir); family (sem'ja); lesson (urok); beginning (načalo); institute (institut); meeting (vstreča); shop (cex); portion (učastok); form (forma); event (sobytie); connection (svjaz); century (vek); club (klub); studies (učëba); concert (koncert); village (selo); cottage (domik); car, train (vagon); congress (s"ezd); school (učilišče); creativity (tvorčestvo); production (proizvedenie); creation (sozdanie); composition (sostav); trolley (tramvaj).

*Group 5*: children (rebjata); boy (mal'čik); mother (mama); woman (ženščina); pupil (učenik); komsomol member (komsomolec); father (otec); son (syn); old man (starik); bird (ptica); child (rebënok); grandfather (djadja); schoolteacher (učitel'nica); brigade leader (brigadir); boy (mal'čiška); inhabitant (žitel'); general (general); army (vojsko).

*Group 6*: side (storona); lecture (lekcija).

*Group 7*: voice (golos); artisan (master); fire (ogon'); master (xozjain); assistant (pomoščnik); leader (rukovoditel'); participant (učastnik); sailor (morjak); autumn (osen'); agronomist (agronom); tractor driver (traktorist).

*Group 8*: room (komnata); courtyard (dvor); corner (ugol); movement (xod); course (kurs); kitchen (kuxnja); dress (plat'e); platform (ploščadka); armchair (kreslo); health (zdorov'e).

*Group 9*: hour (čas); minute (minuta).

*Group 10*: friend (drug); worker (rabočij); boss (načal'nik); chairman (predsedatel'); worker (rabotnik); director (direktor); young child (malyš); soldier (soldat); officer (oficer); authorities (načal'stvo).

*Group 11*: table (stol); cause (pričina); desk (parta).

*Group 12*: road (doroga); happiness (sčast'e); trace (sled).

*Group 13*: view (vid); eyeglasses (očki); cord (verëvka).

*Group 14*: conversation (razgovor); glory (slava).

*Group 15*: shoulder (plečo); request (pros'ba).

*Group 16*: people (narod); fatherland (rodina); river (reka); production (proizvodstvo); development (razvitie); government (gosudarstvo); branch (vetka).

*Group 17*: war (vojna); youth (molodëž'); organization (organizacija); economy (xozjajstvo); kilometer (kilometr); animal (životnoe); militia (družina); grain (zerno); district committee (rajkom).

*Group 18*: soul (duša); wearing (nošenie); struggle (bor'ba); taste (vkus).

*Group 19*: tongue (jazyk); nose (nos); mountain (gora); spirit (dux); elbow (lokot').

*Group 20*: attention (vnimanie); exchange (smena); tea (čaj); bottle (butylka); gratitude (blagodarnost'); academic division (fakul'tet).

*Group 21*: lad (paren'); daydream (mečta); father (papa); doctor (doktor).

*Group 22*: picture (kartina); conversation (beseda); number (cifra); wave (volna); difficulty (trudnost'); fog (tuman); flag (flag); orchestra (orkestr).

*Group 23*: line (očered'); forehead (lob); chin (podborodok).

*Group 24*: image (obraz); satisfaction (udovol'stvie); fist (kulak); leadership (rukovodstvo).

*Group 25*: chest (grud'); bed (krovat').

*Group 26*: memory (pamjat'); number (čislo); appearance (oblik).

*Group 27*: combine (kombinat); undertaking (predprijatie); November (nojabr').

*Group 28*: board (doska); cheek (ščeka).

*Group 29*: half (polovina); ink (černila).

*Group 30*: seven-year plan (semiletka); kilogram (kilogramm); hectare (gektar); May (maj).

*Group 31*: world (svet); public square (ploščad); condition (uslovie); threshold (porog); darkness (temnota); bench (skamejka).

*Group 32*: neck (šeja); lodging (pomeščenie); bed (postel').

*Group 33*: misfortune (beda); girl (devčonka); youth (molodost').

*Group 34*: death (smert'); butter (maslo); smoke (dym).

*Group 35*: knee (koleno); conclusion (zaključenie).

*Group 36*: paw (lapa); sleeve (rukav).

*Group 37*: February (fevral'); March (mart).

*One-member groups*: work (trud); country (strana); back (spina); schoolchild (škol'nik); smile (ulybka); corridor (koridor); staircase (lestnica) surprise (udivlenie);

agitation (volnenie); God (bog); meat (mjaso); silence (tišina); excursion (èkskursija); plant (rastenie); September (sentjabr'); flame (plamja); moment (mig); period (period).

*Program B: Groups after pass 225*

*Group 1*: year (god); house (dom); scale (škala); city (gorod); earth (zemlja); wall (stena); forest (les); shore (bereg); sky (nebo); sea (more); construction (stroitel'stvo); village (derevnja); grass (trava); station (stancija); ship (korabl'); staff (štab); preparation (podgotovka).

*Group 2*: day (den'); time (raz); song (pesnja); answer (otvet); book (knižka); verse (stix); watch (časy); mouth (rot); fish (ryba); period (srok); blanket (odejalo); day (sutki); ticket (bilet); plate (tarelka).

*Group 3*: father (papa); pioneer (pioner); student (student); neighbor (sosed); reader (čitatel'); artist (xudožnik); sportsman (sportsmen); peasant (krest'janin); wild animal (zver').

*Group 4*: word (slovo); look (vzgljad); bread (xleb); technology (texnika); flower (cvetok); worry (zabota); steam (para); laughter (smex); lamp (lampa); tractor (traktor); equipment (oborudovanie); thousand (tysjača); operation (operacija); supper (užin); cloud (tuča); merit (dostoinstvo).

*Group 5*: comrade (tovarišč); truth (pravda); girl (devuška); girl (devočka); mother (mat'); brother (brat); wind (veter); secretary (sekretar'); bell (zvonok); captain (kapitan); commander (komandir); chauffeur (šofër); grandmother (babuška); man (mužčina); author (avtor); silence (molčanie); frost (moroz); aunt (tëtja); daughter (doč').

*Group 6*: leg (noga); help (pomošč'); goal (cel'); tooth (zub); ear (uxo); tone (ton); eyebrow (brov'); pencil (karandaš); length (dlina).

*Group 7*: door (dver'); question (vopros); night (noč'); evening (večer); decision (rešenie); possibility (vozmožnost'); dinner (obed); task (zadanie); sack (mešok); breakfast (zavtrak).

*Group 8*: window (okno); chair (stul).

*Group 9*: strength (sila); spring (vesna); fear (trevoga); speed (skorost').

*Group 10*: end (konec); communism (kommunizm).

*Group 11*: thought (mysl'); machine (mašina); part (čast'); guest (gost'); group (gruppa); number (nomer); thing (vešč'); speech (reč'); game (igra); command (komanda); sound (zvuk); group of ten (desjatok); power (vlast'); bench (stanok); surname (familija); train (poezd); law (zakon); horse (lošad'); dog (sobaka); appearance (vystuplenie); calculation (rasčët); tractor (traktor); stove (peč'); inclination (stremlenie); ship (sudno); pigeon (golub'); corn (kukuruza).

*Group 12*: path (put'); history (istorija); paper (bumaga); garden (sad); character (xarakter); box (jaščik); sheet of paper, leaf (list); row (rjad); shop (magazin); cap (šapka); height (vysota); pillow (poduška); shirt (rubaška); practice (praktika).

*Group 13*: occurrence (slučaj); hall (zal).

*Group 14*: month (mesjac); second (sekunda); academy (akademija); cadre (kadr).

*Group 15*: name (imja); council (sovet); morning (utro); party (partija); army (armija); age (vozrast); minister (ministr); settlement (poselenie); horse (kon');

population (naselenie); fleet (flot); commission (komissija); ministry (ministerstvo).

*Group 16*: sun (solnce); member (člen); wife (žena); engineer (inžener); rain (dožd'); locksmith (slesar); teacher (učitel'); ray (luč); female pupil (učenica); female worker (rabotnica); instructor (prepodavatel'); pine tree (sosna).

*Group 17*: light (svet); friendship (družba); condition (položenie); building (zdanie); brigade (brigada); fate (sud'ba); competition (sorevnovanie); boot (sapog); crowd (tolpa); moon (luna); blood (krov'); ice (lëd).

*Group 18*: week (nedelja); chair (stul).

*Group 19*: joy (radost'); collective (kollektiv); stone (kamen'); sand (pesok); cleanliness (čistota); chorus (xor); cold (xolod).

*Group 20*: district (rajon); collective farm (kolxoz); factory (fabrika).

*Group 21*: air (vozdux); workshop (masterskaja); gathering (sobranie); result (rezul'tat); meaning (smysl); circle (kružok); page (stranica); sleep (son); bus (avtobus).

*Group 22*: Young Communist League (komsomol); ruble (rubl'); ton (tonna); meeting (svidanie); birth (roždenie); percent (procent); July (ijul').

*Group 23*: pocket (karman); edge (kraj).

*Group 24*: union (sojuz); republic (respublika); committee (komitet); culture (kul'tura); meter (metr); society (obščestvo); region (oblast'); management (upravlenie); October (oktjabr'); completion (okončanie); June (ijun'); August (avgust).

*Group 25*: finger (palec); paint (kraska); respect (uvaženie); pride (gordost').

*Group 26*: summer (leto); wing (krylo); tail (xvost).

*Group 27*: builder (stroitel'); enemy (vrag); spectator (zritel').

*Group 28*: holiday (prazdnik); sister (sestra); citizen (graždanin); female neighbor (sosedka).

*Group 29*: love (ljubov'); shadow (ten').

*One-member groups*: hand (ruka); street (ulica); time (pora); field (pole); example (primer); milk (moloko); gate (vorota); telephone (telefon); regret (sožalenie); opinion (mnenie); palm (of hand) (ladon'); measure (mera); center (centr); wish (želanie); name (nazvanie); editorial board (redakcija); fine person (molodec); communist (kommunist); wardrobe (škaf); depth (glubina); card (karta); nape (zatylok); iron (železo); curiosity (ljubopytstvo); hay (seno).

## References Cited

Fillmore, C. J. 1968. "The case for case." In E. Bach and R. T. Harms, eds., *Universals in Linguistic Theory*. New York.

Jakobson, R. 1936. "Beitrag zur allgemeinen Kasuslehre. Gesamtbedeutungen der russischen Kasus." *Travaux du Cercle Linguistique de Prague*, 6: 240–88.

Maher, J. P. 1969. "Italian *serpe*: why not *serpente*?" *Language Science* no. 6, Indiana University.

Sechehaye, A. 1950. *La structure logique de la phrase*. Paris.

Shtejnfel'dt, E. 1963. *Chastotnyj slovar' sovremennogo russkogo literaturnogo jazyka*. Tallin.

# Dynamic Aspects of Word Order in the Numeral Classifier

Some of the synchronic hypotheses proposed in Greenberg 1973 regarding the numeral classifier construction will serve as a point of departure for the present more diachronically oriented study.[1]

Among the conclusions of the earlier discussion which will prove to be relevant in this connection are the following.

1. There are many indications that in the tripartite construction consisting of quantifier (Q), classifier (Cl), and head noun (N), Q is in direct construction with Cl and this complex construction, which will be called the classifier phrase, is in turn in construction with N.[2] We may symbolize these relationships as follows: ((Q ↔ Cl) ↔ N), where the notation ↔ is used to indicate the possibility of both orders of the items connected by it.

2. In consonance with the world-wide favoring of the word order QN in languages without numeral classifiers, there is a heavy statistical predominance of the order Q-Cl as against Cl-Q in the classifier phrase of languages with the numeral classifier construction.[3]

[1] The present study was supported by the Stanford Project on Language Universals founded by the National Science Foundation. I am also indebted to Charles Li for calling to my attention Wang Li 1958 and to Vicky Shu for providing a translation of the relevant chapter on the history of the classifier construction in Chinese.

[2] There are, however, a few instances in which the classifier goes with the noun, but these usually involve the deletion of the numeral 'one'. An example is the Bengali and Assamese 'definitive' mentioned later in the paper, e.g. Bengali *boĭ-khana* 'book-the', in which *khana* functions as a numeral classifier in other constructions. Efik seems to have an incipient classifier system in which the classifier is prefixed to the noun which itself is followed by a numeral. This case seems to involve something like English *two grease spots* as against *two spots of grease*.

[3] See especially Greenberg 1963, Universal 18, which includes AN → DN with far greater than chance frequency.

3. In accordance with the first principle, that of immediate constituency of Q and Cl, orders in which N separates Q from Cl nowhere occur as regular word order types. The remaining possibilities, then, all of which are found, are: (1) (Q-Cl)-N; (2) N-(Q-Cl); (3) (Cl-Q)-N; (4) N-(Cl-Q). In conformity with the second principle, however, orders (1) or (2) are far more frequent than (3) or (4) in numeral classifier languages.

4. A further observation is that, whereas the order within the classifying phrase Q ↔ Cl is, for any language, almost invariably fixed, there is considerable variation in many languages in the order of the Head Noun ↔ Classifier Phrase construction. Thus, many languages have both N-(Q-Cl) and (Q-Cl)-N as regular possibilities in apparent free variation (e.g. Malay).

5. The favoring of Q-Cl over Cl-Q in the classifying phrase does not find its parallel in a corresponding favoring of the order (Q ↔ Cl)-N over N-(Q ↔ Cl). The order in which the classifying phrase is postposed to the noun is at least as frequent as the preposed order. Because of this fact, the Classifier ↔ Head Noun construction was not considered a subtype of the Quantifier ↔ Head Noun construction in regard to word order properties in Greenberg 1963.

6. In numeral classifier languages the numeral classifier construction is almost always identical with the measure construction including rules of word order. This is so much the case that many grammars of such languages consider the numeral classifier construction as merely a subvariety of an overall construction type which includes measures. For example, if the order is five-flat-object-book, a classifier language will almost invariably have the order five-pounds-cheese.

7. It is generally the case that numeral classifier languages will apparently lack a classifier in nouns indicating periods of time, units of distance and the word 'time' in such phrases as 'five times'. It was hypothesized that in these cases, the correct interpretation was not that the classifier is omitted but that words like 'day', 'mile', and 'time' are themselves measures of verbal action so that we have to do with a subtype of the overall classifier or measure phrases. In other words, such phrases as 'five days' are rather to be identified with (Q ↔ Cl) than (Q ↔ N).

8. Finally, it was noted that many classifier languages have constructions in which the classifier appears without a quantifier. The meaning here is invariably singular, and is in some languages specified as definite, in others indefinite, and in still others neither. In some grammars it is explicitly noted that this occurs through deletion of 'one' (the most unmarked number).

The preceding purely synchronic observations suggest certain diachronic hypotheses which may be stated as follows.

First, we may posit that the synchronic order of the Q ↔ Cl classifier phrases is not only synchronically basic but represents diachronically the normal order Q ↔ N before the introduction of the noun classifier construction. It is normally still present in expressions of time, distance, and frequency of verbal action in isolated form and in incorporated form in the measure construction. Since in fact classifiers are always nouns and in a great many instances still function as head nouns, we deduce that the classifier phrase at the beginning is simply a quantifier-noun phrase with a particular syntactic use. It was noted, under conclusion 2 above, that in regard to word order properties, Q ↔ Cl within the classifier construction conforms to generalizations of Q ↔ N in non-classifier languages.

Second, the great variability of order within languages of the classifier phrase itself in construction with the head noun as against the virtual fixity of Q ↔ Cl (point 4 above) suggests that the order of N in relation to the classifier phrase is often in the process of undergoing a shift.

Third, we may further hypothesize that it is likely that in such cases the earlier order is N-(Q ↔ Cl) rather than (Q ↔ Cl)-N. This is because the postposing of the classifier phrase, viewed as a quantifying expression, is deviant in relation to the general tendency of quantifiers to precede nouns. We may conjecture that in later stages with the spread of the general classifier to the point where the language is close to or in some cases reaches a situation in which there is only a single 'classifier', the construction comes to be treated more and more as simply a quantifier and hence moves to the more normal order Q-N as now represented by (Q ↔ Cl)-N.

We may now consider the evidence bearing on the validity of these hypotheses. The most cogent will be direct historical documentation. Here Chinese represents a uniquely valuable case as a numeral classifier language with historical records extending over at least three millennia. At present all Chinese dialects have this construction and also have, as far as I know, the order (Q-Cl)-N. As a further point it is to be noted that they also use classifiers in the demonstrative construction in the singular (Dem-Cl)-N.

The following brief account of the history of the classifier construction in Chinese is based chiefly on Wang Li 1958 and the various works of Dobson on different stages of early Chinese (Dobson 1959, 1962, 1964, 1968).

The earliest written Chinese is that of the only partially deciphered oracle bones of the Shang dynasty (1401–1123 B.C.). Wang Li (1958: II.236) cites two examples from this period in which the classifier is a noun identical with the noun classified, e.g. *rén shí-yoù-liù rén* 'man ten-and-six man', i.e. 'sixteen men'. This "autonymous" construction is found in Burmese, Thai, and other Southeast Asian languages at the present time. However, there is also the use of *rén* 'man' as a classifier in *qīang shí rén* 'Qiang (a tribal name) ten man', i.e. 'ten Qiang'.

As scanty as the evidence is from the Shang period it shows substantial agreement with that of the next period, Early Western Chou, and indicates that the basic pattern of early Chinese in this matter was already established. The points of agreement include the existence of the autonymous construction, the use of *rén* as a classifier, and the word order N-Q-Cl.

The texts of Early Western Chou (11th and 10th centuries B.C.) are of two types which agree in their essential linguistic features. The first of these consists of inscriptions on bronze vessels and the second of certain archaic portions of the *Shu Ching* (*Book of Documents*); Dobson (1962) calls this language Early Archaic Chinese (EAC). His work contains both a summary grammar and a set of texts with translation constituting about one third of the extant corpus of this period.

EAC has a limited set of classifiers and the autonymous construction of the Shang period continues to be frequent. Unlike contemporary Chinese, classifiers do not occur in the demonstrative construction. While the present paper is concerned primarily with word order, it may be pointed out that the later appearance of the demonstrative construction confirms a diachronic hypothesis in Greenberg 1973, namely that the classifier construction starts with expressions of quantity and, if it spreads syntactically, does so first by occurring with demonstratives.

In all, according to Dobson, EAC has three constructions: N-Q-Cl, N-Q, and Q-N. The evidence of this period and of the preceding Shang period confirms our hypothesis insofar as the postposed ordered N-(Q-Cl) occurs rather than (Q-Cl)-N as in present-day Chinese. An examination of the texts edited by Dobson reveals certain other pertinent facts not considered in the grammatical sections of his book. We might expect on the basis of our earlier stated hypotheses that the order Q-Cl incorporated in the full classifier phrase N-(Q-Cl) reflects the earlier basic Q-N order. This is supported by the exclusive occurrence of the order Q-N in time, distance, measure, and currency expressions in EAC. In fact, with countables the Q-N construction without classifiers is still the most usual one. In other words the classifier is not required. It remains then to explain the occurrence of N-Q expressions. An examination of the texts edited by Dobson shows that at least in this part of the corpus, the order N-Q only occurs in lists, e.g. from the *Sheau Yu Diing*: reward /Yū/?/?/bow/one/,/arrow/hundred/,/decorated/bow case/one/,/metal/mail/one/, etc. Forrest (1948: 112) notes this usage of N-Q without classifiers as being specifically in lists in the "Proto-Chinese" language of the *Book of Odes*, equivalent to Dobson's Middle Archaic Chinese.

It is noted by Chao (1968: 272–73) in his grammar of contemporary Mandarin that the order N-(Q-Cl) is found in lists. In Banggais, an

Austronesian language (van den Bergh 1953: 81) in which the normal order is (Q-Cl)-N, lists have the order N-(Q-Cl). The rule is illustrated by the example of a list of contents of a bride price payment. Among non-classifier languages, Biblical Hebrew may be cited in this connection. An interesting example is I Kings 5–7, which contains a detailed description of the building work done for Solomon by Hiram, King of Tyre. Throughout this description the numerals consistently precede the noun. But in 7:40–45 there is a summary which begins, "So Hiram made an end of doing all the work that he made for King Solomon on the house of the Lord: the two pillars . . ." etc. In this summary all the numerals follow the noun. The further significance of this construction will be discussed in a later section.

To summarize, in EAC, outside of the N-Q list construction we have Q-N and N-(Q-Cl). We interpret Q-N as a survival of the earlier non-classifier stage and N-(Q-Cl) as reflecting this form in its Cl-Q constituent.

The "Classical Chinese" literary language of the fourth and third centuries B.C. is called Late Archaic Chinese by Dobson. This language does not use classifiers and the usual construction is Q-N.[4] The *Book of Odes* (11th–7th century B.C.) shows, according to Dobson (1968), an intermediate situation in which all of the EAC alternatives appear but the classifier construction is limited to *rén* 'man'.

The indications are that the classifier construction did not disappear from the spoken language during this period but its non-occurrence is part of the stylistic emphasis on brevity and the omission of redundant items. It reappears in the written language of the Han dynasty (202 B.C.–A.D. 221) but still with the old word order. After the Han period the modern order Q-Cl-N begins to occur. Wang Li conjectures from the frequent appearance of the classifier construction in poetry of the T'ang dynasty (A.D. 618–907) that by this time the construction was compulsory. The shift to the contemporary state of affairs was probably complete by the ninth century, to judge from certain Buddhist texts qualified by Maspero as "popular" (Maspero 1915). These texts are probably specifically Mandarin. They exhibit not only the modern order (Q-Cl)-N but also the use of the classifier with the singular demonstrative and the frequent use of *ko*, the Mandarin general classifier. On the other hand a more literary text of the same period analyzed by Schafer (1948) shows basically the same alternative constructions as those of EAC, namely N-Q-Cl, Q-N, and N-Q.

[4]Wang Li cites some examples of the classifier construction from the classical language, but these are all from the *Ts'o Chuan*. However, its traditional date is disputed and it is generally now assigned to the Han period. It would seem that the occurence of classifier constructions in it lends linguistic support to the hypothesis of its relatively late date. In fact the occurrence of the preposed order as an alternative suggests that it is even post-Han.

Further historical evidence comes from Khmer. Modern Khmer has the order N-(Q-Cl); Old Khmer has the same order. This case is then compatible with our hypothesis in that it does not show (Cl-Q)-N which would contradict it by implying a shift from prenominal to postnominal position.

A somewhat more ambiguous case is Burmese. The present Burmese order is N-(Q-Cl). According to Hla Pe (1965), from the 15th century on, Pali exercised an intensive influence on Burmese, resulting among other things in a construction (Q-Cl)-(linking particle)-N. Presumably, the native Burmese construction is found earlier and has persisted into modern times; the case is thus like that of Khmer except for the intrusion of Pali influence.

Important evidence for a shift of the classifier phrase from postnominal to prenominal position, not based on direct historical evidence, is furnished by Gilyak. In this language there is a rule that with the numbers 1–5 inclusive Q-Cl follows the noun while for numbers larger than 5 the order is (Q-Cl)-N. In the speech of the younger generation, according to Panfilov (1962: 191), the construction with 1–5 now usually exhibits the order (Q-Cl)-N so that this order has been generalized to all numerals. Thus we see the shift from postnominal to prenominal position in actual process in Gilyak at the present time. The hypothesis that this is the last stage of a shift from an earlier general postnominal position, in which the smallest, most unmarked numerals have shown the greatest resistance to an innovation in word order is strengthened by the existence of other similar cases in non-classifier languages. It was earlier suggested that as the general classifier spreads the classifier construction gets treated more and more like an ordinary numeral construction. In Gilyak the younger generation has also virtually accomplished the reduction to a single classifier.

It is planned to treat in more detail in a separate paper cases of the type just referred to. The following examples will indicate what is meant. In the Basque of San Sebastian, the number 'one' always follows the noun, 'two' may precede or follow, and numbers larger than 'two' always precede. In the Basque dialects of France, only 'one' follows. Gavel (1929: 116) notes that in certain dialects in Spain, however, all cardinal numbers are postposed, and he remarks, "Tel était peut-être primitivement l'usage basque général." In Classical Arabic 'one' and 'two' follow the noun, 3–10 may either precede or follow, and for numbers greater than 10, the numeral always precedes the noun. Modern dialects show varying stages of a shift to exclusive Q-N order in Gutman scale or implicational chain fashion as shown in Table 1, in which italics indicate the more frequent occurrence of a particular alternative and F and P mean "follows noun" and "precedes noun" respectively. Examples of stage 1 are Classical, Hassania (Mauretania), and Zanzibar, incidentally a good example of survival at the periphery. Stage 2 is exemplified by Fellahin

*Table 1*

| | 1 | 2 | 3–10 | >10 |
|---|---|---|---|---|
| 1. | F | F | F~*P* | P |
| 2. | F | F | P | P |
| 3. | F | F~P | P | P |
| 4. | F | P | P | P |
| 5. | *F*~P | P | P | P |
| 6. | P | P | P | P |

dialects of Syria (Bauer) and Palestine (Driver). Stage 3 is found in Iraqi (Erwin) and Syrian (Cowell). Stage 4 is exemplified in Tunisian, Syrian, and Palestinian Fellahin. Stage 5 is Moroccan, and stage 6 is Meccan (Schreiber).

Another interesting example is Umbundu, a Bantu language of Angola, described in Valente 1964. The order N-Q is practically universal in Bantu languages and can be confidently reconstructed for Proto-Bantu. In Umbundu, with 1–5 the only permitted order is N-Q; with 6–99 the alternative constructions N-Q and Q-N are found. With numbers >99 only Q-N occurs.

The foregoing examples contribute to the establishing of the hypothesis that when a sequence of the lowest numbers follow the noun, while the higher numbers precede in the same language, it is the former which represents the earlier rule which applied to all numerical phrases. Hence, it also serves to strengthen the hypothesis of a historical change from noun + classifier phrase to classifier + noun phrase in the case of Gilyak.

Thus far, all the evidence adduced for the shift from postposed to preposed classifier phrase has been directly historical or, in the case of Gilyak, an actually observed generational shift. Generally, however, in deciding such questions the most copious source is reconstruction based on the comparison of related languages. There are indeed language families within which some languages have preposed and others postposed order. But to reconstruct postposed order would, of course, be in the present context circular, for this is precisely what we are trying to verify. In phonology we can often reconstruct phonetic features of proto-phonemes because we have independent evidence concerning the relative plausibility of changes. But in the present instance, it is precisely the plausibility of these processes which is at issue.

Two comparative cases of this sort are worth considering here, even if no decisive conclusion can be drawn. One is that of the Thai language family. In respect to word order in the classifier construction disregarding minor variations, these languages may be divided into two groups. One, consisting of Thai proper (Siamese), Laotian, Shan of Burma, and the geographically isolated Khamti of Assam, postposes the classifier construction to the noun. The other group, containing Thai languages of northern Vietnam near the

Chinese border and also languages in China proper (e.g. Dioy of Kweichow province), has the preposed order. I shall with slight arbitrariness call these the Southern and Northern type respectively. The question is whether it is possible to tell which type embodies the earlier pattern. According to our general thesis it should, of course, be the Southern type.

There is one further interesting and relevant fact. All Thai languages exhibit the same pattern of 'one' following while other numbers precede the quantified item which was noted earlier in Basque and Arabic, but within the classifier construction. For example, Laotian has 'orange round-object one' for 'one orange', but for numbers larger than one, 'orange two round-object'. Correspondingly, expressions of time and distance, and others without a noun head show this same pattern, e.g. 'year one' = one year, but 'two year' = two years. Our hypothesis here is that the Thai classifier construction arose at a time before a shift from N-Q to Q-N was complete, i.e. while the most unmarked number still followed the noun. After that it remained, as it were, in a fossilized state within the classifier construction. A language of the Southern type will therefore regularly have 'orange round-object one' and 'orange two round-object' as illustrated above for Laotian. The Northern languages have 'two round-object orange' with the preposed classifier phrase, as described earlier. However, for "one orange" they do not have '*round-object one orange', as might have been expected, but 'round-object orange one'. The Northern languages have, however, the same pattern as the Southern ones in expressions of time, distance, etc., e.g. 'year one', 'two year'.

The argument might be advanced that it is simpler to derive the Northern pattern from the Southern rather than vice versa. In the former instance 'orange two round-object' would change to 'two round-object orange', while 'orange round-object one' would put the classifier before the noun. Given once more a hypothesized greater resistance of the unmarked 'one', the position of 'one' would be unchanged and perhaps also be resistant because of the pattern 'year one' found throughout Thai.

The opposite course of change seems more complex and less plausible. If the Northern pattern were original, 'two round-object orange' would become 'orange two round-object', but 'round-object orange one' would become 'orange round-object one' with the classifier 'round-object' *inserted* between 'orange' and 'one'. This seems less likely, though I hardly consider the argument decisive.

Another relevant comparative case is that of the Indo-Aryan languages, whose classifier constructions are considered by Emeneau (1956) to be the source of similar constructions in Dravidian and Munda languages. The construction is widespread in Indo-Aryan although absent from many of them. It is particularly prominent in the "Gaudian group" (Bengali, Assamese, Oriya, Bihari). In Bengali, as described in Ferguson 1962, the "classifiers," generally called determinatives in the grammars of Bengali and closely related languages, have the following main uses. They are suffixed to nouns and other substantival words such as adjectives and demonstratives to express determination (hence the name "determinative," e.g. *boĭ-khana* 'book-the'). In this usage the meaning can only be singular. For the plural definitive there is only a single possibility, the suffix *-gulo*, which does not figure as a classifier in the numeral construction. The singular definitives are chosen by the criteria common in numeral classifier systems, e.g. shape, human vs. nonhuman, etc. and also appear with the noun in numeral constructions, e.g. *pãc-khana boĭ* 'five flat-object book' with the same classifier *khana* as in *boĭ-khana* 'book-the' cited above. In this construction both Q-Cl-N and N-Q-Cl are possible with the latter being definite, e.g. *boĭ pãc-khana* 'the five books'.[5] Chatterji (1926) has discussed the earlier history of these classifying determiners. Since the determinative use is confined to the singular, one could conjecture that its suffixing reflects the hypothesized earlier postposed order N-Q-Cl with as elsewhere the deletion of 'one'. Chatterji's historical data, however, give no evidence of the former existence of an actually expressed 'one'. His material does, however, seem to show a greater frequency of the postposed construction in the numerical construction in the earlier literature. It would require a careful examination of these texts to verify whether the meaning, when postposed, was always definite in earlier times. In the closely related Assamese, Babakaev (1961) cites the determinative construction as in Bengali, but only refers to Q-Cl-N in the numeral construction. Kakati (1941), however, gives with the numeral 'one' expressed and in the indefinite meaning both Q-Cl-N and N-Cl-Q. This suggests in line with the earlier thesis regarding the greater stability of word order in the most unmarked numeral 'one', the last stages of the posited shift from postposed to preposed position, with 'one' showing free variation while the other numerals precede. All this is admittedly precarious and requires further research, particularly with informants, in these languages.

We may summarize our results on this point, then, by asserting that there are a number of cases of varying probability in which the evidence points to a historical shift from postposed to preposed position and no cogent counterevidence. It should be noted, however, that it is not claimed that the

[5] According to Chatterji (1926), Bengali can have in addition to N-Q-C1 with the connotation of definiteness, and to Q-C1-N, which is the usual construction, additional constructions in which the classifier phrase has the internal order C1-Q rather than Q-C1. In this case the meaning is approximative, e.g. 'about three'. This is parallel to the Russian usage *čelovek p'at'* 'about five men' versus *p'at' čelovek* 'five men'.

construction *always* arises in the postpositive form. Outside of probable cases of borrowing in the preposed form, there are other instances in which the preposed form is found and in which there is nothing to show that it was ever otherwise (e.g. Iranian languages).

It remains, however, to consider the factors involved in the synchronic favoring of the postposed classifier construction such that even consistent SOV languages with preposed nominal modifiers, such as Japanese, have the postposed order as usual or exclusive. Diachronically, also, as has been seen, there is evidence that the construction sometimes originates with this order even though in the non-classifier construction the quantifier precedes the noun.

One line of investigation is to consider languages in which variant orders occur and to investigate what, if any, differences of function are found. The evidence unfortunately is very fragmentary, but there are some useful indications which might be pursued further.

In Palaung, an Austroasiatic language of Burma, described in Milne 1921, there are two quantifier constructions; Q-N, or N-(Q-Cl), e.g. *ār kū* 'two fish' or *kū ār tō* 'fish two classifier'. As can be seen, these are the two basic constructions of Early Archaic Chinese if we exclude the N-Q list construction. No account is given concerning different meanings or functions of the two constructions. However, an examination of accompanying sentences and texts shows a further syntactic difference. In the Q-N construction Q always immediately precedes the noun, being indeed the only modifier which precedes. In contrast, the classifier phrase may follow the noun at a considerable remove, being separated from the noun by intervening elements which are not part of the noun phrase. The following is an example (Milne 1921: 39), *Ta-ang gē leh Yang-ngūn sa-ram ō ār uaī kū*, literally 'Palaung they go Rangoon year this two three classifier', i.e. 'A few Palaung are going to Rangoon this year'. The classifier phrase can be here viewed as adverbial, as though one said, 'The Palaung go to Rangoon this year fewly, or in small numbers'. It could seem natural also to have a pause between 'this' and 'two three classifier'.

In Standard Malay the classifier phrase is compulsory and may precede or follow the noun. Thus one may say either *lima ekor ikan* 'five classifier fish', or *ikan lima ekor* 'fish five classifier'. In general the grammars I have consulted seem to treat this as 'free variation'. I did, however, encounter a statement concerning this in one grammar of Malay, namely Pierce 1944, which contains the following statement (p. 34): "These coefficients (*sc.* classifiers) precede the noun except in the case where emphasis falls upon the numeral." Thus: *ikan, lima ekor*, 'fish, five of them'. Note that here the postulated pause is indicated by a comma.

Although Hungarian does not have numeral classifiers in the usual sense, alongside of the common set of numerals is one which is used optionally, but only with persons. This second set has a suffix *-an* or *-en* depending on vowel harmony considerations. This personal set usually follows rather than precedes the noun. Thus one can say either *három ember jött*, 'three man came' or *az emberek hárman jöttek*. In the latter case, unlike the usual numeral construction which governs the singular, 'man' is morphologically plural and the verb is also plural in agreement with it. Moravcsik (1971) notes that the suffix *-an*, *-en* is the usual one which forms adverbs from adjectives in Hungarian and that this construction shares the same word order possibilities as the adverbial manner phrase. One can also say *hárman jöttek az emberek* just as one says *gyorsan jöttek az emberek*, i.e. 'quickly came the men'. She seeks to convey the feeling of the Hungarian numeral with *-an* or *-en* which she calls adverbial by translating 'the people three-ly came', etc.

Japanese has two alternative constructions in quantifier expressions. One of these involves the classifier expression, a fused word with the order Q-Cl, joined to the following noun by the marker *no*, e.g. *sambiki no inu* 'three-animal *no* dog'. Otherwise *no* is a genitive marker and has a variety of other uses, e.g. it can sometimes be paraphrased 'who is', 'which is'. In the other construction *no* is not involved and the Q-Cl combination usually follows but is much freer in its word order properties. It may, for example, be sentence initial but it usually precedes the verb. Martin (1956: 175) calls this latter type adverbial and tries to convey its peculiarities into English by phrases like 'to the extent of . . .'. It may be further noted that grammars generally say that the *no* construction is more definite in meaning.

Wang Li (1958) notes that whereas in the *Ts'o Chuan* both the preposed and postposed constructions occur, the first is more closeknit while in the latter the noun may be separated from the classifier by additional items, e.g. *mă níu jīe băi pī* 'horse cow all hundred classifier', in which *jīe* 'all' separates the nouns from the classifier phrase.

In a general way, then, there seems to be a parallelism in the languages just discussed in the existence of two constructions. In one of them the quantifying expression precedes the noun. The other is freer in word order, tends to follow, to be associated with the verb or the sentence as a whole, and may have a pause before it. I will hereinafter call the first of these prenominal and the second adverbial.

Where there is a distinction within the language between a classifier and non-classifier construction, the classifier construction is to be ranged with the adverbial. Ainu is such a language. Either the numeral precedes the noun directly without a classifier or it follows with the classifier. In their grammar, Kindaiti and Tiri (1936) regularly translate the Ainu classifier construction by the Japanese pronominal *no* phrase. Unfortunately, they give no account of the difference between the two. Batchelor (1905) states that in Ainu the classifier construction occurs only in an answer to questions and that there it is compulsory.

We hypothesize that the adverbial construction is, at least in those languages in which the classifier construction arises through internal processes, the basis for this construction. Essentially, the classifier expression is in origin a quantifying phrase which serves as comment to the head noun functioning as topic. This is seen most clearly in the list construction where, for example, in Mandarin, Chao describes it as involving a pause and supplying "under one's breath" of *shr* 'is', e.g. 'the oranges, (are) two round-objects; the bananas, (are) three long-objects, etc.' (the example is invented). Chao classifies this 'list construction' as S-P (subject-predicate).

The use of a classifier in these instances can be viewed as a device which avoids the bare predication of numerals which is disfavored in many languages. For example, in English one says 'there are two tables' rather than 'the tables are two'. Dawson (1968: 63) in his work on Classical Chinese, commenting on a passage from *Chuang-Tsu*, makes the following observation: "Notice the word order here. Instead of saying 'the Brigand Chih had nine thousand followers' the normal word order is as here 'the followers (of) the Brigand Chih (were) nine thousand men'." Here 'men' has the role which develops into the classifier in the classifier construction.

The stages would be parallel to the hypothesized sequences of deep structures in some generative accounts of the adjective phrase: 1) predication, 2) relative clause, 3) adjective follows noun, 4) adjective precedes noun. I do not mean to assert that this represents a diachronic sequence in which each is a stage in which one of these constructions predominates. Several may coexist. The relative clause which has not thus far been exemplified here is found in Gilbertese, a Micronesian language which has both N-Q-Cl and Q-Cl-N where related languages have only N-Q-Cl. Alongside of Q-Cl-N is a relative construction: 'book which two flat-object'.

Finally, it may be conjectured that possessive classificational systems arise in much the same way as numeral classifier systems. In the languages, all of them Austronesian or Amerind, which have such systems, it is built on a division between alienable and inalienable possession in which for inalienables (typically body parts and/or kinship terms) we have a direct construction without classifier expressed by possessive affixes, e.g. 'head-my', whereas alienable possession is expressed by a superordinate possessed noun in apposition to the noun designating the actual possessed object, e.g. 'dog my-animal'. One cannot in such languages say 'my-dog' directly. For 'the dog is mine' one says 'the dog is my-animal'. The inalienables here play much the same role as time and length expressions in classifier languages. They retain the earlier construction. There is no "normal" expression such as *'the nose is mine' in answer to the strange hypothetical question *'Whose nose is this?'. These languages all have bound possessives. Hence there is difficulty in expressing possessive predication and this is circumvented by saying 'This dog is my-animal'. In principle the same factors are involved in languages without possessive classification where a single word, usually one meaning 'thing' or 'possession' is used here. An example is the construction in Egyptian Arabic with *bitā'* 'possession'. We have parallel to possessive classifier languages, *elbēt bitā'ī* 'the house possession-my' but with kin terms *ab-ī* 'father-my'.

It is realized that the account given here is in many respects conjectural and that more investigation of these questions is needed. I hope, however, that the testing of the hypotheses advanced here will help to stimulate further work on these questions.

## References Cited


Babakaev, V. D. 1961. *Assamskij jazyk*. Moscow.

Batchelor, J. 1905. *Ainu-English-Japanese Dictionary*. 2nd ed. Tokyo.

Bergh, J. D. van den. 1953. *Spraakkunst van het Banggais*. The Hague.

Chao, Y. R. 1968. *A Grammar of Spoken Chinese*. Berkeley and Los Angeles.

Chatterji, S. K. 1926. *The Origin and Development of the Bengali Language*. Calcutta.

Dawson, R. 1968. *An Introduction to Classical Chinese*. Oxford.

Dobson, W. A. C. H. 1959. *Late Archaic Chinese; A Grammatical study*. Toronto.

———. 1962. *Early Archaic Chinese*. Toronto.

———. 1964. *Late Han Chinese*. Toronto.

———. 1968. *The Language of the 'Book of Odes'*. Toronto.

Emeneau, M. 1956. "India as a linguistic area." *Language* 32: 3–16.

Ferguson, C. A. 1962. "The basic grammatical categories of Bengali." Paper presented to the Ninth International Congress of Linguists 881–90. Cambridge, Mass.

Forrest, R. A. D. 1948. *The Chinese Language*. London.

Gavel, H. 1929. *Grammaire basque*. Bayonne.

Greenberg, J. H. 1963. "Some universals of grammar." In *Universals of Language*, ed. J. H. Greenberg. Cambridge, Mass.

———. 1973. "Numeral classifiers and substantival number: problems in the genesis of a linguistic type." *Working Papers on Language Universals* 9: 1–39. Stanford.

Hla Pe. 1965. "A re-examination of Burmese 'classifiers'." *Lingua* 15: 163–85.

Kakati, B. 1941. *Assamese, Its Formation and Development*. Gauhati.

Kindaiti, K., and M. Tiri. 1936. *Ainu-go hô gaisetsu* (Introduction to Ainu grammar). Tokyo.

Martin, E. 1956. *Essential Japanese*. Rutland, Vt.

Maspero, H. 1915. "Sur quelques textes anciens de chinois parlé." *Bulletin de l'École Française de l'Extrême Orient* 14.

Milne, L. 1921. *An Elementary Palaung Grammar*. Rangoon.
Moravcsik, E. 1971. "Observations on cardinal numbers in Hungarian." Unpublished ms.
Panfilov, V. Z. 1962–65. *Grammatika nivxskogo jazyka*. Moscow.
Pierce, J. 1944. *A Simple but Complete Grammar of the Malay Language*. Singapore.
Schafer, E. H. 1948. "Noun classifiers in Classical Chinese." *Language* 24: 408–13.
Valente, J. F. 1964. *Gramática umbundu*. Lisbon.
Wang Li. 1958. *Hàn-yǔ shǐ-gǎo* (Outline of the History of the Chinese language). Peking.

# How Does a Language Acquire Gender Markers?

## 1. Introduction

By a noun gender system will be meant a system in which the noun stems of a language are divided into a set of genders, this distinction being based on the fact that the choice of a noun belonging to a particular gender determines the choice among a set of alternative "agreeing" forms in one or more other classes of morphemes or words, e.g.: articles, demonstratives, adjectives, unbound anaphoric pronouns, pronouns incorporated in a verb complex, etc. Such systems are often called noun class systems. However, it is not usual to apply this term when sex is among the bases of classification. Structurally, such systems do not differ in any basic way from those in which sex does not figure. 'Gender' ultimately comes from Latin *genus* which simply means "kind," and there is ample precedent for applying the term gender to all such systems. When sex figures among the bases of classification, we will refer to sex gender. There is a further advantage in using the term gender system rather than noun class system. There are at least two systems of noun classification other than gender systems, numeral classifier systems and possessive classifier systems. We are therefore free to use noun class system as the superordinate term which includes all systems of this type.

The present study is based on a broad but by no means exhaustive sample of languages with noun gender systems. The approach is largely in terms of diachronic process. Our ultimate aim is to establish how such systems arise, their typical course of development, and the factors involved in their ultimate extinction. While such an ambitious goal is clearly not attained here, it is hoped that this study at least represents significant progress in this direction. The content of this paper falls into four main sections. The first of these (Sec. 2) poses certain basic questions relevant to the study of nominal gender systems including some fundamental definitional ones. The next (Sec. 3), which constitutes the main body of the paper, develops a processual theory as to how, in languages which already have gender systems, the nouns come to acquire gender markers, whether they were present at an earlier period or not. If the former is the case, we have a "renewal" of old markers which in some cases have been weakened by phonetic attrition. The existence of two historical layers of markers is in such cases usually evident from the existence of double markers. If, however, such did not exist previously, we have a pristine case. Many gender systems, of course, do not have overt markers on the noun, and genders are distinguished only by agreeing forms outside of the noun. For reasons of space the remaining topics are discussed much more briefly, details being reserved for future treatment. The penultimate section (Sec. 4) deals with the spread of syntactic agreement, which is coincident with the process by which the nouns receive overt marking, but which also develops in its absence. The final section (Sec. 5) is devoted to some speculations regarding the rise of gender and the relations of the conclusions of the present study to previous theorizing concerning gender origins. The important topic of the classificational system as such in relation to its semantic bases is only touched on incidentally and is also reserved for future treatment.

## 2. Types of Noun Classification

Our preliminary definition of a noun gender system in the initial paragraph is clearly in need of further specification. It will be repeated here for convenience. By a noun gender system will be meant a system in which the noun stems of a language are divided into a set of genders, the distinction being based on the fact that the choice of a noun belonging to a particular gender determines the choice among a set of alternative "agreeing" forms in one or more other classes of morphemes or words, e.g. articles, demonstratives, adjectives, unbound anaphoric pronouns, pronouns incorporated in a verb complex, etc.

A noun gender system may be regarded, then, as involving the intersection of two basic factors, classification and agreement, the two being in a relation of mutual determination, the gender being defined by the agreements and the agreements being determined by the genders. The mutual determination here defined as constitutive of gender systems is not, however, a logical requirement. Agreement is possible without classification. For example, in Hungarian *ebben a kertben* 'in this garden' there is agreement in case between *eb-ben* 'this' and *kert-ben* 'garden', both being in the locative. Yet Hungarian is not a gender language, since differences in agreement patterns do not divide the noun stems of the language into classes. In Hebrew *yeled tov* 'good boy', versus *hayyeled hattov* 'the good boy', there is agreement in definiteness between *yeled* 'boy' and *tov* 'good', but although Hebrew does have sex gender, it is not shown in this construction because all noun bases behave similarly in regard to it. It would be useful, then, to distinguish the wider notion of concord from agreement, the latter being a subtype in which the choice of alternative concord elements depends on the class to which the stem of the governing item belongs, whether marked by an affix or not.

Noun classification can exist without concord just as concord can exist without noun classes, though whether, synchronically viewed, such a classification can be considered grammatically significant is another question. Of course any number of classifications of nouns, as of any other word class, can be carried out, which are syntactically irrelevant, though some may be relevant from some other point of view, e.g. the declensional classes of Latin. Others might be perfectly arbitrary, e.g. a classification of bases into those with at least one stop consonant. The following, however, turns out to be a kind of classification which, while it does not involve agreement, may be of potential diachronic relevance to the origin of noun classes. In Malay and certain other languages there is widespread and compulsory use of certain superordinate terms in lexicalized phrases parallel in formation to English 'apple tree'. Thus, in Malay one cannot say merely *Djawi* for 'Java' but rather *tanah Djawi* where *tanah* means 'land' and occurs as an independent word, and so for a number of other superordinates. One might say that this constitutes a classification in which each superordinate term defines a class and in which those nouns which do not have such a superordinate term constitute an additional class with a zero marker. In Javanese this type of classification has absolutely no syntactic function, and it might therefore be considered far-fetched to consider it grammatically relevant.

However, just such a system in principle exists in the Daly River subgroup of general Australian, spoken in the northwest of the continent. In some of these languages it seems to have absolutely no syntactic function. Yet, for example, in Tryon's grammar of Maranungku, a language of this group, this type of system is called a noun class system (Tryon 1970). A noun must belong to one of four classes. The first consists of nouns preceded by *awa*, itself a noun meaning 'meat' which can occur independently. These nouns all designate edible animals or insects, e.g. *awa patpat* 'grasshopper'. Similarly, class two consists of nouns always preceded by *yili* 'stick' and comprising tools, weapons, and wooden implements, while class three nouns are preceded by *miya* 'vegetable food' and indicate kinds of vegetable foods. The fourth class which has a zero marker and is highly heterogeneous is noted as being by far the largest. As far as can be seen from Tryon's account, this classification has no syntactic relevance. However, in other subgroups of the

Daly River group, there are languages which have a system of classification clearly related to that of Maranungku in which it forms the basis of agreement phenomena. For example, in Marengar (Tryon 1974: 122) the same four classes are found, but we find, for example, agreement with adjectives. Thus, corresponding to class two in Maranungku are words prefixed by *yeri* 'stick' = Maranungku *yili*. With the adjective *-kati* 'good' we have *yeri-kunt$^y$ikin$^y$ yeri-kati* 'good boomerang'. With nouns in the large class with a zero marker we find, for example, *wat$^y$an kati* 'good dog' in which neither item has a class marker.

In this instance, for reasons discussed at the end of Sec. 3.5, I believe we have to do with a nascent system. At the other end of the development, diachronically, are languages like Lobi in the Voltaic subgroup of Niger-Congo which has paired singular and plural suffix sets, which no longer have syntactic relevance but are historically related to those of Voltaic languages with functioning systems. Viewed synchronically, Lobi simply seems to have a very elaborate system of plural formation by affix replacements, falling into a number of different patterns.

Viewed synchronically, then, and no doubt tautologically, a noun classification system, if it is syntactically relevant, involves some form of agreement. But what of numeral classifier systems? These classify nouns in accordance with the classifier they take, and the classification is clearly a syntactically relevant one. A choice of a particular noun determines the choice of the classifier. There are, however, some differences between such systems and those usually called gender systems. One important difference is that in a full-fledged numeral classifier language, there are a considerable number of nouns which are non-countables and do not take classifiers, whereas in gender languages, literally every noun has a gender. Secondly, in numeral classifier languages, with a few exceptions, agreement is confined to the construction with quantifiers. In spite of these differences and others that will be mentioned later, it will be shown in the final section that there is a possible diachronic connection between numeral classifier and gender systems. What is said here about numeral classifier systems applies *mutatis mutandis* to possessive systems, such as those found in some Oceanic and Amerind languages. Agreement is confined to the possessive construction. Corresponding to non-countables in a classifier language are inalienably possessed nouns which are not subject to classification.

One further aspect of the definition of gender system as stated here is in need of further elucidation. What is meant by the noun stems of a language being divided into a set of genders? Ideally, a classification is supposed to be exhaustive and to divide the universe under consideration into mutually disjoint sets. The latter requirement is probably not fulfilled in any of the languages which are usually considered to have gender systems. To begin with, there are instances of individual stems which belong to more than one class, e.g. Spanish *hij-o* 'son', *hij-a* 'daughter'. This is what is traditionally called 'motion', and insofar as there is a systematic semantic relationship, it becomes one of the objective bases for assigning meaning to classes. More drastically, two inflectionally different classes may share all of their stems. This is frequently the case with paired singular and plural classes. Such classes may be said to be in equipollent relationship, and in a sense, to be considered a superclass. Specialists in Bantu, for example, have differed as to whether in such pairs they are dealing with one class or two. Since viewed as a superclass it does have a distinct membership, we may say that this does not detract from the overall system in classifying the noun stems.

Sometimes, however, the relationship between two inflectionally different classes is not equipollent. This is often true for diminutive, augmentative, and place gender as found, for example, in many Bantu languages. Most, if not all, stems found in such classes are also found in others. There may be a productive rule by which a member of any other class becomes a member of this class by affix replacement or even by addition. In these cases we may say that we are dealing with a derivative gender. Where, as is sometimes the case, a gender does not have a single stem which is unique, it will be called a minor gender. An example is the neuter gender in Nama Hottentot. In view of these considerations, we will mean by a gender classification one in which there are at least two classes, including in the term 'class' also 'superclass', as mentioned above, but excluding minor genders in our count.

## 3. Overt and Covert Systems

In defining agreement, nothing was said about the existence of a gender marker on the noun itself, merely that membership in a particular gender determined selection in agreeing forms. However, in such paradigm cases as Bantu, the noun itself has an overt class marker as, for example, in the Swahili phrase *ki-ti ki-nene hi-ki* 'stool large this', and this is also generally true in Indo-European. Sapir mentions the "relentless rhythm" of Latin *illōrum saevōrum virōrum* 'of those savage men'. Where a marker exists in the noun itself, the system will be called overt; where it is not found, the system will be called covert. Viewed once more diachronically, there are two types of covert systems, those in which overt expression formerly existed, e.g. French, as compared to Italian, and those in which, as far as can be seen, it never existed. There are many examples of this, for instance, the Northern Caucasian languages (except the northwestern group which has no gender).[1]

This is one more point of difference between gender systems and other

[1] However, in most Caucasian languages there are a few words which have class markers. This matter is discussed later at the end of Sec. 3.5.

systems of noun classification. In numeral classifier systems the classifier goes syntactically and is sometimes fused with the numeral and never seems to occur additionally with the noun itself. Similarly, in possessive systems the classifiers go with personal possessive affixes and do not appear on the noun. They thus fail to give rise to phenomena such as the "alliterative concord" of Bantu languages.

*3.1. From covert to overt gender: Niger-Congo languages with simultaneous prefix and suffix marking.* The Niger-Congo languages have an inherited system of noun genders involving the existence of overt class markers on the noun. In some of the major subgroups, these are generally prefixed to the noun (as in the well known instance of Bantu), but in other branches they are normally suffixed. The markers themselves, whether prefixed or suffixed, exhibit clear relationship in phonetic form and semantic function. The West-Atlantic, Kwa, and Benue-Congo branches are basically prefixing, while the Voltaic and Adamawa-Eastern branches are suffixing. The Mande branch, which is the most divergent genetically, shows no clear traces of this system. An example of prefixing is Swahili *ki-ti*, pl. *vi-ti* 'chair' and suffixing, Mossi (Voltaic) *bi-ga*, pl. *bi-se* 'child'. Alongside of this, however, there are a few languages in each major branch except, of course, Mande which have prefixes and suffixes simultaneously. An example is Akasele (Voltaic) *ke-ji-ke/n-ji-m* (< **m-ji-m*) 'knife'. How is this diversity to be explained? One of the suggestions has been that languages with both prefixes and suffixes represent the original state of affairs and that subsequently some languages lost their suffixes and some their prefixes (e.g. Welmers 1973: 209). However, a closer look at languages with double affixing tells a quite different story.

We will start with Gurma, a Voltaic language which is often cited in the literature as a typical example of a language with prefixes and suffixes. However, the detailed grammar of Chantoux, Gontier, and Prost (1968) shows that whereas the suffixes are a normal part of the noun, the prefixes are often omitted. When a prefix is present, it corresponds fairly closely to the definite article in languages like English and French, e.g. *niti-ba* 'men', *ba niti-ba* 'the men'. In fact the authors of this grammar write the "prefixes" as separate words. Furthermore, as we shall see, there can be no reasonable doubt that the preposed article is recent and the suffix old.

Gurma gives its name to the whole subgroup of Voltaic languages of which it is a member. An examination of the other languages of the subgroup shows that in regard to what corresponds historically to the preposed article of Gurma, they fall into a number of typologically distinct groups. To begin with, there is Moba which shows no prefixes at all. It is thus similar to the great mass of Voltaic languages which have class suffixes only. There is Gurma itself in which, as we have seen, the preposed class marker functions as a definite article. Another language, Gangam, has a preposed marker like Gurma, but unlike Gurma, it is not merely a definite article. It combines, roughly speaking, the uses of the English indefinite article when it is [+specific], that is, it involves an existence assumption and can in general be replaced by 'a certain', e.g. 'I am looking for a certain notebook'. Statistically, it occurs with the noun in the vast majority of its textual occurrences. However, there are a minority of constructions, especially generic ones, e.g. as a verb object in negative sentences, in which it does not occur. I shall call this type of "article" a non-generic article. However, as will be indicated in later discussion, by no means all instances of absence of this article involve genericness, and the name is not an entirely appropriate one. Articles of this kind are found in a number of languages in various parts of the world and, as it appears, relatively little attention has been paid to this phenomenon.

Finally, within the Gurma group are the Akasele and Tobote-Basari languages in which there are no contrasts between prefixed and non-prefixed forms. In general, with a few exceptions to be discussed, all nouns have both prefixes and suffixes, and the pair functions basically in the same way as prefixes or suffixes by themselves in the Niger-Congo languages.

We thus have, within the same subgroup, four stages of a process leading ultimately to the development of a new set of prefixed class markers reinforcing the previously existing suffixes. These stages are: (1) no marker, (2) definite article, (3) non-generic article, (4) class prefix.

That this is the order of development is shown in a number of ways. To begin with, the suffixes are representative of a set found through the entire Voltaic subgroup and reconstructible for Proto-Voltaic. They are often irregular phonetically and sometimes reduced to zero or tonal alternations. The prefixes, in contrast, are transparent and in fact identical with the verb subject pronouns which agree with the noun in class. Moreover, that a functional prefix detaches itself from a noun, gradually becomes a definite article, and then disappears is like running the historical camera backwards. Manessy, well-known as a Voltaic specialist, in an article discussing the phenomenon of double affixes in Voltaic languages, comes to the following conclusion: "Thus Tamãri and Ngangam appear to mark an intermediate stage in the development of a process quite comparable to that by which the Latin demonstrative became the French article, a process whose commencement can be discovered in Gurma and of which Akasele illustrates the highest stage of development" (Manessy 1965: 175).

Manessy here mentions, in addition to Ngangam, Tamãri as illustrating the same stage of a non-generic article. However, in subsequent publications he correctly assigned Tamãri to a different genetic subgroup of Voltaic.

But if suffixes can be renewed by prefixes, why cannot prefixes be renewed by suffixes? In fact this process is well attested in the languages of the West Atlantic subgroup of Niger-Congo which are, as noted earlier, basically prefixing. The definite article stage is represented by Dyola which has, in addition to the usual West Atlantic prefix system, a suffixed article which duplicates the prefix, e.g. *fu-nak* 'day', *fu-nak-əf* 'the day' (Sapir 1965). In certain other West Atlantic languages the original prefixes have been reduced to initial consonant alternations and, in the case of Wolof, even these have been reduced to the status of archaic survivals in a few words. The system has been renewed, however, by suffixed class markers which can in certain constructions still be separated from the noun and which function as a definite article. Serer-Non illustrates the stage of the non-generic article. Fula which still has functional initial consonant alternations illustrates the last stage. The class suffixes have become markers on virtually all nouns, and no contrasts exist between constructions with and without the suffix. Wolof, Serer-Non, and Fula are the three members of one subgroup of northern West Atlantic.

Similarly, in the Kwa group which is prefixing, there are languages like Kebu and Avatime in which suffixes are found. In the case of Avatime once more they function like the definite article. In Kebu we have a language in which nouns are normally both prefixed and suffixed and in which, on internal evidence, it appears that the suffixes are more recent, though the evidence is perhaps not decisive.

Among Benue-Congo languages, Tiv which is closely related to Bantu has both prefixes and suffixes. The suffixes are clearly recent. The suffixes essentially exhibit an advanced stage of the non-generic article. Nouns can appear without the suffix mainly in one construction, the locative. As we shall see from a more detailed examination of the non-generic article, this is a typical construction in which the form without the article tends to survive.

But if suffixes can be renewed by prefixes (e.g. Gurma) and prefixes can be renewed by suffixes (e.g. Dyola), why cannot prefixes be renewed by additional prefixes or suffixes by suffixes? Regarding the former of these possibilities, there are examples in Niger-Congo, but I do not know of any instances of the latter.*

In almost all dialects of Temne, a language of the Southern branch of West Atlantic (the other languages already mentioned belong to the Northern branch), the prefixed class marker has an additional marker, usually the same as the vowel of the prefix which functions as a definite article. Wilson (1961: 13) notes that in one dialect, that of Konike, "the nouns in all contexts are in

*Marchese (1988: 333–34) suggests that suffix renewal has taken place in Godié and other Kru languages.—Eds.

what looks like the definite form." This dialect, then, has probably entered into the final stage in which the former definite article has become part of the class marker on the noun.

The most important example of prefixes being renewed by prefixes is that of the Bantu languages, for so, I believe, the well-known pre-prefix vowel found in many Bantu languages should be interpreted.

In the majority of instances the pre-prefix functions as a typical non-generic article and indeed provides the most abundant evidence we have anywhere of the characteristics of this stage. Examples include Luganda, Kirundi, Bemba, Konde, Lamba, Zulu, Xhosa, and Southern Kikongo. Thus far I have noted only one example of a Bantu language with a pre-prefix which functions as a definite article, namely Dzamba. The south-western group of Bantu including such languages as Herero, Ovambo, and Ochin-Donga illustrates the last stage in which the pre-prefixes have become part of the class marker on nouns in general.[2]

*3.2. The development of class markers outside of Niger-Congo. A priori*, there is no reason to expect the process by which a definite article becomes a marker on the noun to be confined to Niger-Congo languages. Secondly, there is no reason why it should only occur in gender systems which do not include sex as a semantic basis for gender. Thirdly, there is evidently no necessity for the process to be one of renewal confined to languages which already have overt markers, as is true with Niger-Congo languages outside of the Mende group. Fourthly, as we shall see, there is no reason even for this process to be confined to languages with gender classification at all.

All of these possibilities can be illustrated from languages in Africa. The languages of the Eastern Nilotic subbranch of the Nilotic languages, which in turn belong to the Eastern Sudanic substock of Nilo-Saharan, all have sex gender. These languages fall into two subgroups, one consisting of Bari and other languages very closely related to it. The other consists of a set of internally more divergent languages including Maasai, Lotuko, and Teso. Bari has a sex gender classification without any marker on the noun. The gender elements appear in certain constructions, e.g. in the demonstratives, pronominal possessives, and relatives. In the other group of languages, there are genetically related prefix markers for sex gender (Teso, in addition, has a neuter) which are typical non-generic articles. As against the Niger-Congo case, these are from all evidence pristine markers, and none of the languages has reached the stage at which the prefix has become a mere classificatory mark on the noun.

[2]However, these languages do have the unarticulated form for the vocative of common nouns so that, strictly speaking, they are still in the stage of the non-generic article, albeit an advanced stage.

A further possibility is exemplified by the Southern Nilotic (Kalenjin) languages which constitute another subbranch of Nilotic. The Nandi-Kipsigis and Pokot (Suk) groups have genetically cognate suffixes for singular and plural, without gender classification. In Pokot these function like a definite article, while in Nandi-Kipsigis they are in the stage of the non-generic article.

Another example of a pristine marker, in this instance without connotations of either gender or number, is provided by the Southwestern Mande languages. We have here a suffixed *-i* which functions as an ordinary definite article in Kpelle, but is a non-generic article in the remaining languages: Mende, Loko, Gbandi, and Loma.

As a final African example, we may cite a main subgroup of languages of the Central group of Southern Khoisan languages including here the various dialects of Hottentot and the closely related languages of the Naron Bushman. These languages have a system of three genders, masculine, feminine, and neuter. They all, with the possible exceptions to be noted, have a pristine non-generic suffixed article as gender-number markers. However, the extinct Hottentot dialects of Griqualand East and West are known from word lists in which the gender-number suffixes do not occur. In languages with the non-generic article, it is usually employed in citation forms. Hence, in these dialects the affixes were probably either definite articles or not used at all (cf. Planert 1905).

The phenomenon under discussion is not confined to Africa, although it seems to be more frequently encountered there than in any other major region. I will not here cite either the numerous cases of languages with definite articles of the usual sort or languages with gender classification in which the noun has an overt marker, but rather those instances in which the telltale and hitherto neglected stage of the non-generic article is known to occur. A particularly interesting case is Aramaic which, in a recorded history of almost 3000 years, has gone through the three stages mentioned here. An *-ā* (< **hā*) suffixed to nouns in the masculine and feminine, singular and plural, which were already provided with sex/number markers based on the inherited Semitic system, functions as a definite article in the earliest inscriptional language (ninth century B.C.) and as late as the Aramaic portions of Daniel and Nehemiah (generally dated second century B.C.). From the early Christian era onward, we have to reckon with two dialect groups, Western and Eastern, in which the former is more conservative in this matter. The Eastern literary dialects (e.g. Syriac, Babylonian Talmudic) have a non-generic article while the Western literary dialects still have a definite article (Christian Palestinian Syriac, Targum Onqelos, etc.). The contemporary dialects of Aramaic still are distinct in this respect, but each group has advanced one further stage. West Aramaic now has a non-generic article while in Eastern Aramaic, it is a general noun marker. One Eastern dialect, that of Ṭūr-Abdīn, has developed a new prefixed article, this time distinguished for gender and number, thus renewing the process which started in prehistoric times at least 3000 years earlier.

Khasi, an Austroasiatic language of Assam, has a three gender system: masculine, feminine, and neuter with a prefixed nongeneric article.

A number of Austronesian languages on New Britain and New Ireland possess non-generic articles. These include Mengen (New Britain) with a suffixed article (Müller 1907) and Tolai (New Britain), and the only dialectically differing Label (New Ireland) with a prefixed article (Franklin 1962 and Peekel 1929).

Native Australia offers interesting examples. Dyirbal in northeastern Australia, a member of the Pama-Nyungan group which comprises most of the continent, has a non-generic article at an advanced stage associated with a classification of nouns into four genders: masculine, feminine, and two inanimate genders, with animals divided between the masculine and feminine (Dixon 1972). In the northwest of the continent there is a concentration of languages belonging to various other subgroups than Pama-Nyungan, most of which have gender classification. An interesting case is that of Worora and the closely related Ungarinyin. Both languages have a system of four genders much like that of Dyirbal, with class markers that are clearly related to each other historically and more remotely to those of Dyirbal. Worora, however, has suffixed class markers on a large proportion of its nouns that have reached the final stage of complete amalgamation and universal use, while these are lacking altogether in Ungarinyin (Love, n.d.), as far as can be made out from the rather sparse information available.

I do not know of any certain instances of the non-generic article in Amerind languages, except possibly Goajiro, an Arawakan language as described by Holmer (1949). This is a sex gender language in which gender marking has been renewed through a set of suffixed non-generic articles. The development, if reliably reported, must have been very rapid, since Celedón less than a century previously, although describing Goajiro as a sex gender language, gives no indication of the existence of the specific markers cited by Holmer. There are a number of Amerind languages with sex gender with markers on the nouns, which indicate that they should have gone through the sequence of stages postulated here, e.g., Chinook, a Penutian language, and Chiquita, a Macro-Ge language of Bolivia.

There are also some instances of what appears to be the last stages of a non-generic non-classifying article, e.g., the *-s* of Klamath and other Plateau Penutian languages of Oregon, which appears on most nouns and in most constructions. The "absolutive" of Uto-Aztecan and other Amerind languages possibly also belongs here. This requires further investigation.

The foregoing review is far from exhaustive. There are doubtless other examples of languages in the stage of the non-generic article or instances of closely related languages which exhibit different stages of the development just outlined.

*3.3. The cycle of the definite article: The initial stage.* In the foregoing sections three stages in the process by which a definite article ultimately may become a noun marker were briefly indicated. It remains to consider this process in greater detail. The three stages were (1) definite article, (2) non-generic article, (3) noun marker. It will be convenient in subsequent discussions to call these Stage I, Stage II, and Stage III articles, respectively.

Each of these stages is initiated by a significant change by means of which it can be defined. However, there are instances of transitional phenomena such that certain languages are on the borderline between two stages. In some cases it is possible to see that a language is well advanced within a particular stage, while in other instances it is clear that it has only entered the stage recently. Hence, the whole development is to be viewed as a single continuous process marked by certain decisive turning points.

Since the most common origin of the definite article is the demonstrative, a development of which there are numerous and well-attested examples, we might speak of the demonstrative as stage zero. The historical development of definite article has been studied in a number of instances in considerable detail. It develops from a purely deictic element which has come to identify an element as previously mentioned in discourse. Such a use is often an additional function of an element which is also a pure deictic, but sometimes there is a particular demonstrative which has assumed this as its basic function. The source deictic is most often one which points to location near the third person rather than the first or second person, e.g. Latin *ille*. The point at which a discourse deictic becomes a definite article is where it becomes compulsory and has spread to the point at which it means "identified" in general, thus including typically things known from context, general knowledge, or as with 'the sun' in non-scientific discourse, identified because it is the only member of its class. Such an article may, as with German *der*, be an unstressed variant of the demonstrative, which continues in its former use in stressed form.

An interesting case in a gender language of a nascent article which is, so to speak, at a point between a zero stage demonstrative and a Stage I definite article is Bwamu, a language which appears to be a genetic isolate within the Voltaic branch of Niger-Congo. In this language the original suffixes have been phonetically eroded to the point at which they no longer exhibit a clear indication of membership in a gender. Moreover, all vestiges of agreement have disappeared with the exception of two demonstrative type elements, both of which precede the noun and indicate previous mention. Unfortunately, our only major source for the language (Manessy 1960) is devoted to noun morphology and says little about syntax. Manessy calls one of the two elements a determinative and the other a demonstrative pronoun. However, even the first of these does not appear to be a definite article. He notes that its presence is "facultative et relativement peu fréquent dans le discours" (Manessy 1960: 93). Moreover, he does not translate it as an article. Yet it is only these two elements which indicate the gender membership of the noun. The determinative is a monosyllabic element, basically similar to the obsolescent class affixes. We have, it would appear then, a case of renewal of gender by a demonstrative element which is not yet an article and whose next stage would presumably be comparable to that of a language like Gurma which has a clear Stage I article.

*3.4. Stage II of the definite article.* Stage II was in the earlier sections of this paper referred to as the non-generic article. We shall see that this is not really an adequate designation. We may define Stage II as the stage in which we have an article which includes, along with possibly other uses, both definite determination and non-definite specific uses. Specific, opposed here to generic, is the use of such an article in contexts in which a specific but unidentified item is referred to, that is, there is a presupposition of reference. Thus, English 'I am looking for a book' is ambiguous as between specific reference, i.e. there is a certain book for which I am looking, and a reading in which there is no such assumption. I might mean any old book, for example, to prop up an unbalanced table leg.

Our definition is minimal. In fact, languages in Stage II generally include instances of non-referential use so that they correspond *grosso modo* to the combined uses of a definite and indefinite article. Frequently, existing descriptions are simply not sufficient for us to decide. We must also include in our definition a maximal condition to distinguish Stage II from Stage III in which the former article is a mere marker. There must be at least one construction in which common nouns regularly appear in their non-articulated forms so that all common nouns have two contrasting forms, one with and one without the article. This may involve minimal contrast as when the non-articulated form of the noun is used in generic sentences like 'I don't like meat', as against an articulated form in 'I don't like the meat', (i.e. some particular specimen which has just been mentioned or can be identified by non-verbal context). However, in languages with Stage II articles the choice of articles is always largely grammaticalized, being determined by the syntactic construction and is thus redundant. For example, most of them have generalized either the articulated or non-articulated as negative object, and they do not express the semantic distinction which has just been noted. This is a large step in the direction of a Stage III article. Languages with Stage II articles show varying degrees of advancement towards a situation in which the distinction between the two forms is completely redundant, being dependent on the construction, e.g. negative objects are always articulated or always non-articulated, the same for nominal predicates, etc. With the attainment of complete grammaticization, the analogical tendency sets in for one or the other form to become universal. If the articulated form, which is the one which has usually spread to more contexts, predominates, we have a Stage III noun marker. If not, the articulated form disappears. I believe this is what has happened in Eastern Bantu languages without pre-prefixes.[3] In the proto-language the pre-prefix was probably a Stage II article which in some languages remained in this stage, in some moved into Stage III, and in some languages disappeared. These varied developments often took place in quite closely related languages of the same subgroup.

In languages with Stage II articles the articulated form has become the normal form of the noun. It is usually the lexical citation form and it heavily predominates in text. Grammars of such languages habitually list not the uses of the articulated form, but rather situations in which it is *not* used. As is evident from the earlier discussion, no more than is the case with the ordinary definite article, or for that matter individual cases in case languages, is there a single overall semantically based definition which will completely delineate the respective uses of the articulated and non-articulated forms. As is usually done in the grammars, however, it is easier to distinguish the relatively limited set of uses of the non-articulated forms and view the articulated forms as an unspecified remainder.

As we may conclude from the earlier discussion, we cannot expect that all languages with Stage II articles will have the same set of uses for the non-articulated forms. However, there is a common core of functions which recur in languages of this type.

Most of the functions of the non-articulated form can be placed in one of two categories. Strangely enough, on a scale of degree of determination, these two categories are at exactly opposite ends. In some instances the article does not occur, because the noun is inherently determined (e.g. proper names) or because it is determined by something else in the particular construction (e.g. a demonstrative modifier). In these instances the noun

[3] There are in some instances, probably, also sociolinguistic factors. Carter (1963) in an interesting article asserts that the Tonga are quite conscious of the distinction between nouns with and without pre-prefixes and consider the excessive use of the former as "undignified." There are in this language considerable variations in frequency of these forms in texts of various styles.

which would not usually have an article in Stage I does not acquire it in Stage II. It is because of these uses that the name 'non-generic article' is not really appropriate. At the other end of the determination spectrum are the generic uses, as in negation and predication. These opposing uses of the non-articulated form bear a certain resemblance to the use of non-articulated forms in languages with both a definite and indefinite article. In such languages proper names do not usually have an article, but the article may also be absent in generic uses, e.g. French *je n'ai pas d'eau* 'I don't have water'; *il est tailleur* 'he is a tailor'. The generic uses of the non-articulated forms in languages with Stage II articles, it may be noted, largely coincide with the totality of two sets of categories enumerated by Moravcsik in her discussion of determination, on the one hand, as inherently definite and on the other, as generic (Moravcsik 1969: especially p. 72).

Instances of automatic definiteness will be considered first. These include proper names, vocatives, and nouns modified by demonstratives and personal possessive pronouns. Of these, proper names, both personal and place, are the group most consistently used in unarticulated form. No exception was found to the rule that in languages with Stage II articles, the article is not found with proper names. This was the reason for the specification of the existence of contrast between articulated and non-articulated in *common* nouns as a part of the definition of a language with a Stage II article. For some of the languages a minimal contrast is reported when the same noun is used both as a common and proper name. For example, in Bemba *amafupa* or *mafupa*, depending on the usual rules for the use of the articulated and non-articulated form, is a common noun meaning 'bones', but as the name of a river it takes the form *Mafupa*, without the pre-prefix. In some languages an animal name, when used to designate a character in a folktale, is in the unarticulated form, but when used as a common name, is articulated or non-articulated in accordance with the general rules for the use of the two forms in the language.

Common nouns, when used in the vocative, commonly occur without the article. In one language of Stage II, Lotuko, both articulated and non-articulated forms occur, but the latter is said to be more emphatic as well as more elegant.

In construction with demonstratives, there is some variability. The predominant tendency is to add the article to the noun redundantly, a tendency already visible in some instances in languages with ordinary Stage I articles, e.g. Arabic and Classical Greek. Sometimes, when the article is not on the noun, it is added to the demonstrative. There are some indications that the principle involved here is that definiteness is a property of the noun phrase as a whole. There are instances of word order variation where, in one order, the marker is on the noun and in the other, on a demonstrative or other modifier.

In Teso and Maasai, with Stage II prefix articles, almost all noun modifiers follow the noun. However, those forms which precede take the article which in that case does not occur with the noun. Cases of alternative word order show clearly that what is involved is that definiteness is marked once only and always initially in the noun phrase in these languages. A Maasai example is *il-kuti tuŋana* 'few people', with its alternative *il-tuŋana kuti* 'people few'.

The interrogative which corresponds to the demonstrative is the specifying interrogative 'which?'. Its usage as request for identification in English is to be distinguished from its employment in the sense of 'what kind of?'. 'Which wine do you want?' illustrates the potential ambiguity. In the identificational sense it is not usually accompanied by an article on the noun in Stage II languages.

The personal possessive construction, like the demonstrative construction, shows a tendency to mark definiteness redundantly on the noun, and once more, this is a tendency which is already visible occasionally in languages with Stage I articles, cf. Italian *la mia casa* '(the) my house'. Kinship terms, as inalienables, however, show far less affinity for the definite article, a point that can also be illustrated from Italian which has *mio padre* and not **il mio padre*.

When, as often, there are two constructions, one for alienables and one for inalienables, it will usually only be the latter in which the possessive pronoun is directly affixed to the noun. Often, also, the kinship term can only occur with possessives so that, e.g. 'John's mother' is always *John his-mother* or the like. In these cases the article is, so to speak, blocked from attachment to the nouns. Whatever the factor involved, kinship terms rival proper names in their resistance to the acquisition of a Stage II article.

We turn now to the instances in which a Stage II article is not used with nouns taken in a generic sense. These may be classified as falling roughly into four main types: (1) negation, (2) predication, (3) adverbial and locative uses, (4) generic verb objects and dependent genitives in compounds. These last two items can be shown to be basically similar.

In regard to negation, two observations can be made. The first is that non-articulated forms are confined to the objects of verbs in negative sentences and to subjects in negative existential sentences. They do not ever seem to occur with definite subjects in negative sentences, e.g. with 'girl' in the sentence 'the girl did not pick the flowers'. With indefinite subjects we are evidently dealing with instances in which an existential sense is involved. The somewhat strange sentence 'a girl did not pick the flowers' is either contrastive and really predicative that is equivalent to 'it was not a girl who picked the flowers', or equivalent to the negative existential 'no girl picked the flowers', 'there was not a girl who picked the flowers'. Such sentences are generally expressed in these two latter ways in languages, in which case they fall under predication and existential negation, in both of which cases non-articulated forms are common in languages with Stage II articles.

The second observation is that verb objects in negative sentences can also be divided into instances with generic and with definite objects, but very few languages in Stage II make a consistent distinction. The languages which I have examined which are closest to making this distinction consistently are Zulu and Xhosa, two closely related Bantu languages. Elsewhere, the rule is generalized so that either negative objects always take the article, or they never do. The latter is more usual.

Two Bantu languages from very different areas, Southern Kikongo and Luganda, show the following variation. A negative object takes the article when it precedes the verb but does not when it follows. A closer consideration of these two cases shows the following. The usual order is for the object to follow the verb. When it precedes, it is always definite in meaning, initial in the sentence, and referred to by a pronominal object on the verb. In other words, it is topicalized and the definiteness of topicalization takes precedence in the linguistic expression. An example from Tucker and Mulira's grammar of Luganda is the following: *toggyawo bitanda* 'don't take away the bedsteads' in which *bitanda* does not have the pre-prefix, but *e-bitanda tobiggyawo* 'the bedsteads, don't take them away' in which we find *e-bitanda* with the pre-prefix, and in addition, the incorporated object pronoun *bi-* in the verb (Ashton et al. 1954: 33).

A second major type of construction in which the articulated form usually does not occur is with nominal predicates in sentences of the type 'the man is an iron worker', but not where the sentence is equational so that the predicate is definite, e.g. 'he is the chief'. Predicative adjectives are treated analogously and usually do not have the articulated form.

The third major type is adverbial under which may be subsumed locative and temporal constructions. These are similar to expressions in English without the article such as 'by hand', 'on foot', 'at home', and 'at night', as well as words which double as adverbs and prepositions like 'behind' and 'above'. There is here, as in other instances, a strong tendency towards grammaticalization which takes the following form. All nouns governed by prepositions are in the non-articulated form even when their meaning is specific, but the articulated form reappears when the noun has a qualifier such as an adjective or dependent genitive, even if the meaning is generic. A rule of this sort occurs sometimes even with a Stage I article as exemplified by Rumanian in which, with a few minor exceptions, all those prepositions, constituting the large majority, which are not themselves articulated nouns followed by the genitive, take the noun without the postposed article. The articulated form is used, however, if the noun has qualifiers. Thus, we have *în grădină* 'in garden' but *în grădină cea mare* 'in the garden the large'.

Since body part nouns are frequently the source of adverbs and their corresponding prepositions, we often see a contrast between body parts as nouns which will in Stage II languages have the articulated forms in most constructions, as against their adverbial and prepositional uses in which they are non-articulated. A grammar of Ateso states that "many prepositions are derived from nouns by dropping the noun prefix" (Hilders and Lawrance 1957: 66).

The last major group is that of generic noun objects and nominal compounds based on a genitive construction. Again, we may cite examples from languages like English in which we have phrases like 'take care' and even occasional object-incorporation as in 'babysit'. An example of a Stage II language in which this occurs extensively is Khasi. In Gunwinggu which is really a Stage III language, nouns in classes III and IV, the two thing-classes, may be incorporated in the verb as objects, in which case they do not have their class-prefixes.

Compounds based on the genitive construction, or genitive expressions on the border of lexicalization, show similar characteristics. The genitive in such cases is taken generically, just as is the noun object of the verb. These expressions can be distinguished from genitive expressions in which the *regens* is non-generic. These are often systematically distinguished. An instance in point is Tamãri, a Voltaic language with older noun class suffixes which has a prefixed Stage II article. From *fa nafa* 'cow' and *li yini* 'horn', we have *li na yini* 'une corne de vache', 'a cow-horn', as against *fa nafa kwa li yini* 'la corne de la vache' or 'une corne de la vache'. The reason *na* occurs in 'cow's horn' without either a prefix or suffix is that in the first round of gender suffixation, the same phenomenon occurred so that the first member of a compound did not acquire the suffix, as can be seen in Voltaic languages which are suffixing only. In fact, because this is a productive contrast, one can say that languages like Tamãri were still in the final stages of a Stage II suffixed article when they began to develop a new prefixed article.

A special case here is that of diminutive constructions which are based, in many languages, on a compound of the form 'child of X'. Since this is highly productive and any noun in principle can have a diminutive, the unarticulated form of the noun sometimes survives in this formation, even when the dependent genitive acquires the article at a later point in the development of Stage II languages.

One further construction should be mentioned in which nonarticulated nouns sometimes appear, namely with numerals. Numerals appear more frequently in indefinite constructions like 'five houses' than in definite constructions like 'the five houses'. However, even the former construction is not generic. Hence, the noun should in Stage II have the articulated form with numerals, and this is generally the case, but there are occasional deviations. Mende, a language without noun-classes with a suffixed Stage II article *-i*, distinguishes indefinite from definite numeral constructions along the lines to be expected in a language with a Stage I article, e.g. *maha felenga* 'chief two', as against *maha feleisia* 'the two chiefs'. In the latter expression, as is normal in Mende, it is the following modifier which takes the definite form. An even more striking example is Aramaic. In modern Western Aramaic, an advanced Stage II dialect, the only productive use of nouns in the non-articulated form which has survived is with numerals. As noted earlier, the development of the article through the stages enumerated here was much more rapid in Eastern than in Western Aramaic dialects.

*3.5. The Stage III article*. It was indicated that during the second stage there is a decreasing set of environments in which there is direct contrast between the articulated and non-articulated form. In general it is the articulated form which spreads until it becomes the normal form of the noun. In the absence of significant contrast, there is an analogical tendency for one of the forms, usually the articulated, to spread to all the remaining environments so that, synchronically, the mass of common nouns now only have a single form, usually the one which is historically the reflex of the articulated form. When this happens, we are in Stage III in which the former article is a pure marker which no longer has any synchronic connection with definiteness or specificity. The line between Stages II and III is somewhat arbitrary. How restricted and non-productive must the alternating forms of the noun be for a language to be assigned to Stage III rather than Stage II? We will not so much be concerned here with the problems of assignment of borderline languages in terms of our somewhat rough and ready definition, as in considering the first stages of the process, and the synchronically non-functional survivals which are characteristic of Stage III languages.

There are two distinct classes of cases to be considered, those in which the original demonstratives which gave rise to the process were classifying so that the final result is a set of gender markers on the noun, and those in which this was not so, so that the final result is rather the existence of an 'empty' marker, a mere sign of nominality on the large majority of common nouns.

Where the original demonstrative was a classifying one, the essential outcome is, of course, that the nouns are now classified by markers, either pristine or renewing an older system (i.e. double affixation). There are, however, always telltale signs of the process by which the markers have come into existence. The first of these is that proper names, kinship terms, and frequently, borrowed nouns which entered the language at a point in the development in which there was no longer a synchronically relevant alternation between articulated and non-articulated forms, all end up without having gender markers. Involved as they normally are in a system with gender agreement, they are assigned gender on a semantic basis.

This is the presumed explanation for the existence of the class 1.a in Bantu languages, a phenomenon which is in fact found throughout Niger-Congo with the exception, of course, of Mande which has no noun classes. Class 1.a typically contains personal proper names and kinship terms, lacks the class affix, and has the agreements of class 1, the singular personal class which in Bantu has the prefix **mu-*.

The second consequence of this process has to do with locative and adverbial expressions in general. It will be recalled that body part terms and other nouns, e.g. 'earth' (= 'down') in Stage II languages, frequently contrast non-articulated forms in adverbial and prepositional uses with articulated forms in nominal uses. Such adverbs and prepositions tend to survive because of the absence of productive alternations. Prepositions and adverbs, being a restricted and fairly closed set, also often survive in the face of lexical replacements of the corresponding common noun. An examination of adverbs and prepositions will generally uncover relict forms without class markers. For example, Ovambo, a Bantu language in Stage III, in which nouns only occur in pre-prefixed form, has *posi* 'under' to be analyzed as *po-* 'on' and *-si* 'earth', the latter without the pre-prefix. The root **-si* is the general Bantu root for 'earth', but in Ovambo and related languages it has been replaced by *edu*.

There are also consequences for the nominal member of locational and other prepositional constructions. It was seen that the noun governed by a preposition does not usually take a Stage II article. A characteristic result in Stage III is the reinterpretation of the preposition as itself a gender marker, since the noun has none, and the development of agreements with it parallel to that of the earlier gender classes. Hence, the rise of so-called place genders as in Bantu languages. A further facilitating factor at work here is that place demonstratives in these languages often have two elements, one meaning 'place' and the other a deictic element found also with the regular gender demonstratives. For example, in Swahili we have *ha-pa* 'here, this place', parallel to *ha-wa* 'these', referring to nouns in class 2 (plural personal class) which have the prefix *wa-*. Syntactically it is plausible, as pointed out in Givón 1976, that such agreement should start with sentences in which place is topicalized. The final chief area of survival of the non-articulated form is, as might be expected, in fossilized nominal compounds and incorporated verb objects. We might also add here that sometimes words like 'person', 'thing', etc. survive in pronominal uses without the article (cf. French *personne*, *pas*, *point*; Italian *cosa* 'what?').

Instances of class 3 noun markers where the original demonstrative article was not classifying are especially intriguing, because we do not have here the guide of gender-agreement. All we have is that virtually every noun in the language has a particular marker which has, as it were, become a sign of nominality as such. Such cases will illustrate in a graphic manner how the study of generalized diachronic process extends the reach of internal reconstruction. Our evidence for the interpretation of such a marker as a former article rests on the fact that it shows the same characteristic survivals as where there is gender classification.

A case in point is Hausa. With rare exceptions Hausa nouns end in a vowel. This vowel is almost always long. A text count of nouns would probably show something like 99% final long vowels. However, forms with short vowels do exist, falling into two main and apparently unrelated types, proper names and adverbial expressions. To take the former, there are, to begin with, minimal contrasts between the same word as a common noun and proper name. Thus, *gàmbóó* designates a child born after twins, but *Gàmbó* is a proper name which may be given to such a child. There is a town *Dáwáákí* contrasting in final vowel length with *dáwáákíí* 'horses', the source of its name. Many proper names have short vowels without such a contrast, e.g. *Kánò*, *Zààríyà*, which are cities. In some instances the reason may be that they are borrowed words, for example, the personal names *Béllò* (from Ful), *ˀÀlhájì* (from Arabic). Borrowed common nouns constitute another short vowel category, e.g. *ˀàngúlú* 'vulture' borrowed from Nupe and *síísì* 'six pence' from English.

With regard to adverbial expressions, there is a whole series of terms, many of them body parts, which have special forms with short vowels when used with the preposition *ˀà*. These forms are called locatives in the grammar. They also exhibit tonal and other differences. Thus, *ˀídòò* is 'eye', but *ˀà ˀídó* 'in the eye'; *bààkíí* 'mouth', but *ˀà bákà* 'in the mouth'. Examples of words that are not body parts are *wútáá* 'fire', but *ˀà wútá* 'in the fire'; *k'ásáá* 'country', but *ˀà k'ásà* or just *k'ásà* 'on the ground, below'. There are also time expressions with the preposition *dà*, e.g. *dáréé* 'night', but *dà dáré* 'at night'. In addition words like *jíyà* 'yesterday', (*ˀà*) *bààrá* 'last year', *yànzú* 'now', etc. have short vowels without contrasting long vowel forms. Those numerals which end in vowels have them short, e.g. *bíyú* 'two', except units, which, as generally in languages, are treated as nouns, e.g. *dáríí* 'hundred'.

None of the adverbial expressions can have modifiers without being replaced by long vowel forms. At present these forms are more and more being replaced by the corresponding long vowel forms as alternatives even without modifiers.[4]

In light of the above account, we can explain the long vowel forms as the resultant of a former article which has reached Stage III, while the short vowel forms are the original forms still surviving in some of their most typical uses. Note that there is no possibility of a unified account of Hausa short vowel forms on a purely synchronic base. Hausa does have sex gender, but it appears that the demonstrative-article which is the presumed source of the long vowel forms, just as with Aramaic *-ā*, did not vary for gender or number.

A somewhat similar case to that of Hausa, namely Tiv, a language of the Benue-Congo branch of the Niger-Congo family, may be mentioned in passing. The old prefix system has here been renewed by suffixes which, however, only appear in those classes which had consonantal affixes. Their presence in the other classes can be detected by tonal changes which parallel those of the consonantal class. The earlier non-suffixed form of the noun, called the prepositional by Abraham (1940), survives after prepositions, e.g. *ḿgérěm* 'water', *šá m̀gěr* 'in the water'. This form may not be used with a preposition if the noun has modifiers. It also survives in diminutives and augmentatives, which are old compounds with the noun as second members, in mostly identical form. A perusal of Abraham's dictionary shows that many other compounds with the non-suffixed form as second member are reflecting an older direct construction without a class marker of the *regens*. There are also adverbial uses of words like 'ground' for 'down'.

Where the article was not a gender classifier, one additional phenomenon may be noted. Since in this case virtually all nouns receive the same mark, it becomes a sign of nominality as such and is used to derive verbal nouns. The *-s* of Plateau Penutian functions this way.

The entire account given here has been on the basis of the category of determination. This seems natural enough, because we are dealing with developments deriving from what is a definite article in its first stage. There is, however, another way of looking at the process which at first blush seems very different, but is in fact ultimately related to the notion of determination, namely case.

If we consider the Stage II article which is the decisive turning point, we can roughly state the matter as follows. The characteristic constructions

[4] Data regarding Hausa final vowel quantity is very inadequate in the existing literature. I am indebted to W. Leben and Mohammed Tairu for checking some cases of final vowel quantity in Hausa.

without Stage II articles include the vocative and adverbial uses corresponding to the locative and instrumental of languages which have these cases. The genitive and accusative are the cases in which real contrast between the articulated and non-articulated form occurs, particularly the latter where negative and generic, sometimes incorporated objects, are without the article which occurs in other uses. The subject case is, par excellence, the case which takes the article. Nominal and adjectival predication has to be considered separately. Here the subject is articulated, but the predicate often is not. However, as with the verb-object, there is the possibility of contrast roughly between permanent properties (articulated) and non-permanent (non-articulated).[5] Proper names do not enter here. For them an account based on determination is primary.

The case hierarchy just sketched is clearly related to definiteness. Subjects, as favorite topics, tend to be definite. In some languages they must be so. The accusative where the contrast is clearest is precisely the case which in some languages, e.g. Turkish, Persian, is the only one which formally distinguishes definiteness by a marker.

All this bears on the origin of case markers. In Indo-European it is striking that the two cases which can be reconstructed with zero inflection are the vocative and the locative. The latter has, in the singular, two variants: zero and *-i*. In the plural it has long been noted that *-sí* (with a variant *-su*) is really *-s* 'plural' + *-i*. In fact a form with just *-s* is also found. In Sanskrit the plural oblique forms for instrumental, dative, ablative, and locative have sandhi forms like that at word boundary, thus being in effect added to the pure base form. Note that the locative and other oblique cases, being marked forms, do not usually remain in the zero form, but acquire prepositions or postpositions as with Hausa *ʔà*, Tiv *šá* and, presumably, Indo-European *-i*. This view also strengthens the case for those who equate the nominative singular *-s* with the demonstrative **so*. Accusatives, on the other hand, often derive from old prepositions marking an indirect object. The case hierarchy just described is obviously related to that discussed in much recent work in regard to subjectivization and topicalization, including relational grammar.

The entire foregoing account of how noun classes acquire markers is subject to two important reservations. One is that sometimes only a few nouns within a class come to have markers, and this by a mechanism which is essentially different from that just described. In almost all such cases we have

[5] The Slavic short and long forms of the adjective, the latter containing a suffixed demonstrative or relative, belong here. The long form starts out as definite and tends to become like a Stage II article plus adjective, until, as for example in Russian, it only serves as a predicate adjective, and here only in certain uses.

"motion," that is, a minimal contrast of the same stem in different classes. This is common in North Caucasian. The nouns here do not in general have markers, but there are instances like Avar *v-as* 'boy', *j-as* 'girl'. I believe that these arise from substantivization of adjectives which do have concord markers.

Another and more fundamental reservation is the following. While the development of markers from the article is no doubt the usual process, there is what at the moment is, to my knowledge, the unique case of the Daly River languages in Australia described in Sec. 2. Here, a new system has been superimposed on an older Australian-wide formation of the usual type. In this new system, as it appears, the source of the marker is a superordinate noun and in some languages of this group concord subsequently has developed in the adjective to produce a gender system in the sense defined here.

## 4. The Spread of Grammatical Agreement

From the account in foregoing sections we see that the demonstrative, as the normal source of Stage I definite articles, plays the rôle of initiator for the whole process described here. It also plays a further rôle in that it constantly generates concordial phenomena, sometimes producing gender agreement where the demonstrative is classifying, and sometimes not. If we look at the impressive tables of concord series often found in grammars of Bantu languages, we can see that for every one of them, there is abundant synchronic and diachronic evidence of the rôle of the demonstrative. A detailed treatment of this process is not within the scope of this paper. We may note, however, a few principal considerations.

The term used up to now has been simply 'demonstrative', but this requires some further specification. If we consider once more our initial example of the Gurma group of Voltaic, we note that the new prefixes which arise match synchronically not the demonstratives of these languages, but the verb subject and object pronouns. This does not exclude the diachronic possibility that they come from earlier demonstratives which, on the one hand, developed into pronouns and on the other, into articles. The present demonstratives also would have these as their source with the addition of new deictic elements. If we look at present day French, the article matches the object pronoun. Historically, both come from the primarily demonstrative *ille* which also had anaphoric uses in Latin.

In fact the synchronic boundary of these forms is a shifting one. In most languages the demonstrative pronoun and demonstrative adjective are identical. In many languages the third person pronoun is identical with a demonstrative, and often an article is identical with one or the other. It is not excluded that the article should arise from what is ultimately a demonstrative, but come more directly from a third person pronoun. It was noted earlier that in the Neo-Aramaic of Ṭur-'Abdīn a new prefixed article has arisen. Nöldeke derived it from the demonstrative, while Siegel, in a more recent treatment, argues probably correctly for a prefixed pronoun. In any event the pronoun and demonstrative are very similar. Hence, when talking about the demonstrative in the present connection, I will not be drawing a strict line between demonstrative and third person pronoun.

We may distinguish in somewhat rough and heuristic fashion three types of concordial phenomena. The first is that of a noun with its immediate modifiers in the noun phrase, e.g. adjective, demonstratives, and numeral. The second is predicate agreement, that of a subject noun with predicate adjective or demonstrative. The third is anaphoric use. We may distinguish under these two types. Where a deleted noun has no modifier, we have a pronominal substitute. Where the noun has modifiers, there may be a substitute, e.g. 'one' in English 'the good one'. Languages with noun classes in such cases, however, usually attach the class marker to the noun modifier. This is probably one of the sources of modifier agreement, as soon as it is redundantly applied when the noun is present also. Another kind of redundant anaphora is intraclausal, but not within the noun phrase, as when the verb compulsorily contains a pronominal mark of the subject or other noun phrase head. The origin here is no doubt in topicalized sentences.

Much of this may be illustrated by the development in Rumanian of two new so-called improper articles which now exist alongside of the earlier suffixed definite articles. The first of these, *cel*, is originally a demonstrative from Latin *ecce illum* 'behold that', the last element of which by itself gave the Rumanian suffixed article. Alongside of *om-ul bun* 'man-the good', one can have *om-ul cel bun* 'man-the that good'. With deletion of the noun, we get *cel bun* 'the good' = Latin *bonum*, *ceí drepţi* 'the just' = Latin *justi*, and with relative-like uses *om-ul cel cu boi* 'the man with cattle'. The second article is *al* in the masculine singular. It derives from the preposition *a* and the same demonstrative *ille* found in the suffixed article and in the first improper article *cel*. Its basic use is possessive and can be seen from such examples as the following:

> *pom-ul bun al vecinu-lui*
> 'apple-the good that-of neighbor-the'
> *pom-ul meu şi al vecinu-lui*
> 'apple-the my and that-of neighbor-the'
> *ai noștri sosiră*
> 'the our (people) have: arrived'.

These parallel Bantu examples in that *cel* goes with the noun modifier, agreeing with the noun in gender and number, and *al*, as with the Bantu genitive, agrees with the *regens* which is followed by the *rectum*. In such a phrase as *femei-le ce-le frumoase a-le satu-lui* 'women-the those beautiful those-of village-the' the basic structure is similar to that of Swahili: *wa-kwe wa-zuri wa m-ji* 'women beautiful those-of village'. In fact, in Tagliavini's grammar of Rumanian, he notes the basic resemblance in such instances to languages like Swahili (Tagliavini 1923: 274).

Demonstratives, then, are constantly producing concord phenomena. However, specific demonstratives, as they become bleached of deixis by anaphoric uses, are constantly being replaced by new demonstratives usually formed from the older ones by the addition of new deictic elements, by reduplication, etc. These in turn lose their deictic force to be replaced by others. In relation to gender there are several possible courses of development. If the demonstratives themselves have gender classification, they will give rise to further phenomena of gender agreement. If they pass through the phases described earlier in the paper, they will end up in the noun, all the while producing concord from diachronically successive layers of demonstratives. The existence of such layers is shown in languages like Bantu in which the varying concords for the same gender exhibit a number of different forms. The persistence of the genders provides the cement which puts together, in the same set of concords, forms which differ phonetically.

The development of the article and that of the other concordial phenomena may not take place at the same pace. If the former proceeds more rapidly, we have languages in which gender is shown with the articulated noun and usually with the anaphoric pronoun also, but not with non-articulated nouns or on noun modifiers. Examples of such languages include Ijo, particularly the Brass dialect, with suffixed Stage I articles which distinguish masculine, feminine, and neuter in the singular and with the same distinction in pronominal reference, but without agreement in the noun phrase. Tunica, a Gulf Amerind language, only shows gender in definite nouns and also has pronominal elements incorporated in the verb, but no agreement in the noun phrase.

If the demonstrative is not a classifying one, it will still produce phenomena which are on the surface concordial, if the same demonstrative is at work, as in Hebrew *hay-yeled hat-tov* 'the-boy the-good'. Where, however, there is no classification and the "concord" elements involve varying forms of deictics of different periods, we will have at best suspicious similarities among some forms as in English 'this', 'that', 'the', 'they', 'them', whereas others, e.g. 'she', though of demonstrative origin, will exhibit no overt connection.

Incidentally, we see from this why it is the noun par excellence which gives rise to classificational systems of syntactic relevance. It is not so much that the noun designates persisting entities as against actions or temporary states of persistent entities. It is that nouns are continuing discourse subjects and are therefore in constant need of referential devices of identification. As soon as we wish to talk about an action as such, we nominalize it; classification is a help in narrowing the range of possible identification.

The theory of the special role of the demonstrative in the development of agreement advanced here is not intended necessarily to encompass concord in case or number. It is plausible in regard to number and is in fact almost always an incidental by-product of gender agreement where that occurs, since gender systems, except in a few instances in Australia, always intersect with the category of number.

## 5. The Problem of Origins

It is the thesis of this paper that, given a classifying demonstrative and the constant tendency of demonstratives to generate agreement, the result will be a gender system. Further, if the demonstrative goes through the stages outlined, the result will be a marker on the noun as well as on the agreeing element. Given the existence of classifying demonstratives, the whole process will unfold with something close to inevitability. However, it has not been explained how classifying demonstratives arise in the first place. This remains for further investigation. There is one possible origin which is just that. That is, it is not asserted that in any actually reconstructible case it occurred this way, nor that there are no other mechanisms.

This possible source is numeral classifier systems. As was pointed out in an earlier study (Greenberg 1972), the first construction to which the numeral classifier spreads is to the demonstrative, as has happened in Chinese, Thai, and other instances. This gives us just what we need, a classifying demonstrative. In fact, in Kiriwina in the Trobriand Islands, it has spread from the demonstrative to some adjectives; in standard Thai it occurs with adjectives in some constructions so that true agreement phenomena begin to appear. In northern Thai languages the classifier functions like an article, and in Jacaltec Maya, as an anaphoric pronoun. It may, however, not be necessary to go so far afield. The fundamental bases of contrast, animate and inanimate, human and nonhuman, male and female, tend to occur in demonstratives, third person pronouns, and interrogatives as a guide to identification.

It is possible that gender systems in their initial stages are of this type. The way in which gender arises need not be the same as that by which the system can expand by the development of new genders. A mechanism by which place gender might develop was described in the course of this paper, namely, through the reinterpretation of a preposition or postposition as a class marker.

Such prepositions frequently derive from locational nouns. Minor genders such as diminutives, and less often augmentatives, probably arise by a similar mechanism involving an element meaning 'small' or 'large'. Three parallel instances may be cited in which it appears that a neuter has just developed or is in the process of developing in a system with masculine and feminine. Boas, in his grammar of Chinook (1911: 602), notes that the neuter in Chinook can be used with any masculine or feminine stem to give an indefinite meaning. He notes also that the neuter is close to being what in the initial discussion was called a minor gender. He states that "the number of words which appear *only* in the neuter gender is so small that we may almost suspect that the neuter was recently indefinite and used to indicate both singular and plural." In Khasi, alongside of a masculine and feminine, there is a neuter which does not distinguish number. Its meaning is diminutive. It is my overall impression that there are *no* stems here which are exclusively neuter. A third case is Hottentot, also with masculine and feminine and a neuter, common gender used for words like 'child' in distinction from 'boy' and 'girl'. As with Khasi, there appear to be no stems which are exclusively neuter. Khasi has *ʔi* as the neuter marker and Hottentot has *-i* for neuter singular, the common sound symbolic vowel for diminutive. A remarkable parallel between Chinook and Hottentot is shown in Meinhof's statement regarding Nama Hottentot. "The *i* of the *genus commune* was originally an indefinite article which had nothing to do with gender and it is still used this way at the present time. It can be added to every substantive whether of masculine or feminine gender to signify an instance of the appropriate class" (1909: 48). Why common gender should arise from indefiniteness, I cannot really say. Meinhof believes that "this indefinite meaning of *i* easily led to the further result that little or no attention was paid to sex in its use so that its use as *genus commune* came into existence."

It has not been possible here, for reasons of space, to treat the relationship between the views presented here and the large and frequently murky literature on the origin of gender.[6] Suffice it to point out that the notion of a special rôle for the demonstrative in the development of gender is far from novel, being found after a fashion even as early as Bopp, who found the origin of inflectional elements in pronouns. In most speculation about gender, it has been assumed that classification starts with the noun, and the problem is to discover how it spreads. If the thesis is valid that the usual course of events is that it starts with the demonstrative and only sometimes ends up in the noun, the statement of the problem should be reversed. There are some

[6] For historical reviews of the literature on gender, see particularly Royen 1919 and Fodor 1959.

examples of earlier speculations which point in this direction, though none of them seem to be very clear. The closest approach encountered was in the writings of that frequently acute but generally neglected thinker Raoul de la Grasserie. After I had arrived at the notion that the Nahuatl absolutive was probably an old determiner, I found in his essay on the article the following statement: "In the Nahuatl language, the substantive ending *tli* is not a derivational suffix, but an indication of determination whose function has disappeared" (1896: 293).

## References Cited

Abraham, R. C. 1940. *The Principles of Tiv*. London.

Ashton, E. O., with E. M. K. Mulira, E. G. M. Ndawula, and A. N. Tucker. 1954. *A Luganda Grammar*. London, New York, Toronto.

Boas, Franz. 1911. "Chinook." *Handbook of American Indian Languages*. Part I: 561–677. Washington, D.C.

Carter, Hazel. 1963. "Coding, style and the initial vowel in north Rhodesian Tonga: A psycholinguistic study." *African Language Studies* 4: 1–42.

Celedón, R. 1878. *Gramática, catecismo i vocabulario de la lengua goajira*, ed. by E. Uricoechea. Paris.

Chantoux, A., A. Gontier, and A. Prost. 1968. *Grammaire gourmantché*. Dakar.

Dixon, Robert W. 1972. *The Dyirbal Language of North Queensland*. Cambridge, Eng.

Fodor, Istvan. 1959. "The origin of grammatical gender." *Lingua* 8: 1–41, 186–214.

Franklin, Karl J. 1962. "Tolai language course." Division of Extension Services, Territory of Papua and New Guinea.

Givón, Talmy. 1976. "Topic, pronoun and grammatical agreement." In *Subject and Topic*, ed. by Charles Li, 149–88. New York, San Francisco, London.

de la Grasserie, Raoul. 1896. "De l'article." *Mémoires de la Société Linguistique de Paris* 9: 285–322, 381–94.

Greenberg, J. H. 1972. "Numeral classifiers and substantival number: Problems in the genesis of a linguistic type." *Working Papers on Language Universals* 9: 1–40. Stanford University.

Hilders, J., and J. Lawrance. 1957. *An Introduction to the Ateso Language*. Kampala.

Holmer, Nils M. 1949. "Goajiro (Arawak) II: nouns and associated morphemes." *International Journal of American Linguistics* 15: 110–20.

Love, J. R. B. N.d. "An outline of Worora grammar." In *Studies in Australian Linguistics*, ed. by A. P. Elkin, 112–24. Sydney.

Manessy, George. 1960. "La morphologie du nom en Bwamu (bobooulé), dialecte de Bondoukuy." Université de Dakar.

———. 1965. "Les substantifs à prefixes et suffixes dans les langues voltaïques." *Journal of African Languages* 4: 170–81.

Marchese, Lynell. 1988. "Noun classes and agreement systems in Kru: A historical approach." In *Agreement in Natural Language: Approaches, Theories, Descriptions*, ed. by Michael Barlow and Charles A. Ferguson. Stanford.

Meinhof, Carl. 1909. *Lehrbuch der Nama-Sprache*. Berlin.

Moravcsik, Edith A. 1969. "Determination." *Working Papers on Language Universals* 1: 64–98.

Müller, Hermann. 1907. "Grammatik der Mengen-Sprache." *Anthropos* 2: 80–99, 241–57.
Peekel, G. P. 1929. "Grammatische Grundzüge und Wörterverzeichnis der Label Sprache." *Zeitschrift für Eingeborenen-Sprachen* 20: 10–33.
Planert, W. 1905. "Über die Sprachen der Hottentoten und Bushmänner." *Mittheilung des Seminars für orientalische Sprachen*, 3 (Berlin).
Royen, Gerlach. 1919. *Die nominalen Klassifikations-System in den Sprachen der Erde*. Mödling bei Wien.
Sapir, J. David. 1965. *A Grammar of Diola-Fogny*. Cambridge, Eng.
Siegel, Adolf. 1968. *Laut- und Formenlehre des neuaramäischen Dialekts des Tûr Abdîn*. Hildesheim.
Tagliavini, Carlo. 1923. *Grammatica della lingua Rumena*. Heidelberg.
Tryon, D. T. 1970. "An introduction to Maranungku, Northern Australia." Australian National University.
———. 1974. "Daly River Languages, Australia." Department of Linguistics, Research School of Pacific Studies, Australian National University.
Welmers, William E. 1973. *African Language Structures*. Berkeley and Los Angeles.
Wilson, W. A. A. 1961. *Temne: An Outline of the Temne Language*. London.

# Generalizations About Numeral Systems

## 1. Introduction

In this study a number of generalizations concerning numeral systems are proposed. Many, but not all of them, are stated here for the first time. The existing literature on this topic can be divided into several quite different sorts of studies. There are first, particularly in the earlier period, general or regional surveys of numeral systems, such works as those of Pott (1849), Conant (1896), Fettweis (1927), Thomas (1897–98, on Mexico and Central America), Dixon and Kroeber (1907, on California), Schmidt (1915, on Africa), and, above all, the immense worldwide collection of Kluge (1937–42). These studies are useful in showing the typological variety and a real distribution of numeral systems in regard to their basic mathematical structure. However, none of these studies is recent. In addition, none gives information regarding the syntax of numeral constructions, which constitutes the basis for many of the generalizations presented here. A second class of works is by mathematicians concerned with the history and evolution of numerical systems, such as Wilder (1953), Smeltzer (1958), and Menninger (1969). These works contain valuable ideas regarding the mathematical aspects, but they tend to concentrate on the development of written notations in the Near East and Europe, and to be cursory and superficial regarding spoken languages, particularly in non-Western and preliterate societies. Finally, there are studies by linguists in the relatively recent period. Brandt Corstius (1968) has edited a collection of formal grammatical analyses of particular systems, most of them transformational generative. An important contribution is that of Hurford (1975), a generatively oriented study which aims at greater generality and considers a number of diverse systems. A number of Hurford's formulations cover some of the same ground as mine, although expressed in a different framework. He notes, for example, that "in languages it is often the case that M's have the properties of nouns" (p. 51) (an M is a base of a numeral system). With this, compare the discussion under generalization 20. His rule of 1-deletion is contained in generalization 36, and his switch rule in my 26 and 27. His "packing principle" is related in a complex way to generalizations 37 and 38 of this paper.

Among non-generative treatments, the pioneer article of Salzmann (1950) deserves to be mentioned. I had already completed most of the present research when Stampe (1977) came to my attention; this article, which is similar in approach to mine, contains a number of generalizations and explanatory suggestions almost all of which, it is gratifying to report, independently corroborate my own conclusions. Among the more significant points are the following: that cardinal numbers are basically defined by their order in counting, that a system based only on addition suffers from "the stringent limit that memory plays on such a counting procedure," that smaller numerals are adjectival in nature and larger nominal, that the preferred order in addition is larger preceding smaller, particularly for larger numbers, that the preferred order in multiplication is multiplier preceding multiplicand, and that this preference is related to the worldwide favoring of QN (quantifier-noun) order as against NQ order, a fact which, as Stampe notes, was earlier stated by me. He also observes the tendency for the smaller, more frequent numbers to be expressed by combinations which are more unified phonetically. On a few relatively minor points, however, his generalizations are not borne out by my evidence. Readers of this article are urged to consult Hurford's book and Stampe's article also.

This study will mainly be concerned with a synchronic treatment of the most unmarked system, cardinal numbers in the attributive construction. Later sections also take into consideration the relation between attributive and other uses of cardinal numerals (e.g. counting, predication) and between cardinal and other series such as ordinals. There is also a section on language contact and one on evolutionary factors in the development of numerical systems.

## 2. Cardinal Numerals in the Attributive Construction

2.1. The Scope of Cardinal Numeral Systems. By the scope of a cardinal numeral system will be meant the set of numbers which can be expressed in it. It is important to distinguish, as is usually done, between a number and a numeral expression. Numeral expressions are always in some particular spoken language or system of written notation. Thus, 'the square root of sixteen,' *vier*, *six moins deux*, and '$2^2$' are all numeral expressions which designate the same number. We must be able to represent numbers as such in abstraction from the numerical expressions by which they can be designated.[1] Hurford (1975) uses strokes for this purpose; thus the number referred to in the above examples would be represented as ////. For larger numbers, this is obviously impractical. Hence like him I will, as a practical device, employ Arabic numerals for this purpose.

It is important to distinguish among numerical expressions in any natural language a special subset, the numerals proper, which constitute the numeral system of the language. Thus, in English 'sixteen' is a numeral expression which is also a part of the numeral system, whereas 'the square of four,' which designates the same number, is a numeral expression which is not. The system of numerals is described by a specific part of the grammar. In general its bounds are clear, but doubts may occasionally arise. For example, is 'nineteen hundred and seventy' as an alternative expression for 'one thousand nine hundred and seventy' part of the numeral system in English? Further examples from English are 'dozen' and 'score'. Reasons for considering expressions of this kind as not part of the system will be mentioned later.

The set of numerical expressions is obviously broader than that of the numerals in any language. The following generalization regarding numeral systems has already been stated by Merrifield (1968):

1. Every language has a numeral system of finite scope.

Thus, corresponding to each of the "grammars for numeral names" contained in Brandt Corstius (1968), there is a specific number which is the largest for which a numeral is generated, and this is true of all formalized treatments which I have examined. Given this result, it will be convenient to define the limit number L for each system as the next largest natural number after the largest expressible in the system. The reason for adding 1 is that this will often give us a convenient round number. Thus, for American English $L = 10^{36}$, assuming that, as in most dictionaries of American English, the lexical item with the highest numerical value is 'decillion'.

As contrasted with the much larger body of numerical expressions, the numerical system proper is generated by the act of counting. We do not normally count 'one, two, three, the square root of sixteen, five . . .' in English. Further, this helps us to eliminate such marginal expressions as 'dozen', 'score', etc. By and large, the numerals used in counting are the same as the set which has been mentioned above as the primary object of the present study, namely cardinal numbers in the form they take when they

[1] In the text of the paper I have tried to distinguish carefully between number and numeral, but I have sometimes used phrases like the 'number *n*' in place of such clumsy expressions as 'the numeral expression designating *n*' when the meaning was clear from the context.

qualify nouns. In some languages, however, they differ from counting forms. However, they always exhibit the same mathematical structure. For example, we never have a language in which the counting forms are decimal while the forms which qualify nouns are vigesimal. This topic will be discussed under generalization 53, at which point this identity of mathematical structure will be shown to extend to other numeral sets as well.

Of course, counting is a matter of competence rather than performance, since presumably nobody will ever count to some very large number. As long as there is a procedure such that given a numeral expression for any number, speakers can produce the next higher number, this is sufficient.

It is a corollary deducible from generalization 1 that no natural language has a place system with the zero principle, such as found in the written system of Arabic numerals. The possibility of expressing an infinity of natural numbers in this way derives from the theorem that for an arbitrary base *b* (in English, of course, $b = 10$), every natural number N can be written in just one way in the form:

$$N = a_n b^n + a_{n-1} b^{n-1} \ldots a_1 b + a_0$$

where $a_n$, $a_{n-1} \ldots a_1$, $a_0$ designate numbers from a set $0, 1 \ldots b - 1$. Mandarin has a term *ling* which means zero and indicates an empty place (in fact it means 'empty'), but it is redundant, is not used consistently and, more importantly, the numbers $b^n$, $b^{n-1}$, . . . (i.e. 10,000, 1,000, etc.) are indicated by a finite set of unanalyzable lexemes rather than by the place principle.

It is not asserted here as a generalization, but it is possible that all natural languages can designate any number, however large, by using numerical expressions which are not part of the numeral system. All that is required is a recursive mechanism involving 'one'. However, what is needed, then, for practical purposes, is some way of keeping track of the 'ones', and this can only be done by counting them, so we are back to the numerical system.

> 2. Every number *n* ($0 < n < L$) can be expressed as part of the numerical system in any language.

We may call this the thesis of continuity. Considering the relation of the cardinal numeral system to the act of counting, we may consider this, strictly speaking, a tautology, since if any numerical expression names a number *n*, the next by definition names $n + 1$. If there is no next numeral, then $n + 1 = L$, the limit number.

However, it is worth stating because contrary assumptions have sometimes been made. For example, Lichtenstein (1811–12: I, 668) stated that Van der Kamp could not find a Xhosa word for 8, although he stayed among them a long time and he himself could not discover Bechuana words for 5 or 9. In more recent times, some Indo-Europeanists have claimed that numerals for the higher decades, since they are not reconstructible, did not exist while a word for 100, which is reconstructible, did (Szemerényi 1960). As we shall see later, there is a relation between historical stability and markedness. In general the higher the numeral, the more marked, but units of the system have a special status and are less marked than would be deduced from their number value alone.

3. Zero is never expressed as part of the numeral system.

Instances in which reference is made to a class with zero members are normally dealt with by negative constructions in natural languages.

This might again be viewed as a tautology, since the numeral system is based on counting, and counting begins with 'one'; we do not count a set without members. However, it is worth stating since a linguistic extension of the numeral system to include 'zero' is not logically excluded. It is also of interest to note that in Peano's famous system of axioms for numbers, the very first postulate is "zero is a number" (Peano 1908: 27).

*2.2. Systems Without Operations or with Addition Only.* In this and subsequent subsections, along with certain generalizations regarding numerical systems, we will develop *pari passu* the notion of the arithmetical analysis of such systems. The most basic concept is the generalized mathematical notion of function.

Every numeral expresses a number as a function with one or more numbers as arguments. For example, in English 'twenty three' expresses 23 as a function $(a \times b) + c$ in which the argument *a* has the value 10, *b* has the value 2, and *c* has the value 3. A limiting case is the identity function which takes on the same value as its single argument, e.g. 'three' in English which designates 3 as the value of the identity function with the argument 3. When this is so, we may say that a particular number receives simple lexical representation.

4. In every numerical system some numbers receive simple lexical representation.

No matter how high L is, it is possible to have a system in which no number receives simple lexical representation. Thus we might construct a system as follows: $(2 - 1, 3 - 1, 2 + 1, 2 + 2$, etc.). Such a system requires the use of subtraction, or perhaps some other non-additive function, at least once, to express 1. Every system, then, has one or more numerals which receive simple lexical expressions. Salzmann (1950) calls the set of such numerals the 'frame' of the system. We shall call them here the atoms. Atoms are of two kinds, simple atoms and bases.

5. No number is ever expressed in any numerical system by means of a function any of whose arguments is ≥ L.

For example, in a system which only goes up to 7 (i.e. L − 8), we could not express 6 by (9 − 3), since 9 > L.

We can typologize systems into those which use only the identity function and thus consist solely of atoms, and those which also employ other functions such as addition or multiplication. Those of the former type are reported from South America, Australia, New Guinea, and South Africa (Bushman).

6. The largest value of L in systems with only simple lexical representation is 5 and the smallest is 2.

An example of L = 5 is Guana, an Arawakan language (Kluge 1937–42: III, 40) with the system 1, 2, 3, 4, 'many'. Such systems are uncommon. There is a single instance of a system L = 2, namely Botocudo, a Macro-Ge language in Brazil with only two terms: 1, 'many'. The most common values for L are 3 and 4. However, even systems with L = 4 often express 3 as 2 + 1. It seems that 2 is never 1 + 1, although rarely, 2 may be the dual of 1. It is of interest to note that these simplest systems parallel that of number in the noun. Corresponding to L = 2 is a singular/plural distinction, and to L = 3, singular/dual/plural. This relationship is graphically illustrated in Worora, an Australian language in which there is only a single numeral root which means 1 in the singular, *iaruŋ*, 2 in the dual, *iaruŋandu*, and 3 or more in the plural, *iaruŋuri* (Love 1933).

It is characteristic of all of these systems and of some with addition only that there is a term which is usually glossed 'many', with the indefinite value ≥ L.

7. The smallest value for L in systems with arithmetical operations is 4. This is a surprisingly low value. An example of a language with this limit is Port Essington Tasmanian, with 1, 2, 2 + 1, 'many'.

This upper limit is rather uncertain for reasons which will soon appear. An example of L = 11 is the language of Dagur and Vatai in New Guinea (Frederieci 1913: 41), with the following system: 1, 2, 2 + 1, 4, 4 + 1, 4 + 2, 4 + (2 + 1), 4 + (2 + 2), 4 + (2 + 1) + 2, 10. The parenthesized sums are represented by single words.

Two instances have been encountered of systems in which counting can be carried on up to 30 and which could be interpreted as involving addition only. These are Mullukmulluk in Australia (Tryon 1974) and Aghu in New Guinea (Drabbe 1957). In the former, for example, 20 is expressed as 'hand one,

one, foot, foot' which could be analyzed as (5 + 5 + 5 + 5). This reflects, of course, the common method of first counting on the hands and then on the feet. However, since 5 is itself expressed as 'hand one,' this could be interpreted as (5 × 1), and the above analysis might be amended to ((5 × 1) + 5 + 5 + 5). For Aghu in New Guinea, however, an account in which any of the numbers are represented by a function which involves multiplication seems to be excluded. In this system, also, counting on the fingers and toes is involved. A typical example is the term for 11: *koto wodo*, which means 'big toe'.

In these and similar instances it seems that numerals are never used without the accompanying gestures, and the gestures are often used without verbalization. It seems doubtful that such expressions are used attributively to nouns in sentences. There are other indications that some of the numerical systems recorded in the literature are simply the names for gestures used in counting. For example, for Auetö, a Tupian language, Steinen (1894: 536) gives the same numeral expression for 4 and 9. This is probably the word for 'index finger'. Even more strikingly, the following "system" is reported by Koch-Gruenberg from the Kaliana in South America: *meyakan* 1, *meyakan* 2, *meyakan* 3 (*meyakan* 'finger').

Another source of uncertainty is revealed by Douglas' statement regarding the Western Desert Language in Australia (1958) in which numerals up to seven are given, the higher ones being formed by addition of 1, 2, or 3: ". . . originally, it appears, these compounds implied only a vague number."

*2.2.1. The arithmetical operations in general.*

> 8. Of the four fundamental arithmetical operations—addition and its inverse, subtraction, and multiplication and its inverse, division—the existence of either inverse operation implies the existence of both direct operations.

This is one of a series of generalizations which point to the marked status of the inverse operations.

> 9. The existence of multiplication implies the existence of addition.

This is a near universal. I have encountered just one instance in which a numerical system has multiplication without addition, whereas there are many examples of addition without multiplication. In one subgroup of the Yuman languages, which are affiliated to the Hokan stock, we find systems in which L = 11 and the numerals may be analyzed as follows: 1, 2, 3, 4, 5, 3 × 2, 7, 4 × 2, 3 × 3, 10.

The only arithmetical operation beyond the four fundamental ones is one which might be called the "going-on" operation.[2] It is found in the Mayan group and in a few Finno-Ugric languages. An example is Ostyak in which 18 is expressed as 8, 20, that is, '8 going-on 20'. Such constructions often involve an ordinal interpretation, as is clear, for example, in Estonian when this same number is to be interpreted as '8 of the second decade'. In other instances, however, the meaning is in fact something like 'going on', e.g. Vogul 23 *vat-nupəl xurm* 'thirty-towards three'. In functional notation the 'going-on' operation may be expressed as follows: $f(x, y, z) = (x - 1)\,y + z$. Then, Ostyak 18 is the value of this function for the arguments $x = 2$, $y = 10$, $z = 8$.

One might argue that exponentiation is also an operation utilized in natural languages, but I believe this is erroneous. For example, English 'hundred' is not to be analyzed as $10^2$ with 10 and 2 as arguments in a function $f(x, y) = x^y$, since, unlike the representation of 200 as $2 \times 100$, 2 is not expressed overtly. A marginal case is English 'billion', 'trillion', 'quadrillion' . . . in which, if we go by the Latin etymology, we can analyze these in their British interpretation as $10^{2\cdot 6}$, $10^{3\cdot 6}$, $10^{4\cdot 6}$. . . .

> 10. Subtraction is never expressed by the mere sequence of the subtrahend and minuend.

In standard arithmetical terminology the subtrahend is the number subtracted, the minuend the number from which subtraction takes place, and the remainder is the result.

As contrasted with subtraction, simple juxtaposition is common for addition and multiplication, e.g. German 13 *drei-zehn* 'three, ten'. There are instances in which subtraction might seem to occur without overt expression, but such instances are generally to be interpreted as involving deletion. For example, in Tarahumara, a Uto-Aztecan language, *ki-makoi* is 9 and *makoi* is 10. One might wish to interpret *ki* therefore as 1. The ordinary word for 1 is *bire* and hence *ki* would be a suppletive allomorph. However, the correct analysis is that *ki* expresses subtraction and *bire* has been deleted. There are three reasons for making this kind of interpretation a general rule. First, the apparent subtrahend is generally suppletive. Secondly, the element to be deleted is always one of a limited set, essentially 1 or the bases of a system, and these are precisely the elements which are subject to deletion, as will be indicated in a later generalization. Thirdly, there are examples in which such a deletion is clearly indicated by the meaning of the element which remains. For example, in Efik 9 is *usuk-kiet* in which *kiet* is the ordinary word for 1, while 10 is *edip*, a base of the system. In this case *usuk* cannot be an

[2] This operation is called "overcounting" by Hurford (1975: 235), following Menninger 1969.

allomorph of *edip*, 10 since it is derived from *suk* 'to be left over'. However, in Tamil and other Dravidian languages, 9 appears to be 'one, ten' and this may be a genuine exception.

> 11. When a number is expressed by subtraction, or when a subtraction occurs as a constituent of a complex expression, the subtrahend is never larger than the remainder.

This generalization would be violated if a language expressed 2 as 10 − 8, since the subtrahend 8 is larger than the remainder 2. It would not be violated, however, if 8 was expressed as 10 − 2, which in fact is found quite often. Note that in the former instance we would be using 8, which had not occurred in the counting series up to that point, to express 2. This is one example of the general tendency to construct numerals on the basis of those which have occurred earlier in the series. Of course, if we are to have subtraction at all, the minuend must not yet have occurred in counting, e.g. 10 in the above example. There is also the fact that in counting a sequence subtractively, we seem to be going backward, a factor noted by Stampe (1977). This may be one reason for the unpopularity of subtraction. Amasoye (1972: 34), a speaker of Kalabari Ijo which has a vigesimal system that makes extensive use of subtraction, in advocating a more "rational" decimal system with addition only, says regarding subtraction: "The effect of this manner of counting is that we progress in our counting not by actually advancing but by retrogressing."

> 12. A subtrahend is always a simple lexical expression.

As noted earlier, a simple lexical expression is one which does not involve any except the identity function. An example of a violation would be the expression of 17 in a language as 20 − (2 + 1). There is no corresponding limitation for addition. For example, in Welsh *pedwar ugain ac un ar bumtheg* 'four twenty and one on five-ten', i.e. (4 × 20) + [1 + (5 + 10)], both addends are complex. Whereas the subtrahend may not be complex, the minuend may be. For example, in Yoruba 65 is [(20 × 4) − 10] − 5 in which there are two complex minuends, (20 × 4) and (20 × 4) − 10.

> 13. If a number $n$ is expressed by subtraction as $y - x$, then every number $z$ ($z > y > n$) is also expressed subtractively and with $y$ as the minuend.

For example, in Latin 18 is *duodēvīginti*, that is 'two from twenty'. Here $n = 18$ and $y = 20$ and $x = 2$. The only number $z$ smaller than $y$ (20) and greater than $n$ (18) is 19. Hence, 19 also will be expressed subtractively with 20 as the minuend, i.e. 20 − 1.

A marginal exception is Zapotec, as described in Córdova's *Arte del Idioma Zapoteco*, reproduced in Thomas (1897–98) in which 55 is (60 − 5), but 56 is either (60 − 4), as predicted by generalization 14, or (60 + 1) − 5, and correspondingly for 57, 75, 76, 95, and 96. In Montagnais, an Athabaskan language, 7 is expressed as either (10 − 3) or (8 − 1), although 9 is (10 − 1) and 8 is (4 × 2). Hence this is also an exception.

> 14. Every minuend is a base of the system or a multiple of the base.

This is evidently what is intended by Salzmann when he states (1950: 82): "Subtractive operation is usually of the Latin type undēvīginti and is bound to the cycle boundary." That is, in Latin 19 expressed as (20 − 1), and 20—the minuend—is a member of what Salzmann calls a cycle, since at regular intervals of ten we get multiples of ten while the intervening numbers are expressed by operating on, i.e. adding to or subtracting from, them. Later base will be defined, but for the moment we will consider it as generally understood.

The above quoted example of Zapotec is obviously an exception to this generalization also, since in the expression of 57 as (60 + 2) − 5 the minuend 62 is not a base or a multiple of a base. There are two further exceptions, one is Arikara, a Caddoan language in which, as reported by Prince Maximilian von Wied, 7 is (8 − 1), 9 is (10 − 1) and 11 is (12 − 1) in a decimal system. The exceptions here are, of course, 7 and 11. The other is Montagnais in which, as noted under generalization 14, 7 may be expressed as (8 − 1).

> 15. Division is always expressed as multiplication by a fraction. Only units or multiples of units are dividends, and the denominator of the fraction is always 2 or a power of 2.

Division is even more "marked" than subtraction and subject to severe limitations. Almost all examples are 50 expressed as (1/2 × 100), usually in a vigesimal system. In Oriya, an Indo-Aryan language, 275 is *pau ne tini šata* 'quarter from three hundred', i.e. (3 × 100) − 1/4 *(100), with the occurrence of 100 which is multiplied by 1/4 being deleted.[3] 'Half' is the "unmarked fraction" and is almost always a simple lexical item, often derived from 'to split', or 'to break' or the like. Even where a full system of fraction is found, the expression of half as 'one second' is excessively rare.

2.2.2. *The commutative and associative laws of addition and multiplication.* As we move from subtraction and division to addition and

[3] The asterisk, here and elsewhere, denotes a deleted expression.

multiplication, it becomes necessary to consider, in a more systematic way, the procedures involved in analyzing numerical systems. This is mainly because of complications related to the commutative and associative laws which apply to addition and multiplication, but not to subtraction and division.

Given that a certain numeral expression in a language designates 8 and that it does so as a function of 10 and 2, we can deduce that subtraction is involved. Whether there is an overt morpheme meaning 'to take away' or the like or not, the minuend is unambiguously 10, the subtrahend 2, and the remainder 8. In regard to addition and multiplication, however, a certain ambiguity obtains, which has no parallel in the corresponding inverse operations. To begin with addition, a distinction is made in arithmetic between the augend, that which is added to, and the addend, that which is added. The result is the sum, and any term of the sum is called a summand, whether it is the augend or the addend. According to the commutative law of addition, a + b = b + a, and this principle can be generalized to any number of summands. Hence in addition, given a language in which 7 is expressed as a function of 5 and 2, we can deduce that the arithmetical function is addition, but these numerical values are insufficient to determine which of the two summands is the augend and which is the addend. These two interpretations correspond to two different pragmatic situations, e.g. putting two objects on an already formed pile of five objects, as against putting five objects on a pile of two objects. Since the numerical result by the commutative law is the same, it might be thought that linguistically this makes no difference. But, as the subsequent discussion will show, there are various indications as to which of the two possible analyses is the correct one and this leads to generalizations regarding the construction of numerical systems.

A similar situation obtains in regard to the commutative law of multiplication. That which is multiplied is called the multiplicand, and that which multiplies, the multiplier. The result is the product, and the term factor is applied both to the multiplicand and the multiplier. The commutative law of multiplication states that a × b = b × a, and this result can be extended to any number of factors. If, in 3 × 10, 3 is the multiplicand, we are to think of ten piles with three objects on each pile, while if 10 is the multiplicand, we have three piles of ten objects each.

Because of the commutative law by which the order of summands or factors does not matter for the final result, standard arithmetical notation does not provide a means for symbolizing these distinctions. Parenthesization is introduced here as a method. In 5 (+ 3) = 8, 5 is the augend and 3 is the addend, whereas in (5 +) 3, 5 is the addend and 3 is the augend. Similarly, for multiplication, in 3(× 10), 3 will be the multiplicand and 10 the multiplier, whereas in (3 ×)10, 3 will be the multiplier and 10 the multiplicand.

Hierarchization will be used as a cover term for the process of determining the augend/addend or the multiplicand/multiplier. The augend and multiplicand are the passive members and the addend and multiplier the active ones.

Where there are three or more addends or factors, an additional process enters, namely grouping. The associative law of addition $(a + b) + c = a + (b + c)$ tells us that whether we combine *b* with *a* to produce a first sum or *b* with *c*, the result is the same. *Mutatis mutandis* the same analysis applies in relation to the associative law of multiplication $(a \times b) \times c = a \times (b \times c)$. Grouping distinctions both for addition and multiplication once more have pragmatic correspondents. Thus, given that $x = 3$, $b = 5$ and $c = 6$, $[a(+b)](+c)$ can be interpreted as follows. We first have a pile of three objects $(a = 3)$, to which we add five $(b = 5)$. We then take six objects $(c = 6)$ and add it to the resulting pile of eight objects to obtain fourteen. Both associative laws can be generalized to *n* summands or factors. In other words, order of operation does not affect the mathematical result.

*2.2.3. Steps in the analysis of numerical systems.* It is not the purpose of this section to give a detailed set of procedures for analyzing numerical systems. However, something like at least a partial ordering of procedures and of definitions seems necessary to provide sufficient clarity in regard to some of the terms to be used in the generalizations. For example, the notion of augend and addend involves a relationship between two numerical expressions, but until grouping has been carried out, we will not be able to apply these concepts to sequences of three or more addends.

The first step in analysis has already been briefly considered in Sec. 2.2.2. To each numeral is assigned one or more numbers based on morphemic identifications, and the arithmetical functions are inferred. For example, in English 'two hundred and three', the numeral which designates 203, is analyzed as containing the arguments 2, 100, 3 and the arithmetical function inferred is $(a \times b) + c$, in which $a = 2$, $b = 100$, and $c = 3$. In the limiting case of simple lexical expression, say 'six', which designates 6, the function is the identity function $f(a) = a$, where $a = 6$.

At this stage, we do not as yet have hierarchization or grouping of summands or factors, but we can automatically infer some parenthesizations from the arithmetical functions themselves. This is so for subtraction and division as well as for combinations of multiplication with addition or subtraction. In the above example of English 'two hundred and three', to derive the correct numerical value we must parenthesize $(2 \times 100) + 3$. If we did not, we would get $2 \times (100 + 3) = 206$.

The identification of phonologically different stretches as representing the same number is of three different kinds. One of these is agglutinal-fusional, as when English *fif-* in *fifteen* is taken to represent the same number as *five* in *twenty-five*. A second is suppletion, as when in Chrau, an Austro-Asiatic language, *mat* indicates 10, but for 20 we find *var jat* where *var* means 2. This leads us to deduce that *jat* is a suppletive alternant for 10. A further type, portmanteau expression, can be illustrated by Russian *sorok* 40. An analysis into (4 × 10) without specific subsequences being assigned meanings 4 and 10 is suggested by the facts about the Russian numeral system, but this requires the notion of base, which has not yet been defined.

We next note that in certain numerical expressions in languages, the arithmetical operations themselves are represented by overt morphemes. Reverting to the earlier English example of 'two hundred and three', we can deduce that 'and' designates the operation of addition. Such an overt morphemic expression of an operation will be called a 'link', in this case a link for addition. Such 'links' are not the only way in which operations are expressed. Word order, prosodic phenomena, inflection, or some combination of them are other methods. In Mandarin 32 is expressed as 3, 10, 2 in which the order is significant. For example, 2, 10, 3 would represent 23. In Classical Sanskrit *aṣṭáçatam* 8′, 100 is 108, but *aṣṭaçatám* 8, 100′ is 800. The use of accent alone, in this case pitch accent, is extremely rare, and I cannot quote any instance outside of Sanskrit. However, accentual phenomena often accompany other methods, but are so sparsely reported in the literature that I refrain from generalizing about them.

An example of inflection is the following. In Classical Arabic 5 is represented as *xams*$^{un}$ (the feminine nominative singular indefinite is used here as the citation form). The plural *xamsūna*, cited in the nominative, represents 50. There are corresponding relations between other digits and the corresponding tens. Here the inflection *-ūna* represents at the same time the operation of multiplication and the multiplier 10. Later it will be shown that there is good reason in instances like this to assume a deletion of 'ten'.

For some links, their very meaning virtually compels a particular hierarchization. Consider addition first. It frequently involves no overt expression, e.g. English 'twenty-five'. Almost as common is a formative, often affixed, meaning 'and' or 'with'. In many languages a single morpheme means both 'and' and 'with'. We may call this a comitative link. Since the basic meaning is association, it may, on occasion, go with either of the two addends. For example, in Galla 103 is *ḍibbā-f sadi* 'hundred-and three', whereas in Classical Arabic the same number is *miʾat*$^{un}$ *wa-thalāthat*$^{un}$ 'hundred and-three'. Later we shall see that in such expressions the augend is universally the hundreds expression while the digit is the addend. It will also appear that the decisive factor here is whether the language is prepositional or postpositional, not the arithmetical relation.

A third type is far less popular, but is still widespread. This is a word or affix meaning 'upon'. It will be called a superessive link. By its very meaning it would seem to go with the augend. If we add three items to ten, then the three are put on the heap of ten and not vice versa. 'Under' never occurs as a link. Unlike the comitative link, the superessive link shows consistency across languages in regard to the numeral with which it is in construction, regardless of the word order of the numerals or whether the language is prepositional or postpositional. For example, in Old Church Slavic 11 is *jedinŭ na desęte* 'one on ten' in which the syntactic connection of 'on' with 'ten' is shown by the fact that it is a preposition which governs the locative case of *desętĭ*, just as it does with other nouns. In Logbara, a Central Sudanic language which is postpositional, 11 is *moodri dri-ni alo* 'ten on-it (lit. its head) one'. We see that once more it is 'one' which is on 'ten', and not vice versa. An invariant relation also holds with the rather rare 'possessive link', e.g. Quechua 11 which is *čunka ukni-yuq* 'ten one-having' which exactly parallels the far-off Mountain Nubian, an Eastern Sudanic language with 11 'ten one-having', i.e. 'ten' which possesses a 'one'.[4]

These facts might be stated as one or more generalizations. However, a more powerful statement becomes possible after we have introduced another fundamental operation, namely serialization. This determination is independent of the semantics or syntax of overt links that we have just been considering, since it depends only on the mathematical structure of the numerical system. In fact it will be applicable whether there are links or not. Whenever there are at least two successive numbers, $x$, $x + 1 \ldots$, such that each is expressed as the sum of some constant $y$ and $z$, $z + 1 \ldots$, respectively, we will say that $y$ is an augend by serialization. We may illustrate this from English. Let $x$ be 'twenty-one', $x + 1$ be 'twenty-two', etc. They are expressed as $(2 \times 10) + 1$, $(2 \times 10) + 2$, etc., respectively. Hence 20 is the augend by serialization in these expressions, and 1, 2 . . . are the addends. The augend may have either simple lexical expression or be internally complex, as with $20 = 2 \times 10$ in this example.

There are some instances in languages in which addition occurs without being part of such a series. An example is Mandjak, a language of the West Atlantic branch of Niger-Congo in which 7 is 6 + 1, but 8 receives simple lexical expression. Such non-serialized sums will be said to be sporadic.

Augends identified by serialization for any particular sum never disagree

[4] In addition to the modes of expressing addition described in the text, there are others. One of these involves the meaning 'to be extra', 'to be added', or the like. An example is Kolokuma Ijo 11 *oi keni fini* 'ten one is-extra'. Another is a form meaning 'to be left', 'remain', as in Anglo-Saxon 12 *twā-lif* 'two remain', Modern English 'twelve'. In both of these the identity of the augend is given by the semantics. In the latter method, the unit is perhaps always deleted.

with those identified by superessive, possessive, or other links which lend themselves to interpretation in this regard. The first notion is, however, the broader one. Further superessive or possessive links never occur in sporadic sums. This probably also holds for the other methods mentioned in footnote 4. We have therefore the following generalization.

> 16. Every superessive or possessive augend is a serialized augend.

We can see that this is an empirical generalization by noting what a language would have to be like to violate it. Let us suppose that in a particular language 8 was expressed as '3 on-5', but 9 was a single lexical expression. We would have a superessive augend 5 which was not a serialized augend.

> 17. A serialized augend is always larger than its addends.

The reader may have noticed that in all the examples given, the augend was larger than the addend. Note that serialization was defined without reference to the relative size of the numbers. For example, if in a language 8 was $2 + 6$, and 9 was $2 + 7$, then 2 would be a serialized augend which was smaller than its addends. In the above statement, a restriction was made to serialized augends to the exclusion of sporadic sums. There is sometimes no way in which the augend can be identified. Even with sporadic augends, however, there are no convincing counter-examples.

Up to now nothing has been said in regard to grouping, a process which becomes relevant where there are more than two addends. Generalizations 16 and 17, which relate to hierarchization and thus assume two addends, will be found to hold for each successive pair of constituents after grouping is carried out.

> 18. Whenever there are three or more summands and at least one is a product, parenthesization starts by separating the summand with the largest numerical value from the rest. The same rule then applies to the remainder, if it consists of more than two summands, and so on.

For example, in English 3423 with the summands $3 \times 1000$, $4 \times 100$, $2 \times 10$, and 3, since at least one summand is a product, generalization 18 applies. Since 3000 is the largest numerical value, we first parenthesize $(3 \times 1000) + [(4 \times 100) + (2 \times 10) + 3]$. We then parenthesize within the second member: $(4 \times 100) + [(2 \times 10) + 3]$. Since the remainder has only two summands, the process is complete.

In every generative account of numerical systems I have seen, the phrase structure tree which results assumes a constituent structure which is in accordance with this generalization.

There are a number of empirical indications which support the preceding generalization and no strong counterevidence. (a) Word order in languages like German which for numbers like 325 *dreihundert-fünf-und-zwanzig* [(3 × 100) + (5) + (2 × 10)] would require discontinuous constituents, were we to group the hundreds and tens as one constituent distinct from the digits. (b) The absence of 'and' in English between twenty and five in the corresponding expressions 'three hundred and twenty-five' tells in favor of (3 × 100) + [(2 × 10) + 5] rather than [(3 × 100) + (2 × 10)] + 5, since coordinating conjunctions generally join constituents. (c) The existence of morphologically fused forms or unification in a single word by accent, for the lower values. As an example of the former we may note in Hindi that complex numerals lower than 100 are all single words whose morphological elements are so irregularly fused that morphemic analysis becomes difficult, whereas multiples of one hundred, one thousand, etc. are separate words. For example, 273 is *dō sau ti-hattar* 'two hundred seventy-three' in which we may compare *ti* with *tin* 'three', and *hattar* with *sattar* 'seventy', and *sāt* 'seven'. This supports a parenthesization {(2 × 100) + [(7 × 10) + 3]}. In Estonian multiples of 10 and 100 are written as single words united by the word accent whereas the thousands are written separately.

The proviso in generalization 18 that at least one of the sums be a product was made for the following reason: there are instances like Welsh *dau ar bum-theg* 'two on five-ten', i.e. 2 + (5 + 10), which grouping clearly does not involve taking the largest value first. The analysis of 17 here as 2 + (5 + 10) is further supported, since, in accordance with generalization 17, (5 + 10) is a serialized augend. Thus, 16 is *un ar bum-theg* 'one on five-ten'. It is characteristic of expressions such as this involving three simple addends that two of them always form a complex which is serialized. This is expressed in the following generalization.

19. The maximum number of sporadic addends is two.

This principle may be further illustrated by the following example. In Kato, an Athabaskan language of California, 9 is *bun-naka-naka* 'five-two-two'. However, *bun* 'five' is a serialized augend, as can be seen from 6 which is 'five-one' and 7 which is 'five-two'. Hence the analysis of 9 here is 5 + (2 + 2). In fact 4 is *naka-naka* 'two-two'.

We now turn to hierarchization and grouping in multiplication. The analysis will in general be parallel to that for addition, but with some important differences. Corresponding to the augend in addition is the multiplicand. Here also, there are instances in which the semantics determines the hierarchization. Unlike addition, overt expression of the operation of multiplication is relatively infrequent, with most examples from North America. A clear type of semantic determination is the use of an adverbial numeral, i.e. a member of the series 'once', 'twice', etc., which is then obviously the multiplier. For example, in Classical Greek 2000 is *dis-khílioi* 'twice-thousand' in which *dis* is the same as the numerical adverb for 'twice'. This immediately suggests an analysis (2 ×) 1000, i.e. 1000 taken twice, not, obviously, 2 taken a thousand times. There are instances in which syntactic considerations play a rôle. Whereas the chief extra-numerical model for addition, namely coordination, is, as we have seen, non-hierarchical, this does not hold for the main syntactic models for multiplication, the numeral-noun constructions and the partitive. Thus, if in a language we find 30 expressed as 'three-ten(s)', we usually find a general syntactic resemblance to construction such as 'three houses'. We shall see later that, in particular, multiplicands are often treated like nouns and multipliers like numerals or like noun modifiers in general. Hence, it is reasonable to equate the multiplicand with the noun and the multiplier with the adjective. In the partitive construction, the multiplicand may be identified with the noun in the partitive as in Wolof 200 *ɲar-i temer* 'two-of hundred', which is completely parallel to *ɲar-i nag* 'two-of cow'.

As with addition, we have the independent criterion of serialization. If we find successive products of the form $n \times m$ and $n \times (m + 1)$, we say that $n$ is the multiplicand by serialization and $m$, $m + 1$ are multipliers. However, the definition of a serialized augend is not completely parallel to that of a serialized multiplicand. One of the ways in which it differs is that we do not require that $n$, $m$, $m + 1$, etc. in the above expression should always have overt lexical expression. Consider, for example, Swahili in which 2, 3, 4 are *mbili*, *tatu*, and *nne*, respectively, whereas 20 is *ishirini*, 30 *thelathini*, and 40 *aroba'ini*, with similar lack of morphological relations between digits and tens up to and including 9 and 90. This is because the tens have been borrowed from Arabic. Still, we wish to say that *ishirini* is (2 × 10), *thelathini* (3 × 10), etc., since, it would be generally agreed, we are dealing with a decimal system. In other words, we allow a "portmanteau" analysis here. Let us call expressions like 'twenty' and 'thirty' in English serialized products. To allow for instances like Swahili we say that a serialized product may have simple morphemic expression. On the other hand, as with the augend, the multiplicand itself may have an arithmetically complex internal structure. For example, in Adyge, a Northwest Caucasian language, 40 is (2 ×) (10 × 2), 60 is (3 ×) (10 × 2), and 80 is (2 ×) (10 × 4). We are evidently dealing here with a vigesimal system in which the base 20 is expressed in a mathematically complex way.

We need one more proviso, namely that every one of our serialized products should be a serialized augend or minuend also. Without this limitation, we could analyze English 'four', 'six', 'eight' as portmanteaus of (2 × 2), (2 × 3), and (2 × 4), respectively. But, of course, they are not augends. We may recapitulate our somewhat complicated definition of a serialized multiplicand as follows. A serialized multiplicand is a number whose successive multiplication by at least two other numbers results in serialized products which are either expressed as simple lexemes or as a product of the multiplicand and multiplier, and such that each serialized product is also a serialized augend or minuend.

Parallel to the earlier generalization 16 regarding augends, we have one regarding multiplicands:

> 20. All adverbially or partitively expressed multiplicands are serialized multiplicands.

That is, in a case like that of Classical Greek *dis-khílioi* 'twice a thousand', it will always be found that the adverbially expressed multiplicand is also a serialized multiplicand. The situation is similar in regard to partitive expressions.

Incidentally, in defining serialized multiplicand, we have also defined the notion of base which up to now has been the sole method of typologizing numeral systems. A serialized multiplicand is a base. Since both multiplication and addition are involved in this definition, a system without these operations cannot have a base. There can be, however, and commonly is, more than one base, e.g. 10; 100; 1000; 1,000,000 in English. The smallest base will be called the fundamental base. If all the bases are powers of the fundamental base, the system will be called "perfect." There are only four numbers which figure as fundamental bases in perfect numeral systems of the world, in order of frequency: 10, 20, 4, and 12. Most systems with 20 as a fundamental base have 100 as the next highest base rather than $400 = 20^2$.

> 21. All the bases of a system are divisible by the fundamental base.

A violation of this produces a very complicated system. At least two such systems do seem to exist, that of Coahuilteco, a Hokan language, as reported in Swanton (1940), which has 3 and 20 as bases, and Sora, a Munda language, with 12 and 20 (Stampe 1977: 601).

The multiplicands which are not serialized multiplicands by the above definition, and therefore not bases, fall into two types. There are first those which fail because they are not augends, even though they are multiplied by successive numbers. The multiplicand here is usually two, and they can be called 'pairing systems'. As far as I know, all examples are from North America. One example is the Wintun branch of California Penutian. For example, the Central Wintun numerals from 1 to 10 can be analyzed as follows 1, 2, 3, 4, 5, 2 × 3, 7, 2 × 4, 10 − 1, 10. Because of the existence of the successive products 2 × 3 and 2 × 4, 2 is a multiplicand, but does not conform to the earlier definition of a serialized multiplicand. We will call it a pseudo-base. It has a further characteristic, namely that the multiplicand is smaller than the multiplier, whereas generally the opposite holds, e.g. English 'twenty' which is (2 ×) 10.

> 22. A multiplicand in a pseudo-base is always smaller than its multiplier.

In a true base, this may also hold for individual numeral expressions. There are decimal systems, e.g. Keres (Kluge 1937–42: III.486) in which, for example, 120 is [(10 + 2)×]10. However, in such cases numbers smaller than the base are also multipliers. Hence we have the following implicational relation.

> 23. If a serialized multiplicand is a factor in some product in which the multiplier is larger than the multiplicand, it is also a factor in some product in which it is smaller than the multiplicand.

The other case in which a multiplicand is not a base by the definition given here is that of sporadic products. For example, in Breton, 18 is *trixwek* 'three six'. Neither 3 nor 6 are ever multiplied by any other number in the numeral system. We can posit that 3 is the multiplicand because Breton has QN word order.

Parallel to generalization 19 about sporadic addends, we have the following:

> 24. The maximum number of sporadic factors is two.

Whenever three or more numbers are multiplied, it will always be found that all except one, the multiplier, form a complexly expressed serialized multiplicand, i.e. a base. For example, in Huastec 200, expressed as 2 × 5 × 20, 5 × 20 is a complex expression for 100 which is a base, as can be seen from 300 which is 3 × 5 × 20, etc. This, incidentally, gives us a grouping and hierarchization [(2×)(5 × 20)].

There is one other interesting fact about multiplication which has no parallel with addition. This is the rôle of the number 1 itself. Structurally, it parallels zero in addition, being what is called in mathematical group theory a 'unity', i.e. just as $n + 0 = n$ for any $n$, so $n \times 1 = n$ for any $n$.

While 0 is, as we have seen, never expressed, 1 sometimes is. Since multiplication of any number by 1 is redundant, it is not usually expressed. However, 1 is always part of the numeral system, while 0 never is. Hence the possibility of its employment always arises. The following will be found to hold:

25. Only a base is ever multiplied by 1.

Thus, in English one says either 'one hundred' or 'a hundred', and similar expressions exist in many languages. It is not difficult to see why this is so. Bases which are often called units are in effect being counted, hence one starts with 'one'. The base is sometimes expressed by some ordinary noun in the language, e.g. 'road' in Yuchi. In some societies when large numbers are counted, the units are represented by stones or some other material object which themselves are counted. For example, Tönjes (1910: 62) in his grammar of Ovambo, a Southwestern Bantu language, notes: "If someone has the task of counting a herd of 37 oxen, one proceeds as described above and if asked regarding the total, he answers: '*ēngobe odi li omilongo nhatu nengobe nhano na mbali.*' That is, these cows are three tens and seven cows." Similar facts are described in Araujo 1975 regarding the Basque counting of sheep. An interesting confirmation of the rôle of counting in the expression of 1 as a multiplier is the fact that in Gujarati 100 is *ek so* 'one hundred' in counting, but simply *so* 'hundred' in context.

*2.3. Order of Elements in Numerical Expressions.* The most important principle underlying the order of addends is that when in a language there are instances of both the larger addend preceding the smaller and of the smaller preceding the larger, the latter construction is found in the smaller numbers, and there is a definite number or a free variation interval at which the order shift takes place. The order is never reversed again for higher numbers.

For example, given in Italian that 16 is expressed as (6 +) 10 *se-dici* in which the smaller precedes the larger, we will predict that all smaller numbers expressed by addition will have the same order, e.g. *quindici* (5 +) 10, *quattordici* (4 +) 10, etc. Given that 17 is *diciasette* 10 (+ 7), we will predict that in all higher numbers expressed by addition, the larger will precede the smaller. For example, 18 is *diciotto* 10 (+ 8) and 23 is *ventitre* 20 (+ 3).

Sometimes there is a free variation interval in which either order occurs. For example, in Welsh, as described by Bowen and Rhys (1960), for numbers up to and including 59, the smaller precedes the larger. From 61 to 99 both orders occur, while over 100 the larger precedes the smaller. In view of generalization 17 which states that a serialized augend is always larger than its addend, the statements in this section could be as easily made regarding augends and addends.

Note that generalization 18 regarding the grouping of addends is logically prior to those of this section. In languages like German in which a number like 243 is *zweihundert-drei-und-vierzig* with the order 200, 3, 40, we can only say that the larger addend precedes the smaller in this expression because it has already been parenthesized as 200 + (3 + 40).

In order to express the additional regularities regarding the free variation interval, the earlier loosely expressed generalization is broken up into two as follows:

> 26. If in a language, in any sum the smaller addend precedes the larger, then the same order holds for all smaller numbers expressed by addition.
>
> 27. If in a language, in any sum the larger addend precedes the smaller, then the same order holds for all larger numbers expressed by addition.

That these two generalizations are logically independent can be shown from a logically possible but in fact nonexistent type of language which conforms to one and violates the other. Consider a language in which the numerals 11–17 are analyzed as follows: 1 + 10, 2 + 10, 3 + 10, 4 + 10, 5 + 10 ~ 10 + 5, 6 + 10, 10 + 7. Such a language would conform to generalization 26 but violate 27.

It will be convenient to define the upper cut-off number for addition as the largest number with the order smaller-larger + 1, and the lower cut-off number as the smallest number with the order larger-smaller − 1. The free variation interval will consist of all the numbers expressed by addition, which are at once less than or equal to the upper cut-off number and greater than or equal to the lower cut-off number.

For example, in Italian where the upper cut-off number is 17 and the lower cut-off number is 16, the cut-off interval will be null. In the Welsh example the upper cut-off number is 100, the lower cut-off number is 60, and the free variation interval is 61–99.

It will then be a corollary deducible jointly from generalizations 26 and 27 that all numerals formed by addition in the free variation interval are in free variation in regard to the order of their summands.[5]

Languages in which for all numerals formed by addition, the larger precedes the smaller are extremely common. Those in which the smaller always precedes the larger are extremely rare. Malagasy is an example. In Classical Arabic it was possible for all numbers, but in free variation with an order in which only digits preceded tens. There is thus a world-wide favoring of the

[5] I have found just one exception to the generalizations about cut-off numbers, namely Trumai, an Equatorial language (Steinen 1894: 542) in which 'three' is (2 + 1) but 'six' through 'nine' and 'eleven' through 'fourteen' are (5 + 1) . . . (5 + 4) and (10 + 1) . . . (10 + 4). The highest numeral given is 'twenty'. However, the expression for 'one' in (2 + 1) is suppletive.

order larger + smaller. In the history of both Indo-European and Semitic, there has been a constant drift towards lowering both the upper and lower cut-off numbers. For example, in Latin the lower and upper cut-off numbers were 20 and 100, while for Spanish they are 15 and 16, respectively. It may be stated as an intragenetic diachronic universal that for any language in either family at $t_1$ and $t_2$, where $t_2$ is later than $t_1$, both the upper and lower cut-off at $t_2$ is less than or equal to the upper and lower cut-off numbers at $t_1$.

There is evidently a cognitive principle involved in the favoring of the order larger + smaller. If I express a large number, say 10,253 in the order 10,000; 200; 50; 3; the very first element gives me a reasonably close approximation to the final result, and every successive item gives a further approximation. The opposite order leaves the hearer in the dark till the last item is reached. He may not know even then, till a noun or an inflection on the last item of a substantivized numeral informs him that the numeral construction is closed. In light of this, we can see also why natural languages do not adopt a place system with zero. Either the powers are in ascending order with the attendant cognitive problem just described, or they are in descending order, in which case the hearer has exactly the same problem, since an initial 6 may indicate 6,000 or 600,000 or 60, and this will not be known till the numeral expression is completed. In natural languages the existence of separate lexical terms such as 'thousand' for powers of the base soon orients the hearer.

> 28. If there are any numerals in which the expression of the multiplier follows that of the multiplicand, the language is one in which the numeral follows the noun.

It will be convenient in discussing ordering within a product, since in most instances the multiplicand is a unit of the system, to use the symbols M for multiplier and U for unit, and talk of MU or UM order. Since, as we have seen, the most common syntactic treatment of multiplication is to equate it with the QN (quantifier-noun) construction, i.e. *three tens* like *three houses* and *tens three* like *knives three* in most languages, the two orders harmonize, MU with QN and UM with NQ. Where there are numeral classifiers, it is the order numeral + classifier that is fundamental and conforms to this generalization and not classifier phrase + noun (cf. Greenberg 1963). Wherever the above harmonization is broken, it is always in favor of MU order which occurs in a number of instances with NQ order, e.g. Lhasa Tibetan and Maori. Thus, as noted by Stampe, MU order is highly favored over UM in languages of the world, being even stronger than the preference for QN order in relation to NQ. The only example encountered of a language with the disfavored order relationship both for addition and multiplication, i.e. smaller before larger and UM is Timucua, an extinct language of Florida (Pareja 1886). Even here, for numerals over 'twenty' the order larger before smaller prevails.

> 29. If the multiplier follows the multiplicand in a particular numeral, it follows in all higher numerals which are expressed by multiplication. Where there is this variability in multiplicand-multiplier order, the language is always one in which the numeral follows the noun.

More frequently in NQ languages than the disharmonic relation with MU permitted by generalization 28 is variability which always takes the form described in the above generalization. The point at which MU is replaced by UM might be called the cut-off point for multiplication, analogous to that for addition described earlier. Here also, there may be a free variation interval.[6]

Margi, a Chadic language of Nigeria which has a decimal system, may serve as an example. The order with multiplier of ten is 2 × 10, 3 × 10, etc., but for hundreds it is 100 × 2, 100 × 3, etc. In this language the numeral follows the noun. Another example which shows that the cut-off point need not be one at which a new base occurs is Nandi, a Southern Nilotic language of the Nilo-Saharan stock. In this language we have 2 × 10, while from 30 through 50 there is free variation, and from 60 on the order is 10 × 6. Here again, the numeral follows the noun. In these and other languages of this type, we have a diachronic process by which starting with the highest units, a former MU construction is changing to UM to harmonize with NQ order. The general principle which underlies this and a number of other generalizations is that the larger the number value of a numeral, the more it resembles the noun in its syntax. In some instances it can be shown that there has been a shift from QN to NQ, which precipitated a change from MU to UM, starting with the highest numerals. A detailed discussion of this phenomenon is reserved for a separate publication since space limitations preclude a fuller treatment here.

> 30. A link for addition is never initial in a numeral.
>
> 31. If a link for addition is final, the language is postpositional.
>
> 32. If a link for addition occurs medially, it always goes with the following numeral in a prepositional language and with the preceding numeral in a postpositional language.

[6] Strictly speaking, because of the free variation interval, this generalization as well as 35 and 46 should be split into two generalizations, as was done with the cut-off for addition stated in generalizations 26 and 27.

These three generalizations may be taken together. It was noted earlier that addition in languages where there is overt expression of this relationship is frequently 'comitative', and is similar in its syntax to nominal coordination. However, although probably all languages have overtly expressed markers of coordination, many languages simply juxtapose numerals without overt coordination, e.g. Turkish.

Where coordinators are found, their order properties are clearly related to whether the language is prepositional or postpositional. Of the two most common types of links, the superessive is itself an adposition, while words for 'and' are the same as for 'with' in many languages. The kinds of deletion, on the whole, parallel those of coordinators in languages of the same adpositional type.

However, generalization 30 seems to transcend this relationship in that initial links might be expected in prepositional languages, and because we have initial coordinators in instances like Latin *et . . . et . . .* and English 'both . . . and'.

The patterns commonly encountered where there is an extended set of addends is shown in the table below, separately for prepositional and postpositional languages. A much more detailed investigation of noun and other coordinate constructions in relation to numeral constructions is required than was attempted for this study and would probably yield further generalizations.[7]

| Prepositional languages | Postpositional languages |
|---|---|
| 1. W C-X C-Y C-Z | 1. W-C X-C Y-C Z |
| 2. W X Y C-Z | 2. W-C X-C Y-C Z-C |
| | 3. W X Y Z-C |
| | 4. W-C X Y Z |

In the above table, W, X, Y, Z stand for numeral expressions and C indicates an overtly expressed coordinator. I have considered fused expressions to be single numeral expressions, e.g. 'fourteen' in English. Sometimes a coordinator is found in petrified form within a complex numeral, e.g. Classical Greek 13 *treiskaídeka*, i.e. *three-and-ten*.

The importance of the adpositional factor is shown vividly by Bedauye, a Northern Cushitic postpositional language which has borrowed *wa* 'and' from

[7] The patterns for the expression of coordinators could of course be considered a kind of gapping, and the results of a fuller study might be fruitfully considered in the light of recent work on this phenomenon, e.g. Sanders 1976. As far as I know, however, all kinds of gapping considered up to now consider coordinations in which the deleted elements are always the non-coordinators, e.g. *John likes fish and Mary meat*.

Arabic, a prepositional language. Whereas in Arabic prepositional pattern 1 is found for *wa* which is prefixed, e.g. Classical Arabic 355 *thalāthu miʾatin wa-xamsu wa-xamsūna* 'three hundred and-five and-fifty', in Bedauye we find variation between patterns 1 and 2 of the postpositional kind for the same element, e.g. 31 *məhei taman-wa gal-(wa)* 'three ten-and one(-and)'.

> 33. When there is word order variation in addition between larger and smaller, and one order has an overt link and the other has not, it is always the order smaller + larger which has the link.

This is one further indication of the primacy of the order larger + smaller in addition.

The following are examples. In Latin 21 was either *ūnus et vīginti* or *vīginti ūnus* (i.e. 'one and twenty' or 'twenty one'). In the later style of Biblical Hebrew (e.g. Chronicles) the same variation existed. In Araucanian, an Andean language of South America, 11 is either *mari quiñe* 'ten, one' or *quiña huente mari* 'one on ten'.

> 34. If a link for subtraction is final, the language is postpositional.

This is, of course, analogous to generalization 32. Unlike addition, subtraction may have an initial link, e.g. earlier Biblical Welsh, as described by Hurford (1975). Subtraction is expressed finally in Somali, a postpositional language, e.g. 19 *labaton mid-la* 'two-ten one-not'.

*2.4. Some Characteristics of Bases.* We have already had one generalization, no. 25, which refers specifically to the bases of a numerical system and which states that only a base is ever multiplied by 1. Further investigation of multiplication by one indicates a further regularity.

> 35. If 1 is expressed as a multiplier with a particular base, it is expressed with all higher bases.

For example, in English we do not say 'a ten' or 'one ten', but given that we do have 'a hundred' or 'one hundred', we predict on the basis of this generalization that we will have 'a thousand', 'one thousand'. There are many confirmatory instances. There may be a free variation interval. For example, in Maori for 10, 'one-ten' is in free variation with 10, whereas for 100, it is stated to be "generally required." One exception was encountered, Ulithi, an Austronesian language, in which 1 is expressed with 10, 100, and 1000 but not with 10,000 and 100,000.

> 36. The only numeral expressions deleted are those for 1 and for bases of the system.

In the discussion of generalization 10 regarding the overt expression of the operation of subtraction, it was noted that 1 is often deleted as a subtrahend. In reference to generalizations 25 and 35, both of which refer to 1 as a multiplier with bases, one might choose to regard its omission, found in most languages, as involving deletion.

Bases also are frequently deleted. An example was noted earlier in the discussion of generalization 15, referring to division where the example of Oriya was cited, in which 100 is deleted in the expression of 275 as (3 × 100) − 1/4 *(100). The lowest base is often deleted in all its occurrences from *b* + *1* up to but not including *(2 ×) b*. This will only occur where there is an overt link for addition and particularly when, as is often the case, this link is different from that employed for higher numbers. This process is at present going on in Hausa in which 11–17 may be expressed according to the model *góómà šáà ɗáyá* 'ten plus one' for simply *šáà ɗáyá*, with the latter being increasingly favored. This does not apply to 18 and 19 because they are expressed by subtraction from 20. In such cases, when the process of deletion is complete, the former link will be reinterpreted as a suppletive variant of 10, thus involving a drastic semantic change. Bases are also deleted as multiplicands, particularly where the digits have number agreement with plural multiplicands. An instance is Efik, with a vigesimal system. Here 20 is *édíp*, but 40 is *àbà* (2 ×) *20, 60 is *àtá* (3 ×) *20, etc.; *àbà* is the plural of *ìbà* 'two', *àtá* of *ìtá* 'three', etc. In Sidamo, an Eastern Cushitic language, 50–90 are the plurals of 5–9. In the light of these examples, the Semitic expression of 30, 40, etc. as the plurals of 3, 4, respectively, which has puzzled Semitists, becomes clear. Originally, 20 was the dual of 10, but has everywhere except in Ethiopian Semitic, in analogy to the other decades, become the plural of 10, whereas in Ethiopic the dual was generalized from 20 to the remaining decades.

There are also examples of the deletion of bases where the "going-on" relation occurs, e.g. Estonian, in which for 11–19 we have expressions which can be interpreted as '1 of the second *10', etc.

*2.5. Some General Organizing Principles of Numerical Systems.* The preceding 36 generalizations obviously put powerful constraints on what constitutes a possible numeral system. Nevertheless, they fail to account for some very general regularities. For example, given the complex mathematical structure and morphological irregularities of the expression of 72 as *soixante douze*, i.e. 'sixty-twelve' with each component further susceptible of a more complex analysis as (6 × 10) and (10 + 2), respectively, we would be quite surprised if we found 372 in French was not *trois cents soixante douze* but say **trois cents septante dix deux*. Yet this is not forbidden by any of the generalizations thus far. Many conventional grammars describe the numeral system by a relatively small series of translation equivalents, giving, for instance, just one example of a complex numeral > 100 and < 1000 in a decimal system and assuming that the reader will be able to form all the others from this single example. This suggests that certain overall consistencies are being taken for granted.

> 37. If a numeral expression contains a complex constituent, then the numerical value of the complex constituent itself in isolation receives either simple lexical expression or is expressed by the same function and in the same phonological shape, except for possible automatic phonological alternations, stress shifts, or overt expressions of coordination. This principle will be called the principle of incorporation.

This generalization, of course, presupposes an analysis into immediate constituents on the basis of generalization 18. A complex constituent contains at least two numerals. The application to the French example is as follows. In 372, to be analyzed as [(3 ×) 100][+ ((6 ×)10) (+ (10(+2))], ((6 ×) 10) (+(10(+2)) is a complex constituent, since it contains four numerals. It has the value 72. In French 72 is expressed exactly the same way as in 372.

There is a still stronger principle which holds for all numerals above a particular base in systems which have more than one base. Such a base may be called the base for predictable expression. Put informally, there are no "surprises" in numerals larger than this base. Thus, in French, we should be surprised when we get to 70 and find that it is expressed *soixante-dix* and not **septante* (which occurs in some forms of French). Above 100 there are no such surprises except that we can never predict at what point a new higher base will appear, or when we will reach L, the limit. Since I have not found it possible to state this principle in a very simple way, instead of stating it in its entirety, followed by explanations and illustrations, it will be given in steps. Those statements which are intended as part of the generalization are italicized.

> 38. *In systems with more than one base, there is a base, the base for predictable expression, above which in all numerals certain regularities hold. Such numerals, when analyzed into their two principal constituents, will fall into two types, simple and complex. In the simple numeral we have a product, or rarely a quotient. In the complex numeral the two constituents are summands.* An example of a simple numeral is 'five hundred', of a complex numeral is 'three hundred' and 'forty-five'. By generalization 18 concerning groupings in a sum, the principal constituents are

'three hundred' and 'forty-five'. *In the simple constituent the factors or elements in a division are expressed in the same way as when they occur in isolation.* For example, in English 'five hundred' conforms to this, but 'fifty' does not. Hence the base for predictable expression in English cannot be 'ten'. *Complex expressions fall into two parts, a product and a remainder.* For example, in English 'three hundred and seventy-two', 'three hundred' is a product and 'seventy-two' is a remainder. *The remainder has the two following properties. It never has a larger value than the next lower base of the total expression.* For example, in 'three hundred and seventy-two', the remainder 'seventy-two' has a value 72, which is smaller than the next lower base of the total expression 'three hundred seventy', i.e. 100. This does not hold for French *soixante-douze* in which the remainder 12 > 10. *Finally, the remainder is expressed by the same mathematical function as when it occurs in isolation.* For example, in 'three hundred and seventy-two', the remainder 'seventy-two' is expressed in the same way as in the numeral expression for 72 in isolation both in its mathematical analysis and phonological expression. In Russian 140 *sto sorok* 'hundred forty' the remainder 40 is expressed in the same way as 40 in isolation. This is not required by the preceding generalization (37) and, along with other facts, shows that 100 is the base for predictable expression in Russian. In decimal systems the base for predictable expression is usually 100. In Mandarin it is 10.

39. The degree of morphological fusion varies inversely with the size of the numerical value.

One of the overall characteristics which we observe in numerical systems is that in general the smaller the numeral, the more we encounter morphological irregularities. This is in conformity with the marking hierarchy in that the larger the numerical value, the more marked, and morphological regularity is a property of marked expressions. This principle is consistent with the two preceding in that it also involves the notion that the greater the predictability in formation, the higher the numerical value.

The foregoing generalization has been stated quite vaguely. It could have been broken down into a whole series of implicational generalizations, e.g. if a product containing a particular base is a single word, so is every product containing a smaller base.

This hierarchy is often finely graded. The following are examples. In Yakut, a Turkic language, *süürbe* 'twenty' shows no resemblance to *ikki* 'two' and *otut* 'thirty' only a vague one to *üs* 'three'. Above 'thirty' all the tens are clearly the digits followed by *uon* 'ten', but 'forty' and 'fifty' show sandhi phenomena not reflected in the orthography, i.e. *tüörduon* and *biehuon* (cf. *tüört* 'four', *bies* 'five'), while above 50 there are no sandhi phenomena. In Efik there are two links for addition, *è* and *yè*. The former is used up to 20. For 21–23, *ye* is in free variation with *y-* and > 24 only *yè* occurs. Many more examples could be cited.

*2.6. The Syntax of Numerical Expressions.* A full-fledged study of the syntax of numeral systems which can on occasion reach heights of complexity (e.g. Russian, Classical Arabic) would require a full-length study in itself. Here only a few of the more obvious regularities are pointed out. The syntax of numeral constructions can be divided at least roughly into those of the internal syntax of complex numeral expressions and the external syntax of the numeral expressions as a whole in the QN constructions. The following discussion is confined essentially to external syntax.

It is well known that in many languages with a singular/plural distinction in the noun, e.g. Turkish, the noun itself is in the singular with numerals designating numbers larger than 1. A more detailed study of this problem reveals certain further regularities.

> 40. In languages in which the expression of plurality is facultative in the noun, the singular may be used with numerals designating numbers > 1.

In most instances the use of the singular is, in fact, compulsory. One of the characteristics of unmarked categories, in this case the singular, is that in many instances it stands for the category as a whole, and hence may be used with the plural, while the marked category of the plural is restricted to actual plurality. Whenever this holds, the cardinal numeral designating numbers > 1 is included in the situations in which a singular form of the noun may, or usually must be used.

> 41. In languages with singular/dual/plural systems in the noun, if the plural is used in any instances where a set of two objects is designated, the plural may be used with the numeral for 2.

This is the counterpart of 40 for systems with duals, in which the dual-plural distinction is neutralized and the relatively unmarked plural appears in the position of neutralization. The best known examples are Indo-European and Semitic. For example, in Homeric Greek the plural is freely used where the dual might be expected and among these instances is that of constructions with *dúō* 'two'.

42. If numeral expressions for the smallest addends take the plural of the noun when they designate numbers > 1, then complex numerals with 'one' as an addend will take the plural of the noun if 'one' is not a separate word.

For example, in English 'two', 'three', etc. take the noun in the plural. So does 'eleven'. When 'one' is a separate word, the whole expression may (e.g. Bantu languages in general) or may not (e.g. English 'twenty one') take the singular.

43. Where there is rule-governed variation between the use of the singular and plural with numerals, the use of the singular is favored with higher numbers, in measure constructions, in indefinite constructions, and with nouns which are inanimate or impersonal.

The following are some examples. In Erza Mordvin the plural is used after 2–10, the singular > 10. In Modern Arabic dialects in general the same rule holds, but for 3–10 in some dialects rather than 2–10 because of the existence of a dual. For Amharic, Armbruster (1908) gives the following complex rule. For animate nouns after 2–99, either the singular or plural is used, over 99 the singular only. For inanimates the singular or plural is used with 2–9, whereas >9, the singular only is used. This evidently combines a preference for the singular both with higher numbers and inanimates. Trumpp in his grammar of Pashto (1873) states that masculine animate nouns are in the plural with numerals >1, whereas for other nouns the singular may occur, although the plural is more usual. In Tlappanec, a Hokan language of Nicaragua, personal nouns are in the plural with numeral >1, impersonal in the singular only. In this case impersonal nouns do not have plurals. It is in fact clear that the rule with regard to numeral constructions is in accord with this tendency in nouns themselves. The following implicational universal probably holds here. Wherever a language has plural forms for any impersonal nouns, it has them for personal nouns, and similarly for inanimates and animates.

The other factors enumerated in generalization 43 can be illustrated from the following examples. In Akkadian the singular of nouns is used with measure expressions while the plural is used with countables. In Kanarese either the singular or plural is used with measures, the plural only with nonmeasures (cf. English 'six foot tall', etc.). In Modern Western Armenian the singular is used with indefinite numeral constructions, the plural with definite. The same rule holds for Ewe, a Niger-Congo language.

44. The order noun-numeral is favored in indefinite and approximative constructions.

Variations in QN order are of two general types. In some languages either QN or NQ may occur with any numeral. The contrast of order may then have a semantic or syntactic function. In the second type, certain numerals precede and others follow the noun.

Illustrations of generalization 44 include the following. In Bengali when the classifier phrase follows the noun the construct is definite, when it precedes it is indefinite. In certain Arabic dialects, e.g. Palestinian and Hassaniya of Mauretania, QN is usual, but when NQ occurs, it is with the indefinite construction. Similar facts hold for Banggais and Samoan, both Austronesian languages, the former having classifiers. In Tamil, NQ is favored when the noun is indefinite. It is worth noting that sometimes this order preference occurs in constructions of descriptive adjectives with nouns. For example, in Bedauye, AN order occurs when the phrase is definite, NA when it is indefinite.

In Russian and in Zyryan, a Finnic language, QN is the usual order while NQ order is associated with an approximative meaning. In Bengali within the numeral classifier construction Q-Cl is usual, but Cl-Q is approximative.

> 45. If a language has NG order in the possessive construction, it has QN order in the partitive construction.

We have seen the partitive is the second major type of construction in QN constructions, the other being adjective-noun. In most languages with partitive constructions, it is assimilated to the genitive construction of the noun in its possessive subtype. In such cases NG generally goes with QN, i.e. 'house of the man' is like 'three of the oranges', and GN with NQ. However, QN is favored over NQ in that there are languages like Lithuanian in which, while the genitive order is GN, the partitive has QN.

> 46. If there is variation in NQ order depending on the identity of the numeral, one of the two orders is used with a continuous series of numbers beginning with 'one', or 'one' and the bases of the system are used with one of the orders. If there is free variation with a particular numeral *x*, the next higher is also in free variation or is in the opposite order to that of *x* with the noun.

The reason for specification of bases in the system as an alternative is based on a very small number of instances like Igbo in which the order is NQ, except for 'one', 'twenty', and 'four hundred'.

Diachronically viewed, I believe the generalization holds that it is the lowest and most unmarked numerals (sometimes 'one' alone) which show the earlier order. In regard to instances in which the numerals with the lowest values follow the nouns, some of the evidence has been discussed in

Greenberg 1975. I believe this principle also holds when the lowest numbers precede the noun, and thus leads to the hypothesis that there has been a shift from QN to NQ with the lowest numerals as the survivors of the earlier order. In the discussion of generalization 29, it was noted that variation of MU order in which UM occurs with higher numerals is also evidence of a shift from QN to NQ. The case for both interpretations is strengthened by instances in which both of these infrequent phenomena occur in the same language, e.g. Adyge and Kabardian, closely related Northwest Caucasian languages, and Masai, an Eastern Nilotic language. In the case of Margi which has an MU-UM switch, some closely related languages of the Bata group have QN order for the lowest numerals.

> 47. If a language has both partitive and adjectival QN constructions, the smallest number which employs the partitive is larger than the largest number which has the adjectival construction.

In general there is a preference for the partitive with larger numbers. The following are a few representative examples. In some dialects of Berber in Morocco (Laoust 1921), 'one' and 'two' are adjectives. Above 'two' all numerals are in a genitive-like construction with the noun and may have the genitive particle *n*. In Rumanian from 20 all numerals are followed by *de* 'of, from' with the substantive. Welsh has both constructions, but the partitive is preferred with higher numbers. In New Egyptian the construction *numeral* + *n 'of'* + *noun* is used particularly with larger numbers. In Lithuanian 1–9 are adjectives, while with larger numbers the genitive plural is used. In Russian and some other Slavic languages, in the direct cases numbers larger than 'four' govern the genitive plural. This generalization is subject to the following limitation. In some languages in complex numbers the construction is determined by the smallest addend, particularly if it is adjacent to the noun. Thus, in Russian 'twenty-one' has the same construction as 'one'.

The preference of the partitive for higher numbers is in accordance with some other generalizations we have already encountered. The higher the number, the more likely it is to be treated as a noun, and the basic noun-noun construction is of the genitive type.

> 48. The construction with the interrogative 'how many?' is usually the same as that with the highest block of numerals.

For example, in English 'how many?' governs the plural. In Russian *skol'ko* takes the genitive plural when the whole phrase is in a direct case. In Amharic, as we saw in the discussion of generalization 43, there is a complex rule which involves a preference for the singular of the noun with higher numerals. The singular is also found with the interrogative. A minor exception is Classical Arabic. The interrogative *kam* governs the accusative singular like numerals 11–99, not the genitive singular like those larger than 99.

## 3. Cardinal Contextual Numerals and Other Numeral Series

The main section of this paper has been restricted to what may be considered the most unmarked series, namely, cardinal numerals as qualifiers of nouns. The overall uses of cardinal numerals may be classified as follows. We may first distinguish discourse uses from nondiscourse uses. The nondiscourse use is in counting which may in turn be divided into concrete and abstract counting. In the former specific items are involved, whereas in the latter the numerals are abstracted from such contexts as when we simply count 'one, two, three. . . .' Such counting is done even in technologically simple societies. There are also sometimes guessing games in which numbers figure as such. The distinction between concrete and abstract counting is particularly clear in numeral classifier languages. If, for example, bananas are being counted, the appropriate classifier is used with each numeral. In abstract counting, the general classifier may be used or no classifier at all. There are a fair number of languages in which there are distinct counting and discourse forms. In such instances we may call the former absolute and the latter contextual. That the absolute forms are the marked category can be seen from the following generalizations.

> 49. Absolute forms of cardinal numbers may have overt markers added to the contextual forms, but not vice versa.
>
> 50. Where there are contrasting forms for the absolute and contextual uses of cardinal numerals, there is always neutralization for some numerals, in which case the contextual form appears.
>
> 51. The existence of a separate absolute form for a particular numerical value implies its existence for the next lower value.

The following are examples. In Chuvash two sets of forms exist for 1–10, the absolute being longer, e.g. *pěr* 'one' (contextual): *pěrre* (absolute). Above ten, the longer form only occurs with the digits in complex numerals. In Gã, a Kwa language of the Niger-Congo family, *eko* is the contextual form for *ekome*, the absolute. The following exceptions have been noted. In Moroccan Arabic from 11–19 the contextual forms are longer, e.g. *ḥdašel* 'eleven' (contextual), *ḥdaš* 'eleven' (absolute). Another exception is Hungarian *két* 'two' (contextual), *kettö* 'two' (absolute). Here the exception is not in the overt marking which is regular, but that in violation of generalization 51, there is no separate absolute form for 'one'. A similar exception exists in regard to the Mandarin forms for 'two'.

52. Where the distinction between absolute and contextual cardinal numerals exists, the use of the contextual form as a multiplier with a lower base implies its use with all higher bases.

For example, in Mandarin there are two forms for 'two', *èr* (absolute) and *liăng* (contextual). Of these, *èr* is used as a multiplier of 'ten', where *liăng* is the usual but not exclusive form with 'hundred', 'thousand', and 'ten thousand'. A similar relation exists in Palaung with *ū* 'one' (contextual) and *hlɛh* 'one' (absolute) in that *ū* is used with bases from 100 up. The use of the contextual form with bases is once more to be referred to the general principle that bases behave like substantives, and the larger their numerical value, the more substantive-like they are.

Within discourse, one may distinguish ordinary from arithmetical discourse. In the latter, so far as I can see, the absolute forms are used when a distinction of contextual and absolute exists. In non-arithmetical discourse, the main uses besides that as noun qualifiers are substantivized forms and predications. In the former a noun is deleted. This is a universal possibility in numeral classifier languages, in which case the classifier is always retained. In case languages, the numeral seems almost always to acquire a case marker if it did not already have it in the non-deleted form. In predication, if a separate absolute form exists, it is used. For more detailed discussion, reference may be made to Greenberg 1974, in which what is there called the A form corresponds to the contextual and the B form to the absolute.

The generally marked character of the ordinals and other numeral series in relation to the cardinals is discussed in Greenberg 1966. The chief phenomena to be noted are overt marking of ordinals in comparison to cardinals, the neutralization of the distinction for higher numbers with the cardinal form appearing in the position of neutralization, and the suppletive irregularities commonly found in the lowest ordinals, e.g. English 'first', 'second', . . . . This latter may be stated implicationally in a form analogous to generalization 52. Other marked series include the adverbial ordinal 'the first time', 'the second time', and distributives 'one at a time', 'one each'. These show relationships to the unmarked cardinals resembling that of the ordinal.

The basic generalization by which the discussion in the body of this paper confined to cardinal forms qualifying nouns becomes valid for all numeral series is the following.

53. All numeral series have the same mathematical structure.

A further distinction not mentioned above is that between specialized and generalized numerals; some languages have terms with meanings such as Khasi *bhar* '32 oranges'. It might be thought that these are exceptions.

However, they merely behave like nouns to which the usual numeral system is applicable, as in English 'one dozen', 'two dozen', etc.

## 4. Numeral Systems and Language Contact

It is a well-known phenomenon that higher numerals are more commonly borrowed than lower ones, usually in a sequence starting at a certain number. There are, however, occasional exceptions, e.g. Swahili which borrows the numerals for 6, 7, and 9 from Arabic, but retains the Bantu term for 8. It is not, however, so much that the terms for numbers over a certain value are borrowed, but rather that the atoms of the source language are borrowed in this order. It will be recalled that by atoms are meant the lexically expressed numbers, and that these in turn can be divided into bases and non-bases. The following is an example. In Tupi indigenous numerals are found for 1–3 and Portuguese terms for 4–20.[8] However, 21 is *vinte mocoi cembyra* 'twenty (Port.), one (Tupi), on-top (Tupi)' and so for all complex numerals over 20, with Portuguese borrowing for the digits 4–9 only. An almost completely parallel case is that of Kui, a Dravidian language in which Indo-Aryan numerals are borrowed from Oriya for 3–20, while above 20 the odd numbers for 'one' and 'two' continue to be Dravidian. Thus, suppletion does not arise in these instances. We therefore have the following diachronic near-universal.

> 54. If an atomic numeral expression is borrowed from one language into another, all higher atomic expressions are borrowed.

In other instances of contact, the result is the replacement of an old system by a new one, with or without borrowing. An interesting example is that of a number of Plateau Benue-Congo languages in Nigeria with an earlier duodecimal system which is being replaced by a decimal system through the influence of Hausa. The process is similar in all these languages. They had atomic expressions up to 12. It might be thought that the old expressions for 11 and 12 would simply be eliminated and a decimal system constructed, either using the old word for 10 or borrowing its Hausa equivalent. However, what happens is that the old word for the unit 'twelve' is reinterpreted as 10, and the old expressions for 10 and 11 eliminated. Similarly, the old word for $12^2 = 144$ is reinterpreted as 100, or in some languages the Hausa word for 100 is borrowed.

This seems to show that for the speakers there is a certain psychological reality attached to the notion base. There are instances in which related or

[8] "Atom" in this connection is meant in terms of the borrowing language in which fused forms analyzable in the source language may be treated as individual lexical items, e.g. Portuguese 11–19 in Tupi.

borrowed words for one base are used with the value of a different base. For example, in Adamawa Fulani, the Hausa *dubu* 'thousand' is borrowed in the meaning 'million'. In northern East Africa there is a widespread root *tam*, *tom*, which sometimes means 10 and sometimes 20. An intricate history of successive replacements of decimal by vigesimal systems and vice versa can be largely reconstructed, but this is not discussed here.

A further indication of the psychological reality of the notion of base as such is that in some languages terms for higher bases are formed from that of a lower base by the addition of a qualifier meaning 'large' or the like. This is also an indication of the relatively marked character of the higher bases. Examples include Nama Hottentot in which 100 is 'large 10', and Yuchi in which 100 is the word for 'road', thousand is 'road large', and million is 'road large old'.

Another interesting possibility is that a complex numeral expression of the older system is reinterpreted as a unit of the new system. An example is Abkhasian, a Northwestern Caucasian language in which an older decimal system is being replaced by a vigesimal system. The expression for the first six decades are as follows: 10, 2 × 10, 3 × 10, 2 × (2 × 10), 2 × (2 × 10) + 10, 3 × (2 × 10), etc. Once more, we note the relative stability of the lower numerals, the vigesimal system having only penetrated down to 40. Here and elsewhere in language contact, we see that the relative marking hierarchy founded on the largeness of the numerical values is as potent as in the internal structure of numerical systems. This principle is also involved in generalization 54 in that the more marked the number, the more likely that its numeral expression will be borrowed. There is further confirmation of this principle in that there are instances in which an irregular ordinal 'first' is borrowed, while 'one' is not. In fact, I do not know of a single instance in which the latter has occurred. It was also shown earlier that the absolute (counting) form is marked as against the contextual form. There is at least one example of borrowed numerals being used in counting, while the indigenous ones are retained in context. This is Malto, a Dravidian language in which Aryan terms for 1, 2 are borrowed for counting, while the indigenous terms are retained in contextual uses.

## 5. Numeral Systems and Cultural Evolution

There has recently been a revival of interest in the evolutionary aspects of language, stimulated principally by the well-known work of Berlin and Kay (1969) on color terminology. Cecil Brown has discussed botanical and body-parts terminology from this point of view (1976, n.d.) and recently, Webb (1977) has discussed the existence of a verb 'to have' in its possible connection with cultural evolutionary factors. The study of numeral systems would seem to have a special value from this point of view for two reasons. Unlike the areas just mentioned, the existence of a connection is not in dispute. Moreover, it is also clear what it consists of, mainly but not exclusively, the size of L, the limit number. Yet as far as I know, there has been no recent work on numeral systems from this point of view. Here, only a few observations are offered.

The typological divisions between systems without bases and those with at least one base has at least a gross correlation with technological level. The building up of systems with more than one base shows a variety of processes, as has been seen at various points in the exposition. Higher bases are sometimes formed from internal linguistic resources. The example of 100 as 'large 10' has already been cited. Another internal method, that of multiplication, can be illustrated from Kutenai in which *yitwu* is 10, *yitwunwu* (**yitwuyitwu*) is 100, *yitwul-yitwunwu* 1000, and *yitwul-yitwul* 10,000. The external method of borrowing is, of course, well-attested and certain terms for higher bases have a vast geographical spread, e.g. Iranian *hazar* for 'thousand'.

The process of building up of higher units is, however, subject to much fluctuation. At a certain middle cultural level, say with agriculture but without writing, the upper portions of the system may be seldom used. One symptom is variability. Different informants give different versions often with differing upper limits. The existence of such a penumbra of the system will also appear in the variation from language to language within the same family in that only lower numerals may be reconstructible, even though each individual language may go well above these smaller numbers. As in Indo-European and elsewhere there may be gaps in what is reconstructible. For example, in Bantu 'ten' is easily reconstructible and in general the systems are decimal, but the numerals 6–9 are not, presumably because they are less frequent than the base. There may be actual regression where a people changes its mode of life through external circumstances. For example, the Bushman languages of South Africa usually have no numeral higher than 3, yet at least 4 seems reconstructible for the larger stock, Khoisan, as a whole suggesting 'secondary primitivity'.

One final observation regarding this aspect of numeral systems may be offered. Less "progressive" methods may for a time out-perform more progressive ones. In parts of New Guinea gesture methods based on body parts starting with the fingers of one hand and then going on to wrist, elbow, etc., and around back to the other hand provide a way of expressing numbers as high as 20 at a point where the spoken language does not go beyond three or four. In regard to writing, something similar holds. In an interesting paper, Boyer (1944) distinguishes iterative methods of graphic symbolization from ciphering. The Roman numerals involve iteration in that 300, for example, is CCC. On the other hand, the Ionian system based on the Greek alphabet in which $\alpha$ symbolized 1, $\beta$ 2, etc. is a ciphering method. The Egyptian Hieroglyphic method and other ancient methods were iterative at a time when spoken language utilized the ciphering principle. It would seem that, as elsewhere in evolution, a new structure which is basically more progressive than an older one may not immediately realize its potential, which requires a period of time for its unfolding.

## References Cited

Amasoye, Boma I. 1972. *The Future of the Ijo Language and Its Dialects*. Vienna.
Araujo, F. 1975. "How the Basque count sheep." *Anthropological Linguistics* 17, 4.
Armbruster, Carl Hubert. 1908. *Initia Amharica*. Cambridge, Eng.
Berlin, Brent, and Paul Kay. 1969. *Color Terms: Their Universality and Evolution*. Berkeley and Los Angeles.
Bowen, John T., and T. S. Rhys. 1960. *Teach Yourself Welsh*. London.
Boyer, C. B. 1944. "Fundamental steps in the development of numeration." *Isis* 35: 153–68.
Brandt Corstius, H. 1968. *Grammars for Number Names*. Dordrecht.
Brown, Cecil H. 1976. "General principles of human anatomical partonomy and speculations on the growth of partonomic nomenclature." *American Ethnologist* 3: 400–424.
———. N.d. "Folk botanical life forms: their universality and growth." Manuscript.
Conant, L. L. 1896. *The Number Concept*. New York.
Córdova, J. de. 1578. *Arte del idioma zapoteca*, ed. by Nicolas León (1886). Morelia.
Dixon, R. B., and A. L. Kroeber. 1907. "Numeral systems of the languages of California." *American Anthropologist* 9: 663–90.
Douglas, W. H. 1958. *An Introduction to the Western Desert Language of Australia*. Oceanic Linguistic Monograph 4. University of Sydney.
Drabbe, P. 1957. *Spraakkunst van het Aghu-Dialect van de Awju-Taal*. The Hague.
Fettweis, E. 1927. *Das Rechnen der Naturvölker*. Berlin.
Frederieci, Georg. 1913. "Wissenschaftliche Ergebnisse einer amtlichen Forschungsreise nach dem Bismark-Archipel im Jahre 1908." *Mitteilungen aus den deutschen Schützgebieten, Ergänzungsheft 7*. Berlin.
Greenberg, Joseph H. 1963. "Some universals of grammar with particular reference to the order of meaningful elements." In *Universals of language*, ed. by J. H. Greenberg, 58–90. Cambridge, Mass.
———. 1966. *Language Universals*. The Hague.
———. 1972. "Numeral classifiers and substantival number: problems in the genesis of a linguistic type." *Working Papers on Language Universals* [WPLU] 9: 1–39.
———. 1974. "Studies in numerical systems: double numeral systems." *WPLU* 14: 75–89.
———. 1975. "Dynamic aspects of word order in the numeral classifier." In *Word Order and Word Order Change*, ed. by Charles N. Li, 27–46. Austin and London.
Hurford, James R. 1975. *The Linguistic Study of Numerals*. Cambridge, Eng.
Kluge, Theodor. 1937–42. *Die Zahlenbegriffe*. Berlin.

Laoust, Emile. 1921. *Cours de berbère marocain: grammaire, vocabulaire, textes. Dialectes du Sous, du Haut, et de l'Anti-Atlas*. Paris.
Lichtenstein, Heinrich. 1811–12. *Reisen im südlichen Africa, in den Jahren 1803, 1804, 1806*. Berlin.
Love, J. R. B. 1933. "An outline of Worora grammar." In *Studies in Australian Linguistics*, ed. by A. P. Elkin. Australian National Research Council, Science House, Sydney.
Menninger, Karl. 1969. *Number Words and Number Symbols*. Cambridge, Mass.
Merrifield, William R. 1968. "Number names in four languages of Mexico," in Brandt Corstius 1968: 91–102.
Pareja, Francisco de. 1886. *Arte de la lengua Timuquana* (original 1614). Bibliothèque Linguistique Américaine 11. Paris.
Peano, Giuseppe. 1908. *Formulario mathematico*. Turin.
Pott, A. F. 1849. *Die quinäre und vigesimale Zählmethode bei Völkern aller Weltteile*. Halle.
Salzmann, Zdenek. 1950. "A method for analyzing numerical systems." *Word* 6: 78–83.
Sanders, Gerald A. 1976. "A functional typology of elliptical coordinations." Reproduced by the Indiana Linguistics Club.
Schmidt, Marianne. 1915. "Zahl und Zählen in Afrika." *Anthropologische Gesellschaft in Wien* 45: 165–209.
Smeltzer, Donald. 1958. *Man and Number*. New York (2nd ed.).
Stampe, David. 1977. "Cardinal number systems." In S. S. Mufwene et al., eds., *Papers from the Twelfth Regional Meeting*, Chicago Linguistic Society, 594–609.
Steinen, Karl von den. 1894. *Unter den Naturvölkern Zentral-Brasiliens*. Berlin (2nd ed. 1899).
Swanton, John Reed. 1940. "Linguistic material from the tribes of southern Texas and northeastern Mexico." *Bureau of American Ethnology, Bulletin 127*. Washington, D.C.
Szemerényi, Oswald. 1960. *Studies in the Indo-European System of Numerals*. Heidelberg.
Thomas, C. 1897–98. "Numeral systems of Mexico and Central America." *Nineteenth Annual Report, Bureau of American Ethnology*, part 2: 853–956. Washington, D.C.
Tönjes, Hermann. 1910. *Lehrbuch der Ovambo-Sprache Osikuanjama*. Berlin.
Trumpp, Ernest. 1873. *Grammar of the Pašto, or Language of the Afghans*. London.
Tryon, D. T. 1974. "Daly Family languages, Australia." Canberra: The Australian National University.
Webb, Karen. 1977. "An evolutionary aspect of social structure and a verb 'to have'." *American Anthropologist* 79: 42–49.
Wilder, Raymond Louis. 1953. *The Evolution of Mathematics*. New York.

# Universals of Kinship Terminology: Their Nature and the Problem of Their Explanation

In seeking a topic which might fittingly initiate a series of lectures in honor of a distinguished linguistic anthropologist, kinship terminology seemed to me a uniquely appropriate choice. Harry Hoijer, and indeed he was the very embodiment of the study of language as part of human culture which is the hallmark of linguistic anthropology, himself wrote a masterly article on Athapaskan kinship systems. Virtually all linguists who have concerned themselves with kinship, including such figures as Sapir, Lounsbury, and Burling, have had academic affiliations with anthropology. At the same time, far from being a topic of exclusive interest to linguistics, kinship terminology has, ever since its study was brilliantly inaugurated by Louis Henry Morgan in the nineteenth century, attracted the interest of many leading cultural and social anthropologists (e.g., Kroeber, Rivers, Lowie, Radcliffe-Brown, Murdock, White, Tax, Eggan, Leach, and Lévi-Strauss). This only partial listing is impressive both in regard to the eminence of the figures involved and the breadth and variety of the theoretical trends they represent.

The study of kinship terminology thus constitutes a major link between the linguists, a highly specialized group all too prone to develop their field in an esoteric and at times even unintelligible manner in isolation from the rest of anthropology, and those more general theorists concerned with that most central of anthropological topics, the manner in which man organizes his social existence.

The reason for its relevance between groups of researchers whose findings in other respects hardly ever impinge on each other is not far to seek. On the one hand, a kinship terminology, consisting as it does of elements of language, is a linguistic phenomenon, one which exercises a special fascination because it constitutes what is perhaps the most highly organized part of the lexicon and is thus susceptible to the formalized analytical approaches dear to the heart of linguists. On the other hand, the referents of these elements are precisely those individual relationships and group structures which are significant in all societies while in some they appear to constitute the very warp and woof of the social fabric.

These two sides of kinship terminology, one from the linguistic point of view inward looking, the other outward looking toward the referents of kin terms, are capable of generating tension and controversy.

However, the field took explicit form only through the brilliant and seminal paper of Kroeber on classificatory systems of relationship (Kroeber 1909). In this article Kroeber advanced the thesis that kinship terminology was primarily a linguistic phenomenon and hence subject to analysis and interpretation by linguistic methods. With this he contrasted what he called the sociological interpretation which, he felt, had up to that time dominated the study of kinship terminologies chiefly in the form of attempts to explain them as reflections of present or past social arrangements, especially forms of marriage and rules of descent. He concluded his article with the statement that "terms of relationship reflect psychology, not sociology. They are determined primarily by language and can be used for sociological inferences only with extreme caution."

The viewpoint expressed here by Kroeber was attacked by W. H. R. Rivers, whose work *Kinship and Social Organization* (Rivers 1914) was designed to refute Kroeber by analyzing instances in which, he maintained, certain characteristics of kinship terminology required explanation by the present or former existence of specific marriage customs, e.g. cross-cousin marriage.

The controversy thus initiated by Kroeber's article dominated theoretical discussions for a considerable period. Although it was inevitably transformed in certain ways in the course of time and has been at times overshadowed by other issues such as that between descent and alliance theories, it has not, I believe, entirely lost contemporary relevance. We see this, for example, in David Schneider's latter-day defense of Kroeber's views, while the social functionalists in their stress on the social correlates of kin terms are in a sense the non-diachronic successors of Rivers.

The controversy in its heyday aroused heat and passion, I believe, because of its connection in the minds of the contestants with an issue of still broader import than kinship matters, one which concerned the very nature of anthropology as a discipline. Rivers believed, for his part, that the scientific status of anthropology was at stake. If there were no lawful connections between social phenomena and kinship terminology and the latter was merely linguistic, then a major phenomenon was being consigned to the realm of caprice and inexplicable variability.

Kroeber did not shrink from this conclusion. Influenced by the notion of *Geisteswissenschaft* of Neo-Kantians like Rickert, he believed that the search for laws of the same kind found in the physical sciences was a vain enterprise and one which, moreover, failed to grasp the basically historical nature of the cultural sciences. What was common to the two contestants was the tacit assumption that if kinship terminology is basically linguistic, it is not subject to lawlike generalization. This can be understood in the light of linguistics of the period but even more in view of the earlier history of the topic in anthropology. Neither Morgan himself, nor his most articulate opponent MacLennan, were interested in explaining terminologies for their own sake. The aim they shared was to reconstruct the course of human social evolution, and kinship terminologies were to be judged in relation to this all-encompassing end. So MacLennan, when it appeared that the evidence from terminologies supported his opponent, sought to impugn their significance by asserting that they were merely linguistic terms of salutation reflecting social status rather than consanguinity, without further significance for the central problem of reconstruction of the temporal course of human societal institutions.

In a subsequent study, Kroeber to some extent modified his earlier extremely negative assessment of the role of social factors (Kroeber 1917). A mediating view began to prevail which while admitting the existence of certain important and valid correlations with social institutions, at the same time pointed to a large residue which could not be explained in this manner. A typical spokesman of this view was Lowie.

As we see from the following statement, just as in previous discussions, the sociological view was equated with lawfulness and the linguistic with the unique and accidental: "The reality of such phenomena militates against any attempt to reduce the whole of kinship terminology to social causes. There will always be residual phenomena resisting interpretation on any but linguistic lines. This means that they are, in a sense, unique facts that can be understood after they are observed but that could not be deduced from general principles" (Lowie 1929: 89).

In what is perhaps the wisest article ever written on kinship terminology, Sol Tax sought to put the quietus on this by now ancient dispute as well as that between diffusion and independent invention by noting that ". . . the problem is less to show that any of these has or has not been instrumental in human history than to show what part each has played and what part each will play" (Tax 1937: 4).

One further observation regarding this controversy is in order. I have presented it as a confrontation between linguistic and sociological interpretations. It was, however, at least as frequently stated in terms of an opposition between psychological and sociological approaches. In Kroeber's article, psychological and linguistic are used virtually as synonyms. The reason for this was no doubt that the relevant aspect of language was the semantics of lexical classification. What was really involved were concepts expressed in language so that the psychological and the linguistic were, so to speak, two sides of the same coin, being indeed the Saussurian *signifiant* and *signifié*.

Kroeber's 1909 article is significant in still another respect, its precocious analysis of kinship terminology by reference to eight categories: generation, lineal versus collateral, age difference in one generation, sex of the relative, sex of the connecting relative, sex of the speaker, consanguineal versus affinal, and condition of the connecting relative, e.g. living or dead. Leaving aside some difficulties and complications, in principle any kin term in any language can be specified by means of them. For example, 'grandmother' in English is consanguineal, lineal, female, and second ascending generation.

This type of analysis in its basic logical structure is identical to that developed twenty years later in phonology by the Prague School of Structural Linguistics, in which features played the same role as the categories of Kroeber. The contemporary technique of componential analysis is simply a further development of this same basic model. It was therefore highly appropriate that, in an issue of *Language* in 1956 dedicated to Kroeber, there appeared two articles, one by Lounsbury and one by Goodenough, which initiated the modern method of componential analysis (Lounsbury 1956; Goodenough 1956). They not only employed the logical model to which we have been referring, which came to be known as the paradigm in the writing of ethnosemanticists, but took the specific categories of Kroeber as the starting point of their analysis.

The categories themselves constitute what in the 1960's came to be called a universal etic framework by means of which individual systems could be described. The parallel is, as recognized, close to the phonemic theory of American structuralism of this period which operated with a universal phonetic theory and a universal set of procedures whose purpose was to analyze each phonemic system as a unique structure with the hope for many that the phonemic analysis would reveal the psychologically real categories which underlay the speakers' linguistic behavior.

There was, for the Prague School at least, another more generalizing aspect as shown, for example, in Trubetskoy's classic "Grundzüge der Phonologie" (1939). Given the existence of universally definable features, systems become comparable by noting the extent and manner in which they employ the same features. This leads, of course, to typology, which was indeed a central concern of the Prague School. For example, there is a feature of nasality for vowels definable on a universal phonetic basis. Any particular language may or may not use contrasts of nasality in its vowel system. On this basis, the languages of the world fall into two types, those with an opposition between nasalized and non-nasalized vowels, and those without.

Kroeber's paper anticipated these developments, too. In his 1909 article he presented a table in which for a number of kinship systems, the number of terms which involved each category were given. He noted that the difference between systems might be conceptualized in terms of whether or not they made use of particular categories and if so, the extent to which they did. In this way he characterized systems typologically. For example, Eskimo is typologically like English in that it makes considerable use of the lineal/collateral distinction, whereas Hawaiian belongs to a different type because it does not.[1]

During the 1960's there took place one of those mysterious swings of the scientific pendulum which gives rise independently to similar developments in distinct but related fields. There was a move toward generalization in place of the relativistic aim of characterizing each system in unique terms. In linguistics the first major evidence of this trend was the Conference on Language Universals held in 1961 at Dobbs Ferry, under the sponsorship of the Social Science Research Council's Committee on Linguistics and Psychology. In cultural anthropology the most obvious indication was probably the appearance in 1969 of the work of Berlin and Kay on basic color terms (Berlin and Kay 1969). These presented basic parallels in method and results which have become explicit in recent developments in fields like botanical classification in the work of Cecil Brown and others.

The methodology of contemporary language universals work, as it developed in conjunction with typology, applies in principle equally to phonology, grammar, and semantics. Historically, however, attention to semantics was in the earlier period confined to the citation of isolated examples from the lexicon to illustrate the viability of such methods in semantics.

The investigation of kinship terminology as probably the most highly organized portion of the lexicon and one already well studied by formal methods, represented an attractive possibility for the more systematic application of the methods developed in earlier language universals research.

[1] In an article, "The Mecca of Continental Chinoise," by Harvey Steiman, I find the following beautiful statement of the same basic principle by Richard Wing, the chef of the restaurant Imperial Dynasty, in Hanford, California: "As he turns the fire under the iron wok, he gives an example. 'If I put the cold oil into the cold wok and add the food, that's one technique. If I put hot oil (from the deep fryer) into the cold wok, turn on the fire and add the food, that's another technique. Cold oil into the hot wok, a third technique. Hot oil, hot wok, fourth technique. Each produces a slightly different taste. Western cooks don't make these distinctions.'" (*San Francisco Examiner and Chronicle* Magazine, *California Living,* November 5, 1978).

The most important requirement for utilizing such methods, however, is the existence of an analytic framework of logically independent feature dimensions such as we find, most conspicuously, in phonology. As we have seen, the Kroeberian categories in principle fulfill this requirement as shown by the role they had already played in the development of componential analysis. By an ironic twist of intellectual history, then, the analysis developed by Kroeber in order to exhibit differences among systems furnished an important foundation for an approach which aimed at lawlike generalizations.

As part of the Forum Lecture series of the Summer Institute of Linguistics held at Bloomington, Indiana in 1964, the present writer delivered a series of four lectures on the general topic of language universals (Greenberg 1966). The last of these was devoted to kinship terminologies.

I shall first summarize and develop somewhat further the results obtained by this approach and then consider what contribution they can make in regard to the controversy concerning the psychological or linguistic versus the sociological interpretation of kinship terminology.

To do so will, however, require a brief discussion of a problem of terminology and a discussion of three key concepts and their interrelations: typology, implicational universal, and marking.

The terminological problem is the ambiguous use of the word 'feature' which can lead to considerable confusion and difficulty of exposition. The nature of this difficulty can be illustrated from phonological theory. A sound can be voiced, that is accompanied by vibrations of the vocal folds, or unvoiced when such vibrations are lacking. Traditionally the term feature has been applied to such alternatives. Hence a sound may be said to have the feature voiced or unvoiced depending on this phonetic factor. On the other hand, the term 'voicing feature' applies to the set consisting of the two mutually exclusive possibilities. For this latter meaning I shall use the term 'dimension' while each alternative on such a dimension will be called a 'value'. Thus a particular sound in a language might have the value unvoiced on the dimension of voicing.

This use of the term 'dimension' is consonant with its meaning in mathematics. The basic property of a dimension is its logical independence from other dimensions in the same overall system. Thus in phonology the dimension of voice is independent of the dimension of bilabiality because any value on one dimension can co-occur with any value on the other, while various values on a single dimension are mutually exclusive. This is so in the present case in that vibration or non-vibration of the vocal fold can be manipulated independently of closure or non-closure of the lips. Just so, in kinship, the kintype *father* has the value masculine in the dimension of sex of referent, and lineal on the dimension lineal versus collateral, and keeping generation constant, four kintypes are possible given two values on each dimension: *father*, *mother*, *uncle*, *aunt*.

The notion of typology follows naturally from that of a set of dimensions, each with a number of values. We can first enumerate all the logically possible combinations of values on different dimensions. Then languages, or whatever are the loci of these values, can be classified typologically on the basis of which of these combinations they possess. Take, for example, nasality versus orality, that is non-nasality in vowels. A language may have nasal vowels as is the case with French, Portuguese, Yoruba, and many other languages, or not have them as is true for English and Russian. There are then two types of languages in the world, one including French, Portuguese, and many others and the other including English, Russian, and a still larger number of languages. This is a typology based on one dimension with two values and therefore defining two types. It is of course not very exciting. Usually, however, typologies involve more than one dimension. In the present instance we may note that whether a language has oral vowels is independent of whether it has nasal vowels. We now have two dimensions of two values each resulting in four logically possible types. The interest of typologies stems from the possibility of generalization from the empirical absence of logically possible types.

Thus, pursuing the above example, we consider the occurrence in languages of the world of the four logically definable types. These are languages with both nasal and oral vowels, languages with oral but without nasal vowels, with nasal vowels but without oral vowels, and languages without either. Of these four types, only two are known to exist: languages which like French have both nasal and oral vowels and those which like English have oral vowels but not nasal vowels. No languages are known to exist which have neither nasal nor oral vowels. Such languages would not have any vowels. This is equivalent to what is called an unrestricted universal, namely that all languages have vowels. The fourth possible type is that which would have nasal but no oral vowels, and no such language is known to exist. This negative statement regarding the non-existence of a type is once more convertible into a positive statement, but in this instance a conditional, or as it is commonly called, an implicational universal. If a language has nasal vowels it also has oral vowels but not necessarily vice versa. An equivalent statement is that the presence of nasal vowels universally implies the presence of oral vowels. With this statement we have reached our second key concept: that of implicational universal. It turns out that valid statements of this kind are numerous and pertain to almost every linguistic phenomenon when it is investigated across languages. It may be and has been objected that it is strange to call something a universal when it does not occur in all languages. What is universal is the logical scope of our statement. For any language whatever, when it has some particular property it always has some other. Such statements are in fact logically like many laws in the physical sciences which hold only under specified limiting conditions.

What is more important is that, first of all, such statements *are* numerous and express law-like regularities concerning many properties of language regarding which at first blush no generalization seems possible. Thus, finding languages like French which have nasal vowels and those like English which do not, our first impulse is to deny the possibility of generalization. However, the construction of an explicit typology reveals, as we have seen, regularities of universal scope which would not otherwise be evident. Their second basic value is that they indicate relations between linguistic variables which are of a hierarchical nature. In some sense, oral vowels are universally preferred over nasal vowels in that the former can occur without the latter but not vice versa. This hierarchical relationship is known as marking. The implying member, that is the hierarchically subordinate one, is called the marked and the implied, the hierarchically superior, the unmarked.

The concept of marking is, however, no mere logically equivalent restatement of an implicational relationship. In such cases, we usually find a whole cluster of logically independent statements of universal scope which support the same hierarchy. Sometimes, as in the example already cited, there are only two values on the same dimension, but often we find more complex hierarchies of more than two values.

The concept of marking derives from Prague School phonology and was first advanced by Trubetskoy (1930). It was soon extended to grammatical categories and to a lesser extent to lexical semantics by Jakobson. Once given its applicability to grammatical categories which involve contrasting meaning values, e.g. present versus past, singular versus plural, its relevance to lexical semantics becomes obvious. Indeed, some semantic categories are capable of both lexical and grammatical expression, e.g. diminutive versus normal size, and display the same marking characteristics in both instances.

The term 'mark' derives from its earliest use in phonology. The marked member is relatively complex in relation to the unmarked. Thus in our previously cited example, the nasal vowel is more complex acoustically than its oral counterpart in that it involves nasal resonances in addition to the oral resonances of oral vowels. This additional element was called the mark.

Some of the further characteristics of marked as against corresponding unmarked categories can be illustrated from the dimension of number in countable nouns in which, for languages with a grammatical contrast between the singular and the plural, the singular is unmarked and the plural is marked. One of these is overt marking, analogous to marking in phonology, in that the marked category often has overt phonetic expression whereas the unmarked is indicated by zero, that is by the absence of any sound sequence. Thus, in English the plural is marked by 's' and other variants while the singular has zero expression. In some languages both are indicated by sound sequences but so far as is known there is no language which overtly marks a singular without marking the plural. This, of course, can be stated as an implicational universal. Overt expression in the singular implies overt expression in the plural.

A second important characteristic is that the unmarked category tends to have more distinctions than the marked category. For example, in German where number intersects with gender, the unmarked singular has three genders (masculine, feminine, and neuter), whereas in the marked plural all these differences are neutralized and there is a single form undifferentiated for gender.

A third characteristic is defectivation of the marked. Sometimes the marked category simply lacks an intersecting category found in the unmarked. Thus the future, which is universally marked as against the present, does not, in French and some other languages, have a subjunctive while the present does. A fourth characteristic is the greater text frequency of the unmarked. Text counts in a number of languages show that the singular tends to be approximately four times as frequent as the plural.

If we investigate these and other marking properties in regard to Kroeber's kinship categories, we find unmistakable evidence of the existence of marking hierarchies. Detailed evidence is presented in the monograph *Language Universals*, cited earlier (Greenberg 1966). Here are a few examples: In English the absence of sex distinction in the collateral term 'cousin' as against its expression in the corresponding lineal terms 'brother' and 'sister' is evidence for the marked status of collateral as against lineal. The absence of a term cousin-in-law as against the existence of brother-in-law and sister-in-law, is further evidence of the same hierarchy by defectivation. The existence of an additional overt mark in the case of grandparental terms as against parental terms, and an overt mark 'in-law' in affinal terms are evidence for the marked character of the second as against the first ascending generation and of affinal as against consanguineal respectively. We may summarize this and a mass of other evidence in the following way. Lineal is unmarked as against collateral, consanguineal is unmarked as against affinal, male is unmarked as against female in regard to sex of referent, older is unmarked in relation to younger. In regard to generation there is a more complex set of relationships. In general, the closer a generation is to ego, the more unmarked it is. Likewise, each ascending generation is unmarked in relation to the corresponding descending generation.

These individual results are not random but show a certain underlying unity from which we can develop a higher level generalization. Two basic factors are evidently at work, seniority and genealogical remoteness from ego. The existence of such broader bases for generalizations is also found in other aspects of language in regard to marking. For example, for adjectival opposites the pole which is closer to the zero point is marked, e.g. short as against long, low as against high.

The results concerning marking relationships in kinship categories just mentioned, possess typological relevance. In particular, the existence of certain types would violate the assumption that the marked category never has more internal differentiation than the unmarked. For example, a system which had terms for male cousin and female cousin but a single sibling term undifferentiated for gender would violate the hypothesis that collateral terms are marked in relation to lineal. As far as I know, no such system exists.

We may now set ourselves the more general goal of developing a set of principles which will define the notion of empirically possible kinship system, by excluding certain logically conceivable systems. The success of such an endeavor would be judged by the extent to which forbidden types do not exist while permitted types do.

In order to accomplish this, we will need other principles beyond those which arise from marking theory. Before considering these, however, something more should be said regarding typology. The exposition up to now has given a too restricted notion of typology. In particular, it might appear that a typology must be based directly on a set of dimensions such as those proposed by Kroeber in regard to kinship terminology and which he himself, as we have seen, used for typological purposes.

An example of another way of proceeding typologically which uses these dimensions in a more indirect way by their intersection in particular kintypes is the well known scheme independently devised by Lowie (1928) and Kirchhoff (1932). This is based on the terms for either the three male or the three female relatives in the first ascending generation, namely the father, the father's brother, and the mother's brother, or the mother, mother's sister, and father's sister. Both Lowie and Kirchhoff distinguished four types which may be illustrated from the female kintypes as follows. The first type is generational, in which there is a single term applied to all three relatives. The second is the bifurcate merging in which there are two terms, one for the mother and the mother's sister and the other for father's sister. The third is the bifurcate collateral in which there are three terms, one for each of these relatives. The fourth is lineal, in which, as in our own system there are two terms, one for the mother and the other for both mother's sister and father's sister, namely 'aunt'.

Just as for the typologies considered up to now, it is possible to enumerate the logically possible types, note if any are empirically absent and, if there are, to derive generalizations, implicational or otherwise. In the present case, there are actually five possible types, although both Lowie and Kirchhoff thought that their four types exhausted the logical possibilities. The possibility of a fifth type which never actually occurs was noted by Murdock (1947), namely one in which there are two terms, one for the mother's sister and the other for the mother and father's sister.

As with other instances in which there are non-occurrent types, this result can be rephrased as an implicational universal. Whenever the same term is used to designate the mother and the father's sister, this same term is used for the mother's sister also. The principle involved is the avoidance of logically disjunctive definitions. There is no way of demarcating by a single set of defining properties a term which embraces the mother and the mother's sister without including in its reference the father's sister. This is because mother's sister shares matrilineality with mother and collaterality with father's sister, but there is no common property of mother and father's sister, the two most different terms, except female, first ascending generation, and this includes mother's sister in its reference.

The calculation of the number of logically possible types based on three kintypes is a special case of the combinational problem of the number of partitions of *n* objects. When *n* is three this is the sum of the number of ways the three objects can be put in one group (1), two groups (3), and three groups (1). As *n* increases, this number soon becomes astronomical. In Greenberg 1966, another study was carried out to test further the idea that kin terms involving logical disjunctions are avoided, that of grandparental terminology. This involves four kin types: father's father, mother's father, father's mother, and mother's mother. With four kintypes there are 15 possible systems. In the original study, about 100 systems were considered. Subsequently, Murdock (1970) published an article which used a sample of 566 systems but which did not include all the systems used in my earlier study and considered, among other topics, grandparental terminology. The following results represent a pooling of these two samples. Of the 15 possible types, there are four which do not occur in either sample. These are exactly those types in which there is a term which includes father's father and mother's mother without including the remaining two kintypes in this reference. The result is, of course, entirely analogous to that of uncle and aunt terminology in that terms are avoided which designate the two most different relatives unless it includes all of the relatives in the set. Four other types are extremely rare, occurring in only one of the two samples or only two or three times in the combined sample. These are terms which designate mother's father and father's mother by the same term without including the other two kintypes. But father's mother and mother's father are also disjunctive, differing both in sex of relative and sex of connecting relative.

A further cognitive principle also appears to be at work here, even if only statistically, which I shall call salience. It is a hierarchical relationship which, unlike marking, does not obtain among values on the same dimension but between dimensions. Sex of referent is more salient than sex of connecting relative in that systems which neutralize the former but not the latter are infrequent, whereas those which neutralize the latter but not the former are extremely common. An example of the former, relatively infrequent kind of system, is one in which there is one term for father's mother and father's father and another for mother's father and mother's mother. An example of the latter is our own system which specifies sex of relative but not that of connecting relative. This is the most popular of the 15 possible types.

We thus have two types of principles which will predict the nonoccurrence or relative rarity of certain types. One is based on marking, the other is exemplified by what I will, for the moment at least, call the cognitive principles of avoidance of logically disjunctive categories and salience. These two types of principles are logically independent of each other since they make distinct predictions regarding the nonoccurrence or low relative frequency of specific types.

A study by Nerlove and Romney (1967), followed by a paper proposing certain emendations by Kronenfeld (1974), applies to sibling terminology the same basic method just outlined, a combination of marking theory and cognitive assumptions. These latter are stated in more explicit terms than in my work and are derived from Bruner, Goodnow, and Austin (1956), but are essentially similar to mine. Given eight kintypes based on the occurrence of three dimensions with two values each (sex of referent, sex of speaker, and age relative to speaker) there are 4140 possible types. The results must, I believe, be considered impressive. Of this vast number of types, only 12 so-called major ideal types, not violating their restrictions, account for 214 of the 240 systems in their sample. Of the remainder, 21 belong to what they call derivative types, that is, those which exhibit an extra complexity which is not usually found but which does not violate markedness or disjunctivity restrictions. There remain only five outright violations, and this small area of indeterminacy is even further reduced in Kronenfeld's follow up study. I am aware that the present exposition does not do justice to some further complicating factors in these studies, but the more detailed discussion they deserve would take us afield from the main points pursued here.

We can recapitulate the results thus far in the following way. By a combination of assumptions from linguistic marking theory and cognitive theory, we are able to predict with considerable success just which among what is sometimes a very large number of logically possible types will actually occur. On the other hand, such a theory cannot, obviously, predict which of these types will be found in particular instances. These would seem rather to correlate with social and cultural factors. Thus, in the uncle/aunt typology the absence of a type in which there is one term for mother and father's sister and another for mother's sister is predictable from logical disjunctivity. On the other hand, the presence of the bifurcate merging type has generally been connected with the existence of exogamous groupings and the lineal type with emphasis on the nuclear family. We would in this way have arrived at a pleasingly simple and precise answer to the question raised by Tax in relation to the relative roles of linguistic-psychological factors and sociological factors in kinship terminologies. However, a number of considerations suggest that such a simple formulation is not adequate for two main reasons. The first is that such general terms as linguistic, psychological, and sociological refer to complex phenomena and it requires some analysis to specify in what aspect and in what way they figure in the explanation of terminologies. The second is that it treats each of these factors in isolation and leaves their interaction out of consideration.

Consider, for example, what is meant here by a linguistic explanation. It was pointed out earlier that there was a tendency simply to equate linguistic with psychological explanation, and that this arose probably from the fact that it was the lexical semantic aspect of language that was involved in the study of terminologies. However, it is not difficult to see that other aspects of language are also relevant to the study of kinship terminology. For example, there is the factor of grammatical sex gender which has, as far as I can see, received at best cursory mention in theoretical discussions of kinship terminologies. Because of its existence in the Romance languages, one of Kroeber's categories, sex of the referent, always receives expression in these languages. We could hardly, it seems to me, argue for social factors to explain the difference between Spanish, which distinguishes sex of cousins, and English, which does not, since the existence of grammatical sex gender in Spanish compels this distinction. Hence, contrary to our earlier thesis, there must be at least some instances in which linguistic rather than sociological factors are required as part of the explanation as to why a particular empirically permissible type occurs in one specific instance and not in another.

We may note that marking theory, since it was developed in and applies to other aspects of language than kinship terminology, reveals regularities in the expression of kinship categories, which are more generally linguistic and therefore cannot be explained by social practices as such. In the foregoing section, marking theory was only utilized to the extent that it excluded certain types of kinterms defined by means of kintypes. This was in accordance with what may be called the lexicographic approach which entirely dominates the analytic literature on kinship. That is, we start with a list of linguistic expressions and their definitions by kintypes and carry on our analysis from there without any attention to the linguistic structure of the terms. Thus 'father-in-law' in English is defined as spouse's male parent but no attention is paid to meaning of 'in-law', which as has been seen is evidence for the marked character of affinal relationships. So in Arabic the fact that there is a single unanalyzed term for grandfather while grandson is expressed by son-of-son is disregarded in a lexicographic analysis, but is once more brought within purview of generalization by marking theory.

Psychology also, not surprisingly, turns out to be more complex in its relationship to kinship terminologies than merely the cognitive aspects of classification. Nerlove and Romney in their paper on sibling terminology realize that their task is not only to show what kinds of systems do not occur but also to explain why certain of the permissible systems occur in specific instances, while others do not. They make a beginning by at least seeking to account for the occurrence of those systems with cross-sex terminology and those which lack it. By a cross-sex term is meant one which is used by males to refer to females and vice versa. They suggest two hypotheses. One is that cross-sex terminology is associated with sibling avoidance, presumably a cultural trait. This turns out to be significant just short of .05 level. A second hypothesis, association with the post-partum taboo, turns out to be much stronger, being significant at the .001 level. Now, although post-partum taboo is no doubt a cultural trait, it has a strongly psychological aura because it involves in its explanatory role a whole series of psychological intervening variables. It is not basically cognitive and presumably no one would call it linguistic. Hence, psychological factors can be involved in the explanation of the occurrence of one rather than another system in specific instances.

The foregoing argument tends, of course, to denigrate the exclusive role of the social even in association with cultural factors in explaining the choice of one empirical possibility in preference to another. However, one can also support an opposite argument to the effect that a proposed cognitive argument is in fact sociological. To consider once more the Lowie-Kirchhoff typology, the non-occurrence of the only logically disjunctive type was attributed to a cognitive principle. However, one might argue that this has rather to do with the nature of social institutions. There are no social arrangements of residence of descent which will align the mother and father's sister against the mother's sister. In general this argument could be used against the purely cognitive explanation of any disjunction. Alternatively, if inclined towards logical positivist type arguments, one could assert that the whole question is meaningless. After all, the lexical items that make up a terminology have defining criteria that refer to the world outside of language and are therefore necessarily external.

There is, however, an argument which is, I believe, decisive for the existence of a purely cognitive factor here, and that is that the same basic principles hold for other terminologies, such as color terms. A similar argument holds regarding marking hypotheses. For these also hold throughout other aspects of language including terminologies with other subject matters. They are therefore not subject to exclusively sociological explanation. Further, there is one cognitive principle not mentioned which surely rests on the nature of human cognitive capacities. This is the avoidance of systems which use all available principles of contrast. For example, uncle-aunt terminology on occasion employs the lineal versus collateral distinction, sex of referent, sex of speaker, and age of uncle or aunt in relation to father and mother respectively. But no system uses all of these simultaneously. Such limits are also found in phonology and seem best explained on the basis of cognitive capacities, although even here one *could* claim that social life couldn't be that complicated either.

The answer to all of this, however, probably lies in the reflection that the human mind might indeed operate very differently, given the same social situation. In Hamlet's phrase, were we indeed "in comprehension like a god" and, in addition, playfully inclined, we might easily devise and live with systems consisting of numerous disjunctive terms.

In addition to all of these considerations, it was noted that the simple view earlier treated cognitive, linguistic, and social factors in isolation without regard to their interaction. For example, we take certain categories, as in Kroeber's analysis, as universally given and make them the basis of our analysis. Generally this works, given certain biological and social fundamentals. However, particular social arrangements can produce new dimensions confined to certain societies. Crow and Omaha systems generally, perhaps always, require matrilineal and patrilineal descent respectively. It has been noted, for example by Lounsbury, that in most instances not a single kin term is in fact confined to relatives in a particular unilinear group. It may also be noted that the speaker's unilineal group always contains more distinct terms than the lineage of the father in a Crow system or mother in an Omaha system. Both of these are understandable in terms of marking theory. The lack of correlation between clan membership and terminology is typically with more remote relatives where there is in all systems obliteration of distinctions. Further, given the importance of unilineal grouping, it will form a basis for distinguishing terminology but again the principle asserts itself that the more remote grouping is less differentiated. There is therefore interaction.

In Aristotelian and scholastic language, the existence of unilineal lineage provides the matter, while the principles of marking contribute the form which molds it.

Several other issues relating to typology require at least passing mention to put the present exposition in perspective. One is that, as scholars hostile to cross-cultural approaches will doubtless have noted, our typologies have all referred to limited sectors of kinship such as grandparental terminology or sibling terminology. In this respect, it is like contemporary linguistic typology which always refers to some limited aspect of language, whereas in nineteenth-century typologizing such terms as inflective and agglutinative were meant to characterize languages as wholes. Just so the Lowie-Kirchhoff typology sought a salient property which was central to the kinship system as a whole.

However, as we extend our typologies to include, for example, the mutual limitations on type which obtain when we consider uncle-aunt typologies along with cousin typologies, we will begin to understand systems more and more as integrated wholes. In fact, here also, it appears that marking theory will be of value. It has long been known that cousin terminology is generally consonant with aunt-uncle terminology. This consonance is defined as the existence of the same terminological distinctions in the first ascending generation and in regard to the offspring of each relative. Thus, if the father and father's brother have the same term, then their children will also. But many exceptions exist. A study of these discrepancies will reveal a marking principle once more at work. The cousins as more remote relatives merge distinctions found in the aunt-uncle terms but almost never the other way around. Thus bifurcate merging systems are often accompanied by Hawaiian cousin terminology. The opposite situation, in which a generational system is accompanied by Iroquois cousin terminology, is far less common.

There is a further connection between the internal structure of kinship systems and cross-cultural generalizations which largely remains to be explored. I believe that the kind of analysis of individual systems which does most justice to the psycholinguistic data in regard to how people actually define kin terms is by relational products and the converse of relations, that is, reciprocals in which more distant kin terms are defined by combinations of more fundamental terms. In doing this, there is a many-to-one mapping. Once a term which covers a set of kintypes is defined, when it functions in the definition of further kin terms it is almost never split up. On the other hand, several different closer kin terms can figure as logical sums in defining more distant relatives. For example, in systems with separate terms for older and younger brother, an 'uncle' term may include father's younger and father's older brother. This is the internal systemic counterpart of marking theory in which distinctions for more distant relatives are neutralized. Thus in Hausa, *kaka* 'grandfather' can be defined as anyone whom my *'uba* 'father' or *'uwa* 'mother' calls *'uba* 'father'. But *'uba* and *'uwa* are themselves defined generationally so that, for example, father's male cousin is 'father'. One does not split up 'father' so that there would be a separate kin term for 'father's father' and another one for 'father's male cousin's father'. This principle is stated by Tax, though not in its full generality.

A major omission in this paper has been a consideration of the diachronic aspect of kinship systems, yet recent work in typology has tended more and more to consider diachronic process in relation to synchronic generalization. The disregard of this factor is not then one of principle but derives from two considerations. One is that even a cursory treatment would require another paper of at least equal length to the present one. The other is that although important work has been done, and indeed Hoijer's paper on Athapaskan kinship (Hoijer 1956) is a model of comparative historical studies in this area, this aspect of kinship has, relatively speaking, been neglected.

What I hope to have accomplished in this paper, in addition to giving some notion of the relevance of contemporary language universals research to kinship terminology, is to highlight once more the unique contribution to anthropological theory that kinship studies can make. They provide the possibility, through the analysis of highly specific and formally manageable phenomena, of disentangling the contribution various causal factors (social, historical, psychological, linguistic and, I should add, evolutionary) make to an important cultural phenomenon.

Considering the magnitude of the topic and the limitation of time, it has not been possible to consider two of those just mentioned, namely, the historical and the evolutionary. The importance of historical, at least historical linguistic factors, was at least hinted at in the discussion of sex gender. In regard to evolution, I believe that Dole in particular has made a good case for its relevance while sensibly admitting that many details of terminology are not susceptible to analysis in evolutionary terms. Thus, in the realm of kinship, to rephrase the prophet Isaiah, the evolutionary lion may lie down with the functional lamb and a linguist shall lead them.

## References Cited

Bruner, Jerome S., Jacqueline S. Goodnow, and George A. Austin. 1956. *A Study of Thinking*. New York.

Eggan, Fred. 1956. *Social Organization of North American Tribes*. Chicago.

Goodenough, Ward C. 1956. "Componential Analysis and the Study of Meaning." *Language* 32: 195–216.

Greenberg, Joseph H. 1966. *Language Universals*. The Hague.

Hoijer, Harry. 1956. "Athapaskan Kinship Systems." *American Anthropologist* 58: 309–33.

Kirchhoff, Paul. 1932. "Verwandtschaftsbezeichnungen und Verwandtenheirat." *Zeitschrift für Ethnologie* 64: 46–89.
Kroeber, Alfred. 1909. "Classificatory Systems of Relationship." *Journal of the Royal Anthropological Institute* 39: 77–84.
———. 1917. "California Kinship Terminologies." *University of California Publications in American Archaeology and Ethnology*.
Kronenfeld, David B. 1974. "Sibling Terminology: Beyond Nerlove and Romney." *American Ethnologist* 1: 489–506.
Lounsbury, Floyd G. 1956. "A Semantic Analysis of the Pawnee Kinship Usage." *Language* 32: 158–94.
Lowie, Robert H. 1928. "A Note on Relationship Terminologies." *American Anthropologist* 30: 263–67.
———. 1929. "Relationship Terms." *Encyclopaedia Britannica*. 14th ed. 19: 84–89.
Murdock, Peter. 1947. "Bifurcate Merging." *American Anthropologist* 49: 59–69.
———. 1970. "Kin Term Patterns and Their Distribution." *Ethnology* 9: 165–207.
Nerlove, Sarah, and Kimball Romney. 1967. "Sibling Terminology and Cross-Sex Behavior." *American Anthropologist* 69: 179–87.
Rivers, William H. R. 1914. *Kinship and Social Organization*. London.
Tax, Sol. 1937. "Some Problems of Social Organization." In *Social Organization of North American Tribes*. Fred Eggan, ed. Chicago.
Trubetskoy, Nikolai S. 1930. "Zur allgemeinen Theorie der phonologischen Vokalsysteme." *Travaux du Cercle Linguistique de Prague* I: 39–67.
———. 1939. "Grundzüge der Phonologie." *Travaux du Cercle Linguistique de Prague*, VIII.

# Some Iconic Relationships Among Place, Time, and Discourse Deixis

That third person pronouns and definite articles often show an important synchronic or diachronic relationship to demonstratives is well known. In many languages there is no separate third person pronoun as distinct from one or more of the demonstratives. In other cases third person pronouns derive historically from demonstratives, though there are other sources, most notably reflexive pronouns. Similarly, definite articles are often synchronically identical with or clearly related to demonstratives and are also in the overwhelming majority of cases derived from demonstratives historically.[1] There are also many instances in which a demonstrative has some article-like uses so that it seems to be a nascent article, e.g. Homeric *ho*. In Moravcsik 1969, a cross-linguistic treatment of determination, there is a table of languages with definite articles. Many entries are preceded by a parenthesis indicating that the article is not compulsory, and others are preceded by a bracket indicating inadequate information. In virtually all of these cases we have to do with demonstratives.

There is a further facet to the relationship between demonstratives on the one hand and third person pronouns on the other, namely, that the

Most of the data contained in this paper were gathered for a study *Diachronic Typology of Pronominal Systems,* funded by the National Science Foundation, grant no. 78-07225, for which I herewith express my thanks. A monograph on the subject is planned which will include a chapter on demonstrative systems. For most of the points made, it would have been possible to extend the examples considerably. A fuller treatment will be contained in the projected study just referred to.

[1] The general numeral classifier is in rare instances the source of a definite article or a third person pronoun. A common alternative source of third person pronouns are identitives, i.e. words meaning 'same' used as reflexive pronouns and/or intensifiers.

demonstrative involved is almost always a distance demonstrative. The paradigm case is Latin *ille*, the most distant demonstrative of a set of three, which is the source of both the article and third person pronouns in Romance languages. Numerous other similar examples could be cited. Apparently, there has been no detailed discussion of the reason for this phenomenon. However, what is presumably the common notion here is that a deictic element simply becomes anaphoric, and this is no doubt a key element in the relationship between the two. But we see, even in this simple formulation, an iconic element. Deictics are seen to be in some sense prior both conceptually and historically. Within text there is metaphorical pointing back so that we are in some sense talking about physical space as an iconic model for discourse. Also past mention is regarded as in some sense distant so that we see already one of the important characteristics of this mapping.

The present paper was written on the assumption, however, that the problem is more complex than would appear from the above account. One reason is that it is stated in terms of a relation between deixis and anaphora. But in this respect third person pronouns and articles are somewhat different. Anaphora is central to the very notion of a third person pronoun. Definite articles, however, involve the broader notion of "identified" which includes anaphora as merely one of a number of ways in which identification takes place. Christophersen (1939) in his discussion of the English article has provided here a convenient terminology. Anaphora proper may be called a contextual basis because it involves previous mention in the speech context. However, the definite article is also used when something previously mentioned has provided a verbal context from which the reference may be derived. Having just mentioned Yale, I may then say that the library is very good and the definiteness derives from the fact that we interpret the library as being the Yale library. We may call this an extended contextual basis. In contrast to the foregoing we may talk of a situational basis if speech is not involved. A restricted situational basis is one in which the specific time and place of the discourse provides an orientation. If for example I am dining with someone and I say "Please pass the wine," the wine need not have been mentioned previously to be identified. Finally, there is a general background of assumed knowledge about the world as when we talk about 'the sun', 'the weather'. I omit here extensions of the article to generic use and its further development to a Stage II and finally a Stage III article (Greenberg 1978). In this last stage the term "article" has, strictly speaking, only diachronic relevance.

A further respect in which we would like to extend the earlier account is the following. If, indeed, perceptual space is employed as an iconic model for discourse space, we would like to ask further questions about the details of this mapping and, if possible, develop a broader basis for it. To note just one important detail, anaphora involves reference to what has been said and this necessarily took place in the past. Hence, some sort of mapping of perceptual space into discourse time is involved which we can obviously compare to reference to actual time as distinct from discourse time. Clark 1973 turned out to be highly relevant in this regard. Based essentially on English and the use of marking theory it arrives at general notions regarding iconic relations of this kind, which were found in all essentials to be consonant with the results of the present cross-linguistic approach.

A third way in which the subject seems to demand more attention is that if we assert simply that a distance demonstrative is the usual source of both definite articles and third person pronouns we have not accounted for certain evidence which indicates that the choice of a particular demonstrative within a demonstrative system shows a certain variability, and this raises problems whose consideration may shed light on the whole process.

The following are the sort of facts that are of particular interest. Sometimes in the same language family, different demonstratives assume one or more of these roles. An example is Slavic. In Old Church Slavonic there were three basic demonstratives involving successive degrees of distance from the speaker, *si*, *toj*, and *onŭ*. There was also a nearer demonstrative *ovŭ* which occurred only in certain restricted contexts. Of these demonstratives, *onŭ* became the source of the third person pronouns in almost all Slavic languages. However, Standard Bulgarian and Standard Macedonian use *toj*, although some dialects of both employ *onŭ*.

That all does not necessarily proceed smoothly is also shown by the fact that there are languages with more than one definite article or more than one third person pronoun. An example of the former in Macedonian which has three articles related to degrees of proximity: *-v*, *-t*, and *-n*. An example of the latter is Hindi which has two third person pronouns *ye* and *vo*, which also function as demonstratives. They are distinguished by proximity but with an admixture of respect in that men are usually referred to by the more distant demonstrative regardless of physical proximity (Pradeep Dhillon, personal communication). Why do such systems exist? Is it clear that from a purely logical point of view anaphora and spatial distance are independent in that the anaphorically referred to, or that assumed as identified, can differ in proximity and hence, be referred to approximately by any of the demonstratives depending on the object in relation to the speech situation.

All this suggests, of course, that we examine demonstrative systems. Some of their characteristics are already evident from examples given and will, of course, be familiar to all linguists. The primary feature involved appears to be visual distance in relation to the speaker. This has been assumed in the use of such terms as near or far demonstrative in which by 'near' is meant 'near the speaker' and by 'far', 'far from the speaker'. Assuming for the moment that this is justified we may isolate several characteristics of the psychological space that mediates between the real world and the linguistic world of anaphora and determination.

First it is a world of visual space and its most fundamental feature is that of relative distance in relation to the speaker. It involves therefore relative visual distance and the speaker as, so to speak, the point of origin. As noted already by Clark the most useful coordinates for such a space is not the Cartesian space of three dimensional coordinates, but a space of polar coordinates in which objects are located by distance and direction from the point of origin. Since we are viewing the speaker as point of origin the line thus generated will have a direction, that is, it will be a vector with a positive value when it goes from the speaker to some point in the space. Even this is not enough. The asymmetry of the human body so that we normally look forward, and the existence of a ground so that the downward direction is very limited, provide other characteristics of this conceptual space. To this we should add that direction is not as important as sheer distance. Thus, far above the speaker will be 'there' just as much as considerable distance on the ground.

The egocentricity of the reference point is perhaps obvious. In fact, the general notion of deixis, pointing, has been extended to the notion of shifters, that is, those items in language which determine reference by relation to the speech act itself, whether to its time, its location, or to the speaker so that tense, for example, is considered a deictic category. These shifters were aptly called by Bertrand Russell 'egocentric particulars'. However, there is some additional linguistic evidence. There are a few languages in which in addition to terms like 'this' (near) and 'that' (far) which pertain to distance and two of which, at least, seem to occur in every demonstrative system, there are additional terms. These always take the speaker as point of reference.

One example is Katu, a Mon-Khmer language of Vietnam (Wallace 1966), which is described as having the following five demonstratives: here, there (nearby), there (level), upward from speaker, downward from speaker. Another is Archin (Kibrik 1977), a Caucasian language which is also stated to have five demonstratives: this (near speaker); this (near hearer), that, that below speaker, that above speaker. Probably the most elaborate system of this kind is in Eskimo which besides the usual place demonstratives has this (to the right), this (to the left), that above, that below, all in relation to the speaker.

There is a further type of evidence, itself iconic, that the speaker is the point of reference in demonstrative systems. Greater distance from the speaker is sometimes indicated by the addition of a marker to the less distant. A well-known instance involving demonstratives of place is the French series *ici*/*là*/*là-bas*. Frei (1944) mentions also the colloquial demonstrative *çui-*

*ci/çui-là/çui-là là bas*. In Japanese there are parallel sets of different classes of demonstratives, e.g. *ko-no/so-no/a-no* 'this', 'that', 'that over there'. For the place demonstratives we find *ko-ko/so-ko/a-so-ko*. Even more striking is Ronga, a Bantu language with *letiya* 'there' (distant); *letiyaa* 'very far'; *letiyaaa* 'that which is at the horizon' (Junod 1896). If we say that speaker is first person, then we have a way of organizing the space correlated to but distinct from sheer distance from the speaker, namely, the participants in the speech act. A few languages have developed systems in which demonstratives are related to person in a quite consistent manner.

The phenomenon was apparently first noted in Wilhelm von Humboldt 1829. His prize example was classical Armenian, in which sets not only of demonstratives, but of articles and third person pronouns were based on the series *-s*, *-d*, *-n* correlated respectively with the first, second, and third person. Brugmann (1904) in his important study of demonstrative pronouns introduced a set of terms which have since become known collectively as person deixis. These are *ich-Deixis*, *du-Deixis*, *jener-Deixis*, and *dér-Deixis*. It will be noted that the last of these is connected neither with person nor with distance from speaker. This latter is described as not distinguishing between near and far but involving only an undifferentiated reference to anything not in the immediate vicinity of the speaker.

Wackernagel (1928: 102–3), in his discussion of Brugmann, proposed the following four terms in place of Brugmann's: 1. *Hic-Deixis*; 2. *Iste-Deixis*; 3. *Ille-Deixis*; 4. *Tó-Deixis*. The first three of these are of course the Latin demonstratives, whose connection with first, second, and third person is particularly strong in the Roman Comic writers Plautus and Terence. The fourth one, however, is the neuter nominative-accusative singular of the Greek *ho* (m.s.); *hē* (f.s.); *tó* (n.s.).

As noted by Wackernagel, the fourth deictic, both in German and Greek, is the source of the definite article. In German, the article is the unstressed form of *dér*. In Homeric Greek *tó* is still a demonstrative but on the way to becoming an article, while in Classical Greek it has become a full-fledged article.

In terms of modern marking theory, we would consider these fourth forms as the unmarked ones. This step was in fact taken by Frei (1944), a structuralist and a member of the Geneva school.

We may note in passing that the use of an accented form in German for the demonstrative, and the same one without stress as an article is one which recurs elsewhere and involves a further iconic factor. Historically, loss of accent and sometimes phonetic reduction in the change from deixis to anaphora, mirrors the loss of prominence which comes with the change from making known to the mere expression of something as already known, a change from new to old information. In Hungarian, stressed *az* (the farther of the two demonstratives) is unstressed as an article and loses final *-z* if the next word begins with a consonant. In Vedic Sanskrit certain oblique forms of the demonstrative *íyam* are demonstrative with the pitch accent, anaphoric without it. A further example is Papago, a Uto-Aztecan language in which the farther of the two demonstratives *heʔg* is a demonstrative when stressed, an article or third person pronoun when unstressed (Mason 1950: 59).

As we see from the examples of *dér* and *tó*, an unmarked demonstrative is a possible source for the definite article, and, it may be added, for a third person pronoun. In what appears to be rivalry between two distance demonstratives, one is the most distant and the other is the unmarked form which includes distance reference as is generally the case with the *-t* demonstrative in Slavic. But how does a demonstrative come to be the unmarked demonstrative?

To see this more clearly let us go back to the situation in which we have a set of three demonstratives clearly associated with person. One may add that there is often good objective evidence for a close association between three demonstratives and the three persons. Thus, according to Vaillant (1958: 379) the Serbians say *ovo meni, to tebi, ono njemu* 'this for me', 'that for you', and 'that yonder for him'. In Greek of the Classical period *hó-de* is clearly connected with the first person as seen from the use of *hód' anḗr* 'this man' in place of the first person pronoun in Tragedy, and such expressions as *tē̂i-de kheirí* 'with this hand of mine'. The second person demonstrative is *hoûtos*, as can be seen in such expressions as *hoûtos tí poieîs* (Aeschylus) 'What are you doing?', literally 'that what you-do' in which *hoûtos* 'that' is nominative and agrees with the second person singular of the verb. The distance demonstrative *ekeînos* is never associated with first or second person in this way.

Objective evidence for the connection between demonstratives and the category of person is also provided by historical data. The three articles of Classical Armenian have clear etymologies involving Indo-European demonstratives and they also have obvious synchronic relationships to them. The three demonstratives, *ays*, *ayd*, and *ayn* parallel the three articles, *-s*, *-d*, and *-n*. In modern Armenian, except for a few marginal uses, the first two of these have become possessive pronouns of the first and second person, respectively, while the third has become an ordinary definite article.

In the Japanese of about A.D. 1200, the middle demonstrative *so* and several complex forms involving *so*, namely *sore*, *soko*, and *sonata*, are used as second person pronouns (Sansom 1928: 78).

Up to this point iconic relationships have been treated very much as metaphor, or at least as one kind of metaphor, that based on similarity of structure. Moreover, these metaphors have been essentially spatial, taking as iconic models the speaker as the point of origin.

The subject of metaphor has, of course, an enormous literature and it is not my purpose to discuss it in any detail here. However, one but not the only kind of metaphor is that involving an analogical relationship. In fact, the earliest discussion of the subject we have, that of Aristotle in the Poetics (we disregard here his discussion in the Rhetoric) puts it in the form of an analogical proportion. If we consider the metaphor of the kind which can be expressed by a proportion, then a logical question can be raised which is relevant to the relation between the demonstratives and persons. This is the question of symmetry. A relation is symmetrical if, whenever it holds between A and B, it also holds between B and A. Thus we tend to think of similarity as symmetrical. If A is similar to B, B is similar to A.

In Aristotle's well-known example the relationship is symmetrical and takes the form of an analogical proportion. The shield is to Ares as the cup is to Dionysus. The relationship is symmetrical because we could as easily say that the cup is to Dionysus as the shield is to Ares.

However, when we actually use a metaphor, as when we call a cup Dionysus' shield, there is a directionality involved, as is indeed suggested by the etymology (<*metaphérein* 'to transfer'). Still it could be used either way. An icon, however, is asymmetrical. The map is not the territory, as the half-forgotten Korzybski used to say.

Intuitively, as it were, in the paper up to this point a directionality has been assumed in each specific instance. But in reference to person and demonstratives, the case is not so clear. Does it make more sense to say that 'here' is where I am or that 'I' am the one who is here?

To me, at least, the second locution seems stranger. That is, it seems more "natural" to say that we map the participants in discourse into space than vice versa so that person becomes the model for place as the icon.

At this point it becomes important to consider the synchronic-diachronic distinction. Going back to proportional analogy, I will take an example from morphology rather than meaning, hence metaphor is not involved.

In Latin, the synchronic proportion *digitus*: *digitī* = *amīcus*: *amīcī* asserts that the genitive singular of *amīcus* 'friend' is derived from its nominative singular after the model of *digitus* 'finger'. But one could as easily have used *amīcus* as a model for *digitus*, or indeed any regular second declension noun. In other words, the relationship viewed synchronically is symmetrical.

If, however, in Late Latin, we assert the proportion *digitus*: *digitī* = *fructus*:*fructī*, it is symmetrical synchronically, but not diachronically. *Fructus* was a fourth declension noun with the genitive singular *fructus*, which was analogically replaced by *fructī*. Hence, the relationship is asymmetrical. *Fructī* was modelled on *digitī* or *amīcī*, but not vice versa.

But the Armenian and Japanese examples show persons derived from demonstratives and thus contradict what seemed earlier the intuitively more satisfactory relationship between person as model and demonstrative as icon. I leave the question at this point, not seeking a solution, but using it to point out that there is no necessary agreement between synchrony and diachrony on this point. It does seem, however, that we must assume that at some point the speakers acted counterintuitively to produce the historical consequences that we found.

Likewise, there is a difference between synchronic and diachronic points of view regarding "unmarked" demonstratives. Once a former demonstrative can refer to just about any space, whether visible or not, and has accumulated many other uses, it becomes perhaps synchronically inaccurate to define it primarily in spatial terms.

However, this paper is basically oriented towards diachrony. Having seen from the foregoing discussion both their distinctness and the intricacy of the relations between the two, we see that there is no basic contradiction if the two types of analysis are not identical.

Returning to the question of the relation between person and demonstrative (which exists in a clear form only in a limited number of languages), we note that it is historically unstable. Thus, in Greek, by New Testament times *hóde* has virtually disappeared except for certain fixed expressions. It has yielded to *hoûtos* which has become the unmarked demonstrative as opposed to *ekeînos*, the marked distance demonstrative. Similarly in the history of Slavic *si*, the near demonstrative of Old Church Slavonic has disappeared except for isolated lexicalized survivals and fixed expressions and has been replaced by *toj*, the second person demonstrative. Since the third person demonstrative *onŭ* became specialized as a third person pronoun, the descendant of *toj* would have remained as the sole demonstrative in some Slavic languages. The system was renewed usually by the addition of place adverbs as in Substandard English 'this here', 'that there'. An example is Polish in which the unmarked demonstrative *ten*, historically a contamination in which *-n* comes from the third person demonstrative, has been supplemented in *ten tu* 'this' in which *tu* means 'here' and *tamten* 'that' in which *tam* means 'there'. In Old Polish *on* was still a distance demonstrative.

The middle distance demonstrative can also absorb the distant demonstrative as in the history of English in which a third degree deictic *yon* only survives in Scotch dialects. As a result, we have only *this* and *that* in which *that*, the successor of both the second and third degree deictics, is the unmarked member.

There are still other courses of development of deictic systems not treated here. The purpose of the foregoing discussion is to indicate that where a third person pronoun or definite article apparently does not derive from a distance demonstrative, its source is an unmarked demonstrative which has spread and replaced other demonstratives. Such demonstratives always include distance reference and may often, in fact, be used freely in place of any other demonstrative including a most distant one if it survives.

There still remain the interesting cases in which there are several rival pronouns or articles one of which may have first person deixis in a threefold system or be the nearer member in a system of two degrees of deixis. I propose to consider only one of the systems in any detail, Macedonian. The reason is that more and better material was available to me in this instance than in any of the others. Macedonian has three suffixed articles inflected for gender and number that correspond to three demonstratives with clear associations with first, second, and third person. The demonstratives are in the masculine singular *ovaj*, *toj*, and *onaj* connected with the first, second, and third person respectively. The articles are in the masculine singular *-v*, *-t*, and *-n* after vowels, *-ov*, *-ot*, *-on* after consonants, e.g. *brat-ov*, *brat-ot*, *brat-on* all translatable as 'the brother'. From now on the Macedonian original will not usually be given but the deictic category of each article will be indicated by a numeral in parentheses following the noun.

By and large the use of the article in Macedonian is similar to its use in English. Of the three forms (2) is clearly the unmarked one. It is used not only when something referred to is visible to the addressee but when it is known but absent. In a historical text, or a grammar, and in the narrative portions of a novel, (2) occurs almost exclusively so that one would hardly suspect that there was more than one article. The one sort of example encountered outside of reported speech was in the preface of books in which one has what is sometimes called autodeixis, as in Greek inscriptions where one finds *tóde mnẽma* 'this inscription'. An example is Koneski 1954, a grammar of Macedonian written in Macedonian. It begins "Concerning the character (2) and purpose (2) of the grammar (1). . . ." Note here that (1) has a slight deictic force. 'This grammar' seems an acceptable English translation. Somewhat later we find "The examples (2) in this (1) part of the grammar (1). . . ." In this instance we have a true anaphoric use of a form other than (2), the article of the word for "grammar."

I now give some examples from the texts in Lunt 1952. The first is from a story entitled "Mother-in-Law, Father-in-Law, and Daughter-in-Law" (no articles in the title). The mother- and daughter-in-law are seated in front of the fireplace. The daughter-in-law, who is pregnant, says "Momma, when the child (1) I am bearing is born to us, what name shall we give him?" The mother-in-law says it should be called Petko. The daughter-in-law asks "Where will we put him?" The mother-in-law (2) answers "here on the hearth (1), next to the fireplace (1)." "But over the shelf (2) which was over the hearth (2), there was then (a) shovel." Note, Macedonian has no indefinite article. "But suppose the shovel (3) falls on him," asked the mother-in-law (2). The mother-in-law says it will crush and kill him. They both begin crying over the dead child. Note that in all the examples of (1), and the single instance of (3), we have not anaphora but what Jespersen following Christophersen called a restricted situational basis. At this point the father-in-law comes and finds the women crying. On hearing the reason he says, "Such stupidity cannot be found anywhere in the world (1)." This would be an example of an unrestricted situational basis.

He leaves in disgust. He encounters four examples of stupid behavior. After each one, he says, "These people are even more stupid than my (3) women" [*moi-ne ženi*]. Note that except for certain close-kin terms the possessive is expressed by an adjective which normally takes one of the three articles. The normative grammars say that (3) is only used when something is distant but visible, but in these instances, the father-in-law is away from home. In one instance, however, for no apparent reason, "my (2) women" occurs.

After seeing such stupidities in the world (2), he returned home because he had found people even more stupid than his own women.

Note that the world in the first passage above is (1), but in the one just quoted is (2). They are actually different words *vek-ov* and *svet-ot*. The reason may be that *vek*, which also means century or eternity, is really to be translated 'in this age' and, as we shall see, time periods during which the speech act takes place regularly take near demonstratives. The other case 'my [2, 3] women' has no real explanation. What we have here is, I believe, the spread of the unmarked form as a general alternative, leading to its universal use as in standard Bulgarian and in certain Macedonian dialects.

I quote a few more examples from another story in Lunt in which the writer is reminiscing about his childhood. At one point he says to someone (direct speech) "I have neither father nor mother. I am hungry. My heart (literally 'the-heart (1) to me') aches." The other person's answer includes 'your heart' expressed as 'the-heart' (2). Macedonian, like German and some other languages, uses a definite article with body parts: "Das Herz tut mir weh." In such cases the articles express possession. This is of interest in that in the case of Armenian, the language most often cited as having three articles, I believe that in the Classical language only the third person form approaches an article in its use (more or less like *ho* in Homer). In modern Armenian the distance article is a true article while the main use of the other two is as possessives.

Finally from the same story of a man's boyhood we find that he encounters a bully concerning whom he says "He frowned and spat at my (2) feet." Although it is the narrator's feet, unlike the example of my (1) heart above, there is no direct quotation. The author is referring to his feet in the past, not in the present speech situation, hence, *moi-te nozi* and not *moi-ve nozi*.

An example of a language with multiple pronouns is Hindi, one of the numerous languages in which demonstratives also function as third person pronouns. There are two degrees of deixis and no grammatical gender. In the nominative case the two forms are *ye* 'this' and *vo* 'that'. In grammars of Hindi it is generally stated that *ye* is used if the person or thing is present. For example, if I were sitting with a friend at a table in a cafeteria and an acquaintance of mine, but one not acquainted with my friend, joined us, I might introduce him or her and then go on to describe him or her to my friend in a sentence such as the following. He (or she) (*ye*) is a graduate student in the linguistics department at Stanford (personal communication, Dhillon).

However, the predominance of *vo*, the farther demonstrative, is shown by the fact that some grammars only mention *vo*, or mention both *ye* and *vo* and only use *vo* in the paradigms and in the sentences given for translation. One grammar (Catchpole 1946: 12) says that "*yeh* is used in place of *wuh* (*vo*) if the person or object referred to is present." It was also noted earlier that *vo* may replace *ye* even if the person referred to is present as a sign of deference or respect.

From the preceding discussion we see that the third person pronoun or article is derived from a distance demonstrative or an unmarked demonstrative which is used so widely that it includes distance deixis as one of its uses. Probably the main factor is that the distance demonstrative is easily extended to that which is absent as in narrative, or present but not visible as far distant or behind the speaker. It is therefore the natural candidate for the expression of that which was previously mentioned which will in most cases not be in the actual speech situation. In the case of the article, besides this anaphoric use, we have rather more frequently reference to what is known from the situational context or general knowledge than speech context. But this knowledge is the result of past experience or refers, in narrative, usually to past events.

Hence, the transition from space to time is quite "natural" and past time, generally referred to metaphorically as behind us, easily assimilates to the distant and invisible. In accordance with the discussion in the initial sections of this paper, the primary metaphor of space is organized in terms of the visual field and the participants in conversation. The projection of this metaphorical space into the dimension of time is now considered.

We can distinguish three aspects of time which are relevant to deixis in the present connection. The qualification "in the present connection" is made because others exist, e.g. tense, which is not discussed in this paper. The first of these aspects is the one which we have been mainly concerned with up to this point, namely reference to specific objects mentioned or known, typically by anaphoric pronouns or by articles used anaphorically or based on previous knowledge whether supplied contextually or from the specific or general situation knowledge of the speaker.

The second is actual references to time, i.e. words like 'now', 'yesterday', 'today', which are deictic in that they are referred to either by their relation to the present speech act, or sometimes by the use of some different zero point of reference as in narrative. Corresponding to this latter are tenses like the pluperfect in verb systems. The third is reference to statements themselves as when we say after or before a quotation that someone said or will say the words comprising the quotation.

We will find in all of these that with varying degrees of clarity there is a general tendency to refer to the past by a distance demonstrative and the future by a near demonstrative. Extending somewhat our initial metaphor one may note that as we walk, and we normally walk forward in order to see where we are going, we face the place at which we will arrive in the future while the place we have just been is behind us. It is consistent with this that the far distant future which is also ahead of us but is not visible should be referred to by a distance demonstrative.

The first of the aspects of time just mentioned, namely that corresponding to anaphora and determination, easily translates into past mention or the application of knowledge acquired in the past. What would be the equivalent for the future rather than the past? With regard to anaphora the corresponding term is cataphora.

There is, however, a basic asymmetry between past and future in relation to knowledge which makes it impossible for cataphora to exist in the same sense as anaphora with a mere change in the order of the relevant constituents. In anaphora there is coreferentiality between the anaphoric substitute and the antecedent which precedes and is therefore identified. If we reverse this, the cataphoric substitute cannot be coreferential at the moment it is used because we do not yet know what it refers to. After the cataphor has been mentioned we can then in retrospect say that it is coreferential or that when the substitute is used it is proleptically cataphoric.

What this means is that a normally anaphoric marker used in this way cannot usually be any more than a sign that some identification will follow, very much as an opening quotation mark tells us that a quotation is coming without it yet being known. For this reason it is always redundant from the specifically referential point of view. Another possibility is that it is really anaphoric, since what will follow has already been mentioned and the apparently cataphoric element is really coreferential with something that preceded and is simply about to give us an additional characterization or identification.

In some instances such elements are, so to speak, grammaticized: they have become part of the conventional grammatical machinery of the language. The closest to a really deictic element pointing forward in discourse are examples like these. (This last sentence actually illustrates the point by its final word 'these'.) In a Greek inscription we find *Athenaíōn hoíde apéthanon*, 'of the Athenians these (1) died'. This is followed by a list of names (Liddell and Scott 1945; s.v. *hóde*). Here English 'these' is the natural translation and so in German and other languages. So in biblical genealogies where the names follow as in Genesis 10: "These are the generations of the sons of Noah, Shem, Ham, and Japheth" in which the Hebrew original, the Greek Septuagint, the Vulgate, and the Douai French version all agree in using the nearer demonstrative. However, in these cases it is arguable that it is the mere proximity in discourse that is involved since a demonstrative which immediately follows will probably be a nearer demonstrative also. It would seem natural immediately after an enumeration of names to refer to them by a near demonstrative.

The difficulty of finding true examples of cataphora, and the commonplace nature of anaphora suggests the unmarked status of the latter. One criterion of the unmarked is the tendency for it to undergo greater elaboration into subcategories which are neutralized in the marked. A striking example of this is the development of whole series of time demonstratives all referring to past mention in Masai (Tucker and Mpaayei 1955: 18). Citing the masculine singular form we find *ola-naaji* 'that man we mentioned a few hours ago'; *ola-duoo* '. . . this morning'; *ola-nole* '. . . yesterday'; *ola-naarri* 'some time ago'; *ola-pa* 'long ago'. Logically we could have a cataphoric 'the man I will talk about tomorrow', although, as noted above, this would not be true co-reference unless he had been already identified in previous discourse which would, of course, be anaphoric.

Regarding actual time expressions, our second category, the near demonstrative, regularly covers the current time period including, however, both that which is past and that which is to come. Brugmann (1904) cites many examples in Indo-European languages of the survival of an *Ich-Deixis* demonstrative in time expressions where it has otherwise gone out of use. Russian *siju minutu* 'this minute, right now' refers to the immediate future. It is a survival of the former first person deixis Old Church Slavonic *si* which is no longer used as an ordinary demonstrative anywhere in Slavic except in the Rhodope dialect of Bulgarian.

A clear example of the survival of the distance demonstrative in relation to past time is in Latvian; the present third person pronoun of standard Latvian *viņš* derives from the former distance demonstrative in a system of three degrees of deixis. It still survives as a regular demonstrative in some dialects. There are a number of survivals in the standard language in fixed time expressions referring to the past, e.g. *viņ gad* 'last year'; *viņ nedel* 'last week'; *viņ dien* 'the other day'.

It was stated earlier that for the "prophetic future" the distance demonstrative is used. An example is Isaiah 4.1 and 4.2: "In that day seven women shall take hold of one man, saying . . ."; 4.2: "In that day shall the branch of the Lord be glorious and beautiful. . . ." In the Hebrew text "that" is *hahu* in both verses; the farther demonstrative in a system of two degrees of deixis. The Greek Septuagint does not use a demonstrative in 4.1 but in 4.2 the farther demonstrative *ekeînos* is used. The Septuagint, like the New Testament, normally employs only two degrees of deixis.

The clearest examples of the association of the distant demonstrative with the past and the near demonstrative with the present is in regard to quoted discourse. In English we can say 'I'll tell you this' but hardly 'I'll tell you that'. If one uses 'this' in regard to past discourse it is pretty sure to involve an imminent repetition for emphasis or reindoctrination. "I told you this already. You better improve your grades or you will fail." In Greek it is practically a regular rule that the unmarked (2) is used of what has just been said, the new demonstrative for what is immediately to follow. A striking example is Herodotus 6.53 in which after giving the Lacedemonian account of an incident he says "*Taûta mèn Lakedaimónioi légousin . . . táde dè egȍ gráphō*." "That (neut. pl. of *hoûtos* (2)) is what the Lacedemonians say . . . but I say (lit. 'write') this (neut. pl. of *hóde* (1))".

It was noted earlier that *hóde* (1) of Classical Greek is not regularly used as a demonstrative by the time we reach New Testament Greek. With one or two exceptions all the uses of *hóde* in the New Testament are in the neuter plural *táde* 'these things' and occur after a verb of saying to introduce a quotation.

Pedersen (1913: 186) gives it as a rule for old Irish that *so* the near demonstrative refers to what follows and *sin* the far demonstrative to what precedes. For Old Church Slavonic, Vaillant (1958: 138) states that *si* the near demonstrative usually describes what one is about to say.

Although there is some variation here, the significant fact is that, to my knowledge, nowhere does a contrary rule exist, namely, that what is said previously is referred to by a near demonstrative and what is about to be said by a far demonstrative.

Finally, a related but distinct iconic mapping concerns relative order of mention in discourse. In one, the order is invariant under the transformation as in English 'the former', 'the latter'. However, a number of languages use demonstratives, in which case the nearer demonstrative refers to what was mentioned later while the distance demonstrative indicates what was mentioned earlier, so that it is relative distance from the present speech act backwards in time which is reflected. Moreover, it is always the nearer demonstrative which occurs first so that one is, as it were, journeying backwards in discourse time from the present. Familiar examples are German *dieser* and *jener* and French *çelui-çi*, *çelui-là*, but the phenomenon is much more widespread, e.g. in Hindi and Avestan.

It has been the general purpose of this paper to show how a particular conception of space derived from the speech situation as structured by human physiology and psychology underlies a series of iconic mappings from space into real time and discourse time. The term 'icon' has in relation to language diverse aspects. Perhaps primarily it has been thought of as a kind of nonarbitrary relation between sound and meaning, so-called sound symbolism. But in the present and other instances the mapping is from a set of relations in the world, psychologically mediated, into a set of linguistic terms and then of these into yet other sets of linguistic terms. The relations may be either paradigmatic, as when we put a system of grammatical person into relation with a set of demonstratives, or syntagmatic, as in mapping of these same terms in an ordered fashion into discourse.

## References Cited

Brugmann, Karl. 1904. "Die demonstrativpronomina der indogermanischen Sprachen." *Königliche Sächsische Akademie der Wissenschaften. Abhandlungen der Phil.-Hist. Klasse* 22: 6.

Catchpole, H. 1946. *Elementary Urdu*. Ipswich: W. S. Cowell.

Christophersen, Paul. 1939. *The Articles, a Study of Their Theory and Use in English*. Copenhagen: Munksgard; London: Oxford University Press.

Clark, Herbert. 1973. "Space, Time, Semantics, and the Child." In T. E. Moore, ed., *Cognitive Development and the Acquisition of Language*. New York: Academic Press, 28–64.

Frei, Henri. 1944. "Systèmes de Déictiques," *Acta Linguistica* IV, no. 3. Copenhagen.

Greenberg, Joseph H. 1978. "How does a language acquire gender markers?" In *Universals of Human Language*, ed. Joseph H. Greenberg. Stanford: Stanford University Press, III: 47–82.

Humboldt, Wilhelm von. 1829. "Über die Verwandschaft der Ortsadverbia mit den Pronomina in einigen Sprachen." *Berlin, Akademie der Wissenschaften, Abhandlungen der Phil.-Hist. Klasse*.

Junod, Henri Alexandre. 1896. *Grammarie Ronga*. Lausanne: G. Bridel.

Kibrik, A. E. 1977. *Opyt Strukturnogo opisanija Arčinskogo Jazyka*. Vol. 2. Moscow: Moscow University Press.

Koneski, Blaze. 1954. *Gramatika na makedonskijot jazik*. Del II, Skopje: Prosvetno Delo.
Liddell, H. G., and R. Scott. 1945. *A Greek-English Lexicon*. Oxford.
Lunt, Horace G. 1952. *A Grammar of the Macedonian Literary Language*. Skopje: Drzavno Knigoizdatelstvo.
Mason, J. 1950. *The Language of the Arizona Papago*. Philadelphia: University Museum, University of Pennsylvania.
Moravcsik, Edith. 1969. "Determination", in *Working Papers on Language Universals*. 1: 64–98. Stanford Universals Project: Stanford.
Pedersen, Holger. 1913. *Vergleichende Grammatik der Keltischen Sprachen, vol. 2 Bedeutungslehre*. Göttingen: Vandenhoek und Ruprecht.
Sansom, George. 1928. *An Historical Grammar of Japanese*. Oxford: Clarendon Press.
Tucker, Archibald N., and J. Tompo Ole Mpaayei. 1955. *A Maasai Grammar*. London, New York, Toronto: Longmans, Green, and Co.
Vaillant, André. 1958. *Grammaire comparée des langues slaves*. Volume 2. *Morphologie*. Lyon: IAC.
Wackernagel, Jacob. 1928. *Vorlesungen über Syntax*, second series, second edition. Basel: Emil Birkhaeuser.
Wallace, Judith M. 1966. "Katu Personal Pronouns." *Mon-Khmer Studies* II. Saigon: Summer Institute of Linguistics, 55–62.

# The First Person Inclusive Dual as an Ambiguous Category

A comparison of languages which have pronouns in the dual number reveals a number of apparently exceptionless generalizations or, in some instances, strong statistical tendencies.[1] One of these is that the first person inclusive is a favored category among duals. Thus Wurm (1972: 62) in regard to Australian languages notes that, "the presence of a dual number, at least in the first person inclusive, is widespread."

In contrast the second person is a disfavored category. The existence of a second person dual pronoun seems to always imply that of a first person dual, whether with or without the inclusive-exclusive distinction, and/or a third person dual. Even the third person is, relatively speaking, a disfavored category. There are only marginal examples of systems with only a third person dual. The two instances I have noted are Tunica, a Gulf Amerind language, in which it only occurs in the masculine, and Old Akkadian in which it is only present in the verb subject inflection. In Forchheimer's sample of 71 languages (1953) there are no languages of this type.

On the other hand, languages in which the only dual form is the first person inclusive are not only fairly frequent in Australia, as noted by Wurm, but are the dominant type in the Philippines and are found in a number of languages in Africa, Oceania, North America, and South America. One example of such a language, Southern Paiute, a Shoshonean language, is found in Forchheimer and in Ingram 1978, a typological survey of systems of personal pronouns based on Forchheimer's sample.

[1] Grateful acknowledgment is made to the National Science Foundation for its grant BNS-78, "Diachronic Typology of Pronominal Systems," and to the Stanford Humanities Center, for their support of the research on which this paper is based.

In contrast to the inclusive first person, I have found no language in which the only dual pronoun is a first person exclusive. It also holds as a strong statistical implication that whenever there is a first person exclusive dual there is also a first person inclusive dual. I have noted just a single exception here, Savo in the Solomon Islands (Todd 1975).

When the sole dual pronoun is a first person inclusive, there is almost always a distinction in the plural between the first person inclusive and exclusive. If this is so, abstracting from other possible distinctions such as different gender forms, there will be just eight pronouns: first person singular, second person singular, third person singular, first person inclusive dual, first person inclusive plural, first person exclusive plural, second person plural, and third person plural.

The following is a list, not intended to be exhaustive, of instances of such systems. Starting in Africa we have Toma (Prost 1967) and Dan (Doneux 1968) of the Mande subgroup of Niger-Congo; Banjoun (Voorhoeve 1967), a member of the Bamileke group, which is particularly close genetically to Bantu proper within Niger-Congo; Duru (Bohnhoff 1986) of the Adamawa-Eastern subgroup of Niger-Congo; Margi (Hoffmann 1963) and Kulere (Jungraithmayr 1967), both belonging to the Chadic branch of Afroasiatic, and Nuer (Crazzolara 1933), a language of the Nilotic sub-branch of the Nilo-Saharan family (in bound forms only). In Austronesian, outside of the Philippines, a system of this kind is found in Muyuw on Kiriwina Island (Lithgow 1976). Australian examples include Njigina (Cappell 1939–40), Melville Island (Cappell *ibid.*), Bardi (Metcalfe 1975), and Uradhi (Crowley 1983). In the Americas, outside of the example of Southern Paiute cited by Forchheimer from Sapir 1930, there is Winnebago (Susman 1943), a Siouan language, Miwok, a Penutian language (Freeland 1951), Carib (Hoff 1968), and Kraho, a Ge language (Shell 1952).

Given the frequency of this type of pronominal system in the Philippines and the fact that the ethnosemantic movement which was so prominent in the 1950's and 1960's included several Philippine specialists, it is not surprising that this kind of pronominal system should have come to their attention. There were successive treatments of Ilocano (Thomas 1955), Maranao (McKaughan 1959), and Hanunoo (Conklin 1962). The analysis most commonly adopted is that of Conklin, which uses three binary features, but already Thomas, who excluded the third person because of important syntactic differences with the other persons, took the decisive step, which was to treat the first inclusive dual as a combination of the first and second person, and the first person plural inclusive as its plural. There is an obvious terminological difficulty here. One wishes to consider the first person inclusive dual "as though" it were a singular, yet it refers to two persons. The feature terminology introduced by

*Table 1*

Ilocano, Showing the Traditional Analysis (left) and Conklin's Analysis (right)

| Ilocano (traditional analysis) | | | | Ilocano (Conklin's analysis) | |
|---|---|---|---|---|---|
| Singular | Dual | Plural | | +restricted | −restricted |
| 1. *-ko* | *-ta* (incl.) | *-tayo* (incl.)<br>*-mi* (excl.) | [+speaker<br>−hearer] | *-ko* | *-mi* |
| 2. *-mo* | | *-yo* | [−speaker<br>+hearer] | *-mo* | *-yo* |
| 3. *-na* | | *-da* | [+speaker<br>+hearer] | *-ta* | *-tayo* |
| | | | [−speaker<br>−hearer] | *-na* | *-da* |

Conklin ± restricted has come into fairly common use while the symbolization of the inclusive first person, even when there is no dual, is quite commonly expressed as 1 + 2 or the like. Moreover Conklin-type analyses have been used for other languages with similar systems, probably arrived at independently, or at any rate not citing Conklin's classic study.

To illustrate this analysis, I will first show the Ilocano system as it was traditionally analyzed before Thomas' article and then how it would be analyzed using Conklin's three features ± speaker, ± hearer, and ± restricted. (See Table 1.) All eight possible combinations of these three binary features occur and in combination account for systems of the Ilocano type.

This analysis was widely viewed as a triumph of ethnosemantic method and, of course, a comparison of the traditional and the ethnosemantic analyses shows the advantages of the latter. Given the prevailing relativistic views of the anthropologists of this period, it would naturally be concluded that an analysis of the Conklin type more truly represents the native's conceptual structure which could only be seen, as it were, through a distorting lens when we imposed our own categories like dual, inclusive, and exclusive. On the other hand, the still dominant anti-mentalism of American linguistic structuralism prevented ethnosemanticists, for the most part, from positing that the ethnosemantic analysis represented more faithfully the actual mental representations of the speakers. Instead, resort was had to such notions as greater economy and internal consistency. A typical statement is that of Thomas (1955: 207–8). "It is also worthy of note that this system, though utterly foreign to the basic concepts of English structuring and thought, yields a pattern in Ilocano which is both consistent and complete." Here English conceptual structure is confronted not with its Ilocano counterpart but with fundamental scientific notions such as consistency and completeness, thus reflecting a basic contradiction. Moreover, the dual and the first person inclusive-exclusive distinctions are hardly notions based on the structure of English. The dual was perhaps best known from ancient Greek, while the inclusive-exclusive distinction was familiar already from languages in Oceania and Africa even in the early nineteenth century.

In fact there are even more striking data outside of the Philippines that seem to indicate the correctness of a Conklin type analysis. It may have been noticed that in Ilocano itself the morphological structure of the pronominal system does not reflect an analysis into three binary features. The only morphological hint we get is indeed in conformity with the notion of some connection between the first person inclusive dual *-ta* and the first person inclusive plural *-tayo*, which differ by only one feature in the analysis. However, the second part of *-tayo* appears to be identical to the second person plural *-yo*. It will be shown in later discussion that this is indeed the correct historical analysis, that is, *-tayo* consists of *-ta* + *-yo*.

On the other hand there are some languages with what we may call Ilocano-type pronominal systems in which the ethnosemantic analysis is far more closely indicated in the morphological structure of the pronoun system than in Ilocano itself. An instance is Winnebago, a Siouan language whose verb subject pronouns are shown below:

| | Restricted | Non-restricted |
|---|---|---|
| 1. | *ha*-V | *ha*-V-*wi* |
| 2. | *ra*-V | *ra*-V-*wi* |
| 1+2. | *hĩ*-V | *hĩ*-V-*wi* |
| 3. | V | V-*wi* |

Here V stands for the verb stem and the restricted and non-restricted contrast is clearly indicated although the speaker and hearer features are not.[2] Another example of a system with the same morphological structure as Winnebago is Kraho, a Ge language. In languages of this sort we may speak of a transparent subtype as against Ilocano. The great majority of languages of the type under discussion do not show the restricted/nonrestricted contrast in their morphological structure and will be called the opaque subtype, while the term Ilocano will be applied to the type as a whole.

The sort of analysis proposed by ethnosemanticists is further strengthened by the case of Bardi in Australia. Here, in a language of the opaque subtype, there is a prefix *r-* which indicates plurality of actors both with nominal and pronominal plurals. However, it is absent when the subject is first person dual

[2] There are instances in which a first person inclusive plural shows by its morphological structure that it consists of the first person plus the second person, e.g. Tokpisin *yumi*, but I have found no instances of a dual inclusive formed in this manner.

inclusive. Hence Metcalfe in his description (which employs a three feature analysis of the Conklin type) instead of + restrictive simply calls all restricted forms + singular including the first person inclusive dual.

It is of interest to note that there are a few examples of languages with the same basic pronominal structure with a third number category which takes the form of a conventional dual in the first person exclusive, second, and third persons. However, this "dual" is actually a trial for the first person inclusive with the meaning 'I, thou, and one other person'. Hence there are twelve forms rather than eight as in the Ilocano type. A language with such a set of pronouns is Weri, a language of New Guinea (Boxwell 1967). The Weri system of independent pronouns is shown below:

| | Singular | Dual | Plural |
|---|---|---|---|
| 1. | *ne* | *tenip* | *ten* |
| 2. | *në* | *arip* | *ar* |
| 1+2. | *tepir* | *tëarip* | *tëar* |
| 3. | *pë* | *pëarip* | *pëar* |

A similar system is found in Ngandi, an Australian language (Heath 1978), except that dual forms only occur in the masculine. Comparable also is the pronoun system of Cayapo (Wiesemann 1986), except that instead of a dual there is a paucal. The Cayapo set of pronouns, unlike that of Ngandi and Weri, but like that of Kraho, a closely related Ge language, may be said to be transparent in the sense defined earlier, while Weri and Ngandi are opaque.

How do systems of the Ilocano type arise? The opaque and transparent subtypes probably arise by different processes. If we once more consider Ilocano itself, an opaque system (see Table 1), we note that whereas the first inclusive dual is morphologically simple, *-ta*, the first inclusive plural is complex *-ta-yo* and *-yo* is identical with the pronoun of the second person plural. If we look at other Philippine languages with the Ilocano type pronominal system we see that this is a valid analysis. The first inclusive dual is always *-ta*, or in its independent form involves historical reflexes of the Proto-Austronesian **kita* to which either the second singular, second plural, or third person plural has been suffixed as a pluralizer.

Now Proto-Austronesian is generally reconstructed as not having a dual while the plural inclusive is **-ta* ~ **kita*. The course of events we reconstruct is the following. A system with an inclusive-exclusive distinction in the plural, but without dual pronouns, comes to restrict the meaning of the inclusive plural to the dual and in the process forms a new inclusive plural by suffixing a second singular pronoun (I have found this only in the Philippines), or more commonly a second plural or third person plural. The latter is often identical with a demonstrative and/or nominal plural. Harmon

1974, which includes a discussion of the historical development of pronouns in the Manobo group of languages in the Philippines, comes precisely to this conclusion. A new first inclusive plural has been formed by suffixing, in this case the second plural, to the older form which has now been confined to the dual.

The composite nature of the new first inclusive plural is shown vividly in a few languages in which the new form of the first inclusive plural has discontinuous constituents, as seen in Muyuw. The forms for "distant possession" in a system with three degrees—intimate, intermediate, and distant—are shown below for Muyuw:

| | Restricted | Unrestricted |
|---|---|---|
| 1. | *guna-* | *ma-* |
| 2. | *mu-* | *mi-* |
| 1+2. | *da-* | *da-...-s* |
| 3. | *na-* | *si-* |

Here the *-s* suffixial part of the first inclusive plural derives from the third plural *-si* functioning as a pluralizer. Another example of discontinuous constituents showing the composite origin of the first person plural inclusive in an opaque Ilocano type system is Duru, in which the pluralizer is *-vi*, which functions independently as the second person plural pronoun. In this case not only the verb and its pronominal objects may intervene between *ba*, the first person dual inclusive, and *-vi*, but even a set of serial verbs (Bohnhoff 1986: 104).

Finally, there is an example of the change we have been discussing in the course of development, namely Bviri (Santandrea 1961), a language of the Adamawa-Eastern subgroup of Niger-Congo. If the inclusive plural becomes confined to the dual, while a new expression of the first inclusive plural arises by the affixation of a pluralizing element, since historical changes do not occur instantaneously, there ought to be a period, however brief, in which the old plural still retains its meaning alongside the new dual meaning as shown by free variation between the old and new methods of indicating the first person plural inclusive. This is exemplified by Bviri:

| | Restricted | Unrestricted |
|---|---|---|
| 1. | *ne* | *ˀdu* |
| 2. | *ngo* | *ra* |
| 1+2. | *nda* | *nda,ra-nda* |
| 3. | *ni* | *ndi* |

The pluralizer here is obviously the second plural, which in this instance has been prefixed.

The preceding discussion has been concerned with the origin of the opaque Ilocano subtype. Wherever there is any definite historical evidence it arises by the process just described. With regard to the much rarer transparent subtype, all of the examples of which appear to be Amerind, we seem to find a different process than that for the opaque subtype, but the same one in all instances. In a system of bound pronominal affixes which was previously indifferent to number, or stated more precisely, had a pluralizer whose use was not compulsory, a situation found in a number of languages, there existed four pronouns: first person, second person, third person, and inclusive dual. From the existing evidence it appears that compulsory pluralization took place as a unitary process giving rise to a system like that of Winnebago shown above.

Thus far we have been considering the origins of the Ilocano type pronominal system. The further diachronic question concerns which types of pronoun systems it gives rise to. Two of these do not involve any really drastic change. One is that the first person inclusive plural once more absorbs the inclusive dual. When this occurs, we have the very common type in which there is an inclusive-exclusive distinction in the plural and no dual. However, the former presence of an Ilocano system can be deduced from internal and comparative evidence. The first person plural inclusive is complex in form and contains an analyzable pluralizer. An example of this is Gaddang, a Philippine language of Northern Luzon, affiliated with the Northern Cordilleran subgroup as outlined in Tharp 1974. It has no dual, but it has the distinction of inclusive and exclusive forms in the first person plural. Hence typologically it resembles Malay and the vast majority of Austronesian languages. However, the first person inclusive plural is *-tam* and is clearly cognate with *tamu* and similar forms in closely related languages of the same subgroup, all of which are of the Ilocano type and all of whose first inclusive plurals are analyzable as resulting from the suffixation of *-mu*, a second singular marker, to the old inclusive plural *-ta* to form a new inclusive plural, thus confining *-ta* to the dual. A process similar to that deducible for Gaddang took place in many Carib languages, except that the pluralizer was a general one found both with nouns and plural pronouns. It is likely that an examination of the morphological structure involving the application of techniques of internal reconstruction and the comparative method would reveal in some instances that languages with the inclusive-exclusive distinction in the plural, but with no dual, once had systems of the Ilocano type. From the data considered up to now, we see that there is a special relationship between the Malay type and the opaque Ilocano subtype in that either can change into the other. There is a further complication, which has only been hinted at in the previous exposition. In some languages the independent pronouns and one or more sets of bound pronouns may have different systems. An example is Nuer, cited earlier as an example of an Ilocano system of the opaque subtype, in which only the bound pronouns have a system of the Ilocano sort whereas the independent pronouns are of the Malay type. We may call differing systems which are found in the same language symbiotic and assume, on general historical grounds, that one of these must be older and the other an innovation. The answer to this question can only be resolved, if at all, by further comparative and internal analysis. Such studies would be part of a more extensive investigation than that attempted here.[3]

For the relatively infrequent transparent Ilocano subtype, a different sort of development, though once more to a very similar system, is exemplified by Dakota and Assiniboine, two closely related Siouan languages. Assiniboine is sometimes considered to be a Dakota dialect. We will illustrate this kind of typological change with reference to Assiniboine (Levin 1964), whose possessive prefixes for body parts are shown below:

| | Singular | Dual | Plural |
|---|---|---|---|
| 1. | *ma-* | | *ũ-...-pi* |
| 2. | *ni-* | | *ni-...-pi* |
| 1+2. | | *ũ-* | |
| 3. | *∅* | | *∅-...-pi* |

We have an inclusive dual form *ũ-*, which with the pluralizer *-pi* has a meaning embracing both 'I and others (excluding second person)' and 'I, thou, and others'. My interpretation is that a former **ma . . . pi* with the meaning first plural exclusive, corresponding to Winnebago *wa- . . . -pi* has been absorbed by *ũ . . . pi*. We may call such a system the Assiniboine type.

In relation to the change of the Ilocano type to the Assiniboine type an instance of symbiosis can be cited. In Bardi the independent pronouns are of the opaque Ilocano type while the various series of bound pronouns belong to the Assiniboine type.

More drastic than the historical developments from the Ilocano type just described are two instances in which, from the evidence available, it appears that the first inclusive dual has in fact been interpreted by speakers as a dual. This is indicated by it becoming the starting point of the development of the dual as a full-fledged category.

One of these is Miwok, a Penutian language of California, which was listed earlier among those of the Ilocano type. However, only some of the dialects of this language conform to the model of Ilocano. There are two dialect groups,

[3] A more detailed discussion will be found in J. H. Greenberg, *Diachronic Typology of Pronomial Systems* (Stanford, Calif.: Stanford University Press, forthcoming).

the eastern consisting of North, Central, and South Sierra, Plains, and the extinct Saclan Miwok, and the western which has as members Lake (near Clear Lake) and Coastal Miwok in Marin County north of San Francisco. The dialect of Bodega Bay may be considered to be a subdialect of the latter.[4]

The independent pronouns of Northern Sierra Miwok (left), an Eastern dialect, and Lake Miwok (right), a Western dialect, are shown below:

| | Singular | Plural | | Singular | Dual | Plural |
|---|---|---|---|---|---|---|
| 1. | *kanni* | *ʔičči* (inclusive)<br>*massi* (exclusive) | 1. | *kani* | *ʔitsi*, *ʔotsi* | *maa*;<br>*maako* (Bodega) |
| 2. | *mi* | *miko* | 2. | *mi* | *mikkots* | *mikko* |
| 3. | *ʔissaki* | *ʔissakko* | 3. | *ʔi* | *ʔikkots* | *ʔikko* |

First it may be noted that neither of these two dialects are of the Ilocano type, which does, however, appear in Central and Southern Sierra Miwok. Attention is directed to the first person of Northern Sierra *ʔičči* which is cognate with *ʔitsi* of Lake Miwok. The form *ʔotsi* of the latter dialect is a variant from a second informant.[5] A comparison of the systems of the two dialects shows that the dual category of Lake Miwok started with *ʔitsi*, while its inclusive meaning in Northern Sierra suggests that it must have been originally an inclusive dual. This is exactly the conclusion of Freeland, the pioneer investigator of Miwok, who states (1949: 35) regarding the pronoun systems of Lake Miwok and, indeed, of Western Miwok in general: "The occurrence of a dual in all persons is interesting. No duals are present in the eastern dialects but the difference between the inclusive and exclusive is sharply marked by the existence of two separate stems. . . . In the western dialects the inclusive has been reinterpreted as a dual and analogous dual forms have been developed for the second and third persons while the idea of inclusive and exclusive has been lost."

There is a "missing link" of course, direct evidence for *ʔitsi* as a first inclusive dual which presumably once existed. However, fairly recently, in Callaghan 1984, a dictionary of Plains Miwok, the westernmost dialect of the eastern subgroup, we find the entries *--či* as a first person dual inclusive probably in the declarative subject paradigm. Miwok has multiple series of bound forms and what is queried is not its status as a dual inclusive but its series membership. There is also an entry *ičči* stated to be the first person dual inclusive free pronoun by one informant, while the other informant is recorded with a query as considering it to be a first person plural inclusive. Unfortunately the dictionary is not accompanied by a grammar.

[4] A map showing clearly the distribution of Miwok dialects is to be found in Callaghan 1970.

[5] Of the two variant forms *ʔitsi* and *ʔotsi* it is clear on comparative grounds that the former represents the inherited form of the dual inclusive and the latter results from contamination with the form for the number 'two'.

A historical development similar to that of Miwok may be posited for the Daly River subgroup of Australian languages but with the difference that the inclusive-exclusive distinction is retained in the plural and extended to the dual. The original system is the opaque Ilocano subtype with, for most of the languages of the group, the phenomenon that we have already encountered so frequently, that the first person plural inclusive consists of the first person inclusive dual with an additional marker which in some of the pronominal series is a suffix discontinuous with the dual marker. In all the languages of the group there is a suffixed dual marker, differing in different languages or subgroups, not resembling the word for 'two' nor etymologizable from our limited data. This dualizer occurs in the first person exclusive, the second person, and the third person, leaving only the first person inclusive as a witness to the earlier system. The separate morphological status of the first person inclusive dual is noted by Tryon (1970: 17; 1974: 107) but without reference to possible historical implications. A typical example of a Daly language pronominal system is shown below in the bound subject pronouns of Marithiel:

| | Singular | Dual | Plural |
|---|---|---|---|
| 1. | *yikin* | *nangki* (incl.)<br>*katipini* (excl.) | *nangki...nim* (incl.)<br>*kati* (excl.) |
| 2. | *nanyu* | *natipini* | *nati* |
| 3. | *nang* (m.)<br>*ngiya* (f.) | *watipini* | *wati* |

It was seen in the earlier part of this paper that the synchronic evidence for analyzing pronominal systems of the Ilocano type in such a manner that the dual no longer figures as a category but that it should rather be described as a combination of + restricted, + speaker, and + hearer is indeed powerful. Yet in at least two instances it seems from diachronic evidence that the speakers interpreted it as a dual making it the starting point for a new system in which the duals may be mapped into the corresponding plurals in a one-to-one relationship. It would appear from this that the "traditional" analysis is not as foreign to the conceptual system of speakers of Ilocano type languages as would appear at first blush.

Thus the first person inclusive dual appears to be an ambiguous category, reminding one of the figure-ground illusions described by Gestalt psychologists. It shows that the human mind has, within certain strong limits, multiple possibilities of organizing the world through the medium of linguistic categories.

There is here a kind of paradox. I first sought to show that a relativistic view in which the conceptual system implied by a three-feature analysis is assumed to be different and perhaps incommensurate with that implied by the "traditional" one is brought into question by diachronic evidence. However in doing this we have sacrificed the notion of a uniform and universally valid set of typological categories by positing an ambiguous one.

In spite of the diachronic connection the two types of analyses do not appear to be stateable by the same set of synchronic universally applicable categories. Yet one is translatable into the other. Metcalfe (1975) in his treatment of Bardi grammar employs a Conklin type analysis, except that, as we have seen, he substitutes + singular for + restricted. Moreover, he is quite aware of Conklin's analysis, which he refers to in a footnote (134). Having used this feature analysis, however, it is quite clear that he is troubled by the problem of lack of comparability with systems of other types. While introducing the Bardi pronoun system by a rewrite rule N → *+I, +II, +singular* within the framework of an *Aspects* type grammar, he then introduces an interesting set of translation rules whose status within this framework is not clear. He introduces them as follows (48): "For simplicity, these combinations of components will be represented by the following conventions which introduce, in particular, the terms Dual, Inclusive and Exclusive." These rules are set forth below:

+I, −II, +Sing → +I, +Singular
−I, +II, +Sing → +II, +Singular
−I, −II, +Sing → +III, +Singular
+I, +II, +Sing → +Dual
+I, +II, −Sing → +Inclusive
+I, −II, −Sing → +Exclusive
−I, +II, −Sing → +II, −Singular
−I, −II, −Sing → +III, −Singular

Note that the translation equivalents are not really stated in a universal system since redundancies peculiar to Bardi are used, e.g. + dual which designates the First Inclusive Dual. This is possible because it is the only dual in the Bardi pronominal system. The same considerations hold for + inclusive and + exclusive.

However, the terms on the right side of Metcalfe's system of conventions are closer to a universal system and point in the right direction. In what follows I will give a brief sketch of how this might be done. What I propose is in some respects like what is done in phonology when relevant features for a particular language are defined by means of a fundamental vocabulary of phonetic terms. In doing something analogous for personal pronominal systems we first define the fundamental elements which make up the logically possible types. The pronouns of each language are defined in terms of these. We can then state synchronic and diachronic universals which range over the actually occurring types, but resorting in a way which we will exemplify to the fundamental underlying 'language'.

Disregarding gender and other complications, which might be incorporated in a further elaboration, our 'language' will consist of an infinite number of sets whose members will be drawn from one or more of the following: 1, 2, 3, signifying first, second, and third person, respectively. These three are the 'primitive ideas' of the system. The totality of these sets is our 'universe of discourse'. It will not be necessary here to enumerate them.

Each one contains one or more of the three elements and there is no limit on the number of members of the sets. There is the further provision that 1 cannot occur more than once in any set. This is because for reasons which are not discussed here, it is assumed that there is only one speaker. Examples of such sets are (1), (3), (2,3,3,3,3). In every language there are a number of expressions, the pronouns, consisting of one or more series, which can be coordinated to these sets in the sense that the meaning of any individual pronoun can be expressed as a set of these sets, which in the limiting case will consist of a single-member set. In this 'language' it will be possible to express the various levels of generalization in and across languages described in Greenberg 1968. Since we require an ascending series of type levels we will call the individual sets characterized above as being of level 1.

To define the meaning of any pronominal form in any language we require expressions of level 2. Examples are English 'I' as ((1)) and 'you' as ((2), (2,2), (2,2,2), etc.; (2,3), (2,3,3), etc.; (2,2,3), (2,2,3,3), etc.). The meanings are given here extensionally by listing the sets but it is usually possible to give an intensional definition by means of the properties common to the constituent sets, and this will be both briefer and more informative. Thus 'I' can be defined as the set of level 2 whose only member is (1) and 'you' as the set of all sets whose members contain at least one occurrence of 2 and no occurrence of 1. We can define significant features or "in language" generalizations over the pronominal systems of individual languages by statements of level 3 which refer to sets of the individual pronominal expressions which, as we have seen, are of level 2. For example, in a language with a dual category consisting of a first person inclusive, first person exclusive, second person, and third person, we can define the dual category extensionally as a third level set (((1,2)), ((1,3)), ((2,2, (2,3)), ((3,3))) or intensionally by noting that all the member sets of level 1 have just two members and these comprise all the sets of sets which have this property in the language in question. This formulation is not identical to the extensional one because it does not specify the complex membership of the third set of sets. This latter would be covered by what appears to be a universal principle, with a few rare and doubtful exceptions, namely that languages do not distinguish in what are usually called second person non-singulars between 2 and 3, as long as at least the sets (2,2), (2,2,2), etc. are present depending on the appropriate number category.

The universal synchonic generalization noted in the initial section of this paper that the presence of a second person dual in any pronominal system implies the presence of either a first person dual, a third person dual, or both can be expressed as follows. Whenever there is a pronominal expression in a language, whose extensional definition involves member sets with just two members, such that 2 is a member of all of them, i.e. ((2,2), (2,3)) then there are pronouns whose extension contains one or more sets of level 2 whose constituent sets have two members and none of which have 2 as a member at level 1. Of course, just as in phonology we write *p* without enumerating all its phonetic properties, one can use the ordinary terminology with qualifications where appropriate. The present purpose is simply to show what I believe the underlying 'language' to be like in which, reverting to the specific topic of the present paper, it is possible to express differing systems in which the same set, in this case (1,2), can be defined by different properties, depending on the structure of the rest of the system, as either the set with the membership (1,2) as its only member or as the set whose only member is the set with two members which has 1 as one of its members. In fact all of Conklin's features can be easily expressed in this language.

It would seem that a change from a set defined as having the membership (1,2) to one in which its cardinal number becomes a part of the definition is a remarkable shift from what would seem to be basic to an incidental property shared by other sets, that is to have two members. Yet such semantic shifts are not unknown in other aspects of language. In Greenberg (1978: 289), a discussion of numeral systems, it is pointed out that in some instances in which a duodecimal system is replaced by a decimal system the old expression meaning 'twelve' shifts its meaning to 'ten'. It would seem that the meaning of successor to eleven is the fundamental meaning of twelve whereas its function as a base would be an accidental property, yet the meaning shift actually occurs. In one way this change is even more unexpected. In the case of the first inclusive dual it is logically true that an expression with the meaning of first + second person will imply that it has two members whereas the function of 12 as a base of a numeral system is not logically required and only occurs in a minority of languages.

## References Cited

Bohnhoff, L. E. 1986. "Yag Dii (Duru) pronouns." In Wiesemann ed. 1986: 108–30.

Boxwell, M. 1967. "The Weri pronominal system." *Linguistics* 29: 34–43.

Callaghan, C. A. 1970. *Bodega Miwok Dictionary*. Berkeley: University of California Press.

———. 1984. *Plains Miwok Dictionary*. Berkeley: University of California Press.

Capell, A. 1939–40. "The classification of languages in North and North-West Australia." *Oceania* 10: 241–72.

Conklin, H. C. 1962. "Lexicographical treatment of folk taxonomies." In Householder and Saporta, eds. 1962: 119–41.

Crazzolara, J. P. 1933. *Outlines of a Nuer Grammar*. Vienna: Anthropos.
Crowley, T. 1983. "Uradhi." In Dixon and Blake, eds. 1983: 307–428.
Dixon, R. M. W., and B. J. Blake, eds. 1983. *Handbook of Australian Languages. Volume 3*. Amsterdam: Benjamins.
Doneux, J. 1968. *Esquisse grammaticale du Dan*. Dakar: Université de Dakar [*Documents Linguistiques* 15].
Forchheimer, P. 1953. *The Category of Person in Language*. Berlin: W. De Gruyter.
Freeland, L. S. 1949. "Western Miwok texts with linguistic notes." *International Journal of American Linguistics* 13: 31–46.
———. 1951. *Language of the Sierra Miwok*. Baltimore: Waverley Press [*International Journal of American Linguistics* Memoir 6].
Greenberg, Joseph H. 1968. *Anthropological Linguistics*. New York: Random House.
———. 1978. "Generalizations about numeral systems." In Greenberg, Ferguson, and Moravcsik, eds. 1978: 249–96.
———. Forthcoming. *Diachronic Typology of Pronominal Systems*. Stanford: Stanford University Press.
Greenberg, Joseph H., Charles A. Ferguson, and Edith A. Moravcsik, eds. 1978. *Universals of Human Language. Volume 3. Word Structure*. Stanford: Stanford University Press.
Harmon, C. 1974. "Reconstruction of Proto-Manobo pronouns and case marking particles." In *Working Papers in Linguistics, Department of Linguistics, University of Hawaii* 6, no. 6: 13–46.
Heath, J. 1978. *Ngandi Grammar, Texts and Vocabulary*. Canberra: Australian National University.
Hoff, B. J. 1968. *The Carib Language*. The Hague: Martinus Nijhoff.
Hoffmann, C. 1963. *A Grammar of the Margi Language*. Oxford: Oxford University Press.
Householder, Fred W., and Sol Saporta, eds. 1962. *Problems in Lexicography*. Bloomington, Ind.: Indiana University Research Center in Anthropology, Folklore, and Linguistics [*Indiana University Research Center in Anthropology, Folklore, and Linguistics, Publ. 21*; *International Journal of American Linguistics* 28, Part 4].
Ingram, D. 1978. "Typology and universals of personal pronouns." In Greenberg, Ferguson, and Moravcsik, eds. 1978: 215–47.
Jungraithmayr, H. 1967. "A brief note on some of the characteristics of 'West Chadic'." *Journal of West African Languages* 4: 57–58.
Levin, H. B. 1964. *The Assiniboine Language*. Bloomington: Indiana University.
Lithgow, D. R. 1976. "Austronesian languages: Milne Bay and adjacent islands." In Wurm, ed. 1976: 441–523.
McKaughan, H. 1959. "Systematic components of pronoun systems: Maranao." *Word* 15: 101–2.
Metcalfe, C. D. 1975. *Bardi Verb Morphology (Northwestern Australia)*. Canberra: Australian National University [Pacific Linguistics B-3].
Prost, A. 1967. *Le Loghoma*. Dakar: Université de Dakar [*Documents Linguistiques* 13].
Santandrea, S. 1961. *Comparative Outline Grammar of Ndogo, Sere, Tagbu, Bai, Bviri*. Bologna: Negrizia.
Sapir, E. 1930. "The Southern Paiute Language." *Proceedings of the American Academy of Arts and Sciences* 65: 1–296.
Shell, O. 1952. "Grammatical outline of Kraho (Ge family)." *International Journal of American Linguistics* 18: 115–29.

Susman, A. 1943. *The Accentual System of Winnebago*. New York: Columbia University [Ph.D. Thesis].

Tharp, J. A. 1974. "The Northern Cordilleran subgroup of Philippine languages." *Working Papers in Linguistics, Department of Linguistics, University of Hawaii* 6, no. 6: 53–114.

Thomas, D. 1955. "Three analyses of the Ilocano pronoun system." *Word* 11: 204–8.

Todd, E. M. 1975. "The Solomon language family." In Wurm, ed. 1975: 805–46.

Tryon, D. T. 1970. *An Introduction to Maranungku (Northern Australia)*. Canberra: Linguistic Circle of Canberra [*Pacific Linguistics* B-15].

———. 1974. *Daly Family Languages, Australia*. Canberra: Linguistic Circle of Canberra [*Pacific Linguistics* C-32].

Voorhoeve, J. 1967. "Personal pronouns in Bamileke." *Lingua* 17: 421–4

Wiesemann, U. 1986. "The pronoun system of some Je and Macro-Je languages." In Wiesemann, ed. 1986: 359–80.

Wiesemann, U., ed. 1986. *Pronominal Systems*. Tübingen: Gunther Narr.

Wurm, S. A. 1972. *Languages of Australia and Tasmania*. The Hague: Mouton.

Wurm, S. A., ed. 1975. *New Guinea Area Languages and Language Studies. Volume 1: Papuan Languages and the New Guinea Linguistic Scene*. Canberra: Department of Linguistics, Research School of Pacific Studies. The Australian National University [*Pacific Linguistics* C-38].

———. 1976. *New Guinea Area Languages and Language Studies. Volume 2: Austronesian languages*. Canberra: Department of Linguistics, Research School of Pacific Studies, The Australian National University [*Pacific Linguistics* C-39].

PART II

# STUDIES IN LANGUAGES OF AFRICA AND THE NEAR EAST

# Review of Guthrie's *The Classification of the Bantu Languages*

This is the third in the valuable series of linguistic works currently being issued by the International African Institute.[1] The author, Malcolm Guthrie, is known for his competent descriptive grammar of Lingala, a Bantu language of the Congo. Moreover, he has a wide first-hand acquaintanceship with Bantu languages. In fact, in the introductory section of the present work, he claims intimate knowledge regarding languages of no less than 14 of the 16 zones into which he here divides the Bantu family and the work itself gives evidence of a wide variety of observations regarding many areas in which published material is meager. Nevertheless, for reasons which I shall state below, one must regretfully conclude that the work does not answer to the expectations aroused and that it represents a relatively small contribution to the subject it treats.

The book is divided into four sections: (I) Introduction, (II) Identifying the Bantu Languages, (III) Methods of Classification, and (IV) The Bantu Languages Classified. It is accompanied by a separate map in which the Bantu languages are numbered in accordance with the system described in the fourth section.

In the brief introductory section certain general matters are treated, such as the establishment of a standard nomenclature for Bantu languages and methods of transcription. The author seems well aware of the problem of phonemic vs. phonetic transcription in dialect area work and one could have wished for a more extended treatment of this interesting topic.

The section on the identification of the Bantu languages which follows is

[1] Malcolm Guthrie, *The Classification of the Bantu Languages* (London, New York, and Toronto: Oxford University Press, 1948).

much the weakest of the work and reflects a curious lack of understanding of the method of genetic classification of languages. The author here chases the will-o'-the-wisp of the discovery of 'criteria' for 'defining' the Bantu languages. The author reflects that it is 'interesting' that Bleek, the pioneer of Bantu linguistics, did not try to define the term Bantu. He also finds it 'interesting' that Meinhof, the father of Bantu comparative work, did not make such an attempt. That the contemporary investigators, Doke and Tucker, have enumerated some characteristics of the Bantu languages strikes him as encouraging but inadequate. We are told that "the most that has been achieved is a more or less complete statement of the characteristic features of Bantu languages, scarcely any one of which is found to apply to all the languages which everyone has accepted as Bantu." This is evidently not enough for Guthrie, who is seeking a full scholastic definition *per genus et differentia specifica*.

At this point we might have expected the writer to reflect that perhaps Meinhof, Doke, and the others had good reason for not attempting such a definition and he might have asked himself whether such definitions exist for Indo-European, Semitic, and other well-known language families. But he presses on. We are now given four sets of criteria, the first two of which are called principal, the latter two subsidiary—not, we are told, because they are less important but because they are more difficult to apply through "contraction and attrition." One criterion is the existence of a set of grammatical genders marked by prefixes involving "no correlation with sex references or with any other clearly defined idea" (a purely gratuitous assumption). Another is the existence of a "balanced vowel" system, that is, the usual Bantu five or seven vowel system. Presumably if any Bantu language were to differentiate the *a* phoneme into separate front and back phonemes, it would cease to be Bantu. The only criterion enumerated which is relevant to historical analysis is his second, "a vocabulary, part of which can be related by fixed rules to a set of hypothetical common roots."

Having at length arrived at an elaborate set of criteria, by their application, he succeeds in excluding some perfectly good Bantu languages. It is perhaps excusable that Bamum, Bafut, and other languages of the Cameroon 'Semi-Bantu'–Bantu borderline are not included, for this is an ingrained, traditional misconception, but what shall we say of his refusal to admit the Manenguba group (Nkosi and others), which even unsophisticated observers like Johnston and Dorsch saw were Bantu? Moreover, these languages show special resemblances to those of the Duala group, and Duala has always been accepted as Bantu and is so classified by Guthrie.

Apparently all four criteria must be present for a language to be Bantu. What, then, of the languages which satisfy some but not all of the requirements laid down by the author? Guthrie solves this problem by the establishment of a number of low caste and outcaste groups (possibly the result of past linguistic miscegenation?).

We are told of languages such as Bira "which are incompletely Bantu" because while they have noun prefix classes, adjective agreement is distinctly fragmentary. These languages are included by Guthrie in his enumeration, but their lack of full status is indicated by the use of italics. Distinct from these, we are told, is another spawn of half-breeds called Bantoid, which are excluded from consideration altogether. These languages have all the Bantu characteristics except a common vocabulary. The example given is Bafut of the Cameroons, but of the six noun root morphemes quoted, three are easily derivable from standard Proto-Bantu forms, not to mention the prefixes. In fact, Bafut is one of the languages of the 'Semi-Bantu'–Bantu area whose Bantu affiliations have been traditionally ignored. What other mythical hybrids may roam the African landscape, we are not told. But whatever they may be, they will not lack congenial companions, Bantoid and Semi-Bantu and the centaur-like Nilo-Hamitic.

In his third section, Guthrie discusses methods of classification. We are offered several, the historical, the empirical, and the practical. The historical method is, according to the writer, the setting up of a genealogical tree of dialects and it is impossible here because "with practically no historical records, true historical study, as distinct from comparative study is impossible." The empirical method is the study of the distribution of isoglosses. The various types, phonetic, lexical, syntactical, etc., each come in for separate discussion. Guthrie considers the empirical method unusable because different isoglosses lead to different classifications. The method which he advocates he calls the practical, that is, "the presence of some arbitrariness is admitted as an essential modification of the empirical method." Evidently, all that the writer means by this is that no one isogloss or restricted set of them can be used as the sole criterion. For we are told somewhat later that at the meeting of zones B, C, and H there is a bunching of isoglosses of different types and that phenomena of this kind determine his classification. The author's technique of classification is set forth in the final section. The Bantu area is divided into sixteen zones, each designated by a letter. Within each zone, each language is numbered, a new decade being employed for each subgroup. Thus the designation of the Sumba language as F 23 places it within the second group of languages in zone F. The problem of the definition of language and dialect is discussed at this point and a 'practical' as opposed to a 'scientific' solution is adopted. By 'practical' is apparently meant non-linguistic. Thus we are told that Sukuma (F 21) and Nyamwesi (F 22) are hardly more than dialect variants of the same language, but "for political and demographic reasons, we have to consider them as separate languages." Since Guthrie never tells us, except for the few examples cited at this point, where these considerations have entered into his classifications, his division into languages becomes almost useless. Besides, what is 'practical' in the usual sense of the word about this procedure is difficult to see. The administrator, for example, wondering whether the same set of school textbooks could be used for Sukuma and Nyamwesi, might be misled by Guthrie's classification into assuming they were far more different than they really are. The opposition of 'scientific' and 'practical' here is altogether unfortunate. The linguist, no more than the chemist, has two separate sets of principles, one for his laboratory and another for practical application.

The final section is concluded by a listing of languages in each zone by subclasses. For each zone, Guthrie gives comparable information concerning a number of important features, e.g., the presence of a gender indicating the diminutive, the presence and formation of negative tenses, etc. This is much the most valuable portion of the work since it enables us to plot the distribution of some important features over the entire Bantu area. Some mapping of lexical isoglosses has been done by other writers, but the field remains on the whole neglected. Yet it is a subject of the highest interest, for here we have a vast dialect area, unique in the primitive world, in which the conclusions of European dialect geography can be tested under very different geographic and cultural conditions. It is as an advance in this direction that the present work makes a distinct contribution.

# The Patterning of Root Morphemes in Semitic

It is an obvious, though little-noted fact, that the characteristic triconsonantal verb morphemes of Semitic languages (the traditional triliteral roots) do not ordinarily contain identical first and second consonants. On the other hand, a pattern of identical second and third consonants is of frequent occurrence, constituting the well-known geminate subtype of Semitic verb. Thus, while sequences such as **mmd* are virtually non-existent in Semitic languages, Arabic *mdd* 'to stretch', *frr* 'to flee', etc. are representatives of a common Semitic type.

The existence of this degree of patterning led to the present investigation of the over-all patterning of the triconsonantal verb morphemes of the Semitic languages, particularly Arabic. The most general conclusions are stated here by way of anticipation in order to orient the reader in the detailed discussion which follows.

> 1. In the first two positions, not only identical but homorganic consonants are excluded. For example, no Semitic language has triconsonantal verb morphemes beginning *bm-*, since this would involve two labials, or *gk-*, since such a form would contain two velars in the first and second positions. The lack of gemination in I-II is therefore seen to be a special case under the rule referring to homorganic consonants in general.
>
> 2. Homorganic consonants are likewise excluded in positions two and three, though not quite as rigorously as in the first two positions. The rule for positions two and three does not preclude identical consonants, as we have seen, so that it should be rephrased as referring to homorganic but not identical consonants.

Thus in Arabic, we have *škk*, 'to split', but **škg*, containing non-identical velars in positions two and three, could not occur. The geminate type is thus clearly an anomaly in terms of the overall patterning of Semitic verbal roots.[1]

3. In positions one and three there is marked, but less rigorous exclusion of homorganic, including identical consonants, than in other combinations of positions. Thus there are few instances of the general type of Arabic *qlq*, 'to be disturbed', with identical first and third consonants, or Syriac *prm*, 'to tear', with homorganic, in this case, labial, consonants in these positions.

The concept homorganic requires some consideration at this point. The articulatory positions arrived at inductively by the present study of pattern phenomena agree well with the statements of the early Arab grammarians regarding the *maxrag* (plural *maxa:rig*) literally 'place of egress'. Perhaps the most striking instance is the classification of *r, l*, and *n* as homorganic on the basis of the data presented here in full agreement with the statements of Sibawaihi and other early Arab grammarians and in contrast with the usual view that *n* is the nasal member of the series containing *d* and *ṭ* just as *m* does, in fact, pattern as a member of the labial series *f* (Arabic *f* < Proto Semitic **p*), *b*, *m*. Not too surprisingly, *w* and *y* do not consistently pattern with any group of consonants. It has long been realized that the so-called weak verbs of Semitic, containing *w* and *y* in various positions, are 'rationalizations' by which older forms containing root *u* and *i* were incorporated into the dominant triconsonantal schema.

Scattered references to various aspects of the phenomena just discussed are found in the writings of Arab and Hebrew grammarians and lexicographers. Lists of incompatible consonants are found in a few instances.[2] The closest to a general formulation that I have been able to discover is the statement

[1] This evidence can be considered relevant to the traditional controversy regarding the former biconsonantal form of the Semitic triconsonantal roots. That during the Pre-Semitic period, the device of gemination was one of the methods of forming triconsonantal roots from former consonantals is probable. On the other hand, the existence of geminates in Egyptian suggests that some geminates go back to the Hamito-Semitic period; cf. also such etymologies as Egyptian *tmm* equals Proto-Semitic **tmm* 'to finish'.

[2] Such lists are to be found for Arabic in the *Muzhir* of Jalāl ad-Dīn Suyūṭī and in the *Khaṣā'iṣ*, II, of Ibn-Jinnī. In the grammar of Erpenius (*Thomae Erpenii Grammatica Arabica*, Lugduni, 1748), p. 18, there is an enumeration of *litterae incompatibiles* based on an Arabic source I have not been able to identify. Erpenius is followed closely by De Sacy in his *Grammaire Arabe*, 2nd ed. (Paris, 1831), p. 31. For Hebrew the only mention of this topic which I have found is in the *Miqnē Abram* of Abraham ben Meir de Balmes (Venice, 1523), pp. 21–22.

I am indebted to Father Herman Merzbach for the reference to Ibn-Jinnī as well as for enlightening discussion of the topics treated in this paper.

of al-Ghawalīqī, echoed by Spitta-Bey, "As regards Arabic formations, the most excellent are those formed by letters which are distant in their points of formation."[3] Some use of this principle is made by Arab lexicographers as a criterion of loan-words. For example, the *Taj al-'Arūs* tells us, under the article *sad̲a:b* 'rue (an herb)', that this form is not genuine Arabic because *s* and *d̲* are never found in the same Arabic root. The only general study of the topic under discussion is that of J. Cantineau, which arrives independently at some of the conclusions described here. However, Cantineau's study is more restricted in scope, only Arabic being considered, and without discussion of patterning in the first and third positions.[4] None of the standard Semitic comparative grammars mention the topic.

The key position in the present study is accorded to Arabic because of the abundance of lexicographical information and the relative archaism of its phonological structure. The composition of 3775 verb roots was investigated based on the lexicons of Lane and Dozy.[5] The results of this study are set forth in the accompanying Tables 1, 2, and 3 describing the patterning in positions I–II, and I–III, and II–III respectively. For example, the figure 6 in row *g*, column *s* of Table 1 indicates that there are six Arabic verb roots of the form *gs*-, while the figure 8 in column *b* row *d* of Table 3 describes the fact that there are eight tri-consonantal verb roots in Arabic with *b* in the second, and *d* in the third position. In addition, coefficients of probability for each square in the three tables were calculated by the formula CR/n, where C equals total occurrences in the column in which the square is located, R equals total occurrences in the row in which the square is found, and n equals 3775, the total number of roots investigated. These tables are not reproduced here. Reference is made to them at the appropriate points in the discussion.

For the Semitic languages other than Arabic, I have not used numerical data. For each feature of patterning, the discussion of the Arabic material is followed by the consideration of evidence from other Semitic languages. For this purpose I have drawn on standard lexical sources chiefly for Syriac, Hebrew, Ugaritic, South Arabic, Ethiopic, and Assyrian.[6] In the absence of a

[3] Al-Ghawālīqwī, *Mu'arrab*, ed. Sachau, p. 7. This passage is referred to by W. Spitta-Bey in his *Grammatik des arabischen Vulgärdialektes von Aegypten* (Leipzig, 1880), p. 15.

[4] "Esquisse d'une phonologie de l'Arabe classique," *BSLP*, 126: 93–140 (1946). See also the discussion in GLECS III, 49–55 (1939).

[5] E. W. Lane, *An Arabic-English Lexicon* (London and Edinburgh, 1863–), and R. Dozy, *Supplement aux Dictionnaires Arabes* (Leyden, 1881).

[6] The chief lexicographical sources utilized for languages other than Arabic were: J. Payne-Smith, *A Compendious Syriac Dictionary* (Oxford, 1903); J. Levi, *Wörterbuch über die Talmudim und Midraschim*, 4 vols. (2nd ed.; Berlin and Vienna, 1924); W. Muss-Arnolt, *A Concise Dictionary of the Assyrian Language* (Berlin, 1905); W. Gesenius, *Hebräisches und aramäisches Handwörterbuch über das alte Testament* (16th ed.; Leipzig, 1915 [ed. F. Buhl]);

*Table 1*

Arabic I–II

| | II | ʔ | h | ḥ | ʕ | x | ɣ | q | k | g | r | l | n | š | ḍ | s | z | ṣ | t | d | ṭ | ṯ | ḏ | ṯ̣ | f | b | m | w | y | |
|---|---|---|---|---|---|---|---|---|---|---|---|---|---|---|---|---|---|---|---|---|---|---|---|---|---|---|---|---|---|---|
| I | ʔ | 0 | 3 | 2 | 0 | 3 | 0 | 1 | 4 | 5 | 13 | 9 | 8 | 2 | 0 | 9 | 9 | 3 | 5 | 6 | 2 | 5 | 2 | 0 | 5 | 11 | 8 | 7 | 9 | 131 |
| | h | 0 | 0 | 0 | 0 | 0 | 0 | 0 | 1 | 10 | 12 | 5 | 1 | 3 | 3 | 0 | 7 | 2 | 6 | 10 | 3 | 1 | 5 | 0 | 4 | 10 | 11 | 13 | 15 | 122 |
| | ḥ | 0 | 0 | 0 | 0 | 0 | 0 | 8 | 7 | 10 | 17 | 11 | 12 | 9 | 5 | 9 | 8 | 9 | 5 | 9 | 4 | 3 | 7 | 4 | 9 | 10 | 11 | 16 | 13 | 196 |
| | ʕ | 0 | 3 | 0 | 0 | 0 | 0 | 10 | 8 | 9 | 15 | 12 | 12 | 5 | 6 | 9 | 9 | 8 | 9 | 7 | 9 | 6 | 7 | 2 | 8 | 12 | 11 | 15 | 14 | 206 |
| | x | 0 | 0 | 0 | 0 | 0 | 0 | 0 | 0 | 1 | 15 | 13 | 8 | 9 | 6 | 7 | 7 | 7 | 4 | 9 | 8 | 1 | 3 | 0 | 8 | 11 | 9 | 11 | 7 | 144 |
| | ɣ | 0 | 1 | 0 | 0 | 0 | 0 | 0 | 0 | 0 | 13 | 11 | 7 | 4 | 7 | 5 | 3 | 3 | 2 | 5 | 6 | 4 | 3 | 0 | 6 | 10 | 13 | 7 | 12 | 122 |
| | q | 1 | 3 | 6 | 11 | 0 | 0 | 0 | 0 | 1 | 18 | 15 | 11 | 8 | 5 | 7 | 0 | 8 | 4 | 9 | 7 | 2 | 6 | 0 | 10 | 12 | 12 | 14 | 10 | 180 |
| | k | 3 | 5 | 4 | 5 | 0 | 0 | 0 | 0 | 0 | 13 | 11 | 8 | 6 | 0 | 10 | 2 | 0 | 6 | 9 | 0 | 4 | 2 | 4 | 7 | 11 | 10 | 15 | 6 | 141 |
| | g | 3 | 7 | 6 | 5 | 0 | 0 | 0 | 0 | 0 | 16 | 9 | 10 | 6 | 0 | 6 | 8 | 1 | 0 | 10 | 0 | 5 | 7 | 1 | 6 | 9 | 8 | 13 | 6 | 142 |
| | r | 7 | 9 | 7 | 10 | 4 | 7 | 13 | 10 | 13 | 0 | 0 | 5 | 9 | 7 | 10 | 9 | 5 | 8 | 12 | 5 | 6 | 2 | 0 | 13 | 15 | 12 | 14 | 16 | 228 |
| | l | 3 | 8 | 12 | 8 | 5 | 6 | 11 | 9 | 8 | 0 | 0 | 0 | 1 | 0 | 4 | 6 | 3 | 3 | 2 | 7 | 4 | 2 | 2 | 10 | 14 | 8 | 16 | 8 | 160 |
| | n | 6 | 14 | 10 | 12 | 10 | 11 | 21 | 15 | 15 | 0 | 0 | 0 | 18 | 9 | 13 | 12 | 10 | 11 | 11 | 8 | 2 | 1 | 3 | 16 | 20 | 9 | 18 | 8 | 283 |
| | š | 4 | 7 | 8 | 7 | 5 | 5 | 7 | 8 | 6 | 15 | 2 | 8 | 0 | 0 | 1 | 2 | 3 | 4 | 6 | 5 | 0 | 4 | 3 | 7 | 11 | 9 | 14 | 12 | 163 |
| | ḍ | 3 | 4 | 4 | 3 | 1 | 3 | 0 | 0 | 4 | 10 | 2 | 5 | 0 | 0 | 0 | 0 | 0 | 0 | 1 | 0 | 0 | 0 | 0 | 3 | 10 | 5 | 9 | 8 | 75 |
| | s | 5 | 8 | 12 | 8 | 9 | 1 | 6 | 6 | 10 | 12 | 17 | 14 | 0 | 0 | 0 | 0 | 0 | 4 | 10 | 5 | 0 | 0 | 0 | 13 | 14 | 12 | 14 | 8 | 188 |
| | z | 1 | 5 | 4 | 7 | 2 | 2 | 1 | 4 | 4 | 7 | 6 | 8 | 0 | 0 | 0 | 0 | 0 | 0 | 0 | 0 | 0 | 0 | 0 | 4 | 7 | 7 | 6 | 9 | 84 |
| | ṣ | 3 | 6 | 7 | 6 | 4 | 3 | 4 | 2 | 0 | 9 | 13 | 6 | 0 | 0 | 0 | 0 | 0 | 0 | 11 | 0 | 0 | 0 | 0 | 8 | 8 | 8 | 14 | 8 | 120 |
| | t | 2 | 1 | 1 | 2 | 2 | 0 | 1 | 0 | 1 | 9 | 6 | 3 | 0 | 0 | 1 | 0 | 0 | 0 | 0 | 0 | 0 | 0 | 0 | 4 | 5 | 3 | 5 | 4 | 50 |
| | d | 4 | 6 | 6 | 8 | 3 | 3 | 3 | 2 | 6 | 11 | 12 | 6 | 0 | 0 | 4 | 0 | 0 | 0 | 0 | 0 | 2 | 0 | 0 | 7 | 10 | 9 | 13 | 8 | 123 |
| | ṭ | 0 | 3 | 6 | 2 | 2 | 3 | 0 | 0 | 0 | 12 | 10 | 7 | 1 | 0 | 1 | 0 | 0 | 0 | 0 | 0 | 0 | 0 | 0 | 8 | 8 | 9 | 10 | 8 | 90 |
| | ṯ | 2 | 0 | 0 | 2 | 1 | 3 | 3 | 1 | 2 | 5 | 6 | 2 | 0 | 0 | 0 | 0 | 0 | 0 | 1 | 1 | 0 | 0 | 0 | 4 | 6 | 5 | 6 | 0 | 50 |
| | ḏ | 6 | 3 | 0 | 4 | 1 | 0 | 1 | 2 | 0 | 9 | 4 | 2 | 0 | 0 | 0 | 0 | 0 | 0 | 0 | 0 | 0 | 0 | 0 | 2 | 4 | 4 | 6 | 6 | 54 |
| | ṯ̣ | 1 | 1 | 0 | 1 | 0 | 0 | 0 | 0 | 0 | 3 | 4 | 1 | 0 | 0 | 0 | 0 | 0 | 0 | 0 | 0 | 0 | 0 | 0 | 1 | 0 | 2 | 1 | 0 | 15 |
| | f | 8 | 5 | 9 | 4 | 5 | 4 | 8 | 4 | 7 | 21 | 11 | 7 | 7 | 6 | 8 | 2 | 7 | 12 | 8 | 6 | 4 | 1 | 2 | 0 | 0 | 0 | 13 | 12 | 181 |
| | b | 2 | 9 | 4 | 7 | 7 | 6 | 5 | 5 | 5 | 15 | 11 | 3 | 4 | 2 | 7 | 7 | 4 | 5 | 8 | 9 | 3 | 6 | 1 | 0 | 0 | 0 | 11 | 6 | 152 |
| | m | 3 | 6 | 10 | 10 | 5 | 5 | 4 | 6 | 5 | 17 | 16 | 5 | 7 | 5 | 8 | 8 | 9 | 5 | 4 | 7 | 3 | 3 | 0 | 0 | 0 | 0 | 10 | 10 | 171 |
| | w | 4 | 9 | 5 | 8 | 7 | 4 | 11 | 13 | 11 | 14 | 13 | 3 | 8 | 7 | 9 | 8 | 8 | 4 | 8 | 4 | 5 | 3 | 3 | 6 | 9 | 4 | 0 | 0 | 188 |
| | y | 1 | 1 | 0 | 0 | 0 | 0 | 2 | 0 | 0 | 0 | 0 | 1 | 1 | 0 | 1 | 1 | 0 | 2 | 0 | 1 | 0 | 0 | 0 | 1 | 2 | 2 | 0 | 0 | 16 |
| | | 72 | 127 | 123 | 130 | 76 | 66 | 120 | 107 | 133 | 301 | 229 | 163 | 108 | 68 | 129 | 108 | 90 | 99 | 156 | 97 | 60 | 64 | 25 | 170 | 239 | 201 | 291 | 223 | |

*Table 2*

Arabic I–III

| | III | ʔ | h | ḥ | ʕ | x | ɣ | q | k | g | r | l | n | š | ḍ | s | z | ṣ | t | d | ṭ | ṯ | ḏ | ṯ̣ | f | b | m | w | y | |
|---|---|---|---|---|---|---|---|---|---|---|---|---|---|---|---|---|---|---|---|---|---|---|---|---|---|---|---|---|---|---|
| I | ʔ | 0 | 6 | 1 | 0 | 2 | 0 | 6 | 5 | 3 | 14 | 11 | 10 | 1 | 3 | 3 | 1 | 0 | 2 | 9 | 4 | 3 | 1 | 0 | 8 | 10 | 10 | 7 | 11 | 131 |
| | h | 10 | 1 | 0 | 6 | 0 | 0 | 2 | 3 | 7 | 12 | 8 | 4 | 5 | 3 | 5 | 2 | 0 | 7 | 6 | 2 | 3 | 1 | 0 | 4 | 11 | 9 | 5 | 6 | 122 |
| | ḥ | 7 | 0 | 1 | 0 | 0 | 0 | 11 | 10 | 6 | 17 | 11 | 11 | 6 | 4 | 7 | 7 | 4 | 2 | 10 | 4 | 4 | 3 | 2 | 12 | 13 | 13 | 17 | 14 | 196 |
| | ʕ | 1 | 5 | 0 | 0 | 0 | 0 | 12 | 5 | 9 | 18 | 17 | 13 | 5 | 3 | 9 | 5 | 4 | 2 | 13 | 5 | 4 | 1 | 0 | 15 | 15 | 16 | 16 | 13 | 206 |
| | x | 5 | 0 | 0 | 7 | 0 | 0 | 7 | 0 | 3 | 15 | 13 | 8 | 5 | 2 | 5 | 3 | 6 | 5 | 6 | 5 | 2 | 0 | 0 | 10 | 10 | 11 | 7 | 9 | 144 |
| | ɣ | 0 | 0 | 0 | 0 | 1 | 0 | 5 | 0 | 2 | 10 | 9 | 6 | 2 | 4 | 5 | 2 | 4 | 3 | 4 | 6 | 5 | 1 | 3 | 7 | 7 | 8 | 14 | 14 | 122 |
| | q | 6 | 1 | 10 | 11 | 2 | 0 | 1 | 0 | 0 | 15 | 9 | 8 | 4 | 5 | 9 | 5 | 8 | 5 | 11 | 10 | 3 | 1 | 2 | 9 | 14 | 14 | 7 | 10 | 180 |
| | k | 8 | 2 | 9 | 4 | 1 | 0 | 1 | 1 | 1 | 11 | 8 | 7 | 6 | 0 | 6 | 3 | 0 | 9 | 11 | 1 | 5 | 2 | 1 | 10 | 14 | 8 | 5 | 7 | 141 |
| | g | 8 | 3 | 6 | 7 | 0 | 0 | 1 | 0 | 0 | 15 | 11 | 5 | 7 | 2 | 5 | 6 | 1 | 0 | 11 | 0 | 2 | 3 | 2 | 11 | 11 | 10 | 8 | 7 | 142 |
| | r | 10 | 2 | 12 | 12 | 5 | 6 | 11 | 4 | 3 | 1 | 15 | 13 | 4 | 7 | 8 | 4 | 5 | 3 | 14 | 4 | 8 | 2 | 1 | 12 | 16 | 18 | 16 | 12 | 228 |
| | l | 11 | 0 | 8 | 7 | 3 | 2 | 9 | 4 | 9 | 1 | 0 | 9 | 4 | 0 | 6 | 4 | 4 | 6 | 7 | 5 | 10 | 3 | 4 | 7 | 12 | 13 | 4 | 8 | 160 |
| | n | 11 | 5 | 16 | 9 | 8 | 2 | 9 | 6 | 11 | 24 | 17 | 2 | 13 | 7 | 13 | 9 | 6 | 14 | 9 | 8 | 8 | 4 | 2 | 11 | 18 | 13 | 14 | 14 | 283 |
| | š | 5 | 6 | 5 | 9 | 5 | 0 | 9 | 4 | 3 | 18 | 8 | 7 | 1 | 0 | 5 | 1 | 4 | 3 | 5 | 6 | 2 | 4 | 1 | 7 | 14 | 9 | 15 | 7 | 163 |
| | ḍ | 4 | 0 | 4 | 7 | 1 | 0 | 1 | 2 | 2 | 8 | 4 | 6 | 0 | 0 | 1 | 2 | 0 | 0 | 3 | 3 | 2 | 0 | 0 | 4 | 3 | 6 | 6 | 6 | 75 |
| | s | 5 | 3 | 10 | 9 | 4 | 3 | 8 | 7 | 8 | 18 | 14 | 8 | 0 | 0 | 4 | 0 | 0 | 7 | 11 | 9 | 0 | 0 | 0 | 13 | 12 | 11 | 12 | 12 | 188 |
| | z | 2 | 0 | 2 | 2 | 4 | 2 | 9 | 0 | 4 | 13 | 9 | 5 | 0 | 0 | 0 | 0 | 0 | 2 | 5 | 0 | 0 | 0 | 0 | 5 | 4 | 8 | 4 | 4 | 84 |
| | ṣ | 2 | 1 | 8 | 10 | 5 | 5 | 4 | 4 | 0 | 11 | 7 | 5 | 0 | 0 | 0 | 0 | 1 | 3 | 8 | 0 | 0 | 0 | 0 | 8 | 10 | 9 | 10 | 9 | 120 |
| | t | 1 | 4 | 3 | 4 | 1 | 0 | 2 | 2 | 0 | 6 | 3 | 3 | 0 | 0 | 3 | 0 | 0 | 0 | 1 | 0 | 1 | 0 | 0 | 3 | 5 | 6 | 1 | 1 | 50 |
| | d | 4 | 2 | 2 | 7 | 3 | 2 | 6 | 5 | 7 | 14 | 10 | 10 | 1 | 1 | 6 | 0 | 2 | 0 | 3 | 0 | 3 | 0 | 0 | 5 | 4 | 8 | 8 | 10 | 123 |
| | ṭ | 3 | 0 | 7 | 5 | 4 | 0 | 5 | 0 | 0 | 6 | 5 | 6 | 3 | 0 | 5 | 2 | 0 | 0 | 2 | 1 | 1 | 0 | 0 | 6 | 5 | 5 | 9 | 10 | 90 |
| | ṯ | 1 | 0 | 0 | 0 | 0 | 0 | 0 | 0 | 4 | 7 | 7 | 5 | 0 | 0 | 0 | 0 | 0 | 1 | 2 | 3 | 1 | 0 | 0 | 1 | 6 | 4 | 4 | 4 | 50 |
| | ḏ | 2 | 0 | 2 | 2 | 0 | 0 | 3 | 0 | 0 | 9 | 6 | 7 | 0 | 0 | 0 | 0 | 0 | 0 | 1 | 0 | 0 | 0 | 0 | 6 | 7 | 3 | 2 | 4 | 54 |
| | ṯ̣ | 1 | 0 | 0 | 1 | 0 | 0 | 0 | 0 | 0 | 4 | 1 | 2 | 0 | 0 | 0 | 0 | 0 | 0 | 0 | 0 | 0 | 0 | 0 | 3 | 1 | 1 | 0 | 1 | 15 |
| | f | 8 | 6 | 13 | 9 | 10 | 3 | 6 | 5 | 7 | 14 | 12 | 4 | 5 | 4 | 6 | 3 | 6 | 6 | 10 | 1 | 3 | 3 | 3 | 1 | 0 | 11 | 12 | 10 | 181 |
| | b | 8 | 4 | 6 | 10 | 4 | 2 | 13 | 2 | 4 | 20 | 15 | 6 | 5 | 4 | 4 | 2 | 3 | 6 | 6 | 3 | 4 | 1 | 1 | 0 | 1 | 5 | 8 | 5 | 152 |
| | m | 6 | 1 | 12 | 8 | 5 | 2 | 7 | 3 | 10 | 16 | 12 | 11 | 4 | 5 | 6 | 3 | 4 | 8 | 12 | 8 | 7 | 2 | 0 | 0 | 0 | 0 | 9 | 10 | 171 |
| | w | 14 | 2 | 9 | 10 | 4 | 2 | 9 | 5 | 5 | 17 | 7 | 4 | 5 | 3 | 4 | 6 | 3 | 5 | 16 | 3 | 5 | 1 | 2 | 7 | 15 | 11 | 0 | 14 | 188 |
| | y | 0 | 0 | 0 | 1 | 1 | 0 | 0 | 1 | 0 | 1 | 0 | 3 | 0 | 0 | 2 | 0 | 0 | 1 | 0 | 0 | 0 | 0 | 1 | 0 | 2 | 3 | 0 | 0 | 16 |
| | | 143 | 54 | 146 | 157 | 73 | 31 | 157 | 78 | 108 | 335 | 249 | 188 | 86 | 57 | 127 | 70 | 65 | 100 | 196 | 91 | 86 | 33 | 25 | 185 | 240 | 243 | 220 | 232 | |

*Table 3*

Arabic II–III

| | III | ʔ | h | ḥ | ʕ | x | ɣ | q | k | g | r | l | n | š | ḍ | s | z | ṣ | t | d | ṭ | ṯ | ḏ | ṯ̣ | f | b | m | w | y | |
|---|---|---|---|---|---|---|---|---|---|---|---|---|---|---|---|---|---|---|---|---|---|---|---|---|---|---|---|---|---|---|
| II | ʔ | 0 | 0 | 0 | 0 | 0 | 0 | 0 | 2 | 2 | 11 | 6 | 5 | 2 | 0 | 4 | 0 | 0 | 2 | 7 | 0 | 1 | 0 | 0 | 3 | 10 | 8 | 3 | 6 | 72 |
| | h | 3 | 3 | 0 | 0 | 0 | 0 | 6 | 2 | 7 | 16 | 11 | 7 | 4 | 2 | 1 | 2 | 0 | 4 | 11 | 2 | 1 | 0 | 1 | 2 | 13 | 12 | 11 | 6 | 127 |
| | ḥ | 0 | 0 | 13 | 0 | 0 | 0 | 4 | 1 | 4 | 6 | 12 | 7 | 3 | 3 | 3 | 1 | 2 | 5 | 5 | 3 | 2 | 1 | 2 | 8 | 7 | 12 | 10 | 9 | 123 |
| | ʕ | 0 | 0 | 0 | 4 | 0 | 0 | 5 | 4 | 6 | 12 | 9 | 6 | 2 | 2 | 4 | 2 | 1 | 3 | 8 | 3 | 7 | 0 | 3 | 8 | 15 | 6 | 11 | 9 | 130 |
| | x | 0 | 0 | 0 | 2 | 8 | 0 | 1 | 0 | 2 | 10 | 4 | 4 | 1 | 1 | 3 | 1 | 4 | 4 | 2 | 3 | 0 | 2 | 0 | 2 | 5 | 9 | 5 | 3 | 76 |
| | ɣ | 0 | 0 | 0 | 0 | 0 | 0 | 0 | 0 | 0 | 8 | 7 | 1 | 2 | 2 | 1 | 2 | 2 | 1 | 4 | 2 | 4 | 0 | 0 | 1 | 7 | 8 | 8 | 6 | 66 |
| | q | 3 | 2 | 6 | 7 | 1 | 0 | 10 | 0 | 0 | 10 | 10 | 5 | 3 | 1 | 2 | 1 | 6 | 3 | 6 | 5 | 2 | 3 | 1 | 6 | 9 | 6 | 6 | 6 | 120 |
| | k | 6 | 1 | 3 | 3 | 0 | 0 | 0 | 9 | 0 | 12 | 10 | 5 | 2 | 1 | 6 | 5 | 1 | 4 | 8 | 0 | 4 | 0 | 1 | 4 | 4 | 9 | 5 | 4 | 107 |
| | g | 6 | 2 | 5 | 8 | 0 | 0 | 0 | 0 | 14 | 17 | 12 | 10 | 1 | 0 | 8 | 5 | 0 | 0 | 6 | 0 | 1 | 2 | 0 | 6 | 8 | 10 | 9 | 3 | 133 |
| | r | 11 | 6 | 13 | 16 | 6 | 2 | 15 | 9 | 13 | 23 | 1 | 6 | 13 | 8 | 16 | 7 | 6 | 6 | 19 | 10 | 8 | 1 | 1 | 15 | 21 | 17 | 12 | 20 | 301 |
| | l | 5 | 5 | 9 | 13 | 5 | 4 | 15 | 9 | 11 | 0 | 22 | 1 | 1 | 1 | 13 | 0 | 4 | 10 | 10 | 8 | 5 | 2 | 1 | 16 | 15 | 15 | 17 | 12 | 229 |
| | n | 11 | 2 | 6 | 7 | 6 | 0 | 12 | 3 | 3 | 3 | 0 | 24 | 1 | 0 | 5 | 5 | 1 | 4 | 6 | 3 | 3 | 1 | 1 | 10 | 10 | 8 | 11 | 17 | 163 |
| | š | 4 | 0 | 5 | 7 | 1 | 1 | 6 | 3 | 3 | 11 | 3 | 3 | 14 | 0 | 0 | 1 | 0 | 0 | 4 | 4 | 0 | 0 | 0 | 6 | 8 | 9 | 9 | 6 | 108 |
| | ḍ | 3 | 1 | 5 | 4 | 4 | 1 | 0 | 0 | 1 | 6 | 4 | 2 | 0 | 10 | 0 | 0 | 0 | 0 | 3 | 0 | 0 | 0 | 0 | 3 | 8 | 3 | 6 | 4 | 68 |
| | s | 8 | 0 | 6 | 6 | 5 | 1 | 5 | 4 | 2 | 12 | 9 | 5 | 0 | 0 | 11 | 0 | 0 | 0 | 8 | 3 | 0 | 0 | 0 | 6 | 8 | 11 | 12 | 7 | 129 |
| | z | 6 | 1 | 3 | 6 | 1 | 3 | 10 | 2 | 3 | 12 | 8 | 4 | 0 | 0 | 0 | 13 | 0 | 0 | 0 | 0 | 0 | 0 | 0 | 4 | 8 | 9 | 7 | 8 | 108 |
| | ṣ | 2 | 0 | 3 | 4 | 1 | 0 | 2 | 1 | 0 | 10 | 9 | 3 | 0 | 0 | 0 | 0 | 12 | 2 | 8 | 0 | 0 | 0 | 0 | 7 | 9 | 5 | 5 | 7 | 90 |
| | t | 6 | 2 | 5 | 4 | 2 | 0 | 4 | 6 | 2 | 10 | 7 | 6 | 2 | 0 | 0 | 0 | 0 | 13 | 3 | 0 | 0 | 0 | 0 | 4 | 4 | 10 | 6 | 3 | 99 |
| | d | 7 | 3 | 9 | 8 | 3 | 4 | 5 | 0 | 5 | 15 | 5 | 8 | 2 | 1 | 8 | 0 | 0 | 0 | 19 | 0 | 2 | 0 | 0 | 9 | 6 | 12 | 12 | 13 | 156 |
| | ṭ | 8 | 0 | 6 | 6 | 2 | 0 | 2 | 0 | 0 | 11 | 8 | 7 | 2 | 0 | 4 | 0 | 0 | 0 | 0 | 11 | 2 | 0 | 0 | 6 | 8 | 6 | 6 | 2 | 97 |
| | ṯ | 5 | 0 | 0 | 0 | 0 | 1 | 2 | 0 | 2 | 10 | 3 | 2 | 0 | 0 | 0 | 0 | 0 | 0 | 2 | 0 | 15 | 0 | 0 | 2 | 1 | 5 | 5 | 5 | 60 |
| | ḏ | 3 | 0 | 2 | 3 | 1 | 0 | 2 | 0 | 0 | 10 | 5 | 2 | 0 | 0 | 0 | 0 | 0 | 0 | 0 | 0 | 0 | 11 | 0 | 5 | 5 | 3 | 5 | 7 | 64 |
| | ṯ̣ | 0 | 0 | 0 | 1 | 0 | 0 | 0 | 0 | 0 | 4 | 2 | 0 | 0 | 0 | 0 | 0 | 0 | 0 | 0 | 0 | 0 | 0 | 7 | 3 | 2 | 3 | 1 | 2 | 25 |
| | f | 7 | 4 | 7 | 7 | 4 | 1 | 11 | 2 | 3 | 19 | 13 | 9 | 2 | 4 | 2 | 3 | 3 | 7 | 7 | 2 | 4 | 1 | 2 | 19 | 0 | 0 | 15 | 12 | 170 |
| | b | 10 | 4 | 10 | 9 | 6 | 5 | 12 | 6 | 5 | 20 | 17 | 14 | 7 | 4 | 8 | 3 | 5 | 9 | 8 | 12 | 10 | 3 | 0 | 0 | 22 | 1 | 15 | 14 | 239 |
| | m | 7 | 2 | 7 | 10 | 5 | 2 | 5 | 4 | 5 | 20 | 17 | 13 | 7 | 4 | 10 | 9 | 4 | 9 | 14 | 4 | 3 | 0 | 1 | 0 | 0 | 23 | 5 | 11 | 201 |
| | w | 11 | 9 | 12 | 12 | 7 | 4 | 14 | 7 | 11 | 21 | 19 | 14 | 8 | 6 | 10 | 7 | 8 | 9 | 13 | 7 | 5 | 6 | 1 | 16 | 16 | 12 | 3 | 23 | 291 |
| | y | 11 | 7 | 11 | 10 | 5 | 2 | 9 | 4 | 4 | 16 | 16 | 15 | 7 | 7 | 8 | 3 | 6 | 5 | 15 | 9 | 7 | 0 | 3 | 14 | 11 | 11 | 0 | 7 | 223 |
| | | 143 | 54 | 146 | 157 | 73 | 31 | 157 | 78 | 108 | 335 | 249 | 188 | 86 | 57 | 127 | 70 | 65 | 100 | 196 | 91 | 86 | 33 | 25 | 185 | 240 | 243 | 220 | 232 | |

Semitic etymological dictionary, one of the great *desiderata* of Semitic studies, the conclusions must be viewed merely as first approximations. I believe, however, that they are correct in all essential matters.

The study is concerned chiefly with verbal roots. In Semitic languages, substantives are, in general, formed from the same set of root morphemes as verbs. There are a few morphemes, some of them biconsonantal, which function as substantives only or from which there are only rare denominative verb formations. These substantival morphemes, which often violate conspicuously the rules of patterning for verbal morphemes, are considered where relevant to the discussion.

It is safe to conclude that there are no triconsonantal verbal roots in Proto-Semitic with identical first and second consonants. A glance at Table 1, with its diagonal line of zeroes, will show that there are no instances in Arabic. There is the noun *dadan* 'plaything' (probably a nursery word) but this is a purely nominal root. There are a few verbs in Assyrian which violate the rule, but these forms have no correspondences outside of Assyrian. Ethiopic has a few instances of verb roots with identical initial and second consonants but these, it is usually assumed, result from quadriconsonantal forms involving reduplication of a biconsonantal nucleus, e.g. Ethiopic *ssl* 'to leave' < *slsl*. The six instances of this type in Ethiopic find no correspondences in other Semitic languages. Hebrew has a single instance *ddh*, a Piel formation meaning 'drive away'.

There is a less rigid exclusion of identical consonants in the first and third positions. In Arabic there are 20 instances. The total expected frequency for roots with identical first and third roots is 154.4 ± 12.4.[7] The number of occurrences are significantly fewer than might be expected. A small number of instances are also found in other Semitic languages, e.g. 14 in Syriac, 9 in Hebrew, 2 in Assyrian. However there is only one certain instance of a Proto-Semitic verbal root of this form, *ntn* 'to give'. It is therefore striking that

C. Conti Rossini, *Chrestomathia Arabica Meridionalis Epigraphica* (Rome, 1931); C. H. Gordon, *Ugaritic Handbook* (Rome, 1947); C. F. Dillman, *Lexicon Linguae Ethiopicae* (Leipzig, 1865); W. Leslau, *Lexicon Soqotri* (Paris, 1938).

[7]The first figure given is the expected frequency on the basis of the formula CR/n mentioned above. The number which follows, preceded by ±, is the size of one standard error ($\sigma$) based on the formula $\sqrt{e - (e^2/n)}$ where e indicates the expected frequency, based on the above formula, and n is the total number of roots, 3775. The number in parentheses gives the number of standard errors of the observed frequency.

Some idea of the significance of the standard deviation may be gathered from the following: 1 S.E. indicates 31.74% (that is slightly less than one chance in three) that the deviation is due to chance; 2 S.E. gives 4.56%; 3 S.E.—0.27%; 4 S.E.—0.0063%; 5 S.E.—0.000057%. Most tables do not give values for over 3.5 S.E. at which points the probability of chance is practically infinitesimal.

so many Semitic substantival roots have identical first and third consonants. Among common Semitic substantives of this pattern are: **šmš* 'sun', **bwb* 'door, gate', **ṯlṯ* 'three', **nwn* 'fish', **tḥt* 'underneath', **lyl* 'might', **šrš* 'root'.

It has been seen that identity in the second and third position, the so-called geminate verb type, is a standard Semitic formation. Such forms abound in all the Semitic languages and in numerous instances they can be referred to Proto-Semitic originals.

The first articulatory position to be considered is that of the laryngal or glottal sounds of which there are assumed to be two, *ʔ and **h*, in Proto-Semitic. The evidence adduced in this study will indicate that the laryngal and the pharyngal series which is next forward to it in articulatory position, behave in the same fashion and should be considered as a single class of consonants on the basis of the patterning displayed in the combinations considered here. There is no doubt, of course, that the two articulatory positions are distinct in existing Semitic languages and, no doubt, in Proto-Semitic likewise.

Regarding the laryngals in Arabic, two of the six possible types of combinations involving ʔ and *h* do not occur, roots with ʔ in the second and *h* in the third position and those with *h* in the first position and ʔ in the second position. Since only 1.0 ± 1.0 (− 1.0 S.D.) roots are expected in the first instance, and 2.3 ± 1.5 (− 1.5 S.D.) in the second, these zeroes are quite without significance. There is a total of 22 instances of roots in Arabic containing both ʔ and *h* in comparison with an over-all expectancy of 19.0 ± 4.4 (+ 0.7 S.D.). We are therefore justified in concluding that ʔ and *h* do not occur any less frequently together in the same root than would be expected on a chance basis. In other words, the rule regarding the non-occurrence of consonants with the same point of articulation does not hold in this instance in Arabic. However, in other Semitic languages, examples of roots involving both laryngals are quite rare, 4 in Hebrew, 1 in Ethiopic, 3 in Syriac. There is only one certain instance of a Proto-Semitic verbal root containing two laryngeals, **hnʔ* 'to be agreeable, sweet, etc.'. A possible Proto-Semitic root is *hmʔ*, depending upon whether one considers plausible the connection in meaning between Arabic 'to tear or wear out a garment' and Syriac 'disregard, neglect'. The root *ʔhb* 'to love' attested from Hebrew and Ugaritic only will be assigned to Proto-Semitic by those who deny the Canaanite status of Ugaritic. Another root *hdʔ* 'to be tranquil' is only known from South Semitic (Arabic and Ethiopic). **ʔhl* 'to dwell' is clearly a denominative from the word for 'tent' (Heb. *ʔóhɛl*). There is likewise the nominal morpheme **ʔlh*, **ʔl* 'God'. Our conclusion then, is that for Proto-Semitic there is only one certain, and two other possible verb root morphemes containing both laryngals. By and large, this state of affairs continues in Semitic languages other than Arabic. In Arabic, however, a number of presumably recent formations has obscured the older pattern.

The next series of consonants in respect to forwardness of articulation are the voiced pharyngal ʕ and the unvoiced pharyngal *ḥ*. Here the general rule clearly holds. There is only one recorded instance in our tables for Arabic whereas the expected frequency for all combinations is 39.7 ± 6.3 (−6.1 S.D.). Instances are rare or non-existent in other Semitic languages and there is no verbal or nominal root which can be plausibly reconstructed for Proto-Semitic which contains both ʕ and *ḥ*.

It was stated above that, with reference to the functioning of the patterns under consideration here, the laryngals and pharyngals behaved as though they were members of the same articulatory series. Part of the evidence for this consists in the fact that laryngals and pharyngals tend not to occur together in the same verb roots. In Arabic there are no instances of verbal roots with laryngals and pharyngals in the second and third position. This is highly significant in view of the expected frequency of 29.2 ± 5.4 (−5.4 S.D.). The total numbers of Arabic verb roots containing both a laryngal and pharyngal is 23 and this is likewise significantly small when compared with the expected frequency of 108.3 ± 10.4 (−8.2 S.D.). There is thus definite evidence of patterning in this direction. In other Semitic languages there is a general absence of laryngals and pharyngals in positions two and three. In other positions such roots are few in number. Hebrew, for example, has a total of eight, with none in the second and third positions, Ethiopic four, of which one is in the second and third position. There are, however, a few instances of roots with both laryngals and pharyngals which are no doubt Proto-Semitic. In positions one and two, we have * *ʕhr* 'be lustful' and * *ʕhd*, Arabic 'be heedful, admonish', Syriac 'recount, remember' as well as the substantival *ʔḥd* 'one'; in positions one and three there are * *ḥṭʔ* 'be sinful, err' and * *ʔnḥ* 'groan'. There are no instances of Proto-Semitic verbal roots with pharyngal and laryngal in the second and third position. There are possibly too few examples to draw conclusions concerning a special tendency of *ḥ* to occur with ʔ, and ʕ to occur with *h* in Proto-Semitic. In the individual languages, however, this phenomenon is quite marked. For example, of the 23 Arabic instances of roots containing a pharyngal or laryngal, 22 conform to this pattern, while all of the 12 Hebrew instances are of this kind, and likewise the 4 Ethiopic. In Syriac, of the six instances not involving final ʔ, five conform. Those with final ʔ are not relevant because there has been coalescence here with verbs containing third radical *w* and *y* and most of the Syriac instances are from forms without original ʔ.[8]

[8] If, following Cantineau, we assume (entirely on the basis of pattern since there is no phonetic evidence to demonstrate it) that ʔ is the voiced counterpart of *h*, it will be noticed that it is

The next set of consonants to be considered are the pair *x* and *ɣ* which I shall call post-velar without meaning to imply anything precise in regard to their point of articulation. The Arab grammarians describe their articulation as farther back than the velars *k*, *g*, and *q*. That they are not merely fricatives in the same articulatory position as the velar stops but are pronounced farther back is shown by their tendency almost everywhere in Semitic to become pharyngals. The present evidence indicates that they pattern in a manner different from the velar stops.

In Arabic, there is a single instance of a root containing two post-velar consonants. The expected frequency is 10.4 ± 3.2 (±2.9 S.D.), so that the occurrence of only a single case is quite significant. Examples of roots of this type in other Semitic languages are extremely rare. It may be confidently concluded that no roots containing two post-velar consonants existed in Proto-Semitic.

The post-velars display a marked tendency not to occur both with consonants in the positions immediately to the back, the pharyngals *ḥ* and *ʕ* and laryngals *ʔ* and *h* and the velars *k*, *g*, *q* to the front. In Arabic there are no roots containing a post-velar and a pharyngal in the first and second position. There are seven in positions one and three and two in positions two and three. As usual, the patterning is least rigid in positions one and three. In all instances we have a *x* followed by an *ʕ*.[9] The total number of occurrences, 9, is significantly small since the expected frequency is 91.1 ± 9.5 (−8.6 S.D.). On the other hand, the 7 instances of roots with initial *x* and final *ʕ* are approximately what would be expected, the expected frequency here being 5.95 ± 2.4 (+0.4 S.D.). In Hebrew *x* has become *ḥ* and *ɣ* has coalesced with *ʕ*. The absence of roots in Hebrew with two pharyngals, noted above in the course of the discussion of pharyngal consonants, is therefore also proof of the non-existence of roots containing both a post-velar and a pharyngal. In Syriac, the same consolidation of the post-velar with the pharyngals has taken place. There are a few instances of roots with pharyngals in the first and third positions in Syriac but it is uncertain whether we have to do with original pharyngals or post-velars which have become pharyngals, because of the absence of cognates from other languages. In Ethiopic *x* remains distinct while *ɣ* becomes *ʕ*. There is a root *xšʕ*, 'to be silent' which is possibly cognate with Arabic *xšʕ* 'to be lowly, submissive, to fear'. If so, the root is still only attested as South Semitic, and need not go back to Proto-Semitic. There are no roots containing both a post-velar and a pharyngal which can be demonstrated to be Proto-Semitic.

---

precisely the combination of a voiced consonant in one position with the unvoiced in the other that occurs.

[9] See note 8 above.

It is a phase of the similar functioning of pharyngal and laryngal consonants, mentioned above, that just as the pharyngals do not occur with the post-velar, likewise the laryngals display a strong tendency not to occur with consonants of the post-velar series. In Arabic, the expected number of roots containing a laryngal and a post-velar is 57 ± 7.5. Actually only 11 instances are found (−6.1 S.D.). There are no examples in II–III where the expected frequency is 12.7 ± 3.5 (−3.6 S.D.). In I–III, however, the patterning is, as usual, weakest with 7 examples of the expected 20.8 ± 4.6 (−2.9 S.D.). Of the total of 11 examples, 10 involve *ʔ* and *x*, while the remaining one contains *ɣ* and *h*.[10] All of the few Proto-Semitic instances involve *ʔ* and *x* only. These are the verbal roots **xbʔ* 'withdraw, hide'; *xṭʔ* 'err, sin'; *ʔxḏ* 'take, seize'; **ʔnx* 'sigh, groan'. There are also the substantive roots *ʔxr* 'other'; *ʔrx* 'path, way' (from which denominative verbs in Northwest Semitic) and **ʔx(w)* 'brother'.

The post-velars likewise tend not to occur with the velar stops *k*, *g*, and *q* which form the next series of consonants toward the front of the mouth. In Arabic there is one such root in I–II, four in II–III, and twenty in I–III. For this latter position the expected frequency is 35.1 ± 5.9 (−2.6 S.D.) so that, as happens frequently, the pattern tends not to hold in this respect. The general coalescence of the post-velars with the pharyngals does not permit an effective estimate of the frequency of roots containing a post-velar and a laryngal in languages other than Arabic. In Ethiopic, where the post-velar *x* remains distinct from the pharyngal *ḥ*, there are five roots containing *x* and a velar stop. The probable Proto-Semitic instances in four of the five instances are in the I–III position. They are **xrq* 'perforate, cut'; **xlq* 'apportion, allot'; **xnq* 'strangle' and **ɣng* 'be coquettish, of dainty habits'. The remaining instance is **nqx*, 'crack, perforate'.

The velar stops, as we have just seen, occur only rarely with the post-velar spirants. Roots containing two velar stops are extremely rare in Semitic languages and probably never existed in Proto-Semitic. In Arabic, I have recorded only four examples, in Hebrew none, in Ethiopic three.

The four series mentioned thus far, laryngals, pharyngals, post-velars, and velars occur freely with all consonants farther forward in their point of articulation. On the other hand, there are rules of non-occurrence among the series themselves, by which they are linked with each other. Such a collection of series within which relationships of this kind obtain I call a section. The four series just mentioned form a section which will be called that of the back consonants. The complex set of relationships among the series of this back section is now to be considered. First we may consolidate the laryngals and

[10] See note 8 above.

pharyngals into one series because of their like behavior, and assign this group the symbol LP. The post-velars, forming the next series forward, may be symbolically put as PV. The velar stops, constituting the most forward of the back consonants will be indicated by V. The rule, then, is that consonants in the same series and adjacent series tend not to occur together, provided the series is still within the same back position. PV consonants occur only rarely with consonants of the series immediately in back, LP, and in front, V. On the other hand, V occurs freely with LP, since these are not adjacent series. Otherwise stated the only combinations of back consonants which occur freely are those in which one member is a velar, and the other a laryngal or pharyngal.

The next series, which is at the same time a section, is that of the liquids *l*, *r*, and *n*. In the I–II position, which will be considered first here, Arabic displays only 5 examples, all of them instances of *r* in the first position and *n* in the second. The absence of any Arabic roots beginning with *rl*, *lr*, *nr*, *nl*, or *ln* is striking in view of the high frequency of liquid consonants. The expected number of roots containing liquids in the first and second position is 83.0 ± 9.1 (−8.6 S.D.), so that the occurrence of only 5 is highly significant. On the other hand, the expected number of roots beginning *rn* is 9.8 ± 3.1 (−1.5 S.D.), so that it cannot be said that these five occurrences are very significantly fewer than the number of instances expected by chance. In other Semitic languages, roots beginning with two liquids are likewise rare. Hebrew has one in *rn*, Syriac only two, both beginning *rn*. Assyrian has a single root in *nl*, and one in *rn* (only verbal noun attested in this case). There is a single authenticated instance of a Proto-Semitic root beginning with two liquids, **rnn* referring to varying types of humanly produced noises 'to cry, whine, shout with joy, etc'.

In the II–III position, patternings are less vigorous, though still conspicuous, particularly in view of the high over-all frequency of the liquid consonants. In Arabic, there are 11 instances, 9 of which involve *r* and *n*, in contrast with an expected frequency of 93.1 ± 9.6 (−8.5 S.D.). Examples of verbal roots of this kind are rare in other Semitic languages. No verbal root containing liquids in the second and third position can be reconstructed for Proto-Semitic. On the other hand, there are several substantival roots of this form, namely, **grn* 'threshing floor', **qrn* 'horn', and **ɤrl* 'uncircumcised'.

In position I–III, patterning is far less rigorous. In Arabic it breaks down almost completely. The only conspicuous instance in which the general tendency of liquids not to occur together asserts itself is in the fact that there is only one example of a root with *l* in the first position and *r* in the third. The total number of roots with liquids in the first and third positions is 79. In comparison with the expected 93.5 ± 9.7, this is not significantly few (−1.5 S.D.). There is evidence, though, that a somewhat greater degree of patterning prevailed in Proto-Semitic. This is particularly true with regard to *l* and *r*. We have seen that in Arabic there is only a single instance of a verbal root with initial *l* and final *r*. No roots of this kind are found in Hebrew, Ethiopic, or Syriac, and none can be attributed to Proto-Semitic. Arabic has numerous roots with initial *r* and final *l*, but none are found in Ethiopic and Hebrew only has two. There are four in Syriac. There appears to be no certain instance of a Proto-Semitic verbal root with initial *r* and *l*. There are, however, the nouns **rgl* 'foot' and **rxl* 'ewe'. Taking the present evidence concerning *r* and *l* together with the results of the discussion regarding liquids in other positions, it is seen that there is no provable instance of a verbal root in Proto-Semitic which contains both *r* and *l*. In positions I–III, roots with initial *n* and final *l* are found in all the Semitic languages and a number of them are Proto-Semitic. On the other hand, those with initial *l* and final *n* are relatively infrequent in the various languages and no verbal root of this form can be traced to Proto-Semitic. Again there are substantival forms **lšn* 'tongue' and **lbn* 'white, milk'. Roots containing *r* and *n*, whether with *r* in the first position and *n* in the third or vice versa, are common in all the Semitic languages and there are a number of attested verbal roots of this type.

On the basis of the facts just cited, it can be seen that of the three liquid consonants, *r* and *l* occur together least, which suggests that these two consonants are the most similar. A somewhat lesser degree of resemblance is found between *l* and *n*, and least between *r* and *n*, using this criterion. The liquids are found to occur freely with all non-liquid consonants, both those in front and in back of their point of articulation. They therefore form a section.

A third large section, within which the relationships are very intricate, is that of the front consonants consisting of sibilant, dental, and interdental series. First to be considered is the status of the much-discussed consonant which, in the present tables, is conventionally transcribed *ḍ*. Its suggested value in Proto-Semitic has varied all the way from Brockelmann's *ḏ̣* to Vilenčik's *ɣy* which would make it a member of the series here called post-velar. A lateral articulation has sometimes been suggested on the basis of certain modern Arabic pronunciations. Cantineau, combining the interdental with the lateral interpretation, suggests that for Arabic, at least, we have "une spirante interdentale emphatique suivie d'un appendice lateral."[11] The present evidence lends no support to Vilenčik's theory that *ḍ* belongs to the post-palatal series. We find *ḍ* occurring with *x* and *ɣ* 32 times in all positions, far more than the expected number of occurrences, 17.6. The data presented here do not lend much support to the lateral theory either. With *l* itself there are 11 occurrences, a rather large number of instances in view of the general low frequency of *ḍ*.

[11] J. Cantineau, *Les Parlers arabes du Horan* (Paris, 1946), p. 101.

This is still less than the expected frequency 22.9 ± 4.8 (−2.5 S.D.). However *ḍ* occurs freely with the other liquids *r* and *n*. A general perusal of the tables accompanying this article will suffice to show that *ḍ* belongs squarely in the section of front consonants although the evidence is not decisive in respect to the position it occupies within this section. With the sibilants *š*, *s*, *z*, and *ṣ*, there are no occurrences in I–II, none in II–III, and only 2 in I–III, where, as we have seen, the patterning is often weak. The total expected frequency of *ḍ* with sibilants in all positions is 44.2 ± 6.6, so that the total actual frequency of 2 is highly significant. The consonant *ḍ* likewise occurs only twice in all positions with the interdentals *ṯ*, *ḏ*, and *ṭ* again in I–III. In view of the very low general frequency of the interdentals this is somewhat less significant than the tendency of *ḍ* not to occur with the sibilants. The total expected frequency is here 14.6 ± 3.8; thus the observed frequency 2 gives −3.3 S.D., a significant figure. *ḍ* occurs somewhat more frequently with the dentals, particularly with *d*. There is 1 example in I–II, 4 in II–III, and 7 in I–III. Of this total 12 instances, 6 are with *d* including all those not in I–III. The expected frequency of *ḍ* with dental stops is 36.6. ± 6.1 and the observed total of 12 gives −4.0 S.D., significantly fewer than the expected number of instances. In all this, *ḍ* behaves like a member of the sibilant or interdental series, since, it will be shown later, sibilants and interdentals occur only rarely together while both combine with somewhat greater frequency with the dental series though still less often than would be expected on a chance basis. The present data, then, support the interpretation of *ḍ*, either as a sibilant or interdental fricative.[12]

Thus far only the Arabic evidence has been considered. *ḍ* is only kept as a distinct phoneme in classical Ethiopic. Elsewhere, except in Aramaic, it merges with *ṣ*. The same general features as those of Arabic concerning the patterning of *ḍ*, are found in Ethiopic. It occurs a total of 5 times with sibilants (which represent either Proto-Semitic interdentals or Proto-Semitic sibilants). Four of the five instances with dentals involve *d*. There is absolute incompatibility between *ḍ* and *s* both in Ethiopic and Arabic. For Proto-Semitic not a single verbal root involving *ḍ* and a sibilant or *ḍ* with an interdental can be reconstructed. We have, however, the substantive **ḍrs* 'molar tooth' with a denominative verb in some languages. Only attested from South Semitic is

[12] On the basis of other types of evidence than that discussed here, it would seem that *ḍ* is a sibilant rather than an interdental in Proto-Semitic and classical Arabic. Its closeness to *ṣ* as evidenced by the fact that it coalesces with it three times independently within Semitic (Canaanite, Assyrian, later Ethiopian languages) and that a diacritic over *ṣ* was chosen to represent it by the Arabs, is far too often ignored in the attempt to explain more unusual developments. The earlier Arab grammarians all assign it the same place of articulation as *š* so that it may well have been an emphatic *š* in the classical period. The place assigned to *ḍ* in the tables accompanying this article is based on this assumption.

Ethiopic *ḍbs* 'to be weak' which we can compare with the Arabic adjective *ḍabi:s*, 'weak' cited by Freytag in his lexicon. With dentals we have Proto-Semitic **ḍbṭ* 'to seize' and **ḍmd* 'to join' and South Semitic **ḍḥd* 'to slip', **qḍd* 'to cut, harvest'.

It is generally assumed that there are five sibilants in Proto-Semitic, *s*, *z*, *ṣ*, *ś*, and *š*. They are all kept apart only in Hebrew and South Arabic. There is great uncertainty regarding the phonetic values of *s*, *ś*, and *š* in Proto-Semitic. I simply use them here as conventional transcriptions of the three sibilants corresponding to the sounds indicated by *samekh*, *śin*, and *šin* respectively in Hebrew orthography.

In Arabic *samekh* and *šin* are represented by *s*, and *śin* by *š*. There are thus four sibilants in classical Arabic: *š*, *s*, *z*, and *ṣ*. There are 6 roots containing two different sibilants in the I–II position. Since Arabic *s* has two origins in Proto-Semitic the possibility must be considered that roots containing two occurrences of *s* represent these two different sibilants of Proto-Semitic, that is *samekh* and *šin*. There are no examples of this in I–II. In II–III there is a single instance of a root containing two different sibilants. Roots containing *s* in both second and third position are of course, common. They are instances of the usual geminate type and doubtless all represent instances of the gemination of the same sibilant. In I–II there are 10 instances of roots with two different sibilants and 4 cases of roots with *s* in both the first and the third positions. It is noteworthy that all of the examples of roots with two different sibilants are of the same type, a *š* preceding some other sibilant. I believe that this is the result of a general rule of change operative in Arabic which can be stated in the following terms. Wherever, in an Arabic root *s*, continuing Proto-Semitic *šin*, was followed by a sibilant, including a second instance of *šin* itself, in the same root, whether verbal or substantival, the *s* is dissimilated to *š*. This is well-known in the instances of the common nouns for 'sun' and 'root'. For 'sun', one reconstructs Proto-Semitic **šmš*, with two *šins*. Instead of the expected **sms* in Arabic, we get *šms*. Likewise for 'root', Proto-Semitic **šrš*. Arabic has *šrs* in place of the expected **srs*. In the few instances where we have two examples of *s* in Arabic in the same root, the first should come from Proto-Semitic *samekh* rather than *šin*. The total expected frequency of roots with two different sibilants in Arabic together with the expected frequency of *s* in the first and third positions is $121.2 \pm 11.0$. The actual frequency of 22, of which 10 in the I–III position, and of these 4 of the form *s-s* is therefore highly significant.

In other Semitic languages roots which might derive from Proto-Semitic forms with different sibilants are likewise rare. In Ethiopic, there are 4 besides one root in initial and final *s* which in view of the similar development of the sibilants to that of Arabic, might be the reflex of a Proto-Semitic root with two different sibilants. In Hebrew there are 13, of which 7 are in I–III. There are a few instances in the other Semitic languages. There are two verbal roots, known from Arabic and Hebrew, which may be Proto-Semitic. If Hebrew *šsʕ* 'to tear (Piel)', is related to Arabic *šsʕ* 'have a gap, be distant', then, in accordance with the sibilant dissimilation law enunciated above for Arabic, we must reconstruct Proto-Semitic **šsʕ*. Likewise, if Arabic *šzr* 'look at askew', 'twist cord from the left', is cognate with Hebrew *šzr* 'to be twisted (Hophal)', it will derive from Proto-Semitic **šzr*.

The sibilants display a marked tendency in Arabic not to occur in the same roots as the consonants of the interdental series. There are 14 instances in Arabic, of which 7 are in I–II, none in II–III, and 7 in I–III. All of these instances are of the same type, a *š* preceding an interdental. It is tempting to assume that a general rule of dissimilation is at work here also, by which Arabic *s* is dissimilated to *š* before a following interdental. Involved also is the possibility of transposition of a sequence interdental-sibilant to sibilant-interdental of the type to be discussed below in connection with sequences of dentals and sibilants.

Since the interdentals remain as an independent series elsewhere only in South Arabic, and partly in Ugaritic, there is little that can be said regarding the occurrence of interdentals and sibilants within the same root in other Semitic languages. No verbal root containing a sibilant and an interdental can be attributed to Proto-Semitic. There is one instance of a substantival root, **šdṯ* 'six'.

While, as has been seen, the sibilants are incompatible with the interdentals, this is not so, in general, with regard to the patterning of sibilants with the dental stops *t*, *d*, and *ṭ*. The facts, however, are complex and deserve a closer analysis.

In Arabic there are 52 examples of roots containing sibilants and dentals in I–II. The total expected would be 82.0 ± 9.1 (−3.3 S.D.). The curious fact is that these 52 occurrences are by no means randomly distributed. Of the 24 possible combinations of the four sibilants with the three dentals in either order, 13 do not occur. Two observations may be offered. There are no combinations involving *z*. Of the missing 13 combinations, 8 involve a dental preceding a sibilant. In fact, of the 52 roots, 45 contain a sibilant followed by a dental and only 7 a dental followed by a sibilant. This can hardly be accidental and is confirmed by data from other Semitic languages. In Hebrew, of 26 roots with dentals and sibilants in the I–II position, 24 have sibilant followed by dental and only 2 dental followed by sibilant. (One must remember, however, that Hebrew sibilants are also the reflex of Proto-Semitic interdentals.) In Syriac, similarly, there are 26 instances of roots beginning with sibilants, followed by a dental and only 3 with the sequence dental-sibilant. Hebrew has no example of a root containing *z* and a dental in I–II, Syriac only one.

This general picture is confirmed for Proto-Semitic. A number of roots can be reconstructed with initial sibilant and following dental, e.g. **šty* 'drink', **str* 'hide, conceal', but not a single instance of a dental followed by a sibilant. Here, again, there is a substantival exception **tšʕ* 'nine'. Likewise, we cannot attribute to Proto-Semitic any root containing a *z* accompanied by a dental in I–II. I can offer no explanation for the non-occurrence of *z*. In regard to the absence of the sequence dental followed by sibilant, however, an obvious hypothesis is at hand. The rule in Proto-Semitic that the *t-* of the reflexive occurs before initial root consonants other than sibilants, but after sibilants, must be the result of a transposition of the sequence dental plus sibilant to sibilant plus dental. If we assume that this rule applied to two initial consonants of the verbal root as well, the present phenomena can be explained. Assuming there were once verbal roots with an initial dental followed by a sibilant in the second position, these roots have become instances of sibilant initials followed by dentals in accordance with this principle of transposition.

In II–III, there are 47 roots in Arabic containing dentals and sibilants. The expected frequency is $77.8 \pm 8.8$ ($-3.5$ S.D.). Thus both here and in I–II, although there are a considerable number of roots in Arabic of this kind, they are still significantly fewer than would be expected on a chance basis. Here again there are no examples of combinations involving *z*. Combinations involving a dental followed by a sibilant occur freely; there are 18 examples. The transposition rule mentioned above only applies to the first two positions in the root.

The other Semitic languages agree with Arabic in all essentials. Hebrew has an equal number of roots with dental preceding sibilant and dental following sibilant. There are no instances with *z*. Similarly in Syriac there are almost equal numbers of roots with the dental preceding or following the sibilant, and there are no roots with *z*.

For Proto-Semitic we reconstruct a number of roots with sibilant following dental, e.g. **lṭš* 'to hammer, whet' and with dental following sibilant **wsd* 'to establish'. Here also there are no examples of *z*.

In positions I–III there are approximately the anticipated number of roots in Arabic, 81, with $81.1 \pm 9.0$ as the expected frequency. The distribution among those in which the dental precedes the sibilant and vice versa is about what would be expected on a chance basis. Of dental preceding sibilant, there are 22 instances; the expected frequency is $23.8 \pm 4.9$. Sibilants precede dentals in 59 cases. Here the expected frequency is $57.3 \pm 7.6$. There are some instances involving *z*. In other Semitic languages roots with dentals and sibilants in I–II are similarly frequent and for Proto-Semitic, a fair number of such roots can be reconstructed, including some with initial dental **dwš*, **dyš* 'tread, thresh,' **drš* 'seek' and some with *z*, **zwd*, **zyd* 'increase', **zbd* 'endow with'.

The series of dental stops consists of *t*, *d*, and *ṭ*. There are no examples in Arabic of roots with dentals in the first two positions. The expected frequencies are 15.8 ± 4.0 (−3.0 S.D.). This is true of the other Semitic languages also. No verbal or substantival root with dentals in the first two positions can be assumed for Proto-Semitic. In II–III, Arabic has only three examples of roots with two different dentals. All of them end in *td*. This is significantly below the theoretical frequency of 23.0 ± 4.8 (−3.0 S.D.). Ethiopic has one root in *dṭ*. Syriac has two in *dt*, but in one of them *t* is the reflex of Proto-Semitic *ṯ*. Hebrew has one verbal root in *td*. For Proto-Semitic, there is one possible verbal root **ʕtd* 'be prepared, ready' but it may be a denominative form from the more common adjectival form *ʕati:d* 'prepared, ready, future'. There are likewise the substantival forms **wtd* 'peg', **ʕtd* 'goat'.

In I–III, as usual, there are more examples. In Arabic, we find 7 where 17.1 ± 4.1 are expected. The standard deviation of −1.4 is not very significant. Instances of dentals in I–III are rare elsewhere. For Proto-Semitic, we have only **ṭrd* 'drive away' as a verbal root and no substantival examples.

The patterning of the dentals with the sibilants has been considered above. The interrelation of the dentals and interdentals remains to be considered. In Arabic, there are 4 cases in I–II, expected frequency 21.0 ± 4.6 (−3.8 S.D.). In II–III we find 6 where the expectation is 22.2 ± 4.7 (−4.3 S.D.). In both these instances, then, we find some occurrences but significantly fewer than would be expected. In I–III there are 12 such roots; the expected frequency is 22.2 ± 4.7 (−2.2 S.D.). This is considerably less significant.

Since elsewhere, outside of South Arabic and Ugaritic, for both of which our lexical resources are slight, the interdentals are not preserved as a series, descriptive evidence for languages outside of Arabic cannot be cited. For Proto-Semitic, there are the following substantival examples: **ṯdy* 'breast', **dṯʔ* 'grass', **šdṯ* 'six'. There is one verb root *ḥdṯ* 'to happen'. Note that all of these examples involve *d* and *ṯ*.

The last series of front consonants to be considered are the interdental continuants *ṯ*, *ḏ*, and *ṯ̣*. Their relationships with the sibilants and dentals have already been treated. Since, as already noted, the interdentals, outside of classical Arabic, have merged with the sibilants or dentals, only the Arabic evidence will be considered here. There are no examples in Arabic of roots with two interdental consonants in any position. Because of the very low frequency of these consonants, this is not as significant as in the case of other series. The total expected frequency is 9.3 ± 3.1 (−3.0 S.D.). There are no verb or substantive roots in Proto-Semitic containing two interdentals.

The fourth and last section consists of a single series, that of the labial consonants *p*, *b*, and *m*. In South Semitic (Arabic and Ethiopic) *p* > *f*. In I–II there are no instances in classical Arabic of roots with two labials. The expected frequency is 54.6 ± 7.3 (−7.5 S.D.), so that this is highly significant. Other Semitic languages also do not have roots with two labials in I–II and no Proto-Semitic verb or noun root of this type can be reconstructed.

In II–III, there is a single Arabic root ending in *bm*. The expected frequency is 71.2 ± 8.4 (−8.4 S.D.), again highly significant. Elsewhere are no verbal roots of this kind and none can be assumed for Proto-Semitic. Hebrew has *ybm* in the Piel form 'perform the levirate', no doubt a denominate from the noun for 'brother-in-law'. Syriac has this verb likewise.

In I–III, instances are more frequent; Arabic has 16 instances of which 11 have initial *f* and final *m*, the other 5 initial *b* and final *m*. The expected frequency is 72.0 ± 8.5 (−6.5 S.D.). Other Semitic languages have roots of this kind virtually all with initial *p* or *b* and final *m*. A few roots of this kind can be assigned to Proto-Semitic: **pṣm* 'split', **prm* 'tear', **bsm* 'be pleasant', **bhm* 'be silent, stupid', and the substantive **pḥm* 'charcoal'.[13]

Our conclusions in regard to Proto-Semitic may be summed up as follows:

1. Outside of *w* and *y*, there are four sections of consonants, back consonants (*ʔ*, *h*, *ḥ*, *ʕ*, *x*, *ɣ*, *k*, *g*, *q*), liquids (*r*, *l*, *n*), front consonants (*ḍ*, *š*, *ś*, *s*, *z*, *ṣ*, *t*, *d*, *ṭ*, *ṯ*, *ḏ*, *ṭ*), and labials (*p*, *b*, *m*). Consonants of any one section occur freely with those of any other section in the formation of triconsonantal verb morphemes.

2. Different consonants of the same order tend not to appear in the same triconsonantal verb morpheme, except that: (a) In the section of back consonants, the velars (*k*, *g*, *q*) occur freely both with the pharyngals (*x̣*, *ʕ*) and the laryngals (*ʔ*, *ḥ*); (b) In the front section, sibilants occur fairly freely with the dental stops *t*, *d*, *ṭ*. In I–II position, the sibilant always precedes the dental (rule of transposition).

3. The rule of the previous paragraph applies with considerable rigor to I–II and II–III. It is less marked in I–III, where it sometimes breaks down completely.

[13] Something should be said at this point about the quadriconsonantal forms. They all display a similar pattern of conjugation in Semitic languages. Yet it would seem that no single

4. There are no Proto-Semitic roots with identical consonants in the first and second positions and probably none with identical consonants in the first and third positions. On the other hand, identical second and third consonants are very common.

5. The above statements only apply to the verb root morphemes. Substantival morphemes frequently violate them. For example, of the numerals from one to ten, no less than four transgress the usual rules applicable to verb morphemes (*ʔḥd* 'one', *ṯlṯ* 'three', *šdṯ* 'six', *tsʕ* 'nine').

It is to be noted that these rules only apply within the morpheme. There is no objection to a sequence of two like consonants where one of them belongs to another morpheme, e.g. a prefix or a suffix. Thus we may perfectly well have in Arabic *narkabu* 'we ride' with an initial sequence of *n–r*, inasmuch as *n* is a separate prefix morpheme indicating the first person plural subject, or *mifta:ḥ* 'key' < *ftḥ* 'to open' where *m-* is a prefix forming nouns of place and instrument. That the state of affairs reconstructed for Proto-Semitic is the result of dissimilative processes applied to adjacent consonants is obvious. The relative absence of patterning in I–III shows that it is consonants in sequence that are chiefly involved. On the other hand, that they be in close juncture without an intervening vowel does not seem to be necessary. Ordinarily, in Semitic languages, the second and third consonants of the verb do not occur in immediate sequence in verbal forms (the verbal noun, however, frequently has the *qatl* form).

The question arises as to whether the dissimilative changes postulated here occurred during the Proto-Semitic period, or whether it is to be referred even further back, at least to the Proto-Hamito-Semitic period. A preliminary investigation of this question was attempted by examining the constitution of verbal roots in Egyptian.[14] Until the phonology of Proto-Hamito-Semitic is reconstructed and the regular developments leading to the earliest forms of Egyptian can be stated with some precision, there must of course, be considerable difficulties in deciding the question on the basis of Egyptian evidence. Berber and other Hamito-Semitic languages outside of Egyptian did not seem suitable, because they are only documented from the recent period.

My conclusion is that, although much remains to be explained, it is probable

quadriconsonantal root can be referred with certainty to Proto-Semitic. In Arabic, allowing for denominatives and loans, the same general patterns of consonantal avoidance appear in the quadriconsonantal as in the triconsonantal forms.

[14] The lexicographical source consulted for Egyptian was A. Erman and H. Grapow, *Wörterbuch der Aegyptischen Sprache*, 6 vols. (Leipzig, 1925–).

that the type of patterning described here for Proto-Semitic was likewise present in Proto-Hamito-Semitic.

The pattern is much obscured in Egyptian because of the coalescence within Egyptian of consonants originally belonging to different and compatible series and sections. Thus Egyptian ʔ frequently corresponds to Proto-Semitic **r*, **l*, and, without doubt, it is Semitic which is conservative and Egyptian which has innovated in this respect. The result is that in Egyptian, ʔ occurs freely with laryngals and pharyngal consonants in the same verb roots.

We may test our hypothesis best where there is a series which has been relatively undisturbed by development of this kind. One example is the labials. Here Czermak has noted that the rule applies. ". . . kommen sonst labiale Konsonanten im Wortstamme in unmittelbarer Nachbarschaft niemals vor, wenn man vom halbkonsonantischen *w* absieht. . . . Es existiert auch für diese Verbindungen kein Lesezeichen."[15] He indicates that there are instances where the labials are separated by some other consonants (the equivalent of the rule that patterning tends to break down in I–III) and that almost all the apparent exceptions can be explained by the fact that one of the consonants belongs to another morpheme. There is one real exception in the verb *mfx* 'to sift'.

The situation is clear likewise in regard to the velars. Egyptian *k*, *g*, *q* correspond *grosso modo* to Proto-Semitic **k*, **g*, **q*. I could discover no instances of Egyptian roots containing two different velars.

The Egyptian sound transcribed *ṯ* (sometimes at present *č*) seems to result from the fronting of an original *k* under circumstances that cannot at present be stated.[16] It is striking therefore, that there are no verb roots in Egyptian containing both *ṯ* and a member of the series of velar stops.

In like manner *ḏ* seems to result from a fronted **g*. Here, however, there are complications insofar as Egyptian *ḏ* also corresponds to Proto-Semitic *ṣ* and *ḍ*. It also appears that *ḏ* does not occur in roots along with a velar stop, though examples where *ḏ* represents an original sibilant might well have been expected to occur.

Another straightforward case is that of the dentals *t*, *d*. There are no instances of Egyptian roots containing both *t* and *d*.

In regard to the liquids, Egyptian apparently usually wrote *l* as *n*. It reappears in Coptic as *l*. In older Egyptian therefore, we only have to do with graphic *r* and *n*. It has been seen that the patterning of *r* and *n* is not very strict. In Egyptian, verb roots with *r* and *n* in adjacent positions are rare. We have one

[15] W. Czermak, *Die Laute der Aegyptischen Sprache* (Vienna, 1931), pp. 27–28.

[16] The traditional transcription *ṯ* and *ḏ* for Egyptian have nothing to do with the similarly transcribed interdentals of Semitic.

instance of initial *nr* (*nry* 'to fear'), a combination which does not occur in Semitic, and of *rn*, *rnn* 'rejoice' possibly cognate with the Proto-Semitic **rnn*, and *rnp* 'to be young'. On the whole, the rules apply to liquids to the same extent as in Semitic.

In regard to the back section, the Semitic rules concerning the non-occurrence of velars and post-velars finds its correspondence in Egyptian. The only certain member of the post-velar series in Egyptian is *x* and it does not occur in the same roots with *k*, *g*, and *q*.

All of the numerous violations of the prohibition against the appearance of post-velars, pharyngals, and laryngals in Egyptian resolve themselves into sequences of some other back consonant with ʔ or ʕ, or combinations of ʔ and ʕ with each other, thus *ḥh*, *hẖ*, *ḥx*, *hx*, etc. are not found, but *ʔḥ*, *ʔh*, *ḥʔ*, *hʕ*, *ʕh*, *ʕʔ*, etc. do occur. The combinations involving ʔ can be understood as the development of *r* and *l*, as noted above. This leaves the sequences with ʕ to be explained. I believe that the generally accepted etymology by which Semitic **wrx* 'moon' is equated with Egyptian *wʕḥ*, *yʕḥ*, with the same meaning, provides a key to the general process which has given rise to these combinations. **wrx* might normally give **wʔx* (the *r* is retained in many instances). We may assume that ʔ > ʕ because of the other back consonant. In this case there is also partial assimilation of both consonants, to the pharyngal position. Another type of shift is involved in the Egyptian *ḥʕb* 'to play', which I do not think we can keep apart from the Semitic **lʕb* with the same meaning. Egyptian-Semitic etymologies are, in general, so sparse that there is not enough material to set up rules. The suggestion may be ventured that in original sequences involving *r* or *l* and a back consonant, after the shift *r*, *l* > ʔ, there took place diverse assimilations and dissimilations resulting in the present combinations.

The sibilants form the other outstanding exceptions. The combination of *ś* and *s* is very rare; I only know of *śsʔ* 'to undress'. On the other hand, *š* occurs commonly both with *ś* and *s*. It may be that *š* is fronted *x* (as indeed happened in later Egyptian) just as *ṯ* comes from *k* and *ḏ* from *g*. I cannot cite any etymologies in support of this thesis, however.

There are a few instances in Egyptian verb roots with identical initial and second consonants. As in Ethiopic, most are demonstrably contractions of quadriconsonantal forms consisting of a duplicated biconsonantal nucleus. Thus *ḥḥy* 'to seek' occurs alongside *ḥyḥy*, and *śśn* 'to smell' appears also as *śnśn*. I do not know that *ssn* 'to punish' can be explained this way, or *ssḥ* 'to conquer' (not known to occur earlier than the Middle Kingdom, however) or *nny* 'be tired' (only from Middle Kingdom on). There is also the biconsonantal *kk* 'to be dark' doubtless a denominative from *kkw*, 'darkness'. Most instances of identical consonants in the first and third positions can be explained in similar fashion as contracted from reduplicated biconsonantal forms. So, *xbx* alongside *xbxb*, etc. The only examples that cannot be so explained are *nxn*, a denominative from *nxn* 'child', and *grg* 'found'.

Egyptian has geminate forms with identical second and third consonants just as Semitic. In general, then, the situation in Egyptian and Semitic is similar in regard to the occurrence of identical consonants within the verb root morpheme.

It is not necessary, of course, for all of the dissimilative changes to have happened during the same period. It would seem that some of them, at least, must date to the Hamito-Semitic period since they occur both within Egyptian and Semitic.

It is obvious that this is in many ways merely a preliminary attempt in a very neglected field. The conclusions stated here are, in many cases, quite tentative. The general subject of the patterning of consonantal phonemes within the morphemes in Hamito-Semitic languages would seem to be a promising subject of investigation and one whose results must be kept in mind for their bearing on the historical analysis of this family of languages.

# Review of Westermann and Bryan's *Languages of West Africa*

This is the most ambitious in the series of handbooks currently being issued by the International African Institute, which are designed eventually to cover the entire continent linguistically.[1] The area treated in the present work is bounded by the Atlantic Ocean on the west and Lake Chad on the east; it extends from the Gulf of Guinea northward approximately as far as the confines of the Sahara. Like the other volumes in the series, this one presents much valuable information, either widely scattered or unavailable in written sources, concerning the size, location, and nomenclature of the numerous linguistic communities of the area; like the others, it is provided with a map and an excellent introductory bibliography. On all of these counts the present work gives evidence of careful and painstaking research, and adds at a number of points to our knowledge of linguistic distributions in the West African area. The information is arranged in terms of a language classification. In view of the previous publications of the joint authors, I assume that the work of mapping nomenclature and population statistics was done primarily by Bryan, while the classification is that of Westermann, who is well known as the author of a whole series of publications on this topic.

The method of classification is described in the introductory section. Instead of the conventional 'family', 'subfamily', etc., a series of terms is employed, most or all of which have already appeared in other publications of this series. On the lowest level, 'language' indicates either a form of speech without recognized dialect variation or a dominant dialect with which others of lesser importance are associated. A number of dialects of which none

[1] Dietrich Westermann and M. A. Bryan, *Languages of West Africa* (*Handbook of African Languages*, Part II; London, New York, and Toronto: Oxford University Press, 1952).

appears dominant is called a 'dialect cluster'. The next higher unit is the 'language group', with a membership of related 'languages' or 'dialect clusters'. Above the 'language group' is the 'larger unit', which apparently designates the widest genetic unit posited in the present work. In addition we have the 'single unit', 'a language or dialect cluster which belongs to a larger unit while not sufficiently related to any other to form part of a language group' (7–8). Thus far all seems clear; Indo-European would be a larger unit, Germanic a language group, and Albanian a single unit. But there are further terms. We have the 'isolated group', a language group which is not part of a larger unit. This would be an independent family not comparable in extent or ramification to a larger unit. An instance in Asia might be the 'Hyperborean family' of Chuckchee, Koryak, and Kamchadal, which form a group but are apparently unrelated to other languages. Finally, there are 'isolated units', which are either languages known to be unrelated to anything else (like Burushaski in Central Asia) or not classified for lack of evidence. These latter are distinguished by the addition of a question mark. An examination of the work reveals, however, that the question mark also occurs in 'isolated language group?' and even 'larger unit?'. These expressions are nowhere explained, but it seems reasonable to assume that what is intended is that the present evidence, though sufficient to show that the languages in the isolated language group and larger unit are related to each other, is insufficient to determine if the group is related to anything else.

Thus armed with what we hope is the correct interpretation of these terms, we are in a position to determine the number and constitution of independent linguistic units in the area. Or perhaps we are not. For as we peruse the work, we come upon the following statement (54) in the chapter devoted to the Kru languages, which are labeled an isolated language group: "Their nearest relations are the Kwa languages." The Kwa languages are the subject of a later chapter; they are called a larger unit. In other words, first we are told that an isolated language group is independent (by definition); then we are told that Kru is an isolated language group; finally we are told that it is most closely related to Kwa, also supposedly independent. Presumably Kru is also related to other unspecified languages, since if there are 'nearest relations', there should also be more distant ones.

I believe that this phraseology is a lapse by Westermann into the beliefs of an earlier period, when, as we shall see, he believed in the genetic unity of most of the languages of West Africa. Indeed, at one period he even considered the Kru languages a subdivision of the Kwa subfamily of West-Sudanic. For the present purpose, in view of the preponderant evidence as to Westermann's meaning in the rest of the work, we disregard this lapse. If we took the statement seriously, it would be impossible to make sense of the present classification; for, in the absence of any other statements of this kind in the work, we would have to regard the various larger units, isolated groups, and isolated units as potentially related, without any guide as to which are related to which. Surely *all* cannot be meant, since Westermann, like everyone else, certainly considers Chad-Hamitic, a larger unit of the present work, to be unrelated to the main West-Sudanic group, and specifically states that Songhai is independent.

Disregarding this lapse, then, our procedure will be to add up the number of larger units, isolated groups, and isolated units which are not accompanied by question marks. This will give us the minimal number of independent linguistic stocks, since resolution of the problems presented by the queried groups can add to the number of stocks but can never decrease it. Applying this method, we conclude that Westermann is asserting the existence of at least ten independent families in the area, of which five are larger units, two are isolated language groups, and three are isolated units. In addition, well over thirty units are queried, suggesting that in Westermann's view there will eventually prove to be well over ten independent linguistic families in the area. My own opinion is that there are three such families in the area covered in this work: Songhai, which is an independent language; the Niger-Congo family, embracing eight of the ten independent units of Westermann's classification and almost all of the queried units; and the Chad branch of Afro-Asiatic (Hamito-Semitic). Of these both the Niger-Congo and Hamito-Semitic are widely represented outside of the area treated here.

I shall deal first with the problems raised by Westermann's treatment of Niger-Congo languages. A brief review of the history of his opinions regarding the classification of these languages may be of assistance in putting the present work in its proper perspective.

In his first work dealing with the problems of language relationships in Africa (*Die Sudansprachen*; Berlin, 1911), Westermann asserted that all the non-Hamitic and non-Bantu languages of that vast Sudanic area were related. He cited forms from five languages of the Western Sudan: Yoruba, Ewe, Efik, Gã, and Twi; and from three languages much farther to the east: Dinka and Nuba in the Anglo-Egyptian Sudan, and Kunama in Ethiopia. By the convenient device of treating the final consonants of the predominant CVC root formations of these languages as later suffixes, it was possible to adduce a good number of etymologies. The method was based on the assumption that the CV root morphemes of languages like Ewe must represent a 'primitive' monosyllabic type from which the others evolved.

Westermann was evidently dissatisfied with these results, and subsequently abandoned the thesis of the genetic unity of all the languages of the Sudan. It was noticeable in his work of 1911 that the five western languages figured frequently in convincing etymologies from which the eastern languages were excluded. In the following years Westermann began to work out the membership and details of a true genetic unit, involving practically all the languages of the western part of the Sudan, and published a series of separate treatments of subgroups in this family. Finally, in his general work *Die westlichen Sudansprachen und ihre Beziehungen zum Bantu* (Berlin, 1927), he presented approximately 300 etymologies involving the entire system of pronouns, all of the lower numerals, and numerous common nouns, verbs, and adjectives. He also demonstrated the essential unity of the system of noun classes marked by pairs of affixes for singular and plural, and pointed out the resemblance of this system to that of Bantu, extending even to specific details. In 110 of his etymologies, the Proto-Bantu forms reconstructed by Meinhof are close to, often identical with, the Proto-West-Sudanic of Westermann. His conviction regarding Bantu and West-Sudanic soon matured to the point where—in his article on African languages in the 14th edition of the *Encyclopaedia Britannica* (1929), he asserted their genetic connection without qualification.

In 1940, in the chapters on language which he contributed to *Völkerkunde von Afrika* (Essen, 1940, under the joint authorship of H. Baumann, R. Thurnwald, and D. Westermann), he has apparently returned in some respects to the earlier general Sudanic conception. The term 'Sudansprachen' is once again used, but we now have four divisions: Nigritic, with Kwa as one of its subdivisions; Mandingo; Semi-Bantu languages; and Inner-Sudanic. These are defined on typological grounds; for example, Nigritic consists of languages without class systems and with CV root morphemes, the Semi-Bantu group has CV root morphemes and noun classes, the Inner-Sudanic languages have CVC morphemes but no noun classes, and so on. The Bantu languages are listed separately as lying outside the Sudanic complex, and so are the Nilotic languages. As might be expected from the criteria involved, each of the four subdivisions (except Mandingo, a true but minor genetic unit) is a hodgepodge of related and unrelated languages. It is quite as though one were to set up three groups on the basis of sex gender: a group with no gender, comprising Basque, Hungarian, and English; a two-gender group, comprising Norwegian and Italian; and a three-gender group, comprising Russian and German. On the other hand, we are warned (*Völkerkunde*, 383) that the term Sudanic "designates languages of a common type whose genetic unity is only partially demonstrable." We are not told for which languages this unity is fully demonstrable. Bantu, which is listed separately from Sudanic, is stated to have many roots in common with the Nigritic, Mandingo, and Semi-Bantu divisions. "This relationship is closest among Kwa, Semi-Bantu and Bantu" (384). It is clear then, from Westermann's own statements, that the language divisions given here are not genetic, and that this is not a language classification in the usual sense: not all the languages in the Sudanic 'family' are related, while on the other hand there are 'related roots' (whatever that may mean) among languages in the separate Sudanic and Bantu 'families'. In its ignoring of West-Sudanic as a unit (the languages formerly assigned to it being split among the Mandingo, Semi-Bantu, and Nigritic subdivisions of a Sudanic family which comprises almost all the languages of the Sudan), this essay foreshadows the classification reviewed here.

The independent units of the present work correspond in general to the subgroups of West-Sudanic in the 1927 work. Reference to the latter also serves to make more intelligible the odd distribution of linguistic knowledge and ignorance implied by the new classification. All the languages qualified as unclassifiable for lack of evidence are in the eastern part of the area, in Nigeria or the Cameroons. Conceivably this might reflect the differential diligence of English and French scholarship; but as a matter of fact the western area contains British, French, Portuguese, and former German territory, while the eastern area contains the same except for Portuguese. The situation becomes understandable, however, if we realize that in *Die westlichen Sudansprachen*, the task of identifying West-Sudanic languages was not continued into the northern and eastern parts of Nigeria or into the Cameroons—the precise area in which every language or language group followed by a question mark is to be found.

For the present drastic step no explanation is offered here or, to my knowledge, anywhere else in Westermann's writings. It is quite as though Franz Bopp in 1860, after completing his comparative Indo-European grammar, had published, without explanation, a work in which the Indo-European family was fragmented into many independent subgroups and unclassified languages. Perhaps this may be looked on as a praiseworthy exercise in caution; but what if the subgroups are incorrect? That the overall membership of a large linguistic family should be more certain than that of its constituent subfamilies may at first blush seem something of a paradox. But the question whether A, B, and C are all related in some manner is often less difficult than the more subtle problem involved in subgrouping: the problem whether A is more closely related to B than to C. Nobody at present doubts that Oscan, Latin, and Irish are all related; but after more than a century of intensive Indo-European research there is still controversy as to whether Oscan is more closely related to Latin or to Celtic. Everything depends on the length of time during which the ancestral language of the branch had a separate development. If this period is short, and the subsequent period during which the innovations have been subject to analogical and other changes is long, the problem becomes difficult and requires a great deal of descriptive analysis and reconstruction.

Westermann's use of typological criteria in these matters leads to inevitable errors. Of the independent units listed in the present work, only Mandingo and the Gur group are in my opinion completely correct as they stand. Any culture historian who accepts the remainder as valid units will do so at his peril. To take one instance, Westermann attributes great significance to the presence or absence of noun gender classification (both sex and non-sex gender). This is evidently his motive for placing Adyukru, which has noun prefix classes, not with the closely related Ari and Abe of the neighboring Ivory Coast lagoons, but with the West-Atlantic languages, which generally have prefix classes. Since these two groups are now considered independent by Westermann, the error is analogous to stating that Dutch is related to Russian but not to German. In a study of the West-Atlantic languages (*Mitteilungen des Seminars für Orientalische Sprachen* 31: 63–86 [1928]), Westermann presented 153 etymologies among various languages, designed to establish the validity of this subgroup within what he then considered to be the West-Sudanic family. In these etymologies, Adyukru figures only twice; and of these two, one is the first person plural pronoun, which is almost universal in Niger-Congo and therefore not a West-Atlantic innovation.

If Westermann had been consistent, he would have put the northern Guang and southern Guang dialects in separate West-Sudanic subgroups and would now treat these as separate families, since the northern dialects have noun classes and the southern have none. But wherever the relationship is this close, Westermann prefers to follow common sense in classing them together. As the dialects move further and further apart, however, precisely that will occur which Westermann apparently does not consider possible: classless and classifying languages of more distant relationship will be members of the same linguistic grouping.

I do not wish to leave the topic of Niger-Congo languages with an appearance of total disagreement. By and large, the languages now classed as members of the same independent unit are members of the same genetic subgroup of Niger-Congo in my classification. In two details, the present work marks an important advance. Fulani is now placed in the West-Atlantic group and its Hamitic status denied; I do not believe that any responsible scholar still regards it as Hamitic—a view first advanced by Meinhof in his *Sprachen der Hamiten* (Hamburg, 1912). And Songhai, which I consider an independent family, is now unequivocally accorded separate status.

The problems raised by Westermann's treatment of the Chad languages are in principle similar to those just discussed. What I consider to be the Chad group of Hamito-Semitic is divided into a Chad-Hamitic larger unit, therefore presumably independent, and a Chadic larger unit which is queried because of its possible relation to Chad-Hamitic. I consider this an arbitrary division with no basis in fact. In setting up a Chadic division as distinct from Chad-Hamitic, Westermann is apparently following Lukas, who did so because these languages lack grammatical gender. However, as Westermann points out, all these languages except Mandara are now known to have gender. In itself I do not consider this fact especially important; what is important is that the feminine is marked by the almost universal Hamito-Semitic *t* and that the masculine of Gider, one of the Chadic languages of Westermann, has *n*, as in Hausa and Masa, both languages included in Chad-Hamitic by Westermann. In a series of Chad etymologies which I have compiled, and in a series of etymologies to be published in which Chad forms are connected with those of other Hamito-Semitic branches, the languages of this Chadic group enter just as frequently as those of the Chad-Hamitic group.

Most surprising of all is the placing of Angas and closely affiliated languages, which I consider part of a western Chad subgroup comprising Hausa, Ngizim-Bade, and the Bolewa group, in an isolated language group. The appearance of Angas in the chapter on the classless languages of Nigeria along with languages formerly considered Sudanic suggests that in Westermann's opinion they have nothing to do with Hamito-Semitic. The resemblances to the 'Chadic' and 'Chad-Hamitic' languages are attributed to borrowings from Hausa. This explanation is inadequate; it leads to improbabilities and contradictions of the sort which arise whenever a language is excluded from a group to which it is affiliated and the resemblances are explained as borrowings from one of the languages of the group. In the Chad etymologies mentioned above, Angas figures approximately 200 times. Hausa appears in about 80 of these etymologies, but in 120 of them does not. A few of the latter may be incorrect, but hardly all of them or even, I think, a major portion. Most of them are semantically straightforward and involve such recurrent correspondences as Proto-Chad **b* > Angas *p*; **p* > *f*; **d* > *t*; **g* > *k*; **ḳ* > *ɣ*/*y* depending on the following vowel. Included are 6 of the 7 possessive suffixes, and 4 of the 6 new subject pronouns. Of these, the third possessive singular *-nyi* is not found in Hausa but is found in scores of 'Chad-Hamitic' and 'Chadic' languages; it is cognate with *ni*, the third person masculine singular pronoun of the central Cushitic languages. The possessive pronouns of Angas may serve as a further illustration. The terms meaning 'mine', 'thine', are formed by the addition of the usual bound possessive suffixes to a base *mi-* ~ *mu-*. Bolewa, which is Chad-Hamitic in Westermann's classification, has *mi-* in the same function; Hausa does not have this formation. The possessive pronouns of Angas and Bolewa are cited here along with the possessive suffixes of Hausa, which correspond to the second elements of the Angas and Bolewa pronouns:

| | Angas | Bolewa | Hausa | | Angas | Bolewa | Hausa |
|---|---|---|---|---|---|---|---|
| 1st sing. | *mina* | *mino* | *-ā* | 3rd fem. | *minyi* | *mito* | *-ta* |
| 2nd masc. | *miɣa* | *miko* | *-ka* | 1st plur. | *munu* | *mimu* | *-mu* |
| 2nd fem. | *miyi* | *miko* | *-ki* | 2nd plur. | *muwu* | *miku* | *-ku* |
| 3rd masc. | *minyi* | *minyi* | *-sa* | 3rd plur. | *muma* | *misu* | *-su* |

The Angas base *mi-* and the suffix of the 1st and 3rd sing. cannot be explained by borrowing from Hausa; if there was borrowing in this case, it must have been from Bolewa. For the 2nd plur. *wu-* we must go to Buduma and other languages of the Kotoko-Logone subgroup of Chad, which show a differentiation between a 2nd plur. possessive with *w-* like Angas *wu-* and a 2nd plur. verb subject pronoun with *k-* like the Angas subject pronoun *kun* = Hausa *kun*. The same distinction, between 2nd plur. pronouns in *w-* and *k-*, which has been erased in Hausa by the analogical spread of the *k-* form, reappears in Berber *-wən* vs. *-kən*.

It is not only the distribution of the resemblances to Angas among the Chad languages that creates difficulty for the view that borrowing from Hausa is an adequate explanation. The forms taken show every evidence of independent development from reconstructed Proto-Chad and Proto-Afro-Asiatic originals. There are the unique, Grimm-like sound shifts mentioned above. One unusual equivalence, *-īn* for non-front vowel + *l* of the other Chad languages, occurs in a number of instances: Angas *kwīn* 'narrow' = Masa *gɔr*, Kotoko *ɣul*, Musgu *gulle* 'short'; *bwīn* = Musgu *bul* 'hip'; *čīn* = Logone *gala* 'drive away'; *tīn* = Bata *dule* 'cloud'; *pīn* = Bolewa *bolu* 'break'; *sīn* = Wandala *šallwa*, Musgu *salawɔŋ*, Hausa *saywa* (with regular loss of *l*) 'root'. If Angas borrowed *sum* 'name' from Hausa *sūnā*, the original Proto-Hamito-Semitic final *-m* was obligingly restored, cf. Proto-Semitic **šim*, Bedauye (Cushitic) *sim*, etc. In other words, to account for all these resemblances by borrowing we must resort not to borrowing from a single language but to a kind of itinerant borrowing. Indeed, for a small number of apparently good etymologies where only Angas among the Chad languages has retained a form found in other Hamito-Semitic branches, we must travel still further afield to North Africa and the Near East. And in a few cases, where cognates are found with Ancient Egyptian, we need a time machine.

The theory is thus highly improbable. Moreover, it is arbitrary: given all the facts about the languages concerned, it would be just as logical to exclude Hausa (or any other language) from the Chad group, include Angas, and then explain the resemblances between Hausa and the remaining Chad languages as the result of itinerant borrowing from Angas and the other languages. Implicit in this approach is the fallacy of tacitly taking certain languages as points of reference—because we learned them earlier or because the people who speak them are more interesting or more important, or for some other nonlinguistic reason. This fallacy was noted long ago by Codrington. Speaking of those who deny the Malayo-Polynesian status of the languages of Melanesia and see in them a 'Malay' element, he declared that if they had started out with the languages of the New Hebrides or some other Melanesian area as an assumed point of reference, they would have seen 'Melanesian elements' in

Malay, placed Melanesian and Polynesian languages in the same family, and excluded from it Malay and other Indonesian languages.

There are at present only two linguists who attempt to give an overall picture of linguistic relationships in West Africa and in Africa generally—Westermann and myself. It is unfortunate that we differ on a number of points. Some linguists, not specialists in African languages, will wish to draw conclusions about these areas, and it is unreasonable to expect that they should examine the many languages at first hand. Before they arrive at conclusions on the questions discussed in this review, I hope that they will examine the evidence presented by Westermann in his 1927 work, and also the evidence presented in my "Studies in African Linguistic Classification" (*Southwestern Journal of Anthropology* 5: 79–100, 190–98, 309–17 [1949], and 6: 47–63, 143–60, 223–37 [1950]).

A last analogy. Suppose that Europe were as much terra incognita to most linguists as West Africa still is, and that two classifications of the languages had been proposed. Linguist A sets up two extensive families, Indo-European and Finno-Ugric, and one isolated language, Basque. (By a happy chance these correspond to Niger-Congo, Afro-Asiatic, and Songhai.) Linguist B sets up ten families and numerous unclassified languages, beginning perhaps as follows: (1) English, German, Dutch, Swedish, Russian; (2) Polish, Czech, Bulgarian; (3) Macedonian?; (4) Greek, Albanian; (5) Hungarian, Slovene; and so on. It is clear that safety does not necessarily lie in numbers. A classification with many families is not ipso facto more cautious than one with fewer families, in the sense of avoiding errors more successfully. In a word, no satisfactory substitute has yet been discovered for examining the evidence.

# Internal *a*- Plurals in Afroasiatic (Hamito-Semitic)

The normal and uncontested reconstructions of the Proto-Hebrew forms of the segholate nouns are: (1) **malk* (sing.) / **malak-i·m* (pl.) 'king'; (2) **nidr* / **nidar-i·m* 'vow'; (3) **qudš* / **qudaš-i·m* 'sanctuary'. As can be seen from these examples, they fall into three types, those with *a, i*, and *u* respectively as the vowel of the first syllable. The plurals are all marked by an *a* between the second and third consonants which does not appear in the singular. There are corresponding feminines which fall into the same three classes: (1) **malk-at* / **malak-a·t* 'queen'; (2) **ḥirp-at* / **ḥirap-a·t* 'reproach'; (3) **ḥurb-at* / **ḥurab-a·t* 'wilderness'. Aramaic likewise preserves traces of this same alternation.[1]

It was early noted and has won general acceptance among Semitists that these Hebrew and Aramaic forms are cognate with certain of the plurals of internal changes, the so-called broken plurals, of South Semitic.[2] The normal methods of historical reconstruction suggest that the plural suffixes in Hebrew and Aramaic are analogical formations inasmuch as all plurals in these languages have suffixes while South Semitic maintains a distinction between plurals by internal change only (broken plurals) and those with suffixes but without internal change (sound plurals). Thus the equation of the Ethiopic forms *bərk* / *bərak* 'knee' (Proto-Hebrew **birk*) and *'əzn* / *'əzan* 'ear' (Proto-Hebrew

[1] For segholates in Aramaic see G. Nöldeke, *Syriac Grammar* (Leipzig, 1898). For non-Semitists it should be explained that segholates are so-called because of the presence of ε (the sign for which in Hebrew is called *seghol*) in the second syllable of the absolute form. Thus the absolute forms of the nouns quoted here are *melex* (< *malk*), *neder* (< *nidr*) and *qodeš* (< *qudš*).

[2] See Brockelmann, *Vergleichende Grammatik* (Berlin, 1908), I: 430, Anm. 2, with the literature cited there.

*'*uđn*) with Hebrew types 2 and 3 above is obvious (Ethiopic *ə* is the normal reflex of Proto-Semitic **i* or **u*). Ethiopic, however, does not have the expected **qatl* / **qatal*, corresponding to Hebrew subtype 1, a point which will be the subject of subsequent discussion.

In Arabic the forms corresponding to the Hebrew segholates are *qatl-at* / *qatal*, *qitl-at* / *qital*, and *qutl-at* / *qutal*, where *-at* is the singular feminine ending. Of these, *qatl-at* / *qatal* is quite rare, a situation resembling that of Ethiopic in which, as has been seen, **qatl* / **qatal* does not occur. Arabic is probably the innovator in having a feminine suffix in the singular, not found in Ethiopic, Hebrew, or Aramaic. There are Arabic feminines which closely parallel the Hebrew feminine segholates quoted above. In Arabic, the plural with internal *a* is optional in these cases and there are variant forms in which the usual Arabic identity of noun bases in the singular and plural in suffixial plurals is presumably restored by analogy. These forms are therefore: (1) *qatl-at* / *qatal-a·t* or *qatl-a·t*; (2) *qitl-at* / *qital-a·t* or *qitl-a·t*; (3) *qutl-at* / *qutal-a·t* or *qutl-a·t*. Examples are: Ar. *ġurf-at* / *ġuraf-a·t* or *ġurf-a·t* 'spoon'; *kisr-at* / *kisar-a·t* or *kisr-a·t* 'piece'.

The general equivalence of the Hebrew and Arabic forms is further guaranteed by the striking agreement in the word for 'earth', a feminine noun in which both languages display a suffix in the plural but none in the singular: Proto-Hebrew *'*arṣ* / *'araṣ-a·t*; Arabic *'arḍ* / *'araḍ-a·t*.

The earlier attempts to explain the alternation between singular and plural in the forms just cited assumed that within Proto-Semitic either the singular base resulted from the plural by loss of an original *a*, or the plural arose from the singular through the development of a Svarabhakti vowel. These explanations are obviously inadequate and have been generally rejected by Semitists. Nöldeke sums up the general attitude when he declares: "Eine irgend plausibel Erklärung dieser Erscheinung ist mir nicht bekannt."[3]

To my knowledge, the existence of similar plural forms in the languages related to Semitic in the Afroasiatic (Hamito-Semitic) family has not heretofore been pointed out.[4] These alternations cannot therefore be explained in terms of Semitic alone. It will also be pointed out that the Hebrew segholate plurals and related forms discussed above are but one instance of a series of formations, which are all without doubt historically connected and share the common

[3] G. Nöldeke, *Zeitschrift für Assyriologie* 18 (1904): 72.

[4] I consider the Afroasiatic (Hamito-Semitic) family to have five coordinate branches: (1) Ancient Egyptian, (2) Berber, (3) Semitic, (4) Cushite, (5) Chad. For a complete enumeration of languages and evidence for the inclusion of the Chad languages, see J. H. Greenberg, "Studies in African Linguistic Classification: IV. Hamito-Semitic," *Southwestern Journal of Anthropology* 6 (1950): 47–63. Since there is no "Hamitic" branch within the family as against a Semitic one, I have sought to replace the traditional name Hamito-Semitic as misleading.

feature of the appearance of an *a* in the plural, usually between the penultimate and the last consonant, which does not occur in the singular. For convenience of discussion, a number of practically self-explanatory terms will be used for various subtypes of the *a*-plural. Where *a* of the plural alternates with zero in the singular, the process will be called *intercalation* (Ethiopic *'əzn / 'əzan* 'ear'). When *a* of the plural alternates with some other vowel in the singular, the term *replacement* will be employed. Plurals in which replacement or intercalation are accompanied by an alternation of *a* in the singular and some other vowel in the plural will be termed *dissimilatory* (Berber *a-baġus / i-buġas* 'monkey'). Forms in which all the vowels of the plural are *a*, involving several intercalations or replacements will be called *general* (Gulfei *gərəm / garam* 'woman'). Plurals involving the reduplication of the final consonant of the singular preceded by *a* will be called *reduplicatory* (Afar *il / ilal* 'eye'). Employing the terminology usual in Berber grammars, plurals involving internal change will be called *internal*, those with suffixes *external* and those with both processes simultaneously *mixed*. It is evident that certain of the above processes can occur in the same formation. Thus Mubi *gip / gabab* 'knee' employs replacement and reduplication simultaneously.

The Semitic forms discussed thus far all involve intercalation. In addition we may cite the Arabic feminine superlatives such as *kubr-a· / kubar* 'largest (fem.)' which have no parallels elsewhere in Semitic. The process of replacement is clear in the biconsonantal root morpheme for 'son', 'daughter' in which the Proto-Semitic forms had *i* in the singular alternating with *a* in the plural. These are mixed forms with feminine and plural suffixes: **bin / *ban-u·ma* 'son'; **bin-t / *ban-a·t* 'daughter'. The isolated Hebrew form **'i·r / *'ar-i·m* 'city' probably belongs here also.

Replacement in a triconsonantal form seems probable in the Semitic word for 'king, prince' and possibly others. The Arabic singular *malik* and the Akkadian construct (i.e. pre-genetival) *malik* suggest PS **malik / *malak* rather than **malk / *malak* as the Hebrew forms would imply. Likewise Akkadian absolute *napiš-tu*, construct *napš-at* 'soul' (with analogical addition of the feminine suffix not found in other Semitic languages in this word) suggests **napiš* rather than **napš* as the PS singular. In fact alternation of *qatl* with *qatil* in the singular, the same word appearing in both forms in different languages, led Brockelmann to remark: "Schon im Urs. wechselten als Druckvarietäten *qatil* und *qatl* miteinander."[5]

The existence in Akkadian of such variant singular absolutes as *miṣiru* ~ *miṣru* 'boundary', *uzunu* ~ *uzun* 'ear' (which may, however, be analogical formations based on the constructs *miṣir*, *uzun*, etc.), the prevalence in

[5]Brockelmann, *Vergleichende Grammatik,* I: 337.

Aramaic of a vowel of the segholate between the second and third consonant rather than between the first and second (Syriac *mlɛx* 'king', *brɛx* 'knee', etc.) and the existence in Hebrew of some segholates of this type (e.g., *dᵊβaš* 'honey'), all suggest that in some instances the singular had a vowel between the second and third consonant which would then be replaced by *a* in the plural. Just which words had such a vowel in the singular as well as the existence and extent of free variation in this matter (i.e. *qatil* ~ *qatl*, *qutul* ~ *qutl*, etc.) is difficult, or perhaps impossible, to determine.

The rarity of the alternation *qatl* / *qatal* in Arabic and its absence in Ethiopic was noted above. There is a tendency to dissimilation in these forms which we shall encounter again in other Afroasiatic languages and which usually takes the form of a replacement of the first vowel while the second *a* is retained as characteristic of the plural in this position. This process is illustrated by such Arabic forms as *badr-at* / *bidar* 'skin', *baḍ'-at* / *biḍa'* 'piece' in which *qital* is found for the **qatal* we would expect on the basis of Hebrew. Such a process is regularly found in Arabic where the second radical consonant is *j* or *w* with dissimilation to *i* and *u* respectively, e.g. *xajm-at* / *xijam* 'tent'; *dawl-at* / *duwal* 'rule'.[6] The Arabic plural *qita·l*, in adjectival formation with singular *qati·l*, is probably to be included in the dissimilatory subtype, e.g. *kabi·r* / *kiba·r* 'large'.

Another subtype, the general, is found only in South Semitic and is always accompanied by a suffix. In Ethiopic we find *qatal-t* chiefly as plural of *qatta·li·* (e.g. *qadda·mi·* / *qadam-t* 'first') but also in other forms without *a* in the singular, e.g. *nəgu·s* / *nagas-t* 'king'; *qədu·w* / *qadaw-t* 'clean'. In Arabic *qatal-at* is plural of the agentive, participial *qa·til*, e.g. *fa·'il* / *fa'al-at* 'workman'; *sa·ḥir* / *saḥar-at* 'conjurer'.

Finally we may note as present in only a few forms in Akkadian the reduplicatory subtype which is, as we shall see, a very frequent formation in certain Cushite and Chad languages. The only examples that can be cited are Akkadian *alak-tu* / *alkak-a·tu* 'road'; *šam-u·* / *šamam-u·* 'sky'; and *m-u·* / *mam-u·* 'water'.

As can be seen, only intercalation is at all frequent in Semitic and even this as a method of forming plurals is of minor importance compared with suffixation.

In Berber, there are three main types of plural, the internal with *a* replacement, the external with suffixation of *-ən* (masc.) *-tin* (fem.) or, less commonly, *-an* (masc.) *-atin* (fem.), and the mixed plural with both *a* replacement and suffixation. The replacement subtype is here a method of plural formation

[6]This is of course dissimilation from the point of view of the classification of subtypes described above. In *duwal* there has doubtless been assimilation from **diwal*.

which is of major importance. Examples from Kabyle Berber are: (a) internal *a-mqərqur* / *i-mqərqar* 'frog'; *a-zurkəṭṭif* / *i-zurkəṭṭaf* 'blackbird'; (b) external *a-rgaz* / *i-rgazən* 'man'; (c) *asəgləf* / *i-səglafən* 'barking'.[7]

The dissimilatory subtype is common in Berber; in fact, it is almost a general rule that nouns with *a* as penultimate vowel in the singular dissimilate to *u* in internal and mixed plurals, e.g. *a-ɣanim* / *i-ɣunam* 'reed'; *a-farəz* / *i-furaz* 'yellow of the egg'. Dissimilation to *i* also occurs, e.g. *a-mazir* / *i-mizar* 'encampment' and the feminine *ṯa-gənbur-ṯ* / *ṯi-gənbar* 'pitcher'. The intercalating, general, and reduplicating types do not occur in Berber.

The numerous Cushite languages of East Africa make up another branch of Afroasiatic and can be separated for convenience into five subgroups—northern, central, eastern, western, and southern. They will be considered in what follows in that order.[8]

The northern branch of Cushite consists of a number of closely related dialects of which Bedauye, the best known, may be taken as representative. The plural in Bedauye is commonly an *a* suffix but a number of monosyllables show replacement: *'or* / *'ar* 'child'; *bok* / *bak* 'goat'; *mek* / *mak* 'donkey'.

The central or Agau group of Cushitic languages utilizes internal modification to only a slight degree, suffixation being the chief method of forming plurals. Some of the few examples that may be cited are: Awiya *biri* / *biar-koa* 'bull'; *diri* / *diar-koa* 'goat'. Bilin sometimes shows internal reduplication: e.g. *šakum* / *šakakum* 'cheek'. It likewise has reduplication of the last consonant fairly frequently but the vowel is *i* or *u* (*naš* / *našiš* 'bone'; *suŋ* / *suŋuŋ* 'name' as has Chamir (*luk* / *lukuk* 'leg').

Among the eastern Cushite languages Galla and the eastern Sidamo only have suffix formations. In Somali reduplicatory forms are prominent, being the normal plural of all masculine biconsonantal nouns: *dab* / *dabab* 'fire'; *tug* / *tugag* 'thief', etc. In Afar-Saho likewise this is a frequent formation. Examples from Afar are: *il* / *ilal* 'eye'; *bo·r* / *bo·rar* 'cloth'. When the vowel of the singular is *a*, there is dissimilation to *o* or *u* in the reduplicatory syllable: e.g. *af* / *afof* 'mouth'.[9] Afar-Saho likewise has replacement plurals in triconsonantal forms, involving *a·* rather than *a*. Examples are: *waki·l* / *waka·l* 'guardian'; *sa·her* / *sa·ha·r* 'magic'; *hosu·l* / *hosa·l* 'arm'. If the vowel between the second and third consonants of the singular is *a* or *a·* there is

[7] The prefixes *a*-, *i*-, *ta*-, and *ti*- are of separate historical origin and indicate masculine singular and plural and feminine singular and plural, respectively.

[8] For the subdivisions of Cushitic, see the map in the above-mentioned article by J. H. Greenberg, *Southwestern Journal of Anthropology*, 6 (1950): 60.

[9] Similar forms with partial reduplication in modern Semitic Ethiopian languages are generally attributed to Cushite influence.

again dissimilation, to *u* and *i* respectively: *faras* / *faris* 'horse'; *dana·n* / *danun* 'ass'. There are likewise instances of intercalation in Afar-Saho: *furd-a·* / *furad* 'port'.

The western Cushite languages (Kafa, Janjero, etc.) have reduplication plurals and plurals by suffixes. There is little data and no full-fledged grammatical description from the small and isolated southern Cushite languages of Tanganyika. However, in the few recorded Mbulugwe plurals, the reduplicatory type is prominent: *ur* / *urar* 'body'; *amu* / *amamu* 'road'.

In the numerous languages of the Chad area, whose status as Hamito-Semitic has not yet won general recognition, plurals of the type under discussion are prominent, in some instances being the normal and most frequent formation, a situation not found elsewhere in the Afroasiatic family. In fact, it was the importance of internal *a*-plurals in some of these languages and their obvious resemblance to the segholate and broken plurals of Semitic which first drew my attention to the present topic.

The Chad languages fall into at least nine subgroups and for many of them the information is too fragmentary to be taken into account.[10] Short vocabularies which give noun plurals in a few phrases permit only a small glimpse into the mechanism of plural formation. Hence, with few exceptions, those languages for which relatively full grammatical information is available will be taken into consideration.

By far the best-known of the Chad languages is Hausa. Hausa has numerous patterns of plural formation, various types of partial reduplication—though not with *a*—being particularly prominent. Whenever internal change is involved, sometimes accompanied by other processes, intercalation or replacement with *a* is prominent. Examples are: *fálké·* (<*fátké·*) / *fátà·ké·* 'merchant'; *túmk-ìyá·* (*túmá·kí·*) 'ewe'; *dó·kì·* / *dáwá·kí·* 'horse'; *kúnčí·* (<*kúmtí·*) / *kúmà·tú·* 'cheek'. There is general replacement in *mijì* / *mázá·* 'man, male'.

Outside of Angas, which suffixes the third person plural pronoun after the manner of surrounding languages of the Niger-Congo family, only fragmentary information for other languages of the western subgroup is available, but there are indications of the existence of the internal *a*-plural. For example, in Meek's vocabulary of Ngizim we find *gimsik* / *gimsak* 'man'; *gəzbir* / *gəzbar-in* 'tall (agreeing with a feminine noun)'.[11]

East of the territory where Hausa is spoken, the important group of languages

[10] For a complete enumeration of Chad languages see the above-mentioned article by J. H. Greenberg in *Southwestern Journal of Anthropology* 6 (1950): 51–52. The grouping given there is tentative and there are a number of languages for which the evidence for classification is insufficient.

[11] C. K. Meek, *Tribal Studies in Northern Nigeria* (London, 1931), II: 263.

of the Kotoko-Logone subgroup are found. Lukas has provided grammatical outlines of several of these languages. In Logone various forms of the internal *a*-plural are prominent, as can be seen from the following examples: *gənəm* / *gənam* 'woman'; *ləyəmi* / *layam* 'river'; *zəvəni* / *zavan* 'lion'; *kalge* / *kalage* 'mouth'; *bəskwan* / *ba·sa·kwan* 'horse'; *xsəni* / *xasan* 'nose'; *zəxti* / *zaxate* 'lion'; *səlkə* / *sa·la·ke* 'star'. A few instances in which the plural suffix *-en* is also present remind us strongly of the mixed plural of Berber: *ŋgun* / *ŋgwanen* 'belly'; *s̰ivi* / *s̰aven* 'grass'.[12]

Buduma, another language of this subgroup, forms most plurals by suffixing but also employs replacement along with suffixation, e.g. *ŋgərum* / *ŋgəram-ai* 'woman'.

Gulfei has general replacement in *gərəm* / *garam* 'woman' with the variant plural *garame*. It has many instances of the mixed *type*: *x̱ir* / *x̱are* 'tooth'; *gəlkə* / *galke* 'old man'; *sulu* / *salle* 'road'; *ləm* / *lame* 'rope'; etc.

Musgu, southeast of Lake Chad, is the only member of another Chad subgroup. Musgu nouns practically all have suffixes, but the mixed type, whether intercalatory, replacive, or general, is common. Examples are *huŋ* / *huaŋ-ai* 'mountain'; *gumuri·* / *gamar-ai* 'shield'; *mirxi* / *mara·x-ai* 'devil'. Adjectives, which have plurals formed by suffixation, generally accompany this with internal change. Only the masculine singular form of the adjective is given here. The plural form is used for both genders, *pidɛm* / *pudam-ai* 'beautiful'; *mɛlfiŋ* / *malfan-ai* 'blind'; *we·l* / *wal-akai* 'large', etc.

In the large eastern subgroup, the best-described language is Mubi. In this language internal *a*-plurals of all the subtypes and with endless variety of combination are the dominant method of forming plurals. Illustrative examples are *f̱úgá* / *f̱àgè* 'dog'; *mélá* / *málè* 'well'; *sìn* / *sànì* 'leg'; *gìr* / *gárè* 'house'; *fírsí* / *fìrá·s* 'horse'; *bɛ̀dígí* / *bátták* 'garment'; *lísí* / *lésás* 'tongue'; *gìp* / *gá·bàb* 'knee'; *bé·lì* / *bá·làl* 'lake'.

The remaining branch of Afroasiatic is Ancient Egyptian. Only for the Coptic period is there direct evidence of vocalization. Most Coptic nouns do not form separate plurals. Those that do often show internal change, with or without suffixation, but such alternations of vowels between singular and plural as are found can almost all be explained on the assumption of differences of vowel quality in open and closed syllables in the earlier stages of the language.[13]

[12] For the Logone examples, see J. Lukas, *Die Logone-Sprache im zentralen Sudan* (Leipzig, 1936); for Gulfei and Mubi his *Zentralsudanische Studien* (Hamburg, 1937); for Musgu his *Deutsche Quellen zur Sprache der Musgu in Kamerun* (Berlin, 1941); and for Buduma his *Die Sprache der Buduma* (Leipzig, 1939).

[13] In accordance with the usual manner of reconstructing earlier Egyptian from Coptic, an internal *a* plural may survive in two words, accompanied by a plural suffix. The word for 'tear'

Our conclusion is that the segholate plurals of Hebrew and Aramaic, the related broken plurals of South Semitic, and the sporadic partial reduplications with *a* in Akkadian are all representative of an old Hamito-Semitic group of patterns of plural formation. Just as the *r*/*n* declension, which survives in a marginal way in Indo-European, is a major form of declension in Hittite, so these forms, which are of relatively minor importance in Semitic, appear as dominant modes of plural formation in Berber and in some of the Chad languages.

It may be objected that since there are so many languages to choose from and many of them have multiple methods of forming plurals, such coincidences as are cited here are inevitable and prove nothing. It can hardly be an accident, though, that in the Afroasiatic languages, whenever there is a question of plural with internal change, it almost invariably takes the form of an *a* appearing in the plural not found in the singular, and that the favorite position for its occurrence is between the penultimate and last consonant of the root.

There are so few cognates among Afroasiatic languages, and the types of formations are so varied, that it does not seem possible to discover in which group of nouns in the parent language internal plurals appeared as opposed to mixed plurals and those involving suffixation.

The present essay may also be looked upon as further confirmation of the reality of the Afroasiatic family, though I believe that the already existing evidence is sufficient to prove its existence beyond any reasonable doubt.

---

Bohairic *ermé·*, Sahidic and Achmimic *ərmié·* has as its plural Sahidic *ərmióue* and Bohairic *ermó·ui*. Likewise Sahidic *təbné·*, Bohairic *tebné·* 'cattle' has the plurals *təbnóue* (Sahidic), *tebno·ui* (Bohairic), and *təbnóu* but also *təbneue* (Achmimic). The *o* and *o·* of these plurals should derive from earlier Egyptian *u* or *a* replacing *e·* (< *i*) of the singular. The word for 'woman', Achmimic *hime*/*hiaame*, with corresponding forms in other dialects is possibly another example.

# The Labial Consonants of Proto-Afro-Asiatic

Excluding *w* from consideration, almost all languages of the Afro-Asiatic family have three labial consonants, a nasal */m/*, a voiced stop */b/*, and a single unvoiced consonant, in some languages the unvoiced stop */p/*, in others a labiodental fricative */f/*. Thus in Semitic, which may be taken as a representative example of the family as a whole, there are three original labial consonants, an **m* which appears everywhere in this form, a **b* which is found in all languages as */b/* and a single unvoiced consonant which is usually written **p*. This latter occurs as */f/* in all South Semitic languages (Ethiopian, North and South Arabic) and as */p/* elsewhere. In Hebrew and Aramaic a distinction between *p* and *f* developed at a later stage based on an originally non-phonemic alternation found also in the other non-emphatic stops, according to which a fricative allophone arose in postvocalic position while the stop was retained elsewhere.

An example of a parallel situation in a non-Semitic language of the family is Berber. Here again there are three labials, */m/*, */b/*, and */f/*, corresponding to Proto-Semitic **m*, **b*, and **p*, respectively.

Egyptian, however, has four distinct labial phonemes, */m/*, */b/*, */p/*, and */f/*. As might be expected, the first two correspond to Proto-Semitic **m* and **b* while the last two correspond to Proto-Semitic **p*. Those who have considered this matter have tacitly or explicitly assumed that Egyptian has innovated here, splitting an original single unvoiced labial into */p/* and */f/*, although a

[1] A representative opinion is that of Marcel Cohen. "La solution adoptée ici est l'existence d'un seul phonème, l'argument principal étant que *p* et *f* correspondent suivant les mots au phonème unique du sémitique; la division en deux phonèmes serait secondaire en égyptien, s'étant opérée dans des conditions qui nous échappent" (*Essai comparatif sur le vocabulaire et la phonétique du Hamito-Sémitique* [Paris, 1947], pp. 166–67).

conditioning factor for this change has never been discovered.[1] In view of the possible effects of vowels, which in the present state of knowledge cannot be reconstructed with certainty for earliest Egyptian, or in view of other unknown, possibly prosodic factors, and particularly in the absence of this distinction in the other languages of the family which have been reasonably well described up to now, this is a justifiable decision.

It is clear, however, that if some language or group of languages does exist in Afro-Asiatic which distinguishes two unvoiced labials and if these sounds correspond etymologically to the two unvoiced labials of Egyptian, then the above interpretation will have to be abandoned and it will be Semitic rather than Egyptian which will have innovated in merging two originally distinct labial phonemes.

It is the thesis of this paper that such a group of languages does exist, the subgroups of Chad languages spoken on the Jos Plateau in Nigeria, which will be called here the Plateau subgroup. The reconstruction of the original consonantal system of this group not only suggests with a high degree of probability that the Egyptian distinction between */p/* and */f/* is original but suggests the possibility of a still more complex labial series in Proto-Afro-Asiatic with similar implications for other series of consonants not considered in detail here, i.e. the dental and velar series.

The data on the Plateau group and other Chad languages presented here are partly based on my own field investigation and partly on other sources.[2] The chief Plateau languages utilized are Angas, Chip, Sura, Ankwe, and Gerka. The languages most closely related to the Plateau subgroup are the Bolewa group of languages, likewise spoken in Nigeria, which includes Bolewa proper, Karekare, Ngamo, Kanakuru, and Tangale.[3] Other Chad languages, particularly Hausa, Logone, Musgu, and Mubi are also occasionally cited.[4]

[2] This material was gathered in the course of a linguistic survey of the Plateau and Bauchi provinces of Nigeria as a Fellow of the Guggenheim Foundation during the period October 1955–August 1956. I am indebted to the Social Science Research Council and the Columbia Council for Research in the Social Sciences for supplementary support in connection with this research.

[3] Citations of Angas, Chip, Sura, Ankwe, Gerka, and Bolewa forms are based on my own investigations unless otherwise indicated. Through the courtesy of the Roman Catholic authorities in Jos, I was permitted to consult the unpublished work of Father Sirlinger on Angas and Ankwe. Both of these contain far more extensive vocabularies than I was able to gather. A further source for Angas is H. D. Foulkes' *Angass Manual* (London, 1915), which likewise has a very extensive vocabulary. Neither of these writers investigated the tonal systems of these languages, but otherwise their work appears reliable and has been reinterpreted here in phonemic terms. Citations from Sirlinger are indicated by (S), from Foulkes by (F). In one instance a form from Ankwe is quoted from the work of J. F. J. Fitzpatrick, "Some Notes on the Kwolla District and Its Tribes," *Journal of the African Society*, 10 (1915): 16–52, 213–21, 490ff.

[4] For a virtually complete bibliography of the Chad languages, see Dietrich Westermann and M. A. Bryan, *Languages of West Africa* (Oxford, 1952).

The Plateau group is characterized in general by monosyllabic morphemes of the form CVC and VC as against CVCV and VCV of the Bolewa group and the remainder of the Chad languages in general. A typical instance is Plateau Angas, Chip, Sura *sár* 'hand' as against Bolewa *sārā*. In all of the Plateau languages thus far recorded, and in Proto-Plateau as it can be reconstructed from these data, the number of distinct consonants which can occur as the final element of the common CVC morpheme type is limited to *p*, *t*, *s*, *k*, *m*, *n*, *ŋ*, *r*, and *l*.[5] As might be expected, Plateau final *p* corresponds to any non-nasal labial of the non-Plateau languages and *m* corresponds to *m*. Thus Angas (Plateau) *rə̄p* 'to divide' is related to Hausa *rábâ* 'to divide, separate', Angas *tə̄p* 'black' to Hausa *dúfù* 'darkness', and Angas *kwōm* 'ear' to Bolewa *kūmō* 'ear'. In similar fashion final *n*, *ŋ*, *r*, and *l* correspond to these same consonants elsewhere. However, final *n* frequently corresponds to the *l* of non-Plateau languages. All sibilants are reflected by *s*, velars by *k*, and dentals by *t*, except that the implosive *d* becomes *r* not *t* in the Plateau languages. Examples of all these will be found in the etymologies cited later in this paper.

In initial position, the Plateau languages have usually shifted the voiced non-imploded stops of the non-Plateau Chad languages and the other Afro-Asiatic languages to the corresponding unvoiced forms. The labials participate in this general shift so that in a number of instances Plateau *p* corresponds to *b* elsewhere. Examples of this sound change are:[6] (1) (a) Ankwe *pìn*, Gerka *pìn*; (b) Bolewa *bìn* 'room, hut', Kanakuru *mina* 'house', Sokoro *be : ni* 'to build'; (c) Proto-Semitic **bny* 'to build', Cushitic Sidamo *min* 'build', *minē*: 'house'. (2) (a) Angas *pār*, Sura *pār* 'night'; (b) Bolewa *bōdì*, Ngamo *bɛdi*, Kanakuru *biri* 'night'; (c) Cushitic Saho *bar* 'night'. (3) (a) Chip, Ankwe *pìt*, Gerka *pə̀t* 'monkey'; (b) Bolewa *bīdò*, Hausa *bírì* 'monkey'. (4) (a) Angas, Chip, Sura *pò*, Ankwe *pùə̀*, Gerka *pàk* 'mouth'; (b) Bolewa *bò*, Hausa *bà:kí:* 'mouth'.[7]

For all Plateau languages from which data at present are available on this point, with the exception of Ankwe, the unvoiced stops which result from this shift merge with the earlier unvoiced stops which correspond to those of the remaining Chad languages and Afro-Asiatic in general. Ankwe, however, alone among the languages thus far studied, has a phonemic distinction between glottalized and non-glottalized unvoiced consonants. The non-glottalized stops issue from the older voiced stops as in those of the etymologies

[5] In a few instances final *š* is found in Sura.

[6] Forms cited under (a) are from Plateau languages, under (b) from Chad non-Plateau languages, and under (c) from branches of Afro-Asiatic other than Chad.

[7] I cannot say whether the two variants seen in the Bolewa and Hausa are etymologically related. There is a common afformative suffix *īki* in Hausa, but I am not certain of its occurrence in other Chad languages.

just quoted in which Ankwe figures. The original unvoiced consonants are preserved in Ankwe in glottalized form. This may be exemplified from the labial series by the following example: (1) (a) Ankwe *p'ás*, Sura *pās*, Chip *pàs*; (b) Bolewa *púzō* 'rainy season'. (2) (a) Ankwe *p'ét*, Angas *pūt*, Chip *pút/pwát*, Sura *pūt*; (b) Bolewa *pēté*, Hausa *fítá* 'to go out'.

There is the further complication among the labial consonants, not paralleled in the other series, that for the single unvoiced labial of non-Plateau languages we find not only /*p'*/ in Ankwe and /*p*/ in languages other than Ankwe but a labiodental fricative /*f*/ in all the Plateau languages. An instance in point is the verb 'to boil' for which we have Angas *fīl*, Chip *fíál*, Sura *fīl*, Ankwe *fíál* as cognate forms to Bolewa *pūlō*.

Further, there are some instances in which the Plateau languages do not shift original *b* to *p* but instead preserve the voiced consonant. This is paralleled by instances of retention of original *d* and *g* in the other series. An example of this is Angas *bí*, Chip *bíì*, Ankwe *bìì* 'thing' related to Hausa *ˀàbù*, pre-genitival *ˀàbí-*. Though not as frequent as the cases in which the change *b* > *p* occurs, there are a fair number of instances of such preservation of the voiced form. As yet no rule seems formulable by which the conditions for the presence or absence of this shift can be stated. We will call the *b* that becomes *p* in the Plateau languages $*b_1$ and the *b* that remains $*b_2$.

Finally, the Chad languages in general distinguish in the labial and dental position between ordinary voiced and imploded voiced consonants, a distinction not found in any other branch of Afro-Asiatic. The voiced implosives of non-Plateau Chad languages are regularly reflected by similar sounds in the Plateau languages and it is found that the implosives are never devoiced. Examples in the labial series are relatively rare and those for related forms in other languages of the Chad subfamily for which the distinction between *ɓ* and *b* has been reliably reported are even fewer. We may cite the example of Angas *ɓur* (S) 'ashes' which is probably cognate with Bolewa *ɓūtó*, and Gerka (Plateau) *ɓəl* 'horn' which is surely related to Bolewa *ɓālū*, Tangale *ɓwàl*.

We thus reconstruct for Proto-Plateau six labial consonants including *m*. In the following table Angas is taken as representative of the Plateau languages outside of Ankwe.

| | Angas | Ankwe | Proto-Chad | Proto-Semitic |
|---|---|---|---|---|
| 1. | f | f | *f | *p |
| 2. | p | p' | *p | *p |
| 3. | p | p | $*b_1$ | *b |
| 4. | b | b | $*b_2$ | *b |
| 5. | ɓ | ɓ | *ɓ | *b |
| 6. | m | m | *m | *m |

The hypothesis, then, with which we will be mainly concerned here is whether the distinction between Proto-Chad **f* and **p*, both of which appear in Semitic as **p*, coincides etymologically with Egyptian **f* and **p*. Since, as has been seen, the distinction of all labial non-nasals is lost in final position in the Plateau languages, we can only make comparisons in initial position. Since the relationship between the Plateau subgroup of Chad and Egyptian is fairly distant, we cannot expect a large number of etymologies involving the not very frequent unvoiced labial. We find five etymologies with initial Plateau *f* in agreement with Egyptian *f* and three with initial *p* corresponding to Egyptian *p*. In considering these etymologies, in addition to the consonantal changes in final position in the Plateau languages, we must also take into account the common correspondence of Egyptian ˀ in non-initial position to *r* in Semitic and elsewhere and the total loss of the laryngeals ˀ, ʕ, *h*, and *ḥ* in the Plateau languages.

With *f* we have the following: (1) Angas *fíír*, Chip *fér*, Sura *féér*, Ankwe *féér*, Egyptian *fdw*, Coptic (Sahidic) *ftów* 'four'. In Bolewa we find *pōɗɗō* and Hausa *fúɗú*. This is a basic Afro-Asiatic etymology with related forms likewise in Cushitic (Bedauye *faḍig*, Somali *afar*, Saho *afar*, Galla *afur*) and in practically all the remaining Chad languages. The change Proto-Chad *ɗ* > Plateau *r* in this position is regular as was pointed out earlier and exemplified in the word for 'night'. (2) Angas *fier* 'largeness', Egyptian *fˀw* 'power, authority'. Here *-w* is a singular abstract suffix in Egyptian and ˀ for Plateau *r* is regular. This etymology is therefore formally acceptable. Its weakness is the apparent absence of related forms in any other language. (3) Angas *fut* (S), Ankwe *fuut* (S) 'to vomit', Egyptian *ft* 'be disgusted' (Erman-Grapow 'sich ekeln'). This is phonetically straightforward and semantically plausible. There is, however, some possibility of sound symbolism. (4) Angas *fì*, Sura *fìì*, Ankwe *fìì*, Gerka *fi*, Egyptian *fˀ* 'to blow'. Here again, with the usual Plateau loss of laryngeal, we have a formally and semantically acceptable etymology, though with some possibility of sound symbolism. (5) Angas *fīl*, Chip *fíál*, Sura *fīl*, Ankwe *fíál*, Gerka *fəl*, Egyptian *ˀfr* 'to boil'. This is another fundamental Afro-Asiatic etymology. The root also occurs in Cushitic Galla *afel* and Berber Shilḥ *flufu* with partial reduplication, both meaning 'to boil'. Egyptian has no written *l*, though it must have existed since it appears later in Coptic. Forms with *l* in related languages are written often with *r*, sometimes with *n*. Semitic here shows related forms with *r*, e.g. Arabic *fwr*, Syriac *fr'*, *fwr*, Ethiopic *nfr* 'to boil'. Sporadic *r-l* correspondences are common in Afro-Asiatic. A further possible etymology is Angas *fét*, Sura *fét*, 'to sweep', Egyptian *fd* 'to wipe'. These were the Angas and Sura forms which I elicited. However, Sirlinger has both these forms and Ankwe *pat* 'to wipe, to sweep', Angas *pet* 'broom, to sweep'. There were then apparently doublets with initial *p* and *f*.

Correspondences involving *p* are: (1) Angas *piar* (S) 'to jump, to leap', Ankwe *p'aar* ( S) 'to jump', Egyptian *pʔ* 'to fly'. Here Egyptian ʔ corresponds to *r* elsewhere as noted earlier. The semantic transition is shown in Buduma (Chad) *fər* which has the meanings 'to jump, to dance, to fly'. There is also the probably related Angas *pir* (S) 'to stretch the wings'. This is a widespread Afro-Asiatic root. Other examples are Cushitic Bedauye *fār* 'to hop, to jump', Berber Shilḥ *firri* 'to fly'. The common Semitic root 'to flee', Arabic *frr*, Syriac *prr* is doubtless likewise connected. (2) Angas *pūs*, Chip *pùs*, Sura *pūs* 'to shoot, to sting', Angas *pās*, Chip *pás*, Sura *pās* 'arrow'; Egyptian *pzḥ* 'to bite, to sting'. The Plateau loss of the laryngeal *ḥ* and change *z* > *s* are regular. Unfortunately, the absence of this form in Ankwe does not permit us to decide for Proto-Plateau *p* as against $b_1$ on Plateau evidence alone. (3) Angas *pok* 'to peel, to strip' (F), 'to remove grains from the stalk' (S); Egyptian *pgʔ* 'shell'. Here the Hausa *fī́gà* 'to strip a guinea corn stalk' gives welcome evidence that we are dealing with **g* and not **k*.

There are no plausible etymologies, of which I am aware, that involve Plateau *p* and Egyptian *f* or Plateau *f* and Egyptian *p*. Although, as has been noted, not all the above etymologies are equally likely, their combined effect is such that the correspondence of Plateau *p* and *f* to Egyptian *p* and *f* is highly probable; if this is so, it follows that this distinction is original in Afro-Asiatic.

Regarding $*b_1$ and $*b_2$, there is some evidence that the distinction is Proto-Afro-Asiatic and that $*b_2$ may have been a prenasalized voiced stop, */*mb*/. The word for 'thing', quoted earlier, Angas *bí*, Chip *bìí*, Ankwe *bìì* appears in Logone, another Chad language, as *mbi*. Further, if it is Angas *be* (S) 'side, direction', Ankwe *be* (Fitzpatrick) 'place' which is to be connected with Egyptian *bw*; Cushitic Sidamo *ba'a*, Gudella *beyo*, rather than Angas *pí*, Ankwe *pèé*, then we have once more a correspondence with Logone *mb* in *mba* 'place'. Further, Egyptian *bw* appears later in Coptic as *ma*. Finally, there is Angas *būl*, Chip *búl*, Sura *ñbūl*, Ankwe *bél* 'dove' which occurs in Bolewa as *mbōlè* and is related to Egyptian *mnwt* 'dove'. The final *t* in Egyptian is the feminine singular suffix.

As against this evidence, we have a number of cases without *m* or *mb* in non-Plateau languages. An example is Angas *bə́s*, Chip *bís*, Sura *bíš* 'bad', related to Cushitic Quara *bisā*, Sidamo *buššo*, and found in Semitic as **bʔs* (e.g. Arabic *biʔsa* 'it is bad', Akkadian *bīšu* 'bad'). The variants with *m* in the forms connected with Ankwe *pìn* 'room, hut' cited above in a form which goes back to initial $*b_1$ is presumably due to assimilation to the following nasal.

Regarding the distinction between *ɓ* and *b*, for which there is at present no support outside of the Chad languages, it is safer to assume, until such evidence is forthcoming, that they both continue a single original Proto-Afro-Asiatic phoneme. This conclusion is based on the same methodological considerations which justified the inference that the difference between *p* and *f* in Egyptian was secondary until the contrary thesis became highly probable because of the evidence presented in this paper.

# The Origin of the Masai Passive

There are two methods by which facts concerning the unrecorded past of a language may be recovered. The first may be labelled the external method. By confrontation with comparable facts of other languages to which it is related, we may reconstruct in some measure the past of a particular language. This is the familiar comparative method. Sometimes, however, another procedure, that of internal reconstruction, may be applied, independently or as a supplement to the comparative method.[1] The facts of the language as described at a given time suggest certain hypotheses regarding its own past. The present study involves a combination of these two methods. An interpretation strongly suggested by the Masai language in its present form receives further confirmation and elucidation by the subsequent application of the comparative method.

It has long been realized that in the Masai passive the apparent subject is historically the object and that an additional original subject pronoun of the third person is implied. Thus the Masai word *aa-dɔl-i*, in which *-i* is the mark of the present passive, is justifiably translated 'I am seen' on the basis of present usage. Historically, however, it represents something like '*X sees me*' where, for the moment, nothing further is asserted about *X* except that it is of the third person. A. C. Hollis, to whom we are indebted for the first systematic grammar of Masai, labels the formation as passive but translates the paradigm of the model verb *svj* 'to follow' as 'it is followed to me', 'it is followed to you', etc.[2] The recent grammar of Tucker and Mpaayei similarly

[1] For discussions of the theory of internal reconstruction, see G. Bonfante, "On Reconstruction and Linguistic Method," *Word* 1 (1945): 83–94, 132–61; and Henry M. Hoenigswald, "Sound Change and Linguistic Structure," *Language* 22 (1946): 138–42.

[2] A. C. Hollis, *The Masai, Their Language and Folklore* (Oxford, 1905), p. 67.

makes the following observation: "From the point of view of verb conjugation, the Passive could be regarded as a specialized form of *3rd person active* in that it takes a contained object (compare French *on vous appelle* for 'You are called')."[3]

The grammar of Tucker and Mpaayei contains the interesting discovery that in Masai the subjective and objective forms of substantives have distinct tonal patterns. In the instance of the passive, they note that "the noun agent, when used, has the tone patterns of the subject."[4] This indicates that the subject of the passive is treated as a true subject in the present-day Masai language and not as an object, as might be expected on historical grounds. Tucker and Mpaayei paraphrase the passive as '(something) follows me, (something) follows you', etc.[5]

The basic reason for the agreement of previous writers on the Masai language on the hypothesis that the apparent subject is historically the object is to be found in the set of prefixes by which the Masai passive is conjugated for person and number. In general, in Masai person and number, whether of the subject only (intransitive verbs) or subject and object (transitive verbs), are indicated by prefixes. The prefixes of the passive do not agree with those of the active verb of the corresponding person and number. Thus *a-dɔl* is 'I see (him/her/them)' but 'I am seen' is not **a-dɔl-i* with the passive *-i* suffix, as might be expected; it is rather *aa-dɔl-i*. The second person singular active is *i-dɔl* but the passive is *ki-dɔl-i* not **i-dɔl-i*. These passive prefixes, however, agree in every detail, including tonal pattern, with those forms of the active verb in which the *object* is of the corresponding person and number and the subject is third person singular or plural, no distinction being made in number in these forms. Thus *aa-dɔl* is 'he/she/they see me' with the same prefix as *aa-dɔl-i* 'I am seen', and *ki-dɔl* is 'he/she/they see thee' with the same prefix as *ki-dɔl-i* 'thou art seen', and so on through the whole conjugation.

This can hardly be an accident, and the assumption of previous writers on the Masai language has been that the apparent subject of the 'passive' is historically the object and that a third person subject is implied throughout. The question considered here is whether anything more precise can be determined regarding the meaning and form of this third person subject variously paraphrased as 'it' by Hollis, 'something' by Tucker and Mpaayei, and left undetermined as '*X*' by the writer in the earlier portion of this paper.

Can the number of this third person element be discovered? In view of the fact that the forms of the prefix for third person singular and third person plural subject are identical throughout, this does not seem possible at first

[3] A. N. Tucker and J. Mpaayei, *A Maasai Grammar* (London, 1955), p. 79.

[4] *Ibid.*

[5] *Ibid.*, n. 1.

appearance. But other evidence exists. First, it may be noted that the Masai infinitive distinguishes a singular and plural form in which the number always agrees with that of the subject of the clause or sentence. For example, the verb *dɔl* 'see' has a singular infinitive *a-dɔl* and a plural *aa-dɔl*.

The use of these infinitives can be illustrated from the following examples:

| | | | |
|---|---|---|---|
| *atareto* | *ɔltʋŋani* | *a-mʋk* | *ɛnaišo* |
| I helped | the man | to brew (sg.) | beer |
| *kitareto* | *ɔltʋŋani* | *aa-mʋk* | *ɛnaišo* |
| we helped | the man | to brew (pl.) | beer |

Here the singular infinitive agrees with the singular subject 'I' and the plural infinitive with the plural subject 'we'. For the moment, we make this statement with the mental note that if we could discover a construction in which a passive verb governed a following infinitive, the number of the infinitive would agree with and thus reveal the number of the concealed subject of the passive verb.

There is a further relevant observation. A few Masai verbs have two distinct stems, one used in all persons with a singular subject and the other in all persons with a plural subject. An example is the verb 'to be dead', with the singular stem *tua* and the plural *tuata*. Unfortunately, all the verbs with two stems are intransitive, as in the example just cited. Therefore, they are not normally employed in the passive.

There is, however, a construction in Masai which gives us exactly what we want. The passive of the intransitive verbs 'come', 'go', and 'sit', all three of which have distinct singular and plural stems, are used in the passive followed by an infinitive in an idiomatic construction which may be literally translated as 'I am come to be followed', 'I am gone to be followed', and 'I am sat to be followed'. The first two are periphrastic ways of rendering the future passive. The last may be more freely translated 'one stays to follow me'.

In this construction a twofold choice between singular and plural must be made, first in employing the singular or plural stem of the auxiliary verb 'come', 'go', or 'sit', and secondly in regard to the form of the infinitive. In all instances the choice is unequivocally plural. To take one example, 'I shall be followed' is rendered in Masai by *aa-puo-i aa-sʋj*, literally 'I am gone to be followed'. Here the verb 'go' which has the singular stem *lo* and the plural *puo*, uses the plural and the infinitive is the plural infinitive *aa-sʋj* rather than the singular *a-sʋj*.

We now see that the concealed subject pronoun is plural, and since we already know that it is third person, our *X* is third person plural and is to be translated 'they'. The above construction may now be literally translated as 'me-go-they to-follow (pl.)', where *aa-puo-i* is now analysed as *aa-* 'prefix denoting action of third person subject on first person singular object', as elsewhere in Masai, *-puo-* is the stem of the verb 'go' used with a plural subject, and *-i* is now revealed as the pronominal mark of the plurality of the subject in the third person and can therefore be translated as 'they'. This particular construction has a semantic parallel in some Romance languages, e.g. in Italian, where 'they are going to follow me' can be expressed as *mi vanno seguire* 'me go-they to-follow' where, just as in Masai, the pronoun has become the object of the normally intransitive verb 'go'.

To sum up, in the ordinary passive construction in Masai, the present-day forms translated as 'I am followed', 'you are followed', etc., are, historically, 'they follow me', 'they follow you', etc. It may be observed that this is a very wide-spread method of expressing the passive in African languages. Thus, to cite but one out of many possible examples, in the Temne language of far-off Sierra Leone *a dif ko* 'they kill him' is the normal method of expressing the passive 'he is killed'.

As far as the form of this third person plural element is concerned, the examples thus far cited have all been in the present where the suffix is *-i*.[6] In tenses other than the present and continuative, and in the derived forms of the verb, the passive suffix is some consonant followed by *-i* rather than *-i* alone. Since the ending *-i* is thus common to all passive forms and since it appears as such in the present, where the active has no suffix, there is a descriptive basis for positing the passive morpheme as *-i*. Where the *-i* is preceded by some consonant it is not difficult to see that this consonant is a mark of the particular tense or derivational form which has survived in the passive before *-i* but has been lost in the active when in final position and not protected by a following vowel. For this there is, in most cases, internal evidence from Masai as well as the evidence of related languages. One example will reveal the principle underlying the others and be sufficient for our purposes.

The Masai verb has a derived form with the signification 'motion towards the speaker'. This form is marked by a suffixed *-u* in the present and *-uni* in the present passive. That *-uni* is to be analysed not as *-u-* 'motion towards' + *-ni* 'passive' but *-un-* 'motion towards' + *-i* 'passive' is shown both by the Masai and comparative evidence. In Masai itself the final consonant of *un* is restored before other derivational suffixes in compound derivational forms. When the 'neuter' suffix *-ye* is added to that of the 'motion towards', we have *-un-ye* in the active and not **-u-ye*. Likewise Bari, a closely related language, has an *-un* suffix for motion towards.

[6]The 'Nilo-Hamitic' and the Moru-Madi branch of Central Sudanic have highly similar systems of vowel harmony. Here, as elsewhere, when there are two variants of the same morpheme with differing vowels based on rules of vowel harmony, the form with the high vowel will be quoted.

This is likewise the interpretation adopted in these cases by Tucker and Mpaayei. Regarding the suffix discussed above, they remark: "Since the 'Motion Towards' suffix is *-un* in Bari, with final *-n* (see Spagnolo, p. 143) one may postulate here a 'Neuter' vowel suffix restoring this *-n-* in Masai. Compare the Passive form in § 161."[7]

We conclude, therefore, that the form of the suffix which distinguishes the passive from the active, and which is, therefore, historically a marker of the third person plural, is *-i*. Before turning to the comparative evidence, we shall consider more closely the function of this suffix. Strictly speaking, it does not, by itself, indicate the third person plural. Rather, it distinguishes the plural from the singular within the third person since it is always accompanied by a prefix which marks the third person subject without regard to number. The term sometimes employed for such an element is a 'pluralizer'. Therefore, *-i* is a third person pluralizer by the addition of which a form which otherwise would be of the third person but indeterminate in regard to number becomes more closely defined as a plural.

We may conjecture that this *-i* was formerly added to the active third person in Masai, whether optionally or compulsively, to distinguish plurality of the third person subject which is at present ambiguous and can only be specified by the addition of an independent pronoun or understood from the presence of a plural substantive subject.

The Lotuho language, which is closely related to Masai, has an *-i* suffix which is always added in the third person to indicate plurality and is accompanied by a prefix which is identical for the third person subject whether singular or plural. The existence of *-i* as a compulsory third person pluralizer in the active in a language closely related to Masai is a strong confirmation of the general correctness of interpretation of the Masai passive offered here.

In the large Chari-Nile family, of which Masai is a member, most languages conjugate exclusively by prefixes. Barea, however, a member of the Eastern Sudanic branch of the family which includes Masai, conjugates exclusively by suffix. In this language almost all tenses and derived conjugations suffix *-i* as the normal method of expressing the third person plural.

A further instance is found among the Central Sudanic languages which constitute another branch of the Chari-Nile family. In the Moru dialect cluster, a suffixed *-i* is the optional mark of plurality in the third person.[8]

For the Chari-Nile family as a whole, then, we may tentatively reconstruct

[7] Tucker and Mpaayei, p. 149, n. 2. See also p. 150, n. 2 and p. 152, n. 1 for the same reasoning regarding other derivative formations.

[8] A. N. Tucker, *The Eastern Sudanic Languages* (London, 1940), p. 245.

the history of the verbal suffix *-i* as follows: it is originally a third person pluralizer, probably optional. This is the usage still found in the Moru dialects. In Barea, which developed a suffix conjugation, it has become the most frequent suffix of the third person plural. Lotuho has maintained the original state of affairs except that *-i*, from being merely optional, has become a compulsory pluralizer. Finally, in Masai, the *-i* became specialized ultimately to the construction in which the third person plural subject served as a means of expressing the passive. The non-appearance of this element in so many Chari-Nile languages is not difficult to account for in the present theory. Being only optional, it could be more easily lost than a compulsory inflection of the normal type. Further, since the original system was apparently a prefixing one, such a suffix would tend to be lost because of its lack of conformity with the overall system.

The interpretation presented here as to the function of *-i* as an optional third person pluralizer is believed to account more adequately for the observed facts than any alternative hypothesis. However, its rejection in this specific form would not entail the abandonment of the main thesis of this paper, namely, that the Masai passive marker *-i* was originally a third person plural subject element and that it is cognate with the corresponding forms in Lotuho, Barea, and Moru.

Finally, a number of related topics, whose detailed discussion is not within the scope of this paper, may be briefly mentioned. In addition to the *-i* suffix there is apparently a second pluralizer or plural suffix consisting of *-k* followed by some vowel. In Barea *-k* suffixes are found in the third person plural in those instances where *-i* is not found. In the first and second person plurals of Barea only *-k* forms are found; in Dagu in the first person only. In Lugbara and Keliko of the Moru-Madi subgroup of the Central Sudanic branch, *-ki* is used in all three persons of the plural, and in Madi in the third person only. Since *-i* is found only in the third person, it may be conjectured that the *-k* forms were proper to the first and second person and in some cases analogically extended to the third. Alternatively, *-k* is original in all three persons but confined to certain verbal formations. This matter requires further investigation.

Moreover, it cannot be accidental that the two verb plural afformatives discussed here are also the two most frequent nominal plurals in the Chari-Nile languages in general. Indeed, in Moru, in a plural sentence, *-i* may be added either to the nominal subject or the verb, but not to both.[9]

The resemblance of the Nandi passive to that of Masai may also be mentioned. This is a semantic parallel but the forms themselves are not

[9] According to one observer, Mrs. Frazer, all plural sentences must have this *-i*, whether suffixed to the noun or the verb. Tucker, p. 137, n. 1.

related. Just as in Masai, the verb afformatives of the passive are the same as those of the third person active with the object in the same person as the passive subject. However, the Nandi construction differs from that of Masai in that the concealed third person subject is a prefixed *ki-* rather than a suffixed *-i*, and that there is apparently no internal evidence regarding the number of this element. It may be related to a subject *k-* element, usually indifferent to number, which is widespread in Chari-Nile languages, often confined to certain tenses or certain constructions: for example, in Shilluk, Lango, Suk, Kunama, Momvu, Miza, and in Nandi itself.

# Linguistic Evidence for the Influence of the Kanuri on the Hausa

The present study is intended both as a substantive historical contribution, and as an illustration of the possibilities and the limitations of one particular type of historical inference that can be drawn from language, namely, the study of words borrowed from one language into another. Two other basic linguistic sources for cultural-historical conclusions are not considered here, those based on the relationships and distribution of languages as such, and those based on the reconstructed vocabularies of particular *Ursprachen*, that is, the ancestral speech-forms of specific groups of genetically related languages. These latter two methods are not excluded either for dogmatic or methodological reasons, but simply because they do not yield relevant results for the particular problems being considered, although they are very useful in other connections. It should, however, be mentioned that, as will appear at a number of points in the discussion, a valid linguistic classification furnishes an indispensible framework for nearly all inferences drawn from linguistic data including the interlinguistic contact phenomena which are the subject of the present study.

The specific problems treated here arose out of certain questions raised by an earlier study concerning Arabic loan words in Hausa.[1] In view of the undoubted fact that the Hausa could not have possessed a knowledge of writing before the coming of Islam and the further fact that such words as those for 'book', 'pen', 'ink', etc., are all borrowed from Arabic, the writer was puzzled to note that the word for 'write' itself could not be derived from Arabic, while that for 'read', while doubtless of ultimate Arabic origin, displayed certain features which were unusual in words borrowed from

[1] J. H. Greenberg, "Arabic Loan-Words in Hausa," *Word* 3 (1947): 85–97.

Arabic. Subsequent investigation showed that beyond any reasonable doubt the word for 'write' had been borrowed from Kanuri, while the word for 'read', while of ultimate Arabic origin, had been borrowed via this latter language. A systematic investigation of the general question of linguistic contacts between the speakers of Hausa and Kanuri showed the existence of borrowings from Kanuri into Hausa for a number of other words of key cultural importance. It is not my purpose here to consider the documentary historical evidence. It will merely be pointed out that the borrowing of these terms from Kanuri into Hausa, although involving relatively few terms, points to an important role for Kanuri speakers in the introduction of Islamic and other cultural features of Mediterranean origin. The usual view, based primarily on the *Kano Chronicle*, is that Islam was introduced from the Empire of Mali in the fourteenth century.[2] At least one evidence of a contrary tradition of derivation from Bornu has been noted.[3] Since Islam seems to have been established among Kanuri speakers already in the eleventh century, and the Kanem Empire was an important political power during the next several centuries, it seems, on the face of it, likely that it would have exercised important cultural influence on the relatively weak and disunited Hausa states immediately to the west. This is, of course, not to deny the importance of the western factor or the reality of Mali and, later, of Songhai influence. There is nothing contradictory here. As Trimingham has pointed out, the typical history of Islamicization in the Western Sudan has been that of initial conversions, usually among the socio-political elite, with subsequent revivals and gradual spread to the remaining population, marked by episodes of renewed Islamic impulses of both internal and external origin.[4] In fact, there is linguistic evidence of western influence, chiefly Songhai, on the Hausa language, though less extensive than that of Kanuri. This topic merits a separate parallel study to the present one which the writer hopes to carry out at some future date.

The body of the paper is divided into two sections. The first is a systematic statement of the methodological principles involved. The second is the application of these principles to a selected set of examples in which borrowing of Kanuri terms of cultural-historical significance into Hausa seems certain, or in certain cases, highly plausible.

The Hausa language belongs to the Chad branch of the Afroasiatic (Hamito-Semitic) language family.[5] Kanuri belongs to a genetically different

[2] For example, D. Westermann, *Geschichte Afrikas* (Cologne, 1952), pp. 127, 129; and J. D. Fage, *An Introduction to the History of West Africa* (Cambridge, Eng., 1955), p. 34.

[3] R. S. Rattray, *Hausa Folk-Lore, Customs, Proverbs* (2 vols., Oxford, 1913), vol. 2, p. 6.

[4] J. S. Trimingham, *Islam in West Africa* (Oxford, 1959), p. 47.

[5] For details, see J. H. Greenberg, *Studies in African Linguistic Classification* (New Haven, Conn., 1955).

group of languages, Central Saharan, which includes Daza-Teda, Berti, and Zaghawa. More recent investigations, the details of which have not been published, show that Central Saharan is one branch of a much larger stock which includes Maban, Furian, Chari-Nile (Macro-Sudanic), and, in all probability, Songhai and Koman. This wider group, here called Sudanic, becomes relevant at at least one point of the subsequent analysis.

Conclusions regarding borrowing may be classified into two-language inferences and multilanguage inferences. The two-language inferences, which are considered first, involve considerations based on the comparison of the sound systems, semantics, and grammars of the two languages concerned without regard for outside evidence. When the term which we suspect has been borrowed occurs only in the two languages considered, we are in principle confined to such methods. We may classify the methods involved into those which concern phonology, grammar, and semantics.

Comparison of the sound systems of two languages will almost always show certain differences of structure which will affect the phonetic form of borrowed words in such a way as to give evidence regarding the direction of the borrowing. For example, Hausa has both a non-glottalized *k* and glottalized *k'* as distinct phonemes, while Kanuri has only the unglottalized *k*. Hence we will expect that in words borrowed from Hausa into Kanuri the unglottalized *k* of Kanuri will replace the glottalized *k'* of Hausa. If both languages have *k*, then no inference can be drawn from this fact, but Kanuri as the source language is at least not refuted. An example here is the Hausa word 'small' *k'àrámí:*, whose resemblance to Kanuri *kərámì* 'younger sibling' is probably not accidental, and which on the basis of this criterion has probably been borrowed by Kanuri from Hausa. A more complex situation regards *r* sounds in Kanuri and Hausa. Here again Hausa has two distinct sounds, a flapped *r* and a rolled *R*, while Kanuri has a single *r* sound, phonetically apparently closer to the Hausa rolled sound. Both the internal evidence of Hausa itself and comparison with related languages shows that the flapped *r* typically occurs in words inherited from Proto-Chad and Proto-Afroasiatic and corresponds in general to *r* sounds in other languages of the same family.[6] On the other hand, *R* has developed within Hausa itself from the dentals *t*, *d*, *s*, *z* in final position in the syllable—that is, when not followed by a vowel or when final in the word. This is evident from reduplicated forms in Hausa itself, e.g. *kwâRkwátà* (**kwâtkwátà* <**kwátàkwátà*). Here the falling tone on the first *a* shows that a syllable has been lost. Again, we have *k'àRk'áší* 'underneath', a reduplicated form related to *k'ásà* 'earth'. Further, the pregenitival feminine particle, e.g. *ˀúwá-R-*

[6]Examples include Hausa *sár-(kí:)* 'king' = Akkadian *šarru* 'king', Egyptian *śr* 'high official'; Hausa *fùré:* 'flower' = Hebrew *pəri* 'fruit'; Hausa *k'á:rá:* 'cry out' = Semitic **qaraˀa* 'call'.

'mother (of)' as opposed to the masculine *n* in *ˀùbá-n-* 'father (of)' is clearly derived from the general Afroasiatic *t* feminine and in Hausa itself the longer forms for 'of' are the obviously parallel *tá* and *ná*.

The rolled *R* has, however, come into Hausa in other positions via loan-words. Thus Arabic *r* seems invariably to be rendered as *R*. The occurrence of *R*, therefore, in other than syllable final position may be considered an indication of probable foreign origin while the occurrence of *r* in any position is usually an indication that we are dealing with an inherited word. Note, for example, that in the instance of Hausa *k'àrámí:* 'small', cited earlier as being the source of Kanuri *kərámì*, both the criterion of *k'* and flapped *r* lead to this same conclusion. It likewise bolsters our confidence in this criterion to see that a number of terms for political offices ending in the Kanuri suffix *-ma*, and universally admitted to be loan words from Kanuri, have *R* in non-final position in the syllable, e.g. Hausa *číRò:mà* and *yàRí:mà*.

An important, in most instances a decisive criterion is that of grammatical analysability in the source language and lack of such analysability in the borrowing language. In the examples of names for political offices, these forms all contain the common Kanuri suffix *-ma* 'possessor' and the first part can usually be interpreted as a place name or otherwise in Kanuri, while no analysis is possible in Hausa. Finally, among two-language inferences, the criterion of semantic clustering may sometimes be employed. We would consider it unlikely that a particular language would borrow terms for 'stirrup' and 'saddle' from another language but that the term for 'bridle' should have moved in the other direction. This is, of course, in itself a weak criterion, to which we resort only when other methods have failed.

We turn now to multiple language methods. Whenever a form occurs elsewhere than in the two languages we are considering, this wider distribution is relevant. It also raises the possibility that the form has not been borrowed by one of the two languages we are investigating, but has been derived independently from the same or different sources. Thus forms that are found in Kanuri, Hausa, and Arabic may have been borrowed from Arabic independently or have passed from Arabic into Hausa via Kanuri, or from Arabic into Kanuri via Hausa. Often the additional evidence from other languages will enable us to distinguish the source language and the borrowing language in cases where the two-language criteria are not, of themselves, sufficient to decide the case.

In multilanguage cases we have, in part, a wider sphere of application for the two-language criteria mentioned, simply applied to more pairs of languages. Partly, however, new methods can be brought into play. One such new criterion is semantic nearness to the meaning in the source language. For example, Hausa *kúllùm* 'always' must be connected with Kanuri *kúllùm* 'every day'. None of the two-language criteria mentioned gives any basis for decision as to the direction of borrowing. However, the meaning of the Kanuri form is the same as that of Arabic colloquial *kull yu:m* 'every day'. Therefore, the direction of borrowing is Arabic→Kanuri→Hausa. Otherwise we would have to assume that Kanuri had, by a strange accident, changed the meaning from 'always' to 'every day' so that it happened to coincide with the original Arabic meaning.[7]

A second and very important criterion is based on comparative linguistic method. If a form is found in languages related to one of the languages, and in such a manner as to indicate that it is a cognate form, but not in languages related to the other, then it must be older in the first language, which must then be adjudged the source language. This criterion will be abundantly illustrated in the examples discussed later in this paper. It is tacitly assumed in many instances where our knowledge of the general situation of contact and the existence of earlier literary sources for Arabic make us assume Arabic origin almost automatically. If we had to rely on synchronic linguistic evidence only, the criterion of occurrence of cognate forms in related languages would usually in itself suffice. Consider, for example, the Swahili word *kitabu*, which is known to be borrowed from Arabic *kita:b*. The interesting fact here is that the criterion of morphological analysability, which is usually decisive, gives the strange result that the form is analysable in *both* languages. For, by the process called folk etymology by linguists, *ki-tabu* has been analysed as containing the frequent *ki-* class prefix and forms the plural *vi-tabu*. In the absence of written records, the criterion of cognate forms in related languages would be decisive, for there is no common Bantu root **-tabu*, whereas *k-t-b*, which is the root of *kita:bu* in Arabic, is found in other Semitic languages, e.g. Hebrew and Aramaic.

Finally, there is the criterion of geographic distribution of the form as a whole. Thus Hausa *wànzá:mì:* 'barber' and Kanuri *wànzâm* 'profession of barbering', *wànzàmmá* 'barber' must be connected and are probably ultimately from Arabic *ḥajja:m*. However, none of the criteria thus far mentioned is sufficient to decide the direction of borrowing as between Hausa and Kanuri. The whole question is put in a different light when we find that Songhai has *wandjam* 'barber', while apparently no language east of Kanuri has the form. Hausa then becomes the probable source for the Kanuri form.

A selected number of examples of cultural-historical terms are now considered in which the Kanuri provenance of Hausa terms seems certain

[7] However, F. W. Parsons, of the School of Oriental and African Studies, London, to whom I am indebted for comments regarding this paper, informs me that, contrary to the dictionaries available to me, *kullum* can mean 'every day' in Hausa. In this case, the methodological point still stands, but the specific example cited here is invalid since no decision can be made.

or highly probable. The list is, of course, far from exhaustive, nor is the existence of important loan words which moved in the opposite direction, from Hausa into Kanuri, denied.

1. Hausa *Rùbù:tú:*, Kanuri (Lukas) *rə̀vòtə́* 'writing'.[8] A number of independent criteria all indicate the Kanuri origin of the Hausa word for 'writing' beyond any reasonable doubt. Hausa has here the rolled *R* in non-syllable final position, normally an indication of foreign origin as mentioned earlier. Likewise, on the phonetic side, Kanuri has the high central unrounded vowel *ə*, which is phonetically between *i* and *u* and does not exist in Hausa. It appears as *i* and *u*, occasionally as *a*, in Hausa words taken from Kanuri. Since Kanuri has *i* and *u* in addition to *ə*, while Hausa has only *i* and *u*, the appearance of Kanuri *ə* in suspected borrowings is usually an indication of Kanuri origin. The argument is in principle similar to that concerning Hausa *k'* and *k* versus Kanuri *k*, considered earlier, with the roles of the two languages reversed.

More decisive than either of these phonetic arguments is the morphologic one. The suffix *-tə* in Kanuri is a regular method of forming verbal nouns from verb roots. In this instance, it forms the verbal noun in regular grammatical fashion from the verb root *rə̀bò-* 'to write'. There is no such grammatical formative in Hausa.

Finally, the age of the root *rə̀bò-* in Kanuri is guaranteed by the existence of a verb *arbu* in the related languages Teda and Daza with the meaning 'to draw'. Thus, just as with Anglo-Saxon 'write', originally 'to scratch', an indigenous word has been semantically extended to cover the new notion of writing.

There are, then, four independent arguments for Kanuri origin. We might add a fifth, the fact of semantic clustering, as indicated by the next word to be treated, that for 'reading'.

2. Hausa *kàRà:tú:*, Kanuri *kə̀ràtə́* 'reading'. The parallelism of these forms to the words for 'writing' is obvious. Here again the presence of the regular Kanuri verbal noun suffix *-tə́* is decisive for Kanuri origin in Hausa.[9] There is, however, a difference in that the verb stem *-kə̀rà-* in Kanuri is obviously a borrowing from Arabic *qara'a* 'to read' and is therefore not an indigenous root as in the case of the verb 'to write'.

3. Hausa *kà:súwá:*, Kanuri *kàsúgù* 'market'. In the Kanuri dialect

[8] Intervocalically the phoneme *b* appears as a voiced bilabial continuant in the dialect of Kanuri described by Lukas. This sound is written *v* by Lukas. The transcription used in all other Kanuri examples in this paper is phonemic and transcribes this phoneme as *b* in all positions.

[9] A borrowing into Hausa directly from the Arabic verbal noun *qira:ʔat-* is highly unlikely since this would be taken over normally as **kìrá:'ʔà* and because of the parallelism with the noun for 'writing'.

described by Lukas, from which the above form is cited, the phoneme *g* is pronounced as a voiced continuant between vowels. In the Kanembu dialect it disappears, so that we have *kàsû:* 'market', *kàtû:* 'lie' equivalent to Kanuri *kàtúgù*, etc. The Hausa reinterpretation of the final *u*, not a very common noun termination, by the common ending *-wa:*, is therefore easily understood. At any rate, that the Kanuri and Hausa forms are connected is not in doubt. The Kanuri *kàsúgù* is from Arabic *su:q* 'market', with the Kanuri noun-forming prefix *ka-*. The treatment of Arabic *q* in non-initial position as *g* is normal in Kanuri. The Kanuri noun-forming prefix *ka-* is at present obsolescent, but is found in a number of loan words as well as in several derivative formations in Kanuri itself. In several instances, nouns with *k-* prefix occur in Kanuri where the related Teda or Daza have the same root without this prefix. The *k-* noun-forming prefix is widespread in Sudanic, and its occurrence in Kanuri is an important piece of grammatical evidence linking Central Saharan with the general Sudanic family.

Clear examples of *k-* prefix in internal Kanuri formations include *gala-* 'to put in office', *kagala* 'a political office' (Barth), Kanembu *soto-* 'to give hospitality' compared to *kusoto* 'guest' (Koelle). Comparative examples are Kanuri *kágəl* 'anvil' as against Daza *agele* 'masse servant à frapper sur l'enclume' and Kanuri *kəmálì* 'ant' compared to Daza *melle* with the same meaning. Most relevant for the present purpose are examples of the *k-* prefixed to loan words, particularly from Arabic. Examples are *kənásàr* 'victory' < Arabic *naṣr*; *kùlúlù* 'bead' < Arabic *lu'lu'*; *kàlìgímò* 'camel' < Berber *alɣem*. Sometimes the *k-* is prefixed to the Arabic article. This explains the *kal-* in *kàlgə̀tàn* 'cotton' as against Arabic *quṭn*; Kanembu *kalgama* 'wheat' < Arabic *qamḥ*.

The evidence is therefore conclusive that Kanuri *kà-súgù* is borrowed from Arabic *su:q* 'market' and then passed into Hausa as *kà:súwá:*.

4. Hausa *gà:Rú:* 'wall of compound; at Katsina, town wall', Kanuri *gàrú* 'wall'. The sole linguistic reason for considering this a loan from Kanuri into Hausa is the presence of the rolled *R* in non-final position in the syllable. In all other examples considered, however, this has been shown to be a reliable criterion. The argument for Kanuri as the source language would be decisively strengthened if Daza *guru* 'mur en pierre ou terre' is cognate. However, it may well be a borrowing from Kanuri. Hausa *bíRní* 'walled city' is probably also borrowed from Kanuri *bə́rní*.[10] Here the sole linguistic criterion is the presence of a *ə* in the Kanuri form and this evidence is not definitive.

[10] H. R. Palmer, *Sudanese Memoirs* (3 vols., Lagos, 1928), vol. 3, p. 89, assumes that *birni* in Hausa is a loan-word from Arabic. Its use as a proper name for the Bornu capital that was established after the center of the empire shifted from Kanem suggests that it is originally a Kanuri word.

5. Hausa *bíndígà*, Kanuri *bə́nə́dgə̀* 'gun'. This is of ultimate Arabic origin and specifically from the Libyan, probably Tripolitanian or Murzuk, variant *bindega* as opposed to Egyptian and modern Classical *bundu:q*, *bunduqiyya*, all from the Arabic word for 'Venice'. All these are different from the terms for 'gun' current in Tunisia and the western Maghrib. The linguistic evidence for Kanuri as the source of the Hausa form is again the presence of *ə* in Kanuri. There is independent historical evidence that guns first appeared in this area in Bornu towards the end of the sixteenth century.[11]

6. Hausa *síRdì*, Kanuri *sə́rdə̀* 'saddle'. The source is Arabic *sarǰ*. The rendition of Arabic *ǰ* by *d* is rare, perhaps unique. This fact precludes independent borrowing from Arabic. The argument rests again on Kanuri *ə*. In this instance, it is particularly plausible since Hausa *i* for Arabic *a* would be very unusual, but with Kanuri *ə* as the intermediate becomes readily explicable.

7. Hausa *dàbí:nò* 'date, date palm', Kanuri *dìbínò*. The Kanuri word is derived from late Egyptian (Coptic) *ti-bine* 'date, date palm' in which *ti-* is the prefixed feminine singular article. A parallel instance of borrowing with the feminine article is Arabic *timsa:ḥ* 'crocodile' from Coptic *ti-msah* 'the crocodile'. Nubian has also borrowed the Coptic word as *benti*, without the Coptic article and with its own noun-forming suffix *-ti*. Coptic may also be the source of Berber *tini*, *tiini* (<*tiwini*<*tibiní*?). The form of the article *ti-* suggests the Delta dialect Bohairic as the source, although *ti-* occurs in Upper Egypt alongside of *ta-*. The argument for its being of Kanuri origin in Hausa is largely based on geographical distribution. The Egyptian origin of this term does not exclude a post-Islamic origin. The absence of similar forms in Wadai and Darfur and the existence of independent borrowing in Nubian suggests a northern route via the Libyan oases to Egypt.

8. Hausa *bá:bà:ní:*, *bá:bà:*, Kanuri *bábà* 'father's sister'.

9. Hausa *Rá:fà:*, *Rá:fà:ní:*, Kanuri *rábà* (Koelle *rafa*) 'mother's brother'. These may be considered together. The argument for Kanuri origin rests on the presence of rolled *R* in non-final syllable position in Hausa in *Rá:fà:*, on the existence of variants with *-ní:* which in all probability reflect the Kanuri first person possessive suffix *-ní* and the existence of cognate forms for both of these words in Teda and Daza. These are Teda, Daza *baha* 'father's sister' and Teda *dihi*, Daza *dehi* 'mother's brother'. In Daza and Teda *h* and *f* vary with each other intervocalically and our existing sources sometimes give alternative forms of the same word, e.g. Daza *efire*, *ehire* 'wing'. Again Teda and Daza have *lehille*, *lefille* < Arabic *al-fiḍḍa* 'silver'. Hence *-f-* as the earlier form is reasonable. The *-h-* in *baha* is probably analogical with

[11] Guns were acquired by Idris Alooma from Tripoli. Cf. S. J. Hogben, *The Muhammadan Emirates of Nigeria* (Oxford, 1930), pp. 39–40.

the semantically connected form for 'mother's brother'. Further, Teda, Daza *d-* regularly corresponds to Kanuri *r*, e.g. Daza *dag-* 'to love' and Kanuri *rag-* 'to love' and likewise in other cognate forms. The case for the Kanuri forms being cognate to the Teda and Daza forms is thus a strong one, and in conjunction with the phonetic and grammatical factors cited earlier, the evidence is conclusive for Kanuri origin.

In addition to the examples treated in detail here, there is the whole series of names for political titles, ending in the Kanuri suffix *-ma*, whose Kanuri origin is not in dispute.[12] In summary, it may be said that a relatively small number of basic nouns having to do with the religious, political, economic, and social spheres of Hausa culture are certainly, or in some instances, with high probability, borrowed from Kanuri and bear witness to a long continued and important influence upon the Hausa of their eastern Kanuri-speaking neighbors.

[12] For a list of these terms and their occurrences in other languages in Nigeria, see Westermann, *Geschichte Afrikas*, pp. 159–60.

# The Interpretation of the Coptic Vowel System

Coptic, the late form of Egyptian written in the Greek alphabet with the addition of certain letters adopted from Demotic, became extinct as a spoken language probably in the seventeenth century.[1] The language is known in five dialect variants: (1) Bohairic, the language of the Delta; (2) Fayumic, the language of the Fayum; (3) Sahidic, the main literary dialect of Upper Egypt, probably originally the dialect of Thebes; (4) Achmimic, the dialect of Achmim in Upper Egypt; (5) Subachmimic, in many ways intermediate between Sahidic and Achmimic, but with its own distinctive linguistic characteristics. Of these five dialects, Bohairic came into exclusive use during the course of the Middle Ages and is at present the sole liturgical language.

All the Coptic dialects use the seven vowel letters of the Greek language, but [u], except in Greek loanwords, is always preceded by another vowel letter.[2] The normal sequence is [ou], which evidently represents /u/ in all the dialects. The diphthongs in *-u* are likewise usually written with [ou], e.g. [aou] for /au/, but in certain dialects and for certain diphthongs only the second element is symbolized by [u], for example Sahidic [eu] for /eu/. Similarly but less commonly [ei] is used for /i/, usually in diphthongs but also in word initial position in Sahidic. Thus, in Sahidic [eine] represents /íne/ 'to bring'. A conspicuous characteristic of all the dialects except Bohairic is the existence of geminate writings of certain vowels. Thus Sahidic [šeere]

[1] The Dutch traveller Vansleb, *circa* 1680, found people who still spoke Coptic.

[2] Transliterations from the Coptic alphabet are enclosed in brackets. Phonemic transcriptions are put between slant lines. The vowel letters *alpha*, *epsilon*, *eta*, *iota*, *omicron*, *omega*, and *upsilon* are transliterated [a], [e], [ē], [i], [o], [ō], and [u]. The supralinear stroke over a consonant is transliterated by *ə* preceding the consonant.

corresponds to Bohairic [šeri] 'daughter'. Such a doubled vowel may occur only once in a word.

The accepted interpretation of this vowel system as found in Steindorff's standard grammar of Sahidic and as embodied in practically all transcriptions of Coptic is as follows. The Greek letters [a], [e], and [o] always stand for short vowels. The letters [ē] and [ō] represent long vowels of the same quality as [e] and [o], respectively. Of the remaining vowel symbols, [i] and [ou], indicating /i/ and /u/, respectively, are sometimes long and sometimes short, presumably long when stressed and short when unstressed. The difference of length in /i/ and /u/ would therefore not be phonemic. The double-vowel symbols found in all the dialects except Bohairic stand for vowel clusters. It is not clear whether these clusters are to be interpreted as two syllables with separate peaks, and if so whether stress occurs with one or the other, or possibly both.

It is clear that a system of transcription based on this interpretation will be virtually identical with the most common system of transliteration of classical Greek. Indeed, Steindorff asserts that the pronunciation of Coptic is not to be understood from the phonetic values of the Greek spoken *koine* of the second century A.D., the period in which Coptic was first written, but is rather that of classical Greek as taught in the schools of the time.[3]

What seems to strengthen at least that part of the standard interpretation which concerns the length of [ē] and [ō] is its conformity with the usual doctrine regarding vowels in Ancient Egyptian as set forth in Sethe's classic article on the subject.[4] According to this analysis, originally identical vowels of the earliest period developed a long variant in stressed open syllables and a short variant in stressed closed syllables perhaps as early as the Old Kingdom. Later the loss of certain consonants and various analogical formations produced phonemic contrast. Since [ē] and [ō] in all Coptic dialects go back to forms with original open syllables, while the corresponding vowels in closed syllables appear as Sahidic, Bohairic [a], Fayumic, Achmimic, Subachmimic [e] and Sahidic, Bohairic [o], Fayumic, Achmimic, Subachmimic [a], respectively, it seemed as though [ē] and [ō] continued old long vowels and [e], [o], [a] old short ones. This theory also explains the reason for the double treatment of [i] and [ou], which in stressed syllables represent vowels in earlier open syllables but in unstressed position are reductions of old consonantal *y* and *w*. Thus Sahidic [ounou] 'hour' is interpreted as */unú:/* < Old Egyptian **wənắwət*.

[3] G. Steindorff, *Lehrbuch der Koptischen Grammatik* (Chicago, 1951), p. 13.

[4] K. Sethe, "Die Vokalisation des Ägyptischen," *Zeitschrift der Deutschen Morgenländischen Gesellschaft*, 77 (1923): 145–208.

However, the interpretation of the vowels in original open syllables as long and in original closed syllables as short in the Ancient Egyptian period is by no means as certain as is sometimes assumed. A careful examination is required of the cuneiform and, for a later period, the Greek transcriptions, which constitute the main evidence. This is not attempted here. That a difference of quality, however, did develop between closed and open syllables is certain on any showing since, as has been seen, the vowels *e* and *o* in closed syllables appear in certain Coptic dialects as [a]. Further, the lapse of time is enormous, and to argue directly from Old Egyptian conditions to Coptic is as perilous as interpreting the modern English vowel system from Proto-Germanic.

The standard interpretation described here has never been challenged, at least in regard to the length of Coptic [ē] and [ō] as against the shortness of [e] and [o], except by Kuentz in a paper delivered orally.[5] Kuentz apparently felt so uncertain of his ground that he never published his results. Actually Kuentz only presents a small proportion of the evidence which can be adduced against the standard interpretation. In the present paper some of Kuentz's arguments are reproduced, but a number of additional considerations are presented which support Kuentz's basic position.

The analysis offered by Kuentz is as follows. The difference between [e] and [ē] on the one hand and [o] and [ō] on the other is not one of length but of quality, [ē] and [ō] being closed and [e] and [o] being open. The geminate vowels of the dialects other than Bohairic are simply long vowels. Thus, for Kuentz [ee] is /ɛ:/ while [ēē] is /e:/. The standard interpretation for Sahidic as represented by Steindorff as contrasted with Kuentz's analysis can be seen from Table 1.

It should be noted that there are two somewhat independent questions involved. The first relates to the nature of the difference between [e] and [ē] on the one hand and [o] and [ō] on the other. The other concerns the interpretation of the geminate vowel writings in the dialects other than Bohairic. For the first of these questions, Worrell has interpreted [e] and [o] as open against [ē] and [ō] as closed but still retains the traditional hypothesis of the shortness of the first and the length of the latter.[6] Hitherto only Kuentz has questioned this assumption. Worrell's conclusion seems to be based purely on the general assumption that in systems of vowel length the short vowel is always more open than its long partners, and he mentions no specific Coptic evidence. For the geminate vowels only Kuentz has advanced the thesis that this writing

[5] C. Kuentz, "Quantité ou timbre? A propos des pseudo-redoublements de voyelles en copte," *Compte Rendus du Groupe Linguistique d'Études Chamito-Sémitiques*, 2 (1934): 5–7.

[6] W. H. Worrell, *Coptic Sounds* (Ann Arbor, Mich., 1934).

*Table 1*

| Transcription | Steindorff | Kuentz | Transcription | Steindorff | Kuentz |
|---|---|---|---|---|---|
| a | a | a | i | i, i: | i |
| aa | aa | a: | o | o | ɔ |
| e | e | ɛ | oo | oo | ɔ: |
| ee | ee | ɛ: | ō | o: | o |
| ē | e: | e | ōō | o:o: | o: |
| ēē | e:e: | e: | u | u, u: | u |

*Table 2*

| Transcription | Steindorff | Kuentz | Till | Worrell |
|---|---|---|---|---|
| e | e | ɛ | e | ɛ |
| ee | ee | ɛ: | eˀ | ɛˀ |
| ē | e: | e | e: | e: |
| ēē | e:e: | e: | e:ˀ | e:ˀ |
| o | o | ɔ | o | ɔ |
| oo | oo | ɔ: | oˀ | ɔˀ |
| ō | o: | o | o: | o: |
| ōō | o:o: | o: | o:ˀ | o:ˀ |

indicates length. However, Till presents an alternative hypothesis to the conventional one, a theory adopted by Worrell also. He proposes that this manner of writing indicates a still existing laryngeal or pharyngeal following the vowel.[7] He cites the parallel of the Western spelling of Kaaba for Arabic *ka'ba*. There is something to be said for this interpretation as against the accepted theory of vowel clusters, and Till's hypothesis will be discussed later. The views of Worrell and Till in regard to the *e* and *o* vowels as compared to Steindorff and Kuentz are summarized in Table 2.[8]

Since Coptic is no longer spoken, all of the data which can be utilized to decide the questions raised by these variant analyses of the Coptic vowel system are of necessity indirect. In the present instance, there are four main lines of available evidence, internal phonologic, internal morphological, the external implications provided by transcriptions into and from foreign languages, and finally the traditional pronunciation of Coptic in the liturgy. Of these, Kuentz has virtually confined himself to the first, the internal phonologic.

[7] W. Till, "Altes 'Aleph und 'Ajin im Koptischen," *Wiener Zeitschrift für die Kunde des Morgenlandes*, 36 (1929): 186–96.

[8] Till apparently believes in the survival of both a pharyngeal ʕ and a laryngeal ˀ. Worrell only uses ˀ in his transcriptions. I have represented both here by ˀ.

It is always a suspicious circumstance when a language known only indirectly displays characteristics not found in any directly attested instance. From this point of view, the conventional interpretation of the Coptic vowel system is highly implausible. As has been seen, the exact value to be assigned to the double vowels is not quite clear. There are two possibilities. If the double vowel sequences are intended to form single syllables then, in the case of *e*, for example, we have the four following written forms all to be interpreted as forming a single syllable and without difference of quality [e], [ē], [ee], [ēē]. These four written sequences would presumably have one, two, two, and four moras, respectively. In this case there is nothing to keep apart [ē] and [ee], which should be identical both in quality and length, and correspondingly [ō] and [oo] would represent the same sounds. But in fact these pairs are practically never confused in writing. This difficulty of the standard theory is pointed out by Kuentz. Outside of this, a language with three vowel lengths of one, two, and four moras is not known in any directly attested case. Indeed the only system with three degrees of length is Estonian. This is now usually interpreted in other terms, but at any rate Estonian has no vowel with four moras.

If alternatively we assume that [ēē] and [ōō] have two syllable peaks, then any reasonable correlations with the well established stress system become impossible.

All the internal and external evidence leads to the undisputed conclusion that every Coptic word has a single stressed vowel. Outside of Greek loan words, where this is quite possibly orthographic conventions, unstressed syllables only have [a], [e], [i], or [u]. No indigenous Coptic word, excluding the double vowels being considered here, ever has more than one of the remaining vowels [ē], [ō], or [o], which are therefore always stressed. Hence the assumption of two syllables for a sequence such as [ēē] leads to the following alternatives with regard to stress, each one a violation of well established rules based on the remaining cases. If both are stressed, the rule regarding only one stress in a word is broken. If either one is stressed and the other unstressed, we have the otherwise unexampled occurrence of unstressed *ē* and *ō* in indigenous words. If neither are stressed, then we have a transgression of the rule that [ē], [ō], and [o] are stressed wherever they appear.

Therefore the other facts about the Coptic vowel system, particularly those relating to stress, strongly suggest that the written geminate vowels form a single syllable peak. But in this case, as has been seen, [ē] becomes identical with [ee]. However, as we shall soon see, there is considerable evidence to show that [e] differed from [ē] in quality, as did [o] from [ō], and hence they would not fall together. Further, the supposed difference in quantity between [e] and [ē] as well as [o] and [ō] has no solid basis.

*Table 3*

| | Regular verb | With final laryngeal |
|---|---|---|
| 1. Infinitive | [bōl] | [moh] |
| 2. Infinitive with third person singular masculine object | [bol-f] | [mah-f] |
| 3. Qualitative | [bēl] | [meh] |

We turn now to the second line of evidence, the morphological system. Here we will be concerned with the plausibility of certain phonologic assumptions as against others in interpreting morphophonemic alternations. Since the possibility of certain types of alternation as against others largely depends on the kind of sound changes involved in producing them, the considerations involved will be both historical-comparative and purely synchronic.

There are here three groups of phenomena which suggest that the differences between [e] and [ē], [o], and [ō] are qualitative and not quantitative, and that [ē] and [ō] represent high vowels while [e] and [o] symbolize low vowels. These are: (1) the alternation of vowels before existing and previous laryngeal and pharyngeal consonants; (2) the Bohairic and Fayumic *-i* and *-u* diphthongs; (3) the Fayumic correspondence of [ē] with the so-called accented shwa (*Murmurvokal*) of the other dialects.

The chief inflected forms of the Bohairic biliteral verb with stressed short vowel will show the modifications in verbs with final laryngeal *h* as contrasted with the majority of verbs without laryngeals. (See Table 3.)

The tendency of vowels to be lowered before laryngeals and pharyngeals is well-known and particularly well attested from Semitic languages. For example, in Arabic we regularly have *a* in the second syllable of the imperfect of verbs in place of *u* or *i* in verbs with second or third laryngeal root consonants, i.e. *yaftaḥu* 'he opens' as contrasted with *yaqtulu* 'he kills'. In the present instance the alternation [bol-f] 'to unloose him' / [mah-f] 'to fill him' is one of vowel quality with the low vowel *a* before the laryngeal on any theory. Hence it accords better with both the Coptic data and general linguistic theory to assert that, correspondingly, /e/ and /o/ have been lowered to /ɛ/ and /ɔ/, respectively, before the laryngeal. That the same conditioning factor, the following laryngeal, produced vowel lowering in the undisputed case but vowel shortening in the others is improbable.

The alternation *o* ~ *a* is found in the other dialects. Further, in Bohairic, unlike *e* ~ *ɛ* and *o* ~ *ɔ*, this alternation also occurs before *x* and *š*, reflexes of other earlier pharyngeal or laryngeal consonants (š < Old Egyptian *ḫ*; x < Old Egyptian *h*, *ḥ*). This change is therefore older than the *e* > *ɛ* and *o* > *ɔ* shift, the latter of which is confined to Bohairic. Fayumic and sometimes Sahidic have *ε* for *e* before final laryngeal in qualitative of the biliteral verb class: Fayumic, Sahidic /mεh/ 'filled'.

On general phonetic grounds the opposite effect from lowering is to be expected in the first element of *-i* and *-u* diphthongs. The tendency to shorten the tongue movement leads to the raising of the first or lower element and the lowering of the final *-i* or *-u*. The final result is often a monophthong approximately equal in distance from the two original endpoints. In Coptic itself this has happened to the original diphthong **au* in Achmimic, e.g. Achmimic *no*, Bohairic, Sahidic *nau* 'to see'. In Bohairic [ōou] is found where [oou] would have been expected on the basis of morphologically related forms in Bohairic itself and where other dialects have either *o* or the vowel which corresponds regularly to Bohairic *o*. Thus Bohairic [erof] 'to him' but [erōou] 'to them' in place of the expected *[eroou]. With this we may compare Sahidic [eroou] 'to them'. Similarly Bohairic has [ōi] where other dialects have *o* or whatever vowel corresponds to Bohairic [o] in other contexts. Thus Bohairic has [ōik] as compared to Sahidic [oeik] 'bread'. In the Sahidic form [ei] is the regular orthography for *i* in this diphthong. Similarly Bohairic and, in this case, Fayumic also have [ēi] where *[ei] would have been expected: Bohairic [mēini], Fayumic [mēin] but Achmimic [meeine], Sahidic [maein] 'sign'. In all these cases a raising of the first element of the diphthong is on general linguistic principles far more plausible than its lengthening.

Finally, before turning to the external evidence, we may note that Fayumic correspondence of [ē] to what is either phonetically a syllabic sonant or a short central vowel of the *ə* type in Sahidic, Achmimic, and Subachmimic (probably phonemic /έr/, /έm/, etc. in these latter dialects). The supralinear stroke over the consonant before which no vowel is written is here transliterated as *ə* before the consonant. Bohairic has /e/ in these cases. For example, Fayumic [šēmši] corresponds to Sahidic, Achmimic, Subachmimic [šəmše], Bohairic [šemši] 'to serve'. The assumption here that Fayumic [ē] represents a long vowel is obviously implausible from the phonetic point of view.

The most important external evidence regarding the pronunciation of Coptic is a series of medieval texts in which Arabic technical terms are transcribed in Coptic letters in a Coptic text, or an Arabic text is transcribed in the Coptic alphabet, or vice versa. This extremely interesting group of documents provides further evidence which decisively favors the interpretation of the Coptic vowel system presented here and gives virtually no support to the commonly held theory.

Considering these materials in approximate chronological order, we have first the Coptic medical papyri written in Sahidic published by Chassinat and by Stern, both of which date from the ninth or tenth century.[9] Since Arabic has vowel quantitative distinctions, if the standard theory is correct it would be expected that Coptic [a], [e], and [o] should transcribe Arabic short vowels, and [ē] and [ō] should be used to express the Arabic long vowels. That this is not so can be seen from the following representative examples:

| Coptic | Arabic |
|---|---|
| [haulen] | [ḥawla:n] |
| [sapēr] | [ṣbir] |
| [mērəh] | [milḥ] |

In general the transcriptions in the Chassinal document are just about what would be expected if the quality of Arabic vowels was represented by the Coptic and if [ē] and [ō] were closer vowels than [e] and [o]. Thus Coptic [e] renders both Arabic *a* and *a:* particularly where no emphatic or pharyngeal consonant is adjacent to the vowel. This corresponds to the well known Arabic *imāla* or fronted *æ*- type pronunciation of *a* and *a:* under these conditions. Coptic [a] transcribes either *a* or *a:* in the vicinity of emphatics and pharyngeals. Coptic [ē] stands most commonly for Arabic *i* or *i:*. Coptic [o] corresponds to Arabic *u* (actually lower than *u:* in classical pronunciation). Coptic [ō] transcribes both *u* and *u:*, once again without regard to Arabic quantity.

The Stern papyrus shows the same state of affairs but with the further important fact that Arabic *a:* is sometimes written [aa] in Coptic, and Arabic *u:* sometimes as [oo]. If Till's theory that the Coptic doubled vowels are vowel + laryngeal, or pharyngeal, were correct, and if this pronunciation still survived, we would expect Coptic [aa], etc. to stand for Arabic [aʕ] or [aʔ], but this never occurs.

The document published by Casanova and Sobhy is somewhat later in date. In it an Arabic text is written in the Coptic alphabet. In general the same conditions obtain as in the earlier texts. As Casanova observes, Arabic *a* and *a:* are both written [e] with *imāla* and [a] in the vicinity of emphatic and back consonants.[10] In this text [ē] and [ō] are not used. The correspondences of the remaining Coptic vowels are as follows:

[9] Chassinat, "Un papyrus médical copte." *Mémoires de l'Institut français d'archéologie orientale du Caire*, 22 (1921); and Stern, "Fragment eines koptischen Traktates über Alchemie," *Zeitschrift der Ägyptischen Sprache*, 23 (1885): 104, 120.

[10] These are parts of the same original text: P. Casanova, "Un texte arabe transcrit en charactères coptes," *Bulletin de l'Institut français d'archéologie orientale du Caire*, 1 (1901): 1–20; and G. Sobhy, *New Coptic Texts from the Monastery of Saint Macarius by H. G. E. White* (New York, 1926), Appendix I.

| Coptic | Arabic |
|---|---|
| a | a and a: with emphatic and back consonants |
| e | a and a: with *imāla*, and i |
| i | i: |
| o | u |
| ou | u: |

It should be recalled that classical Arabic *i* and *u* are phonetically close to *e* and *o* in colloquial pronunciation. In this and subsequent documents there is no question of Coptic double vowels being used to represent Arabic long vowels since the dialect in general use is Bohairic, which has no doubled vowels.

Finally the Galtier manuscript containing Coptic hymns in the Arabic alphabet may be mentioned.[11] Commenting on this text, Worrell states, "Quantity is disregarded."[12] Here again Coptic [e] and [a] are usually written as [a:] in Arabic; [ē] is either [a:] or [i:], and both [o] and [ō] are transcribed as [ụ:].

The fullest and most reliable source for the traditional pronunciation of Bohairic as used in the Coptic church is Rochemonteix.[13] These data were collected in 1876–77 in several localities. There is much variation, but the general picture which emerges suggests a pronunciation of Coptic similar to that derivable from the earlier documents. Bohairic [a] is usually *a*; [e] is *a* or *a:* (thus Bohairic [xɛn] is rendered *ha:n*); [ē] is *a* or *i* according to Rochemonteix, "les deux voyelles . . . dont il formait sans doute intermédiaire" (at Siut sometimes close *e* in foreign words *erodas* and *irudas* are both reported for [ērōdas]); the back vowels [o], [ō], and [ou] may at this point be merely orthographic variants rendered variously as *ɔ*, *o*, and *u*. Once again there is complete indifference to supposed differences in quality. Mallon reports a greater consistency in the modern pronunciation, [ō] being pronounced *o* and [o] being pronounced as *ɔ*, which is, of course, in accordance with the theory presented here.[14]

The evidence presented here has not been intended merely as a citation of everything which favors the present thesis while contrary indications are

[11] E. Galtier, "Coptica-arabica III," *Bulletin de l'Institut français d'archéologie orientale du Caire*, 5 (1906): 91ff.

[12] Worrell, *Coptic Sounds*, p. 133.

[13] M. Rochemonteix, "La pronunciation moderne du Copte dans le Haute-Égypte," *Mémoires de la Société Linguistique de Paris*, 7 (1890): 245–76. See also George Sobhy, "The Traditional Pronunciation of Coptic in the Church of Egypt," *Bulletin de la Société d'Archéologie Copte*, 7 (1940): 109, 117.

[14] A. Mallon, *Grammaire Copte* (3rd ed., Beirut, 1926), p. 12.

ignored. Almost nothing can be found to support the standard theory. No arguments were originally advanced in its favor. It was simply taken for granted. A conventional transcription of the Greek alphabet appeared to be confirmed by Sethe's theory regarding the Coptic vowel system for a period nearly a millennium earlier than the earliest written Coptic records. This theory itself is far from certain as regards the length of the vowels in open syllables. In fact the existing traditional assumption of the length [ē] and [ō] in Coptic probably played an important role in drawing this conclusion about the earlier period.

While neither the supposed length of [ē] and [ō] as against the shortness of [e], [o], and [a] nor the traditional theory of vowel gemination can be accepted, it was pointed out in the earlier discussion that Till's theory regarding vowel gemination has some degree of plausibility. The most important evidence for Till's view is the fact that in Achmimic the word-final sequence double vowel plus sonant has a final [e], just as consonant plus final sonant. Therefore vowel doubling is treated in Achmimic in the same manner as vowel followed by consonant. That this consonant is either *'alef* or *'ain* is known from earlier Egyptian and Demotic. In general written double vowels only occur in Achmimic and elsewhere where a pharyngeal or laryngeal followed a stressed vowel in closed syllables. It does not occur in word final even in these conditions. Sometimes the pharyngeal or laryngeal is originally the initial consonant of the following syllable. In these cases it may have been metathesized.

If, as I think more probable, the doubled vowel symbols represent vowel length, then length except for a few analogic extensions developed from the loss of a pharyngeal or laryngeal after the vowel. This is closely parallel to the now generally accepted theory regarding the origin of the Indo-European long vowels. In a reconstructed Proto-Coptic based on a comparison of the five dialects, we would in all probability assume that these consonants still existed in the Proto-Coptic period. That they may have survived in Achmimic is possible. There are even cases of the writing of *h* in this dialect in syllable initial apparently to represent such a consonant.[15] At any rate the evidence of the Stern papyrus, cited above, shows that at a later period length was present rather than a pharyngeal or laryngeal consonant, even though the influence of Arabic would work rather for their retention than their loss.

In conclusion, the probable vowel systems of the Coptic dialects are presented with the proviso that, particularly in Achmimic, the posited long vowels were possibly a sequence of short vowel followed by a pharyngeal or laryngeal. It will be noted that those dialects with double vowel symbols have

[15] For example, see W. Till, *Achmimisch koptische Grammatik* (Leipzig, 1928), p. 39.

in every case fewer long than short vowels. There are well established instances of such systems elsewhere, e.g., Hungarian and British English as described by Daniel Jones.

Bohairic: /a/, /ɛ/, /e/, /i/, /ɔ/, /o/, /u/.
Sahidic and Subachmimic: /a/, /ɛ/, /e/, /i/, /ɔ/, /o/, /u/, /a:/, /ɛ:/, /e:/, /ɔ:/, /o:/.
Achmimic: /a/, /ɛ/, /e/, /i/, /ɔ/, /o/, /u/, /a:/, /ɛ:/, /i:/, /ɔ:/, /o:/, /u:/.
Fayumic: /æ/, /e/, /i/, /ɑ/, /o/, /u/, /æ:/, /e:/, /ɑ:/, /o:/.

The correspondences with the written forms except for Fayumic will be obvious from the text discussion. Here the absence of written [o] gives a six-vowel system for which the most probable phonetic values are given. For Fayumic [e] is /æ/, [ē] is /e/, [i] is /i/, [a] is /ɑ/, [ō] is /o/, and [ou] is /u/.

The probable phonetic value of [ē] as *e* will serve to explain why Fayumic has [ē] as the stressed reduced vowel rather than [e], since this would be phonetically closest to the [e] of other dialects.

# Review of Fodor's *The Problems in the Classification of the African Languages*

The linguist who is not an African specialist impelled by a sense of duty is likely, after casual examination, to be put off from reading the present work if only because of its English, which is consistently quaint and at times leaves the reader genuinely puzzled.* As an example of the former, the following not unrepresentative sentence may be quoted: "This sketch can be of very general character only because the material is practically not worked up and hence puzzling, the languages concerned are of many kinds and, for this reason, several exceptions can be found to the recited features" (19). An instance where this reviewer, at least, is uncertain of the meaning is the following: "Greenberg's classificatory system and comparisons can be accepted as a working hypothesis only, and it is the duty of further investigation and comparison to examine, prove or reject his statements by lots" (43). It turns out to be a key to other puzzling passages to realize that 'should' is being used like German *sollen* 'is supposed to'; for example, "Apart from grammatical allusions, a comparative word list should to reinforce the proofs" (40).

However, the work has to be considered seriously (especially by this reviewer) because it is an attempt to discuss in detail a subject which has become the focus of attack in the last few years: the question of sound correspondences—cf. Guthrie 1962, Oliver 1966, Winston 1966.[1] This is indeed the central point of Fodor's book and the sole theoretic basis for what

*István Fodor, *The Problems in the Classification of the African Languages: Methodological and Theoretical Conclusions Concerning the Classification System of Joseph H. Greenberg*. (Studies on developing countries, 5.) Budapest: Center for Afro-Asian Research of the Hungarian Academy of Sciences, 1966.

[1] Regarding Winston, it should be noted that he is in other respects sympathetic, and is in basic agreement with my results in areas where he is acquainted with the evidence.

is essentially a hostile critique. Thus, after discussing my statements regarding the methodological principles of language classification, Fodor writes:

> A very important requirement is missing, however, in the right principles of Greenberg and—as we shall see later—by this omission the value of the entire method is vitiated, in fact, annihilated. The neglect of this postulate also misled many illustrious forerunners of Greenberg. The indispensable postulate in question is the existence of phonetic laws, which is the standard of all comparisons of genetic purpose. It was the phonetic laws by which Meinhof definitely proved the common origin of the Bantu languages and deduced the elements and structure of Proto-Bantu (24).

The bulk of the book is taken up by a very simple procedure. There are numerous citations from the etymologies or tables of related grammatical elements in Greenberg 1963, all of which take the following form: In one comparison, language A has a phoneme *x*, corresponding to phoneme *y* in language B. In another etymology containing phoneme *x* in language A, we find that B has not *y*, but *z*. E.g., Fodor selects the following pairs of etymologies from two languages within the Saharan subgroup of Nilo-Saharan: Berti *su*, Teda *ču* 'two', Berti *sing*, Teda *samo* 'eye'. According to Fodor, "If the counter-parts of 'two' are regular, then that of 'eye' are not, because then the Teda form ought to be *čamo*. If, on the other hand, the counter-parts of the word 'two' [sic! it should of course be 'eye'] are regular then those of 'two' are not, because the Teda form ought to be *su* in this case" (48). What Fodor evidently does not realize is that every assumption about an admissible or non-admissible type of correspondence can be mapped into an assumption about permissible types of historical change. By excluding an example such as the above, Fodor is going beyond even the most extreme neo-grammarian requirements. The diachronic counterpart of Fodor's requirement is that if any merger takes place in one language and not in the other, the result is an irregular correspondence, and we must reject either the etymologies involving the merger or those which do not. Thus, by Fodor's method, since Slavic has merged PIE **d* and **dh* by a change **dh* > *d*, while Sanskrit has preserved the distinction, we must reject one of the following universally accepted etymologies: OCS *dě*(*ti*) = Skt. *dhā* 'to place'; OCS *da*(*ti*) = Skt. *dā* 'to give'. In fact, the vowels are also 'wrong' because of the Indic merger **ē* > *ā*. Examples could be indefinitely multiplied. I cannot refrain from one more example. Using Fodor's assumptions, we must choose between New York English [bɔ:d] = Philadelphia English [bɔrd] 'board' and New York English [bɔ:d] = Philadelphia English [bɔ:d] 'bawd'! Fodor is evidently demanding a one-to-one correspondence between phonemes of two languages for all valid cognates, since even a many-to-one mapping *y*:*x* and *z*:*x* is not acceptable to him. This means that *any* change which is not purely phonetic in either language will destroy valid etymologies. There are, of course, a whole series of processes in addition to merger, admitted by even the most rigid neo-grammarians, which must produce greater and greater variety of correspondences as time goes on. Thus, it takes only one conditioned change in one language and one in a related language under differing conditions to produce four different correspondences of the same original phoneme. Besides this, there are the sound changes produced by morphological analogy, by sporadic assimilation and dissimilation, contamination, etc., all of which are accepted by the most conservative comparativists, and which, in the real world, produce a picture far more complex than that implicit in Fodor's simple procedure.

From this it does not follow, of course, that my classification is necessarily right; but the main weapon in Fodor's arsenal has no reasonable relation to the requirements of the situation. In fact, let loose in all its irrelevant power, it would destroy Indo-European, Fodor's own Finno-Ugric stock, and, as I shall demonstrate, even Bantu—which has been, according to Fodor, 'proved' by Meinhof.

There is a difference between Meinhof's Bantu and my presentation of the evidence for Niger-Congo and similar groupings. Meinhof has reconstructed proto-forms and, for a small number of languages, has stated the reflexes of the sounds he posits as elements in the Proto-Bantu sound system. This does not mean, however, that every form quoted by Meinhof in his etymologies has been explained by regular and invariant developments from the posited original sound system. If Fodor had looked with any care at the classic studies of Meinhof (1910, 1932), he would have found examples like the following which would be sufficient, given any equality of justice, to condemn Meinhof's attempts along with my own. But if on this basis we must reject even Bantu, a group roughly on the same level as the Romance languages, we would be back virtually to the individual language as the highest genetic unit attainable for Africa by the comparative method.

In Table 1, the forms are from three Bantu languages, Swahili, Konde, and Sango—all cited in etymologies in Meinhof (1932: 215 ff.) as containing the same proto-phoneme, Meinhof's *$\gamma$ (here written *g*). After each citation I give the sounds which are the reflexes of *g* in the three languages.[2] Most of these correspondences occur only once, and the addition of other languages would multiply the number of correspondences vastly. Nor has Meinhof explained any of these deviations in the text of his work. It is now generally

[2] I have modified Meinhof's symbolization of Proto-Bantu, and also some of his transcriptions of individual languages, for purposes of simplicity and greater conformity with present practices. These changes have no relevance to the point at issue.

*Table 1*

| Swahili | Konde | Sango | Meinhof | Gross | Correspondence |
|---|---|---|---|---|---|
| *imba* | *imba* | *lu-yimbo* | **gimba* | sing | 0/0/*y* |
| *mw-ona* | *gɔna* | *ɔna* | **gona* | sleep | 0/*g*/0 |
| *gumu* | *uma* | *yuma* | **guma* | hard | *g*/0/*y* |
| *ganja* | *iky-anja* | *li-ganja* | **ganja* | lake | *g*/0/*g* |
| *uki* | *ʊl-ʊki* | *iny-usi* | **guki* | sweetness | 0/0/0 |
| *gawa* | *ya'ba* | — | **gaba* | divide | *g*/*y*/— |
| *el-eza* | *gɛla* | *jela* | **gela* | measure | 0/*g*/*j* |
| *gwa* | *gwa* | *gwa* | **gua* | fall | *g*/*g*/*g* |
| *fyag-ia* | *phyag-ila* | *fyaj-ila* | **pîaga* | sweep | *g*/*g*/*j* |
| *m-kuyu* | *uŋ-khuyu* | — | **kugu* | fig tree | *y*/*y*/— |

accepted that, as first suggested by Homburger 1913, there are two protophonemes involved, which are usually symbolized **g* and **y*. But in addition to this, a very large proportion of the Bantu roots presumed to have **g* have completely sporadic variants which show reflexes of **y* and vice versa. In addition, there is an even greater variation between **j* and **y*. In his recent work on comparative Bantu (1967: 114), Guthrie has to reconstruct no less than eighteen etymologies in which there is variation between **j* and **y*, nine with variation between **g* and **y*, five with variation between **g* and **j*, and one with reflexes of all three consonants. In addition, **d* varies with both **j* and **y* in a number of cases. Nor are problems of Bantu reconstruction limited to these consonants. Guthrie reconstructs no less than six ancestral forms for the word 'day': **cîku*, **cûgu*, **cûku*, **tîku*, **tûku*, and **tûkû*. In fact, from the indications in Guthrie, it appears that somewhere between 20 percent to 30 percent of his reconstructed forms required multiple protoforms—and this, of course, within a group of closely related languages whose unity is not doubted by anyone.

Hence, Fodor's assignment of a different status to Bantu on the basis of Meinhof and other comparative work can only result from a confidence engendered by the presence of asterisks. Had he looked at Westermann 1927, he would have found reconstructed forms for Western Sudanic preceded by asterisks, in general with not much greater variations than the proto-Bantu of Meinhof.[3] Since most of my Niger-Congo etymologies, which are presumably rejected by Fodor, are based on those of Westermann for Western Sudanic, which covers a large proportion of the same languages, I am sure that an etymology preceded by a form with an asterisk in Westermann would meet

[3] Since the relationship among Niger-Congo languages is more distant than that within Bantu, there will obviously be a longer period of time for all the processes that produce diversification of correspondences to take place.

with Fodor's approval, while its placement in my book would lead to its rejection.

In general one does not, as Fodor seems to imply, reject wholesale numerous etymologies, strong on other grounds, merely because they are not completely consistent in their correspondences. By definition, an accident is something that occurs rarely. The numerous "near misses" which are a commonplace of comparative work do not normally result in the rejection of any large number of etymologies. Rather one seeks to explain them by other processes such as those mentioned earlier, or by revisions and more complex statements regarding sound changes. Even Guthrie, for all his emphasis on rigor, does not reject 20 percent to 30 percent of his etymologies on such grounds. He in fact resorts to "mutations," which is merely a polite term for irregular changes, in preference to the exclusion of these cases as accidents.

In addition to his main point about sound laws, Fodor has a chapter entitled "Some Deficiencies in the Documentation of Greenberg" (79–82). This is designed to show that even a spot check will reveal serious inaccuracies in my citations. In order to demonstrate this, Fodor compares my quotations from Mande languages with Prost 1953. But in regard to Mande vocabulary, Prost is a secondary source, who gives single equivalents in the various Mande languages for items on a fixed word list presented in tabular form. When Fodor did not find the item in Prost, he assumes I merely invented it; but all of the presumed imaginary forms are found in Westermann (which, incidentally, is not in Fodor's bibliography), and can be located in existing dictionaries and word lists. Thus, Bambara *dumu* 'to eat', considered to be my invention by Fodor, is found in Bazin (1906: 143) and Travélé (1913: 160). The other Mande forms are also in Westermann and came from Koelle's *Polyglotta Africana*. Fodor also uses Prost 1956 for Songay, again not realizing that there are other sources. For example, *gani* 'animal breast' is criticized as non-existent, but it is to be found in Dupuis Yakouba (1917: 149) glossed as *mamelle d'un animal*. I do not deny that there are some inaccuracies in my work. In the multiple transfer from original source—copying in a notebook, citing in a handwritten manuscript, typing, typesetting, etc.—in handling literally thousands of items, there are bound to be some errors. I do not think they are disproportionately numerous, and they certainly do not affect my argument on any significant point. The number of errors of citation in Fodor's own book, which handles only a minute fraction of the material found in my work, should produce some feeling of charity toward me on the part of the author. For example, in a comparative table (97) to be discussed below, Fodor gives the Fulani number 'five' as *yoɔi* when it should be *jowi*. Perhaps he thought that *j* here was a semivowel; but in the usual Fulani orthography it

*Table 2*

| English | French | Russian | Sanskrit | Swahili | Vai | Fulani | Nubian (Dongola) |
|---|---|---|---|---|---|---|---|
| *one* | *un* | *odin* | *eka* | *moja* | *dondo* | *gɔɔ* | *wērum* |
| *two* | *deux* | *dva* | *dva* | *mbili* | *fera* | *didi* | *owun* |
| *three* | *trois* | *tri* | *trayah* | *tatu* | *sagba* | *tati* | *toskin* |
| *four* | *quatre* | *četyre* | *čatvarah* | *nne* | *nani* | *nahi* | *kemsin* |
| *five* | *cinq* | *p'at'* | *pañča* | *tano* | *soru* | *yɔɔi* | *diĵin* |

stands for an affricate. Fulani *nahi* 'four' should be *nai*. There is a length mark missing on the second *a* in the Sanskrit equivalent for 'four'; etc.

As a final item I should like to discuss the table just alluded to. It contains the numbers from 'one' through 'five' in four European and four African languages. We are told that, "In the former case the relationship is obvious, in the latter the collated forms can much less be called resembling" (96). I reproduce it as Table 2.

There would seem to be no point in such a comparison if the African languages are not also asserted to be related. But the first three languages on the African side are Niger-Congo, while the fourth, Nubian, is a Nilo-Saharan language, for which no relationship to the first three is claimed by myself or anyone else. Indeed, a grouping of the first three against the fourth begins to appear even in this small sample of material. And how is it that, in Indo-European, English /f/ corresponds to French /k/ in *quatre*, but to French /s/ in *cinq*?

I agree with Fodor that "the time has come to begin the study of the theory of Greenberg in detail and after leaving off the one-sized praises or the mere quotations, the experts of the African studies have to prove or to reject his statements" (138). Unfortunately, the naïveté of Fodor's approach is such that it cannot make a significant contribution to this desirable goal.

## References Cited

Bazin, J. 1906. *Dictionnaire bambara-français*. Paris.
Dupuis Yakouba, A. 1917. *Essai de méthode pratique pour l'étude de la langue songoï ou songaï*. Paris: Leroux.
Greenberg, J. H. 1963. *The Languages of Africa*. Bloomington: Indiana University.
Guthrie, M. 1962. "Bantu Origins: A Tentative New Hypothesis." *Journal of African Languages* 1: 9–21.
———. 1967. *Comparative Bantu: An Introduction to the Comparative Linguistics and Prehistory of the Bantu Languages, I.* Farnborough: Gregg Press.
Homburger, L. 1913. *Étude sur la phonétique historique du bantou*. Paris: H. Champion.

Meinhof, C. 1910. *Grundriss einer Lautlehre der Bantusprachen*. 2d ed. Berlin: D. Reimer.
———. 1932. *Introduction to the Phonology of the Bantu Languages*. Berlin: D. Reimer.
Oliver, R. 1966. "The problem of Bantu expansion." *Journal of African History* 7: 361–76.
Prost, A. 1953. *Les langues mandé-sud du groupe mana-busa*. Dakar: IFAN.
———. 1956. *La langue soṅay et ses dialectes*. Dakar: IFAN.
Travélé, M. 1913. *Petit dictionnaire français-bambara et bambara-français*. Paris: Paul Geuthner.
Westermann, D. 1927. *Die westlichen Sudansprachen und ihre Beziehungen zum Bantu*. Berlin: W. Gruyter.
Winston, F. D. D. 1966. "Greenberg's Classification of African Languages." *African Language Studies* 7: 160–70.

# Linguistic Evidence Regarding Bantu Origins

In a previous issue of this journal, Roland Oliver, dealing with the problem of Bantu origins and expansion, devoted considerable attention to the linguistic evidence.[1] The discussion refers almost exclusively to my own work and that of Professor Guthrie. The present article has two principal aims. The first is to clarify certain points regarding my own methodology and conclusions in a few instances in which I believe that a misleading impression is conveyed by Professor Oliver's exposition. The second purpose is more general: to survey the problem as a whole with special reference to those assumptions of Guthrie on the basis of which Oliver draws some of his own conclusions. These two aims should, in my view, be left somewhat separate, since it is clear that in certain respects Oliver is staking out a middle position, as indicated by the following: "As I said, one has not to think of Greenberg's conclusion and Guthrie's conclusion as contradictory. It is a perfectly sound interpretation to think of them as referring to successive stages in time."[2]

As a convenience to the reader, so that he can follow the argument without referring back to the publications being discussed, a number of passages are reproduced here *in extenso* and referred to by number in the course of the exposition.

I shall begin by citing and commenting upon several passages from the article of Oliver referred to earlier.

**(1)** Working from a lexical comparison of the equivalents for about fifty common words in a large number of Western Sudanic and Bantu languages, Greenberg had

[1] Roland Oliver, "The Problem of the Bantu Expansion," *Journal of African History*, 7 (1966): 361–76. I wish to acknowledge here my indebtedness to Professor Oliver for comments and suggestions regarding an earlier version of this paper.

[2] *Ibid.*, p. 367.

reached the conclusion that Bantu belonged to the Western Sudanic language family. He concluded that the Bantu languages, for all their vast extension, did not even form a single district subgroup within this family, but that, taken all together, they merely formed a subgroup which included also most of the languages spoken in the central Cameroons and East-Central Nigeria.[3]

I should like to comment on several points raised in the foregoing passage.

1. The initial phrase "working from a lexical comparison . . ." certainly suggests that only lexical evidence was employed and that grammatical evidence was disregarded. Any reasonably careful reading of my work should dispel this notion. At every point grammatical as well as lexical evidence is cited.[4]

It is not too much to state that in at least one instance, that of Niger-Kordofanian, grammatical resemblances were treated as more decisive than lexical ones. On the specific question of Bantu, a point-by-point comparison was made between the noun-class systems of Bantu and those of the rest of Niger-Congo.[5] In addition, in seeking to demonstrate that such resemblances as those between Tiv and Bantu could not be the result of mere secondary contacts, but bespoke common origin, a set of remarkable agreements in the tonal behavior of Tiv and Bantu noun classes were pointed out.[6]

2. It is stated in (**1**) that about fifty words were used for purposes of linguistic comparison. I do not know the source for this assertion. It may possibly rest on the fact that there are 49 etymologies in the word list comparing the Adamawa-Eastern languages to the remainder of Niger-Congo.[7] However, other lists are longer and one of these, for the Nilo-Saharan languages, contains 161 entries. Further, individual etymological entries often contain words with different but related meanings, e.g. 'water' and 'rain'. There will, it is evident, be a larger number of distinct words involved in each list than the total number of etymological entries.

In fact, the notebooks in which I have compiled systematic vocabulary

[3] *Ibid.*, p. 366.

[4] Examples from *The Languages of Africa* (2nd ed.; The Hague: Mouton, 1966), include pp. 9–13, discussion of resemblances of the noun class system of the Adamawa-Eastern languages with the remainder of Niger-Congo; 31, comparisons of the noun class system of Bantu with the rest of Niger-Congo; 35, grammatical innovations of Bantu; 46–48, Afroasiatic grammatical features found in the Chadic languages; 68–71, grammatical resemblances of Hottentot to the rest of Khoisan; 73–75, grammatical resemblances of Hatsa to the rest of Khoisan; 86–89, common grammatical features of the Nilotic and 'Nilo-Hamitic' languages; 109–17, grammatical features of the Eastern Sudanic languages found in the remainder of the Chari-Nile group; 130–33, grammatical evidence for the unity of Nilo-Saharan; 149–52, grammatical resemblances between the Kordofanian and the Niger-Congo families.

[5] Greenberg, *The Languages of Africa*, p. 31.

[6] *Ibid.*, p. 35.

[7] *Ibid.*, pp. 13–24.

information have columns for over 400 items. Of course, for many languages, existing sources do not contain the equivalents for all these items, but all those which are available were entered. In many instances, I went well beyond such data, searching whole dictionaries for cognates. For example, in regard to Afroasiatic, I had been assembling materials for the possible ultimate publication of an Afroasiatic etymological dictionary for a number of years, a task in which I combed all dictionaries and word lists which were known to me. In addition, I incorporated in the word lists of my general work on African languages the results of previous etymological work by other linguists in so far as they appeared sound in my judgment.

3. One other statement in (**1**) calls for some further elucidation, namely that "Greenberg had reached the conclusion that Bantu belonged to the Western Sudanic language family." That is correct as far as it goes, but is seriously incomplete in failing to point out that Westermann's original conception of Western Sudanic as extending eastward only as far as the Nigeria-Cameroons border received a major amplification in the course of my work. Evidence was presented to show that a large number of languages, including those as distant from West Africa as Zande and Baka, were to be considered as part of the same linguistic stock as Bantu and Westermann's Western Sudanic. This, and not any desire to introduce terminological innovations, was the main reason for proposing the name Niger-Congo in place of the no longer appropriate Western Sudanic. In regard to these more easterly languages which comprise the Adamawa-Eastern branch of Niger-Congo, even A. N. Tucker and M. A. Bryan, who can hardly be accused of being prejudiced in favor of my work, make the following observation: "In boldly taking these languages out of the nebulous 'Sudanic' family in which they had been tentatively placed by Tucker, he has made a great advance in African language classification, for there is no doubt that there is a fair basic vocabulary common to all these languages, and that furthermore many words have roots in common with Bantu."[8]

The existence of many languages not only northwest of Bantu in the Western Sudan, but also directly north of even the most easterly Bantu languages, has an important bearing on later discussion in which Guthrie's attempt to explain resemblances to Bantu in West African languages as 'Bantuisms' will now bear the additional heavy burdens of accounting for the "roots in common with Bantu" mentioned by A. N. Tucker and M. A. Bryan with languages far to the east of West Africa.

(**2**) The next piece of evidence is again linguistic, and it is not, in my view, fundamentally contradictory of Greenberg, although it modifies Greenberg's very

[8] A. N. Tucker and M. A. Bryan, *The Non-Bantu Languages of North-Eastern Africa* (London, New York, and Capetown: Oxford University Press, 1956), pp. 144–45.

simple hypothesis in a very important way. This is the evidence from Professor Malcolm Guthrie's work on the classification of Bantu languages. I have said that Greenberg's work is based on a comparison of about fifty common meanings over the languages of Africa as a whole. Guthrie's work is of an altogether different order of detail. It is based on a comparison of about 22,000 related words in some 200 Bantu languages.[9]

At this point, I wish to beg the reader's indulgence in discussing once again the number of comparisons. The contrast of Greenberg's 50 versus Guthrie's 22,000 certainly does convey the impression of a "different order of detail." To provide comparable figures, Oliver should have at least counted up every cited form in my etymologies. For Guthrie, it must be assumed, he is giving the total number of related forms over all the languages, while for me he merely gives the number of English glosses, each counted only once. On a conservative estimate, I looked at an average of 200 words in 800 languages, that is, about 160,000 words. Of course, there are far fewer forms cited in the etymologies. There are two reasons for this. One was that in order to keep my work to a reasonable length in its published form I generally cited only one example from each relevant subfamily. The second was that I was dealing with more distant relationships. There will be more Bantu etymologies than Niger-Congo etymologies, just as there will be more Romance etymologies than Indo-European etymologies. I would like to terminate my discussion of this "numbers game" by quoting a remark of the eminent Hebraicist, Alexander Sperber, directed to Paul E. Kahle: "Do I have to tell a scholar of his rank that evidence is weighed, not counted?"[10]

From these questions of detail in Oliver's article, I now turn to the more fundamental points at issue between Guthrie and myself. It was noted earlier, and will bear repetition in the present context, that Professor Oliver is evidently taking some kind of middle ground between my position and that of Guthrie. Since this position is not spelled out in detail, I cannot tell how much of Guthrie's arguments against my views is in fact accepted by Oliver. Hence, the points raised here are not intended to refute Oliver's views, since on most of these matters I do not know in any detail what they are, but to develop the evidence for my own views as against Guthrie's.

The questions involved here are complex, but can be divided into three main topics. These are: (*a*) The internal linguistic evidence regarding the probable area of origin of the Bantu-speaking peoples; (*b*) the non-linguistic, chiefly geographic, evidence; and (*c*) the external, i.e. non-Bantu, linguistic evidence regarding Bantu origins.

[9] Oliver, "The Problem of Bantu Expansion," p. 366.

[10] Alexander Sperber, *A Historical Grammar of Biblical Hebrew* (Leiden: Brill, 1966), p. 54.

Logically, perhaps, the last of these should be treated first, but I find it more convenient to discuss them in the order listed.

From my overall theory regarding the linguistic relationship of Bantu within the more inclusive Niger-Congo linguistic stock, it follows for reasons which will be discussed in detail under point (**3**) that the ultimate origin of Bantu should be approximately in the middle Benue area of Nigeria, hence to the north-west of the vast bulk of indisputably Bantu languages.[11]

Guthrie argues that the internal Bantu linguistic evidence is contrary to this assumption. His procedure is the following. He first compiles a set of roots which he calls Common Bantu. These are the roots which occur in at least three of the twelve zones into which Guthrie divided the Bantu languages in his work on Bantu classification.[12] He then calculates for a number of languages their "Common Bantu Index," by which is meant the percentage of these Common Bantu roots which they have retained. According to Guthrie, there is a "Central group" or "nucleus" with retention rates of 43 percent or over. He goes on to state the following.

(**3**) The only case where there is any appreciable difference in the rate of diminution [*sc.* as one moves away from the nuclear area] is to the north-west, where there is a sharp drop from the groups of figures in the forties to the figures in the twenties.[13]

At this point in Guthrie's exposition a footnote is appended which I now cite:

(**4**) . . . It is apparent that it has a bearing on the validity of the Greenberg hypothesis of a migration from a point to the north-west. If the progenitors of the speakers of the Bantu languages had really come from that direction some indication of that should have appeared in these figures. In fact, however, the sharp drop on the north-western side of the nucleus is the exact opposite of what would have been expected if Greenberg's speculations corresponded even remotely to what actually did happen.

Guthrie is assuming that the greatest conservatism, i.e. retention of original roots, is at the point of origin, which, on this basis, would be the central, rather than the north-western part of the Bantu area. There happens to be empirical evidence on this point. If we accepted Guthrie's assumption, we would hypothesize that Iceland, known to have been settled mainly from Norway in the late ninth century A.D., was the place of origin of Germanic, since it indisputably retains the largest proportion of proto-Germanic roots

[11] The phrase "indisputably Bantu languages" is employed here because there is at least one group of languages, the Jarawa, which I consider to be Bantu and which is in the central part of Nigeria, north and west of the area which I posit as the ultimate point of Bantu origin.

[12] M. Guthrie, *The Classification of the Bantu Languages* (London and New York: Oxford Press, 1948). There are, of course, some differences of detail regarding these zones in the more recent work of Guthrie.

[13] M. Guthrie, "Bantu Origins: A Tentative New Hypothesis," *Journal of African Languages*, 1 (1962): 9–21, at p. 15.

and is indeed also the most archaic Germanic language in its grammatical structure.[14] Similarly, a study of contemporary Romance languages would most probably, using Guthrie's assumption, arrive at the conclusion that the point of origin was not Rome, but Sardinia. In fact, the Italian "areal" school of linguistics, the *Neolinguistica*, elevated the opposite assumption into a general principle. They talked about the *area centrale innovatrice* as against the archaic periphery. While all their conclusions have not met with general acceptance, it seems highly unlikely that a school whose central doctrine had to do with the geographical distribution of linguistic phenomena, and hence studied these matters in great detail, should have set up a basic hypothesis unless it held in at least a fair number of instances.[15]

It should be made clear that I am not making a claim opposite to Guthrie's, namely, that it is always the least conservative area which is the point of origin. In fact, we know little of the presumably non-linguistic factors which make certain dialect forms of a language more conservative than others. The most cautious view would be to refuse to draw any far-reaching conclusions from patterns of degree of retention of lexical items from the ancestral language.

Some additional remarks are in order regarding the Icelandic example cited above. It was likewise adduced by R. Wescott in the proceedings of the third conference on African History and Archaeology as reported in this journal.[16] Guthrie's reported reply was that in Icelandic the fall-off was sudden, whereas in Bantu it was gradual. This is belied, however, regarding the north-west group, which is the decisive one for my argument, by Guthrie's own repeated statements on this point, one example of which is found in the passage (**4**) cited above in which he talks of "the sharp drop on the north-western side of the nucleus."

Up to now I have been assuming that Guthrie's method of arriving at a set of Common Bantu roots and of using these as a basis for measuring the degree of conservatism of individual languages is a valid one. I have merely disputed the hypothesis that the geographical location of the most conservative languages is a reliable guide to the point of origin. It is in fact my contention that while Guthrie's method no doubt identifies many roots of the original Bantu speech community, it does not truly delimit this set as a whole and therefore constitutes an illusory basis for measuring relative conservatism and archaism. The relevant principles have been known for a considerable time to historical linguists, and they can be well illustrated from English.

In order to make our parallel with English more like the Bantu situation, let

[14] Evidence concerning the lexical archaism of Icelandic is presented by Bergsland and Vogt in their article "On the Validity of Glottochronology," *Current Anthropology*, 3 (1962): 115–29.

[15] For a general exposition of the doctrine of the Neolinguistica, see G. Bertoni, *Breviario di neolinguistica* (Modena, 1928).

[16] *Journal of African History*, 3, no. 2 (1962): 186–87.

us suppose that English, now spoken essentially in the British Isles, United States and Canada, the Republic of South Africa, Australia and New Zealand, were to continue another thousand years and that, as has been true in the past of the human race, its local dialects would diverge more and more, so that there would result a number of distinct but very obviously related languages. Suppose also that we had nothing but the linguistic evidence to decide the place of origin of this far-flung family.

The fact that the British Isles was the place of origin rather than, for example, Australia, would appear in the following fashion. Since English was spoken there first and only spread to other places at a much later date there was time for many local dialects to develop. The later spread was confined in the main to the diffusion of a linguistically relatively restricted and standardized form. It is indeed true that at the present time dialect differences within the British Isles are far deeper than in any other English-speaking areas. If then we employed a method comparable to Guthrie's, namely, to determine Common English by breadth of distribution within the whole English community, we would arrive not at Proto-English, so to speak, but at the roots of the particular form of English that spread elsewhere. There would be a sensational falling off of the proportion of these roots to the total lexicon precisely in Britain. A Greenberg-like linguist would note the specially close relationship of English to Frisian, a language corresponding to Tiv in the Bantu picture, and the somewhat more remote relationship to Germanic and then to Indo-European as a whole. He would classify the vast English group as a subgroup of a subgroup of Indo-European, and posit the British Isles as the point of origin, while a Guthrie-like linguist would claim that the low retention rate in the British Isles shows that this could not be the original area.

The more exact genetic subgroupings of Bantu would obviously be of central importance in bearing on this question. I am pleased to report here an essential point of agreement between myself and Guthrie. Some years ago I—and it now appears, others—all working in essential independence from Guthrie and each other, arrived at the notion of a basic East-West division within Bantu and with very similar assignment of languages to the two groups. If this is the most fundamental division within Bantu, then a central area for the differentiation of Guthrie's Western and Eastern Bantu is indicated, and this is well in accord with Oliver's position that there are two successive stages, an ultimate northwestern origin for Bantu as a whole and a subsequent differentiation in a more central nuclear area. I consider this a real possibility. However, in my opinion much more remains to be accomplished in determining the genetic subclassification of Bantu. The Western group seems more internally diverse than the Eastern. The Benue-Congo Working Group of the West African Linguistic Society is tending towards the notion of a fundamental division between North-western Bantu, or even a portion of North-western

Bantu as against all the others, and then a further more recent subdivision between the remainder of Western Bantu and Eastern Bantu. All of this, however, is still very tentative.

I now come to the geographical argument. Guthrie indicates his surprise that neither the present writer, nor, in his opinion less excusably, Murdock, as a non-linguist, did not discuss

**(5)** . . . how the large number of Bantu immigrants could have traversed the inhospitable and large impenetrable forest between the rivers Ubangi-Congo and the Atlantic.[17]

The validity of this objection has obviously to be judged by paleobotanists and allied specialists rather than linguists. If the linguist's conclusions are to be of any value to the historian they must be independent and based on linguistic considerations. Hence, had I considered this factor, which I did not, it would not have prevented me from presenting certain conclusions as highly probable inferences from linguistic premises.

Nevertheless, the following observations may be offered. Guthrie himself feels impelled to develop a special theory to account for the striking resemblances between Tiv in Nigeria and Bantu. It should be borne in mind that the Tiv language is one of those which I classify along with a few other languages as comprising the Bantoid sub-branch of the Benue-Congo branch of Niger-Congo. It is on the basis of the location of the Tiv and the other Bantoid languages in the Middle Benue that I conjecture this area as the most probable one of ultimate Bantu origin.

Guthrie accounts for the resemblance of Tiv to Bantu as the result of "an overshoot of the northward movement of the Proto-Bantu A," Proto-Bantu A being his term for the ancestral dialect of Western Bantu. This means that Bantu speakers reached the very area that I have hypothesized as the point of origin, but going in the opposite direction back to it. If there is a road from New York to Chicago, there has to be a road from Chicago to New York.[18]

Further, the difficulty of traversing this area is perhaps not as great as Guthrie supposes. In this regard, I should like to quote an observation of the archaeologist M. Posnansky, whose authority in such matters should be greater than that of linguists such as Guthrie or myself.

**(6)** The lack of real concrete archaeological evidence still allows, according to the interpretation put on the limited data, just as convincing a case to be made in support of the Greenberg hypothesis of Bantu origins in the Nigerian-Cameroons borderland

[17] Guthrie, "Bantu Origins," p. 11 n.

[18] It should be noted that I nowhere speculated regarding the route taken by the Bantu in reaching their present location.

area as in the Guthrie southern woodland belt, though an interpretation connecting the two hypotheses, as has been made by Oliver, is more plausible, with perhaps a greater emphasis being placed on the first stage of movement of peoples and ideas through the forest to the woodland belt than Oliver has allowed.[19]

I now turn to the problems of external evidence. Here the lines are clearly drawn. I maintain that Bantu is merely a group within the vast Niger-Congo family and can in fact be placed within that family in the Benue-Congo branch and can be further pinpointed as a member of the Bantoid sub-branch of Benue-Congo. The considerations that would lead me, if not to this specific hypothesis, at least to the general notion that Bantu should be a relatively recent offshoot of some more extensive family, are described by Oliver with model clarity, as follows:

**(7)** . . . and the Bantu family must be regarded as a distinctly *new* family, the speakers of which must have expanded very rapidly indeed in order to have achieved such a wide geographical dispersion along with such a small degree of linguistic divergence.[20]

In dealing with Guthrie's views regarding the linguistic position of Bantu, my original intention was to deal with it as I understood it from his article of 1962 on Bantu origins from which all the earlier citations are drawn, namely, that Bantu is not related to what I consider to be the rest of Niger-Congo, and the resemblances to Bantu which Guthrie acknowledges and which he calls Bantuisms, are the result of borrowing from Bantu. This view seems to be expressed in the following passages of the 1962 article.

**(8)** The importance of his observations [*sc.* Westermann's], however, was to show that any discussion of Bantu origins must take into account certain features of West African languages. . . .[21]

**(9)** . . . the most likely appears to be that Bantuisms are due to the incorporation of Bantu features into languages of a quite distinct origin . . .; the apparent reflexes of Bantu roots might be acquired as loan words. In other words, we have to postulate that speakers of an alien Bantu-type language arrived in West Africa as introducers into an already developed situation of a different kind. . . . [S]plinter groups speaking a language or languages related to Proto-Bantu reached West Africa and were absorbed and this would sufficiently account for the situation as it now exists.[22]

I am now aware that Guthrie's views are more complex than this, and moreover, have probably changed and developed over time. In his monumental

[19] M. Posnansky, "Bantu Genesis: Archaeological Reflexions," *Journal of African History*, 9, no. 1 (1968): 11.

[20] Oliver, "The Problem of the Bantu Expansion," p. 361.

[21] Guthrie, "Bantu Origins," pp. 9–10.

[22] *Ibid.*

*Comparative Bantu* he discusses the particular problem of Bantuisms in an excursus contained in a part of this work which is in press but has not yet appeared. I have obtained a copy of this excursus and will consider it later in this paper.[23] It is also clear to me now that even in 1962, Guthrie did not consider direct borrowing from Proto-Bantu itself an adequate explanation, as evidenced, first by his phraseology in (**9**) regarding "a language or languages related to Proto-Bantu" as the source of Bantuisms, and secondly by a footnote at the end of the article in which he advances a theory of Pre-Bantu rather than Proto-Bantu as responsible for such features in non-Bantu languages. However, even though it is in a sense a straw man, I should like to discuss first the untenability of explaining these resemblances to Bantu as resulting from borrowing from Proto-Bantu. A clear view of why this is inadequate likewise has a negative bearing on the more complex theories of Guthrie as contained in his Pre-Bantu theory and on the analysis contained in his excursus on the subject in his *Comparative Bantu*.

There is a further matter which I had hoped to avoid discussing because of its more technical linguistic nature, but it is so much a part of Guthrie's argumentation that I believe it must be dealt with, namely, his view that these resemblances involve, to repeat the phrase used in (**9**), "apparent reflexes." I entertain the hope that their discussion, since they involve the nature of historical processcs in a very broad sense, will be of some independent interest to non-linguistic readers.

Let us consider then the hypothesis of borrowing from Proto-Bantu as an explanation for the resemblances of Bantu to the languages which in my view comprise, along with Bantu, the Niger-Congo family of languages.

The cause is here so disproportionate to the effect that it is difficult to see how this explanation could be seriously considered. Guthrie requires a separate migration, postulated *ad hoc* just to account for the resemblances of Bantu to Tiv, a single language of Nigeria. How could mere "Bantu influence" produce resemblances in the pronouns, the most basic vocabulary, and such a fundamental grammatical characteristic as the noun class system, in hundreds of languages extending from Wolof in Senegal to Baka in the Republic of the Sudan, practically the entire breadth of the Sudan?

I have detailed elsewhere some of the purely linguistic arguments against the adequacy of such a theory.[24] Since this appeared in a work not likely to be consulted by historians, I shall repeat here an example of one of the main types of argument in its specific application to the noun class system.

[23] I wish to express my thanks to Eric Hamp for making a copy of this excursus available to me. I am also indebted to Professor Hamp for a critical reading of the final version and particularly for his remarks on my Indo-European examples cited later in this paper.

[24] Greenberg, *The Languages of Africa*, pp. 33–37.

As is well known, one of the salient grammatical characteristics of Bantu languages is the system of noun classes, each of which is marked by a characteristic prefix. These classes are, in general, paired off so that one of each pair is used for a particular set of nouns in the singular and the other for the same set in the plural. These sets have, to varying degrees, unitary semantic properties. For example, in Ciluba of the Kasai, we have such pairs as *muntu*, 'man'/*bantu*, 'men'; *mukaji*, 'woman'/*bakaji*, 'women'; *mulunda*, 'friend'/*balunda*, 'friends'; etc. In this language, as in most Bantu languages, the class with prefix *mu-* has as its plural the class with the prefix *ba-*, and all members of the class denote persons. Moreover adjectives, subject and object pronouns, and various other items agree in class with the noun to which they refer. Thus, in Ciluba, 'tall man' is *muntu munene*; 'tall men' *bantu banene*; 'tall woman' *mukaji munene*; 'tall women' *bakaji banene*. There are instances, however, in which the concord elements are not identical with the noun prefix. To illustrate once more from Ciluba, 'the man takes' is *muntu u-kwata*; 'the men take', *bantu ba-kwata*, where in the first sentence we might have expected **mu-kwata* rather than *u-kwata*. This class system has been reconstructed for Proto-Bantu and there is a standard numbering. All of these facts are probably so familiar even to non-linguists that there is no need to repeat them here.

Noun class systems basically similar to Bantu are found in many Niger-Congo languages, a fact already noted in detail by Harry H. Johnston in his well-known work on Bantu and Semi-Bantu languages. In his work on Western Sudanic, Westermann gives a detailed table of correspondences of these classes with those of reconstructed Proto-Bantu. The coincidences here are so massive that they can hardly be a matter of dispute. However, the Bantu classes show certain peculiarities in comparison with the overall pattern. (So, for that matter, does any other single language or restricted language group.) One of the peculiarities is that, as far as is known, for the *mu-* singular personal class (Class 1) for which examples from Luba were cited above, only Bantu languages have forms with initial *m-*.

Corresponding to Class 1 and its plural Class 2, we have then such examples as *u-pi* 'child'/*ba-pi* 'children' in Lefana, a language of Togo. In the earlier discussion of Ciluba, it was noted that the subject pronoun corresponding to Class 1 was *u-* and not *mu-* as might have been expected. This reflects a general Bantu fact. Class 1 has *mu-* in the noun, adjective, and object pronoun, but *u-* elsewhere.

The question that may be raised is the following. How is it that, as if by a vast conspiracy, of the two indicators of Class 1, *mu-* and *u-*, it was always *u-* that was borrowed by non-Bantu and never *mu*? Similar questions may be raised in a number of other instances, both in regard to the noun class system, in regard to lexical items, and elsewhere. I shall call the type of explanation required to account for these facts by external influence of Bantu on non-Bantu languages the "conspiracy theory."

If we assume, however, that Bantu is a particular offshoot of Niger-Congo, then these and similar facts become understandable. During its period of special development, Bantu went through certain changes, one of which was the development and spread of *m-* forms in Class 1 as well as in certain other classes.[25] It is a normal expectation that when an earlier unified language splits up, the various individual branches each undergo certain independent changes, and it is the sharing in each group of the reflexes of these changes that gives it its distinctive character within the larger family.

In fact, one should not be required to develop arguments of the above type. The hypothesis of a special role for Bantu is, from the linguist's point of view, an arbitrary one. Objectively, what is given is a vast network of recurring resemblances among a large group of languages in which Bantu is conspicuous simply because of the large area it occupies and the correspondingly large number of individual languages and populations speaking it. The fallacy involved may be called that of the "arbitrary point of reference." One starts with a particular language or language family, either conspicuous for its practical importance, or particularly well studied and known to the investigator. One then interprets resemblances to other languages or language families by its influence on other languages. But why should one not start from Akan, for example, and explain Bantu resemblances to Akan as Akanisms rather than resemblances of Akan to Bantu as Bantuisms?

The nature of this argument was apprehended long ago by that remarkably astute observer, Bishop Codrington, in regard to the status of the Melanesian languages in the Pacific. Two citations from his work on the Melanesian languages will show how strikingly parallel the situation is to that in Africa.

**(10)** The view of the Melanesian languages here proposed is, in the first place, that they are homogeneous; and secondly that they belong to a common stock with the Ocean tongues generally—those of the Indian Archipelago and of Polynesia. The view which is opposed is one which would make the Melanesian languages originally distinct from that to which Malayan and Polynesian languages belong and would pronounce all that is found in Melanesian languages common with Malay and Polynesian to be borrowed from these tongues as due to influence received from them.[26]

**(11)** Any observer of the Melanesian languages who approaches them from the West and sees in them much that is the same with Malay calls that a Malay element, and

[25] A possible source for the spread of this *m-* form in Bantu is the following. The object pronoun of Class 1 is *mu-* not only in Bantu but elsewhere (e.g., Fula *mo*). It could have spread analogically from the object pronoun to the noun and adjective and then to other classes. It is perhaps unnecessary to remark that the force of the argument against the conspiracy theory is not dependent on the validity of this specific theory to account for the Bantu situation.

[26] R. H. Codrington, *The Melanesian Languages* (Oxford, 1885), p. 10.

*Table 1*

| | two | three | four | tongue | tooth | mouth | ear | head | hand | bone | water | fire |
|---|---|---|---|---|---|---|---|---|---|---|---|---|
| 1. | didi | tati | nai | dem(gal) | nyi(re) | hundu(ko) | nof(ru) | ho(re) | junggo | ʔiʔ(al) | ndiy(am) | gite |
| 2. | yi | ta | nase | zelem(de) | nyen(di) | no(re) | tube(re) | zu(gu) | nu(gu) | kobe(re) | ko(m) | buge(m) |
| 3. | yi | ta | naase | zellen(ne) | nyen(ne) | noo(re) | tube(re) | zu(o) | nu(o) | kobe(re) | koo(m) | bugu(m) |
| 4. | inyo | ete | nne | (li)nyemi | (le)nyi | (ke)nye | (ko)tu | (ku)li | (ko)nu | (u)kubi | nutu | oja |
| 5. | ova | ota | one | (ki)nemi | (li)-ne | (o)nugu | (ku)tokpa | (ku)ni | (o)wala | (li)xwa | (ku)ni | (ki)fu |
| 6. | inyõõ | ite | inaa | (o)nyã-gemi | (i)-nye | (ka)nyã | (ku)chui | (i)ti | (ku)rõ | (e)kui | (n)du | otoo |
| 7. | (abi)en | (abi)esa | anan | tekrema | ese | ano | aso | oti | nsa | dompe | nsu | ogya |
| 8. | eve | etõ | ene | ade | adu | ngoti | to | ta | abo | vu | tsi | dzo |
| 9. | eji | eta | erĭ | ede | eyí | enu | eti | ori | owo | egũgũ | omi | ina |
| 10. | abuo | ato | ano | ire | eze | onu | nti | ishi | aka | okpukpu | miri | oku |
| 11. | repu | taru | nanzi | (ri)lem | (ri)nyini | (u)nu | tito | (ra)kpə | (ru)wərə | (ru)gu | (m)ene | (wu)la |
| 12. | (m)va | (n)tad | (n)na | (u)lema | (u)nyĭ | (u)mu | (u)tu | (i)si | (u)bog | (u)kub | (a)me | (u)ved |
| 13. | iba | ita | inang | edeme | edet | inua | utong | ibuot | ubok | okpo | mmong | ikang |
| 14. | uhar | utar | unyĩĩ | nombor | (i)nyi(gh) | zwa | to(gh) | (i)tyou(gh) | wegh | kuhe | (m)gerə(m) | usu |
| 15. | bali | tatu | nai | (lu)lem | (li)yino | (ka)nyua | (ku)to | (li)twe | (ku)boko | (li)kupa | (ma)gi | (mu)got |
| 16. | fa | tat | naas | lem | dzine | anu | tsoro | to | wo | kup | nen | bo |
| 17. | hwia | tsia | ni | le | (ri)nyi | (ko)nu | (u)tsu | (ri)chi | (m)va | ku | (ri)shi | ro |
| 18. | uwe | (biya)ta | (biya)ma | mira(se) | linde | ngbwa | tue | li | be | meme | hime | we |

| | | | | | | | | | | | | |
|---|---|---|---|---|---|---|---|---|---|---|---|---|
| 19. | se | ta | sio | menga | tē | nyō | ma | li | ti | bio | ngu | wa |
| 20. | bua | tare | nare | lefe | nini | nu | jara | ju | ko | gbālā | li | we |
| 21. | mala | mahei | fadig | kwire | midab | yaf | angwil | girma | eyi | mitat | yam | nˀe |
| 22. | lama | zadi | afur | arab | ilk(an) | afa(n) | gurra | mata | harka | lafe | bizhan | ibida |
| 23. | laba | saddeh | afar | çarrab | ilig | af | deg | madah | gagan | laf | biyo | dab |
| 24. | lame | sasse | shole | arraba | hinko | afo | machche | umo | anga | mikichcho | wuha | gira |
| 25. | sen | kared | akkiz | (a)lis | (a)sin | (a)mi | (a)sim | (i)ghaf | (u)fes | (i)ghes | (a)m(an) | (u)fa |
| 26. | shn(ayyim) | shalosh | ˀarbaʕ | lash(on) | shen | pe | ˀozen | rosh | yad | gerem | m(ayyim) | ˀesh |
| 27. | snau | shomənt | ftou | las | najhe | ro | maaje | jo | tore | kas | mo(u) | sate |
| 28. | biyu | uku | fudu | (ha)rshe | (ha)kori | baki | kunne | kai | (ha)nnu | kashi | ruwa | wuta |
| 29. | baap | kwan | fiir | liis | aas | po | kwom | kee | sar | gis | am | wus |
| 30. | bollo | kunu | poddo | lisi | udu | bo | kumo | koˀi | sara | osoki | amma | wosi |
| 31. | oieng | somok | unguan | ngelyep | kel(da) | kut | iit | met | ẽ | kowet | peik | maa |
| 32. | are | uni | onguan | ngejep | alai | kutuk | ki(ook) | dukunya | ai(na) | oi(to) | are | kima |
| 33. | ərrexai | xunixo | angwan | ngədyef | xala | xutuk | xiyyok | xosi | xani | xotyu | xari | ximə |
| 34. | öri | sala | ingwan | ngedep | kele | kutuk | swat | kwe | kanin | katyu | piong | kimang |
| 35. | rou | dyak | ngwan | lyep | lech | thok | yich | nhom | chin | ywom | piu | mach |
| 36. | (a)ryau | (a)dek | (a)ngwan | lep | lejo | dhok | yith | wich | chino | chogo | pi | mach |
| 37. | ramˀa | iyˀo | wech | axat(wa) | nigi(at) | otok | itat | o | adhi(t) | emen | mam | gwo |
| 38. | arega | sane | shone | hagga | nihi | aulo | tuso | kele | ad | ketti | emba | shitta |
| 39. | owu | tosku | kemsu | hed | nel | agil | ulug | ur | i | kid | essi | ig |
| 40. | dak | oda | yieza | kalat | yigud | ag | wint | ol | os | am | fik | mo |

calls that which he does not recognize the Melanesian or Papuan. But suppose an observer to begin with the Melanesian languages, and, being familiar with them, advances on the one side to the Polynesian and on the other to the Malayan. . . . He will say that they speak a kind of Melanesian dialect.[27]

It would indeed be preferable, if linguists could approach language classifications in abstraction from the non-linguistic factors, as, for example, if the languages were simply numbered. This is just what I have undertaken in Table 1.[28]

Examination of this table will show a clear break between languages 20 and 21 and between 30 and 31. Languages 1–20 are Niger-Congo, 21–30 Afroasiatic, and 31–40 from the Eastern Sudanic branch of Nilo-Saharan. The number of words and languages involved in this table gives less than one half of one percent of the lexical evidence for these basic divisions. Proto-Bantu is language 15. The theory of Proto-Bantu as the source language then amounts to the claim that number 15 is not related to the other languages in group 1–20, and that it is the source of all resemblances to it in the rest of the languages in 1–20, and that any resemblances they have to each other not attributable to 15 are the result of other diverse and separate origins.

The languages in Table 1 are the following: 1. Fulani (West Atlantic); 2. Mossi (Voltaic); 3. Grunshi (Voltaic); 4. Lefana (Kwa); 5. Avatime (Kwa); 6. Akpafu (Kwa); 7. Twi (Kwa); 8. Ewe (Kwa); 9. Yoruba (Kwa); 10. Igbo (Kwa); 11. Anaguta (Benue-Congo); 12. Yeskwa (Benue-Congo); 13. Efik (Benue-Congo); 14. Tiv (Benue-Congo); 15. Proto-Bantu (Benue-Congo); 16. Ganawuri (Benue-Congo); 17. Irigwe (Benue-Congo); 18. Zande (Adamawa-Eastern); 19. Ngbandi (Adamawa-Eastern); 20. Gbeya (Adamawa-Eastern); 21. Bedauye (Cushitic); 22. Galla (Cushitic); 23. Somali (Cushitic); 24. Sidamo (Cushitic); 25. Ghadames (Berber); 26. Hebrew (Semitic); 27. Coptic (Egyptian); 28. Hausa (Chadic); 29. Angas (Chadic); 30. Bolewa (Chadic); 31. Nandi (Eastern Sudanic); 32. Masai (Eastern Sudanic); 33. Lotuxo (Eastern Sudanic); 34. Bari (Eastern Sudanic); 35. Dinka (Eastern Sudanic); 36. Shilluk (Eastern Sudanic); 37. Didinga (Eastern Sudanic); 38. Barea (Eastern Sudanic); 39. Mahas Nubian (Eastern Sudanic); 40. Tabi (Eastern Sudanic).

The above argument, as noted earlier, refers specifically to the hypothesis of Proto-Bantu as the source language for "Bantuisms" in other Niger-Congo languages. The untenability of the conspiracy theory when stated in terms

[27] *Ibid.*, p. 11.

[28] In Table 1, I have avoided diacritics wherever possible, and have in other ways simplified the transcription. The only phonetic explanation required is that ʔ stands for the glottal stop and ʕ for a voiced pharyngeal. Grammatical elements such as prefixes and suffixes not belonging to the root are enclosed in parentheses.

of Proto-Bantu has resulted in a series of maneuvers by Guthrie to avoid its implications. These arguments may be classified into three types, and I shall discuss them in order. They may be stated as follows: 1. The source of Bantuisms is not so much Proto-Bantu as Pre-Bantu, a still earlier stage. 2. It seems to be the case that often non-Bantu languages show morphological resemblances to Bantu but not lexical, while in other instances, the resemblances are lexical but not morphological. This is elaborated in the above-mentioned excursus in Guthrie's work, *Comparative Bantu*. The general conclusion would be that the whole matter of Bantuisms becomes problematical. 3. The doctrine of "skewed" reflexes is also advanced: that is, that certain resemblances are irregular, i.e. not in accordance with regular sound correspondences. Hence, these also are not subject to normal historical interpretation.

Let us consider, then, the question of Pre-Bantu. The recourse to Pre-Bantu already occurs in the 1962 article which has furnished the basis for the foregoing analysis. On the usual view of how languages differentiate, the Bantu that can be reconstructed from existing languages as their immediate source, namely, Proto-Bantu, must have had a past development of its own and this earlier period may be called Pre-Bantu. In my view, this would be a reasonable name for the language during the time that it was already distinguishable from the most closely related languages such as Tiv, but during which internal divisions on a marked scale had not yet occurred.

In a footnote at the end of the 1962 article to which repeated reference has been made, Guthrie, in order to counter the conspiracy argument, reasons as follows.

**(12)** It is also conceivable that some elements of Pre-Bantu may have been lost in Proto-Bantu, but preserved in some Western African languages. In particular a resemblance, such as that noted by Greenberg between the 'original' West African **bí*, 'child' and the first part of the Proto-Bantu root **-bíada* 'give birth' might be accounted for in this way.[29]

If *bíada* is Proto-Bantu and *bí* is West African (i.e. goes back to Proto-Niger-Congo) then once more the conspiracy argument holds in the following form. How does it come about that in so many Niger-Congo languages we have *bí* meaning 'child' and never the derived verb *bíada*, 'give birth'? They must all have analysed the Bantu verb form, extracted the noun and discarded the verb. Such a proposed sequence of events, reversing the usual derivational process, gives a similar effect to that of an inept cinema projectionist who runs a film backward, or of a narrative history in which a decisive battle is preceded by a peace treaty and followed by a declaration of war.

Guthrie seeks to avoid such an account by arguing, apparently, that Bantu

[29] Guthrie, "Bantu Origins," p. 21, n. 3.

influence in this case stemmed from an earlier Pre-Bantu period in which the noun *bí* 'child' still existed in Bantu and the derived verb *bíada* had not yet been formed from it. Of course, this specific hypothesis cannot be disproved by me, but neither can it be proved by Guthrie.

But note the consequences. As the Pre-Bantu explanation is adopted for *each* case, Pre-Bantu gradually acquires all the features of Proto-Niger-Congo minus, of course, those features not reflected in Bantu at all. This procedure, besides its improbability, is purely *ad hoc* and lies under the same imputation of arbitrariness as the earlier Proto-Bantu theory. Suppose, for example, a dedicated Akanist seeks to explain all resemblances to Akan in other Niger-Congo languages, including Bantu, as Akanisms. Faced with the argument that his theory cannot explain those instances in which for some feature of grammar, lexicon, or phonology, all the other languages show one variant and Akan another (in other words, in the normal view, Akan innovations), he resorts to the expedient of asserting that the source in these cases is not Proto-Akan, but the same language in an earlier stage, Pre-Akan, in which it had just those widespread characteristics which are found elsewhere and thus constituted their source. He likewise cannot be either corroborated or refuted, but his theory is just as good or bad, and just as arbitrary as a theory of pre-Bantu, or depending on one's background and predilections, pre-Mossi, pre-Zande, or pre-what-not.

The next question to be considered is that regarding the supposed situation which Guthrie finds in a number of West African languages in that some show grammatical without lexical resemblance, and some lexical without grammatical resemblances. This view is elaborated in the above-mentioned Excursus to Volume II, Part 2, of *Comparative Bantu* entitled "Bantuisms in non-Bantu Languages," apparently still in press.

Before considering the details of this excursus, a few general observations are in order. There is, it would seem, a real shift in ground involved here in that Guthrie, by actually examining cases beyond the Tiv example which figures in his earlier publications, has been led to the conclusion that in certain instances at least, the resemblances to Bantu have what he calls genealogical significance, which I would interpret to mean genetic. For example, in considering the noun class system of Dyola in Senegal, he notes that "there is a high likelihood that the agreement system of the language is genealogically related to the Bantu system." Again in regard to Lokə in Nigeria, "it would seem to be reasonable to regard these classes as direct reflexes of the Proto-Bantu system."

At this point, I can only be sure of one thing: that Guthrie does not accept the theory that these other languages are simply related to Bantu as part of Niger-Congo. On the normal view, one cannot speak of genealogically related parts of grammar or vocabulary items unless the languages are related. Such specific related forms are at once the reflexes in the real world of items derived from a common source, namely, the ancestral language and, to the investigator, evidence that the languages have a common origin. I can only assume that Guthrie now believes that some of these languages are genetically mixed, that is, have at least two genetic sources. What process this represents in the real world has never been made clear, but it would seem to be a further approach to my view, in that these languages are at least related to Bantu in some way.

There are somewhat similar issues involved in Guthrie's earlier enunciated theory that the much greater resemblances between Bantu languages and Tiv represent an "overshoot" of Proto-Bantu A, that is, the Bantu offshoot ancestral to the Western Bantu languages. If this means anything, it means that Tiv derives from Proto-Bantu A and is therefore some sort of Western Bantu language. In this case, it must share in the same ancestry as the rest of Proto-Bantu A and be a Western Bantu language in the ordinary sense. But both Guthrie and myself agree in denying this. I do this by putting Tiv, the Bantu group, and a few other languages in a particular subgroup of the Benue-Congo branch of Niger-Congo.

Another preliminary observation is in order. While it would indeed be strange if certain languages resembled Bantu in a particular aspect of their grammar like the noun class system, without showing lexical resemblances, the opposite case, namely, lack of a noun class system altogether, along with numerous lexical items in common, is an expectable phenomenon and in fact exists. This is because while vocabulary involves a large number of basically independent elements, any specific aspect of morphology forms an interconnected system which tends to stand or fall as a unit like some lexical item. Just so, in regard to the case system of Indo-European, German, and Icelandic still retain such a system and a comparison with Slavic would show significant points of resemblance, while English, which basically lost the entire system in the period between Anglo-Saxon and Middle English, would not show this, but still retains numerous points of vocabulary resemblance.

Let us now turn to the excursus in some detail. It would exceed the bounds of this paper to examine every case. Guthrie considers the following languages: Temne in Sierra Leone, Dyola in Senegal, Dakarkari, Lokə, and Efik in Nigeria, and Nkonya in Ghana. I will consider here only two typical analyses, that of Lokə and of Dakarkari. In regard to Lokə he concludes that "Although there is no difficulty in establishing correspondences . . . , it would seem reasonable to regard these classes as direct reflexes of the Proto-Bantu system." "Most of the pairings of these classes into singular/plural genders is also not very divergent from what is found in Bantu languages. . . ."

However, he concludes "It must remain an open question for the present whether the presence of a concord system like that in Lokə is by itself of direct relevance to the genealogical relationship of such a language to the Bantu family. This is because possible Bantu reflexes seem to be almost non-existent in the vocabulary. . . ."

This last statement is simply inaccurate, indeed astonishingly so, in view of the evidence to be presented. Guthrie's source for Lokə is an article by Winston on the noun classes of that language.[30] There are therefore only incidental vocabulary items. After some initial discussion and citation of a few sentences, there is on pp. 63–64 the only substantial vocabulary data presented in the article, 30 nouns arranged according to class. There are a few terms such as 'mushroom' and 'roof' for which, as far as I am aware, no Proto-Bantu forms have been reconstructed. Among the remainder we find the following:[31]

(1) Lokə (*lè*)*tú* 'head'; Proto-Bantu *tú* 'head' (*túè*, *túì*, *yùtú*)
(2) Lokə (*k*)*ɔ̀bɔ́* 'arm'; Proto-Bantu *bókò* 'arm'
(3) Lokə (*è*)*bú* 'goat'; Proto-Bantu *búdi* 'goat'
(4) Lokə (*lɛ̀*)*bɛ́* 'breast'; Proto-Bantu *béédè* 'breast'
(5) Lokə (*kì*)*tí* 'tree'; Proto-Bantu *tí* 'tree' (*yìtí*)
(6) Lokə (*kò*)*tûŋ* 'ear'; Proto-Bantu *tú*, 'ear' (*túé*, *túí*, *kùtú*, *yàtú*)
(7) Lokə (*yì*)*nòn* 'bird'; Proto-Bantu *nòní* 'bird' (*nòdí*, *nòní*, *nùní*, etc.)
(8) Lokə (*yà*)*yì* 'blood'; Proto-Bantu *gìdá* 'blood'
(9) Lokə (*ɛ̀*)*bàl* 'axe'; Proto-Bantu *bàd* 'to split'
(10) Lokə (*ò*)*sèn* 'stranger'; Proto-Bantu *gènì* 'stranger'

Two additional items might be cited among the thirty items in Winston's list as quite possible cognates. Note the perfect agreement in tone in the above list. I refrain from discussion of details, such as the noun class affiliations of the nouns in Bantu, which would add further evidence. So far, then, from Proto-Bantu reflexes being "almost non-existent," at least one-third of the items in Winston's list of thirty nouns show obvious resemblances to Proto-Bantu.

The other language cited in his excursus by Guthrie which I would like to discuss is Dakarkari. Unlike Lokə, Guthrie finds here a noun class system which cannot be related with any degree of certainty to the Proto-Bantu system. Again unlike Lokə, Guthrie finds a number of vocabulary resemblances.

[30] F. D. D. Winston, "The Nominal Class System of Lokə," *African Language Studies*, 3 (1962): 49–70.

[31] Noun class prefixes are enclosed in parentheses. Proto-Bantu forms are cited, where possible, from Guthrie's *Comparative Bantu*, Part II. Where Guthrie gives multiple forms, I have cited the most common first and included some of the others in parentheses. (The grave accent indicates low tone, the acute high tone, and the circumflex falling tone.)

He lists 26, but concludes that it is an instance in which "it is doubtful whether any useful conclusion can be drawn . . . it seems that no regular correspondences can be set up." It is an example, in fact, of those languages in which one must view "all the apparent Bantu reflexes as skewed. . . ." As already noted, the question of so-called skewed reflexes will receive separate treatment at a later point in this paper. For the moment, I wish to discuss the question of noun classes in Dakarkari, which, it will be recalled, is stated by Guthrie not to be relatable to the Bantu system. Guthrie's data for Dakarkari are drawn from an article by Hoffman.[32] I reproduce the relevant excerpt from Guthrie's excursus *in toto*.

**(13)** In other languages, however, there are patterns of agreement that operate by concord prefixes throughout the nominal system, although in many cases there are no verbal agreements. Two different types of such agreement have been observed, in one of which it is difficult to correlate the concord element with the Bantu prefixes, while in the other some correlation seems possible. The following selected pairs from Dakarkari (N. Nigeria) will serve as an example of the first type.

| | |
|---|---|
| d\|rẹmȩ / c\|rȩmẹ 'tongue' | k\|dɔmɔ / c\|dɔmɔ 'lip' |
| v\|cȩ / s\|cẹ 'stick' | a\|nwə / c\|nwə 'mouth' |
| a\|cu̧ / s\|cu̧ 'face' | v\|ni̧nə / ni̧nə 'tooth' |

In the case of these concord elements it would be tempting to equate some of them with the Bantu classes in this way: Cl. 6 a-; Cl. 7 k-; Cl. 8 v-; Cl. 10 s-; Cl. 13 c-. This, however, is nothing more than guesswork, and since the pairings this would produce are quite unlike anything found in Bantu languages, it seems of little relevance for questions of genealogical relationship.

Here, as in the rest of the excursus, when dealing with non-Bantu noun class systems, each system is treated in abstraction, without reference to either the internal or external linguistic context of the system. In the case of Dakarkari, Guthrie only looks at the phonological forms of each prefix, and asks whether there is a class with a similar sounding prefix in Bantu. By absence of reference to the internal context, I mean that there is no reference to the meanings of the classes as indicated by the words contained in them, and by absence of reference to the external context, I mean that each language is considered in complete isolation from the comparative data provided by the more closely related languages which often furnish a key to their historic understanding. Even so, and looking at the noun class system of a mere handful of languages of the hundreds which have noun class systems, Guthrie arrives at positive conclusions regarding Lokə, as has already been seen. In regard to Dyola, after dividing the nominal prefixes of that language into two

[32] "An Outline of the Dakarkari Noun-Class System," in *La classification nominale dans les langues négro-africaines* (Paris, 1967), pp. 237–61.

approximately equal groups, the former characterized as involving "putative direct reflexes" and the latter "concord elements with more obscure correspondences," he concludes that "there is a high likelihood that the agreement system is genealogically related to the Bantu system, while some, at least, of those in the second list would be skewed reflexes." For Nkonya he states "there would be some justification for regarding these pairs of prefixes as comparable with the respective genders 1/2, 3/4, 5/6, 5/10, 11/10, since they are in fact very similar to the independent nominal prefixes of Kọyọ (.22) (see this language in the Bantu inventory)." Only for Dakarkari, of the four languages, is the result really negative.

In Westermann's treatment of the subject, on which I built, but which I believe I have a right to say that I developed and expanded, there is a good understanding of the internal and external contexts of these systems in the sense which I have briefly discussed above. It may not be generally realized that Westermann did *not* proceed by taking the Bantu class markers and then looking for correspondences in West Sudanic languages. His *Westliche Sudansprachen*, with its table of West Sudanic noun classes and their point-for-point agreement with those of Proto-Bantu as reconstructed by Meinhof, was preceded by a whole series of studies of subfamilies such as Gur (Voltaic), Kwa, and West Atlantic. In each he considered the totality of the then existing evidence. In terms of such comparison within each subfamily, he characterizes the noun class system in terms of those classes which are truly general within them. It is by this procedure of step-by-step comparison, first within each subfamily and then among the subfamilies, that he arrived at a characterization of the Western Sudanic system. It then turned out, evidently to his surprise, that this system coincided closely with that of Proto-Bantu. It is obvious that Westermann started with the assumption of Bantu independence, and was forced to the conclusion that there was a genetic connection both because of the noun-class system and the vocabulary. However, as I have pointed out elsewhere, this ran so contrary to his prepossessions that, while he at times used the word "genetic," he never really stated the case unequivocally.

There is every difference between studying four cases at random and going through the vast mass of evidence as Westermann did. I reviewed Westermann's data, using additional more recent material as well as evidence from the languages of the Adamawa-Eastern branch of Niger-Congo not considered by Westermann.

Westermann also took into account the semantics of the classes. When this is included, the evidence becomes even more overwhelming. For example, it is already striking to find a West Sudanic pair of classes *u* (sing.)/*ba* (pl.) corresponding to Bantu *mu*/*ba* where Bantu has *u*- for the singular pronoun.

When we add that this set everywhere includes human beings as its basic class membership, we have obviously added powerfully to an already strong case.

Let us return to Dakarkari in the light of these considerations. For reasons of space, I will restrict myself to the very first pair cited from Hoffman, *d*|*ręmę*/c|*ręmę* 'tongue'. For reasons I cannot fathom, Guthrie has not equated the singular *d* prefix with Proto-Bantu *di-*, the prefix of class 5, which normally has as its plural *ma-* (class 6). Moreover, the noun *-ręmę*, as pointed out by Guthrie himself in his discussion of the lexical data, obviously resembles Proto-Bantu *-démè* 'tongue'. In fact, most Bantu languages have forms like *-deme* or *-reme*, and the noun frequently belongs to classes 5/6 in Bantu.

The plural, of course, with the prefix *c-* (phonetically [*č*], approximately as in English *church*) deviates from the Bantu nominal prefix *ma-*, and indeed the general Benue-Congo *a-*, which appears commonly as *a-* in Bantu with pronominal function.

An examination of the Dakarkari system as a whole will show that a whole series of singular classes have either *c* or *s* as their plural. It is a common phenomenon in class languages that the number of distinct plural classes is fewer than in the singular. Dynamically considered, there is a process of spread or generalization of one or two plural classes at the expense of the rest, so that classes which are diverse in the singular come to share the same plural class. It is evidently this process that has been at work in Dakarkari.

A comparison of the class system in the languages most closely related to Dakarkari will show this. Dakarkari belongs to a group which includes Duka, Kambari, and Kamuku. Rowlands, in an article on this group, states the situation as follows:

(**14**) While it is confirmed that Dakarkari, Daka, Kambari, and Kamuku form a fairly closely related group, it is clear that the relationship between Dakarkari and Duka is much closer than any other relationship within the group.[33]

It should also be noted that various dialect forms of Kamuku have been treated in the literature under such names as Bassa, Bassa Kontagora, and Gurmana. Unfortunately, Rowlands does not give plural forms for the words in his list, but he does help in supplying further data regarding the membership of the *d-* class, thus extending the very limited information in this regard to be found in the article of Hoffman cited earlier. For plurals in Duka, Kambari, and Kamuku, we have a number of citations from Duka and Central Kambari originating with Hoffman and published in the report of the Benue-Congo Working Group of the West African Linguistic Society. Unfortunately, there

[33] E. C. Rowlands, "Notes on Some Class Languages of Northern Nigeria," *African Language Studies*, 3: 71–81.

are only a few nouns involved and the volume does not go beyond glosses in English beginning with K. It turns out, in fact, that our most useful source is Koelle's *Polyglotta Africana*, which contains plural forms from practically all the nouns which he cites from Kamuku, as well as a much more limited set of plurals from Bassa.

A comparison of all these sources shows the following. The singular class transcribed with a *d-* prefix by Hoffman, and which is, as a matter of fact, phonetically *də-* before consonants, recurs in all of the other languages, but with *r* or *l*, rather than *d*. That it is the same class is shown by the almost identical membership. For example, corresponding to Hoffman's *d-hyi* 'head' in Dakarkari, we find Dakarkari *ədə-hi* (Rowlands), Duka *ərə-hi* (Rowlands), and Bangawa *ələ-hi* (Rowlands). (Bangawa is another dialect of the Dakarkari-Duka group.) These phonetic variations between *l*, *d*, and *r* are very common in Africa. In fact, Proto-Bantu *d*, which occurs in *di-*, the prefix of class 5 with which we are concerned here, generally appears as *l* or *r* in Bantu languages, except in the nasal combination *nd*, and Meinhof used *l*, rather than the *d* which is now current.

The purpose of this digression is to indicate that when, in Koelle's Kamuku, we find a *li-* prefix in a group of nouns, largely cognate with the *d-* nouns of Dakarkari, there is no reason for hesitation on phonetic grounds to equate the classes in question.

Now Koelle's Kamuku, which, as has been seen, contains the most solid data on noun plurals in this group of languages, has the expected plural in *a-* corresponding to Bantu class 6, with its *ma-*, nominal, and *a-*, pronominal, markers. For example, corresponding to Hoffman's Dakarkari *d-isə*, 'eye', and Bangawa (Rowlands) *əl-iši*, Koelle gives as the Kamuku word for 'eye' *li-šie*, plural *a-šie*. Corresponding to Dakarkari *ədə-gya*, 'egg' (Rowlands), we find in Koelle Kamuku *le-ŋge/a-ŋge*, and Bassa *re-nje/a-nje*, 'egg'. A comparison of materials from all these sources will show that this class contains a series of words which characteristically belong to class 5 of words in Bantu, a class with poorly defined overall semantic characteristics. These include the words 'eye' and 'egg' cited above, as well as 'breast', 'tooth', and 'tongue' (the latter also frequently in class 11 in Bantu). Some of these are not only semantically similar, but are obvious cognates with Bantu—e.g. 'eye', Dakarkari (Rowlands) *ədə-isə*, Kambari *liusu* (Rowlands) (Proto-Bantu **dį-įso*); 'egg', Dakarkari (Rowlands) *ədə-gya*, Kamuku of Ngwoi *ɛ-ɛgi* (Rowlands) (Proto-Bantu **di-gi*); and 'tongue', Dakarkari *ədə-reme* (Rowlands) (Proto-Bantu **di-deme* or **du-deme*).

The case, then, for identifying Hoffman's *d-* singular class with Proto-Bantu *di-* (class 5), is decisive in that a broader comparison shows that the group to which Dakarkari belongs shares the expected plural in *a-*. A number of nouns semantically peculiar to this class are sometimes actually cognate with Bantu and, it should be added, in place of the reduced vowel of Dakarkari, we find in Koelle's Kamuku the expected vowel *i* (Kamuku *li-*).

Finally, I come to the problem of what Guthrie variously calls indirect, false, or skewed reflexes. The questions involved here are even more purely linguistic than those of the immediately preceding section, and anything like an adequate treatment of the issues involved would require easily as much space as all that precedes, and would obviously be inappropriate for a readership consisting predominantly of non-linguists. Nevertheless, I believe that the issue cannot be completely avoided, since it is fundamental to the present problem. This is because Guthrie considers the irregular nature of the resemblances between non-Bantu Niger-Congo and Bantu to require some theory other than common genetic origin. This is made clear, I believe, in the following citations from his 1962 article on Bantu origins:

(**15**) . . . [M]ost of the words that are reminiscent of Bantu roots have to be treated as false reflexes, since the supposed relationship usually involves irregularities, or is based on similarity of shape and not on the regular operation of sound shifting. . . .

The quantity of Bantuisms consisting of possible true reflexes is very restricted, the total number of Bantu roots involved rarely exceeding twenty, although false reflexes may amount to four times this figure. . . .[34]

(**16**) In the first place, if Bantuisms in West African languages are to be attributed to the same source as the common features of the Bantu family, there must have been more than one kind of process of development, since the sound shifting which occurs with absolute regularity in the latter cases is not present except sporadically in the former.[35]

In criticism of my work as not involving the requirement that cognates show absolute regularity of sound shifting, Guthrie is not alone. For example, Fodor has directed an entire book at me which is concentrated chiefly on this one point.[36] And it must indeed appear on the surface that since I admit many resemblances as being very probably related forms which would be rejected by Guthrie, that the latter's methods are more rigorous and hence scientifically more reliable.

But let us consider the question more closely. The impression conveyed in (**16**) is that in Bantu as defined by Guthrie "sound shifting . . . occurs with absolute regularity," but for what he calls Bantuisms this is not the case, and examples which can be accounted for this way are in a small minority.

[34] Guthrie, "Bantu Origins," p. 18.

[35] *Ibid.*

[36] I. Fodor, *The Problems in the Classification of the African Languages: Methodological and theoretical conclusions concerning the classification system of Joseph H. Greenberg* (Budapest, 1966).

Yet one page later in the same source we learn that whereas false reflexes in West African languages account for 52 percent of the cases, in Bantu zones A, B, and C, they constitute about 11 percent. It would seem that "false reflexes" are not confined to Bantuisms in non-Bantu languages, but also occur within Bantu itself, though in a smaller proportion of instances.

But what are these false reflexes? They are, we might say, "near misses," instances which deviate, usually in only one respect, from what would be expected had the postulated sound laws acted entirely without exception. Are such forms mere historical accidents, that is, forms which do not go back to a common source, but rather represent new, historically independent forms which happen by chance to resemble the forms in other languages? They cannot be accidents, at least the mass of them cannot be, in the sense we have just elucidated. There are far too many of them, even in closely related languages. In fact, Guthrie, in his *Comparative Bantu*, after apparently excluding them resolutely, admits them later on and includes them in his etymological index of roots. Sometimes they are "extraneous" items, that is, they have been borrowed from other Bantu languages, but most of them are considered to be genetically connected. In the context of Guthrie's method, there are actually two types to be considered. In the first type, two or more "comparative series" have to be constructed which have the same meaning, but differ partially in form. These are among the so-called osculant sets. For example, no less than five comparative series are postulated to account for the reflexes of the Bantu word for 'honey': *juki, jiki, yoki, yuki,* and *yukį*. In these instances, Guthrie seeks by various methods to arrive at a single Proto-Bantu form from among these possibilites, and derives the others by what he calls "mutations," a polite term for irregular sound change. In the second type, where the deviant forms are not frequent enough to form a separate osculant series, they are listed separately at the end of the entry. In general, I would judge that these forms are historically connected also, exactly as the former, by "mutations." However, the mutational change is here so recent that it only affects one or two languages, as contrasted, say, with the two osculant series for 'two', *bade* and *bede*, in which reflexes of the latter, considered a mutation by Guthrie, are dominant throughout all of Eastern Bantu.

But what are these mutational changes? We must distinguish here between so-called regular sound changes and a whole series of other processes of change which are far from haphazard and display their own type of coherence and, in fact, are recognized by historical linguists in Indo-European and other areas as perfectly normal, even though they cannot be subsumed under statements of invariant phonetic change under phonetically stateable conditions.

By a regular change (or, better, an invariant change, since the other types show certain kinds of regularity), one means a change in which every instance of a particular sound in a language changes to some other sound, either in all of its occurrences (unconditional sound change) or only under phonetically stateable conditions (e.g. *k* becomes *č* before *e* and *i*, a change which occurred in the prehistory of Sanskrit).

Let us consider a change which does not fall under this rubric. For example, the Spanish word for 'tree' is *arbol*, whereas Portuguese has *arvore* and French *arbre*. No Romance linguist doubts that all of these stem from Latin *arbor* and that *arbol* is its continuation in Castilian Spanish. The "mutation" from *r* to *l* belongs to a class of changes known as dissimilation in which one of the two identical sounds, here *r*, changes to a different sound. Now, there is no general sound law that in Spanish *r* always becomes *l* when an *r* precedes. Yet the change is regular in that such changes characteristically involve liquids and nasals, and that *r* itself generally changes to another liquid *l*. This is but one of a whole series of types of non-invariant changes. A very important group involves grammatical analogy. Thus English *r* usually corresponds to German *r*, but in the word 'hare', German has *Hasen*. Guthrie would doubtless call this a false reflex. In fact, *r* and *s* have the same ultimate origin. Long ago in Pre-Proto-Germanic, certain consonants by regular sound change developed two variants in accordance with what is usually called Verner's Law. The condition for this change was the position of the Indo-European pitch accent in relation to the consonant. This accent later was replaced by regular root stress within Proto-Germanic. The accent is basically reconstructable only from Ancient Greek and Vedic Sanskrit. The result was that where the accent shifted within the same paradigm, some forms had *r* and some had *s*. There is still a remnant of this in English *was/were*. In the instance of *hare/Hasen*, English by analogy generalized the *r* variant and German the *s*.

Now as time goes on, more and more of these non-invariant changes accumulate. Hence, the more distantly languages are related, the greater the proportion of true cognates which have gone through these changes, and hence the larger the proportion of what Guthrie calls indirect or skewed reflexes. There are fewer of these between English and German than between English and Persian. Hence, when Guthrie finds a smaller proportion of skewed reflexes in Tiv than in other languages he examines, this is entirely explicable and expectable on the theory that Tiv is more closely related to Bantu within Niger-Congo than are the other languages discussed by him. What Guthrie then calls indirect reflexes are, in the vast majority of instances, forms just as truly cognate as his direct reflexes, but involving other processes which are heavily documented in the history of language change where there is literary evidence, and which are accepted as perfectly normal by comparative linguists.

Up to now, I have been tacitly accepting a certain assumption made by Guthrie and others who have discussed this topic in relation to African language classification, namely, that invariant sound changes are proved by the existence of regular, i.e. recurrent, sound correspondences. It is important to realize that we are here dealing with two distinct levels, actual historical events such as sound changes, and phenomena such as sound correspondences which are being used as evidence for positing these events. Guthrie, Fodor, Winston, and others have been assuming that invariant sound change invariably produces regular correspondences. Hence, in criticizing me, they consider these two phenomena as practically interchangeable, so that I am sometimes accused of disregarding sound correspondences and regular phonetic change almost in the same breath, as though they were equivalent. In fact, they are only highly correlated when languages are very closely related, and even then, this correlation is not perfect.

It is easy to see, for example, that if a particular phoneme in the proto-language was relatively rare, it might easily survive in only one cognate between two languages, and therefore not be recurrent. Since Guthrie directly compares particular languages in isolation with Proto-Bantu, the two-language situation is the one we are appropriately concerned with here.

Even a more frequent phoneme might have very limited occurrences in the specific phonetic environment required for conditioned changes. Documented evidence shows that these conditioned changes are much more frequent than the unconditioned ones. If, for example, an original *f* becomes *h* only before *u*, the number of possible occurrences is limited by the presumably low frequency of a specific sequence such as *fu* in the proto-language.

It is not even true, conversely, that all examples of the same recurrent correspondence always go back to the same original sound. For example English *head* is cognate with French *chef*. To restrict ourselves to the consonants, English *h* corresponds to French *ch* [š] in a few other instances, e.g. 'hound'/*chien*. There is also an English-French correspondence of *d*/*f* found, for example, in 'do'/*faire* going back to a proto-Indo-European **dh*. However, the final consonants of *head* and *chef*, which seem on the surface to be a recurrence of this same correspondence, have nothing to do with the case. In fact, English *d* corresponds to the *t* of Latin *caput* 'head', which has been lost in French, but is still found in the Rumanian plural *capete* 'heads', while *f* in French continues the *p* of Latin *caput* corresponding to the *p* of German *Haupt* and the *f* of Dutch *hoofd*. Thus the form originally had three consonants, and English *d* comes from the third while French *f* comes from the second.

I have also been making another unjustifiable assumption all along, that there is always a clear and determinate distinction which we can arrive at on the evidence concerning which correspondences are direct, which are indirect, and, one should add, which resemblances must be entirely rejected because they cannot be considered to be connected by any sequence of invariant and non-invariant changes. Once more, the distinction between events and evidence is crucial. This relationship may change over the course of time as our knowledge advances. For example, there are a very few words in which Greek has an initial vowel while other Indo-European languages, except in some instances Armenian, do not. Thus, Greek *onoma*, 'name', has an unexplained initial vowel when compared to Latin *nōmen* or English *name*. I presume that Guthrie would at best consider this the result of a mutation, at worst an illusion, so that the connection of the Greek forms to the others would be rejected. In recent years, the theory, first voiced by Saussure in 1879, that Proto-Indo-European had a series of sounds now generally called laryngeals, has won general acceptance. One of the decisive factors was the discovery that some of these occurred in Hittite, a language which was not known in Saussure's time. The initial vowel of Greek is found in words where there are other reasons for positing an initial laryngeal, and is considered to be the reflex of a transition vowel between the laryngeal and the following consonant. Hence, what was formerly considered to be, in Guthrie's terminology at least, an indirect reflex, is now widely considered to be explained by regular sound change. It is worth noting that before this explanation was advanced, Indo-Europeanists did not reject the connection between *onoma* and *nōmen*. They rather put it on the shelf as one of many still unexplained phenomena. Nor do those who at the present time reject the laryngeal explanation deny this connection.

If one actually compares, for example, English and French—and I did this once as an exercise—it is clear that an attempt to apply a method comparable to that which Guthrie uses in regard to Bantuisms would lead to completely negative results. *All* the reflexes would be indirect and one could never get started. Note that if even one of the comparable sets of sounds is non-recurrent, the entire etymology is rejected as belonging to one of his "comparative series." In order to avoid accident, he even demands that recurrence should be found not just in two forms, but in at least three. Let us consider one of the most promising groups of words, namely, those in which initial French *p* = English *f*. I find five of these, so that the initial correspondences can give us a start. The examples are: *pied* = foot; *père* = father; *poisson* = fish; *plein* = full; and *pour* = for. The first must be rejected because in my list of 82 items there is only one occurrence of French [*je*], that in [*pje*], and because English final *t* never corresponds to zero in any other case. For *père* we find the French vowel ɛ does not correspond to the English vowel of 'father' in any other example. In *poisson*, the French diphthong [wa] only occurs in this cognate corresponding to English [i]. In fact in my list, French [wa] in its six recurrences corresponds to six different English vowels. In *plein*, 'full', there has been metathesis of *l* and the adjacent vowel, and nothing corresponds to the French nasalized vowel. In *pour*, the French vowel [u:] corresponds to the vowel of *for* only in this example.

But, it might be objected, granted that the historical processes of change in language are indeed so complex that phenomena such as those just cited are the routine and expected result, does this not leave us open to such free-wheeling procedures that anything goes?

To answer this would be to explain why, in fact, Indo-Europeanists do accept the equations between English and French just given and would be far beyond the reasonable scope of this article. However, one can point to the following main considerations. In regard to non-invariant processes, we do not accept just anything. For example, the change of *r* to *l* in Spanish *arbol* becomes plausible because of the preceding *r* and because the liquid sounds are known from many examples to behave in this fashion, while certain other sounds do not. A second factor, already mentioned in regard to morphological comparison, is crucial. The comparative method is appropriately so called, in that it involves broad range comparisons not confined to two languages. When we see the wider picture, many etymologies become virtually certainties which might not seem so if we restrict ourselves to comparisons of two languages in isolation. When, for example, we find in literally hundreds of languages in West Africa forms for 'three' such as *tato*, *tat*, *tar*, *taro*, and *ta*, often in the same languages which contain members of comparable series for other items, e.g. for 'four' *na*, *ne*, *nai*, etc., one or two might be an accident, but hundreds cannot be. Hence, the probability of some single occurrence being valid is correspondingly increased. We have seen that in the case of the most advanced area of comparative linguistics, Indo-European, such instances are not rejected, even when they have not yet been satisfactorily and completely explained.

As a concluding observation, I should like to pay tribute to Guthrie's work on comparative Bantu, which marks an enormous advance. Comparative Niger-Congo studies, which are in their infancy, must obviously use the results of such studies as the single most important basis for their own comparative studies. On the other hand, much that is puzzling and irregular in Bantu can receive an explanation in a wider context. For example, the remarkable variation in the initial consonants of 'three' and 'five' can now be shown to result from the fact that the forms with *t*- originally belonged to forms agreeing with any class except 10 (the plural of the so-called 'animal class'), while *c*- reflects a palatalization in that class which is found in the noun also in certain Plateau languages of the Benue-Congo.[37] Once the untenable theory of Bantu autogenesis is rejected in favor of a theory in which Bantu finds its proper place in a broader picture, exciting prospects are opened for mutually valuable results. To this end, the outstanding contributions of Guthrie to Bantu proper are bound to make important contributions either with or without his own participation. One hopes for the former.

[37] This alternation still survives in Bantu itself in Kirundi and a few other languages, but the palatalization explanation becomes confirmed, and strengthened by the evidence of other Benue-Congo languages. I presented these results in a talk at the West African Language Congress at Ibadan in 1964. They were never published, but in 1965, Stappers published a paper which contains essentially identical data and conclusions. (See L. Stappers, "Het Hoofdtelwoord in de Bantoe-Talen," *Africana Linguistica* [Tervuren, 1965], vol 2, pp. 177–99.)

# Nilo-Saharan Moveable *k*- as a Stage III Article (with a Penutian Typological Parallel)

Among the grammatical elements of Nilo-Saharan listed in Greenberg (1966: 132) was moveable *k*- (no. 36). This is a prefix which occurs, basically on nominals, in an apparently capricious manner. In the same etymology, forms with and without *k*- may occur as free variants in the same language (e.g. Keliko *karι* ~ *arι* 'blood'), in closely related dialects or languages (e.g. Maasai *ol-oioto*, Teso *a-koit* 'bone'), or in different subfamilies of Nilo-Saharan (e.g. Turkana *a-kiriŋ*; Mangbetu *ri, riŋi* 'meat'). Each etymology usually shows an idiosyncratic distribution of the variants with and without *k*- across dialects and languages, although some languages tend to show a definite preference for one form or the other. Moreover, virtually every Nilo-Saharan nominal etymology shows this variability.

The name moveable *k*- was chosen because of its resemblance to a phenomenon well-known to Indo-Europeanists under the name moveable *s*-. This is an initial *s*- which is present or absent in a similarly capricious fashion in certain roots. Brugmann believed that *s*- in these instances was originally part of the root but was dropped after words ending in *-s*. There would thus develop sandhi variants depending on context and these were selected in a random fashion across languages or even in different derivational formations in the same language. An example is Classical Greek *steg*- 'cover' alongside of both *tégos* and *stégos* 'roof'; Latin *teg*- 'to cover'; Lithuanian *stogas* 'roof'; German *Dach* 'roof'; English 'thatch'. "Hence," says Brugmann (1888: 446) "it often happens that several languages concurrently show loss of *s*- without a sufficient reason for its loss being discovered by the sound

This paper was presented at the 12th Conference on African Linguistics, Stanford University, April 1981.

laws of separate languages." It was suggested by others that *s*- was not part of the root but a prefix. However, no one has been able to assign it a function, for which reason the phonological interpretation seems more plausible.[1]

The examples from Indo-European just cited show an important difference between Indo-European *s*- and Nilo-Saharan *k*-. In Indo-European the moveable element appears indifferently on nominal and verbal forms while in Nilo-Saharan it is, in principle, confined to nominals. A more genuine parallel to Nilo-Saharan is a suffixed -*s* in Penutian languages, which is purely nominal and which in Greenberg (1978: 60) was conjectured to be what was there called a "Stage III article." The Penutian parallel will be discussed in a later section of this paper. In the present study a similar theory is advanced regarding Nilo-Saharan *k*-.

Regarding Stage III articles, the reader is referred to Greenberg (1978). A brief summary is offered at this point in order to clarify the present exposition. In the expression "Stage III article," the term "article" is to be taken diachronically. Thus Nilo-Saharan *k*- is nowhere functionally an article but is rather postulated to have arisen ultimately from a definite article and still more remotely from a distance demonstrative, by far the most common source of definite articles.[2] By a Stage I article is meant a definite article of the type familiar from many European languages, e.g. English 'the'. A Stage II article, a particularly common phenomenon in Africa, is one which has acquired, roughly speaking, the combined uses of both a definite and indefinite article. At this stage the articulated form is heavily predominant in text, but there still remain a number of constructions with the non-articulated form so that most nouns may occur in both forms. These non-articulated uses derive from the two ends of the determination spectrum. They may lack the article because they are automatically definite, e.g. vocatives, proper nouns, and possessed—particularly inalienably possessed—nouns, such as kinship terms. On the other hand, the unarticulated form often survives in various generic uses, typically as negative objects, as predicate noun or adjective, in adverbial, particularly locative, expressions, e.g. 'on foot', as incorporated noun objects, and as dependent members of nominal compounds. Among Nilo-Saharan languages some have typical Stage II articles (e.g. Maasai *ol*- [masc.], *en*- [fem.] with their plurals) which have developed at a later time than the posited Stage III article, Nilo-Saharan *k*-.

The line between Stage II and Stage III articles is in some instances a fine one, but the latter stage may be defined as one in which productive contrasts

[1] For discussion of alternative theories regarding moveable *s*- with the relevant references, see Szemerenyi (1970: 87–88).

[2] Another infrequent source of the definite article is a generalized numeral classifier, that is one which has spread analogically replacing all the others. For an example see Greenberg (1972: 6).

between articulated and non-articulated forms in a substantial body of nominals no longer exist. There are two common outcomes. Either the articulated form spreads analogically so that it becomes universal except for certain survivals, e.g. kinship terms, proper names, or adverbial expressions in which the original noun may have undergone lexical replacement. The other possibility is that the non-articulated form spreads universally. Even closely related dialects may contrast in its general presence or absence, as is the case frequently with the Bantu preprefix.

There are two types of phenomena here. If the original demonstrative varied for gender, whether sex or non-sex, the Stage III article becomes a marker either redundantly renewing an older one, as in Niger-Congo languages with double class affixes, or producing a set of pristine class markers. If the original demonstrative was not classifying, then it becomes a general marker found on almost all nouns, indicating, as it were, mere nominality. The terms "nominal" and "noun" have been used interchangeably in this exposition. In the Nilo-Saharan case almost only nouns are involved, but in infrequent instances (e.g. Nyimang) adjectives also.

It was noted that the normal course of events was that in particular languages either the articulated form spread to all forms formerly containing articulated and non-articulated variants, or the non-articulated form dominated everywhere. There remains a third possibility, namely random survival of one form or the other in each specific lexical form. This is a reasonable possibility if the ancestral language at the time of dialect differentiation was just entering Stage III with free variation of the two alternants.

The value of the Indo-European case of moveable *s-* is that, although it is probably of phonological origin and is not confined to nominals, it is a generally accepted instance of essentially the same type of random survival of alternants hypothesized here for Nilo-Saharan moveable *k-*.

Our hypothesis, then, is that Nilo-Saharan *k-* was a prefixed non-classifying Stage III article which no longer had a function, but that virtually all nouns had variants with and without this *k-*. Even where the noun, e.g. a kinship term, may never have had an articulated variant, it would tend to acquire one because of the well-nigh universal and now functionless variation.

Thus far the formant with which we have been concerned has been considered to be simply *k-*. However, a variety of evidence suggests that there were phonologically determined variants, probably *ki-* before consonant stems (*ki-* or *kɩ-* in languages with vowel harmony) and *k-* before vowel and semivowel initial stems. There was possibly also a variant *ku-* (or *ku-* ~ *kʊ*) when the stem began with a consonant followed by a back vowel.

A comparison between Western and Eastern Nilotic here proves enlightening. There are a number of instances in which the Eastern Nilotic languages have *ki*- or *kɩ*- prefixed to a consonant stem as contrasted with *k*-less forms in Western Nilotic, e.g. Maasai *ki-nyaŋ* 'crocodile' compared with Nuer *nyoŋ*, and *kɩ-ma* 'fire' as contrasted with Nuer *mac*. An example of *ku*- with a back vowel is Maasai *ku-tuk* 'mouth', Dinka *thok*. Bari and Lotuxo likewise have *ku*- but Teso has *ki*-. Whether this is a relatively late vowel assimilation and does not go back to Proto-Nilo-Saharan is difficult to decide. As we shall see later, Zaghawa provides independent evidence for an original back vowel variant.

Before considering further evidence for the *ki*- ~ *k*- alternation, an additional factor needs to be considered. It is a well-known phenomenon in linguistic change that an opaque alternation tends to secondarily acquire new function. An obvious case in the present instance, given the fact that *k*- is confined to nominal forms, is that *k*- becomes a productive mark of nominal derivation from verb roots. This is so widespread in Nilo-Saharan that it may have existed in Proto-Nilo-Saharan. In Greenberg (1966: 132) a Nilo-Saharan grammatical formative *k*- with the function of nominal derivation was listed as a separate item (no. 35), but with the conjecture that it was fundamentally the same element as moveable *k*-, an interpretation I now fully accept. With this additional factor in mind, we can legitimately consider as corroborative of the posited alternation the existence in Sara Mbay, a Central Sudanic language, of a regular alternation in verbal nouns between a *k*- prefix before verb stems beginning with vowels and *ki*- before consonants (Fortier 1953: 54).

A further phonological observation relates to Songhai. In Nilo-Saharan etymologies we find sometimes *h*- and sometimes *k*- in noun roots beginning with zero or *k*- elsewhere. In Songhai itself almost no words begin with a vowel except loan words and a few grammatical formatives. Hence it is reasonable to posit that *h*- has been added to words originally beginning with vowels and that hence *hV*- corresponds to *V*- elsewhere and *kV*- to *kV*-.[3]

In the derivation of verbal nouns we sometimes find that *k*- combines with other derivational elements usually of more specific meaning, the latter being either prefixed, suffixed, or occasionally both prefixed and suffixed. This process by which new and historically complex derivational elements are formed is well-known in Indo-European and elsewhere. We can observe such a process *in statu nascendi* in Ngambay Mundu, a Sara language described by Vandame (1963: 66, 75). Here verbal roots beginning with vowels form verbal nouns meaning 'act of . . .' by prefixing *k*-, as so often in Nilo-Saharan. (Consonant-initial roots do not add a prefix.) An example is *usa* 'eat', *k-usa* 'act of eating'. By prefixing *nje*, which still can function as an

[3] A similar change of initial *V* to *hV* has been noted for Hausa by Newman (1976).

independent noun meaning ‘owner’, we get the agent noun *nje-k-usa* ‘eater’, and with *ne* ‘thing’, the complex prefix seen in *ne-k-ai* ‘a beverage’ from *ai* ‘to drink’.

An older instance of the same process is found in the formation of agent nouns by prefixing *k-* to *a-* listed as no. 34 among the Chari-Nile grammatical elements in Greenberg (1966: 115) with the meaning ‘abstract’, ‘participial’, ‘agentive’, thus producing *k-a-*. The relatedness of the forms without *k-* (Maasai) and with *k-* (Teso, Karimojong, Lotuxo, Bari) is guaranteed both by the identical agentive meaning and by the existence of simultaneous and related suffixes involving a shared alternation for number. These are Maasai, Karimojong, Teso *-an*/*-ak*; Lotuxo *-ani*/*-ak*, and Bari *-nit*/*-k*. The Bari form has in the singular a widespread *-t* ‘singulative’. Southern Nilotic Nandi doubtless has the same formation in the agentive circumfix *ka-in*/*ka-*.

Lukas (1928: 214), who was probably the first to note the existence of the *k-* prefix, though only in Saharan, described alongside of its occurrence as *k-*, a process of amalgamation in Kanuri with a separate prefix element *n-* to produce *kən-*. In this language both *n-* and *kən-* form abstracts. This has an exact parallel in Tubu. In Maba, a presumably related *n-* with similar meaning occurs but without *k-*.

In at least one instance, *k-* has acquired the function of distinguishing otherwise homonymous forms. This occurs in the Moru-Madi subgroup of Central Sudanic. Some of the languages distinguish *arι* ‘bird’ from *karι* ‘blood’ while others have forms without *k-* for both words but add ‘child’ in a diminutive meaning to the word for ‘bird’ (Tucker 1940: 31).

In a few instances *k-* has received an apparently secondary interpretation as singular, or perhaps better singulative in relation to a collective. This was already noted by Lukas in regard to Kanuri *kam* ‘person’; *am* ‘people’ (cf. Daza *am* ‘person’). There is a whole series of consonant stems in Karimojong and Lotuxo in which the singular has *ki-* and the plural zero, e.g. Karimojong *kitwani*/*twani* ‘scorpion’. Very striking here is Bari *kite*/*kisuk* ‘cow’ but *teŋ*/*teŋon* ‘herd’ (Spagnolo 1933: 35).

In view of these facts it is not impossible that the prefix under discussion was originally a singulative; but if this is the case it would have had to spread almost everywhere to the plural also. On the other hand given the random nature of its survival it would take only a single instance of its occurrence in a singular but not a plural to provide the basis for an analogical pattern in the few attested instances.

A further property of *k-* is its occasional prefixing to borrowed nouns, e.g. Lotuxo *xa-taba* < *ka-taba* as contrasted with Bari *taba* ‘tobacco’. In Kanuri *k-* is sometimes prefixed to Arabic loan words, some of which also contain the Arabic article, e.g. *k-al-gutən* ‘cotton’ but *ka-sugu* ‘market’ < Standard Arabic *sūq*.

If nominal *k*- ultimately derives from a demonstrative, then it is reasonable to conjecture that, just as the Latin demonstrative *ille* became on the one hand the source of the Romance definite article and on the other of the Romance third person pronouns, a similar development of Nilo-Saharan *k*- from its originally hypothesized demonstrative meaning to that of third person pronoun could have occurred.

The strongest case for such a development can be made for the third person prefixes of the "basic" conjugation of verbs in the Saharan languages, e.g. the Kanuri *-skin* verbs. This may be called the basic or "strong" conjugation because of its irregularity and lack of productivity as contrasted with the verbs which in Kanuri are formed by suffixing **nəskin* 'do' or 'say'. The most striking characteristic of the strong conjugation in the Saharan languages is that whereas the first and second person subject markers are suffixed, that of the third person is prefixed, thus indicating a separate history. In Kanuri itself the third person prefix is *c*- or *s*- but it clearly derives from *k*- as can still be seen in Teda. The most powerful evidence within Saharan is, however, from Zaghawa. Here we have the posited alternation in the past tense of the "strong" verb in the form *k*- before vowel, *ki*- before consonant, but *ku*- when a back vowel occurs after the first stem consonant. Examples from the singular are: 'ride' *orgi/orli/kor*; 'kill' *ligi/lili/kili*; and 'eat' *bugi/bulu/kubui*.

Another probable survival of a third person *k*- in the verb is in the complex subject-object pronominal prefixes of certain Eastern Nilotic languages. In Teso we find *k-a*- 'third person singular acts on first person singular' and *k-i*- 'third person singular acts on second person singular'. In Maasai there is *k-i*- 'third person singular or plural acts on second person singular'. These may be extended to plural meaning by the addition of plural markers. In the forms just cited we recognize *a*- 'first person' and *i*- 'second person', found not only in these languages but widely in Nilo-Saharan (Greenberg 1966: 130–31, nos. 1 and 2).

Less certain are the following: Tucker and Bryan (1966: 347) in regard to Kunama note a *k*- prefix on Class II verbs. The Class II verbs have an *i*- prefix and are generally transitive, and the *k*- indicates a third person subject functioning usually but not always when the verb is preceded by anything except a noun or pronoun with the accusative ending *-si*. It also occurs in the same class of verbs with imperatives after a noun object without the accusative ending, e.g. *deda k-ikida* 'the boy call!'. In the examples cited by Tucker and Bryan with the imperative, the object always seems to be definite. Both these uses seem plausible historical outcomes of the original *k*- definiteness marker.

Tucker and Bryan themselves compare Kunama *k*- to Maasai *k*- before vowel, *ei*- before consonant, which may precede the subject prefix for emphasis and is much used in questions and answers to questions. This might stem from the hypothesized *k-* having assumed the function of a sentence initial focusing element, a possible development from a demonstrative.

Finally it may be proposed that Nandi *kɔ-* and Pokot *kɔ-*, prefixed as a subject marker of the dependent form but only in the third person, may be, or contain, the *k-* under discussion. This same prefix may also occur in the irregular Nandi verb 'to be'. Here the agreement with Saharan in prefixing for the third person but suffixing for the first and second person is indeed striking. As given by Hollis (1909: 219) the relevant forms are *ki-a* 'I am'; *ki-i* 'thou art'; *ki* or *ko-ki* 'he, she, it is'; *ki-ki* 'we are'; *ki-o* 'you are'; *ki* or *ko-ki* 'they are'.

In the initial section, a typological parallel with Penutian *-s* was mentioned. Once more, as with Nilo-Saharan *k-*, instances in individual languages have been noted while its extensive distribution in Penutian as a whole has not been recognized. Thus Sapir (1922: 225) in his grammatical treatment of Takelma, an Oregon Penutian language, describes *-s* as a nominal derivational element "in a fairly considerable number of words." Barker (1964) in his grammar of Klamath, a Plateau Penutian language, notes *-s* as a highly frequent ending on nouns, which also productively derives verbal nouns. Frachtenberg, in regard to Coos, an Oregon Penutian language, remarks (1922: 326): "In the same manner it may be stated that *-s* was the general suffix indicating nouns and that all nominal suffixes in *-s* eventually go back to this nominal suffix."

The following are some parallels with Nilo-Saharan *k-*. Penutian *-s* often appears on cognate nouns in some languages and not in others or even varies among dialects of the same language. An example of the former is Tsimshian *lok*; Klamath *loloks*; Yakima *eloks* (Plateau Penutian) all meaning 'fire'. An instance of the latter is from various dialects of Costanoan, a California Penutian language. From San Jose and Santa Clara we have *tuxi* and from San Juan Bautista *tuxi-s* all meaning 'day'. There are many similar instances in Costanoan.

As with *k-*, *-s* is widely used to form verbal nouns, e.g. Coos *waa* 'to speak', *waa-s* 'speech'. In Wintun, a California Penutian language, this is its only use, but it is universally productive, e.g. *hara* 'to go', *hara-s* 'act of going'. Parallel to the Nilo-Saharan use of *k-* as a singulative we find in Coos *humi-s* 'a woman', pl. *humake*, and in a parallel fashion Lutuami (Plateau Penutian) *eu-s*, pl. *ewak* 'lake'.

In Klamath it appears on loan words, e.g. from English, *ʔe·pal-s* 'apple', *ʔalyan-s* 'onion'. Of course this might be the English plural although the meaning in Klamath is singular.

In Klamath noun forms without *-s* are used as incorporated generic objects. This is presumably a survival of Stage II characteristics.

Besides seeking an explanation of a specific hitherto puzzling Nilo-Saharan affix, this paper is also intended as an illustration of the fruitfulness of dynamic comparison, that is of the investigation of parallel diachronic processes in historically independent cases.

## References Cited


Barker, M. A. R. 1964. *Klamath Grammar.* Berkeley: University of California Press.

Brugmann, Karl. 1888. *Elements of the Comparative Grammar of Indo-European Languages.* (Translated by Joseph Wright.) Vol. 1. New York: Westermann and Co.

Fortier, Joseph. 1953. *Dictionnaire Mbay-Français.* Moissala (Tchad).

Frachtenberg, Leo. 1922. "Coos." In *Bureau of American Ethnology, Bulletin* 40, pp. 297–430.

Greenberg, Joseph H. 1966. *The Languages of Africa.* 2nd. ed. The Hague: Mouton.

———. 1972. "Numeral classifiers and substantival number: problems in the genesis of a linguistic type." *Working Papers in Language Universals* 9: 1–39. Stanford: Language Universals Project, Committee on Linguistics, Stanford University.

———. 1978. "How does a language acquire gender markers?" In *Universals of Human Language*, ed. J. H. Greenberg, vol. 3, pp. 47–82. Stanford: Stanford University Press.

Hollis, Alfred Claud. 1909. *The Nandi, Their Language and Folk-lore.* Oxford.

Lukas, Johannes. 1928. "Transition und Intransition in Kanuri." *Wiener Zeitschrift für die Kunde des Morgenlandes* 35: 213–14.

Newman, Paul. 1976. "The origin of Hausa /h/." In *Studies in African Linguistics*, Supplement 6 [Welmers Festschrift], pp. 165–75.

Sapir, Edward. 1922. "The Takelma language of Southwestern Oregon." In *Bureau of American Ethnology, Bulletin* 40, pp. 1–296.

Spagnolo, L. M. 1933. *Bari Grammar.* Verona: Missioni Italiane.

Szemerenyi, Oswald. 1970. *Einführung in die vergleichende Sprachwissenschaft.* Darmstadt.

Tucker, Archibald N. 1940. *The Eastern Sudanic Languages.* London: Oxford University Press.

Tucker, Archibald N., and M. A. Bryan. 1966. *Linguistic Analyses: The Non-Bantu Languages of North-Eastern Africa.* London: Oxford University Press, for the International African Institute.

Vandame, Charles. 1963. *Le Ngambay-Moundou: phonologie, grammaire, textes.* (Mémoires de l'IFAN, 69.) Dakar: IFAN.

# Some Areal Characteristics of African Languages

## [1]

General surveys of African languages often list a series of traits which are said to be characteristic of Sub-Saharan Africa as a linguistic area.[1] These enumerations tend to be fairly similar and to include: (1) phonological items such as tone, click sounds, implosives, prenasalized stops, labiovelar stops, and the prevalence of open syllables; (2) morphological traits, e.g., noun class systems and complex verb derivational systems; and (3) syntactic phenomena such as the use of a verb 'to surpass' to express comparison, serial verb constructions, and what Welmers calls semantic ranges. These include idioms such as 'fruit' = 'child of the tree', the use of body part terms as prepositions, and the existence of a verb whose primary meaning is 'to eat' but which includes a wide range of further meanings such as 'to conquer', 'to win an adversary's piece in a game', and 'to have sexual intercourse'.

Of these characteristics, many are in fact found extensively in other major world areas. These include tone, a preference for open syllables, and the use of body part terms as prepositions. A few, however, are confined to Africa but are not always of wide distribution within it, for example, click consonants.[2] Others are common in Africa and are found elsewhere, but only infrequently. An example is labiovelars, both stops and nasals. Ideally, if what is meant by an African areal characteristic is one which is found everywhere in Africa but nowhere else, then clearly none exists.

For present purposes then, we will define areal properties in less stringent terms, as those which are either exclusive to Africa, though not found

[1] Examples include Welmers 1974 and Gregersen 1977.

[2] By Africa is meant here and in subsequent mention Sub-Saharan Africa, unless otherwise specified.

everywhere within it, or those which are especially common in Africa although not confined to that continent.

The justification for these two definitions is that they give rise to similar questions which we may say are of an areal type. What is the actual distribution geographically within Africa of each such trait? How can these distributions be explained historically? Do diverse areal characteristics show at least roughly similar distributions so that an areal classification of African languages themselves becomes feasible? Are the traits which seem most particularly African on a worldwide basis concentrated within certain areas within Africa itself?

In an article published in 1959, the present writer conjectured that this was so. It was stated in the following terms. "It is noticeable that various sections of the continent differ in the intensity with which they partake of such common characteristics. There is a large central area in which all of these characteristics are found in most languages. This core consists mainly of the Niger-Congo languages, Songhai, the Central Sudanic subgroup of Macro-Sudanic, and, to a certain degree, the Chad subgroup of Afro-Asiatic" (1959: 24).

Although since that time there have been a number of further listings accompanied sometimes by brief discussions in general works, outside of Heine's work on word order in African languages, to my knowledge no attempt has been made to map areal traits systematically or account for their distribution.

As a set of preliminary studies in this direction, I will consider here four traits in regard to their areal and genetic distributions in Africa. Since the number of traits is limited and the survey of the data is far from complete, any conclusions regarding them will necessarily be highly tentative and made largely in the hope of stimulating further discussion and research in a rather neglected but important set of topics in African linguistic studies. In the theoretical discussion, I will be interested particularly in the resolution of what might be called the isolation-contact paradox. Given the existence of certain linguistic phenomena over vast and often quite continuous areas, one is tempted to explain them in terms of equally extensive linguistic contacts. If so, how can such explanations be reconciled with the enormous linguistic diversity and genetic differentiation which is also characteristic of Africa from the linguistic point of view?

Of the four topics considered here, two are phonological, namely labiovelar stops and labiodental flaps. The third is the use of a verb meaning 'to surpass' to express comparison. The fourth is a problem of semantic range, the use of a single term meaning both 'meat' and 'animal'.

[2]

The labiovelar articulations with which we will be concerned are mainly coarticulated stops. Most commonly languages have either an unvoiced or a voiced stop or both. The corresponding nasal is far less common and is almost always found in languages which have at least one non-nasal stop. The labiovelar stop has occasionally been reported as implosive. Labiovelar fricatives also occur, though only rarely.

The coarticulated stops and the corresponding nasals are sometimes said to be West African but are, in fact, more extensively distributed. The most detailed statement that I have found is that of Welmers (1973: 47–48):

> There is an interesting geographical distribution of doubly articulated stops in Africa. They occur primarily in languages grouped in a strip from the Atlantic into the Central African Republic, across the West African bulge and somewhat farther east. A number of the coastal languages do not have double stops, and to the north they extend only irregularly beyond the forest into the grassland. Thus northern Bambara does not have either /kp/ or /gb/, but southern Bambara and Maninka have /gb/. Senari (a Southern Senufo language) has both, but Suppire (a very closely related language to the north) has neither; Senari /kp/ corresponds to /b/ or /bb/ in Suppire, while Senari /gb/ is of secondary origin.

There is one area outside of Africa in which these sounds are found. The Kate-Ono group of non-Austronesian (Indo-Pacific) languages in northeastern New Guinea and some Austronesian languages of Melanesia have these sounds.[3]

The following survey of the distribution of labiovelar stops in Africa is in certain respects incomplete or perhaps even inaccurate. My own review of the literature is far from exhaustive. In addition there are certain sources of inaccuracy or incompleteness which are inherent in the literature itself. Since, as was noted by Welmers, even dialects of the same language may differ on this point, it is not safe to conclude from their absence or presence in a description to a corresponding situation in dialects other than those on which the description is based. Indeed, it is often not possible to deduce which dialect or dialects are involved from the description itself. Moreover, for many languages, we still have only word lists. In the absence of an accompanying systematic phonology, the non-occurrence of these sounds cannot with certainty be deduced from their absence in a specific list, only their existence from their occurrence.

[3] For labiovelars in non-Austronesian languages in northeastern New Guinea see especially Pilhofer 1927. Codrington in his classic work on the Austronesian languages of Melanesia noted (1885: 211) that labiovelars are "common in Melanesia," though apparently only the unvoiced non-nasalized stop. He noted that in many languages they lose either the velar or the labial element, a development also common in Africa, as we shall see.

Nevertheless, certain general conclusions can be drawn. As noted by Welmers, these sounds are found in a largely continuous but at certain points fairly narrow east-west band starting with the Atlantic and ending roughly at the Nile-Congo divide (Map 1a). Of the four major stocks in Africa, they are lacking entirely only in Khoisan. There are instances of continuous distributions involving several major stocks or subgroups. An example is the eastern section in which there is a solid block embracing languages of the Adamawa-Eastern branch of Niger-Congo, northeastern Bantu languages, Central Sudanic languages of the Nilo-Saharan family, and finally a few languages of the Eastern Sudanic branch of the same stock (Alur and Kakwa).

The chief pockets of non-occurrence within the large zone of almost continuous distribution, outside of numerous areas of Fula settlement, are Twi (but not the rest of Akan), most Chadic languages of the Jos Plateau and Bauchi in Nigeria, and, finally, a very considerable area farther east in Nigeria and Cameroun consisting of some Bantu languages of zone A (e.g. Duala), a large number of Grasslands Wide Bantu languages (e.g. Ngwe, Bamun), and the Bantoid Mambila and Vute. Whether this corridor is itself continuous I cannot determine because of lack of information concerning certain Grassland languages.

The opposite of such pockets of non-occurrence is the existence of islands of labiovelar speech outside of the main area. The most important of these from the historical point of view is Katla, the only Kordofanian language with labiovelars, at a distance hundreds of miles from the nearest occurrence elsewhere.

If we consider the distribution just sketched in closer detail it is clear that in spite of its appearance in three major stocks, it is a predominantly Niger-Kordofanian phenomenon both in regard to territorial extent and more importantly breadth of occurrence in relation to subgroupings. These sounds appear in every substock of Niger-Congo and also, as has been seen, one Kordofanian language. It has a substantial or even dominant distribution within each subgroup. These facts may be summarized as follows.

In the West Atlantic group, the entire southern subgroup has labiovelars.

It is likewise found in Bijago of the Bissao Islands, which should probably be assigned separate genetic status within West Atlantic. In the northern subgroup of West Atlantic, on the other hand, it is mostly lacking. It seems to be found only in Balante and Nalu, which are closest geographically to the Southern subgroup.

In the Mande languages, the entire southern subdivision of the western languages (Mende, Kpelle, etc.) has the sounds under discussion. The northern subdivision of the western languages likewise has labiovelars except for Soninke and the northern dialects of the Malinke-Bambara-Dyula

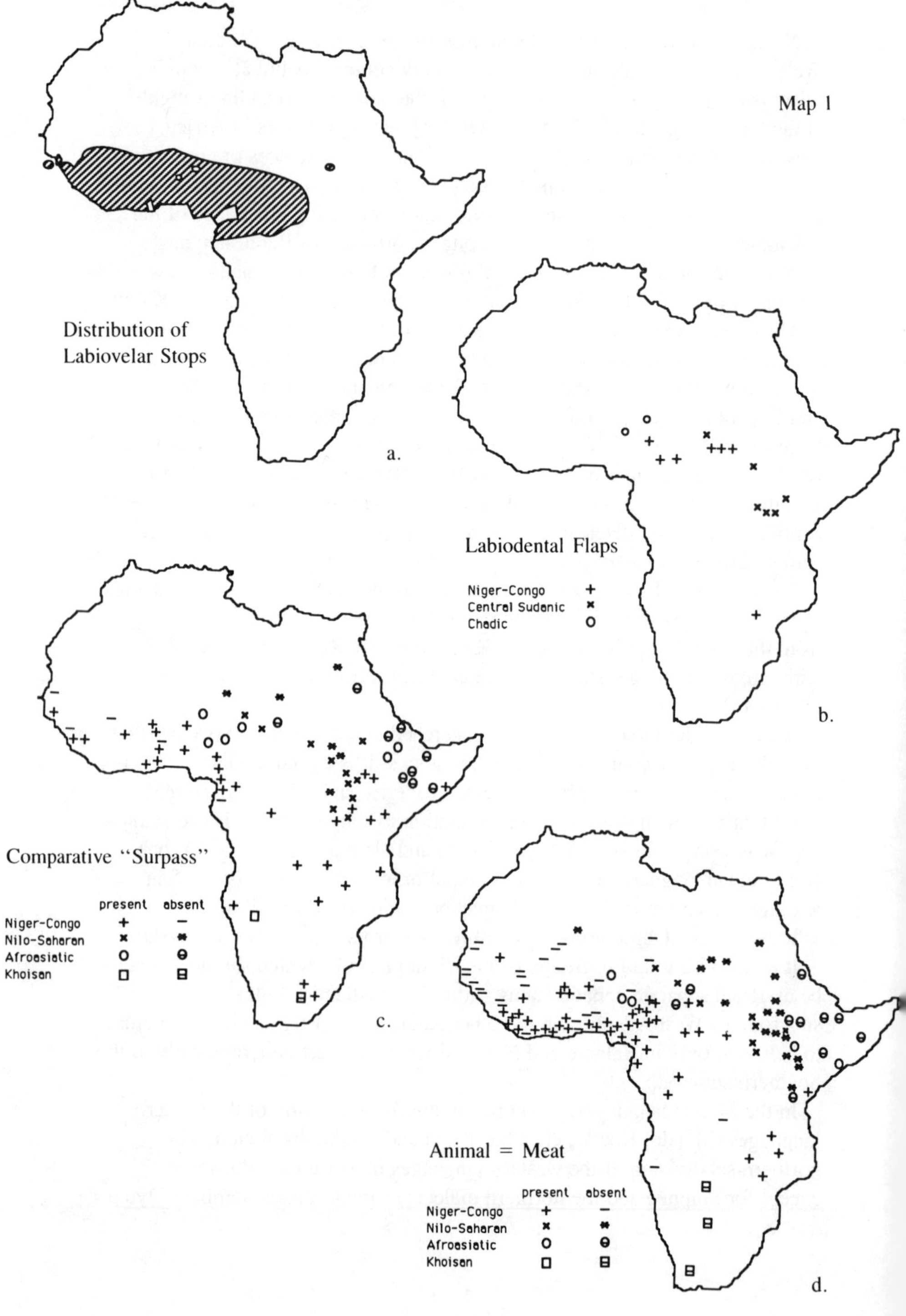

Map 1
Distribution of
Labiovelar Stops
a.
Labiodental Flaps
Niger-Congo
Central Sudanic
Chadic
b.
Comparative "Surpass"
present
absent
Niger-Congo
Nilo-Saharan
Afroasiatic
Khoisan
c.
Animal = Meat
present
absent
Niger-Congo
Nilo-Saharan
Afroasiatic
Khoisan
d.

complex. Further, all of the Eastern Mande languages (e.g. Mano, Busa) have these sounds except Bisa and Samo, both of which are well within the northern non-labiovelar zone.

Most Voltaic languages have labiovelars, so that it will be easier to list the exceptions. These include a few Gurunsi languages (Kassena, Lyele, Nunuma), Mossi, Northern Senufo, and Dogon. Here once more it is the northern languages which lack labiovelars.

The Kwa languages will be treated here separately although it is generally agreed that the boundary between Kwa and Benue-Congo is an artificial one. It appears likely that all Kwa languages except Twi and Igbira possess labiovelars.

In Benue-Congo, all the Plateau languages except Kambari, all the Cross-River languages, and all the Jukunoid languages possess this feature. Among non-Bantu Bantoid languages it is lacking only in Mambila and Vute. In Wide Bantu, it is found in Ekoi, Nyang, Mbe, and some Mbam-Nkam languages. In Narrow Bantu it is, of course, generally absent. However, there are a substantial number of languages in Guthrie's zone A in the northwest which possess labiovelars (e.g. Yaunde, Bafia). It is also found in some languages in zone C and many in zone D (e.g. Kibira) in northeastern Zaire.

In Adamawa-Eastern, all Adamawa languages except the Nielim-Bua-Koke subgroup and possibly Tula along with Dadiya, which are in another subgroup, have labiovelar stops. These two subgroups are both north of the main group of Adamawa languages. It seems that all Eastern languages have these sounds without any exceptions.

It has already been noted that one Kordofanian language, Katla, has labiovelars.

In Nilo-Saharan the picture is very different. Labiovelars are dominant in only one subgroup, Central Sudanic, where they are found everywhere except the Sara-Bagirmi languages in the west.[4] These latter are well within the main non-labiovelar area. The only other occurrences within Nilo-Saharan are in two languages of the Eastern Sudanic subfamily. One of these is Alur, a Western Nilotic language situated between Logbara and Lendu, both Central Sudanic languages with labiovelars. The other is Kakwa, an Eastern Nilotic language of the Bari cluster, in contact with Logo and Madi, both Central Sudanic languages.

In the Afroasiatic family, labiovelars are found only in a few Chadic

[4] Stimulated by an observation of Goodman (1970), I reviewed the evidence for subgrouping in Nilo-Saharan and am now of the opinion that Chari-Nile is not a valid grouping. Central Sudanic and Eastern Sudanic are no closer to each other than either is, for example, to Saharan. However, Kunama and Berta are clearly closer to Eastern Sudanic than they are to Central Sudanic, and either or both are perhaps simply Eastern Sudanic languages.

languages. These include Gwandara, the closest relative to Hausa, the Ron language of the Jos Plateau, Gerka, the Basharawa dialects in the vicinity of Kanam, some languages of the Bata group, and Kotoko.

We should also add that one Indo-European language, Krio, the English-based Creole of Freetown, has labiovelars. On the other hand, the Portuguese-based Creole, at least as spoken in the Casamance area of Senegal, does not. In both of these instances we have conformity with the general distribution of these sounds in West Africa.

The preceding review of the evidence should be sufficient to show that coarticulated labiovelars are basically a Niger-Congo feature. I propose that at least one labiovelar ought to be reconstructed for Proto-Niger-Kordofanian. Regarding Niger-Congo there are a number of widespread etymologies, e.g. *kpa* 'kill', 'die', involving labiovelars. In a number of reconstructions of subgroups, one or more of these sounds have been posited as original for the intermediate proto-language, e.g. by Manessy for Voltaic and Wolf for Benue-Congo.[5]

With reference to Niger-Kordofanian there seem to be a number of etymologies in which various branches of Kordofanian generally show *b* corresponding to Niger-Congo labiovelars.[6] The occurrence of a labiovelar sound in Katla would then be a lone survival within Kordofanian. Unfortunately there are no Katla cognates for the Niger-Kordofanian etymologies just referred to. Thus its appearance in a lone language in Kordofanian in geographical isolation from the main labiovelar area might be explained genetically as a survival.

The sounds under discussion are surely not to be posited for Proto-Nilo-Saharan, although they may well be Proto-Central-Sudanic. In Thayer's comparative study based on Bongo, Kresh, and Sara, she reconstructs a single labiovelar for the ancestral language.[7] In that case their non-appearance in Sara-Bagirmi would be a secondary loss.

For Chadic and Indo-European we are dealing with what are obviously instances of recent contact.

We may conjecture, then, the basic course of events in something like the following terms. Labiovelars in Africa originated in the Niger-Kordofanian languages in which, however, they were lost almost everywhere in Kordofanian and in Niger-Congo across a broad band north of the forest belt in West Africa as well as sporadically elsewhere. Their absence in Proto-Bantu had as a consequence that they are largely lacking in the southern third

[5] See Manessy 1979 and Wolf 1971.

[6] Greenberg 1963. See especially items 21, 26, 31, 35 on the etymological list p. 453ff.

[7] Thayer 1976.

of Africa. From Niger-Congo these sounds spread at an early date to Central Sudanic in the Nilo-Saharan family probably from Adamawa-Eastern. This resulted in a solid bloc of such languages from which a further diffusion from one or another or both led to the appearance of labiovelars in Bantu languages and a few Eastern Sudanic languages. We are referring here in the case of Bantu to zones C and D where they are probably secondary. In zone A further investigation is required. Considering the separate genetic status of this zone within Bantu, it is possible that it was inherited here.

Elsewhere, in Chadic and in Krio, it is again a phenomenon based on contact with Niger-Congo languages.

If the basic theory just outlined is accepted, then insofar as Niger-Kordofanian is concerned, the problem is in general to account not for its presence but its loss. The mystery is why it disappears over an essentially contiguous area in the northern part of the West African bulge. This would be less difficult to explain if it always changed to the same sounds. We are familiar with instances of the propagation of sound changes across dialect and even language boundaries, e.g. the High German consonant shift. But in the present instance, the changes are various except, apparently, for the Kordofanian change to *b*. The coarticulated stops change most commonly to labialized velars, velars, or labials, and often to more than one of these in the same language depending on adjacent, usually following vowels.

In reconstructing at least one labiovelar stop for Proto-Niger-Kordofanian, a theory is proposed which is incompatible with that of Westermann, who assumed that labiovelar stops in his Western Sudanic languages were not original but arose everywhere from labialized velars, i.e., sounds of the $k^w$ type.[8] I believe, in this instance, like his parallel theory regarding the independent origin of noun classes in various West Sudanic languages from originally classless languages, that we are dealing with an inherently implausible hypothesis, namely that a sound which is unusual on a worldwide basis should arise again and again independently in the same area. Particularly in view of its occurrence in Kordofanian, it becomes more plausible to look for a single genetic origin followed by widespread loss and occasional spread by contact. Nevertheless, that labiovelar stops can arise from labialized velars will be indicated in later discussion.

One kind of evidence that the movement is rather from coarticulated stops to labialized velars than vice versa will be direct historical attestation, but of course in Africa this is usually lacking. Our one major source is Koelle's *Polyglotta Africana*, and there are a few instances in which he recorded labiovelar stops in Niger-Congo languages which have since been replaced by

[8] Westermann 1927.

other sounds. There are, apparently, no contrary instances. One example is Bambara. Koelle states explicitly that his informant was from Segou, and he records *gbe* 'white', *gbasi* 'flog', and *gbalo* 'skin'. Musa Travelé from the same city, in his dictionary published in 1913, gives the corresponding words as *g'e*, *gosi*, and *golo* with a variant *wolo*. This last form suggests a labialized velar as a possible intermediate stage, at least before back vowels.

Igbira (now called Ebira in Dalby's atlas) is a language of the Nupe group. Koelle's Egbira-Hima has four words with *gb*. Ladefoged in his general work on the phonetics of West African languages records its sound system as lacking labiovelars.[9] A word list recorded by the former in the *Journal of West African Languages* gives two of the four words found in Koelle, *ɛpa* 'root' for Koelle's *egba* and *ɔbɛ* 'neck' for Koelle's *ogbe*.[10] It is of interest to note that Ebira is spoken at the confluence of the Niger and Benue, completely surrounded by languages with labiovelar stops, so that this change cannot be attributed to language contact.

A third instance from Koelle is Vute for which he records labiovelar stops, whereas Hofmeister in his work on that language does not record any and gives a table of sounds in which it is lacking. Unfortunately, none of the specific words recorded by Koelle as containing these sounds is found in Hofmeister.[11]

As we have seen, however, there is evidence for the acquisition of these sounds by contact with languages that have them, the most obvious mechanism being, of course, loan words. Much more remarkable are a few instances in which what may be called convergent sound change occurs. In all of these instances it is labialized velars which are replaced by stops in indigenous words. One instance is the Chadic language Gwandara, closely related to Hausa but spoken farther south and in contact with Gade and Koro, Benue-Congo languages with labiovelar stops. An example is Hausa *tagwaye* 'twins' for which the Karshe and Kyankyan dialects of Gwandara both have *tegbe*. Another dialect, Nimbia, however, has *tagwəy*.[12]

A second instance of this process is the Zugu dialect of Zaberma, of the Songhai subgroup of Nilo-Saharan. Zugu is in Benin and in close contact with Voltaic languages with labiovelar stops. Among the examples cited by Funke are *kpe* 'king' corresponding to *koi*, and the identical forms meaning 'to go' and *kpili* 'blood' compared to *kuli* and *kpara* 'city' to *kwara*. The latter forms of each pair are found in other dialects of Zaberma.[13]

[9] Ladefoged 1964a.
[10] Ladefoged 1964b.
[11] Hofmeister 1918.
[12] Matsushita 1947.
[13] Funke 1915

A third example is mentioned by Westermann and Ward in Kakwa, a Western Nilotic language closely related to Bari. The instances cited are Kakwa *kpen* 'bird' = Bari *kwen* and *iŋman* 'four' = Bari *iŋwan*.[14] Except for some of the Zugu examples which simply have *ku* in related dialects, one can conjecture a substitution mechanism by bilingual speakers who might replace the labialized velars with stops and from whom it might then spread to monolingual speakers.

Much more difficult to interpret is the presence of labiovelar stops in some Chadic languages of the Kotoko-Logone group. They occur frequently in Gulfei and Affade, infrequently in Makari, but not at all in the closely related Logone.[15] As in the previously discussed instances they have developed through internal change from labialized velars or from *ku* or *gu* (cf. Zugu). Those languages are not in contact with any languages with labiovelars.

[3]

The second areal property of African languages which will be discussed is the labiodental flap *ʋ*. In contrast to the labiovelar stops that we have been discussing which, as has been noted, are also found in the Pacific, these sounds are, as far as present knowledge extends, found exclusively in Sub-Saharan Africa.[16] Moreover, it is a far more infrequent sound. In spite of its rarity, it has, like labiovelars, been reported as occurring in Niger-Congo, Nilo-Saharan, and Afroasiatic languages. The largest concentration of examples appears to be in the Central Sudanic branch of Nilo-Saharan. (Map 1b). Tucker and Bryan report its occurrence in Mangbetu, Asua, Mamvu, and Lese, all within one branch of Central Sudanic. It is also stated, in the same source, to be very common in Kresh and to occur sporadically in Baka and Morokodo, which are likewise Central Sudanic languages.[17] In all of these languages it occurs in common words. It is not reported elsewhere in Nilo-Saharan.

In Niger-Kordofanian almost all known examples are from Adamawa-Eastern. Once more Tucker and Bryan describe it as most common in the Ndogo-Sere group, examples being given from Sere, Mundu, Ndogo, and Bai, and once more in common words. Particularly interesting is its occurrence in Ndogo, Sere, and Bai in the word 'child' *ʋi*, an obvious cognate of the widespread Niger-Congo root *bi*. Richardson gives an example from the Adamawa language Kapere, a southern dialect of Mbum, in which it occurs in

[14] Westermann and Ward 1957.

[15] Paul Newman, personal communication.

[16] This is confirmed by the Phonology Archive at Stanford.

[17] Tucker and Bryan 1966, especially pp. 29, 63, and 86.

the second person plural pronoun *vi*. He also notes its occurrence in Ngbaka Mabo, a form of Mbaka Limba, and in the Yangere dialect of Banda, both of these once more languages of the Eastern division of Adamawa-Eastern.[18]

The one instance of this sound being reported from a Niger-Congo language which is not a member of the Adamawa-Eastern subgroup is indeed a startling one. This is its occurrence far to the south in Shona, a Bantu language group in Zimbabwe. According to Fortune it occurs only in ideophones and rarely even in those. In Hannan's *Standard Shona Dictionary* an example is cited from the Zezuru dialect, where it expresses the "idea of flicking an object."[19]

The only other occurrences are in Chadic languages. In my own fieldwork I encountered it in Gerka in the word for 'buffalo'. The same example is reported in print by Jungraithmayr as *kavin*, the reflex of a common Chadic root.[20] Its existence is also attested in two further Chadic languages, Tera (Newman) and Margi (Hoffmann). In both of these languages it only occurs in ideophones.

As can be seen from the foregoing exposition, the labiodental flap bears in its distribution an important though only partial resemblance to that of labiovelar stops. In Nilo-Saharan it is once more concentrated, this time exclusively, in Central Sudanic. Once more it shares a trait, most probably through contact, with the Adamawa-Eastern branch of Niger-Congo. However, in this case it appears absent from the rest of Niger-Congo except for the lone instance of Shona. Once more, also, its occurrence in Afroasiatic is confined to the Chadic branch. Since it sometimes occurs only in ideophones which are likely to be omitted or poorly reported in grammars and dictionaries, one may suspect that fuller information in the future may fill in some of the gaps in its apparently sporadic distribution. If it does have a single origin, as seems likely, the choice would seem to be between Central Sudanic and Adamawa-Eastern as the ultimate source, without a convincing basis for choice.

## [4]

For our third topic we turn to the expression of the comparative, and usually the superlative also, by means of a construction using a verb meaning 'to surpass'. In many of the languages for which it is described in Africa it coexists with other constructions, but in these cases it is usually the dominant method, and often it is the only one mentioned. There are two chief variants which may be literally translated as follows: (1) 'X is large, surpasses Y'; (2) 'X surpasses Y (in) largeness'. In the latter type we most often have an

[18] Richardson 1956, p. 80.

[19] Fortune 1967, Hannan 1961.

[20] Jungraithmayr 1965.

abstract noun or an infinitive. The superlative is usually expressed by a parallel construction in which Y is substituted by 'all', e.g. for the first variant 'X is large, surpasses all'. Sometimes the comparative occurs in this construction without the superlative or vice versa. Often our information is incomplete.

Clearly this is a very widespread construction in Sub-Saharan Africa, more extensive in fact in its distribution than labiovelar stops. (Map 1c). Although many languages of the world can express comparison by such locutions as 'she surpasses me in intelligence', it is clear that in English and indeed almost everywhere outside of Africa this is only an occasional method and not the basic way of expressing comparisons. The only other linguistic area in which I have encountered this as a usual construction is that of Native American languages and here it is not common. An example is the Zamuco language of Bolivia.[21]

It is much more difficult to obtain an accurate notion of the distribution of this feature in Africa and to explain this distribution historically than in the case of the phonological features we have just been discussing.

The first problem simply arises from the lack of relevant published data. Even a short word list will frequently indicate the presence of coarticulated labiovelars, even though its absence, without a more formal phonological description, is harder to establish. For the comparative construction we need grammars and lexicons. Even these are frequently of no assistance, particularly, it should be noted, if written in accordance with recent models. A traditional grammar organized according to parts of speech will almost always have a section on comparison, since Classical times viewed as an "accident" of the adjective. As for lexicons, even if there is an entry meaning 'to surpass', unless it is a very full dictionary with examples, it will often be of no assistance. Even if the word is present and the examples do not express comparison, this is of course not decisive regarding the absence of the construction.

In regard to historical interpretation of the data, there are certain difficulties inherent in the topic itself as compared with phonology. A construction of this kind can spread from language to language by loan translation, or *calque* as it is sometimes called. Here, unlike the situation in phonology, such as presence in loan words only, which can often tell us the direction of transmission, there is no corresponding method. Further, it is far more difficult to distinguish between genetic persistence and language contact. This is because it may represent the continuation of an inherited construction, but with lexical replacement of the key term 'to surpass', not a highly stable item.

With all of these difficulties it is still possible to describe in broad terms its

[21] Chome and Lussagnet 1958.

distribution in Africa and to attempt a historical explanation. The construction we are discussing is found in all four major stocks of Africa as well as in Krio. It is also apparently common in the various Creoles of the Caribbean where it presumably has an African origin. However, discussion of this aspect has been excluded from the present discussion.

In Niger-Congo it is found in some languages of each major branch. Unfortunately I could not discover any data for Kordofanian. We can make the following general observations regarding its distribution in Niger-Congo when compared to that of labiovelars. Like the latter it is found throughout the West African forest belt as shown by occurrence in most Mende, Kwa, and Benue-Congo languages, and it likewise extends eastward into the Adamawa-Eastern group. It shows, however, two chief differences. It extends farther north, occurring for example in a number of languages of the northern branch of West Atlantic, such as Fula. It is likewise found in some Voltaic and Mande languages north of the labiovelar line. On the other hand it is by no means as continuous in its distribution. In every region in which it is found there are significant gaps. Thus it is apparently absent in Serer-Sin in West Atlantic, Susu of Guiné in Mande, and Tem in Voltaic. This is probably to be attributed to a general tendency for it to be superseded independently and through internal factors by constructions which are more common on a worldwide basis.[22] A further instance of more widespread distribution than labiovelars is its prevalence in Bantu areas. I have recorded 23 occurrences in almost all of Guthrie's zones. Bujeba was the only contrary instance which was encountered.

At the same time we cannot reconstruct the construction as such for Proto-Bantu. Three different roots are the most commonly found: *pit-*, *dut-*, and *kid-*, all of which mean 'pass' in some languages and 'surpass' in others and have different regional distributions. One possibility is that this semantic change has occurred independently in a parallel fashion in different lexical items, but of course this does not preclude its spread by loan translation through calques of different words meaning 'to pass' in different areas. Another possibility is that it was Proto-Bantu and persisted through the change of lexical expression. Of course, and perhaps more likely, both factors may have been at work in different individual cases.

The distribution of this construction in the Nilo-Saharan languages is much wider than that of labiovelars. It extends well beyond Central Sudanic, including for example Songhai and Kanuri in the west and Eastern Sudanic and the Coman languages in the east. It is not, however, found as far north as

[22] Thus in Zamuco, as described in Chome's "*Arte*," which was written about 1750, the construction based on 'to surpass' is the only one mentioned. A modern study (Kelm 1964: 501) shows that this construction has been replaced by the use of a preposition meaning 'in relation to'

Barea, Nubian, Maba, or Daza. As in Niger-Congo there are important gaps, e.g. its non-occurrence in Mangbetu in Zaire, a Central Sudanic language with labiovelars.

As for Afroasiatic languages, it is found not only in some Chadic languages but in Cushitic and even some Semitic languages in Ethiopia. In regard to Chadic, its distribution is wider than that of labiovelars, occurring for example in Hausa, but it is again not found in the Chadic languages east of Lake Chad. Regarding Ethiopia, Bender in his outline sketch of Gumuz, a Coman language, noted the prevalence of this construction "in most Ethiopian languages."[23]

Finally, in Khoisan it occurs in !Kung, a Northern Bushman language in which its presence might be reasonably interpreted as resulting from contact with Bantu.[24]

If the comparative construction we have been discussing is a single historically connected phenomenon, as seems likely from its rarity in other parts of the world, it would seem that we could eliminate Khoisan and Afroasiatic as original sources because of its marginality in both cases. Although found in Chadic, Cushitic, and Ethiopian Semitic, it is lacking in Chadic in precisely those eastern languages which seem most exempt from Niger-Congo contacts. Likewise, in the Ethiopian area it is marginal to its occurrence in Nilo-Saharan. Although found in Amharic it is here an alternative to the typically Semitic use of 'from', and is not found in Ge'ez or Tigrinya. It is also lacking in many Cushitic languages, e.g. Somali, Beja, and Sidamo.

The choice, then, seems to lie between Niger-Congo and Nilo-Saharan, within both of which it occurs extensively and, as has been seen, well north of the labiovelar area in West Africa, and east and north of it in East Africa, as well as in almost all the Bantu area.

For judging both the origin and age of this construction in Africa, it is regrettable that no evidence could be found regarding its presence in Kordofanian. Still, though much more tentatively than for the labiovelars, the existence of this construction in all branches of Niger-Congo and far more extensively than for labiovelars, and its absence in Nilo-Saharan languages like Maba, Daza, Barea, and Nubian, which are remote from Niger-Congo contacts, suggests an ultimate Niger-Congo origin.

## [5]

The final question of this sort considered in this paper is a problem of semantic range, the existence of a single term meaning both 'animal' and 'meat'. I do not have any solid evidence for this anywhere outside of Sub-

23 Bender 1979.

24 J. W. Snyman, personal communication.

Saharan Africa. Before considering the question of its distribution in Africa, however, it will be necessary to consider first what is meant semantically by this equation. What is most common in languages of the world is that there should be a word meaning 'edible flesh' and that this same word should mean 'human flesh', as is the case, unlike English, with German *Fleisch*, which is of course cognate with English 'flesh'. There is often a separate word for 'animal', which in its unmarked or central meaning is 'quadruped', so that, for example, there is either a separate word for 'fish' or a phrase such as 'animal of the water' is used when 'fish' is meant specifically. It is also very common that the same word should be used for 'hunted animal' and food from such animals, e.g. French *gibier* or English *game*, or that the same word should be used for a particular animal and the meat from that same animal whether wild or domesticated, e.g. French *mouton* which means both 'sheep' and 'mutton'.

What is found very commonly in Africa, and apparently never or at least not commonly elsewhere, is that the same word should be used for 'animal' in general, whether wild or domesticated, and for animal food in general. Of the two meanings 'meat' and 'animal', 'meat' seems to be in some sense primary or unmarked and 'animal' secondary and marked. The reasons for asserting this are the following. There is a widespread Niger-Congo root *nam*, *nyam* which often has this double meaning and may well be reconstructible as having both meanings. When, however, there are two separate terms in Niger-Congo languages, if, as is often the case, one is the *nam* root, then the presumed innovation is almost invariably the word for 'animal'. The most conspicuous exception is the Grasslands languages where the form *bep* or the like is found in many languages with the meaning 'meat' while the *nama* root survives as 'animal'. The other indication is that sometimes the two terms are separate but involve the same root. In Niger-Congo languages which have class affixes it sometimes happens that the earlier form remains in the meaning 'meat' but the same root with an additional affix of class 1, 'human', 'animal' has the meaning 'animal'. An example is the Bantu language Tonga in which 'meat' is *nyama* in class 9 while 'animal' is *munyama* in class 1. In instances of this kind I have considered the language as having the equivalence 'meat' = 'animal'.

As with the other African areal properties we have been considering, there are instances in Niger-Congo (I have no information in regard to Kordofanian), Nilo-Saharan, and Afroasiatic languages. Regarding Khoisan the evidence is sparse and somewhat confusing. I tend to draw a negative conclusion there. I have not investigated the question in regard to Indo-European based pidgins and Creoles in Africa and the Caribbean in detail, but believe it to be generally present.

In regard to Niger-Congo, the distribution of the trait we are considering, with the exception of its prevalence in Bantu, is very much like that of labiovelars, in that it tends to be concentrated in the forest zone of West Africa rather than in the savannah to the north (Map 1d). Thus in West Atlantic it is found in the languages of the southern branch that I have investigated but in none of the northern branch. Again in Mande it is reported from the southwestern languages except for Susu while it is found exceptionally in Soninke farther north. As in some instances of the comparative construction which is influenced by the Arabic construction employing a preposition or postposition 'from', there are a number of examples of Arabic influence in Islamic areas in which the marked term 'animal' is borrowed from Arabic *ḥayawa:n* while the older word is retained in the meaning 'meat'. It may therefore have once extended farther north. The semantic equation we are discussing is present in many Voltaic languages, being on the whole less frequent in the northern part of the area. It is found in most Kwa languages but with a few conspicuous exceptions, e.g. the whole Togo group, Twi, and Adangme. Again it is found in most Benue-Congo languages including many Bantu languages. The facts regarding Adamawa-Eastern are interesting. All the Adamawa languages for which I have information possess it, but most of the Eastern languages do not. Those which do not frequently retain the *nyam* root in the meaning 'meat' with various other terms for 'animal'. The few that do, e.g. Ngbandi, generally have a term *sa* or *za* which seems to be a loan word from Central Sudanic, e.g. Logo, Madi *za*, Lendu *eza*, *za*.

It was noted earlier that there was a widespread Niger-Congo root *nyam* or *nam* meaning 'meat', 'animal'. However, this root does not apparently occur in West Atlantic or Mande, even though many of these languages have the semantic equation 'animal' = 'meat'.

In Nilo-Saharan the distribution is much more restricted than in Niger-Congo. Thus Didinga is the only Eastern Sudanic language in which I have found it. In Nubian, the word for 'animal' is borrowed from Arabic. This is also the situation in Maba. For the rest it is present in a fair number of Central Sudanic languages though also absent in quite a few. In Central Saharan it is found only in Kanuri and it is not found in the Songhai of Gao.

In Afroasiatic it is once more found in the Chadic languages of Nigeria but is absent in the languages spoken east of Lake Chad. It is mostly absent in Cushitic except for Elmolo and Boni, and it seems not to occur in Ethiopian Semitic.

Once more the basic facts of distribution, and in this case the existence of a widespread inherited root, suggests an ultimate Niger-Congo if not Niger-Kordofanian origin. We see that in this case as in the others there is significant evidence for linguistic contact between languages of the Eastern branch of Niger-Congo and the Central Sudanic subgroup of Nilo-Saharan.

[6]

The present study then tends to confirm the notion of a sort of nuclear area in Africa in which areal characteristics are most intense. It also suggests that some or most of these originated in Niger-Congo languages and that their present distribution is an outcome of processes both of genetic survival and spread by contact. The incompleteness of these studies and the tentative nature of the conclusions cannot be too strongly stressed. It is hoped, however, that the present paper will serve to stimulate further work on areal phenomena both on the traits discussed here and on others which have been mentioned by various investigators.

## References Cited

Bender, M. 1979. "Gumuz: A sketch of grammar and lexicon." *Afrika und Übersee*, 72, no. 1: 38–69.

Chome, I., and S. Lussagnet. 1958. "Arte de la lengua Zamuca." *Journal de la Société des Americanistes* 47: 121–78.

Codrington, R. H. 1885. *The Melanesian Languages*. Oxford: Clarendon Press.

Dalby, D. 1977. *Language Map of Africa and the Adjacent Islands*. London.

Fortune, G. 1967. *Elements of Shona: Zezuru Dialect*. Salisbury: Longmans.

Funke, E. 1915. "Die Sprachverhältnisse in Sugu, Dahomey, Franz. Westafrika." *Zeitschrift für Kolonialsprachen*, 5: 257–69.

Goodman, Morris. 1970. "Some questions on the classification of African languages." *ISAL* 36, no. 2: 117–22.

Greenberg, Joseph H. 1959. "Africa as a linguistic area." In *Continuity and Change in African Cultures*, ed. W. R. Bascom and M. J. Herskovits, pp. 15–27. Chicago: U. of Chicago Press.

———. 1963. *The Languages of Africa*. The Hague: Mouton.

Gregersen, E. A. 1977. *Language in Africa: An Introductory Survey*. New York: Gordon and Breach.

Hannan, M. 1961. *Standard Shona Dictionary*. London: Macmillan.

Heine, B. 1976. *A Typology of African Languages, Based on the Order of Meaningful Elements*. Berlin: Reimer.

Hofmeister, J. 1918. "Kurzgefasste Wute-Grammatik." *Zeitschrift für Kolonialsprachen*, 9: 1–19.

Jungraithmayr, H. 1965. "Materialen zur Kenntnis des Chip, Montol, Gerka, und Burrum (Südplateau, Nordnigerien)." *Afrika und Übersee*, 48: 161–82.

Kelm, H. 1964. "Das Zamuco—eine lebende Sprache." *Anthropos*, 95: 457–516.

Koelle, S. W. 1854. *Polyglotta Africana*. London: Missionary Society.

Ladefoged, P. 1964a. *A Phonetic Study of West African Languages*. Cambridge: University Press.

———. 1964b. "Igbirra notes and word-list." *JWAL* 1: 27–38.

Manessy, G. 1979. *Contribution à la classification généalogique des langues voltaïques*. Paris: SELAF.

Matsushita, Shuji. 1947. *A Comparative Vocabulary of Gwandara Dialects*. Tokyo: Institute for the Study of Languages and Cultures of Asia and Africa.

Pilhofer, G. 1927. "Formenlehre von zehn Mundarten und Nachbarsprachen des Kate." *Zeitschrift für Kolonialsprachen*, 18: 196–231, 298–315.
Richardson, J. 1956. *Linguistic Survey of the Northern Bantu Borderland*. Vol. 2. London, New York: Oxford U. Press.
Thayer, L. J. 1976. *A Comparative-Historical Phonology of the Chari Languages (Nilo-Saharan Languages of Central Africa)*. Supplemento n. 9 agli *Annali*, vol. 36. Naples: Instituto Orientale di Napoli.
Travelé, M. 1923. *Petit dictionnaire Français-Bambara et Bambara-Français*. 2nd ed. Paris: Guethner.
Tucker, A. N., and M. A. Bryan. 1966. *Linguistic Analyses. The Non-Bantu Languages of North-Eastern Africa*. London, New York, Capetown: Oxford U. Press.
Welmers, W. E. 1974. *African Language Structures*. Berkeley: U. of California Press.
Westermann, D. 1927. *Die westlichen Sudansprachen und ihre Beziehungen zum Bantu*. Berlin: de Gruyter.
Westermann, D., and I. C. Ward. 1957. *Practical Phonetics for Students of African Languages*. London, New York: Oxford U. Press.
Wolf, Paul de. 1971. *The Noun Class System of Proto-Benue-Congo*. The Hague: Mouton.

# Were There Egyptian Koines?

Ferguson in a now classic article (1959a), noting many common features of most forms of contemporary Arabic which cannot be derived historically from Classical Arabic, posited as the source of these characteristics a koine. This koine, it was hypothesized, arose as the result of contact among speakers of different Arabic dialects, both those of the original seventh and eighth century invaders of the Near East and North Africa and those of subsequent migrants.

In choosing the term koine Ferguson doubtless had in mind the situation with regard to Greek in the Hellenistic period which followed the conquests of Alexander the Great. Koine is itself a Greek word meaning 'common', and its use in reference to language is an abbreviation of the phrase *koinḕ diálektos* 'common dialect'. Parallel to the case of Arabic we had a widespread supradialectal form of spoken Greek which contrasted with a standard classical norm.

In another major contribution (Ferguson 1959b), on the concept of diglossia, the widespread occurrence of such contrasts between L and H (i.e. 'low' and 'high') forms of the same language was discussed and analyzed. In the broader context of diglossia, the L form need not arise as a koine; it might, for example, be a Creolized form of H (e.g. Haitian) or an artificial H variety based on an earlier written standard as with the modern Greek *katherevusa* 'purified' whose contrast with *dhemotike* 'popular' is the source of the term 'diglossia', itself once more a Greek word.

A further consideration of the Hellenistic koine reveals other important points of comparison with the Arabic situation but also suggests additional factors. One obvious resemblance is that the Greek koine, like the Arabic, was used as a second language by native speakers of other languages and soon became the essential vehicle of interlinguistic communication over a large area. The members of many of these communities eventually became first language speakers of Greek.

Unlike the Arabic koine, however, Hellenistic Greek itself became a literary language. To take one instance, the Jews of Alexandria who no longer spoke Hebrew or Aramaic translated the Old Testament into Greek (the Septuagint). The Arabic koine on the contrary never became a literary language.

The relation of the Greek koine to contemporaneous and earlier Greek raises additional important questions. In the Pre-Hellenistic period Greek was spoken in the form of local dialects whose differences were in some instances considerable. The Athenian form of Attic, no doubt because of Athenian cultural preeminence as well as the importance of Athens as a military power before the Macedonian conquest, had a special position that made it the basis of the koine.

The koine was described in Moulton (1966: 34) as including important contributions from various dialects, but with Attic as the basis, although the exclusive peculiarities of Attic make but a small show in it.

This writer also notes (*ibid.*: 31) in talking of Alexander's army that in this process naturally those features which were peculiar to a particular dialect would have the smallest chance of surviving and those which most successfully combined the characteristics would be surest of a place in the resulting koine.

In the case of Greek the non-Attic dialects survived for several centuries though under strong koine influence. Indeed one of them, the Tsakonian of Sparta, is generally considered to have survived until the present day. In regard to Arabic, we know too little about the linguistic situation in the Pre-Islamic period to identify the dialectal basis of the koine. Concerning the survival of non-koine dialects, Ferguson is appropriately cautious but, as he hints, there is much to suggest that some present day varieties of peninsular Arabic, or even of Bedouin dialects outside of Arabia itself may continue many features of earlier dialects contemporary with the koine.

In the light of these considerations, we can see that in some instances the koine participates in two types of contrasts. On the one hand it is the general spoken form as opposed to a literary language of greater prestige and on the other hand it contrasts with still surviving earlier dialects. It is interesting to note that in later Greek the term *koinḗ* was used in these two senses. It might mean the general language as opposed to the local dialects, or it designated colloquial 'vulgar' Greek as against the literary standard.[1] Our own word 'common' also has these two meanings, 'general' as against 'particular' and 'vulgar' as distinct from 'cultivated'.

[1] The Greek grammarians also use the word *koinḗ* in these two senses. For references see Liddell and Scott 1925–46, s.v. *koinós*.

Viewed dynamically what we have in a community which retains its linguistic identity over an extended period is the following typical course of events. An original basically unified language develops regional dialects which if unimpeded will diverge in the course of time into mutually unintelligible languages. However because of social and political factors one of the dialects, in modified form, becomes the basis of a new common language, a koine which tends to supersede the original dialects. In a community with writing the common language acquires the additional prestige which accrues to literary use. In the course of time the spoken koine will of course change while the literary form remains relatively stable. In addition the spoken koine develops local dialects so that ultimately, if linguistic unity is to be preserved, a new common language must develop on the basis of a dominant dialect of the old koine.

Thus over a long period of time a linguistic community may develop a koine a number of times. This introduces a further complication. A koine may or may not develop on the same regional basis as the previous one. For example, Old English was based on West Saxon but Middle English developed in the Midlands although with important contributions from other dialects. We may call this the succession problem and distinguish direct from collateral succession depending on whether a particular common language develops on the same regional basis as the previous one. The linguistic criteria involved in making such a judgment are considered at a later point in this discussion.

With the foregoing considerations in mind, we turn to the history of Egyptian. At present, of course, Egypt is Arabic-speaking but Coptic, still used in the liturgy of the Coptic Monophysite Church, is the latest form of a language whose earliest records date from the very beginning of Egyptian written records (circa 3100 B.C.E.).[2] Even after the Arab invasion of the seventh century, Egyptian in its Coptic form continued to be spoken by a substantial majority of the people of Egypt but by the fourteenth century it is estimated that it was only spoken by a tenth of the population.[3] The last report of its being spoken is that of Vansleb, a seventeenth century Dutch traveler who reported that he had encountered Coptic speakers in Upper Egypt who still employed it.

Egyptian thus has a longer recorded history than any other language, something over four thousand years. Until the coming of Arabic it had only one serious rival, Greek under the Ptolemies and in the Roman and Byzantine Empires, but even then it was not spoken as a first language by Egyptians or even as second language in most of Upper Egypt. The initial effect of the

[2] All dates given in this paper are in accordance with those in the Cambridge Ancient History.
[3] For a detailed account of Coptic after the Arab conquest, see Wiet 1927.

Arabic invasion was to strengthen Egyptian as against Greek, the language of the Byzantine Empire it succeeded. During the long period in which it was spoken Egyptian was able to assimilate linguistically numerous Libyans, Semites of Western Asia, and Nubians who had immigrated into the country.

Egyptian constitutes one of the five branches of the Afroasiatic linguistic stock, the others being Semitic, Berber, Cushitic, and Chadic. The genetic position of Egyptian will figure in an essential manner at a number of points in the following argument.

From all that we know of linguistic change, given the distance of about 750 miles from the southern apex of the Nile delta to the First Cataract at the Elephantine, the traditional southern boundary of Egypt, the Egyptian language would inevitably develop strongly differing local dialects. Without non-linguistic factors, social and political, leading to linguistic unification, the extremities of the Egyptian speech area would have in the course of four thousand years or so become at least as different as present day Hindi and Persian. The question at issue then is not whether there were koines at different times but how many there were, when they arose, and what their basis in local speech was in each instance.

That Egyptian had at various times sharply differing local dialects is not merely a conjecture based on our general knowledge of linguistic change. One indication is a text dating from the thirteenth century before our era in which it is stated that a man from the Delta and one from the Elephantine could not understand each other (Erman 1928: 6). The second is that its latest stage, Coptic, which was written in an alphabet which for the first time indicated vowels systematically and reflected contemporary spoken language, had a number of significantly different literary dialects.

That Egyptian was not exempt from diglossia either is shown from the comment of Herodotus (II, 36) that the Egyptians had two sorts of language, 'sacred' (*hirá* the Ionic form of *hierá*) and 'common' (*dēmotikḗ*, cf. *dē̂mos* 'people'). Herodotus uses the word *grámmata* 'letters' as the modified noun so that he is probably referring to two kinds of written language generally known as Hieroglyphic and Demotic, the latter of which is historically more recent.

The same distinction is mentioned about two centuries later by Manetho, an Egyptian priest of the early Ptolemaic era who wrote a number of works in Greek which have only come down to us in excerpts from later writers. One of these was the *Aegyptiaca* whose numbering of the Egyptian dynasties is still in general use. Josephus in his *Contra Apionem* I.14.82 as part of an extended excerpt from Manetho gives the latter's interpretation of the word *Hyksos* which he glosses in Greek as 'shepherd kings'. The Hyksos constituted the 16th Dynasty (1684–1567) who ruled in the eastern Delta during part of the period between the Middle and New Kingdom when there was no united rule over the country. Josephus identified the Hyksos with the Hebrews. Manetho in his etymology of the word says it has two parts. The first is *hyk* which means 'king' in the 'sacred language' (*hierà glôssa*) and the second is *-sos* which means 'shepherd' in the 'common speech' (*koinȇ diálektos*). Here the contrast between a written standard and a spoken form is clear since *diálektos* is normally spoken language in Greek and *koinḗ* is being used in its meaning of 'vulgar' alluded to earlier. In fact *hyk* is easily identified with the hieroglyphic *ḥḳ?* 'ruler'[4] while *šōs* occurs in the meaning 'shepherd' in Coptic in all the dialects except Bohairic, that of the Delta. While it does have hieroglyphic antecedents it does not occur until New Egyptian as *š?s-w* but means 'Bedouins northeast of Egypt and their country' not 'shepherd' in general.

In considering the history of the Egyptian language, we may note that most writers of this topic recognize five periods which in some instances are initiated by changes in the writing system as well as in the spoken language. A few including Sethe and Grapow distinguish a sixth and earliest period exemplified chiefly in the language of the Pyramid texts. In the present context I will consider six periods as providing a richer basis for discussion. They may be rather briefly and in somewhat oversimplified fashion be characterized as follows.

*1. Earliest Egyptian*. This is chiefly the language of the Pyramid texts which appears in hieroglyphic form on the walls of the pyramids of five kings of the 5th and 6th dynasties (2494–2181) at the end of the Old Kingdom. Although their first written attestation is later than that of Old Egyptian, there is general agreement that the archaism of their language indicates an earlier linguistic stage.

*2. Old Egyptian*. This is the literary language of the Old Kingdom from the 3rd through the 6th dynasties (2688–2181). No consecutive texts are known from the two first dynasties constituting the Proto-Dynastic period and what there is is often difficult to interpret. Old Egyptian occurs written in hieroglyphics on monuments. Alongside of it there is hieratic used for writing on papyrus. Hieratic characters are written in detached form and there is an essential one-to-one correspondence between the individual characters written in each script. Hence hieratic texts are often published in hieroglyphic transcription. There are also no differences in vocabulary or grammar between the two forms.

*3. Middle Egyptian*. After the First Intermediate Period, of uncertain

[4] Hieroglyphics are transcribed in the usual manner, with the consonants only, because the vowels are not indicated, and with a dot to denote the boundary between morphemes in the word.

length and during which no central authority existed, national unity was restored under the 11th Dynasty and continued under the 12th (2233–1786). This period is called the Middle Kingdom, and the literary language which came into use in this period Middle Egyptian. There followed the Second Intermediate Period, during which there was once more no single centralized authority. The period of Hyksos rule in the eastern Delta is part of this period. National unity was once more restored under the New Kingdom (Dynasties 18, 19, and 20, 1567–1085). During the earlier part of the New Kingdom, Middle Egyptian with hardly any detectable change continued to be used as the ordinary literary language, except for a few instances to be mentioned later.

Middle Egyptian is generally considered to be the "Classical" form of the language and a grammar simply called that of Egyptian will be primarily concerned with this form of the language. Like Old Egyptian it concurrently used hieroglyphic and hieratic systems of writing.

*4. New Egyptian*. The famous religious innovator of solar monotheism Akhenaten, who reigned 1364–1347, was also an innovator in matters of language. No doubt as part of his cult of "naturalness" he introduced what was primarily the form of Egyptian that he himself spoke. It differs considerably in grammar and vocabulary from Middle Egyptian but continues to be written in the hieroglyphic script and its accompanying hieratic form. However, Middle Egyptian still enjoyed such prestige that it continued in use, however artificially, until the time of the Roman Emperor Diocletian in 296 C.E.

*5. Demotic*. There followed another period of internal Egyptian disunity, the Third Intermediate Period. This included two Dynasties of Libyan origin and several native dynasties which were partially concurrent and none of which ruled the entire country. National unity was restored under a foreign, but culturally Egyptianized ruler, Piankhi of the 25th, or Kushite, Dynasty (715–656). This was followed by the national restoration which began under the Saite or 26th Dynasty and during which the entire country was under indigenous rule. It was however interrupted by an initial period of Persian conquest (525–404) and, after a second period of native rule, by the Persian reconquest under Artaxerxes III in 341. After a brief interval there followed the conquest by Alexander the Great in 332. Thereafter Greek rule was continued under the Ptolemies until the incorporation of Egypt into the Roman Empire.

After a transitional period of "Abnormal Hieratic" (dated by Grapow [1944: 213] as occurring about 1100), there appears beginning in the Kushite period during the eighth century a highly abbreviated script involving numerous ligatures of previously separate hieratic characters and known as Demotic. It began in business but was officially adopted during the Saite restoration and even used for monumental purposes. Demotic writing follows the same basic principles as hieroglyphic and hieratic writing, being partly ideographic and partly phonetic, but the forms, abbreviated from hieratic, have been in some instances so drastically altered that the hieratic source is uncertain.

Demotic also represents a new stage linguistically. It continued in general use until the third century of our era. It is one of the three languages of the Rosetta stone alongside Middle Egyptian and Greek.

*6. Coptic*. The last stage of the Egyptian literary language involves the use of the Greek alphabet supplemented by a few consonantal signs of Demotic origin to represent sounds not occurring in Greek. Biblical translations into Coptic began in the third century at a time when Demotic was still in active use by pagan Egyptians. However the use of the Greek alphabet to represent Egyptian antedates its employment by Christians. At least a century earlier we find the Greek alphabet used on mummy labels and in magical papyri in which it was believed that the efficacy of the spells depended on their being pronounced exactly. The language of these glosses is called Old Coptic.

Coptic is divided into a number of literary dialects. There has been much discussion of the number of distinct dialects to be recognized and their localization, but something approaching a general consensus has been reached.[5] From south to north in the Nile valley there are Achmimic, Subachmimic, Oxyrhynchus, and Saidic. In the Faiyum, that is, the area on and near Birket Qarun (the ancient Lake Moeris), and probably extending to the west bank of the lower Nile at this point, is Faiyumic. Finally there is Bohairic, the dialect of the Delta. By the fifth century Saidic had apparently replaced all the other dialects of the Nile valley but not Faiyumic. It was the vehicle of an original Christian literature, not merely translations from the Greek. Later, Bohairic assumed greater importance, and about 1000 it became the official liturgical language of the Coptic Monophysite Church and continues in this function alongside of Arabic up to the present day.

How is the relationship among these six successive stages to be envisioned? As the starting point we may take the discussion in the important paper of Sethe (1925). This study, in spite of its title (which refers to the relationship of Demotic and Coptic) and its main content (which considers the relative similarities of Demotic to New Egyptian which preceded and Coptic which followed), concludes with the first overview of the entire historical development of Egyptian. It is accompanied by a diagram which takes the following forms. The spoken language is represented as a single dotted line

[5] For a discussion of the various proposals concerning the classification of Coptic dialects see Vergote 1973, I: 88–89; II: 8–11, which includes maps.

indicating a continuous and gradual development from the Earliest Egyptian of the Pyramid texts to the last stage, that of Coptic. At intervals, as the gap between the written and spoken form became intolerable, new literary languages are introduced quite abruptly and they continue virtually unchanged until the separation between the literary and spoken language once again becomes unbearably great. There is just one exception: Sethe considers Demotic to be a direct continuation of New Egyptian in a new orthography while deemphasizing the resemblances between Demotic and Coptic which were central in the standard grammar of Demotic by Spiegelberg (1925).

Sethe's theory was dubbed "cataclysmic" by Gunn (1924: ix) since each literary language was portrayed as having a period of sudden birth from the spoken language at specific intervals. Sethe's theory is somewhat modified in Stricker (1945) who tends to see each form of the literary languages as assimilating some of the features of the spoken language over time. Stricker also takes into account the earlier occurrences of Late Egyptian forms in the literary language before the period of its official use by Akhenaten.

What strikes a linguist, however, is not that Sethe's theory is "cataclysmic" but rather that the spoken language is conceived as a single and continuous though changing entity for thousands of years. Nowhere in either Sethe's or Stricker's treatment is there any mention of dialect variation. Others, however, have taken this factor into consideration. Of these the first seems to have been Edgerton, and later others as, for example, Edel and Callender. Thus Edgerton (1951: 11) states that he considers it quite possible that Middle Egyptian and New Egyptian may represent different parts of Egypt as well as different time periods.

In what follows I shall try to present, at least in rough outline, what I consider to have been the course of development of the Egyptian language. Virtually all of the individual points have already been made by other writers who will be referred to at the appropriate points in the discussion. My own conclusions have been arrived at by an independent evaluation of the evidence. To my knowledge this is the first attempt since Stricker to give an overall view beyond the usual enumeration to successive periods of the language.

As a preliminary step it will prove useful to discuss some of the main factors and assumptions, both linguistic and nonlinguistic, which need to be taken into account in the construction of an overall theory.

One of these is the realization that Egypt, when it was politically united, which holds for most of the long period we are considering, was a highly centralized state which utilized labor on a vast scale in royal constructions and in national military expeditions and supervised a complex irrigation system. All of this required a constant flow of emissaries delivering instructions and receiving reports from provincial centers and also required a vast and ubiquitous army of scribes. Not only was writing essential but a central language of administration was virtually indispensable. One would expect the language of the political capital to play the central even if not the exclusive role in the development of successive official languages.

A further major factor in Egyptian history that has to be taken into frequent account is the fundamental division of the country into the Nile valley (Upper Egypt) and the Delta (Lower Egypt). The beginning of the Dynastic period is marked by the conquest of Lower Egypt by Upper Egypt under the leadership of Menes. This is based on Manetho's account but has been verified by the discovery of the Narmer tablet and by other evidence.[6] According to Breasted (1908: 119), the kings of the 5th Dynasty still felt themselves to be southerners ruling the north. The king of Egypt wore a double crown combining that of Upper and Lower Egypt, and the treasury and other departments had southern and northern divisions. Egypt was often called "the two lands," a designation which lasted until the Coptic period. The persistence of the distinction can, however, be noted in Coptic itself. It is clear that the Coptic dialects can be classified into two groups, one consisting of Bohairic alone, the speech of the Delta, and the other of the remaining dialects.

Before proceeding further one linguistic problem requires discussion, what was earlier called the succession problem. Does a particular stage in a literary language continue an earlier stage of the same dialect or does it stem from a different region and dialect? A characteristic and usually decisive phenomenon may occur when there are three successive periods, say A, B, and C when C derives from the same area as A but B has a different provenance. What we may get is an apparent reversal in historical change. A linguistic feature *x* in stage A is replaced by *y* in stage B but then reappears as *x* in stage C.

The following is an example from morphology. The oldest attested form of Ethiopian Semitic is Geez, also known as Classical Ethiopic. Various writers on comparative Semitic have either considered the present Semitic languages of Ethiopia all to have been the direct descendents of Geez (Wright 1890: 29) so that Geez is in effect Proto-Ethiopic or that Geez is the direct ancestor only of Tigrinya in the northern subgroup of Ethiopian Semitic and spoken in the same general area as Geez while the other contemporary languages descend from a sister dialect of Geez (Brockelmann 1961: I, 31). However, there is at least one feature of Geez which suggests strongly that it cannot be the direct ancestor of any present day Ethiopian Semitic language, an opinion in which I am in agreement with a leading specialist in this group of languages, W. Leslau.

[6] Egyptologists are in disagreement concerning the identity of the figure on the Narmer palette. For a discussion see Emery 1961: 14.

The Semitic verb had a derived, so-called intensive, form which involved the doubling of the second consonant in the dominant triconsonantal pattern. However it also used gemination of the same second consonant in a particular tense-aspect form, the present or continuative which only survives in Ethiopic Semitic and in Akkadian but whose Proto-Semitic status is further assured by its occurrence elsewhere in Afroasiatic (Greenberg 1952).

From this twofold function of the geminated second consonant there arises an ambiguity in that the present continuative, usually called the imperfective in grammars of Ethiopian languages, is identical in both the simple and intensive forms of the verb. This ambiguity was removed in Geez by an innovation of unknown origin; the *a* preceding the geminated consonant was replaced by *e* in the intensive form. However in all present day Ethiopian Semitic languages either the ambiguity persists or is eliminated in some other manner; nowhere outside of Geez is this *e* found. Had Proto-Ethiopic left written records it would presumably show ambiguity in these two forms. Hence we would have Proto-Ethiopic *a*, Geez *e*, and once more modern *a* and there would be an apparent reversal in the course of change.

The most powerful evidence of this kind is probably phonological. When there is a complete merger of two originally distinct sounds they cannot be unscrambled to produce the former state in the normal course of change. In Ferguson's article (1959a) on the koine he notes the merger of *ḍàd* and *ḏ̣āʔ* which never have distinct reflexes in any of the koine forms of Arabic but which are distinguished in Classical Arabic. However, the dialects of the Arabian peninsula do in general retain this distinction and in the same lexical items as Classical Arabic. This is strong evidence that they are not the direct descendent of the ancestral koine language. Should the peninsular dialects ever become the basis of a new koine, an utterly improbable occurrence on sociolinguistic grounds, we would have an apparent reversal in the course of change from unmerged (Classical) to merged (present day koine languages) to unmerged in the hypothetical new koine.

With these considerations in mind we consider the six successive stages of Egyptian in their relationship to each other using both linguistic and non-linguistic evidence. The first stage is generally agreed to be Earliest Egyptian, the language of the Pyramid texts, which exhibits clearly archaic features not found in Old Egyptian. It must therefore precede Old Egyptian which, as we shall see, is to be identified with the language of the Old Kingdom and the First Intermediate Period. Earliest Egyptian would then be Proto-Dynastic (1st and 2nd Dynasties) or, as some have thought (e.g. Sethe and Breasted), Predynastic, belonging to the period before the unification of Upper and Lower Egypt. However, as Erman pointed out long ago (1891), the Pyramid texts already portray the king as wearing the double crown of Upper and

Lower Egypt. There is, however, as Erman also indicated, the possibility that the Pyramid texts are not all of the same age but, as far as I know, this question has never been subject to serious investigation.

Manetho tells us that Menes, the first king of a united Egypt, came from the Thinite nome in Upper Egypt. Its center was Abydos and it was here that the tombs of the kings of the Proto-Dynastic age were discovered. The religious and perhaps the older capital of the southern kingdom was Nekheb, called Hieraconpolis by the Greeks and the center of worship of Horus, who was always identified with kingship in Egyptian religion. Whether Abydos or Nekheb, we have in either case to do with an Upper Egyptian dialect. In a subsequent section I shall adduce certain further linguistic evidence for this identification.

By Old Kingdom times the capital had shifted to the more strategically placed Memphis on the southeastern border of the Delta and from which the Delta could be more easily controlled. Edel (1955: 11), the author of the standard grammar of Old Egyptian, commits himself, though somewhat cautiously, to the view that Old Egyptian was based on a dialect of Lower Egypt. He states that the position of Memphis as capital of the Old Kingdom and the existence of the Pyramids and of most burial sites of officials in the necropolises in the vicinity of Memphis shows that a Lower Egyptian dialect played an important role in the formation of Old Egyptian. Similarly Edgerton (1951: 11–12) states that Standard Old Egyptian was perhaps based on the local speech of the region of the Pyramids.

The degree of linguistic similarity between Old and Middle Egyptian suggests that the latter was the continuation of the former even though the political center of the Middle Kingdom was Thebes in Upper Egypt, a dialect which only much later at the time of Akhenaten attained general literary currency.

The foregoing opinion is the one expressed by Callender in his grammar of Middle Egyptian (1975: 1) in which he asserts that Middle Egyptian texts are written in a language closely related to that of the Old Kingdom adorned with inherited linguistic material from Old Egyptian. He voices his suspicion that Middle Egyptian was actually the spoken language of the late Old Kingdom and of the First Intermediate Period.

It may be noted that Thebes was, as it were, an upstart city whose god Ammon was identified with the more prestigious Re in the compound form Ammon-Re. Re was the god of Heliopolis who played a special role in the rise of the 5th Dynasty of the Old Kingdom.

Linguistically New Egyptian may be considered the critical point in the long development of Egyptian in that it marks what is probably the most thorough change in its long history (Paull 1975, citing Korostovtsev's views).

It is generally agreed that its use as a spoken language long precedes its first introduction into general, including monumental use by Akhenaten. In the Carnarvon tablet, Kamose of the 17th Dynasty, whose reign ended in 1567, at least two hundred years earlier than Akhenaten, talks to his advisers about the campaign against the Hyksos, as Erman observes (1968: 2) in the "purest New Egyptian." Sometimes workmen are represented as speaking New Egyptian early in the New Kingdom, but if Kamose speaks to his closest advisers in New Egyptian he could have only spoken Classical Middle Egyptian to the gods!

A considerable body of Egyptological opinions believes that in fact New Egyptian was already the ordinary spoken language of the Middle Kingdom, e.g. Vergote (1973: II, 9) who cites Stricker (1945) approvingly to this effect. New Egyptian would then be a dialect based on that of Thebes in Upper Egypt, which was the capital during both the Middle and New Kingdom, but would not have attained general literary currency until late in the 18th Dynasty. In fact it never completely displaced Middle Egyptian, which continued to be used even into the Roman period.

The view presented here is already found in Grapow (1944: 211–12) who called the triumph of New Egyptian the breaking out of the folk language of Thebes in Upper Egypt through the crust of the old dominant high language (*Hochsprache*) of Memphis, without however completely eliminating the latter.

The next major change in the standard literary form of Egyptian takes us once more to Lower Egypt. After the Third Intermediate Period a new kind of writing, Demotic, involves with it a new stage of the Egyptian language. Piankhi, the Kushite (i.e. Nubian) king of the 25th Dynasty, established his capital at Memphis, and the Saites of the 26th Dynasty had their capital in the Delta. It is generally believed that the Demotic script was invented in Lower Egypt (Lloyd 1983: 333). Coptic is to be viewed simply as the linguistic continuation of Demotic in a different form of writing. This is contrary to Sethe's views, but others disagree with him. Demotic documents can often be identified as reflecting particular Coptic dialects, and Lexa (1934: 162) maintained that such dialect differences could be traced as far back as the middle Ptolemaic period during the third century before the present era.[7] The period before this would be one in which the original Lower Egyptian koine had not yet developed sufficient differences to be observed in Demotic. Given the nature of Demotic writing it would not be surprising if they existed but could not be detected.

[7] Johnson 1972, which might add to this discussion, is an unpublished dissertation of the University of Chicago which was not available to me.

We may summarize the foregoing review of Egyptian linguistic history as follows. Four linguistic periods are posited. I. Earliest Egyptian, whose main records are the Pyramid texts, is based on an Upper Egyptian dialect and is coincident with the first two dynasties (ca. 3100–2686). II. Old and Middle Egyptian, with its linguistic basis in Lower Egypt, most probably with the dialect of Memphis playing the major role in its formation (Old Kingdom, First Intermediate Period, 2686–2133). III. New Egyptian, based mainly on the dialect of Thebes in Upper Egypt, dominant as the spoken language already in the Middle Kingdom and probably lasting through the New Kingdom and the Third Intermediate Period until the 25th (Nubian) Dynasty or the Saite Restoration (2133–ca. 750). IV. The language, of Lower Egyptian origin, which underlies written Demotic and continues as Coptic until Egyptian ceased to be a spoken language. Although there is no direct evidence for this, we conjecture from what we know of linguistic history in general that each of these was a koine rather than a local dialect which spread in pure form without any characteristics drawn from other dialects.

If the foregoing hypotheses are valid, then I and III would both be Upper Egyptian in origin, while II and IV would be Lower Egyptian. There would then be three instances of collateral rather than direct descent, the replacement of I by II, of II by III, and III by IV. We could look for the types of reversals which were discussed earlier in the sequences I–II–III and II–III–IV. These would show themselves in the recurrence in period III (New Egyptian) of some features of I (Earliest Egyptian) and missing in the intervening period of Old and Middle Egyptian. Similarly we might expect resemblances between II and IV not found in III. The first set of recurrences (I and III) would be Upper Egyptian and the second (II and IV) Lower Egyptian.

In fact, and without any reference to an overall scheme of the development of Egyptian such as that presented here, Edgerton (1951) notes a number of linguistic peculiarities which occur in what he calls Old Egyptian, but which, it is clear from the context, refer to the language of the Pyramid texts, and recur in New Egyptian without appearing in the intermediate period of Old and Middle Egyptian (II). Edel (1954: 12) both modifies and amplifies Edgerton's examples. Edel's version is cited with approval by Vergote (1973: II, 9). As Edel puts it, these phenomena could be explained by assuming that the colloquial language of Upper Egypt retained some elements of the old language of the Pyramid texts which then resurfaced in New Egyptian. The two most prominent of these features are grammatical, the occurrence of a prosthetic ʔ in certain verbal forms and the distinction of gender and number in the demonstrative functioning as a copula which is replaced in period II by an unchanging masculine singular.

Edel (1954: 11) notes the variant forms of the word for 'master, lord'

Pyramid texts *nbw* as well as *nb* (*w* is often omitted in spelling) as against the exclusive writing *nb* in this extremely common word in Old and Middle Egyptian.[8] This contrast seems to be reflected in the Coptic period in which the reflex of *nbw* appears in Upper Egypt while that of *nb* is seen in Bohairic, the dialect of the Delta. Parallel differences in other words with regard to final *w* in noun forms are cited in other instances (*ibid.*: 96). In fact, reconstructions based on a comparison of the non-Bohairic dialects sometimes result in forms incompatible with Bohairic, suggesting the retention of earlier dialect features in the latter. The lapse of time is of course enormous and suggests caution.

The schema presented here may, with the application of the principles of dialect geography, assist in solving what has by writers concerned with the phonological history of Egyptian been considered a strange phenomenon of "reversal." An earlier *ẖ* (a back voiceless fricative whose exact phonetic nature is uncertain) while remaining in certain words, is replaced in others by *š* in the Pyramid texts but then is replaced again by the earlier *ẖ* in Old and Middle Egyptian. There are two roots, however, which continue to be written with *š*, *šmm* 'to be hot' and *sš* 'scribe' and with different vocalization 'to write'. That the *š* in these two roots is merely graphic is shown by the fact that they reemerge as *x* in Bohairic and Achmimic and as *h* in the other forms of Coptic.

The apparent reversal *ẖ* > *š* > *ẖ* is called remarkable by Erman (1928: 46); Albright calls it "the elusive *h* problem," while Edel seeks to eliminate it as a problem altogether by calling it purely graphic (1955: 52).

In regard to this change it is important to take into account, as has been noted generally by students of the history of the Egyptian sound system, that the partial shift of *ẖ* to *š* while *ẖ* remains in other words is paralleled by the partial shifts of *k* to *ṯ* and *g* to *ḏ*. The *ṯ* and *ḏ* were probably palatalized velars which became palatalized alveolars later and then became *t* and *d* in most instances during the late Old Kingdom.

The conditioning factor for the fronting of *k* and *g* was in all probability vocalic and, as we have seen, vowels are not indicated in hieroglyphic writing. A striking indication of the vocalic factor is the second person singular masculine possessive and verb subject suffix *k* as against the feminine *ṯ* which is found in the Earliest Egyptian and continues into later periods. These forms agree exactly with the second person singular masculine-feminine contrast in Semitic *ka* versus *ki* with similar forms in Chadic (e.g. Hausa).

Given the parallelism of the changes in the three consonants, it is clear

[8] In order to avoid the problem of representing hieroglyphics in text I have referred to them in accordance with the sign list in the appendix of Gardiner 1957 and with his accompanying description.

that we have here a general sound shift like those stated in Grimm's First and Second laws in Germanic although involving different phonetic features. In such instances we may find, as with Grimm's second sound shift, that the various sounds do not change simultaneously and that the entire shift originates in one region and is propagated to others. It is in the region of origin that the shift is carried out most completely.

For example, as part of Grimm's second sound shift *t* > *ts*, *p* > *pf* and *k* > *kx*. The phonetic completeness and the order of their origin and spread are stated here with the most complete first. The shift started in the south so that, for example, Swiss German has *kx* where standard German has *k*. None of these changes spread to the northern, Low German, part of the German linguistic area. Now if the modern standard literary language had earlier been Swiss German and then were replaced by the more northern dialects of High German which underlie the present literary language we would have an apparent reversal from pre-Grimm *k* to Swiss *kx* and back to more northern *k*. Such a reversal would not occur with regard to the change from *t* to *ts* which had spread to all of High German.

If we hypothesize that the Egyptian palatalization affected *h̲* later than *k* and *g* and that, in accordance with the general thesis presented here, the Earliest Egyptian of the Pyramid texts which shows the *h̲* > *š* shift was based on an Upper Egyptian dialect from which the palatalization spread north, we can explain the restoration of the *h̲*, which did not affect the words that had an original *š* and therefore involves the unscrambling of an earlier merger, by the development of a new standard language based mainly on Memphis in the North to which the change *h̲* > *š* had never spread.

Finally, we ask whether the Upper Egyptian Proto-Dynastic language was the earliest form of Egyptian concerning which we have any evidence. That such earlier forms would be spoken in Egypt is stated by Butzer (1976: 11) who asserts that there is no reason to doubt that the Predynastic peoples of the Egyptian Nile valley spoke Egyptian. He bases this conclusion both on the linguistic separateness of Egyptian within Afroasiatic and the cultural continuity revealed by the archeological record.

The Egyptian writing system itself at the earliest time that we find it gives evidence of a fairly long previous development. A blank piece of papyrus has been found in a tomb of the Second Dynasty showing that even at that time hieratic must have existed as a writing system alongside of hieroglyphic. James (1979: 464) argues that this is an indication that long texts could have been written as early as the initial part of the First Dynasty.

The most powerful indications, however, derive from the earliest hieroglyphic writing itself. Certain symbols have phonetic values which are different from the ideas they represent as expressed even in the language of the Pyramid texts. That these phonetic readings actually expressed the sounds of words that existed in Predynastic Egyptian is shown by the fact that several of them have cognates in other branches of Afroasiatic. Among these are *d* 'hand' (Gardiner 1957: D 46) with which we may compare Akkadian *idu*, Arabic and Hebrew *yad*, etc., whereas throughout the historic period the word for hand was *ḏrt* which survives with the usual phonetic changes into Coptic. Another is Gardiner F 21 'ear of ox' with the phonetic value *ʔdn* cognate with Arabic *ʔudn*, Hebrew *ʔozen*, etc. all meaning 'ear', whereas the historic word is an obvious new derivative formation *m.sḏr* literally 'place of lying down or sleeping'.[9] To these and others cited in Vycichl (1934) we may add the symbol for 'foot' (Gardiner D 58) to indicate the sound *b*, a probable cognate to the root *bV* 'come' or 'go' found in all other branches of Afroasiatic (Greenberg 1963: 54, no. 20 'to come'). In historic times the Egyptian word for 'foot' is *rd*.

Assuming on the basis of the foregoing indications the existence of an earlier form of Egyptian we may ask where it was spoken. Both linguistic and non-linguistic arguments suggest that the earliest form of Egyptian stems from the Delta and that it was here that the system of writing was invented. Because of the 35 feet or so of alluvium deposited in the last 6,000 years or so it is not surprising that there are no surviving Predynastic records from the Delta proper. Because of the relatively advanced nature of the latest Predynastic culture, the Gerzean or Naqada II as it has more recently been called, it is widely assumed that the Delta was more advanced culturally than Upper Egypt in the immediate prehistoric period; some even propose (e.g. Sethe) that before the unification of the country from the south by Menes there was an earlier conquest of Upper Egypt by Lower Egypt.

A further piece of linguistic evidence, already cited in Vycichl (1934) points to Lower Egypt as the region in which the writing system was invented. In Egyptian hieroglyphs there is no symbol for *l*. Where in the Pyramid texts and in all later forms of hieroglyphic we would expect *l* from Afroasiatic cognates we get *r* in some words and *n* in others. It is difficult to see why the inventors of the script would not have a symbol for *l* if it existed in their speech. The writing system was evidently designed by speakers of a dialect in which *l* had become *r* in some instances and *n* in the others. The fact that *l* survived in some dialects is shown by the fact that a sign was invented for it in the Demotic of the Ptolemaic period by adding a short diacritic stroke to the *r* and by its emergence in Coptic which used the Greek alphabet which had a sign for *l*. Among the words which had *l* in Demotic and Coptic are

[9]The consonant transcribed as *ʔ* is probably a semivowel and corresponds etymologically to both *y* and the glottal stop of Semitic.

some which have Afroasiatic cognates with *l*, e.g. the word for 'tongue' Sahidic *las* related to forms in all other branches of Afroasiatic except Cushitic.

Vycichl already pointed out that the very name of the old religious capital of Upper Egypt, Nekheb, spelled *nxb* in hieroglyphic Egyptian, actually had an initial *l* as can be seen from the name of the present village which is on the same site, *Al-kāb*, in which the initial consonant has been reinterpreted as part of the Arabic definite article. Hence the dialect without *l* in which the writing system originated would be in Lower Egypt. There is a further indication. The word spelled *bnr* 'outside' first occurs in the New Egyptian of the 19th Dynasty which, as was seen earlier, is based on the Upper Egyptian dialect of Thebes. That the sequence *nr* was an attempt to spell *l* by using the two most similar consonants to *l* is shown by the occurrence of *bal* 'outside' in Sahidic Coptic with corresponding forms in other Coptic dialects. In the light of the foregoing evidence I consider it reasonable to posit a Predynastic form of Egyptian spoken in and near the Delta which was replaced in the Protodynastic period by a koine based on the speech of Upper Egypt.

The difficulties and uncertainties of the problems with which this paper has been concerned are obvious. It is presented simply as a set of working hypotheses in need of further corroboration or even major correction in the light of future investigation.

## References Cited

Albright, William F. 1946. "Review of *Phonétique Historique de l'égyptien* by J. Vergote," *Journal of the American Oriental Society* 66: 316–20.

Breasted, James Henry. 1908. *A History of the Ancient Egyptians*. New York: Scribner.

Brockelmann, Carl. 1961. *Grundriss der vergleichenden Grammatik der semitischen Sprachen*. Hildesheim: Olms.

Butzer, Karl W. 1976. *Early Hydraulic Civilization in Egypt*. Chicago: Chicago University Press.

Callender, John B. 1975. *Middle Egyptian*. Malibu: Undena.

*Cambridge Ancient History*. 1970–82. 3 vols. 2nd and 3rd editions. Cambridge: Cambridge University Press.

Edel, Elmar. 1955. *Altägyptische Grammatik*. Rome: Pontificium Institutum Biblicum.

Edgerton, William F. 1951. "Early Egyptian dialect interrelationships." *Bulletin of the American School of Oriental Research*, Nr.122: 9–12.

Emery, Walter B. 1961. *Archaic Egypt*. Edinburgh: Penguin Books.

Erman, Adolf. 1891. "Zur Erklärung der Pyramidentexte," *Zeitschrift für ägyptische Sprache und Altertumskunde*, 29: 39–44.

———. 1928. *Ägyptische Grammatik*. 4th revised edition. Berlin: Von Reuther and Reichard.

———. 1968. *Neuägyptische Grammatik*. 2nd edition revised by W. Erichsen. Hildesheim: Olms.

Erman, Adolf, and Hermann Grapow. 1931–59. *Wörterbuch der ägyptischen Sprache*. Berlin: Akademie Verlag.
Ferguson, Charles A. 1959a. "The Arabic koine," *Language* 35: 616–30.
———. 1959b. "Diglossia," *Word* 15: 325–40.
Gardiner, Alan. 1957. *Egyptian Grammar*. 3rd revised edition. London: Oxford University Press.
Grapow, Hermann. 1938. "Vom Hieroglyphischen-demotischen zum Koptischen." *Sitzungsberichte der Preussischen Akademie der Wissenschaften* (Berlin. Phil. Hist. Klasse): 322–49.
———. 1944. "Ägyptisch. Vom Lebensverlauf einer afrikanischen Sprache," in Hans H. Schaeder, ed., *Der Orient in deutscher Forschung*, pp. 205–16. Leipzig: Otto Harrassowitz.
Greenberg, Joseph H. 1952. "The Afroasiatic Present," *Journal of the American Oriental Society* 72: 1–9.
———. 1963. *The Languages of Africa*. The Hague: Mouton.
Gunn, Butiscombe. 1924. *Studies in Egyptian Syntax*. Paris: Geuthner.
James, Thomas G. H. 1979. "Egypt, History of," in *Macropaedia* 6: 463–65. Chicago: Encyclopaedia Britannica.
Johnson, Janet H. 1972. "Demotic Verbs and Dialects." Ph.D. diss., University of Chicago.
Lexa, František. 1934. "Les dialectes dans la langue démotique," *Archív orientální* 6: 161–72.
Liddel, Henry G., and Robert Scott. 1925–46. *A Greek-English Dictionary*. Oxford: Oxford University Press.
Lloyd, Alan B. 1983. "The Late Period," in Trigger et al. 1983: 279–348.
Moulton, James H. 1966. *A Grammar of New Testament Greek*. Edinburgh: T. and T. Clark.
Paull, C. H. S. 1975. "Review of M. Korostovtsev, *Grammaire du néoegyptién*," *Journal of Egyptian Archeology* 61: 285–86.
Sethe, Kurt. 1925. "Das Verhältnis zwischen Demotisch und Koptisch und seine Lehren für die Geschichte der ägyptischen Sprache." *Zeitschrift der deutschen morgenländischen Gesellschaft* 79: 290–316.
Spiegelberg, Wilhelm. 1925. *Demotische Grammatik*. Heidelberg: Winter.
Stricker, Bruno Hugo. 1945. *De indeeling der Egyptische taalgeschiedenis*. Leiden: Brill.
Trigger, Bruce, et al. 1983. *Ancient Egypt, A Social History*. Cambridge: Cambridge University Press.
Vergote, J. 1973. *Grammaire Copte*. 2 vols. Louvain: Peeters.
Vycichl, Werner. 1934. "Hausa und Ägyptisch." *Mitteilungen des Seminars für Orientalische Sprachen (Berlin)*, 37, no. 3: 36–116.
Wiet, G. 1927. "Qibṭ," in *Encyclopedia of Islam*, ed. M. T. Houtsma, et al. Leyden: Brill.
Wright, William. 1890. *Lectures on the Comparative Grammar of the Semitic Languages*. Cambridge: Cambridge University Press.

PART III

# VERSE PROSODY

# Swahili Prosody

The present discussion of the formal characteristics of Swahili poetry is based on the considerable volume of published poetic and musical material, while for related linguistic problems, use was made of the existing studies of the Swahili language, particularly its phonetics.[1] It would, no doubt, have been desirable to utilize the services of a Swahili-speaking informant acquainted with the native poetry. This did not prove possible; it is believed, however, that the available material is sufficient in accuracy and volume to permit the drawing of trustworthy conclusions.

The bulk of this study will be devoted to the spoken poetry. This is to be distinguished from the *wimbo*, 'song' (pl. *nyimbo*) by its much greater length (the poetry often runs to hundreds of stanzas), its regular division into stanzas, its circulation in written form, and its attribution to a known author. Such poems are called *šairi* (pl. *mašairi*) and many specimens are also known as *utenzi* (pl. *tenzi*).

Swahili poetry invariably employs a stanza form, the most common of which exhibits a rhyme scheme *aaax*, *bbbx*, *cccx*, etc., the rhyme *x* extending through the entire poem. The unit of rhyme is the final syllable of the line. Each line normally contains the same number of syllables. By way of example, and as a basis for discussion the first three stanzas of the "Secret of Secrets" are here quoted.[2]

aχi phani kwa upesi
ilo ali karatasi

[1] I wish to express my thanks to Zellig Harris for his kindness in putting at my disposal the manuscript of his article on the phonemes of Zanzibar Swahili, prepared in collaboration with Nathan Glazer. I am indebted to George Herzog for references to Swahili music.

[2] Dammann 1940, p. 214.

na wino mwema mweusi
utulizao maozi

na kalamu mahabubu
ilo njema ya Arabu
nowe ina la wahabu
Mola wethu Muawazi

nowe ina la wadudi
'bismilla' ni butadi
ndiye pweke wa abadi
mfalume mwenye ezi

1. My brother, give me good paper quickly and good black ink which comforts the eyes.
2. Besides the beloved penholder, the fine one of the Arabs, that I may write the name of the Munificent, our merciful Lord.
3. I shall write the name of the Beloved; I shall begin "in the name of God." He is the unique one from eternity, the King, the Possessor of Power.

The successive units which may be distinguished on analysis are the syllable, the line, and the stanza. They will be considered here in that order. The line may be defined as the unit whose final member participates in the rhyme scheme. In any particular poem it has a fixed number of segments which may be roughly equated to syllables. Swahili is a language of considerable dialectic variation. The poetry is written in a dialect known as Kiongozi, distinct from any of the spoken dialects, and considered to be archaic. The segments into which the line is divided are probably to be identified with the syllable in Kiongozi, assuming it was ever an actual speech form. For purposes of the present discussion, these segments will be called by the more neutral term mora. In the above example, each line contains eight morae.

In the case of native Bantu words the determination of the number of morae is simple; the mora is equivalent to the syllable, or, what comes to the same thing, the number of morae is the same as the number of vowels. All, or practically all, the syllables in Bantu words end in a vowel.[3] The syllable consists either of a vowel alone, a vowel preceded by a single consonant, or a vowel preceded by a consonant cluster. We may distinguish three positions in the cluster, any one or any combination of which may be filled. If none are filled, then we have the type of syllable consisting of a vowel only, as already mentioned. Position one can be filled only by the nasals, m, n, or ŋ. If position two is filled, then this nasal must be homorganic with it. Position two may be

[3]Ashton and Tucker 1942, p. 77, "The Swahili syllable is an open one; i.e. it normally ends in a vowel."

filled by any consonant except a nasal or the semivowels y and w. If position one is occupied by a nasal as we have seen, position two can only be filled by a voiced consonant. Position three may be filled only by y or w. Y may only follow a labial in the second position.[4] All the possibilities, with examples, are indicated in the following tabulation:

| 1 | 2 | 3 | examples | 1 | 2 | 3 | examples |
|---|---|---|---|---|---|---|---|
| – | – | – | a, u | * | * | – | mba, ndi |
| * | – | – | mi, na | * | – | * | mya, nwa |
| – | * | – | bo, tu | – | * | * | pya, kwe |
| – | – | * | wa, ye | * | * | * | mbwa, ŋgwa |

In Arabic, clusters of two consonants not conforming to the Bantu pattern abound. When such words are borrowed into Swahili, the first member of the cluster counts as an extra mora. For instance, *markabu* 'ship' from the Arabic *markab* counts as four morae, *ma- r- ka- bu*. A vocalic release of the consonant which counts as an extra mora is clearly indicated by Harris and hinted at by other students of the language.[5] The Arabic diphthongs ai and au also count as two morae. Thus *sautu*, 'voice' from the Arabic *sautu* makes three morae *sa- u- tu*. In such words, according to Harris, a non-phonemic w- or y- glide is heard and the Swahili, when employing the Arabic alphabet, generally write *sawutu*. The following poetic line, which counts as eight morae, will illustrate this treatment of the Arabic diphthongs.

auladi šaitani, 'the children of Satan'.[6]

This treatment of clusters foreign to the Bantu pattern extends to borrowings from languages other than Arabic. During the period of German rule in Tanganyika, Swahili poets composed poems in praise of Kaisari Virhamu (Kaisari here counts as four morae and likewise Virhamu) and the German

[4] I am here following the standard orthography. Harris analyzes č = ky, š = sy, ž = dy. ɲ = ny is implied in the ordinary writing ny and is so analyzed by Harris. Unless it is taken to be a unit phoneme, the combination ɲw, found in ɲwa 'to drink' does not conform to the syllabic patterns set forth here. The special treatment of ɲ in Arabic writing as ي (ya) rather than as na (otherwise in the combination nasal plus semivowel it is the nasal which is expressed in writing) also suggests its treatment as a unit phoneme. See the discussion of the Arabic alphabet as applied to Swahili below.

[5] So Harris "We state that in a consonant cluster, where the first member of the cluster is not nasal, a vowel-colored release is heard between consonants." Sacleux 1909, p. 7, implies a vowel glide between the consonants of the cluster in such words as *hesma* 'honor', from the Arabic *ḥišma*, accented *'hešima* by the "arabisants," presumably *he'šima* by ordinary mortals. Ashton and Tucker state (p. 84) "many Arabic words, when borrowed into Swahili are given an extra vowel." They give as an example the variants *aɣala:bu* and *aɣla:bu*.

[6] PR, No. 7, stanza 16, line 2 (no pagination).

colonial leader Weissman, transcribed variously as Vissmani and Vismani counts as four morae (*vi- s- ma- ni*) as in the eight mora line

bwana wetu Vismani, 'our master, Weissman'[7]

Arabic clusters which conform to the Bantu pattern form a single mora with the following vowel. *Banduku*, 'gun', from the Arabic *bandūq*, counts as three morae, *ba- ndu- ku*.

When once these principles of mora counting are understood almost all the apparent exceptions to the uniformity of the number of units in all the lines of a given poem disappear and the qualifications which have been made by previous students concerning the employment of a system of syllabic or mora counting in Swahili verse become unnecessary.[8]

It is interesting to note how the native manner of writing Swahili in Arabic letters reflects this system of mora-counting. In writing the Bantu clusters, only a single one of the consonants is expressed. Position two, when filled, is always written. Thus the Arabic letter b stands for Swahili b, mb, bw, by, mbw, etc. If positions one and three only are filled, it is the consonant in position one which is written. Thus the Arabic letter m stands for m, my, mw. The combination ny of the ordinary orthography, phonetically ɲ, is written with the Arabic y, however. The first members of non-Bantu clusters have over them the *sukūn*, in Arabic the mark of vowellessness. Arabic *fetha* (a) indicates Swahili a, *kesra* (i) indicates e or i, *ḍamma* (u) indicates o or u. A letter of prolongation is written sporadically after the penultimate vowel of the word (this syllable always bears the stress), for instance *yubani* or *yubāni* are the written forms of *nyumbani* 'in the house'.

The geminate consonants of Arabic are always simplified in pronunciation. The *tashdid*, the sign of gemination, can either be written or omitted; in any event it never counts as a mora. For example *kulu* 'all' written *kulu* or *kullu* from the Arabic *kullu*, counts as two morae. Vocalic m is written as Arabic mu or m and vocalic n as ni or n.

The result of this system is that a mechanical count of the vowel marks and *sukūn* in a line of Swahili poetry will indicate the number of morae. Some manuscripts, however, put a *sukūn* over the letter of prolongation accompanying a stressed vowel. Such a *sukūn* would have to be disregarded in counting. The opening lines of the Kitabu Maulidi will serve to illustrate this principle. Each line has 15 morae.[9]

[7] Seidel 1900, p. 193.

[8] Thus Sacleux (1909, p. 327): "le nombre de syllables n'est pas toujours de rigeur," quoted approvingly by Werner (1918, p. 116).

[9] Neuhaus 1935, p. 145.

baada humidi na salati ntawahubiri[10]
kwanda kutukuza maulidi ni Mzaffari
alikaghirimu laki tatu za dananiri
wakamwuliza[11] na fuuye wakiiona

1. After praise and prayer I shall inform you.
2. The celebrator of the Maulid is Ja'far.
3. He spent 300,000 dinars.
4. They asked him what use it was and they looked upon him.

The analysis by mora count reveals an interesting divergence between the poetic dialect and the language of prose in the treatment of the syllabic nasals.[12] The distribution of the vocalic form of m in the poetry coincides with that noted in the grammars and phonetic descriptions of the language. The case of syllabic n is quite different. In the poetry it is only found in disyllabic words, for example, *n̥ta*, 'wax'; in all other instances it is non-syllabic. Thus the poetic treatment of n is different from that reported for the present speech in all the numerous polysyllables which show the nasal prefix, either as the singular or plural of the nasal class or as the plural prefix of the class which has u- as its prefix in the singular. Thus we have *ŋgu- ru- we* 'hog', counting three morae in the poetry, but prose *ŋ̥- gu- ru- we,* and *ndi- wa* 'dove' in poetry, but prose *n̥- di- wa.*[13]

It has already been stated that the eight mora line is by far the commonest in Swahili poetry. It is also the shortest line (shorter lines are found in the songs). All the longer types of lines have one or more caesuras marked by word juncture.

A ten mora line with caesura after the fourth syllable is found in the Gungu Dancing Song. Though actually a song, in its length and consistent use of rhyme it approaches the poetry. The first four lines are quoted here. The caesura is indicated by a comma.[14]

| | |
|---|---|
| pani kiti, nikae kitako | Give me a chair that I may sit down, |
| tumbuize, wangu mananazi | and soothe my Mananazi, |

[10] Both the mora count and the Arabic original text show that the transcription should be *t'awahubiri*, with an aspirated t arising from nt.

[11] The Arabic original shows that the transcription should be *makamuuliza*.

[12] In the absence of adequate descriptions of dialects other than the standard Zanzibar dialect, it is quite possible that the treatment of syllabic nasals stated here to be characteristic of poetry may be found in some of the dialects.

[13] The syllabic value of the nasal prefix is noted by Harris, by Ashton (1944, p. 5), and Ashton and Tucker (1942, p. 77). In addition to many other instances of the poetic treatment of the nasal prefix, I have noted the scansion of *ndiwa* as two morae no fewer than 16 times (no contrary instances) in Dammann 1937a.

[14] Steere 1889, p. 172.

| | |
|---|---|
| tumbuize, wangu mwanamke | that I may soothe my wife, |
| mpangua, hamu na simanzi | who takes away my grief and heaviness. |

An infrequent type of line is that of 11 morae with caesura after the sixth syllable. An instance is the Inkishafi poem. The first four lines of the poem extant in the northern version are as follows.[15]

| | |
|---|---|
| tatunga kifungo, kwa kukisafi | So broidering my poem till daintily it trips |
| nikapange lulu, kula tarafi | All threaded on with pearly grain up to the very tips, |
| naina nikite, inkishafi | The Inkishafi I name it by which Apocalypse, |
| kizacha thunubi, kinipukiye | Shamefastly sin's gloom shall appear. |

Next to the eight mora line by far the most common type contains 15 morae and has caesuras after the sixth and tenth morae. Thus the line is divided into three segments of six, four, and five syllables respectively. For an example of this type, reference is made to the quotation from the Kitabu Maulidi given above.

A line of sixteen morae with a caesura after the eighth mora was noted in one instance[16] but this example appears to be a song (in which this type of line is frequent) rather than a poem.

The employment of the caesura as a formal poetic device introduces a new principle in addition to those of mora-counting and rhyme. Swahili words are invariably accented on the penult and the vowel of this syllable is usually also marked by additional length. Thus a fifteen mora line with caesura after the sixth and tenth syllables will invariably have stressed fifth and ninth syllables, while the other word-stresses will be variable and differ from verse to verse.

– – – – –́ –, – – ·–́ –, – – – –́ –

The question arises as to whether these are the only fixed stresses. Possibly other syllables than the pre-caesural are regularly stressed. Such a verse-stress would, of course, sometimes conflict with the word-stress on the penult. That such a verse-stress, distinct from the word-stress, actually exists is suggested by Taylor's statement[17] that "the tonic accent falling on the penultimate syllable is necessarily sometimes distinct from the modulation of the verse." A disregard of word-stress in favor of verse-stress for songs is suggested by Baumann's remark,[18] "als Besonderheit mag erwähnt werden dass im Gesange der Ton einzelner Worte im Gesange auf eine andere Silbe als gewöhnlich fällt, wie man aus der im Anhange abgedruckten Suaheli-Lieder ersehen

[15] Stigand 1915, p. 84.
[16] Buettner 1892, p. 131.
[17] Stigand 1915, p. 84.
[18] Baumann 1891, p. 50.

kann." Finally Sacleux[19] speaks of "accents rhythmiques," two, three, or four in number, depending on the length of the verse, but he gives no information as to where they are placed.

The number of conflicts between such verse-stresses and the normal word-stress will be seriously reduced if we take into consideration Ashton and Tucker's statement[20] that "in the middle of the phrase or sentence the penultimate syllables of words lose their length and very often their stress as well, unless there is a shift of emphasis." They cite the examples:

nitaku: fa 'I shall come'
nitakufa ke: ʃo 'I shall come tomorrow'

In the absence of any studies on this point, it is impossible to decide where these accents occur. The evidence of the songs indicates that the last syllable of words before the caesura may be among those stressed. The most common musical phrase ending involves two long notes, one for the penultimate word-stress and the other for the final syllable which is either prolonged by a hold or followed by a rest.[21] This again has a prose parallel in the phenomenon mentioned by Ashton and Tucker[22] that in questions and subordinate clauses, the final syllable is lengthened and stressed. The examples given are

nile·te: 'shall I bring it?'
alipofi·ka: 'when he arrived'

Another candidate for stress is the first syllable of each of the segments into which the line is divided by the caesuras. So in Taylor's accentuation of the Inkishafi, for which he gives a two line specimen, we find both initial and pre-caesural stress

áimi za wapí, wákizíndíwá
zítuzo wa mató, wásizá ngówá[23]

The musical setting given by Baumann for the Gungu Dancing Song is also suggestive:[24]

pa-ni ki - ti, ni-ka-e ki - ta - ko|| tu-mbu-i - ze, wa-ngu ma-na-na-zi||

[19] Sacleux 1909, p. 327.

[20] Ashton and Tucker 1942, p. 83.

[21] For example, in the elaborate "chant des porteurs de Marongo," transcribed by Tielmans (No. 41 in Chauvet 1929), almost all the musical phrases corresponding to poetic lines end ♩♩, ♩♩𝄾, or ♩♩♩.

[22] Ashton and Tucker 1942, p. 84.

[23] Stigand 1891, p. 84.

[24] Baumann 1891, p. 350.

A. Werner gives a sample accentuation of the 15-mora line. Of the examples given, the first includes a stress on the first syllable of the final segment of the line, the second has a stress on the second syllable of the final segment, while the third has no stress in this part of the verse at all. The other stresses all coincide with the word stresses of words in caesura-final position. Here is the first of Werner's examples:[25]

ai muhamádi, ni uwóngo, yáke khabári.

This problem of verse stress is obviously in need of further investigation.

It has been noted above that stress in Swahili is accompanied by length. A few students have therefore wished to analyze Swahili poetry on a quantitative basis. The anonymous author of the "practical guide to the use of the Arabic alphabet in the writing of Swahili, etc." published by the Zanzibar mission suggests the following scheme for the eight-mora line:[26]

$$\underline{\smile\smile} - \mid \overline{\dot{\smile}} \parallel \underline{\smile\smile} - \overline{\dot{\smile}}$$

Substantially the same pattern is suggested by Zache[27]

$$\overline{\smile\smile} - \smile, \overline{\smile\smile} - \smile$$

while the same writer[28] also gives

$$\overline{\smile\smile} - \overline{\smile\smile} - \overline{\smile\smile}\,\overline{\smile}$$

and

$$- \smile\smile - \smile\smile\,\overline{\smile}$$

for various eight-mora line poems published by Büttner.

The supposed phenomenon of the replacement of two short syllables by a long one, as given in all these quantitative schemes, disappears when the rules of mora-counting are taken into account. If this is not done, such a word as *markabu*, 'ship' is counted as three syllables to occupy the place of four in other verses and we have an apparent replacement of two short syllables by one long one. Of course this phenomenon can occur not only in the first and second or fifth and sixth position in the eight-mora line, as suggested in Zache's scheme, but may occur anywhere in the verse. Moreover, long syllables, that is, the penultimate stressed syllables of words, will occur irregularly in the line, as we have seen, except, of course, the word stress of words immediately

[25] Werner 1918, p. 18. The caesura marks are mine. Werner does not recognize them and, in fact, considers these lines to contain 14 syllables. This may account for her inconsistencies towards the end of the line.

[26] PR, poem no. 26 (no pagination).

[27] Zache 1898, p. 84.

[28] Zache 1887, p. 374.

before a caesura or the end of a line. Thus, it is not possible to interpret Swahili verse in quantitative terms with any consistency.

Rhyme in Swahili is based on the identity of the last syllable or mora in the line. This identity is a graphic one according to the rules for the writing of Swahili in Arabic characters. Thus ba and mba rhyme, likewise me and mi, to and tu, etc. However, in the common rhyme a, the nature of the preceding glide, which by the exigencies of Arabic writing must be expressed, whether phonemic or not, is disregarded, so that graphic 'a, ya, and wa all rhyme.[29]

Of the Swahili rhyme schemes by far the most frequent is aaax.[30] The type aaaax is found occasionally. Rare types with two distinct rhymes in the body of the stanza and one rhyme extending through the poem are abababx and ababaz. Other kinds of stanzas, also infrequent, have two rhymes running through the entire poem. Examples of rhyme-schemes are:

axaxax*xy*
axaxaxx*y*
axaxaxxy

A pattern with three identical lines throughout the poem was found in one instance:

abcbdb*xyz*

The songs differ from poetry in the absence of stanza forms. Most frequently a single rhyme is carried throughout the whole song. Sometimes we find axbxcxdx, etc., where it would be more proper to consider a, b, c, etc. not as independent lines but as caesural separations. In the songs we often find a line of sixteen syllables divided into two segments of eight syllables each by a caesura after the eighth syllable. The number of syllables per line in the songs is frequently less than eight, six being quite common. We sometimes find lines of differing length in a repetitive pattern, for example, 6, 6, 9, 6, 6, 9, where each half of the poem is sung to the same melody. There are songs, particularly women's and children's songs which, in conformity with the general African pattern where no Arabic influence is involved, lack rhyme.[31]

It is not proposed to discuss here at any length the problem of Arabic

[29] According to Harris, these glides in some instances vary freely with zero or are dependent on the nature of the preceding and following vowel, in which case they are non-phonemic, while in other surroundings we find significant contrasts between w and y. The writing ', of course, does not represent a glide.

[30] In symbolizing these rhyme schemes, I use letters from the beginning of the alphabet to indicate rhymes which do not recur through the poem, those from the end of the alphabet for those that do. An italicized letter indicates the repetition of the entire line rather than that of the rhyming syllable alone.

[31] See Tiling 1927.

influence on Swahili verse. The purpose has been to furnish a descriptive treatment of Swahili metrics as a preliminary to such an historical study.

The best statement of the general extent of this influence is contained in Meinhof's statement, made in passing, that "der hier auftretende Reim und die gleiche Länge der Zeile wie überhaupt die Form der Strophen sind auf arabischen Einfluss zurückzuführen."[32]

The most striking fact about the manner in which Arabic influence has been exerted in the absence of the classical *qaṣīdah* found elsewhere in Africa (because of the nature of the Swahili language which precludes the employment of quantitative verse?), and the dominance of the post-classical *tasmīṭ* or strophic rhyme forms with the rhyme extending through the entire poem. That the Swahili, whose intelligentsia show considerable acquaintance with Arabic literature in general, were ignorant of classical forms, is unlikely. Meinhof[33] has demonstrated how the Swahili author of the Liongo poem has followed the Arabic practice of *takhmīs* "making five" (the term is mentioned by the Swahili writer several times in his poem). This process involves the taking of an Arabic *qaṣīdah* and the intercalation of three new lines into each verse rhyming with the first hemistich of the original. From the original *qaṣīdah* which, if we count each hemistich as a separate verse, has the rhyme scheme axbxcx, etc., we produce the strophes aaaax, bbbbx, ccccx, etc. It is possible, too, that the songs with their rhyme axbxcx are a survival of a period when the *qaṣīdah* was being introduced in Swahili.

The almost exclusive use of the aaax strophe is not surprising in view of its general popularity among the Arabs; the more complex forms with double and triple rhymes extending through the poem find close, though not exact, parallels in some of the *zajals* of Ibn Quzmān.[34] The predominance of 8- and 15-syllable lines in Swahili poetry requires explanation. The 8-syllable line is common enough in the present popular poetry and in the earlier post-classical collections, but rather less so than, for example, the 7-syllable line which is not found in Swahili poetry at all.[35] The extremely frequent 15-syllable line in Swahili with its division into segments of 6, 4, and 5 syllables finds no parallel that I know of in Arabic practice, while the much rarer 11-syllable line divided into two segments 6, 5 occurs once in Ibn-Quzmān but is by no means frequent in Arabic poetry. There would appear to be some connection between these two Swahili types of lines which only differ by the inclusion or omission of a four-syllable segment in the middle of the line.

[32] Meinhof 1909, p. 25.

[33] Meinhof 1924.

[34] An example is Ibn-Quzmān's no. 39 with a rhyme scheme abababxy. Considerable popularity for the eight-syllable line is suggested by such medieval Latin instances as the hymns Dies Irae and Stabat Mater, whose form is identical with the standard Swahili eight-syllable aaax

Swahili rhyme clearly shows its derivation from Arabic in that it involves the last syllable of the line, an obvious simplification of the classical rules and one normally found in popular Arabic poetry.

A study of the Arabic origins of Swahili verse, still to be made, would be of interest in showing the manner in which Arabic forms have been adapted to a different linguistic and cultural milieu to result in the characteristic Swahili type of verse.

## References Cited


Ashton, Eric Ormerod. 1944. *Swahili Grammar (including intonation)*. London and New York.

Ashton, E. O., and A. N. Tucker. 1942. "Swahili Phonetics," *African Studies*, 1, pp. 77–104.

Baumann, Oscar. 1891. *Usambara und seine Nachbargebiete*. Berlin.

Büttner, C. G. 1892. *Suaheli Schriftstücke in arabischer Schrift*. Berlin.

———. 1894. *Anthologie aus der Suaheli-Literatur* (*Gedichte und Geschichten der Suaheli*). Berlin.

Chauvet, Stephen. 1929. *Musique Nègre*. Paris.

Dammann, Ernst. 1937a. "Eine Suaheli-Dichtung über Moses, den Habicht und die Taube," *Zeitschrift für eingeborenen Sprachen*, 28, p. 1.

———. 1937b. "Bemerkungen zur Suaheli-Dichtung," *Forschung und Fortschritte*, 13.

———. 1940. *Dichtungen in der Lamu-Mundart des Suaheli*. Hamburg.

Heinitz, W. 1932. "Lied aus Dar es Salam transkribiert" in *Festschrift H. W. Augustin*. Gluckstadt.

Ibn Kuzman. 1933. *Cancionero del šeiḥ, nobilisimo visir, maravilla del tiempo, Abu Bakr ibn Abd-al-Malika aben-Guzman*. Madrid.

Ingrams, W. H. 1931. *Zanzibar: Its History and Its People*. London.

Krapf, L. 1887. "Gedichte im alten Suahili aus den Papieren des L. Krapf," *Zeitschrift für afrikanischen Sprachen*, 1, pp. 1–42, 124–37.

Meinhof, Carl. 1909. *Die Sprachen des dunkeln Weltteils*. Stuttgart.

———. 1924. "Das Lied des Liongo," *Zeitschrift für Eingeborenen-Sprachen*, 15, pp. 241–65.

Neuhaus, G. 1935. "Kitabu Maulidi," *Mittheilungen des Seminars für orientalische Sprachen*, 38, abt. 3, pp. 145–201.

"Practical Guide to the use of the Arabic alphabet in writing Swahili according to the usage of the East Coast of Africa, with facsimiles of Mss. in Arabic characters, notes and explanation." Zanzibar, 1891 (quoted as PR).

Sacleux, Charles. 1909. *Grammaire des dialectes swahilies*. Paris.

Seidel, A. 1900. *Suahili Konversations-Grammatik*. Heidelberg.

Steere, Edward. 1889. *Swahili Tales as Told by Natives of Zanzibar*. 2nd ed. London.

Stigand, C. H. 1915. *A Grammar of the Dialect Changes in the Kiswahili Language*. Cambridge, Eng.


---

form. In the Aug. 10, 1946, issue of the *New Yorker* I find a poem entitled "Ovibos," by Robert Hale, in this same form. Diffusion or independent invention?

Tiling, Maria von. 1926. "Suaheli-Lieder," *Zeitschrift für Eingeborenen-Sprachen*, 17, pp. 295–304.
———. 1927. "Frauen- und Kinderlieder der Suaheli" in *Festschrift Meinhof*, pp. 288–300.
Velten, C. 1917. "Suaheli Gedichte," *Mittheilungen des Seminars für orientalische Sprachen*, 20, abt. 3, pp. 64–182.
———. 1918. "Suahili Gedichte," *Mittheilungen des Seminars für orientalische Sprachen*, 10, abt. 3, pp. 135–83.
Werner, Alice. 1918. "Swahili Poetry," *Bulletin of the Society for Oriental Studies*, 1, pp. 113–27.
———. 1921. "Utenzi wa Ayubu," *Bulletin of the Society for Oriental Studies*, 2, pp. 85–115, 297–319, 347–416.
———. 1924. "The Fowl and the Cat: A Swahili Poem in the Tikuu Dialect," *Bulletin of the Society for Oriental Studies*, 3, pp. 527–31.
———. 1928. "The Native Poetry of East Africa," *Africa*, 1, pp. 348–57.
Zache, Hans. 1887. "Review of Buettner's *Anthologie aus der Suaheli-Literatur*," in *Zeitschrift für afrikanische Sprachen*, 1, pp. 373–76.
———. 1898. "Das Makuganya-Lied," *Mittheilungen des Seminars für orientalische Sprachen*, 1, pp. 84–114.

# Hausa Verse Prosody

The published poetic material in Hausa can be divided into two main categories (see Table 1).[1] There is first the poetry of religious inspiration composed by the Mohammedan learned men, the 'Malams' (sing. *mắlamī́*, pl. *mālamấy*). This poetry is circulated in written form and employs classical Arabic meters. It is usually sung without instrumental accompaniment. The other main type is that of the itinerant individual singer and drummer who sings in the intervals between the dances. This poetry is unwritten; the subject matter is nonreligious, comprising the three genres of *yabṓ* 'song of praise', *zambṓ* 'satire', and *bēgḗ* 'love song'. It is sung with instrumental accompaniment. Though the rhythm is quantitative, Arabic meters are not employed. As in classical Arabic poetry each verse is divided into two hemistichs, but they are shorter than in Arabic poetry, averaging seven or eight syllables. Moreover, rhyme is never employed systematically; where found it is accidental or used as a special effect for a few verses only.

Between these two types a middle position is occupied by the *zắbiyắ*, 'singing master', a Malam who seeks gifts from the pious by performing songs of a religious nature. Each verse is punctuated by a chorus of pupils singing a constant refrain. The verses are longer than those of popular poetry though the meters employed are not Arabic and there is no rhyme. This poetry is also unwritten.

## I. Linguistic Factors

The recognition of the quantitative nature of most Hausa poetry[2] has been delayed by an incorrect doctrine of vowel length in final open syllables. I have

[1] In this study, each poem is referred to by two letters indicating the collection, followed by the individual reference, usually a single letter, which the collector has given the poem cited.

[2] For previous discussions of Hausa poetic form, see P. Prietze, "Dichtung der Hausa," *Africa*,

*Table 1*
*Published Collections of Hausa Poetry*

| | |
|---|---|
| RA | C. H. Robinson. *Specimens of Hausa Literature*. Cambridge, 1896. |
| RB | ———. *Hausa Grammar*. London, 1930. |
| FA | E. Funke. "Einige Tanz- und Liebeslieder der Haussa." *Zeitschrift für eingeborenen Sprachen*, vol. 11, pp. 259–78 (1920). |
| PA | R. Prietze. *Haussa-Sprichwörter und Haussa-Lieder*. Kirchhain, 1904. |
| PB | ———. "Hausa Sänger, mit Übersetzung und Erklärung." *Königliche Gesellschaft der Wissenschaften zu Göttingen. Nachrichten. Philologisch-historische Klasse*, pp. 163–230 (1916). |
| PC | ———. *Ibid.*, pp. 552–604. |
| PD | ———. *Lieder fahrender Haussaschüler. Mittheilungen des Seminars für orientalische Sprachen (MSOS)*, vol. 19, abt. 3, pp. 1–115 (1916). |
| PE | ———. *Gesungene Predigten eines fahrenden Haussalehrers. MSOS*, vol. 20, abt. 3, pp. 1–41 (1917). |
| PF | ———. *Haussa-Prieslieder auf Parias. MSOS*, vol. 21, abt. 3, pp. 1–52 (1918). |
| PG | ———. *Lieder des Haussavolks. MSOS*, vol. 30, abt. 3, pp. 5–172 (1927). |

NOTE: I refer to a few unpublished items collected by myself as follows: GA, a *qaṣīdah* History of Kano; GB, the Song of Šu'aybu, a song in praise of a local headman; GC, the Song of 'Umaru and Musa, a song in praise of a local headman; GD, a song accompanying the Bodo dance.

discussed this question elsewhere, but only in regard to substantives.[3] In view of the relevance of this topic for Hausa verse scansion, a few general statements will be given here with regard to the final quantities of non-substantival forms to amplify this former treatment.

1. Prepositions, conjunctions, and sentence-modifying particles usually have short final vowels. Exceptions include *bísā* 'upon' and *ammā́* 'but'.

2. The essential rules with regard to verbs are as follows: (a.) All active participles have long final vowels, but the 'stative' participles found only in intransitive verbs end in a short vowel (*yánā*

vol. 4 (1933), pp. 86–95, and pp. 169–74 in the same author's "Haussa-Sänger mit Übersetzung und Erklärung," *Königliche Gesellschaft der Wissenschaften zu Göttingen. Nachrichten. Philologisch-historische Klasse* (1916).

[3] "Some Problems in Hausa Phonology," *Language*, vol. 17 (1941), pp. 316–23. My treatment of final vowel quantities differs slightly from that of C. T. Hodge and H. E. Hause. However, this divergency can possibly be attributed to dialect differences since their materials are from Katsina and mine from Kano.

záwnāwā́, 'he is sitting down'; yánā zawné, 'he is seated'). (b.) Before noun objects the final vowel of the verb is short except in monosyllables ending in -ā, -ē, -ō, and polysyllables ending in the directional morphemes -ō 'motion toward', -ē 'motion away' (*yā́ kāma mutûm* 'he seized the man'; *yā́ ḍawkí kā́yā́* 'he lifted the load'; *yā́ kā́wṓ kúḍī́* 'he brought the money'). (c.) All verbs have long final vowels before pronoun objects (*yā́ kāmā ší* 'he seized it'; *yā́ ḍawkḗši* 'he lifted it'; *yā́ kā́wṓ ši* 'he brought it').

3. When not followed by an object and not participial, the usual rule is that transitive verbs have long vowels and intransitive verbs short vowels (*yā́ sánī* 'he knows'; *yā́ tafí* 'he went').

These rules of quantity, based on an investigation of the language in the field,[4] find ample support in the quantitative scansion of Hausa verse. In fact, without them it is difficult to bring any order to the metrical schemes employed.

In modern treatments of the language, vowel lengths have been noted accurately in the case of final high-tone syllables, but the vowels of final low-tone syllables have been uniformly considered short (so in all of R. C. Abraham's grammatical treatments of the language and in P. G. Bargery's *Dictionary of the Hausa Language*). This rests on the phenomenon of the reduction of long vowels in pausal position. Moreover, in the native writing of Hausa in the Arabic script, in general high-tone final vowels are written long and low-tone vowels short, though great inconsistency reigns. This graphic habit has a striking parallel in the neighboring Kanuri language of Bornu where, according to J. Lukas,[5] in the native writing of the language in Arabic characters high-tone syllables are written long and low-tone vowels short. It appears, however, that vowel length is not significant in Kanuri.

The syllable in Hausa has three basic patterns closely paralleling those of Arabic and providing favorable ground for the adoption of Arabic quantitative verse. These three forms of the syllables are CV̆, reckoned as short, and CVC and CV̄, reckoned as long.[6]

There is now general agreement as to the presence of three phonemes of tone in Hausa, high (here marked with an acute accent), low (no accent), and the much rarer compound tone which results from the coalescence of a high and a following low tone (marked with a circumflex accent). The tones are

[4] This research was done in the course of an ethnological investigation in Northern Nigeria as a Field Fellow of the Social Science Research Council in 1938–39. The present investigation was carried out as a Demobilization Fellow of the same institution.

[5] This observation is to be found on page 6 of his "Lautlehre des Badawi-Kanuri in Bornu," *Zeitschrift für eingeborenen Sprachen*, vol. 25 (1934), pp. 3–30.

[6] For discussion of this topic see p. 282 of A. Klingenheben's "Die Silbenauslautsgesetze des Hausa," *ZfES*, vol. 18 (1928), pp. 272–97, and my "Some Problems in Hausa Phonology."

indicated in the texts cited here as exemplifications of metrical schemes, although they are not marked in any of the original sources. It is unlikely that they play any role in the prosody, though, of course, this possibility is not entirely to be excluded.

## II. The Learned Poetry

The material is here arranged in order, starting from those poems which are closest to Arabic models and going on to those that are successively more and more unlike them. The deviations from Arabic patterns are found to be features of Hausa popular verse. A coherent progression obtains, that is, a feature which disappears at one point in the series does not usually reappear later in the series and a new feature, once it occurs, is found in all the later members of the series. The two extremes may be characterized in the following manner. The most 'Arabic' of the poems only deviate in two points from the pattern of the *qaṣīdah*. The lengthening of final vowels is allowed not only in verse close but also at the end of each hemistich. The rhyme does not completely follow the rigid rules of the *qāfiya*. In particular, little attention is paid to the rules governing the syllable preceding the *rāwī*, or main rhyming letter. Equally close to classical forms as the more usual *qaṣīdah* is the unique strophic poem of Mohammed Bello (RB-A War Song),[7] the only recorded instance of the *tasmīṭ* in Hausa. This form does not divide the verse into hemistichs so that the only deviation from Arabic practice in Bello's poem is the presence of such rhymes as *sarākī́*, *gúmkī*. At the other end of the scale of learned poetry we find (a) that there is no rhyme, (b) that a non-Arabic meter is employed, (c) that the hemistichs, and consequently the verses, are shorter.

In what follows, I have normalized the transcriptions since the originals were for the most part written down before the modern period of linguistic investigation. In regard to the system utilized, it may be noted that *c* represents the glottalized dental affricate. Always palatalized are *k*, *ḳ*, and *g* before *e*, *ē*, *i*, *ī* and labialized before *o*, *ō*, *u*, *ū*; but this has not been indicated. Palatalization and labialization have been indicated before *a* and *ā* where we have the contrasts *ka*, *k*$^{y}$*a*, *k*$^{w}$*a*, etc.

The poems RA-F and GA are both in *Wāfir* meter, and rhyme in *-wā*. As is in the classical *qaṣīdah*, the first hemistich of the poem, the *'arūḍ*, ends in the verse rhyme. Of these two poems, RA-F is much stricter in its rhyme. The verse ending is usually *-āwā*, but *-ēwā* and *-ōwā* also occur. The rhyming of *ā*, *ē*, and *ō* is an understandable practice analogous to the Arabic liberty of rhyming *ī* and *ū*. Since the vowels *e* and *o* do not occur in classical Arabic there is no precedent in the classical rules for the treatment of these

[7] For this system of reference see footnote 1.

vowels. Moreover the vowels *a*, *e*, and *o* are closely related in Hausa, being in morphophonemic alternation in their short form. In the other poem, GA, both closed and open syllables precede *wā*. When the syllable is open we have *ā*, *ē*, *ī*, and *ō*. Here are 44–45 of GA:

mu nū́nā mā̂ da súnka táfṓ da fā́rī
súkay sā́rā́ súnā kúma dándacāwā́
sá'annán sáy rúwán bázárā́ yá sáwkṓ
súkay šū́kansu tā́ fitá bā̂ máḳēwā́

∪−−−|∪−∪∪−|∪−−||
∪−−−|∪−∪∪−|∪−−.
∪−−−|∪−∪∪−|∪−−||
∪−−−|∪−∪∪−|∪−−.

We have told you that these were the first to come; they cut down the trees and chopped up the wood.
Then the first rains descended; they did their sowing and the crops came forth plentifully.

The previously mentioned poem of Mohammed Bello (RB-A War Song) is a *tasmīṭ mukhammas*,[8] the rhyme scheme of which is aaaax, bbbbx, ccccx, etc. Each line has two *ramal* feet (−∪−−). The rhyme is of the same free type as that of GA above. The first two stanzas of the poem are as follows:

yán 'úwā́ mún gṓde 'állā
mún yí 'ī́mánčī da sállā
hár jihā́dī dón ka jálla
mún ḳášē dángī́ ná Dálla
sún sánī sū́ sún yí sárkī́

mún ḳášē 'álkā́fírā́wā́
sū́ súwā́ nē Gṓbírā́wā́
sún táfṓ dón Ḳā́dírā́wā́
sū́ da sā́šin 'Ásbínā́wā́
sún táfṓ sū́ dúk da sárkī́

Brethren we thank God;
We perform acts of faith and prayer
Even holy war for Thee the Exalted One:
We slew the breed of dogs,
They know (now) that their task was beyond their strength.

We have slain the heathen;
Who were they? The men of Gobir.

[8] For the *tasmīṭ*, see pp. 404ff. of G. W. Freytag's *Darstellung der arabischen Verskunst* (Bonn, 1880).

They came (to fight) the followers of Abd-el-Kadr
They and half the men of Asben.
They came, all of them, together with their king.

RA-A and RA-C both employ the *Kāmil* meter. The first hemistichs of both poems lack the verse rhyme. RA-C rhymes in *-yā*, most of the verses ending in *-iyā* with some in *-uyā*, a permitted rhyme. There is just one instance of a verse ending in *-ayā* in violation of the classical rules. RA-A rhymes in *-rī*, but very negligently. We find *-ray*, *-rā*, and even *-wā*, *-mā*, and *-may*. There is no consistency in the structure of the penultimate syllable of the verses. Lines 5–6 of RA-C:

ḍán jāhilī̇ dábbā fá nē wā́wā fá nē
yā́ cōcí kây nása bay sánī bá ga dū́níyā
ḍán jā́hilī́ gā́wā́ fá nē tún bay mútu
wāyánsa banzā́ nē zámánsa ná dū́níyā

— — ◡ — | — — ◡ — | — — ◡ — ||
— — ◡ — | ◡◡ — ◡ — | ◡◡ — ◡ —.
— — ◡ — | — — ◡ — | — — ◡ — ||
— — ◡ — | — — ◡ — | ◡◡ — ◡ —.

The son of the ignorant man is a beast and a fool; he destroys himself; he knows nothing in this world.

The son of the ignorant man is a corpse before he dies. He has no sense as long as he remains in the world.

RA-E is in the *Wāfir* meter but without rhyme. Lines 2–3 are quoted here. They are actually the first two lines of the poem since the editor counts the opening *bismillāh* as a line. In regard to the short final *-i* in the noun *'aṣṣalāti* 'prayer', it should be noted that Arabic words and phrases which are fairly frequent in the religious poetry keep the original Arabic quantities. The noun *sállā*, which is the ordinary Hausa word for prayer, always has the long final vowel.

mu gṓde 'ubángíjī sárkī́ saráwtā
da yā́ 'áykṓ muhámmádu ḍán 'amī́na
múnā zúba 'aṣṣalā́ti bísā fiyáyyḗ
da 'ummātán muhámmádu yā́ fí kṓwā́

◡ — ◡◡ — | ◡ — — — | ◡ — — ||
◡ — — — | ◡ — ◡◡ — | ◡ — —
◡ — ◡◡ — | ◡ — — — | ◡ — — ||
◡ — — — | ◡ — ◡◡ — | ◡ — —

Let us thank the Lord, ruler of the kingdom, who sent Mohammed, the son of Amina.

We pray in behalf of the superior one and for the family of Mohammed who surpasses everyone.

RA-D is apparently in *Mustaṭīl*, an uncommon post-classical meter obtained by reversing the *Ṭawīl*. There is no rhyme. There are some irregularities in the scansion particularly in the first foot of each hemistich, where instead of the expected ⏑––– we often find –––, ⏖––, or ⏑––. This variation at the beginning of the hemistich is reminiscent of Hausa popular poetry. Verse 6 illustrates some of these peculiarities. The seventh foot is irregular.

tṓ mā́tā́mu 'almājirāy 'á ku máyda hímmā
kúnā zíkrī kúnā 'addū́'ā kúnā salā́tī

––– | ⏑–– | ⏑–⏖– | ⏑–– ||
⏑––– | ⏑–– | ––⏑– | ⏑––.

Ye, too, O women, my disciples, do you show diligence; invoke the name of God and offer supplications and prayer.

RA-B is in a non-Arabic meter of the following pattern:

⏓–⏑–⏑–⏕–– ||
⏓–⏑–⏑–⏕––

There is no rhyme in this poem. The accumulation of long syllables at the end of each hemistich is frequently found in popular verse. Another popular characteristic of this poem is an occasional extra syllable at the beginning of the hemistich.

## III. The Popular Poetry

The chief formal characteristic of popular poetry which differentiates it from the learned variety is the presence of an indefinite number of syllables (usually from zero to three) at the beginning of each hemistich which do not count as part of the metrical scheme. Another feature of some of this poetry, which is not found in any of the religious poems, is the differentiation of the two hemistichs of the verse in length and meter. Occasionally we find the verses divided, either sporadically or systematically, into three or even four sections, in contrast to the constant employment of the division into two hemistichs in the religious poetry. Rhyme is never employed as a consistent device in the popular poetry.

A number of the published poems could not be fitted into any metrical system, while in others the irregularities are very considerable. There can be no doubt that most of the popular poetry is quantitative but there remains the possibility that some of it employs other principles, perhaps tonal, or no formal principle at all. It appears also that the spoken praise verses, known as *kirari*, do not involve any quantitative principle.[9]

In what follows each of the meters of popular poetry is given a number, the poems in which it appears are listed, and a few verses with their scansion are given as illustration. In the scansion, the first few syllables of the line which are outside the metrical pattern are separated from the essential part of the line by a comma. The meters are arranged according to cadence. Those ending in ⏑– have been put first, then those ending in ⏑––, etc. Those meters in which the two hemistichs have different meters are treated after those which have the same meter in each hemistich.

Meter 1. ⏕–⏕–⏑– PA-34; PB-A, B, C, D (partly), E, F, G, H, N (irregular), P, Q, T (partly); PC-C; PG- Dam Maduga, Dudua

*PB-B, lines 1–3*

'abînda ná bây wā Šā-wuyá bā́ na bây wā Dōdángabá
'abînda na bây wā Rā́matú bā́ na bây wā Yár Gṓje bá
sā́'anda ná kē sôn Rā́matú rīgán kírkī táy wuyā́

⏑–, ⏖–––⏑– || –⏑, ––––⏑–.
⏑–, ⏖–––⏑– || –⏑, ––––⏑–
––, ⏖–––⏑– || –, ––––⏑–.

That which I give to Ša-wuya, I do not give to Dodangaba.
That which I give to Ramatu, I do not give to Yar Goje.
Since I have been in love with Ramatu, it has been difficult for me to obtain a decent gown.

Meter 2. ⏕–⏑–⏑– PG-Ka A, Ka B, Ka C (partly), Ga (irregular)

*PG-Ka, line 20*

Būdel wā́wan Ba'abzinī yā́ jēfí kūrā da ķarfatā

––, ––⏑–⏑– || ––⏑, ––⏑–⏑–.

Budel, the foolish Tuareg, threw the hyena with its shoulder blade.

Meter 3. ⏑––⏑– PG-Ai

*PG-Ai, line 6*

ỵán bírnī súnā sôṇ Mare yán ķáwyē súnā sôn Mare

––, –⏑––⏑– || ––, –⏑––⏑–.

[9]The *kirari* is a short verse characterizing a person, political office, species of animal or plant, etc. A great many of them are recorded in R. Prietze's "Pflanze und Tier im Volksmunde des mittleren Sudan," *Zeitschrift für Ethnologie* (1911), pp. 865–914.

The men of the city love Mare; the men of the countryside love Mare.

Meter 4. – ω̲ – ω̲ – ⏑ – PG-Dudua

*PG-Dudua, lines 1–2*
kḗ barí kū́kā́ církíyā́ ba ki gá gídán maybā́bu bá
maybā́bu da zā́fín zū́čiyā́ kṓ kútúrū́ bay fī́ši bá

–, ω – – – ⏑ – || ω, ω – – – ⏑ – .
– –, ω – – – ⏑ – || –, ω – – – ⏑ – .

Thou bowstring, leave off weeping; thou hast not seen the house of the destitute man.
The destitute man has a bitter heart; even the leper is not more bitter.

Meter 5. – ω̲ – – ⏑ – – PA-5, PB-T (partly)

*PA-5, lines 1–2*
zā́ni Kánō zā́ni Ḍawrā́
zā́ni fátáwčī másōyī́

– ⏑ ⏑ – – ⏑ – – ||
– ⏑ ⏑ – – ⏑ – – .

I am going to Kano; I am going to Daura.
I am going on a trading journey to find a lover.

Meter 6. – ω̲ – ⏑ – – FA-12, I 3 (partly)

*FA-12, lines 15–16*
súnā yánkē ’áwā́kī́
su sáy šinkā́kā́ da nṓnō

⏑, – – – ⏑ – – ||
⏑ –, – – – ⏑ – – .

They are slaughtering sheep.
They sell rice and milk.

Meter 7. – ⏑ – – PA-2; PE-I, II; PG-Ka C (partly)

*PE-I, lines 7–8*
da ḍán garī́ da bā́wā da ḍán gídā́ da bā́wā
ku táttárṓ mu tū́bā da’áykin ma’ā́sī́

⏑ – ⏑, – ⏑ – – || ⏑ – ⏑, – ⏑ – – .
⏑ – ⏑, – ⏑ – – || ⏑ –, – ⏑ – – .

Men born in the city and slaves, men born in the house and slaves,
Gather together and let us all repent of adultery.

Meter 8. ∪——∪—— FA-III.2

*FA-III.2, lines 10–13*
'indán tá čí rī́bā tá kṓmṓ
'indán tá jí dā́ḍín garī́ nē
'indán tá čí rī́bā da dā́mā́
yārā́ náta nā sáyda kṓmī́

——∪,∪——∪——
——∪,∪——∪——
——∪,∪——∪——
——∪,∪——∪——

If she makes a profit, she returns,
If she is fortunate in the city,
If she makes a splendid profit,
Her hired help sell everything.

Meter 9. ω̲—∪——— FA-1, 5, 6; PG-ItA, ItB, GC

*FA-1, lines 4–7*
ga samārī́ súnā wāsā́
ga ỵán mā́tā́ súnā wāsā́
ga ỵán tákardā́ súnā kállṓ
mā́tán 'árnā́ súnā kállṓ

∪∪,——∪———||
∪—,——∪———.
∪—∪,——∪———||
——,——∪———.

The young men are playing.
The young women are playing.
The learned men are looking on.
The pagan women are looking on.

Meter 10. —ω̲—∪—ω̲—— PG-Nada A, B, C

*PG-Nada A, line 12*
nī́ mákaḍín mázā́ nē kún sán bā́ na káḍā mā́tā́ 'abín wṓfī́ bá

—ω—∪——————ω,———∪————

I am a drummer for men, as you know. I do not drum for women who are worthless.

Meter 11. —∪—ω̲—— PB-K (partly); PC-A, B, E, H, K, L, M, N, O, P, Q, R

*PC-A, lines 1–3*
garḗ yánā ḍáka mā́lam 'ín yā́ fítṓ wajḗ nā́mā nḗ

ḱā́rī̄yar kádō tó rúwā́ čē 'ín yā́ fítṓ wajḗ nā́mā nḗ
ḱā́rī̄yar májāčíkī sáy kōgō 'ín yā́ fítṓ wajḗ šī́ kē nán

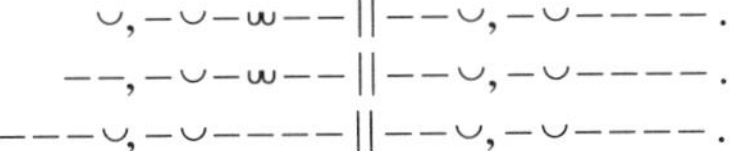

The Malam remains at home; if he comes out, he becomes meat.
The water is the crocodile's protection; if he comes forth, he becomes meat.
The only protection of the snake is the cave; if he comes forth, he is finished.

Meter 12. ——⏑—⏖——— GB

*GB, lines 1–4*

nā́ gṓde rā́yin maybā́ni
maybā́ka šī́ nē sárkínka
dṓle zân yabí maybā́ni
maybāni šī́ nē sárkī́nā́

—, —⏑————— ||
—, —⏑—————— .
—⏑—⏖——— ||
—, —⏑—————— .

I praise the life of the one who gives me.
The one who gives you is your king.
I must needs praise the one who gives me.
The one who gives me is my king.

Meter 13. —⏑—⏖——||—⏑—⏖———. PC-F, G (irregular), I. (The first line of this meter is identical with meter 11.)

*PC-F, lines 59–62*

dū́níyā gíšírī̄ čē da ḍánḍanā́ kan ḱā́rēta
dū́níyā ná dunā́nā kárē yá čē yám mā́gārā́
kṓ dū́níyā tā́ ḱārē kāzā́ ba tā ḍáw táykī bá
kṓ dū́níyā tā́ ḱārē kū́sū ba zây háḱa rā́mī bá

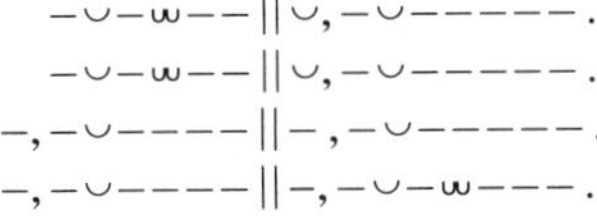

The world is like salt; if you taste it, it is finished.
'The world is sinking away,' says the dog to the dancers.
Even if the world were to end, the chicken could not lift a bag of grain.
Even if the world were to end, the rat could not dig a hole.

Meter 14. —⏑—⏖——||⏖—⏑—⏑—. PD-A, B, C, D; PF-A, D. (The first line is identical with meter 11 and the last line with meter 2.)

*PD-A, lines 13–14*

mā́lam yā́ gáyā míni 'ā́yā barí sáwnal šigā́ dáwā
bā zā́kī bá, bā kū́rā́ bá kó da rāḳúmín dáwā

– –, – ⏑ – ⏔ – – || ⏑ ⏑, – – ⏑ – ⏑ – .
– –, – ⏑ – – – – – || ⏔ – ⏑ – ⏑ – .

The Malam has recited a verse to me. Cease fearing to enter the forest.
There is no lion; there is no hyena; there is not even a giraffe.

Meter 15. – ⏑ – ⏔̲ – – || – ⏑ – ⏔̲ – – ⏔̲ – . PF-B

*PF-B, lines 20–21*

'Ā́li dārívyálka ná kē sō kó da ba zā́ka bā́ni wúrī́ náwa bá
'Ā́lı yá ti ḳártín rárgō̄ rárgō bā́ ya kan yí kamál tása bá

– ⏑, – ⏑ – ⏔ – – || ⏔ ⏑, – ⏑ – ⏔ – ⏔ – .
– ⏑, – ⏑ – – – – – || – –, – ⏑ – ⏔ – ⏔ – .

Ali, I love your laughter even if you do not give me a bit of your money.
Ali is stronger than the shiftless man; the shiftless man does not act as he does.

Meter 16. – – ⏑ – ⏑ – ⏔̲. PG-Galezi A. (In this meter the extra syllables occur at the end of the line.)

*PG-Galezi A, lines 1–2*

ḍám mā́lamī́ da zā́ši káratū́ mīnḗ yá káyši wā́ḳal Galēji
ḍawkṓ táddawā́ ka ḍáwkṓ kúndī́ wā́ḳal galēji bā tā́ka čḗ bá

– – ⏑ – ⏑ – ⏔, – – || – – ⏑ – ⏑ – –, ⏑ – – .
–, – – ⏑ – ⏑ – –, – – || – – ⏑ – ⏑ – –, ⏑ – – .

The son of the Malam who is going to study,
  what has brought him to the song of Galeji?
Take away the ink and take away the book;
  the song of Galeji is not for you.

Meter 17. – ⏑ – ⏔̲ – ( – ) || – ⏑ – ⏑ – ⏔̲ – ( – ). GD

*GD, lines 1–3*

yāyā́ 'á kē bōḍṓ bán gánṓ rábin čínyā bá
ḍán zánan bōḍṓ ḳanḳánē 'á kē ḍáwrāwā́
'a bā́mu bā hasā́rā bá 'ín 'án hánā hasā́rā čḗ

–, – ⏑ – – – || – ⏑ – ⏑ – – – – .
– ⏑ – – – || – ⏑ – ⏑ – – – – .
⏑ – ⏑, – ⏑ – – – || –, – ⏑ – ⏑ – – – .

How is the Bodo dance done? I do not see half of the thigh.
A tiny cloth for the Bodo, one is girded with a small cloth.
If one gives us a present, that is no loss! If someone is prevented
  from giving, that is a loss.

## IV. Historical Problems

In regard to popular Hausa quantitative verse, there are two possible theories of historical origin. Either it is a native African verse form or it is an historical derivative of Arabic meters. The latter alternative appears to be the correct one. The mere existence of transitional forms of religious poetry, as noted above (under II), is not relevant; these transitional forms clearly result from the influence of native popular verse on the learned religious poetry, but the popular verse might either be native African or itself have resulted from an acculturation of Arabic verse to Hausa conditions in the past.

The strongest arguments in favor of an Arabic origin for Hausa popular verse depend on resemblances in form. First is the very fact of the quantitative nature of this verse which is unparalleled, as far as we know, among African peoples not subject to intensive Islamic influence. In matters of detail, we may note the division of the line into hemistichs. Among Africans, this is unknown except for the Fulani, and here too we have to do with quantitative meters among a people under strong Mohammedan influence.[10] As we have seen, Hausa popular poetry most commonly divides the line into two hemistichs, both of the same metric pattern, precisely as in Arabic poetry. Another point of close resemblance is in the meters themselves. As was observed long ago by Freytag,[11] Arabic verse avoids sequences of short syllables, a succession of three being rare and that of four almost unheard of. This same characteristic holds for Hausa popular poetry. In this connection, it is remarkable that all of the Arabic meters whose use has been noted among the Hausa (the *Wāfir*, the *Kāmil*, and the *Mustaṭīl*) involve the alternative use of a long syllable or two short syllables, giving rise to the characteristic patterns ⏕–⏑– and ⏑–⏕–

| | |
|---|---|
| *Wāfir* | ⏑–⏕–\|⏑–⏕–\|⏑–– |
| *Kāmil* | ⏕–⏑–\|⏕–⏑–\|⏕–⏑– |
| *Mustaṭīl* | ⏑–⏕–\|⏑––\|⏑–⏕–\|⏑–– |

All of the popular Hausa meters allow the substitution of two short syllables for a long in the second long syllable preceding or following a short, unless a short syllable precedes, for in that case we should have three short syllables in succession (⏕⏑–⏑–). The reckoning of final syllables as long for metrical purposes is another specific trait common both to classical Arabic and popular Hausa poetry.

The very specific resemblances just noted between the two types of

[10] The hemistich division (in Fulani *feṭṭere*) of the line in Fulani verse is mentioned by H. Gaden in his *Dialecte Peul du Fouta Senegelais* (Paris, 1914), vol. 1, p. 320.

[11] Freytag, *Darstellung der arabischen Verskunst*, p. 14.

versification make it highly probable that the popular quantitative poetry of the Hausa is historically derived from Arabic sources.

## V. Musical Evidence

Musical data might throw considerable light on the problems just discussed. In particular, we should like to compare the music of Hausa religious poetry with what we know of the musical performance of Arabic classical poetry. Likewise the comparison of the music of Hausa popular poetry with that of the religious poetry would furnish evidence relevant to the problem of the historical connection between these two types. Unfortunately, as far as is known, the music of both the Hausa religious and secular poetry is as yet unrecorded. While in the Sudan, the writer did transcribe the music of the song accompanying the Bodo dance (an excerpt is given above in section III under meter 17). While it is not possible to draw any conclusion with regard to the historical problem on the basis of one example, it does throw some light on the structural problems of Hausa poetry. Each of the hemistichs into which the verse is divided has a distinct musical phrase, the two hemistichs being separated by a distinct pause, with the approximate length of about two beats. The end of the verse carries a longer pause, of approximately three or four beats. This pattern of two musical phrases is repeated for each verse with minor changes to allow for the changes in scansion. Here are the first two lines of the Bodo dance:

This example confirms the basic importance of the hemistich division in this type of verse. In other examples which were not transcribed, the writer remembers the constant repetition of two musical phrases separated by a pause. The above example also suggests a division of the metric pattern into subordinate divisions, which we may call feet; it will have been noticed that no such division was attempted in the enumeration of popular meters in section III above.

preliminary syllables + –, ⏑–, ––
preliminary syllables + –, ⏑–, ⏑–, ⏑⏑̲––

This suggests the rule that no foot may end in a short syllable or in a long syllable resolvable into two short syllables. The hemistich and verse pause, which are *a fortiori* the end of a foot, become a special instance of this general rule.

An examination of the above musical quotation will show that there is no correspondence between the musical pitch of the notes and the prose tonal levels of the syllables which are sung to them. In each 'foot', all the syllables are on the same musical tone level regardless of prose pitch differences.

On the other hand, in two Hausa melodies transcribed by Moloney,[12] apparently the only Hausa melodies which have ever been published, considerable attention is paid both to quantity and tone of the text in the musical version, while the prose text of the songs cannot be fitted into any quantitative metrical scheme.

The widespread African practice of drum signaling finds its analogue among the Hausa in two types of 'communications' by instruments. Here, as usually elsewhere, the texts employed are confined to a small number of conventionalized expressions whose contents are already familiar to most of the hearers, a necessary provision in view of the limited resources of these types of communication. The first of the two musical instruments employed by the Hausa for this purpose is the *kākākī́*, a long metal horn, whose use is confined to the royal houses of the various states. It announces the emergence of the king on state occasions and recites his *kirari* 'praises'. The *kākākī́* has two notes, a fifth apart, obtained by blowing the second and third overtones of the fundamental. These two notes represent the two main tones, high and low, of the spoken language. Long syllables are distinguished from short by sustaining the note for approximately twice the time length of a short syllable. There is a tendency, however, exemplified several times in the examples below, to give a long note to a short syllable when the following syllable is on a different tone; possibly extra time is needed to change the lip pressure for the change of note. The final tone of each phrase is long regardless of the quantity of the spoken syllable. The first two syllables of *sarākī́* are consistently represented by one note of the instrument.

It might be well to summarize at this point all the instances of the lengthening of final vowels which have been noted; it appears to be a general prosodic feature of the language.

> 1. Final short vowels in ordinary speech are lengthened in pronunciation and have the same close, tense quality as long vowels. The differences are not entirely effaced; long vowels are still longer than short ones in this position.

[12] C. M. G. Moloney, "On the Melodies of the Volof, Mandingo, Ewe, Yoruba, and Hausa," *Journal of the Manchester Geographical Society*, vol. 5 (1889), pp. 276–98.

*kirari* of 'Abdullahi, the Present Ruler of Kano

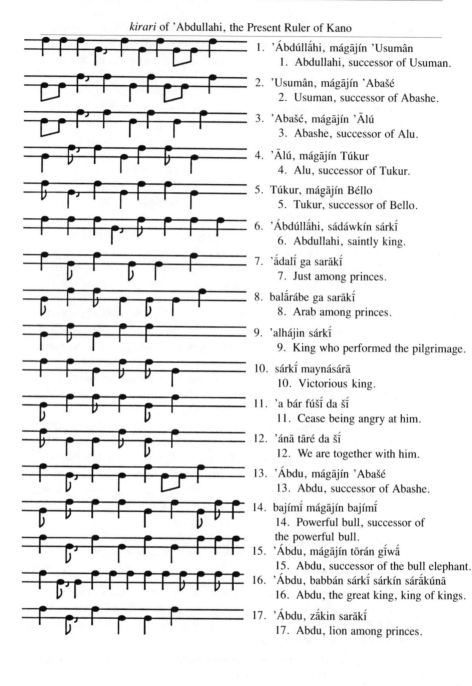

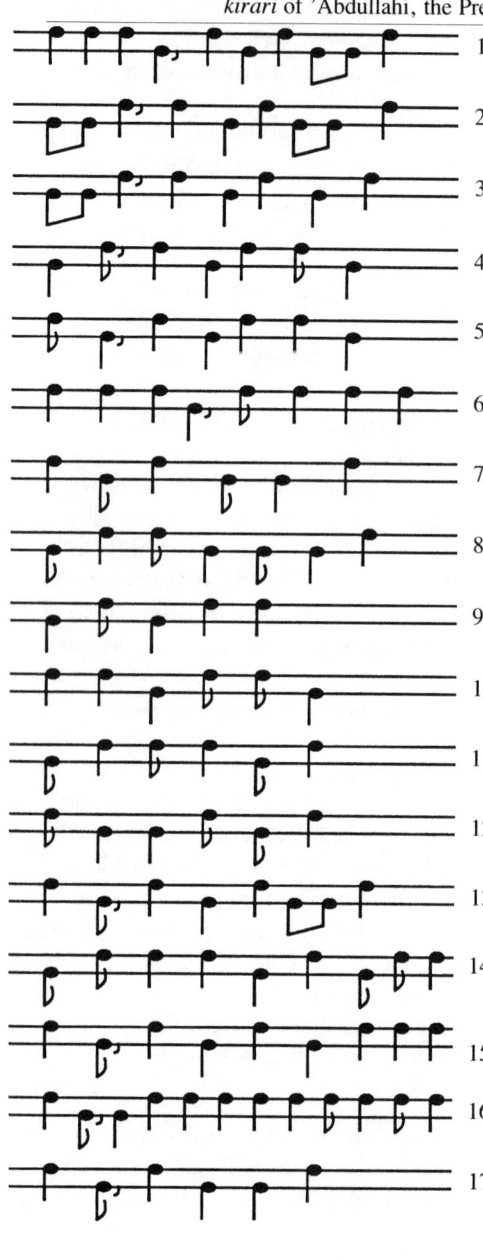

1. 'Ábdúllā́hi, mágājín 'Usumân
   1. Abdullahi, successor of Usuman.
2. 'Usumân, mágājín 'Abašé
   2. Usuman, successor of Abashe.
3. 'Abašé, mágājín 'Ālú
   3. Abashe, successor of Alu.
4. 'Ālú, mágājín Túkur
   4. Alu, successor of Tukur.
5. Túkur, mágājín Béllo
   5. Tukur, successor of Bello.
6. 'Ábdúllā́hi, sádáwkín sárkī́
   6. Abdullahi, saintly king.
7. 'ā́dalī́ ga sarākī́
   7. Just among princes.
8. balā́rábe ga sarākī́
   8. Arab among princes.
9. 'alhájin sárkī́
   9. King who performed the pilgrimage.
10. sárkī́ maynásárā
    10. Victorious king.
11. 'a bár fúšī́ da šī́
    11. Cease being angry at him.
12. 'ánā tāré da šī́
    12. We are together with him.
13. 'Ábdu, mágājín 'Abašé
    13. Abdu, successor of Abashe.
14. bajímī́ mágājín bajímī́
    14. Powerful bull, successor of
    the powerful bull.
15. 'Ábdu, mágājín tōrán gī́wā́
    15. Abdu, successor of the bull elephant.
16. 'Ábdu, babbán sárkī́ sárkín sárā́kúnā
    16. Abdu, the great king, king of kings.
17. 'Ábdu, zā́kin sarākī́
    17. Abdu, lion among princes.

2. Short vowels are lengthened in hemistich and verse pause both in learned and popular quantitative poetry.

3. In songs not based on quantitative meters, the short phrase-final vowel is sung long.

4. In horn signaling, a short final vowel is represented by a long note of the horn.

The other instrument used for signaling is a drum over whose membrane a cord is drawn dividing it into two unequal portions, producing two different pitches; the drum is then referred to as *maybā́kī bíyú*, 'two-mouthed'. The drummer drums out the *kirari*'s of the young girls of the localities. Following the playing of the verse in her praise, any young man may indicate his interest in her by putting a coin on the drum as a gift to the performers. After this, the young girl does a solo dance in front of the drum. The other occasion on which this drum is employed is cooperative farm labor, the *gayyā́*. The *kirari*'s of the various family heads of the community are played to spur them on in their agricultural labor. Both the quantity and tone of the spoken text is indicated very consistently in this type of drumming so that all that will be necessary is the citation of the texts fully marked in regard to tone. Since length of syllables is conveyed by the length of the pause which follows the drum beat (no sustained tone, of course, is possible on a percussion instrument) there is no way of indicating the quantity of the last syllable of the phrase.

*kirari*'s of Young Girls

kúččíyár máyšēḳā́ da 'alharī́nī
da mālamáy tákē ṭafí 'ā tá šā́ tá' wánkā́
silíkī záran ḳawnā́
musúlmin ḳárfē 'zurfā́

The dove of Mecca with a silken nest,
She goes with a Malam; she drank and washed herself
(that is, she bought a medicine).
Silk is the thread which is desired,
Silver is the Muslim metal.

*kirari*'s of Family Heads

gātárī́ másōmín 'áykī
bā mā́ganī́ nē bá sábōda 'áykī nḗ
hádárī yā́ tásṓ
gadā́ mū́gun nā́mā

An ax with which to begin work.
It is not because of medicine; it is through work.
The thunderstorm has risen.
The boar is bad to eat.

The material cited in this section is representative of original African types of poetic expression still surviving among the Hausa alongside of patterns imported from the Islamic world. In addition we might have cited the songs performed to call spirits in the native possession rites known as Bori. Although these performances have incorporated some Mohammedan elements, they are essentially African in content. We have no record of the music employed, but the songs are considered to be *kirari*'s of the respective spirits. The spoken forms of the text reveal no quantitative pattern upon analysis.

From the evidence adduced here, we may tentatively draw a contrast between the poetry of Islamic origin which displays quantitative patterns and in which the tone levels of the spoken text are ignored in musical performance, and the African poetry which does not exhibit quantitative patterns and which incorporates both quantitative and tonal distinctions into the musical settings.

# A Survey of African Prosodic Systems

This is the first attempt at a general survey of the prosodic verse forms of African poetry. It is therefore quite possible that certain phenomena have been overlooked—prosodic systems may exist of which the writer is ignorant. In addition to describing the facts, some historical analysis is likewise attempted. Here, too, the author is aware that certain of the results are merely tentative. Where such is the case, the appropriate qualifications and the existence of alternative hypotheses are indicated.

Only the basic facts concerning the prosodic systems are considered. Discussion of more subtle issues, comparable to such problems of classical metrics as the interrelation of stress and quantity in Latin verse, is not attempted here. It is believed that a general survey of the African terrain such as is attempted here must in most cases precede such detailed work. Moreover, in many instances our linguistic data are not sufficient for such problems at the present stage. Another omission concerns relations of literary dependence of specific poetic productions. Such data are obviously relevant to questions of historical relations among prosodic systems. Here again, except in a few instances, this field is as yet uncultivated. Therefore an attempt to evaluate evidence from this source would have extended greatly the already broad scope of the present paper. Considerations from this area have, therefore, been only infrequently utilized, although their importance is realized.

A mapping of prosodic verse forms in Africa shows a far from random distribution. Almost all examples occur in the northern half of the continent and in many of these, the borrowing and adaptation of Arabic models by peoples under Islamic influence is demonstrable. In certain other instances, notably in the Ethiopia-Somaliland area, one cannot always be certain of the direct or indirect Arabic origin of the existing verse forms. In addition to these and other instances in which Arabic influence, while possible—or even probable—is not certain, there are at least two authenticated instances of verse forms which are to all appearance indigenous, and not the result of Arabic influence.

Where Arabic origin is assured, it will be convenient to distinguish those instances in which the classical pre-Islamic forms, notably the standard *qaṣīdah* or "ode" have been adopted, from those in which postclassical medieval or modern Arabic forms are involved.

The descriptive sections of the present paper are accordingly divided into four parts: (1) indigenous African forms; (2) the influence of Pre-Islamic Arabic verse; (3) the influence of postclassical Arabic verse; (4) instances of possible though not certain Arabic influence. The main descriptive-historical treatment of African verse forms is preceded by a brief discussion of fundamental notions having to do with the nature and types of prosodic systems.

It is probable that there exists, in all human society, beyond the everyday use of language, a body of verbal tradition, written or unwritten which is distinguishable from ordinary language by differences in vocabulary, grammar, and other purely linguistic characteristics. Among the linguistic features which define such non-casual utterances, we find in certain instances adherence to rules which can be stated in terms of the sound structure alone within grammatically given stretches, such as the sentence. In such cases we talk of prosodic systems. Since the rules of prosodic systems can be stated in terms of the sound structure alone, it is feasible, in principle, to discover the existence of such systems without a knowledge of the grammar and semantics of the language. Thus, in the following text, certain regularities might be detected by an analyst entirely ignorant of the language, provided only that the transcription of sound units (phonemes) is accurate and that the boundaries of the relevant grammatical units are likewise given.

axi phani kwa upesi ilo ali karatasi na mwino mwema mweusi utilizao maozi na kalamu mahabubu ilo njema ya arabu nowe ina la wahabu mulu wethu muawazi.

If we divide the foregoing text into units (syllables), each consisting of a member of the class *a*, *e*, *i*, *o*, *u* (vowels), together with any non-vowels which precede up to but not including the preceding vowel, then the following phenomena may be noted. The syllables numbered 8, 16, 24 are the same (*si*); so are syllables 40, 48, and 56 (*bu*); syllables 32 and 64 are also identical (*zi*). All of these syllables have a number divisible by 8, and each is the final syllable of a grammatical unit, the word.

The language is Swahili and it would usually be stated that the poem is divided into lines of 8 syllables each and that the rhyme scheme is a a a b c c c b.

Such prosodic systems appear to be entirely absent among American Indians and to be confined to certain parts of Europe, Asia, and Africa.

The preceding was an example of the principle of syllable count, the occurrence of a certain number of syllables in each line. Relative to the line, which is the fundamental division in terms of which the pattern can be stated, one may classify the prosodic devices as follows: rhyme, alliteration, syllable count, quantity, stress, and tone.

*Rhyme* may be defined as similarity of sound sequence at some determinable place within the line, usually at the end. By *alliteration* is meant the recurrence of particular single sounds at certain fixed places, or merely a certain number of times within the line. A *quantitative* system is one in which syllables are classified as short or long and certain limitations of sequences are applied in terms of this division. A *stress* system involves a division of syllables into stressed and unstressed, again, with certain limitations on their sequence of occurrence. Similarly in *tonal* poetry, we classify syllables into types based on pitch characteristics and regulate the line in accordance with the permitted sequence of tonal types.

The application of any of these principles requires a numerical statement regarding the number of occurrences of the relevant characteristic in the line. This characteristic of prosodic systems may be called its metrical aspect. Thus, in the Swahili example cited, the occurrence of 8 syllables in a line is a metrical characteristic.

Metrical characteristics may be more or less rigid. On this basis they can be classified as fixed, alternative, bounded, maximal, or minimal. These may be illustrated as follows. The requirement that every line have 6 syllables is a fixed metrical characteristic; that it may have either 6 or 8 an alternative; that it have no more than 8 or less than 5 bounded; that it have at most 6, a maximal, and that it have at least 6 syllables a minimal. An example of a minimal characteristic occurs below in the instance of Somali alliteration where the requirement is merely that every line have at least one occurrence of the basic consonant.

Quantity, stress, and tone can only be used as prosodic principles in those languages which have the required phonological characteristics. On the other hand, syllable count, alliteration, and rhyme can be applied in any language. This is an important factor in the consideration of the historical relationships of prosodic systems. Universally applicable principles like that of syllabic count can always be borrowed from one language to another, whereas quantitative patterns cannot be borrowed by a language which does not possess the linguistic distinction between short and long vowels.

It appears safe to conclude that except for possible recent influences of European rhymed poetry, the vast majority of African peoples south of the Sahara, including here the non-Moslem peoples of West Africa and all the Bantu peoples except the Islamicized Swahili, do not possess prosodic systems. The most conclusive evidence is the statement of a native speaker whose training would enable him to detect such a system did it exist. Several instances of such statements have been found. Babalola (1957: 7) says "Yoruba poetry has neither rhyme or regular metre. The 'line' of Ijala poetry is the sense group and its length varies." Nketia (1955: 77), a professionally trained musicologist and linguist, arrives at the same conclusion regarding the Akan languages of Ghana.

There are two exceptions, it would appear, to this general rule. One of these is the occurrence of tone riddles among the Efik in Nigeria, and the other is a system of alliteration among the Somali. Particularly in the former instance, Arabic influence is entirely excluded by the nature of the system which involves significant pitch—a linguistic feature not found in Arabic.

The existence of tone-riddles among the Efik was discovered by Simmons (1955). The tone-riddle is here a specific subtype of riddle for which the indigenous name is *ukabade ikɔ* 'change of words'. The answer to the riddle has the same number of syllables and the same sequence of tones as the question. An example follows (Simmons 1955: 423):

| | | | | |
|---|---|---|---|---|
| Query: | *àfák* | *ɔ́kɔ̀k* | *kéták* | *útɔ̀ŋ* |
| | putting | chew-stick | under | ear |
| Response: | *èsín* | *ényìn* | *kéŋkpɔ́* | *ówò* |
| | putting | eyes | in thing | of person |

It is quite possible that tone-riddles, hitherto unreported, are found elsewhere among African peoples, particularly those in the same general area as the Efik.

The prosodic system of the Somali is about the minimum conceivable. The only requirement is that one particular consonant shall occur at least once in every line of the poem. All of the poetry seems to be sung. Kirk (1905) mentions three genres. Of these the *gerar*, sung on horseback, deals with warlike subjects; the *gabei*, usually sung around the fire, has a non-warlike, often amatory subject matter; and the *hes* is a dancing song with alternating men's and women's parts. In addition, there is the *hoyhoytan* or satire, mentioned by Cerulli (e.g. 1913, no. 16). The prosodic form described above occurs in all of these genres and in practically all published examples. It occurs likewise in the songs which occur in a narrative context in the folklore collection edited by Reinisch (1900).

The following is an example of a *gerar* in *g* (Kirk 1905: 172).

| | |
|---|---|
| Ma sidi galoga | Like the bustard |
| o guluf mel ka daremei | Who has seen an enemy somewhere |
| yan gamʕi wai haben | I cannot sleep at night. |
| sidi arka iyo gosha | Like the lion and the lioness |
| o gabnihi laga layei | Whose young have been slain |
| gurhan ma igu bote | I pace about distraught. |

In some poems phonetically similar consonants are treated as equivalents for the purpose of alliteration. These are: *d* and *ḍ* (the latter a voiced apical stop); *s* and *š*; *h* and *ḥ* (*ḥ* being an unvoiced pharyngeal); ɣ and *g*. In one extended example (Cerulli 1913, no. 15) the liquids *l*, *r*, and *n* are treated as equivalents and there is at least one probable example of *w* and *y* as rhymes.

We turn now to a consideration of classical Arabic prosody as a source of verse forms in a number of African languages. There exist extensive collections of Arabic poetry from the period immediately preceding and contemporary with Muhammad (570–632). These were all written down at a later period. Even if, as is probably the case, many examples are not authentic, the forms employed are certainly pre-Islamic.

The predominant type in these collections is the *qaṣīdah* or "ode," and it is the *qaṣīdah* which provides almost exclusively the basis for the descriptive science of prosody whose invention in the eighth century is attributed to Khalil b. Ahmad. The *qaṣīdah* employs two prosodic principles simultaneously, quantity and rhyme. Each verse (*bayt* 'house, tent') consists of two hemistichs (*miṣraʕ*, 'one of the two flaps of a tent door').

The rhyme which occurs at the end of each verse is identical throughout the poem. In addition, the first hemistich of the first verse (*ʕarūd* 'central tent-pole') usually but not always participates in the verse rhyme. If our unit is the hemistich, then the typical rhyme scheme is a a b a c a d a. If the *ʕarūd* does not rhyme we have a b c b d b e b. Every verse consists of a fixed sequence of long and short syllables which, with certain allowed substitutions, is constant throughout the poem. The last syllable of each hemistich is considered long regardless of its length in prose. A syllable is considered long if it consists either of a long vowel or of a vowel (normally short) followed by a consonant. There are 16 standard quantitative schemes, each of which has a name.

The quantitative and rhyme scheme of the *qaṣīdah* is illustrated here from the first two lines of the poem of Ṭarafah. The end of each first hemistich is indicated by a comma and that of a verse by a period.

> lixawlata ʔaṭlālun biburqati thahmadi, talūhu kibāqi lwashmi fī ẓāhiri lyadi.
> wuqūfan bihā ṣaḥbī ʕalayya maṭayyahum, yaqūlūna lā tahlik ʔasan watajalladi.

There are traces yet of Khaula in the stony tract of Thahmad, apparent like the tattoo-mark seen on the back of a hand.

There my companions halted their beasts awhile over me, saying "Don't perish of sorrow; bear it with fortitude."

The quantitative scheme of these two verses, which are in the meter *Ṭawīl* 'the long one', is as follows.

1. ∪−∪/∪−−−/∪−∪/∪−∪−, ∪−∪/∪−−−/∪−−/∪−∪−.
2. ∪−−/∪−−−/∪−−/∪−∪−, ∪−−/∪−−−/∪−∪/∪−∪−.

The rules of rhyme are rather complex. The following account omits certain refinements which are irrelevant for comparative study. Rhymes are of two types called "fettered" or "free." The "fettered" rhyme ends in a consonant. The vowel which precedes may, in practice, be any of the three short vowels of classical Arabic, *a*, *i*, or *u*. The "free" rhyme ends in a vowel. This final vowel and the preceding consonant must always be the same. The preceding syllable must be one of the four following types and this type remains the same through the poem. These are: (1) *ā* only; (2) *ī* or *ū*; (3) a short vowel followed by any consonant ("closed syllable"); (4) a short vowel *a*, *i*, or *u* not followed by a consonant in the same syllable. An example of the first type would be a rhyme *-ānū* which would have to be maintained unchanged through the entire poem. An example of the second type would be a poem in which every verse ended either in *-īlū* or *-ūlū*. In the third type *-ahmū*, *-ismū*, *-urmū*, etc. would rhyme. The fourth type is illustrated by the poem just cited in which the rhymed lines end in *-adī*. Lines ending in *-idī* and *-udī* might occur in such a poem.

A second pre-Islamic type is the *rajaz*. In this form the line is not divided into hemistichs. As in the *qaṣīdah* the same end rhyme occurs throughout the poem. The quantitative basis of each line, which is usually shorter than a hemistich of the *qaṣīdah*, is the *rajaz* foot −−∪−, which may be doubled or extended in other ways. Occasionally other feet are employed. *Rajaz* poets did not usually compose *qaṣīdahs* and vice versa. Its subject matter was typically satire.

The following is an example of *rajaz* (Ibn Hishām 1858: 562):

in tuqbilū nuʕāniq
wanafrushu nnamāriq
ʔin tudbirū nufāriq
farāqa ghayri wāmiq

If you advance we will embrace you
And spread out the cushions.
If you retreat we will separate from you
A separation without love.

— — ∪ — ∪ — —
∪ — ∪ — ∪ — —
— — ∪ — ∪ — —
∪ — ∪ — ∪ — —

A still simpler form is *sajʕ* or rhymed prose. In *sajʕ*, each line is marked by end rhyme but there is no quantitative or other internal regulation. This form was characteristic of the *kāhins* or soothsayers. It was likewise employed by Muhammad in the Koran. In later times, it was cultivated as an art form as, for example, in the famous Assemblies (*maqāmāt*) of Al-Harīrī in the twelfth century.

Writers on Arabic prosody have often assumed that *sajʕ*, *rajaz*, and *qaṣīdah* constitute a historical progression with the *sajʕ* as the simplest coming first. This is quite possible, though it cannot be conclusively proven. In English, free verse, which is formally simpler, is more recent than rhymed form.[1]

Since the classical *qaṣīdah* employs the quantitative principle it can only be borrowed by languages in which there exists a linguistic distinction between short and long vowels. Such borrowings have occurred among two Mohammedan peoples of the Western Sudan—the Fulani and the Hausa.

The employment of the *qaṣīdah* form in Fulani is confined to learned poetry. There are apparently only two published instances, Reichardt (1859) and Gaden (1935). Both of these poems are written in Arabic script and are by known authors. The former is a poem of religious exhortation in the *mutadārik* meter, one of the standard sixteen but only known from postclassical examples. The latter is an account of the war of El Hadj Omar against the French, written in *Kāmil*, a common classical meter. The Fulani language possesses a distinction of short and long vowels and contains the same syllable types as Arabic. It therefore lends itself without difficulty to the Arabic quantitative forms. Outside of the two examples cited, all published instances of Fulani songs or recited poetry are in the traditional African style, without prosodic rules. The occurrence of the *qaṣīdah* form in Fulani is then a learned exercise which has not been fully assimilated into Fulani culture.

Among the Hausa, there is likewise a distinction between learned and popular poetry. The former employs classical Arabic forms and is religious in subject matter. Unlike the Fulani instance, however, the quantitative principle in modified form has been thoroughly adopted and forms the basis of popular

[1]Complexity, which is in general an imprecise and difficult notion, can for prosodic forms be given objective, measurable meaning. One prosodic form is more complex than another, if the probability of choosing a conforming example by random choice from a set of utterances of the requisite length is less.

poetry. Even here, however, the indigenous African type without prosodic structure is retained in the songs of the spirit-possession cult and in the signal drumming which occurs in a variety of cultural contexts.

As in Fulani, the syllabic structure of the language is essentially like that of Arabic so that it lends itself without difficulty to quantitative schemes. Whereas the Arabic quantitative patterns are employed with great consistency in the learned poetry, the other chief device of the *qaṣīdah*, namely rhyme, tends to be used loosely. In some poems a considerable number of lines do not rhyme and in still others rhyme is not employed at all. In the popular poetry, rhyme does not occur except as an occasional device; it is not a constituent of the prosodic form. Where rhyme is found in the learned poetry, the rules are simpler than those of classical Arabic. Since final syllables ending in a consonant are uncommon in the language, the rhyme is always equivalent to the "loose" rhyme of Arabic. No attention is paid to the phonetic structure of the syllable preceding the last or rhyme syllable. The rhyme, then, always consists of identity of the final syllable consisting of a consonant followed by a vowel.

Popular poetry makes use of quantitative sequences which are generally shorter than those of the classical Arabic meters. The lines are always paired, each corresponding functionally to a hemistich, or half-line of Arabic verse. In some poems, the first of each pair has a meter different from the second throughout. As in classical Arabic poetry, the last vowel is always treated as long. In any line, preliminary syllables up to four in number may be found which are not part of the quantitative pattern. A great variety of metrical forms occur in popular use.

The following is an example of Hausa popular verse in which the odd numbered lines have a different meter from that of the even numbered lines. Preliminary syllables which are not part of the metrical scheme are set off by commas in the scansion (Prietze 1916: no. 6).

dūniyā giširī čē
da ḍanḍanā kan ķārēta.
dūniyā na dunānā
karē ya cē yam māgārā.
kō dūniyā tā ķārē
kāzā ba tā ḍaw taykī ba.
kō dūniyā tā ķārē
kūsū ba zay haka rāmī ba.

The world is like salt; if you taste it, it is finished.
"The world is sinking away" says the dog to the dancers.
Even if the world were to end, the chicken could not lift a bag of grain.
Even if the world were to end, the rat could not dig a hole.

–∪–∪∪––,
∪,–∪––––––.
–∪–∪∪––,
∪,–∪––––––.
–,–∪––––,
–,–∪––––––.
–,–∪––––,
–,–∪–∪∪–––.

This metrical scheme may be summarized as follows:

–∪–⏓/⏓––,
–∪–⏓/⏓–––.

We now turn to a consideration of postclassical Arabic verse forms. In the early Islamic period there arose the practice of improvisation by the insertion of new verses within some already well-known *qaṣīdah*. A fixed number of hemistichs, two or more, was added after the initial hemistich of each line of the original poem and rhymed with it. This process, known as *tasmīṭ* 'the stringing [of pearls]', produces a stanza form of rhyme. As noted earlier, if each hemistich of the *qaṣīdah* is considered a line, then the rhyme scheme of a poem which has the *ʕarūd* or first hemistich rhyme is a a / b a / c a / d a / . . . . If now we insert two new hemistichs in each line rhyming with the first hemistich we obtain the rhyme scheme a, a a, a / b, b b, a / c, c c, a / d, d d, a . . . where commas are used to set off the new inserted lines. Where the original *qaṣīdah* did not contain the initial hemistich rhyme the scheme became a a a b / c c c b / d d d b / . . . . The inserted lines were, of course, in the same quantitative meter as that of the original poem. Soon original poems were being composed in stanzas of this type. An example from the latter part of the eighth century is found in the *Dīwān* or collected poems of Abū Nuwas.

Later the basic *tasmīṭ* scheme was elaborated in Spain by the devising of new nonclassical meters, by varying the meters of different lines in the same stanza and by the development of more complex rhyme schemes. In this form it was called the *muwaššaḥ* ('girdled'). When written in the colloquial rather than classical meter it was called the *zajal*. From Spain, the *zajal* spread throughout the Moslem world. It was also imitated in Spanish, Provençal, and Italian. It was through the *zajal* that rhyme was introduced into Western Europe.[2]

[2]The Arabic origin of rhyme in Europe has been disputed by some Romance scholars. The *prima facie* case for Arabic derivation appears very strong. Menendez Pidal (1943) the well-known Romance specialist, considers and rejects the arguments against Arabic origin.

The *tasmīṭ* and its later derivatives continue in use up to the present in both learned and popular poetry and examples are to be found in almost every collection of contemporary Arabic poetry.

One published example of the *tasmīṭ* in the Hausa language occurs alongside of the more common *qaṣīdah*. This is the "War Song of Abdallah dan Fodio" (Robinson 1930: 133–44). Each line consists of two classical *ramal* feet (–◡––/–◡––) and the rhyme scheme is a a a a b, c c c c b, d d d d b. . . .

The first two stanzas follow:

yan ʔuwā mun gōde ʔallā
mun yi ʔīmančī da sallā
har jihādi don ka jallā
mun ķašē dangī na Dallā
sun sanī sū sun yi sarkī

mun ķašē ʔalkāfirāwā
sū suwā nē Gōbirāwā
sun tafō don ķādirāwā
sū da sāšin ʔAsbināwā
sun tafō sū duk da sarkī

Brethren we thank God;
We perform acts of faith and prayer
Even holy war for Thee the Exalted one:
We slew the breed of dogs,
They know (now) that their task was beyond their strength.

We have slain the unbelievers:
Who were they? The men of Gobir
They came against the followers of Abd-el-Kadr
They and half the men of Asben.
They came, all of them, together with their king.

Among the Kanuri, an important Moslem people immediately to the east of the Hausa, a single example of the *tasmīṭ* rhymed stanzas is forthcoming (Duisberg 1913: 169–85). It can hardly be accidental that, as in the Hausa example quoted above, we have the five-line stanza in place of the more common four-line scheme. Since the Kanuri language does not have significant distinctions of vowel length, the quantitative aspect of the *tasmīṭ* cannot be reproduced. The lines are of different length and it does not appear that any other prosodic principle is employed. The poem is an isolated example of rhyme in Kanuri. All the rest of the published poetry is in the traditional African style without prosodic organization.

It is among the Swahili that the *tasmīṭ* has scored its greatest success. It is by far the most common form in both learned and popular poetry, whether sung or recited. Swahili does not possess vowel quantitative distinctions. This principle has been replaced by that of syllabic count. By far the most popular variant is the four-line stanza in which each line contains eight syllables. Since all Swahili syllables end in a vowel, the rhymes would all be classified as "loose" in the Arabic terminology. As in Hausa, the rule of rhyme is identity of the last syllable. For Swahili, this simplification is practically inevitable on linguistic grounds. Since closed syllables and vowel length do not exist, the fourfold classification of Arabic penultimate syllables falls together in a single type. In the last syllable the phonetically similar vowels *e* and *i* are permitted to rhyme as well as the pair *o* and *u*.

The following is an example of the very common four-line stanza with eight syllables per line (Dammann 1940: 214). The first three stanzas are as follows:

axi phani kwa upesi
ilo ali karatasi
na wino mwema mweusi
utilizao maozi

na kalamu mahabubu
ilo njema ya Arabu
nowe ina la wahabu
Mola wethu Muawazi

nowe ina la wadudi
'bismilla' ni butadi
ndiye pweke wa abadi
mfalume mwenye ezi

My brother, give me good paper quickly and good black ink which comforts the eyes, and the beloved pen, the fine one of the Arabs, that I may write the name of the Munificent, our merciful Lord. I shall write the name of the Beloved; I shall begin "in the name of God." He is the unique one from eternity, the King, the Possessor of Power.

In addition to the more common four-line stanza, five-line stanzas are occasionally found. In one example, the "Song of Liongo" (Meinhof 1924), the conscious following of Arabic models is evidenced by the author's mention of the technical term *taxmīs*, literally 'making five'. The predominance of the four-line stanza in Swahili is not surprising in view of other evidences of its popularity.[3] Occasional examples of more elaborate rhyme schemes

[3]Thus Hartmann (1897: 214) calls it the *tasmīṭ* par excellence. It was this form, moreover, which was introduced in Hebrew in the early tenth century (*ibid.*: 113). Likewise, the only

reminiscent of the *zajal* of medieval Spain are found, for example, the following: a b c b d b e e e, f g h g i e e e, etc.

Besides the common eight-syllable line, longer types are sometimes found with internal caesuras, that is, obligatory word boundaries at certain fixed points. Among these are a ten-syllable line with caesura after the sixth syllable, an eleven-syllable line with caesura after the sixth syllable and, most elaborate of all, a fifteen-syllable line with two caesuras, one after the sixth and the other after the tenth syllable. An example of the latter follows. The caesuras have been marked by commas inserted in the text (Neuhaus 1935: 145).

baada humidi, na salati, ntawa hubiri
kwanda kutukuza, maulidi, ni mzaffari
alikaghirimu, laki tatu, za dananiri
wakamuuliza, na fuuye, wakiiona.

After praise and prayer I will inform you. The celebrator of the Maulid (i.e. feast of Muhammad's birthday) is JaʕfarHe spent 300,000 dinars. They asked him what use it was and they looked upon him.

There is also at least one published example of a Berber *tasmīṭ* (De Calassanti-Motylinski 1885).

Whereas in all of the examples previously considered, there can be no reasonable doubt of direct Arabic influence, there are a number of other prosodic systems in which the historical problem is more complex. Particularly in the Horn of Africa (Ethiopia and the Somalilands), a number of languages use rhyme as a principle of versification, sometimes in combination with other principles. The languages concerned are Geᶜez (Classical Ethiopic), Amharic, Tigre, Tigrinya, Saho, and Galla. It will be convenient to refer to these as constituting an East African rhyming area.

The earliest examples of Geᶜez verse, all apparently unpublished and dating from the fourteenth century when Geᶜez was no longer a spoken language, appear from the descriptions to consist of lines of irregular length and without any principle of internal regulation. All the lines of the same poem have the same end rhyme consisting of identity of the last syllable. As a system this is equivalent to Arabic rhymed prose (*sajʕ*) and Cerulli at least has no doubt regarding its Arabic origin.[4] The writers of this verse all probably spoke

rhymed poem in Coptic, the *Triadon* (Lemm 1903), consists of quatrains with the *tasmīṭ* rhyme scheme.

[4] Cerulli (1956: 85) states, "Certainly the introduction of rhymed prose in Ethiopic was an imitation of Arabic." Moreover, the use of rhymed prose in the introductory section of the prose biography of Lalibala (Perruchon 1892) is quite in the Arabic style. An alternative theory is that rhymed prose is an old South Semitic tradition brought into Ethiopia by the Semitic migrants from South Arabia and continued independently in both Arabic and Ethiopic. In this case, South

Amharic as their first language. Alongside of external indications we have the fact that consonants are considered equivalents for rhyme when they have fallen together in the Amharic consonantal system and this in turn coincides with the Amharic tradition of pronouncing Geᶜez.

The first recorded examples of Amharic poetry, the so-called Royal Songs—a collection of twelve poems celebrating the martial exploits of Ethiopian kings in their battles with the Moslems and dating from about the same period as the Geᶜez poetry considered above—are likewise in rhymed prose, with the same rule of rhyme. As a further indication of the connection of the two traditions, we have a particular feature in regard to rhyme which characterizes both Geᶜez and Amharic poetry down to the present day. A final consonant of the line which in prose would be pronounced without a following vowel is followed by a central unrounded high vowel *ə* thus producing, in these cases, the identity of final syllable which is the rule of rhyme in both languages. In the Ethiopic syllabary a consonant which is not followed by a vowel and a consonant followed by *ə* are written with the same symbol. It is possible on the evidence of related languages that at the time when this syllabary was invented the final position consonant was actually followed by a vowel *ə* in the spoken language. It would then continue to be pronounced in poetic recitation, thus maintaining the identity of final syllable consisting of a consonant followed by a vowel as the principle of rhyme. This practice continues up to the present in Amharic poetry constructed on the more recent principle of rhyme combined with syllabic count. A final consonant which in spoken Amharic prose would not be followed by a vowel, is followed by *ə* in reading poetry and counts as a separate syllable.

The Amharic Royal Songs mentioned above differ from Geᶜez in rhyme only in that *r* and *l* freely rhyme, and while in some of the poems the same rhyme is maintained throughout, in others a new rhyme may be introduced at certain points. Thus, the seventh poem of this collection consists of 22 lines with the following rhymes *q(ə)*, *q(ə)*, *q(ə)*, *q(ə)*, *q(ə)*, *q(ə)*, *ra*, *la*, *la*, *ra*, *la*, *ra*, *ra*, *la*, *ra*, *la*, *ra*, *la*, *la*, *la*, *ra*, *la*.

In the fifteenth century strophic poems make their first appearance in Geᶜez liturgical poetry and they continue to be cultivated up to the present day. Three and five line strophes predominate with the same end rhyme according

---

Arabic, a language distinct from Northern classical Arabic, known from a large inscriptional literature and still spoken in several forms on the South Arabian coast and on a few islands in the Indian Ocean, becomes of special importance inasmuch as it is more closely related to Ethiopic than North Arabic is. Mehri has rhyme but with a fixed number of stresses per line (Jahn 1902). The South Arabic dialect spoken on the island of Soqotri shows, most surprisingly, syllabic count but no rhyme (Mueller 1905). Of course, rhymed prose may have existed and been superseded. The case for Arabic origin, then, seems stronger than for a common South Semitic tradition.

to the rules of the earlier rhymed prose in each strophe. The rhyme schemes are thus a a a b b b c c c . . . and a a a a a b b b b b c c c c c . . . . As in the earlier rhymed prose there is no metrical regulation of the line. The most famous early example of this form is the fifteenth-century *Weddase Maryam* or "hymns in praise of Mary," whose literary origin has been discussed in the literature. Ethiopian tradition attributes the original to Ephrem Syrus, a well-known Syriac writer, but the theory of Arabic origin has been advanced. The latter is not an evidence of Moslem influence in this case, since by this time the various Christian churches of the Near East were using Arabic, the dominant spoken language, for literary purposes.

The relations of the Monophysite Ethiopian church to that of the Syrian Monophysites is well documented. Regardless of the literary origins of the poem, the strophic rhyme scheme is similar to that of the later Syriac poetry. Since the Syriac use of rhyme is derived from Arabic this would, in the ultimate instance, be an example of the indirect influence of Arabic. Earlier Syriac poetry utilized the principle of syllabic count which existed before the Arabic principle of rhyme was superimposed. As has been noted, Geᶜez poetry does not involve the principle of syllabic count. The most probable explanation of the Geᶜez strophic forms is that the Syriac principle of rhymed stanzas was amalgamated in Ethiopic with the earlier practice of rhymed prose resulting in the typical strophic forms of Geᶜez ecclesiastical poetry.

In Amharic, as in Geᶜez, there is a contrast between earlier and later prosodic systems. The rhymed prose of the Royal Songs, the earliest surviving example of Amharic poetry, is succeeded by the principle of syllabic count combined with the rhyme of the earlier form. In the existing collections, short sung couplets consisting of two lines, almost always of twelve syllables each with a caesura after the sixth syllable, are very common. Longer poems sometimes consist of sequences of such rhymed couplets and therefore have the rhyme scheme a a b b c c. . . . In other examples, a single rhyme is found throughout the poem, or there is occasional change of rhyme, just as earlier in some of the Royal Songs. Some published examples do not employ syllabic count and when monorhymed, coincide completely in form with the early rhymed prose.

The source of the principle of syllabic count in modern Amharic poetry is uncertain. It is possibly derived from the modern Arabic quatrain (*ʕarobi*) as described for Tunis by Stumme (1893). The *ʕarobi* is a four line stanza with rhyme pattern a b c b, or sometimes a b a b. In the Tunisian examples, syllabic count has replaced the classical quantitative meter as it has in much modern Arabic popular poetry, particularly from North Africa. Most of the *ʕarobis* in Stumme's collection have six syllables per line. In a collection of Berber poetry from the Riff, almost all the examples are twelve-syllable rhymed couplets with caesura after the sixth syllable (Renisio 1932). These two instances suggest a wide extension for this form, particularly in North Africa. The difference between a rhymed couplet of twelve-syllable lines with caesura after the sixth, and a quatrain of six-syllable lines with the rhyme pattern a b c b is, of course, purely graphic, so that the most common Amharic verse form coincides completely in its prosodic rules with the *ʕarobi*. It is the absence of this form in published collections of popular verse of Arabic speaking areas nearer to Amharic than North Africa that suggests caution in accepting the *ʕarobi* as the model for modern Amharic verse. There is the further fact that languages other than Amharic in this area have syllabic count along with rhyme, and the historical connection of these verse forms to Amharic would have to be accounted for.

One example is Saho, a Cushitic language of Eritrea. The total published poetic material is apparently very small, being confined to a small collection of songs collected by Reinisch (1889–90, vol. I). These are usually rhymed, though often only sporadically. However, numbers 4 and 7 of the collection show great regularity. Each is of six lines with rhyme scheme a b c b d b and with the same number of syllables in each line, five in the first instance, and four in the second. Again if we consider the lines as equivalent to Amharic hemistichs the resemblance is close, the main differences being in the number of syllables and the fact that the poems have six hemistichs rather than four. There are, however, occasional examples of six hemistichs or more in Amharic verse, the Tunisian *ʕarobi*, and among the Beni Iznassen Berbers of the Riff. Besides, Amharic occasionally employs a ten-syllable line with caesura after the fifth syllable.

Number 7 of Reinisch (1889–90) will illustrate the form in Saho.

sūm silēmān
nō dēsamā
lubāk belli
dat haššamā
ginni Falūm
kä Gazāmā

Prince Sileman, our protector, like the lion is his black hair. He is like the Jinn of Falum and Gazama.

The extensive collections of Galla poetry display in their versification a general resemblance to the Amharic couplet and the Saho examples just discussed. Galla poems are usually divided into four-line strophes with rhyme schemes a b a b or a b c b. The number of syllables in each line is fixed and is the same throughout the poem as a general rule. Poems with four-syllable lines are rare, with five frequent, with six or seven the most common of all, and with eight syllables likewise frequent. The examples with six syllables and rhyme scheme a b c b are, of course, formally identical with the usual Amharic couplet. There are cases of longer lines with a regular caesura. Thus there is one poem consisting of eleven-syllable lines with a caesura after the fourth syllable.

Rhyme is somewhat sporadic in Galla poetry but the number of syllables is fixed practically without exception. An occasional device of Galla poetry is vowel harmony between the first and third lines and between the second and fourth lines of the quatrain. In the following example this is carried out completely:

| | |
|---|---|
| lensan lon gusa | Lensa [a kind of grass] causes the cattle to dry up |
| bia garati | On the mountain; |
| densan lon busa | Flight exposes cattle, |
| iya nafati | To screams of desperation. |

Tigrinya is an Ethiopian Semitic language spoken to the north of Amharic and in the same general region as the extinct Geʿez, or classical Ethiopic. Unlike Amharic, Saho, and Galla, there is no regular use of the rhymed couplet. Rhyme shifts at irregular intervals, as in some of the medieval Amharic Royal Songs, but these changes are more frequent, every four to seven lines on the average, with occasional unrhymed lines. In much of the poetry there seems to be no internal metrical regulation of the line but in other cases the principle of syllabic count is unmistakably present. In most of Conti Rossini's extensive collection (1903–5) we have a ten-syllable line with caesura after the fourth syllable. A single, quite long poem on the battle of Addi Cheleto (Conti Rossini 1906) has five-syllable lines with the usual change of end rhyme at irregular intervals.

Tigrinya does not share the Geʿez-Amharic tradition of adding *ə* after a final consonant in recitation. The rhyme therefore, which consists in principle in identity of the last syllable, may be either CV or CVC. The equivalence of similar consonants for purposes of rhyme is carried very far, as in the neighboring Tigre. Not only are *r* and *l* treated as equivalents but also *k*, $k^h$, and *h*, and likewise the pairs *q* and $q^w$, *g* and $g^w$, *n* and *ñ*, and the laryngeals ʕ and ʔ. In certain poems, much as in Tigre, all voiced stops *b*, *d*, *j*, *g*, and $g^w$ are treated as equivalents. The rhymes of Conti Rossini (1903–5, no. 157) will illustrate this: *gar*, *gar*, *$g^w$al*, *$g^w$al*, *$g^w$al*, *$g^w$al*, *jor*, *gar*, *bar*, *bar*, *gar*.

The remaining language of the Ethiopian area for which extensive poetic collections exist is Tigre, another Semitic language, spoken northeast of Tigrinya. In Tigre poetry each line is divided into two hemistichs. There does not appear to be any principle of metrical organization within the line. As in Arabic and as in the earliest Geʿez poetry, the same rhyme is maintained throughout the entire poem.

The rule of rhyme is in principle close to that of Arabic classical poetry in that there is some regulation of the penultimate syllable in the line. Unlike Amharic and Geʿez no *ə* is added after final consonants. A marked feature of Tigre rhyme is the degree to which phonetically similar consonants are equated for purposes of rhyme; this has led previous observers to the conclusion that the consonants do not participate in the rhyme.[5] As a matter of fact, the rules are quite exact. Because an *ə* is not added to a final consonant in recitation, rhymes fall into two classes as in Arabic, "fettered," ending in a consonant and "free," ending in a vowel. In "fettered" rhyme the final consonant which must always belong to the same class of phonetically similar consonants is always preceded by the same vowel. In "free" rhyme the final vowel must always be the same, the preceding consonant must belong to the same consonant class and the preceding syllable is likewise subject to some restrictions. If the syllable is open, i.e. ends in a vowel, it must be open through the whole poem and have the same vowel. If not, it must be closed through the whole poem with no restriction on the particular consonant which closes the penultimate syllable. Sometimes we have a rhyme in which the same final vowel is always preceded by two consonants, but there are no restrictions on the combinations allowed.

For purposes of rhyme the consonants fall into a number of almost mutually exclusive classes. These classes are the liquids (*r*, *l*, *n*, and occasionally *m*), the labials (*b*, *m*), the laryngeals (*ḥ*, ʕ, ʔ, and *h*), *y*, which forms a class by itself, and the obstruents consisting of the remaining consonants except *w*, for example *t*, *d*, *t*ʾ, *s*, *z*, *f*, *k*, *q*, *ǰ*, *š*, etc. The consonant *w* never seems to be used in rhyme.

These rules of rhyme may be illustrated as follows. An example of fettered rhyme consisting of a final liquid always preceded by *a* is found in Littmann (1913–15), poem 71, which rhymes *-an*, *-ar*, *-ar*, *-ar*, *-al*, etc. The rule of loose rhyme in which the penultimate syllable is open and always has the same vowel is exemplified by poem 7 in the same collection. The rhyme here consists of final *a*, preceded by an obstruent, preceded by the vowel *ä*. The rhymes of this eight-line poem are *-äka*, *-äta*, *-äsa*, *-äta*, *-äta*, *-äsa*, *-äša*, *äta*. An example of loose rhyme with penultimate closed syllable is poem 32 of Littmann, another eight-line poem in which the final vowel is *e* always preceded by an obstruent which is always preceded by a consonant without limitations as to class. The rhymes are *-mde*, *-rqe*, *-ǰǰe*, *-zze*, *-dde*, *-nte*, *-sse*, *-dde*.

Except for the hemistich division, the resemblance of Tigre verse prosody to Arabic rhymed prose is patent. Even the extensive substitution of similar

[5] Thus Noeldeke (1917–18: 14) remarks "This rhyme is more careful than appears at first glance. Still it pays little attention to the identity of consonants."

consonants for each other in the rhyme has its parallel in the relative frequency of this practice, called *ʔikfā* by the Arabs in rhymed prose and *rajaz*.[6] The Tigre are Moslems and subject to strong Arabic cultural influence. As with the earliest Geʿez and Amharic rhymed prose we may hesitate between the alternative explanations of Arabic origin and continuation of a common South Semitic tradition.

In addition to the languages already mentioned, Beja should probably be included in the East African rhyming area. The small collection of Roper (1923) seems to be the only published material. These all are divided into four-line stanzas without any apparent metrical system. Rhyme is frequent but sporadic. Several poems, however, are rhymed throughout. The form, therefore, again approximates the rhymed prose of Tigre and the earlier Geʿez and Amharic poetry.

Two other peoples in Northern Africa have prosodic systems, the Nubians and the Berbers. The Nubians inhabit the Nile Valley of the northern part of the Sudan. There are also speakers of related dialects in the hills of Kordofan and still farther west. We are only concerned here with the Nile Nubians. But a small amount of poetic material has been published—much of it incidental to ethnologic texts in the form—for example, marriage songs. Except for some songs appended by Lepsius to his grammar (Lepsius 1880), none of these show prosodic regulation. In Lepsius' material, the songs are all divided into stanzas of four lines each with rhymes a b a b or a a b b in each stanza and differing from stanza to stanza. The rhyme usually consists of repetition of the same word.

An example follows (Lepsius 1880: 256):

galaban šaǰan tōd wēki
ekk aminsu dīkol wēki
en anīsa mutta bōgsun
sāla-būn olmisseg bōgsun

A son of worry and of sorrow we considered you. We considered you as one who died. Your friend cut her hair and threw it away. She is sick and has been weeping.

The eight-syllable line, of course, is reminiscent of Swahili although a direct influence from this quarter seems unlikely. The Nubians are Moslems and universally bilingual in Arabic. In one Nubian text, an Arabic poem of three lines occurs with end rhyme and eight syllables in each line (Junker and Schaefer 1921–22: 90). Such eight-syllable lines, usually but not always quantitative, are common in Egyptian popular poetry. The knowledge of Egyptian Arabic poetry shown by this quotation in a Nubian text is very

[6]Goldziher (1896–99): part 1, p. 79.

strong evidence for the Arabic origin of the principle of rhyme and the line of eight syllables in Nile Nubian poetry.

The Berber language is spoken widely in North Africa and the Sahara in many distinct dialectal variations, some of which deserve to be ranked as separate languages. We are dealing here with a number of largely independent local poetic traditions. The absence of any recorded poetic literature from many areas makes it difficult to draw valid conclusions of a historical nature at the present stage of our knowledge. Three main types of prosody can be distinguished in the existing material. These are: (1) absence of any prosodic principle; (2) rhyme unaccompanied by metrical regulation of the line; (3) rhyme combined with syllabic count.

The first of these types, the absence of any prosodic principle, seems particularly characteristic of the Shilḥ and Beraber group of southern and central Morocco. One poem recorded by Boulifa in the Demnat area of southern Morocco (Boulifa 1908: 63) has end rhyme, shifting at intervals in the course of the poem. In the absence of rhyme, this form therefore approximates that of the medieval Amharic Royal Songs. There is some possibility that the poetry of this part of Morocco has a fixed number of stresses per line, but our linguistic knowledge is insufficient to verify the hypothesis.

The Riffian area of northern Morocco is one in which rhyme is normal. Biarnay's examples (1917) from the Ait Temseman are generally rhymed couplets, though a few are longer—the longest example running to eight lines. Renisio's Riffian material which shows two or sometimes three-line poems with rhyme, is drawn from three tribes, the Ait Ouriaghel, the Beni Tuzin, and the Beni Iznassen. Of these examples, a majority for all three tribes consists of 12-syllable lines with caesura after the sixth syllable. In the rest, the line does not appear to be metrically regulated. The typical form, as has been noted earlier, is therefore identical prosodically with the common modern Amharic couplet form.

The Zenaga of Mauretania, to judge from Nicolas's data, fall into the second category as defined above—that is rhyme without syllabic count. The typical form is here the single quatrain or a string of quatrains each with the rhyme scheme a b a b.

Tuareg poetry, of which Foucauld (1925–30) has made an extensive collection for the Ahaggar region, is characterized by poems of varying length, some quite long, with the same end rhyme throughout. Foucauld himself describes the poetry as quantitative. However, since there are so many inconsistencies in the application of the schemes as described, and since no linguistic basis in vowel quantitative distinctions has been reported in any other Berber dialect or indeed, by other students of the Tuareg languages, it appears that provisionally at least, we should deny a quantitative basis for this poetry. What does occur is syllabic count with regular caesura. Each type has an indigenous name, which is applied to the melody to which it is sung. The types found are a nine-syllable line with caesura after the fourth syllable, a ten-syllable line with caesura after the fifth syllable, and a ten-syllable line with caesura after the sixth syllable.

The remaining area for which extensive collections exist is that of the Kabyles in Algeria. The typical rhyme scheme here is a a b a a b a a b . . . or a a b a b a a b a b a a b a b. . . . In longer poems the rhyme may shift at irregular intervals. This poetry, unlike that of the Riffian Berbers and the Tuaregs, is not sung. Much of it is by known individual poets. In some instances, syllabic count is not employed. In others (e.g. Luciani 1899), the three lines of the stanza have seven, five, and seven syllables respectively. In the poetry of Sid Mojand (1914), each poem consists of three tercets, that is of nine lines, with the syllabic count seven, five, and seven for each tercet as in Luciani's collection.

There is also a single published example of the *tasmīṭ murabbaᶜ* from the island of Djerba (De Calassanti-Motylinski 1885). The apparent rarity of this form as compared to others with no direct Arabic parallel makes one hesitate to accept this as proof of the Arabic origin of Berber prosody. It is more likely a later case of local influence on an already established prosodic tradition, whether of ultimately Arabic provenance or not.

From the data just reviewed, the outstanding impression is that of the great prosodic variety of various Berber regional poetic traditions. In one matter, at least, there is agreement, suggesting a common basis for these local developments. This is the rule of rhyme. Unlike any other known African system, the rhyme involves phonetic similarity or identity from the last vowel until the end of the verse. If the final sound of the line is a vowel, this means that the only requirement is vocalic identity and there are no restrictions on the previous consonant. If the lines end in one or more consonant then both this consonant and the previous vowel are involved in the rhyme. Everywhere the pairs *n* and *m*, *r* and *l* are treated as equivalents for purposes of rhyme. Among the Tuareg these equivalences are carried much further. The unvoiced stops form one group, the voiced stops another. The unvoiced fricatives *f* and *s* rhyme with each other. A final cluster of two consonants may rhyme with a single consonant, if the final consonant of the cluster is a permitted rhyme in itself. As an example, we cite Foucauld (1925–30), no. 28, in which the rhyme consists of *a* followed by an unvoiced stop, most frequently *t*: *at*, *art*, *at*, *ayt*, *art*, *art*, *aq*, *ant*, *at*, *alt*, *at*, *ak*, *ak*, *at*.

A further evidence of the basic unity of Berber poetic tradition is the common term *izli* for a two- or three-line poem, regardless of the regional differences in prosodic form.

The possible origin of the Riffian couplet of twelve-syllable lines with caesura after the sixth syllable in the Arabic *ʕarobi* has already been mentioned. There is likewise a possible Arabic source for the common Kabyle rhyme scheme a a b a a b. . . . In Fuad (1939), a manuscript collection from Egypt possibly dating from the seventeenth century, a single long stanzaic poem (no. 30) has the following elaborate variant of the basic fourfold *zajal*: a a b, a a b, a a b, c c d, e e f, e e f, e e f, c c d, etc. In each tercet, the first and third lines consist of two *rajaz* feet (– – ⏑ – / – – ⏑ –) and the second line of one (– – ⏑ –). The syllabic count is thus 8, 4, 8. The common Kabyle type likewise has a different and smaller number of syllables for the second line as opposed to the first and third (7, 5, 7). Moreover, Sid Mojand always uses three of these tercets producing a nine-line poem whose rhyme scheme is identical with the portions of the above poem which have non-recurrent rhyme. In the actual singing of the *zajal* these recurrent and non-recurrent parts are separated by an instrumental interlude.

In general, since the Berbers are all Moslems, large numbers are bilingual in Arabic, and their language contains a very large number of Arabic loan words—there is a real basis for assuming Arabic influence in this, as in many other cultural features.

As was indicated in the opening section, this paper has been of a survey nature and many of the conclusions are merely of a tentative nature. The great variety of prosodic systems in Africa is apparent. It is hoped that the gaps in synchronic material and both synchronic and diachronic analyses that it reveals, will be a stimulus to further work in this area. The outstanding impression in the historic dimensions is the vast reach of certain and, in many cases highly probable, Arabic influence in the northern part of Africa—an influence well documented for many other aspects of the culture of the area.

Some further observations on the question of rhyme may be of interest. Unlike syllabic count which may arise independently through the mechanism of a varying text set to a constantly repeated melodic line, and quantitative verse which may originate in the same fashion when the language contains quantitative distinctions, it is not easy to discern any obvious way in which systematic rhyme can arise. Sporadic rhyme, particularly through the literary device of repetition of the same word, occurs almost everywhere but its utilization as a prosodic principle is another matter. In Africa, the single ultimate origin of all rhyme either in a common South Semitic tradition, or, far more likely, through the direct or indirect intermediary of Arabic, is highly probable. Outside of the area considered here, the eventual Arabic origin of rhyme in western European languages and in Hebrew, Syriac, and Coptic has been indicated. To this should be added Persian and certain languages influenced in turn by Persian literary forms. With the possible exception of Chinese, it is likely that all rhyme has a single origin.

We perhaps never think of rhyme as an invention. To speakers of English with its tradition of rhymed poetry, rhyme appears as something "natural." It seems likely rather that rhyme is one of those devices whose invention by no means lies on the surface, but whose inherent esthetic expressiveness and applicability to all languages leads to its facile adoption in almost all instances where a people become acquainted with the possibility of its employment.

## References Cited

Babalola, Adeboye. 1957. "Ijala: The Poetry of Yoruba Hunters," *Black Orpheus.* (Ibadan, Nigeria), no. 1, pp. 5–7.

Basset, H. 1920. *Essai sur la littérature des Berbères*. Algiers.

Biarnay, S. 1917. *Étude sur les dialectes Berbères au Rif*. Paris.

Bloch, A. 1946. *Vers und Sprache im Altarabischen*. Basel.

Boulifa, Said. 1908. *Textes Berbères en dialecte de l'Atlas*. Paris.

———. 1934. *Recueil de poésies Kabyles*. Algiers.

Cerulli, E. 1913. "Conti e proverbi somali nel dialetto degli Habar Auwāl," *Rivista degli Studi Orientali* (Rome), 7: 797–836.

———. 1919–20. "Somali Songs and Little Texts," *Journal of the African Society*, 19: 135–40.

———. 1956. *Storia della letteratura etiopica*. Milan.

Chaine, M. 1920–21. "La poésie chez les Ethiopiens: Poésie amharique," *Revue de l'Orient Chrétien*, pp. 306–26; 401–25.

Conti Rossini, C. 1903–5. "Conti populari tigrai," *Zeitschrift für Assyriologie*, 17: 23–52; 18: 320–86.

———. 1906. "Poemetto lirico tigrai per la battaglia di Addi Cheleto," in *Orientalistische Studien Noeldeke gewidmet*, 2: 925–39.

Dalman, G. A. 1901. *Palästinischer Diwan*. Leipzig.

Dammann, E. 1940. *Dichtungen in der Lamu-Mundart des Swahili*. Hamburg.

De Calassanti-Motylinski, A. 1885. "Chanson berbère de Djerba," *Bulletin de Correspondance Africaine* (Algiers), pp. 461–64.

Desparmet, J. 1905. "La poésie Arabe actuelle à Blida et sa métrique," *Actes du XIVe Congress Internationale des Orientalistes* (Algiers), 3: 437–602.

Duisberg, A. von. 1913. *Grundriss der Kanuri-Sprache in Bornu*. Berlin.

Elder, E. E. 1926. *Egyptian Colloquial Arabic Reader*. Oxford.

Faitlovitch, J. 1910. "Versi abissini," *Giornale della Societa Asiatica Italiana*, 23: 1–88.

Foucauld, C. E. 1925–30. *Poésies touareges: dialecte de l'Ahaggar*. 2 vols., Paris.

Freytag, G. W. 1880. *Darstellung der Arabischen Verskunst*. Bonn.

Fuad, Hasanein Ali. 1939. "Ägyptische Volkslieder," *Veröffentlichungen des Orientalischen Seminars der Universität Tübingen*, heft 10.

Gaden, H. 1935. "La Vie d'el Hadj Omar, Qacida en Poular," *Travaux et Mémoires, Institut d'Ethnologie*, vol. 21.

Gies, Hermann. 1879. *alfanūnu ssabʕatu*: *Ein Beitrag zum Kenntnis sieben neuerer arabischen Versarten*. Leipzig.

Goldziher, I. 1896–99. *Abhandlungen zur Arabischen Philologie*. Leiden.

Greenberg, J. H. 1947. "Swahili Prosody," *Journal of the American Oriental Society*, 67: 24–30.

———. 1949. "Hausa Verse Prosody," *Journal of the American Oriental Society*, 69: 125–35.
Grohmann, A. 1919. "Äthiopische Marienhymnen," *Sächsische Akademie der Wissenschaften, Abhandlungen, phil.-hist. Klasse*, vol. 23.
Guidi, I. 1889. "Le canzoni geez-amarina in onore di Re Abissini," *Reale Academia dei Lincei, Rendiconti* (Rome), pp. 52–66.
Hartmann, M. 1897. *Das arabische Strophengedicht: I. Das Muwaššah*. Weimar.
Ibn Hishām. 1858. *Das Leben Muhammads nach Muhammad Ibn Ishak*, ed. by F. Wüstenfeld. Vol. I, Göttingen.
Jahn, A. 1902. *Die Mehri-Sprache in Südarabien: Texte und Wörterbuch*. Vienna.
Junker, H., and H. Schaefer. 1921–22. *Nubische Texte im Kenzi-Dialekt*. 2 vols., Vienna.
Justinard, L. 1925. "Poemes Chleuhs Recueillis au Sous," *Revue du Monde Musulman*, 60: 63–107.
———. 1928. "Poésies en dialect du Sous Marocain d'après un manuscrit arabico-berbere," *Journal asiatique* 213: 217–51.
Kirk, J. W. C. 1905. *A Grammar of the Somali Language*. Cambridge, Eng.
Kolmodin, J. 1912. "Traditions de Tsazzega et Hazzega, Textes tigrigna," *Archives d'Études Orientales*, 5: 1.
Lemm, O. von. 1903. *Das Triadon, ein Sahidisches Gedicht mit Arabischer Übersetzung*. St. Petersburg.
Lepsius, K. R. 1880. *Nubische Grammatik, mit einer Einleitung über die Völker und Sprachen Afrikas*. Berlin.
Littmann, E. 1907. "Canzone tigre in onore del Governatore italiano," *Rivista degli Studi Orientali*, 1: 211–15.
———. 1913–15. "Lieder der Tigre-Stamme," *Publications of the Princeton Expedition to Abyssinia*, vols. 3, 4. Leiden.
———. 1914. *Die altamharischen Kaiserlieder*. Strassburg.
———. 1925. *Galla Verskunst; ein Beitrag zur allgemeinen Verskunst nebst metrischen Übersetzungen*. Tübingen.
Luciani, D. 1899. *Chansons Kabyles de Smail Azikkiou*. Algiers.
Meinhof, C. 1924. "Das Lied des Liongo," *Zeitschrift für Eingeborenen-Sprachen*, 15: 241–65.
Meissner, Bruno. 1902. "Neuarabische Gedichte aus dem Iraq," *Mitteilungen des Seminars für orientalische Sprachen*, 5: Abt. 2: 77–131; 249–301.
Menendez Pidal, R. 1943. *Poesia arabe y poesia europea*. 2d ed., Buenos Aires.
Mueller, David H. 1905. *Soqoṭri-Texte*. Vienna.
Neuhaus, G. 1935. "Kitabu Maulidi," *Mitteilungen des Seminars für orientalische Sprachen*, 38, no. 3: 145–201.
Nicolas, F. 1953. *La Langue Berbère de Mauretanie*. Institut Français d'Afrique Noire, Mémoires no. 33.
Nketia, J. H. 1955. *Funeral Dirges of the Akan People*. Achimoto, Ghana.
Noeldeke, T. 1917–18. "Tigre-Lieder," *Zeitschrift für Assyriologie*, 31: 1–25.
Perruchon, J. 1892. *Vie de Lalibala, Roi d'Ethiopie*. Paris.
Prietze, R. 1916. "Haussa-Sänger mit Übersetzung und Erklärung." *Königliche Gesellschaft der Wissenschaften zu Göttingen, Nachrichten, Phil.-hist. Klasse*, pp. 163–230, 552–604.
Reichardt, C. J. 1859. *Three Original Fulah Pieces*. Berlin.

Reinhardt, C. 1894. *Ein arabischer Dialekt gesprochen in 'Omān und Zanzibar*. Berlin.
Reinisch, L. 1889–90. *Die Saho-Sprache*. 2 vols., Vienna.
———. 1900. *A. W. Schleichers Somali-Texte*. Vienna.
Renisio. 1932. *Étude sur les dialectes Berbères des Beni Iznassen, du Rif et des Senhaja de Srair*. Paris.
Robinson, C. H. 1896. *Specimens of Hausa Literature*. Cambridge, Eng.
———. 1930. *Hausa Grammar*. 5th ed., London.
Roper, E. M. 1923. "Poetry of the Hadendiwa," *Sudan Notes and Records*, 10: 147–58.
Serjeant, R. B. 1951. "South Arabian Poetry." Vol. I, *Prose and Poetry from Ḥadramawt*. London.
Sid Mojand. 1914. *El Jardin de los Deseos, poesias berberiscas de Sid Mojand*, trans. and ed. by Isaac Munoz. Madrid and Buenos Aires.
Simmons, D. C. 1955. "Specimens of Efik Folklore," *Folklore* 66: 417–24.
Socin, A. 1900. "Diwan aus Centralarabien," *Königliche Sächsische Gesellschaft der Wissenschaften, Abhandlungen, Phil.-hist. Klasse*, 19, nos. 1–3.
Sonneck, C. 1902–6. *Chants arabes du Maghreb. Étude sur le dialecte et la poésie populaire de l'Afrique du Nord*. 3 vols., Paris.
Stumme, Hans. 1893. *Tunisische Märchen und Gedichte*. Leipzig.
———. 1895. *Dichtkunst und Gedichte der Schluh*. Leipzig.
———. 1896. *Märchen und Gedichte aus der Stadt Tripolis in N.A.* Vol. 1. Leipzig.
Vito, L. de. 1893. *Esercizi di lettera in lingua tigrigna*. Rome.

PART IV

# PSYCHOLINGUISTICS

# Studies in the Psychological Correlates of the Sound System of American English

*with James J. Jenkins*

## I. Measuring Linguistic Distance from English

It is a linguistic commonplace that the sequences of phonemes in English, as probably in all languages, are subject to powerful constraints. For initial and final consonant sequences rules have been formulated by a number of linguists.[1] One of the consequences of these rules as formulated by these writers, is that they allow for the generation of many sequences which do not occur in English, e.g. */strib/. It is reasonable to hypothesize that such a sequence will elicit a response from English-speaking subjects different from that of an existent sequence, e.g. /strʌk/, but different also from such a sequence as */gvsurs/ which cannot be generated from rules of English consonant sequences. One would conjecture that on some psychological dimension of strangeness or distance from English */strib/ would be located between /strʌk/ and */gvsurs/. Indeed we are likely to be dealing with a dimension more complex than a three-point scale consisting of existing sequences, generatable sequences, and non-generatable sequences. Consider, for example, the sequence */stwip/. Here the prevocalic sequence of three consonants conforms to the general rule of sequence /s/, unvoiced stop (in this case /t/), and liquid or semivowel (in this case /w/). However, it is less

These studies were begun at the Center for Advanced Study in the Behavioral Sciences, where both authors were fellows in 1958–59 and 1964–65. We are grateful to the Social Science Research Council and to the Carnegie Corporation of New York, who have directly and indirectly supported our work. We wish to thank Mr. Duane Martin for his assistance with computations and with the programming and running of the subsequent factor analyses. We would also like to thank the Psychology Department of the University of Minnesota for the use of its facilities. The four studies in this series were originally published in two parts.

[1] L. Bloomfield, *Language* (New York, 1933), pp. 127–38; B. Whorf, "Linguistics as an Exact Science," *Technology Review* 43 (1940): pp. 61–63, 80–83, reprinted in *Language, Thought and Reality*, ed. John B. Carroll (Cambridge, Mass., 1956), pp. 220–32.

close to the pattern of English than the above-mentioned */strib/. This is because /stw-/ does not occur as an initial sequence in any English word although it can be analogically deduced from, say, *skr-*:*skw-*, = *str-*:*x*, where *skr-*, *skw-*, and *str-* all occur. Here we have, so to speak, a combination which is not as possible as */strib/ but more possible than */gvsurs/. We would predict, therefore, that it should take a correspondingly intermediate position on our hypothetical scale of nearness to English.

Faced with the present problem, the reaction of the psychologist and linguist is characteristically different. The psychologist immediately thinks of experiments and subject reactions. The linguist reaches for pencil and paper and works for refinement of definition based on logico-mathematical manipulation of the structure of existent forms in the language. These two procedures are logically independent. The possibility of devising a mathematical scale based on the structure of English, to be presently described, and then measuring subject reactions on the basis of psychological dimensions such as those just mentioned, makes this an area of possible psycholinguistic investigation. Much as in classical psychophysics, we have an objectively derivable dimension which can be investigated in relation to its psychological correlates.

A common linguistic procedure which might be employed here is substitution. Thus, for example, */lʌt/ is close to English because we can reach existent English words by single substitutions in each position, e.g. *but*, *let*, *luck*. In the case of *stwip*, we can get 'strip' by substituting *r* for *w*, but since no existent word begins with *stw-* it is clear that no substitutions in the fourth or fifth position can give an English word. However, if we move to substitutions in two places simultaneously, we can, for example, by substituting *-kr-* for *-tw-* get *scrip* whereas such measures will still be of no avail in sequences such as *gvsurs*. It is clear that length plays a role also. The longer the sequence, the more difficult it becomes to produce English words by substitutions. It seems advisable, therefore, to hold the factor of length constant. For the experiments described here, sequences of four phonemes all of the form *CCVC* were chosen. If we have a sequence of length *n*, we can substitute from zero up to *n* at a time and each such number of substitutions can be done in $\binom{n}{i}$ ways where *i* takes on values from 0 to *n*. The total will, of course, be $2^n$, in this case 16. By zero substitution we will mean leaving the word as it is, in which case it will only qualify if it already exists in English. At the other end of the scale any sequence of four letters can become English by substitution in all places simultaneously. Since we wish our scale to reflect distance so that the larger numbers will be given to words farther from English we will subtract the total number of successful substitutions from 17. In this way a word which can only become English by a single type

*Table 1*

| A | B | C | |
|---|---|---|---|
| 0 | 1 | 0 | |
| 1 | 4 | 4 | (e.g., slab, crab, club, clam) |
| 2 | 6 | 6 | |
| 3 | 4 | 4 | |
| 4 | 1 | 1 | |

of substitution, that is in all four places, will have a rating of 17 − 1 = 16 and a word which exists in English will allow of all 16 substitutions and have the value 17 − 16 = 1. To illustrate with a syllable used in Experiment A, /klæb/ was rated as 2, that is, as very close to English, in the following way. In Table 1, the first column gives the number of simultaneous substitutions, the second column the number of ways $\binom{n}{i}$ in which this can be done and the third column the number of these which give English words.

The total in column C is 15 and the rating of /klæb/ is 17 − 15 = 2. The identity substitution is allowed. Thus any existent word automatically receives all possible substitutions. Substitution by zero is not allowed. For example, by substituting zero in the second place of *klæb* we would get *kæb*. Usually it makes no difference to the rating which decision is taken in regard to identity and zero substitution.

The linguist then devised a list of 24 sequences of the form *CCVC* designed to sample the sixteen-point scale just described. This list, hereafter referred to as List 1, contained the items in Table 2. The linguistic substitution scale will hereafter be referred to as S.

Experiment A, designed as a preliminary exploration, was carried out at the Center for Advanced Study in the Behavioral Sciences in the early months of 1959. The words of List 1 were recorded by the linguist on a Revere tape recorder in two random orders.

Each syllable was pronounced twice with a three-second delay between repetitions and an interval of fifteen seconds between the last occurrence of each word and the first occurrence of the next word. The technique used was free magnitude estimation. Each of the six subjects was tested individually.[2] The instructions were as follows:

This is an experiment on the relationship of one-syllable foreign words to English. You will hear each of these words repeated two times, so that you can hear each word clearly. Some of these words are from languages that are very close to English, some not so closely related, and some from languages that are very distant from English.

[2] For those unacquainted with free magnitude estimation, the instructions for subjects which follow should provide sufficient indication.

*Table 2*

| Syllable no. | S | Syllable no. | S | Syllable no. | S |
|---|---|---|---|---|---|
| 1. stɩk | 1 | 9. klɛb | 4 | 17. žwʊp | 12 |
| 2. græs | 1 | 10. swæč | 4 | 18. ðyʌŋ | 12 |
| 3. spɛl | 1 | 11. srʌm | 5 | 19. vrüɤ | 13 |
| 4. trʌk | 1 | 12. θlæš | 5 | 20. žlöp | 13 |
| 5. slʌk | 2 | 13. θwæǰ | 8 | 21. ðgᵼx | 16 |
| 6. swɩt | 2 | 14. trʊg | 8 | 22. zbüɤ | 16 |
| 7. klæb | 2 | 15. træx | 9 | 23. mböł | 16 |
| 8. brʌd | 2 | 16. žrɩk | 9 | 24. mzœç | 16 |

Your task will be, when you hear one of these words, to give me a number, as a judgment as to how far this seems to be from being an English word. Use this first word and score as a basis for your next judgment. If that seems to be twice as far from English, you would give me a number that is twice as large. If the word seems to be half as far from English, give a number that is half as large. If it is ten times as far, give a number that is ten times as large, and so on. Remember, you can use any system of numbers. Just choose some numbers that you feel comfortable with. Are there any questions?

Let's try a word to see how it will go. (Put on tape for one word.)

How far would you say that is from English?—That's fine. Now if the next word seems to be twice as far away, you would say ______. If it is half as far away, you would say ______. If it is ten times as far away, ______. O.K.?

Let's try it from the beginning and run through the sequence.

(Put the tape on for all 24 words and record the responses.)

Now I would like to have some personal information. (Personal questionnaire administered.)

We will now go through the list in a different order. You can change your scale if you like, but that is not necessary, and it does not matter if you do not give the same response to the same words. The reason we repeat the list of words is to help you get more familiar with the procedure and to get away from any order effects that might exist due to chance pairings of different words.

(Continue the tape and leave it on for the rest of the experiment.)

An overall impression of the results of Experiment A can be gathered from Figure 1, in which the results of the two trials for the six subjects are given. For the abscissa, the values are those of the linguistic rating scale S as described above. The set of 24 words are divided into six groups of four words each with the mean values 1, 2, 4.5, 8.5, 12.5, and 16, respectively. The ordinate values are the means of each set of four words on the magnitude estimation scales for the six subjects. The mean for each word is the mean of the six subjects, with each subject's ratings equated at a mean of 50. The result is, except for a threshold effect at the value of 1 of the linguistic rating,

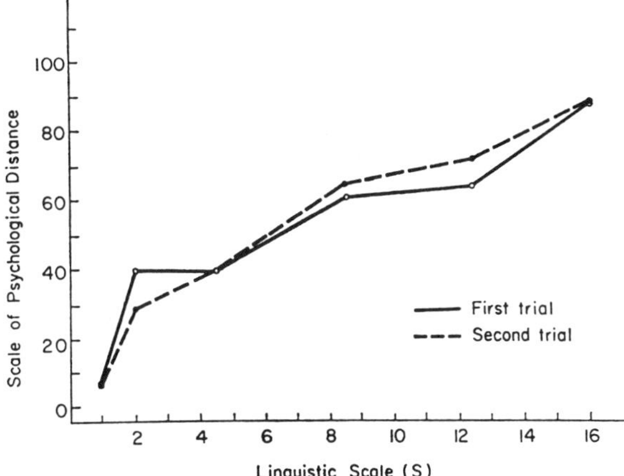


*Figure 1*

*Table 3*

| S | First trial | Second trial |
|---|---|---|
| 1 | 8.21 | 7.81 |
| 2 | 39.24 | 29.03 |
| 4.5 | 39.09 | 39.33 |
| 8.5 | 62.40 | 64.76 |
| 12.5 | 64.47 | 72.22 |
| 16 | 86.77 | 86.99 |

very nearly linear. For the second trial, a line $D_{50} = 20.75 + 4.14\ S$ very nearly coincides with four of the six points. The values of these means for each of the two trials are contained in Table 3. The means for individual words of List 1 for the second trial are contained in Table 4. Quite large deviation from the expected result may be noted for a few individual words, notably *θlæš* ranked as closer to English than was hypothesized and *brʌd* and *srʌm* farther away. It turned out that several subjects had misheard *θlæš* as *flæš* 'flash' on a recording of only mediocre fidelity. The deviation away from English in the items *brʌd* and *srʌm* are both possibly attributable to the fact that the linguist, a New York City native, has an *r* sound which is different from that of Midwestern and Far Western speakers and that his vowel *ʌ* is farther back than that of most dialects of American English.

A discussion of the results of this experiment as described by the linguist to a Linguistics Department Seminar at Columbia University raised the issue of foreign sounds as against English sounds in the judgment of the subjects. It was pointed out that such items as *zbüɣ* contained two non-English sounds. The objection might be boldly stated as follows: Subjects are confronted with

*Table 4*

| Word | S | Means | Word | S | Means | Word | S | Means |
|---|---|---|---|---|---|---|---|---|
| 1. stɩk | 1 | 6.60 | 9. klɛb | 4 | 42.53 | 17. žwʊp | 12 | 64.28 |
| 2. græs | 1 | 10.35 | 10. swæč | 4 | 32.48 | 18. ðyʌŋ | 12 | 66.07 |
| 3. spɛl | 1 | 7.17 | 11. srʌm | 5 | 62.58 | 19. vrüɤ | 13 | 77.82 |
| 4. trʌk | 1 | 7.17 | 12. *θ*læš | 5 | 19.70 | 20. žlöp | 13 | 80.73 |
| 5. slʌk | 2 | 33.08 | 13. *θ*wæǰ | 8 | 70.43 | 21. ðgɫx | 16 | 106.95 |
| 6. swɩt | 2 | 22.63 | 14. trʊg | 8 | 42.12 | 22. zbüɤ | 16 | 89.93 |
| 7. klæb | 2 | 21.7 | 15. træx | 9 | 72.92 | 23. mböł | 16 | 67.25 |
| 8. brʌd | 2 | 38.55 | 16. žrɩk | 9 | 73.58 | 24. mzœç | 16 | 83.82 |

*Table 5*

| Word | S | Word | S | Word | S |
|---|---|---|---|---|---|
| 1. stɩk | 1 | 9. klɛb | 4 | 17. čwʊp | 12 |
| 2. græs | 1 | 10. swæč | 4 | 18. ðyʌŋ | 12 |
| 3. spɛl | 1 | 11. srʌm | 5 | 19. zml̩p | 13 |
| 4. trʌk | 1 | 12. knæp | 5 | 20. vrüɤ | 13 |
| 5. slʌk | 2 | 13. θwæǰ | 8 | 21. ðgöh | 16 |
| 6. swɩt | 2 | 14. trʊg | 8 | 22. ðgɫx | 16 |
| 7. klæb | 2 | 15. træx | 9 | 23. zbüɤ | 16 |
| 8. brʌd | 2 | 16. žrɩk | 9 | 24. žgr̩ɤ | 16 |

stimuli some containing sounds which are in English and some containing some sounds which are not. It is hardly surprising that the latter are judged as more different from English. Of course this will not account for the consistent difference of judgment in the intermediate range.

Since the linguistic scale used will give the same result for words with non-English sounds or English sounds in positions in which they do not occur in actual English words, it is possible to make up syllables with the same S value which differ in this respect. Hence a revised list, hereinafter to be called List 2, was devised for the subsequent experiment.

The words of List 2 are contained in Table 5. In this list, *θlæš* of List 1, which, as was noted, was misheard as *flæš*, has been replaced by *knæp* (item 12) and new items 17, 19, 21, and 24 have been so constructed that of the two items with S = 12, number 17 has one non-English sound while 18 has none, of the two items with value 13, number 19 has no non-English sound while number 20 has one, and of the four items with value 16, two (22, 23) have two non-English sounds while two (21, 24) have only one such sound. Subsequent experiments using List 2 showed that this made no significant difference. In other words, English sounds in strange combinations or strange positions were judged to be just as foreign as words with foreign sounds.

Instructions for Experiment A were identical with those of Experiment B except for the following additional paragraph:

O.K. we will hear the list one more time. Again, you can change your numbers if you like, and don't worry if you do not give the same response to the same stimuli. This is a check on the experiment and the ordering effects, rather than for your reliability.

Experiment B utilized List 2 and employed the same basic design and instructions as Experiment A. Seventeen students in an introductory psychology course at the University of Minnesota were individually tested. This time an Ampex recording of high fidelity was used and there were three trials instead of two as in Experiment A. As before, each word was said twice with a three-second interval between repetitions and a 15-second interval between words. The last trial was taken for analysis as being most free of experimental artifacts, but the data are very similar for all three trials.

The results of this experiment were very similar to those of Experiment A (see Table 7). Again, if the words are grouped in sets of four, the result is very nearly linear with a threshold effect for words in English (S = 1). For Trial 3 the results are contained in Table 6 with the individual rating scales once more equated, with their means at 50:

The coefficient of linear correlation based on values for individual words between the S scale value and the magnitude estimation means for Trial 3 was

*Table 6*

| S | Means of ME ratings |
|---|---|
| 1 | 3.145 |
| 2 | 28.955 |
| 4.5 | 35.478 |
| 8.5 | 56.198 |
| 12.5 | 71.146 |
| 16 | 102.417 |

*Table 7*

| Word no. | S | Means | Word no. | S | Means | Word no. | S | Means |
|---|---|---|---|---|---|---|---|---|
| 1 | 1 | 2.90 | 9 | 4 | 32.92 | 17 | 12 | 87.97 |
| 2 | 1 | 3.06 | 10 | 4 | 29.25 | 18 | 12 | 46.49 |
| 3 | 1 | 2.90 | 11 | 5 | 46.12 | 19 | 13 | 66.62 |
| 4 | 1 | 3.71 | 12 | 5 | 33.90 | 20 | 13 | 84.63 |
| 5 | 2 | 29.16 | 13 | 8 | 63.19 | 21 | 16 | 82.68 |
| 6 | 2 | 25.10 | 14 | 8 | 41.16 | 22 | 16 | 111.87 |
| 7 | 2 | 28.15 | 15 | 9 | 62.14 | 23 | 16 | 98.57 |
| 8 | 2 | 33.40 | 16 | 9 | 67.59 | 24 | 16 | 111.56 |

.94. The means for individual words obtained on the third trial of Experiment B were those listed in Table 7.

Experiment C once more utilized List 2. However, instead of free magnitude estimation, an 11-point rating scale was used. The purpose here was to evaluate the reliability of free magnitude estimation as a rating technique by the use of the more commonly employed rating scale as well as to test further the nature and reliability of the phenomena investigated in Experiments A and B. Experiment C used 15 subjects at the University of Minnesota and as in Experiment B there were three trials. The same recording was used as in Experiment B. The instructions to the subjects were as follows:

This is an experiment sponsored jointly by Dr. Joseph Greenberg, a linguist at Columbia University, and Dr. James Jenkins of our department. We are interested in developing a measure of the degree of differences that exist between languages. This experiment is designed to see how people perceive differences between languages. I am going to present some words to you with the tape recorder. Some of these words are common English words; some are from languages closely related to English, some not so closely related to English; some distantly related, and some that are very, very distantly related to English. All of these words are short, one syllable words, and they will each be presented two times, so that you will be sure to hear them clearly.

Now this is what I would like you to do:

Look at the booklet that I handed you. Write your name and trial 1 on the top line. You will notice that there are numbers going down the page, and by each number there is a line that is numbered from one to eleven. When you hear a word you are to decide how close it is to being an English word. If you think it is an English word you are to circle the mark above the number one. If you think it is as far from English as it can possibly be you are to circle the mark over the eleven, if it is relatively near English circle the smaller numbers, and if it is relatively far from English circle the larger numbers. Try to make use of the whole scale. Are there any questions? If not I'll play the first word to see how it goes.

If there are no further questions I will play the list throughout. Listen to the number of the word and then listen to the word repeated twice, rate the word accordingly and wait for the next word.

*Second time*. Turn the page to a new rating scale and number this trial two. You are now going to hear the list in a different order. Now you have an idea of the range of stimuli, and therefore your responses may change accordingly. Do not attempt to rate a word a certain way because that is the way it was rated the last time.

*Third time*. Number the next rating scale trial three. This is a still different order of the same words. Listen carefully and rate appropriately.

Now we would like you to fill out the information blank on the last page. If you do not know the answer of any of the questions, just leave it blank. But please answer honestly.

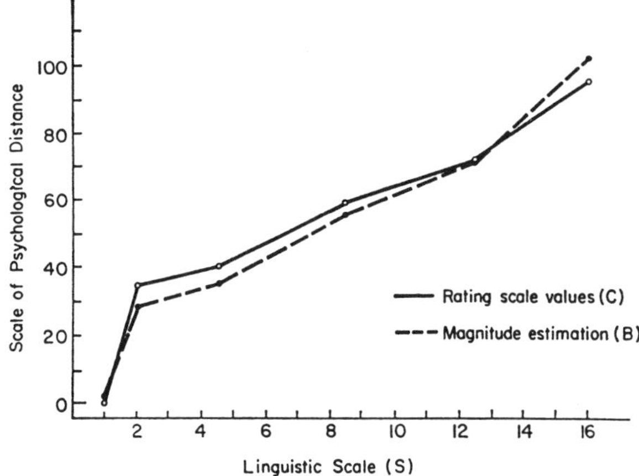


*Figure 2*

The results of C were extremely close to those of Experiment B, as shown in Figure 2. The coefficient of correlation between rating scale medians and magnitude estimation medians was +.98. The correlation between the results of C (medians) and linguistic measure S was +.95, insignificantly different from the value +.94 for the results of B and the linguistic measure as mentioned earlier. The rank order correlation between the rating scale of Experiment C and magnitude estimation of Experiment B was +.94. The correlation between the rating-scale median and means for the third trial was +.99 indicating essential identity of the measures for scaling purposes.

If the first category on the rating scale is assigned a value of zero and each successive interval increases by one unit, the mean rating scale value is 4.86. The results may then be compared to the magnitude estimation values by multiplying by 10.30. While such a comparison is crude, since it makes no assumptions about the nature of the scales whatsoever, it can be seen that it yields good agreement. Table 8 gives the resulting values for the rating scale experiment.

The finding that the magnitude estimation procedure and the category rating scale produce virtually identical results is of more general importance than is superficially apparent. Psychophysical scales may be divided into two general classes which Stevens has termed "prothetic" and "metathetic."[3] The first class seems to characterize continua having to do with *how much* (loudness, length, numerousness, duration, etc.) while the second seems typical of continua concerned with *what kind* and *where* (visual position, angular

[3] S. S. Stevens, "On the Psychophysical Law," Psychological Review 44 (1957), pp. 153–81.

*Table 8*

| List 2 | | | |
|---|---|---|---|
| 1 0.00 | 7 29.56 | 13 51.50 | 19 74.88 |
| 2 0.00 | 8 37.80 | 14 46.66 | 20 66.64 |
| 3 0.00 | 9 39.14 | 15 65.92 | 21 93.42 |
| 4 0.07 | 10 35.74 | 16 72.10 | 22 96.10 |
| 5 43.98 | 11 50.78 | 17 87.86 | 23 89.92 |
| 6 26.78 | 12 35.02 | 18 57.68 | 24 98.16 |

inclination, proportion, pitch, etc.). Category scales of the first class of stimuli are usually of quite different form from magnitude estimation scales. For the second class, the two forms of scaling tend to agree, as they do in this case. One of the implications of this finding is that the perceptual sensitivity of the subjects is uniform across the entire length of the scale as opposed to being highly sensitive for small departures from English and less and less sensitive for differences between very distant "words" as one might initially suppose to be the case. The writers believe that the agreement of the scaling methods and the linear relation which both bear to the linguistic scale constitute indirect evidence for the correspondence of the psychological comparison process and the linguistic substitution analysis which led to the development of the scale. Subjects appear to match this substitution procedure when asked to make distance or category ratings and match it equally well at all points on the continuum tested. This consideration leads directly to the next study.

Experiment D, the last of the group, was a word association test with the 24 words of List 2 as the stimuli. The test was given at the University of Minnesota in June 1960 to 117 subjects. The time allowed each subject for writing down the associations was 15 seconds. The instructions for Experiment D were as follows:

You are about to participate in one of the Minnesota studies in verbal behavior. This particular study is sponsored by Professor James Jenkins of the Psychology Department here and Professor Joseph Greenberg, Professor of Linguistics at Columbia.

Please put your name, age, sex, and date on the cover of the blue books that have been passed out to you. Now open the book and put a number 1 in the middle of the first line of the first page. About halfway down the first page put the number 2. Then fold back the page and put a three on the back of the first page. Continue numbering in this manner until you reach 24.

I have on this tape recorder a list of words. Some of these words are English, but most of them are from foreign languages so you probably have never heard them before. The speaker will give the number of each word, and then he will say the word two times. When you hear the word you are to write down as many other words as this one makes you think of in the time allowed. The words that you write down might be things, places, ideas, events, or whatever you happen to think of when you hear the key word.

For example, the speaker might say, 'Number one, horse, horse'. You might think 'horse-cow', write 'cow', then you might think 'horse-race', write 'race' below 'cow'. Be sure to think back to the original word after each word you write down because the test is to see how many words *that* word makes you think of. A good way to do this is to think of the key word over and over as you write. In the example above we do *not* want you to respond to 'horse': 'cow', 'calf', 'leg', 'arm', a chain of associations, but respond to the stimulus word 'horse' itself.

Another stimulus word might be 'ketch', in which case you might write 'ketchup', or 'boat', or you might not think of any word before the speaker gives the next number. In that case you are to leave the space blank. But work as rapidly as you can in the interval given and get ready for the next word when the speaker gives the number. Are there any questions?

The mean number associates for each word across all the subjects is given in Table 9. Correlations between these results and those of Experiments B and C which likewise utilized List 2 were as follows: The coefficient of linear correlation between the median number of associations and medians of the magnitude estimation results of Experiment B was −.86; with the rating-scale medians of Experiment C it was −.84; and with measure of linguistic distance S it was −.75. Rank-order correlations between the inverse order of number of associations and the rank of magnitude estimation medians was +.81; with the rating-scale medians +.80.

As was to be expected, the correlations here are somewhat lower than that between magnitude estimation and rating scales, since the latter two require the same judgment by the subject. At the same time, that high correlations would be obtained was hypothesized on the basis of a general meaningfulness dimension such as has appeared in psychological investigation of both nonsense syllables and real words varying in frequency of usage.[4] The three most popular associates to each of the syllables of List 2 are given below:

1. stɩk: tree 27; wood 19; hit 14
2. græs: green 85; lawn 30; soft 10
3. spɛl: words 34; word 28; write 17
4. trʌk: car 33; truck 18; road 17
5. slʌk: slug 22; mud 12; slow 10
6. swɩt: sweat 39; sweet 39; swift 20
7. klæb: clap 23; hands 12; clam 11

[4] For a discussion of meaningfulness, see B. J. Underwood and R. W. Schulz, *Meaningfulness and Verbal Learning* (Philadelphia: Lippincott, 1960).

*Table 9*

| Word no. (List 2) | S | Associates | Word no. (List 2) | S | Associates |
|---|---|---|---|---|---|
| 1 | 1 | 2.68 | 13 | 8 | 1.44 |
| 2 | 1 | 3.05 | 14 | 8 | 1.74 |
| 3 | 1 | 2.62 | 15 | 9 | 1.85 |
| 4 | 1 | 3.14 | 16 | 9 | 1.58 |
| 5 | 2 | 1.83 | 17 | 12 | 1.52 |
| 6 | 2 | 2.25 | 18 | 12 | 1.91 |
| 7 | 2 | 2.22 | 19 | 13 | 1.37 |
| 8 | 2 | 2.22 | 20 | 13 | 1.58 |
| 9 | 4 | 1.72 | 21 | 16 | 1.95 |
| 10 | 4 | 1.91 | 22 | 16 | 1.76 |
| 11 | 5 | 1.96 | 23 | 16 | 1.35 |
| 12 | 5 | 2.45 | 24 | 16 | 1.06 |

8. brʌd: bread 48; brother 42; blood 26
9. klɛb: club 28; clip 14; cliff 9
10. swæč: switch 26; swatch 14; hit 14
11. srʌm: strong 19; sarong 12; strum 10; guitar 10
12. knæp: nap 31; canoe 17; knapsack 9
13. θwæj: thatch 23; thrash 20; whip 5
14. trʊg: truck 22; trudge 13; true 12
15. træx: track 41; trash 16; train 7
16. žrɩk: jerk 12; giraffe 9; shriek 7
17. çwʊp: whip 8; hoop 8; whoops 6; whoop 6
18. ðyʌŋ: young 54; old 13; girl 8; boy 8
19. zml̩p: milk 26; smooth 19; smoke 9
20. vrüɣ: room 16; broom 11; rim 5
21. ðgöh: girl 21; good 15; go 8
22. ðgɵx: baby 26; good 22; girl 9
23. zbüɣ: German 10; bird 6; book 6
24. zgr̩ɣ: girl 19; good 10; go 8

The following additional observation may be made in regard to the results of Experiment D. It was noted earlier in reference to Experiment A, that the greater than hypothesized linguistic distance from English of two syllables, *brʌd* and *srʌm*, might be attributable to the relative strangeness of the *r* and *ʌ* sounds of the linguist's New York speech to subjects of Midwestern or Far Western speech background. This seems to find some confirmation in the fact that in Experiment D, 18 subjects, as noted above, responded to /trʌk/ with the association 'truck' whereas, e.g. no subject responded to the stimulus /spɛl/ with 'spell'.

Examination of the actual responses of subjects to the 24 stimuli shows that a very large number of responses were single substitutions, or, for words with lower S values, multiple sound substitutions, including zero substitutions.

For example, among the responses to /*swɩt*/ as a stimulus were: *wit* 2; *quit* 2; *sit* 2; *spit* 1; *slit* 1; *sweat* 39; *sweet* 39; *swat* 17; *Swiss* 1; *swish* 2; *swim* 4; *swig* 2; *switch* 17; *swing* 3; and even a non-existent **swip* 1, besides a large number obviously mediated by one of the foregoing. It seems then that the high agreement found between the S scale and subject reactions is to be attributed largely to the fact that subjects do in fact substitute and that S is a measure of the possibilities offered by substitutional procedures. At the same time reliable differences are found among words having the same S ratings. It may be hypothesized that, in large part, these differences may be explained in terms of three other related factors. First, it should be noted, that in calculating S a single substitution is all that is required in order to score a plus for any one of the $2^n$ possibilities. Thus, of two words with the same S rating, one might have total substitutional possibilities greater than the other. Second, those substitutions are more frequent in which the sound substituted in the response is phonetically similar to the sound of the stimulus. Thus, among the substitution responses to /swɩt/ listed above, the possible substitution *skit* with *k* for *w* does not occur, whereas *spit* and *slit* do. In these two latter examples, *p* resembles *w* as being bilabial and both *w* and *l* are sonants. On the other hand, *k* has no basis of similarity with *w* other than sheer consonantality. A third factor is certainly associational strength of the substituted form. In principle it should be possible to evolve a finer measure than S, in which the associational strength and phonetic similarity of individual substitutions are taken into account and which might explain some of the remaining variance.

Finally, it may be noted that in a few cases there was undeniable mediation by the graphic form although the immediate stimulus was purely auditory. This was particularly noteworthy in the case of the stimulus /knæp/. It is clear that the responses with initial *n* which were favored were those which are spelled *kn-*. It even led to misspellings with *kn-* of words whose standard spelling begins with *n-* or even with *gn-*, e.g. *knat* 3; *knap* 2; *knick* 5; *knip* 1. In a further study to be reported elsewhere, in which methods similar to those already discussed are applied to the meaningfulness values of nonsense syllables,* it will appear that auditory mediation of the visual stimulus presented to subjects in the usual nonsense syllable experiments carried out by psychologists is of fundamental significance.

## II. Distinctive Features and Psychological Space

The results of the preceding paper, with its unusually high intercorrelations between successive applications of free magnitude estimation and between free magnitude estimation and other techniques, encouraged the application of

*The study referred to is the following paper in the present volume, "A Linguistic Approach to the Meaningfulness of Nonsense Syllables"—Eds.

this technique in further instances. A series of experiments was carried out in the summer of 1960, with students at the University of Minnesota as subjects, designed to explore the psychological correlates of distinctive features in phonology. These experiments involved the method of paired comparisons. In this method, from a set of *n* stimuli all possible non-identical pairs are presented in both orders. Thus if the original set contained three basic stimuli A, B, C, the following six sets of paired stimuli would result: AB, BA, AC, CA, BC, CB. It is evident that the number of pairs resulting from *n* basic stimuli will be $2 \times \binom{n}{2}$. Thus with the six basic stimuli employed in the experiments reported in this section there were

$$30 = 2 \cdot \binom{6}{2} = 2 \cdot \frac{6 \cdot 5}{1 \cdot 2} = 30$$

sets of paired stimuli. Since the addition of further members to the basic set increases in number of paired stimuli at an increasing rate, it is not feasible to present, for example, the entire consonantal or vocalic system of a language such as English since it presents an excessively difficult and time-consuming task for the subject.

The basic stimuli chosen were the six consonants p, b, t, d, k, g, since these constitute a neatly structured subsystem of the overall sound system of English. The actual stimuli in the four experimental runs to be described were oral and/or visually presented instances of these consonants with a following *a*, e.g. *pa*, or with [a] in oral presentation. The subjects were asked to assign a number as a measure of distance for each pair, e.g. to estimate the distance between PA and BA.

The following are some of the questions to which such a series of experiments might furnish answers. Are pairs which differ in two features consistently rated as more distant from each other than those which are only one feature apart (e.g. PA–GA vs. PA–KA)? Among those which are one feature apart, are pairs agreeing in manner rated as closer or more distant than those which agree in position (e.g. PA–KA vs. PA–BA)? Is the greater articulatory distance between the peripheral labial and velar position as against labial-alveolar and velar-alveolar distance reflected in the results (e.g. PA–TA vs. PA–KA)?

In the first experiment (A), five subjects were presented with the set of 30 paired stimuli as described above in three different random orders on three successive trials. In this, as in the other experiments of this series, only the results of the third trial were employed in formulating the results statistically. In experiment A subjects were presented with the stimuli on tape and recorded their distance estimates in a space beside the written representation of what they heard. There were thus both aural and visual stimuli.

The instructions for Experiment A were as follows:

This is one of a series of studies in the psychology of language sponsored by Professor James Jenkins in our department and Professor Joseph Greenberg of the Department of Anthropology at Columbia University. The aim of this research is to knit together the sciences of psychology and linguistics. We regard it as important research and would appreciate your wholehearted cooperation.

We are interested in your impressions as to how much speech sounds differ.

I am going to ask you to listen to some syllables on the tape recorder and I shall ask you to give an estimate in numbers as to how different the sounds are. This, of course, is subjective and there are no right or wrong answers. We just want to know how far apart *you* think the sounds are.

I know that this is an unusual task, so in order to clarify what I would like you to do, I will give you an analogous situation. See the dots on this sheet of paper? (Hold up sheet with six randomly arranged dots.) They would be representative of bacteria seen through a microscope, just dots on paper, or galaxies viewed through a giant telescope. If I were to ask you to tell me how far apart these two dots are (pointing), and did not give you any more information, you could say any number you chose, 5, 10, 36, 100, etc. But if I then asked you to give me a number estimating how far apart *these two* are (pointing to two dots twice as far apart as the first two), in relation to your first number, you would be more restricted. If your first number had been 5, you would probably now say 10 or 11. If the first were a 10, you would probably say 20. Now look at these two (pointing to two dots about half as far apart as the initial pair). If my first were 5, I would probably say 2 or 2½. If the first were 10, I would say about 5, and so on. For this distance (pointing again), I would probably say about the same as my first value.

You see how it works? If they are twice as far apart, give them a number twice as big, if ten times as far apart, a number ten times as big, half as far apart would warrant a number half as big, and so forth.

What we would like in *this* experiment is this: When you hear the first pair of syllables, give them a number as to how far apart they sound to you, your own subjective judgment. If the next pair sounds twice as far apart, give a number twice as large; half as far apart, give a number half as large, and so on.

We are not interested in how different the letters look, or how far apart they are in the alphabet, but how different the sounds of the syllables seem to be in your estimation. You may worry that your scale is changing or that you have forgotten what you said before, and so on. Don't let this worry you; you can do this task better than you think you can. And you will get better and better as we go along.

Are there any questions at this point?

Before we begin the actual rating, I would like you to be familiar with the speaker's voice. The syllables that are to be used in the actual rating are listed on this sheet in alphabetical order. (Hand out paper.) Just circle the syllable as it is spoken. Any questions?

(*Gives familiarization list.*)

Now the speaker will say the syllables in pairs, and he will repeat the syllables once. You are to listen carefully, give the first pair a number representing how far apart they sound to you, and use this judgment as a basis for later ones.

Write the number of your estimate on the dashed line immediately following the listed pair of syllables. The cardboard shield with the window in it will allow you to concentrate on one pair at a time. Just slide it down and make your responses through the window.

(*Present first randomization.*)

This part of the experiment is like the last except that the order of the pairs is different. You have warmed up to the procedure and know what it is like. You can shift your scale or have it remain the same, whichever you prefer.

(*Present second randomization.*)

Now, one more time through the list in a new order and we will be through.

The accompanying sheet for Experiment A had the following form:

1. pa ba _____
2. ga pa _____ etc.

In Experiment B there were likewise five subjects and the procedures were the same as for Experiment A except that there was no visual presentation; only identifying numerals each followed by a blank space were on the instruction sheet in place of the numerals followed by the syllable pair followed by a blank space. The results would presumably be more free of orthographic effects but the subject was more likely to mishear the syllables. The instructions for Experiment B were exactly like those for Experiment A, already given, except that the third paragraph from the end, beginning "Write the number of your estimate on the dashed line . . ." was replaced by the following: "Write the number of your estimate on this paper after the number of the syllable pair read."

Since a preliminary comparison of the results of Experiments A and B indicated considerable variability among subjects, particularly in the case of B, it was decided to repeat the procedures of B on another group of five subjects in order to increase the size of the sample. This repetition is called here Experiment C and is identical with Experiment B except for the identity of the subjects.

Finally, for the same reason as in the first group of experiments, namely to investigate the reliability of magnitude estimation by comparison with other methods, five subjects were used in essentially the same experiment but with a rating scale substituted for magnitude estimation as the technique. This set is here called Experiment D. The instructions for D were as follows:

This is one of a series of experiments in the psychology of language sponsored by Professor James Jenkins in our department and Professor Joseph Greenberg of the Department of Anthropology at Columbia University. The aim of this research is to knit together the sciences of psychology and linguistics. We regard it as important research and would appreciate your wholehearted cooperation.

We are interested in your impression as to how speech sounds differ.

I am going to ask you to listen to some syllables on the tape recorder and I shall ask you to rate on this scale (holding sample scale up) how similar the consonants of the syllables sound to you. The vowel is always the same; it is merely to carry the sound of the consonant.

This task is, of course, subjective. There are no right or wrong answers. We just want to know how far apart *you* think the sounds are.

Before we begin the actual rating, I would like you to be familiar with the speaker's voice. All of the syllables to be used in the actual rating are listed in this sheet in alphabetical order. (Hand out paper.) Just circle the syllable as it is spoken. Are there any questions?

(Familiarization list is presented here. Subject has a list of 30 items, each of which lists the six syllables. As each item is spoken he circles the correct syllable.)

(Hand out rating sheets.)

Now the speaker will read the syllables in pairs. You are to listen carefully and rate on this sheet by circling the colon above the similarity rating you would like to give the speech sounds. Are there any questions?

(Present the first list of pairs on the tape.)

This part of the experiment is like the first except that the order of presentation is different. Do not try to give a response just because you gave that response before. Just rate how similar the sounds are.

(Present second randomization.)

We will go through the list one more time in a different order and then we will be through.

(Present third randomization.)

The instruction sheet for Experiment D had the following appearance:

| 1. : | : | : | : | : | : |
|---|---|---|---|---|---|
| extremely similar | decidedly similar | pretty similar | somewhat similar | slightly similar | not similar |

| 2. : | : | : | : | : | : |
|---|---|---|---|---|---|
| extremely similar | decidedly similar | pretty similar | somewhat similar | slightly similar | not similar |

Experiment D resembled B and C in that there was no visual stimulus.

As with the group of experiments reported in the first paper of this series, it was, of course, necessary to calibrate the differing scales of individual subjects on the free magnitude estimation Experiments A, B, C, and to calibrate the results of free magnitude estimation with those of the rating scale of Experiment D. In this present instance, instead of equating all the results to an arbitrary mean, statistical comparisons were based on the rank order of distance estimates. This seemed adequate since the subjects generally restricted themselves to a narrow interval in magnitude estimation and to generally equal intervals.

For each pair of syllables differing in order only, e.g. pa-ta and ta-pa, the two raw scores were averaged to give a single measure of distance. For each subject these 15 scores were ranked, the smallest number representing the smallest judged distance being assigned the number 1. For the rating scale, the number 1 was assigned as raw score for the judgment 'very similar' implying the smallest distance and each successive point on the scale received the next larger natural number up to 6 for the judgment 'not similar'. As with the magnitude estimation data, these scores were averaged for each pair of syllables differing in order only and the 15 resultant scores ranked with the lowest receiving rank order 1.

The set of raw scores, i.e. actual numerical judgments for one subject in experiment A, will serve as an illustration of the method employed. (See Table 10.) For example, this subject rated the distance between *ka* and *ta* as 3 when presented in that order but as 4 when presented in the order *ta* followed by *ka*.

For this subject, the pair *ka-ta* was rated as closest (average of the two orders 3.5) and this pair was therefore given the rank order 1. The next closest judgment, 4, was given both for DB and BG. The usual procedure in cases of tied ranks was followed. The sum of the ranks 2 and 3 were averaged so that both DB and BG received a rank of 2.5. A similar procedure was employed for the rating scale experiment (D) utilizing the numbers 1 to 6 for raw scores as described above.

That the subjects found this a more difficult task than the rating of distance from English in the first set of experiments is shown by the lower intercorrelations among the four experiments as set forth in Table 11. A correlation of .514 or greater is significant at the 5 percent confidence level and of .641 at the 1 percent level. Thus the results of A (magnitude estimation with aural-visual presentation) correlates significantly at the 5 percent levels with all the others and B and C correlate with each other and with A while D (rating scale) only correlates significantly with A. This suggests that future tests with larger samples should concentrate on the technique employed in test A, the only test involving aural-visual stimuli.

The results of these tests show great internal consistency from the linguistic point of view. As a point of departure we may take the rank of each pair of syllables when averaged across the 20 subjects in the four experiments. Thus if a particular pair had been rated as closest by every subject, it would receive an average rank of 1, if last, an average rank of 15. These average results ranked in turn in order of average judgment of closeness are to be found in Table 12. Alongside of these results are the averages for five subjects in Experiment A only, since this was the method which correlated most highly with the others. The last column gives the rank order of the averages for

*Table 10*

| | p | b | t | d | k |
|---|---|---|---|---|---|
| b | 6,5 | — | — | — | — |
| t | 6,4 | 6,7 | — | — | — |
| d | 7,7 | 3,5 | 5,6 | — | — |
| k | 4,5 | 5,4 | 3,4 | 4,7 | |
| g | 5,6 | 3,5 | 3,7 | 4,4 | 4,4 |

*Table 11*

| | A | B | C | D |
|---|---|---|---|---|
| A | — | .6923 | .6170 | .7640 |
| B | .6923 | — | .7216 | .2880 |
| C | .6170 | .7216 | — | .1715 |
| D | .7640 | .2880 | .1715 | — |

*Table 12*

| | Total averages | Rank order | Test A averages | Rank order |
|---|---|---|---|---|
| BD | 3.225 | 1 | 3.3 | 1 |
| GD | 4.750 | 2 | 3.8 | 2 |
| PB | 5.850 | 3 | 5.9 | 3.5 |
| KG | 6.075 | 4 | 7.9 | 7.5 |
| BG | 6.500 | 5 | 5.9 | 3.5 |
| PT | 6.575 | 6 | 6.0 | 5 |
| KT | 7.575 | 7 | 6.1 | 6 |
| TD | 8.000 | 8 | 7.9 | 7.5 |
| PD | 9.475 | 9 | 9.5 | 11 |
| PK | 9.975 | 10 | 10.0 | 12 |
| TB | 10.025 | 11 | 11.1 | 13 |
| TG | 10.150 | 12 | 9.1 | 9 |
| KD | 10.275 | 13 | 11.7 | 14 |
| KB | 10.350 | 14 | 9.2 | 10 |
| PG | 10.600 | 15 | 12.2 | 15 |

Experiment A, which differs in some respects from the results of an overall pooling of the results of the four experiments.

Measures summarizing the relative importance of agreements or disagreements in particular features can be easily obtained by averaging the above results. For example, a measure of the importance of agreement in point of articulation can be obtained by averaging the distance measures of the pairs PB, TD, and KG; agreement in possession of the voicing feature by averaging the results for BD, BG, and DG. Again the measure of alveolar-labial distance as against alveolar-velar distance can be measured by averaging the distances of the set TP, TB, DP, and DB against those of the set TK, TG, DP, and DG, etc. Results for a number of such factors of agreement or contrast are shown in Table 13.

The following are the main conclusions which emerge from an examination of the above results. 1. Sounds agreeing in all but one feature are consistently judged as closer than those differing by two features. 2. Distances between points of articulation are ranked as follows: labial-alveolar, alveolar-velar, labial-velar, conforming fairly closely to articulatory facts. 3. Agreement in voicing is a much greater factor in judgments of similarity than agreement in lack of voicing. In fact, it is the most important factor of all those measured in the experiment. This perhaps not unexpected result presumably reflects the greater psychological weight of marked as against unmarked features and, it might be conjectured, would hold at least as strongly for agreement in nasality as against agreement in non-nasality.

A schematic representation of the "psychological" space of p, t, k, b, d, g, is portrayed in Figure 3.

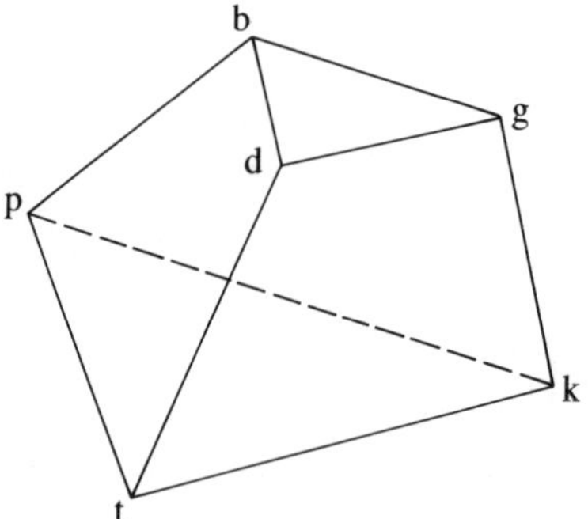


*Figure 3*

*Table 13*

| | Total for all experiments | Experiment A only |
|---|---|---|
| A | | |
| 1. agreement in presence of voicing | 4.825 | 4.333 |
| 2. agreement in non-voicing | 8.042 | 7.366 |
| 3. agreement in presence or absence of voice | 6.433 | 5.849 |
| 4. agreement in point of articulation | 6.642 | 7.233 |
| B | | |
| 5. alveolar-labial contrast | 7.325 | 7.475 |
| 6. alveolar-velar contrast | 8.187 | 7.675 |
| 7. labial-velar contrast | 9.356 | 9.325 |
| C | | |
| 8. difference in one feature | 6.503 | 6.266 |
| 9. difference in two features | 10.146 | 10.466 |

In general, the linguistic coherence of the results obtained by this series of experiments suggests that it would be useful to extend them to other sets of consonants or vowels, employing the technique of experiment A on a larger sample of subjects.

## III. Descriptive Ratings of Selected Consonants

As a further means of investigating the class of problems considered above, it seemed worthwhile to explore the possibilities of applying the well-known method of the semantic differential. The semantic differential consists of a set of rating scales, each scale being defined by two adjectives, customarily polar opposites, used as labels for each end of the scale. The scale itself usually has seven points. A set of stimuli are presented one by one to the subject. He rates each stimulus on each scale, the same set of scales being used in connection with each stimulus.[5] In the study reported here the stimuli were individual English sounds. The mathematical method of evaluating the results has been most commonly some form of factor analysis. By this technique, a series of mathematically independent factors are isolated which provide an economic representation of the interrelationships of stimuli and scales. Usually scale relationships are examined to answer the question as to how many independent rating dimensions are of importance over the set of stimuli. To the extent that judgments on two different scales are similar over the stimuli evaluated, the scales may be viewed as measuring the same factor.

In a previous section we reported relations among a subset of English consonants obtained by direct pairwise comparisons when subjects were asked to attend to the differences between them. That the present procedure will tap other dimensions than those found earlier is to be expected. Both approaches, of course, yield measures of similarity of speech sounds. In the present case, those sounds which are similarly located on the various scales will receive a smaller "distance" measure than those which are evaluated differently. Yet this measure of similarity does not result from a direct comparison of the sounds themselves, as earlier, since each sound is judged in some absolute sense against the polar scale being considered at the moment. Direct comparison, on the other hand, is responsive to the interactions of the characteristics of the items being judged. Such a method is especially sensitive to changes in the configuration when the set of elements is added to or changed so that individual distances in a new context will be differently evaluated. That particular effect is presumably minimized under the present procedure. Further, the kinaesthetic similarity of two sounds formed at the

[5] For a detailed account of the semantic differential, see Charles E. Osgood, George J. Suci, and Percy H. Tannenbaum, *The Measurement of Meaning* (Urbana, 1957).

same point of articulation presumably plays a direct role in judgments in a comparison study, whereas in a semantic differential study such factors will be expected to appear only insofar as the various sounds at the same point of articulation display an acoustic or motor similarity which can be verbalized in terms of the polar adjectives used in the scales. It is evident, also, that the results of the semantic differential will be richer, as it were, in semantic content in that verbal characterizations of the bases of judgment will be derivable from the results, whereas direct comparison techniques will only give "abstract" distances among the sounds.

In the experiment represented here, a series of consonants was rated along 26 scales. The consonants were *p*, *k*, *b*, *d*, *s*, *z*, *m*, *n*, *l*, and *r*. The particular consonants selected were designed to sample the English system in that stops, fricatives, nasals, and liquids were all represented, and among the obstruents both unvoiced and voiced sounds. It was also thought advisable to include only sounds which would be unambiguous stimuli when presented orthographically to phonetically naive subjects. The scales included many of those utilized in previous studies employing the semantic differential in order to provide comparability with these studies, since one question to be investigated was whether the same factorial structure would appear as that found where meaningful verbal materials were used as stimuli. In addition to the scales typical in such studies, it was thought to be of special interest to include scales involving current acoustic or traditional articulatory terminology (e.g., *compact–diffuse*, *back–front*, and *liquid–solid*).

Experiment A was conducted in the summer of 1960. Nine undergraduates of the University of Minnesota served as subjects. The instructions were as follows:

This is a study of speech sounds. You have been given a series of rating scales on which we would like you to judge the speech sounds. You should have ten rating sheets; each with a different speech sound written at the top. We want you to rate the sounds on the basis of how they seem to you. Place a checkmark on *each* of the scales wherever *you* feel the sound should be rated. Work as fast as you can; don't take too long to make any rating and rate your first impression of the sounds. Don't hesitate to use the extreme ends of the scales where they seem appropriate.

Here are some examples of the way you should do this task:

Suppose you were rating the sound "AAACK" and you came to the rough-smooth scale. You would probably consider the sound "AAACK" as more rough than smooth. If you felt it was *very* rough you would rate it here; if you thought it was *quite* rough you would rate it here; if you thought it was just *somewhat* rough you would rate it here. (Illustrate on board.)

If next you were rating the sound "MMUMM" and came across the rough-smooth scale, you might feel that "MMUMM" was more smooth than rough. If you felt that it was *somewhat* smooth you would rate it here, if you felt that it was *quite* smooth you would rate it here, and if you felt that it was *very* smooth you would rate it here. Of course you would make only one mark.

Some of the ratings will not be very literal. When you are rating "AAACK," for example, you might come to the scale hot–cold. (Indicate on board.) There is no obvious "correct" answer here—so rate it as *you* feel it should be rated. Does "AAACK" seem more hot or cold or in between? We want your *impressions* of the sounds. In some cases you may wonder how a certain scale can apply to the sound you are rating, but we have found that you will be able to make decisions quite easily if you follow directions, rating quickly on first impressions.

The speech sounds we want you to rate are on each page at the top. We want you to rate the sound of the first letter, the consonant. We have put the same vowel (AH) with each one to carry the sound so you can say it to yourself. (Examples) Don't attend to the vowel; it is the consonant sound we want you to rate.

Are there any questions? Remember, rate the sound printed at the top of each sheet. Put one check mark on each scale, do not skip any scales. Finish all of one sheet before going on to the next one.

All right, go ahead and do the sounds in the order that the sheets are in your folder.

The results of this experiment are set forth in Table 14, in which the average rating for each consonant on each scale is presented. The point on the left end of the scale is scored as 1, that on the right as 7, and the intervening points are assigned the integral values between 1 and 7. Thus, if for a particular consonant on the scale *weak–strong*, all of the subjects had marked the extreme left end of the scale (i.e., the end labeled *weak*), the number 1 would appear in the table at the appropriate point.

A distance measure among consonants can be calculated by the generalized Euclidean distance formula

$$D = (\Sigma_1^{26} d_{ij}^2)^{1/2},$$

where $d$ is the difference between the average judgments for two consonants, $i$ and $j$, on a particular scale. This is a generalization to 26 dimensions of the well-known distance formula for two-dimensional space based on the Pythagorean theorem, whereby the length of the hypotenuse equals the square root of the sum of the squares of the other two sides. Thus, in the present instance, the distance between $P$ and $K$ is calculated beginning the summation with scale 1 as follows:

$$\sqrt{(3.3 - 2.7)^2 + (3.2 - 3.4)^2 + (3.4 - 3.0)^2 \ldots \text{etc.}}$$

The measures of distance among the consonants arrived at in this manner are set forth in Table 15.

An examination of this table shows a cluster of low values (i.e., similarities) involving the four stops *p*, *k*, *b*, *d*. For every stop, the closest two consonants are likewise stops. For three of these, *p*, *k*, and *d*, the three most distant are *l*, *s*, and *m* in that order. For *b*, the same three are

*Table 14*

| | P | K | B | D | S | Z | M | N | L | R |
|---|---|---|---|---|---|---|---|---|---|---|
| 1. Inhibited–Free | 3.3 | 2.7 | 3.2 | 4.1 | 5.6 | 4.9 | 4.1 | 3.9 | 5.3 | 3.4 |
| 2. Closed–Open | 3.2 | 3.4 | 3.3 | 3.8 | 4.4 | 4.6 | 3.3 | 4.1 | 5.0 | 4.0 |
| 3. Bad–Good | 3.4 | 3.0 | 4.2 | 4.4 | 3.9 | 3.4 | 5.0 | 3.8 | 4.3 | 4.0 |
| 4. Warm–Cool | 4.3 | 5.3 | 3.1 | 3.3 | 3.3 | 4.1 | 2.6 | 4.1 | 3.8 | 3.3 |
| 5. Liquid–Solid | 5.4 | 5.6 | 4.9 | 5.3 | 2.8 | 3.9 | 3.2 | 4.2 | 2.1 | 3.7 |
| 6. Delicate–Rugged | 5.3 | 5.1 | 5.0 | 5.4 | 3.1 | 4.1 | 4.1 | 4.0 | 2.8 | 4.9 |
| 7. Tight–Loose | 2.6 | 3.1 | 3.8 | 2.4 | 4.7 | 4.2 | 4.8 | 3.1 | 5.4 | 3.9 |
| 8. Empty–Full | 4.9 | 3.3 | 5.7 | 4.6 | 4.3 | 4.9 | 5.0 | 4.7 | 4.4 | 4.2 |
| 9. Masculine–Feminine | 3.1 | 3.6 | 3.6 | 2.3 | 4.8 | 3.3 | 4.1 | 3.7 | 5.0 | 2.8 |
| 10. Passive–Active | 4.4 | 4.6 | 4.4 | 4.1 | 4.7 | 5.0 | 4.6 | 3.3 | 4.0 | 5.4 |
| 11. Dark–Bright | 4.1 | 4.3 | 3.9 | 3.8 | 5.6 | 3.9 | 3.3 | 3.3 | 5.0 | 3.6 |
| 12. Back–Front | 5.1 | 3.8 | 5.1 | 4.2 | 5.6 | 4.8 | 4.7 | 4.7 | 4.3 | 4.3 |
| 13. Easy–Difficult | 4.6 | 5.1 | 3.7 | 3.9 | 3.8 | 4.9 | 4.0 | 4.4 | 3.2 | 4.2 |
| 14. Angular–Rounded | 4.3 | 3.3 | 4.4 | 4.1 | 3.6 | 2.9 | 5.3 | 4.3 | 5.1 | 4.1 |
| 15. Thick–Thin | 3.4 | 3.7 | 2.9 | 3.3 | 5.6 | 3.8 | 3.1 | 4.0 | 4.2 | 3.0 |
| 16. Weak–Strong | 5.1 | 5.3 | 5.3 | 5.6 | 3.9 | 4.8 | 4.7 | 4.3 | 3.4 | 5.3 |
| 17. Harsh–Mellow | 3.3 | 2.8 | 4.6 | 4.4 | 3.6 | 3.0 | 5.3 | 4.8 | 5.8 | 2.8 |
| 18. Abrupt–Continuous | 1.8 | 2.9 | 3.2 | 3.2 | 6.0 | 4.7 | 5.0 | 4.6 | 5.6 | 4.0 |
| 19. Large–Small | 3.3 | 4.3 | 2.8 | 3.3 | 4.8 | 3.6 | 3.6 | 4.4 | 3.9 | 3.2 |
| 20. Diffuse–Compact | 5.1 | 5.4 | 4.7 | 4.4 | 3.0 | 3.2 | 4.3 | 4.1 | 3.7 | 4.0 |
| 21. Sharp–Dull | 4.3 | 3.4 | 4.3 | 3.8 | 3.1 | 3.3 | 5.1 | 3.9 | 4.8 | 4.9 |
| 22. Hazy–Clear | 4.8 | 4.8 | 4.0 | 4.6 | 4.0 | 3.4 | 3.3 | 4.3 | 3.8 | 3.9 |
| 23. Vibrant–Still | 3.6 | 4.0 | 3.3 | 3.9 | 2.9 | 3.2 | 3.3 | 4.4 | 3.0 | 2.3 |
| 24. Heavy–Light | 2.8 | 3.4 | 2.7 | 2.4 | 5.4 | 4.1 | 3.2 | 3.9 | 4.9 | 2.4 |
| 25. Smooth–Rough | 3.8 | 5.3 | 3.7 | 4.7 | 3.1 | 4.2 | 2.3 | 3.2 | 2.7 | 5.6 |
| 26. Hard–Soft | 3.4 | 2.1 | 3.7 | 2.8 | 5.0 | 4.1 | 4.6 | 3.9 | 5.1 | 3.2 |

*Table 15*

| | P | K | B | D | S | Z | M | N | L | R |
|---|---|---|---|---|---|---|---|---|---|---|
| P | — | 3.96 | 3.29 | 3.31 | 8.60 | 5.60 | 6.52 | 4.83 | 8.83 | 4.72 |
| K | 3.96 | — | 5.71 | 4.67 | 8.88 | 5.86 | 8.19 | 5.69 | 9.61 | 5.25 |
| B | 3.29 | 5.71 | — | 3.30 | 7.69 | 5.06 | 4.20 | 4.22 | 7.23 | 4.11 |
| D | 3.31 | 4.67 | 3.30 | — | 8.42 | 5.31 | 6.08 | 4.46 | 8.46 | 4.10 |
| S | 8.60 | 8.88 | 7.69 | 8.42 | — | 4.86 | 6.37 | 5.76 | 4.36 | 7.70 |
| Z | 5.60 | 5.86 | 5.06 | 5.31 | 4.86 | — | 5.55 | 4.13 | 6.19 | 4.36 |
| M | 6.52 | 8.19 | 4.20 | 6.08 | 6.37 | 5.55 | — | 4.34 | 4.74 | 5.67 |
| N | 4.83 | 5.69 | 4.22 | 4.46 | 5.76 | 4.13 | 4.34 | — | 5.46 | 5.51 |
| L | 8.83 | 9.61 | 7.23 | 8.46 | 4.36 | 6.19 | 4.74 | 5.46 | — | 7.81 |
| R | 4.72 | 5.25 | 4.11 | 4.10 | 7.70 | 4.36 | 5.67 | 5.51 | 7.81 | — |

most distant, but the order is *s*, *l*, and *m*. This establishes a phonetically comprehensible scale of judgment with stop sounds on one end and continuants on the other. There are indeed four scales in which the first four consonants reckoning from one end are stops and the remainder are continuants. Putting the value for the stop end of the continuum first in each case, these are scale 5, *solid–liquid*, scale 6, *rugged–delicate*, scale 18, *abrupt–continuous*, and scale 20, *compact–diffuse*. Except for scale 6, where the most rugged is *d*, the unvoiced stops *k* and *p* always have the extreme values among the stops on these particular scales.

The importance of the stop versus continuant dimension can also be shown by a procedure analogous to that employed in the previous study in this series, which consolidates individual results on the basis of sound features. The mean value of all distance measures involving stop with stop is 4.04; continuant with continuant, 5.52; and stop with continuant, 6.34. On the other hand, a similar calculation using presence and absence of voicing as the criterion leads to less clear-cut results. The mean value of distances among voiced obstruents is 4.56; of voiced with unvoiced, 5.49, and of unvoiced with unvoiced, 7.15.

While the overall significance in this study of the stop-continuant opposition is thus well established, the position of *r*, phonetically reckoned as a liquid, is of interest. In Table 15, *r* is closer to *k* than one of the stops, *b*, and *r* is, correspondingly, closer to *b* than *k* is to *b*. It is also closer to *d* than *k* is to *d*. It thus shows a tendency to gravitate toward the stop end of the continuum. It is also farther from the most polarized continuant, *l*, than one of the stops, namely, *b*. An examination of its distance to *l* on individual scales shows the greatest separation on scale 17, *harsh–mellow* (3.0); scale 25, *smooth–rough* (2.9); scale 24, *heavy–light* (2.5); scale 9, *masculine–feminine* (2.2); and scale 6, *delicate–rugged* (2.1). Thus, *r* appears as harsh, rough, heavy, masculine, and rugged, as against *l*, which is mellow, smooth, light, feminine, and delicate.

In the system of Jakobson and his associates, *r* is opposed to *l* as interrupted to continuant. They are referring, however, to the rolled or tapped *r*, which in fact does not fit logically into a stop–continuant dichotomy because it consists of repeated constrictions.[6]

Linguistic considerations suggest a further complexity to be superimposed on the stop-continuant dichotomy. It was noted above that in those scales in which the stops were at one end and the continuants at the other, the unvoiced stops generally showed the greatest distance from the continuants. This is understandable if it is assumed that voicing acts as a sonority component which moves these sounds closer to the continuant extreme. It may be further noted that of the four voiced stops, the bilabial *b* is closer to the polar *l* than

[6]The majority of subjects in these experiments were from the Minneapolis–St. Paul region and presumably had a "medio-palatal *r*" that should be classified phonetically as a continuant. The agreement, however, on such judgments as male–female with Fonágy's subjects, who were Hungarian and presumably had a rolled *r*, cited later in this article, is remarkable and suggests a degree of psychological unity among the phonetically diverse *r* sounds.

*d*, and that the bilabial *p* is closer than the other unvoiced stop, *k*. Similarly, the bilabial *m* is consistently near the continuant pole and sometimes shows the extreme value, while the other nasal *n* tends to intermediate values. This suggests that the bilabials, with their larger resonance cavity than alveolars or velars, add a component in the direction of the more sonorous continuant end of the scales.

As was mentioned earlier, a common statistical method of evaluating results for the semantic differential is factor analysis. For Experiment A, the so-called Thurstone diagonal method was employed, using the average scores over subjects as the raw scores to which the diagonal method is applied.[7] In this method, the scale with the largest deviations from the mean of 4.0, calculated as the sum of the squares of each deviation, is selected as the "pivot." Other scales are said to be loaded positively or negatively according to the extent of agreement between these scales and the pivot scale. The squares of these "loadings" having been subtracted from the total variance, the scale with the largest remaining variance is the second "pivot," and so on. In the present instance, loadings for the first, second, and third factor were calculated.[8]

The general semantic characteristic of factor 1 is suggested by the five scales with the highest loading on this factor: *abrupt–continuous* (positive), *liquid–solid* (negative), *tight–loose* (positive), *delicate–rugged* (negative), and *inhibited–free* (positive). In addition it was observed that *diffuse–compact*, a scale with small variance, contributes almost all of it to this first factor. We have, therefore, a contrast between abrupt, solid, tight, rugged, inhibited (and compact) on the one hand and continuous, liquid, loose, delicate, free (and diffuse) on the other. This is evidently a factor not easily identifiable with any of those which have appeared in the investigation of verbal concepts. The two poles might be characterized as involving a concentration versus dispersion of matter. An examination of the values for the consonants on the scales with the heaviest loading for this factor shows the stops, particularly the unvoiced stops, at the concentration pole and the continuants at the dispersion pole.

The scales with the highest loadings on the second factor are *harsh–mellow* (positive), *smooth–rough* (negative), *angular-rounded* (positive), *passive–active* (negative), *easy-difficult* (negative), *sharp–dull* (positive), and *bad–good* (positive). We have, thus, a contrast of harsh, rough, angular, active, difficult, sharp, and bad with mellow, smooth, rounded, passive, easy,

[7] The Thurstone diagonal method is explained in Osgood, Suci, and Tannenbaum, *The Measurement of Meaning*, pp. 332–35. A standard treatment of methods of factor analysis in general is Harry H. Harman, *Modern Factor Analysis* (Chicago, 1960).

[8] The tables of data for this and subsequent analyses are to be found in Tables 19–23.

dull, and good. In general, a similar arrangement for consonants is found for those with heavy loadings on factor 2 as for factor 1, except that *s* and *z* do not pattern with the continuants *l*, *m*, and *n*, but are closer to the stops. Except for *r*, which takes an intermediate position, we have, then, a contrast between obstruents (stops and fricatives) and sonants (nasals and liquids). This contrast seems to be appropriately described by the scale with the highest loading on this factor as harsh (obstruents) versus mellow (sonants).

The scales with the highest loadings on the third factor are *weak–strong* (positive), *heavy–light* (negative), *empty–full* (positive), *vibrant–still* (negative), *delicate–rugged* (positive), *back–front* (positive), and *masculine–feminine* (negative). Thus, it contrasts weak, light, empty, still, delicate, back, and feminine with strong, heavy, full, vibrant, rugged, front, and masculine. This seems identifiable with "potency," which figures regularly as the second factor on tests with verbal concepts as stimuli. The ratings of the consonants on scales with heavy third factor loadings is less clear than for the first two factors, but, in general, the stops and *r* are at the strong end and *n*, *l*, and *s* at the other. Except for *r*, this distribution resembles that for the first factor and seems substantially identical with the potency factor identified on inspection earlier involving an *r*/*l* dichotomy.

The most conspicuous result of comparisons between the present data and those employing verbal stimuli is the absence among the three factors enumerated here of anything that can be reasonably equated with the *good–bad* dimension which regularly figures as the first factor in verbal studies. A potency factor does appear with some admixture of activity as the third factor in the present study. This corresponds, by and large, with the second and third factor of verbal tests. On the other hand, the *concentration–dispersion* and *harsh–mellow* factors, so important here, do not seem directly comparable with any found in studies employing verbal stimuli.

Since Experiment A employed only 9 subjects, it was decided to repeat the study with a larger number of subjects and with more elaborate analysis. This resulted in Experiment B, in which 61 undergraduates at the University of Minnesota participated in the winter quarter, 1961. The scales, the consonant stimuli, and the instructions were exactly the same as in the first experiment.

The results of Experiment B are found in Table 16, containing the means of each consonant on each scale. It is thus directly comparable to Table 14, which gives the corresponding results for Experiment A.

The overall coefficient of correlation between the set of scale values obtained in Experiment A and in Experiment B was +.814, a generally satisfactory result according to the standards of reliability accepted by psychologists. The correlations of the scale values given for each consonant in Experiment A with the scale values given in Experiment B are set forth in the first column of

*Table 16*

| | P | K | B | D | S | Z | M | N | L | R |
|---|---|---|---|---|---|---|---|---|---|---|
| 1. Inhibited–Free | 4.3 | 3.6 | 3.7 | 3.7 | 4.7 | 4.5 | 4.5 | 4.1 | 5.1 | 4.7 |
| 2. Closed–Open | 3.7 | 3.1 | 3.4 | 3.2 | 4.0 | 3.8 | 3.6 | 3.3 | 5.0 | 4.1 |
| 3. Bad–Good | 4.3 | 3.5 | 3.6 | 3.6 | 4.1 | 3.5 | 5.1 | 3.6 | 5.1 | 3.9 |
| 4. Warm–Cool | 3.6 | 4.8 | 3.6 | 4.0 | 3.8 | 4.2 | 2.4 | 3.9 | 3.4 | 3.6 |
| 5. Liquid–Solid | 4.6 | 4.9 | 4.7 | 5.2 | 3.4 | 4.0 | 3.6 | 4.0 | 2.6 | 4.9 |
| 6. Delicate–Rugged | 5.0 | 5.0 | 4.4 | 5.2 | 3.9 | 4.8 | 3.0 | 4.3 | 2.6 | 5.2 |
| 7. Tight–Loose | 3.4 | 3.0 | 3.8 | 3.1 | 4.2 | 3.8 | 4.4 | 4.1 | 5.3 | 3.5 |
| 8. Empty–Full | 4.1 | 4.4 | 4.5 | 4.7 | 3.9 | 4.2 | 4.8 | 4.1 | 4.1 | 4.5 |
| 9. Masculine–Feminine | 2.9 | 3.0 | 3.7 | 2.7 | 3.9 | 3.6 | 4.9 | 4.0 | 5.4 | 2.9 |
| 10. Passive–Active | 3.9 | 4.9 | 4.1 | 3.9 | 4.0 | 4.6 | 3.6 | 3.8 | 3.6 | 4.9 |
| 11. Dark–Bright | 3.6 | 3.6 | 3.6 | 2.7 | 4.0 | 4.1 | 4.3 | 3.5 | 5.1 | 3.4 |
| 12. Back–Front | 3.8 | 3.6 | 3.6 | 3.5 | 4.0 | 4.1 | 4.5 | 3.6 | 4.4 | 3.9 |
| 13. Easy–Difficult | 4.1 | 4.7 | 3.6 | 4.2 | 3.6 | 3.7 | 2.9 | 3.6 | 2.9 | 4.2 |
| 14. Angular–Rounded | 4.0 | 2.8 | 4.5 | 3.8 | 4.1 | 3.3 | 5.1 | 4.2 | 4.6 | 4.3 |
| 15. Thick–Thin | 3.2 | 3.2 | 2.9 | 3.0 | 4.3 | 4.2 | 3.3 | 3.9 | 4.4 | 3.1 |
| 16. Weak–Strong | 5.0 | 4.9 | 4.8 | 5.3 | 4.3 | 4.4 | 4.2 | 3.9 | 3.6 | 5.5 |
| 17. Harsh–Mellow | 3.7 | 2.5 | 3.8 | 3.5 | 3.8 | 3.6 | 5.5 | 4.0 | 5.4 | 3.0 |
| 18. Abrupt–Continuous | 3.3 | 2.4 | 3.6 | 3.4 | 4.6 | 3.8 | 5.3 | 4.2 | 5.2 | 3.6 |
| 19. Large–Small | 3.6 | 3.3 | 3.4 | 3.1 | 4.2 | 3.7 | 3.7 | 3.9 | 4.0 | 2.8 |
| 20. Diffuse–Compact | 4.6 | 4.8 | 4.9 | 4.5 | 3.3 | 3.3 | 3.8 | 4.2 | 3.8 | 4.3 |
| 21. Sharp–Dull | 3.8 | 2.7 | 4.1 | 4.4 | 3.5 | 3.0 | 4.6 | 4.1 | 4.4 | 3.2 |
| 22. Hazy–Clear | 4.2 | 5.0 | 4.1 | 4.3 | 3.9 | 4.1 | 4.1 | 3.7 | 4.0 | 4.3 |
| 23. Vibrant–Still | 3.8 | 3.1 | 3.9 | 4.0 | 3.4 | 2.9 | 4.0 | 3.6 | 4.3 | 3.0 |
| 24. Heavy–Light | 3.2 | 3.3 | 2.8 | 2.9 | 3.7 | 3.9 | 3.9 | 3.4 | 4.8 | 2.8 |
| 25. Smooth–Rough | 4.3 | 4.9 | 4.2 | 4.5 | 3.3 | 3.8 | 2.7 | 3.5 | 2.3 | 4.3 |
| 26. Hard–Soft | 3.6 | 2.6 | 3.4 | 2.7 | 4.1 | 3.8 | 5.1 | 4.0 | 5.1 | 2.9 |

*Table 17*

| | *r* | S.D. | | *r* | S.D. |
|---|---|---|---|---|---|
| L | .905 | .929 | S | .731 | .364 |
| K | .853 | .927 | P | .724 | .534 |
| D | .841 | .791 | R | .717 | .794 |
| B | .769 | .537 | Z | .657 | .460 |
| M | .761 | .835 | N | .168 | .278 |

Table 17, while the standard deviations of the scale values in Experiment B are to be found in the second column. It is obvious that the consonants which have large dispersions of values are in the main responsible for the consistencies in the two experiments while those which deviate little from the mean scale values tend to be less reliable. This may be in part attributable to the fact that some consonants are by their nature polar and distinct with respect to the others and in part to the fact that we may have failed to provide scales appropriate to the verbal description of the distinctive attributes of some of the consonants (e.g., *z* and *n*), if such attributes do indeed exist.

A purpose analogous to that served by the generalized Euclidean distance measure (Table 15) in Experiment A is here represented by the coefficient of correlation for each pair of consonant sounds for Experiment B given in Table 18 below.

Each correlation may be viewed as representing the extent to which the ratings for each pair of consonants co-vary as one proceeds across the rating scales. As opposed to the distance procedure employed earlier, this statistic does not reveal how much the absolute scale values are alike; rather, it shows whether the changes in value from scale to scale are relatively similar for each pair of consonants.

Table 18 shows results similar to those in Experiment A in that each stop is highly and positively correlated with every other stop and the largest negative correlation of each stop is with *l*. That the detailed pattern is similar is further borne out by the fact that all the stops have low negative correlations with *s* and zero or negative correlations with *m*. As in the first study, *r* is seen to be similar in rating to the stops. The mean ratings for *r* correlate highly positively with *p*, *k*, *b*, and *d*, but negatively with *l*.

The source of these salient correlations is clearly seen in the table of means (Table 16). On 9 of the 26 scales the stops, together with *r*, constitute the first 5 entries at one pole or the other. In 7 of these cases *l* is the most polar consonant on the other end of the scale and is usually accompanied by *m* and *s*. The stops and *r* are described as being solid, thick, strong, abrupt, large, compact, heavy, rough, and hard, while *l*, *m*, and *s* are the most polar sounds on scales described as liquid, delicate, loose, continuous, smooth, and soft.

The discrepancy in descriptive terms between *r* and *l* is obvious in the general polarity above. There are, however, still scales on which they receive similar ratings (e.g., both are described as free, warm, and somewhat rounded). Scales on which the sounds differ by more than two full scale units describe *r* as solid, rugged, masculine, harsh, heavy, rough, and hard, as

*Table 18*

| | P | K | B | D | S | Z | M | N | L | R |
|---|---|---|---|---|---|---|---|---|---|---|
| P | — | .687 | .756 | .858 | −.205 | .268 | −.235 | .182 | −.627 | .838 |
| K | .687 | — | .530 | .717 | −.352 | .514 | −.668 | −.070 | −.828 | .730 |
| B | .756 | .530 | — | .812 | −.330 | .005 | .003 | .462 | −.483 | .704 |
| D | .858 | .717 | .812 | — | −.385 | .186 | −.334 | .276 | −.762 | .771 |
| S | −.205 | −.352 | −.330 | −.385 | — | .437 | .389 | .233 | .515 | .036 |
| Z | .268 | .514 | .005 | .186 | .437 | — | −.321 | .061 | −.283 | .542 |
| M | −.235 | −.668 | .003 | −.334 | .389 | −.321 | — | .291 | .768 | −.263 |
| N | .182 | −.070 | .462 | .276 | .233 | .061 | .291 | — | .007 | .179 |
| L | −.627 | −.828 | −.483 | −.762 | .515 | −.283 | .768 | .007 | — | −.574 |
| R | .838 | .730 | .704 | .771 | .036 | .542 | −.263 | .179 | −.574 | — |

opposed to *l* which is called liquid, delicate, feminine, mellow, light, smooth, and soft. This result, of course, is straightforward confirmation of the relevant findings in Experiment A.

Experiment B fails to reveal the tendency for *k* and *p* to occupy the most polar position among the stops which was seen in Experiment A. Thus, the argument that voiced stops are rated in absolute values as more like the sonorous continuants than are the unvoiced stops must be regarded as unverified. However, it is still clear that within each class of stop, the bilabial stops are described as being more like the continuants than the dental or alveolar stops. Ratings of *d* correlate −.76 with ratings of *l*, while ratings of *b* correlate only −.48. Similarly, ratings of *k* are seen to be more highly negatively related to *l* (−.83) than are the ratings of *p* (−.63). The same pattern holds for the intercorrelations between the same pairs of stops and the ratings of *s* and *m*. It may further be noted that the bilabial nasal *m* is clearly identified with the continuant pole, while the dental nasal *n* shows no relation to the continuants. This appears to be the same kind of resemblance found in the distance ratings of Experiment A; the greater sonority of the bilabials, resulting from their larger resonance cavity, it may be hypothesized, diminishes their opposition or increases their similarity to sounds drawn from the continuant end of the scales. See Table 19.

In Experiment B, machine techniques of factor analysis were employed. Principal factors were extracted, and a Varimax solution of the rotation of axes was obtained. Roughly speaking, the principal factor solution describes the correlation matrix in terms of a minimum number of dimensions run through the "center of gravity" of the multidimensional spatial representation of the correlations. It attempts to place axes so as to extract as much relationship as possible with each one and provides a concise description of a space which can represent the correlations observed. Varimax analysis consists of an analytic solution of the problem of rotating the axes in this space in an attempt to describe it in accordance with specified criteria defining a particular kind of optimal solution.

Since it is not clear that the Varimax assumptions apply or that we know the criteria for an optimal solution of the kind of study attempted here, the writers inspected both principal factor solutions and Varimax solutions to see which offered the most interesting results. In addition, the data were considered from two viewpoints. First, the intercorrelations between consonants (across scales) were taken as the base for analysis. Results are shown in Tables 20 and 21. Second, the intercorrelations between scales (across consonants) were used as the starting point. These results are shown in Tables 22 and 23.

When the intercorrelations among consonants were considered, the

*Table 19*
Experiment A: Diagonal Factor Analysis

| | F1 | F2 | F3 | Total variance | Remaining variance | Remaining as Pct. of total |
|---|---|---|---|---|---|---|
| 1. Inhibited–Free | 2.39 | .01 | −.27 | 8.27 | 2.49 | 30% |
| 2. Closed–Open | 1.34 | −.26 | −.58 | 3.55 | 1.34 | 38 |
| 3. Bad–Good | .68 | 1.11 | .14 | 3.06 | 1.35 | 44 |
| 4. Warm–Cool | −.96 | −.80 | −1.27 | 6.08 | 2.91 | 48 |
| 5. Liquid–Solid | −3.22 | −.32 | .80 | 12.85 | 1.74 | 14 |
| 6. Delicate–Rugged | −2.40 | −.25 | 1.72 | 8.94 | .16 | 2 |
| 7. Tight–Loose | 2.41 | .20 | −.87 | 9.32 | 2.71 | 29 |
| 8. Empty–Full | .06 | .91 | 1.88 | 7.14 | 2.78 | 39 |
| 9. Masculine–Feminine | 1.70 | .49 | −1.71 | 7.69 | 1.64 | 21 |
| 10. Passive–Active | .08 | −1.19 | 1.51 | 4.99 | 1.28 | 26 |
| 11. Dark–Bright | .83 | −.47 | −.34 | 4.86 | 3.83 | 79 |
| 12. Back–Front | .53 | −.10 | 1.70 | 6.86 | 3.68 | 54 |
| 13. Easy–Difficult | −.56 | −1.14 | .65 | 3.36 | 1.33 | 40 |
| 14. Angular–Rounded | .35 | 1.84 | .35 | 5.12 | 1.49 | 29 |
| 15. Thick–Thin | 1.40 | −.69 | −1.47 | 6.60 | 2.00 | 30 |
| 16. Weak–Strong | −1.48 | −.41 | 2.84 | 10.43 | .00 | 0 |
| 17. Harsh–Mellow | 1.32 | 2.98 | .00 | 10.62 | .00 | 0 |
| 18. Abrupt–Continuous | 3.97 | −.01 | .00 | 15.74 | −.02 | 0 |
| 19. Large–Small | .94 | −.49 | −1.20 | 4.28 | 1.72 | 40 |
| 20. Diffuse–Compact | −1.90 | .59 | .66 | 5.65 | 1.25 | 22 |
| 21. Sharp–Dull | −.01 | 1.14 | .37 | 4.55 | 3.11 | 68 |
| 22. Hazy–Clear | −1.10 | −.05 | .12 | 2.63 | 1.40 | 53 |
| 23. Vibrant–Still | −.83 | .61 | −1.76 | 7.05 | 2.89 | 41 |
| 24. Heavy–Light | 2.28 | −.37 | −2.25 | 12.04 | 1.64 | 14 |
| 25. Smooth–Rough | −1.82 | −1.97 | .13 | 10.94 | 3.73 | 34 |
| 26. Hard–Soft | 2.26 | .74 | −1.10 | 8.73 | 1.86 | 21 |

*Table 20*
Experiment B: Principal Factor Matrix from Intercorrelations Among Consonants

| | F1 | F2 | F3 | Variance accounted for |
|---|---|---|---|---|
| P | −.874 | .242 | −.073 | .828 |
| K | −.901 | −.231 | .204 | .907 |
| B | −.757 | .426 | −.415 | .926 |
| D | −.921 | .151 | −.220 | .919 |
| S | .372 | .570 | .675 | .919 |
| Z | −.392 | .128 | .864 | .916 |
| M | .545 | .690 | −.259 | .840 |
| N | −.153 | .754 | −.163 | .618 |
| L | .871 | .357 | .015 | .887 |
| R | −.855 | .313 | .241 | .887 |

*Table 21*
Experiment B: Varimax Solution for Intercorrelations Among Consonants

| | F1 | F2 | F3 | $h^2$ |
|---|---|---|---|---|
| P | −.893 | −.147 | .093 | .828 |
| K | −.676 | −.639 | .207 | .907 |
| B | −.933 | .147 | −.184 | .926 |
| D | −.933 | −.210 | −.070 | .919 |
| S | .265 | .488 | .782 | .919 |
| Z | −.210 | −.270 | .894 | .916 |
| M | .169 | .897 | −.079 | .840 |
| N | −.461 | .629 | .099 | .618 |
| L | .649 | .681 | .043 | .887 |
| R | −.834 | −.155 | .409 | .887 |

*Table 22*

Experiment B: Principal Factor Matrix from Intercorrelations Among Scales

| | F1 | F2 | F3 | F4 | Variance accounted for |
|---|---|---|---|---|---|
| 1. Inhibited–Free | .693 | −.293 | .370 | −.139 | .723 |
| 2. Closed–Open | .817 | .254 | .354 | .141 | .879 |
| 3. Bad–Good | −.675 | −.592 | −.286 | .236 | .945 |
| 4. Warm–Cool | −.948 | .293 | .047 | −.079 | .993 |
| 5. Liquid–Solid | −.944 | −.095 | −.026 | −.248 | .962 |
| 6. Delicate–Rugged | .967 | −.067 | −.015 | .015 | .941 |
| 7. Tight–Loose | −.261 | .717 | .422 | .159 | .787 |
| 8. Empty–Full | .944 | .022 | .000 | .221 | .941 |
| 9. Masculine–Feminine | −.703 | −.483 | .446 | −.009 | .927 |
| 10. Passive–Active | .845 | −.317 | .231 | .283 | .949 |
| 11. Dark–Bright | .828 | −.105 | .500 | .030 | .948 |
| 12. Back–Front | −.949 | −.185 | .034 | .055 | .940 |
| 13. Easy–Difficult | .680 | .603 | .114 | −.312 | .938 |
| 14. Angular–Rounded | .660 | −.694 | −.217 | −.067 | .970 |
| 15. Thick–Thin | −.841 | .246 | .347 | −.229 | .942 |
| 16. Weak–Strong | .929 | .332 | .000 | .077 | .981 |
| 17. Harsh–Mellow | .954 | .124 | .035 | −.189 | .962 |
| 18. Abrupt–Continuous | .738 | −.354 | −.485 | .072 | .913 |
| 19. Large–Small | −.637 | .521 | −.081 | .320 | .788 |
| 20. Diffuse–Compact | .562 | .752 | −.266 | −.029 | .953 |
| 21. Sharp–Dull | −.647 | −.066 | .438 | .597 | .972 |
| 22. Hazy–Clear | .526 | .673 | −.264 | .242 | .860 |
| 23. Vibrant–Still | .841 | −.373 | .060 | .321 | .955 |
| 24. Heavy–Light | −.992 | .006 | −.013 | .023 | .985 |
| 25. Smooth–Rough | .979 | .028 | −.010 | .035 | .961 |
| 26. Hard–Soft | .744 | −.337 | .394 | −.340 | .939 |

principal factor analysis yielded a readily interpretable solution. The first factor, accounting for 51 percent of the variance, showed significant loadings for all consonants except *n*. Positive loadings were observed for *l* (.87), *m* (.54), and *s* (.37), with negative loadings for the remaining consonants, the strongest being *b* (−.76), *r* (−.85), *p* (−.87), *k* (−.90), and *d* (−.92). Clearly, this is the major dimension already discussed above with the stops and *r* versus *l*, *m*, and *s*.

The second factor appeared to be highly identified with nasality, with the following significant loadings: *n* (+.75), *m* (+.69), *s* (+.57), and *b* (+.43). There were no significant negative loadings.

The third factor had the highest loadings for the sibilants, *z* (+.86) and *s* (+.68), with *b* (−.41) as the only significant negative loading.

The Varimax solution looks very much the same, except that on the first factor *l* is most clearly opposed by the voiced stops (i.e., *b* and *k* change places), on the second factor nasality is opposed to the voiceless stop *k* (−.64), and on the third factor the voiced stop *b* is not significantly negatively loaded. The difference between the solutions may be largely accounted for in terms of the shift in axes which makes the voiced stops polar on the first factor and minimizes their role elsewhere. There is little to choose from between the two solutions. They are essentially similar and their linguistic interpretation is clear.

The factor methods were then applied to the matrix of intercorrelations between scales. (These correlations must be regarded as somewhat unstable, since each of them is based on only ten pairs of scale values, whereas each consonant correlation was based on 26 pairs of values.) The principal factor analysis yielded three factors of appreciable magnitude. Factor 1, accounting for 64 percent of the variance, was most clearly defined by the adjectives (all loadings greater than .93) hard, tight, abrupt, masculine, harsh, rugged, solid, difficult, and rough. The factor was quite pervasive, and 25 of the

*Table 23*

Experiment B: Varimax Solution for Intercorrelation Among Scales

| | F1 | F2 | F3 | F4 | Variance accounted for |
|---|---|---|---|---|---|
| 1. Inhibited–Free | .784 | −.222 | −.035 | −.243 | .724 |
| 2. Closed–Open | .769 | .048 | −.533 | .030 | .879 |
| 3. Bad–Good | −.502 | −.281 | .715 | .321 | .945 |
| 4. Warm–Cool | −.713 | .612 | .332 | .035 | .994 |
| 5. Liquid–Solid | −.690 | .325 | .603 | −.134 | .963 |
| 6. Delicate–Rugged | .689 | −.457 | −.499 | −.100 | .942 |
| 7. Tight–Loose | −.049 | .831 | −.252 | .179 | .787 |
| 8. Empty–Full | .686 | −.387 | −.556 | .108 | .941 |
| 9. Masculine–Feminine | −.091 | .290 | .913 | .046 | .928 |
| 10. Passive–Active | .855 | −.405 | −.168 | .165 | .950 |
| 11. Dark–Bright | .942 | −.088 | −.214 | −.094 | .949 |
| 12. Back–Front | −.597 | .304 | .682 | .164 | .941 |
| 13. Easy–Difficult | .380 | .174 | −.783 | −.389 | .939 |
| 14. Angular–Rounded | .471 | −.850 | .077 | −.144 | .971 |
| 15. Thick–Thin | −.446 | .741 | .418 | −.141 | .942 |
| 16. Weak–Strong | .588 | −.184 | −.775 | −.029 | .981 |
| 17. Harsh–Mellow | .644 | −.293 | −.609 | −.301 | .963 |
| 18. Abrupt–Continuous | .288 | −.853 | −.320 | .003 | .913 |
| 19. Large–Small | −.583 | .528 | −.074 | .404 | .788 |
| 20. Diffuse–Compact | .045 | .056 | −.971 | −.073 | .954 |
| 21. Sharp–Dull | −.079 | .504 | .542 | .647 | .973 |
| 22. Hazy–Clear | .072 | .016 | −.903 | .200 | .861 |
| 23. Vibrant–Still | .757 | −.551 | −.185 | .211 | .955 |
| 24. Heavy–Light | −.706 | .409 | .547 | .142 | .985 |
| 25. Smooth–Rough | .680 | −.399 | −.577 | −.080 | .961 |
| 26. Hard–Soft | .821 | −.251 | −.014 | −.450 | .940 |

26 scales had significant loadings on it. This brief list of the very highest scales includes all but one of the scales found on factor 1 of Experiment A, concentrated versus dispersed, hence this may be viewed as the same factor.

Factor 2, accounting for 16 percent of the variance, was defined much less well by the following adjectives (loading between .60 and .75): sharp, empty, vibrant, angular, and thin. This appears to be a factor somewhere between factors 2 (harsh vs. mellow) and 3 (potency) of Experiment A.

The third factor was only weakly defined (loadings between .45 and .50) as back, passive, and small. It seems much like the third factor (potency) of Experiment A.

The Varimax analysis permits a sharper definition of factors by splitting up the first principal factor and redistributing the variance. Under this analysis, all factors may be defined by loadings above .70. The first factor is described as front, bright, free, open, good, light, smooth, and liquid; the second is empty, weak, thin, and small; and the third is passive, warm, mellow, rounded, still, and dull. These seem most readily identified with the first, third, and second factors of Experiment A, respectively.

In all analyses we seem to find a general opposition of the stops plus *r* versus the nasals, sibilants, and *l*. This is the most salient characteristic of the data by inspection as well as by factor analysis of the consonants and the scales. It is the most important factor on all analyses. Smaller but distinctive descriptive differences are observed when scales are examined on which the sibilants are more polarized, as well as those on which the nasals are more polarized. These characteristic descriptive differences again may be found in each kind of data, but they emerge most clearly in the factor analysis of the consonants. In the analysis of scales they show themselves (less clearly) in the clusters of scales such as *empty–full*, *weak–strong*, and *thin–thick* for the sibilants, and *mellow–harsh*, *rounded–angular*, *smooth–rough*, *passive–active*, and so on for the nasals.

The principal factor technique seemed most adequate for disclosing relations among the consonants themselves, but the Varimax analysis seemed superior in making clear scale relationships. (This seems a reasonable outcome given the two very different kinds of sampling problems involved in selecting consonants from a small fixed population and scales from some arbitrarily large and heterogeneous population.)

The results arrived at in these studies are in good general agreement with the relatively few results of sound-symbolic studies which are directly comparable (studies of vowels having been far more frequent). In an appendix to *Die Metaphern in der Phonetik*, Fonágy gives the results of tests in which 95 Hungarian speakers were given choices, usually between pairs of sounds, in terms of a comparative judgment regarding certain qualities.[9] Some of these were consonants, and in most instances these could be reasonably equated with certain scales of the present study. Asked which was softer ("Welcher ist weicher?") of *r* and *l*, 77.42 percent responded with *l* and 22.58 percent with *r*. In Experiment A on the *hard–soft* scale, *r* was rated 2.9 and *l* was 5.1, and in Experiment B, *r* was 3.2 and *l*, 5.1. To the question "Which is the man?" ("Welcher ist der Mann?") 91.3 percent of Fonágy's subjects chose *r* over *l*. This may be compared with the *masculine–feminine* scale on which in Experiment A *r* was 2.8 and *l* was 5.0, and in Experiment B *r* was 2.9 and *l* was 5.4. To the question as to which is harder ("Welcher ist harter?") of *k* and *l*, 91.55 percent responded that *k* was harder. In Experiment A, on the *hard–soft* scale, *k* was rated 2.1 and *l* was 5.1; in Experiment B, *k* was 2.6 and *l* was 5.1. These, which were the only comparable results, are all confirmatory. Fonágy seems intuitively to have chosen consonants which tended to extreme values on these scales, as can be seen by comparing these results in more detail with the data on Tables 14 and 17.

The present results may also be compared to those of Newman's study.[10] His technique, which followed that of Sapir's earlier study, was different from that employed in the present studies. Subjects were given pairs of nonsense sequences which differed in only one sound and in one experiment were asked which was larger and which smaller (141 subjects), and in another which was dark and which was light (136 subjects). Some of the consonants used by Newman coincided with those utilized here, and his results may be compared with our *large–small* and *dark–bright* scales. To illustrate with an example, .775 of Newman's subjects judged *p* smaller than *b*. On Experiment A, *p* was rated 3.3 on the *large–small* scale and *b* was rated 2.8. Hence, *b* was rated larger, and this may be considered an agreement. For 22 such comparisons of Newman's *large–small* with the same scale on Experiment A, there were 14 agreements and 8 discrepancies; the results were the same with Experiment B, although the agreement or disagreement was not in every case on the same pair. For the *dark–light* experiment of Newman, there were 14 agreements and 6 disagreements with Experiment A and 2 cases in which the consonants in our study had the same rating. With Experiment B there were 11 agreements, 7 disagreements, and 4 instances with equal ratings. These relatively unsatisfactory results may be attributed to three factors.

[9] Ivan Fonágy, *Die Metaphern in der Phonetik; ein Beitrag zur Entwicklungsgeschichte des wissenschaftlichen Denkens* (The Hague, 1963).

[10] Stanley S. Newman, "Further Experiments in Phonetic Symbolism," *American Journal of Psychology*, 45 (1933): 53–75.

First, the technique used was different in many ways. Newman's subjects had a direct comparison offered to them; our subjects rated each sound independently. Newman's subjects were forced to make a discrimination or choice; our subjects could assign equal values if they chose. Newman presented consonants in different complex acoustic environments; ours were presented in a constant environment. We believe that all of these differences have important effects on what aspect of the stimulus is selected for judgment and what the subject is free to do with the judgment.

Second, the Newman experiment, unlike the Fonágy experiment, employed many consonants which had intermediate, as opposed to polar, values on the dimensions being judged. This technique, as we have seen in our own study, readily leads to unreliable ratings.

Third, the rating scales of the present study necessarily preserve transitivity. Given that the mean value of *p* on a particular scale is less than that of *b* and the mean value of *b* in turn is less than that of *d*, it must follow that *p* is less than *d*. Newman's technique forces no such transitivity on the data, and, indeed, the data are often found to be nontransitive. Hence, even at best there could not be perfect agreement between the studies.

These are the only directly comparable experimental results of which we are aware. A study by Tesmer, approaching the question from an aesthetic viewpoint and asking German subjects for preferences in monosyllables consisting of consonant–vowel, shows results in agreement with the present study in that the aesthetically preferred agrees in general with the ratings along such scales as *harsh–mellow* and *smooth–rough*. This shows that with the vowel factor constant, voiced consonants are preferred over unvoiced. The *l* was judged positively and the *r* negatively.[11] A study by Givler, reported in 1915, may be cited in which for speakers of American English consonantal preferences showed the following order (the more preferred first): *r*, *l*, *n*, *v*, *m*, *b*, *d*, *z*, *č*, *f*, *t*, *w*, *j*, *k*, *s*, *t*, *š*, *h*, *g*, and *θ*.[12] The general preference for continuants and voiced sounds thus appears once again.

Finally, a study by Roblee and Washburn involving judgments of *VC* combinations on a seven-point scale of *pleasant–unpleasant* shows the following order from most unpleasant to most pleasant: *g*, *k*, *š*, *t*, *ž*, *b*, *d*, *f*, *p*, *z*, *s*, *θ*, *ð*, *v*, *n*, *m*, and *l*. There was no rating for *r*. Not only does the stop–continuant hierarchy make its appearance here, but the rating of the labial as pleasant compared to other points of articulation, particularly the

[11] Hermann Tesmer, *Experimentalle euphonische Untersuchungen einzelner Vokale und Silben* (Halle, 1933).

[12] Robert C. Givler, "The Psycho-physiological Effect of the Element of Speech in Relation to Poetry," *Psychological Monographs*, 19, no. 2 (1915).

velar, is clearly also a factor. This study, which contained consonants not included in the present experiments, also suggests that among the fricatives those with the lowest and most concentrated frequency are judged the least pleasant. Except for *s* and *z*, the unvoiced–voiced preference noted earlier is superimposed on this series.[13]

It may be legitimately concluded from this study and from comparison with earlier studies that there exist reliable psychological phenomena, particularly for the extreme ratings, for consonants along certain scales of judgment. These phenomena might be further explored by adding to the number of consonants investigated, eliminating scales which on the basis of the present analysis largely duplicate each other and adding different scales which may probe other factors not appearing in the present set.

## IV. Descriptive Ratings of Selected Vowels

Parallel to the preceding study of this series, in which the semantic differential technique was applied to the description of a set of consonants, two experiments were carried out in which subjects were asked to rate a set of vowels. These experiments involved descriptive judgments on 23 bipolar scales, only 15 of which were identical with scales used in the consonant experiments. Some scales felt to be largely descriptive of consonants were discarded (e.g., *liquid–solid* and *abrupt–continuous*) and scales believed to be especially appropriate to vowels were added (e.g., *high–low* and *falling–rising*). In addition, color scales (e.g., *red–green* and *yellow–blue*) were employed in view of the repeated findings in the previous literature regarding vowel-color synaesthesia.

Experiment A, which was intended as a preliminary exploration of the problems involved, employed nine subjects and used as stimuli seven simple vowels or diphthongs. The instructions were identical with those reported for the consonant experiment, except for the portion referring to the graphic symbols on the top of each page, which represented the stimuli for the subjects. The section substituted for the corresponding one in the consonant study was as follows:

The speech sounds we want you to rate are on each page at the top. Here (on board) is the way the sounds are read:

AY read as *a*, as in *pay*, *say*, *day*, etc.
AH read as *ah*, as in *ah*
EE read as *e*, as in *reed*, *speed*, etc.

[13] Louis Roblee and M. F. Washburn, "The Affective Values of Articulate Sounds," *American Journal of Psychology*, 23 (1912): 579–583.

IE read as *i*, as in *pie*, *lie*, etc.
OH read as *o*, as in *oh*
OO read as *oo*, as in *boot*, *loot*, etc.
OW read as *ow*, as in *cow*, *now*, etc.

These vowels are, of course, all of the type found in unchecked syllables in English. They will be referred to in the following discussion as *EJ*, *A*, *IJ*, *AJ*, *OW*, *UW*, and *AW*, respectively. The subjects were predominantly from the Minneapolis-St. Paul area and would presumably have minimal or no diphthongization in *IJ* and *UW* and little or even none for *EJ* and *OW* also. This sample, then, involves the five traditional long vowels and the back and front rising diphthongs *AJ* and *AW*.

The results of Experiment A are given in Table 24, which reports the mean rating for the nine subjects for each vowel on each scale.

A preliminary notion concerning the general patterning of the vowels with reference to the scales employed can be obtained from the generalized distance formula described in the immediately previous article in the series. The distance measure for each pair of vowels in Experiment A is set forth in Table 25. It will be noted that the greatest single distance is between *IJ*, the highest front vowel, and *A*, the lowest back vowel (11.10). The most

*Table 24*

| | IJ | EJ | A | OW | UW | AJ | AW |
|---|---|---|---|---|---|---|---|
| 1. Weak–Strong | 2.7 | 4.2 | 4.4 | 4.8 | 3.7 | 4.9 | 5.2 |
| 2. Heavy–Light | 5.8 | 4.2 | 3.2 | 3.4 | 3.9 | 4.3 | 3.3 |
| 3. Thick–Thin | 6.2 | 3.8 | 3.1 | 3.1 | 3.8 | 4.8 | 2.8 |
| 4. Dark–Bright | 5.7 | 4.6 | 3.4 | 4.2 | 4.7 | 5.3 | 4.4 |
| 5. Oblong–Round | 2.4 | 3.4 | 4.6 | 5.7 | 4.9 | 2.9 | 5.1 |
| 6. Hard–Soft | 2.9 | 2.8 | 4.4 | 4.8 | 4.8 | 2.9 | 3.4 |
| 7. Back–Front | 4.7 | 3.9 | 3.6 | 4.8 | 5.0 | 3.8 | 3.4 |
| 8. Narrow–Wide | 2.1 | 3.3 | 5.6 | 5.3 | 4.3 | 3.4 | 4.9 |
| 9. White–Black | 3.0 | 3.4 | 4.8 | 4.1 | 4.1 | 2.8 | 3.4 |
| 10. Falling–Rising | 5.0 | 4.3 | 2.7 | 3.0 | 4.0 | 4.1 | 3.1 |
| 11. Red–Green | 4.2 | 3.4 | 3.9 | 4.0 | 4.2 | 3.9 | 3.2 |
| 12. Sharp–Dull | 1.1 | 3.2 | 5.2 | 5.1 | 4.0 | 2.2 | 4.1 |
| 13. High–Low | 1.1 | 3.4 | 5.2 | 5.2 | 3.9 | 2.0 | 5.0 |
| 14. Smooth–Rough | 4.3 | 3.7 | 2.8 | 2.8 | 2.0 | 4.2 | 3.1 |
| 15. Passive–Active | 5.8 | 5.0 | 3.2 | 3.8 | 3.8 | 4.6 | 3.3 |
| 16. Masculine–Feminine | 5.8 | 3.4 | 2.9 | 3.9 | 5.2 | 4.2 | 3.7 |
| 17. Bad–Good | 3.9 | 3.8 | 4.8 | 5.0 | 5.0 | 3.6 | 3.6 |
| 18. Warm–Cool | 4.3 | 4.0 | 2.9 | 3.2 | 4.9 | 4.6 | 3.7 |
| 19. Closed–Open | 3.4 | 4.2 | 5.6 | 5.9 | 3.6 | 4.1 | 4.2 |
| 20. Empty–Full | 3.3 | 3.9 | 5.4 | 5.0 | 4.6 | 3.1 | 4.3 |
| 21. Yellow–Blue | 3.7 | 3.2 | 4.0 | 4.6 | 5.3 | 3.2 | 4.0 |
| 22. Diffuse–Compact | 4.9 | 3.6 | 2.6 | 3.3 | 5.0 | 4.3 | 4.2 |
| 23. Large–Small | 5.2 | 4.2 | 2.3 | 2.6 | 4.1 | 4.7 | 3.0 |

*Table 25*

| | IJ | EJ | A | OW | UW | AJ | AW |
|---|---|---|---|---|---|---|---|
| IJ | — | 6.09 | 11.10 | 10.53 | 7.81 | 4.83 | 9.55 |
| EJ | 6.09 | — | 6.13 | 5.60 | 5.36 | 3.27 | 4.45 |
| A | 11.10 | 6.13 | — | 2.65 | 6.17 | 8.52 | 4.05 |
| OW | 10.53 | 5.60 | 2.65 | — | 4.82 | 7.96 | 3.79 |
| UW | 7.81 | 5.36 | 6.17 | 4.82 | — | 6.08 | 4.84 |
| AJ | 4.83 | 3.27 | 8.52 | 7.96 | 6.08 | — | 6.23 |
| AW | 9.55 | 4.45 | 4.05 | 3.79 | 4.84 | 6.23 | — |

polarized vowel is *IJ*, which shows a greater mean distance from all other vowels than any other.

In general, the overall pattern which shows most decisively is one which aligns the front vowels or those that have a front component as the second diphthongal element against the back vowels defined in analogous fashion. If we study the intervowel distances on the basis of this grouping (front vowels, *IJ*, *EJ*, and *AJ*; back vowels, *A*, *OW*, *UW*, and *AW*), it is immediately clear that this constitutes an important factor in accounting for similarity or dissimilarity. The back vowels are judged quite similar to each other, the mean distance between these vowels taken pairwise being 4.39 (range: 2.65–6.17). The front vowels are likewise seen as similar, with the mean interpair distance of 4.73 (range: 3.27–6.09). Interpair distances between front and back vowels, however, show much larger values, with a mean of 7.44 (range: 4.45–11.10). In this conceptual space, then, the back vowels are seen to be crowded together, as it were, in one locus, with the front vowels clustered together some distance away; *IJ* is most distant from the back vowels in general, with *AJ* next and *EJ* least. Among the back vowels *A* is consistently most distant from each front vowel, and *UW* is least distant.

This description, of course, does not give any indication of the specific scales which contribute to these similarities and differences, nor does it afford a verbal description of the attributes associated with the coordinates of the extreme distances observed in Table 25. More light is shed on these aspects of vowel judgments by some form of factor analysis. For this experiment, given the small number of subjects and the preliminary nature of the study, more elaborate factor analyses were not attempted. However, as in the parallel case of the consonants, a diagonal factor analysis was carried out to determine the extent to which the scales could be grouped as measures of independent components of judgment. In addition, the position of the vowels on each of these components was considered. Results of the diagonal analysis are given in detail in the Appendix. The five scales with the greatest absolute variation on the first factor are *high–low*, *sharp–dull*, *narrow–wide*, *thick–thin*, and *oblong–round*. Of these, all except *thick–thin* have positive loadings. Thus, this factor contrasts high, sharp, narrow, thin, and oblong with low, dull, wide, thick, and round. We may, perhaps, best summarize this opposition as *acute* versus *grave*, employing more traditional terms not found among the adjectives of the present scales.

One method of relating this factor to the vowels is to calculate the mean rating for each vowel over the scales with the highest loadings just cited. In this calculation, ratings were translated into positive or negative deviations from the midpoint of the seven-point scale. Thus, a rating of 3.2 was entered in the form −.8. The vowel *IJ* has the largest mean rating on the negative side (acute), −2.34, and then, in order, *AJ* (−1.26), *EJ* (−0.58), *UW* (+0.26), *AW* (+0.86), *A* (+1.10), and *OW* (+1.24). Thus, all the front vowels were on the left side of the scale (acute) and all the back vowels were on the right side (grave). Again, *IJ* was the most polarized (largest mean distance from the midpoint).

The second factor had the highest loadings on the scales *smooth–rough*, *bad–good*, *oblong–round*, *dark–bright*, and *empty–full*. All loadings were negative, except for *smooth–rough*; so the factor yields a contrast between smooth, good, round, bright, and full on the one hand and rough, bad, oblong, dark, and empty on the other. This may be summarized as a *pleasant–unpleasant* contrast, once more using adjectives not on our scales. Using the same method of calculation as for the first factor, the strongest deviations are found to be on the negative side (pleasant), with the vowels ranged in the following order: *OW* (−1.04), *UW* (−1.02), *A* (−.68), *AW* (−0.62), *EJ* (−0.02), *IJ* (+0.14), and *AJ* (+0.26). Once again, front vowels are aligned against back vowels, but here in a somewhat different fashion.

The third factor has the largest loadings on *closed–open*, *diffuse–compact*, *warm–cool*, *large–small*, and *masculine–feminine*, with negative loadings on all except the first. We thus have closed, compact, cool, small, and feminine against open, diffuse, warm, large, and masculine. On the whole, this appears to represent size and strength and may be called *potency* or *expansiveness*.

Using once more the same technique, we find the strongest deviations this time in the positive direction (potency), with *A* having the largest positive deviation and *IJ* the largest negative, as follows: *A* (+1.38), *OW* (+0.98), *AW* (+0.32), *EJ* (+0.20), *AJ* (−0.34), *UW* (−0.56), and *IJ* (−1.00). For this factor the *back–front* distinction, while still present, is evidently subordinate to the *high–low* dimension, the lowest vowel *A* being the most potent or expansive and the two highest, *UW* and *IJ*, being the most constricted.

We may briefly summarize the results of Experiment A by stating that it shows most strongly an overall contrast between front and back vowels, with

*AW* patterning with the back vowels and *AJ* with the front. The most polarized vowel is *IJ*. At the other extreme, the ordering of vowels is less fixed; in general, *A* is the most distant from *IJ*, but for certain combinations of scales either *OW* or *UW* has this role.

Experiment B consisted of judgments on the same scales as for Experiment A, but two additional vowels were included as stimuli: *I* as in *bit*, and *E* as in *met*. The subjects were 44 students in Introductory Psychology at the University of Minnesota. All subjects rated all the vowels, except that through inadvertance two subjects failed to give judgments concerning *E*, so that for this vowel there are only 42 subjects. The instructions were identical to those for Experiment A, except that to the list of stimuli were added:

IH read as *i*, as in *it*, *hit*, *bit*, etc.
EH read as *e*, as in *bet*, *met*, etc.

We have, thus, two "short" vowels of the kind which occur in checked syllables.

The results of Experiment B are set forth in Table 26. This table of mean ratings on each scale for each vowel may be directly compared with the results for Experiment A given in Table 24. A measure of reliability between experiments A and B can, of course, be based only on comparisons of results for those vowels employed in both experiments. The product-moment correlations for each of these vowels is given in Table 27. The overall correlation between the ratings for the seven vowels in both experiments is .746. This outcome, while highly significant statistically, is somewhat lower than that obtained in the experiments with the consonants (.814) and indicates that there is less reliability than one would desire in the vowel rating procedure. As was to be expected, the vowel of greatest polarity, *IJ*, showed the highest reliability (.874), while the vowels which show little dispersion in ratings, *UW* and *EJ*, have poor reliabilities.

It is not clear from this single study why the reliabilities are not more satisfactory. It may be that the psychological characteristics of these particular vowels are not marked or not commonly agreed upon; or that appropriate scales for these particular vowels were not chosen; or that the representation of the vowels being judged by each subject were somewhat different, vowels being notoriously slippery stimuli. Examination of the raw data suggests that further study of the source of variation might be fruitful. Even for the most stable vowel, *IJ*, there were a few major shifts of ratings from Experiment A to Experiment B, notably on the *weak–strong* scale, for which a mean rating of 2.7 was obtained in the first study, but 4.8 on the second. The distribution of ratings in this particular case appears bimodal, indicating that two different views of the vowel with respect to this scale are popular.

*Table 26*

| | IJ | EJ | A | OW | UW | AJ | AW | I | E |
|---|---|---|---|---|---|---|---|---|---|
| 1. Weak–Strong | 4.8 | 4.6 | 3.6 | 4.5 | 3.7 | 4.7 | 5.0 | 3.0 | 3.5 |
| 2. Heavy–Light | 4.6 | 3.6 | 3.9 | 3.7 | 3.7 | 4.3 | 3.1 | 5.1 | 4.2 |
| 3. Thick–Thin | 5.1 | 3.8 | 3.3 | 3.2 | 3.4 | 4.7 | 3.1 | 4.8 | 4.3 |
| 4. Dark–Bright | 5.2 | 4.7 | 3.9 | 4.2 | 3.5 | 4.9 | 3.5 | 4.4 | 3.7 |
| 5. Oblong–Round | 3.1 | 3.4 | 3.9 | 5.8 | 4.2 | 3.4 | 4.8 | 3.2 | 3.5 |
| 6. Hard–Soft | 2.7 | 3.8 | 5.2 | 4.9 | 5.1 | 3.6 | 3.4 | 3.4 | 3.4 |
| 7. Back–Front | 4.6 | 3.9 | 3.5 | 4.4 | 3.8 | 4.3 | 4.2 | 4.3 | 3.8 |
| 8. Narrow–Wide | 3.2 | 3.8 | 4.6 | 5.5 | 4.5 | 3.6 | 5.2 | 2.7 | 3.4 |
| 9. White–Black | 3.6 | 3.6 | 3.9 | 4.3 | 3.6 | 3.2 | 4.1 | 3.6 | 4.2 |
| 10. Falling–Rising | 4.5 | 3.9 | 3.2 | 3.8 | 3.5 | 4.3 | 3.7 | 4.2 | 3.6 |
| 11. Red–Green | 3.6 | 3.6 | 4.3 | 3.4 | 4.6 | 3.8 | 3.6 | 4.3 | 4.3 |
| 12. Sharp–Dull | 1.8 | 3.2 | 4.8 | 4.7 | 5.2 | 3.2 | 3.7 | 3.7 | 3.8 |
| 13. High–Low | 2.0 | 3.4 | 5.1 | 4.7 | 4.7 | 3.7 | 4.4 | 3.8 | 4.4 |
| 14. Smooth–Rough | 3.6 | 3.4 | 2.3 | 2.5 | 2.5 | 3.2 | 4.2 | 1.5 | 5.1 |
| 15. Passive–Active | 5.7 | 4.2 | 3.0 | 3.4 | 3.6 | 5.0 | 4.2 | 4.1 | 3.7 |
| 16. Masculine–Feminine | 5.4 | 3.4 | 4.4 | 4.2 | 4.5 | 3.6 | 3.4 | 4.3 | 3.8 |
| 17. Bad–Good | 3.6 | 4.5 | 4.2 | 4.3 | 4.4 | 4.3 | 3.3 | 3.4 | 3.6 |
| 18. Warm–Cool | 4.7 | 3.7 | 2.7 | 3.9 | 4.0 | 3.9 | 3.5 | 4.6 | 4.3 |
| 19. Closed–Open | 4.0 | 4.4 | 4.8 | 4.9 | 4.5 | 4.3 | 4.4 | 3.6 | 3.4 |
| 20. Empty–Full | 3.6 | 4.5 | 4.6 | 4.8 | 4.9 | 4.5 | 4.7 | 3.2 | 3.4 |
| 21. Yellow–Blue | 3.4 | 3.6 | 4.1 | 3.5 | 4.7 | 4.0 | 3.7 | 4.2 | 3.9 |
| 22. Diffuse–Compact | 4.2 | 4.4 | 3.3 | 4.2 | 3.8 | 4.8 | 3.8 | 4.2 | 4.2 |
| 23. Large–Small | 4.8 | 4.1 | 3.7 | 2.9 | 3.0 | 4.6 | 3.1 | 5.5 | 5.0 |

*Table 27*

| | *r* | S.D. | | *r* | S.D. |
|---|---|---|---|---|---|
| IJ | .874 | 1.032 | UW | .502 | .686 |
| EJ | .592 | .447 | AJ | .680 | .573 |
| A | .730 | .756 | AW | .709 | .621 |
| OW | .837 | .799 | | | |

*Table 28*

| | IJ | EJ | A | OW | UW | AJ | AW | I | E |
|---|---|---|---|---|---|---|---|---|---|
| IJ | — | 4.14 | 7.50 | 7.39 | 7.24 | 3.65 | 6.29 | 4.47 | 5.21 |
| EJ | 4.14 | — | 4.24 | 4.38 | 4.18 | 1.85 | 3.40 | 4.35 | 3.62 |
| A | 7.50 | 4.24 | — | 3.36 | 2.10 | 5.05 | 4.31 | 6.08 | 5.04 |
| OW | 7.39 | 4.38 | 3.36 | — | 3.05 | 5.14 | 3.39 | 6.86 | 5.76 |
| UW | 7.24 | 4.18 | 2.10 | 3.05 | — | 4.78 | 4.08 | 5.92 | 4.98 |
| AJ | 3.65 | 1.85 | 5.05 | 5.14 | 4.78 | — | 4.34 | 3.87 | 3.81 |
| AW | 6.29 | 3.40 | 4.31 | 3.39 | 4.08 | 4.34 | — | 5.81 | 4.36 |
| I | 4.47 | 4.35 | 6.08 | 6.86 | 5.92 | 3.87 | 5.81 | — | 2.16 |
| E | 5.21 | 3.62 | 5.04 | 5.76 | 4.98 | 3.81 | 4.36 | 2.16 | — |

Some of the main points of similarity and difference between the results of experiments A and B can be noted by a comparison of the same kinds of measures on the two studies. The results of the application of the generalized distance formula are given for the nine vowels in Experiment B in Table 28.

The values for distances among the seven vowels used in Experiment A are directly comparable to the corresponding values for that experiment found in Table 25. Looking only at these vowels, we note that once again the greatest single distance is between *IJ* and *A* (7.50). We also note immediately that in this case and in all others the distances in the table are less extreme than they were in the first experiment. This is probably due to the greater number of subjects in the second study; with the small sample of Experiment A, more extreme values are to be expected. The relative distances between *IJ* and the three back vowels *A*, *OW*, and *UW* are in the same order, but with the differences much diminished.

Front and back articulation continued to be the most obvious single ordering principle evident on inspection of the table. If, as in Experiment A, we compare the interpair distances, back to back, front to front, and back to front, the outcomes remain the same as for that experiment. Mean distances and ranges were: back vowels 3.48 (2.10–4.31), front vowels 3.21 (1.85–4.14), and back to front 5.33 (3.40–7.50).

The addition of *I* and *E*, both of course front vowels, provides new evidence for the importance of the *back–front* distinction. Since both, in addition to being front vowels, are the only "short" vowels also, we would expect them to pattern similarly. In fact, the distance between them, 2.16, is the third smallest of the entries in the tables of distance. If we include *I* and *E* in the calculations of front and back interpair distances, the earlier findings are maintained. The number of front vowel pairings increases appreciably (from three pairs to ten pairs), but the mean distance between the pairs is only 3.71 (range: 1.85–5.21). The number of pairings of front and back vowels increases also, of course (from 12 to 20 pairings), and yields a mean distance of 5.44 (range: 3.40–7.50). The results with *I* and *E* thus corroborate the role of the back/front dichotomy as an important distinction affecting judgments on the given scales.

An additional measure of resemblance among vowels was calculated for Experiment B, the coefficient of correlation. This coefficient was used both as a means of measuring the resemblance between the vowels and the degree of relationship between scales and as the basic material for the factor analyses. The matrix of correlations describing the relationship between the vowels is given in Table 29. This measure is partially independent of the distance measure just presented and, in this case, gives striking results. Of the 16 coefficients of correlation between vowels which *agree* in frontness or in

Table 29

| | IJ | EJ | A | OW | UW | AJ | AW | I | E |
|---|---|---|---|---|---|---|---|---|---|
| IJ | — | .443 | −.589 | −.455 | −.599 | .675 | −.270 | .454 | .071 |
| EJ | .443 | — | −.070 | .058 | −.157 | .802 | .107 | −.190 | −.355 |
| A | −.589 | −.070 | — | .623 | .829 | −.268 | .117 | −.539 | −.466 |
| OW | −.455 | .058 | .623 | — | .634 | −.248 | .568 | −.840 | −.744 |
| UW | −.599 | −.157 | .829 | .634 | — | −.308 | .142 | −.613 | −.580 |
| AJ | .675 | .802 | −.268 | −.248 | −.308 | — | −.158 | .203 | −.126 |
| AW | −.270 | .107 | .117 | .568 | .142 | −.158 | — | −.697 | −.397 |
| I | .454 | −.190 | −.539 | −.840 | −.613 | .203 | −.697 | — | .786 |
| E | .071 | −.355 | −.466 | −.744 | −.580 | −.126 | −.397 | .786 | — |

Table 30
Experiment A: Diagonal Factor Analysis

| | F1 | F2 | F3 | Total variance | Remaining variance | Remaining as Pct. of total |
|---|---|---|---|---|---|---|
| 1. Weak–Strong | 1.11 | −.36 | .76 | 4.87 | 2.92 | 60% |
| 2. Heavy–Light | −2.04 | .28 | −.18 | 4.87 | .60 | 12 |
| 3. Thick–Thin | −2.74 | .54 | −.10 | 8.62 | .81 | 9 |
| 4. Dark–Bright | −1.97 | −1.14 | .16 | 5.99 | .78 | 13 |
| 5. Oblong–Round | 2.69 | −1.17 | −.04 | 9.40 | .79 | 8 |
| 6. Hard–Soft | 1.68 | −.30 | −.32 | 5.66 | 2.65 | 47 |
| 7. Back–Front | −.44 | −.87 | −.10 | 2.70 | 1.74 | 64 |
| 8. Narrow–Wide | 2.81 | −.84 | .64 | 9.61 | .59 | 6 |
| 9. White–Black | 1.50 | .24 | −.15 | 3.82 | 1.49 | 39 |
| 10. Falling–Rising | −1.70 | .72 | −.82 | 4.60 | .52 | 11 |
| 11. Red–Green | −.24 | .15 | −.04 | 1.10 | 1.02 | 93 |
| 12. Sharp–Dull | 3.76 | .18 | .08 | 14.95 | .77 | 5 |
| 13. High–Low | 4.08 | .00 | .00 | 16.66 | .00 | 0 |
| 14. Smooth–Rough | −1.14 | 2.57 | .00 | 7.91 | .00 | 0 |
| 15. Passive–Active | −2.18 | .04 | .32 | 5.81 | .96 | 16 |
| 16. Masculine–Feminine | −1.74 | −.74 | −.89 | 6.39 | 2.02 | 32 |
| 17. Bad–Good | .70 | −1.19 | .34 | 3.01 | .98 | 33 |
| 18. Warm–Cool | −1.16 | −.14 | −1.14 | 3.20 | .53 | 17 |
| 19. Closed–Open | 1.44 | −.84 | 2.00 | 6.78 | .00 | 0 |
| 20. Empty–Full | 1.72 | −1.07 | .45 | 4.72 | .42 | 9 |
| 21. Yellow–Blue | .87 | −.91 | −.72 | 3.42 | 1.31 | 38 |
| 22. Diffuse–Compact | −1.32 | −.28 | −1.43 | 4.55 | .68 | 15 |
| 23. Large–Small | −2.38 | .84 | −1.05 | 7.83 | .35 | 4 |

backness, 13 are positive and 3 are negative. The three negative correlations all involve a checked vowel, *E* or *I*, with a front nonchecked vowel. Moreover, the third highest positive correlation in the entire matrix is between *E* and *I* (.786). It appears, then, that in addition to back versus front, there is likewise evidence that the opposition *checked* versus *unchecked* ("short" vs. long or diphthongal) exercises a coherent influence on the results. Of the 20 correlations between front and back vowels, 18 are negative and 2 are very low positive. Here again, then, we find confirmation of the earlier findings.

Finally, Experiments A and B can be compared by reference to the outcomes of the diagonal factor analysis. In order to obtain direct comparability, *E* and *I* were excluded from this analysis for Experiment B. Results of the factor analysis are given in Table 31, which may be compared with the results of Experiment A, presented in Table 30.

The scales with the highest absolute variation on factor 1 are *sharp–dull*, *high–low*, *passive–active*, *hard–soft*, and *thick–thin*. Of these the third and the fifth had negative loadings. Thus, we have a contrast between sharp, high, active, hard, and thin on the one hand and dull, low, passive, soft, and thick on the other. This is evidently to be equated with the first factor of the diagonal analysis for Experiment A, which it will be recalled was named *acute* versus *grave*. Twenty-one of the 23 scales have loadings of the same sign on this factor in the two experiments. Three of the five scales with the highest loadings are identical. Employing the same technique as previously, that is, relating the factors to the vowels by calculating the average deviation

*Table 31*

Experiment B: Diagonal Factor Analysis

| | F1 | F2 | F3 | Total variance | Remaining variance | Remaining as Pct. of total |
|---|---|---|---|---|---|---|
| 1. Weak–Strong | −1.16 | −.55 | .91 | 2.99 | .51 | 17% |
| 2. Heavy–Light | −.55 | .08 | −.54 | 1.52 | .92 | 60 |
| 3. Thick–Thin | −1.48 | .38 | −.73 | 4.04 | 1.18 | 29 |
| 4. Dark–Bright | −1.45 | −.78 | −.14 | 3.29 | .56 | 17 |
| 5. Oblong–Round | 1.39 | −.14 | 1.87 | 5.46 | .00 | 0 |
| 6. Hard–Soft | 2.17 | −.89 | −.20 | 5.71 | .17 | 3 |
| 7. Back–Front | −.64 | −.11 | .59 | .95 | .18 | 19 |
| 8. Narrow–Wide | 1.35 | −.70 | 1.49 | 5.14 | .61 | 12 |
| 9. White–Black | .49 | .62 | .56 | 1.23 | .30 | 24 |
| 10. Falling–Rising | −.86 | .46 | .04 | 1.37 | .42 | 31 |
| 11. Red–Green | .68 | .17 | −.80 | 1.33 | .20 | 15 |
| 12. Sharp–Dull | 2.96 | .00 | .00 | 8.78 | .00 | 0 |
| 13. High–Low | 2.43 | −.22 | .29 | 6.80 | .76 | 11 |
| 14. Smooth–Rough | −.77 | 2.83 | .00 | 8.59 | .00 | 0 |
| 15. Passive–Active | −2.18 | −.01 | −.06 | 5.49 | .74 | 13 |
| 16. Masculine–Feminine | −.35 | −.93 | −.19 | 3.29 | 2.26 | 69 |
| 17. Bad–Good | .44 | −.56 | −.41 | 1.28 | .61 | 48 |
| 18. Warm–Cool | −.74 | .59 | .14 | 2.54 | 1.62 | 64 |
| 19. Closed–Open | .40 | −1.26 | .43 | 2.11 | .18 | 8 |
| 20. Empty–Full | .67 | −1.22 | .42 | 2.96 | .84 | 28 |
| 21. Yellow–Blue | .78 | .19 | −.68 | 1.36 | .25 | 18 |
| 22. Diffuse–Compact | −.67 | −.12 | .13 | 1.45 | .97 | 67 |
| 23. Large–Small | −1.44 | .53 | −1.04 | 4.12 | .69 | 17 |

of each vowel from the midpoint of the scale over five scales, the distribution of the vowels is seen to be similar. As for the first factor in Experiment A, the extreme negative deviation (*acute*) and the most polar vowel is *IJ* (−1.64), and then moving from left to right across the scale, *AJ* (−0.32), *EJ* (−0.32), *AW* (+0.04), *OW* (+0.74), *UW* (+0.80), and *A* (+0.96). Once again all the negative deviations are for the front vowels and all the positive for back vowels. The shifts in relative order as compared to Experiment A involve only the back vowels. In the first experiment the order was *IJ*, *AJ*, *EJ*, *UW*, *A*, and *OW*. In the second experiment *A* and *UW* have moved to a relatively more polar position.

The second factor is most strongly represented by the scales *smooth–rough*, *closed–open*, *empty–full*, *masculine–feminine*, and *hard–soft*. Of these, all but the first had negative loadings. The contrast is thus between smooth, open, full, feminine, and soft at one extreme and rough, closed, empty, masculine, and hard at the other. Both *smooth–rough* and *empty–full* appeared among the top five scales on the second factor in Experiment A, and it appears obvious that this factor is to be identified with the factor that we tentatively labeled *pleasant–unpleasant* in the first experiment. Nineteen of the 23 scales have loadings of the same sign on the second factor in the two experiments, and the cases which disagree in sign have minimal loadings.

The rating of the vowels on the relevant scales shows a greater shift in absolute order between the experiments than the ratings for the first factor, but the nature of the distribution is essentially the same. The same three vowels are seen as being most pleasant, *A* (−0.94), *UW* (−0.90), *OW* (−0.86), and the remaining vowels are seen as near the zero point: *AJ* (−0.16), *EJ* (−0.02) and *AW* (−0.06). The only appreciable shift is that of *AW* from moderately pleasant to neutral.

The highest loadings for factor three are *oblong–round*, *narrow–wide*, *large–small*, *weak–strong*, and *red–green*, of which the third and the fifth have negative loadings. Thus, a contrast between oblong, narrow, small, weak, and green, and round, wide, large, strong, and red is involved. The earlier characterization of the third factor as *potency* or *expansiveness* still seems appropriate, though only one scale, *large–small*, is found in common among the first five scales in the two experiments; the identification of this factor must be somewhat doubtful. As should be expected, identification of the less important factors is less sure. In the comparisons here, for example, the first factor had three scales in common between the experiments, the second had two scales in common, and the third has only one scale in common. Similarly, the number of scales with identical sign in the loadings on the factors decreases as we proceed from the first through the third.

The resemblance of the placement of the vowels on the third factor is also smallest. The largest positive deviation (*potent* or *expansive*) is for *OW*, while the largest negative deviation is for *IJ*. In the first experiment *OW* had the second largest positive deviation, while *IJ* had the greatest negative. The placements of the vowels are: *OW* (+1.10), *AW* (+0.50), *UW* (+0.16), *EJ* and *A* (+0.02), *AJ* (−0.14), and *IJ* (−0.26). The ordering on the first experiment was *A*, *OW*, *AW*, *EJ*, *AJ*, *UW*, and *IJ*.

Two types of machine factor-analysis (Principal Factor and Varimax) were performed on each correlation matrix, one consisting of the correlation of the ratings over the scales, taking the vowels pairwise, and the other consisting of the correlation of the ratings over the vowels, taking the scales pairwise. The analysis of the first matrix added little to what had already been shown, with both the Principal Factor and the Varimax analyses showing a first factor which opposed front and back vowels and a second factor which appeared to separate "short" vowels and diphthongs.[14]

The factor analysis of scales included, of course, the ratings of *E* and *I* and therefore is not directly comparable to related analyses discussed earlier. It was felt that these analyses should be given in some detail, however, since the findings may be of some importance in selecting scales for future studies. The results of the Principal Factor analysis are in Table 32 and those of the Varimax analysis are in Table 33.

The first factor in the Principal Factor analysis was characterized by seven scales of almost equal loadings (all greater than .85): *thick–thin*, *falling–rising*, *hard–soft*, *sharp–dull*, *large–small*, *high–low*, and *narrow–wide*. The opposition is between thick, falling, soft, dull, large, low, and wide on the one hand, and thin, rising, hard, sharp, small, high, and narrow on the other. Substantial agreement with the first factor (*acute–grave*) discussed in each of the diagonal analyses appears to exist. The pattern of signs is in exact agreement with the first diagonal factor on the distance data for the same experiment and agrees in 21 of the 23 cases with the pattern in Experiment A for the same diagonal factor. Four of the scales, *sharp–dull*, *high–low*, *thick–thin*, and *large–small*, occur among the first seven on all three analyses and three other scales appear on two of the three analyses. The mean deviation across the seven scales for the vowels is, beginning from the *acute* end: *IJ* (+1.24), *I* (+0.70), *AJ* (+0.50), *E* (+0.27), *EJ* (+0.33), *AW* (−0.49), *UW* (−0.73), *A* (−0.79), and *OW* (−0.86). It is once again striking to see the front vowels, including *I* and *E*, with positive placements and the back vowels with negative placements.

The second factor on the Principal Factor analysis has its highest loadings on *weak–strong*, *red–green*, *yellow–blue*, *back–front*, and *closed–open* (all with loadings above 0.50). The first, fourth, and fifth have negative loadings,

[14] These analyses and the corresponding diagonal analyses based on vowels as variables with scales as observations are available from the writers.

*Table 32*
Experiment B: Principal Factor Matrix

| | F1 | F2 | F3 | F4 | F5 | Variance accounted for |
|---|---|---|---|---|---|---|
| 1. Weak–Strong | .051 | −.945 | −.070 | −.147 | .150 | .946 |
| 2. Heavy–Light | .753 | .439 | .225 | .281 | −.152 | .913 |
| 3. Thick–Thin | .955 | .153 | .191 | .039 | −.031 | .975 |
| 4. Dark–Bright | .729 | −.434 | .420 | .047 | .043 | .901 |
| 5. Oblong–Round | −.721 | −.396 | −.338 | .261 | −.368 | .996 |
| 6. Hard–Soft | −.876 | .136 | .370 | .173 | −.148 | .976 |
| 7. Back–Front | .611 | −.554 | −.159 | .332 | −.354 | .943 |
| 8. Narrow–Wide | −.857 | −.441 | −.195 | .124 | −.057 | .988 |
| 9. White–Black | −.479 | .007 | −.763 | .257 | −.018 | .880 |
| 10. Falling–Rising | .879 | −.372 | .119 | .072 | −.212 | .975 |
| 11. Red–Green | −.164 | .924 | .245 | .024 | .014 | .943 |
| 12. Sharp–Dull | −.867 | .374 | .068 | .075 | −.306 | .997 |
| 13. High–Low | −.864 | .357 | −.135 | −.101 | −.208 | .947 |
| 14. Smooth–Rough | .610 | .396 | −.624 | −.247 | −.072 | .986 |
| 15. Passive–Active | .825 | −.432 | .121 | −.011 | .119 | .897 |
| 16. Masculine–Feminine | .261 | .108 | .279 | .885 | .192 | .979 |
| 17. Bad–Good | −.448 | −.238 | .733 | −.182 | −.170 | .857 |
| 18. Warm–Cool | .779 | .096 | −.121 | .260 | −.421 | .877 |
| 19. Closed–Open | −.732 | −.539 | .339 | .146 | .056 | .967 |
| 20. Empty–Full | −.787 | −.487 | .285 | −.132 | −.038 | .958 |
| 21. Yellow–Blue | −.306 | .715 | .408 | −.069 | −.201 | .817 |
| 22. Diffuse–Compact | .638 | −.336 | .135 | −.390 | −.522 | .965 |
| 23. Large–Small | .855 | .420 | .012 | −.135 | .049 | .929 |

so that strong, red, yellow, front, and open contrast with weak, green, blue, back, and closed. While this factor is not readily identifiable with either of the remaining two factors in the previous analyses, the balance of indicators seems to suggest that this ought to be regarded as related to the factor of potency or expansiveness previously discussed. The position of the vowels in terms of mean deviation scores is from most potent or expansive to least potent or constricted *OW* (−0.58), *IJ* (−0.48), *AW* (−0.46), *EJ* (−0.34), *AJ* (−0.30), *A* (+0.10), *UW* (+0.26), *E* (+0.30), and *I* (+0.32). The position of the "short" checked vowels on the extreme weak and constricted pole is striking. The presence of these extremes may well be the source of the shift in this factor, of course.

The third factor of the Principal Factor analysis has its heaviest loadings on the scales *white–black*, *bad–good*, *smooth–rough*, *dark–bright*, and *yellow–blue*, of which the first and third are negative. Thus, black, bad, rough, dark, and yellow contrast with white, good, smooth, bright, and blue. This seems to be identifiable with the second factor of the diagonal analysis of Experiment A in that three of these five scales are among the five loading

*Table 33*
Experiment B: Varimax Factor Matrix

| | F1 | F2 | F3 | F4 | F5 | Variance accounted for |
|---|---|---|---|---|---|---|
| 1. Weak–Strong | −.020 | −.887 | .348 | −.195 | −.009 | .947 |
| 2. Heavy–Light | .535 | .230 | −.473 | .416 | −.421 | .913 |
| 3. Thick–Thin | .713 | −.121 | −.501 | .215 | −.393 | .976 |
| 4. Dark–Bright | .692 | −.506 | .050 | .190 | −.357 | .901 |
| 5. Oblong–Round | −.883 | −.101 | .434 | −.040 | −.130 | .996 |
| 6. Hard–Soft | −.336 | .550 | .713 | .074 | .165 | .976 |
| 7. Back–Front | .029 | −.630 | −.152 | .239 | −.682 | .944 |
| 8. Narrow–Wide | −.753 | −.137 | .593 | −.095 | .203 | .988 |
| 9. White–Black | −.892 | −.051 | −.207 | .043 | .192 | .880 |
| 10. Falling–Rising | .512 | −.518 | −.239 | .130 | −.610 | .976 |
| 11. Red–Green | .147 | .913 | −.179 | .130 | .201 | .944 |
| 12. Sharp–Dull | −.556 | .710 | .409 | −.083 | .103 | .998 |
| 13. High–Low | −.617 | .612 | .265 | −.261 | .234 | .948 |
| 14. Smooth–Rough | .042 | −.016 | −.956 | −.228 | −.137 | .987 |
| 15. Passive–Active | .586 | −.641 | −.212 | .117 | −.290 | .898 |
| 16. Masculine–Feminine | .154 | .022 | .002 | .974 | −.085 | .979 |
| 17. Bad–Good | .207 | .201 | .860 | −.180 | −.053 | .858 |
| 18. Warm–Cool | .221 | −.098 | −.529 | .246 | −.691 | .877 |
| 19. Closed–Open | −.298 | −.141 | .905 | .050 | .189 | .967 |
| 20. Empty–Full | −.308 | −.064 | .874 | −.247 | .186 | .959 |
| 21. Yellow–Blue | .121 | .887 | .124 | −.025 | .031 | .818 |
| 22. Diffuse–Compact | .431 | −.312 | −.096 | −.409 | −.711 | .966 |
| 23. Large–Small | .626 | .070 | −.701 | .051 | −.195 | .929 |

most heavily on that factor, which we there called *pleasant–unpleasant*. While it is clear that this factor is somewhat shifted from its presumed counterpart in the other analyses, it seems reasonable to continue the terminology. The placement of the vowels on this factor (from *pleasant* to *unpleasant*) is: *AJ* (+0.56), *UW* (+0.50), *A* (+0.40), *EJ* (+0.36), *OW* (+0.24), *IJ* (+0.20), *I* (−0.14), *AW* (−0.36), and *E* (−0.42).

A consideration of the Varimax analysis of scales (see Table 33) raises again the question of the fruitfulness of this analytic solution for this kind of problem. As was mentioned in regard to the same technique in connection with the consonantal analysis, it is not certain that the assumptions underlying this procedure are applicable to studies in this domain. At any rate, in contrast with the relatively high agreement of the other procedures and the ease in conceptualizing the factors, the Varimax procedure yields a set of factors of a quite different sort and factors which resist easy classification in either psychological or linguistic dimensions.

The first factor contrasts white, oblong, narrow, thin, and bright with black, round, wide, thick, and dark (all relevant scales loading greater than

.69). This result seems to involve some elements of the factor which we have called *acute–grave* and a *bright–dark* dimension. Mean deviations of the vowels on these scales are: *IJ* (+0.84), *I* (+0.74), *AJ* (+0.68), *EJ* (+0.40), *E* (+0.18), *A* (−0.24), *UW* (−0.28), *AW* (−0.70), and *OW* (−0.84). The *IJ* end is white, oblong, and so on. Once again we have the striking result that the deviations in one direction are all front vowels and the deviations in the other are all back vowels.

The second Varimax factor has its largest loadings (all above .64) on the scales *red–green*, *yellow–blue*, *weak–strong*, *sharp–dull*, and *passive–active*. The third and fifth of these are negative, thus creating an opposition between red, yellow, strong, sharp, and active on the one hand and green, blue, weak, dull, and passive on the other. This most closely resembles the factor we have called *potency* or *expansiveness*. The ratings of the vowels from least to most potent are: *IJ* (−1.14), *AJ* (−0.54), *AW* (−0.46), *EJ* (−0.40), *OW* (−0.06), *E* (+0.16), *I* (+0.22), *A* (+0.52), and *UW* (+0.66).

The third Varimax factor has the highest loadings on the scales *smooth–rough*, *closed–open*, *empty–full*, *bad–good*, and *hard–soft*. All loadings are greater than .70 and the first loading is negative. This seems closest to the *pleasant–unpleasant* factor treated earlier, showing high overlap in the scales with maximum loading on the second factor of both of the diagonal analyses. The mean values for the vowels on this factor, ranging from unpleasant to pleasant, are: *I* (−0.70), *E* (−0.66), *IJ* (−0.34), *AW* (−0.08), *AJ* (+0.30), *EJ* (+0.36), *OW* (+0.88), *UW* (+0.88), and *A* (+0.90). It is noticeable here that in addition to the general tendency for the front vowels to be judged unpleasant as opposed to back vowels, the short front vowels exhibit this tendency to a marked extent.

We may summarize these results by noting that except for the first factor, which seems to be a mixture of *acute–grave* and *bright–dark*, the three most readily distinguished factors are *acute–grave*, *potency*, and *pleasant–unpleasant*. Of the 12 factorial dimensions we have considered here (under one treatment or another), 11 are distributed across the vowels so that a front vowel, almost always *IJ* or *I*, is at one extreme, and a back vowel, usually *A* or *OW*, is at the other. The front vowels are always found at the acute, the unpleasant, and the weak or constricted end of the scale and the back vowels at the other. Vowel height is evidently involved also, in that *IJ* is the highest front vowel, and *A* and *OW* are in the low and central back area. Indeed, a general comparison with the results of the previous study on consonants suggests itself in that examination of the scales in common to both studies shows that the abrupt consonants tend to the same side of the scale as the front vowels, while the continuants, of which *l* is the most polarized, tend to be identified with judgments similar to those given the back vowels.

These results accord in general with the results of previous studies. The brief review of the literature which follows makes no claim to completeness. Emphasis is on experimental studies or individual introspective reports which furnish material comparable to that of the present study.

To our knowledge the first experimental study was that by Roblee and Washburn in 1912.[15] All *VC* combinations of a set of 13 vowels and 17 consonants, except those that were meaningful, were judged on a seven-point *pleasant–unpleasant* scale. The result for each vowel was calculated by averaging all the points on the scale in which it appeared with any consonant. There were two trials, with 15 of those on the first and 13 of those on the second given after an interval of months. The extreme values were *u*, as in *mud*—2.9 on both trials (*most unpleasant*)—and *a*, as in *father*—4.3 on both trials (*most pleasant*). In our study no *pleasant–unpleasant* scale was used, but we may perhaps take the mean values over the five most highly loaded scales given earlier for the factor described as *pleasant–unpleasant*, namely, $F_2$ in both diagonal analyses and $F_3$ on the Varimax. Roblee and Washburn's order for means over the two trials on those vowels common to both studies is *IJ*, *UW*, *I*, *AJ*, *EJ*, *OW*, *E*, and *A* from unpleasant to pleasant. Our orders are: Diagonal–Experiment A: *AJ*, *IJ*, *EJ*, *A*, *UW*, and *OW*; Diagonal–Experiment B: *IJ*, *EJ*, *AJ*, *OW*, *UW*, and *A*; and Varimax: *I*, *E*, *IJ*, *AJ*, *EJ*, *OW*, *UW*, and *A*. There is obvious general agreement, but there is a striking discrepancy in the judgment of *E* as pleasant in the Roblee-Washburn experiment and unpleasant on the Varimax third factor.

In 1929, Sapir introduced the technique of using pairs of nonsense words differing in only one sound and asking subjects for categorical comparative judgments.[16] Thus, a subject might be told that of *zin* and *zan* one designated a large table and one a small table, and he was to choose. One group of Chicago high-school students was asked to judge among pairs which differed by having a different front vowel. There were 100 word pairs to be judged for size. Each pair contrasted two different front vowels from the set: *a*, as in *Mann*; *ä*, as in *hat*; *ɛ*, as in *met*; *e*, as in *été*; and *i*, as in *fini* held constant for quantity. Sapir reports the results of *a* versus *i* for four (randomly chosen?) pairs of stimuli. The subjects were 485 Chicago high-school students, 21 university students, 8 American adults, and 7 Chinese adults. The results in all groups indicate the choice for *i* to symbolize *small* and *a* to symbolize *large*. Sapir also reports the results for each pair of these vowels for four different age groups. Without exception, the lower front vowel is judged as larger and in general proportionate to the phonetic distance (e.g., a larger proportion of subjects agree that *i* is smaller than *a* and that *i* is smaller than

[15] Roblee and Washburn, "The Affective Values of Articulate Sounds."

[16] Edward Sapir, "A Study in Phonetic Symbolism," *Journal of Experimental Psychology*, 12 (1929): 225–239.

*e*) in every group. Sapir's vowels were all phonetically different from ours, except that our *E* equals his *ε*. Making the obvious equations, in our first experiment the judgment on the *large–small* scale among the relevant vowels from small to large was *IJ* (5.2), *EJ* (4.2), and *A* (2.6). On Experiment B in the same scale, we have *IJ* (4.8), *EJ* (4.1), and *A* (3.7). However, *E* was rated at 5.0, even smaller than *IJ*. The reason is no doubt that suggested already by Newman in a similar instance: the shorter length of the *E*. In Sapir's study, as noted above, the vowels were held constant for quantity.

The same technique was used by Newman, who extended its use by including back vowels[17] (Sapir included these as a group but never reported his results), and by using two bases for judgment instead of one: *large–small* and *dark–bright*. On the former of these, Newman's results confirm those of Sapir and extend them to the back vowels. Newman used vowels of actual American English (presumably Chicago) speech. His scale values start from *i* as in *bit* as the extreme rating and on the small side. His order with 141 subjects is as follows: *ι*, *i*, *ei*, *ai*, *ä·*, *yu·*, *u·*, *a·*, and *ɔ·*. This agrees well with our results on the *large–small* scale, making the appropriate equations. For Experiment A we found *IJ*, *AJ*, *EJ*, *UW*, *OW*, and *A*, and for Experiment B we found *I*, *IJ*, *AJ*, *EJ*, *A*, *UW*, and *OW*. Of course, our equation of *OW* with Newman's *ɔ·* is not satisfactory.

For the *dark–bright* comparisons Newman got the same general contrast of front vowels (*bright*) versus back vowels (*dark*), but the anchor vowel is now *i·* rather than *ι*, evidently because shortness is irrelevant here, and at the other extreme *u·* rather than *ɔ·*. The order is now as follows: *i·*, *ι*, *ai*, *ei*, *ä·*, *yu*, *a·*, *ɔ·*, and *u·*. Our *dark–bright* scale starting from the bright end is, for Experiment A, *IJ*, *AJ*, *UW*, *EJ*, *OW*, and *A*. This evidently does not agree with Newman regarding *A* and *UW*, whose places are, so to speak, exchanged. Our second experiment gives *IJ*, *AJ*, *EJ*, *I*, *OW*, *A*, and *UW*. This, with a larger number of subjects, corresponds fairly closely with Newman's results.

This *dark–bright* dimension in vowels is further explored through a series of experiments in a study by Chastaing with results close to those of Newman and of our Experiment B.[18] In one experiment, 30 Parisian subjects rated five vowels on a seven-point scale of *luminosité–obscurité*. This is, of course, identical with our technique. The vowels were, from bright to obscure, *i*, *e*, *a*, *o*, and *u*. Other experiments gave similar results. In a particularly interesting one in which subjects chose vowels for a nonsense word, of the six vowels allowed—*a* (back *a*), *e*, *i*, *o*, *u*, and *y*—the most frequent vowel chosen for 'daylight' was *i*, 'dawn' *e*, 'dusk' *o*, and 'darkness' *u*.

From these data and those of Newman, but only partly corroborated by our

[17] Newman, "Further Experiments in Phonetic Symbolism."

[18] Maxime Chastaing, "La Brillance des voyelles," *Archivum Linguisticum*, 14 (1962): 1–13.

own results, it appears then that there may be two different hierarchies: one of size in which *i*, as small, polarizes with *a*, and one for brightness, in which it polarizes with *u*. In this connection, it is of interest to note a report by Sapir of the reactions of a subject to successive changes in the vowels of *mīla*, which was assigned the meaning 'brook'. These were as follows: *mūla* 'fairly large, rather rambling brook at night'; *mōla* 'ocean at midnight'; *mɔ̄la* 'ocean in the daytime'; and *māla* 'bright ocean'. Sapir only reports this subject among many, presumably because his responses corresponded to Sapir's own intuitions.

These data suggest a connection with sound–color synesthesia. We would expect that, since front vowels are judged bright and back vowels dark, light and dark colors should be assigned analogously. In the data assembled by Reichard, Jakobson, and Werth for five subjects, this is borne out in general.[19] Thus, *i* is associated with white by two subjects, silver-white by one, canary yellow by one, and yellow by one, while for *u*, of four subjects with associations, two report black-brown, one dark-blue, and one blood-red. For *a* three report red and one reports tan. A further report of personal synesthesia by Masson shows a rather systematic pattern, with *i* as white, and at the other extreme the low-back rounded vowel [ɑ] as black, while *u* is cobalt or royal blue.[20]

Chastaing reports studies of vowels on other dimensions than *dark–bright* in another publication.[21] Of particular interest, as a further crosscultural extension of the evidence, is his report of a number of experiments carried out by Ohwaki and Sato, utilizing Japanese vowels on Japanese subjects.[22] Asked to choose vowels for nonsense names for angular figures with broken lines, the order of choices was *i*, *e*, *o*, *a*, and *u*; for rounded figures, *a*, *o*, *u*, *e*, and *i*. For thin figures the order was *i*, *e*, *a*, *o*, and *u*; for thick figures *a*, *o*, *u*, *e*, and *i*; for small figures *i*, *e*, *o*, *u*, and *a*; and for large figures *a*, *o*, *u*, *e*, and *i*. It is of interest to note that the order is not exactly the opposite for the second member of any of these pairs of polar adjectives and that the uncertainties are all among the back vowels, just as in our own results.

Finally, we may note a series of experiments reported by Fonágy.[23] One-hundred and fifteen Hungarian subjects were asked which is smaller, fatter, and so forth, of the two vowels, *i* and *u*. Of the two, *i* was judged the smaller, thinner, faster, sharper, happier, friendlier, brighter, weaker, more

[19] Gladys A. Reichard, Roman Jakobson, and Elisabeth Werth, "Language and Synesthesia," *Word*, 5 (1949): 224–33.

[20] David I. Masson, "Synesthesia and Sound Spectra," *Word*, 8 (1952): 39–41.

[21] Maxime Chastaing, "Le Symbolisme des voyelles, significations des 'I,' Part II," *Journal de Psychologie Normale et Pathologique*, 55 (1958): 461–81.

[22] *Ibid.*, p. 470.

[23] See n. 9.

beautiful, sweeter, and less hollow. These results are in agreement in the appropriate cases for both Experiment A and Experiment B on the *small–large*, *thick–thin*, *sharp–dull*, and *dark–bright* scales. On the *weak–strong* scale, there was a reversal from Experiment A to B. Fonágy's results agree with those on our first experiment, in which *i* was judged weaker than *u*. It may be noted that this was the most conspicuous reversal of our results between the two experiments and that this was the category among Fonágy's subjects in which the results were least clear-cut.

It has not, of course, been possible to cite in detail all the studies reported in the literature, but no case of marked discrepancy between our results and those of others of which we were aware was left unmentioned here. We believe that an unprejudiced review of this evidence, as well as of our own study, is sufficient to show a body of quite reliable phenomena in this area. Moreover, as far as can be seen, it holds in general crossculturally among speakers of such diverse languages as English, French, Chinese, Japanese, and Hungarian.

We have not considered the articulatory and acoustic bases of the phenomena reported here. Newman has already suggested the connection of the size of the resonance cavities in judgments of size, as well as the role of length. It would appear from our results that, other things being equal, the more forward and the higher a vowel, the more it is judged small and in general as acute, weak, and unpleasant on our main factors. The most extreme vowel is *IJ*, the most forward and highest, and the one with the highest $F_2$ and lowest $F_1$. The smaller articulatory and acoustic differences among the back vowels are shown by the lesser reliability of their ordering at the other end of the scale from *IJ*. The role of rounding as distinct from backing is difficult to judge until more unrounded back vowels and some rounded front vowels are included. In general, the results of these studies should be extended and further tested by the presentation of a larger variety of auditorily presented stimuli. Further crosscultural studies are also obviously called for.

# A Linguistic Approach to the Meaningfulness of Nonsense Syllables

Ebbinghaus, the inventor of nonsense syllables, was also the first to note that these presumably meaningless sequences were not in fact equally meaningless.[1] As he states (Ebbinghaus 1913: 23):

> . . . the homogeneity of the series falls considerably short of what might be expected of it. These series exhibit very important and almost incomprehensible variations as to the ease and difficulty with which they are learned. It even appears from this point of view, as if the difference between sense and nonsense material is not as great as one would be inclined a priori to imagine.

Since the time of Ebbinghaus psychologists have learned to rate nonsense syllables with considerable reliability on a scale of "meaningfulness," M, based on the responses of subjects in terms of associations to their use as stimuli.

In the present study methods are described by which the M value of nonsense syllables can be deduced through purely linguistic methods with measures which correlate as well with experimental results as the experimental results do with each other. A consideration of these linguistic methods will suggest an explanatory theory to account for the variations of nonsense syllables along the meaningfulness dimension.

Since the linguistic procedures involve, as one of their fundamental considerations, the notion of a scale for the distance of any sound sequence to English (or, in the general case, to any natural language) for purposes of

[1] This study was supported by a grant from the Social Science Research Council which enabled Professor James J. Jenkins and me to carry out joint research at the University of Minnesota during the summer of 1960. It was completed at the Center for Advanced Studies in the Behavioral Sciences during the academic year 1964–65 and the summer of 1965.

preliminary orientation, the nature of such a scale already utilized in a series of published experiments will first be described (Greenberg and Jenkins 1964). Ebbinghaus's intuition in the above-quoted passage that "the difference between sense and nonsense material is not nearly so great as one would be inclined a priori to imagine" receives expression in scaling of this kind insofar as English itself becomes merely the limiting case of distance to English, namely the one in which the distance becomes zero.

In English, and probably in all languages, the sequences of phonemes are subject to powerful constraints. Suppose that we were to draw at random from a box containing wooden squares such as those used in the game of anagrams and inscribed with symbols representing the phonemes of spoken English. If we drew sets of six symbols and preserved the order in which they were originally drawn, the overwhelming majority would not represent existing English sequences. Let us suppose that in one such set we draw *g*, *v*, *s*, *u*, *r*, and *s* in that order.

This sequence, of course, is not found in English. Something further can be said, however, namely that in a certain sense it is an "impossible" combination in English. Thus we would not be tempted to look it up in a dictionary to discover whether it was a rare word with which we happened not to be acquainted. We would, moreover, confidently predict that no soap manufacturer would use it as a brand name for his product. In fact it means 'we love' in Georgian. Let us draw a second time, now choosing three phonemes and let us suppose that we draw *d*, *i*, and *b* in that order. Let us further assume that we are unacquainted with any word *dib*, so that it appears to be a non-occurring sequence just as was the case with *gvsurs*. However, unlike the earlier instance, we will be willing to look it up in a dictionary or assume that it might be coined as a brand name or a slang expression in the future. In fact, the Oxford English Dictionary does list a word *dib* meaning, among other things, 'a counter used in playing cards, etc., as a substitute for money'. Let us now draw a third time, taking three counters. On this occasion we obtain *lʌt*. Here again we are willing to entertain the possibility of a real word, with which we are unacquainted, perhaps spelled *lut* or *lutt*. But even the unabridged Oxford English Dictionary in this case gives no result. It seems, then, that some "words" which are not in English, e.g. *lʌt* are more possible than others which are not, e.g. *gvsurs*.

Linguists have established rules regarding the phonetic structure of English syllables based on the sound sequences of existing forms (e.g. Hultzen 1965). Thus *gvsurs* would immediately be declared impossible, because, along with other considerations, all English syllables which begin with three consonants, which is the upper limit, have an initial *s*, a medial unvoiced stop *p*, *t*, or *k*, and a final liquid or semivowel *r*, *l*, *w*, or *y*.

A sequence *stræb* would not be excluded by the rules just noted and in fact it obeys these and all other rules concerning the structure of English syllables.

Based on the foregoing examples, we have a simple threefold division. Every sound sequence will be "possible" if it conforms to the rules established by linguists concerning the structure of English sound sequences or "impossible" if it does not. Among the possible combinations, some are found to exist in English and some are not. Thus we have impossible sequences, possible but not actual, and actual, as exemplified by *gvsurs*, *stræb*, and *strʌk* ('struck') respectively.

In fact the situation is not that simple as we can see from the following example. Returning to our game of anagrams, let us suppose that we draw *s*, *t*, *w*, *i*, *p*. Here the first consonant group *stw-* conforms to the rule for initial sequences given earlier, consisting, as it does, of *s*, followed by an unvoiced stop followed by a semivowel, yet in this case we will not be tempted to look it up in the dictionary. The reason is that *stw* does not occur as an initial sequence in any English word although it conforms to the general rule cited earlier. It can, however, be deduced analogically from *skr-* : *skw-* = *str-* : *X*, where *skr-*, *skw-*, and *str-* all occur (e.g. *script*, *square*, and *strap*). In the instance of *stwɩp*, it appears, we have something which is, so to speak, not as possible as *stræb* but more possible than *gvsurs*.

From these examples we can construct a scale of distance from English in which at one extreme we have sequences actually found in English and at the other instances which deviate most drastically as in the case of *gvsurs*.

The whole question can be approached systematically by devising a scale of distance from English based on the well known procedure of sound substitution.

Thus /*lʌt*/ (pronounced as though spelled *lutt*) is close to English because it is possible to obtain actual English words by single substitutions in each of its three positions, for example *but*, *let*, *luck*. In the case of *stwæp* we can get *strap* (in which the vowel is pronounced as *æ*) by substituting *r* for *w*, but since no word in English begins with *stw*, it is clear that no substitution in the fourth or fifth position will give an English word. However, if we move to substitutions in two places simultaneously we can, for example, by substituting *-kr-* for *-tw-* get *scrap* whereas such substitutions will not be available in the instance of *gvsurs*. It is clear that length plays a role here also. The longer the sequence, the more difficult it becomes to produce English words by substitution. In constructing a scale therefore, the length must be held constant and also, for comparability, the syllabic structure in terms of vowels and consonants.

For any given length *n*, we can substitute from zero up to *n* at a time. The total number of substitutions, given length *n*, will be the sum of *n* taken zero at a time, one at a time, two at a time, up to *n* at a time, that is $2^n$. By substituting zero at a time we will mean leaving the sequence alone. In this case it will give something in English only if it is already in English. At the other end of the scale, any sequence of the given length and syllabic structure can be generated by simultaneous substitution in all of the positions. We allow the identity substitution by which anything is allowed to be substituted for itself. In this way a sequence already in English will allow all of the $2^n$ possible substitutions while the sequences which are the most deviant will only allow a single substitution, one which takes place simultaneously in all the positions.

The scale is defined by means of the portion of the $2^n$ possible substitutions which give an English word. Since we wish our scale to reflect distance from English with larger numbers reflecting greater distance, we subtract the number of valid substitutions from $2^n + 1$. The scale will thus run from 1, where the sound sequence exists in English ($2^n$ substitutions; value $(2^n + 1) - 2^n = 1$), to the most distant (only 1 substitution valid; value $(2^n + 1) - 1 = 2^n$).

The experiments carried out in Greenberg and Jenkins (1964) will now be briefly summarized since the present study is its natural extension. In these experiments syllables were constructed of the form CCVC. The scale thus ran from 1 to $2^n$, i.e. from 1 to 16. Twenty-four syllables were constructed to sample this scale. All the substitutions were those of individual sounds and the stimuli were all auditory. Subjects in a number of experiments were asked to estimate the distance from English on a freely constructed scale (free magnitude estimation) with zero point for zero distance to English; to rate the syllables on an eleven point scale in which the extreme left position indicated zero distance from English, and finally to give associates for each stimulus syllable. Both the number of responses in this last test and the associates themselves were recorded.

Before summarizing the results of these experiments and considering their relevance to the present study, an example of one of the stimulus syllables will be given to show how a rating is assigned on the sixteen point scale.

The syllable *klæb* was rated 2. This is of course the lowest rating a syllable may receive if it is not actually found in English. In the following table, column A gives the number of simultaneous substitutions, column B the logically possible number of ways in which this number of substitutions can be made, and column C the number of these which give at least one English word. English words produced by the substitutions are then given.

| A | B | C | klæb |
|---|---|---|---|
| 0 | 1 | 0 | (klæb) |
| 1 | 4 | 4 | (slæb, kræb, klʌb, klæm) |
| 2 | 6 | 6 | (slæb, slæb, slæb, kræb, kræb, klæm) |
| 3 | 4 | 4 | (slæb, slæb, slæb, klæm) |
| 4 | 1 | 1 | (kræb) |

In no instance is the substitution given the only one possible. All that is required is that there be at least one.

In Experiment B of the study being discussed, on the third trial with 17 subjects, the coefficient of linear correlation between ratings on the substitution scale of the 24 invented syllables and the free magnitude estimations of the subjects was + .94. On the eleven point scale of distance from English utilized by the subjects, the correlation of the rating scale medians with the linguistic substitution measure was + .95 and between the rating scale medians and the free magnitude estimation, both of which are, of course, based on subject responses, + .99. The last correlation corroborates the validity of free magnitude estimation as a technique of rating, while the first two indicate that the linguistically derived substitution scale maps very closely the psychological dimensions involved in judgments of closeness to English.

The last experiment of the series was a word association test with the 24 syllables functioning as stimuli for 117 subjects. The time period was 15 seconds. The linear correlation between the median number of associations per syllable and the medians of free magnitude estimation was − .84, with rating scale medians − .84, and with the linguistics distance measure − .75. Since the number of associations elicited in a standard time period is one of the operational definitions for the meaningfulness of nonsense syllables, it was clear that the linguistic rating scale based on substitutions corresponded not only to judgments of distance to English but also, though less closely, to the dimension M of nonsense-syllable studies.[2]

In view of these results, an obvious step was to construct a set of linguistic ratings for CVC syllables, based on the same principles as those utilized in the CCVC experiments just described, which might be expected to correlate in a satisfactory manner with the association value of the CVC syllables used in the studies of such psychologists as Glaze, Krueger, Archer, and Noble. One obvious difference is that the linguistically constructed scale would have $2^3$ or 8 points rather than the $2^4$ or 16 points of the scale derived from CCVC syllables. However, a far more fundamental difference must be taken into account. Whereas the experiments carried out with CCVC syllables utilized purely auditory stimuli and the scale values were calculated on the basis of phonetic substitutions, all the psychological experiments concerning the

[2] Where the syllables already existed in English in the same written forms and therefore had a rating of 1, the associates were practically all based on semantic association. Where they were close to English they partly rested on semantic association and partly on sound similarity. When they were farthest away sound similarity figures along with metalinguistic judgments. Examples of the last are *zbüɤ* whose most common associate was 'German' and *ðgɐx* which had 'baby' (i.e. sound made by a baby) as the most frequent response.

meaningfulness dimension of CVC stimuli were visual (graphic) or were auditory only insofar as they sometimes employed the spelling out loud of the letters of the trigram.

It should be pointed out that professional psychologists concerned with the meaningfulness of CVC syllables have completely identified the written and the auditory stimuli, although it can be easily shown that they are by no means equivalent. Thus Underwood and Schulz (1960: 9) define a nonsense syllable as "a vowel between two consonants giving a three letter combination. . . ." We read later in the same source (1960: 10), that "No syllable was used which had the same final and initial letter, and the letter *y* was considered a vowel."

It is clear to begin with that the notion of syllable is basically a phonetic one, and not a graphic one. It is most commonly defined as involving a single peak of sonority or sound prominence (the vowel) and margins of lesser sonority or prominence (the consonant or consonants). We may say indeed that *A*, *E*, *I*, *O*, and *U* 'represent' vowels graphically and that *B*, *D*, *F*, etc. 'represent' consonants, but we would never arrive at such a classification from their visual shapes. Moreover *Y* represents a vowel in *GYM*, exactly the same one as in the homonymous *Jim*, but a consonant in *YET*—hence the problem it poses to psychologists as to whether it is a vowel or a consonant. Further, the letter *X* in its most common occurrence as non-initial in a word represents two consonants /ks/, so that to call *VAX* a CVC combination is neither fish nor fowl. In fact *TAX* is homonymous with *TACKS*. In one case, two consonants are represented by the letter *X* and in the other by three letters *CKS*. Because of all these considerations the CVC formula of the psychologist could most accurately be described as a sequence of three letters in which the first and third position are occupied by graphic symbols which most frequently represent a single consonant while the second is occupied by a symbol which usually represents a vowel sound.

A further indication of the difference is the following. We may have a graphic stimulus like *XAN* called a CVC syllable by psychologists. However no sequence *X* + (graphic) vowel + (graphic) consonant occurs in written English. The graphic symbol *X* most frequently represents the biconsonantal sequence /ks/ leading to *ksæn* as a deducible 'pronunciation'. But the initial sequence *ks* is not generated by the formulas for permissible initial consonant sequences in English. Hence for the normal speaker it is 'unpronounceable'. However, an unpronounceable syllable is a contradiction in terms.

From these considerations we see that the CVC graphic formula called a syllable by the psychologist is not equivalent to the auditory stimulus consonant + vowel + consonant which would correspond to the CVC stimulus in the psycholinguistic experiments just outlined. Hence to account for the responses in the meaningfulness dimension to graphic CVC's as stimuli involves additional complexities. One conjectures that a phonetic interpretation of the visual stimulus plays a role and that the importance of this intervening variable depends on the possibility of a phonetic interpretation, its degree of conformity to the phonetic patterns of English syllable formation if interpretable, and the meaningfulness of the sequence when pronounced. Consider the following example. Presented with the trigram *KOT* and applying pronunciation rules deduced from actual words, a subject would presumably pronounce [kŏt] which coincides in sound with the word 'cot'.[3] He might therefore rate it as meaningful. Presented, however, with *COT* as a graphic stimulus, we would conjecture that even a larger proportion of subjects would consider it to be meaningful. In fact, 86 percent of Archer's subjects rated *KOT* as meaningful while 100 percent did so for *COT*.

Hence it will not do simply to convert all the graphic trigrams into derivable auditory stimuli and then apply a measure of nearness to English such as those used in the CCVC experiments. The intervention of pronunciation of the trigram between the original graphic stimulus and the subject's response suggests that the subject in responding to trigrams may go through a sequence of successively more recondite procedures. If only the most obvious one is required, virtually all subjects will perform it and it will rate 100 percent or very close to it. The more devious and complex the processes involved, the smaller the proportion of subjects will be who resort to it and the smaller the meaningfulness rating. From the high correlations of operationally different methods such as the report of any associations (Glazer, Krueger), the mean of actually reported associations (Mandler), and the scaled estimate by the subjects themselves (Noble, Stockwell, Pryor), it appears that the subject does essentially the same thing in all cases. Even rated pronounceability seems to involve the same basic subject strategy, as will be indicated later.

Let us hypothesize the following sequence. If the trigram spells an English word, provided that the word is familiar to the subject, it will be reacted to as meaningful and he will seek no further. Being meaningful it will suggest associations along a number of semantic dimensions. If it does not spell an English word, many subjects will try to pronounce it. Here there will be degrees of difficulty. Certain letters or letter sequences are non-existent or extremely rare in certain positions in the graphic word. Even if pronunciations can be assigned, they may result in sound sequences which are not part of the

[3]From this point on the pronunciation symbols of the American College Dictionary published by Random House are employed. A list of these symbols is found in Appendix B.

normal spoken language and will therefore be considered unpronounceable by most subjects. If they are unpronounceable, then a fortiori they cannot be assigned meaning, except for a few marginal cases of alphabetic sequences (e.g. *XYZ*). For example *KOT*, as indicated above, is easily assigned a meaning on the analogy of English spelling rules; [K] as in 'kin', [O] as in 'hot', and [T] as in 'pit'. However *XYM* is not easily assigned a pronunciation since the analogy of *X* in 'six' will produce initial /ks/ which does not occur in English words and furthermore -*Y*- is rare in words of the graphic form CVC.

If the trigram is pronounceable without difficulty but does not mean anything when pronounced, it may still give rise to associations by phonetic similarity. For example *FOD* is straightforwardly pronounceable by rules derivable from actually occurring words spelled by trigrams but when pronounced does not coincide with any real word. Still it may suggest 'fed' or 'God'.

The foregoing discussion suggests that we would expect successively lower meaningfulness ratings for (1) nonsense syllables which coincide with some actual English word in its standard orthography (e.g. *CAT*); (2) those pronounceable and meaningful when pronounced but not spelled in this manner (e.g. *KOT*); (3) those pronounceable, but not meaningful when pronounced (e.g. *FOD*); and (4) those not pronounceable (e.g. *XYM*).

It is of interest to note that instructions in Archer's experiment (1960: 5) somewhat parallel this presumed sequence of difficulty. "Is it a word? Does it sound like a word? Does it remind me of a word? Can I use it in a sentence?" If we disregard the last question, then an affirmative answer to the first question puts the syllable in the first of the above categories. An affirmative answer to the second question after a negative one to the first would put it in the second category. An affirmative answer to the third question after negative replies to the first two would put it in the third category, since if it is pronounceable it should always be phonetically similar to one or more actual words. A negative answer to all three would put it in the fourth category, the unpronounceable.

This fourfold classification, with a further elaboration explained below, yielded a five-point scale which will be called the PM or pronounceability-meaningfulness scale. The highest number, 5, was assigned to the category hypothesized to be the highest in meaningfulness. The points on this scale may be described as follows.

> 5. Trigrams which exist as words in their conventional spelling. At this point the need for some objective procedure for determining this was not realized and this judgment was made by the author. Example: *CAT*.

4. Any trigram which is fully pronounceable or analogically pronounceable and is a word when so pronounced was given this rating. The concept of analogical pronounceability is explained below under 2. Examples of trigrams with the rating 4 are *BAJ*, *KAP*.

3. Any trigram which was not rated 2 or 1, as described below, and which was pronounceable but when pronounced was not an English word was given the rating 3. An example is *FOD*.

2. A rating of 2 was assigned to a trigram if it was analogically pronounceable but was not an actual word when so pronounced. If it was meaningful it was rated as 4 in accordance with the rule given above under 4.

Trigrams were considered analogically pronounceable if the spelling pattern did not conform at all, or only rarely, to that of actual words in English spelled by CVC trigrams, provided that a pronunciation could be deduced from values in non-CVC spellings which when so deduced did not violate rules regarding the permissible sound sequences of English. For example, no word in English spelled CVC ends in the letter *F*, but the phonetic value /f/ can be deduced from non-CVC spelled words such as *safe*. If the final *F* of a trigram is given this phonetic value, it will sometimes be pronounceable as a word which is actually English. When this is so, it is assigned a rating 4 as illustrated above. An example is CUF. If it is not an English word when analogically pronounced it is given a value 2. An example is *KAG*.

The following categories were assumed to be analogically pronounceable: trigrams with final *F*, *J*, *K*, *S*, *V*, and *Z* and/or with medial *Y* as well as those ending in *AH*.

1. The lowest category consisted of syllables called unpronounceable because the analogic pronunciation assigned produced a forbidden sound sequence. Initial *Q* was likewise considered unpronounceable because it occurs almost exclusively in the combination *QU* which has a phonetic value /kw/ so that the assignment of a pronunciation /k/ to *Q* requires a complex process of reasoning.

All unpronounceables were assigned a value of 1. The following types of trigrams were considered unpronounceable: those with initial *Q* or *X*, final *Q*, or ending with any of the sequences *EH*, *IH*, *OH*, *UH*, *YH*, *IY*, *IW*, *UW*, or *YW*.

The method just described lacks precision in certain respects as was noted in the discussion. More elaborate scales are described in the remainder of the paper. However, as a preliminary test regarding the validity of the type of analysis just described, values on the PM 5-point scale were calculated for all the trigrams used by psychologists in nonsense syllable experiments. The means of Archer values for each of the points was then calculated and gave encouraging results. They were as follows:

| PM | Archer value |
|---|---|
| 1. | 23.48 |
| 2. | 38.68 |
| 3. | 50.22 |
| 4. | 72.19 |
| 5. | 96.05 |

The means of the Archer deciles in terms of the PM scale are as follows:

| Archer decile | PM (mean) | Archer decile | PM (mean) |
|---|---|---|---|
| 1–10 | 1.37 | 51–60 | 2.90 |
| 11–20 | 1.73 | 61–70 | 3.13 |
| 21–30 | 2.00 | 71–80 | 3.38 |
| 31–40 | 2.18 | 81–90 | 3.69 |
| 41–50 | 2.54 | 91–100 | 4.19 |

Except for an expected threshold effect seen in the large increase in the PM values from the ninth to the tenth Archer decile the latter function, when plotted, closely approximates a straight line.

A number of special studies gave further evidence of the importance of meaningfulness when a pronounceable trigram was an English word and when it was not. Thus all trigrams with final J except for those rated as 1 (unpronounceable), e.g., *XAJ*, were divided into two groups, those which were meaningful when pronounced and those which were not. For example, *BAJ* was in the meaningful group whereas *DAJ* was not. Of the 107 trigrams, there were 19 meaningful with an Archer mean of 32.43 and 88 meaningless with an Archer mean of 16.01.

Another study was that of Archer trigrams with initial *Q*. It will be recalled that all such trigrams were considered unpronounceable and received a PM value of 1. But might there not be distinctions in the association values of the 120 trigrams with initial *Q*, reflecting the rest of the PM scale, if we abstract from *Q*? For example, since the trigrams ending in *-YH* were rated as 1, *QYH* might be expected to rate lower than *QEM* since the former was rated 1 for two reasons, initial *Q* and final *YH*, whereas *QEM* was rated 1 for only one reason.

The initial *Q* was assigned two pronunciations /k/ on the analogy of *Iraq* and /kw/ because *Q* in non-final position is always followed by *U* and this sequence is almost always (except for 'quay') pronounced /kw/. We may thus parallel the original PM 5-point scale among the trigrams with initial *Q*. For example, *QYH* will be rated 1 (unpronounceable) because of the earlier rules. The trigram *QUJ* was rated 2 because trigrams in final *J* were rated as analogically pronounceable and even with pronunciation with initial /k/ or /kw/ is not a word. The trigram *QIB* was given a rating 3, since with *Q* as /k/ or /kw/ it is pronounceable non-analogically but it is not a word. The trigram *QAB* was rated 4, since with the pronunciation /k/ it gives the word 'cab'. The trigram *QIP* was rated 5 because it gives the word 'quip' and it is also correctly spelled with the insertion of *-u-*.

The results of the study for the 120 trigrams were as follows:

| PM | n | Archer mean |
|---|---|---|
| 1 | 9 | 9.22 |
| 2 | 25 | 11.62 |
| 3 | 16 | 17.94 |
| 4 | 65 | 31.03 |
| 5 | 5 | 53.00 |

The foregoing results which showed that different meaningfulness values occurred in a consistent way among syllables all rated as 1 in the PM scale, suggested that a more complex procedure might be employed to account for variability in M.

It is evident that the pronunciation and meaningfulness aspects of the PM scale are at least partially independent. For example, a trigram such as *BAJ* is considered analogically pronounceable based on a classification of trigrams into three classes: unpronounceable, analogically pronounceable, and fully pronounceable. It is assigned a PM value of 4 instead of 2, because when analogically pronounced it gives an actual word, that is, it is meaningful. Meaningfulness is, as it were, an additional vector which adds to the association value predicted from pronounceability alone.

In view of this, if two separately calculated scales could be devised, one to measure pronounceability and one to measure meaningfulness, and if they could then be combined, a more subtle and powerful instrument would result than the original PM five-point scale. The remainder of this study is devoted to the description of two scales $V_1$ and $V_2$, the former a measure of pronounceability and the latter of meaningfulness.

It is evident that a trigram or any letter sequence is more or less pronounceable insofar as it conforms to the rules of English spelling. Thus, in the discussion of the PM scale, trigrams ending in *V* were classified as only analogically pronounceable because there is no trigram ending in *V* on which a pronunciation could be based.

These considerations lead to the definition of $V_1$ by applying the distance-to-English substitution method described in the initial section of this paper in relation to the CCVC syllables used in Greenberg and Jenkins (1964). To consider once more trigrams with final *V*, it is clear that no single substitution in the first or second position nor any double substitution in the first and second position simultaneously can produce an English trigram.

We would like to have a fairly restricted set of normally spelled words of CVC graphic form on which to base our measure. The reference set chosen was simply those omitted by Krueger in his study, since he wished to exclude CVC sequences which actually represented words. Such excluded trigrams will be called Krueger trigrams. Our $V_1$ scale will have $2^3$ or 8 points and its values will be calculated as ($2^3 + 1 = 9$) minus the total number of substitutions zero, one, two, or three at a time that will produce at least one Krueger trigram. For example *CAT*, which is a Krueger trigram, will receive a rating of $9 - 8$ or 1 (i.e. closest to English). *SAN*, which allows of all three types of substitutions one at a time, e.g. *FAN*, *SIN*, and *SAP*, and hence by the rule allowing the identity substitution, also the three types of substitution two at a time and, like all trigrams the single substitution three at a time, permits a total of 7 of the 8 possible substitutions (only the substitution of none at a time being excluded) and therefore has the value $9 - 7$ or 2. The trigram *XYH* only allows the substitution of three at a time, giving the maximum value $9 - 1$ or 8 on the 8-point scale.

Although the measure just described is called one of pronounceability, it is clear that meaningfulness enters into it also. A particular substitution is accepted if it produces a trigram which is meaningful when spelled in the way allowable by substitution. Nevertheless, there is a difference. Thus *XYZ* will be rated very low on the pronounceability index just described but a fair number of subjects will consider it meaningful. On the other hand, the trigrams *BAJ* and *LAJ* will both be rated 5 on the $V_1$ scale, whereas the former will rank higher on the meaningfulness vector $V_2$ which will now be described.

The basic notion of this second vector is to define a notion of target word not confined to those spelled by trigrams. A quantitative measure results by rating the graphic "distance," defined by the number and assumed psychological difficulty of the steps involved in reaching it. A trigram is always rated by its distance to the nearest target. For example 'cot' is the target word for *KOT* and it is reached by a single letter substitution.

Since on the second vector, we wish to allow sufficient scope for the undoubted imaginativeness of some subjects as noted in the associates recorded in Greenberg and Jenkins (1964), we will draw up rules such that every trigram will be assigned at least one possible pronunciation. This will be compensated for by the number and complexity of graphic manipulations that will be required to reach a target word, if indeed one exists. Similarly the use of "far-out" targets from more easily pronounceable trigrams will require more numerous and complex operations which will be reflected in the value on the $V_2$ scale. In place of the free-wheeling procedures used earlier in regard to the PM scale, all the operations are precisely described so that researchers following them independently would arrive at the same results. In principle the whole procedure could be programmed on a computer.

Evidently the following must be included in the specifications: pronunciation rules for trigrams, definition of what is in English (i.e. what are legitimate target words), a standard pronunciation for these words, and a scoring procedure depending on the relation of the trigram to the target word.

In order to assign one or more pronunciations to every trigram, a dictionary in which each entry is accompanied by its pronunciation and interpreted in accordance with a pronunciation key. That of the American College Dictionary (1965–66) was the one utilized. As an example we may take the entry 'cat' after which is found the pronunciation (kăt). The pronunciation key gives *a* as the vowel of 'act' or 'bat'.

In fact, there are important regional and class phonetic differences among speakers of American English which doubtless influence their pronunciation of the trigrams. One reason for selecting the codification found in this dictionary, and approximately the same form in other dictionaries of American English, is that it provides a reasonable compromise among divergent dialects although perhaps not representing the speech of any particular individual. Also, very importantly, it provides the basis for an objective, replicable procedure.

In Appendix A, the pronouncing key of the ACD is given for reference purposes and then the rule types which in their totality provide an algorithm for deriving pronunciation rules. The rule types are, as it were, a set of metarules for deriving rules. Under each successively more complex rule type are given the rules which derive from their application. Each rule maps a particular orthographic symbol or a sequence of such symbols into a symbol or sequence of symbols in the pronunciation key of the initial section of Appendix A. The result of applying all relevant rules to a specific trigram is to assign one or more pronunciations to each one. For example, by applying rules 1, 56, and 34 the trigram *BEZ* is mapped into two pronunciations [bĕz] and [bēz].

The next step is to determine the target word or words. Thus [bĕz] does not give a target but [bēz] is pronounced in the same way as the word 'bees'. We can now compare the trigram *BEZ* with the target word 'bees' in accordance with rules described later to obtain a value on $V_2$.

In order to identify target words objectively use was made of Moser, Dreher, and Oyer (1957). In this work all monosyllables of American English are given in accordance with the usual dictionary pronunciation and thus are easily equated to the key of the ACD. Thus for the two pronunciations [bĕz] and [bēz], one would first look under B and then scan the columns beginning Bĕ and Bē respectively for final z. Under the first one would find a blank but under the second the word 'bees' in standard orthography.

The next step is to find all the targets for each of the one or more pronunciations of each trigram. Wherever more than one target exists, the ones chosen give the smallest value (i.e. are closest to English) according to the scaling procedure which follows.

If the trigram itself spells a word, e.g. *CAT*, then the pronunciation rules are so designed that they will map the actual pronunciation along with others possible. Thus *CAT* will give [kăt] in accordance with the pronunciation rules of Appendix A. Under the pronunciation [kăt] in Moser, Dreher, and Oyer one will find the target word 'cat' which when compared to the trigram *CAT* will show a zero difference. This provides a natural zero point for the $V_2$ scale.

A study of the relation of target words to the trigrams shows that the addition of a letter, particularly at the end, tends to produce a higher association value than the substitution of a letter. For example *BAL* has as one pronunciation [bôl], which provides its nearest target 'ball' which is reached from the original trigram by adding a letter at the end. For *KAP*, the pronunciation [kăp] gives its nearest target 'cap' which is reached from *KAP* by the substitution of 'c' for 'k'.

The following rule was adopted. Add 1 for every external addition (initial or final), 2 for every internal addition, and 3 for every substitution or deletion. Substitutions are allowed only when the substituting and substituted letters have the same pronunciation in at least one case, as for 'k' and 'c'. If several operations have to be carried out the numbers assigned to each are added. Thus to reach the target 'badge' from *BAJ*, we need the substitution of 'g' for 'j' (permissible because they may have the same phonetic value [j] under the pronunciation rules), the internal addition of 'd' and the external addition of 'e'. This gives a total of 3 (substitution) + 2 (internal addition, or insertion) + 1 (external addition) for a value of 6 on $V_2$.

The value 9 was adopted as a natural maximum for $V_2$ since by three substitutions, rated as 3 each, an English word of three letters could be reached for any trigram. Hence, if when pronounced in any of the ways allowable by the rules of Appendix A, no target existed, the trigram was rated as 9. Also if the nearest target had a value larger than 9, the value 9 was assigned. We thus have a ten-point scale from zero when the target and the trigram are identical to a maximum of 9.

One other factor was introduced. Moser, Dreher, and Oyer give many rare monosyllables, e.g. 'Zu', presumably the Sumerian storm god of that name. Targets were divided into two categories, major and minor. A major target is one which has a frequency of more than one in a million in the Thorndike-Lorge general count or which is the abbreviation of a personal common name, since these are inadequately represented in Thorndike-Lorge. Any other monosyllable found in Moser, Dreher, and Oyer is a minor target. A minor target is assigned a value of 1 for $V_2$, rather than the zero reserved for major targets. The distance measure for additions, deletions, and substitutions was then added to 1 for minor targets rather than to 0 as for major targets. Since Moser, Dreher, and Oyer omit obscene terms these were added as major targets.[4]

Taking $V_1$ and $V_2$ as separate measures, the linear correlations of these with the experimental results of Krueger (K), Glazer (Gl), Noble's m (m), and Archer (A) are as follows:

| | K | Gl | m | A | $V_1$ | $V_2$ |
|---|---|---|---|---|---|---|
| K | 1.000 | .784 | .844 | .853 | −.442 | −.660 |
| Gl | .784 | 1.000 | .808 | .781 | −.411 | −.580 |
| m | .844 | .808 | 1.000 | .936 | −.667 | −.749 |
| A | .853 | .781 | .936 | 1.000 | −.665 | −.805 |
| $V_1$ | −.442 | −.411 | −.667 | −.665 | 1.000 | .508 |
| $V_2$ | −.660 | −.580 | −.749 | −.805 | .508 | 1.000 |

It is clear from this tabulation that $V_1$ and $V_2$ are fairly independent of each other so that a combined measure might be expected to correlate better with experimental results than either in isolation. It is encouraging that $V_2$ correlates with A more highly than A does with Gl. Moreover $V_1$ correlates most highly with A and Nobles' m which appear to be the most reliable experimental measures. In general $V_2$ correlates with experimental measure better than $V_1$ and this was also to be expected.

Multiple correlations of $V_1$ and $V_2$ with the experimental measure are given in the following tabulation. The intercorrelations of the experimental studies are repeated from the preceding tabulation for purposes of comparison.

| | K | Gl | m | A | $V_1V_2$ |
|---|---|---|---|---|---|
| K | 1.000 | .784 | .844 | .853 | .706 |
| Gl | .784 | 1.000 | .808 | .781 | .635 |
| m | .844 | .808 | 1.000 | .936 | .824 |
| A | .853 | .781 | .936 | 1.000 | .857 |
| $V_1V_2$ | .706 | .635 | .824 | .857 | 1.000 |

It is apparent that a multiple correlation of the two vectors does about as well as some of the experimental measures. In three instances it shows higher

[4] A sample of twenty-five trigrams with their PM ratings, values on $V_1$ and $V_2$, and target words for the latter vector may be found in Appendix B. A complete set is obtainable from the author.

correlations with some experimental result than this result with that of some other experiment, namely it correlates more highly with m than does Gl, more highly with A than either K or Gl. Moreover it tends to correlate most highly with A and m which themselves show the highest correlations with other experimental studies.

Both $V_1$ and $V_2$ were rated separately against the Archer deciles, in which each individual value was assigned the value of the midpoint of its decile. The deciles were 0–9, 10–19, 20–29, 30–39, 40–49, 50–59, 60–69, 70–79, 80–89, and 90–99, with 100 rated as a separate value. For the eight values of the $V_1$ scale the Archer means reckoned in this fashion were 96.59, 69.16, 61.92, 57.96, 46.51, 29.58, 21.47, and 8.62, respectively. The means for each of the Archer decile values as just described were 6.39, 5.43, 5.00, 4.64, 4.42, 4.41, 3.88, 3.68, 2.38, 1.13, and 1.10. The Archer values calculated in the same manner for the ten values of the $V_1$ scale were 95.42, 81.97, 71.71, 59.14, 44.35, 41.24, 46.40, 28.10, 30.90, and 27.10. The means of $V_2$ Archer deciles beginning with 0–9 are as follows: 8.61, 8.14, 7.03, 6.45, 5.64, 4.83, 4.00, 2.96, 2.12, 0.65, and 0.05.

It should be emphasized that the two metrics described are offered merely as approximate measures based on the more general notion of nearness to English. Moreover, because each allows a much smaller number of values than those of the experimental tests a perfect correlation with them is a mathematical impossibility. That in spite of these and other factors to be mentioned it produces correlations in the same range as experimental measures with each other shows that it offers a good approximation to the experimental results and we can legitimately infer that it must be taking into account the most significant factors at work in subjects' responses in the psychological experiments.

Some of the defects relating to one or both of the vectors have been mentioned in passing. They may be summarized as follows. The reference set, Moser, Dreher, and Oyer, from which the targets were drawn is obviously unrealistic in that it includes many words not known to the average college student. Other sources, such as Thorndike and Lorge, err in the other direction in that they do not include personal names and colloquial and slang terms. The method of major and minor targets is obviously an approximation and the metric is somewhat arbitrary as is indeed the whole assumption of additivity of the various operations in reaching the target words.

Other factors not taken into account in calculating $V_2$ are the number of target words at a minimum distance to the stimulus trigram, the existence of additional targets at greater distance from the trigram, and the frequency of the target words. It has, however, been contended that if a word is in the speaker's normal language its frequency is so high that differences in this property are of no significance in the learning situation and it might be expected that a similar situation holds in regard to M (Cofer 1961: 3). This matter is discussed later. Finally our methods do not take into account the undoubted fact that longer sequences than those generated by our methods are used by subjects as target words. Thus a trigram *BOT* might be judged meaningful because it could be associated with 'botany'. Most such trigrams have closer targets with the methods employed here.

Further sources of variance which have been mentioned in the literature are variations, largely local, in slang terms and individual differences in knowledge and background experience of English. One linguistic factor has evidently not been considered by psychologists: the phonological systems of the subjects, normally predictable from a knowledge of the place in which they grew up. Again sacrificing validity to reliability, so-called General American as recorded in normative dictionaries was employed. However, since this approximates Midwestern American English and most of the experiments took place in this region, the effects here were probably minor.

If the dialects of all the subjects were known, then we could set up different rules of pronunciation depending on this factor. Thus for New York City subjects *CAH* would have 'car' as an acceptable target, but not for Minneapolis or Chicago speakers.

Since frequency is the variable most frequently discussed by psychologists as a possible explanation for M, it deserves a more detailed discussion. It will be useful to distinguish, as is common in the practice of linguists, between text and lexicon frequency. Psychologists have only used text frequency. Moreover they have used calculations of their own, as in the case of Underwood, or that of others based on frequency in running texts in which position in the word or syllable is not taken into account and in which words of all lengths and syllabic structures are included even though the results are to be correlated with responses of the graphic form CVC. The two methods commonly employed have been to sum letter frequencies for each trigram or to use trigram frequencies. To consider the first, it is obvious that the sum of individual frequencies will fail to account for many significant differences in M. To take a simple example, the summed frequencies of *HER* and *REH* will be the same, but the former will clearly be expected to, and in fact, does have on all studies a much higher M value than the latter. Trigram frequency may be expected to give much better results.

The most elaborate collection of trigram frequency data is that of Underwood and Schulz (1960: 336–69). Their procedure is as follows (pp. 65–76). They used three sources, the Thorndike-Lorge word frequency count, a count made by Underwood, and that found in Pratt (1939), a work on cryptography. All of these are based on the frequencies of individual words in running text. In order to convert these into trigram counts, all words of three or more letters were broken up into trigrams. Thus a single occurrence of the word *learning* in a text would be analyzed as containing single occurrences of *LEA*, *EAR*, *ARN*, *RNI*, and *ING*. Such trigram frequencies were summed across their occurrences in the sources used. From Thorndike-Lorge in the list of 20,000 most frequent words, the top five words in each column was used (416 columns). The Underwood (U) count was made on approximately 15,000 words of written passages. Pratt's data consists of 20,000 words of text material. For each trigram its frequency in the words from these three counts was summed. In the view of the authors, "it would seem that the most stable values would result if the frequencies of all three samples were summed."

Trigram frequencies may be expected to give much better results than the summation of individual letter frequencies. However, the occurrence of CVC trigrams word internally will be largely irrelevant to the stimulus value of the same trigram given in isolation, e.g. the *HER* in potsherd. Even the trigrams which spell English words in isolation will produce irrelevant weightings since their M values in experiments, as long as they are recognized as part of the linguistic repertory of the subjects, receive a rating of 98 to 100 regardless of text frequency. However, since trigrams found in words which appear in text are likely to be pronounceable in isolation and since three letter words will obviously be meaningful, a slight positive correlation with experimental measures of M is to be expected. This is just what we find. If we take the frequency of those trigrams in Underwood and Schulz which conform to the patterns used in experiments, a linear correlation coefficient with the Archer values of + .090 was calculated.

Finally it is of interest to note that the measures based on the principles described here are applicable to any language with a standard orthography. However, the appropriateness of the specific measures proposed here will depend on the syllabic and word structure of individual languages and the relation between the sounds and the orthography. For example, $V_1$ will be inapplicable to languages without CVC syllables such as Hawaiian though an analogous measure might be devised if CVCV were used as experimental stimuli. In languages with very straightforward relationships between spoken and written forms the correlation between $V_1$ and $V_2$ will be much higher than in English. Of course, even in English measures following the same principles could be devised for stimuli which are of differing syllabic structures. The present study has been based on CVC syllables because of their wide use by psychologists.

## Appendix A

The following is the pronunciation key of the American College Dictionary:

| | | | | | |
|---|---|---|---|---|---|
| ă | act, bat | m | my, him | ŭ | up, love |
| ā | able, cape | n | now, on | ū | use, cute |
| â | air, dare | ng | sing, England | û | urge, burn |
| ä | art, calm | ŏ | box, hot | v | voice, live |
| b | back, rub | ō | over, no | w | west, away |
| ch | chief, beach | ô | order, ball | y | yes, young |
| d | do, bed | oi | oil, joy | z | zeal, lazy |
| ĕ | ebb, set | ŏŏ | book, put | zh | vision, azure |
| ē | equal, bee | ōō | ooze, rule | ə | (unaccented vowel, occurs in *a*bove, syst*e*m, eas*i*ly, gall*o*p, circ*us*) |
| f | fit, puff | ou | out, loud | | |
| g | give, beg | p | page, stop | | |
| h | hit, hear | r | read, cry | | |
| ĭ | if, big | s | see, miss | | |
| ī | ice, bite | sh | shoe, push | | |
| j | just, edge | t | ten, bit | | |
| k | kept, make | th | thin, path | | |
| l | low, all | *th* | that, other | | |

In what follows the word 'letter' will indicate a symbol in standard English orthography. All letters will be cited in capitalized Roman form while symbols from the pronunciation key will be called phones. Complex symbols, such as *oi* in the above key will be considered simple phonemes. Thus JOY has three letters and joi has two phones, j and oi. The phones in the above key can be classified into consonants and vowels on a phonetic basis. The vowels are ă, ā, â, ä, ĕ, ē, ĭ, ī, ŏ, ō, ô, oi, ŏŏ, ōō, ou, ŭ, ū, û, and ə. All the rest are consonants.

Consider the subset of dictionary entries in which the number of letters equals the number of phones. For example, JOY does not belong to this subset because it has three letters and two phones but CAT does. Then any letter is a vowel letter if the initial phone in its pronunciation is a vowel phone in at least one case and it is a consonant letter if the initial phone is a consonant in any case. By this operation A, E, I, O, U, and Y (from YTTERBIUM, for example) are determined as vowel letters. All the remainder and Y are consonant letters. Thus Y is both a vowel and consonant letter. *C* and *V* will symbolize variables whose values are consonant letters and *c* and *v* phones whose values are vowel sounds.

Rules are unconditional if they map every occurrence of a letter or letter sequence into a particular phone or phone sequence in a specified position in the trigram. Rules are conditional if they map letters or letter sequences into phones or phone sequences in a specified position in the trigram only when preceded or followed by some other letter. Rules are variable if there is more than one mapping into phones under specified conditions. A rule is idiosyncratic if it only applies to a letter or letter sequence in a single trigram.

Rule Type 1. *Unconditional initial and final rules*. Take the set of all dictionary entries which begin *CV* and divide it into subsets each of which all contain the same initial *C*. For example DANCE and DUCK will be in the same subset but CRIB will be in another.

If for any subset, every pronunciation begins with the same phone or phone sequence, the initial letter which defines the subset is unconditionally mapped into the initial phone or phone sequence of the pronunciation. For example, since every member of the subset DANCE, DUCK, . . . has a pronunciation which begins with the phone d the mapping D → d is established. A parallel operation on the set of dictionary entries which end *VC* gives unconditional final mappings.

By this type the following specific rules are generated:

Initial B → b (1);
D → d (2);
F → f (3);
H → h (4);
J → j (5);
K → k (6);
L → l (7);
M → m (8);
N → n (9);
P → p (10);
Q → k (11);
R → r (12);
T → t (13);
V → v (14);
W → w (15);
X → z (16);
Y → y (17);
Z → z (18).

Final B → b (19);
C → k (20);
D → d (21);
F → f (22);
G → g (23);
K → k (24);
L → l (25);
M → m (26);
N → n (27);
P → p (28);
Q → k (29);
R → r (30);
T → t (31);
V → v (32);
X → ks (33);
Z → z (34).

Rule Type 2. *Unconditional Digraph Rules*. Take the set of ACD entries which are spelled *CVC* and have two symbols in their pronunciation and for which *C* has already been mapped by a rule of Rule Type 1. For example, PAY → pā is in this set because it is spelled *CVC*, because P → p by Rule 10 and because the pronunciation has two phones. Now extend this set to include all *CVC* entries which end in the particular *VC*. For example, MAY will be in the same set with PAY. If all the members of the set end in the same phone then there is a tentative mapping of the digraph into the phone. For example, since all digraphs of the form *-AY* have a pronunciation ending in ā, AY is mapped into ā, but there is a further manipulation of these mappings in certain instances described in the next paragraph.

If the phone into which the tentative mapping has been made (e.g. ā) occurs somewhere in the ACD flanked by two consonant phones and the corresponding orthography has the vowel letter of the digraph flanked by consonant letters which map the consonant phones by rules of Type 1, then the vowel letter maps into the vowel phone and the consonant letter maps into zero.

For example, the phone ā occurs in FADE ↔ fād in which ā is flanked by F and D and F → f by Rule 3 and D → d by Rule 21. Hence in AY → ā, A is mapped into a and Y is mapped into zero.

Rule Type 2 produces the following specific rules: AH → ä, H → zero (35); AW → ô (36); AY: A → ā, Y → zero (37); OY → oi (38); UY → ī (39).

Rule Type 3. *Initial-final transfer rule.* If a particular C does not appear in any ACD entry beginning *CV* or in any ending *VC*, it is mapped into the same phone as corresponding initial or final if such a mapping of Rule Type 1 exists. By this rule type the mapping of final J → j (40) is established by transfer from Rule 5.

Rule Type 4. *Variable and idiosyncratic digraph rules.* If in the extended set defined in the second paragraph under Rule Type 2 there are one or more than one final phones which are found more than once in pronunciations of this set, this value or these values are extended to all members of the set. For example ou occurs in at least two instances of the pronunciation of the set of trigrams ending in the digraph OW (COW → kou; HOW → hou), as does o (ROW → rō; LOW → lō). Hence all trigrams ending in OW map this letter sequence variably into both ou and ō. Hence, for example, by an application of a rule of this rule type and by Rule 12 the trigram ROW is mapped into the two pronunciations rou and rō.

If any pronunciation is found in only one member of the set, it is an idiosyncratic mapping for that trigram alone (alongside of unconditional or variable mappings if they exist). By this rule type the following rules are established: EW → ū and ōō variably and ō idiosyncratically only in SEW (41); EY → ā and idiosyncratically ē in KEY (42); OW → ou and ō variably (43).

Rule Type 5. *Initial and final variant, conditional and idiosyncratic rules.* Take the set of all ACD entries beginning *CV*. If any *C* not given an initial mapping by a rule of Rule Types 1 or 3, when followed by some particular vowel symbol has the same initial phone in all its occurrences, the consonant letter is mapped into that phone conditionally when preceding that vowel letter. For example, initial CA words all have initial k in their pronunciation; hence, C is initially mapped into k before A. If before a particular vowel symbol two or more phones are each found in at least two instances, then these are variant values under the given condition. If a particular value only occurs in one case, it is idiosyncratic for that instance. Taking the set of all ACD entries ending in *VC*, corresponding rules are set up for the pronunciation of final *C*.

The following are the rules of Rule Type 5: Initial C → k before A, O, or U (conditional) (44); Initial C → s before E (conditional) and → ch (idiosyncratic) in CEL (because of CELLO) (46); Initial G before A, O, U → g (conditional) (47); Initial G before Y → j (conditional) (48); Initial G before E, I → g, j (variant, conditional) (49); Initial S before A, E, I, O, Y → s (conditional) (50); Initial S before U → s, sh (variant, conditional) (51); Final S after any vowel s, z (variant, unconditional) (52).

Rule Type 6. *Unconditional, conditional, and idiosyncratic medial values.* Take the set of all ACD entries beginning *CVC* or ending *CVC* excepting all those whose *VC* sequence is a digraph assigned under a rule of Type 2 and providing the accent mark for an entry with initial *CVC* does not occur later than the second vowel phone of the pronunciation and for final *CVC* does not occur earlier than any vowel phone (i.e. is an accented vowel). For example, CITY → sĭtē and PREFER → prĭfur are in this set.

Now form an ordered set in which the first member is any *V* which occurs in either an initial or final *CVC* and the second member is any vowel phone which occurs as the second symbol of the pronunciation for an initial *CVC*. Thus I → ĭ and E → û are among the ordered pairs. Now for any ordered pair consider the class of those consonant letters which precede in any occurrence of the class and the class of consonants which follows. Thus, from the examples of the preceding paragraph, C is a member of the m′ class of the ordered pair I:ĭ and T is a member of its m″ class.

Then if both m′ and m″ for any ordered pair has at least two members, the mapping of the letter into the phone is unconditional. For example, since the ordered pair I:ĭ has at least two members of its m′ class (e.g. P in PIT ↔ pĭt and C in CITY ↔ sĭtē) and in its m″ class (e.g. T in PIT ↔ pĭt and N in SKIN ↔ skĭn), I → ĭ unconditionally.

If the m′ class of an ordered pair has only one member in the m″ class, then the mapping is conditional on the member of m′ preceding.

If the m″ class of an ordered pair has only one member and the m′ class more than one, then the mapping is conditional on the member of m″ following.

As an example of a rule derived from this last rule type, consider the ordered pair E:û which has at least two members in its m′ class (e.g. F in PREFER ↔ prĭfur and H in HER ↔ hûr) but only one member in its m″ class, namely R. Hence the mapping E → û is conditional before R.

If the m′ class and the m″ class each have only a single member, the mapping is idiosyncratic to the trigram containing the member of the m′ class as its first member and that of the m″ class as its second member.

By rule Type 6, the following specific rules are generated: A → a, ā, ä, and ô (variant, unconditional) (53); A → â before R (conditional) (54); A → ŏ after W (conditional) (55); E → ĕ and ē (variant, unconditional) (56); E → ĭ and û before R (variant, conditional) (57); E → ä in SER (idiosyncratic because of SERGEANT) (58); I → ĭ and ī (unconditional) (59); I → û before R (conditional) (60); O → ŏ, ō, ŏŏ, and ōō (unconditional) (61); O → ô before R (conditional) (62); U → ŏ, ō, ŭ, and ōō (unconditional) (63); U → û before R (conditional) (64); Y → ĭ and ī (unconditional) (65); Y → û before R (conditional) (66).

Rule Type 7. *Additional digraph zero mappings*. Where a final *C* is by a rule of Type 2 in any instance assigned a zero mapping (this applies in fact only to H and Y) this zero value is extended to all -*VC* trigrams with such final members in sequences which do not occur as final -*VC* in any dictionary entry. The vowel is mapped into the pronunciation(s) assigned unconditionally by rules of Type 6.

Thus no ACD entries end in IH. By rule 35, of Type 2, H is assigned a zero value in the sequence AH. A zero value is extended to H in the sequence IH while I is mapped into the unconditional values specified in rule 59 of Type 6. Under this rule type we obtain the following rules: EH: E → ĕ, ē; H → zero (67); IH: I → ĭ, ī; H → zero (68); OH: O → ŏ, ō, ŭ, ōō; H → zero (69); UH: U → ŭ, ū, ŏŏ, ōō; H → zero (70); YH: Y → ĭ, ī; H → zero (71); IY: I → ĭ, ī; Y → zero (72).

Rule Type 8. Under the preceding seven rules all trigrams excepting those ending in UW, IW, and YW have been assigned at least one pronunciation. By phonetic considerations U is mapped into u and oo by sound absorption since ū and ōō are juw and uw phonetically. Thus juww, uww > juw and uw respectively. By shift of syllabic boundary IW and YW give juw which equals u of the pronunciation key. Hence the rules: UW → ū, ōō (73); IW → ū (74); YW → ū (75).

## Appendix B

Values for Selected Syllables on $V_1$ and $V_2$ with Target Words

| | $V_1$ | $V_2$ | Target word | | $V_1$ | $V_2$ | Target word |
|---|---|---|---|---|---|---|---|
| 1. BAC | 5 | 1 | back | 14. KIP | 3 | 9 | — |
| 2. CAT | 1 | 0 | cat | 15. LEK | 5 | 2 | leak |
| 3. CEW | 3 | 8 | sue | 16. LOQ | 5 | 4 | lock |
| 4. CUG | 3 | 9 | — | 17. MOL | 4 | 2 | (moll) |
| 5. DIQ | 5 | 4 | Dick | 18. NAQ | 5 | 5 | knack |
| 6. DOX | 3 | 5 | docks | 19. PUL | 3 | 1 | pull |
| 7. FAV | 5 | 9 | — | 20. QOF | 7 | 7 | cuff |
| 8. GEP | 2 | 5 | jeep | 21. QYJ | 8 | 9 | — |
| 9. HAF | 5 | 2 | half | 22. RYL | 6 | 4 | rill |
| 10. HYL | 6 | 4 | hill | 23. SUL | 4 | 9 | — |
| 11. JER | 2 | 2 | jeer | 24. TUH | 5 | 6 | to |
| 12. KAR | 4 | 3 | car | 25. VEW | 2 | 2 | view |
| 13. KYW | 6 | 9 | cue | 26. WIZ | 5 | 4 | wise |
| | | | | 27. ZOT | 4 | 9 | — |

## References Cited


Archer, E. James. 1960. "A re-evaluation of the meaningfulness of all possible CVC trigrams." *Psychological Monographs* 74, no. 10.

Cofer, Charles N., ed. 1961. *Verbal Learning and Verbal Behavior*. New York: McGraw Hill.

Ebbinghaus, H. 1913. *Meaning: A Contribution to Experimental Psychology*. Translated by H. A. Ruger and C. E. Bussenius. New York: Teacher's College, Columbia University.

Glazer, J. A. 1928. "The association value of nonsense syllables." *Journal of Genetic Psychology* 35: 255–69.

Greenberg, J. H., and J. J. Jenkins. 1964. "Studies in the psychological correlates of the sound system of American English, Part I." *Word* 20: 157–77.

Hultzen, L. S. 1965. "Consonant clusters in English." *American Speech* 40: 5–19.

Krueger, W. C. F. 1934. "The relative difficulty of nonsense syllables." *Journal of Experimental Psychology* 17: 145–53.

Mandler, G. 1955. "Associative frequency and associative prepotency as measures of response to nonsense syllables." *American Journal of Psychology* 68: 662–65.

Moser, H. M., J. J. Dreher, and H. J. Oyer. 1957. "One-syllable words." *Technical Report by the Ohio State University Research Foundation, R.F. Project 664*. Columbus.

Noble, C. E. 1961. *Measurement of Association Value (a) Rated Association (a) and Scale Meaningfulness (m) for the 2100 CVC Combinations of the English Alphabet*. Missoula: Montana State University.

Noble, C. E., F. E. Stockwell, and M. W. Pryor. 1957. "Meaningfulness (m′) and association value (a) in paired-associate syllable learning." *Psychological Reports* 3: 441–52.

Pratt, F. 1939. *Secret and Urgent*. Indianapolis: Bobbs-Merrill.

Thorndike, E. L., and I. Lorge. 1944. *The Teacher's Word Book of 30,000 Words*. New York: Columbia University Press.

Underwood, B. J., and R. W. Schulz. 1960. *Meaningfulness and Verbal Learning*. Chicago, Philadelphia, New York: Lippincott.

# PART V

# LINGUISTIC MODELS AND LINGUISTIC EXPLANATION

# On the 'Language of Observation' in Linguistics

Encountering such an expression as 'the language of observation', the linguist will immediately conclude that the 'language' in question is not a natural language, but one of those artificial postulational constructions typically produced by philosophers of an analytic bent. Such 'languages' are generally formalized and their value is presumed to lie in the clarification of concepts which results, or at any rate is intended to result from the use of formalization.

In the present instance, however, we will be concerned with something too inchoate to submit easily at the present time to formalization. The justification, however, for using a term with 'formal language' overtones, is that we will not be describing natural languages directly but will rather be concerned with the analysis of a certain kind of discourse which occurs in the shop-talk of linguists themselves, something perhaps not unlike the 'language stratum' of certain ordinary language philosophers.

The purpose in doing this is to call attention to the existence of such a stratum of discourse, to assay its significance in overall linguistic theory and to suggest lines along which a more systematic treatment might eventually proceed.

In spite of a certain vagueness which seems inseparable from the subject in its present state and the inconclusive nature of much of the present argument, the questions raised here are, I think, worth raising. Moreover, notwithstanding their rather rarefied and abstract nature, they relate fairly directly to the general topic of languages of the world with which this conference is concerned. For such an enterprise, a central question is the comparability of linguistic descriptions constructed in accordance with differing theoretical models. If there is, indeed, an underlying language of observation in the sense to be

This is a revised version of a paper presented at the Conference on Languages of the World held at the Center for Applied Linguistics in April 1970.

discussed here, then one of the essential functions that it can fulfill is to provide a universal basis for the comparability of language descriptions.

In fact such a basic language exists in practice and is constantly utilized but without receiving explicit recognition. The following is an illustrative example.

In one of the introductory chapters of Emmon Bach's excellent book, *An Introduction to Transformational Grammars*, the student is presented with two alternative descriptions of the phonological system of a hypothetical language X, labelled Description 1 and Description 2, respectively. These two descriptions are formalized in the sense that they are presented, largely in Description 1 and completely in Description 2, by sequences of symbols rather than words in ordinary language. In neither instance is the description discursive. That is, they do not consist of sequences of sentences with syntax structure of ordinary English sentences, which would still be possible even with the employment of a technical terminology couched in symbols. Bach then adduces arguments to show that Description 2, which consists of ordered rewrite rules, is superior to Description 1, which consists of unordered 'taxonomic' statements.

The linguist has become so inured to formalized modes of expression that unless it has been specifically pointed out, he will probably not have realized in reading Bach's text that, in fact, not two but three formulations have been presented. One of these three has not been explicitly recognized, nor is it in the running in the debate regarding the relative merits of Description 1 and Description 2.

The third, silent contender is a discursive verbal description of language X which is presumably there because without it the elementary student for whom the book is intended would, no doubt, find Descriptions 1 and 2 unintelligible. Even the professional would probably find this discursive description of some assistance and he certainly would be unable to understand Descriptions 1 and 2 without this verbal prelude, had he not in his previous training mastered a technical terminology on the basis of statements explaining them in ordinary English. The situation here is no different in principle from the introduction of basic mathematical concepts or, more generally, scientific concepts, in ordinary language which must have been mastered before it becomes possible to understand the technical languages of mathematics and the sciences.

Bach himself evidently considers this initial discursive statement as different in some fundamental way from the rival "scientific" descriptions which follow. Thus, he prefaces his consideration of language X with the following remarks (p. 20): "I shall state the facts for the language in ordinary English and then give two descriptions, the first in a form familiar to students in modern linguistics, the second as a set of rewrite rules."

The example just given resembles many others that might have been cited in the following respect. The possibility of such factual-level statements is taken for granted and utilized in practice without according it any explicit theoretical recognition. The point of view that I will seek to outline in a very preliminary fashion here is that the existence of this level and its characterization is a matter of some theoretical significance. It goes well beyond its pragmatic contribution on the psychological side to the intelligibility of higher-level discourse in that it is related in a fundamental way to two of the basic criteria of scientific theory construction, empirical verifiability and completeness.

It is generally agreed that any scientific description must be rejected if it has as a consequence the logical derivation of consequences which are in conflict with observed fact or if all the facts are not accounted for in the theory. The foregoing statement requires certain qualifications. First, agreement with fact is relative to a somewhat vague norm in accordance with which certain violations are tolerated if they are sporadic, or, where the observations are quantitative, if there is reasonably close approximation to the theoretically expected values. Still, gross violations are not easily accepted and even small or sporadic deviations can eventually lead to revision of theory if it can be shown that these deviations can themselves be accounted for systematically, e.g. Verner's law as accounting for the exceptions to Grimm's law.

The requirement of completeness also calls for some comment. It does not necessarily refer to the language as a whole. It can, and in practice most often does, relate to some subpart defined in advance of the investigation, e.g. the system of verbal conjugation, the segmental phonologic system, etc. Such presystematically drawn boundaries are often vague at certain points but there is a body of data which by general agreement must be accounted for.

Besides these two criteria of agreement with fact and completeness, that of generality with its much discussed and evidently complex relation to simplicity is the third basic criterion. Yet the former two notions seem to have a kind of priority in that a description which violates them, however well endowed in respect of elegance, simplicity, generalizing power, and insightfulness, will be subject to rejection.

This level will hereafter be referred to as O, the language of observation. It is far broader in scope than appears in the foregoing example in that it is not confined to phonology, to the writings of a single school in linguistics, or to the sole purpose of making clear for pedagogical reasons for elementary students the underlying facts which are being subjected to theoretical analysis.

Thus, there are numerous examples in the literature of differing analyses of morphological systems, e.g. that of the Russian verb conjugation in terms of alternative models such as traditional paradigms, morphemes and their distribution, or generatively, in which all the participants are in essential agreement regarding the 'facts'.

As appears from such examples, and also from that in Bach's book, in some way O seems to provide a language which is neutral in relation to the various schools and their rival analyses, or even between members of the same school when presenting different analyses. Thus Bierwisch and Ross, both members of the TG school, present differing theories regarding underlying word order of subject, verb, and object in German. However, both agree that the basic facts which have to be accounted for are that in main clauses German has 'normal' SVO order, and in subordinate clauses SOV. Once again these facts are taken for granted as an area of agreement by the participants, and the facts in question are of the kind that can be learned from standard grammars of German which make no particular claim to theoretical sophistication.

As we have seen, a striking element common to all these instances is lack of explicit reference to O as a level. It is a kind of background phenomenon apparently never brought into the forefront of consciousness. The closest to overt recognition in the context of contemporary theory is probably in Chomsky's well-known theory of the three adequacies, though even here, as elsewhere, it characteristically lurks in the background. For the first of the three adequacies, 'observational adequacy' would seem to have no locus in reality unless there were statements embodying observed 'facts' to which we might refer in evaluating the observational adequacy of a description.

Let us grant, then, the existence of such a level of factual statements based on observation of the actual practice of linguists and involving, it would seem, a rather surprising consensus in the specific data even among linguists of different schools. How can this level be characterized from a theoretic point of view and whence does this consensus arise? Perhaps we may, for purposes of initial discussion, characterize the kind of discourse with which we are dealing in the following way. It consists of statements regarding individual languages which rest in some reasonably direct way on a body of observations, that is, it consists of 'observation statements'. The difficulty, however, of distinguishing descriptive from purely observational statements is notorious, if indeed the latter exist at all. What is being aimed at can be expressed by two criteria: (1) particularity, i.e. absence of generalization, (2) the use of terms based directly on physically observable characteristics which are not defined by means of logically more primitive concepts within some theory. That statements presented as factual in linguistic discussion do not satisfy these criteria any more than in another science will soon appear and is, in fact, not at all surprising.

The general point is indeed far from novel. Thomas Kuhn states it cogently in his well-known work, *The Structure of Scientific Revolutions*. Alluding to the 'natural history approach' he notes (pp. 16–17): "No natural history can be interpreted in the absence of at least some implicit theoretical and methodological belief that permits selection, evaluation, and criticism." We may revert for illustrative purposes to the example from Bach's book, *An Introduction to Transformational Grammars*, cited earlier. The following are two of the statements included in his account which, as we recall, are stated to be "facts for the language in ordinary English."

> 1. Every syllable consists of a nucleus, an optional string of consonants, and an optional final consonant.
>
> 2. The phonemes have the following conditional variants (allophones): /p k/ are voiced between vowels, /a/ is [o] except where stressed.

Regarding the first of the two ideal criteria for observation, lack of generality, the very occurrence of the word 'every' in the first statement, "every syllable . . ." is an overt indication of generality. Regarding the second criterion, the use of terms based directly on observation and not definable by means of more primitive terms in some theory, both statements abound in terms which are not 'primitive' and are defined within a framework of theory. This is particularly striking in the second statement with such giveaway terms as allophone, phoneme, and the technical use of brackets for the first and slashes for the second. Thus, to spell out the obvious, 'allophone' is a theoretical concept which presupposes such other concepts as environment and phonetic similarity, which in turn presuppose 'feature' in the traditional phonetic sense. If two phones are similar they must be similar in certain "respects" stateable in phonetic terminology. Moreover, 'allophone' is itself a relational term involving in its own definition the term 'phoneme'. There is no such thing as an allophone in isolation. It is always an allophone of some phoneme.

While, in light of the previous remarks regarding the nonexistence of pure observational statements in science, these results are in general not unexpected, one aspect does seem worthy of being noted. The body of theory presupposed by these 'statements' of fact is essentially classical phonemic theory. Thus, as so often in the history of human thought, the theoretical statement of yesterday is the factual observation of today. One is reminded of Bloomfield's remarks concerning the "nature of such terms as subject, object, and predicate" (1933: 3): "Like much else that masquerades as common sense, it is in fact highly sophisticated and derives, at no great distance, from the speculations of ancient and medieval philosophers." In the present instance, however, the time interval is to be measured in decades rather than centuries.

It should be understood that the foregoing remarks are not intended in any fashion as a hostile critique of Bach's excellent and sophisticated book. What

Bach has done here is normal for the practicing scientist who is quite capable of moving his subject matter ahead without worrying about the epistemological basis for what, at any particular point in the history of science, passes for its lowest-level observational statements.

What we might, in light of the foregoing example, call the 'relative' nature of the distinction between an observational and a theoretic level, calls for further analysis. Does it not put into doubt the assertion made earlier in this paper that O, the language of observation, provided a common basis which was neutral in relation to differing theoretical schools? If, for example, we consider a typical instance of classical phonemic analysis such as Bloch's analysis of Japanese this relativity becomes particularly clear. Bloch's exposition, in accordance with the pattern being sketched here, and in this case quite overtly, is based on two levels. There are first numerous statements regarding the phones of Japanese and their distribution, and the set of these statements obviously constitutes for Bloch a lower 'factual' level which is then accounted for theoretically by assigning the phones to higher-level units, the phonemes. Yet these latter 'theoretical' statements of Bloch could easily, *mutatis mutandis*, pass muster as factual-level statements in an analysis such as Bach's.

However, examples of this sort do not destroy the notion of an absolute basic level O. The following considerations would seem to apply. It would still be true that from an analysis of Japanese based on a model like that of Bach, one could *deduce* a whole series of statements quite like those of Bloch's lowest-level distributional statements, and that these would in principle be identical. One would here have to distinguish two different contexts of exposition in the transformational generative literature. One of these might be called the pedagogical. The preliminary factual statements by Bach regarding his hypothetical language X is but one example. They abound in such works as Koutsoudas' *Writing Transformational Grammars* and Harms's *Introduction to Phonological Theory*. In this latter work the equation, structuralist's theoretical level = transformationalist's factual level, occurs at times in a highly explicit way. The data for an exercise in theoretical analysis is an actual 'phonemic' statement taken from the structuralist literature. In these instances the reduction to the structuralist's factual level involves simply a reversal of the pragmatic order of the structuralist's exposition. The structuralist presents phonetic "facts" and constructs phonemic statements on their basis. From the phonemic statements thus presented the phonetic facts can be recovered. The other context is that of actual grammars. Here the relationship is far more indirect. Nevertheless it is clearly possible to deduce such low-level distributional statements from the total phonology. What is most important, it is possible, or perhaps more accurately put, there is usually sufficient clarity in the use of theoretical terms to ascertain, given two descriptions (whether from the same or different schools), which differences rest on discrepancies in fact and which on differing theoretical analyses.

The second observation that might be offered in regard to this relativity of theoretical and observational levels is that the lowest-level distributional statements of the structuralist no more satisfy the ideal criteria for pure observation statements than those of Bach with regard to the facts concerning his hypothetical language X. Their generality is obvious, for example, in statements such as: "The phone *č* never occurs before *a*, *o*, and *u*." Such statements are based on generalizations over an already "edited" corpus. Moreover, there is a framework of theoretical terms, namely those of phonetic theory which exhibit a comprehensive logical organization.

The phenomenon discussed in the foregoing section as exhibiting the relativity of observational and factual levels may be considered, from another point of view, as a difference in linguistic usage by linguists themselves, i.e. their usage of such terms as 'fact' and 'theory'. If we view our task here as a theoretical explication of the term 'fact' as used by linguists, then such discrepant meanings are the normal raw material of differing pre-systemic usages which are typically encountered in attempts at explication. A preliminary criterion intended to guide such efforts was mentioned earlier, namely, that the language we are seeking to characterize "rests in some reasonably direct way on a body of observation." Such a criterion is meant merely as a guide, and its vagueness as so stated is obvious, yet it has an overriding role, once it has been adopted, as against the uses of such terms as 'fact' by linguists in actual practice. In what follows I shall try to outline one possible approach in terms of which greater precision can be given to this criterion, and in terms of which the relativity of usage just discussed can be accorded its proper place.

One form such a reconstruction might take would be use of the well-known axiomatic method. I do not mean by this that a full axiomatization should be carried out. It quite probably would not prove desirable even if it were feasible. It is rather that a consideration of the problems arising in axiomatization might provide a framework for ordering and clarification.

The axiomatic method involves in its essentials the construction of a calculus which in its initial phase is uninterpreted and in which more complex notions are defined in terms of logically more primitive notions until the most primitive terms are reached which are undefined in the calculus. The terms of this calculus are, of course, not chosen in an arbitrary manner.

Most of them will ultimately, when the calculus is interpreted, stand for concepts which are already used in the working technical vocabulary of the science, and the connection will be exhibited normally by a choice of symbols whose reference to these concepts will be obvious (e.g. letters which abbreviate the usual designation of the concept). Ultimately, the primitive terms receive definitions of a quite different sort, definitions which provide the connection of the whole system with empirical observations. These definitions have traditionally been called coordinating definitions, but since they provide the basis for interpretation of the system as a whole, I shall call them interpretive definitions; in fact, they are not unconnected with the tasks of the interpretive components as set forth in contemporary transformational-generative grammatical theory. These two parts of the theory, the calculus itself and the interpretive definitions, involve rather different considerations so that it will be convenient to refer to them as C and I respectively.

The notion of C provides a convenient method of accounting for the relativity of levels discussed earlier. However differently either the word 'fact' or some synonymous expression is being used by different linguists or, what is more frequent, however different the types of statements that are being employed as the lowest level, we will say that those concepts and statements provide the axiomatic basis of O from our point of view, which cannot be defined in terms of other concepts. Hence, when Bach uses a term like allophone in what he is in practice treating as lowest level in his discourse, we will consider that these terms are not primitive in this discourse, even though they are not defined explicitly, as long as their understanding can be said reasonably to involve more primitive terms such as environment, phone type, etc. Assuming for the moment an axiomatization in which this reduction takes place, we may say that although Bach uses terms like allophone and phoneme and Bloch uses such terms as environment and phone, they are, so to speak, 'speaking the same language' insofar as the underlying axiomatization might well turn out to be identical. I shall call this reduction to lower-level concepts resolvability. The thesis of a common O advanced earlier would then come to this: that there is an agreement among linguists regarding the underlying calculus of axiomatization, were this axiomatization to be carried out.

Undoubtedly the discussion so far has tended to a kind of optimistic overstatement which I shall now try to counteract to some extent, and in the process bring in considerations inextricably connected with I. This accentuation of the positive, which was purposeful, seems justified since the central point, which I believe to be a valid one, is that there is, in general, a common basis of observation statements on which linguists agree and which they seek to account for in various manners by higher-level theories.

One source of this optimism has been the concentration in the present discussion on phonology, obviously an area of relatively high agreement in regard to observation statements. Yet even here it would, of course, be incorrect to assert complete unanimity regarding such a level. There are two major areas of indeterminacy, one relating to I and the other to C. In regard to I, we may distinguish two main types of interpretation which may be called physical and phenomenological, respectively. By physical interpretation rules are meant those in which it is possible to specify in a reasonably satisfactory way either physiological or acoustic parameters. In other instances we are not in a position to do so. What we have is rather the kind of intersubjective agreement based on perception found in everyday life in relation to such concepts as 'red'. Notions relating to syllabicity doubtless belong here. In such cases, while there is typically a large area of agreement there may also exist a not inconsiderable range of uncertainty. In the case of the syllable, a conspicuous instance is the determination of syllable boundaries. Perhaps we should include here still a third class of primitive terms whose interpretation shares a lack of physical specification with the second type, but which probably cannot be reduced to perceptual agreement. Here we might include such shadowy but indispensable concepts as phonological word boundaries. The other major problem area belongs to C. The basic issue here can be conveyed by the question: how fine-grained should the observations be? The area of possible maneuver for any particular language description would seem to have a lower bound in the limits of consistent perceptual discriminability and an upper bound in actual contrastiveness in the language. That the extent of phonetic specification is an unsolved problem is recognized in present-day phonological theory. At the very least, though, it might be pointed out that the relation between finer- and coarser-meshed descriptions is highly structured. Thus, to pursue the mesh metaphor, two descriptions might be called congruent if all the wires of the coarser mesh coincide with some of those in the finer, and such congruence is usually found in practice.

A basic question which has not yet been raised concerns the status of O in regard to the relationship between individual language descriptions and cross-language generalization. In considering the question, it is essential to distinguish several types of discourse, or 'language-strata'. We have considered O itself, up to now, as containing observation statements regarding specific languages. Such statements clearly belong to a different kind of discourse from that in which concepts occurring in O are reconstructed, whether axiomatically or otherwise. Such a language is essentially a metalanguage for O. Unlike O itself it is nonempirical in that it is entirely postulational in form and consists of analytic sentences, even though the system itself has been devised in such a manner that its terms can be applied to individual language observations. While it consists of definitions and tautologies, it is of course corrigible in the sense that it becomes subject to modification if it ceases to give the desired results when applied to individual natural languages.

In contrast, O itself is synthetic in that by means of the interpretive definitions of Meta-O, its statements receive meaning in individual language statements capable of empirical truth or falsity. That these concepts are intended to be applicable to all languages, not just to certain individual languages, is in general clear. The example of the use of terms like allophone in describing the phonological facts of Bach's hypothetical language X provides a kind of *a fortiori* evidence for the thesis of general applicability.

The preceding is a particularly straightforward example; such straightforward instances of universal applicability are especially characteristic of phonology, or at any rate, of segmental phonology. Regarding grammar the situation is more complicated in a number of ways. One set of complications arises from the fact that we are dealing here with form and meaning. One type of situation encountered can be illustrated from the description of case systems. Here it would seem that the two aspects lend themselves to two fairly independent types of analyses, corresponding with reasonable exactitude to the traditional areas of morphology and syntax. The first is the organization of the formal structure in which the names of individual cases are as it were mere labels for distinguishable entities abstracted from the semantics of case use, but not from phonological shape. In regard to the second aspect, the semantics of case, the situation is in principle probably parallel to that of phonology in that description could be carried out for individual languages by means of concepts ultimately resolvable into primitive ideas stated in the metalanguage of O and applicable to all languages. However, the difference in practice is that the kind of analysis which could be incorporated into Meta-O has not yet progressed very far. It is, I believe, a result congruent with the proposals of Ferguson in his paper for this meeting,[1] that the most promising resolution would seem to be in the direction of positing individual 'case uses', e.g. agent, separation, accompaniment as the logical primitives of Meta-O in terms of which such terms as 'instrumental', 'dative', etc., in individual languages could be defined as more complex entities. However, if we compare this situation with that in phonology we see that a comparable achievement would require the distinction of such uses as but a first step. There is, it is true, once more a level O of observation insofar as there are certain facts about case usages in particular languages readily stateable in traditional terminology. What is lacking, when compared with phonology, is an overall descriptive framework, one which for phonology was already provided by traditional phonetics and which systematically defines a universe of possible speech sounds. Viewed in

[1] Published as Charles Ferguson, "Grammatical Categories in Data Collection." *Working Papers on Language Universals*, Vol. 4, 1970.

this light, Hjelmslev's study of case was a pioneer attempt to provide just such a systematization.

The relatively greater complexity of problems in this area is shown by a further class of facts which can probably be cited from any case language and which is exemplified by rules of case government by verbs. Some of these can probably be covered by generalized statements, e.g. 'verbs of wishing', but some are usually the specific property of individual lexical items. These do represent, once more, examples of specific O since they involve facts on which various observers can agree. However, while there is a reasonable expectation that such concepts as 'agent', etc., can be formulated in Meta-O with the potential of cross-linguistic applicability, it would seem that individual lexical items figuring in such rules are irreducibly individual language facts.

The language stratum that might be called generalizing O is that form of discourse in which universals are stated, again using terms definable by means of the primitive ideas of Meta-O. Logically such discourse is empirical like specific language O. Its basic difference is that it contains variables whose values range over individual languages. That there is a body of such generalizing statements in phonology at least, which have thus far received empirical verification, should not be a matter of dispute, although their theoretical significance has been contested by some. Such universals stateable on the basis of O-level facts of individual languages, some unrestricted and others implicational in form, are found in Postal's *Aspects of Phonological Theory*, and are the basis for the marking conventions in Chomsky and Halle's *The Sound Pattern of English.*

Exceptionless implicational syntactic and semantic universals arrived at by the straightforward comparison of surface observation are perhaps less widely accepted, though again I would contend that the evidence for them is indisputable. Thus, to cite but one example, languages with a trial number in the pronoun always have the dual. Those which have an inclusive/exclusive distinction in the first person plural have it in the trial, if it exists, and in the dual if it exists. What is perhaps even less often realized is that there are in all probability some unrestricted universals of surface grammar also. For example, I have noted, thus far without exception in a variety of languages of differing fundamental order types, that when a personal pronoun is in apposition with a noun phrase (as in English *we, the people*) the pronoun always precedes. Such examples, should they be verified, have, it would seem, considerable theoretical significance. They are in fact akin to 'conspiracies' noted in recent work regarding individual languages, but differ in that they belong to universal O. To set up, as has been suggested, a metaprinciple distinct from the grammatical rules themselves which would select precisely those alternatives among deeper-level rules which lead as it were to the foreordained surface result would not obscure the fact that the metarule itself is a generalization based on surface observations.

This paper has been devoted essentially to a discussion of the 'language of observation'. Nothing has been said regarding higher-level theoretical discourse. It has received an implicit negative definition in that it would not "rest in some reasonably direct way on a body of observation." That present TG grammar provides such a theoretical level is clear and it is, indeed, one of its great accomplishments. What is often called 'abstractness' of theory refers precisely to the existence of theoretical constructs which do not possess a direct and simple relation to the body of observed facts. Obviously such a vague phrase as 'direct and simple relation' is in need of more careful explanation. Once again the situation in regard to phonology is reasonably clear. In various writings on phonological theory by Halle and Chomsky, certain requirements of classical phonemic theory are rejected which would limit theoretical elements such as phonemes to a relation in which any particular phone would in all its occurrences be assigned to the same phoneme. In traditional phonemic theory, at least as practiced in the United States, which does not allow such overlapping, the relation between phone and phoneme was then a very simple one, merely class membership.

The considerations just adduced are intended merely to give some idea of what is meant by directness and simplicity of relationship. They do not apply with any literalness to grammar, and even for phonology they do not do justice to the variety of structuralist practice which quite often tolerated a fair degree of 'indirectness'. For example, certain phonetic properties of segments, even though contrastive, were often not assigned to the same phoneme as other phonetic properties of the same segment, but rather to junctures which should be considered as true theoretical constructs. Also, the process approach in morphophonemics practiced by some American structuralists involved setting up theoretical base forms whose relation to the observed facts was complex. It is clear, however, that whereas in structuralism all such departures from direct and simple relation to the level of observed fact were resorted to only out of necessity and then usually with some opposition (e.g. Bloch's objections to juncture, and the attempts to maintain item and arrangement models in morphophonemics), TG grammar freely employs theoretical constructs and considers them a virtue rather than a *pis aller*.

It is not within the scope of this paper to consider developments in linguistics in their relation to the broader trends of scientific methodology. It can be noted incidentally, however, that the criterion for theoretical concepts that they be constructed from observables is often considered the essential characteristic of positivistic approaches. Thus, Harré (1961: 19), summarizing the views of Mach, the classic source of modern positivism, says among other things, "The only propositions which are worth enunciating are those stating concomitances of observables."

It is now clear that theories in physics, the science with which the great majority of the philosophers of science have been concerned, do not have this simple structure. On the other hand, it does not seem reasonable to attempt to impose conclusions derived from the nature of physical theory to linguistics in a literal way. Linguistics should rather pursue the kinds of theory that are most fruitful from their point of view without being constrained by the requirement of either conformity to, or transcendence of, positivistic limitations.

It seems to me not unreasonable to assert that historical explanation of the traditional kind possesses the same kind of indirectness in relation to the data of observation and explanatory power as transformational grammar. The resemblance between the two which is generally agreed, however, not to be an identity is therefore not really surprising. Once again, the picture in phonology is reasonably clear, compared with other aspects of language description. Far more work needs to be done on historical syntax, for example, to ascertain to what extent syntactic deep structures represent earlier historically attested surface structures.

In closing, the question might be raised whether these are not, in fact, rival types of explanatory theory. If so, historical explanation in the traditional sense of accounting for surface linguistic facts of $t_2$ by principles of change (i.e. processes) of lesser or greater degree of generality operating on the surface linguistic facts of $t_1$ where $t_1$ preceded $t_2$ would be a worthy alternative. Recently it has become more and more apparent that there are alternative views of the nature of syntactic deep structure which differ in fundamental ways, with no convincing way at present of choosing among them, e.g. Chomsky, Fillmore, McCawley. Even within what is essentially the same model, differing accounts of the same surface phenomenon occur. Since this situation exists to a far greater degree in syntax and semantics than in phonology, any statement regarding the relationship between historical grammar and deep structure is relative to the particular interpretation of deep structure which is being employed. This point arises repeatedly, for example, in the very thoughtful paper of E. C. Traugott, "Towards a Grammar of Syntactic Change." This relative lack of constraint on theories of deep structure would seem to contrast with the determinateness both of earlier historic states and of the corresponding principle of change involved in the derivation of later states. The ultimate test should, it is submitted, be empirical and rest mainly on their respective abilities to provide a basis for fruitful generalizations concerning language.

## References Cited

Bach, Emmon. 1964. *An Introduction to Transformational Grammars*. New York: Holt, Rinehart & Winston.

Bloch, Bernard. 1950. "Studies in colloquial Japanese IV: Phonemics." *Language* 26: 86–125.

Bloomfield, L. 1933. *Language*. New York: H. Holt.

Chomsky, Noam, and Morris Halle. 1968. *The Sound Pattern of English*. New York: Harper and Row.

Harms, R. T. 1968. *Introduction to Phonological Theory*. Englewood Cliffs, N.J.: Prentice-Hall.

Harré, R. 1961. *Theories and Things*. London and New York: Sheed and Ward.

Koutsoudas, A. 1966. *Writing Transformational Grammars: An Introduction*. New York: McGraw-Hill.

Kuhn, Thomas S. 1962. *The Structure of Scientific Revolutions*. Chicago: University of Chicago Press.

Postal, Paul. 1968. *Aspects of Phonological Theory*. New York: Harper and Row.

Traugott, Elizabeth C. 1969. "Towards a grammar of syntactic change." *Lingua* 23: 1–27.

# Rethinking Linguistics Diachronically

One of the major developments of the last decade or so in linguistics has been a revived and apparently still expanding interest in historical linguistics. External signs abound, the most obvious being the holding of the First International Conference on Historical Linguistics in 1973, followed by two other such meetings. Textbooks and symposium volumes appear in increasing numbers. Such a phenomenon must surely both arise from and in turn affect general linguistic theory. In fact, in comparison with the immediately preceding period, recent years have been marked by an increased perception of the relevance of diachronic studies for the basic problems of linguistic science. At a minimum, the strict separation of synchronic and diachronic studies—envisaged by Saussure, but never absolute in practice—is now widely rejected.

For generativists, the appearance of Chomsky and Halle 1968 seems to mark a turning point in this regard. An explicit statement to this effect is to be found in Stockwell and Macaulay (1972: vii), a volume embodying the results of a conference held in 1969: "The publication in 1968 of *Sound Pattern of English* marked the end of one period in generative phonology and the beginning of another. The earlier period was characterized by a Saussurean separation of synchronic and diachronic description; in the later approach such a dichotomy has appeared unpractical."

It was, of course, the uncanny resemblance—at times, identity—between

The text represents, with minor changes, my LSA Presidential Address, delivered on 29 December 1977. I am indebted to Charles Ferguson, Henry A. Gleason Jr., Paul Kiparsky, Elizabeth Traugott, and William H. Jacobsen Jr. for comments and suggestions. The title of the address contains an allusion to Leach 1961, a re-assessment of anthropological theory after the decline of the functional school of British social anthropology.

generative rules in phonology and historical changes, both in their substance and their ordering, that provoked this reaction. In the same year that *SPE* was published, a book by Heeschen appeared in Germany, devoted to basic problems of generative phonology. This work explicitly mentions two equations—one static and one dynamic—between generative phonology and linguistic history. For the first, Heeschen points to the fact that "the systematic phonemic representation shows a startling resemblance (*verblüffende Ähnlichkeit*) to the phonetic representation of an older linguistic state" (1968: 167). With regard to the dynamic aspect, he notes that "sound laws and rules then have a direct action. The sound law produces changes which are described and explained by a rule" (168).

Increasing attention to diachronic factors has also characterized recent work in typology and universals. In the still dominantly structuralist milieu of the 1961 Dobbs Ferry Conference on Universals (cf. Greenberg 1963), it was natural that the viewpoints expressed were almost completely synchronic. (The only real exception was a paper on nasals which included several diachronic generalizations, though not labeled as such; Ferguson 1963.) Several years later, in my Summer Linguistic Institute Forum lectures at Bloomington in 1964 (cf. Greenberg 1966a), I brought in diachronic process in a partly explanatory role to account for the cluster of synchronic generalizations which constitute marking theory. Later, somewhat more systematically (Greenberg 1966b), I sought to broaden typological theory to encompass linguistic change through the key concept of change of type, and to define such notions as implicational universal in a diachronic context. The last few years have seen an increasing concern in typological studies with diachronic process. An example is the Conference on Word Order and Word Order Change held in Santa Barbara in 1974, the results of which were published in Li 1975. Fully half the papers presented at this conference dealt with the reconstruction of earlier word orders and the processes of word order change. During recent years a number of scholars both in phonology (e.g. Hyman, Bell, Chen) and syntax (Keenan, Comrie, Lehmann, and Venneman, to name just a few) have been largely concerned with a processual approach to typological problems.

The rise of sociolinguistics, roughly during the same period, has contributed in a vital way to this burgeoning interest in processes of change. Here another and related Saussurean dichotomy, *langue* vs. *parole*, has been undergoing a parallel weakening. Variation within the language community, conceived as on-going change, is a central topic of this new sociolinguistics.

However, merely to say that the strict dichotomy between synchronic and diachronic linguistics is breaking down is an essentially negative formulation.

The developments just sketched would seem to raise once again, in a fundamental manner, the question of the nature of the relationship between the synchronic and diachronic aspects of language—a relationship which has been a central problem of linguistic theory in the modern period. Are we perhaps witnessing a swing away from the structuralism which has dominated most of twentieth-century linguistics, in which the separation of the synchronic from the diachronic and the pivotal importance of synchrony for linguistic theory have been the most basic doctrines, transcending differences among schools and individual researchers?

Such suspicions have been voiced, e.g. by Traugott (1976: 502): "In recent years the prospect that the assumed relationship between diachrony and synchrony might change has been shadowy but present." But of course we should not expect a mechanical swing of the pendulum back to its former position. It is perhaps already possible to discern two major characteristics of such a renewed diachronic emphasis. One of these is the development of a thoroughly dynamic framework for synchronic description. This is foreshadowed by the Prague notion of dynamic synchrony, and the even earlier interest of some Neogrammarians in the study of on-going changes; it is now receiving extensive implementation both in the theory and the practice of such scholars as Labov and Bailey. A second characteristic, related to the contemporary interest in linguistic universals, is the emphasis on processual generalizations, particularly implicational hierarchies and marking relationships as they unfold through time—whether actual, as in historical linguistics, or inferred from social and regional variation, as in sociolinguistics.

If, in accordance with these developments, a fundamental re-assessment of theory is underway, one might expect to find evidence for it in recent discussions of the nature of scientific explanation in linguistics. Presumably, in linguistics as elsewhere, theories are formulated for their explanatory value. To me, at least, the expression "explanatory theory" contains a redundancy: to say that one has a theory, but it doesn't explain anything, is an odd locution.

Of course, numerous incidental observations and even extended discussions regarding linguistic theory and its explanatory role can be found in the recent literature. However, I am aware of only one book entirely dedicated to the topic of scientific explanation in linguistics. That is Cohen 1974, which consists of the papers presented at a meeting on the subject. However, a glance at the index shows no entry under historical explanation or historical linguistics. In the body of the work, I find two passing references to the topic, but no serious discussion of it. One is in the thoughtful introductory paper by Sanders, in which he states (1974: 17): "For a linguistic theory to have scientific significance and conceptual value, therefore, it must provide explanations for facts about the essential properties of all languages and their range of possible variation and change."

In the same volume, Dretske, a philosopher, asks (23) whether one should "take history as one's paradigm and think of linguistic explanation on the model of historical explanation." Speaking of professional linguists, he notes: "some are engaged in what might properly be called historical studies—investigating the way languages have evolved, the causes, conditions and consequences of linguistic change. Certainly here we would expect our explanations to resemble those of the historian." He concludes this part of the discussion by stating that "One is likely to find as many different types of explanation as we have specialists devoted to the study of language."

This raises an interesting question as to whether the same linguistic phenomenon might have two different, equally valid, explanations—say a synchronic and a diachronic one. Such an assumption is in conflict with the common view that, if two different theories are advanced to explain the same fact, at least one of them must be wrong. This is a question to which I will return later.

Much more representative of the Cohen volume is a whole series of papers which make the now familiar assumption that a synchronic grammar of a language is a theory of that language. The problem is two-fold: (a) to investigate the explanatory role of such grammars in the linguistic behavior of those who speak it, and (b) to discover the universals governing the selection of an optimum grammar compatible with the data—the so-called selection problem. In these discussions the historical dimension of language is simply ignored.

Before describing my own views on the place of diachronic linguistics in general linguistic theory, I will briefly characterize a few of the concepts of the relationship between the synchronic and diachronic aspects of language that have been espoused at various times.

There is, of course, the view generally held in the nineteenth century before the rise of structuralism, according to which explanation was simply to be equated with historical explanation. The possibility of synchronic explanations (the word synchrony was, of course, not used before Saussure) was simply not entertained. There is the by now famous remark of Paul (1909: 20): "It has been alleged that there is yet another scientific view of language than the historical. I must reject this. What is described as a non-historical, yet scientific, view of language is basically nothing but an incompletely historical one." (Paul was referring to a review of the first edition of his work by Misteli, a typologist in the Humboldtian tradition; 1882: 382ff.) As has occurred several times in the history of linguistics, Paul considered *his* type of theory explanatory, while previous linguistics was regarded as merely descriptive. As he put it, "historical grammar arose from the older, merely descriptive grammar" (23).

As we know, the coming of twentieth-century structuralism completely reversed the view held by Paul and the other Neogrammarians. Of course, not all structuralists agreed in detail on this, any more than on other issues. Still, one thing common to all structuralist approaches was the autonomy of synchronic structure, i.e. the notion that it could be studied independently of language history—and, beyond this, that it was the primary object of linguistic theory. Synchrony was, so to speak, where it was at.

In the Prague and American structuralist schools, at least, this did not mean a complete separation of the two fields. The situation might instead be described as noblesse oblige. Whatever structuralist school was dominant was in the position of offering new synchronically derived insights to the study of linguistic change. As noted by Weinreich, Labov, and Herzog 1968, this was, in the first instance, a new classification of linguistic changes—in American structuralism, into phonetic vs. phonemic types; or, more generally, into those which changed language structure vs. those which did not; or, in generative theory (on the view that a synchronic grammar is a system of rules) into rule addition, deletion, re-ordering, etc.

In all this, however, it was not clear what relevance, if any, historical linguistics had to the basic theoretical concerns of linguistic science. It seemed rather to be viewed as a field worth annexing, perhaps because of its still-lingering prestige. As to why it should be cultivated at all, except as a philological instrument for text interpretation, I do not see what answer there could be except the famous and fatuous remark of the mountain-climber, namely that it was there.

In more recent generative theory, particularly following the seminal article of Kiparsky 1968, we find a more integral role for diachrony in linguistic theory. It is now capable not only of receiving help but also of giving it. As Kiparsky states later (1971: 578), "We cannot simply take the theory of grammar for granted and hold it constant while we apply it to change." Rather, historical evidence is relevant in deciding questions of synchronic theory, e.g. whether the use of curly brackets represents linguistically significant generalizations. However, synchronic theory still remains the basic goal of linguistics. The relationship envisioned between the diachronic and synchronic might be likened to the medieval view of the role of philosophy in relation to theology: *Philosophia famula theologiae*, "Philosophy, handmaiden of theology."

What I shall assert here, however, is that diachronic factors enter at a number of levels and often in a complex way, as an integral and at least equal partner with synchronic factors, in the over-all explanatory-theoretic structure of linguistic science. Naturally, given the broad scope of the topic and the limited time at my disposal, the exposition will be somewhat sketchy, and will not to do justice to the many complexities involved.

The viewpoint presented here grew out of my interest in typology and universals, and initially developed within a strictly synchronic framework. Attention to diachronic factors arose in a natural manner from attempts to explain synchronically determined generalizations, and thereafter played an ever-increasing role. There is always a temptation in such matters to go to an opposite extreme. This I shall seek to avoid. Scientists in their habitual sublimation are capable, in Freudian language, of object cathexis onto abstract ideas. It might also seem that, in a period when equal rights for various minorities is the order of the day, diachronic linguistics might qualify for equal rights with synchronic linguistics. What we *should* seek, of course, is an assessment of the relationship which will most adequately account for the facts with which linguistic science must deal.

Before embarking on more concrete matters, a further preliminary is in order. There is, of course, an enormous literature in the philosophy of science discussing such concepts as 'theory', 'scientific law', and the nature of scientific explanation. To consider all the major issues raised in this literature, in their application to linguistics, is beyond the scope of the present paper. However, for the sake of clarity in the subsequent discussion, it will be advisable to consider, even if only briefly, a few main points.

I will start by citing what I consider to be a commonsensical view of explanation as stated by Bach (1974: 154): "We might take as necessary ingredients of an act of explanation (1) some phenomenon, (2) some puzzlement about the phenomenon, (3) some hypothesis about the phenomenon, (4) some grounds for feeling that the hypothesis is correct." With regard to the first of these, I see no reason for us to restrict ourselves in advance regarding the type of linguistic phenomenon to be explained. Thus we will include, among other things, synchronic facts about individual languages, specific linguistic changes—and (on a higher level) synchronically-derived universal implicational relationships, and facts and generalizations about language contact.

Bach's statement regarding scientific explanation raises a further issue which requires discussion—namely his third point, that an explanation requires "some hypothesis about the phenomenon." Discussion of this matter in the philosophy of science has tended to revolve around the thesis concerning explanation which was first advanced by Hempel in 1942, commonly called the deductive-nomological, or sometimes the "covering law" model. Briefly stated, the *explanandum* or "the thing to be explained" is explained if it can be deduced from a base, the *explanans*, which contains at least one law. The explanans or deductive basis will also, in explaining individual events, include one or more particular statements, often called initial conditions.

I, like many others, find this a reasonable notion; but of course it contains the highly ambiguous term 'law', which has itself been the subject of wide-ranging discussions. In particular, there are differences in levels of generalization, and many attempts have been made to distinguish empirical generalizations from laws which are genuinely explanatory.

One property which has often been considered a hallmark of laws is unrestricted generality. Whatever conditions exist on their application should themselves be stated in general terms, i.e. without proper names which ultimately rest on specifications of time and place. So measured, certain common types of linguistic explanation, both synchronic and diachronic, fail the test. Thus, if we ask why the plural of Eng. *book* is *books*, we may cast the explanation in the deductive-nomological mode as follows: The explanans contains the general rule that, whenever the singular ends in an unvoiced sound, the plural is formed by adding *-s*. Further, *book* ends in *k*, which is an unvoiced consonant. From these elements of the explanans, we deduce that the plural of *book* is *book-s*, which is thus explained. (Here, as is sometimes the case, the deductive-nomological explanation bears an uncanny resemblance to the Aristotelian syllogism.) But of course the rule that I have cited lacks generality, in that it holds for English only within a specified historical period. Diachronic linguistic principles, traditionally called laws, suffer from the same defect. If the explanandum is the *f* of the word *foot*, then Grimm's first law may be cited as the general principle in the explanans; but this is also restricted to a specific time-period and a specific speech-community.

However, some philosophers of science do not wish to withhold the designation 'law' from generalizations of this sort. To me, at least, it seems reasonable to apply the term 'explanation' even to low-level statements of restricted generalization, and to relativize the notions of law and empirical generalization. On this view, the degree of generality at which we begin to use the term 'law' ceases to be a central issue.

The reason for being willing to apply the term 'explanation' to deductions from statements of restricted generality is twofold. They are, on the face of it, reasonable answers to *why* questions—since, once we understand them, we cease to ask the particular question. If we pursue the matter further, we ask higher-level questions. The second reason is that an answer to such a higher-level question (by no means always forthcoming) may well be a statement of unrestricted generalization. Hence restricted generalizations belong, even if at a low level, to a comprehensive chain of deductive reasoning.

We now turn to the respective roles of synchrony and diachrony at successively higher levels of generality. It seems natural to begin with individual language irregularities, e.g. the plural formation of Eng. *foot* as *feet*. It is especially in such cases that a historical genetic explanation is convincing. Such a historical account is in a certain sense very simple, and might be likened to an etiological myth: Once upon a time there was an *-i* suffix in the plural. The vowel of the preceding syllable was affected by this suffix, so that *fōti* > *fȫti*. Then final *i* was lost. Next, *ȫ* was unrounded to *ē*, so that the Old English nom./acc. sg. was *fōt*, and the pl. was *fēt*. Add the subsequent vowel shifts and we obtain modern *foot/feet*.

One of the ways in which this account is satisfying is that it begins with a situation in which the plural has an overt mark, a suffix *-i*. This seems more understandable than a mechanism of internal change. In this respect we can again compare this account to etiological stories which explain an anomaly by positing an earlier period of normality, and then a sequence of events which produced the anomaly. Thus the absence of tails in rabbits is explained by the hypothesis that the rabbit formerly had a tail, and then lost it in some incident.

Of course, the linguistic account is superior to the folkloristic in a number of ways. First, there is both direct and comparative evidence as to its truth. Further, the events involved—e.g. umlauting and loss of final vowels—are instances of changes of a general nature, covering in principle all the cases that come under them, even though restricted in time and space. As a consequence, the same generalization can also be utilized to explain other phenomena, e.g. the remaining internal vowel-change plurals, the vowel alternation in *old/elder* and *long/length*, and still others. However, it is obvious that such devices as rule features (e.g. [−Rule 26] in the lexicon under *foot*) are no sort of explanation, since all they do is state that an item does not undergo a certain rule, which is simply another way of stating that it *is* an exception.

Sometimes, we can encapsulate a whole sequence of changes in a set of ordered synchronic rules; but while this seems more explanatory, it is surely the earlier events which figure in the explanation of what resulted later, not their statement in symbols. However, the latter has been assumed by many linguists in recent times. Thus, through familiarity it may have escaped attention that, in my citation from Heeschen above, precisely this is asserted: "The sound law produces changes which are described and *explained* by a rule" (emphasis supplied). In other words, when we describe an event by words or other symbols, it is explained.

Pursuing the rabbit comparison, we might say that the parallel to considering synchronic rules as explanatory is the following: The rabbit only superficially appears not to have a tail. In deep structure it really has one, but it has been subject to a tail-deletion transformation. Thus there are no real exceptions to the rodent-tail-possession-generalization.[1]

The foregoing does not, of course, mean that there are no explanatory generalizations in individual languages on the synchronic plane. The instance of the *-s* plural was given earlier. Such generalizations are themselves the outcomes of historical processes; they are thus susceptible of diachronic explanation, just as irregularities are. The following is an example.

In those languages of the Niger-Congo family which have a noun classification system, some nouns usually belong to what is conventionally called Class 1a. It takes the agreements of Class 1, the singular personal class. It differs, however, from Class 1 (and indeed from all the other classes) in that it has no overt class-marker affix. The nouns belonging to this class are typically proper names and certain kin terms. In some languages, there is an exceptionless rule of class assignment on this basis, which can then be used as part of the deductive base of a deductive-nomological explanation.

The reason for this rule itself—i.e., why it is precisely the class which contains proper names and kin terms—is not statable in purely synchronic terms. However, it can be accounted for by a consideration of how nouns in languages with noun classes acquire overt markers—a process which has taken place a number of times in Africa, and less frequently elsewhere. This process is treated in some detail in Greenberg 1978. It may be summarized as follows: A classifying demonstrative becomes a definite article. The origin of definite articles from demonstratives is, of course, well attested in Indo-European and elsewhere. The next stage, far less common, is what may be called a Stage II article—one which, roughly speaking, combines the uses of a definite and indefinite article, but is typically lacking in certain constructions. In the final stage, practically no nouns remain with a contrast between the articulated and non-articulated forms. For the vast majority of nouns in this last stage, the only form of the noun contains the former article, which has thus become a mere classifying marker. However, a minority of nouns are found without any marker. This is because they did not, in the first instance, occur with the definite article which is the ultimate source of the marker. One such group of nouns is proper names, because they are by definition definite. Another group is certain kinship terms which are inalienably possessed in Bantu languages, are therefore always accompanied by a personal pronominal marker, and are therefore likewise definite.

In the light of this example, we can consider the proposal mentioned earlier

[1] It is true that rabbits are dock-tailed rather than tailless. However, there are folktales that seek to explain this condition as a result of some incident in which the tail is severed (cf. Parsons 1923: 15, 61).

in this paper, derived from Dretske, that the same linguistic phenomenon might be explained in several different ways—more specifically, that there might be simultaneous yet non-contradictory diachronic and synchronic explanations. The answer appears to be positive. Two apparently different explanatory principles are not contradictory if one is logically deducible from the other, in which case the deduced one is at a lower level. They are no more contradictory than Kepler's laws of planetary motion are to Newton's more general law from which they are deducible. In the present instance, a specific proper name in a particular Niger-Congo language is explained by the synchronic rule of Class 1a, while the rule itself is deduced from diachronic process.

A further possibility is that a synchronic language-particular rule can be deduced from a synchronic universal. For example, the presence of prepositions rather than postpositions in Classical Arabic can be derived from the synchronic universal implication that, if a language is VSO, it has prepositions. With this type of explanation, it seems to me we have reached a level which deserves on any showing to be called a law. Its applicability is subject to a general principle, determined not by space-time restrictions but by the defining properties of language. This point has been clearly enunciated by Hurford 1977. Regarding such universals as those of word order, he notes (584): "Even if we examine all the languages known today, we still cannot know whether or not some new language discovered tomorrow will provide a counter-example, or whether some known language will at some time in the future have changed in such a way as to falsify the generalization. In brief, we cannot examine all possible natural languages."

Even higher-level theories from which synchronic universals may be deduced have already begun to emerge. The most familiar, no doubt, is marking theory. The relationship of the marked to the unmarked is defined by the co-occurrence of a set of properties. Thus if we find, in a particular aspect of language, that one category has greater text-frequency than the contrasting one, we hypothesize that it is the unmarked. Here 'unmarked' is simply a cover term for the complex of properties found in unmarked categories. From this hypothesis, we can deduce the existence of whatever other properties of the unmarked categories can be appropriately applied, and these are in turn empirically testable; e.g., the existence of an overt indicator for the unmarked category in any language should imply its existence in the marked.

If we now raise the further question as to why the particular properties characteristic of the unmarked (as against the marked) tend to co-occur, diachronic principles will play a key role in providing—generally along with certain synchronic conditions—the deductive base for their explanation.

At all levels, it may be noted, diachronic principles exhibit a characteristic well-known to historians. Langlois and Seignobos 1898 called these the multiple 'traces', i.e. the consequences of an event or a class of events. Superficially unconnected phenomena receive a common explanation as different outcomes of the same event. We have seen this in the case of English irregular plurals and in that of Class 1a in Niger-Congo languages.

In the instance of marking theory, a diachronic process explanation of a highly general type is at least discernible in phonology. Marked features usually arise from conditioned assimilative changes of unmarked features in restricted environments. Hence the unmarked feature, barring other processes that might destroy it, survives in the remainder—normally, the majority—of the original environments. Moreover, when merger occurs, it is the marked feature which is once more re-absorbed. We thus obtain a general explanation, based on diachronic process, for the typical implicational relationship by which marked features in phonology imply the corresponding unmarked. The lesser text-frequency of the marked category results from its origin in restricted environments. Likewise, the fact that the phonemes in a marked series are generally fewer than the unmarked, or equal in number to them, follows from the fact that each marked member arises from a corresponding unmarked, and from the further diachronic tendency of members of marked series to merge with each other. Certain synchronic generalizations will also figure in terms of initial conditions; e.g., to begin with, the number of members of the unmarked series should not be greater in the environments in which the change to marked occurs.

In the preceding sections, I have given examples in which diachronic and synchronic phenomena figure together in explanation, and also cases in which purely synchronic generalizations account for synchronic facts. There are also generalizations across purely diachronic phenomena. Thus, to revert to the example *foot/feet*, a comparison of other instances in which internal change can be investigated historically suggests the following generalization: Except for reduplication, infixes are always historically secondary, and develop from prefixes or suffixes.

On an even more abstract level, one can seek generalizations over state-process models. Is it true, e.g., that for the existent types in any typology, one can ultimately get from any one to every other one? I conjecture that this is true. If it is not, one of the possible alternatives is what, in general systems theory, is called a sink; i.e., there is one type from which there is no egress, and every other type is connected with it by changes.

A case in point is Ferguson's suggestion that there is no new source for nasals. If this were true (I believe it is not), the few languages like Quileute, which have lost their nasals, could never acquire them again. Moreover, the near universality of nasals would be, as it were, the accidental outcome of the fact that, assuming monogenesis, the protolanguage of humankind had nasals. If it didn't, there would be no nasals anywhere—as there is no way, *ex hypothesi*, in which they could arise from any other sound.

The preceding exposition is intended to show in broadest outline that the answer to the question raised earlier, regarding the respective parts played by the synchronic and diachronic aspects of languages in over-all explanatory theory, is that both enter in essential ways, that they are sometimes involved simultaneously in the explanation of a single phenomenon, and that diachronic factors are, if anything, more prominent. If so, this may be because diachrony involves the comparison of more than one state, and from a greater investment you get a greater return.

The deepest level of all, however, is likely to call upon psychological principles—including physiological factors in relation to phonology—in an effort to account for both dynamic and static generalizations about language. In the present period, there is a tendency to equate an interest in psychology with synchrony, in terms of a statically conceived 'psychological reality'. But change also involves psychology, to at least the same degree. In this connection, it is of interest to note that it was the historically oriented Neogrammarians of the nineteenth century who initiated psycholinguistics. The first important collaborative psycholinguistic experiments were those of Thumb, a Sanskritist, and Marbe, a psychologist (e.g. 1901); and the weighty tomes of Wundt 1900 on language, which would probably repay study at the present time, were concerned, to a considerable extent and naturally enough, with accounting for the historical data accumulated by the then dominant school of the Neogrammarians.

In the remainder of this paper, I shall explore the possibility that diachronic factors are involved at another still more abstract level, that of metatheory. Metatheory is, of course, discourse—or, if you will, theory—about theory. Hence, how metatheory is conceived varies with what is meant by theory. For example, if by a theory we mean a synchronic grammar of a particular language, then metatheory is something like what has been called the theory of linguistic description—more simply, linguistic theory.

In the present instance, I am concerned with what might be called descriptive rather than pure metatheory, and this only with regard to phonology. By *pure* metatheory I mean an analysis of the logically-possible phonological theories. This would, I think, be a valuable but arduous exercise—in constant danger, moreover, of being outflanked by human ingenuity capable of inventing kinds of theory not contemplated in one's original scheme. By *descriptive* metatheory I mean analysis within a common theoretical framework of historically-given theories. In what follows, I can merely suggest a few lines of investigation, by which we can see how diachronic facts have constrained theories which were in their overt statement purely synchronic; and how intuitively-held criteria of analysis, which could have been stated in a fairly straightforward fashion in diachronic terms, have required complex, unnatural (and sometimes unsuccessful) synchronically-formulated definitions and procedures. In spite of the recent exposition of new theories in phonology, I shall be mainly concerned with what might be called classical structuralist phonology, e.g. Prague, American, and British-prosodic; I believe that the considerations advanced here are also more broadly applicable.

One way of approaching our topic is the following. While most structuralist phonologists were solely occupied with synchronic analysis, several attempts were made, notably by Jakobson 1931 and Hill 1936, to classify sound changes into those which altered the system and those which did not. The results of such an analysis will differ with differing synchronic concepts of system. Thus, for Jakobson, a change in distinctive-feature specifications was a phonemic change; to Hill, such a change would not be phonemic unless it produced new contrasts.

Now, by a Gestalt-like shift of focus, we may note that every analysis of change in terms of what it does to the system can be mapped into an analysis in which the phoneme itself is defined in terms of change. For any particular synchronically-stated theory, we can say that the phoneme is the kind of unit which subsists through certain sorts of changes but not through others.

What might be called the over-all strategies of Prague and American structuralism were, in one important respect, similar. The successive splits of an original sound by conditioned change (the most common kind) show the same abstract structure, branching evolution, that occurs in a number of other fields—both non-linguistic (e.g. speciation in biology) and linguistic (e.g. linguistic genetic differentiation)—though each exhibits important further peculiarities. Whenever a sound changed in a certain environment but remained in others, the two sounds were regarded as phonetically different (allophones in American terminology, variants in Prague terminology), but as instances of the same phoneme at least, as long as their distribution was not obscured by further changes.

If phonetic change conformed to the simple model used by the creationists of pre-evolutionary biology, a phoneme would be like a species and its allophones like varieties, and no real difficulties would arise. The creationist model was clearly stated by Prichard, the leading British anthropologist of the early nineteenth century (1813: 7): "Providence has distributed the animated world into a number of distinct species and has ordered that each shall multiply according to its kind and propagate the stock to perpetuity, none of them ever transgressing their own limit, or approximating in any degree to others or ever in any case passing into each other. Such confusion is contrary to the established order of nature." But, of course, this is exactly what does often happen in the course of phonetic change. The "transgression of limits" which Prichard denied in biological change can be compared to the partial and complete mergers of one sound with another, giving rise to such characteristic phonological problems as neutralization and phonemic overlapping.

Note that, contrasted with American and Prague structuralism, British prosodic analysis is fundamentally different, in a way which can be captured by considering the very different consequence of conditioned change for it. Both American and Prague structuralism attributed no theoretical significance to the phonetic characteristics of the environment of conditioned change. That the allophone is generally assimilative in relation to its environment is mentioned by Pike, but only as a heuristically valuable consideration in carrying out a phonemic analysis. A prosodic analysis, however, abstracts that which is different after the change whenever it is assimilative to the environment, as it usually is. It becomes a prosody extending over the conditioning segment and the segment which has acquired the feature from it. But what is invariant, in terms of features over an extended period, is a phonematic unit.

The foregoing is, of course, just a small part of what would be considered in a more extensive analysis which took into account other kinds of phonetic change in particular mergers, along with their theoretical consequences for phonological analysis. What I have called strategies, then, are generalized statements as to how accomplished changes affect the phonemic analysis after the event. The analysis moves forward in time, so to speak. It is also possible to move backward in time. Given a particular strategy and a phonological analysis after a change has taken place, what can we deduce regarding the situation before the change? This involves reconstruction, and we can talk about the implied reconstructive power of a particular theoretic approach—which could be zero in the limiting case.

It thus becomes possible, within the metatheory of phonology, to produce a partial ordering of theories on the basis of the historic depth of their implied reconstruction. The following much-discussed example from Classical Sanskrit may serve as an illustration: *k* and *c* are often in morphophonemic alternation, e.g. in *vāk* 'voice' (nom. sg.) *vācás* (gen. sg.). Historically, *c* derived from *k* before the front vowels *e* and *i*. Subsequently, *e* merged with *a*, producing minimal contrasts of *ka* (< **ka*) vs. *ca* (< **ce* < **ke*).

Generative phonology here derives surface forms with *c* from an underlying *k*. Structuralists would be unanimous in assigning *k* and *c* to different phonemes because of the surface minimal contrast. Here the implied reconstruction is deeper in the generative analysis. However, various approaches within generative phonology will themselves vary in regard to depth. Thus, in reference to the above example, it has been proposed that the *a* which occurs after surface *c* be assigned to an underlying *e* which will first palatalize *k* to *c*, and then itself change to *a*, thus recapitulating the historic course of events. The case of *e*/*a*, however, is different from *k*/*c*, in that Sanskrit actually has a phonetic *k*, but not a (short) *e*. Those who accept such 'abstract' analyses have, then, a deeper theory than those who reject them. It is important to note that such terms as 'deep' and 'shallow' are not meant here to imply value judgments to this extent, although they almost inevitably do. No one, presumably, *strives* to be shallow.

A further Sanskrit example is of interest. The palatal *ñ* of Sanskrit occurs only in contact with a preceding or following palatal stop. Since it is in complementary distribution with dental *n*, it is very likely to be assigned by structuralist theory to the same phoneme as the latter. Why, in cases like this, it should be grouped with *n* rather than some other nasal (also in complementary distribution with *ñ*), and why the phoneme which has *ñ* as an allophone should be symbolized as *n*, are further questions which I cannot deal with here. This structuralist analysis is obviously deeper than the one implicit in the Sanskrit alphabet, in which *n* and *ñ* are symbolized differently, or that found in the Sanskrit grammarians, who treat *n* and *ñ* as separate units. Thus a linguist of the stature of Pāṇini, with presumably native-speaker intuitions, in this instance, espoused (or at least acquiesced in) an exceedingly shallow analysis. A consistently phonetic analysis in which the phone and phoneme are extensionally and intentionally identical might be said to be of zero depth.

I used the phrase "partial ordering" earlier in regard to phonological theories. This was done because, in regard to two theories A and B, there might be one class of cases in which A presented a deeper analysis, and another in which B did. But if it is always the case that the implied reconstructions of A are deeper than those of B, the former theory as a whole may be said to be deeper. It is probable that any generative theory is deeper than any structuralist theory. However, the deepest of all was probably that of Kruszewski and Baudouin de Courtenay—often considered early forerunners of structuralism, since they included a frankly comparative-historical component.

Thus far I have been talking about over-all strategies of theories. One may also talk of tactics, by which I mean more specific procedures, proposed to deal with certain recurrent problems in a uniform way. The division between strategy and tactics—without, of course, using these terms—is expressed by Trubetskoy (1969: 46): "After ascertaining the definition of the phoneme in the preceding chapter, we now give the practical rules by which a phoneme can be distinguished from phonetic variants on the one hand and from combinations of phonemes on the other." We might call this the case-book approach. Thus there was the case of *h*/*ŋ*, that of the Danish intervocalic stops, etc. Each of these problems arises in a variety of languages as the result of parallel diachronic processes, and uniform solutions were proposed within a synchronically statable set of procedures. There was usually an intuitively favored solution which could not be derived from the highly general statements defining the phoneme. The favored solution was implicitly reconstructive. Most decisively, if procedures or aspects of the definition of the phoneme, though otherwise favored, resulted in implicit reconstruction that ran contrary to reasonable history, they would be replaced in the particular instance by other procedures.

Besides strategy and tactics—and, as it were, between them in point of generality—there were, particularly in American practice, what might be called principles. These were to some extent inherent in the tactical procedures, but might be called upon in a quasi-independent manner to justify particular solutions. Examples of such principles are phonetic similarity, economy, and patterning. I believe that each of these can be shown on closer analysis to be useful in justifying, on nonhistorical grounds, the grouping together of historically related sounds. They were sometimes used to justify procedurally drastic but intuitively satisfying solutions, such as the analysis of a single phonetic segment of very limited distribution into a sequence of phonemes. For example, in some Bantu languages, the sequence *mu* has changed to syllabic *m̩* before consonants. If this *m̩* of limited distribution could be interpreted phonemically as its historic source *mu*, then (a) we would have one less phoneme than if *m̩* were considered a separate phoneme; (b) we would have one less syllabic type—both of these involve economy; and (c) morphophonemic alternation would be eliminated, since *mw* before vowel stems (e.g. in Class 1 nouns) and *m̩* before consonant stems could both be interpreted phonemically as *mu*.

This last source of support for a biphonemic solution would, of course, be rejected by those who insisted on a strictly autonomous phonology; in the example just cited, one could dispense with it in view of the other considerations. It is of interest, however, in showing how problems of levels arise from the nature of historical phonetic change. In the case of changes which occurred fairly long ago, in which the resultants have themselves had an eventful history, morphological alternations might be the sole surviving evidence.

In general, the allophone of today is the phoneme of tomorrow and the morphophoneme of the day after tomorrow; by the same token, the morphophoneme of today is the phoneme of yesterday and the allophone of the day before yesterday. Corresponding roughly to these degrees of depth, we may distinguish a number of problems arising from the relationships among differing sounds which have the same historic source.

Time will permit discussion of only one problem which occurs at the most superficial of these levels. It may be called the *crux* of free variation. There are quite possibly cases of what might be called perpetual free variation, e.g. of languages in which stops freely vary in extent of aspiration, in the same environments, for an indefinite period. More commonly, however—particularly where there is a phonetic discontinuity, as when the stop *p* is in free variation with a labiodental *f*—what we have is a change in progress. This free variation within a single person's speech is, of course, only an aspect of ongoing change as shown by the distribution of these variants across age, social class, etc. But the great majority of phonological descriptions have been based on a very few speakers. Bloch (1948: 24) defined free variation as a relationship between two phones such that either might substitute for the other—unconditionally, or with conditioned free variants in specified environments. Since the two variants cannot in such cases be distinctive, even a maximally shallow phonological theory which operates with phonemic units must assign them to the same unit.

Since phonetic change is normally from one sound to a similar sound, both the American principle of phonetic similarity of allophones and the Prague definition of a phoneme by means of exclusive common features will usually work. The American doctrine, because of the very vagueness of the term 'phonetic similarity', is less subject to the hazards of sound change than that of the Prague school. The phonetic product of sound change and its source sound need not possess the exclusive common features that defined their source (e.g. *s* > *h*). During the period of free variation, then, their functional redundancy would require their affiliation to the same phonological unit, while their phonetic specification would exclude it.

But a definition in terms of exclusive common features is basically like the traditional mode of definition *per genus proprium et differentiam specificam*. If phonetic change did follow the model of the species of the creationists, there would be no problem. This suggests the more general point that, since discovery procedures are essentially chains of definitions, their failure arises from the attempt to grasp a dynamic phenomenon statically. Daniel Jones talked of the allophones as a family of sounds. If we follow further the implications of this metaphor, we arrive at Wittgenstein's well-known characterization of the different senses of a word as bearing a family resemblance. Indeed, in ordinary language some terms such as 'sibling' have what might be called a historic definition: they are defined, not in terms of contemporary exclusive common features, but in terms of past events which produced the relationship.

One may suspect that this is also what lies behind problems in defining theoretical terms elsewhere in linguistics. For example, the borderline cases which produce difficulties in defining the word can be viewed dynamically in terms of the process by which word boundaries are obscured or new boundaries created. I will take one instance of limited scope—meant merely as an illustration, since the facts require further investigation. In languages with both word stress and vowel harmony, these two criteria occasionally give different results, thus producing so-called borderline cases. In such languages it would seem that, in the incorporation of adpositions or in compounding, one element first becomes unstressed, and then develops vowel harmony with the stem. If this holds generally as the diachronic order of development, it limits the kinds of borderline cases that may be found; thus we would not find instances of vowel harmonization without loss of stress. The investigation of such processes would, in other words, result in diachronic implications; it would predict what kinds of borderline cases can be found and how they arise. Once we understand this, the question of a definition which resolves all cases loses some of its saliency.[2] One theoretical approach is superior to another, if it can predict when the second will get in trouble.

I am well aware of the merely suggestive nature of some of the considerations I have advanced in this paper. In some cases, this is because of limitations of time; in others, because the investigation is still in its initial stages. What I do hope to have accomplished is at least to raise the possibility that full and systematic consideration of diachronic factors can help to put a number of fundamental problems of linguistics in a new light, and can contribute to its development as a truly explanatory science.

## References Cited

Bach, Emmon. 1974. "Explanatory inadequacy." In Cohen, ed. 1974: 153–72.

Bloch, Bernard. 1948. "A set of postulates for phonemic analysis." *Language* 24: 3–46.

Chomsky, Noam, and Morris Halle. 1968. *The Sound Pattern of English*. New York: Harper and Row.

Cohen, David, ed. 1974. *Explaining Linguistic Phenomena*. New York: Wiley.

Dretske, Fred I. 1974. "Explanation in linguistics." In Cohen, ed. 1974: 21–42.

Ferguson, Charles A. 1963. "Assumptions about nasals." In Greenberg, ed. 1963: 42–47.

Greenberg, Joseph H., ed. 1963. *Universals of Language*. Cambridge: M.I.T. Press.

———. 1966a. *Language Universals, with Special Reference to Feature Hierarchies*. (Janua linguarum, series minor, 59.) The Hague: Mouton.

[2]This discussion, of course, suffers from circularity in that the notion of word boundary is assumed. In a fuller treatment, it could be shown that there are two ways of treating this. One is to formulate two working definitions: one for situations in which a word boundary exists on any showing, and the other when it does not. A second approach is to use a set of comparative concepts defining 'more like a word boundary', and based on such criteria as word accent, syntactic immediate constituency, and participation in vowel harmony.

———. 1966b. "Synchronic and diachronic universals in phonology." *Language* 42: 508–17.

———. 1978. "How does a language acquire gender markers?" In *Universals of Human Language*, ed. by J. H. Greenberg, 3: 47–82. Stanford: Stanford University Press.

Heeschen, Claus Friedrich Eugen. 1968. Einführung in die Grundprobleme der generativen Phonologie. Bonn; Inaugural-dissertation.

Hempel, Carl G. 1942. "The function of general laws in history." *Journal of*

Hill, Archibald A. 1936. "Phonetic and phonemic change." *Language* 12: 15–22.

Hurford, James R. 1977. "The significance of linguistic generalizations." *Language* 53: 574–620.

Jakobson, Roman. 1931. "Prinzipien der historischen Phonologie." *Travaux du Cercle Linguistique de Prague* 4: 247–66.

Kiparsky, Paul. 1968. "Linguistic universals and linguistic change." In *Universals in Linguistic Theory*, ed. by Emmon Bach and Robert T. Harms, 171–202. New York: Holt, Rinehart & Winston.

———. 1971. "Historical linguistics." In *A Survey of Linguistic Science*, ed. by William O. Dingwall, 577–642. College Park: Linguistics Program, University of Maryland.

Langlois, Charles B., and Charles Seignobos. 1898. *Introduction aux études historiques*. Paris: Hachette.

Leach, Edmund Ronald. 1961. *Rethinking Anthropology*. London: Athlone Press.

Li, Charles N., ed. 1975. *Word Order and Word Order Change*. Austin: University of Texas Press.

Misteli, Franz. 1882. "Review of Paul's *Prinzipien der Sprachgeschichte*." *Zeitschrift für Völkerpsychologie und Sprachwissenschaft* 13: 376–409.

Parsons, Elsie Clews. 1923. *Folklore of the Sea Islands, South Carolina*. (Memoirs of the American Folklore Society, 16.) Cambridge, Mass.

Paul, Hermann. 1909. *Prinzipien der Sprachgeschichte*. 4th ed. Halle: Niemeyer.

Prichard, James Cowle. 1813. *Researches into the Physical History of Man*. London: J. & A. Arch.

Sanders, Gerald. 1974. "Introduction." In Cohen, ed. 1974: 1–20.

Stockwell, Robert P., and Ronald K. S. Macaulay, eds. 1972. *Linguistic Change and Generative Theory*. Bloomington: Indiana University Press.

Thumb, Albert, and K. Marbe. 1901. *Experimentelle Untersuchungen über die psychologischen Grundlagen der sprachlichen Analogiebildungen*. Leipzig: Engelmann.

Traugott, Elizabeth Closs. 1976. "Review of *Variation and Linguistic Theory*, by Charles-James N. Bailey." *Language* 52: 502–6.

Trubetskoy, Nikolai S. 1969. *Principles of Phonology*. Translation by Christiane A. M. Baltaxe of *Grundzüge der Phonologie*, 1939. Berkeley and Los Angeles: University of California Press.

Weinreich, Uriel, William Labov, and Marvin I. Herzog. 1968. "Empirical foundations for a theory of language change." In *Directions for Historical Linguistics*, ed. by Winfred P. Lehmann and Yakov Malkiel, 97–195. Austin: University of Texas Press.

Wundt, Wilhelm Max. 1900. *Völkerpsychologie: eine Untersuchung der Entwicklungsgesetze von Sprache, Mythus und Sitte*. Vol. 1–2: *Die Sprache*. Leipzig: Engelmann.

# Types of Linguistic Models in Other Disciplines

"In France, structuralism is today a panacea. From linguistics it passed into anthropology. From there it has not ceased to spread, at least if one believes the general rumor. It has, it seems, reached philosophy. According to an editorial writer in a recent issue of *L'Arc*, 'it has even become the dominant philosophy'" (Bouden 1968: x).

The statement regarding the origin in structural linguistics of what has become, particularly in France, but to a great extent elsewhere also, a major trend in a number of humanistic and social science disciplines, could be paralleled by a number of other such pronouncements and is in its basic outlines historically correct. The by now numerous readers and book-length treatments of structuralism almost invariably begin with the *Cours de Linguistique Générale*, the seminal work of Ferdinand de Saussure, the Swiss pioneer of modern structuralist linguistics, which appeared posthumously in 1916. Beginning approximately with the second quarter of the twentieth century, structuralism became the dominant approach in linguistics. It is itself a complex phenomenon and a number of major schools and trends can be distinguished. Of these, the most important for our purposes are the Prague school, whose most influential representatives were the Russians Trubetskoy and Jakobson, and the American structuralist school, which has included such well-known figures as Bloomfield, Bloch, Hockett, and Harris. It has indeed been argued, in my opinion correctly, that the revolution in linguistics produced by generative-transformational grammar initiated with the publication of Chomsky (1957), himself a pupil of Harris, has been basically within the

I wish to express my appreciation to Renato Rosaldo and David Pingree for their comments on an earlier version of this paper.

framework of twentieth-century structuralism.[1] Of the two figures outside of linguistics who have probably been the most conspicuous structuralists, Levi-Strauss in anthropology and Barthes in literary criticism, the former's immediate influence has been chiefly that of the Prague school and only mediately Saussure, while the latter goes more directly to Saussure for his inspiration. In American anthropology, the influential school of ethnosemantics, which flourished particularly in the 1960's, is most clearly affiliated to American structural linguistics.[2]

Clearly a movement of such scope can hardly be covered in a single volume, much less within the bounds of a brief paper. Rather, and in a somewhat summary fashion, the case of contemporary linguistics will be treated in the framework of a more general problem in the history and philosophy of science, namely the reasons for and nature of the influence of one area of investigation on others. Further, attention will be focused mainly on a similar phenomenon of the influence of a linguistic model, namely that of comparative-historical linguistics in the nineteenth century. This emphasis can be justified by several considerations. The earlier case has been far more neglected and indeed, in contrast to the influence of structuralism, has never been subject to comprehensive treatment. Further, the addition of a second major example will be of value in providing additional evidence relevant to the conceptual analysis of the broader problem already mentioned.

It may have been noted that all of the fields thus far mentioned have belonged to the humanities and social sciences. Such phenomena do not seem to occur in the natural sciences, at least in the more obvious form of one discipline taking another as a model. Perhaps for this reason this phenomenon has been discussed hardly if at all in the contemporary literature in the philosophy of science.[3]

We may begin by noting that the influencing, or as I shall henceforth call it, the model science has a certain prestige, and gives the appearance of greater success. This is, of course, not in itself sufficient. It must in some sense be relevant to the influenced field, that is, it must provide a potential model which furnishes both a new way of conceiving its object and, more concretely, at least some specific methods flowing from this conception that seem applicable to the other discipline in a way which promises to be fruitful.

[1] On this point see, for example, Bach (1974: 167), and Koerner (1976: 703).

[2] Excellent general treatments of structuralism include Lane 1970; Pettit 1975; and Culler 1975.

[3] However, those who stress the role of analogy in the construction of scientific theory (e.g. Hesse 1966; Harré 1970) analyze examples such as the role of wave models of sound in the development of wave theories of light. These are, of course, within the bounds of a single discipline.

This relationship may be couched as a metaphor. The object of study in the other field is in some sense "like a language," hence the methods which have proven successful in linguistics can be appropriately employed.

With regard to the first point, the prestige and success of linguistics, it will be sufficient to quote from Levi-Strauss (1963: 33):

> But, after all, anthropology and sociology were looking to linguistics only for insights; nothing foretold a revelation. Not only did it renew linguistic perspectives; a transformation of this magnitude is not limited to a single discipline. Structural linguistics will certainly play the same renovating role with respect to the social sciences that nuclear physics, for example, has played for the physical sciences.

A distinction was made earlier between the general point of view and the specific methods contributed by one science when it becomes the model for another. For the moment we will be concerned with the former as the more fundamental. What Saussure was the first to articulate was indeed a new way of looking at language. In terms made popular in the well-known and influential work of Kuhn (1962), it involved a shift of paradigm, or what he has more recently preferred to call, "exemplars" (1972: 187). Saussure himself stated these differences by means of a series of dichotomies. Of these the most fundamental is that between diachronic and synchronic approaches, terms introduced by Saussure which have become common coin in theoretical discussions in humanistic and social studies. A diachronic approach to language is concerned with its change through time and explains linguistic phenomena as outcomes of their historical antecedents. A synchronic approach abstracts from change and considers language as a system at a particular time. To Saussure it seemed that the previous diachronic linguistics was not concerned with the nature of what was conceived of as in a process of change, namely language itself. Thus he states, "The first thing that strikes us when we study the facts of language is that their succession in time does not exist insofar as the speaker is concerned. He is confronted with a state. That is why the linguist who wants to understand a state must discard all knowledge of what produced it and ignore diachrony. He can enter the minds of the speakers only by suppressing the past. The intervention of history can only falsify his judgment" (1959: 81).

This brings us to another key Saussurian distinction: that between *langue* 'language' and *parole* 'speech'. The former is social and constitutes a system. It is the true object of linguistic science. The latter is the individual employment by its users on specific occasions and lacks stability. Moreover, the system of language is basically a network of relations rather than a set of individual linguistic forms.

Thus the paradigm provides a new mode of explanation. A linguistic phenomenon is explained by its relationships within a system, not genetically as a result of the previous phenomena of which it is the historical outcome.

From the viewpoint, however, of a paradigm replacing an old one the situation is very different from that of the physical sciences. Structural linguistics did not replace historical linguistics in the way that, say, Copernican astronomy annulled the Ptolemaic system. It continued to be practiced widely and recent developments have led many linguists to assert that the strict separation between the two insisted on by Saussure has broken down and the integration of these two points of view in linguistics is indeed a conspicuous contemporary trend.

From the present point of view it is of interest to note that this earlier paradigm of historical linguistics which dominated the nineteenth century and succeeded a still earlier one of *grammaire générale*, likewise enjoyed high prestige in its time and furnished a model for other humanistic and social studies. The hallmark of this approach was that it was comparative. In contrast to all previous linguistics, it developed a systematic method for comparing diverse languages.

It is possible to distinguish three ways in which comparative linguistics was successful and thus provided a model for other disciplines. As against the earlier static view, it explained the relatively greater resemblance of certain languages to each other as the result of historical development and differentiation over time by the constantly increasing divergence of what were originally mere dialect variations of a single language. Further, more remote similarities among whole groups of languages were explained by the postulation of still earlier languages and earlier differentiations. The metaphor of a family tree was employed. Thus, resemblances among English, Frisian, German, Dutch, and the Scandinavian languages were explained as the result of an earlier language, a postulated proto-Germanic. In turn the resemblance of Germanic, Celtic, Slavic, Romance, Greek, Armenian, Indo-Iranian languages, and still others as against, say, Semitic was explained by the hypotheses that these in turn descended from dialects of Proto-Indo-European.

A second achievement was that as a by-product of such hypotheses, many specific linguistic forms could be explained as resulting from systematic changes from the common ancestral language.

The third great achievement was that by this process of comparison among the descendant languages it was possible to reconstruct with a high degree of probability a substantial portion of the vocabulary and grammatical structure of hypothesized ancestral language.

One particular case, already mentioned, was particularly impressive to educated men of the nineteenth century, namely the demonstration that most of the languages of Europe were related to those of a large portion of those of

Asia, particularly to Sanskrit, the language of the sacred books of Hinduism, and along with this its further success in penetrating beyond documented history to reconstruct the very words and grammatical structures of the ancestral Indo-European languages. Applications of the methods of comparative philology, as it was then called, to other fields followed, e.g. mythology, religion, and law. An example is that of the distinguished jurist, Sir Henry Maine, who sought to found a comparative jurisprudence on the linguistic model. As with Levi-Strauss, though in less extravagant terms, he voices the contemporary belief in the superiority of linguistics. Thus he remarks (Maine 1871: 8): "I should, however, be making very idle pretension if I held a prospect of obtaining, by the application of the Comparative Method to jurisprudence any results which in point of interest or trustworthiness are to be placed on a level with those which, for example, have been accomplished in Comparative Philology."

Now one might assume that in these various applications of the comparative method deemed so successful in linguistics, one could transfer its methods into a new field by employing the same method of classification into groups of related phenomena corresponding to the linguistic families, construct broader genealogies of such groupings, reconstruct the hypothetical earlier forms and explain later ones genetically as developments from them. Such a mode of application may be called formal in that the methods of the field to be initiated are transfused into new materials while retaining their original form. But, in fact, the methods actually employed were in far more direct dependence on the actual data and results of comparative linguistics. This type of model I shall call the material, as opposed to the formal.

If, to take the example of Indo-European, there existed an ancestral Indo-European language, it was spoken by a population which of course had nonlinguistic institutions. These must have developed into their contemporary form along the same lines of population differentiation as the languages themselves. In fact, the reconstructed vocabulary, insofar as it referred to such institutions, could be utilized in tracing those developments. Hence Maine confines himself to Indo-European speaking peoples and seeks to reconstruct through comparison their earliest legal institutions.

The use of comparative linguistics as a formal model also occurred, but much later and unconsciously as it were. That is, those who originated it were unaware of linguistic methodology and the resemblance was noted either by later practitioners or even outsiders.

One example is that of the Culture-Historical school of ethnography of Germany and Austria which first became prominent in the first decade of the twentieth century. The essential similarity of method of comparison of cultural traits of peoples throughout the world and the reconstruction of a set of original cultures from which they developed was first pointed out in

Greenberg (1957) and was subsequently acknowledged explicitly in Leser (1977: 4) in an issue of the journal *Anthropos* celebrating the hundredth anniversary of Fritz Graebner, the founder of this school.

Another instance is that of the Finnish folklore school, which by a method called the geographical-historical collected all variants of a story, classified them into groups and sought to reconstruct the original form of the story by systematic comparison. The resemblance of this method to that of comparative linguistics is not noted by the earliest expositors of the method (e.g., Krohn 1910, Aarne 1913). It does, however, receive explicit statements in Stith Thompson's standard work *The Folktale* (1951). While not actually a member of this school, Thompson is very sympathetic to it and appreciates the value of its contributions. He notes (p. 431), "If he succeeds in avoiding the many pitfalls awaiting him and always uses good judgment, he should have arrived at a close approximation of the archetype of the story he is studying. His task has been not unlike that of the student of Indo-European languages who has worked out the theoretical Indo-European form of a word. He has constructed this by first studying the word in each of the Germanic languages and, by the application of the general laws of change, positing a primitive Germanic form which would normally produce these words. In like manner, he works out theoretical constructions for primitive Celtic, primitive Slavic, etc. Then from all these primitive forms for the main branching of the language family he arrives at a hypothetical work which would serve as a common ancestor of them all. This method of working back to primitive local forms and from them to an ultimate archetype is applicable not only to language but to traditional narrative."

It is particularly likely to be true of the formal as opposed to the material model that because it refers to the more general and abstract features of method, it is applicable to a much broader range of fields and is less likely to arise from the explicit influence of its success in one particular field. It represents as it were a broad set of similar paradigms which are part of the general climate of opinion at a particular time. Thus, the representation of relationships of languages as a branching family tree which was first carried out by Schleicher (1860) is attributed by Hoenigswald (1963) to Schleicher's training in classical philology under Ritschl who depicted the relationship of manuscripts of the same work as a stemma, or family tree, and employed a method parallel to that of comparative linguistics in restoring the original text. Timpanaro (1963) has pointed out that such a diagram was first employed by Zumpt in 1831 and soon after by Ritschl (in 1832) and Madvig (in 1834). In linguistics proper Friedrich Schlegel (1808: 318) called for a representation of linguistic relationships by a family tree without actually constructing one. For textual criticism the basic principle was enunciated much earlier in New Testament criticism, apparently first by Bengel in 1734, though he did not actually construct family trees of manuscripts, an activity which he considered premature in the state of knowledge then existing (Timpanaro 1963: 20).

In the more recent period Maas (1950) has consciously and systematically applied the linguistic principle that independent agreement in two or more branches of the same linguistic stock implies that the form has been preserved from their common ancestor to textual criticism based on genealogies of manuscripts.

One can, however, go much further afield to find the same model in the nineteenth century.

It has perhaps not escaped the mind of the reader that the same basic scheme is involved in the evolutionary interpretation of biological taxonomies. Darwin himself in *On the Origin of Species* noted this analogy at two points (pp. 40, 422–23), in the latter instance in some detail. In the *Descent of Man* (p. 70) he states, "The formation of different languages and of distinct species and the proof that both have been developed through a gradual process are curiously parallel." He refers here in a footnote to an entire chapter devoted to this topic in Lyell's *Antiquity of Man* (1863).

This resemblance was also noted in earlier writings from the linguist's side. Schleicher, who apparently never mentioned the analogy of linguistic family ties to manuscript genealogies discussed earlier (Koerner 1976: 696), wrote an extensive letter to Haeckel published in 1863 under the title *Die Darwinische Theorie und die Sprachwissenschaft* which contains a family tree of the Indo-European languages and asserts that the principle was known in linguistics before biology. Addressing Haeckel, he states, "I hope that the proof that the main characteristics of Darwin's doctrine can be applied to linguistic development or rather, as one may say, were already there unconsciously will not be entirely unwelcome to you, the zealous proponent of Darwin's basic ideas."

In contrast to what is usually, as we see in Schleicher, an unconscious convergence of basic ideas, the material application is always a conscious one and may in fact be first suggested by a practitioner of the science which is taken as a model. Thus the first material application of the comparative historical method was that of the Grimm brothers in their famous collection of German folktales. Of the two brothers, one, Jacob, was primarily a linguist, the other, Wilhelm, a folklorist. In the third volume, Wilhelm Grimm specifically asserts the Indo-European origin of the folktales in the collection from "broken-down myths" which have developed along different lines among different branches of the Indo-European language family (Thompson 1951: 372).

If we turn to twentieth-century linguistic structuralism, most of what has been said about the earlier paradigm of historical comparative linguistics holds true. A material application (what Pettit in his general work on structuralism calls "straight" analysis) is simply to apply structural linguistics to the analysis of literary language. As Pettit (1975: 40) puts it, "here the linguistic model of language is used to provide a model, of precisely, language."

The Russian school of formalistic criticism which flourished in the 1920's included both linguists and literary critics and in the prominent instance of Jakobson someone who was both. On the linguistic side it is clearly a forerunner of the Prague School. The latter, from its first period of prominence in the late 1920's, had as a main interest the application of linguistics to literary language. Thus Vachek (1966: 131), in his history of the Prague School of Structural Linguistics, notes regarding Mukařovsky, a leading member of the school, "His main interest is centered on the structure of literature with special regard to the part played in this structure by linguistic devices."

Formal applications of linguistic structuralist methodology developed somewhat later and have most frequently employed a set of concepts first found in Saussure. Language is viewed as having two dimensions, both involving relations. The first is paradigmatic, the relation of any linguistic element to others which might have but did not appear at a specific point in the sentence. For example, in "the boy struck the cat," "girl," "man," etc. are in paradigmatic relationship to "boy." The syntagmatic relationship is that of one element to another which appears alongside it in text, e.g. the relationship of "boy" to "struck." In formal applications, one or both of these are frequently applied to some nonlinguistic subject matter, e.g. by Barthes (1967) to women's fashions. A simple example is the way meals are arranged in the western tradition. The various courses that follow each other are in syntagmatic relationship, whereas the various alternatives which might function as the same course, e.g. "cake" versus "fruits" as desserts are in a paradigmatic relationship.[4]

As with nineteenth-century comparative philology, structuralism is allied to a larger movement which is part of the general climate of opinion. The emphasis on synchronic system and structure and even the formal analogue of paradigmatic versus syntagmatic relationships appears, of course without this terminology, in the pioneer work of the Russian folklorist Propp on the morphology of the folktale (1928). Once again, the movement in its most general outlines is even broader, as some have pointed out, embracing anthropological functionalism and Gestalt psychology, in historical

[4] A further elaboration of this method which has also been influential is not discussed here. This is the additional analysis of the paradigmatic dimension, originating in Prague school phonology, in terms of underlying features typically binary, e.g. voiced versus unvoiced, continuant versus noncontinuant. These, by their intersection, produce the phonemic units of the language which function on the paradigmatic level in phonology.

independence of linguistics. Piaget (1970: 9) takes this broader view defining structuralism as analysis in which "the logical procedures, or natural processes by which the whole is formed are primary, not the whole, which is consequent on the system's law of composition of the elements."

It was stated at the beginning of this paper that the use of models from a prestige science was characteristic of the humanities and social sciences, but not of the natural sciences. This is no doubt true, but if we go back far enough we find similar processes at work. For the Greeks, mathematics, particularly geometry, is the model science while physics has not yet developed a generally accepted paradigm. We find a material application of mathematics to physics in the Pythagorean doctrine that the physical world consists of numbers and in Plato's Timaeus in which the four elements of Empedocles—fire, air, water, and earth—are identified with the regular solids, all of whose faces are regular polygons and which in turn are constructed from two kinds of triangles as still more fundamental (Cornford 1937: 210–39).

It was not until late antiquity that the Neo-Platonist Proclus sought in *Elements of Theology* (*Stoicheíōsis theologikḗ*) to use the axiomatic methods of geometry in a non-mathematical field. Once again, in the seventeenth century we find the Euclidian method in Descartes' version of general scientific method. It is even applied to ethics, as we see from the very title of Spinoza's famous work, *Ethica more geometrico demonstrata*.

It has not been possible in a brief paper either to make explicit the numerous qualifications to which the broad picture presented here is subject, nor a logical analysis of the two kinds of models, material and formal. It is to be hoped, however, that it may stimulate interest in what has been a relatively neglected aspect of the history of linguistics itself and one which is of general relevance to the history and philosophy of science.

## References Cited

Aarne, Antti. 1913. *Leitfaden der vergleichenden Märchenforschung*. Folklore Fellows' F. F. Communication no. 13, Hamina, Suomalaisen tiedeakatemian Kustantama.

Bach, Emmon. 1974. "Explanatory Inadequacy." In *Explaining Linguistic Phenomena*. David Cohn, ed. Cambridge, Mass., Wiley and Sons, pp. 153–72.

Barthes, Roland. 1967. *Système de la mode*. Paris: Editions du Seuil.

Boudon, Raymond. 1968. *A quoi sert la notion de "structure"?* Paris: Gallimard.

Chomsky, Noam. 1957. *Syntactic Structures*. The Hague: Mouton.

Cornford, Francis Macdonald. 1937. *Plato's Cosmology; the Timaeus of Plato, translated with a running commentary*. London: K. Paul, Trench, Trueborer & Co.; New York: Harcourt Brace & Co.

Culler, Jonathan D. 1975. *Structuralist Poetics*; *Structuralism, Linguistics and the Study of Literature*. Ithaca, N.Y.: Cornell University Press.

Curtius, Georg. 1858. *Grundzüge der griechischen Etymologie* I. Leipzig: Teubner.

Darwin, Charles E. 1959. *On the Origin of Species*. 1st edition. London: J. Murray.

———. 1871. *Descent of Man*. London: J. Murray.

Greenberg, Joseph H. 1957. *Essays in Linguistics*. Chicago: University of Chicago Press.

Harré, Romano. 1970. *The Principles of Scientific Thinking*. Chicago: University of Chicago Press.

Hesse, Mary B. 1966. *Models and Analogies in Science*. Notre Dame: University of Notre Dame Press.

Hoenigswald, Henry M. 1963. "On the History of the Comparative Method." *Anthropological Linguistics* 5 (1): 1–11.

Koerner, G. F. K. 1976. "Towards a Historiography of Linguistics: Nineteenth and Twentieth Century Paradigms." In *History of Linguistic Thought and Contemporary Linguistics*. Hermann Parret, ed. Berlin and New York: W. de Gruyter, pp. 658–78.

Krohn, Kaarle L. 1910. *Die folkloristische Arbeitsmethode*. Oslo: H. Aschehoug.

Kuhn, Thomas S. 1962. *The Structure of Scientific Revolutions*. Chicago: University of Chicago Press.

———. 1972. *The Structure of Scientific Revolutions*, 2nd ed. Chicago: University of Chicago Press.

Lane, Michael, ed. 1970. *Structuralism: A Reader*. London: Cape.

Leser, Paul. 1977. "Fritz Graebner: eine Würdigung." *Anthropos* 72: 1–55.

Levi-Strauss, Claude. 1963. *Cultural Anthropology*. Translated by Claire Jacobson and Brooke Grundfest Schoepf. New York: Basic Books.

Lyell, Charles. 1863. *The Geological Evidences of the Antiquity of Man*. London: J. Murray.

Maas, Paul. 1950. *Textkritik*, 2nd edition. Leipzig: Teubner.

Maine, Sir Henry James Summer. 1871. *Village-Communities in the East and West*. London: J. Murray.

Pettit, Philip. 1975. *The Concept of Structuralism; A Critical Analysis*. Berkeley: University of California Press.

Piaget, Jean. 1970. *Structuralism*. Translated by Chaninah Maschler. New York: Basic Books.

Propp, Vladimir. 1928. *Morfologija Skazki*. Leningrad: Academia.

Saussure, Ferdinand de. 1916. *Cours de linguistique générale*. Lausanne, Paris: Payot.

———. 1959. *Course in General Linguistics*. Translated by Wade Baskin. New York: Philosophical Society.

Schlegel, Friedrich von. 1808. *Über die Sprache und Weisheit der Indier*. Heidelberg: Mohr und Zimmer.

Schleicher, August. 1860. *Die deutsche Sprache*. Stuttgart: J. G. Cotta.

———. 1863. *Die darwinische Theorie und die Sprachwissenschaft*. Weimar: H. Böhlau.

Thompson, Stith. 1951. *The Folktale*. New York: The Dryden Press.

Timpanaro, Sebastiano. 1963. *La genesi del metodo del Lachmann*. Florence: F. Le Monnier.

Vachek, Josef. 1966. *The Linguistic School of Prague*. Bloomington: University of Indiana Press.

# Two Approaches to Language Universals

Although there have been few published discussions, linguists have, since at least the mid-60's, been aware of two distinct approaches to language universals. One of these has been most closely associated with the name of Noam Chomsky and with generative grammar while the other took its start with my paper on word order (Greenberg 1963), was characteristic of most of the work of the Stanford Project on Language Universals, and is now continued by individual researchers as well as centers at Cologne and elsewhere.

Among the earlier discussions of the two approaches may be mentioned Bell (1971), Bugarski (1972: 126–28), Lehmann (1972), and Ferguson (1978). These discussions are all by non-generativists, some not committed to either approach (e.g. Bugarski), or typologically oriented scholars such as Bell, Lehmann, and Ferguson. They are all moderate in tone and state either that a synthesis of the two approaches is desirable (Bugarski), is already underway (Lehmann), or that there has been a degree of convergence chiefly because of changes in the generativist approach (Ferguson).

From about 1978 on, however, a group of Italian generativists have been actively engaged in integrating typology into generative grammatical theory. A conference on this subject was held in Bologna in 1980 and resulted in a series of papers in *Lingue e Stile* in the same year. The basic point on which almost all agree is that if it is the task of universal grammar to define "possible human language," then typological considerations must enter because research of this kind leads to the discovery of strong limitations on possible human languages not discoverable by any other method.

This paper was originally written in 1981–82 and was presented at the University of Minnesota in 1983. Minor revisions were made in 1985.

Ramat (1980: 314) in the introductory paper states that "there is no real contradiction between the principles of generative grammar and the typological approach." Rizzi (1980: 354) concludes that "If the work is well done, there is of necessity a fundamental convergence of results as is the case with Greenberg's word order universals and X-bar theory."

More recently, however, there have been several attacks by generativists on the typological approach to universals. The most active has been Coopmans (1983, 1984) the former of which was an attack on Comrie (1981) and the latter on Hawkins (1983).

In the summary which accompanies Coopmans (1984) he asserts "Finally, it shows how the study of language typology might proceed within a generativist framework." This is to be done, as he says, by using Greenberg-type language surveys to form initial hypotheses, but they will have to be followed by careful analysis within a restrictive theory of grammar. There seems to be here a basic circularity. If one has an adequate restrictive theory of grammar to begin with, why should one have to resort to typological data in order to discover restrictions to be incorporated in the grammar? Having presumably discovered a sort of preliminary pre-theoretic value for typology he then goes on to state that "the two approaches differ greatly and cannot be compared or related in any way" (*ibid.*: 67).

Another hostile critique of typology is that of Smith, once more a review of Comrie (1981). He states (1982: 255) that one of the few praiseworthy features of Comrie's book is that it is "extremely rare in even raising and discussing the issues which separate Greenberg and Chomsky." These reviews of Comrie and Hawkins elicited rejoinders (Comrie 1983, 1984), Hawkins (1985) and even one surrejoinder (Smith 1983).

A further critical attack is Lightfoot (1981), devoted once more to word-order typology. Finally a recent work of Stassen (1985), a cross-linguistic study of the comparative construction, provides in its initial chapter the most extensive exposition of the typological approach to universals since Comrie (1981). Like Comrie he asserts that the typological method can make a contribution to universal grammar, an expression which even figures in the title of his book.

Two general observations may be made regarding this recent controversial literature. Topically it centers on word order typology especially in the attacks by generativists who seem practically to equate typology with word-order or more accurately, constituent order typology. This is partly understandable in the context of the discussions revolving around Hawkins (1983), a work devoted to word-order. But typology is a far broader notion and by now I and others have treated a considerable number of other topics (cf. Stassen 1985: 2 for a partial enumeration). Even if all the conclusions of word-order typology were to be refuted, and this is clearly not the case, there remains a large body of additional work which has not been subject to critical analysis by generativists. The second general observation to be made is that typologists, e.g. Hawkins and Stassen, in their desire to show that typology can make contributions to linguistic theory, have uncritically accepted the equation of linguistic theory with universal grammar whereas, as I shall try to show, the notion of theory in linguistics has a far wider domain than the general principles utilizing the construction of synchronic grammars.

My purpose in this discussion is not polemic. It is rather to clarify the issues at stake, but given the limitations of an article length treatment and the vastness of the topic, many important aspects will be omitted or treated only cursorily. Further, I will concentrate on setting forth my own views which differ in certain respects even from those of some individuals with whom I share much common ground (e.g. Comrie, Seiler). For generativist views I will rely mainly on Chomsky, but here an even greater variety of opinion and attitudes exist ranging from a considerable receptivity to the typological approach (e.g. Bach, Ramat) to outright rejection (Coopmans, Lightfoot). In addition there are now numerous competing varieties of generative grammatical theories. Also, there have been important changes during the period under consideration so that the treatment is, of necessity, to some degree historical.

I will first discuss some characteristics of the two approaches. Secondly, since there is general agreement that the significance of universals is in their explanatory role, I will discuss my own views regarding the structure of explanation in linguistics. Finally, I will consider very briefly some implications of these views in their relation to the present climate of theory in linguistics.

Three characteristics are often mentioned as distinguishing the typological approach from that of the generativists, looking at many languages as against looking at very few, or in principle perhaps at only one, a concentration on surface as against deep structure and the use versus non-use of typological methods. To a degree these three contrasts can be summarized as an emphasis on breadth as against depth. Human energy being finite, a combination of breadth and depth is beyond any single researcher's capacities. Moreover, not enough languages are known in depth to make this possible at our present state of knowledge. I believe that both strategies should be employed. Undoubtedly they appeal to different predilections of researchers.

The three characteristics of the broad approach are connected in various ways. Typology, which seeks lawful relations among properties of languages, necessarily requires fairly large areal and genetic samples of languages and hence inevitably emphasizes easily available and comparable data, thus tending to exclude the idiosyncratic characteristics which inevitably appear when any single language is investigated in very fine detail.

These three factors, though thus interrelated, deserve separate treatment. With regard to breadth of linguistic coverage, it is clear that Chomsky himself since his first published discussion of universals (1965) has tended to believe that one language was probably sufficient to arrive at universals. During the initial period at MIT it was generally held that it was impossible to write a grammar of a language unless one had native speaker intuitions. Since the first generation of generativists were English speakers, this inevitably led to a strong concentration on English. This notion has generally been abandoned and, of course, generative grammar has spread beyond the English-speaking world. More significantly, data from a variety of languages are now frequently advanced in support or refutation of proposals in grammatical theory. However, Chomsky himself states as late as 1976 "Deep analysis of a single language may provide the most effective means for discovering non-trivial properties of universal grammar" (1976: 56). More recently he has somewhat relaxed his stance. While noting that "intensive studies of particular languages is likely to give a deeper insight into UG [Universal Grammar] than less far-reaching study of a wide variety of languages," he goes on to cite approvingly a 1981 dissertation by Marantz that "combines coverage of a wide variety of language types with construction of a well articulated theory of UG" (1982: 92).

There remains, however, a difference between citing data from several languages in regard to a particular issue and systematically pursuing a linguistic topic by examining a broad and representative sample of languages to arrive at generalizations.

The question of one versus many languages is more than just a matter of tactics. As pointed out in Comrie (1981) it is in principle impossible to arrive at implicational universals by looking at just one language. If, for example, I find a language like Sindhi with both front and back implosives, it is only by comparing it with other languages that it becomes possible to discover the universal implication that whenever a language has back implosives it has front implosives. A further difficulty is the following. In earlier discussion of universals by the MIT school a classification into substantive and formal universals was made. Both Katz and Postal (1964) and Chomsky (1965) give as examples of substantive universals the Jakobsonian set of universal phonological features. However, it is not asserted that all languages employ all of them. In fact, no single language makes use of the total set. Hence one could never discover them by investigating only one language.

The second issue mentioned earlier is attention to surface structure as against deep structure. According to Chomsky (1965: 118):

> [T]here is no reason to expect uniformity of surface structures, and the findings of modern linguistics are thus not inconsistent with the hypotheses of universal

> grammarians. Insofar as attention is restricted to surface structures, the most that can be expected is the discovery of statistical tendencies, such as those presented in Greenberg (1963).

Chomsky then further remarks (*ibid.*: 209–10): "In general it should be expected that only descriptions concerned with deep structure will have import for proposals concerning linguistic universals." In accordance with this view, notions of a universal deep structure, now abandoned, were fairly widely held in the sixties.

That regularities in surface structure were unexpected during this period may also be gathered from the following statement (Lakoff 1968: 7–9):

> This is not to say that it is unprofitable to look at a wide range of linguistic data given our present knowledge of what grammar is like. . . . A case in point is . . . Greenberg (1963). Greenberg took a very superficial look at thirty languages. He considered only the surface structure of certain types of sentences in these languages. . . . Of course, Greenberg could not have done anything more sophisticated along these lines since there do not exist thirty diverse languages that have been studied extensively beyond the level of surface structure. But considering the limited scope of his study, there was no reason why he should have come up with any interesting facts at all. . . . What is remarkable is that Greenberg did come up with some results. . . . Considering the impoverished theory of grammar that he was working in—phrase structure grammar—it is remarkable that he was able to describe any universal facts at all that are of interest. But though Greenberg was able to *describe* these facts in terms of phrase structure grammar, he could not *explain* them within that theory. Indeed, there exists no known theory of grammar in terms of which they can be explained.

It is of interest to note in regard to the foregoing statement that Lakoff believes that one *must* have a theory of grammar before investigating linguistic phenomena. Since I was obviously not a generativist, he assumed that I must be working in the theory of phrase structure grammar that dominated American structuralism before the rise of generative grammar. In fact it was not that I was espousing either surface or deep structure theories. I was simply indifferent to the distinction between the two, often relating surface phenomena which in a generative account would at that period require a derivation in deep structure of one from the other, or both from a different structure.

This whole question now appears to be moot. About 1970 Chomsky began to develop his Extended Standard Theory as an answer to generative semantics. This involved both phonological and semantic interpretation at the level of surface structure. The very term 'deep structure' was ultimately abandoned to be replaced by 'initial phrase marker' which had much more modest functions than the earlier 'deep structure'.

Thus by 1975 Chomsky observed regarding deep structure (1975: 82):

The term 'deep structure' had unfortunately proved to be misleading. It has led a number of people to suppose that it is the deep structures and their properties that are truly 'deep', in the non-technical sense of that word, while the rest is superficial, unimportant, variable across languages, and so on.

One may further observe that certain generalizations are only stateable as surface phenomena. These began to be noted as 'conspiracies'. A whole series of deeper rules of varied types, 'conspired' to produce a surface regularity. For example in Yurok, Classical Arabic, Hausa, and other languages a highly restricted set of syllable types, namely CV̆, CV̄, CV̆C, identical for all these languages, resulted from a diversity of rules. But universal conspiracies also exist. Thus, as far as I am aware, whatever order properties a language may possess, a first or second person pronoun always precedes its apposition as in English, "We, the people of the United States. . . ." Finally, in recent years, in addition to the Chomskyan model, a whole series of generative grammatical models have arisen, all oriented towards surface structure.

The third characteristic mentioned initially was the use of typology. In my view, typology is indispensable but it is not the sole basis for principles of linguistic explanation. Typology is inextricably bound up with universals among which the implicational type figures prominently.[1] It is also related to marking theory in ways to be mentioned presently. The term 'marking' in this context is used essentially in its Prague School meaning of hierarchical relations among categories and not as a set of conventions in universal grammar such that the extent to which a grammar deviates from such conventions the more marked and less highly valued it is.

The interconnection of typology, universals, and marking may be stated as follows. The absence of certain logically possible types is equivalent to particular kinds of universalist statements, depending on the pattern of the typology and the missing types. In practice, the most common situation is that of four logically possible types, based on the presence or absence of two properties. Of the four, one is frequently absent or statistically rare. This can be restated as a universal implication. For example, the non-existence of languages with back implosives but without front implosives is logically equivalent to the statement that the presence of back implosives universally implies the presence of front implosives. In turn, when such an implicational relation exists, the unmarked category is the implied one. But marking involves a whole cluster of other characteristics such as non-zero expression of the marked category in morphology, its lesser text frequency in both morphology and phonology, etc. (cf. Greenberg 1966).

[1] I am indebted to Roman Jakobson for first calling to my attention the importance of implicational universals.

Chomsky himself never seems to use the term 'implicational universals' and until recently the term 'typology' was also excluded. However, it is not difficult to see that these concepts, especially after the initial period of generative grammar, are in fact employed. Thus in the famous ninth chapter of Chomsky and Halle (1968), a work on the phonology of English, a whole series of marking conventions are set forth so that certain feature combinations are designated as *u* and it costs a rule to change them to a marked combination, thus making the grammar less highly valued. But what is the source of the conventions themselves? They can't be derived from generative grammars because they are logically prior and intended to be utilized in writing the grammars themselves. The answer is clear. The unvoiced nasal, for example, is universally marked because of its relative rarity in languages and the implicational universal that the presence of unvoiced implies the presence of voiced nasals. These facts in turn are known because of earlier cross-linguistic typological surveys of investigators like Trubetskoy and Hockett.

A further value of marking hierarchies of the Prague type was proposed by Jakobson (1941), namely that the unmarked precedes the marked in first language acquisition. An important contribution of Chomsky is the immense stimulus he gave to research on child language acquisition. But we find here again an important change of position without explicit acknowledgment. In their work on the sound patterns of English, Chomsky and Halle say (1968: 331):

> We have been describing acquisition of language as if it were an instantaneous process. Obviously, this is not true. A more realistic model of language acquisition would consider the order in which primary linguistic data are used by the child . . . To us it appears that this more realistic model is much too complex to be taken up in any meaningful way today and that it will be far more fruitful to investigate in detail, as a first approximation, the idealized model outlined earlier, leaving refinements to a time when this idealization is better understood.

However, more recently Chomsky states (1981: 95):

> Universals of the sort explored by Joseph Greenberg and others have obvious relevance to determining just which properties of the lexicon have to be specified in this manner in particular grammars—or to put it in other terms, just how much must be learned as grammar develops in the course of language acquisition.

In an EST account, the lexicon contains unmarked categories that are then changed to marked categories in specific grammars, and the assumption is being made that these rules are learned by children after a period of using the unmarked form.

The most obvious example of the tacit use of implicational universals is, however, the X-bar convention introduced in 1970. Originally it was posited as a variable which could be rewritten as head, modifier or head, complement and then specified as noun, verb, or prepositional phrase. However in its initial form there was no ordering of head and modifier complement in universal grammar. Later a convention was introduced by which, for any particular grammar the order of head and non-head was the same for all X-bar constructions. The obvious connection with word order typology was first pointed out in Riemsdijk (1978).

There remains a deeper difference between my approach and that of others which has been much more rarely noted. I refer to the generativist assumption that linguistic theory is to be equated to the principles involved in the construction of synchronic grammars, and that, correspondingly, universals are the study of the basic properties underlying such grammars. A representative statement is Chomsky (1965: 28) that "the study of universals is the study of the properties of any generative grammar for natural language." For a considerable period, Sanders was almost alone in seeing that there is even an issue here. He noted (1974: 17) that "Facts about natural languages can be accounted for, in principle, either directly—by laws quantified over the set of all possible languages—or indirectly—by laws quantified over the set of all possible grammars of such languages." But then without supporting argument he asserts that it is preferable, perhaps necessary, that all facts and laws about languages be specified in terms of facts about grammars. A further limitation that these should be synchronic grammars is simply taken for granted.

Later, Lieb and Seiler took note of this issue. The former (1978: I: 61) states "A language universal is a property of languages, not grammars, and does not depend on grammar." Further, regarding the approach through grammars, "the extent to which this has been accepted uncritically is stunning."

In more recent discussion this issue has become more prominent. Smith (1982: 256) in his criticism of Comrie, talks about the Chomskyan paradigm which he supports as characterized by "its emphasis on *grammars* rather than *languages*," while Comrie in the very title of his paper of 1978 "Linguistics is about Languages" took the opposite stance. However, both Comrie and Hawkins in their replies to critics seem to accept the notion that linguistic theory is the same as universal grammar and seek to show that the typological approach can make a contribution to linguistic theory by contributing to the theory of grammar.

I shall deal first with the question of generalizing over grammars rather than languages and secondly, the limitation to synchronic grammar. My objection to both is basically similar. They constitute arbitrary restrictions both on the range of relevant data to be explained and the nature of the explanations themselves.

Regarding the first, there are many important properties of languages which will not appear in grammars. They may be classified into three types: grammar-derived, transgrammatical, and non-grammatical. By grammar-derived properties will be meant ones that can be logically derived from grammars but are not explicitly stated in them. The following is an example. Nowhere in any grammar based on current models could it be stated that the French noun had two genders, although one could no doubt derive it from the rule specifying that all nouns in the lexicon must be marked as masculine or feminine. However, present theories give no motive for deriving such a statement.

Now it turns out that if one compares two-gender languages typologically there are some interesting limits on possible types. The only features that ever appear are animacy or sex. There is, however, a third type in which feminine is grouped together with inherently sexless items so that the contrast is masculine versus non-masculine. However, as far as I know, there is no system with a basically [ ± feminine] contrast.

More serious in my view are what I shall call transgrammatical facts. These involve a relationship between the facts of two languages which will appear in both grammars but the relationship between which will not be found in either. A typical example is when a large number of words have been borrowed from a language A into a language B and these borrowed words show different phonological constraints or derivational formations from native words. An attempt has been made to deal with such situations by positing lexical features such as [+ French] in English or [+ Arabic] in Turkish. However what this will not show is the systematic changes which occur in the process of the transfer from A to B which may give further evidence regarding, for example, sound similarity as shown in substitution and which can be compared with evidence from other sources regarding the same subject.

Finally, there are certain types of facts which will not appear in grammars at all and yet have theoretic significance. If a grammar is a model of linguistic competence, I fail to see how the fact that in languages with morphological plurals the singular is used about four times as frequently as the plural in text can or should be included in the grammar. It is well-known that frequency data play an important part in marking theory which in turn has significance for cross-linguistic generalizations.

In many instances whether facts are stated directly about languages or about grammars will make no real difference. But if a rule or other property of a grammar is wedded closely to a particular theory it will be an artifact of that theory and not related to languages' capacities. An example is that Katz and Postal in the first published discussion of universals by generativists, enunciate a distinction between substantive and formal universals. In attempting to exemplify the latter they state (1964: 160) "[O]ne of the most detailed formal universals is a specification that certain rules must be found in the syntactic component of any linguistic description—for example the rule Rel→ md." The rule given here means that Relative is to be rewritten as matrix dummy. But matrix dummy was a purely theoretical constraint to allow recoverability of the place of insertion of a relative clause. A year later it was no longer a universal.

The other major limitation on explanatory theory is the restriction to synchronic factors. Here there has been some broadening of scope in that we have witnessed a revival of interest in historical linguistics. The seminal events here were Kiparsky (1968) and King (1969). However, the generativist approach took two main forms which follow predictably from the equation of theory with synchronic grammatical theory. One of these is that historical change becomes theoretically relevant insofar as a particular complex synchronic rule is strengthened as a valid generalization if it resulted from a unitary historic change (the problem of curly brackets). The other is the conception of linguistic change as the replacement of one grammar by another. This resulted in a classification of changes under such rubrics as rule addition, rule deletion, rule reordering, etc. On a broader view, it was claimed that the general trend of historical change was towards grammatical simplification. After the initial excitement, the weakness of this approach, it is fair to say, became generally evident.

In Cohen (1974), one of the very few book length treatments of explanation in linguistics, only Dretske, a philosopher of science, takes any note of the possible explanatory role of historical linguistics. Noting that perhaps not all linguists are doing the same things, he raises the possibility that there might be corresponding types of linguistic explanation. He asks (1974: 23) "Or should one take history as one's paradigm and think of linguistic explanations on the model of historical explanations?"

It is my view that historical explanation must play an autonomous and not merely auxiliary part in the overall structure of linguistic explanation. Moreover, it is not confined to the explanation of facts of individual languages but generalizable through the concept of diachronic process as a class of similar but historically independent changes and through the notion of recurrent patterns of change of type.

I shall seek to clarify these notions by a brief sketch of how I conceive of the overall structure of explanation in linguistics. There is, of course, an enormous literature on scientific explanations. In linguistics, in addition to numerous incidental but relevant discussions scattered throughout the literature, there are also several collections of papers devoted to this topic (Cohen 1974; Hornstein and Lightfoot 1981; Butterworth, Comrie, and Dahl 1984).

It is obviously not possible to discuss all the issues raised in this literature. In the present context, however, a few general observations are in order. One is that the concept of explanation is inextricably intertwined with that of theory. This is so much so that the expression 'explanatory theory', often encountered in the linguistic literature, may be considered redundant. What would a theory be that didn't explain or at least seek to explain anything? Another indication of the close connection between theory and explanation is that discussions of explanation generally center about problems of theory construction. Germane to the present discussion is that by considering a grammar as a theory of a language, by a tacit transition it becomes the explanation of a language.

Besides its connection with explanation, a further observation may be made concerning the term 'theory'. We expect it to have a certain degree of comprehensiveness and generality to deserve the name of theory. Often two basic levels are proposed, a lower one of empirical generalizations and a higher level from which empirical generalizations are deduced. Such a higher level statement is frequently called a law.

I believe it is possible within the linguistic data to demarcate two basic levels. In each there are various sublevels. Although there seems to be an eternal regress of questioning, since it is always possible, like a pesky child, to ask for an explanation, it is nevertheless possible to say that on a particular level something has been explained when we no longer ask that question but move to a higher level one.

One other preliminary observation is in order. To begin the explanatory ascent we need a lowest level as a starting point. It has been claimed that there are no facts which do not presuppose a theory; the term theory-laden is sometimes used. However, there does seem to be a lowest level of sheer facts. Without it we would never get started and without it there would be no laws for the lowest Chomskyan level of adequacy, observational adequacy.

It is characteristic of this level that although it may employ theoretic terms it never explains anything else but is itself in need of explanation. Moreover, any theory which contradicted it would be rejected. An example would be the fact that in Latin the dative singular of *puer* ('boy') is *puerō*. No doubt dative and singular are theoretic terms, but that *puerō* is the dative singular of *puer* does not explain any other fact about Latin.[2] Moreover, any grammar which gave different results would fail at the level of observational adequacy.

[2] This requires further elaboration (cf. Greenberg 1970). There is no absolute lowest level. The level discussed here is that of citation forms in grammars and dictionaries and sentences

At a higher level we may indeed ask questions which stem from the theory itself. Whether transformations change meaning makes sense in the framework of earlier generative grammatical theory. Are all types in a typology connected in the sense that ultimately, if not directly, any type can change into any other, what I call the hypothesis of connectivity? As a question this only makes sense in the context of diachronic typological theory.

To illustrate the problem of types and levels of explanation I will start with some Turkish examples. Suppose that we are told that the plural nominative of *adam* ('person') is *adamlar* but that the corresponding form of *el* ('hand') is *eller*, so that in one instance the plural mark is *-lar* and in the other *-ler*. If we answer that all singular nominative nominal forms with *-a-* in the last syllable take *-lar* while those with *-e-* take *-ler* we will stop asking about the plurals of *adam* and *el*. If we then ask why all nouns in *-a-* take *-lar* and all those in *-e-* take *-ler*, we can be told that there are eight vowels in Turkish and that nouns whose final vowels are *a*, *ɨ*, *o*, or *u* take *-lar* and those with *e*, *i*, *ö*, or *ü* take *-ler*. Once we know this we stop asking about *a* and *e*, but we may ask the reason for this particular division of vowels and it can be pointed out that the first set are all the back vowels and the second set all the front vowels. At this point we can give all the basic rules of the Turkish vowel harmony system, which works throughout the language, not only in nouns. There are also a certain number of easily specified exceptions which are either loan words (especially Arabic) or certain affixes. We can thus answer literally thousands of lower level questions by a sample set of rules.

All of this is, of course, synchronic and we would certainly say that a grammar of Turkish which provided maximally generalized statements about vowel harmony was more explanatory than one which did not. However, we must call even this an empirical generalization rather than a theory. A theory contains one or more laws. What we have talked about is only true of Turkish. Expressed in law-like terms we would have to say 'whenever a language is Turkish all the vowels in a word are back vowels, or all are front vowels'.

It is characteristic of laws that although they hold only under stated conditions, these conditions are expressed in general not under proper name conditions. This seems a natural point at which to separate empirical generalizations from laws. We have grown so accustomed to the view of a grammar of a language being a theory of that language and hence explanatory, that this point has not been generally appreciated. One of the dissenting voices is once again Sanders (1974: 16):

---

in languages which are cited in theoretical discussion, basically the level of *langue* rather than *parole*. In *langue* each example is a type of which tokens occur in actual discourse (at the pragmatic level).

> [I]f a grammar is a theory about a particular language, . . . then it is a theory which has a grossly unnatural domain—no less unnatural than a theory about a particular cat (as opposed to a theory about all cats, or all animals). The domain of all languages, on the other hand, is a perfectly natural one relative to the present state of scientific knowledge and its presently foreseeable developments.

What all this suggests is that the natural next step is not to look within Turkish itself, but rather at vowel harmony systems typologically across languages. In such investigations we generally find that there are logically possible types which do not occur and such results are stateable in universalistic, often implicational form, from which they can be deduced.

In the present context this attempt is not made since it would require a separate and extensive study. A general notion, however, may be given thus of three of the basic dimensions of vowel quality, namely height, the back-front opposition, and lip rounding. The subordinate or marked status of the last is evident from the fact that it is never the sole principle of any system. There are, in addition, other generalizations about vowel systems that point in the same direction.

In instances like Turkish vowel harmony, generalization within a language will to a degree be an explanation. However there are many phenomena, e.g. unique or small groups of exceptions, for which synchronic generalization in the usual sense is ruled out. English plurals by internal vowel change is an example. The plural *men* is a unique example of the alternation of *a* and *e* to express the singular-plural distinction. There are, of course, other instances of vowel change plurals in English, e.g. *tooth/teeth*; *goose/geese*; *mouse/mice*; *louse/lice*.

Lakoff, in a work based on his interesting dissertation on syntactic irregularity (1970), calls such instances minor rules even when they cover only one case and suggests rule features in the lexicon for the entries involving these cases. It is difficult to see in what sense one can talk about a rule when there is no common property for the instances which fall under it. We must say that *a* of the singular is replaced by *e* in the plural when the lexical item is *man*.

One is tempted to quote Romans 2: 14, in which Paul talking of the pagans who are not under the Jewish law says ". . . these not having the law, are a law unto themselves."

But a historical account shows that all of these plurals fall under a generalized account since they arose from a former suffix *-i* which umlauted the previous vowel and was then lost or reduced. Here once more there is a kind of explanation, in that we stop asking specifically about *man/men*. Moreover our explanation leads to further generalization in that alternations like *old/elder* can be shown to result from the same sequence of changes.

We can, of course, ask still higher level questions but they will refer to similar umlauting or vowel modification in other historically independent instances. Which vowels produce such changes and how are they grammaticized? These are diachronic typological and universalistic questions.

Generativists have shown little or no interest in explaining exceptions or language-specific rules. For example, Chomsky and Halle state (1968: ix):

> Counterexamples to a grammatical rule are of interest only if they lead to the construction of a new grammar of even greater generality or if they show some underlying principle is fallacious or misformulated. Otherwise, citation of counterexamples is beside the point.

Katz and Postal (1964: 160) seem to exclude language-specific facts from the scope of explanatory theory:

> In short, one must distinguish between those features of a language that it has by virtue of being English, French, Chinese, etc., as opposed to one of the others from those features it has by virtue of being a natural language. A full specification of the latter is a theory of structure of natural language and the features are the universals of language.

This excludes an enormous mass of language-specific facts from explanatory theory, yet typological and diachronic factors will explain a substantial portion of them. The efficacy of diachronic explanation is not limited to language-specific irregularities. Whole clusters of synchronic cross-linguistic generalizations, of which those of marking theory are perhaps the most conspicuous, can sometimes be deduced from diachronic, often in conjunction with synchronic premises.

Let us consider the example of vowel nasality. The following synchronic generalizations may be noted: (1) There are languages without nasal vowels but there are no languages without oral vowels. (2) The text frequency of nasal vowels is smaller than that of oral vowels. (3) The number of nasal vowel phonemes is never greater than the number of oral vowel phonemes. (4) In conditions of external neutralization of oral and nasal vowels, only oral vowels appear. By external neutralization is meant that the conditions do not involve adjacent nasal consonants.

We can deduce these generalizations from a set of diachronic principles.

1. Nasal vowels arise from oral vowels by conditioned change in nasal consonant environment.

Since nasal vowels arise from oral vowels under restricted conditions, in the remaining environments the oral vowel remains. From this we deduce the first synchronic universal. We also require a further diachronic principle that vowels never completely disappear from a language. If such a language existed—and none is known—the regularity would be reduced to the implication that whenever a language has oral vowels it has nasal vowels.

A further consequence of the origin theory of nasal vowels is that since the conditioning environments are restricted and less extensive than the nonconditioning environments, the text frequency of nasal vowels is smaller (our second synchronic universal). Strictly speaking we once more need an auxiliary hypothesis, in this instance synchronic, about the relative frequency of nasal consonant environments compared to all others. Of course the conditioning consonant may be only the following or only the preceding nasal consonants or only affect certain vowels making the conditioning environments even smaller.

2. Merger of oral vowels implies the previous merger of the corresponding nasal.

Since nasal vowels arise from oral vowels they are equal or even smaller in number than their oral counterparts when they arise. By the diachronic principle just mentioned they have a greater tendency to merge and thus become fewer in number. This explains the third synchronic generalization regarding the equal or greater number of oral vowel phonemes in comparison with nasal vowel phonemes.

3. In externally conditioned merger, e.g. in word final, it is rather that the nasal vowel loses nasality than that the oral vowel acquires it.

This explains the fourth synchronic universal concerning neutralization. In the environment of generalization, only the unmarked oral vowel appears since the nasal vowel has merged with it.

Analogues of the three diachronic principles just enunciated hold in general for marked features in phonology. They thus can account for a large number of observed regularities which derive from synchronic marking theory.

Another aspect of diachronic processual explanations is that highly language specific, often unique rules, become understandable as part of the mechanism of change of synchronic type. An example from numeral noun order is the following. Since I first encountered it in Margi, a Chadic language of Nigeria, it may be called the Margi rule. In Margi the numeral follows the noun as does the adjective. However, there is a worldwide favoring of the order numeral preceding noun. Even Welsh, a strong VSO language with NA order, has the numeral preceding the noun (hereafter QN). Whenever, contrary to this, the numeral follows the noun, with very few exceptions NA order also holds so that we have the universal statistical implication NQ → NA. We may therefore hypothesize that NQ order arises from QN on the analogy of NA order in languages which have the latter.

Although as we have seen, in Margi the numeral follows the noun, as does the adjective, within the numeral construction this only holds for higher units. Thus one says 'thousands two', 'hundreds two', but for multiples of 10 the order is 'two tens', 'three tens', etc., the opposite of that with nouns. As idiosyncratic as the rule may seem, an identical one occurs in Kabardian, a Northwest Caucasian language which, like Margi, has NA order.

Similar phenomena, though differing in details appear in certain Nilotic languages, e.g. Nandi and Masai. In all these cases the languages are NA and NQ. Comparison within all of the genetic groups allows us to interpret QN order as a survival in the most unmarked lower numerals of the earlier order under the influence of NA order.[3]

The point here is that we can often make sense out of highly idiosyncratic phenomena, sometimes found in only a single language, as part of the mechanism of changes of type when we examine synchronic typologies from a dynamic point of view.

Of course all explanations call for still higher levels and more comprehensive explanations. In our search for these we must, I believe, go outside of linguistics proper to psychology, the physiology of sound production, the nature of the world and of the speech situation (pragmatics). This question has been raised in recent years in terms of a distinction between "strong universals," that is, those explainable on purely linguistic grounds, and "weak" universals, those involving non-linguistic factors. I consider the question open but there must be, I believe, at least some weak universals. This is particularly obvious in phonology. For example, even in a work on generative phonology, the author notes (Schane 1973: 121) that "in the end, the true explanations for naturalness are likely to be extralinguistic, physiological and/or psychological."

An example of a universal that may be plausibly imputed to psychological processing relates once more to numeral systems. There is a strong tendency in languages in higher numerals to put the higher units before the lower. For example, in English we say 'three thousand four hundred and sixty-five'. Up to twenty however, lower precedes higher (e.g., eighteen = 8 + 10) but after twenty the higher precedes, e.g. 'twenty-one'. Let us call this a switch point. There is never more than one switch point and as we ascend in the numeral system the switch is always from lower following higher to higher following lower. In many languages the higher units always precede—e.g. Mandarin. I am only aware of one language with the opposite order and no switch point,

[3] For a more detailed discussion see Greenberg 1978.

Malagasy, and Keenan (personal communication) informs me that Malagasy speakers encounter processing 'difficulties' with higher units. The advantage of higher units preceding lower is obvious. If I start with 'three thousand' I immediately know that the number is between 3,000 and 4,000 and the next expression 'four hundred' further determines the limits as between 3,400 and 3,500, etc. If smaller units are placed first and if I begin with five, all I can see is that the number is 5 or more and I approximate the ultimate value much more slowly.

I have sketched successive levels of explanation from single language synchronic generalizations and specific diachronic explanations to synchronic typological, diachronic processual and, ultimately, extra-linguistic explanations. Of course, an enormous amount of concrete work remains to be accomplished, but at least a start has been made within the last twenty years.

I have concentrated on my own approach with which I am naturally enough better acquainted than with those of others. I have also sought to be constructive. In comparing the generative approach to the one I have just described there is a further fundamental difference which flows from what I have said. To generativists it would appear that the topic of language universals is simply a synonym for the general enterprise of constructing a formal explanatory theory of grammar. As we have seen, diachronic and typological explanatory principles seem in principle to be excluded, although this limitation is often tacitly overcome in practice. Whereas the problem of universals is central to me, for more orthodox generativists there is, in a sense, no separate area of universals research. Many generativist textbooks do not even have the term 'universal' in the index. In recent years Chomsky no longer talks about linguistic universals but rather of UG (universal grammar).

A remarkably frank statement is that of a participant in the first conference on universals organized by generativists (McCawley 1968: 125):

> My conscience demands that I begin by pointing out that I am writing under false pretenses. I do not purport to have any universals in semantics to propose. . . . Accordingly, let me for the bulk of this paper forget that this is a conference on language universals and simply talk about semantics as it relates to English.

There may be at present signs of what Kuhn has called a paradigm crisis (cf. Ramat 1979). We have numerous competing theories of grammar and apparently no generally accepted way of choosing among them. It is sometimes the case in such situations not that one is false and the rest are true but that they all unconsciously share the same assumptions about the questions to be answered. The problems of synchronic grammatical theory are no doubt important but they are not to be identified with linguistic theory as a whole.

It is my hope that the broader base of method and explanation sketched here can with further specific investigations and theoretical exploration make a contribution towards a more comprehensive and explanatory body of linguistic theory.

From all indications it is likely, however, that the two approaches sketched here will continue for a considerable period, distinct, but influencing each other. On the one hand, the often brilliant and insightful analyses of specific grammatical phenomena in the generative literature can be helpful to the typologist. On the other, the broad cross-linguistic approach can often uncover phenomena which need to be taken account of in a theory of universal grammar.

## References Cited


Bell, Alan. 1971. "Acquisition- and transmission-significant universals." *Working Papers in Language Universals* 5. Language Universals Project, Stanford University.

Bugarski, Ranko. 1972. *Jezik i lingvistika*. Belgrade: Nolit.

Butterworth, Brian, Bernard Comrie, and Östen Dahl, eds. 1984. *Explanations for Language Universals*. Berlin: Mouton.

Chomsky, Noam. 1965. *Aspects of the Theory of Syntax*. Cambridge: M.I.T. Research Laboratory of Electronics. Special Technical Report no. 11.

———. 1975. *Reflections on Language*. New York: Pantheon Books.

———. 1976. "On the Nature of Language." In *Origins and Evolution of Speech*, ed. by Stephen R. Hornad, D. Steklis, and Jane Lancaster. Annals of the New York Academy of Sciences, vol. 280.

———. 1981. *Lectures on Government and Binding*. Dordrecht: Foris.

Chomsky, Noam, and Morris Halle. 1968. *Sound Patterns of English*. Cambridge: M.I.T. Press.

Cohen, David, ed. 1974. *Explaining Linguistic Phenomena*. New York: Wiley.

Comrie, Bernard. 1978. "Linguistics is about languages." *Studies in the Linguistic Sciences* 8: 221–36.

———. 1981. *Language Universals and Linguistic Typology*. Oxford: Basil Blackwell.

———. 1983. "On the validity of typological studies: A reply to Smith." *Australian Journal of Linguistics* 3: 93–96.

———. 1984. "Language universals and linguistic argumentation: A reply to Coopmans." *Journal of Linguistics* 20: 155–63.

Coopmans, Peter. 1983. Review of Comrie 1981. *Journal of Linguistics* 19: 455–57.

———. 1984. "Surface word-order and universal grammar." *Language* 60: 55–69.

Dretske, Fred I. 1974. "Explanation in linguistics." In Cohen, ed. 1974: 21–41.

Ferguson, Charles. 1978. "Historical background of universals research." In Greenberg, ed. 1978: I: 7–31.

Greenberg, Joseph H. 1963. "Some universals of grammar with special reference to the order of meaningful elements." In *Universals of Language*, ed. by Joseph H. Greenberg. Cambridge: M.I.T. Press.

———. 1966. *Language Universals, with Special Reference to Feature Hierarchies*. The Hague: Mouton.

———. 1970. "On the language of observation in linguistics." *Working Papers in Language Universals* 4. Language Universals Project, Stanford University.
———. 1978. "Generalizations about numeral systems." In *Universals of Human Language*, ed. by Joseph H. Greenberg. II: 249–95.
Hawkins, John A. 1983. *Word Order Universals*. New York: Academic Press.
———. 1985. "Complementary methods in universal grammar: A reply to Coopmans." *Language* 61: 569–87.
Hornstein, Norbert, and David Lightfoot, eds. 1981. *Explanation in Linguistics: The Logical Problem of Language Acquisition*. London: Longmans.
Jakobson, Roman. 1941. *Kindersprache, Aphasie und allgemeine Lautgesetze*. Uppsala: Almqvist & Wiksell.
Katz, Jerrold J., and Paul H. Postal. 1964. *An Integrated Theory of Linguistic Descriptions*. Cambridge: M.I.T. Press.
King, Robert D. 1969. *Historical Linguistics and Generative Grammar*. Englewood Cliffs, N.J.: Prentice-Hall.
Kiparsky, Paul. 1968. "Linguistic universals and linguistic change." In *Universals in Linguistic Theory*, ed. by Emmon Bach and Robert T. Harms, 171–204. New York: Holt, Rinehart & Winston.
Lakoff, George Philip. 1968. *Deep and Surface Grammar*. Bloomington: Indiana University Linguistics Club.
———. 1970. *Irregularity in Syntax*. New York: Holt, Rinehart & Winston.
Lehmann, Winfred. 1972. "Converging theories in linguistics." *Language* 48: 266–75.
Lieb, Hans-Heinrich. 1978. "Universals and linguistic explanation." In *Universals of Human Language*, ed. by Joseph H. Greenberg. I: 157–202.
Lightfoot, David. 1981. "Explaining syntactic change." In Hornstein and Lightfoot, eds. 1981: 209–40.
McCawley, James. 1968. "The role of semantics in a grammar." In *Universals in Linguistic Theory*, ed. by Emmon Bach and Robert T. Harms: 125–70. New York: Holt, Rinehart & Winston.
Ramat, Paolo. 1979. "Crisi del formalismo? Teoria della grammatica e dati empirici." *Lingua et Stile* 14: 271–83.
———. 1980. "La nozione di 'tipo' e le sue articulazioni nelle discipline del linguaggio; Introduzione." *Lingua e Stile* 15: 311–28.
Riemsdijk, H. C. van. 1978. *A Case Study in Semantic Markedness*. Lisse: Von Ridder.
Rizzi, Luigi. 1980. "Il programma chomskiano e la tipologia linguistica." *Lingua e Stile* 15: 347–70.
Sanders, Gerald A. 1974. "Issues of explanation in linguistics." In Cohen, ed. 1974: 1–20.
Schane, Sanford A. 1973. *Generative Phonology*. Englewood Cliffs, N.J.: Prentice-Hall.
Smith, N. V. 1982. Review of Comrie 1981. *Australian Journal of Linguistics* 2: 255–61.
———. 1983. "A rejoinder to Comrie." *Australian Journal of Linguistics* 3: 97–98.
Stassen, Leon. 1985. *Comparison and Universal Grammar*. Oxford: Basil Blackwell.

# Bibliography of the Published Works of Joseph H. Greenberg

# Bibliography of the Published Works of Joseph H. Greenberg

The list that follows is complete as of the summer of 1989. The arrangement is chronological by year, but no effort has been made to determine the order of appearance of items within a given year. Asterisked entries have been reprinted or translated elsewhere, as detailed in the Appendix following the "In Press" heading at the end of the main chronological listing. The following abbreviations have been used throughout:

| | |
|---|---|
| *AA* | *American Anthropologist* |
| *Afr Stud B* | *African Studies Bulletin*, African Studies Association/Hoover Institution |
| *IJAL* | *International Journal of American Linguistics* |
| *J Afr L* | *Journal of African Languages* |
| *JAF* | *Journal of American Folklore* |
| *JAOS* | *Journal of the American Oriental Society* |
| *Lg* | *Language* |
| *MSLL* | *Georgetown University Monograph Series on Language and Linguistics* |
| *Southw J Anthrop* | *Southwestern Journal of Anthropology* |
| *WPLU* | *Working Papers in Language Universals*, Stanford University |


*1940*

1. The decipherment of the Ben-Ali Diary, a preliminary statement. *Journal of Negro History* 25: 372–75.

*1941*

*2. Some aspects of Negro-Mohammedan culture-contact among the Hausa. *AA* 43: 51–61.
3. Some problems in Hausa phonology. *Lg* 17: 316–23.

*1946*

*4. *The Influence of Islam on a Sudanese religion.* New York: J. J. Augustin. ix + 73 pp.

*1947*

5. Arabic loan-words in Hausa. *Word* 3: 85–97.
6. Islam and clan organization among the Hausa. *Southw J Anthrop* 3: 193–211.
7. Swahili prosody. *JAOS* 67: 24–30.

*1948*

8. The classification of African languages. *AA* 50: 24–30.
*9. Linguistics and ethnology. *Southw J Anthrop* 4: 140–47.
10. The tonal system of Proto-Bantu. *Word* 4: 196–208.
11. Review of *The cow-tail switch and other West African tales*, by H. Courlander and G. Herzog. *JAF* 51: 99–100.

*1949*

12. Hausa verse prosody. *JAOS* 69: 125–35.
13. The logical analysis of kinship. *Philosophy of Science* 16: 58–64.
*14. The Negro kingdoms of the Sudan. *Transactions of the New York Academy of Sciences*, Series II, 11: 126–34.
15. Studies in African linguistic classification: I. Introduction, Niger-Congo family. *Southw J Anthrop* 5: 79–100.
16. Studies in African linguistic classification: II. The classification of Fulani. *Southw J Anthrop* 5: 190–98.
17. Studies in African linguistic classification: III. The position of Bantu. *Southw J Anthrop* 5: 309–17.
18. Review of *The classification of the Bantu languages*, by Malcolm Guthrie. *Word* 5: 81–83.
19. Review of *Le Bura-Mabang du Ouadai*, by Georges Trenga. *AA* 51: 485–86.
20. Review of *A Treasury of Jewish folklore*, by Nathan Ausubel. *JAF* 62: 440–41.

*1950*

21. Studies in African linguistic classification: IV. Hamito-Semitic. *Southw J Anthrop* 6: 47–63.
22. Studies in African linguistic classification: V. The Eastern Sudanic Family. *Southw J Anthrop* 6: 143–60.
23. Studies in African linguistic classification: VI. The Click languages. *Southw J Anthrop* 6: 223–37.
24. Studies in African linguistic classification: VII. Smaller families; index of languages. *Southw J Anthrop* 6: 388–98.
25. Review of *Africanisms in the Gullah dialect*, by L. D. Turner. *JAF* 63: 381–82.
26. Review of *The distribution of the Nilotic and Nilo-Hamitic languages of Africa*, by M. A. Bryan. *Lg* 26: 173–75.

27. Review of *Mohammedanism*, by H. A. R. Gibb. *JAF* 63: 120.
28. Review of *The Negro African languages*, by L. Homberger. *Lg* 26: 170–73.
*29. Review of *Selected writings of Edward Sapir in language, culture, and personality*, ed. D. Mandelbaum. *AA* 52: 516–18.
*30. The patterning of root morphemes in Semitic. *Word* 6: 162–81.
31. Review of *The Bantu of North Kavirondo, Vol. 1*, by Gunter Wagner. *AA* 52: 255–56.

*1951*

32. Vowel and nasal harmony in Bantu languages. Zaire, *Revue Congolaise* 8: 813–20.
33. Review of *Grundzüge einer vergleichenden Grammatik der Bantusprachen*, by Carl Meinhof. *JAOS* 71: 94–95.
34. Review of *Manuel de Tshiluba (Kasayi, Congo Belge)*, by A. Burssens. *Lg* 27: 438–39.
35. Review of *Wörterbuch der Djaga-Sprache (Madjame-Mundart) gesprochen am Kilimandjaro in Ostafrika*. *JAOS* 71: 194.

*1952*

36. The Afro-Asiatic (Hamito-Semitic) present. *JAOS* 72: 1–9.
37. Review of *The sculpture of Negro Africa*, by Paul S. Wingert. *JAF* 65: 104–5.

*1953*

38. An application of New World evidence to an African linguistic problem (Hausa). *Mémoires de l'Institut Français d'Afrique Noire* 27: 129–31.
*39. Historical linguistics and unwritten languages. *Anthropology Today*, ed. A. L. Kroeber. Chicago: University of Chicago Press. Pp. 265–86.
40. (With Morris Swadesh.) Jicaque as a Hokan language. *IJAL* 19: 216–22.
41. Review of *The ethnographic survey of Africa*, 6 vols. *AA* 55: 162–63.
42. Review of *Recueil de Textes Falashas*, by A. S. Aescoly. *AA* 55: 445.
43. Review of *Dictionnaire Ngbandi*, by P. B. Lekens, and *Dictionnaire Français-Lomongo*, by H. Hulstaert. *Lg* 29: 576–77.
44. A reply to W. Leslau: The imperfect in South-East Semitic. *JAOS* 73: 167–68.
45. Comments in *An appraisal of anthropology today*, eds. Sol Tax et al. Chicago: University of Chicago Press. Pp. 59–60, 117, 120, 224–25, 232–33, 266–67, 292, 352.

*1954*

*46. The linguistic approach; the word as a linguistic unit; language change. *Psycholinguistics*, eds. C. E. Osgood and T. A. Sebeok. Baltimore: Waverly Press. (Second edition. Bloomington: Indiana University Press, 1965.) Pp. 8–19, 66–70, 146–65.
*47. A quantitative approach to the morphological typology of language. *Method and Perspective in Anthropology: Papers in honor of Wilson D. Wallis*, ed. R. F. Spencer. Minneapolis: University of Minnesota Press. Pp. 192–220.

48. Studies in African linguistic classification: VIII. Further remarks on method; revisions and corrections. *Southw J Anthrop* 10: 405–15.

*49. Concerning inferences from linguistic to nonlinguistic data. *Language in culture*, ed. H. Hoijer. Chicago: University of Chicago Press. Pp. 3–18.

50. Comments in *Language in culture*, ed. Harry Hoijer. Chicago: University of Chicago Press. Pp. 130–31, 133–34, 136, 138, 142–44, 156, 160–61, 172–73, 177–78, 188, 200, 203, 211–12, 214, 224–29, 241, 245, 274–75.

51. Review of *Les Langues du monde*, by A. Meillet and M. Cohen. *AA* 56: 1133–34.

52. Review of *Languages of West Africa*, by D. Westermann and M. A. Bryan. *Lg* 30: 302–9.

53. Review of *The nature of culture*, by A. L. Kroeber, and *Culture: A critical review of concepts and definitions*, by A. L. Kroeber and C. Kluckhohn. *AA* 56: 568–71.

54. Review of *La Langue berbère*, by A. Basset. *AA* 56: 148.

55. Review of *Die Tasmanischen Sprachen*, by W. Schmidt. *Word* 10: 117–19.

56. Review of *Unkhoswe Waanyanja*, ed. by Guy Atkins. *Word* 10: 117.

*1955*

*57. *Studies in African linguistic classification*. New Haven, Conn.: Compass Press. 116 pp.

58. Internal *a*-Plurals in Afroasiatic (Hamito-Semitic). *Afrikanistische Studien* [zum 80.en Geburtstag Diedrich Westermann gewidmet], ed. Johannes Lukas. (Veröffentlichungen des Instituts für Orientforschung der Akademie der Wissenschaften der DDR 26.) Berlin: Akademie-Verlag.

59. Review of *Languages in contact*, by U. Weinreich. *AA* 57: 167–68.

*1956*

*60. The measurement of linguistic diversity. *Lg* 32: 109–15.

61. Review of *Baba of Karo: A woman of the Moslem Hausa*, by M. F. Smith. *AA* 58: 749–50.

62. Review of *The economy of Hausa communities of Zaria*, by M. G. Smith. *AA* 58: 931–33.

63. Review of *Geschichte der Erforschung der Nilotischen Sprachen*, by Oswin Köhler. *Lg* 32: 563–67.

64. Review of *A Maasai grammar with vocabulary*, by A. N. Tucker and J. T. ole Mpaayei. *Word* 12: 487–89.

*1957*

*65. *Essays in linguistics*. Chicago: University of Chicago Press. vii + 108 pp.

*66. The nature and uses of linguistic typologies. *IJAL* 23: 68–77.

67. Nilotic, 'Nilo-Hamitic' and Hamito-Semitic: A reply. *Africa* 17: 364–78.

68. Review of *A Bushman dictionary*, by Dorothea F. Bleek, *Lg* 33: 495–97.

*1958*

69. The labial consonants of Proto-Afro-Asiatic. *Word* 14: 295–302.

*1959*

70. An axiomatization of the phonologic aspect of languages. *Symposium on sociological theory*, ed. Llewellyn Gross. New York: Harper & Row, Inc. Pp. 437–82.
71. Africa as a linguistic area. *Continuity and change in African cultures*, ed. W. R. Bascom and M. J. Herskovits. Chicago: University of Chicago Press. Pp. 15–27.
*72. Current trends in linguistics. *Science* 130: 1165–70.
*73. Language and evolution. *Evolution and anthropology: A centennial appraisal.* Washington, D.C.: The Anthropological Society of Washington. Pp. 61–75.
74. The origin of the Masai passive. *Africa* 29: 171–76.
75. Review of *Fundamentals of language*, by R. Jakobson and M. Halle. *AA* 61: 157–58.
76. Review of *An introduction to the Western Desert languages*, by W. H. Douglas. *Lg* 35: 382–85.
77. Review of *A short description of item categories in Iraqw*, by W. H. Whiteley. *AA* 61: 163–64.

*1960*

78. An Afro-Asiatic pattern of gender and number agreement. *JAOS* 80: 317–21.
*79. African tongues and tribes. *Rotarian* 96: 35, 61–62.
80. The general classification of Central and South American languages. *Selected Papers of the Fifth International Congress of Anthropological and Ethnological Sciences*, ed. A. Wallace. Philadelphia: University of Pennsylvania Press. Pp. 791–94.
81. Linguistic evidence for the influence of the Kanuri on the Hausa. *Journal of African History* 1: 205–12.
82. A method of measuring functional yield as applied to tone in African languages. *MSLL* 12: 7–16.
83. A survey of African prosodic systems. *Culture in history*, ed. Stanley Diamond. New York: Columbia University Press. Pp. 925–50.
84. Review of *Language change and language reconstruction*, by H. M. Hoenigswald. *AA* 62: 1108–10.
85. Comments in *Style in language*, ed. Thomas A. Sebeok. Cambridge, Mass.: M.I.T. Press. Pp. 102–3, 426–28.

*1961*

86. (With John B. Carroll.) Two cases of synesthesia for color and musical tonality associated with absolute pitch ability. *Perceptual and motor skills* 13: 48.
87. Review of *A course in modern linguistics*, by C. F. Hockett. *AA* 63: 1140–45.
88. Review of *Die demonstrativen Bildungen der neuarabischen Dialekte*, by W. Fischer. *Word* 17: 63–66.
89. Review of *Hausa literature and the Hausa sound system* and *The Language of the Hausa people*, by R. C. Abraham. *AA* 63: 452.

*1962*

90. On the African affiliation of Hebrew and the Semitic languages. *Jewish Social Studies* 24: 79–85.
91. Is the vowel-consonant dichotomy universal? *Word* 18: 73–81.
92. The interpretation of the Coptic vowel system. *J Afr L* 1: 22–29.
93. Africa: IV: Languages. *Encyclopedia Americana* 1: 223g–223h (1962–66 editions).

*1963*

94. Editor, *Universals of language*. Cambridge, Mass.: M.I.T. Press. 269 pp. Preface, iii–iv. (2nd edition, 1966.)

*95. Some universals of grammar with particular reference to the order of meaningful elements. *Universals of language,* ed. J. H. Greenberg. Cambridge, Mass.: M.I.T. Press. Pp. 58–90 (2nd edition, 1966, pp. 73–113.)

*96. (With Charles Osgood and James Jenkins.) Memorandum concerning language universals. *Universals of Language*, ed. J. H. Greenberg. Cambridge, Mass.: M.I.T. Press. Pp. 255–64.

*97. *The languages of Africa. IJAL* 29: 1 (Part II). vi + 171 pp. (Publication of the Indiana University Research Center in Anthropology, Folklore and Linguistics, 25.) Bloomington: Indiana University; The Hague: Mouton.

98. The Mogogodo, a forgotten Cushitic people. *J Afr L* 2 (Part I): 29–43.

*99. Language and linguistics. *The Voice of America Forum Lectures, Behavioral Science Series* 11.

100. Vowel harmony in African languages. *Actes du Second Colloque Internationale de Linguistique Negro-Africaine*. Dakar: Université de Dakar, West African Languages Survey. Pp. 33–38.

101. History and present status of the Kwa problem. *Actes du Second Colloque Internationale de Linguistique Negro-Africaine*. Dakar: Université de Dakar, West African Languages Survey. Pp. 215–17.

102. Langues et histoire en Afrique. *Présence Africaine* 45. Pp. 33–45.

*1964*

*103. The study of language contact in Africa. *Symposium on multilingualism*. Second meeting of the Inter-African Committee on Linguistics, Brazzaville, 1962. London, CCTA/CSA Publications Bureau. Publication No. 87. Pp. 167–75.

104. Historical inferences from linguistic research in Sub-Saharan Africa. *Boston University Papers in African History*, Vol. 1, ed. J. Butler. Boston: Boston University Press. Pp. 1–15.

*105. Nekotoryje obobschchenija kasajushchixsja vozmozhynx nachal'nyx i konechnyx posledovatelnostej soglasnyx. [Some generalizations concerning initial and final consonant clusters.] *Voprosy Jazykoznanija* 4: 41–65.

106. (With James J. Jenkins.) Studies in the psychological correlates of the sound system of American English, I and II. *Word* 20: 157–77.

107. Preface to *Cultural dynamics*, by Melville J. Herskovits. New York: Alfred A. Knopf. Pp. v–viii.
108. Foreword to *A phonetic study of West African languages: An auditory instrumental survey*, by Peter Ladefoged. Cambridge, Eng.: Cambridge University Press. Pp. ix–x. (Shortened version, p. ix in the 2nd edition, 1968).
109. Reply to H. K. Schneider: Confusion in African linguistic classification. *Current Anthropology* 5: 56–67.
110. Some universals of word order. *Proceedings of the Ninth International Congress of Linguists*, ed. Horace G. Lunt. The Hague: Mouton. Pp. 418–20.

*1965*

111. Linguistics. *The African world: A survey of social research*, ed. Robert A. Lystad. New York: Praeger. Pp. 416–41.
*112. Urbanism, migration, and language. *Urbanization and migration in West Africa*, ed. H. Kuper. Pp. 50–59, 189.
*113. The history and present status of African linguistic studies. *Proceedings of the First International Congress of Africanists*, Accra, University of Ghana, 1962. London: Longmans. Pp. 85–96.
114. The evidence for */mb/ as a Proto-Afroasiatic phoneme. Symbolae Linguisticae in Honorem Georgii Kuryłowicz, *Bulietyn Towarzystwa Językoznawczego*, Krakow. Pp. 88–92.
115. Foreword to *Ekoid Bantu: Languages of Ogoja, Eastern Nigeria, Part I, Introduction, phonology and comparative vocabulary*, by David W. Crabb. Cambridge, Eng.: Cambridge University Press. Pp. ix–x.

*1966*

116. Polyglotta evidence for consonant mutation in the Mandyak languages. *Sierra Leone Language Review* 5: 106–10.
117. Synchronic and diachronic universals in phonology. *Lg* 42: 508–17.
*118. Interdisciplinary perspectives in African linguistic research. *Afr Stud B* 9, no. 1: 8–23.
*119. (With Jack Berry.) Sociolinguistic research in Africa. *Afr Stud B* 9, no. 2: 1–9.
*120. Language universals. *Current trends in linguistics: Volume III: Theoretical foundations*, ed. T. A. Sebeok. The Hague: Mouton. Pp. 61–112.
121. (With James J. Jenkins.) Studies in the psychological correlates of the sound system of American English, III and IV, *Word* 22: 207–42.

*1967*

122. The first (and perhaps only) nonlinguistic distinctive feature analysis. *Word* 23: 214–20.
*123. The science of linguistics. *Readings in anthropology*, ed. Morton H. Fried, 2nd edition, 1: 347–63. New York: Thomas Y. Crowell.
124. (With James J. Jenkins and Donald J. Foss.) Phonological distinctive features as cues in learning. *Journal of Experimental Psychology* 77: 200–205.

125. Reply to *CA* Book Review of Greenberg's *Language Universals* (1966), *Current Anthropology* 9:168–71.

*1968*

126. Hausa. *Encyclopaedia Britannica* 11: 163.
127. Nubian language and writing. *Encyclopaedia Britannica* 16: 690–91.
128. Anthropology: The field. *International Encyclopedia of the Social Sciences* 1: 304–13.
* 129. Culture history. *International Encyclopedia of the Social Sciences* 6: 448–55.
130. Ferdinand de Saussure. *International Encyclopedia of the Social Sciences* 14: 19–21.
* 131. *Anthropological linguistics: An introduction*. New York: Random House. 212 pp.

*1969*

132. African languages. *Encyclopaedia Britannica* 1: 312–14.
133. Some methods of dynamic comparison in linguistics. *Substance and structure of language*, ed. J. Puhvel. Berkeley: University of California Press. Pp. 147–203.
134. Review of *The problems in the classification of the African languages*, by I. Fodor. *Lg* 45: 427–32.
* 135. Language universals: A research frontier. *Science* 166: 473–78.
136. Preface to *WPLU* 1: iv–vi.
* 137. African languages. *Collier's Encyclopedia* 1: 243–47.

*1970*

* 138. Some generalizations concerning glottalic consonants, especially implosives. *IJAL* 36: 123–45.
139. The role of typology in the development of a scientific linguistics. *Theoretical problems of typology and the Northern Eurasian languages*, eds. L. Dezsö and P. Hajdú. Budapest: Akadémiai Kiadó. Pp. 11–24.
140. On the 'language of observation' in linguistics. *WPLU* 4: G1–G15.
141. Chadic languages. *Encyclopedia Americana* 6: 231.
142. Click languages. *Encyclopedia Americana* 7: 67.
143. Cushitic languages. *Encyclopedia Americana* 8: 353.

*1971*

144. *Language, culture and communication: Essays by Joseph H. Greenberg*, selected and introduced by Anwar S. Dil. Stanford: Stanford University Press. 367 pp.
* 145. Linguistics as a pilot science. *Linguistics in the 1970s*, Fourth Annual Smithsonian Symposium, 1970. Co-sponsored by the Linguistic Society of America, Center for Applied Linguistics, and the Smithsonian Institution, Washington, D.C. Pp. 1–14.

* 146. Is language like a chess game? First Distinguished Lecture of the American Anthropological Association, 1970. *Annual Report* 4: 53–67.

147. (With A. D'Anglejan, W. E. Lambert, and G. R. Tucker.) Psychological correlates of the French sound system. *Perception and Psychophysics* 9(3B): 356–57.

* 148. Nilo-Saharan and Meroitic. *Current Trends in Linguistics* 7: 421–42. The Hague: Mouton.

149. The Indo-Pacific hypothesis. *Current Trends in Linguistics* 8: 808–71. The Hague: Mouton.

150. A biographical memoir—Melville Jean Herskovits. *Biographical Memoirs* (National Academy of Sciences) 42: 65–93. New York, N.Y.: Columbia University Press.

*1972*

151. Linguistic evidence regarding Bantu origins. *Journal of African History* 13: 189–216.

152. On the identity of Jungraithmayr's Mimi. *Africana Marburgensia* 2: 45–49. Marburg: Universitätsbibliothek.

* 153. Numeral classifiers and substantival number: Problems in the genesis of a linguistic type. *WPLU* 9: 1–39.

*1973*

154. Typological method. *Current Trends in Linguistics* 11: 61–112. The Hague: Mouton.

155. *Language typology: A historical and analytic overview*. (Janua Linguarum Series Minor 184.) The Hague: Mouton.

*1974*

156. Studies in numerical systems, I: Double numeral systems. *WPLU* 14: 75–89.

157. Bantu and its closest relatives. *Studies in African Linguistics*. Supplement no. 5 (Oct.), pp. 115–24.

158. A method for measuring the degree of overt expression of grammatical categories applied to the Sanskrit of the Rigveda. *WPLU* 16: 1–19.

159. The relation of frequency to semantic feature in a case language (Russian). *WPLU* 16: 21–45.

160. (With Chris O'Sullivan.) Frequency, marking, and discourse styles with special reference to substantival categories in the Romance languages. *WPLU* 16: 47–73.

*1975*

161. Dynamic aspects of word order in the numeral classifier. *Word order and word order change*, ed. Charles N. Li. Austin, Texas: University of Texas Press. Pp. 27–43.

162. Research on language universals. *Annual Review of Anthropology* 4: 75–94. Palo Alto, Calif.: Annual Reviews.

*1976*

163. (With Dorothea Kashube.) Word prosodic systems: A preliminary report. *WPLU* 20: 1–18.

*1977*

164. Niger-Congo noun class markers: Prefixes, suffixes, both or neither. *Studies in African Linguistics*, Supplement 7: 94–104.
165. *A new invitation to linguistics*. Garden City, N.Y.: Anchor Press/Doubleday. 147 pp.

*1978*

166. Foreword to *L' Expansion bantoue. Viviers, 4–16 avril 1977. Colloques Internationaux du Centre National de la Recherche Scientifique*. Pp. 9–12.
167. Chief Editor, *Universals of human language*, 4 vols. Stanford: Stanford University Press.
168. (With Charles A. Ferguson and Edith Moravcsik.) Preface. *Universals of human language*, ed. J. H. Greenberg et al. Stanford: Stanford University Press. 1: v–xi.
169. Introduction. *Universals of human language*, ed. J. H. Greenberg et al. Stanford: Stanford University Press. Volume 1: 1–5.
170. Typology and cross-linguistic generalization. *Universals of human language*, ed. J. H. Greenberg et al. Stanford: Stanford University Press. Volume 1: 33–59.
171. Diachrony, synchrony, and language universals. *Universals of human language*, ed J. H. Greenberg et al. Stanford: Stanford University Press. Volume 1: 61–91.
172. Introduction. *Universals of human language*, ed. J. H. Greenberg et al. Stanford: Stanford University Press. Volume 2: 1–8.
173. How does a language acquire gender markers? *Universals of human language*, ed. J. H. Greenberg et al. Stanford: Stanford University Press. Volume 3: 47–82.
174. Generalizations about numeral systems. *Universals of human language*, ed. J. H. Greenberg et al. Stanford: Stanford University Press. Volume 3: 249–95.

*1979*

175. Rethinking linguistics diachronically. *Lg* 55: 275–90.
176. The classification of American Indian languages. *Papers of the Mid-America Linguistic Conference at Oklahoma*, eds. Ralph Cooley et al. Norman, Okla.: University of Oklahoma, Interdisciplinary Linguistics Program. Pp. 7–22.

*1980*

177. Types of linguistic models in other disciplines. *Proceedings of the American Philosophical Society* 124: 35–40.
178. Universals of kinship terminology: Their nature and the problem of their explanation. *On linguistic anthropology: Essays in honor of Harry Hoijer*, ed. Jacques Maquet. Malibu: Undena Publications. Pp. 9–32.
179. Circumfixes and typological change. *Papers from the 4th International*

*Conference on Historical Linguistics*, ed. Elizabeth C. Traugott et al. Amsterdam and Philadelphia: John Benjamins. Pp. 233–41.

*1981*

180. African linguistic classification. *General history of Africa I. Methodology and African prehistory*, ed. J. Ki-Zerbo. Berkeley: University of California Press. Pp. 292–308.
181. Nilo-Saharan moveable *k-* as a stage III article (with a Penutian typological parallel). *Journal of African Languages and Linguistics* 3: 105–12.
182. Christmas as a festival in earliest Hinayana Buddhism. *Journal of Irreproducible Results* 27: 7–8.

*1983*

183. Some areal characteristics of African languages. *Current approaches to African linguistics*, ed. Ivan Dihoff. (Publications in African Languages and Linguistics 1.) Dordrecht and Providence, R.I.: Foris. Pp. 3–21.

*1985*

184. (With C. G. Turner II and S. Zegura.) Convergence of evidence for peopling of the Americas. *Collegium Antropologicum* 9: 33–42.
185. Some iconic relationships among place, time, and discourse deixis. *Iconicity in syntax*, ed. John Haiman. (Typological Studies in Language 6.) Amsterdam and Philadelphia: John Benjamins. Pp. 271–87.
186. A new interpretation of the so-called "violence texts" based on the new discoveries from Upper Tell–el–New York III. *Journal of Irreproducible Results* 30: 7–8.

*1986*

187. (With C. G. Turner II and S. Zegura.) The settlement of the Americas: A comparison of the linguistic, dental, and genetic evidence. *Current Anthropology* 25: 477–97.
188. Introduction: Some reflections on pronominal systems. *Pronominal systems*, ed. Ursula Wiesemann. Tübingen: Günter Narr Verlag. Pp. xvii–xxii.
189. On being a linguistic anthropologist. *Annual Review of Anthropology* 15: 1–24.
190. The realis-irrealis continuum in the Classical Greek conditional. *On conditionals*, eds. Elizabeth Traugott et al. Cambridge, Eng.: Cambridge University Press. Pp. 247–64.
191. Were there Egyptian koines? *The Fergusonian impact*, Vol. I, eds. Joshua A. Fishman et al. Berlin, New York, Amsterdam: Mouton de Gruyter. Pp. 271–90.

*1987*

192. *Language in the Americas*. Stanford: Stanford University Press.
193. Author's precis and reply to reviews of *Language in the Americas*, *Current Anthropology* 28: 647–52, 664–66.

*1988*

194. The first person inclusive dual as an ambiguous category. *Studies in Language* 12: 1–18.
195. The present status of markedness theory: A reply to Scheffler. *Journal of Anthropological Research* 43: 367–74.

*In Press*

196. Two approaches to language universals. *New vistas in grammar: Invariance and variation*, ed. Linda Waugh and Stephen Rudy. Amsterdam and Philadelphia: John Benjamins.
197. The methods and purposes of linguistic classification. *Language transmission and change*, ed. W. S.-Y. Wang. London and New York: Blackwell.
198. Some problems of Indo-European in historical perspective. *Sprung from a common source*, ed. Sydney Lamb. Stanford: Stanford University Press.
199. Relative pronouns and PIE word order type in the context of the Eurasiatic hypothesis. In a volume edited by Winfred Lehmann.
200. The last stages of grammatical elements: Degrammaticalization and regrammaticalization. *Aspects of Grammaticalization*, eds. Elizabeth Traugott and Bernd Heine. Amsterdam and Philadelphia: Benjamins.
201. Comments at session on Typology and Universals at Conference on Second Language Acquisition and Linguistic Theory, ed. Thomas Huebner.
202. Review of *Archaeology and language: The puzzle of Indo-European origins*, by Colin Renfrew. *Quarterly Review of Archaeology*.
203. The logical bases of linguistic prescriptivism: A parallel between classical grammarians and Moslem legal theorists. In a Festschrift for Robert Politzer.

## Appendix: Reprints, Translations, Revised Versions

*2. Reprinted in *Cultures and societies of Africa*, ed. Simon and Phoebe Ottenberg. New York: Random House, 1960. Pp. 477–88.

*4. Monographs of The American Ethnological Society, X.

*9. Excerpt in French translation reprinted in *La Lexicologie*, ed. Alain Rey. Paris: Klincksieck, 1970. Pp. 176–77. Reprinted in *Language in culture and society*, ed. Dell Hymes. New York: Harper & Row, 1964. Pp. 27–35. Reprinted in *Language, culture, and communication: Essays by Joseph H. Greenberg*, selected and introduced by Anwar S. Dil. Stanford: Stanford University Press, 1971. Pp. 1–10.

*14. Reprinted in *The making of Black America,* ed. August Meier and Elliott Rudwick, 1. New York. Atheneum, 1969. Pp. 3–13. Reprinted as BC 112, Bobbs-Merrill Reprint Series in Black Studies.

*29. Reprinted in *Edward Sapir: Appraisal of his life and work*, ed. Konrad Koerner. Amsterdam and Philadelphia: John Benjamins, 1984. Pp. 62–64.

*30. Reprinted in *Readings in Arabic linguistics*, ed. Salman H. Al-Ani. Indiana University Linguistics Club, 1978. Pp. 431–56. Reprinted in *Comparative Semitic* *linguistics*, ed. M. H. Goshen Gottstein. Jerusalem: Hebrew University Institute of Languages and Literatures. Pp. 146–55.

* 39. Reprinted in *Language, culture, and communication: Essays by Joseph H. Greenberg*, selected and introduced by Anwar S. Dil. Stanford: Stanford University Press, 1971, Pp. 11–46.
* 46. Reprinted in *Readings for the history of the English language*, ed. C. T. Scott and J. L. Erickson. Boston: Allyn and Bacon, 1968. Pp. 7–20. Reprinted as Introduction, the linguistic approach. In *Communication and culture: Readings in the codes of human interaction*, ed. Alfred G. Smith. New York: Holt, Rinehart and Winston. Pp. 121–29.
* 47. Reprinted in *IJAL* 26: 178–94, 1960. Translated into Russian in *Novoje v Lingvistike*, ed. V. J. Rozentzveig. 3: 60–94, 1963. Italian translation, Un approccio quantitativo alla tipologia morfologica della lingua, in *La tipologia linguistica*, ed. Paolo Ramat. Bologna: Mulino, 1976. Pp. 171–92.
* 49. Reprinted in *Psycholinguistics: A book of readings*, ed. Sol Saporta, New York: Holt, Rinehart and Winston, 1961. Pp. 468–80. Reprinted in *Language, culture, and communication: Essays by Joseph H. Greenberg*, selected and introduced by Anwar S. Dil. Stanford: Stanford University Press, 1971. Pp. 49–67.
* 57. French translation appearing in the *Bulletin de l'Institut Français d'Afrique Noire*, Tome XVI.
* 60. Reprinted in *Language, culture and communication: Essays by Joseph H. Greenberg*, selected and introduced by Anwar S. Dil. Stanford: Stanford University Press, 1971. Pp. 68–77. Translated into Russian in *Novoje v Lingvistike*, ed. V. J. Rozentzveig. 6: 204–14, 1972.
* 65. Also issued as *Viking Fund Publications in Anthropology, No. 24*, New York: Wenner-Gren Foundation for Anthropological Research, 1957. vii + 108 pp. Chapter 5, Language and evolutionary theory, reprinted in *Readings in anthropology* 1: 408–29, ed. Morton H. Fried. 1968. Chapter 3, Genetic relations among languages, reprinted in *Readings for the history of the English language*, ed. by C. T. Scott and J. L. Ericson. Boston: Allyn and Bacon, 1968. Pp. 35–47. Pp. 27–31 reprinted in French translation in *La Lexicologie*, ed. Alain Rey. Paris: Klincksieck, 1970. Pp. 111–16.
* 66. Portuguese translation, *Sobre a natura e o uso das tipologias linguisticas. Revista de Antropologia* 6: 1–14. São Paulo, 1958.
* 72. Reprinted in *Cultural and social anthropology: Selected readings*, ed. P. B. Hammond. New York: Macmillan, 1964. Pp. 369–78.
* 73. Reprinted in *Man in adaptation: The cultural present*, ed. Y. A. Cohen. Chicago: Aldine, 1968. Pp. 29–40. Reprinted in *Language, culture, and communication: Essays by Joseph H. Greenberg*, selected and introduced by Anwar S. Dil. Stanford: Stanford University Press, 1971. Pp. 106–25. Reprinted in Bobbs-Merrill Reprint Series (A-95).
* 79. Reprinted in *Language, culture, and communication: Essays by Joseph H. Greenberg*, selected and introduced by Anwar S. Dil. Stanford: Stanford University Press, 1971. Pp. 137–42.

*95. Reprinted in *A Reader in historical comparative linguistics*, ed. Allan R. Keiler. New York: Holt, Rinehart and Winston, 1972. Pp. 306–37.

*95. German translation (excerpts only) in *Sprachwissenschaft: Der Gang ihrer Entwicklung von der Antike bis zur Gegenwart*, ed. H. Arens. Freiburg: Alber, 2nd ed. 1969. Pp. 702–7. (Translated as *La Linguistica*. 1975. Madrid: Editorial Gredos.)

*95. Italian translation in *La tipologia linguistica*, ed. Paolo Ramat. Bologna: Mulino, 1976. Pp. 115–54.

*95. Russian translation in *Novoje v Lingvistike*, ed. V. J. Rozentzveig. 5: 114–62, 1970.

*95. Chinese translation in *Guowai yuyanxue* (Linguistics Abroad) 2: 45–60, 1984.

*96. Russian translation in *Novoje v Lingvistike*, ed. V. J. Rozentzveig. 5: 31–44, 1970

*96. German translation in *Sprachwissenschaft: Der Gang ihrer Entwicklung von der Antike bis zur Gegenwart*, ed. H. Arens. Freiburg: Alber, 2nd ed. 1969. Pp. 713–20. (Translated as *La Linguistica*. 1975. Madrid: Editorial Gredos.)

*97. Revised edition, 1966. The Hague: Mouton. vi + 180 pp. Reprinted in *Problems in African history*, ed. Robert O. Collins. "Niger-Congo," 70–75 from 1963: 6–7, 30–33, 35–38; "The languages of Africa," 124–33 from 1963: 42–43, 49–51, 85–86, 89–94. Englewood Cliffs, N.J., 1968.

*99. Reprinted in *The behavioral sciences today*, ed. B. Berelson. New York: Basic Books, 1963, Pp. 126–38. Reprinted in *Language, culture, and communication: Essays by Joseph H. Greenberg*, selected and introduced by Anwar S. Dil. Stanford: Stanford University Press, 1971. Pp. 156–67.

*103. Reprinted in *Language, culture, and communication: Essays by Joseph H. Greenberg*, selected and introduced by Anwar S. Dil. Stanford: Stanford University Press, 1971. Pp. 185–97. Russian translation in *Novoje v Lingvistike*, ed. by V. J. Rozentzveig. 6: 130–40, 1972.

*105. English version: Some generalizations concerning initial and final consonant clusters. *Linguistics* 18: 5–34, 1965. Revised version in *Universals of human language*, ed. Joseph H. Greenberg et al. Stanford: Stanford University Press, 1978. Vol. 2, pp. 243–80.

*112. Reprinted in *Man in adaptation: The biosocial background*, ed. Y. A. Cohen. Chicago: Aldine, 1968. Pp. 259–67. Reprinted in *Language, culture, and communication: Essays by Joseph H. Greenberg*, selected and introduced by Anwar S. Dil. Stanford: Stanford University Press, 1971. Pp. 198–211.

*113. Reprinted in *Language, culture, and communication: Essays by Joseph H. Greenberg*, selected and introduced by Anwar S. Dil. Stanford: Stanford University Press, 1971. Pp. 212–27. Polish translation, Historia i obecny stan Afrykanistycznych badan lingwistycznych, in *Problemy Afrikanistyki*, ed. Stefan Strelcyn. Warsaw: Panstwowe Wydawnictwo Naukwe. Pp. 120–33.

*118. Reprinted in *Language, culture, and communication: Essays by Joseph H. Greenberg*, selected and introduced by Anwar S. Dil. Stanford: Stanford University Press, 1971. Pp. 228–48.

* 119. Reprinted in *Language, culture, and communication: Essays by Joseph H. Greenberg*, selected and introduced by Anwar S. Dil. Stanford: Stanford University Press, 1971. Pp. 249–59.
* 120. Revised edition: *Language universals with special reference to feature hierarchies*. The Hague: Mouton, 1966. 89 pp.
* 123. Reprinted in *Language, culture, and communication: Essays by Joseph H. Greenberg*, selected and introduced by Anwar S. Dil. Stanford: Stanford University Press, 1971. Pp. 274–94.
* 129. Reprinted in *Language, culture, and communication: Essays by Joseph H. Greenberg*, selected and introduced by Anwar S. Dil. Stanford: Stanford University Press, 1971. Pp. 168–84.
* 131. Chapter, The nature and definition of language, reprinted in *Language, culture, and communication: Essays by Joseph H. Greenberg*, selected and introduced by Anwar S. Dil. Stanford: Stanford University Press, 1971. Pp. 260–73. Translated into Japanese by M. Ando. Tokyo: Charles E. Tuttle, 1973.
* 135. Reprinted in *Language, culture, and communication: Essays by Joseph H. Greenberg*, selected and introduced by Anwar S. Dil. Stanford: Stanford University Press, 1971. Pp. 295–313.
* 137. Reprinted in *Language, culture, and communication: Essays by Joseph H. Greenberg*, selected and introduced by Anwar S. Dil. Stanford: Stanford University Press, 1971. Pp. 126–36.
* 138. Also appeared in *WPLU* 1: iv–vi (1969).
* 145. Reprinted in *Language, culture, and communication: Essays by Joseph H. Greenberg*, selected and introduced by Anwar S. Dil. Stanford: Stanford University Press, 1971. Pp. 314–29. Reprinted in *Themes in Linguistics: The 1960's*. The Hague: Mouton, 1972. Pp. 45–60.
* 146. Reprinted in *Language, culture, and communication: Essays by Joseph H. Greenberg*, selected and introduced by Anwar S. Dil. Stanford: Stanford University Press, 1971. Pp. 330–52.
* 153. Also published in *Proceedings of the Eleventh International Congress of Linguists* (Bologna-Florence, Aug. 28–Sept. 2, 1972), ed. Luigi Heilmann. Bologna: Mulino, 1974. Vol. I, pp. 17–37. Reprinted in *Linguistics at the crossroads*, eds. Adam Makkai et al. Padua: Liviana Editrice, 1977. Pp. 276–30.